THE HANDBOOK OF

WEST EUROPEAN
PENSION POLITICS

THE HANDBOOK OF
WEST EUROPEAN PENSION POLITICS

Edited by

ELLEN M. IMMERGUT
KAREN M. ANDERSON
AND
ISABELLE SCHULZE

OXFORD
UNIVERSITY PRESS

OXFORD
UNIVERSITY PRESS

Great Clarendon Street, Oxford OX2 6DP

Oxford University Press is a department of the University of Oxford.
It furthers the University's objective of excellence in research, scholarship,
and education by publishing worldwide in

Oxford New York

Auckland Cape Town Dar es Salaam Hong Kong Karachi
Kuala Lumpur Madrid Melbourne Mexico City Nairobi
New Delhi Shanghai Taipei Toronto

With offices in

Argentina Austria Brazil Chile Czech Republic France Greece
Guatemala Hungary Italy Japan Poland Portugal Singapore
South Korea Switzerland Thailand Turkey Ukraine Vietnam

Oxford is a registered trade mark of Oxford University Press
in the UK and in certain other countries

Published in the United States
by Oxford University Press Inc., New York

© The Several Contributors, 2006

The moral rights of the author have been asserted
Database right Oxford University Press (maker)

First published 2006
First published in paperback 2009

All rights reserved. No part of this publication may be reproduced,
stored in a retrieval system, or transmitted, in any form or by any means,
without the prior permission in writing of Oxford University Press,
or as expressly permitted by law, or under terms agreed with the appropriate
reprographics rights organization. Enquiries concerning reproduction
outside the scope of the above should be sent to the Rights Department,
Oxford University Press, at the address above

You must not circulate this book in any other binding or cover
and you must impose the same condition on any acquirer

British Library Cataloguing in Publication Data

Data available

Library of Congress Cataloging in Publication Data

Data available

Typeset by SPI Publisher Services, Pondicherry, India
Printed in Great Britain
on acid-free paper by
CPI Anthony Rowe, Chippenham, Wiltshire

ISBN 978–0–19–929147–2 (Hbk)   978–0–19–956247–3 (Pbk)

1 3 5 7 9 10 8 6 4 2

For Jens and Michael; Katja; Marlene, Iris and Herbert

Preface

This book was meant to be deductive; and it was meant to be contemporary. The original idea was to test the "veto points" perspective that I had developed during an historical study of the development of national health insurance programs in Sweden, France and Switzerland. My plan was to undertake a new comparative study, but this time on "pension politics" in place of "health politics." The idea would be to consider more than three cases this time, but still to select critical cases for comparison.

In the course of the research—and even during the drafting of my grant proposal to the German Research Council (*Deutsche Forschungsgemeinschaft*, DFG)—I began to notice that something was wrong. It was not the case that some nations efficiently passed pension reform, while others were blocked by myriad veto points. Instead, most governments in Western Europe had indeed tried to grapple with their pension problem in some fashion, thus producing a much more complex pattern of policy outcomes than the simple black-and-white dichotomy of "success" versus "failure." Further, as I worked through the findings of existing studies, it seemed that the factors that seemed to be important to pension politics varied enormously with the choice of cases. This undermined my belief in the enterprise of "case selection." I gave up, and started anew, now seeking to investigate a complete universe of cases—all 15 EU nations, as well as Switzerland—and went back to my funding agency, and asked for more money, bringing a much larger group of people than planned on board.

This book represents the first concrete result of this broad comparison. What we found was that neither "veto points" nor "veto players" provides a compelling answer to the riddle of pension politics. These approaches are helpful, but they must be supplemented by a theory of *political competition*. Indeed, for all of our efforts to focus on contemporary policies, the historical development of the welfare state proved to be of considerable importance. The fight for votes was central to the introduction and expansion of pension programs. Similarly, the intensity and strategy of competition is critical to reform efforts. Both the incentives to expand, and the difficulties that governments face in proposing cuts, depend upon their electoral system, and also on political parties' strategies for competition. Thus, political competition is a complex variable which depends upon a number of features of political systems, and on what we call "electoral maps." Moreover, the impact of competition is also complex: if there is too little competition, governments have little incentive to reform; too much, and they become paralyzed, because they fear the electoral costs linked to cuts in popular government benefits. Certainly, the theme of political competition is not new. But we do think that we have made a first step in combining various aspects of competition into a more holistic concept. Thus, once again, the contribution in this book is inductive. Our next step will be to refine it further; and finally to get on to that deductive test.

We have tried to aim this book at three distinct audiences, and to structure it in such a way that each group can focus on the sections in each chapter most relevant to them. To start with, for those interested in welfare states and institutional change, the first section of the Editors' Introduction reviews the theoretical issues, then each case study provides a complete narrative account of pension politics in their particular country, (in section IV and Table 3 in each case study chapter); these can be read singly, or in any combination. Second, for students and practitioners of social policy, we have tried to provide complete information on debates on pension policy in section II of the Editors' Introduction, as well as on existing pension systems across Europe in section III and Fig. 2 for each case study chapter, and in the Appendix (see Ch. 18). Finally, for readers interested in comparative and European politics, we assess the impact of political institutions on governments' abilities to introduce policy change in a systematic cross-national comparison in Chapter 1 and sections I, III, and V of each case study chapter. As the basis for this comparative evaluation, we provide descriptions of the political institutions and governmental majorities in all "old" EU nations, and discuss how to assess the veto points and veto players in each case (in Tables 1 and 2, Fig. 1, and section II of each case study). We believe that by looking at these political systems "in action," as governments, political parties and interest groups contest the pension issue, the working of political institutions becomes more interesting and more compelling, and thus pension politics provides a good window into how these political systems work in practice.

In our acknowledgements, we thank a number of individuals and institutions, without whose help this project would never have been possible. But here, I as the initiator of this project, would like to give my whole-hearted thanks to Karen Anderson and Isabelle Schulze, my co-editors and co-investigators. Without their help, this project and this book would never have come into being. I would also like to express here my (up to now) inadequately-expressed appreciation of the loving support I received from my husband, Jens Alber, throughout the project.

Ellen M. Immergut
Berlin, March 2006

Acknowledgements

For financial support—and especially for the precious gift of time—we thank the German Research Council (*Deutsche Forschungsgemeinschaft*, DFG) and the Hanse Institute of Advanced Study (*Hanse-Wissenschaftskolleg*, HWK) as well as Friedrich Breyer, who was the co-principal investigator of the main grant that included the pensions politics sub-project, and Martin Kolmar, who was originally part of the grant application; Michael Schuster, our patient and flexible DFG administrator; Frau Schenk, the administrator for the University of Konstanz; Stephan Leibfried, who made the stay at HWK possible and served as sponsor; and Gerhard Roth, the Rektor of the HWK, as well as the HWK Staff. We also thank both the Humboldt University Berlin and the University of Konstanz for various institutional and personnel resources. Schulze is grateful for the additional support given to her dissertation by the *Forschungsnetzwerk Alterssicherung des Verbands Deutscher Rentenversicherungsträger*, now the *Deutsche Rentenversicherung Bund*.

For various intellectual inputs, including comments and sharing of data, we thank Jens Alber, Stefano Bartolini, Hilke Brockman, Eugénia da Conceição-Heldt, Tom Cusack, Bernhard Ebbinghaus, Peter Flora, Richard Hauser, Karl Hinrichs, Alexander Jäger, Sven Jochem, Bernhard Kittel, Wolfram Lamping, Lutz Leisering, Joakim Palme, Manfred G. Schmidt, Nico Siegel, Wolfgang Strengmann-Kuhn, Bart van Riel, Torbjörn Strandberg, Peter Taylor-Gooby, George Tsebelis, Margaret Weir, as well as of course, the anonymous reviewers of the DFG and OUP. A number of master's-degree students at the University of Konstanz participated in research discussions, and some wrote their theses in conjunction with the project: Simone Grimmeisen, Dorothée Haag, Anika Rasner, Daniela Rieker, Saskia Richter (now Jung), and Martin Schludi. For research assistance we thank Stefan Lhachimi, Miriam Leis and especially, Heiko Giebler, Lisa Hoffmann, Niklas Schrader and Aiko Wagner; for language editing and substantive comments, Alex Street; for secretarial assistance, Martina Rudolph.

We would also like to thank our editors Dominic Byatt and Lizzy Suffling, as well as the staff at Oxford University Press who put their faith in our project, and for all the work they put into our manuscript.

Last but not least, we extend a warm round of thanks to our many authors who worked so hard and so enthusiastically to produce the chapters and tables that follow.

E. M. I., K. M. A., I. S.

Contents

List of Figures	xx
List of Tables	xxii
List of Appendix Tables	xxv
List of Contributors	xxvii

1 **Editors' introduction: the dynamics of pension politics**   1
   Ellen M. Immergut and Karen M. Anderson

I	The political-institutional framework for pension politics	4
	The impact of political institutions on public policies	4
	Veto points and veto players	7
	Political institutions and the welfare state	8
	The new politics of the welfare state	10
	Bringing labor back in	13
	Varieties of capitalism	14
	Demographic and budgetary pressures	16
	Ideas, learning and discourse	17
II	The policy framework for pension politics	18
	Contours of the pension problem and favored solutions	18
	The structure of pension systems: tiers and pillars	21
III	Pension politics	23
	An institutional approach to pension politics	23
	Pension politics in Western Europe	24
	Single veto player governments; no veto points	24
	Multiple veto points	26

Many partisan veto players	28
Moderate veto points and veto players	30
Closed veto points, moderate veto players, unusual electoral configurations	34
Political competition	36
The future of pension politics	37

PART I SINGLE VETO PLAYER GOVERNMENTS; NO VETO POINTS

2 United Kingdom: pension politics in an adversarial system — 49
Isabelle Schulze and Michael Moran

I	Introduction	49
II	Political system	51
III	Pension system	59
IV	Politics of pension reform since 1980	66
	Overview	66
	The Social Security Act 1986	67
	The Pensions Act 1995	74
	The Welfare Reform and Pensions Act 1999	76
	The Child Support Pensions and Social Security Act	79
V	Conclusion	82

3 Greece: political competition in a majoritarian system — 97
Polyxeni Triantafillou

I	Introduction	97
II	Political system	98
III	Pension system	109
IV	Politics of pension reform since 1980	117
	Overview	117
	The 1980s: a period of expansion	122
	1990: the Souflias Reform (Law 1902/90)	123
	1991: the Fakiolas Committee and Law 1976/91	130
	1992: the Souflias Reform (Law 2084/92)	131
	1997–1999: the Spraos Report and the "Mini Reform Package" (Law 2676/99)	135

		The attempt that failed: the Giannitsis Proposals of 2001	137
		The Reppas Reform (Law 3029/02)	139
V		Conclusion	140

4	France: the importance of the electoral cycle	150
	Eugénia da Conceição-Heldt	

I	Introduction		150
II	Political system		151
III	Pension system		166
IV	Politics of pension reform since 1980		173
	Overview		173
	The Mauroy Reform of 1982: retirement at age 60 and minimum contributions		177
	The Balladur Reform of 1993: the reform of private sector pensions		178
	The 1995 Juppé Plan: a first attempt to reform the special schemes		182
	The stillborn Thomas Law of 1997: the controversial establishment of private capital-funded plans		184
	The 2003 Raffarin Reform: a further attempt to reform the special schemes		187
V	Conclusion		190

PART II   MULTIPLE VETO POINTS

5	Switzerland: the impact of direct democracy	203
	Giuliano Bonoli	

I	Introduction	203
II	Political system	205
III	Pension system	217
IV	Politics of pension reform since 1980	223
	Overview	223
	The adoption of a law on occupational pensions 1982	226
	The 10th AHV/AVS Revision	230
	The 11th AHV/AVS Revision	233
	The 1st BVG/LPP Revision	235
	The stock market crisis of the early 2000s and occupational pensions	237
V	Conclusion	239

6	Finland: labor markets against politics *Olli Kangas*	248

    I Introduction   248
   II Political system   251
  III Pension system   264
  IV Politics of pension reform since 1980   273
       Overview   273
       The introduction of employee contributions 1992   274
       The 1992 harmonization of private and public sector pensions   280
       The 1995 reform of the income base for calculating employment pensions   281
       The 1995 reform of national pensions   282
       Reforms of private sector pensions in 2002 and public sector pensions in 2004   284
   V Conclusion   287

7	Belgium: linguistic veto players and pension reform *Karen M. Anderson, Sanneke Kuipers, Isabelle Schulze and Wendy van den Nouland*	297

    I Introduction   297
   II Political system   298
  III Pension system   312
  IV Politics of pension reform since 1980   317
       Overview   317
       Incremental reforms   321
       Reform of early retirement 1982   323
       The Mainil Reform of 1984   323
       The St Anna Plan 1986   325
       Flexible pension age and repackaging early retirement 1990   327
       Attempts at comprehensive reform   329
       The 1996 pension reform   332
   V Conclusion   338

PART III MANY PARTISAN VETO PLAYERS

8 Sweden: after social democratic hegemony   349
    Karen M. Anderson and Ellen M. Immergut

   I   Introduction   349
  II   Political system   351
 III   Pension system   360
 IV   Politics of pension reform since 1980   367
       Overview   367
       The 1980s: political competition and policy stability   367
       The 1990s   370
       The 1994/98 reform   372
       Sticking to the agreement and working out the details   380
  V   Conclusion   386

9 Italy: a narrow gate for path-shift   396
    Maurizio Ferrera and Matteo Jessoula

   I   Introduction   396
  II   Political system   398
 III   Pension system   415
 IV   Politics of pension reform since 1980   422
       Overview   422
       The 1980s: "Much Ado About Nothing"   422
       The 1992 Amato Reform   431
       The 1994 Berlusconi Reform   434
       The 1995 Dini Reform   436
       The 1997 Prodi Reform   439
       A new multi-pillar architecture for Italian pensions   440
       The Berlusconi–Tremonti Reform: 2001–2005   443
  V   Conclusion   445

10	Denmark: a "World Bank" pension system	454
	Christoffer Green-Pedersen	

I	Introduction	454
II	Political system	456
III	Pension system	464
IV	Politics of pension reform since 1980	470
	Overview	470
	Tax on interest gains of funded pension scheme 1982	474
	Improvements to the national pension 1986–1990	476
	The introduction of occupational pensions 1986–1991	479
	ATP for recipients of cash benefits	484
	Increased means testing of the national pension 1993	486
	Introduction of the Special Pension scheme (SP)	488
V	Conclusion	489

PART IV MODERATE VETO POINTS AND VETO PLAYERS

11	Spain: between majority rule and incrementalism	499
	Elisa Chuliá	

I	Introduction	499
II	Political system	501
III	Pension system	514
IV	Politics of pension reform since 1980	520
	Overview	520
	1985 Reform: Law of urgent measures for the rationalization of the structure and protective action of the Social Security system	522
	1987 Reform: Law on regulation of pension plans and funds	529
	1990 Reform: Law on non-contributory pensions of the Social Security system	532
	Excursus: the guidelines of Spanish pension policy since 1995 – The Toledo Pact	534
	1997 Reform: Law on consolidation and rationalization of the Social Security system	538
	2002 Reform: Law on measures for the establishment of a system of gradual and flexible retirement	541
	The institutional solidity of the Toledo Pact	542
V	Conclusion	544

12	Austria: from electoral cartels to competitive coalition-building	555
	Isabelle Schulze and Martin Schludi	
I	Introduction	555
II	Political system	556
III	Pension system	566
IV	Politics of pension reform since 1980	570
	Overview	570
	Pension reform 1984: 40. ASVG Novelle	574
	Pension reform 1987: 44. ASVG Novelle	576
	Pension reform 1993: 51. ASVG Novelle	578
	Pension reforms 1995 and 1996: Strukturanpassungsgesetze	580
	Pension reform 1997: ASRÄG and 1. Budgetbegleitgesetz	584
	Pension reform 2000: Sozialrechts-Änderungsgesetz (SRÄG)	587
	Pension reform 2003: Budgetbegleitgesetz	590
	Pension reform 2005: Pensionsharmonisierungsgesetz	593
V	Conclusion	593

13	Portugal: in search of a stable framework	605
	Elisa Chuliá and María Asensio	
I	Introduction	605
II	Political system	607
III	Pension system	624
IV	Politics of pension reform since 1980	633
	Towards comprehensive social security: The creation of the non-contributory regime in 1980 and the Social Security Framework Law of 1984	633
	The creation of the second and third pillars of the Portuguese pension system in the second half of the 1980s	639
	1993: cutting the costs of pensions and preventing strategic behavior by pensioners-to-be	641
	The White Paper Commission 1996–1998	642
	The 1999 measures to introduce a flexible retirement age, and to improve the benefits for dependent pensioners	644
	Restructuring Social Security: the 2000 and 2002 Social Security Framework Laws and the issue of the "plafonamento"	645
V	Conclusion	650

14	**Germany: beyond policy gridlock**	**660**
	Isabelle Schulze and Sven Jochem	
I	Introduction	660
II	Political system	662
III	Pension system	671
IV	Politics of pension reform since 1980	676
	Overview	676
	Blüm I reform 1989: Pension Reform Act 1992	679
	Blüm II reform 1997: Pension Reform Act 1999	682
	The Riester reform 2001	686
	The Rürup reform 2004 (RV-Nachhaltigkeitsgesetz)	693
V	Conclusion	695

PART V CLOSED VETO POINTS, MODERATE VETO PLAYERS, UNUSUAL ELECTORAL SYSTEMS

15	**The Netherlands: political competition in a proportional system**	**713**
	Karen M. Anderson	
I	Introduction	713
II	Political system	714
III	Pension system	724
IV	Politics of pension reform since 1980	729
	Overview	729
	Cost containment of the AOW in the 1980s	732
	Supplementary pensions	733
	Adapting to European equal treatment law	734
	The EU and occupational pensions	736
	Supplementary pensions: improving coverage	737
	AOW cost containment in the 1990s	738
	The 1994 election	740
	The introduction of the AOW reserve fund	742
	Reforming occupational pensions	744
	The stock market downturn	746
	Revision of the PSF	748
V	Conclusion	749

16	Ireland: pensioning the "Celtic Tiger"	758
	Isabelle Schulze and Michael Moran	
I	Introduction	758
II	Political system	759
III	Pension system	769
IV	Politics of pension reform since 1980	775
	Overview	*775*
	Social Welfare Act 1988: PRSI for the self-employed and farmers	*778*
	The Pensions Act 1990	*782*
	The Pensions Amendment Act 1996	*787*
	The Pensions Reserve Fund Act 2000	*789*
	The Pensions (Amendment) Act 2002	*792*
V	Conclusion	794

17	Luxembourg: an electoral system with panache	804
	Isabelle Schulze	
I	Introduction	804
II	Political system	805
III	Pension system	815
IV	Politics of pension reform since 1980	820
	Overview	*820*
	The 1984 reform	*823*
	The 1987 reform	*828*
	The 1991 reform	*832*
	Public sector reform 1995–1998	*833*
	The 2002 reform (Rentendësch 2001)	*838*
V	Conclusion	842

18	Data Appendix: Pension systems in Western Europe	854
Index		905

List of Figures

Figure 1.1	A generic description of pension systems	22
Figure 2.1	Party system in the United Kingdom	55
Figure 2.2	Pension system in the United Kingdom	63
Figure 3.1	Party system in Greece	104
Figure 3.2	Pension system in Greece	113
Figure 4.1	Party system in France	159
Figure 4.2	Pension system in France	170
Figure 5.1	Party system in Switzerland	213
Figure 5.2	Pension system in Switzerland	223
Figure 6.1	Party system in Finland	258
Figure 6.2	The structure of Finnish pension schemes before and after the 1996 reform	269
Figure 6.3	Pension system in Finland	270
Figure 7.1	Party system in Belgium	304
Figure 7.2	Pension system in Belgium	316
Figure 8.1	Party system in Sweden	356
Figure 8.2	Pension system in Sweden post-1998	363
Figure 8.3	Pension system in Sweden pre-1994	364
Figure 9.1	Italy's reform sequence in the 1990s: the explanatory model	398
Figure 9.2	Party system in Italy (1980s)	406
Figure 9.3	Party system in Italy (1990s)	408
Figure 9.4	Pension system in Italy	419
Figure 10.1	Party system in Denmark	460
Figure 10.2	Pension system in Denmark	469
Figure 11.1	Party system in Spain	509
Figure 11.2	Pension system in Spain	518
Figure 12.1	Party system in Austria	562
Figure 12.2	Pension system in Austria	568
Figure 13.1	Party system in Portugal	617
Figure 13.2	Pension system in Portugal	632

Figure 14.1	Party system in Germany	667
Figure 14.2	Pension system in Germany	674
Figure 15.1	Party system in the Netherlands	719
Figure 15.2	Pension system in the Netherlands	727
Figure 16.1	Party system in Ireland	765
Figure 16.2	Pension system in Ireland	772
Figure 17.1	Party system in Luxembourg	811
Figure 17.2	Pension system in Luxembourg	819

List of Tables

Table 2.1	Political institutions in the United Kingdom	53
Table 2.2	Governmental majorities in the United Kingdom	57
Table 2.3	Overview of proposed and enacted pension reforms in the United Kingdom	68
Table 3.1	The electoral system introduced in 1989 in Greece (applicable to three elections: June and November 1989 and October 1990)	100
Table 3.2	The electoral system in 1990 in Greece (in force for 1993, 1996 and 2000 elections)	101
Table 3.3	Political institutions in Greece	103
Table 3.4	Governmental majorities in Greece	107
Table 3.5	Greek pension system	114
Table 3.6	Overview of proposed and enacted pension reforms in Greece	119
Table 3.7	Greek legislation that led to system expansion in the 1980s	124
Table 4.1	Political institutions in France	154
Table 4.2	Governmental majorities in France	162
Table 4.3	Overview of proposed and enacted pension reforms in France	174
Table 5.1	Political institutions in Switzerland	210
Table 5.2	Governmental majorities in Switzerland	215
Table 5.3	Overview of proposed and enacted pension reforms in Switzerland	224
Table 6.1	Political institutions in Finland	254
Table 6.2	Governmental majorities in Finland	261
Table 6.3	Proportional shares (%) of different pension schemes of total pension expenditure in Finland 1950–2000	271
Table 6.4	Overview of proposed and enacted pension reforms in Finland	275
Table 7.1	Political institutions in Belgium	301
Table 7.2	Governmental majorities in Belgium	307
Table 7.3	Overview of proposed and enacted pension reforms in Belgium	318
Table 8.1	Political institutions in Sweden	354
Table 8.2	Governmental majorities in Sweden	358

Table 8.3	Overview of proposed and enacted pension reforms in Sweden	368
Table 9.1	Political institutions in Italy	400
Table 9.2	Governmental majorities in Italy	411
Table 9.3	Overview of proposed pension reforms in Italy 1980–1992	424
Table 9.4	Overview of proposed and enacted pension reforms in Italy 1992–2005	427
Table 10.1	Political institutions in Denmark	458
Table 10.2	Governmental majorities in Denmark	463
Table 10.3	Overview of proposed and enacted pension reforms in Denmark	471
Table 11.1	Political institutions in Spain	504
Table 11.2	Governmental majorities in Spain	512
Table 11.3	Indicators of the Social Security contributory pension system 1980–2003	521
Table 11.4	Overview of proposed and enacted pension reforms in Spain	523
Table 12.1	Political institutions in Austria	558
Table 12.2	Governmental majorities in Austria	564
Table 12.3	Overview of proposed and enacted pension reforms in Austria	571
Table 13.1	Political institutions in Portugal	613
Table 13.2	Governmental majorities in Portugal	620
Table 13.3	Number of Portuguese pensioners by scheme and regime (September 2002)	628
Table 13.4	Changes in the eligibility criteria for old-age pensions	628
Table 13.5	Differences in the amount of pensions between private sector employees and state employees 2003	629
Table 13.6	Overview of proposed and enacted pension reforms in Portugal	635
Table 14.1	Political institutions in Germany	663
Table 14.2	Governmental majorities in Germany	668
Table 14.3	Overview of proposed and enacted pension reforms in Germany	677
Table 15.1	Political institutions in the Netherlands	716
Table 15.2	Governmental majorities in the Netherlands	721
Table 15.3	Overview of proposed and enacted pension reforms in the Netherlands	730
Table 16.1	Political institutions in Ireland	762
Table 16.2	Governmental majorities in Ireland	767
Table 16.3	Overview of proposed and enacted pension reforms in Ireland	776
Table 17.1	Political institutions in Luxembourg	807

Table 17.2 Governmental majorities in Luxembourg   813
Table 17.3 Overview of proposed and enacted pension reforms
            in Luxembourg   821

List of Appendix Tables

Table A.1	Demographic, fiscal, and labour market indicators for Western Europe	855
Table A.2	Current pension system in the United Kingdom	856
Table A.3	Current pension system in Greece	860
Table A.4	Current pension system in France	863
Table A.5	Current pension system in Switzerland	866
Table A.6	Current pension system in Finland	869
Table A.7	Current pension system in Belgium	874
Table A.8	Current pension system in Sweden	876
Table A.9	Current pension system in Italy	879
Table A.10	Current pension system in Denmark	882
Table A.11	Current pension system in Spain	885
Table A.12	Current pension system in Austria	887
Table A.13	Current pension system in Portugal	889
Table A.14	Current pension system in Germany	891
Table A.15	Current pension system in the Netherlands	893
Table A.16	Current pension system in Ireland	896
Table A.17	Current pension system in Luxembourg	899

List of Contributors

Karen Anderson is Associate Professor in the Department of Political Science at Nijmegen University. She received her Ph.D. in political science from the University of Washington. Her research focuses on the comparative political economy of the welfare state, particularly the role of unions and social democratic parties in welfare state restructuring processes. Her work has appeared in *Comparative Political Studies, Zeitschrift für Sozialreform, Canadian Journal of Sociology*, and the *Journal of Public Policy*. She is currently completing a book about the restructuring of the Swedish welfare state during the 1990s.

Maria Asensio is a researcher at the Research and Development Department of the Portuguese Instituto Nacional de Administração (since 1997) and Professor in the Department of Public Administration at the Faculty of Law in the University of Coimbra (Portugal, since 2001). She holds a BA in Sociology from the Universidad Complutense de Madrid and a doctorate in Political Science from the Universidad Autónoma de Madrid. She obtained a Master's degree in the Center for Advanced Study in the Social Sciences of the Instituto Juan March de Estudios e Investigaciones in Madrid and she is a Doctorate Member at the same Institute. She wrote her doctoral thesis under the supervision of Professor Vincent Wright and Professor Andrew Richards. Her current work focuses on policy change and institutional reform in the public sector and on the intra-organizational forces that promote different patterns of interest groups-state relations.

Giuliano Bonoli is Professor in the Swiss Graduate School of Public Administration (IDHEAP) in Lausanne. He received his Ph.D. at the University of Kent at Canterbury for a study on pension reform in Europe. He has been involved in several international research projects on the process of welfare state transformation, in particular on pension reform. He has published extensively on these issues, including "Social policy through labour markets. Understanding national differences in the provision of economic security to wage-earners", *Comparative Political Studies*, vol. 36, no. 9, Nov. 2003; Two Worlds of Pension Reform in Western Europe," *Comparative Politics*, vol. 35, no. 4, July 2003; and *The Politics of Pension Reform. Institutions and Policy Change in Western Europe*, Cambridge University Press, 2000.

Elisa Chuliá is Professor of Political Science in the Department of Political and Administrative Science at the Universidad Nacional de Educación a Distancia in Madrid. She received her MA in Communications at the Johannes Gutenberg University of Mainz and in 1997 completed her doctorate at the Center for Advanced Studies in the Social Sciences of the Instituto Juan March, and Complutense University, Madrid. She is author of the book *El poder y la palabra* ("The Power and the Word", Biblioteca Nueva/UNED, 2001) on press policy during the Francoist dictatorship; and co-author, with Víctor Pérez Díaz and other Spanish social scientists, of several books on pensions, family policy and immigration in Spain. Her current work focuses on the politics of pension reform in the Iberian Peninsula.

Eugénia da Conceição-Heldt is Assistant Professor in the Department of Social Sciences at the Humboldt University of Berlin. Her publications include *The Common Fisheries Policy in the European Union: A Study in Integrative and Distributive Bargaining* and *Decentralisation Tendencies in Western European Countries: A Comparative Analysis of the Territorial Reforms in Belgium, Italy, and Spain.* She has received a fellowship from the German *Studientstiftung des deutschen Volkes* and was awarded with the "Europe Prize." Her current work focuses on negotiation analysis, the impact of interest groups on policy outcomes, decision-making in the European Union, and comparative analysis of political institutions.

Maurizio Ferrera is Professor of Comparative Public Policy, Department of Welfare and Labour Studies, University of Milan; Director of "URGE," Research Unit on European Governance, Collegio Carlo Alberto, Moncalieri, Turin; Director of "Poleis," Centre for Comparative Political Research, Bocconi University, Milan. He did his graduate work in Political and Social Sciences at the European University Institute–EUI, Florence. He was appointed Full Professor at the University of Pavia; Co-director (with M. Rhodes) of the European Forum on "Recasting the European Welfare State", Robert Schuman Center, EUI; and Visiting Professor in several European and US universities. His latest books are: *The Boundaries of Welfare. European Integration and the new Spatial Politics of Social Protection*, Oxford University Press, 2005; *Welfare State Reform in Southern Europe*, Routledge, 2005; and *Rescued by Europe? Italy's social policy reforms from Maastricht to Berlusconi* (with E. Gualmini), Amsterdam University Press, 2004. He has authored various articles on comparative welfare states, the South European model of social protection, and the process of European integration in the field of social policy. In addition to pension politics, his current work focuses on the territorial restructuring of Europe's socio-political space; and challenges to, and prospects for, the welfare state in Italy, Spain, Portugal and Greece.

Christoffer Green-Pedersen is a research professor of public policy at the Department of Political Science, University of Aarhus Denmark, where he also earned his Ph.D. He is the author of *The Politics of Justification. Party Competition and Welfare-State Retrenchment in Denmark and the Netherlands from 1982 to 1998* (Amsterdam University Press, 2002) as well as several articles on welfare state reforms, social democracy, party competition and pension politics. He is currently working on a research project on agenda setting and policy dynamics in comparative perspective.

Ellen M. Immergut is Professor of Comparative Politics at Humboldt University Berlin, in the Institute for Social Sciences (*Institut für Sozialwissenschaften*). She did her graduate work in Sociology at Harvard University, was appointed as Assistant and Ford Career Development Associate Professor in the Department of Political Science at the Massachusetts Institute of Technology, Visiting Professor at the Instituto Juan March in Madrid, and Professor of Political Theory at the University of Konstanz. She is author of the book *Health Politics* (Cambridge University Press, 1992), as well as various articles on the new institutionalism, institutional design and health policy. In addition to pension politics, her current work focuses on the crisis of governance models in negotiated economics and the politics of constitutional reform.

Matteo Jessoula is a researcher in the Department of Social and Political Studies at the University of Milan. He received his Ph.D. in Political Science from the University of Pavia with a dissertation entitled, "The development of supplementary pensions in the reconfiguration of the Italian pension system." His recent publications include, "Reconfiguring Italian pensions: from policy stalemate to comprehensive reforms" (with M. Ferrera) in Bonoli and Shinkawa (eds.), "Ageing and Pension Reform Around the World: Evidence from Eleven Countries." His current research interests are comparative pension politics, comparative social policy and, multi-level governance of social policies.

Sven Jochem is Lecturer in comparative politics and political theory at the Department of Politics and Management at the University of Konstanz and the Department of Political Science at the University of Berne. He did his graduate work at Heidelberg and is author of the book *Skandinavische Wege in die Arbeitslosigkeit* and co-editor of the book *Konzertierung, Verhandlungsdemokratie und Reformpolitik im Wohlfahrtsstaat*. In addition to German pension politics, his current work focuses on the politics of welfare state reforms in comparative perspective.

Olli Kangas is currently Research Professor at the Danish National Institute for Social Research in Copenhagen. He defended his Ph.D. at the University of Helsinki, was nominated Visiting Research Fellow at the Swedish Institute for Social Research in Stockholm and appointed Professor of Social Policy, University of Turku. He has been visiting professor at the University of Stockholm, the Social Policy Research Centre in Sydney, the Center for Social Policy in Bremen and Eovtos Loránd University in Budapest. He is author of *The Politics of Social Rights* and various books in Finnish. His main research interest is the comparative study of causes and consequences of social institutions. He recently published an edited book (with Joakim Palme) on social policy and economic development in the Nordic countries (Palgrave/Macmillan 2005) and he is currently completing a book on social policy, labour markets and poverty dynamics in the EU countries.

Sanneke Kuipers is postdoctoral researcher in the Department of Public Administration at Leiden University. Her research interests include policy reform, policy evaluation, and the institutionalization of public organizations. She wrote her doctoral dissertation on Belgian and Dutch social policy reform. She recently published an edited book on institutional crisis (with Arjen Boin and Marc Otten, 2000), and co-authored articles on the politicization of policy failures in *Government and Opposition* (with Annika Brändström, 2003), on EU decision-making (with Torsten Selck, forthcoming, *Journal of European Public Policy*), and a chapter on the politics of policy evaluation in the *Oxford Handbook of Public Policy* (with Mark Bovens and Paul 't Hart, 2006).

Michael Moran is Professor of Government at the University of Manchester, UK. He has been a visiting fellow at the University of Konstanz, the European University Institute, Florence, and the Australian National University. His publications include *The Politics of the Financial Services Revolution* (1991), *Governing the Health Care State* (1999) and *The British Regulatory State: high modernism and hyper-innovation* (2003). He teaches in the fields of British politics and comparative public policy.

Martin Schludi is Publications Manager at the Institute for Employment Research (IAB) in Nuremberg. He studied "Politics and Management" (*Verwaltungswissenschaft*) at Konstanz University and Gothenburg University with a focus on social policy. He was research associate at the Max Planck Institute for the Study of Societies in Cologne where he contributed to an international conference project about the adjustment of national employment and social policy systems to economic internationalization. His work in this project resulted in several articles co-authored with Anton Hemerijck such as "Sequences of Policy Failures and Effective Policy Responses" (Oxford University Press, 2000). He earned his doctorate at Humboldt University in Berlin and worked as visiting researcher at the Amsterdam Institute for Advanced Labor Studies at Amsterdam University. He is author of the book "The reform of Bismarckian Pension Systems. A Comparison of Pension Politics in Austria, France, Germany, Italy and Sweden," (Amsterdam: Amsterdam University Press, 2005).

Isabelle Schulze was a researcher at the Mannheimer Zentrum für Europäische Sozialforschung (MZES) at the University of Mannheim and is now Coordinator of the Zukunftskolleg for Younger Scholars at the University of Konstanz. Schulze's dissertation (Humboldt University Berlin) considers the role of electoral threat in pension politics; her MA thesis (University of Konstanz) analyzed the impact of farmers' interests in agricultural politics in Britain and Germany. She was awarded a dissertation fellowship from the Forschungsnetzwerk Alterssicherung of the Federation of German Pension Insurance Institutes (Verband Deutscher Rentenversicherungsträger; now Deutsche Rentenversicherung Bund).

Polyxeni Triantafillou received her Ph.D. from the Department of Political and Social Sciences of the European University Institute in Florence, and is now a financial analyst. She has worked for the European Commission and has received a scholarship from the Greek Scholarship Foundation (IKY). She is the author of articles on welfare reform and corporatism in Greece. Her research focuses on the politics of welfare state reform (in Greece and in Europe) and the evaluation of policy outcomes. Other research interests include corporatist theory and post-1974 politics in Greece.

CHAPTER 1

EDITORS' INTRODUCTION: THE DYNAMICS OF PENSION POLITICS

ELLEN M. IMMERGUT
KAREN M. ANDERSON

For more than two decades, governments in the advanced industrial states have been grappling with pension reform. The pressures for reform are well-known: increasing life expectancy, falling birthrates, and decreasing employment and economic growth. These developments constrain the financing of public pension systems because fewer contributors finance growing numbers of pensioners. The pressures on public pension systems are not only financial, however. Indeed, political actors have begun to question the fundamental normative and political assumptions underlying public pension arrangements. This is surprising, given that public pension schemes, from their inception in the late nineteenth and early twentieth centuries, to their full development in the post-World War II era, served both as a solution to old-age poverty and to the political problems associated with class and other forms of social inequality. As T. H. Marshall wrote in an essay that can be said to embody the philosophy of the post-war settlement, the social rights and the social citizenship that the welfare state made possible constituted the culmination of a centuries-old process of expansion of rights and democratization (Marshall 1963).

It is worth considering the political origins of the welfare state when analyzing the recent period of retrenchment and restructuring in public pension provision. Even in the United States, not known for the generosity of its welfare state, Franklin Delano Roosevelt declared "Freedom from Want" to be one of the "Four Freedoms" to be guaranteed to all citizens (Brody 1975: 301). In France, Sweden, Switzerland and even in many of the countries defeated in World War II such as Germany, the commitment to social equality and social policy was discussed, enacted and implemented after the war. And in the non-democratic nations of Western Europe, authoritarian regimes significantly expanded social rights.[1]

As the vast literature on the comparative history of the welfare state demonstrates, there were historical precedents for these post-war social programs, as well as great variation in the politics of the post-war welfare state. Nevertheless—and in contrast to other areas of the welfare state, such as health care, unemployment, education and family policy—old-age security emerged as a universal social right in Western Europe, despite differences in design and coverage, and the extent to which the public sector played a dominant role in the "public–private mix." Moreover, this political commitment to provide for citizens' economic security in old-age embodied some common assumptions that cut across national and partisan lines, and that differed from those of previous decades. First, the economic turmoil of the decades preceding World War II had shown both capital and equities to be unreliable investments. Second, as the Keynesian model spread, pension benefits were viewed as a useful tool of demand stimulus, whereas high levels of pension savings were seen as a threat. Third, the perception of demographic developments had shifted from concern with population decline in the 1930s to appreciation of a baby boom by the end of the 1940s. Consequently, most public pension programs were based on pay-as-you-go (PAYG) financing: current contributors would finance the pensions for current retirees. Furthermore, as the post-war era developed into one of unprecedented economic growth, many countries expanded their public programs to provide more generous income replacement in old age. In other countries, similar expansion took place through government mandating or collective bargaining. Thus, in an era of economic and population growth, political parties throughout Western Europe—and even in the United States—developed a multi-partisan political commitment to old-age security as a basic social right.

Today, in an age of globalization and European integration, these commitments and assumptions stand on shakier ground.[2] Porous borders have undermined the conditions for both state sovereignty and Keynesian policies—at least at the national level. At the same time, the changed age distribution has called the "generational contract" into question, as future pensioners are often both numerous and wealthy in comparison to the younger cohorts that finance their retirement.[3] As a result, one of the mainstays of the post-war welfare state—public pension programs—has become the object of political contestation and institutional re-negotiation.

Our focus in this book is on the *politics* of these contemporary pension reforms. We find it helpful to draw on Lowi's (1964) distinction between "regulatory," "distributive," and "redistributive" types of policy. Each of these policy types generates a distinct pattern of political conflict and mobilization, and it is precisely these distinct patterns in the realm of pensions that are the focus of this book. Public pension policies are a strong case of "redistributive policies." They involve broad swathes of voters in questions of generational fairness and both class and gender equality. Consequently, it is not a simple matter to adapt public pension programs to changed economic, demographic and social circumstances. We ask whether there are important differences in how governments across Western Europe respond to similar reform pressures. We examine and evaluate competing explanations for differences in the capacity of national governments to reform their public pension arrangements. In particular we investigate whether the type of government itself—that is, its constitution and political configuration—makes a difference for a nation's capacity for pension reform. Are different structures of government or constellations of partisan forces particularly conducive to enacting and implementing policy change? Are others beset by policy blockages and veto points? We consider also the reactions of voters and interest-groups to plans for pension reform: is it true that voters will punish politicians who propose cuts? If so, why do politicians who want to be re-elected propose reforms? Similarly, what have been the reactions—or proposals—regarding pension reforms coming from unions, employers and business groups? What about banks, insurance companies and other financial interests? Finally, we consider the role of ideas and policy discourses—could this variable help to explain divergent reactions to the public pension problem? In sum, each of the chapters in this book uses "structured, focused comparison" to investigate the politics of pension reform (George and Bennett 2005).

The chapters that follow are the outcome of a collaborative research project funded by the German Research Foundation (*Deutsche Forschungsgemeinschaft*). This external funding allowed us to collect similar information about a relatively large number of countries (all 15 "old" EU members, plus Switzerland). The authors of the country chapters present detailed information about the constitutions and political institutions, party and electoral systems as well as voting results in the country at hand—the *political-institutional* framework for pension politics. They also provide an overview of the current pension system and its history—the *policy* framework for pension politics. But the core of each chapter is concerned with the *politics* of reform: what was proposed and why? How did various political actors respond? And how we can explain these policy outcomes?

Each chapter author provides an answer to these questions for his or her particular case but, here, we as editors would like to present an overview of our empirical findings and their theoretical relevance. As we will elaborate, our main argument is that theories of political institutions fail to explain variations in the capacity of European governments to reform their public pension programs, because they neglect the variable of political competition. By "political competition," we mean the strategy and intensity with which politicians compete for votes. Depending upon the formal electoral system, but also on the distribution of voter preferences, and the party system, the total pattern and intensity of political competition varies across political systems and, indeed, within a given political system, even over time. Whether politicians compete directly with one another to win the allegiance of the same voters, the frequency and closeness of elections, the probability of a change in government, and the likelihood that concentrated pockets of voters can unseat particular politicians, all factor in to the character of "political competition" in a given polity. Consequently, institutionalist theory must be radically reconsidered and revised. To make our case, we discuss, first, theories about the impact of political institutions on public policies in general, and, next, theories about pension politics in particular. We describe in some detail the various methods of measuring political institutions, since this is relevant for the argument of the *Handbook*, and the analyses in the chapters that follow. The subsequent sections outline major differences in existing pensions systems and the array of proposed policy options. The chapter closes with a survey of pension politics and pension policy outcomes in Western Europe.

I THE POLITICAL—INSTITUTIONAL FRAMEWORK FOR PENSION POLITICS

The impact of political institutions on public policies

Debates about the impact of political institutions on public policies are the continuation of a centuries-old debate in normative political philosophy. Classical thinkers, such as Hobbes and Rousseau argued that the functions of the state could be fulfilled only if executive power were concentrated. In contrast, liberals such as Locke and Montesquieu argued that executive power should be divided, and hence, controlled. These arguments are the basis for contemporary scholarship about which system of government results in the "best" governance and political stability. Three typologies in particular have substantially influenced the direction of scholarship about the impact of political institutions on public policy: Lijphart's distinction between "majoritarian" and "consensus" democracies; Powell's "visions of democracy" and Persson and Tabellini's classification scheme based on "executive" and "parliamentary" types.

In a series of pioneering works, Arend Lijphart (1984, 1999) divided democracies into two groups: majoritarian and consensus democracies. These systems differ in the extent to which executive power is concentrated or dispersed. In a majoritarian system, political power is concentrated in the executive, and indeed, government control tends to be concentrated in the hands of one party. The United Kingdom is the prime example of the majoritarian form of government, which, consequently, is often referred to as the "Westminster" system of government. At the other extreme, we find the consensus democracies. Here, executive power is divided by the separation of executive, legislative and judicial power; bicameralism; federalism;

and multi-party government. Switzerland and Belgium are important examples. Historically, the framers of the constitutions in these countries designed extensive "checks-and-balances" to respond to societies that were extremely divided—for example along religious or language cleavages. Such institutions allowed minorities to veto policies which they opposed, a pre-requisite for their agreement to join the polity. Lijphart argues that these divided societies with their multiple veto points have nevertheless found ways to achieve consensus on policies, and thus can be termed the consensus democracies. In such systems, myriad checks-and-balances mean that political decisions are possible only if a wide variety of political actors can agree on them; decades of such agreements have produced a political culture of compromise and accommodation.

The political institutions that result in majoritarian versus consensus democracy are not just about different ways of doing the same thing. Rather, the most radical part of Lijphart's argument is that these different political forms produce policies with different substantive contents. Countries classified as consensus democracies have a better record in managing inflation, protecting the environment, more generous social and foreign aid policies, lower rates of incarceration, and tend to reject the death penalty. Thus, "consensus democracy tends to be the 'kinder, gentler' form of democracy," (Lijphart 1999: 275).

This basic contrast between concentrated versus dispersed executive power is also at the heart of G. Bingham Powell's (2000) important work on competing "visions of democracy." The majoritarian vision calls for electoral rules that produce clear majorities and legislative procedures that allow this majority to enact legislation with minimal institutional interference. The majoritarian blueprint aims to achieve decisive government action and clear political accountability. By contrast, the proportional vision values political inclusiveness more highly than decisiveness and accountability. From this viewpoint, elections serve the purpose of choosing delegates who will then form governments and draft policies. Its blueprint for political institutions includes proportional representation for the electoral system, and many sorts of power-sharing arrangements, such as bicameralism and representation of the parliamentary opposition in legislative committees. Majoritarian governments should be more effective in introducing reform; but proportional governments better reflect the wishes of voters.

Persson and Tabellini (2002; see also Persson et al. 2000) propose yet a third typology, reducing relevant institutional features to just two variables: the electoral system (single member districts versus all forms of proportional representation); and the executive regime (presidential versus parliamentary). They argue that these institutions provide very different incentives to politicians, and hence result in very different public policies. In a single-member district electoral system, politicians belonging to a given political party need to maximize the number of districts won by their party in order to take control of the government. This is achieved most efficiently by offering constituents targeted benefits, such as pork barrel projects, agricultural subsidies or protective tariffs—the type of policy that Lowi (1964) termed "distributive." In a proportional electoral system, on the other hand, politicians must maximize votes rather than districts, so they pursue "redistributive" policies such as public pensions and other social policies that appeal to broad strata of voters, rather than merely to pockets of concentrated voters in particular electoral districts. Redistributive policies cost more, however, so government spending should be higher in proportional systems. Furthermore, government spending must be paid for by taxes, and this is where presidentialism versus parliamentarism becomes relevant. Presidents are directly elected, so voters will hold them more accountable for tax increases than they do parliaments. (Indeed, the direct election of representatives in a single-member district system also increases accountability, and hence the "tax sensitivity" of elected officials.) Consequently, government spending should be (*ceteris paribus*) lower in presidential as compared to parliamentary regimes, and in single-member districts than in proportional representation electoral systems.

These path-breaking typologies are the starting point for any analysis of the impact of political institutions on government policies. Yet, for all their merits, they suffer from several common shortcomings. First, any given political system is a composite of many different institutional components. To some extent, these institutional features may cluster together, because constitutional architects tend to be influenced by historical events and political constellations that increase the appeal of a particular institutional design and vision of democracy. Nevertheless, political conflicts and political bargains about institutions, as well as the continuous amendment of political systems over time, mean that constitutional structures are almost never the products of a fully coherent and consistent conscious design. Thus efforts to classify political systems are plagued by the presence of institutional features that do not neatly fit the typologies. Indeed, most typologies fit one or two cases well, but cannot fully accommodate the many cases that fit only awkwardly.

Second, the ways in which political institutions work in practice depend upon the distribution of political preferences and political majorities. Whether or not a presidential system results in "divided government," for example, is contingent on whether the President belongs to the same party as his/her legislature. Similarly, the workings of bicameral parliaments depend upon the partisan leanings of the representatives in the two chambers. Consequently, a country may pass through phases of very different "political configuration" even though its political system has not undergone constitutional revision.

Third, it is not clear how these typologies can explain the problem we investigate in this book. Pension reform entails a change in policy. Unless the political system has changed, why would an institutional set-up that promotes expansive government and social programs result in social policy cutbacks? Furthermore, in turning from the general problem of the impact of political institutions on public policy to the specific problem of pension reform politics in Western Europe, it is clear that the majority of Western European political systems are "consensus democracies" informed by a "proportional vision." Yet, there is considerable variation in pension reform outcomes within Western Europe (as we shall discuss). The classification of political systems into ideal types does not appear sufficient for explaining the dynamics of pension policy change.

Veto points and veto players

Veto points and veto players theory attempts to remedy these shortcomings by conceptualizing political systems as integrated wholes and leaving more scope for the role of political preferences. Both perspectives are particularly relevant for understanding the dynamics of pension reform because they emphasize the ways in which political institutions obstruct policy-making. Veto point theory views the legislative process as a chain of political decisions taken in a series of political arenas (Immergut 1990; 1992a; 1992b). Formal constitutional rules and de facto electoral results shape the likelihood that a legislative proposal will be vetoed during the decision-making process. In a parliamentary system, the probability of legislative veto hinges on whether agreement by the legislature is constitutionally necessary for passage (it is, unless the executive enjoys special powers, such as emergency powers or the right to legislate by decree), and on whether the legislative majority supports the executive (as in the case of majority government). Similarly, the probability that proposed legislation will be vetoed by Presidents, second chambers, referenda or constitutional courts depends upon the partisan composition of these potential "veto points." The likelihood of veto is significant for two reasons. First, it indicates how difficult it is to pass legislation—and hence to introduce policy change. Second, the more difficult it is to change existing policy, the more opportunities there are for interest groups opposed to particular legislation to demand concessions. This link between veto points and interest group power is thus dependent upon the group's willingness to block the proposed policy as well as on its access to the decision-makers at different decision points. Veto point theory provides insight into the dynamics of policy change and the sources of bargaining power among affected groups, but it does not reveal much about how legislative proposals reach the political agenda or about government preferences. The theory simply estimates the probability of veto once legislation has been proposed, as well as the potential for interest group influence.

As with the veto point theory, the veto players approach emphasizes the ways in which political decision-making institutions structure attempts to change the legislative status quo. Tsebelis (1995; 1999; 2002) defines a "veto player" as institutional or partisan political actors whose agreement is necessary for the passage of legislation. "Institutional veto players" include actors whose power flows from constitutional rules, such as Presidents, second chambers, and constitutional courts. These "institutional veto players" are roughly equivalent to "veto points," and, like the veto point approach, Tsebelis considers partisan majorities in deciding whether or not institutional veto players are politically significant. The German second chamber (*Bundesrat*), for example, would count as an institutional veto player only when its majority differs from that of the lower house or *Bundestag*, which invests the government. "Partisan veto players" are the parties that comprise the government. The greater the number of partisan and institutional veto players, the greater the barriers to new legislation, and hence to policy change.

A second step in veto players theory rests on policy preferences. The greater the distance between the policy preferences of the veto players, the more difficult it is to change the status quo. Policy preferences can be measured by content analyses of party programs (party manifestos), expert surveys about the ideological positions of the political parties, or following the legislative process regarding a particular policy issue ("process tracing," Hall 2003; George and Bennett 2005), as we do in this *Handbook*. The "coherence" of each veto player's set of preferences also influences the likelihood of agreement. To the extent that the members of a parliamentary group prefer a narrow range of policy options, compromise with other political parties will be more difficult. Tsebelis hypothesizes that the probability that legislation will be adopted is inversely related to the number of veto players, their maximal policy distance, and their policy cohesion.

The veto points and veto players perspectives are useful starting points for understanding the dynamics of pension reform because both predict the potential sources of resistance to reform proposals in any given political system. Indeed, pension reform politics provides a good test for the explanatory power of this perspective, because pension reform has been a recurring item on the political agenda across West Europe, not necessarily because of partisan pressures, but because of demographic and financial constraints. Thus pension politics can serve as a "natural experiment" for theories about the relationship between government structure and government action. We emphasize here that successful reform is not merely a matter of the formal political institutional constraints, but is the result of the interplay between political institutions and electoral majorities. This requires an examination of the specific political configurations, and this approach should be considered "*political*–institutional" rather then merely "institutional."[4]

As the following chapters demonstrate, the veto points and veto players perspective provides a simplified approach to conceptualizing a wealth of detail about how political institutions shape the policy process. However, the chapters also show that the analysis of pension politics raises some troubling issues for veto points/veto players theory. Simply put, the institutional incentives for and constraints on government activity are inadequately theorized by the political-institutional approach. Indeed, previous work on pension politics and the politics of welfare state retrenchment has put many of these issues on the research agenda, as we discuss in the next sections of this Introduction.

Political institutions and the welfare state

There is by now a large literature illuminating how political decision-making institutions influence pension reform processes and other kinds of welfare state restructuring. Huber, Ragin and Stephens (1993) were among the first to quantitatively analyze the impact of "constitutional structures" (such as federalism, bicameralism, direct democracy and single-member electoral districts) on both the growth and development of welfare state expenditures and pension expenditures.

They concluded that institutional barriers slowed the growth of the welfare state in previous periods, but have little effect on current cutbacks. M. G. Schmidt (2001; see also 2002) also found a statistical relationship between political partisanship and welfare state expansion and retrenchment but argues that partisanship interacts with constitutional structures and institutional veto points and veto players—including the existence of central banks and membership in the EU.[5] By contrast, Swank (2001) finds that centralized governments (and proportional representation systems) are associated with greater resistance to welfare state contraction. Kittel and Obinger (2003) try to make sense of these seemingly-contradictory findings by combining various sources of data into a meta-quantitative analysis of the determinants of social expenditures. They conclude that Flora's "growth to limits" thesis best explains the social policy developments of the 1990s: countries that already had very generous welfare states—such as Sweden, Denmark and New Zealand—stopped expanding, whereas less generous welfare states (the US, Switzerland, and Japan) had more scope for topping up their social policy programs. Taken together, these studies argue that politics and political institutions may not matter much for the current period of welfare state retrenchment—or that they may matter in ways that quantitative analysis is not equipped to uncover.

Part of the problem here has to do with the measures of politics and policies used in quantitative studies. As many scholars point out (Esping-Andersen 1990; Korpi and Palme 2003; Myles 1989; Palme 1990), social expenditures are not the best way to measure political reactions to social problems. More retirement and more unemployment will increase social expenditures, but this does not necessarily indicate a fair, just or effective welfare state. Moreover, effective governance may mean cutting welfare benefits, if the resources required to pay for public programs are contracting. It may also be equally important to adapt welfare state institutions to new social risks rather than simply to defend the status quo (Bonoli 2004; Esping-Andersen et al. 2002; Levy 1999; Taylor-Gooby 2005; Armingeon and Bonoli 2006). Thus, to measure the impact of politics on welfare state reform, we need good measures of the extent of social protection and how governments prioritize among different social risks (Kitschelt 2001; Lynch 2001; 2006).

The most recent wave of institutional research goes beyond the earlier emphasis on expenditure by developing more reliable measures of pension policy change. Brooks (2002) develops a measure of pension privatization by simulating the impact of recent reforms on the average worker's pension at system maturity. Bridgen and Meyer (2005) also use a simulation model to track changes in the structure of occupational pension entitlement in the UK, drawing on economic sociology to explain these shifts. Simulation models for measuring welfare state change constitute the cutting-edge of research on policy outcomes.

The historical institutionalist paradigm has inspired a large number of studies that investigate the effects of institutions on pension policy-making. Kent Weaver's (1998; Weaver and Rockman 1993) work is especially important here, because it was among the first to investigate systematically the relationship between political-institutional structure and policy change. Others have drawn on these basic insights to explain reform dynamics in a variety of geographical settings. For example, Kay (1999) finds that Latin American governments that could introduce reforms by decree (Chile and Argentina) radically changed their pension systems, whereas in Brazil precarious parliamentary majorities blocked reform. Bonoli (2000; 2001), too, finds that the presence or absence of veto points was critical for the passage of reforms in Britain, France and Switzerland. On the basis of a comprehensive study of social and economic policy reforms across the advanced industrial nations, Scharpf (2000) also concludes that institutional veto points and veto players hindered successful welfare state adjustment to the international economy.

Thus, studies focusing directly on the politics of reform find that political institutional configurations make a difference for the scope and success of governmental action. At the same time, however, all of these studies point to weaknesses in the political-institutional approach and the importance of additional variables for explaining how welfare state reform reaches the political agenda. Bonoli, for example, shows that the effects of institutions are not uni-directional. While the ability of the executive government to push through reforms was important in predicting the passage of reforms, reforms that passed through a more consensual and conciliatory process (made necessary by the existence of veto points) were ultimately more successful. Moreover, he points to competitive pressures engendered by different sorts of electoral systems, as well as the timing of the electoral cycle, in explaining the motivations of governments in proposing pension reforms. Levy (2005), too, emphasizes the factor of political competition in explaining why French welfare state retrenchment has not gone very far despite the absence of veto points. Other studies point to the impact of the party system on the dynamics of electoral competition and hence, the likelihood of welfare state reform. Green-Pedersen (2001) argues that centrist pivot-parties that can choose to cooperate with either left or right parties can better withstand electoral resistance to social welfare cutbacks than parties competing across a left–right divide in a two bloc system. Kitschelt (2001) argues that welfare state retrenchment is impeded by party systems cross-cut by a confessional or ethnic dimension, and facilitated by the presence of strong liberal or social democratic parties. In sum, there is substantial evidence that political institutions in combination with governing majorities and political competition affect the politics of policy-making, and hence policy outcomes. Yet, there is no consensus in the literature about the exact ingredients necessary for social policy reform.

The new politics of the welfare state

The work of Paul Pierson changed academic debates about the welfare state by claiming that the politics of welfare state retrenchment is fundamentally different from the politics of welfare state formation and expansion. Whereas the introduction of new social rights allowed politicians to compete for votes by taking credit for these new programs, social policy cutbacks are unpopular. For example, even when politicians such as Reagan and Thatcher came to power by promising to roll back the welfare state, their retrenchment efforts met with much political resistance. Thus, the retrenchment era is one of a "new politics" of the welfare state, where partisan differences matter less than voter loyalty to the public programs from which they benefit (Pierson 1994; 1996; 2001).

The new politics perspective has been very important in placing voters and electoral politics more centrally in the analysis of welfare state politics. Yet, there has been some confusion about which aspects of the new politics approach are most important and what exactly this approach predicts in terms of outcomes.

One important aspect of the new politics perspective is the "blame avoidance" thesis first proposed by Weaver: given public resistance to cuts in popular spending programs, politicians will attempt to avoid blame by making cuts less transparent (Weaver 1986, Pierson and Weaver 1993). This can be achieved by hiding cuts in obscure changes in benefit formulas or benefit taxation ("obfuscation") or even by long transition periods and grandfather clauses that delay cuts into the future, when voters will hopefully have forgotten which politicians were responsible for policy change. A second strategy of blame avoidance might be better termed "blame *sharing*." If government cooperates with opposition in drafting retrenchment legislation, it is more difficult for voters to punish a particular party since they all share the blame. A similar strategy of sharing or "blame *buffering*" is to enlist the support of independent experts or interest groups with credibility as defenders of the welfare state (such as unions or pensioners' organizations). Blame on politicians will be "buffered," if these neutral arbiters or staunch supporters agree that reform is necessary to sustain the long-term viability of these public programs (see Schludi 2005).

The new politics approach emphasizes the political effects of *policy legacies*. As Esping-Andersen (1990) and others have also argued, social policies themselves help to shape political processes by providing normative and material resources to various social strata and groups. More broadly, the organization of the welfare state creates lasting patterns of political solidarity and political mobilization that shape definitions of what is just, how groups define their interests, and the political coalitions that are likely to emerge (Pierson 1993; Skocpol 1985). One type of policy legacy that is particularly important in pension policy is "lock-in" effects. Pension arrangements necessarily involve long-term planning, and both policy-makers and politicians are loath to interfere in this process. Markets, too, respond to public policies; the existence of an extensive public pension system will crowd out employee benefit plans and private pension insurance. Conversely, if public pension provision is low, collective bargaining and private plans will fill the gap, as we discuss later. Politically, the dynamics of pension reform should look different if all citizens stand united behind a single universal plan, or if pensioner interests are divided by a myriad of different schemes (Esping-Andersen and Korpi 1984; Klass 1985; Rothstein 1998). Thus, the new politics take on policy legacies is that the institutionalization of social programs means that many voters count on existing welfare state provisions and will prefer the status quo to retrenchment, and that the pattern of support should vary according to program structure.

Finally, several scholars interpret the new politics approach to mean that class politics and organizations representing the working class have declined in importance. Efforts to expand the welfare state beyond a narrow working-class base as part of "catch-all" political strategies result in broad and general support for social programs. Hence, unions and social democratic parties (so central to the "working-class power" view) are not essential for the defense of the welfare state in the face of retrenchment pressures (see criticism by Korpi and Palme 2003). Indeed, taken together, the reliance on administrative decisions to hide welfare state retrenchment, the importance of policy legacies, and the decline in class conflict link the new politics approach to quantitative studies that argue that there has been a decline in the importance of politics for the welfare state.

These various strands of argument make it a bit difficult to know exactly what the new politics approach predicts in terms of welfare state cutbacks and how to measure welfare state retrenchment (Alber 1996). Initially, the focus appeared to be one of policy stability. This broadly fit the pattern of pension policy reform in the 1980s, when few reforms took place. However, the pattern of the 1990s was different, with high levels of reform and retrenchment activity in many social welfare areas, including pensions. Moreover, the absence of legislative change does not necessarily indicate policy stability. If programs are not adapted to meet changing needs, the social safety net becomes frayed (Clayton and Pontusson 1998). This is especially true for pensions, because benefits lose real value if they are not indexed to inflation or wages. Furthermore, the tendency of politicians and program administrators to avoid blame or the pitfalls of the legislative process may lead to policy "drift"—changes in policy implementation that have repercussions for the distribution of social risks, and the quality of social protection (Hacker 2002; 2005).

Another puzzle for the new politics thesis is the number of reforms that have been introduced even at the cost of voter punishment at the next elections (Visser and Hemerijck 1997)—why has blame avoidance been inoperative? Moreover, since estimates of both the threat of pension crisis and potential pension policy solutions are based on models that forecast future benefits and contributions in relationship to hypothetical assumptions about demographic and labor market developments (more on this below), lack of transparency may simply be in the nature of pension politics rather than the result of a deliberate strategy of obfuscation.

The new politics approach has set the agenda for the current generation of welfare state research. In light of our discussion of different types of political institutions, however, we want to emphasize here that the new politics approach does not generate consistent predictions about the relationship between forms of government and pension policy reform. As Pierson (1996) himself points out, majoritarian governments are more effective at passing legislation, yet are more exposed to blame than governments in consensus democracies, where power and accountability are shared. In short, we still do not have clear hypotheses about which type of government we should expect to respond more effectively to the pension crisis, and about how government legislative capacity is related to opportunities for blame avoidance. As we will show, the type of electoral system and the structure of political competition are critical for understanding both the willingness and effectiveness of governments in introducing pension reforms.

Bringing labor back in

A number of scholars trace differences in the willingness of key interest groups to accept reform to variations in policy feedback effects. This type of argument is an important amendment to the new politics approach because it highlights the conditions under which key stakeholders are willing to accept retrenchment. Labor unions are political actors for which such feedback effects are particularly relevant, and several recent studies both challenge the class neutrality of the new politics approach, at the same time that they support its basic premiss about the explanatory importance of policy legacies. Anderson (2001) compares the politics of welfare state retrenchment across different policy areas in Sweden in the 1990s—notably pensions and unemployment benefits—and argues that variation in the intensity of labor preferences concerning reform is an important variable for explaining differences in reform outcomes across policy sectors. Retrenchment in Sweden was possible only when important union groups supported reform, and this pattern of support depended on how highly unions valued core features of the programs targeted for retrenchment. Differences in preference intensity are linked to different feedback processes generated by different types of social policies. The key insight here is that different types of social policies provide different types of benefits and resources to unions as organizations. Pensions can be conceptualized as "deferred wages," which helps explain the sources of union pension policy preferences. Seen this way, unions may be willing to accept modest cuts in future pensions that reduce privileges to well-protected groups if these reductions enhance the financial sustainability of the pension system and its capacity to deliver on its deferred wage promise (see also Anderson and Lynch forthcoming; Anderson and Meyer 2003). Specific aspects of program design also provide organizational resources to unions, particularly arrangements that give unions an institutionalized role in administration. This explains the resistance of Swedish unions to retrenchment in union-administered unemployment insurance at the same time that they accepted cuts in future pensions. Similarly, in other nations, self-administration may be a source of jobs for union officials, as in France (Bonoli and Palier 1997; Béland 2001), or provide union leaders with a power base for political influence, as well as a means of administrative influence, as in Germany (Ebbinghaus and Hassel 2000; see also Brugiavini et al. 2001).

Finally, in line with the blame avoidance thesis, union cooperation and a conciliatory government stance towards unions may be a critical element in successful reforms. Italian policy-makers and politicians that cooperated with the unions in drafting reforms may have been more successful in bringing the legislative process to a successful close than those that pursued a combative course. More generally, Ferrera and Rhodes (2000) have pointed to the resurgence of "corporatism" in

Southern Europe, with intensified union–government–employer cooperation through "social pacts" (see also Regini 2000; Regini and Regalia 1997; Rhodes 2001; Visser and Hemerijck 1997).

The implication of these arguments about the centrality of labor for the politics of welfare state reform is clear. In the corporatist political economies of Western Europe, organized labor is still a major actor in the politics of welfare state reform, not least because of the effects of policy legacies. In many Western European countries, unions are still the main defenders of the pension policy status quo, even if they face competition from new interest groups like pensioners' organizations. Each of the chapters that follows asks how unions influence reform politics, and the picture that emerges is that outcomes can rarely be read off aggregate measures of "labor power." Instead, unions co-exist and compete with many other important affected interests in the pension political arena, and as the "new politics" approach suggests, union preferences and bargaining power are shaped by the feedback effects of existing pension arrangements.

Varieties of capitalism

Research on the role of unions and employer associations has been given a new twist by the "Varieties of Capitalism" (VoC) approach. The VoC perspective focuses on the sources of comparative advantage in different kinds of economies. (Berger and Dore 1996; Crouch and Streeck 1997; Hall and Soskice 2001) and has potentially much to say about the politics of pension reform. First, the VoC approach suggests that discussions about the objective need for cutting pension benefits requires more critical scrutiny. Most West European nations are characterized as "coordinated market economies." In contrast to "liberal market economies", such as Britain or the United States, these nations compete economically on the basis of high quality production not low wages. Consequently, social benefits (such as pensions) are part of the package of inducements that encourages workers to invest in skills, and employers to provide high-quality training, and thereby add value to the economy (Ebbinghaus and Manow 2001; Estévez-Abe et al. 2001; Estévez-Abe 2002). This means that in order to evaluate the need for reform, one must analyze the "embeddedness" of pension policies within economic and social institutions that include the financial and banking sectors, the industrial relations system, and the organization of employers and industries, including the mechanisms and politics of coordination and cooperation within and across these groups, corporate actors and sectors. Further, this very connectedness of social and pension policies with wage formation, capital provision and product markets—the "complementarities" as this approach calls this web of relationships—means that policy change may either be very difficult, as the particular changes to the pension system may not conform well to the overall logic of the political economy in a particular nation, or that even small changes may have quite large disruptive "spillover" effects (Streeck and Thelen 2005; Thelen 2003).

The VoC approach suggests a second important insight as well: the pension system is embedded in the banking system, and the organization of the pension system has repercussions for the scope for private investments and the market for private equities in a nation. Consequently, we should not be surprised that groups representing the financial sector as well as the insurance industry have been active in pension reform discussions (Bonoli and Shinkawa 2005). Indeed much of the debate about pensions is probably connected to a larger shift towards economic integration and financial deregulation. On the one hand, European pension policy-makers hope to solve their pension problems by taking advantage of the growth and potential investment returns in global financial markets. On the other hand, efforts to incorporate pension savings—both public and private—into financial markets may be a strategy to improve the internationally competitive position of European regional and national financial markets (Clark 2003; Clark and Whiteside 2003). In the language of the VoC approach, efforts to "privatize" or "marketize" European public pensions, may be part of an effort to move coordinated market economies closer to liberal market economies, as well as to reap the benefits of European economic integration by creating expanded market opportunities for European-wide investment markets.[6]

While a full evaluation of the economic motives and limits on pension reform is beyond the scope of our project, the "varieties of capitalism" and "economic geography" perspectives tell us that we must incorporate employer, industry and financial interests and organizations into our analysis, as well as sensitivity to historical and spatial variation. Here we feel it is important to emphasize that a focus on formal political institutions does not preclude a discussion of this type of interest group politics. Indeed, political institutions provide the "rules of the game" within which politicians, economic interest groups, and other actors attempt to influence policy outcomes. In other words, we view the role of economic interest groups as essential components of our analytical framework, even if the primary focus of that framework is political institutions and electoral competition.

Nevertheless, we conclude that while an analysis of the politics of pension reform does not preclude an appreciation of the economic interests at stake, the dynamics of pension politics in Europe cannot be reduced to a pure politics of economic interest, and interests cannot be simply read off an actor's location in the production structure. Political conflicts about pension policy reform involve a multitude of participants whose opportunities to dominate the political process depended upon political institutions and electoral pressures. We include many cases (such as Spain, Sweden, the UK, and even France) where governments passed reforms despite union opposition; we have others (such as Luxembourg, Belgium, and Switzerland) in which the demands of business, insurers and financial interests were ignored or overridden. Thus, pension policy outcomes do not result directly from economic preferences, interests or pressures—whether these take the form of formally organized interest groups, "fractions of capital," the "third face of power" or the like.[7]

Demographic and budgetary pressures

No discussion of pension politics would be complete without a discussion of the objective "problem pressure" driving pension reform. Population aging—tied to declining birth rates and longer life spans—means that costs of pension programs will increase, causing financial problems for pension schemes. These problems are particularly severe for certain types of pension programs, but none are exempt—as will be discussed in the following section on "contours of the pension problem and favored solutions." Similarly, changing rates of economic growth and comparative rates of return to different types of investments change the economic context for pension policy. Demographic and economic changes, in turn, have repercussions for the financial sustainability of pension schemes. For the West European nations under consideration here, European integration and the Maastricht criteria increase budgetary pressures by making even pre-existing deficits take on new political and economic relevance.[8]

Many economists and social scientists—including Gruber and Wise (1999b), Börsch-Supan and Miegel (2001), Disney and Johnson (2001), Feldstein and Siebert (2002), Rein and Schmähl (2004), and Clark, Munnell, and Orszag (2006), to name but just a few of many examples—have discussed the need for pension reform.[9] Similarly, many international organizations and national social security authorities, including the World Bank, the IMF, the OECD, MISSOC (Mutual Information System on Social Protection in the Member States of the European Union), the Social Security Administration of the United States and the German VDR (*Verband Deutscher Rentenversicherungsträger*)[10] have reported on the economic, demographic and budgetary problems facing contemporary pension systems. Indeed, Bonoli and Shinkawa (2005) argue that this objective problem pressure—together with the type of pension system, which shapes the political repercussions of these financial pressures—is the most important factor in explaining the type and amount of pension reform undertaken in a range of European, North American and Asian nations.

We do not deny the importance of these objective pressures.[11] Nevertheless, our evidence shows that problem pressure alone cannot explain the pattern of pension reforms in Western Europe. Countries such as Germany, which certainly has its share of demographic, economic and budgetary problems, have been slower to introduce radical reforms than countries such as Sweden and Italy, or even Ireland, which has the best demographic outlook in Europe. (For comparative statistics please refer to Appendix Table A1, p. 855.) Further, even if pension reforms are indeed ultimately motivated by problem pressure, political decisions made during the course of the reform process change the final policy outcomes. Reform blueprints must survive democratic political decision-making processes before they become law. Many reform ideas change shape or are dropped completely in this political decision-making process. Thus, pension "politics" are central to pension reform.

Ideas, learning and discourse

At the other extreme, a number of studies emphasize the importance of conceptual "framing." Citizens view the issue of pension policy cutbacks very differently depending upon the types of questions they are asked on surveys (Kitschelt 2001), or the information they are given (Boeri et al. 2002). V. Schmidt (2000) argues that the discourse used to justify retrenchment—and in particular, the link between retrenchment and national values—is essential for retrenchment efforts. Other scholars have also considered the impact of ideational legacies and social, economic, and pension policies (Berman 1998; Hall 1986; Nullmeier and Rüb 1993; Weir 1992). Indeed Hugh Heclo (1974) argued some time ago that pension politics may be influenced more by civil servants learning about this policy sector— "puzzling," as he called it—than by partisan struggle and executive governments "powering" their way to solutions.[12]

Because our study is based on qualitative case studies, we have been able to pay close attention to the peculiarities of national discourses and the ways in which ideas and processes of ideational construction have affected pension politics in these particular cases. However, we must report that we did not find an overall impact of "ideas" or "learning" per se. Policy-makers in the countries we investigated were certainly influenced by the international debate about public pensions promoted by an epistemic community of pension experts, and given form by international organizations and international networking initiatives (such as the European Observatory on Aging or the World Bank). But rather than observing either a process of national policy-makers suddenly discovering new ideas about how to solve their pension policy problems, or a process of regional diffusion of policy ideas, we observed national policy-makers drawing on ideas and solutions from the history of their own country, using pre-existing policies and existing policy ideas as institutional templates, and combining these with internationally-discussed proposals. Thus, we witnessed national proposals emerging as a kind of "collage" pasted together from national and international proposals, which in turn were revised and modified during the political process.

During these political processes, communication to the public was indeed important. Here, widespread, common-sense "public beliefs" did set limits to the plans of policy-makers. Expert assessments of the problems of national pension systems could be made convincing in some nations but not others. In Sweden, the long-term sustainability of the system—the need to develop a pension system that would last until the next "Ice Age"—and in Italy, the importance of Europe (respectively) found widespread public support. In Spain and Greece, by contrast, the general public did not find the arguments of experts politically credible: in Spain, demographic arguments failed to excite citizens, because the rate of employment was increasing; in Greece, the use of international experts to pave the way for pension cuts completely backfired when the public interpreted the experts as stooges of the government.

II The policy framework for pension politics

Contours of the pension problem and favored solutions

In a recent publication, "Pensions at a Glance," the OECD (2005) emphasizes two main functions of public pension schemes: first, to protect against old-age poverty and, second, to maintain income after retirement. Public schemes need not shoulder this entire burden, but it is the role of pension policy to ensure that these two functions are met by the combination of public and private schemes—which Rein and Rainwater (1986) describe as the "public-private mix"—found in a particular country. Although our focus is on changes in pension policy introduced by law—that is either changes in the public programs themselves, or in the legal rules for private pension schemes, whether part of collective bargaining agreements or individual—the pre-existing pension system constitutes the starting point for any changes in pension policy.

In comparing pension systems, we focus on the division of labor between public and private, as well as the ways in which these two functions are addressed by different parts of the pension system. As a first step in describing the public programs, we focus on four important aspects: *coverage, benefits, financing* and *administration*. That is, public pension programs (as well as private and occupational coverage) differ with respect to the percentage of the population that is covered for retirement benefits; the generosity and type of benefit that is offered; the way in which these benefits are financed; whether pension benefits are administered by private or by governmental agencies, and the extent to which different population groups or different social insurance benefits are grouped together under a single administrative scheme.

Historically speaking, coverage and administration have been extremely important issues. Today, however, most political conflicts and policy recommendations regarding pension policy have focused on benefits and financing. To be sure, shifts in benefits and financing, as we shall see, may bring issues of coverage and administration back to the fore. The two most hotly debated issues are "pay-as-you-go" financing and "defined-benefit" versus "defined-contribution" benefit formulae. In a pure PAYG system, the working-age population pays social insurance contributions that finance current pension payments. Several variations of this model are possible. For example, PAYG schemes may include "buffer funds" to cover fluctuations in costs caused by varying numbers of beneficiaries, contributions and changes in benefits. The design of buffer funds differs across systems, but the basic idea is to have a financial reserve for meeting a portion of current or future pension payments. Few contributory public pension schemes are fully contribution-financed. Governments often provide a subsidy financed from general revenues to the public pension scheme to cover deficits, lower contribution rates, or pay for the contributions of those who are unemployed, sick, or caring for children.

In a "defined-benefit" scheme, the benefit payments are determined by a formula based on the number of years of contributions and the average yearly contributions or annual income. There are usually ceilings on the earnings subject to contributions, as well as the level of pension-carrying earnings. In some systems, the benefit depends upon the annual income earned in each year of employment; in others, benefits are calculated based on the best of a particular number of earnings years (usually ranging from 5 to 20 years); in yet a third group, benefits depend upon the final salary. Furthermore, once the benefit has been calculated at retirement, pension pay-outs are usually indexed to either prices or wages. Regardless of these sources of variation, however, "defined-benefits" systems define in advance the level of future benefits, even if some parts of the benefits formula depend on factors such as inflation, which cannot be determined in advance.

In a "defined-contribution" system, by contrast, only the level of contributions is specified in advance, whereas the level of future benefits depends on the value of contributions. Defined-contribution schemes can either be funded, or based on "notional accounts." In the former case, contributions are invested in an individual account, and benefit pay-outs simply reflect the growth of the capital in the account until retirement, as well as the type of payment plan chosen for the benefits. In "notional" systems, benefits are calculated on the basis of contributions to "notional" accounts. This means that pension plan administrators make calculations as if the contributions actually existed in an individual account and had been invested, assuming a predefined rate of return on contributions. In some systems, financial reserves are individually or collectively invested, in others they are not invested at all. The individual country chapters that follow explore these issues in more detail.

The demographic and economic developments discussed in previous sections of this chapter make the issues of PAYG financing and defined-benefit versus defined-contribution systems increasingly important. As the ratio of beneficiaries to contributors grows, PAYG financing implies that in order to continue to pay benefits at previous levels, contribution rates must increase—in several European nations contributions are forecast to double by the year 2050 (Feldstein and Siebert 2002: 2). In order to avoid either cutting benefit levels significantly or substantially increasing contributions, many policy-makers look to some form of funding as a way to make future pension payments more affordable. However, the shift from a PAYG to a fully- or partially-funded system is difficult, because current contributors in a PAYG system are already paying for the pensions of current retirees. Thus, in order to introduce funding, current workers would have to pay higher contributions in order to fund both current PAYG pensions and their own future funded pensions. This double burden of the transition cohort of pensioners is known as the "double-payment problem" (see Pierson 1994) and it is one of the primary mechanisms that "locks" policy-makers into maintaining PAYG financing.

Defined-benefit schemes are vulnerable to similar problems. Promises to pay a particular benefit in future are easier to keep when the number of new contributors is increasing faster than the number of retirees. As populations age, and as the nature of employment has changed (with industrial, life-time employment significantly diminished), public and private pension plans based on defined benefits have become financially less stable. In the private sector, we can currently observe a rapid movement from defined benefit to defined contribution plans over the last decades (Bridgen and Meyer 2005). In the public sector, however, efforts to change the rules of the game for pension benefits are more explicitly political and tend to involve more overt political conflict. Regardless of whether the decision to convert a benefit scheme from defined benefit to defined contribution is made by governmental authorities, is an outcome of collective bargaining, or is the result of what the private market is willing to offer in terms of individual pension policies, the shift from defined benefit to defined contribution exposes individuals to more market risk. If returns to investments are high, such a risk may prove beneficial; if not, pensioners will experience lower retirement income (see also Anderson 2004).

Although debates about PAYG and defined-benefit versus defined-contribution plans have garnered the most public and scholarly attention, there are many other proposals for reducing future pension costs and increasing financial sustainability. One general tendency has been to try to tighten the link between benefits and contributions. This means changing benefit formulas so that benefits depend more directly on contributions, hence reducing the redistributive effects of pension benefits. Examples include increasing the reference period for the calculation of benefits and requiring longer qualifying periods. Other ways to reduce pension costs include changing the basis for the benefit calculation from gross to net wages (Disney and Johnson 2001), lowering the replacement rate, changing the formulas for benefit indexation or the tax status of benefits, or even simply skipping or delaying benefit up-rating.

A related tendency has been to increase both "negative" and "positive" gender equality. On the one hand, and often as a result of European Court of Justice decisions,[13] many governments have reduced privileges for women, such as lower retirement ages, shorter qualifying periods, and contribution rates equal to men's despite longer life expectancies.[14] The constraints of EU law were particularly important in the Netherlands and Belgium in this regard. Reductions in widows' and dependants' pensions are also under discussion in many European nations. Further, since women work disproportionately in the public and white-collar sectors, cuts in privileges to white collar employees or civil servants often affect women disproportionately. On the other hand, in order to compensate against the economic barriers women face, governments have also proposed increased credits for child-rearing years. Similarly, efforts to increase the universality of pension plans and the social safety net for low-income earners and those with irregular career paths (again, disproportionately women) tend to benefit women.

A different approach to addressing the financial sustainability of public pension systems has been to increase the revenues of pension systems, for example by increasing the contribution made by general tax revenues or special taxes (VAT or energy taxes, for example) to pension systems—although these approaches, obviously, increase the general tax burden. Governments have also proposed fusing separate special pension schemes in order to eliminate inequities, reduce administrative costs and increase the coverage of the system to include greater proportions of higher-income persons, such as by rolling civil servants into the general pension schemes or eliminating special privileges for public sector workers.

Some policy measures have a potentially large policy impact because they reduce lifetime pension benefits and increase lifetime contributions. This can be achieved by increasing the standard retirement age or by tightening provisions for early retirement (Ebbinghaus 2006). Similarly, increases in fertility or immigration would counteract the demographic impact of population aging (Esping-Andersen et al. 2002).

The structure of pension systems: tiers and pillars

Many "liberal" economists view the reduction of PAYG financing as the most important issue in pension policy reform, and advocate structural reform.[15] First, generous PAYG programs, with attractive provisions for early retirement, constitute an incentive for early exit and an implicit tax on work. Consequently, such programs exacerbate the effects of population aging, further decreasing the proportion of the population that is economically active and thus reducing economic growth (Gruber and Wise 1999a). Second, economists view taxes—payroll or other kinds—as an economic deadweight that slows economic growth and reduces work incentives (Feldstein and Siebert 2002). As pension programs are generally the largest portion of government budgets for social expenditures, these taxes could be reduced if pension programs were reduced. Further, payroll taxes disproportionately increase the marginal costs of low-wage work and thus increase unemployment, causing a vicious cycle of increased social need and higher taxes. Moreover, many economists discourage large public pension programs—even when funded—because they are concerned by the potential for political influence on financial markets, and they believe in the virtue of individual initiative.

For these reasons, the World Bank (1994) argued in its key pension policy statement "Averting the Old-Age Crisis," that nations should strive for a three pillar model. The first pillar should provide minimal obligatory PAYG public pensions in order to prevent old-age poverty; the second pillar (which could be public or private) should provide income security in old-age through earnings-related, funded pensions; and the third pillar would top up the first and second pillars with individual, private, voluntary retirement savings plans.[16] Critics of the World Bank approach argue, however, that it is not possible to simply unload the implicit public pension debt onto the second and third pillars. As social scientists increasingly emphasize, psychological and framing effects are very important for public policies. Unfortunately, human beings seem systematically to "discount" the future. That is, people tend to overvalue the current benefit of spending their money in comparison to the future benefit of enjoying a higher standard of living in retirement. Consequently, they tend not to save enough for retirement. Government pension programs or government-mandated pension programs are necessary if this tendency is to be

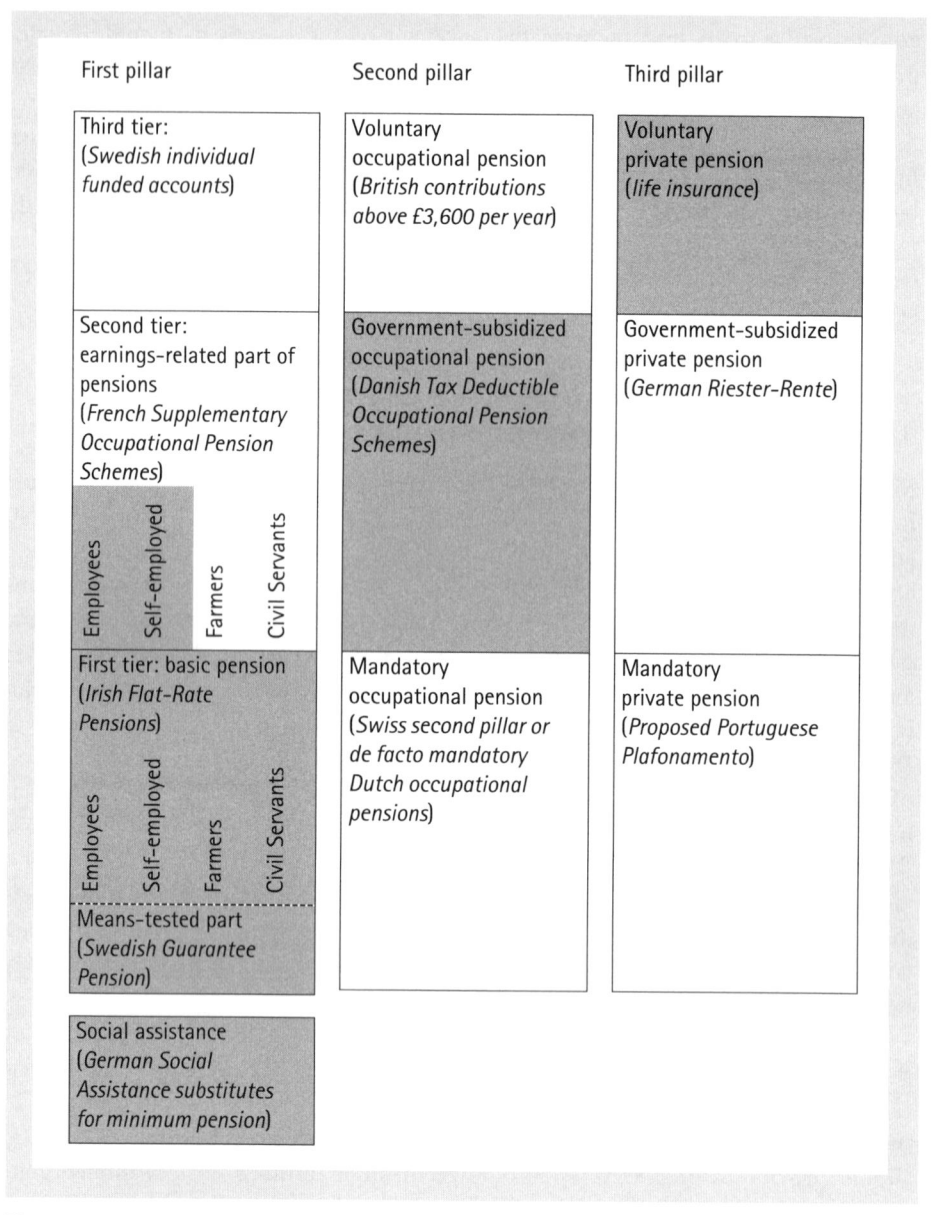

First pillar	Second pillar	Third pillar
Third tier: (*Swedish individual funded accounts*)	Voluntary occupational pension (*British contributions above £3,600 per year*)	Voluntary private pension (*life insurance*)
Second tier: earnings-related part of pensions (*French Supplementary Occupational Pension Schemes*) [Employees, Self-employed, Farmers, Civil Servants]	Government-subsidized occupational pension (*Danish Tax Deductible Occupational Pension Schemes*)	Government-subsidized private pension (*German Riester-Rente*)
First tier: basic pension (*Irish Flat-Rate Pensions*) [Employees, Self-employed, Farmers, Civil Servants]	Mandatory occupational pension (*Swiss second pillar or de facto mandatory Dutch occupational pensions*)	Mandatory private pension (*Proposed Portuguese Plafonamento*)
Means-tested part (*Swedish Guarantee Pension*)		
Social assistance (*German Social Assistance substitutes for minimum pension*)		

Fig. 1.1 A generic description of pension systems

counteracted. Further, the ease with which individuals can contribute to second and third pillar plans, as well as the market supply of second and third pillar plans, varies with economic status. Low-income earners find it difficult to finance a private plan, and for financial institutions, these plans are largely unprofitable because administrative costs are relatively fixed, and thus very large in comparison to the invested savings. Aside from forcing individuals to save, governments can provide tax incentives for second and third pillar plans, but these of course benefit higher income earners disproportionately. Indeed, if one takes this sort of tax expenditure into account, it is not clear that privatizing pensions eliminates as much government debt as is often claimed.

In sum, pension politics entail political choices both about the structure of pension systems as wholes and the details of formulae for allocating both pension benefits and the taxes that finance them. In order to keep track of these proposed and enacted changes, we rely on the language of pillars and tiers used in the literature, but want to clarify here our specific use of these terms. We use the term "pillar" to describe the sector in which the pension program is located: the first pillar is the public sector; the second, the occupational sector; the third, individual private sector. We use the term "tiers" to indicate the type of pension benefit, whether targeted, minimum, flat-rate, earnings-related, or defined-contribution in an individual account, as well as whether these benefits are mandatory or voluntary. We also use vertical divisions to indicate special schemes for different occupational groups (see Fig. 1.1, p. 22).

III Pension politics

An institutional approach to pension politics

As we have seen, decisions about which types of pension policy change are most effective and most desirable are not merely technical but also political matters. Politics enters into judgments about pension policy proposals because these judgments are based on political priorities and political feasibility. Our approach to the problem of pension reform has been to study the politics of pension reform itself. In contrast to quantitative studies, which must perforce simplify both dependent and independent variables in order to look for systematic effects, we rely on detailed institutional information on both the pension policy proposals and the configuration of political systems at specific points in time. In contrast to most qualitative studies, however, which are usually restricted to one, two or at most five cases, and are thus subject to the difficulties of case selection, we have elected to study pension politics in a complete universe of cases. That is, we include all 15 "old" EU member states, as well as Switzerland. Any generalization we make is obviously limited to this group of countries. But we can be sure that we are not emphasizing factors that are relevant to a specific sub-group of those nations, and which would be falsified if even one additional case were added. In addition, we narrow the questions that we address to a set of "political" questions. Does the structure of government affect the dynamics of pension politics? Are some forms of government better than others at grappling with policy problems? Do some polities privilege some interest groups or voters at the expense of others? How do nationally-distinct notions of fairness and justice affect the dynamics of pension politics?

We begin each chapter with a description of the political system which follows the veto players and veto points approaches, indicating the number of partisan veto players (number of parties in the government coalition) and the institutional veto points (political arenas with the constitutional right and political interest in vetoing proposed laws). Next, the chapters move to the pension system. Here, we present the structure of the current pension system using the language of pillars and tiers, and review public pension schemes in terms of coverage, financing, administration and benefits. The main sections in each chapter describe and analyze the dynamics of pension politics from the 1980s to the present.

Pension politics in Western Europe

We began this comparative study with the assumption that governments in countries with greater numbers of veto players or effective veto points would be impeded in their efforts to introduce significant pension reforms. But this is not what we found. Instead, we were puzzled that some countries with few veto players and no veto points—such as the UK, Greece, and France—pulled back from controversial pension reforms when they encountered voter resistance. At the other extreme, countries with many veto players and effective veto points—such as Finland and Switzerland—adopted significant legislation. We argue that "political competition" can explain such deviations from the predictions of veto points and veto players theory.

Single veto player governments; no veto points

The United Kingdom

The British system of government exemplifies the Westminster model of "majoritarian" government. Single-party governments supported by stable parliamentary majorities (manufactured in part by the single-member district electoral system) contain only a single partisan veto player, and are not impeded by institutional veto points, because the House of Lords cannot veto but only delay legislation. And indeed, the Thatcher government (as well as its successors) succeeded in drastically expanding the second and third pillars in British pension provision in the 1980s—and in undermining the universal nature of the first pillar by expanding already extensive opting-out provisions. Nevertheless, even such strong governments were not able to achieve their original policy goals. Threatened by competition from the Liberal–SDP Alliance in Britain's southern electoral districts, Tory backbenchers insisted on concessions to middle-class constituents as well as business and pension industry interests. Thus, Thatcher was not able to eliminate State Earnings-Related Pensions entirely, but instead reduced benefits and increased the incentives for contracting out. Similarly, in 1999, the Blair government's more stringent eligibility conditions for disability pensions were softened in response to protests from Labour backbenchers and Labour Peers in the House of Lords. Moran and Schulze argue in their chapter that the breakdown of party discipline on specific policy issues results from the intensity and pattern of electoral competition in particular constituencies.

Greece

Likewise, the Greek political system contains no veto points, and the electoral system generates decisive parliamentary majorities, with governments usually based on one-party majorities, and thus one partisan veto player. Nevertheless, it is precisely these disproportionalities that make the political system extremely competitive—elections can be won or lost by a few hundred votes in a few districts, and hence politicians are hostage to even small groups of disgruntled voters. Consequently, the development of the Greek pension system has been shaped by clientelistic politics and electoral rewards to special interests, while efforts to cut benefits and to eliminate some of the largest inequalities have met with effective resistance from both the political opposition and the trade unions. As Triantafillou shows in her chapter, the conservative New Democratic government was able to use its one-seat parliamentary majority—as well as the "urgent procedure" rule and passage of legislation during the summer session when fewer MPs were present—to introduce significant benefit cuts in the early 1990s. The government stuck to its plans, despite widespread strikes to protest its legislation, but ultimately shelved those for more far-reaching reforms.

Reform blockage continued under the left-wing PASOK governments in the 1990s and 2000s. Despite the pressures of trying to qualify for EMU—and several expert commissions calling for deep structural changes—the PASOK governments withdrew several proposals in the wake of union opposition, and so met the EMU budget criteria only by creative bookkeeping. Indeed, even when the left attempted to introduce reforms similar to those proposed by conservatives, the conservative opposition placed electoral gain above policy cooperation and abstained from the parliamentary debates. Although the reforms improved the financial sustainability of the pension system somewhat, structural reform remained elusive. The merger of several pension schemes was left to voluntary agreements, and modest cuts in already generous public sector benefits, were outweighed by improvements in private sector benefits.[17]

France

The Constitution of the French Fifth Republic was introduced to remedy the defects of the Fourth Republic, with its weak and unstable governments. Presidential politics has stabilized the party system into two ideologically distinct blocs, such that coalition partners no longer have an interest in defecting from the government. Nevertheless, as the President cannot veto social policy legislation, s/he is not a veto point or veto player for this policy domain. Consequently, French governments are strong, stable and armed with an array of institutional mechanisms—such as the "Guillotine" and the *vote bloquée*—to push legislation through parliament. Indeed, several French governments did just that. In 1993, the Balladur government increased the qualifying and reference period for public pensions, changed the indexing rules, increased contribution rates, and created a special fund for non-insurance benefits. In 2003, the Raffarin government further increased the contribution period, added incentives for working past 60 years of age, and "harmonized" several aspects of public sector pensions to the less favorable conditions in the private sector. By contrast, the Juppé government—enjoying the same 82 percent parliamentary majority as Balladur and not facing a hostile President—introduced legislation in 1995 to extend the pension reforms to the public sector and to create optional individual retirement plans in the private sector. Although both proposals passed into law—and were thus not impeded by veto points or veto players in any way—the government backed down in the face of massive strikes called to protest the reforms. The critical difference between the reforms—Conceição-Heldt argues in her chapter—was the intensity of electoral competition: during the "honeymoon period" reforms could be imposed without fear of electoral backlash; later in the electoral cycle, politicians were more vulnerable, particularly when they proposed direct cuts in privileges to particular groups (railway and transportation workers) who could easily punish individual politicians in single-member districts. Thus, political competition can explain the deviation from the predictions of veto points and veto players theories—not only in France, but also the UK and Greece.

Multiple veto points

Switzerland

Swiss political institutions are perhaps the most "consociationalist" in Western Europe, having emerged through conflicts across both religious and language divisions. The collegial executive necessitates broad party consensus before legislation can even be proposed; the bicameral parliament has the power to revise and even block governmental legislative proposals; and at the end of the legislative process, the possibility of vetoing legislation through referenda allows interest groups to make credible threats throughout the legislative process. Although Swiss election results have been unusually stable during the twentieth century, with almost no change from election to election, and only rarely a change in government, voters have become more volatile in recent years, leading to increased political competition. This has made the parties more restive and parliamentary decision-making both more difficult and more responsive to voters' demands. As Bonoli shows in his chapter, the many veto points of the Swiss system did indeed slow the expansion of the public pension system. In the 1980s and 1990s, however, veto points provided opportunities for opponents of cuts—in particular unions and the Socialist party—to demand modernizing compromises as the quid pro quo for fiscal consolidation. In addition, the other instrument of direct democracy—the popular initiative—has been used to place demands for social policy expansion on the political agenda. Consequently, Switzerland introduced a compulsory second pillar of occupational pensions, and improved both basic and occupational pension coverage for non-core workers, such as women. Some retrenchment measures, such as a higher retirement age for women and a lower accrual rate for occupational pensions have been introduced. In contrast, other proposed cuts, such as a further increase in the female retirement age and the use of VAT revenues to improve the finances of the pension system, have been blocked by referendum challenges. Thus, Swiss veto points do not preclude policy adaptation, but they do make politicians extremely sensitive to interest groups and voters willing to block legislation.

Finland

Constructed through conflicts between conservative landowners and revolutionary socialists, Finnish political institutions included two veto points: the President (a substitute for the previous power of the Czars) and the Parliament, where a one-third minority could veto legislation. These veto points were crucial for the development of the Finnish pension system in the twentieth century, since they allowed, initially, agricultural interests to insist on universal flat-rate pensions, and later, a coalition of unions and employers to add a second tier of mandatory earnings-related pensions administered by private sector institutions. In order to close off these veto points, however, Finnish political actors developed various consociational and corporatist practices. Surplus majority governments tried to neutralize the parliamentary veto point, while recourse to corporatist negotiations between the labor market partners—in one famous instance instigated by the President after he used his veto prerogative—helped to overcome the difficulties of cross-party agreement.

In the late 1980s and 1990s, constitutional reforms eliminated these veto points, but surplus majority government remained the rule, so political decision-making stayed in the hands of large numbers of partisan veto players. Nevertheless, in a series of step-wise reforms, Finnish political parties have introduced major structural changes. They converted the universal flat-rate national pension into a residual, means-tested program; introduced pension contributions for employees; extended the pension benefit formula to career earnings, lowered the accrual rate, added greater penalties for early retirement and a flexible retirement age, reduced the privileges of public sector workers, and added a demographic factor to dampen expenditure growth. Kangas argues that the key to these reforms was the use of agreements negotiated by the labor market partners to outflank reform opponents who might otherwise be compelled by the pressures of political competition to veto reforms that imposed losses on their main constituents: farmers in the case of the Center party, and industrial workers in the case of the Social Democratic Party and the Left Party.

Belgium

Constitutional reform in bicameral Belgium, as in Finland, reduced the number of veto points in parliament. The Senate was converted to a chamber of "reflection," and hence eliminated as a veto point entirely. The Chamber of Deputies was made irrelevant as a veto point by the introduction of a constitutional rule requiring a two-thirds majority rule for government formation, thus both cementing the practice of consociationalism and forcing it to new levels. The executive's room for maneuver was increased by provisions for special powers legislation, where parliament could grant the executive the right to legislate by decree in a given policy area. The introduction of a constructive vote of no confidence further strengthened the stability of the executive government. Finally, Belgium's transformation from a unitary to a federal state was intended to reduce areas of political disagreement by devolving them to the state level. However, the bifurcation of the party system along linguistic lines, as well as mechanisms for protecting language groups (the alarm bell procedure in parliament and the linguistic parity rule in cabinet decision-making) re-entrenched the linguistic cleavage in governmental decision-making. Thus, the closing-off of the parliamentary veto point did not reduce the number of *partisan* veto players; in fact, their number increased as *linguistic* veto players became more important.

Fragmented political authority in both the executive and legislative branches—within the context of increasing electoral competition from new parties—places unions in a favorable bargaining position. Anderson, Kuipers, Schulze and van den Nouland thus argue that it is not surprising that pension policy-making in Belgium has been marked by incremental rather than radical reform, despite the very heavy problem pressure created by high budget deficits in the context of the EMU requirements. Nevertheless, the liberal parties have used political competition to propose some significant reforms, including a "silver fund" designed to soften the future impact of population aging on the Belgian welfare state.

Many partisan veto players

Sweden

The extent of reform in Sweden and Italy is even more surprising than the reforms adopted in veto-heavy polities like Switzerland, Finland and Belgium. Indeed, by any comparative measure, the most substantial pension reforms in the 1980s and 1990s were introduced in these two nations, despite the presence of many partisan veto players. The 1994/1998 Swedish pension reform has attracted much international attention because it converted a defined benefit PAYG system into a notional defined-contribution system supplemented by mandatory individual funded accounts. The reform also replaced the old universal flat-rate basic pension with a pension-tested guaranteed minimum pension. This outcome is surprising given that Sweden was governed by a four-party minority government when the first part of the reform was adopted (1994) and was thus characterized by a parliamentary veto point and four partisan veto players. The non-socialist government introduced far-reaching reform by gaining the cooperation of the opposition Social Democrats (SAP) shortly before an election the SAP was forecast to win. Anderson and Immergut argue that the pressures of the highly competitive electoral system pushed the SAP to regain its position as the natural party of government by moving toward the middle of the political spectrum and demonstrating that it could solve pressing policy problems. Keeping pension reform out of electoral competition was key to this strategy, because the SAP did not want to antagonize their core voters on the left even as they looked to pick up votes in the middle. Thus, even when faced with union opposition and demands from the party base to rescind the reform after the 1994 election, the SAP stayed the course and worked out the implementing legislation for the reform in cooperation with the then non-socialist opposition.

Italy

In Italy as well, major changes in pension politics were enacted in the 1990s by governments composed of many partisan veto players—four partisan veto players in the case of the d'Amato Reform in 1992, and six partisan veto players and a parliamentary veto point (the *Camera dei deputati*) in the case of the Dini reform in 1995. The background to both reforms was an emerging consensus that the pension system was beset with high costs, inequities and labor disincentives. Nevertheless, Italian policy-makers had been unable to introduce reforms because high levels of partisan competition resulted in parliamentary maneuvering and unstable governments that made pension policy a tempting area for clientelistic appeals to voters. As Ferrera and Jessoula show, however, the transition from the First to the Second Republic in the 1990s gave executive governments some tools to contain political competition, and hence to become more effective in policy-making. The new mixed-member electoral system, with its predominantly majoritaritarian elements, provided incentives for electoral alliances and strengthened the position of the Prime Minister. Consequently, governments became more stable (as there was no longer and incentive to defect from the coalition in order to improve one's relative share of the spoils of office), and Italy experienced for the first time real changes in government with alternation between government and opposition. To be sure, however, single-member districts did not end the vulnerability of politicians to concentrated groups of voters, nor did the collapse of government coalitions necessarily lead to new elections, as in a pure majoritarian system—as was the case when the Lega Nord withdrew from the governing coalition when the Berlusconi government threatened the "seniority pensions" so dear to its core voters.

External pressures were important as well. In particular, the requirements of EMU changed the perceptions and attitudes of political actors. As international markets reacted to political inaction with radical devaluation of the Lire, politicians empowered technocratic governments to find a solution to the financial sustainability of the pension system as part of budget consolidation efforts. Unions, as well (notable in Italy for their high representation of retired workers), began to accept the need for reform and worked together with governments to hammer out pension reform agreements. The result was a series of significant cost-cutting measures and structural reforms that shifted the Italian pension system from a single to a multi-pillar system. The d'Amato and Dini reforms tightened eligibility conditions and benefit rules considerably, and introduced a notional contribution-defined benefit formula incorporating economic and demographic factors to assure continued cost control.

Denmark

Denmark, too, is a political system characterized by many partisan veto players and a parliamentary veto point. The Danish electoral system is highly proportional and its party system relatively fragmented. Minority governments are the rule, which means that the governing party or parties (the partisan veto players) face a parliamentary veto point, and as Green-Pedersen argues in his chapter—contrary to the predictions of veto player theory—the logic of policy-making is one of assembling a legislative coalition to support government proposals. Here, the "issue" ownership on which the political parties base their electoral strategies is critical. Social Democrats will not support conservative governments on welfare state cuts, and conservatives will not support left governments in raising taxes. The reverse coalitions, however, are possible—Social Democratic support for conservative tax increases and conservative support for Social Democratic welfare retrenchment, because "issue" ownership is not compromised.

During the course of partisan conflicts about both the expansion of the pension system in the 1950s and 1960s, and subsequent debates about retrenchment and social security in the 1980s and 1990s, the pattern of veto point politics led to stalemate. Consequently, Denmark, in sharp contrast to Sweden, never went beyond a basic flat-rate pension, although benefits were relatively generous. This provided a window of opportunity for pension policy expansion in the 1980s, but economic crisis, weak Social Democracy, a divided labor movement, and liberal resistance to public or union control of pension savings pushed pension politics onto the path of private occupational pensions through collective agreements. Thus, Denmark's multi-pillar system emerged from accidents of sequence and timing, in combination with the political constraints of cobbling together legislation majorities stretching across partisan veto players. As in the other countries with many partisan veto players, successful reform depended upon agreements to hold political competition in abeyance, in order to allow policy cooperation.

Moderate veto points and veto players

Spain

The Spanish case clearly shows the advantage of majoritarian political institutions for introducing significant policy change. Designed to produce majority governments and combat excessive fragmentation, the electoral system (and the closed party lists) buffers the largest parties somewhat against political competition, an effect which is strengthened by the protections enjoyed by the executive government, particularly the constructive vote of no confidence. Thus Spain has extremely stable governments, and exclusively *single-party* if not always *majority* governments. This institutional set-up results in two patterns of political decision-making: majoritarian rule and parliamentary legislative-coalition politics. In the first type, governments based on absolute parliamentary majorities and unfettered by institutional veto points were able to pass important cuts and structural changes despite union opposition. The 1985 pension reform (which tightened eligibility and benefit conditions considerably) and the 1987 law on pension plans (which introduced framework legislation for a second and third pillar) were extremely controversial politically, and the Socialist governments could only pass them because of their comfortable parliamentary majority.

As Chuliá shows in her chapter, however, there is a second pattern of decision-making. The electoral system also favors the small regional parties, and these become important veto players when the winning parties do not achieve an absolute majority, thus making parliament a veto point. Under precisely such a political configuration, the Catalonian regional party—the CiU—initiated the negotiations with trade unions and political parties that laid out the de facto "rules of the game" for pension politics in the "Toledo Pact." Indeed, this set of normative guidelines continued to restrain conservative governments even when the parliamentary veto point was no longer operative. Further, public beliefs set boundaries on government action, as pension cuts and privatization required public credibility to be accepted as legitimate. Since Spanish social security expenditures were well below those of other European nations, and the demographic problem was compensated by immigration and labor market expansion, governments were restrained in their proposals for restructuring—even when pushed by international organizations such as the OECD. Furthermore, the rapid expansion of the relatively weak welfare state during the transition to democracy meant that their welfare state was linked with democratization in the collective memory of Spanish citizens, making it very difficult for the center-right *Partido Popular* to pursue any measures that could be considered anti-welfare-state, for fear that the party would be labeled anti-democratic or neo-conservative. Instead, the Party pursued expansion of the third pillar more subtly, using the tax code.

Austria

The Austrian political configuration is in the process of transition from a consociationalist–corporatist to a more conventional pattern of coalition government. With majority (and generally surplus majority) governments, the only veto point is the Constitutional Court, which may be overruled by a two-thirds parliamentary majority. Despite proportional representation, the Socialist and People's Parties have long dominated the party system. These parties governed for many years in a "grand coalition," supported by an array of corporatist chambers in which political decisions related to economic matters were made. Consequently, the executive government remained relatively weak in relation to the parliamentary fractions and the corporatist chambers. The latter ensured their veto power by sending their own representatives—most prominently trade unionists—into parliament.

Even when the Socialist party eventually gained the electoral strength to govern alone, these consociational and corporatist practices continued. This pattern was interrupted, however, by the Freedom Party's successful strategy of competing as a radical right-wing populist party. Both by defining itself as an anti-establishment party, and by taking votes from the two dominant parties, the Freedom Party forced the larger parties back into their traditional grand coalition. This time, however, in place of the old system of cartelization of votes according to the *Lager* or social milieu, the parties faced much higher levels of electoral competition. Political competition had heated up, not only because of the change in the party configuration, but also because of the change in the electoral formula, which increased political competition at the level of individual candidates, and hence, candidates' sensitivity to concentrated constituencies. As Schulze and Schludi show, the result was a series of attempted cost-cutting and structural reforms that were eviscerated by the dominant parties' efforts to protect their electoral clientele—farmers, public sector workers and civil servants for the Austrian People's Party (ÖVP), and blue-collar unions for the Socialists (SPÖ). Trade unionist MPs and the parliamentary representatives of the state-level parties were also willing to defy party discipline to veto legislation. Only after a second political re-alignment to form a conservative/right-wing (FPÖ–ÖVP) government—for whose parliamentary majority the dwindling number of trade union MPs were no longer relevant—were a series of more radical measures introduced, including a higher retirement age for women, penalties for early retirement, an increase in the benefits reference period to 40 years, and the incorporation of the separate schemes for civil servants and public sector workers into the general scheme.

Portugal

The veto points in the Portuguese system were introduced in order to ensure political stability after the transition to democracy in 1974–6: the President and the Constitutional Court were to provide political direction and boundaries to the legislative process in the case of weak or unstable governmental majorities. Chuliá and Asensio argue in their chapter that although over time larger and more stable parliamentary majorities have produced stronger governments, these veto points require consensual politics for large-scale pension and social legislation. When this condition is absent, governments often fall. Political competition makes such cross-party agreement difficult to obtain, because the two largest parties contest elections based on competing partisan visions of the good society and social justice. The Socialists emphasize the need for social policy expansion and the just distribution of the costs of social security by combating contribution evasion, whereas the center-right Social Democrats promote actuarial fairness and privatization. Since each of these dominant parties is flanked by competitors to their left or right (respectively), too much moderation on either side might benefit, ironically, the competing dominant party. Nevertheless, electoral competition does not appear so extreme as to allow particular interests to veto policy proposals entirely: the electoral formula provides only moderate proportionality, which helps the two largest parties to maintain their dominant position in government formation. Disproportionalities are not sufficient to provide opportunities for pockets of voters to veto policies; the two largest parties are not mainly competing for the same voters. Consequently, Portuguese pension politics have produced both moderate expansions of pension coverage and some progress toward a multi-pillar system with some funding. Thus, although domestic critics urge more radical reform, by international standards Portugal has introduced some significant retrenchment and funding measures.

Germany

As in Spain, Austria, and Portugal, the veto point of the German system—the second chamber, or *Bundesrat*—is critical for legislative bargaining because it determines which concessions need to be made to the parliamentary opposition and/or to regional branches of the parties in the governing coalition. As Jochem and Schulze argue in their chapter, however, neither the existence of a veto point nor the pattern of coalition government (which means that two partisan veto players must agree on legislative proposals) has blocked German pension policy-making. While veto player bargaining has indeed resulted in some inconsistencies and contradictions in policy, the main problem facing policy-makers has been the constraints of electoral competition, which has dramatically increased since German unification. Previous governments were able to maintain cross-party consensus both for the expansion of the pension system in the 1970s and early 1980s and the first steps towards retrenchment in the 1990s. But with the new regional cleavage (because of unification) and increasing competition for votes, politicians have so far feared the electoral fallout from pension cuts: the party base does not want to take the fall for the reform ideas of the leadership.

Since the large catch-all parties compete for some of the same voters, they are tempted to exploit the pension issue in the electoral arena. Morever, with single member districts and the importance of regional electoral results for the *Bundesrat* majority, specific groups of voters—such as real-estate interests, for example—can make pointed electoral threats. Thus, the Social Democratic Party (SPD) promised to eliminate the cost-cutting demographic factor in the 1998 election, only to have to lower the replacement rate by other means after the election. At the same time, the overall proportionality of the electoral system—despite the relatively high threshold of 5 percent—has allowed new entrants to change the nature of pension politics discourse. The Green Party was important in pushing the Social Democrats towards a more pragmatic view of pension reform and opening up the door for a paradigm shift concerning the expansion of the second pillar. More recently, the merger of the ex-state socialist PDS with a West German electoral alliance into the Left Party has given opponents of welfare state reform a stronger voice in the German parliament. Whether the "grand coalition" government that took power in late 2005 becomes a mechanism for limited political competition, as in the days of the politics "of the middle way" (Schmidt 1987), or whether it succumbs to political pressures remains to be seen. Thus, moderate numbers of veto points and veto players do not block successful policy-making. Instead, the pattern and intensity of political conflict set the parameters for retrenchment.

Closed veto points, moderate veto players, unusual electoral configurations

The Netherlands

The Dutch electoral system stands out as the most proportional in Western Europe. The entire country comprises one electoral district, so the effective threshold of representation is less than one percent. Not surprisingly, electoral competition is intense, and it has been relatively easy for broadly-based interests to gain parliamentary representation. When the state pension (AOW) was frozen in the 1980s and early 1990s, for example, two pensioners' parties were formed and made it into parliament. In response, the Labor Party and even the Liberals outbid each other defending pensioners' interests, and indexation was restored.

The Dutch political configuration is conducive to welfare state expansion because of proportional representation, frequent alternations in government, and competition between Christian Democrats (CDA) and the Labor Party for the working class vote. However, as Anderson demonstrates in her chapter, in the field of pensions this expansionist tendency has been countermanded by two peculiarities. First is the influence of confessional parties in Dutch politics. When public and occupational pensions were established after World War II, Catholic corporatist ideology was very influential. The Catholic Party's (one of the forerunners of the CDA) insistence on corporatist administration (for example by Catholic employers' organizations and unions) contributed to the emergence of a strong occupational pension sector, as well as the establishment of an "insurance-based" basic pension. The emergence of this dual system means that the public pension budget is lower than it might otherwise have been in such a competitive system—although the tax deduction for the occupational pensions is also a heavy budget item.

Second, as the dominant party and in its position as pivot, CDA-led governments responded to the need for budgetary consolidation, and were able to impose their views on coalition partners—although at a steep electoral price. This political decision caused huge losses for the CDA in 1994, resulting in the first government since 1918 without confessional party representation.

The combination of political competition and corporatist accommodation has produced a public–private mix in pensions that provides generous and nearly universal coverage. Moreover, occupational pensions are funded. The responsive electoral system has provided incentives for the parties to pick up new issues and respond to new needs—such as gaps emerging in the coverage of the elderly, the need for funding, and EU legislation concerning gender equality. At the same time, however, political competition has made it difficult to impose cuts. In addition, this dual-track nature of pension politics tempts both government and neo-corporatist bargaining partners to offload the pain of budgetary consolidation and wage-restraint onto other actors. The government wants the labor market partners to restrain both wage bargains and occupational pensions, while the labor market partners object when government cost-saving measures call for them to increase the benefits paid by contractual pension schemes.

Ireland

The veto points of the Irish system have been largely irrelevant for pension politics. Instead, as in the Netherlands, the key to understanding Irish pension politics is the electoral method and party system. Although Ireland's electoral system is highly proportional, political competition is held in check by the existence of a dominant party (a product of the Irish Republic's political history and class structure) and the single transferable vote electoral method. Because the single-transferable vote encourages electoral alliances and competition between candidates of the same party, political campaigns tend to focus on local issues rather than broad-based class redistribution. Consequently, pension policy has not been prominent as a tool of political competition, and as Moran and Schulze show in their chapter, pension expansion has been limited. In the post-war period, the limited political incentives for expansion—together with a number of other factors, including the Irish party system (which is based on the question of nationhood rather than socio-economic cleavages), the weak Left, the Catholic Church's traditional opposition to state intervention—resulted in a minimal pension system. Despite the tremendous economic expansion of the 1990s, public pension growth continued to be minimal, and was subjected to the needs and logic of the "Celtic Tiger." For example, as part of the series of corporatist pacts of the late 1980s and 1990s, unions agreed to low but steady wage increases, and cuts in public spending, especially in the health sector. Rather than increasing public pension benefits, pension reforms brought the self-employed into the public system, thereby increasing revenues and restoring fiscal balance to the system.

The goals of these pacts were non-inflationary economic growth, higher profits, economic restructuring from agriculture to the tertiary sector, and consolidation of government budgets whose deficits (and consequent public debt) were causing economic crisis. Pension policy focused on improving public finances by increasing the revenue base for the first pillar pension by extending mandatory coverage to farmers and the self-employed. This was an important quid pro quo for the sacrifices made by labor—although to be sure, these important constituencies were integrated into the system on very advantageous terms. Even as economic growth took off, and despite the very favorable demographic situation, politicians did not seek popularity by expanding public pensions. Instead, the profits of economic growth were plowed back into the system to provide partial funding for the future. To promote expansion of coverage, policy-makers introduced vesting rules for occupational pensions, subsidized personal pensions, and better regulation of both the second and third pillars through a national pension board. Thus, throughout, political competition did not promote pensions as an electoral issue; nor did it provide particularistic interests with veto power over policy proposals.

Luxembourg

Luxembourg has a highly-proportional electoral formula with a low electoral threshold. Not coincidentally, together with the Netherlands, it is one of only two countries in Western Europe that has witnessed the emergence of a pensioners' party. At the same time, however—following the Lijphardt rule of proportionality—the low number of parliamentary seats (60) radically reduces the system's proportionality.[18] In addition, there are only four electoral districts, with numbers of seats that very considerably, and, consequently, large disparities in representation among the regions, not to mention the large number of persons (immigrants and cross-border workers) who are not entitled to vote. Finally, the electoral rules provide for multiple votes (as many as the seats in the district) and allow votes to split their votes (*panachage*) and to allot more than one vote to particular candidates (accumulation).

This particular set of institutional rules has allowed politicians to target pension politics to particular voter groups with surgical precision. Faced with increasing left-wing competition in the late 1970s (and following its first electoral loss since 1919), the dominant Christian Socialist Party (CSV) consolidated the pension schemes of blue-collar workers, farmers and the self-employed at the cost of white-collar employees—as well as non-voting cross-border workers and immigrants—by converting the capital-based pension system with government notional contribution guarantees to a PAYG system. Although this reform addressed the financial problems of the occupationally-organized pension schemes, it did not address large inequalities between private and public pension schemes. This was the impetus for the rise of the Party for Pension Justice (ADR), which was able to make pensions the dominant political issue for all five electoral campaigns of the 1980s and 1990s.

As a result, as Schulze shows, successive Luxembourgian governments have expanded public pensions and reduced their actuarial basis—harmonizing public and private pensions by transferring civil servants and public sector workers to the private scheme while at the same time extending the generous 5/6 of last salary rule to all workers. Political competition, not veto point or veto player politics, is the key to understanding pension politics in Luxembourg.

Political competition

This comparative overview of pension politics in Western Europe shows that institutional theories based on veto points and veto players must be revised to account for the impact of political competition. Veto points and veto players provide a good guide to the logic of the policy-making process—particularly in the systems with many institutional veto points or veto players—but this view of the legislative process must be supplemented, we believe, with a theory of political competition.

By "political competition" we mean aspects of the political battle that are more overarching than "electoral" or "party" competition alone. Although much work remains to be done, the intensity of political competition and its effects on policy-making seem to depend upon a number of features of the political system. The electoral system and the pattern of distribution of political preferences—who votes for whom in which electoral district—what one could call the "electoral map"—affect the incentives to politicians to compete for votes by expanding public pensions programs, as well as their electoral risk when they decide to propose cuts. Single-member districts (or other disproportionalities) may allow politicians to overlook some political problems or interests. But, as we have seen, they may also make them extremely vulnerable to concentrated groups of "veto voters."[19] More proportional electoral systems, on the other hand, provide incentives for universal benefits expansion and impede cuts—but they do not lend themselves to targeted privileges. At the same time, however, proportional systems with low electoral thresholds allow the entry of new parties and thus new issues—which include both proposals for more "liberal" welfare states, as well as pension "justice." Finally, while political competition forces politicians to respond quickly to voters, overheated competition may cause policy blockage precisely by making politicians so vulnerable that they are afraid to propose policy change. All in all, the exact incentives and vulnerabilities of politicians depend upon the precise conditions of political competition, and thus upon the interaction of political preferences, party strategies, and the electoral method. Further conceptual analysis is needed to specify this variable more precisely—but we hope here to have made the case, at least, that the veto points and veto players do not provide an adequate explanation for the dynamics of pension politics.

The future of pension politics

While we have pointed to significant differences in the intensity and pattern of political competition as a key variable in explaining pension politics, we conclude this introduction with two caveats. First, politics in Western Europe in the twentieth century has been shaped by long-term processes of religious conflict, state and nation-building, urbanization and democratization, which left institutions and values in place that constrained political competition. Rokkan's famous cleavages, Lijphart's consociational practices, Schmitter and Lehmbruch's patterns of interest-intermediation are just some of the mechanisms that held political competition in check, and allowed politics in Western Europe to settle into somewhat stable patterns that could be compared. Today, it is not just globalization and European integration that have unsettled the post-war social and political order, but the erosion of many of these underlying social moorings have made voters more volatile and politics less predictable. The re-negotiation of the twentieth century welfare state is thus taking place in an era where political competition promotes change, but may also make it more difficult to construct coherent policies, or to achieve consensus among conflicting interests.

Second, no mono-causal explanation can do justice to an area of policy-making as complex as pension policy. While we have focused here on the role of political institutions, and political competition as a common cross-cutting theme, we have also tried to point to the role of nationally-specific historical trajectories, policy templates, as well as the political construction of interests and the framing of political discourse. It is precisely these processes that can be uncovered by the case studies that follow, and it is to those that we now turn.

Notes

1. See, for example, Alber 1982; Baldwin 1990; Flora 1986; Guillén 1997; Mares 2003; Orloff 1993; Palme 1990; Skocpol 1992.
2. On the impact of globalization and European economic integration on the welfare state, see, for example, Esping-Andersen et al. 2002; Huber and Stephens 2001; Leibfried and Pierson 1995; Rhodes 1996; Scharpf and Schmidt 2000.
3. On the pensions crisis see, for example, Bonoli and Shinkawa 2005; Börsch-Supan and Miegel 2001; Clark 2003; Clark and Whiteside 2003; Clark et al. 2006; Disney and Johnson 2001; Feldstein and Siebert 2002; Gruber and Wise 1999b; Myles 2002, 2003; Myles and Pierson 2001; Rein and Schmähl 2004; Schokkaert and Parijs 2003.
4. Other important contributions to a political-institutional understanding of politics are: Armingeon 2002, Colomer 2002, and Kaiser 1997.
5. Veto points and veto players hamper Social Democratic and Christian Democratic attempts at expansion, as well as liberal attempts at cutbacks. See also Birchfield and Crepaz 1998; Hicks 1999; Hicks and Swank 1992.
6. See Ziegler 2000 for an example from the United States.
7. For a discussion of these terms and issues, see Block 1984 [1977]; Lukes 1974.
8. On pension politics at the European level, see De la Porte and Pochet 2002; Anderson 2002.
9. There is also an enormous literature within economics on the political economy of pension reform. See overview in Breyer 1994; Breyer and Craig 1997. Such works have informed our study, but we have focused on studying pension politics empirically, rather than on the basis of abstract models.
10. The VDR merged with another public pension authority in 2005 to become *Deutsche Rentenversicherung* (German Pension Insurance).
11. In fact, it may be that in debates about the politics of the welfare state, political scientists and political sociologists may have tended to overstate their case. By trying to show that there is scope for political choice even within seemingly narrow constraints—that "politics" can be used against "markets"—we, as well as others, may have sounded as though politics might overcome all odds. A more nuanced way to put this might be to focus on the ways in which politics do matter in national responses to similar problems, without asserting that politics is *more* important than the contours of the policy problem at hand.
12. Marier 2005 returns to this focus on civil servants. Recent literature has increasingly stressed the role of policy learning and policy diffusion. See, for example, Brooks 2005.
13. See Directive 79/7/EEC of 19 December 1978 on the Progressive Implementation of the Principle of Equal Treatment for Men and Women in Matters of Social Security and the 1990 *Barber* decision that extended the meaning of Article 119 (on equal treatment) to

include age requirements in occupational pension schemes. This includes both the age of entrance into a scheme and the age of retirement.
14. However, the European Parliament has recently decreed that womens' and men's contributions must be the same (Directive 2002/73/EC).
15. Examples include Feldstein 1998; Feldstein and Siebert 2002; Holzmann 2000; and Holzmann and Stiglitz 200.
16. Later publications argued that the three pillar approach must be adjusted for particular national situations and policy traditions. See Holzmann 2000; Holzmann and Stiglitz 2001.
17. Here one must note, however, that these relatively generous pension benefits compensate for the relative lack of other income maintenance programs.
18. Lijphart 1999: 154; Wagner 2005.
19. The term "veto voters" is taken from Isabelle Schulze's dissertation (2006), which examines the impact of credible "electoral threat" on pension politics (electoral district by electoral district) in Austria, Luxembourg, Germany, and the United Kingdom.

References

ALBER, JENS (1982). *Vom Armenhaus zum Wohlfahrtsstaat: Analysen zur Entwicklung der Sozialversicherung in Westeuropa.* Frankfurt: Campus Verlag.
—— (1996). *Selectivity, Universalism, and the Politics of Welfare Retrenchment in Germany and the United States.* Prepared for 92nd Annual Meeting of the American Political Science Association. San Francisco, 08/31/1996.
ANDERSON, KAREN, M. (2001). "The Politics of Retrenchment in a Social Democratic Welfare State: Reform of Swedish Pensions and Unemployment Insurance." *Comparative Political Studies.* 34, 9 (November): 1063–91.
—— (2002) "The Europeanization of Pension Arrangements: Convergence or Divergence?" In de la Porte, C. and Pochet, P. (eds.), *Building Social Europe Through the Open Method of Co-ordination.* Brussels: Peter Lang, 251–84.
—— (2004). "Pension Politics in Three Small States: Denmark, Sweden, and the Netherlands," *Canadian Journal of Sociology,* 29(2): 289–312.
—— and MEYER, TRAUTE (2003). "Social Democracy, Unions and Pension Reform in Germany and Sweden." *Journal of Public Policy,* 23(1): 23–54.
—— and Julia F. LYNCH (forthcoming). "Internal Institutions and the Policy Preferences of Organized Labor: The Effects of Workforce Ageing on Union Support for Pension Reform," *Comparative Politics.*
ARMINGEON, KLAUS (2002). "The Effects of Negotiation Democracy: A Comparative Analysis." *European Journal of Political Research,* 41, 1 (January): 81–105.
—— and BONOLI, GIULIANO (eds.) (2006). *The Politics of Post-Industrial Welfare States.* London: Routledge.
BALDWIN, PETER (1990). *The Politics of Social Solidarity: Class Bases of the European Welfare State 1875–1975.* Cambridge: Cambridge University Press.
BÉLAND, DANIEL (2001). "Does Labor Matter? Institutions, Labor Unions and Pension Reform in France and the United States." *Journal of Public Policy,* 21(2): 153–72.
BERGER, SUZANNE and DORE, RONALD (eds.) (1996). *National Diversity and Global Capitalism.* Ithaca, NY: Cornell University Press.

BERMAN, SHERI, E. (1998). *The Social Democratic Moment: Ideas and Politics in the Making of Interwar Europe.* London, Cambridge: Harvard University Press.
BIRCHFIELD, VICKI and CREPAZ, MARKUS M. L. (1998). "The Impact of Constitutional Structures and Collective and Competitive Veto Points on Income Inequality in Industrialized Democracies." *European Journal of Political Research,* 34, 2 (October): 175–200.
BLOCK, FRED (1984 [1977]). "The Ruling Class Does Not Rule: Notes on the Marxist Theory of the State." In Ferguson, T. and Rogers, J (eds), *The Political Economy.* Armonk, NY: M. E. Sharpe, 32–46.
BOERI, TITO, BÖRSCH-SUPAN, AXEL and TABELLINI, GUIDO (2002). "Pension Reforms and the Opinions of European Citizens." *American Economic Review,* 92(2): 396–401.
BONOLI, GIULIANO (2000). *The Politics of Pension Reform: Institutions and Policy Change in Western Europe.* Cambridge: Cambridge University Press.
—— (2004). "Switzerland: Negotiating a New Welfare State in a Fragmented Political System." In Taylor-Gooby, P. (ed.), *New Risks, New Welfare. The Transformation of the European Welfare State.* Oxford: Oxford University Press, 157–80.
—— and PALIER, BRUNO (1997). "Reclaiming Welfare: The Politics of French Social Protection Reform." In Rhodes, M. (ed.), *Southern European Welfare States. Between Crisis and Reform.* London: Frank Cass, 240–59.
—— and SHINKAWA, TOSHIMITSU (eds.) (2005). *Ageing and Pension Reform Around the World: Evidence from Eleven Countries.* Cheltenham, UK: Edward Elgar.
BÖRSCH-SUPAN, AXEL, H. and MIEGEL, MEINHARD (eds.) (2001). *Pension Reform in Six Countries: What Can We Learn from Each Other?* Berlin: Springer.
BREYER, FRIEDRICH (1994). "The Political Economy of Intergenerational Redistribution." *European Journal of Political Economy,* 10 (1): 61–84.
—— and CRAIG, BEN (1997). "Voting on Social Security: Evidence from OECD Countries." *European Journal of Political Economy,* 13 (4): 705–24.
BRIDGEN, PAUL and MEYER, TRAUTE (2005). "When do Benevolent Capitalists Change their Mind? Explaining the Retrenchment of Defined-benefit Pensions In Britain." *Social Policy and Administration,* 39 (7): 764–85.
BRODY, DAVID (1975). "The New Deal and World War II." In Braeman, J., Bremner, R. H., and Brody, D. (eds.), *The New Deal. Volume 1. The National Level.* Columbus: Ohio State University Press, 269–309.
BROOKS, SARAH, M. (2002). "Social Protection and Economic Integration: The Politics of Pension Reform in an Era of Capital Mobility." *Comparative Political Studies,* 35, 5 (June): 491–523.
—— (2005). "Interdependent and Domestic Foundations of Policy Change: The Diffusion of Pension Privatization Around the World." *International Studies Quarterly,* 49(2): 273–94.
BRUGIAVINI, AGAR, EBBINGHAUS, BERNHARD, FREEMAN, RICHARD et al. (2001). "Learning from Welfare Reforms: The Case of Public Pensions" and "Unions and Pensions: Theory, Evidence, and Implications." In Boeri, T., Brugiavini, A., and Calmfors, L. (eds.), *The Role of Unions in the Twenty-First Century. A Report for the Fondazione Rodolfo Debenedetti.* New York: Oxford University Press, 187–233.
CLARK, GORDON L. (2003). *European Pensions and Global Finance.* Oxford: Oxford University Press.
—— and WHITESIDE, NOEL (eds.) (2003). *Pension Security in the 21st Century. Redrawing the Public-Private Debate.* Oxford: Oxford University Press.
—— MUNNELL, ALICIA H. and ORSZAG, J. MICHAEL (eds.) (2006). *The Oxford Handbook of Pensions and Retirement Income.* Oxford: Oxford University Press.

CLAYTON, RICHARD, and PONTUSSON, JONAS (1998). "Welfare-State Retrenchment Revisited: Entitlement Cuts, Public Sector Restructuring, and Inegalitarian Trends in Advanced Capitalist Societies." *World Politics*, 51 (October): 67–98.

COLOMER, JOSEP M. (ed.) (2002). *Political Institutions in Europe*. London: Routledge.

CROUCH, COLIN and STREECK, WOLFGANG (eds.) (1997). *Political Economy of Modern Capitalism*. London: Sage.

DE LA PORTE, CAROLINE and POCHET, PHILIPPE (eds.) (2002). *Building Social Europe Through the Open Method of Co-ordination*. Brussels: Peter Lang.

DISNEY, RICHARD, and JOHNSON, PAUL (eds.) (2001). *Pension Systems and Retirement Incomes across OECD Countries*. Cheltenham, UK: Edward Elgar.

EBBINGHAUS, BERNHARD (2006). *Reforming Early Retirement in Europe, Japan and the USA*. Oxford: Oxford University Press.

—— and HASSEL, ANKE (2000). "Striking Deals: Concertation in the Reform of Continental European Welfare States." *Journal of European Public Policy*, 7, 1 (March): 44–62.

—— and MANOW, PHILIP (eds.) (2001). *Comparing Welfare Capitalism. Social Policy and Political Economy in Europe, Japan and the USA*. London: Routledge.

ESPING-ANDERSEN, GØSTA (1990). *The Three Worlds of Welfare Capitalism*. Princeton: Princeton University Press.

—— and KORPI, WALTER (1984). "Social Policy as Class Politics in Post-War Capitalism: Scandinavia, Austria, and Germany." In Goldthorpe, J. H. (ed.), *Order and Conflict in Contemporary Capitalism*. Oxford: Clarendon Press, 179–208.

—— et al. (eds.) (2002). *Why We Need a New Welfare State*. New York: Oxford University Press.

ESTÉVEZ-ABE, MARGARITA (2002). "Negotiating Welfare Reforms: Actors and Institutions in Japan." In Steinmo, S., and Rothstein, B. (eds.), *Institutionalism and Welfare Reforms*. New York: Palgrave, 157–83.

—— IVERSEN, TORBEN and SOSKICE, DAVID (2001). "Social Protection and the Formation of Skills: A Reinterpretaion of the Welfare State." In Hall, P., and Soskice, D. (eds.), *Varieties of Capitalism*. Oxford: Oxford University Press, 145–83.

FELDSTEIN, MARTIN (ed.) (1998). *Privatizing Social Security*. Chicago: University of Chicago Press.

—— and SIEBERT, HORST (eds.) (2002). *Social Security Pension Reform in Europe*. Chicago: University of Chicago Press.

FERRERA, MAURIZIO and RHODES, MARTIN (2000). "Recasting European Welfare States: An Introduction." *West European Politics*, 23(2): 1–10.

FLORA, PETER (ed.) (1986). *Growth to Limits: The Western European Welfare States Since World War II*. Berlin: Walter de Gruyter.

GEORGE, ALEXANDER L. and BENNETT, ANDREW (2005). *Case Studies and Theory Development in the Social Sciences*. Cambridge, MA: MIT Press.

GREEN-PEDERSEN, CHRISTOFFER (2001). "The Puzzle of Dutch Welfare State Retrenchment." *West European Politics*, 24(3): 135–50.

GRUBER, JONATHAN, and WISE, DAVID A. (1999). *Social Security and Retirement Around the World*. Chicago: University of Chicago Press.

GUILLÉN, ANA MARTA (1997). "Welfare state development in Spain. A historical and explanatory approach," in Palier, B. (ed.), *Comparing Social Welfare Systems in Southern Europe*. Paris: MIRE, 67–91.

HACKER, JACOB S. (2002). *The Divided Welfare State: The Battle over Public and Private Social Benefits in the United States*. Cambridge: Cambridge University Press.

HACKER, JACOB, S. (2005). "Policy Drift: The Hidden Politics of US Welfare State Retrenchment." In Streeck, W., and Thelen, K. (eds.), *Beyond Continuity: Institutional Change in Advanced Political Economies.* New York: Oxford University Press, 40–82.

HALL, PETER, A. (1986). *Governing the Economy: The Politics of State Intervention in Britain and France.* Oxford: Oxford University Press.

—— (2003). "Aligning Ontology and Methodology in Comparative Politics." In Mahoney, J., and Rueschemeyer, D. (eds.), *Comparative Historical Analysis in the Social Sciences.* Cambridge: Cambridge University Press, 373–404.

—— and SOSKICE, DAVID (eds.) (2001). *Varieties of Capitalism.* Oxford: Oxford University Press.

HECLO, HUGH (1974). *Modern Social Politics in Britain and Sweden.* New Haven: Yale University Press.

HICKS, ALEXANDER (1999). *Social Democracy & Welfare Capitalism.* Ithaca, NY: Cornell University Press.

—— and SWANK, DUANE H. (1992). "Politics, Institutions, and Welfare Spending in Industrialized Democracies, 1960–82." *American Political Science Review*, 86, 3 (September): 658–74.

HOLZMANN, ROBERT (2000). "The World Bank Approach to Pension Reform." *International Social Security Review*, 53(1): 11–34.

—— and STIGLITZ, JOSEPH E. (eds.) (2001). *New Ideas About Old Age Security: Toward Sustainable Pension Systems in the 21st Century.* Washington, D.C.: World Bank.

HUBER, EVELYNE, RAGIN, CHARLES, C. and STEPHENS, JOHN, D. (1993). "Social-Democracy, Christian Democracy, Constitutional Structure, and the Welfare-State." *American Journal of Sociology*, 99(3): 711–49.

—— and STEPHENS, JOHN, D. (2001). *Development and Crisis of the Welfare State: Parties and Policies in Global Markets.* Chicago: University of Chicago Press.

IMMERGUT, ELLEN, M. (1990). "Institutions, Veto Points, and Policy Results: A Comparative Analysis of Health Care." *Journal of Public Policy*, 10(4): 391–416.

—— (1992a). *Health Politics: Interests and Institutions in Western Europe.* Cambridge: Cambridge University Press.

—— (1992b). "The Rules of The Game: the Logic of Health Policy-Making in France, Switzerland and Sweden." In Steinmo, S., Thelen, K., and Longstreth, F. (eds.), *Structuring Politics: Historical Institutionalism in Comparative Perspective.* Cambridge: Cambridge University Press, 57–89.

KAISER, ANDRÉ (1997). "Types of Democracy: From Classical to New Institutionalism." *Journal of Theoretical Politics*, 9(4): 419–44.

KAY, STEPHEN, J. (1999). "Unexpected Privatizations: Politics and Social Security Reform in the Southern Cone." *Comparative Politics*, 31, 4 (July): 403–22.

KITSCHELT, HERBERT (2001). "Partisan Competition and Welfare State Retrenchment: When Do Politicians Choose Unpopular Policies?" In Pierson, P. (ed.), *The New Politics of the Welfare State.* Oxford: Oxford University Press, 265–302.

KITTEL BERNHARD and OBINGER, HERBERT (2003). "Political parties, institutions, and the dynamics of social expenditure in times of austerity." *Journal of European Public Policy*, 10(1): 20–45.

KLASS, GARY, M. (1985). "Explaining America and the Welfare State: An Alternative Theory." *British Journal of Political Science*, 15 (October): 427–50.

KORPI, WALTER and PALME, JOAKIM (2003). "New politics and class politics in the context of austerity and globalization: Welfare state regress in 18 countries, 1975–95." *American Political Science Review*, 97(3): 425–46.

LEIBFRIED, STEPHAN and PIERSON, PAUL (eds.) (1995). *European Social Policy. Between Fragmentation and Integration.* Washington, D.C.: The Brookings Institution.

LEVY, JONAH, D. (1999). "Vice into virtue? Progressive politics and welfare reform in continental Europe." *Politics and Society*, 27 (2): 239–73.

—— (2005). "Redeploying the State: Liberalization and Social Policy in France." In Streeck, Wolfgang and Thelen, Kathleen (eds.), *Beyond Continuity: Institutional Change in Advanced Political Economies.* Oxford: Oxford University Press, 103–26.

LIJPHART, AREND (1984). *Democracies: Patterns of Majoritarian and Consensus Government in Twenty-one Countries.* New Haven: Yale University Press.

—— (1999). *Patterns of Democracy: Government Forms and Performance in Thirty-Six Countries.* New Haven: Yale University Press.

LOWI, THEODORE, J. (1964). "American Business, Public Policy, Case-Studies, and Political Theory." *World Politics*, 16 (July): 677–715.

LUKES, STEVEN (1974). *Power: A Radical View.* London: Macmillan.

LYNCH, JULIA (2001). "The Age-Orientations of Social Policy Regimes in OECD Countries." *Journal of Social Policy*, 30(3): 411–36.

—— (2006). *Age in the Welfare State. The Origins of Social Spending on Pensioners, Workers, and Children.* Cambridge: Cambridge University Press.

MARES, ISABELA (2003). *The Politics of Social Risk: Business and Welfare State Development.* Cambridge: Cambridge University Press.

MARIER, PATRIK (2005). "Where did the Bureaucrats Go? Role and Influence of the Public Bureaucracy in the Swedish and French Pension Reform Debate." *Governance*, 18(4): 521–44.

MARSHALL, T. H. (1963). "Citizenship and Social Class." In Marshall, T. H. (ed.), *Class, Citizenship, & Social Development.* Chicago: University of Chicago Press, 71–135.

MYLES, JOHN (1989). *Old Age in the Welfare State: The Political Economy of Public Pensions.* Kansas: University Press of Kansas.

—— (2002). "A New Social Contract for the Elderly." In Esping-Andersen, G. (ed.), *Why We Need a New Welfare State.* Oxford: Oxford University Press, 130–72.

—— (2003). "What Justice Requires: Pension Reforms in Ageing Societies." *Journal of European Social Policy*, 13(3): 264–69.

—— and PIERSON, PAUL (2001). "The Comparative Political Economy of Pension Reform." In Pierson, P. (ed.), *The New Politics of the Welfare State.* Oxford: Oxford University Press, 305–33.

NULLMEIER, FRANK and RÜB, FRIEDBERT, W. (1993). *Die Transformation der Sozialpolitik: Vom Sozialstaat zum Sicherungsstaat.* Frankfurt am Main: Campus.

OECD (2005). *Pensions at a Glance: Public Policies Across OECD Countries.* Paris: OECD.

ORLOFF, ANN SHOLA (1993). *The Politics of Pensions: A Comparative Analysis of Britain, Canada, and the United States, 1880–1940.* Madison: University of Wisconsin Press.

PALME, JOAKIM (1990). *Pension Rights in Welfare Capitalism: The Development of Old-Age Pensions in 18 OECD Countries 1930 to 1985.* Stockholm: Swedish Institute for Social Research.

PERSSON, TORSTEN, ROLAND, GÉRARD and TABELLINI, GUIDO (2000). "Comparative Politics and Public Finance." *Journal of Political Economy*, 108(6): 1121–161.

—— and TABELLINI, GUIDO (2002). *Political Institutions and Policy Outcomes: What are the Stylized Facts?* [Internet]. August 2002 [cited February 2003]). Available from ftp://ftp.igier.uni-bocconi.it/homepages/tabellini/tp0208161.pdf

PIERSON, PAUL (1993). "When Effect Becomes Cause: Policy Feedback and Political Change." *World Politics*, 45 (July): 595–628.

—— (1994). *Dismantling the Welfare State? Reagan, Thatcher and the Politics of Retrenchment.* Cambridge: Cambridge University Press.

—— (1996). "The New Politics of the Welfare State." *World Politics*, 48 (January): 143–79.

—— (ed.) (2001). *The New Politics of the Welfare State.* Oxford: Oxford University Press.

—— and WEAVER, R. KENT (1993). "Imposing Losses in Pension Policy." In R. K. Weaver, and B. Rockman (eds.), *Do Institutions Matter?* Washington, D.C.: Brookings Institutions, pp. 110–50.

POWELL, G. BINGHAM (2000). *Elections as Instruments of Democracy: Majoritarian and Proportional Visions.* New Haven: Yale University Press.

REGINI, MARINO (2000). "Between Deregulation and Social Pacts: The Response of European Economics to Globlization." *Politics and Society*, 28(1): 5–33.

—— and REGALIA, IDA (1997). "Employers, Unions and the State: The Resurgence of Concertation in Italy?" *West European Politics*, 20(1): 210–30.

REIN, MARTIN and RAINWATER, LEE (eds.) (1986). *Public/Private Interplay in Social Protection: A Comparative Study.* Armonk, NY: Sharpe.

—— and SCHMÄHL, WINFRIED (eds) (2004). *Rethinking the Welfare State: The Political Economy of Pension Reform.* Cheltenham: Edward Elgar.

RHODES, MARTIN (1996). "Globalization and West European Welfare States: A Critical Review of Recent Debates." *Journal of European Social Policy*, 6(4): 305–27.

—— (2001). "The Political Economy of Social Pacts: 'Competitive Corporatism' and European Welfare Reform." In Pierson, P. (ed.), *The New Politics of the Welfare State.* Oxford: Oxford University Press, 165–94.

ROTHSTEIN, BO (1998). *Just Institutions Matter.* Cambridge: Cambridge University Press.

SCHARPF, FRITZ, W. (2000). "Economic Changes, Vulnerabilities, and Institutional Capabilities." In Scharpf, Fritz W. and Schmidt, V. A. (eds.), *Welfare and Work in the Open Economy: From Vulnerability to Competitiveness.* Vol. 1. Oxford: Oxford University Press, 21–124.

—— and SCHMIDT, VIVIEN, A. (eds) (2000). *Welfare and Work in the Open Economy: From Vulnerability to Competitiveness.* 2 Vols. Oxford: Oxford University Press.

SCHLUDI, MARTIN (2005). *The Reform of Bismarckian Pension Systems: A Comparison of Pension Politics in Austria, France, Germany, Italy and Sweden.* Amsterdam: Amsterdam University Press.

SCHMIDT, MANFRED G. (1987). "West Germany: The Policy of the Middle Way." *Journal of Public Policy*, 7 (2): 135–77.

—— (2001). "URSACHEN und FOLGEN wohlfahrtsstaatlicher Politik. Ein internationaler Vergleich." In Schmidt, M. G. (ed.), *Wohlfahrtsstaatliche Politik. Institutionen, politischer Prozess und Leistungsprofil.* Opladen: Leske + Budrich.

—— (2002). "Political Performance and Types of Democracy: Findings from Comparative Studies." *European Journal of Political Research*, 41 (1): 147–63.

SCHMIDT, VIVIEN, A. (2000). "Values and Discourse in the Politics of Adjustment." In Scharpf, F. W. and Schmidt, V. A. (eds.), *Welfare and Work in the Open Economy: From Vulnerability to Competitiveness.* Vol. 1. Oxford: Oxford University Press, 229–309.

SCHOKKAERT, ERIK and PARIJS, PHILIPPE VAN (2003). "Social Justice and the Reform of Europe's Pension Systems." *Journal of European Social Policy*, 13(3): 245–63.

SCHULZE, ISABELLE (2006). *Der Einfluss von Wahlsystemen auf Politikinhalte: 'Electoral Threat' in der Rentenpolitik.* Dissertation. Berlin: Humboldt Universität zu Berlin.

SKOCPOL, THEDA (1985). "Bringing the State Back In: Strategies of Analysis in Current Research." In Evans, P. B., Rueschemeyer, Dietrich, and Skocpol, T. (eds.), *Bringing the State Back In.* Cambridge: Cambridge University Press, 3–37.

—— (1992). *Protecting Soldiers and Mothers: The Political Origins of Social Policy in the United States.* Cambridge: Harvard University Press.

STREECK, WOLFGANG and THELEN, KATHLEEN (eds.) (2005). *Beyond Continuity: Institutional Change in Advanced Political Economies.* Oxford: Oxford University Press.

SWANK, DUANE (2001). "Political Institutions and Welfare State Restructuring: The Impact of Institutions on Social Policy Change in Developed Democracies." In Pierson, P. (ed.), *The New Politics of the Welfare State.* Oxford: Oxford University Press, 197–237.

TAYLOR-GOOBY, PETER (ed.) (2005). *New Risks, New Welfare.* Oxford: Oxford University Press.

THELEN, KATHLEEN (2003). "How Institutions Evolve: Insights From Comparative Historical Analysis." In Mahoney, J. and Rueschemeyer, D. (eds.), *Comparative Historical Analysis in the Social Sciences.* Cambridge: Cambridge University Press, 208–40.

TSEBELIS, GEORGE (1995). "Decision Making in Political Systems: Veto Players in Presidentialism, Parliamentarism, Multicameralism and Multipartyism." *British Journal of Political Science,* 25, 3 (July): 289–325.

—— (1999). "Veto Players and Law Production in Parliamentary Democracies: An Empirical Analysis." *American Political Science Review,* 93, 3 (September): 591–608.

—— (2002). *Veto Players: How Political Institutions Work.* Princeton: Princeton University Press.

VISSER, JELLE and HEMERIJCK, ANTON (1997). *A Dutch Miracle.* Amsterdam: Amsterdam University Press.

WAGNER, AIKO (2005). *Die Disproportionalität der Bundesländerwahlsysteme. Eine Analyse mittels Fuzzy-Set/Qualitative Comparative Analysis.* Bachelorthesis. Berlin: Humboldt-Universität zu Berlin.

WEAVER, R. KENT (1986). "The Politics of Blame Avoidance." *Journal of Public Policy,* 6 (4): 371–98.

—— (1998). "The Politics of Pension Reform: Lessons from Abroad." In Arnold, R. D., Graetz, M., and Munnell, A. (eds.), *Framing the Social Security Debate: Values, Politics, and Economics.* Washington, DC: National Academy of Social Insurance, 183–229.

—— and ROCKMAN, BERT (1993). "When and How do Institutions Matter?" In Weaver, R. K., and Rockman, B. (eds.), *Do Institutions Matter?* Washington, DC: Brookings Institution, pp. 445–61.

WEIR, MARGARET (1992). *Politics and Jobs: The Boundaries of Employment Policy in the United States.* Princeton: Princeton University Press.

WORLD BANK (1994). *Averting the Old Age Crisis.* Oxford: Oxford University Press.

ZIEGLER, NICHOLAS, J. (2000). "Corporate Governance and the Politics of Property Rights in Germany." *Politics & Society,* 28(2): 195–221.

PART I

SINGLE VETO PLAYER GOVERNMENTS; NO VETO POINTS

CHAPTER 2

UNITED KINGDOM: PENSION POLITICS IN AN ADVERSARIAL SYSTEM

ISABELLE SCHULZE

MICHAEL MORAN

I Introduction

BRITISH pension politics are marked both by the executive authority of the Westminster system of government and by partisan political conflict. The result has been a pension system that has moved decisively further down the path of private sector pensions, but with significant concessions to key electoral constituents along the way.

The greatest achievement—and the most distinctive feature—of the British state pension system is its financial sustainability. The system is considered effective, targeted, non-distortive for the labor market, and projections for expenditure development estimate state pension costs of approximately 4 percent of GDP in 2050 (Kral 2001: 5). The decreasing value of basic pensions and declining number in State

Earnings Related Pension Scheme (SERPS), thanks to provisions of the pension reform of 1986, keep the costs for the state pension system low and at the same time promote the expansion of privatization. A comparative, macroeconomic advantage of the British pension system is the big share of capital funding through private pensions. Investment of occupational and personal pension funds account for a large share at the stock market and assets equal 60 percent of GDP (Disney et al. 1999: 120).

Nevertheless, the UK pension system faces some serious problems. Despite the positive picture of the state of finances of the UK pension system, the projections for public pension expenditure have to be considered with care. Projections for state pension costs development most often do not bear in mind the increasing costs for means-tested social assistance benefits (Disney et al. 1999: 121). But due to the constant decline in real value of the pension benefits, the basic pension lies below the level for social assistance if supplements are taken into account. In other words, pension benefits from the first pillar alone do not provide an adequate standard of living, while occupational pensions and private pensions have not hitherto been available or worthwhile to low-income earners due to high administration costs. Recent reforms, such as the introduction of Stakeholder Pensions in 1999, and the substitution of State Earnings Related Pension Scheme (SERPS) with State Second Pensions (SSP), have been first steps to remedy the two main problems of the UK pension system: old age poverty and inequality (Bertelsmann Stiftung 2002: 2).

Governmental reform proposals in British pension policy have been radical and straightforward both under Conservative and under Labour governments. But the Thatcher government in 1986, as well as the Blair administration in 1999, had to back down from their initial proposal due to intra-party disaffection. The Conservatives made concessions to their supporters in the pensions industry and the business community, while the Labour Party conceded to backbenchers and Labour peers' claims to the benefit of beneficiaries of incapacity pensions. However, the extent to which the government had to lower its initial goals was much more significant in 1986. The financial difference between abolishing the State Earnings Related Pensions Scheme—as initially proposed—and SERPS benefit reduction—as finally enacted—was immense. The following description of the reform processes provides evidence that suggests that the Thatcher government in 1986 faced a much greater party competition constraint than Labour did, despite its large parliamentary majority. In particular, the British quasi two-party system, and thus the Conservative government, were threatened by the rise of the Liberal/Social Democrat Alliance of the early 1980s. It is a central argument of this chapter that the 1986 reforms were less radical than superficial appearances might suggest. The government was forced to retreat, moreover, by changes in the wider character of the party system. In particular, the need to face new pressures of party competition shaped the Conservative Party in pension policy, notably the need to respond to the emergence of the Liberal/Social Democrat Alliance as a major new force in British politics in the mid-1980s.

II Political system

Constitutional history and nation-building

The UK is famous for its "unwritten" constitution, a product of development over several centuries. Though often described as unwritten, in fact numerous elements of the constitution are contained in written statute. The constitution does, however, have the distinction of being uncodified in a single document, and is therefore a combination of written rules and understood conventions. Moreover, even the written statutes have required nothing more than a simple parliamentary majority to be changed. Based on the principle of parliamentary sovereignty all powers reside with the parliament. After the Glorious Revolution of 1688, which finally extinguished the claims of the monarchy to supreme sovereign power, the division of power between the Crown, the House of Lords and the House of Commons constituted a system of checks and balances. But modern constitutional practices have been less marked by checks and balances than by the extraordinary authority of an executive with a majority in the House of Commons.

Although the UK is still a unitary, centralized state, there has been some decentralization in the last decade. Referenda among the Scottish and the Welsh populations in 1997 approved the creation of a Scottish Parliament and Executive, and a Welsh Assembly. The Belfast Agreement also led to the re-establishment of a parliament in Northern Ireland in 1998, though its operations are presently suspended (Plöhn 2001: 172; Hazell 2003).

Economically, Britain was marked indelibly by its role as the historical pioneer of industrialism. One economic legacy is profound inequality in the economic fortunes of different regions, notably a significant North–South divide. Northern England has been the traditional home of mining, steel production and shipbuilding. However, the importance of the heavy industry began to decline in the 1970s culminating in the recession, and high unemployment rates. The South of England started out as an agricultural region and then developed a steadily growing service sector. Today the City of London and the South-East of England is dominated by the financial sector. The 1980s in particular was the decade when a structurally depressed North was confronted by a prospering South-East with high growth rates and a booming financial services sector.

The socio-economic and demographic composition of the British population also has a regional aspect. The Southern coast of England, for instance, is a popular senior citizens' area of residence, sometimes referred to as the "Costa Geriatrica" (Green 1998: 97). Between 1921 and 1971 a concentration process of elderly people led to clusters of over-65-year-olds in Sussex, South-West England, and Wales (Allon-Smith 1982: 38). As we shall see, some of these demographic patterns turn out to be important in accounting for the course of pension policy.

Institutions of government

The Head of State is the Queen whose functions are mainly symbolic. There is some possibility for informal Crown influence over policy discussions, such as in the confidential weekly briefings of the Prime Minister to the Queen (Bogdanor 1995; Norton 2004).

Real political power lies with the governing party and its leader, who becomes Prime Minister. The Prime Minister may be subject to a vote of no-confidence but he has the right to ask the Queen to dissolve parliament at any time. Prime Ministers are expected to dominate cabinet, and to provide the principle guidelines of governmental policy. The extent to which this really happens depends heavily on prime ministerial style, and the extent to which prime ministers can dominate colleagues—who are also, potentially, rivals for the prime minister's job. Most of the cabinet work is done outside the normal cabinet sessions in an elaborate network of committees, some permanent, some created ad hoc to deal with particular policy issues (Burch and Holliday 1996, 2004).

These structural features have one important consequence for policy debate: they tend to ensure that the most important arguments about policy occur inside the executive, where the most powerful players are lodged, rather than in more formal arenas of competition, such as the floor of the House of Commons.

The House of Lords and the House of Commons are the two chambers of the British Parliament. The members of the House of Lords are appointed by the Prime Minister or—until 1999—inherited their peerage. The House of Lords had equal powers to the House of Commons until 1911. Today, the veto power of the upper chamber is reduced to the right of delay for a maximum of one session but the Lords actively participates in amending bills during the legislative process.[1] The Lords typically contain members often independent of party and with high technical expertise. One result is that the Lords is often a more serious obstacle to government proposals than is a House of Commons controlled by the governing party.

The principle formal tasks of the lower house—the House of Commons—are legislation and monitoring the executive. In reality, the single most important function of the Commons, especially in its deliberations in the chamber, is to advance the partisan battle. Government backbenchers are there primarily to support the Prime Minister and his/her government, both by votes and argument. Opposition backbenchers are there to attack the government. While debates on policy proposals are superficially about the merits of proposals, their most important purpose is to pursue the partisan struggle.

Electoral system

The 646 members of the House of Commons are elected by plurality vote in single member districts for a term of five years. This electoral system leads to a de facto entrance barrier into parliament of approximately 35 percent and causes a chronic

Table 2.1 Political institutions in the United Kingdom

Political arenas	Actors	Rules of investiture	Rules of decision-making	Veto potential
Executive	Queen	Hereditary	Gives royal assent to legislation	Not a veto point
	Prime Minister	Appointed by the Queen; needs support of majority of members in the House of Commons	Proposes legislation	—
Legislative	House of Commons	5-year term; 646 members elected in single-member districts; first-past-the-post plurality vote; House can be dissolved on Prime Minister's request	Government majority can decide on agenda (except for opposition days), closure (i.e. end of debate for certain parts of the bill) and guillotine (i.e. majority decides on allocation of time and thereby determines the end of the debate)	Not a veto point, as majority government
	House of Lords	Life-time appointment; 666 members (in 2004); majority of new appointments on nomination of Prime Minister	May object a bill with the effect of suspension of the legislation for the maximum of one session i.e. one year (no delaying power in money bills)	Not a veto point
Judicial	Law Lords in the House of Lords	12 Law Lords appointed by the Prime Minister	Highest Court of Appeal; because of unwritten constitution and Common Law there is no risk that legislation taken by majority would conflict with constitutionality	Not a veto point
Electoral	Referendum	Government majority in House of Commons can decide to consult the electorate on a certain question in a referendum	Non-binding	Not a veto point, as controlled by government majority
Territorial units	National Parliaments in Scotland, Wales and Northern Ireland	Separate, independent elections in each country (Scotland mixed majority and proportional electoral system)	Scotland: legislative competences in health, education, sports, farming, community and transport policy; power to rise or lower income tax by 3%; Wales: only secondary legislative competences i.e. statutory instruments	Not a veto point, as cannot veto legislation, but resulting in diversification of policy

under-representation of small parties without geographical strongholds (Lijphart 1994: 17; Blackburn 1995; Denver 2002). If a member of parliament dies or retires from his mandate, by-elections become necessary that have a tendency to be used as protest votes against the current government but often do not reflect the trends in the next general election.

Legislative process

Most legislative initiatives, and virtually all important legislation, originate in the executive and are "managed" through parliament by the government of the day. Usually, the responsible ministry, on behalf of the government, publishes a White Paper with "fairly definite legislative intentions" (Prime Minister's Office 2003). The White Paper is then transformed into a legislative bill and introduced to one of the chambers—most of the time to the House of Commons. If the government wants to test opinion first, a Green Paper with an invitation to comment on the governmental objectives precedes the White Paper. Experts, unions, employers' organizations, government bodies and other ministries are included in the consultation stage. More important still, powerful procedural norms encourage extensive consultation with affected interests well in advance of even preliminary publication of proposals. Both the Green and the White Paper may be discussed in parliament. Government lawyers (*Parliamentary Counsel*) draft the bill in the responsible department before it is submitted to the house (Davies 2000: 14; Prime Minister's Office 2003).

The first reading in the House of Commons (or the House of Lords) is a pure formality. The bill and its underlying principles are debated in general in the second reading. The government majority sets the agenda, chooses the timetable, length (*closure*) and end (*guillotine*) of debates of the house (Punnett 1994: 257). A positive vote on the bill transfers it to the committee stage at the end of the second reading.

The standing committees are groups of 18 to 25 deputies created ad hoc for each separate legislative proposal. Members are not chosen for any special expert knowledge in the sector under consideration, as is the case in committees of Continental-style working parliaments. However, the responsible minister for the bill and his counterpart of the Shadow Cabinet are always part of the Committee. The Committee deliberates the bill clause by clause and may suggest amendments. As committee composition reflects partisan strength of the plenary, only government amendments, or at least those acceded to by the government, have a serious chance of being passed. During the report stage (*Consideration*) clauses and amendments of the committee stage can be reviewed again.

In a third and final reading, the members of the chamber vote on the bill which is then sent to the other house, where it passes through identical stages. However, the House of Lords usually holds committee stage in the full house. If the Lords amends the Commons' proposals, they are generally remitted to the House of Commons. This procedure is continued until the chambers find a common version. If no agreement is attainable the House of Lords can block the reform for the current

Party family affiliation	Abbreviation	Party name	Ideological orientation	Founding and merger details	Year established
Right	Conservative	Conservative Party	Center-right	Successor of the pro-monarchist Tories	17th century
Left	Labour	Labour Party	Party with strong socialist tendencies until the late 1980s; restructured under Michael Foot, Neil Kinnock and Tony Blair	Founded as Labour Representation Committee as political wing of the unions; renamed in 1906	1900
Center Parties	SDP	Social Democratic Party	Attempted to replace Labour Party as the dominant left party; support mixed economy, welfare state, and EU-membership	Founded by four former Labour Party ministers; fusion with Liberal Party into LDP in 1988	1981
Center Parties	LDP	Liberal Democratic Party	Liberal	Liberal Party (L) as the successor of the anti-monarchist Whigs in the 17th century; Fusion of the Liberal Party with the Social Democratic Party in 1988	(1861) 1988
Nationalist Parties	SNP	Scottish National Party	Committed to Scottish independence		1934
Nationalist Parties	PC	Welsh Nationalist Party (*Plaid Cymru*)	Left-nationalist; preservation of cultural and linguistic Welsh roots		1925
Northern Ireland Parties	UUP	Ulster Unionist Party	Conservative; close links to Tories		1905
Northern Ireland Parties	DUP	Democratic Unionist Party	Radical protestant; working-class electorate		1971
Northern Ireland Parties	SDLP	Social Democratic and Labour Party	Nationalist; non-violent fight for independence from Britain	Successor of the Nationalist Party	1970
Northern Ireland Parties	SF	We Ourselves (*Sinn Féin*)	Extremist catholic; Political wing of the IRA		1905

Fig. 2.1 Party system in the United Kingdom

Sources: Becker (2002: 153–200), Munzinger (1999), Sturm (1999: 235–236).

parliamentary session. In other words, the upper chamber has the power to suspend the enactment of the bill for the maximum of one year. The Lords is not empowered to deal with finance laws. The Queen's signature on the act (*Royal Assent*) concludes the legislative process (Punnett 1994: 256).

Three features of the legislative process should thus be highlighted. First, the House of Commons has poor institutional capacities to deal with technically complex policy proposals. Second, policy proposals are shaped within the executive, and through extensive, continuous consultation and bargaining with "affected interests"—this notion in turn being an important mechanism by which some institutions and interests are incorporated into the policy process, and others excluded. Third, the open discussion of legislation is largely a means by which government and opposition in the British Westminster system can pursue their wider adversarial struggle.

Parties and elections

The electoral system, which historically has confined the electoral battle to two major parties—Conservatives and Labour—has resulted in the conventional characterization of the British as a two-party system. However, on average 5.6 parties per constituency take part in national elections, and the nationalist parties are of growing importance in Scotland and Wales (Sturm 1999: 234).

The origins of the Tories—the Conservative Party—go back to the seventeenth century. They successfully made the transition to full formal democracy in the twentieth century, and were the dominant party of government for much of that epoch. In the post-war period the Conservatives controlled government from 1951 to 1964, from 1970 to 1974 and from 1979 to 1997. The Conservatives are a center-right party strongest in rural and suburban constituencies. Their electoral span encompasses the self-employed, managers, and skilled workers—but also a share of unskilled workers (Ingle 1987: 88; Jacobs 1989: 381–2).

The Labour Party evolved from the trade union movement that established the *Labour Representation Committee* in 1900. The first Labour MPs entered the Commons in 1906, and in the 1918 General Election it emerged as the Conservative Party's main rivals. The first Labour government was formed in 1924. Labour was weak in terms of share of votes in the 1980s at a time when the party drifted to the left. After the 1997 national election, Labour regained power after 18 years in opposition and controlled a majority of 419 out of 659 seats. The Labour Party is strong in urban, industrial areas in Northern England, Wales and Scotland. Its electoral base is dominated by working-class and public sector middle-class voters (Denver 2002).

The Liberals were a constitutionally radical party attached to some sections of business, and were the Conservatives' main opponents until 1918. After the rise of the Labour Party in the 1920s, the Liberals declined in importance but re-gained significant electoral support in the late 1970s and 1980s. In the two elections 1983 and 1987 the Liberal Party competed together with the Social Democratic Party

Table 2.2 Governmental majorities in the United Kingdom[a]

Election date	Start of gov.	Head of gov. (party)	Governing parties	Gov. majority (% seats) House of Commons	Gov. electoral base (% votes) House of Commons	Gov. majority (% seats) House of Lords[b]	Institutional veto points	Number of veto players (partisan + institutional)
05.03.1979	05.05.1979	Thatcher I (Con)	Con (339)	53.4%	43.9%	No majority	None	1 + 0
06.09.1983	06.12.1983	Thatcher II (Con)	Con (397)	61.1%	42.4%	No majority	None	1 + 0
06.11.1987	06.13.1987	Thatcher III (Con)	Con (376)	57.8%	42.3%	No majority	None	1 + 0
	11.28.1990	Major I (Con)	Con (373)	57.4%	42.3%[c]	No majority	None	1 + 0
04.09.1992	04.11.1992	Major II (Con)	Con (336)	51.6%	41.9%	46.3%	None	1 + 0
05.01.1997	05.02.1997	Blair I (Lab)	Lab (419)	63.6%	43.2%	15.1%	None	1 + 0
06.07.2001	06.08.2001	Blair II (Lab)	Lab (412)	62.5%	40.7%	28.7%	None	1 + 0
05.05.2005	05.06.2005	Blair III (Lab)	Lab (355)	55.0%	35.2%	No majority	None	1 + 0

[a] Note that these majorities do not take into account changes due to by-elections!
[b] No exact data available for the years 1979 until 1991 and 2005.
[c] Electoral base in 1990 refers to the 1987 election and, again, does not take into account by-elections.

Sources: www.parliament.uk/faq/elections_faq_page.cfm#elec1uk; www.election.demon.co; House of Lords Information Office (personal communication with Isabelle Schulze on 23.03.2004); http://www.parliament.uk/commons/lib/research/rp2005/rp05-033.pdf

(SDP)—founded by right-wing Labour dissidents in 1981—as the Alliance. The two parties merged in 1988 into the Liberal Democratic Party. Scotland and Wales have nationalist parties—the Scottish National Party (SNP) and the Plaid Cymru (Party of Wales). The party system in Northern Ireland is completely different from the rest of Britain. The main parties are Ulster Unionist Party (UUP), Democratic Unionist Party (DUP), Social Democratic and Labour Party (SDLP), and Sinn Féin.

Interest groups

The Trades Union Congress (TUC) has been the umbrella organization of unions since 1868. Today, it includes 76 individual unions with a membership density of approximately 27 percent. Member unions are principally autonomous. Consequently, corporatist networks that would enable the TUC to commit its members to centrally negotiated pacts have been very difficult to establish in Britain. The union landscape is highly fragmented; even within individual unions there are often strong traditions and institutions of decentralization. However, there is a trend towards merging unions to mitigate the great fragmentation in unionism. Margaret Thatcher defeated any beginnings of corporatism in the 1980s with her legislation on unions. Legislative changes required the notification of the employer of planned strikes, allowed collective dismissal of striking employees, and prohibited union sanctions against employees not willing to strike. The largest union is the public sector UNISON with 1.2 million members followed by the Transport and General Workers' Union (TGWU) with 880,000 members (Wilson 1993: 47–8; Plöhn 2001: 175; Becker 2002: 205–8).

The main national association representing pensioners is the National Pensioners Convention (NPC). Formally separate from the trade union movement, the convention nevertheless originated in 1979 as the brainchild of Jack Jones, a leading trade unionist of the period, and continues to rely heavily on union activists. Although in reality pensioners have highly diverse interests, the platform of the NPC is heavily shaped by trade unionism, notably by public sector trade unionism.

The Confederation of British Industry (CBI) is the main representative association of employers of all sectors. The CBI lobbies in parliament and in cabinet for its members' interests but is not involved in wage negotiations. Whereas the CBI membership is made up of companies, the Institute of Directors (IoD) is a club for individual employers and top managers, founded in 1903. The Institute of Directors gave very strong support of the Thatcher government at a time when the CBI, with its much more diverse membership, was often ambivalent about the Conservatives' liberal economic policies (Wilson 1993: 48; Becker 2002: 207). As the interests of employers and the financial business of the City of London do not always match, the financial sector has its own representative bodies such as the British Bankers' Association (BBA) and the Association of British Insurers (ABI). The rate of organization among special sector business associations is high.[2]

In the pensions industry sector, the National Association of Pension Funds (NAPF) constitutes the association of employer-sponsored occupational pension funds. The NAPF participates actively in pension policy-making by commenting on governmental proposals and lobbying. The Life Offices Association (LOA) and Associated Scottish Life Offices are trade associations which represent the interest of life assurance industry, approximately 90 percent of ordinary life assurance business in the UK. The lobbying power of the pensions industry, and its ability to participate in pensions policy networks, is very great. The pensions industry, although sometimes internally divided, is well integrated into the City of London—perhaps the single most effective constellation of interests in British society.

III PENSION SYSTEM

Historical overview

A Liberal government established the first state old-age pension system in Britain in July 1908, under pressure from the union movement and the Labour Party. Despite a lengthy process and numerous adversaries including the friendly societies, the government was able to introduce a law on non-contributory pensions, which provided for tax-financed, means-tested benefits at a retirement age of 70 years (Heclo 1974: 178; Ogus and Barendt 1982: 189; Secretary of State for Social Security 1998: 15).

As the benefits were extremely low, a Conservative government passed the *Widows', Orphans', and Old Age Contributory Pensions Act* in July 1925, establishing a contributory system. This insurance system provided pensions to employees between 65 and 70 years. After the insured turned 70, he or she received the full benefits provided by the non-contributory pensions scheme, but without a means test. The Act also provided for wives' supplements to husbands' pensions, for those of age 65 and above. But as women were frequently younger than their husbands, coverage was often inadequate until the wife turned 65. To remedy this, the female retirement age was reduced in 1940 from 65 to 60 years in the *Old Age and Widows' Pensions Act, 1940* (Heclo 1974: 207–209; Equal Opportunities Commission 1978: 6; Ogus and Barendt 1982: 43, 190).

Following World War II, the Beveridge Report suggested a unitary national contributory insurance system providing for a subsistence income for old age, disability, unemployment and widowhood. The Labour government passed the introduction of flat-rate benefits for flat-rate contributions in 1946 as the *National Insurance Act* (Heclo 1974: 254, 257).

But pension benefits were low and did not prevent old age poverty. Between the late 1950s and the early 1970s subsequent governments made proposals for superannuation. Each failed—or was not implemented due to new elections and change of government. After the return of Labour in 1974, parliament passed in cross-party consensus the

Social Security Pensions Act 1975. The act established a State Earnings-Related Pensions Scheme (SERPS) on top of the flat-rate basic pensions with the aim of providing pension entitlements amounting to 25 percent of income for all insured with earnings above the Lower Earnings Limit. SERPS benefits were calculated on the basis of the average earnings of the best of 20 years, and benefits were indexed to inflation. Concurrently, indexation of the flat-rate pensions was guaranteed in line with either price or wage inflation, whichever was greater. Due to the transition period, the SERPS only fully matured in 1998. Employers had the possibility of contracting-out of SERPS, thereby receiving a rebate of the state pension contribution, if the occupational scheme they offered guaranteed benefits at least equal to the SERPS (Perry 1986: 223; Barr and Coulter 1990: 279; Minns and Martin 1996: 222; Rechmann 2001: 65).

Thus, the *Social Security Pensions Act 1975* was not only a major step in the provision of state-earnings-related pensions, but it also set new incentives for the private, occupational pension market. However, occupational pensions in the UK had a long tradition even before the contracting-out rebates made them more attractive. The first occupational pension system for civil service was set up in 1810 for disability. This was expanded to a contributory old age pension for civil servants who had served at least 45 years in 1834. Big companies in the private sector followed the public sector in mid-nineteenth century and established occupational pension schemes mainly for their white-collar workers. The *Finance Act 1921* regulated that contributions to occupational pension funds and the return from investment was exempt from taxation. By 1936, 6,544 employers offered occupational pension schemes to approximately 1.6 million employees. The occupational pension coverage expanded continuously up to the 1970s and reached 10.6 million in 1987. By the 1970s most occupational pension benefits were based on final salary. The tax treatment of occupational pensions was revised by the *Finance Act 1970* offering 1.5 times final salary as tax-free lump sum in approved pension schemes. The *Social Security Pensions Act 1975* secured pension entitlements of early leavers (Goode 1993: 55–69).

Thus, as it had developed by 1975, the British Pension System comprised a "Beveridgean" low benefits tier and supplemental pensions that could be located in either the first or second pillars. The Thatcher revolution greatly enhanced the attractiveness of the second and third pillar options, but was not ultimately successful in eliminating supplemental pensions from the first pillar entirely. Nevertheless, even subsequent Labour governments did not propose public pension expansion, but rather focused on making occupational and private alternatives more widely available to low-income earners, and in strengthening the minimum social safety net in old age.

Description of the current pension system

Coverage

Today, the consequence of these past political decisions is a pension system composed of three pillars. (See Fig. 2.2 on p. 63 and Table A2 in the Appendix.) The first tier in the first pillar is the flat-rate Basic State Pension and covers the entire working population aged 16 to 65 with a minimum income of £94 per week (in 2005–2006). For coverage through the Basic State Pension employees and employers as well as self-employed pay contributions—so-called National Insurance Contributions (NICs). NICs are general social security contributions, that is they not only cover old age pensions but also health service, sickness, disability and incapacity benefits and job seeker's allowance. In 2004, 11.4 million pensioners received Basic State Pensions.[3] Although the Basic State Pension is based on the principles of employment and contribution payments it also creates derived rights to dependent, surviving or divorced spouses (Blake 2002: 1).

The second tier of the first pillar is an earnings-related component of the pension. The *Child Support, Pensions and Social Security Act 2000* recently replaced the State-Earnings-Related Pension Scheme (SERPS) with the State Second Pension (SSP). All salaried employees who pay National Insurance Contributions are covered by the State Second Pension at the same time. Although the self-employed contribute to the Basic State Pension Scheme they are covered neither by the former SERPS nor by the new State Second Pension. The ultimate goal of redesigning SERPS into SSP was to extend coverage to low-income earners, disabled persons and caregivers, turning the earnings-related element of SERPS into flat-rate benefits by April 2007 (Blake 2002: 7).

Insured employees may contract-out of SSP into approved occupational pension schemes—*Contracted-out Salary-related Schemes* (COSRS), *Contracted-out money-purchase Schemes* (COMPS), *Contracted-out Mixed Benefit Schemes* (COMBS) and *Contracted-out Hybrid Schemes* (COHS)—or personal pension plans—*Appropriate Personal Pension Schemes* or *Stakeholder Pension Schemes*.[4] Contracting-out is made attractive by the National Insurance rebate, as well as favorable tax treatment: contribution payments are not subject to income tax and employees receive part of their occupational pension as a tax-free lump sum (up to 25%). Moreover, the returns on investment are not liable to corporation tax or capital returns tax (Devetzi 1999: 59). In addition, since 2001, employers with more than five employees are required to provide access to at least one Stakeholder Pension Scheme(s) to their workforce if they do not offer suitable occupational pension arrangements.[5]

Administration

The structure of the state pension does not follow occupational lines, as it does in many other European countries, but the Basic State Pension revenues are administered and disbursed under the roof of the Inland Revenue National Insurance Office (NICO). NICO is in charge of over 65 million National Insurance accounts and provides services to insured persons (www.inlandrevenue.gov.uk/nic/aboutus.htm). The Department for Work and Pensions (DWP) (formerly Department for Social Security, DSS) takes responsibility for and monitors the Basic State Pension and SERPS/SSP entitlements and benefits. Dependent agencies divided into regional and local offices pay out pensions benefits (DWP 2002a: 42).

The Basic Pension System itself is divided into two categories: Category A entails pensions based on personal contributions to the National Insurance while Category B refers to deferred pension rights of a dependent spouse. Category D benefits go to people older than 80 years (and not entitled to either Category A or B) (DWP 2002a: 3).

The UK features a great diversity of private pension schemes—occupational and personal pensions. In the mid-1990s insured persons could chose among 150,000 pension schemes. Until now the Occupational Pensions Regulatory Authority (OPRA) regulated occupational pension arrangements and monitored the compliance of occupational and stakeholder pension schemes with the legislative requirements. Where the security of assets was in danger, OPRA had the power to appoint an independent trustee to the board of the respective pension fund. The *Pensions Act 2004* replaced OPRA with the so-called Pensions Regulator (HoL, 24.01.1995: col. 986; www.opra.gov.uk).

Occupational, private, and stakeholder Pension schemes are organized as trusts with boards of trustees as decision-making body. The schemes' pension funds are managed and invested usually by investment firms, banks or insurance companies known as fund managers. The Boards of Trustees are required to monitor the fund manager. The pension funds are invested in national or foreign shares, government securities and property. The distribution of pension funds in the UK is highly concentrated. Minns and Martin found that "63 percent of total pension fund accumulated assets are owned by organizations and companies with their headquarters in the southeast of England" and in return two-thirds of the "investments are invested in the shares of the top 90 companies based or headquartered in the southeast" (Minns and Martin 1996: 221–4, 226, 229; see also Minns 2001).

Membership organizations such as unions, financial service companies or employers may provide stakeholder pensions. Administrative charges for stakeholder pensions are limited to 1 percent of the personal fund value per year. Personal Pensions are offered and administered by finance companies or life insurance companies. The Financial Services Authority (FSA), which is the statutory regulator for financial services since 2001, monitors the field of private pensions (Devetzi 1999: 59; Blake 2002: 1, 8; www.inlandrevenue.gov.uk/pensionschemes/orgs.htm#1).

The Pension Protection Fund (PPF) was established only recently by the *Pensions Act 2004*, after several scandals revealed that occupational pension schemes were being underfunded. The PPF is financed through levies on defined-benefit occupational pension schemes and its aim is to protect the members of such schemes in case of the employer's insolvency (DWP 2004).

Financing

The Basic State Pension as well as SERPS and SSP are contribution-based, pay-as-you-go systems. Contributions for the flat-rate, basic pensions and the SERPS/SSP are paid to the National Insurance Fund (NIF). It is important to note that the National Insurance Contributions not only contribute to the financing of pensions but the NIF covers all social security benefits, and therefore, revenues of the pension systems cannot be extracted. Contribution rates follow a categorization of classes.

First pillar	Second pillar	Third pillar
Third tier: none	Voluntary occupational pension: all contributions above £3,600 per year (CISRS, CIMPS)	Voluntary private pension: all contributions above £3,600 per year
Second tier: State Earnings-Related Pensions Scheme (SERPS) (1978-April 2002) and State Second Pensions (SSP) (since April 2002) [Employees, Self-employed, Farmers, Civil Servants]	OR Stakeholder pensions: mandatory offer by employer; voluntary for employees and self-employed	
First tier: basic state pension [Employees, Self-employed, Farmers, Civil Servants] Means-tested Part for > 80-years	OR Contracting-out to approved occupational pension schemes instead of SSP (either defined-benefit or defined-contribution: COSRS, COMBS, COHS, COMPS)	OR Contracting-out to Appropriate Personal Pensions (instead of SERPS or SSP)
Tax-financed, means-tested Income Support for pensioners plus housing benefits, council tax Benefits, winter fuel payment (Pension Credit since Oct. 2003; previously MIG)		

Fig. 2.2 Pension system in the United Kingdom

Class 1 contributions are shared between employees and their employers: employees pay 11 percent and employers pay a rate of 12.8 percent for all gross earnings between the Earnings Threshold of £94 per week, and the Upper Earnings Limit of £630 per week (in 2005–06).[6]

Employers pay the full rate for the entire earnings without upper limit. However, starting in 2003, employee's contributions also fall due for income above the Upper Earnings Limit—namely 1 percent of earnings. Wages lower than the Earnings Threshold are not subject to Class 1 contribution payments—neither for the employee nor for his employer. "However, once earnings reach the Lower Earnings Limit (LEL) (set at £77 per week for 2003–04) contributions will be treated as having been paid on earnings from the Lower Earnings Limit up to and including the ET" (Inland Revenue 2003: 5). Employees who have more than one job pay National Insurance Contributions in each job up to a maximum of 53 times Upper Earnings Limit minus Earnings Threshold.[7]

Employees who contract-out from SSP by means of an occupational pension scheme receive a rebate in National Insurance Contributions of 1.6 percent, their employers a rebate of 3.5 percent for salary-related schemes and a rebate of 1.0 percent for money-purchase schemes (www.hmrc.gov.uk/rates/nic.htm). Although Appropriate Personal Pensions are another possibility for contracting-out they do not reduce the National Insurance Contribution rate. Instead the Inland Revenue National Insurance Contributions Office (NICO) will transfer the corresponding sum of payments to the insured's Appropriate Personal Pension Scheme at the end of each year (Inland Revenue 2003: 9).

Self-employed people with a yearly income above £4,345 (2005–06) pay a flat-rate part and a profits-related part of contributions. Class 2 contributions are £2.10 per week. Additionally the self-employed have to disburse 7 percent of all gains between the Lower Profits Limit of £4,895 per year and the Upper Profits Limit of £32,760 per year (in 2005–06). Starting in 2003, gains above the Upper Profits limits are subject to a contribution rate of 1 percent. Voluntary contribution payment to National Insurance is possible in Class 3. It is an opportunity for non-working people or citizens living abroad to build up pension entitlements by contributing a flat-rate of £7.35 per week (2005–06). Parliament has the right to assign a Treasury Grant to the National Insurance Fund since 1993 in order to sustain the Fund's finances (Kral 2001: 24; Mayhew 2001: 2; Inland Revenue 2003: 12–13).

Occupational and private pensions are mostly funded, except for the occupational scheme of the public sector. As the Green Paper for the pension reform of 1999 points out "... the market value of the financial assets of all funded occupational pension schemes and personal pensions is about £830 billion. With such amounts at their disposal, pension funds are a major player in domestic and overseas financial markets, and are an important element in the stability and growth of the wider UK economy" (Secretary of State for Social Security 1998: 22).

Benefits

Basic State Pension benefits are flat-rate and do not depend on income. In order to be eligible for a full basic pension, the insured person needs to have contributed for 90 percent of the entire potential working career between 16 and 65—that is to say 44 possible years (for women, only 39 years until 2020). Eligibility to the basic pension requires a minimum qualifying period of 10 years; the share of flat-rate benefits is adjusted according to the number of years of insurance. Several conditions create entitlement to pension credits even if no contribution payments to National Insurance are made.[8] Unemployed persons, people suffering from illness or disability, or persons who are receiving Maternity Allowance or Carer's Allowance or Working Tax Credit, or who are taking approved training, receive credits at the weekly Lower Earnings Limit (Inland Revenue 2003: 17–18). Retirement age is 65 years for men and 60 years for women. However, equal retirement age of 65 years has already been passed in parliament (*Pensions Act 1995*) and will be phased-in between 2010 and 2020. Early retirement or partial pension does not exist. Late retirement is possible between 42 days and five years after standard retirement age. Each year of deferred retirement leads to a benefit bonus of 7.5 percent of the flat-rate Basic State Pension benefit now changed to a bonus of 10.4 percent (*Pensions Act 2004*; DWP 2002a: 3).

The full basic pension flat-rate benefit is £79.60 (April 2004) per week.[9] Supplements of £47.65 ($\approx$ €70) are paid for dependent spouse. Pensioners above 80 years get a supplement of 25p ($\approx$ 37 cents) per week (DWP 2002 a: 5; MISSOC 2002). This means "that if a person is attempting to live on the state pension alone then that person is living in the very greatest poverty" (Baroness Seear in HoL, 24.01.1995: col. 986).

Means-tested, tax-financed income supplements have always been available to augment the primary flat-rate pension. The so-called Income Support provides benefits of £55.65 ($\approx$ €82 in 2004) but savings, real estate and other incomes are taken into account. Persons who qualify for Income Support also benefit from extra payments such as Winter Fuel Payment, Cold Weather Payment and Housing Benefits (MISSOC 2002). However, employees with incomes below the minimum income limit did not acquire entitlements for the state pension in the past, neither did people with an unsteady working life. A Minimum Income Guarantee (MIG) was replaced by the Pension Credit in October 2003 guaranteeing a minimum of £105.45 ($\approx$ €154) a week for singles or £160.95 ($\approx$ €236) for couples in 2004 (www.dwp.gov.uk/publications/dwp/2004/gl23_apr.pdf).

Drawing second tier first pillar SERPS/SSP pensions benefits is only possible on reaching standard retirement age, and there is a minimum qualifying period of one year of contribution payments. SERPS benefits are calculated as 20 percent of average revalued lifetime earnings.[10] The SSP uses different accrual rates for lower income bands during a transition period (see Appendix Table A2). After the transition period SSP will be flat-rate benefits, calculated as if everybody had earned the Lower Earnings Threshold (Bill HC 9/1999: EN Part II 211.–212.).

SERPS/SSP benefits are reduced for each year of a contracted-out occupational pension scheme or appropriate personal pension. Widows and widowers had received the full amount of the SERPS pensions benefit of the deceased spouse in the past. With effect from 5 October 2002, the rate for the survivor was reduced from 100 percent to 50 percent. Both Basic Pension and SERPS/SSP pension benefits are fully indexed with inflation beyond 2.5 percent. Adjustment is decided by parliamentary act on a yearly basis (Budd and Campbell 1998: 109; Inland Revenue 2003: 29).

Concurrent employment while drawing pension benefits is possible and men over 65 and women over 60 years do not have to pay National Insurance Contributions

(*Certificate of Age Exception*), only the employer's share falls due (Budd and Campbell 1998: 25; MISSOC 2002; Inland Revenue 2003: 25). Basic Pension and SERPS benefits are subject to income tax with a tax-free lump sum[11] but no social security contributions have to be made.

Benefit regulations of private pensions are dependent on whether the scheme qualifies for contracting-out or Stakeholder Pensions. Those occupational schemes and private pension plans that cannot substitute SERPS/SSP are free to define contribution conditions, qualifying criteria and benefit calculation formula. In contrast, contracted-out occupational pension schemes, appropriate personal pension plans and Stakeholder Pensions have to comply with a number of requirements: first, until April 2005 these schemes had to adjust pension entitlements and benefits to price increases up to 5 percent per year, and since April 2005 up to 2.5 percent per year.[12] Second, the benefits to be expected have to be as high as SERPS/SSP benefits. Third, the contribution rate must not be below the National Insurance Contribution rebate. The most frequently used occupational schemes (COSRS) calculate pension benefits on the assessment-base derived from the average salary of the last three years prior to retirement multiplied by the number of years of insurance (maximum 40 years) times 1/80th (Blake 2002: 2).

IV Politics of pension reform since 1980

Overview

To understand British pension politics one must begin by recalling some of the key historical and institutional features covered in our sketch of the system. Some of these are the product of the pension system itself; some reflect the wider institutional setting of that system in the structure of the British welfare system. Esping-Andersen (1990) points out that the residual character of a British system means that collective public provision functions as a floor on which private arrangements are erected. This residual character historically influenced the development of pensions policy. Neither universalist coalitions (like those in Scandinavia) nor powerful corporatist institutions (as in Bismarckian welfare systems) were obstacles to pension reform. Moreover, there existed by the beginning of the 1980s a uniquely close connection between the pension system and financial markets, through the system of occupational pension schemes. That connection also intersected with a key institutional feature of British economic life: the dominant place occupied by the financial markets of the City of London in not only the British financial system but also in the wider economy. Pension funds were controlled from the financial services economy of the South-East, and were invested heavily in enterprises also controlled from the South-East, in particular from London. The dominant position of the City-based markets was magnified by the development of policy throughout the 1980s: by the decline of the manufacturing sector in the economy, and by the development, especially after the "Big Bang" deregulatory reforms on the Stock Exchange in 1986, of a financial services boom.

It is therefore no surprise to discover that British pension policy in the 1980s and 1990s involved a continuous strengthening of the private and capital-funded pillars of the pension system. One of the first cost-saving changes in the British Pension System was the change in pension adjustment to price index in 1980. Previously, pensions were indexed either to price or wage increase whichever one was higher (Pierson 1994: 59; Bonoli 2000: 62).

The most important reform of the decade was the *Social Security Act 1986*. How we judge the magnitude of the reform depends on whether we evaluate the extent to which it actually retrenched benefits, or whether we measure it by comparing what was eventually enacted with the initial proposals. The 1986 Act not only cut SERPS benefits but also created incentives to stimulate further privatization of supplementary pensions.

After an almost 20-year long discussion of equal retirement ages for men and women the *Pensions Act 1995* increased women's retirement age to 65. At the same time a comprehensive regulatory framework was set up to protect early leavers' pension rights and to guard pension funds from fraud and mismanagement.

In order to close remaining gaps in occupational and/or private pension coverage the *Welfare Reform and Pensions Act 1999* introduced Stakeholder Pensions. One year later the *Child Support, Pensions and Social Security Act 2000* replaced SERPS with a phased-in flat-rate State Second Pension intending first to upgrade low-income earners benefits and second to reinforce incentives for high-income earners to contract-out.

The Social Security Act 1986

Background: changes in the early 1980s

It is striking that while the Conservatives were elected with a secure parliamentary majority in 1979, their landmark reform did not pass until six years, and one general election triumph, later. The reason for this has partly to do with the internal politics of the Conservative Party, and partly to do with way even the new government in 1979 was still mired in a wide range of apparently intractable problems concerning the pension system.

In pension policy itself, the government had to face the problems of reducing the public share in pension costs and of regulating preservation of occupational benefit entitlements of early retirees. In February 1981, the Thatcher government established the Scott Committee which was supposed to analyze the difference between public and private sector occupational pensions. Civil servants' pensions were

Table 2.3 Overview of proposed and enacted pension reforms in the United Kingdom

Year	Name of reform	Reform process (chronology)	Reform measures
1983	Equal Retirement	• 1975 Equal Opportunity Commission • July 22, 1981 Social Service Committee	• Equal retirement age for men and women – failed
1986	Social Security Act 1986	• 1981 Scott Committee • 1981 Occupational Pensions Board Report • 1983 Inquiry Commission "Provision for Retirement" • June 1985 Green Paper • December 1986 White Paper (major modifications) • April 1986 passage in both houses	• Introduction of private pension plans as subsidized contracting-out possibility; • Extension of reference period for SERPS benefits from 20 years to life-time career; reduction of replacement rate of SERPS from 25% to 20% of assessment base; • Reduction of widow's pension from 100% to 50% of deceased's benefits
1995	Pensions Act 1995	• June 1992 Pension Law Review Committee ("Goode Committee") • June 1994 White Paper • July 1995 passage in both houses	• Regulations to protect occupational pension funds against fraud and mismanagement; • Regulation on vesting of pension entitlements for early leavers; • Abolishment of requirement for occupational pensions to provide Guaranteed Minimum Pensions; • Increase in female retirement age from 60 to 65
1999	Welfare Reform and Pensions Act 1999	• 1997 Pension Provision Group • December 1998 Green Paper "A New Contract for Welfare: Partnership in Pensions" • Labour peers signal opposition → modifications in incapacity benefits • November 1999 passage of in both houses	• Introduction of means-tests for incapacity benefits; • Introduction of Stakeholder Pensions

2000	Child Support, Pensions and Social Security Bill 2000	• December 1998 Green Paper "Partnership in Pensions" • December 1999 governmental bill • July 2000 passage of bill in both houses • Low-income earners with income above lower earnings limit are treated as if they earned the lower earnings threshold • Replacement of earnings-related SERPS benefits with flat-rate State Second Pensions (SSP) benefits
2004	Pensions Act 2004	• December 2002 Green Paper • June 2003 Green Paper • February 2004 Green Paper • May 12, 2004 bill • November 18, 2004 passage • Establishment of the Pension Protection Fund to protect members of defined-benefit schemes if employers become insolvent and pension funds are underfunded • Replacement of OPRA by Pensions Regulator • Change in indexation requirements for occupational defined-benefit schemes (reduction from 5% to 2.5% cap) • Introduction of rewards for late retirement (plus 10.4% per extra year of employment) • Refunding early leavers' contributions if vesting period was not fulfilled

inflation-proofed, and in times of high inflation they caused unprecedented costs. But instead of proposing abolition of indexation for civil service pensions, the Scott Committee suggested the extension to the private sector of the public sector regulations. The government ignored the recommendations.

The Occupational Pensions Board, which had been commissioned to scrutinize the problem of early leavers in occupational pensions, in 1981 suggested preserving and adjusting early retirees' pension benefit to inflation—a proposal that, according to Nesbitt, employers simply could not afford (Nesbitt 1995: 36, 38).

The harmonization of men's and women's retirement age was another prominent policy issue from the late 1970s. With the establishment of the Equal Opportunities Commission in 1975, the gender difference in standard retirement age advanced to the top of the political agenda. Trades Union Congress and the Labour Party pledged for a reduction of men's retirement age and thus a common age of 60 years (Equal Opportunities Commission 1978: 2; Social Services Committee 1982: xxi). Retirement at 60 would also slightly benefit the labor market and help to reduce unemployment (GMWU 1982: 337–338; ISTC 1982: 348; TUC 1982: 127, 132). The Department for Health and Social Security (DHSS) rejected the lowering of men's retirement age because not only did it imply greater immediate cost in terms of men's benefits at a younger age but the department was afraid that people's additional private old age provisions were not laid out for a longer period in retirement. Consequently, the Department feared that after the private assets were exhausted the pensioners would claim supplementary benefits from the state. A reduction of men's retirement age would cost £2,500 millions per year, financed, for example, through an increased contribution rate of +1.2 percent. In contrast, estimated net savings, if the female retirement age was increased, amounted to £400 millions per year (Equal Opportunities Commission 1978: 13; Social Service Committee 1982: 457–61).

The diverging preferences and the financial and legal problems associated with the retirement age led to further suspension of appropriate legislation. The government assigned the Social Services Committee to investigate and recommend options for the equalization of retirement age on 22 July 1981. The Committee suggested a flexible retirement age with reduced benefits from 60 years on, which was also favored by the CBI, the Conservative Party, and the Liberal Party.[13] Both employers (CBI) and private insurance industry (LOA and NAPF) requested long periods for phasing-in new retirement ages (CBI 1982: 275, 283; LOA 1982: 192; NAPF 1982: 104; NFSE 1982: 294–95). But before any legislative action was taken national elections were scheduled.

The situation of the Thatcher government was critical in the early 1980s both in political and in economic terms. On the one hand the Conservative Party faced a new challenging party formation, on the other hand unemployment was rising. But when inflation rates were ameliorating and the Falkland war improved the Conservative standing in opinion polls, Prime Minister Margaret Thatcher called an early election on June 9, 1983. On election day, the Conservative Party lost in terms of votes but it achieved—in terms of seats—a majority of 144.

The Green Paper

Although Thatcher guaranteed prior to the 1983 elections that the earnings-related pensions would not be touched, an Inquiry Commission "Provision for Retirement" was set up in the fall of 1983 to scrutinize the three pillars of the British pension system with special attention to the portability of pension rights for employees who changed employers, and the recommendations on retirement age by the Select Committee on Social Services (TUC 1984: 1; HoC, 15.04.1986: col. 750–51). According to Bonoli, it was surprising that the Commission was built mainly of ministers, but that neither pensioners nor employees were represented. Interest groups were only given a short two-month period to comment on the Commission's report in November 1984 (Bonoli 2000: 66).

This method of producing policy proposals was indeed surprising by the conventional standards of British government. But it was not a surprise given the new thinking which increasingly emboldened the Conservatives in government. Before 1979, the notion that policy should only be made after extensive consultation with affected interests was engrained in the British policy-making system—a core institutional value. Thatcherism, especially Thatcherism after the victory of 1983, marked a great departure, not only in policy content, but also in policy style. It turned away from consensus and cooperation with affected interests to decision-making through small task forces, drawn from the core executive, and often indeed drawn from a small number of trusted senior ministers and Conservative policy advisors. The autonomous manner of producing the pension proposals thus arose from a fundamental institutional change in British government: the rise of a policy-making style which asserted the autonomy of the core executive from institutions of civil society.

One of the aims of the 1986 reform was to improve portability of occupational pension rights (Bonoli 2000: 61–6). The government intended to introduce personal pensions as a contracting-out option alternative to occupational pensions. Secretary of State Norman Fowler envisaged offering the opportunity to transfer occupational pension entitlements to new individualized pensions annuity plans if an employee changed or left employment (early leavers). The personal pensions would be based on a money purchase principle.

The DHSS issued a Green Paper on 3 June, 1985 to sound out the positions of all relevant actors in pension policy. Pierson refers to this proposal as an "undeniable bombshell" (Pierson 1994: 60). Although the Green Paper was quite general and did not include precise estimations of expected savings, it was clear that the aim of the government proposal was significant long-term savings (Fowler (C) in HoC, 03.06.1985: col. 42). The Chancellor of the Exchequer planned to save £1 billion (HoC, 06.06.1985: col. 465). The press even predicted that the increase in National Insurance contributions would boost revenues by £1.5 to 2 billions per year (*Financial Times* 13.05.1985). The Green Paper suggested replacing SERPS with compulsory contributions of 4 percent either to an occupational pension scheme or to a personal pension scheme. The employers of all employees with earnings above a certain limit would have to contribute at least half of the 4 percent contribution rate. This change would affect the National Insurance in as far as the total contribution rate would be reduced from 19.45 percent to 16.5 percent of earnings, but at the same time the contracted-out rebate of 6.25 percent was to be phased out over a three-year period. Men above 50 years and women above 45 years would not be affected by the new system but their pensions would be calculated according to the old SERPS or contracted-out scheme's provisions (DHSS 1985b: 5, 8; HoC, 03.06.1985: col. 37–8).

Notwithstanding the recommendations of the Equal Opportunity Commission and of the Social Services Committee Report of 1982, and despite the government's desire to economize, the Green Paper did not make any suggestions to raise female retirement age or to equalize the pension age in any other way (DHSS 1985b: 10).

The Green Paper was briefly debated in the House of Commons on June 3, 1985. The debate followed the stylized form of parliamentary adversarial combat in a legislature with a weak grasp of the technical details of policy. The Labour opposition attacked the government for being the "pension snatcher" and for "dismantling the welfare state" (Meacher (Lab) and Faulds (Lab) in HoC, 03.06.1985: cols. 40, 50).

Outside parliament the Green Paper met almost unified opposition.[14] The Trades Union Congress (TUC) rejected the extension of money purchase schemes mainly because of high administrative costs and because the dependence on the rate of return from investment was insecure and hampered planning for old age. The TUC was also strongly opposed to the abolition of SERPS. It argued that positive aspects would be lost: for example, SERPS was an attractive alternative for persons with irregular working careers, and women, because of the 20 best years rule. The TUC further argued that there was no independent Royal Commission to prepare and consult on the pension reform but that unilateral action by the government produced the reform draft. The complaint showed how far the unions were, even after six years of Conservative government, still attached to the old ways of making policy by extended consultation with, and conciliation of, affected interests—a method that, as we have seen, Thatcherite Conservatism was abandoning (TUC 1984: 3–6; TUC 1985a: 9; TUC 1985c: 16, 38).

Beyond these arguments the TUC also tried to mobilize its membership. It is striking how symbolic and ineffectual these were—the typical tactics of pressure groups operating from a point of weakness in the British system. The experience shows once again how far policy-making was controlled by an increasingly autonomous core executive. It called on union members to write protest letters to their MPs, to the Minister of Social Services and to alert local newspapers and radio stations. It also called for participation in a national march in London on October 27, 1985 and made the government proposals known both by textual Green Paper summaries and by anti-reform propaganda with posters, stickers and leaflets (TUC 1985a: 16–17; TUC 1985b; TUC 1985d: 13; TWGU 1985a, b).

The Green Paper also provoked protests from employers and the pension industry. The NAPF favored the existing regulations because the system based on the 1975 all-party consensus assured planning reliability. Continuity in legislation was one of the top priorities for the pension industry. NAPF and CBI promoted a modification of SERPS that would significantly reduce the costs rather than involve its abolition (DHSS 1985a: 3, 12; TUC 1985a: 5, 9). Employers argued that a coherent state system was to be replaced by a fragmented assemblage of occupational and private schemes, that administration costs to set up an occupational scheme were too high for small- and medium-sized employers and, last but not least, they flinched from the transition costs and double payment problem to the new system (Pierson 1994: 61; Rechmann 2001: 69–70).

The National Pensioners' Convention also opposed the Green Paper. As they defended the rights of existing pensioners their attention was focused more on the abolition of supplementary benefits than on the SERPS (NPC 1985: 10).

Gallup opinion polls showed that the Conservatives fell from 44 percent in July 1983 to 34 percent in June 1985, and another 10 percentage points between mid-June and mid-August 1985. In September 1985, the Alliance took the lead for a second time after December 1981 to February 1982 in the opinion polls.[15]

The White Paper

In reaction to the fierce opposition, the government deviated from the Green Paper proposal when it published a White Paper in December 1985. The White Paper contained major concessions to the employers' and pension industry's claims. On the precondition that Exchequer costs for pensions would be reduced, and incentives for personal pensions created, the government now agreed to maintain SERPS. Changes that were part of the White Paper included the provision that contracted-out occupational schemes would not have to guarantee full inflation-proofing but only up to 3 percent per year. With respect to SERPS benefit calculation, the benefit assessment base was extended from 20 best years to lifetime earnings (i.e. 44 years for men and 39 years for women) and the pensioners could only expect 20 percent instead of 25 percent of the assessment base as pension benefits. The transition period was scheduled from 1998 to 2009 with a reduction of 0.5 percentage points a year. Widows and widowers' pensions would be reduced from 100 percent to 50 percent of the deceased's benefits. The expected savings would amount to £12.5 billion by 2033 equaling 50 percent of the costs of pensions without reform (DHSS 1985a: para 1.15, 1.16, 1.17).

The most important change that promised to make occupational pension schemes much more attractive for employers was that they were allowed to offer defined-contribution schemes, whereas previously, under the *Social Security Pensions Act 1975*, only defined-benefit schemes were allowed to contract-out. Moreover, all new occupational schemes and take-ups of personal pension plans would be rewarded by an additional rebate in National Insurance contributions of 2 percent for the first five years after the new arrangements took effect (DHSS 1985a: para 1.18). The additional rebate would prove to be a fatal decision later on—a major subsequent source of cost escalation. The provisions enacted rose short-term cost—via forgone revenues—by estimated £9.7 billions for the period 1987 to 1993 (Wain 1995: 329).

Parliamentary process

The second reading in the House of Commons on January 28, 1986 showed that not only the opposition parties rejected the reform proposal, but also Conservative backbenchers had reservations even after the modifications between the Green Paper and the governmental bill (HoC, 15.04.1986: col. 751).

Some of the Conservative dissent reflected the presence on the backbenches of a style of Conservatism that Thatcherism had displaced. Thus, Francis Pym—the Conservative member for South-East Cambridgeshire, a constituency where the SDP candidate C. J. Slee ran second in the 1983 election[16]—demanded that the government should not insist on their proposal, but should set up a Royal Commission to produce an independent report and to base a new bill on up-to-date evidence and calculations (Pym in HoC, 28.01.1986: cols. 840–2).

In fact, the parliamentary debate was dominated by wrangling over time allocations for debate. This reflects the essential character of parliamentary scrutiny—which is less about debating the merits of an issue than advancing the partisan battle.

The Pensions Act 1995

Background: pre-parliamentary stage

On November 5, 1991, Robert Maxwell, head of the Maxwell affiliated group, died in mysterious circumstances. After his death, it was discovered that £400 million had been taken out of the group's occupational pension funds. Employees who had lost their occupational pension entitlements, due to the Maxwell transactions, were partly compensated through a £2.5 million relief fund set up by the Department of Social Security in 1992 (Nesbitt 1995: 136–7). But the scandal showed that legislative action was necessary to safeguard pension entitlements, which meant to imposing minimum funding standards on occupational and private pension funds, and improving control mechanisms.

The government of John Major (who unexpectedly won the General Election of 1992, having succeeded Margaret Thatcher as Prime Minister in 1990) was responsible for dealing with the aftermath of this scandal. Thus, the government established a *Pension Law Review Committee* on June 8, 1992 with representatives from the pensions industry and the research community as committee members, and Professor Goode as committee chairman (Davies 2000: 20). The Committee was assigned

> (t)o review the framework of law and regulation within which occupational pension schemes operate, taking into account the rights and interests of scheme members, pensioners and employers; to consider in particular the status of ownership of occupational pension funds and the accountability and roles of trustees, fund managers, auditors and pension scheme advisers; and to make recommendations (Goode 1993: iii).

The Committee published its report in 1993 and recommended enacting a separate pensions act which would further regulate the pre-existing trust law. A way of controlling funding standards, including restrictions on the withdrawal of surpluses and a change in appointment of trustees, was designed to safeguard the occupational pensions to a greater degree (Nesbitt 1995: 138).

The government published a White Paper in June 1994 and eventually a governmental bill in December 1994. The bill envisaged measures to improve monitoring and control of private and occupational pension funds in the wake of the Maxwell scandal. At the same time, the bill introduced changes in several other areas of the pension system: The cost-saving measures entailed the following:

1. An increase in retirement age for women from 60 to 65 combined with an increase in required contribution years for full benefit from 39 to 44 from 2010 to 2020.
2. Annualization of the SERPS entitlement calculation changed, i.e. entitlements were calculated per year and not as a sum at the point of time retiring. In other words, years with earnings below the minimum income limit could not be neutralized by an average of the entire working life above the lower income limit.
3. Contribution reductions to the National Insurance Funds were to be out-phased for younger people in favor of reductions as incentives to older people (Budd and Campbell 1998: 111; Davies 2000: 20).
4. The bill facilitated the requirements for contracting-out significantly.

Prior to the *Pensions Act 1995*, occupational salary-related schemes had to provide a Guaranteed Minimum Pension that would at least equal the sum a person would have received if he or she had not contracted-out but stayed in SERPS. The occupational pension provider had to adjust the Guaranteed Minimum Pensions to inflation up to 3 percent. If inflation rose above 3 percent, the state covered for all adjustment cost above the 3 percent rate (Blake 2002: 4). In other words, the reform measure, the abolishment of the Guaranteed Minimum Pensions, increased not only the incentives for employers to offer occupational pension schemes but also reduced state expenditure at the same time as extra inflation adjustment costs ceased to exist.

After years of discussions on flexible retirement age or retirement age at 60 the government had settled for the 65-year option. The Trades Union Congress mobilized against the increase in female retirement age and sent out a campaign pack with model letters to lobby with one's local member of parliament. The unions also met with Labour Party front bench members to elaborate their position (TUC 1994; 1995: 64; TUC 1995: 63). But it is important to note that no consultations between Conservatives and the TUC were mentioned.

Parliamentary stage

The bill was first debated in the House of Lords on January 24, 1995 (HoL, 21.01.1995: cols. 974–1052). During parliamentary debates an issue of controversy was the staffing of the boards of trustees. In addition, Labour and Liberals further pledged for flexible retirement, namely, a "decade of retirement" between 60 and 70 (HoC, 24.04.1995: col. 545). Overall, the *Pensions Bill 1995* was widely supported in the House of Lords as well as in the House of Commons (*The Times*, 25.01.1995). The reformed regulation of the system in the context of Maxwell met hardly any opposition. In spite of unions' protests and campaigns against other measures—such as the harmonization of the retirement age—and rejection of the proposal by the Labour opposition the law passed both houses in early July 1995.

The act achieved not only equal retirement age but also passed measures for better protection of the members of defined-benefit occupation pension schemes. The *Pensions Act 1995* introduced a minimum solvency requirement for defined-benefit occupational funds. That is to say, if the pension scheme's liability coverage fell below 90 percent, the employer would have to increase the assets (Bill 87/1995: clause 50–54). It enrolled the pension funds to index occupational pensions and Appropriate Personal Pensions annually (increase with inflation up to 5 percent). With respect to the composition of pension boards, members of schemes received the right to select one-third of the trustees (HoL, 24.01.1995: col. 975). With regards to monitoring, the act established a new body, the Occupational Pensions Regulatory Authority, and introduced personal punishment (fines and imprisonment) of pension board trustees for mismanagement (Bill 87/1995: clause 1-28). A Pensions Ombudsman was established. The act set up a compensation scheme for underfunded pension funds and introduced age-related rebates of National Insurance Contributions for those contracted-out of SERPS into Appropriate Personal Pensions and Contracted-Out Money Purchase Schemes (PT 1994).

Although the *Pensions Act 1995* include several features to improve the protection of pension fund mismanagement, and of pension fund insolvency, it did not regulate or cap administrative charges for private pensions—an element that still turned private pensions quite unprofitable for low-income earners (Fawcett 2002: 15).

The passage of the 1995 Act thus presents us with a political riddle: why was the political opposition of the unions sufficient to block an increase in the female retirement age in 1986, but not in 1995? In addressing this question, once again, we highlight the changes in the party constellation. In the 1983 General Election, female voters were slightly over-represented in the Conservative and in the Alliance electorate, and thus constituted a credible electoral threat (Butler and Kavanagh 1984: 296). By 1995, this threat had faded, and so the retirement age could be raised without electoral repercussions.[17]

The Welfare Reform and Pensions Act 1999

Background: 1997 election and pre-parliamentary stage

On March 5, 1997, Secretary of State for Social Security presented a plan to reform the state basic pension. His proposal foresaw that employees should build up their own "Basic Pension Plus." The incentive to fund such personal basic pensions was an additional rebate on the National Insurance Contributions. The implementation of this proposal would have led to the incremental disappearance of the state pension pillar (DSS 1997; ICPR 1997). But before any further steps could be taken elections took place, and in May 1997 Labour returned with a landslide Commons majority.

According to the government, by the late 1990s there were two obvious gaps in the British pension system: people outside the labor market or with very low earnings (i.e. below £3,300 a year) were not covered; and people with income between £3,300 and £9,000, carers and disabled people usually did not belong to a private funded pension scheme as administrative costs were too high in proportion to the low contribution payments they could afford. The shortcomings in personal pensions that had to be solved by legislative action were to prevent mis-selling, to reduce start-up and administrative costs, and to improve the quality of information provided. Another problem was that within the group of the poorest were many pensioners who would be entitled to Income Support but did not claim it.[18]

As early as 1996, the Labour Party unveiled its intentions in pension policy. Labour planned to establish a new kind of supplementary pension open to those employees who did not have access to an occupational scheme (approximately 12 million people). SERPS would be available for carers or low-income earners unable to build up a private retirement savings scheme. Labour further promised to consider the issue of a minimum pension for the poorest pensioners to relieve them from means-tested Income Support (TUC 1996: 4–6).

In June 1997, the government published a consultation document which invited interest groups to comment and to make proposals. A Pension Provision Group, chaired by Tom Ross, was installed in order to reach consensus on the perception of current pension levels and future trends (Secretary of State for Social Security 1998: 15).

In December 1998, the Labour government issued a Green Paper: *A New Contract for Welfare: Partnership in Pensions*, which argued that occupational pensions legislation should respond to changing labor market conditions and marital stability. These included increasing numbers of part-time jobs; frequent changes of employers; rising employment in small- and medium-sized companies; unsteady working careers; and sharing of pension rights in cases of divorce. The objective was to enlarge the coverage for sufficient total pension income for low-income earners through the means of a State Second Pension (SSP), which was to replace SERPS. Furthermore, coverage was improved as low contributions and low administrative costs of new Stakeholder Pensions made contracting-out more attractive for low-income earners. The bill aimed at ensuring "that more people take out a funded second pension" in making Stakeholder Pensions more appealing to employees with incomes between £9,000 and £18,500 per year (Secretary of State for Social Security 1998: 5; HoC, 23.02.1999: col. 230). The Stakeholder Pensions were envisioned to cover, within the existing framework of occupational and personal pensions, approximately 35 percent of employees whose employers did not offer an occupational pension scheme, and to cover also the self-employed. Voluntary continuation of contributions to Stakeholder Pensions with tax relief would be possible for five years after stopping work (Secretary of State for Social Security 1998: 25–26, 48, 62; Bill 44/1999: 5).

Stakeholder Pension schemes were to be organized as trusts under the leadership of a board of trustees. They had to meet minimum standards concerning costs, access and terms, and their governance structure had to be approved and registered.

Administrative charges were to be paid as a percentage of contributions, or of personal entitlements, but not as a lump sum. Members had to be offered the possibility "to stop and re-start contributions without penalty"; transfer of entitlements to different schemes was to be easily accessible; and annual information on expected pension benefits had to be guaranteed (Secretary of State for Social Security 1998: 52–4).

The paper further recommended providing a guaranteed minimum income in retirement, and transforming SERPS into State Second Pensions (Act c. 30 of 1999). The State Second Pension also was intended to motivate contracting-out as benefits would be flat-rate in the long-run, while contributions remained earnings-related (Disney et al. 2001: 10).

The Trades Union Congress, in its response to the Green Paper, considered occupational pension schemes the best way to provide for supplementary pensions and therefore the unions' top goal was to broaden the range of occupational pensions and, in the best of all cases, to make them mandatory. Nevertheless the TUC welcomed the proposal to complement the basic state pension with Stakeholder Pensions as private, supplementary pensions; but Congress requested a contribution rate of 10 percent to ensure that Stakeholder Pensions might realistically alleviate poverty in old age. Moreover, the TUC would have preferred that the employers be required to contribute to Stakeholder Pensions. However, the provision of access by employers and the limitation of charges on Stakeholder Pensions found TUC approval (TUC 1998: 2; TUC 1999a: 89–90; Ward 2000a).

Parliamentary stage

The government laid the *Welfare Reform and Pensions Bill 1999* before the House of Commons on February 10, 1999 (Bill 44/1999; HoC, 11.02.1999). Even before the consultation process was over, the bill was deliberated in detail in a second parliamentary reading scheduled for February 23, 1999 (HoC, 23.02.1999: col. 231). Controversy in parliament did not revolve around Stakeholder Pensions but around disability pensions. Incapacity benefits had been used to keep the number of long-term unemployed low. But the rising number of people claiming this benefit and concurrently drawing occupational pensions necessitated legislative action. The precondition envisaged for eligibility to incapacity benefits was that the person applying for such benefits had to have paid at least four weeks of National Insurance contributions within the last two years. Furthermore, the bill included the introduction of means-tests for incapacity benefits, implying that benefits of people with occupational pensions were cut. When the bill reached the House of Commons report stage in May 1999, it became clear that Labour backbenchers would rebel against the provisions cutting the incapacity benefits (*The Times* 17.05.1999; 19.05.1999). Sixty-seven Labour members of parliament had signed an amendment to reject the benefits cuts.[19] Peers led by Labour member Lord Ashley of Stoke promised to continue the opposition to the bill started in the House of Commons. But Tony Blair announced that the government would proceed with the disability benefit cuts "even if they caused the biggest revolt since he came to power"

(*The Times* 18.05.1999). A Labour National Policy Forum in July passed a Transport and General Workers' Union resolution that the policy should be reviewed (*The Times* 05.07.1999).

Newspaper coverage of the report stage in the House of Lords pointed out that "the Government *was forced* to offer concession on its Welfare Bill after suffering a series of crossbench defeats in the House of Lords" (*The Times* 05.07.1999, our emphasis). Sixty-six out of 180 Labour peers did not take part in the voting on amendments on report stage which demonstrates the resentment with the bill within Labour rank-and-file.

By the fall of 1999, the government was under time pressure. It intended to pass a series of bills before the end of the parliamentary session on November 17, 1999. When Labour peers signaled defection from the government party line in disability pensions, the Blair government threatened to revise the constitutional reform of the House of Lords that had been agreed on the previous week: thus, the 92 hereditary peers were in danger of losing the concession of keeping their seat in the upper chamber (*The Times* 08.11.1999).

In reaction to the intra-party disaffection, however, the government made some concessions: it increased the limit for means-tests and consecutive benefit reduction from £50 to £85 per week. Peers such as Labour ex-MP Lord Ashley of Stoke still demanded greater concessions. Lord Ashley tabled an amendment that the period of National Insurance contributions relevant for eligibility was extended to seven years and the Lords adopted the amendment with 260 to 127 votes. Another issue of controversy was the war widow's pension. A Lord's amendment allowing war widows to keep their husband's pension after remarrying was passed in the House of Lords with 153 to 140 votes (*The Times* 04.11.1999; 09.11.1999).

In the final vote on the *Welfare and Pensions Reform Bill* the majority of the House of Lords agreed to the version as passed by the Commons. However, 45 Labour backbenchers voted against the bill (HoC, 09.11.1999: col. 924–53; HoL, 09.11.1999: col. 1435; *The Times* 10.11.1999).

The Child Support Pensions and Social Security Act

Pre-parliamentary stage

The government's Green Paper *Partnership in Pensions* of December 1998 aimed to increase SERPS for low-income earners and for carers in replacing SERPS by State Second Pensions with effect from April 2002 (Bill HC 9/1999: EN Part II 202). Between 2002 and 2007, the system of earnings-related pensions would be substituted by a system of flat-rate benefits, but contributions would stay earnings-related. As people with a yearly income below £9,500 would be unlikely ever to join a funded, private supplementary pension scheme, incentives to do so had to be legislated. The introduction of the State Second Pension would be divided into a transition period and a final period. During the transition period, the idea of State Second Pensions was to treat carers without income, or persons with income between the Lower Earnings Limit (£3,432 in 1999/00) and the Lower Earnings Threshold (£9,500), as if they had earned the Lower Earnings Threshold for pension benefits. Qualifying conditions for being treated as carers are either receiving Child Benefits for children under six years or Invalid Care Allowance or caring for a sick or disabled person. For everybody earning more than £21,600 pension benefits would stay the same as under SERPS. For anybody with earnings below this, threshold benefits would increase. In the final period after 2007—that is, for all persons younger than 45 years—State Second Pensions would be flat-rate benefits. The flat-rate benefits were to be calculated as if everybody had earned £9,500 (Bill HC 9/1999: EN Part II 211.–212.). The unions welcomed the proposal to replace SERPS with State Second Pensions because low-income earners would profit, and because it "would be free from political interference from future Conservative governments" (TUC 1999b: 13). But the TUC leadership demanded to index State Second Pensions to wage increase instead of price increase.

The Association of Consulting Actuaries (ACA) opposed the restructuring of the rate of rebate on National Insurance for occupational pensions. The reduced rebate, combined with the new option of Stakeholder Pensions and the regulated occupational sector, would turn occupational pension schemes less attractive and less affordable for employers (ACA 1999: 1).

Parliamentary process

The bill presented to the House of Commons on December 1, 1999 was composed of four parts. The first part introduced new measures in child support: it simplified and strengthened the child support regime, for example, the formula to assess the child support liability was changed (Bill HC 9/1999: EN Part I Clause 1). Part two contained the replacement of SERPS by State Second Pension, and regulating measures for occupational, personal and war pensions. The third part dealt with social security administration and the fourth part referred to National Insurance Contributions (Bill HC 9/1999).

In the second reading in the House of Commons, Secretary of State for Social Security (Alistair Darling of the New Scottish Labour Party) pointed out that Labour government proposals on pensions "have been welcomed almost universally" (HoC, 11.01.2000: col. 161). However, the Conservative spokesman, Willetts, drew a quite different picture. He considered "the proposals, particularly on pensions, ... actively damaging" and "invite[d] the House to vote for [the Conservative's] reasoned amendment" (Willetts (C) in HoC, 11.01.2000: col. 174). Within Labour's own ranks members would have preferred to keep the earnings-related component of SERPS (Cousins (Lab) in HoC, 03.04.2000: col. 718). They also questioned whether an increase in the basic pension would not have had the same effect as the State Second Pension but would have been less complex (Jones (Lab) in HoC, 11.01.2000: cols. 162; and in HoC, 03.04.2000: cols. 713–714).

The pension industry blamed the government for increasing pension complexity in phasing-in State Second Pensions in two stages (LCP 2000). And according to the opposition, there was a danger that the increased complexity in contracting-out would hamper contracting-out to funded schemes (Willetts (C) in HoC, 11.01.2000: col. 172).

On November 29, 1999, the government published the consultation paper, *The Structure of Rebates for the State Second Pension*, and invited interest groups to comment. But only in late January, after the second reading had already taken place, did the government release additional information on the financial implication of State Second Pensions on National Insurance contributions. The flat-rate benefits of State Second Pensions would turn contracting-out more attractive. But the expected costs for National Insurance rebates to encourage contracting-out were estimated at £12 to £15 billion (HoC, 03.04.2000: col. 714). Baroness Barbara Castle tabled an amendment in the House of Lords to re-establish the link between basic pensions and earnings. The amendment was accepted in the Lords and by government majority in the Commons (HoC, 24.07.2000: col. 801). Further, the Lords suggested in amendment No. 18 to allow full concurrent tax-deductible membership in Stakeholder Pension and occupational pension schemes. State Secretary Rooker, on behalf of the government, rejected this idea. However, in a first concession to the pensions industry on July 5, 2000, the government had already accommodated to allow concurrency for yearly incomes up to £30,000. This modification implied that about 90 percent of occupational pension scheme members could also make contributions of £3,600 a year tax-free into Stakeholder Pensions. Despite numerous divisions during the parliamentary process, the Pension Reform 2000 passed the House of Commons. The Lords did not insist on its amendments but agreed to the Commons version of the bill on July 26, 2000 (HoC, 24.07.2000: cols. 792–824; HoL, 26.07.2000: cols. 421–33).

Pension Reform 2004

Following new scandals that occupational pension schemes turned out to be underfunded when the employer went insolvent, the government drafted a new proposal to improve the protection of members of defined-benefit occupational pension schemes.[20] The Green Paper of December 2002 established a Pensions Commission to review private pensions in the UK. The first report of October 12, 2004 set the framework for the new pension reform (Pensions Commission 2004).

The *Pensions Act* 2004, passed on November 18, 2004, established a Pension Protection Fund that pays compensation to members of defined-benefit schemes that are unable to deliver benefits after the employer's bankruptcy. Furthermore, the act replaces the Occupational Pensions Regulatory Authority (OPRA) by a new Pensions Regulator. The act regulates that members of occupational pension schemes that have gone insolvent in the past will be compensated through the Financial Assistance Scheme granting £400 over 20 years. With respect to the State Pension, the act extended the benefits for late retirement: it provided that the State Pension is drawn at least 12 months after standard retirement, and the weekly pension benefits are increased by 10.4 percent for each year of deferred retirement. Alternatively, these extra benefits may be paid out as lump-sum "based on pension foregone plus an annual rate of return of 2 percent (DWP 2004). The act committed employers to refund contributions to occupational pension schemes if the vesting period had not yet been fulfilled. Previously, these contributions were lost.[21]

V Conclusion

Summary of the magnitude of changes

The history of pension reform in the UK since the early 1980s is complex, but the centerpiece of reform is undoubtedly the Thatcher government's legislation of 1986.

The 1986 Pension Reform in the UK was intended to reduce public expenditure on pensions in the long term and to strengthen the private component within the pension system. The original proposal to realize this goal—abolition of SERPS—did not survive the law-making process. It was replaced by a more modest measure: tightening the benefit criteria and setting greater incentives for contracting-out through the establishment of Appropriate Personal Pensions. Viewed in hindsight, the *Social Security Act* 1986 did not save any public expenditure in the short run. On the contrary, due to the extra National Insurance rebates and the surprisingly high uptake of Appropriate Personal Pensions the costs exceeded the savings by far.[22] It did make long term control of pension spending more effective but, as we noted at the beginning of this chapter, it did two things by in part shifting the demands on spending to another part of the public purse: (i) the rebates reduced revenues to the National Insurance Fund and consequently transfers from the Treasury were still necessary; (ii) the inadequacy of the basic pension shifted to demand pressures to the system of means-tested public assistance.

Although the British 1986 Pension Reform is often cited as an example of a successful pension reform, much depends on how we measure success. If we compare the impact of the final legislation with the government's original intentions in the Green Paper, what is striking is the extent of retreat from original radical aims. As SERPS remained in operation, the act created no structural change. The extension of the reference period and the reduction of the assessment base to calculate future SERPS benefits—although significant for the level of individual benefits—was a modification within the principles of the existing system. The relative losers in the reform were persons with gaps in their insurance career, for example, women or the unemployed. The beneficiaries in the reform were the private insurance industry and stock corporations, as the act opened a potentially big market for contracted-out personal pensions, and consequently boosted available assets for investment and re-investment. At the same time, employers' scope of action with respect to occupational pensions was enlarged. The option to offer not only defined-benefit but also defined-contribution schemes reduced the employers' risk in guaranteeing pensions.

Pensioners and employees close to retirement were not affected by the reform due to the transition period.

The *Pensions Act 1995* was mainly a piece of legislation aimed at protecting pension entitlements of early leavers, and protecting pension funds assets against fraud and mismanagement in the wake of the Maxwell scandal. These provisions were of major importance to the soundness and sustainability of the British pension system but they were provisions for incrementally reforming the system, not for pension retrenchment. The second part of the *Pensions Act 1995* —the equalization of retirement age—was indeed a cost saving measure, although the impulse came from the European Union and the necessity of equal treatment of men and women. Against the opposition of Labour, Liberals, unions and parts of the business sector who all supported a lower, or at least more flexible, retirement age, the government brought forward, and passed, a female pension age of 65 years.

The *Welfare Reform and Pensions Act 1999*, and the *Child Support, Pensions and Social Security Act 2000*, further strengthened the market for private pensions and created more incentives to contract-out of the state pillar. Although Stakeholder Pensions are open and attractive to groups of persons previously outside the scope of supplementary private pensions, only future analysis will show their real impact on supplementary pension coverage, because compulsory insurance in the second or third pillar of the pension system was not enacted. The concessions made by government were to structurally marginal features: for instance, benefits to war widows and incapacity pension benefits.

By 1980, the UK already had a strong private occupational pension sector. The trend of policy since then has strengthened this key structural feature. Reforms throughout the last two decades have made private, capital-funded old age pensions more secure and easier to access. Compared to the provisions of the *Social Security Pensions Act* of 1975, British pension legislation by 2002 had reduced the financial risk for employers who establish occupational pensions. The single most radical reform proposals during our period came in the 1985 Green Paper; but it was precisely these radical proposals from which government made a dramatic retreat. Structurally, what is most striking is the way a historically entrenched feature, a powerful private sector, was strengthened over the period.

Impact of the political system on pension politics

The conventional view of pension politics is inspired by a particular view of the Westminster model of democracy and by a view of the British government as an exemplar of that model. On this view, once a government has a secure majority at Westminster then it can act unilaterally (Pierson 1994: 33). That view implies that the larger the Westminster majority, the easier it should be for government to push through radical measures. However, this assumption is open to question if we look at the relationship between seat distribution in the House of Commons and the different measures discussed in this chapter. Between 1983 and 1987, that is, in the legislative term during which the Pension Act of 1986 was negotiated and enacted, the Conservative party had a 144 seats majority. From 1992 to 1997 the Conservatives could count only on a 21-seat majority in the lower house, and this was being eroded over the parliament by by-election losses. Surprisingly, however, the Thatcher government in 1986 neither equalized retirement age for men and women nor abolished SERPS completely, whereas the narrow majority in 1995 sufficed to transfer the governmental proposal more or less unchanged into law. Recent reforms, however, reversed the picture: the large majority of the Blair government since 1997 had little difficulty in passing the main provisions of the 1999 and 2000 legislative changes. But the large Thatcher and Blair majorities of 1983 and 1997 respectively were embedded in different party contexts and have to be seen in relation to competition.

Other analyses of the British 1986 Pension Reform seek to explain the successful passage of the Social Security Act 1986 in two terms: by the divided opposition (Labour and Alliance versus governing Conservatives); and the large majority in the House of Commons.[23] But we argue that the changing character of the party system, and notably of party competition, had a more subtle and important role in this period. The split opposition and, more precisely, the triumphant rise of the Alliance intensified the party competition for the Conservatives as election outcomes became much less predictable. A first-past-the-post electoral system combined with a divided opposition does not automatically reduce or neutralize the accountability effect for the governing party. It depends on the geographical distribution of interests. Whereas the national Conservative government had a buffer of 72 seats in 1983,[24] the buffer at the constituency level depended on the vote distribution between the individual competing candidates. Prior to the 1980s, the Labour and Conservative Party ran first and second in almost all constituencies in England. But in 1983 there were more than 300 constituencies where the Alliance were in second place, after the Conservatives. The country was divided into two-party systems with Alliance and Conservatives competing against each other mainly in Southern England, with Labour and Conservatives being the main rivals in industrial Northern Britain (Denver 1983: 100; Berrington 1988: 117). Intra-party documents are hardly publicly available to provide evidence for a party split between the Northern and the Southern wings of Conservatives in England. Nevertheless, Gallup polls observed the Conservative Party as overwhelmingly divided at the time of the publication of the 1985 Green Paper which make the proposition of a geographically split government party more plausible (King et al. 2001: 39). Since the Alliance faded away later in the decade, it is easy to forget that in the aftermath of the 1983 General Election it seemed set to emerge as a major rival to, if not replacement of, the Labour Party as the Conservatives' main opponents (Crewe and King 1995: 465).[25]

The division of the anti-Conservative vote does not reduce electoral risks for the Conservative government in any way if the anti-Conservative parties are geographically concentrated and stand for different policy positions. At constituency level, the government party still runs against only one dominant competitor, and on the aggregated level the opposition divide does not change the requirement to win more than 50 percent of the seats. Although a dramatic swing and a Labour return to government was highly unlikely, the loss of the 50 percent mark of seats would have given a pivotal position to the Alliance in any future government-making.

One of the Alliance partners—the newly-founded Social Democratic Party—appealed to Conservative core constituency in the 1980s—the financial and business community. According to Crewe and King, the business sector had an interest in a party that could prevent Labour from returning to government in times when the Thatcher government experienced great unpopularity. Moreover, the SDP had the potential to hold the balance of power and reduced the effects of "the pendulum swing of two-party politics and excessive, often partisan legislations as one party follows the other by rotation into office", as well as to moderate the neo-liberal policies to prevent "the electorate to swing substantially to the left" (Stephenson 1982: 89–90; Crewe and King 1995: 247–8). The Conservatives' drive to contract-out and privatize the pension system becomes even clearer if we consider the geographical distribution of interests in the private pension industry. As we noted earlier, the majority of UK pension funds were situated, administered and invested in South-East England, exactly the same area where the Liberals were second strongest party in almost all electoral districts in 1983 (Jacobs 1989: 398; Minns and Martin 1996; Minns 2001). The Conservative government thus adopted an electorally rational strategy: the Reform Act 1986 appealed to business interests in the South-East, simultaneously pre-empting the Alliance policy and at the same time conciliating the pensioners and elderly who were key swing voters in the crucial South-East constituencies.

After the Social Democratic hype died down, the Alliance dissolved and the two parties merged into the Liberal Democratic Party. The regional divide in the character of party competition became less pronounced. When hopes that voters across all opposition parties would unite to displace the Tories in 1987 were not fulfilled (Berrington 1988: 120), party competition became more predictable again. This reduced the risk for the Major government of being punished by voters for the pension reform of 1995.

The pension changes in 1999 and 2000 under Labour expanded the pension system rather than imposing cuts on pensioners. The groups that were affected by retrenchment measures, such as the war widows and disabled persons, lobbied successfully through the House of Lords. Only by invoking a threat to dissolve the Chamber in its present form was the Government able to bring the Lords to heel.

Interest group influence

We have noted that as the Thatcher government became more securely entrenched after the 1983 election victory it increasingly turned to modes of decision-making that ostentatiously ignored the interests of civil society in many critical policy proposal episodes. Something of this pattern is apparent in the pension politics of the 1980s. But this did not mean that policies ignored all interests. The main losers seem to have been the trade unions.

Union support was no prerequisite for the parliamentary adoption of a reform either in the 1980s or 1990s. Although the Trades Union Congress protested against the 1986 reform and the female retirement age increase in 1995 with demonstrations and campaign packs, and would have preferred a stronger emphasis on occupational pension schemes, in 1999, all acts passed the Houses.

By contrast, interest groups of employers and the pension industry seem to have had much influence on policy. As we have argued, the drift of policy over the two decades has been to strengthen the interests of the private pension industry. One explanation for this, particularly in the landmark reforms of 1986, lies in the changed character of party competition after the rise of the Alliance. It helps explain why the NAPF and CBI were able to "force" the government to back down from many of the original reform proposals in the Green Paper.

Constraints of policy design

The history of pension policy in the last two decades of the twentieth century is testimony to the importance of policy legacies; and these shape path dependency in policy choices. The long history of occupational pensions in the UK provided favorable pre-conditions for further strengthening of the second and third pensions pillar in the 1980s and 1990s. The existing structure of contracting-out schemes since 1975, and investment regulations favoring the maximization on returns (e.g. the possibility of investing in shares and in assets abroad) were comparative advantages in reinforcing and improving capital-funded, private old-age provisions.

The SERPS was not yet mature in 1986. Only put into force with the *Social Security Pensions Act 1975*, less than a decade of accrued pension rights hindered the radical reconstruction of the state system. Although the double payment problem would have been small, and public outcry should have been expected to be smaller than in a scheme that has acquired legitimacy over decades, the Thatcher government was still unable to abolish SERPS.

The low pension benefits in the UK suggest that retrenchment was difficult as there are few "vices" to slash. According to Pierson "British pension policy must have seemed a dubious target for reform" in the 1980s "because existing benefits were ungenerous by international standards, cutbacks were hard to justify" (Pierson 1994). Nevertheless, pension reform reached the agenda because cutbacks would produce savings for the government budget.

Policy design and historical legacy certainly influenced the reform options and, more importantly, shaped the actors and the interest group coalitions in the first place. But they do not fully explain British pension politics. Just important was the role of ideas, a subject to which we now turn.

Role of ideas and historical context

The 1970s proved both a policy and an ideological watershed in British policy-making. The British trajectory is well known. For virtually three decades after the end of the Second World War interventionist ideologies guided both economic and welfare policy-making. At the same time, the "glorious thirty years" of sustained economic growth across the advanced capitalist world buoyed a weak British economy. The ending of the long boom pitched the economy into crisis, caused a corresponding crisis of interventionist ideology, and by the end of the 1970s resulted in the rise of very different policy configurations and ideological assumptions. The change can be summarized as the passing of the Keynesian ideological hegemony and its displacement by neo-liberal ideologies. With the election of Margaret Thatcher neo-liberal ideology began to dominate the policy-making system, leading to an emphasis on privatization and welfare state retrenchment. This in turn had repercussions for pensions policy. Above all, it provides the key to the ideological environment in which the long drift of pensions policy over the two decades is to be understood: that drift strengthening private pension interests, and linking pension provision closely to the fortunes of securities markets. Ironically, as the crisis in the rate of return caused by a falling stock market at the start of the new millennium shows, these long-term changes were also at the root of the emerging crisis of the present occupational pension system in the United Kingdom.

Abbreviations

ABI	Association of British Insurers
ACA	Association of Consulting Actuaries
APEX	Association of Professional, Executive, Clerical and Computer Staffs
BBA	British Bankers' Association
BMA	British Medical Association
C	Conservative Party
CBI	Confederation of British Industry
CIMPS	Contracted-in Money Purchase Schemes
CISRS	Contracted-in Salary-related Schemes
COHS	Contracted-out Hybrid Schemes
col.	column
COMBS	Contracted-out mixed benefit schemes
COMPS	Contracted-out money-purchase Schemes
COSRS	Contracted-out Salary-related Schemes
DHSS	Department for Health and Social Services
DSS	Department of Social Security
DUP	Democratic Unionist Party
DWP	Department for Work and Pensions
FSA	Financial Services Authority
GMWU	General and Municipal Workers' Union
HMSO	Her Majesty's Stationery Office

HoC	House of Commons
HoL	House of Lords
ICPR	International Center For Pension Reform
IoD	Institute of Directors
ISTC	Iron and Steel Trades Confederation
L	Liberal Party
Lab	Labour Party
LDP	Liberal Democratic Party
LOA	Life Offices Association
MIG	Minimum Income Guarantee
MP	Member of Parliament
MPA	Metropolitan Pensions Association
NAPF	National Association of Pension Funds
NFSE	National Federation of Self-Employed
NI	National Insurance Scheme
NICO	Inland Revenue National Insurance Office
NICs	National Insurance Contributions
NIF	National Insurance Fund
NPC	National Pensioners Convention
OPRA	Occupational Pensions Regulatory Authority
PC	Plaid Cymru
PPF	Pension Protection Fund
SDLP	Social Democratic and Labour Party
SDP	Social Democratic Party
SERPS	State Earnings Related Pension Scheme
SNP	Scottish National Party
SSP	State Second Pension
TGWU	Transport and General Workers' Union
TUC	Trades Union Congress
UK	United Kingdom
UUP	Ulster Unionist Party

Notes

1. See for example Public Bill Office (HoL) 2001a, b.
2. For example, BBA represents "90% of the UK banking sector's assets and represent[s] 95% of all banking employment in the UK" (www.bba.org.uk/bba/jsp/polopoly.jsp?d=103&a=1559 Access on 28.04.2005).
3. www.hmrc.gov.uk/rates/nic.htm and www.dwp.gov.uk/asd/asd1/state_pension/SP_summ_stats_Mar04.asp
4. Apart from these fairly formalized types of occupational and personal pensions there are a variety of voluntary occupational (*Contracted-in Salary-related Schemes*, CISRS, and

Contracted-in Money Purchase Schemes, CIMPS) and personal pensions mainly used by high-income earners paying contributions of more than £ 3,600 per year (Blake 2002: 2; DWP 2002b: 10).

5. In April 2002—only one year after the new regulation had taken effect—Stakeholder Pension Schemes covered 840,000 members (www.inlandrevenue.gov.uk/stats/pensions/03IR75F.pdf).
6. www.hmrc.gov.uk/rates/nic.htm Access on 25.04.2005.
7. Further employer's contributions—so-called Class 1A contributions—may fall due for material benefits provided by the employer "which are available for private use. For example, company cars" (Inland Revenue 2003: 11).
8. The technically correct expression of the minimum qualifying period is 25% of 90% of working life, i.e. full working life career is 45 years; 90% thereof are 40.5 years; 25% thereof are approximately 10 years.
9. www.dwp.gov.uk/publications/dwp/2004/gl23_apr.pdf (19) Access on 25.04.2005.
10. Note that pre-1988 entitlements are multiplied with the rate of 25% (change after *Social Security Act 1986*; The Pension Service 2004: 39).
11. Tax-free lump sum of £4,615 (≈ €6,758) per year for pensioners younger than 65 years, of £6,100 (≈ €8,933) per year for pensioners between 65 and 74 years and of £6,370 (≈ €9,329) per year for pensioners older than 74 years. Supplements are granted for dependent spouses and children (http://europa.eu.int/comm/employment_social/missoc/2003/uk_part6_en.htm Access on 25.04.2005).
12. Complete abolition of indexation requirements for defined-contribution schemes (DWP 2004).
13. Social Services Committee 1982: lxxxii–lxxxiii; Equal Opportunities Commission 1978: 8–10; see also Ogus and Barendt 1982: 196.
14. "... the Secretary of State has managed to generate a consensus of hostility which I would have thought must be unprecedented in modern times. The CBI as well as the Child Poverty Action Group, the Law Society as well as the pension and insurance industries, have all opposed it. ... The only bodies that lined up behind him were the Monday Club and the Institute of Directors" (Meacher (Lab) in HoC, 15.04.1986: col. 785–6).
15. In September 1985 29% of voters indicated to support the Conservatives in the next election, 29.5% Labour and 39% Alliance (King et al. 2001: 15).
16. Pym (C) 57.6% of votes, Slee (SDP) 29.8% and Jackson (Lab) 12.6% (Crewe and Fox 1984).
17. Surprisingly, Labour was the party that was believed to address the issue of the status of women best of all the parties between 1990 and 1996 with high values as 45% of the polls in 1995 (King et al. 2001: 113). Furthermore we have to take into account that only women born after March 6, 1955 (i.e. 39 years old at the time of the publication of the governmental draft) were to be affected fully by the increase in pension age (Salt 1994: 4).
18. Reasons for not claiming Income Support were that benefits are stigmatized, people are unaware of Income Support payments, or people believe that the process of claiming was difficult and complex (Secretary of State for Social Security 1998: 23–35).
19. Among the rebels was Frank Field, the first Minister for Welfare Reform under the Blair Government (*The Times* 17.05.1999).
20. Several review commissions and reports preceded the legislation: Myners Report, Pickering Report, Sandler Review, Quinquennial Review of OPRA, followed by the Green Paper "Simplicity, Security and Choice: Working and Saving for Retirement" in December 2002 (Cm 5677) and "Working and Saving for Retirement: Action on Occupational

Pensions" in June 2003 (Cm 5835) and "Simplicity, Security and Choice: Action on Occupational Pensions" in February 2004 (Cm 6111); Pensions Bill (12 May 2004) (www.dwp.gov.uk/lifeevent/penret/penreform/2_bill.asp Access on 25.04.2005).

21. In November 2005, pensions for once entered high politics in Britain with the publication of the main report of the Pensions Commission, a three person Commission established to report on the long term future of private pensions and savings. The main thrust of the Report (Pensions Commission 2005) was to combine a proposed rise in the age of pension entitlements (in most cases, eventually, to 67) with the extension of universal entitlement to a more generous state pension. The effect would be to reverse much of the efforts at targeting pursued by Mr Brown as Chancellor since 1997. The days before and after publication were accompanied by media briefings for and against the proposals, notably involving the Treasury. At the time of writing it is simply impossible to judge what the long term impact of the Report will be.

22. "5.5 million people, far more than the original estimates, took up the offer after some very aggressive marketing by insurance companies. The cost of this was, according to the Government's National Audit Office, £9.3bn in all over six years while the savings were estimated as £3.4bn, leaving a net cost of £5.9bn (National Audit Office, 1990, para 3.27)" (Ward 2000b: 140).

23. See, for example, Bonoli (2000), Nesbitt (1995) or McAllister and Rose (1984: 202). Bonoli claims that the combination of first-past-the-post electoral system and "a division of in the anti-conservative camp contributed substantially to neutralizing the potential impact of electoral punishment and as a result to reducing the weight of the accountability effect" (Bonoli 2000: 47). Nesbitt claims that the re-election of the Thatcher government and the large parliamentary majority provided a "sense of immortality" and led the Conservative government to act in an uncompromising, long-term perspective rather than with looking at the next election cycle (Nesbitt 1995: 57–58). Yet, taking into account three lost by-elections in the early 1980s, opinion polls, and a loss in terms of votes in the 1983 election compared to 1979, it is questionable whether the Conservative Party really felt "immortale" and the proposition would require further evidence. Philip Norton suggests a very different course of reasoning. According to his analysis, backbench behavior in the House of Commons changed in the late 1970s and intra-party dissent in legislative voting became much more common. For the first Thatcher term he asserts "the number of backbenchers who made it clear to the whips that they were prepared to vote against the government was such as to threaten the government's majority. Rather than run the risk of such defeat, the government conceded the dissenters' point, either wholly or in part" (Norton 1985: 29). Even in the aftermath of the 1983 election the Conservative government faced 15 occasions of MPs voting against the government bill in the 1983/1984 session (see Norton 1985: 34 table 32.36). Norton (1985: 39) attests Prime Minister Thatcher: "Public impressions notwithstanding, she has been careful to try to maintain her contact with backbenchers" and "her government have been prepared to offer concessions on a number of sometimes significant issues". Another instance casting doubt on Thatcher's cocksure majority is the voting on the *Shops Bill* in April 1986. Only three months before the passage of the *Social Security Act 1986*, the Thatcher government was defeated "when 72 Conservative MPs voted against and 15–20 abstained" (Cowley and Stuart 2004: 2) as small retailers, "trade unions and Church organizations that were opposed to the Government's proposal for Sunday trading, … were able to capitalize on divisions among Conservative backbenchers" (Punnett 1994: 155). At the time it was "the only Government with a secure majority in the entire twentieth century to lose a Second Reading vote" (Cowley and Norton 2004; see also Norris 1997: 45). The *Shops Bill* example shows that a

defeat of the *Social Security Act 1986* could have been possible if it had been prosecuted in its Green Paper version.
24. Provided the opposition would act as a unitary actor and half of the 144 majority deputies would change sides.
25. Asked which parties had the best policies at the time of the negotiations on the 1985 Green Paper most interviewed persons mentioned the Alliance (29%) in September 1985, closely followed by the Conservatives (28%), and Labour (23%) (King et al. 2001: 126).

Bibliography
Primary sources and government documents
Acts and bills
Act c. 30 of 1999. *Welfare Reform and Pensions Act 1999: Explanatory Note*, (11.11.1999).Bill 87/1995. *Pensions Bill (HL)*, 1994–95, (21.03.1995).
Bill HC 9/1999 EN. *Child Support, Pensions and Social Security Bill: Explanatory Notes*, 1999–2000, (01.12.1999).
Bill 44/1999. *Welfare Reform and Pensions Bill as presented to the House of Commons: Explanatory Notes*, 1998–99, (10.02.1999).

Parliamentary debates
House of Commons Weekly Hansard:
Issue No. 1350, (06.06.1985): col. 464–498.
Issue No. 1350, (03.06.1985): col. 34–51.
Issue No. 1369, (28.01.1986): col. 819–894.
Issue No. 1379, (15.04.1986): col. 746–794.

House of Commons Hansard:
Vol. 258, (24.04.1995): col. 525–621.
Vol. 325, (11.02.1999): col. 470.
Vol. 337, (03.11./09.11.1999): col. 297–450, 924–953.
Vol. 326, (23.02.1999): col. 214–290.
Vol. 354, (24.07.2000): col. 792–824.
Website:
(11.01.2000): www.publications.parliament.uk/pa/cm/cmvote/00111v01.htm
(03.04.2000): www.publications.parliament.uk/pa/cm/cmvote/00403v01.htm

House of Lords Hansard:
Vol. 560, (24.01.1995): col. 974–1052.
Vol. 606, (08.11./09.11.1999): col. 1154–1230, 1323–1435.
Website:
(26.07.2000): www.publications.parliament.uk/pa/ld199900/ldhansrd/vo000726/index/00726-x. htm

Other governmental and parliamentary documents
CBI (1982). "Memorandum submitted by the Confederation of British Industry", in Committee, Social Services (ed.), *Third Report of the Social Services Committee: Age of Retirement*. London: House of Commons, 273–83.
DHSS (1985a). *Reform of Social Security: Programme for Action (White Paper)*. Cmnd. 9691. London: Department of Health and Social Security.
DHSS (1985b). *Reform of Social Security: Programme for Change*. Cmnd. 9518 (Vol. 2). London: Department of Health and Social Security.

DSS (1997). *Guaranteed, Secure Pensions for All Says Peter Lilley.* Department of Social Security (05.03.1997[cited 27.11.2003]). Available from http://www.newsrelease-archive.netØ coiØdeptsØ GSSØ coi7412c.ok

DWP (2000a). *State Pension (SP) Summary of Statistics.* [web-site]. Department for Work and Pensions, (September 2002 [cited 22.08. 2003]). Available from http://www.dwp.gov.uk/asd/asd1/state_pension/rp902.pdf

DWP (2000b). *United Kingdom National Strategy Report on the Future of Pension Systems.* [web-site]. European Commission, (September 2002 [cited 11.08. 2003]). Available from http://europa.eu.int/comm/employment_social/soc-prot/pensions/uk_pensionreport_en.pdf

DWP (2004). *Guide to the Pensions Act 2004.* [web-site]. Department for Work and Pensions, (November 2004 [cited 25.04. 2005]). Available from http://www.dwp.gov.uk/lifeevent/penret/penreform/guidepensionsact04.pdf

GMWU (1982). "Memorandum submitted by the General and Municipal Workers' Union." In Committee, Social Services (ed.), *Third Report of the Social Services Committee: Age of Retirement.* London: House of Commons, 337–41.

GOODE, ROY (1993). *Pension Law Reform: The Report of the Pension Law Review Committee.* Command Papers Cm 2342 (Vol. I). London: House of Commons.

ISTC (1982). "Memorandum submitted by the Iron and Steel Trades Confederation." In Committee, Social Services (ed.), *Third Report of the Social Services Committee: Age of Retirement.* London: House of Commons, 348–50.

LOA (1982). "Memorandum submitted by the Life Offices' Association and the Associated Scottish Life Offices." In Committee, Social Services (ed.), *Third Report of the Social Services Committee: Age of Retirement.* London: House of Commons, 191–2.

NAPF (1982). "Letter to the Clerk to the Committee from the National Association of Pension Funds." In Committee, Social Services (ed.), *Third Report of the Social Services Committee: Age of Retirement.* London: House of Commons, 104–5.

NATIONAL PENSIONERS CONVENTION (1985). *Response to the Consultative Document on "The Reform of Social Security".* Command Papers Cmnd 9581: House of Commons.

NFSE (1982). "Extract from a Letter to the Clerk of the Committee from the National Federation of Self Employed and Small Businesses Limited." In Committee, Social Services (ed.), *Third Report of the Social Services Committee: Age of Retirement.* London: House of Commons, 294–5.

PENSIONS COMMISSION (2004). *Pensions: Challenges and Choices: The First Report of the Pensions Commission: Executive Summary.* [website]. Pensions Commission, (12.10.2004 [cited 17.10. 2004]). Available from http://www.pensionscommission.org.uk/publications/2004/annrep/exec-summary.pdf

PUBLIC BILL Office (HoL) (2001a). *House of Lords Public Bill Sessional Statistics for Session 1999–2000.* London: House of Lords.

PUBLIC BILL Office (HoL) (2001b). *House of Lords Public Bill Sessional Statistics for Session 2000–01.* London: House of Lords.

SECRETARY OF STATE FOR SOCIAL SECURITY (1998). *A New Contract for Welfare: Partnership in Pensions.* Green Paper Cm 4179. London: Department for Social Security.

SOCIAL SERVICE COMMITTEE (1982). "Appendices to the Minutes of Evidence Taken Before the Social Service Committee." In Committee, Social Services (ed.), *Third Report of the Social Services Committee: Age of Retirement.* London: House of Commons, 457–61.

SOCIAL SERVICES COMMITTEE (1982). *Third Report of the Social Services Committee: Age of Retirement.* House of Commons Papers Vol. IX, HC 26. London: House of Commons.

Newspapers

The Times. Various issues.

Secondary sources

ACA (2000). *The Structure of Rebates for the State Second Pension: Response to the Consultation Paper dated 29th November 1999.* [website]. Association of Consulting Actuaries, (January 2000 [cited 18.12. 2003]). Available from www.aca.org.uk/Public_content/Reponse_rebates.doc

ALLON-SMITH, RODERICK D. (1982). "The Evolving Geography of the Elderly in England and Wales." In Warnes, A. M. (ed.), *Geographical Perspectives on the Elderly.* Chichester/New York/Brisbane/Toronto: John Wiley & Sons, 35–52.

BARR, NICHOLAS and COULTER, FIONA (1990). "Social Security: Solution or Problem?" In Hills, J. (ed.), *The State of Welfare: The Welfare State in Britain since 1974.* Oxford: Clarendon Press, 274–337.

BECKER, BERND (2002). *Politik in Großbritannien: Einführung in das politische System und Bilanz der ersten Regierungsjahre Tony Blairs.* Paderborn: Schöningh.

BERRINGTON, HUGH (1988). "The British General Election of June 1987: Have We Been Here Before?" *West European Politics*, 11(1): 116–21.

BERTELSMANN STIFTUNG (2002). *International Reform Monitor: Social Policy, Labour Market Policy and Industrial Relations: United Kingdom.* [web-site]. Bertelsmann Stiftung, (March 2002 [cited 01.11.2003]). Available from www.reform-monitor.org/pdf-cache/doc_reports_2-id-999.pdf

BLACKBURN, ROBERT (1995). *The Electoral System in Britain.* New York: St. Martin's Press.

BLAKE, David (2002). *The UK Pension System: The Current System and the Reforms since 1980.* Commentary: Pensions Institute.

BOGDANOR, VERNON (1995). *The Monarchy and the Constitution.* Oxford: Oxford University Press.

BONOLI, GIULIANO (2000). *The Politics of Pension Reform: Institutions and Policy Change in Western Europe.* Cambridge: Cambridge University Press.

BUDD, ALAN and CAMPBELL, NIGEL (1998). "The Roles of the Public and Private Sectors in the U.K. Pension System." In Feldstein, M. (ed.), *Privatizing Social Security.* Chicago: University of Chicago Press, 99–127.

BURCH, MARTIN and HOLLIDAY, IAN (1996). *The British Cabinet System.* London: Prentice Hall.

—— and HOLLIDAY, IAN (2004). "The Blair Government and the Core Executive." *Government and Opposition*, 39(1): 1–21.

BUTLER, DAVID and KAVANAGH, DENNIS (1984). *The British General Election of 1983.* London: MacMillan.

COWLEY, PHILIP and NORTON, PHILIP (2004). *What if they Lose? The Consequences of Government Defeats in the Commons.* [web-site (briefing paper)]. 26.01.2004 [cited 28.04. 2005]). Available from www.revolts.co.uk/And%20what%20if%20they%20lose.pdf

—— and STUART, MARK (2004). *A Damn Close Run Thing: The Voting on the Higher Education Bill.* [web-site]. Economic and Social Research Council (ESRC), (28.01.2004 [cited 30.01. 2004]). Available from www.revolts.co.uk/A%20damn%20close%20run%20thing%20II.pdf

CREWE, IVOR and FOX, ANTHONY (1984). *British Parliamentary Constituencies: A Statistical Compendium.* London: Faber and Faber.

—— and KING, ANTHONY (1995). *SDP: The Birth, Life and Death of the Social Democratic Party.* Oxford: Oxford University Press.

DAVIES, BRYN (2000). "The Structure of Pension Reform in the United Kingdom." In Reynaud, E. (ed.), *Social Dialogue and Pension Reform.* Geneva: International Labour Office (ILO), 11–24.

DENVER, DAVID, T. (1983). "The SDP-Liberal Alliance: The End of the Two-Party System?" *West European Politics*, 6(4): 75–103.

—— (2002). *Elections and Voters in Britain.* Basingstoke: Palgrave Macmillan.

DEVETZI, STAMATIA (1999). "Großbritannien." In Verband Deutscher Rentenversicherungsträger (ed.), *Rentenversicherung im internationalen Vergleich.* Frankfurt am Main: Verband Deutscher Rentenversicherungsträger, 43–76.

DISNEY, RICHARD, EMMERSON, CARL and TANNER, S. (1999). *Partnership in Pensions: An Assessment.* Commentary No. 78. London: Institute for Fiscal Studies.

—— —— and SMITH, SARAH (2001). *Pension Reform and Economic Performance in Britain in the 1980s and 1990s.* [web-site]. National Bureau of Economic Research, (2001 [cited 30.11.2003]). Available from www.nber.org/books/bcf/pension3-2001.pdf

EQUAL OPPORTUNITIES COMMISSION (1978). *Sex Equality and the Pension Age: A Choice of Routes.* Manchester: Equal Opportunities Commission.

ESPING-ANDERSEN, GØSTA (1990). *The Three Worlds of Welfare Capitalism.* Princeton: Princeton University Press.

FAWCETT, HELEN (2002). *Pension Reform in the UK: Re-casting the Public/Private Mix in Pension Provision 1997–2000.* Prepared for ECPR Workshop, "The Politics of Pension Reform". Turin, 22–27 March 2002.

GREEN, ANNE E. (1998). "Sozioökonomischer und sozialgeographischer Überblick." In Kastendiek, H., Rohe, K., and Volle, A. (eds.), *Länderbericht Großbritannien: Geschichte, Politik, Wirtschaft, Gesellschaft.* Bonn: Bundeszentrale für politische Bildung, 89–115.

HAZELL, ROBERT (2003). *The State of the Nations 2003: The Third Year of Devolution in the United Kingdom.* Exeter: Imprint Academic.

HECLO, HUGH (1974). *Modern Social Politics in Britain and Sweden.* New Haven: Yale University Press.

ICPR (1997). *The UK Attempt to Privatize Basic State Pensions.* [web-site]. International Center For Pension Reform, (1997 [cited 27.11.2003]). Available from http://www.josepinera.com/icpr/pag/pag_tex_ukpension.htm

INGLE, STEPHEN (1987). *The British Party System.* Basil Blackwell: Oxford/New York.

INLAND REVENUE (2003). *National Insurance Contributions for Employees. National Insurance Contribution Series CA01.* [website]. Inland Revenue, (April 2003 [cited 26.08.2003]). Available from http://www.inlandrevenue.gov.uk/pdfs/nico/ca01.pdf

JACOBS, FRANCIS (1989). "United Kingdom." In Jacobs, F. (ed.), *Western European Political Parties: A Comprehensive Guide.* Harlow/Detroit: Longman, 374–440.

KING, ANTHONY, WYBROW, ROBERT, J. and GALLUP, ALEX (2001). *British Political Opinion 1937–2000: The Gallup Polls.* London: Politico's.

KRAL, JIRI (2001). *The United Kingdom Pension System.* Prepared for "Learning from the Partners": World Bank/IIASA Conference. Vienna, April 6–7, 2001.

LCP (2000). *Government Proposals for State Second Pension.* [website]. Lane Clark & Peacock, (01.02.2000 [cited 18.12.2003]). Available from http://www.lcp-actuaries.co.uk/information/press_release.asp?ID=41

LIJPHART, AREND (1994). *Electoral Systems and Party Systems: A Study of Twenty-Seven Democracies 1945–1990.* New York: Oxford University Press.

MAYHEW, LES (2001). *A Comparative Analysis of the UK Pension System Including the Views of Ten Pension Experts.* [web-site]. PEN-REF, (2001 [cited 07.06. 2001]). Available from ftp://ftp.iccr.co.at/spa/penref-d2country-gb.pdf.

MCALLISTER, IAN and ROSE, RICHARD (eds.) (1984). *The Nationwide Competition for Votes: The 1983 British Election.* London/Dover: Frances Pinter.

MINNS, RICHARD (2001). *The Cold War in Welfare: Stock Markets versus Pensions.* London/New York: Verso.

—— and MARTIN, RON (1996). "Pension Funds in the United Kingdom: Centralization and Control." In Reynaud, E. et al. (eds.), *International Perspectives on Supplementary Pensions: Actors and Issues.* Westport, CT/London: Quorum Books, 221–32.

MISSOC (2002). *Trends in Social Protection: Comparative Tables: Chapter VII Old age: United Kingdom.* [web-site]. European Commission, (01.01.2002 [cited 26.08.2003]). Available from http://europa.eu.int/comm/employment_social/missoc/2002/uk_part6_de.htm

MUNZINGER (1999). *Großbritannien, Nordirland: Parteien und Verbände.* [web-site]. Munzinger Online, (April 1999 [cited 30.11.2003]). Available from http://www.munzinger.de/

NESBITT, STEVEN (1995). *British Pensions Policy Making in the 1980s: The Rise and Fall of a Policy Community.* Aldershot: Avebury.

NORRIS, PIPPA (1997). *Electoral Change in Britain since 1945.* Oxford: Blackwell.

NORTON, PHILIP (1985). "Behavioural Changes: Backbench Independence in the 1980s." In Norton, P. (ed.), *Parliament in the 1980s.* Oxford/New York: Basil Blackwell, 22–47.

—— (2004). "The Crown." In Jones, B. (ed.), *Politics UK.* Harlow: Pearson, 360–387.

OGUS, A. I. and BARENDT, E. M. (1982). *The Law of Social Security.* 2nd edn. London: Butterworths.

PENSIONS Commission (2005). *A New Pensions Settlement for the 21st Century.* London: Department of Work and Pensions.

PENSION SERVICE (2004). *A Guide to State Pensions.* [web-site]. Department for Work and Pensions, (April 2004 [cited 03.05.2005]). Available from http://www.thepensionservice.gov.uk/pdf/np46/np46apr04.pdf

PERRY, RICHARD (1986). "United Kingdom." In Flora, P. (ed.), *Growth to Limits: The Western European Welfare States Since World War II. Volume 2: Germany, United Kingdom, Ireland, Italy.* Berlin: Walter de Gruyter, 155–240.

PIERSON, PAUL (1994). *Dismantling the Welfare State? Reagan, Thatcher and the Politics of Retrenchment.* Cambridge: Cambridge University Press.

PLÖHN, JÜRGEN (2001). "Großbritannien: Interessengruppen im Zeichen von Traditionen, sozialem Wandel und politischen Reformen." In Reutter, W., and Rütters, P. (eds.), *Verbände und Verbandssysteme in Westeuropa.* Opladen: Leske & Budrich, 168–96.

PRIME MINISTER´S OFFICE (2003). *Guide to legislation.* [website]. HMSO, (2003 [cited 27.08.2003]). Available from http://www.pm.gov.uk/output/page 29.asp

PT (1994). "The Queen's Speech". *Pensions Today,* 17(12): 1–2.

PUNNETT, R. M. (1994). *British Government and Politics.* 6th edn. Aldershot: Dartmouth.

RECHMANN, SUSANNE (2001). *Alterssicherung in Großbritannien und Irland: Eine institutionelle und empirische Analyse.* Berlin: Duncker & Humblot.

SALT, HILARY (1994). *Equalisation of State Pension Ages Report on Costs of Changes: Prepared for the Trades Union Congress.* Swinton: Institute of Actuaries Associate of the Pensions Management Institute.

STEPHENSON, HUGH (1982). *Claret and Chips: The Rise of the SDP.* London: Michael Joseph.

STURM, ROLAND (1999). "Das politische System Großbritanniens." In Ismayr, W. (ed.), *Die politischen Systeme Westeuropas.* Opladen: Leske + Budrich, 217–53.

TUC (1982). "Memorandum submitted by the Trade Union Congress." In Committee, Social Services (ed.), *Third Report of the Social Services Committee: Age of Retirement.* London: House of Commons, 126–46.

—— (1984). *Submission to Secretary of State on "Portable" Pensions.* Memorandum. London: Trades Union Congress.

—— (1985a). "Commentary: Breaking the Consensus." *Pension Briefing* (1 (August)): 5–26.

—— (1985b). *Delegates' Campaign Pack.* Campaign Pack. London: Trades Union Congress.

TUC (1985c). *Government Review of Social Security: TUC Memorandum of Comments*. Memorandum. London: Trades Union Congress.

—— (1985d). "TUC Response to the Government Green Paper 'Reform of Social Security.'" *Pension Briefing* (2 (December)): 13–19.

—— (1994). *State Pensions for All at 60: A TUC Campaign Pack*. Campaign Pack. London: Trades Union Congress.

—— (1995). *General Council Report 1995*. Annual Report. Brighton/London: Trades Union Congress.

—— (1996). "The Labour Party's Plans for Pensions." *TUC Pensions Briefing* (10 (November)): 4–7.

—— (1998). *Pensions Review: Stakeholder Pensions: TUC Submission to DSS Consultation Document*. London: Trades Union Congress.

—— (1999a). *Congress 1999: General Council Report*. Annual Report. Brighton/London: Trades Union Congress.

—— (1999b). *Report of Congress 1999*. Trades Union Congress.

TWGU (1985a). "Hands Off Pensions." *T & G Record* (September): 7.

—— (1985b). "Rallies Against Pension Robbers." *T & G Record* (August): 12.

WAIN, BARBARA (1995). "A Disaster Foretold? The Case of the Personal Pension." *Social Policy and Administration*, 29(4): 317–34.

WARD, SUE (2000a). "Fighting Talk." *Pensions World*, (March): 53–4.

—— (2000b). "Personal Pensions in the UK, the Mis-selling Scandal and the Lessons to be Learnt." In Hughes, G., and Stewart, J. (eds.), *Pensions in the European Union: Adapting to Economic and Social Change*. Bosten: Kluwer, 139–46.

WILSON, GRAHAM (1993). "Changing Networks: The Bureaucratic Setting for Government Action." In Budge, I., and McKay, D. (eds.), *The Developing British Political System: The 1990s*. London/New York: Longman, 30–51.

CHAPTER 3

GREECE: POLITICAL COMPETITION IN A MAJORITARIAN SYSTEM

POLYXENI TRIANTAFILLOU

I Introduction

PENSION reform in Greece has been difficult because consensus is elusive. When political actors attempted to reform the pension system in the context of extra-parliamentary legitimacy (i.e. through extensive dialogue with the trade unions) they encountered the following obstacles: (a) the conflictual nature of Greek politics; (b) a lack of a corporatist tradition, and as a consequence, the lack of consensus-building mechanisms; and (c) the strong attachment of the trade unions to existing arrangements, which favor workers with the highest unionization rates. In most cases, unions have been able to mobilize against reforms, leading to either failure or the watering down of the proposals.

The structure of political competition in Greece is a major constraint on policy-making. The Greek political system is essentially a two-party system dominated by the center-right New Democracy (ND), and the center-left Pan-Hellenic Social

Movement (PASOK). Thus consensus is practically impossible, because by disagreeing with the government's plans the major opposition party improves its prospects of winning the next election. This means that reforms are almost always piecemeal and incremental. Even when the government is backed by a majority in Parliament, union opposition to reforms often has the potential to derail even the best-planned incremental cuts. To avoid union opposition and potential strikes, governments on some occasions have departed from normal policy-making routines and used the "urgent procedure," or passed legislation during the summer session when many MPs were absent.

II POLITICAL SYSTEM

Constitutional history and nation-building

Greece gained independence in 1829 and became a constitutional monarchy in 1843, which lasted until 1909. Thereafter, Greece witnessed a period of liberal politics marked by the leadership of the reformist Eleutherios Venizelos. In 1915, the conflict between Venizelos and the King concerning Greece's foreign policy led to a political crisis that lasted until 1920, and resulted in the emergence of a new political elite recruited mainly from Greece's middle class. From 1936 to 1940 a military dictatorship ruled Greece, which was followed by a four-year period of German occupation (1941–1944). However, soon after the country's liberation, civil war broke out between the royalist Greek army and the communist-dominated resistance forces, which ended in 1949 with the defeat of the latter. In the subsequent years, a democratic (but also exclusionist and anti-Communist) political system was established that reflected pre-existing tensions between politicians, the monarchy and American political agents.[1] Mounting dissatisfaction with government performance and heated conflicts between the executive and the King led to the establishment of another military dictatorship. The dictatorship collapsed in 1974 after student protests.

The restoration of democracy triggered a process of institutional and political change. In November 1974, the center-right party New Democracy (ND), led by Konstantínos Karamanlís, took power. The new government was charged with the task of shaping the emerging political system and quickly showed its resolve to try to break with the past by introducing new elements to the political system (i.e. the legalization of the Communist Party, KKE) and a referendum in December 1974 on the form of the state which produced a large majority in favor of a presidential democracy). In 1975 Parliament adopted a new Constitution establishing the "Hellenic Republic." Some of the Constitution's provisions were inspired by the 1949 Constitution of West Germany and the 1958 Constitution of France (especially those concerning the powers of the President).

Since 1975, political life has stabilized, political institutions have been consolidated and political parties have become the foci of political life. Building party democracy was the major aim of the first post-1974 governments. At the time, political parties were expected to perform "the double function of incorporating the once again mobilizing masses and accommodating them in the new democratic design" (Pappas 1999: 37). However, the process of incorporation was sometimes similar to the pre-Junta regimes, and involved the creation of extensive clientelistic, party-controlled networks. In consequence, post-1974 governments were transformed into patrons that served their clienteles' interests by using the state bureaucracy. This meant that economic and social policies were often designed to satisfy political ends. Political costs came before the interests of society as a whole, again resulting in piece-meal policy-making with negative consequences for the economy. Reversing these policies, however, is an extremely risky political exercise for any government that wishes to maintain its political *raison d'être*.

Institutions of government

Greece has a presidential-parliamentary system. Parliament (*Βουλή*) elects the President of the Republic every five years with a two-thirds majority. If this fails, the vote is repeated five days later. If the second vote fails, a third vote occurs for which a three-fifths majority is needed. If this third vote fails, Parliament is dissolved and new elections are held. The new Parliament can elect the new President with a three-fifths majority. If this proves impossible the vote is repeated, and the President is elected by the absolute majority of MPs (Constitution Arts 31, 32). In recent years Parliament has been able to elect the President of the Republic without holding new elections.

Executive power rests mainly with the government. The President of the Republic has limited powers, as a result of constitutional changes introduced in 1986.[2] Legislative power rests with the President and Parliament. Parliament passes laws, and these are promulgated and published by the President. Among the Parliament's other functions are the right to review the Constitution, to pass the budget and to exert more general control over the government.

In Greece, the Prime Minister and the government dominate political life. The Prime Minister ensures the unity of the government, directs government and civil service activities, and presides over 19 ministries. Policy-making is centrally coordinated, with lower levels of government responsible only for local matters.

As this chapter will show, the government largely controls the formulation of pension policy. The Prime Minister typically sets the main lines of policy in co-operation with the Ministry of Labor and Social Security, which drafts legislation. However, given the high political costs involved in pension reform, governments have had to consult with trade unions to increase their legitimacy before proposing legislation. In many cases, the government's attempts to establish social dialogue with the unions have ended in conflict and strikes.

Electoral system

The Greek electoral system has remained fairly stable since the re-introduction of democracy, but the method for allocating parliamentary seats has changed several times. After the 1974 restoration of democracy, the electoral system promoted political stability by facilitating strong governments. Over time, however, majority parties have used electoral reforms to ensure that they stay in power.

Parliamentary elections are held every 4 years. There are 300 seats in Parliament, of which twelve are national seats. The country is divided into 56 minor constituencies and 13 major constituencies. The number of seats per minor constituency varies from 1 to 38. The most important recent changes concerning the number of seats per constituency are the following: first, the number of single seat constituencies increased from 3 in 1974 to 5 in 1977 and 6 in 1996. Second, the number of seats for central Athens (Athens A) decreased from 22 in 1974 to 19 in 1996, whereas the number for greater Athens (Athens B) increased from 28 in 1974 to 38 in 1996.

First-tier seat allocation is based on a quota calculated by dividing the number of valid votes by the number of seats plus one in each minor constituency. Seats are

Table 3.1 The electoral system introduced in 1989 in Greece (applicable to three elections: June and November 1989 and October 1990)

Distribution of seats	Seats	Electoral districts	Method for allocating seats
National seats	12 (closed list)	Nation-wide	All parties participating in 2nd distribution
1st distribution		56 electoral districts[a]	Quota resulting from dividing the total number of valid votes by the number of seats per constituency plus 1
2nd distribution	288 seats	13 major electoral districts	Quota method applies; distribution of seats not "used" on the basis of votes not used in the first distribution
3rd distribution		National	3rd distribution used in previous elections was abolished
Special provisions	Parties with more than 1% at the national level get one seat; political parties with more than 2% at the national level that would get fewer than 3 seats are given an extra seat		
Barriers	No barriers apply		

[a] First-past-the-post system applies to single seat constituencies.
Source: Mendrinou: 2000, p. 105.
Note: Table based on Greek source translated and compiled by the author.

allocated to each party or coalition of parties by dividing the total number of votes cast for each party, or coalition of parties, by the quota. In single-seat constituencies the candidate that receives the most votes wins the seat.

The allocation of seats in the second distribution takes place in the thirteen major constituencies on the basis of the votes "not used" in the first distribution (votes not used in single seat constituencies are not included). In the second distribution the quota is calculated by dividing the total number of votes cast in each major electoral district by the number of seats not distributed in the first distribution. The total number of votes for each political party nationwide is then divided by this quota, resulting in the number of seats for each party. If some seats cannot be allocated on the basis of the quota, they go to the political parties with the greatest number of remaining (not used) votes (usually smaller parties). There was no third distribution on the district level in the electoral system according to the 1989 reform.

All political parties participate in the national distribution of seats. The number of nationwide votes for all political parties is divided by 12. Seats are allocated to each political party by dividing the total number of valid votes cast for each party by this number. If fewer than 12 seats are allocated by this method, the remaining seats go to those political parties that have the greatest average number of votes per "national seat" nationwide. To calculate the average, the total number of votes cast for each party is divided by the number of national seats already allocated plus one. Remaining seats are allocated starting with the political party that has the highest average number of valid votes per national seat.

Table 3.2 The electoral system in 1990 in Greece (in force for 1993, 1996 and 2000 elections)

Distribution of seats	Seats	Electoral districts	Method for allocating seats
National seats	12 (closed list)	National constituency	As in 1989
1st distribution		56 electoral districts[a]	As in 1989
2nd distribution	288 seats	13 major electoral districts	Distribution on the basis of the total number of votes
3rd distribution		National	3rd distribution re-established
Special provisions	Normalization procedure: provisions for parties with 3% of the national vote; these parties get 70% of the number of seats that corresponds to their share of the vote (i.e. a political party that gets 3% at the national level is allocated 6 instead of 9 (3% of 288 seats)		
Barriers	To be allocated a seat a political party or a coalition of parties must get a minimum of 3% of the votes at the national level		

[a] First-past-the-post system applies to single seat constituencies.
Source: Mendrinou: 2000, p. 116.
Note: Table based on Greek source translated and compiled by the author.

The 1989 electoral reform can be seen as a strategic attempt by the PASOK government to prevent the formation of a solid ND government (center-right) after the 1989 elections. Riven by internal conflicts resulting from its failure to implement its economic policies from 1985 onwards, damaged by the corruption scandals that emerged at the end of the 1980s, and threatened by ND, which had moved to the center, PASOK tried to reduce the power of the expected winner of the 1989 elections by strengthening smaller political parties. The changes of the 1989 electoral reform led to the formation of the first post-1974 coalition government (a case of an "ends against the middle" government, i.e. consisting only of right and left parties) in Greece (Mendrinou 2000: 106–111).

Electoral reform in 1990 re-introduced the so-called "reinforced proportionality" system used until 1989. The main features of the reform are summarized in Table 3.2.

First- and second-tier seat distribution stayed the same as under the 1989 electoral law, but a third-tier distribution was introduced. Seats remaining after subtracting the seats already allocated in the first and second round were allocated as follows: the total number of votes is divided by the number of seats that have not been distributed. The total number of votes of each party is then divided by this quota. The result is the number of seats awarded to each party. If after this process there are still undistributed seats, they go to the party that received the most votes nationwide. The electoral reform also included the so-called "normalization clause," which means political parties that pass the threshold of 3 percent are entitled to a number of seats not fewer than 70 percent of the number of seats that would correspond to the number of votes cast for these parties nationwide, if the system were fully proportional. The same procedure as in 1989 is followed for the distribution of national seats. Thus, the electoral reform of 1990 aimed at accommodating two conflicting goals: political stability and pluralism. The law strengthened the political party with the most votes and prevented the formation of dysfunctional coalition governments (like the ones in power in 1989–90). At the same time, the law provided for a "controlled" representation of smaller parties in Parliament by establishing the 3 percent entry rule.

Legislative process

The Government and Parliament have the right to propose legislation. The President can issue legislative acts ($πράξεις$ $νομοθετικού$ $περιεχομένου$) if requested by a government minister, but this usually happens only in extraordinary situations. In such cases, the texts issued by the President must be presented to Parliament within 40 days, to get Parliament's approval (Constitution, Art. 44). The President also issues decrees, which provide details on the implementation of an existing law. Decrees are always signed by the relevant minister (Constitution, Arts. 43, 35).

Table 3.3 Political institutions in Greece

Political arenas	Actors	Rules of investiture	Rules of decision-making	Veto potential
Executive	President (*Próedros tis Dimokratías*) (Limited executive powers)	5-year term; elected by Parliament (several ballots with different majority requirements)	Promulgates and publishes laws; right to send a bill back to Parliament for further discussion	Not a veto point
	Prime Minister (*Prothypourgós*)	Appointed by President followed by vote of confidence in Parliament; relative majority sufficient	Can ask President for dissolution of Parliament; initiates legislation	——
Legislative	Parliament (*Vouli*/Βουλή)	4-year term; 300 seats; 56 multi-member constituencies integrated into 13 electoral districts; weighted proportional representation with 3-tier distribution of seats (12 mandates on national level); 3%-entrance hurdle; may be dissolved by President on government's request for issues of major importance for the country.	Three parliamentary readings; urgent legislation may be passed with three sessions only; special rules during summer sessions with only 1/3 of parliamentary members participating	Not a veto point due to government majority
Judicial	Constitutional Court/Highest Special Court (*Ανώτατο ειδικό δικαστήριο Anótato idikó dikastírio*)	Highest Special Court: 11 members; appointed by the government	Surveys the constitutionality of legislation upon appeal; audits elections and referendums	Not a veto point
Electoral	Referendum	Referendum called by President upon request of 3/5 majority of Parliament in the case of bills regulating critical social issues (absolute majority in the case of important "national issues"); government has the right of initiative	Decision by absolute majority	Not a veto point
Territorial units	57 Prefectures (*Νομοί/nomoí*) 13 regions approx. 6,000 communities	Elections are called every four years to choose the heads of prefectures; heads of regions are appointed	Responsible for policy specific to their respective areas; responsibilities are regulated by law	Not a veto point

Government bills concerning pensions are submitted to Parliament by the Minister of Finance after consultation with the Court of Auditors. For pensions financed by local authorities' budgets or other legal entities governed by public law, the proposal is presented to Parliament by the minister in charge of the relevant institution and the Minister of Finance (Constitution Art. 73, par. 2).

Two aspects of the legislative process are particularly relevant to this chapter, as the government resorted to these practices in 1990–92. First, certain laws can be passed during the summer sessions of Parliament (July, August, and September). In other words, the Greek Parliament does not go completely into recess during the summer like Parliaments elsewhere. Given that only one-third of MPs participate in these summer sessions, this is a major opportunity for bypassing regular parliamentary decision-making. Second, legislative proposals the government considers to be urgent can be discussed in Parliament in a shorter period of time than usual, (three sessions), leaving less time for debate. The number of sessions can be increased to five by a proposal submitted by at least thirty MPs (Parliamentary Regulation Art. 76, par. 6).

Party family affiliation		Abbreviation	Party name	Ideological orientation	Founding and merger details	Year established
Left parties	Social democratic parties	PASOK (ΠΑΣΟΚ)	Pan-Hellenic Socialist movement (Πανελλήνιο Σοσιαλιστικό Κίνημα)	Center Left		1974
		DIKKI (ΔΗΚΚΙ)	Democratic Social Movement (Δημοκρατικό Κοινωνικό Κίνημα)	Center Left	PASOK off-shoot (dissolved in 2004)	1995
		SYN (ΣΥΝ)	Coalition of the Left (Συνασπισμός της Αριστεράς και της Προόδου)	Left	Coalition of small parties of the left	1989
		KKE (KKE)	Communist Party of Greece (Κομμουνιστικό Κόμμα Ελλάδος)	Extreme Left		1974
Right wing		ND (ΝΔ)	New Democracy (Νέα Δημοκρατία)	Broad Right		1974

Fig. 3.1 Party system in Greece

Parties and elections

Since the restoration of democracy in 1981, the Greek political system has been fairly stable, with two political parties, ND and PASOK, dominating politics, with an average vote share of about 85 percent between them from 1981 to 2004. Electoral competition is strong, and has intensified due to a convergence towards the center in recent years (Diamantopoulos 1997: 297).

As Diamantouros (1995: 553) argues, the short transition to democracy in Greece lacked strong social and institutional foundations, so politics was prone to populism and confrontation. Before 1981, Greece experienced several political transformations, the most important of which was the rise of the Pan-Hellenic Socialist Movement (PASOK). PASOK was framed as a modernizing force that would make the sorts of changes that would free political life from the legacies of the past (e.g. patronage and extreme centralization), by establishing "new models of economic development and a new civic consciousness that would respect the distinctiveness and autonomy of civil society organizations" (Petras et al. 1993: 160). The party's rise to power and government performance have often been explained with reference to the party's ability to promote its objectives by using populist discourse. Greek populism was based on a simplistic division of the social space into two camps, the privileged and the under-privileged (Lyrintzis 1987: 683). This worldview reflected the contradictory nature of the Greek middle classes, PASOK's main supporters. However, the reconciliation of contradictory interests was not unproblematic in terms of economic modernization and rationalization, a fact that the PASOK leadership was aware of (Tsakalotos 1998: 117). In contrast to other European countries, PASOK governments chose to implement Keynesian policies at a time when the model of post-war economic growth had reached its peak in Greece. As in other social democratic experiments, in its second term (starting in 1985) PASOK was forced to move right and adopt a five-year stabilization program, which was brought to a halt in 1987 because it seriously threatened the party's re-election prospects. In the late 1980s, political corruption involving high-ranking members of government further weakened the PASOK government. After a short period of political instability,[3] due in large part to the electoral reforms passed in 1989, ND (Νέα Δημοκρατία/New Democracy) formed the government in April 1990.

The ND government faced several internal and external challenges, which led to its early demise. ND's difficulties in improving public finances, combined with the fierce opposition of both PASOK and the PASOK-led trade unions, as well as ND's handling of foreign policy issues (developments in the Former Yugoslav Republic of Macedonia), led to the government's fall in 1993 and the return of PASOK to power.

The need to choose a new leader after the death of PASOK's founder (Andreas Papandreou) in 1996 exposed the tensions between the modernizing and the conservative-populist factions within the party. The 1996 election of Kostas Simitis was a victory for the modernizers; Simitis won on a program aimed at modernizing the public sector and improving public finances in preparation for EMU. Greece's subsequent success in meeting the EMU budget requirements helped him secure another majority in 2000.

Several other aspects of the Greek party landscape deserve mention. To start with, distinctions such as those between Christian democracy and social democracy are hardly applicable in Greece because many of the societal actors crucial to the formation of these parties (i.e. trade unions or religious organizations) were either absent or state-manipulated during the formation of the existing parties. In fact, today's party system is, above all, a product of the period following the fall of the dictatorship. This means that allegiances (and the Right–Left division) were formed on the basis of societal rather than ideological cleavages—specifically, on views about the need to break with the political traditions of the pre-Junta period, and the necessity of incorporating previously excluded groups (Moschonas 1994). In the years following the fall of the military regime in 1974, party competition was structured around these claims. Once democracy was firmly established, however, political parties found themselves without some of the tools that helped them face electoral competition such as the Right–Left division. As Pappas (1999) writes: "When PASOK actually came to power, the differences between Right and Left blurred. But it took society some time before it realized that the division between 'stagnation' (the Right) and 'progress' (the Left) had little to do with which party was in power (188)." Due to the de-ideologization of Greek politics, the two major political parties have to compete in a radically reduced arena, which means they have to move away from the cleavages of the past and re-invent themselves. Given the bipartite structure of Greek politics and the increasing similarity of the two major parties, political competition often takes place along the lines of strategic disagreement. Each party will denounce the policies of the other even if the policies are not substantially different from its own, to improve its electoral standing (Schludi 2001: 21).

According to Diamantopoulos (1997: 280–4), there have been few changes in the Greek political system since 1974. Small shifts in the allocation of power following the first years after the democratic transition only confirmed the bipolarity of the party system. Two factors contribute to this stability. First, the stability that can be observed today is due to developments in the organization of party machinery and the establishment of clientelistic networks. The two political parties have established their own clienteles whose allegiance is difficult to shift to new political formations, because the two biggest parties have more or less the same chances of coming to power and serving the interests of their clienteles. Contextual factors, however, such as the need to balance public finances and comply with the Stability and Growth Pact, leave limited room for clientelistic practices and deprive political parties of this source of stability. It is no wonder, therefore, that new tendencies were observed both inside PASOK and ND, along with some short-lived opportunistic attempts to capture the disappointed voters of both these parties (i.e. offshoots such as DIKKI (PASOK) the short-lived POLAN and KEP, both ND offshoots). Second, the centralization of the major political parties means that the party leadership has been in firm control of developments within the party, and able to prevent schismatic tendencies.

Table 3.4 Governmental majorities in Greece

Election date	Start of gov.	Head of gov. (party)	Governing parties	Gov. majority (% seats)	Gov. electoral base (% votes)	Institutional veto points	Number of veto players (partisan + institutional)
11.20.1977	11.28.1977	Karamanlis V (ND)	ND (171)	57.0%	41.8%	None	1 + 0
	05.09.1980	Rallis (ND)	ND (171)	57.0%	41.8%	None	1 + 0
10.18.1981	10.21.1981	Papandreou I (PASOK)	PASOK (172)	57.3%	48.1%	None	1 + 0
06.02.1985	06.02.1985	Papandreou II (PASOK)	PASOK (161)	53.7%	45.8%	None	1 + 0
	07.26.1985	Papandreou II (PASOK)	PASOK (161)	53.7%	45.8%	None	1 + 0
06.18.1989	07.02.1989	Tsanetakis (ND)	ND (145), SYN (28)	57.7%	57.4%	None	2 + 0
	10.12.1989	Grivas (Ind.)	Technocratic government	–	–	None	–
11.05.1989	11.23.1989	Zolotas (Ind.)	ND (148), PASOK (128), SYN (21)	99.0%	97.8%	None	3 + 0
04.08.1990	04.11.1990	Mitsotakis (ND)	ND (150)	50.0%	46.9%	None	1 + 0
10.10.1993	10.13.1993	Papandreou III (PASOK)	PASOK (170)	56.7%	46.9%	None	1 + 0
09.22.1996	09.24.1996	Simitis I (PASOK)	PASOK (162)	54.0%	41.5%	None	1 + 0
04.09.2000	04.25.2000	Simitis II (PASOK)	PASOK (158)	52.7%	43.8%	None	1 + 0
03.07.2004	03.10.2004	Karamanlis I (ND)	ND (165)	55.0%	45.4%	None	1 + 0

Interest groups

Trade unions in Greece are organized somewhat differently than elsewhere in Europe. At the lowest level, unions are divided into sectoral, firm-level, and general (mixed) unions. The second organizational level includes both sectoral federations and so-called "labor centers" that amalgamate first-level unions in a given geographical area (normally within a prefecture). Primary level unions can be members of one federation and one labor center. At the highest level, labor is organized in two confederations, the General Confederation of Greek Workers (GSEE/$\Gamma\Sigma EE$), which covers workers under private contracts, and the Civil Servants' Confederation (ADEDY/$A\Delta E\Delta Y$).

Trade unions in Greece are structured such that some of the groups favored by the pension system (particularly workers of the public sector) are over-represented in the trade union confederations that participate in policy-making. As Mavrogordatos (2001: 80) notes, despite its status as a representative of the private sector, GSEE essentially represents the interests of public sector employees (the wider public sector and utilities) who are the backbone of the confederation. With civil servants represented by ADEDY, it is clear that private sector employees are left with limited space for representation. Given these considerations, reforms should be expected to disadvantage those categories of workers that are either under-represented (private sector employees, younger workers) or not represented at all (e.g. future generations).

As far as the distribution of membership between the private and the public sectors is concerned, and keeping in mind the difficulty in defining GSEE as an exclusive representative of the private sector, unionization rates in the public sector remain much higher: rates range from 80–98 percent (European Foundation for the Improvement of Living and Working Conditions, 2003). Ioannou notes a decline in union density for GSEE (from 564,000 voting members in 1992 to 442,000 in 1998) and a slight increase for ADEDY (from 236,000 voting members in 1992 to 241,000 in 1998) (Ioannou 1999: 16).

Trade unions in Greece are commonly considered to be weak, for two reasons: the strong presence of the state in union affairs and the weak position of the left especially in the past (the parties of the left were not recognized until the 1970s (Mavrogordatos 2001)). The numerical weakness of Greek unions does not mean that unions lack mobilizing capacity, however. Indeed, unions have organized massive strikes in recent years, contradicting the "weak unions" argument.

Another particular feature of the Greek trade unions is their high degree of politicization. In the years following the return to democracy, labor organizations did not play a large role in the shaping of the new polity, which remained the prerogative of the political parties. Controlled modernization from above between 1974 and 1981 was undertaken by right-wing governments and did not preclude a party-sponsored syndicalism, which was also promoted by PASOK especially during its first term in government (Kioukias 1997: 308–9). The influence of political parties on trade union issues is still strong, with many union leaders holding high-ranking party leadership positions.

The most important employers' organisation is the SEV (Federation of Greek Industries). As with the trade unions, this top federation is not representative of the business sector. The SEV represents Greece's largest companies, excluding the smaller businesses which are the backbone of the Greek economy (Lavdas 1997: 84–5).

SEV has been the government's counterpart in all recent attempts to establish social dialogue practices in the area of labor market and employment policies.

However, concerning pensions, SEV has maintained a discreet presence in the background of the negotiations. Apart from making occasional calls for a sustainable, conflict-free solution to the crisis of the pension system, SEV has not played the role that GSEE and ADEDY have played in the pension reforms. This is explained, first by the fact that the employers' priority is to avoid increases in contribution rates (Featherstone and Tinios (2003) manuscript: 10). Given that contributions rates are already high, employers can be fairly sure that their interests are represented in the policy-making process. Second, any additional labour costs would act as obstacles to employment creation which any government would prefer to avoid, given consistently high Greek unemployment rates. Finally, governments try to avoid a strong employer presence in the policy-making process because appearing to be employer-friendly may create major problems with the trade unions, which are the government's main source of extra-parliamentary legitimacy (Schludi 2001:19).

Let us close this section by briefly referring to the place of Greece in the literature concerning corporatism. It is fair to say that Greece is a case of "disjoined corporatism" (Lavdas 1997: 17; Triantafillou 2003). This means that Greece is a case of state corporatism in which the state promoted the political incorporation of the working classes by conferring privileged status to certain interest groups (creating an interest group "oligopoly" through a top-down process, which is still closely linked to the state). But the Greek state does not exhibit concertation (i.e. institutionalized consensus-seeking policy-making processes) with regard to policy-making (other types of interaction have developed instead throughout the years: i.e. clientelist exchange, confrontation through strikes), which implies problems for the system of conflict resolution, and indeed, due to the lack of concertation practices in Greece, the favorable economic outcomes that are usually associated with corporatism have been absent.

Thus, there is no institutionalized consultation in Greek policy-making, and the degree of union integration in the policy-making process depends on the willingness of the government. This means that consultation is sometimes a façade that legitimizes decisions already taken. This does not mean, however, that the social partners have failed to influence policy-making. In fact, the 2002 pension reform has very often been portrayed as one of the few cases of successful social dialogue between the government and the trade unions (see p. 139).

III PENSION SYSTEM

Historical overview

The year 1861 saw the emergence of the first Greek social security funds. Civil servants and those working under arduous conditions were the first categories to be covered.

In the subsequent years, social insurance coverage increased unevenly, resulting in a mosaic of insurance regulations covering various occupational groups.

Legislation passed in 1922 recognized social insurance as a responsibility of the state. The government formed by the Liberals in 1928 in the midst of a general strike took up the issue and passed legislation establishing the IKA (Social Insurance Organization/Ίδρυμα Κοινωνικών Ασφαλίσεων). Its founding law, passed in 1932, reflected the characteristics of the continental model of social security. In 1937 the IKA started operating in the three biggest Greek cities (Athens, Piraeus, and Thessaloniki), covering large employers. Soon coverage was extended to other cities and smaller firms. However, the scheme still excluded many groups, including farmers and rural laborers. Limited coverage of these categories was introduced with Law 694 passed in 1937. The "universalization" of coverage was a gradual process that was only achieved at the beginning of the 1980s.

The post-war period has been shaped by a 1951 law (Law 1846/51), which served as the basis of all social security legislation for almost forty years. The law extended coverage, introduced new calculation formulae that favored lower income classes and provided for indexing mechanisms to protect benefits from inflation. The law also established the levels of minimum pensions and made provisions for state financing. It is surprising to see that in the preamble extensive reference is made to the Beveridge report, and special emphasis is placed on the idea of national solidarity, expressed through the new formulae used for the calculation of benefits. To achieve the double aim of improving protection and promoting economic growth, the government opted for a PAYG system. At the time, it was thought that capitalization created large reserves whose investment would be problematic given Greek economic conditions. In order to free resources that could be channeled to the restructuring of the economy, contributions were fixed at relatively low levels.

Most of the legislation passed in the 1950s consisted of small modifications to legislation passed in 1951—in most cases to increase the privileges of certain groups (especially civil servants). Reforms only went so far as to regulate the eligibility conditions for pensions paid to a handful of people.[4] At the end of the 1950s the social security system was oriented to the Beveridgean ideal of universal coverage. The extension of coverage, however, was not coupled with a change in financing that was intended to achieve this aim, namely the IKA. Harmonization remained an expression of intent. New inequalities among those insured at IKA were created and the differences between the general scheme and occupational funds remained. As Venieris (1994: 184) notes, the governments of the time (although aware of the seriousness of the problems IKA was facing) "...preferred short-run electoral benefits" favoring those groups that had easier access to the state machinery, "to long-run social benefits, which reflects much of the individualistic character of their voters".

The most important development in social protection in the 1960s was the creation of OGA (*OΓA*), the organization providing social insurance benefits to farmers. OGA was financed by contributions,[5] a 10 percent levy on income taxes, a 15 percent levy on company taxation, stamp duties and taxes levied on cigarettes and luxury products (Law 4169/61, Art. 11). If benefit expenditures exceeded receipts, funds could be transferred from the other two insurance branches of the organization (health and crop insurance) if these were in surplus, otherwise benefits were reduced accordingly. Benefits were not indexed but could be increased by ministerial decree. Legislation passed in 1967 (Law no. 29, 14.06.1967) increased benefits and provided for new sources of funding.

When the IKA law 1846/51 was first brought to Parliament, the government made it clear that a deficit would arise in 1962, which should be covered by raising contributions. The fund went into deficit sooner than planned, though, and in 1960 the government extended qualifying periods to increase IKA's receipts.

Apart from some small changes concerning minor occupational funds, there were no significant developments in social insurance legislation in the 1960s and most of the 1970s. As Katrougalos (1996: 52) argues, welfare policies in this period consisted of providing some limited services and special privileges to some parts of the population (especially in the public sector), "always in response to the electoral needs of the moment."

Description of the current pension system

Coverage

The main characteristics of the Greek pension system are its strong emphasis on a fragmented first pillar. Due to the lack of coherent planning the system developed gradually, with many small groups enjoying their own funds. Since the creation of the major pension fund covering wage-earners (IKA) in the 1930s, efforts have been made to combine funds insuring similar occupational groups, but with limited success.

High fragmentation of the system means that the insured population is not equally distributed among the funds. In fact, most pensioners belong to the following funds (Ministry of Labor and Social Security 2002: 411): (a) IKA: 33.96 percent (insures most private sector wage earners); (b) OGA: 46.25 percent (covers farmers); and (c) TEVE: 5.79 percent (provides pensions for many of the non-agricultural self-employed).[6] There are other funds covering smaller occupational groups. Civil servant pensions are financed out of general revenues. Public sector enterprises have their own funds. In the paragraphs that follow we focus on IKA, the largest social security organization in Greece.

IKA today provides benefits to 872,000 pensioners (Ministry of Labor and Social Security 2002: 417), mainly private sector wage earners. IKA also insures public sector employees if they are not covered by any other pension fund for their main pension. IKA also covers wage earners working in non-EC countries, provided that the employer operates in Greece, and persons who work fully or partly under work-contracts (if they are not insured elsewhere for a main pension). IKA also covers immigrants, and various groups of workers who are not permanently employed by the same employer, as well as some groups of self-employed workers.

IKA was created to cover the gaps resulting form the "occupationalization" of the pension system and to prevent further fragmentation. In 2001, there were 170 social security funds, 63 of which provided main and supplementary pensions (Ministry of Labor and Social Security 2002: 349). As a result of this fragmentation there are striking discrepancies in eligibility conditions and the level of benefits. The system is fragmented both horizontally across sectors of employment and economic activity, and across levels of protection (primary, supplementary pension, separation payments). In the 1990s, some efforts were made to reduce the number of organizations providing social security benefits (Law 2676/99, these efforts mainly focused on funds providing supplementary pensions). Further provisions concerning the unification of social security funds were introduced after the last reform in 2002 (Law 3029/02).

In Greece, the role of first pillar supplementary pensions is very peculiar. For those insured by IKA, supplementary pensions are part of the main pension paid by IKA. The fact that membership in the supplementary fund of IKA (TEAM) is compulsory, and that it is run on a PAYG basis mean that it is not much different from the main scheme. Furthermore, revenues from the supplementary fund are often used to cover the deficits of the fund providing the main pension. At the same time, there are several funds that provide supplementary pensions to groups of workers that receive their main pension from IKA. Finally, lump sum payments are provided by several provident funds (mainly covering the public sector).

For the second pillar, legislation from 2002 provides for the creation of occupational funds based on capitalization for the first time, administered by workers and supervised by the state (Law 3029/02, Art. 7). Tax exemptions apply for the contributions to these funds (Law 3029/02, Art. 7, par.17).

Greece has no minimum income scheme, but there are three types of benefits that perform this function. OGA pensions (pensions usually paid to farmers but also paid to the uninsured population over 65), the minimum pensions provided by IKA consisting of a contribution-linked (organic) part and a top-up (welfare) part, and finally the Pensioners' Social Solidarity Supplement (EKAS/$EKA\Sigma$), a means-tested benefit provided to low-income members of all pension funds, which was introduced in 1996.

Administration

The managing board of IKA is headed by a government-appointed Governor. Six board members represent workers, three represent employers, two represent pensioners and there are 13 IKA personnel specializing in financial and administrative issues. The managing board serves for three years, and the Ministry of Labor oversees the fund.

Financing

IKA provides old-age, invalidity, and survivors' pensions. Benefits are financed on a PAYG basis, with contributions paid on gross wages. Additional revenues come from social taxes and assets held by the fund (for 2002, revenue by source was distributed as follows: employers' and workers' contributions 78.3% social taxes 13.74% state contribution 4.5% assets 0.5%, other: 2.93%).[7]

First pillar	Second pillar	Third pillar
Third tier[a] Separation payments (mostly civil servants and public sector employees)	Voluntary occupational Pension	Voluntary private pension
Second tier: Earnings-related part of pensions[a] Private sector employees (IKA+TEAM) / Self-employed / Public Sector Employees and civil servants	Subsidized occupational pension: occupational funds established with the 2002 reform (voluntary)	Subsidized private pension: none
First tier: basic pension[a] Employees (IKA) / Self-employed (OAEE) / Farmers (OGA) / Civil servants EKAS (*ΕΚΑΣ*) Pensioner's Social Solidarity Supplement (*Επίδομα Κοινωνικής Αλληλεγγύης Συνταξιούχων*)	Mandatory occupational pension: none	Mandatory private pension: none
Social assistance: OGA pensions paid to persons with insufficient contribution records		

Fig. 3.2 Pension system in Greece
[a]Indicates a multitude of funds covering various groups within the same occupational category.

Table 3.5 Greek pension system

Population category	Benefits	Fund	Financing
1. Uninsured over 65 and farmers	Universal pension. A new subsidized contributory scheme was put in place for farmers in 1997 to replace the universal scheme	OGA	Universal Scheme: State subsidy New Scheme: Contributions, state subsidy calculated on the basis of the total amount of contributions
2. Civil servants, military staff and autonomous state organizations	Primary pension, supplementary pension, separation payment. In some cases the pensioner may be receiving two supplementary pensions	Pensions are paid either through the Budget or through IKA (main pension) and several funds paying supplementary benefits.	Pensions are Financed through the Budget contributions and earmarked taxes (the so called "social taxes")
3. Private sector employees: IKA	Workers in this category receive either: Primary pension Or Primary pension + supplementary pension Or Primary pension + supplementary pension + separation payment	Primary pension is paid by IKA. Supplementary pensions are paid either by TEAM or smaller funds. Smaller funds also pay separation payments.	Depending on the case pensions are financed by contributions, state subsidies, deficit financing and earmarked taxes.
4. Sailors	Primary pension + supplementary pension + separation payment	NAT and other small funds.	Pensions are financed through contributions, state transfers and earmarked taxes
5. Public sector enterprises, banks	Primary pension + supplementary pension + separation payment	Special, enterprise funds IKA + special fund for supplementary pension	Contributions (falling mainly on the employer). The employer finances deficits too.
6. ΔEH – Public Power Corporation	Primary pension + supplementary pension + separation payment	ΔEH budget	Contributions. The enterprise covers deficits too.
7. Self-employed	Either primary pension only or Primary pension + supplementary pension	Main pensions are paid by TEVE, TAE, TSA. Supplementary pensions are paid by smaller funds.	Pensions are paid through fixed contributions, state transfers and earmarked taxes

| 8. Professions- Self-employed | Workers in this category receive either a primary pension (sometimes two) or a primary pension and a supplementary pension | Special funds (i.e. lawyers, doctors, engineers etc) | Earmarked taxes, fixed monthly amount, income from property. |

Additional features.

For workers that started working from 1993 onwards the following provisions apply:
- Uniform retirement age (65).
- Maximum replacement rates: 60% for main pension, 20% for supplementary pension.
- The State contributes to the financing of their pensions.

A means-tested benefit is paid to low income pensioners since 1996 (EKAS-Pensioners Social Solidarity Supplement).

Source: Based on "The Greek Report on pension strategy": Appendices, Athens: Ministry of Economy and Finance, Ministry of Labour and Social Security, 2002, p. 9.

On the basis of Law 2084/92, workers' contributions for a main pension are 13.33 percent of monthly gross wages, and employers' contributions equal 6.67 percent. Contributions rise by 2.2 percent and 1.4 percent respectively for occupations falling under the category "hard and arduous work." For workers entering the labor market as of January 1, 1993 the state provided additional financing equal to 10 percent. However, according to recent legislation this form of state contribution is to be replaced by an annual subsidy to the fund of 1 percent of GDP for the years from 2003 to 2032. If any other funds merge with IKA the state will cover any deficits. Contributions for the main supplementary pension scheme (TEAM) amount to 6 percent and are equally shared between workers and employers.

One of the most important problems concerning the financing of the Greek pension system is the high rate of contribution evasion. Contribution evasion occurs either because workers are not insured or because they are insured for shorter periods than those worked, or are placed in a lower insurance class (hence lower contributions) rather than the one that corresponds to their earnings (this is mostly the case with the self-employed). Moreover, it is possible for employers to deduct contributions from workers' salaries but not to pay them to the insurance fund, since conditions are rather loose. Limiting contribution evasion was one of the objectives of the reforms passed from 1990 onwards.

Benefits

An old-age IKA pension consists of two parts: the basic amount and, potentially, supplements. The basic amount depends on two factors: the number of contribution years and the reference income. The reference income is based on an "insurance class" (ασφαλιστική κλάση), which corresponds to an imputed daily wage (τεκμαρτό ημερομίσθιο; Spyropoulos 1996: 28–35).

In order to calculate the imputed wage one has to calculate the average daily wage for the five years preceding retirement.[8] This is done by adding the worker's monthly wages during the five years before retirement and then dividing by the number of days for which contributions were paid during these five years (at least 1,000 days, if less, the reference period is extended). Once the average daily wage has been calculated, the worker is assigned to one of the 28 insurance classes (for example for the year 2004 an average daily wage of €50 corresponded to the 17th insurance class and the imputed daily wage used for the calculation of the benefit was €48.93).

The basic part of the benefit is calculated by multiplying the imputed daily wage by 25 and then by the coefficient corresponding to each insurance class (the coefficient is higher for lower insurance classes). For example, for an imputed salary corresponding to the 4th insurance class the coefficient is 0.5, whereas for an imputed salary in the 20th insurance class the coefficient is 0.3.

The basic component of the old-age pension is increased by an amount equal to 1.5 times the daily wage of an unskilled worker in cases where the pensioner has a non-working spouse or one who does not receive a pension. Further increases are provided if the worker has young children (20% for the first child, 15% for the second and 10% for the third) and for periods spent in employment classified as hard and arduous.

Whenever the amount produced by the calculation formula is below the minimum limits that apply for each year, a minimum pension is paid. The same increases apply in the case of dependants. An increase is provided in the case that the worker has paid contributions for more than the minimum period required (the increase is equal to 1% for every 300 days over the minimum qualifying period, i.e. 4,500 days—15 years).

A different system applies to those who entered the system after 1993: each contribution year equals 1.714% of the monthly imputed salary (the calculation formula is: 1.714% × monthly imputed salary × years of contributions. The replacement rate of a full pension equals 35 years times 1.714 = 60%, Law 2084/92, Art. 28). The imputed monthly salary used for the calculation of the benefit results from adding the monthly salaries received in the 5 years preceding the claim (Christmas and Easter bonuses as well as vacation allowances are excluded) divided by the number of months for which contributions were paid.

In addition to periods spent in employment, periods of military service also qualify for pension rights, provided that contributions were paid. If a wage earner fails to meet the eligibility criteria, periods of military service can be included for the calculation of an old-age pension, provided that the wage earner has a contribution record of at least 3,600 days (12 years) and is older than 58. The number of days is reduced to 900 in the case of a disability pension (minimum degree of disability: 67%).[9]

Finally, the calculation of benefits may also include periods of unemployment. Under current legislation only 250 days spent in unemployment in the last 10 years count for the calculation of a pension. Furthermore, according to Law 2874/2000, the long-term unemployed insured in IKA can continue to be insured in IKA to fulfill the conditions for an old-age pension. Contributions are financed by a special account (LAEK/*ΛΑΕΚ*—Special Account for Employment and Vocational Training) administered by the agency providing unemployment benefits, OAED (*ΟΑΕΔ*). Pensions are indexed according to the salary of public sector employees, which in turn depends on the government's income policy.

IV Politics of pension reform since 1980

Overview

In contrast to most other European countries, the 1980s was a period of expansion for the Greek welfare state (Katrougalos 1996: 47). Benefits rose, eligibility conditions for some categories of workers were relaxed, and coverage was extended to new groups of workers. In the early 1980s Greece spent 12.4 percent of GDP on social protection.

The income policies implemented in 1981–82 and the expansion of coverage between 1982 and 1987 raised expenditure to 20.8 percent of GDP by the end of the 1980s (Guillén and Matsaganis 2000: 121). In particular, expenditure on pensions grew from roughly 7 percent during the 1970s to 15 percent of GDP in 1989 (OECD 1990: 45).

The reform of the Greek pension system in the early 1990s can be seen as part of a larger set of changes in economic governance from the mid-1980s onwards, in response to mounting fiscal imbalances. Pension reform was one of the top priorities of the Conservative government elected in 1990. Reform was originally planned to take place in two phases. The first stage would aim at correcting the fiscal imbalances of the system, and major structural changes (merging of funds, expansion of private insurance) would be left for the second phase. Reform, however, never progressed beyond the first stage. Three laws passed between 1990 and 1992 (Law 1902/90, Law 1976/91, Law 2084/92) stabilized the finances of the pension system for roughly 20 years, introduced greater equality between the private and public sector benefits, and reduced the number of invalidity pensions recipients.

Taking advantage of the "breathing space" provided by its conservative predecessor, the socialist government, in power from 1993 to 2004 adopted a different approach to social policy issues and has slowly tried to rationalize the system. An expert committee (the Spraos Committee) was established in 1996 to study the problems of the Greek economy and suggest reform options in several policy areas. The Committee published its report on social security in October 1997. Although the report echoed the conclusions of earlier committees, once the government realized that reactions to the Committee's findings could be very controversial, it sidestepped the committee it had itself created (Featherstone et al. 2001: 474).

In 1997, the government initiated debate on the future of social insurance. Again, the proposal envisaged change in two phases; the idea was first to provide short-term support for existing schemes, and then to proceed with the substantial reform of the system. This process led to a small package of measures, focusing on contribution evasion, in 1998. Unwilling to confront the unions again, the government decided that the larger issues of pension reform could be postponed to earlier in the next electoral cycle. In 1999, legislation was passed to reorganize some of the funds (Law 2676/99).

The most recent piece of legislation concerning the pension system was passed in June 2002. The final decision was difficult, and the risk of failure was always present. The law contains some "traditional measures" (e.g. uniform retirement age for the members of all funds, gradual reduction of replacement rates for public sector employees to 70 percent starting from January 2008, provisions for the merging of nine funds insuring mainly workers of the public sector with IKA, changes in reference periods) with some "non-traditional" ones (i.e. original by Greek standards. These include fixed state contributions to the expenses of IKA, measures to support mothers, measures for workers with short contribution records etc.). With these measures the government aims to reduce some of the inequalities among various categories of workers, and to adapt the social security system to labor market changes.

It is difficult to give a thorough evaluation of these measures. With regard to the financial sustainability of the system, one could expect that the (limited) cuts

Table 3.6 Overview of proposed and enacted pension reforms in Greece

Year	Name of reform	Reform process (chronology)	Reform measures
1990	Souflias Reform (Law 1902.90)	• April 1990 ND government announces intention of pension reform • meetings with opposition parties and social partners • employers reject increase in contribution rate • September 6, 1990 government proposal • September 10, 1990 first strikes • strike wave that lasts until the law is passed in Parliament • September 25–October 4, 1990 urgent process in Parliament • October 4, 1990 passage of bill in Parliament	• increase in retirement age to 60 (women) and 65 (men) • increase in minimum contribution periods • tightening eligibility for invalidity pension • increase in reference period from 2 to 5 years • increase in contribution ceiling • pension indexation changed from ATA to public employees' wage increase • introduction of benefit reductions for early retirement • re-introduction of contributions for public servants • introduction of minimum retirement age for civil servants: 60 for men, 58 for women and 50 for mothers with young children • abolition of special funds for banks, telecommunication, electricity and public transport was not enacted as originally envisioned
1991	Fakiolas Committee Law 1976/91	• June to October 1991 expert committee chaired by Fakiolas set up • November 13, 1991: passage of minor modification in Parliament • May 1992 publication of Fakiolas report; unions reject report as basis for negotiations • government rejects Fakiolas suggestions	Fakiolas report • higher retirement age for women and women with young children • extension of reference period to the whole working career • changes in the level of invalidity pensions • reduction of benefit ceilings Law 1976/91 • tightened eligibility conditions for pensions paid to members of the National Resistance • modifications for people that were "trapped between" law 1902/90 and previous legislation

(Continued)

Table 3.6 (Continue)

Year	Name of reform	Reform process (chronology)	Reform measures
1992	Sioufas Reform (Law 2084/92)	• June 1992 unofficial meetings between Minister of Economy and unions • government secretly asks IMF to provide an expert study • September 8 to 18, 1992 debate in seven parliamentary summer sessions • September 22, 1992 passage in Parliament	• Harmonization of eligibility conditions to IKA standards • changes in financing: increase in contribution rates • harmonization of male and female retirement ages to 65 • new system for all entering labor market after 1.1.1993 • contribution increase for civil servants and self-employed • introduction of maximum replacement rate of 60% for main pension and 20% for supplementary pensions • exclusion of special bonuses from benefit calculation
1996	Spraos Report Law 2676/99	• Oct 1996 establishment of the Spraos committee • Dec 1998: passage in Parliament	Initial goals failed! Law 2676/99: • merger of several insurance funds for self-employed and in the public sector • changes in survivors' pension • changes in pension accumulation rules • increase in minimum pensions • increase in female retirement age to 65
2001	Giannitsis Proposals	• April 2001 Report of the British actuarial agency on the sustainability of the Greek pension system • April 20, 2001 publication of government proposal without prior consultation with the unions • April 26, 2001 general strike • withdrawal of the proposal	Failed! measures envisioned: • rise in retirement age to 65 for all funds • seniority pension after 40 instead of after 35 years of insurance • abolition of retirement age of 50 for mothers with young children • extension of reference period to best 10 out of last 15 years

| 2002 | Reppas Reform (Law 3029/02) | • Consultations between Minister of Labor Reppas and unions
• June 18 to 20, debate in Parliament
• June 2002 passage of the government bill | • voluntary merger of special funds with IKA
• introduction of fixed state participation in the expenses of IKA
• creation of occupational capital-funded pension insurance managed by the social partners
• harmonization of replacement rate to 70 percent for both private and public sector
• extension of reference period for public sector from last salary to best 5 of last 10 years
• establishment of the National Actuarial Authority |

resulting from the reduction of the replacement rates of civil servants and the extension of the reference periods will be offset by the increase in private sector replacement rates. The merger of funds is expected to eliminate some of the inequalities that exist between various categories of workers.[10] The law also includes some elements of de-*étatisation* of the social insurance system by allowing for the creation of independent occupational funds.

The 1980s: a period of expansion

When PASOK came to power in 1981, it promised "social change here and now," thereby creating expectations about the speed and quality of social policy developments. Benefit improvements and the extension of coverage were attempts to increase PASOK's popularity and demonstrate the party's intention to shift to a social assistance system (Petmesidou 1991: 42) that reflected the party's ideology at that time. However, if such a shift has been realized, this has been at the expense of further fragmentation, inequalities, and deficits. Whenever change occurred, it was not as the result of a coherent plan.

During this period pensions were increased, coverage was extended to new groups of the population (uninsured persons over 70), and the level of minimum pensions provided by IKA was fixed at 20 times the minimum wage of unskilled workers.

As a result of the incomes policies pursued before PASOK's stabilization program was implemented in the mid-1980s, the value of pensions increased significantly during this period. At this time, pensions were indexed according to ATA (an automatic indexation mechanism which penalized high salaries and pensions), so increases were more significant for those receiving low pensions, who are typically insured with the biggest funds.[11] Pensions paid to public sector employees grew at a slower pace, reflecting the fact that pensions paid to this group were already high (OECD 1987: 55).

Nevertheless, benefit differentials between "mass" and "elite" funds persisted due to the relaxed eligibility conditions pertaining to the latter group of funds. Inequalities were more striking if supplementary pensions are considered, because benefits ranged from 12 percent to 108 percent (accumulation of more than one supplementary pension) of previous earnings for 35 years of contributions, and were provided mostly to public sector employees (including social security fund employees, the fund insuring trade unionists and the personnel of workers' organizations; KEPE 1988: 86–7).

In order to secure universal minimum pensions, pension rights were extended to people who either had poor contribution records, or no record at all, such as farmers (Law 1287/82), political refugees and returning immigrants (Laws 1469/84 and 1539/85), as well as members of the National Resistance (Law 1543/85). Eligibility conditions for invalidity pensions were relaxed as well. By Law 1759/88, benefits equal to 50 percent of a full pension were granted to beneficiaries with a degree of disability between 33.3 percent and 50 percent. These measures, along with the strong incentives for early retirement, the slower increase in average earnings and the small increases in the number of people employed, caused the pension costs/GDP ratio to double within one decade. The number of employed per pensioner fell from 2.8 in 1979 to about 2 in 1989 and the budgetary deficit for the pension system (excluding government contributions to civil servants) rose from less than 1 percent of GDP in 1980 to 9 percent in 1989 (OECD 1990: 47–8). Both IKA and OGA (the two biggest funds) were in serious financial difficulty. In contrast, most of the funds insuring privileged professional categories were in surplus thanks to state contributions.

1990: the Souflias Reform (Law 1902/90)

Social security reform was one of the top priorities of the government formed by ND (Conservatives) in April 1990, after a short period of political instability following the corruption scandals of the late 1980s. Due to a change in the electoral law (see section "Electoral System") in 1989, ND had a majority of only one seat in Parliament, despite its high share of the popular vote. Except for pensions, the government dealt with all the items on its reform agenda (privatization, tax evasion, the labor market) immediately after the elections. Pension reform was a major issue that had to be negotiated through extensive dialogue with the interested parties, so the government was prepared to co-operate with the opposition and the trade unions.

Given the fiscal crisis and the pressures coming from international organizations (IMF, EEC), the Ministry of National Economy started elaborating reform proposals based on a report on the state of the Greek economy commissioned by the previous government (the Aggelopoulos Report), which mainly recommended increasing the revenues. Although the government had clearly stated its commitment to reform, it was difficult to agree on a strategy. Whereas the Minister of National Economy, Georgios Souflias, insisted on measures with immediate results—including contributions increases—affecting all groups, the Minister of Health and Social Security pushed for a more comprehensive solution that would apply only to new entrants to the labor market, and insisted that no final decisions could be taken because of uncertainty about the extent of the system's financial problems. At the same time, the Prime Minister announced during the discussion of the budget in Parliament the government's intention to increase the retirement age from 58 to 62. Disagreement within the government caused confusion and led to an increase in applications for early retirement.[12]

Before taking action, the government sought opposition support. At a meeting with the leaders of the two main opposition parties, the Prime Minister secured their support for the government's efforts to elaborate on commonly accepted solutions to prevent the system from collapsing, on the condition that decisions would be the result of extensive dialogue. At this point the Prime Minister made no clear reference to the nature of the reforms under consideration (in any case, at this stage the government itself had not got further than establishing some basic principles such

Table 3.7 Greek legislation that led to system expansion in the 1980s

Year	Content of legislation
1982	
Law 1239/82	New arrangements were introduced for the payment of contributions. Amounts due until 31. 10. 1981 were exempted from additional fees and interests and could be paid in 48 monthly instalments.
Law 1275/82	Increases in pensions provided by TEVE (30% from 01. 01. 1981 and 25% from 01. 01. 1982), TAE (20% from 01. 01. 1982) and TSA.
Law 1287/82	Increases in pensions provided by OGA (50% from 01. 08. 1981); pensions were provided to the wives of farmers; to cover additional expenses OGA was subsidized from the general budget.
Presidential decree 633/82	TEAM coverage (supplementary pensions, fund established by law 997/79) extended to all IKA members (or members of any other main fund) not yet covered by a supplementary fund.
Law 1296/82	Pensions provided to persons older than 70 who did not receive any pension; the benefits were equal to the old-age pensions paid by OGA; the age limit was later lowered to 68 (Law 1422/84).
Law 1305/82	Changes in insurance classes; the minimum old-age and invalidity pension paid by IKA was fixed at 18 times the daily wage of unskilled workers (survivors' pension: 16); minimum pensions increased further in 1986 (equal to 20 times the daily wage of an unskilled worker, Law 1543/85 Art. 42); changes in the imputed wages (on the basis of which insurance classes were structured) were linked to the CPI (Art. 2, p.1244).
1983	
Law 1358/83	Time spent in military service taken into consideration in benefit calculation.
Presidential decree 258/83	Temporary benefits equal to 50% of the minimum old-age pensions provided by OGA were paid to insured people whose applications for a pension were pending.
Law 1405/83	Ceilings imposed on benefits (Art. 8).
Law 1469/84	Pensions paid to returning immigrants; persons older than 65 who had paid contributions for at least 2,700 days could buy off the missing time for their retirement.

1985	
Law 1539/85	Pensions paid to political refugees returning to Greece; eligibility conditions for invalidity pensions loosened (applying to persons younger than 35).
Law 1543/85	Pensions paid to members of the National Resistance movement (more favourable conditions pertaining to this category were introduced by Law 1813/88) and those who fought against the 1967–1974 junta regime.
1987	
Law 1745/87	Creation of a scheme providing supplementary coverage to farmers.
1988	
Law 1759/88	Degrees of invalidity were reviewed; benefits were now paid for invalidity exceeding 33.3%; new arrangements were introduced for the payment of contributions.

as the harmonization of conditions applying to public and private sector employees, an increase in retirement age, and the tightening of conditions pertaining to invalidity pensions). According to the government's plan, the Minister of National Economy would meet trade union and employers' representatives during the initial phase of the reform to inform them about the state of the social security system, and to ask them to submit their own suggestions. The governing boards of the pension funds would be asked to submit their own proposals as well. Once the proposed new legislation was drafted, the issue would be discussed further in Parliament.

The first round of the Souflias meetings with the social partners produced no clear results. As expected, trade unions whose members were insured in the funds facing the greatest problems appeared more concerned. GSEE proposed a small increase in contributions in return for institutionalized state contributions to the system and debt settlement. The insurance period for a minimum pension (4,050 days—13.5 years) and age limits were not negotiable. On the contrary, GSEE agreed to the abolition of some provisions favoring certain groups and the tightening of the eligibility criteria for invalidity pensions. As far as the public sector was concerned, the discussions revealed two potentially divisive issues: the re-introduction of contributions for public servants and the conditions for early retirement (especially those concerning women retiring after 15 years of service (Newspaper *To Vima* 29 July 1990; 5 August 1990).

As expected, employers rejected contribution increases, arguing that these would harm competitiveness. Instead, employers pushed for increased state social security subsidies, especially since the system was being used to address problems that were the state's responsibility. Employers proposed reform in two stages: in the first stage measures should address the short-term needs of the system, while the measures taken in the second phase should guarantee the long-term sustainability of the system.

The government's proposals were announced on September 6, 1990. Most of the measures concerned public sector employees, who were favored by the existing system. In effect, on the basis of previous legislation, public sector employees could receive a pension regardless of age, as long as they had been in service for long enough to meet the requirements for a full (after 35 years) or a reduced pension. According to the proposed measures, public sector employees would have to satisfy two criteria (age limits and years in service). Furthermore, the changes in the calculation formulae would lead to lower benefits for public sector employees. The funds insuring those employed in banks, OTE (Telecommunications Organization), DEI (Public Power Corporation) and public transport would lose their special status, and new entrants would have to be insured in IKA (i.e. higher contributions and age limits), whereas contributions for those already insured in these funds would be increased to equal those of IKA.

Proposals affecting the IKA included contribution increases, longer reference periods (from two to five years), an increase in the income ceilings for contributions from Drs. 222,000 (about €650) to Drs. 280,000 (about €820), and the introduction of six new insurance classes. Pensions would no longer be indexed to ATA but would follow increases in public employees' wages (which in turn were adjusted according to the government's inflation objective). For 1991, increases in pensions would be half the increase in public sector wages. The retirement age for those working under arduous conditions was to be increased by two years (to 57 for women and 62 for men). Eligibility for invalidity pensions would also be tightened.

It was estimated that the new measures would reduce the annual rate of increase in IKA's deficit by 50 percent. Increases in contribution rates would increase revenues by Drs. 55 billion (about €161.5 million), changes in the indexation of minimum pensions would add another Drs. 80 billion (about €235 million), and changes in the conditions pertaining to hard and arduous occupation and invalidity pensions would create savings of Drs. 50 billion (about €146 million) (Newspaper *To Vima* September 9, 1990).

The announcement of the measures produced one of the biggest strike waves in fifteen years, which lasted almost three weeks and brought the economy to a halt. It quickly became clear that under these circumstances the prospects for social dialogue were poor, not only because the government would not compromise on any of its main positions but also because its interlocutors (both political parties and workers' organizations) were not convinced of the sincerity of the government's intentions. Their responses to the perceived intransigence of the government were extreme. As expected, during the strikes the highest participation rates were observed in the public sector. As a result of these strikes, the government was forced to reconsider some of its original plans.

The discussion in Parliament

The bill brought to Parliament contained some changes compared to what had been initially announced. These had to do with groups of workers in the public sector such as women with young children employed before January 1, 1983[13] who would be "trapped" between the old and the new systems. According to the proposal, those workers in the public sector, who, according to the new provisions had to continue working, would not be forced do so for more than seven years, regardless of whether they fulfilled the age criterion or not.

The bill was discussed during the summer session of Parliament for five days, under the "urgent" procedure (September 25, 26, 27, 28; October 4, 1990). During the discussion, the opposition parties accused the government of introducing what they considered a law that increased taxation, and underlined the problems on the revenue side of the social security system (i.e. contribution evasion, the use of the funds' reserves). Objections were also expressed about the lack of substantial negotiations with the social partners before the bill was brought to Parliament.

The opposition parties did not make detailed alternative suggestions. PASOK MPs often referred to the creation of a minimum benefit—"a national pension"—but this was a proposal that ND had previously endorsed (Parliamentary proceedings, 26 September 1990: 2514). Other points that were raised were the distinction between civil servants employed before and after 1983[14] as well as some disadvantages created for some categories of workers who were "trapped" because of the transition (especially mothers of under-age children).

There were few amendments made during the discussion in Parliament. Those that were made concerned the calculation of benefits for some specific groups of workers (i.e. university professors, and doctors of the National Health Service, Art. 5), the deficits of the special funds (a paragraph was added to the article on the financing of these funds (Art. 11) stating that the employer has to cover any deficits) and, finally, workers in the category of "hard and arduous work" were insured in special funds (retirement age applied as established by each of these funds). The most important "deviation" from the original proposals announced at the beginning of September 1990 concerned the provisions regarding future members of the special funds. Specifically, public sector enterprises would continue to insure their personnel with the special funds, instead of IKA as was originally suggested. All ND MPs voted for the legislation, producing a majority of one. Only 100 MPs were present during the summer session.

The content of the Law

Law 1902/90 introduced several important changes. For old-age pensions, the retirement age was fixed at 65 for men and 60 for women, and the minimum contribution period raised from 4,050 to 4,500 days (i.e. 13.5 to 15 years by adding 150 days annually as of 01.01.1992). Men who were 63 years old by 31.12.1991, and women who were 58, were excluded from these provisions. The insured could also retire at the age of 62 (men) or 57 (women) after 10,000 days (33 years) of contributions. Early retirement was possible as long as the contribution criterion was fulfilled (but in any case not before the age of 60 for men and 55 for women). In this case the pension was reduced by 1/200 of a full pension for each month preceding the standard age.

Women older than 50 with young or disabled children were entitled to a reduced pension if they had a contribution record of 5,500 days. The benefit was reduced by 1/200 of the full pension for each month preceding age 55, but could not be lower than the minimum pension.

The retirement age for those working under arduous conditions was fixed at 60 and 55 for men and women respectively, provided that they fulfilled the contribution criterion (4,500 days—15 years). This provision did not apply to those who were older than 58 (men), and 53 (women) by January 1, 1991. Groups of workers in this category to whom other age criteria applied were not affected by this provision. A committee was set up to revise the list of professions falling under this category.

Invalidity pensions

According to the new law, the insured was entitled to an invalidity pension under the following conditions. One way was to fulfill the contribution criterion for old-age pensions (4,500 days—15 years). Other conditions apply if disability occurred before the insured reached the age of 21, in which case contributions were reduced to 300 days and increased by 120 for every year after 21 up to 4,200 (14 years). Finally, workers were eligible for an invalidity benefit if they had made 1,500 days of contributions (5 years), 600 of which had to be in the five years preceding retirement. In either of the first two cases, 300 of the days of contributions required had to be made in the year preceding the claim.

The legislation also changed the definitions of invalidity. According to the new definitions, to qualify as suffering from "severe invalidity," the degree of incapacity had to be 80 percent, where it had previously been 66.7 percent. Those in this first category were entitled to a full old-age pension. "Moderate invalidity" applied to those considered to suffer from 66.7 percent to 79.9 percent incapacity, whereas before the range had been from 50 percent to 66.6 percent; these people were entitled to three quarters of the value of an old-age pension. "Partial invalidity" was considered to cover those suffering 50 percent to 66.6 percent incapacity, where the boundaries had previously been 33 percent to 50 percent, and entitled one to half of an old-age pension.

Public sector and special funds

According to previous legislation, the retirement age for public sector employees depended only on the number of years of employment. Men and unmarried women could retire after 25 years of service (or 35 for a full pension) and married women, widows and unmarried single mothers with young children could retire after 15 years of employment. The new law introduced age limits and made a distinction between those who were employed before and after 1983. For those who had been employed before January 1, 1983 and chose to retire before December 31, 1997, a link was established between age and the worker's contribution record (the limits being 55 for men 53 for women, and 42 for women with young or disabled children). For those employed after January 1, 1983, the retirement age increased to 60 for men, 58 for women and 50 for women with under-age or disabled children. The 15-year clause was abolished. To reduce the instances of unjust treatment under the new provisions, no age limit applied to those who chose to continue working for seven years having fulfilled the old criteria based on employment duration (Arts 2, 3). For those who chose to retire after 35 years of service (full pension), the age limit was fixed at 60.

On the basis of the old provisions, a full pension was paid after 35 years of service and was equal to 80 percent of the salary and the seniority increment received during the last month preceding retirement, multiplied by the annual ATA value (automatic indexation mechanism). Under the proposed measures, the pension was calculated differently, which would lead to lower benefits and was thus expected to reduce the numbers taking early retirement. After 25 years of service the pension would be equal to 25/50 of the full benefit (1/50 added for each year of service). Each additional year of service up to 30 years counted for 2/50 (3/50 up to 35 years) (Law 1902/90, Arts 5, 6). In addition, those employed from 1 October 1990 onwards started paying contributions equal to those paid for IKA (5.25 percent until 01.07.1991 and 5.75 percent from then onwards, Arts 6 and 25).

The 1990 reform introduced the same age conditions and calculation formulae[15] for the members of the special funds (main and supplementary funds of those working in banks, the public power corporation (DEI), the telecommunications organization (OTE), and public transportation (ISAP), Art. 10) with the exception of those members working under hard and arduous conditions. In addition, the members of these funds had to start paying insurance contributions, which by 1996 (1993 for those employed in OTE) would be at least 7.5 of their salaries.[16] Employers would still be responsible for covering any deficits in the funds. From January 1, 1991 the primary pensions paid by these funds were indexed to public sector wages.

Management of the funds' assets

The 1990 reform also included provisions for the management of the funds' reserves. Contrary to past practice (Law 1611/50), the interest rate on funds' deposits with the Bank of Greece were to equal the savings deposits of commercial banks (Art. 13). Furthermore, pension funds were given the right to form mutual funds and invest part of the assets. Further specifications were provided by ministerial decree. The new provisions were the government's response to the trade unions' arguments about the mismanagement of the assets. From this moment onwards the funds were "... the owners of their reserves, so that money is invested in the most profitable way" (Parliamentary Proceedings, September 27, 1990: 2616).

In sum, the ND government secured passage for the 1990 law, but at a high price. Despite the government's attempts to secure union support, unions mounted a three week strike against key provisions of the reform legislation, prompting the ND government to water down parts of the reform. The ND government refused to back down, however, and used the "urgent" procedure in Parliament to allow voting during the summer session of Parliament. The revised legislation passed by only one vote with only about one-third of MPs present.

1991: the Fakiolas Committee and Law 1976/91

With the first stage of reform out of the way, the ND government embarked on the second set of reforms. Eager to not repeat the mistakes of the last round of reform, the government started a new round of talks with the social partners. An independent expert committee (the "Fakiolas committee," named after its coordinator, Prof. Rossetos Fakiolas), was appointed in June 1991 to study the problems of social security. Final decisions were to be taken in close cooperation with the interested parties.

The experts had little time to prepare their report, which had to be ready by early October 1991. Trade union representatives expressed their skepticism about the role of the committee. The unions thought that the government had already formulated its proposals—concerning the reduction of the number of funds, further changes for public sector pensions, the introduction of tripartite financing and of private insurance—that the committee would simply have to rubber-stamp. Shortly after the committee was established, trade union representatives withdrew.

Two months after the Fakiolas committee was established, the Prime Minister announced that the government had decided to postpone far-reaching reforms and would focus on minor changes instead. Soon a document stating the government's intentions was distributed to the committee members that emphasized the following issues: the weak link between contributions and benefits, the need for a clear distinction between social security and social assistance policies, the state's financing responsibility, the need to re-examine issues relating to the transferability of social security benefits, and finally the need to review issues relating to the accumulation of benefits. No proposals were made on the minimum income scheme, which was expected to be introduced at a later date.

The reactions of the committee members whose work was being undermined notwithstanding, the government drafted a bill and introduced it in Parliament (Law 1976/91) without consulting the social partners. The law complemented existing legislation and included minor modifications of Law 1902/90 in response to problems that had arisen with its implementation, and made additional specifications concerning the calculation of benefits. It also provided for the re-examination of the conditions under which pensions were issued according to the provisions regarding the members of the National Resistance movement, which constituted another example (along with invalidity pensions) of the transfer payments included in the system.

The Fakiolas report was published in May 1992, but with inconclusive results. The report contained no quantitative estimate of the impact of the proposed measures due to lack of data, so the committee argued that it should be allowed to continue its work. The text revealed partial agreement with the trade unions' conclusions on the causes of the problems facing the pension system. However, the Fakiolas report went further by raising issues about the role of pensions in pre-election periods, the abuse of invalidity pensions and the lax conditions pertaining to those working under hard conditions.

Public reaction to the report was largely negative. GSEE representatives criticized it for yielding to government pressure for immediate measures and for lacking a scientific approach to the problems of social security. According to GSEE, the report could not be the basis for any negotiations because it forced trade unions to provide a simple "yes" or "no" answer (INE-GSEE 1992: 6). In the wake of such criticisms, the government refused to support the Fakiolas report and insisted that its conclusions were not indicative of government intentions.

1992: the Souflias Reform (Law 2084/92)

Despite the failure of the Fakiolas report, the ND government had not given up on reform. In June 1992 the Minister of National Economy, Stefanos Manos[17] (in office since February 1992) held his first meetings with trade union representatives. The minister insisted on two points: first, that the government did not intend to surprise its interlocutors during the dialogue process, and second that it was prepared to contribute more to the financing of the system, responding in this way to one of the unions' constant demands.

As noted, the ND government avoided taking a clear stance with regard to the Fakiolas report. In reality, the government was looking for reliable information elsewhere. While discussing with the trade unions, the Ministry of National Economy called a group of IMF experts to study the problem and provide solutions. This was not only a clear sign of the government's mistrust of national technocrats but also an attempt to weaken opposition to the reform by appealing to the work of a prestigious international organization. This decision, however, did not help reduce union skepticism. On the contrary, by choosing not to provide any information about its intentions to involve the IMF in the reform process, the government was set to provoke the enmity rather than the cooperation of its partners.

At that early, unofficial stage of the discussions, the government focused on the following points (Newspaper *To Vima* 28 June 1992): the harmonization of eligibility conditions to IKA standards; changes in financing mechanisms; the transformation of supplementary pensions and separation payments into optional schemes; the harmonization of retirement ages for men and women (65 years).

The government chose to focus first on the measures concerning new entrants to the labor market. Once decisions had been taken in this area the government expected to obtain some concessions concerning current workers. GSEE, however, insisted that such a distinction should not be made, and that any discussion should draw on the conclusions of its own report. ADEDY (the civil servants' confederation) on the other hand, made its participation in the dialogue conditional on the Minister's commitment not to change the 35-year rule in the public sector.

Despite these disagreements, some consensus seemed to emerge after the third meeting between the Ministers of National Economy and Labor, and GSEE representatives (ADEDY representatives refused to participate). In exchange for a new system covering those entering the labor market after January 1, 1993, GSEE was given the guarantee that the government would settle the debts of the insurance organizations and that the transition periods for those affected by previous legislation (Law 1902/90) would not change. After the meeting, the Minister of National Economy announced that a solution that would guarantee the sustainability of the system for 20 years had just been found.

Soon, however, the outcome of the meeting was questioned by GSEE officials who, under pressure from the opposition parties,[18] rejected the government's proposals. This U-turn undid any progress achieved thus far and made further developments dependent on the usual rhetoric about a neo-liberal government attacking workers' rights, illustrating that workers' organizations still did not have their own voice in the policy-making process. Again the government found itself in conflict with the unions. Despite its efforts to rescue the dialogue process, the government had to start preparing itself for a new round of strikes and implement its policy without union support.

The discussion in Parliament

The parliamentary discussion of the bill took place in the summer session in September. To increase revenues, contribution increases were planned for civil servants and the self-employed, and a tax was imposed on pensions (1–5 % depending on the benefit level). Measures to cut spending included a reduction in replacement rates for both main (60%) and supplementary pensions (to be limited to 20 %), an extension of reference periods, and the exclusion of Christmas and Easter bonuses from the calculation of benefits.

Again the parliamentary discussion emphasized issues similar to previous debates. Whereas the government justified the law in terms of problems on the expenditure side, opposition parties referred to the problems on the revenue side. PASOK repeated its proposals for establishing a national pension (providing a minimum income), increasing state subsidies, amortizing the debt of social security organizations, proceeding with new measures to improve the management of the funds' assets, and limiting contribution evasion (Parliamentary proceedings, 9 September 1992: 1136). The proposals submitted by SYN (The Coalition of the Left party) only repeated union demands, and in neither case was any effort made to provide concrete and quantifiable alternatives to what was being proposed.

Overall, the changes made during the parliamentary discussion were limited: most of the planned cuts in the survivors' pension were removed, provisions regarding the employment of pensioners insured through a public sector fund were removed, and pensions up to Drs. 100,000 (€300) were exempted from the 1 % tax.

The outcome of this second phase of reform fell short of the original goals. Indeed, the second phase was intended to introduce radical changes. Instead, the reform created a "breathing space" of about 15 years for the system, but the changes were only parametric. There are many reasons for this outcome. Although issues of political cost should not be ignored—indeed, the government had been "overburdened" with trying to reform major aspects of the economy (i.e. taxation, public sector enterprises) in just two years—other factors are of equal relevance. Issues of party unity (the threat of some MPs leaving ND to form a new party under the minister of Foreign Affairs, A. Samaras, was already present) as well as developments in foreign policy (i.e. events in the former Yugoslavia and the handling of the conflict with the Former Yugoslav Republic of Macedonia) further limited the government's room for maneuver.

The content of the Law

Law 2084/92 introduced a series of parametric changes designed to increase the financial sustainability of the pension system and harmonize eligibility conditions across schemes. The new rules applied to workers entering the labor market with the necessary "grandfather clauses" applying to current cohorts of workers.

In terms of financing, contributions rose to 6.67 percent of wages (previously 5.75%) for workers and 13.33 percent for employers (previously 11.5%) for those insured at IKA as of January 1, 1993. The state contributed 10 percent of gross wages for new labor market entrants. Contribution rates for other funds providing main pensions increased gradually over the next three years to equal IKA contributions. Civil servants are a special case: those employed from 30 September 1990 onwards started paying contributions for a main pension equal to 3 percent from January 1, 1993, 5 percent from January 1, 1994 and 6.67 percent from January 1, 1995. The rates for arduous occupations increased by 1.40 percent (employer) and 2.20 percent (employee). Finally, a tax was imposed on all pensions amounting to 1 percent for the part of pensions up to Drs. 100,000 (€300), 2 percent for the part from Drs. 100,000–200,000 (from €330–585) and so on up to 5 percent for pensions over Drs. 500,000 (about €1,470).

Eligibility was also tightened:

- a full pension was provided at 65 after 4,500 days (15 years) of contributions;
- a reduced pension was paid to claimants after 4,500 days of contributions and if the last 750 days (2.5 years) fell within the five years preceding retirement;
- the benefit was reduced by 1/200 for each month of retirement before the standard age;
- workers retiring under these conditions could not be younger than 60;
- the option of early retirement was still available to women with disabled children if the claimant was older than 55 and had paid contributions for 6,000 days (20 years); or was older than 50 with at least 750 days (2.5 years) of contributions within the five years preceding retirement (the pension was reduced by 1/200 for each month preceding standard retirement age);
- finally, women with three or more children could retire at 50 after 6,000 days of contributions.

Invalidity pension rules were also changed. An invalidity pension was paid: First, if the insured is younger than 21 and has a contribution record of 300 days (1 year). Contributions increase by 120 days (5 months) for each year after 21 up to a maximum of 1,500 days (5 years). Second, if the insured has a contribution record of 1,500 days, 600 of which were paid during the five years preceding retirement. The third possibility is if the insured has a contribution record of 4,500 days. The definitions regarding degrees of invalidity remained unchanged.

The most significant cuts were expected to result from the changes in the benefit calculation for workers employed after 1993. Although the reference period remained at five years (Law 2084/92, Art. 28), Christmas and Easter bonuses were not included in reference income. Pensions were calculated on the basis of 35ths for those employed until 31 December 1982 (each year of contributions was equal to 1/35th of the benefit), and on the basis of 50ths for those employed from January 1, 1983 to December 31, 1992. For those employed from January 1, 1993 each year of qualifying service equals 1.714 percent of the reference salary (replacement rate 60 percent). Replacement rates for supplementary pensions were fixed at 20 percent.

Finally, a small fund was created (LAFKA/ΛΑΦΚΑ, "Solidarity account for social security funds") to finance funds in deficit. LAFKA would be funded by freezing revenues from social taxes received by certain funds at their nominal 1992 level and shifting the excess receipts to this pool.

1997–1999: the Spraos Report and the "Mini Reform Package" (Law 2676/99)

The PASOK government elected in October 1993 based its election campaign on the need for a new "social contract," emphasizing social dialogue and concertation, and won 46.9 percent of the vote. Indeed, after the three-year term of the ND government, which had opted for what was then considered a Greek version of Thatcherism, the new approach promoted by the socialists was expected to generate the consensus needed for the major economic reforms required to qualify for EMU. PASOK's first term in government in the 1990s ended without any substantial change in the pension system, however. Reform only reached the agenda during PASOK's next term (from 1996).

In October 1996, the government established a committee to investigate the long-term prospects of the pension system. The committee's report was part of a larger study on the Greek economy in the context of EMU, which was coordinated by Professor Giannis Spraos, and the study of the pension system was drafted by a group of experts who reported to Spraos. The report's findings were to be used by the government in the process of social dialogue on the pension system, which was expected to start in June 1997. Discussions of pension reform were planned to take place in two phases. Initial discussions would focus on contribution evasion and asset management, and the funds' relations to the public, administrative modernization, assistance benefits and health insurance. Changes in eligibility conditions and the financing of the social security system would be discussed after the Spraos report had been completed.

The Spraos Committee report was published in October 1997, although some details had already been leaked to the press. In contrast to the Fakiolas report, the Spraos Report contained a detailed analysis of the "pensions problem." Overall, the Spraos Report promoted the creation of a three-pillar system, and its proposals can be summarized as follows:

1. On the revenue side, the committee argued that contribution rates were already too high (with the exemption of public sector employees) so contributions increases should be a last resort. In fact contributions could even be reduced for some categories of workers (i.e. young people, and sectors where contributions were already too high) if contribution evasion were curbed (Spraos Committee 1997: 38).
2. Concerning retirement age, the report emphasized the gap between the statutory retirement age and the effective retirement age. To reduce early retirement the committee suggested that there should be incentives to increase the period

spent in employment, to harmonize retirement ages for men and women, to re-examine those instances where pensions are paid regardless of age, and to review the occupations falling under "hard and arduous work," for which a lower retirement age applies (Spraos Committee 1997: 52–53).

3. Concerning the state's subsidy to the system, the committee expressed its doubts on the provisions regarding tripartite financing contained in Law 2084/92 and pointed to the need to replace state subsidies to the system with new sources of financing (Spraos Committee 1997: 44).
4. The Committee argued that benefits should be more closely linked to contributions and suggested that the provisions pertaining to the minimum pension (nearly 60% of pensions paid by IKA at the time were minimum pensions) should be reviewed. Given that minimum pensions play the role of assistance benefits, the committee suggested that assistance objectives should be achieved by strengthening means-testing (as it is done with EKAS for example, which was introduced in 1996) (Spraos Committee 1997: 51).
5. The Committee emphasized the need to unify funds to avoid the "financial absurdities" created by fragmentation, and pointed to the pressing need for administrative modernization, which would help reduce the incidence of multiple pensions (Spraos Committee 1997: 62, 67–72; 46–8).

Overall, the report promoted the creation of a three-pillar system consisting of a flat rate pension ("national pension"), an employment-related benefit financed on a PAYG basis and a top-up benefit based on capitalization. The report did not, however, provide a detailed analysis of the transition to such a system, and it did not adopt a single detailed model but presented several alternatives. Final choices would be subject to consultation between the government and the social partners. Despite its informative content and reasoned arguments, the Spraos report created new deadlocks. The report's proposals were hardly different from other studies, and neither were the reactions. The trade unions rejected the report and so did all the parties to the left of PASOK (Featherstone et al. 2001: 474). Most importantly, the report's publication revealed the reluctance of the PASOK government to proceed with radical reform, as well as the limited role reserved for technical knowledge in providing the basic guidelines for the reform process.

Once the initial reactions to the report had subsided, the government initiated dialogue with the social partners, which would cover only such issues as the unification of funds,[19] the management of the funds' assets and contribution evasion (the so-called mini-reform) which resulted in the passing of Law 2676/99.

The law contained several important changes.

(a) Three of the biggest funds insuring the self-employed, TAE (Storekeepers' Insurance Fund), TEVE (Fund for Craftsmen and Small Entrepreneurs), and TSA (Fund for Motorists)) were merged into OAEE (Organization for the Insurance of Liberal Professionals, Law 2676/99, Arts 1–13). The new fund covered the post-1993 members.

(b) Twelve civil servants' supplementary funds were merged into TEADY (Fund for Civil Servants' Supplementary Insurance, Arts 14–24). Here as well, provisions applied to the post 1993 entrants.
(c) New provisions were introduced regarding survivors' pensions (Art. 62).[20]
(d) Provisions were made regarding the accumulation of pensions and income from employment (Art. 63).
(e) Minimum pensions provided to the post-1993 entrants were increased by 50 percent (Art. 64).
(f) EKAS (the pensioners' social solidarity supplement) was increased by 50 percent (Art. 70).

In sum, the PASOK government elected in 1993 waited several years before it even attempted pension reform, and backed down quickly when the party membership and unions opposed key elements of the Spraos report. In the end, the PASOK government adopted several incremental changes that fell short of the proposals outlined in the Spraos report.

The attempt that failed: the Giannitsis Proposals of 2001

Changes in the pension system were one of the aims of the PASOK government re-elected in April 2000. According to PASOK's election campaign, the main pension policy objective of a future PASOK government would be to move to a three-pillar system. This pre-supposed the establishment of a long-awaited minimum income scheme in the form of a "national pension" provided to those who were uninsured or failed to fulfill the eligibility conditions to claim a pension.

To avoid the controversies that expert reports had caused in the past, the new PASOK government hired a British actuarial agency to study the sustainability of the social insurance system. The report was submitted in April 2001. As with any study of this kind, it contained estimates on the development of basic parameters affecting the system (trends in the population, unemployment and economic activity) and their future financial implications for the system. On the basis of these estimates, several scenarios for reform were provided ranging from simple parametric changes on the revenue or the expenditure side of the system, to structural changes (i.e. introduction of a flat-rate pension combined with a reduced-level earnings-related pension, or a shift from a defined-benefit to a defined-contributions scheme). The suggestions were not binding; the final choice lay with the government.

Following the submission of the report, the government elaborated its proposals. The measures that were finally announced by the Minister of Labor and Social Affairs, Anastasios Giannitsis, on April 20, 2001 consisted of parametric changes that were hardly comparable to the various scenarios included in the GAD (Government Actuary's Department) report. The proposals aimed to increase equity between generations of workers.

According to the government's proposals, the retirement age for a full pension would be gradually raised to 65 for all funds (the transitional period starting in 2007) and seniority pensions would be paid after 40 years of contributions (currently 35) regardless of age. The retirement age for women (currently 60) would be raised gradually to 65 as of 1 January 2007. Conditions pertaining to the retirement of women with young children were also expected to change. The proposal was for this group to retire at the age of 50 after 25 years of contributions. From 2007 onwards the retirement age for this category of women was planned to rise progressively to 65. Instead of retiring early, women would get a "bonus" of two years of pension rights for each child.

Although there were no plans to change the eligibility conditions for arduous occupations, the list of occupations falling under this category was to be reviewed.[21] For those retiring after 2007, replacement rates would be fixed at 80 percent of previous earnings (main pension: 60 percent, supplementary pension: 20 percent; PASOK had removed this provision during Simitis' first term in government). It was expected that the period taken into consideration for the calculation of benefits would be extended (best 10 out of the last 15 years for all workers).[22] Reference income would be indexed to wages.

As far as the financing of the pension system is concerned, the idea was for state contributions to remain as established in Law 2084/92 (10 percent of gross wage for each worker entering the labor market from 1993 onwards), whereas social taxes (earmarked taxes financing pension funds) would be abolished. Finally, existing funds providing main and supplementary pensions were to be unified in eight schemes.

These reform proposals were similar to the measures taken during 1990–92: the government decided to use the available room for parametric changes to reduce some inequalities. In fact, the idea was that the new system would lead to a harmonization of eligibility conditions for many funds and categories of workers and would eliminate some of the remaining distortions of the existing schemes.[23] Although much "lighter" than the measures proposed in the GAD report and indeed far from PASOK's pre-election commitment to establish a three-tier system, the Giannitsis proposals generated heated reactions. When the proposals were announced (April 19, 2001), tempers ran high. Union representatives reacted not only to the content of the measures but also to the government's decision to present some reform measures before consulting the unions. A general strike a few days later (April 26, 2001) prompted the government to change its approach and led to the withdrawal of the proposals.

The announcement of the measures created major problems for the government since it was forced to fight on two fronts simultaneously. First, it had to re-establish communication with the unions (i.e. GSEE, the biggest union confederation) who were the indisputable winners of this first confrontation with the government. According to some members of the cabinet and high-ranking PASOK politicians, the withdrawal of the proposals had practically cancelled the reform. After the withdrawal of the measures, the trade unions were much stronger, which meant that any further discussion of the issue would have to respond to the unions' demands for increased state participation in the financing of the system, an issue that the government preferred to avoid given the state of the Greek economy. In order to bring the trade unions back to the discussion table, the government appointed an expert committee to use the British report prepared for the government as well as the findings of the study by GSEE researchers, to produce a commonly accepted "diagnosis" of the problem.

Secondly, the government had to guarantee the unity of PASOK. Soon after the announcement of the proposals, the two people in charge of the reform, the Prime Minister and the Minister of Labor, found themselves at odds not only with the trade unions but also with many of their own party members, for whom the political cost of such decisions weighed more heavily than the necessity of reform.[24]

The Reppas Reform (Law 3029/02)

The policy-making process

After some unsuccessful attempts to induce unions to engage in dialogue, the Minister of Labor was replaced by the former spokesman of the government, Dimitris Reppas, who was expected to bridge the communication gap between the government and the trade unions. In his effort to bring his interlocutors back to the discussion table, the Minister of Labor was assisted by the new Minister of National Economy, who was committed to exploring the option of increasing state participation in financing the system. This, however, would be a very difficult task given the requirements of the Stability and Growth Pact and the high Greek public deficit, estimated at almost 100 percent of GDP (IMF 2002: 3).

In the months that followed the withdrawal of the Giannitsis proposals, the new Minister of Labor engaged in frequent and extensive consultation with the unions (mainly GSEE). A final decision was difficult to reach, but these renewed efforts at consensus (Law 3029/02 passed in June 2002) resulted in a compromise between the government's preferences for increased sustainability and equity, and the unions' demand for increased state financing.

The discussion in Parliament

The bill was brought to Parliament in June 2002 and discussed in three sessions (18, 19, 20 June). ND MPs chose to abstain from the debate, although they did participate in the discussion during the first session. The Law was passed by 144 votes to 131 (275 MPs present). The only significant modification made during the discussion in Parliament concerned the merging of special funds (public sector enterprises and banks) with IKA. Merging was made voluntary rather than compulsory (Law 3029/02, Art. 5, para. 2).

The content of the Law

The law contained some "traditional measures" (e.g. uniform retirement age for the members of all funds, gradual reduction of replacement rates for public sector employees to 70 percent starting January 2008, the merger of nine funds insuring mainly public sector employees) with some "non-traditional" ones (by Greek standards). These included fixed state participation in IKA financing, the creation of funded occupational schemes, measures to support mothers, measures for workers with short contribution records and so on. With these measures the government aimed to reduce some of the inequalities between various categories of workers, and to adapt the social security system to labor market changes.

As far as the structure of the pension system is concerned, provisions were made for the creation of a single fund for all wage earners for both main and supplementary pensions. Merging, however, is on a voluntary basis (Law 3029/2002, Art. 5, para. 2). In addition, for the first time in Greece, the law allows for the creation of occupational funds based on capitalization (Art. 7), managed by the social partners.

The law also introduced some parametric changes that will take full effect after 2007. Total replacement rates will be fixed at 70 percent (main and supplementary pensions) for both private and public sector employees (Art. 1, para. 14; Art. 2, para. 10; Art. 3, para. 2), and reference periods will be increased to the best five out of the final ten years (previously five years for IKA and last salary for public sector). As outlined by the government in 2001, the list of occupations considered to be hard and arduous work, will be reviewed. Furthermore, increases in benefits will be provided to those who decide to continue working after the minimum retirement age (Art. 3, para. 1) and at the same time smaller reductions will be made for those with 35 years of contributions who retire early (1/267 per month).

Women who bear children as of January 1, 2003 were to get a 1-year credit for the first child, $1\frac{1}{2}$ years for the second and 2 years for the third (Art. 4, para. 7; this provision helps women fulfill the eligibility conditions more easily). As far as the financing of the system is concerned, previous state participation in the financing of IKA was replaced by an annual subsidy fixed at 1 percent of GDP. Finally, a new independent body, the National Actuarial Authority was established to provide actuarial studies and assist the Ministry of Employment and Social Security with its planning.

It is difficult to provide a reliable evaluation of the measures at this early point, as the details of the merger of the funds and the functioning of the occupational funds are yet to be defined.[25] However, as stated in the preamble to the Law, the measures do not solve the problem but simply create the conditions and the institutional basis for a future reform.[26]

V Conclusion

Summary of the magnitude of changes

The central trend in pension reform in Greece since the 1980s is one of limited progress. Several years after the first attempt to reform the Greek pension system, reform remains "unfinished business." The changes introduced since the early 1990s did not provide a permanent solution to the problems created by demographic and labor market changes. How well do Greek reforms perform in terms of financial sustainability, equity (intra and inter-generational) and efficiency (i.e. the response of the pension system to changes in the labor market)?[27]

Although the effects of the reforms introduced in the early 1990s should not be underestimated, the problem of the financial sustainability of the Greek pension system remains unresolved. According to recent data, expenditure on pensions stands at 12.6 percent of GDP and is expected to increase to 24.8 percent of GDP by 2050, the highest proportion in Europe (European Commission 2001: 22).

The legislation passed since the beginning of the 1990s has had some significant effects in terms of equity. However, the burdens implied by the reforms are disproportionately allocated, with younger cohorts and private sector wage earners (i.e. the post-1993 cohorts) bearing the costs of adjustment. Older cohorts (i.e. pre-1983 workers) and public sector workers experienced few cuts. The improvements in terms of equity will be visible first when legislation concerning these cohorts takes full effect, and second when the mergers of the funds foreseen in the 1999 and 2002 legislation take place. In the second case, however, progress is likely to be extremely slow given that most mergers are voluntary.

Finally, concerning effectiveness, the improvements made in recent years (probably with the exception of the provisions included in the Reppas reform concerning mothers and workers with short working careers) were not included in the reform negotiations described above, but were introduced separately (i.e. EKAS as a response to old-age poverty and the provisions concerning the long-term unemployed included in Law 2874/2000). Although this can be seen as an instance of piecemeal policy-making (i.e. the limited capacities of political actors to combine aspects of various policy areas in a single package deal) it is also an indication of the limited space left for the interests that would benefit most from such changes (i.e. the unemployed, younger people).

Impact of the political system on pension politics

Given the long-term problems facing the Greek pension system and the available solutions, it is hardly surprising that the need for reform has been recognized by all political actors. The positions of the two main parties today display common characteristics but the de facto two-party structure of the political system makes straightforward agreement impossible for electoral reasons. Since either of the two major parties could be in power after the next elections, neither has an interest in constraining their capacity to criticize as the party of opposition, which also explains why there have been so few attempts to secure even the tacit consensus of the opposition when introducing a reform.

As this chapter shows, in most cases bills were passed with minor modifications, whereas more important changes (i.e. the Souflias reform) were made in response to pressure from non-parliamentary political actors. Furthermore, the solid majorities achieved in the passing of reform legislation reveal the importance of assuring the agreement of party members before introducing a pension law (which was lacking in 2001 when the Giannitsis proposals were announced).

In this respect, the ND government proved more resistant to union pressures in the 1990–92 reform process. The ND government's success in passing more politically costly measures is explained by two related factors: first, the critical state of the Greek economy in the early 1990s, and secondly, the cohesion that the government majority was able to display despite its fragile parliamentary position.

This was not the case with PASOK, however. Each time Simítis decided to handle the "hot potato" of pension reform, he had to contend with hostile reactions from within his party and from unions. Whereas ND could be said to have passed pension reforms by achieving internal cohesion thanks to the economic crisis, PASOK was unable to do so when faced with another external constraint, the Maastricht criteria for entry to EMU.

Interest group influence

In recent years, unions have been actively involved in pension reform although it is virtually impossible to translate union mobilization into an effective political obstacle against the adoption of government proposals (laws are passed in Parliament after all). Given that most West European pension systems are financed by contributions, unions have a large stake in these programs. Additionally, unions have increasingly shown interest in social policy issues in order to assert their role in social policy-making. Mobilizing against government proposals usually helps unions prove their strength, which has been falling in recent years due to lower rates of membership. As discussed, Greece lacks a tradition of consensual, tripartite policy-making. However, retirement is an important issue for the unions, and any proposal to change retirement conditions is bound to invoke their interest and their protest along with claims for their direct involvement in policy-making.

Unions played a significant role in each of the reforms discussed in this chapter, either through protest (i.e. the Souflias reform, the Giannitsis proposals) or through collaboration with the government (i.e. the Reppas reform). This is also reflected in the content of the legislation since this content relates to the organizational features of unions (i.e. membership). Therefore, along with the "grandfather clauses" that are always included in pension reforms, which aim to prevent current workers from mobilizing, some concessions have been made to the groups that the unions that could mobilize most easily (i.e. public sector workers during the 1990 reform, some provisions in 2002 legislation).

Especially during the last reform (the Reppas reform), the unions played an active role in policy-making. Compared to the proposals presented in 2001, the 2002 reform contained more concessions to the unions, which satisfied some of their most insistent demands (i.e. increased state financing). Part of the unions' success is also due to the fact that for the first time, unions were able to provide a technically feasible alternative to the government's proposals (see p. 144 on the role of ideas), which increased public support.

Constraints of policy design

Like other mature public pension systems, the "contract-like" status of pension commitments in Greece mean the system is highly resistant to change, even though dissatisfaction with the system is widespread (O'Donnell and Tinios 2003). In other words, voters may be unhappy with certain aspects of the current system, but there is little support for structural change.

The measures necessary to curtail pension expenditure are more or less known. If the financing method is to remain unchanged, a choice (or a combination of options) must be made between increasing contributions, reducing the number of beneficiaries (i.e. by increasing retirement age and limiting early retirement) or cutting benefits. The negative implications for each one of these choices are clear: contributors may not be willing to pay higher contributions (this may not be an attractive option for the government either: high contribution rates have negative effects on employment), and in the latter two cases current workers might either need to prolong working life to acquire pension rights, or see their benefits significantly cut in the future. All this can lead to widespread protest that may include possible winners, given also the fact that the complex technicalities involved in the calculation of benefits are not easily understood by the public.

Greece is no exception to this rule. Greece, however, has one more feature that weakens governments' arguments about the need to reduce expenditure (Triantafillou 2003b: 6–7): In Greece, like many other countries, the state regulates the functioning of the pension system and ultimately acts as a guarantor of its sustainability. In Greece, the state has not acted as a sound manager of the system and has very often abused its power to interfere with the funds' finances. For many years, governments have essentially appropriated the revenues of the social insurance system by allowing reserves to be invested either in state securities or to be deposited with the Bank of Greece at a low interest rate. Although in the past the reserves were used to boost economic development, this has been done without Labor's consent and—most importantly—for a very long period of time. Second, the pension system has often been used to perform redistributive functions without a parallel increase in state financing, that is, without the revenue coming from general taxation. As a result, any attempt to introduce changes to the pension system that will improve its sustainability meets with arguments about the state's neglectful role, and any reform will have to find a compromise between the need for further cuts and the need to rationalize the financing of the system by increasing non-contribution revenue.

Let us close this section by referring briefly to an additional constraint which is due not to the structure of the pension system, but to the design of the Greek welfare state in general. As shown in the sections on the history of the Greek pension system and its current structure see pp. 111–12, pensions in Greece are used as a substitute for other policies (mainly assistance policies—a feature of Mediterranean welfare states; see Ferrera 1996). Due to the underdevelopment of other policy sectors, pensions are often the only source of income for many households, which also explains the fierce reactions that can be observed each time a government decides to attempt pension reform.

Role of ideas and historical context

Although a highly technical issue, pension reform in Greece has not been ear marked by a prominent role for those with academic or financial expertise, those who could have acted as "policy brokers" in this highly conflictual constellation of political actors. There are two reasons for this. First, there is a limited number of people who have the necessary technical knowledge. Furthermore, even if policy experts manage to convince policy-makers of the necessity of certain measures, the final decisions are always affected by considerations about the political costs involved. The same applies in the case of models proposed by international organizations (i.e. the three-pillar system proposed by the World Bank and later endorsed by other international organizations).

Second, it is difficult to distinguish expert studies from the agency that commissions them. Therefore, technical knowledge loses its objectivity and is not trusted. In 1997 and 2001, both the government and the social partners appeared better equipped in terms of the technical evidence used to support their arguments, than at the time of the 1990–92 reforms. However, the technical reports commissioned by the government (the Spraos reports and the GAD reports as well as the Fakiolas report in 1992) lacked political backing, and the reliability of the information provided each time was questioned. The studies commissioned by the government in 1997 and 2001 provoked widespread suspicion and were rejected by the unions as covert attempts to justify *faits accomplis*, which overshadowed their scientific content. In other words, expert knowledge in Greece falls victim to the highly politicized process of policy-making where strategic disagreement and incremental decisions are not the exception but the rule, and where particularistic, clientelistic demands prevail over the needs of those who cannot take part in policy design.

Abbreviations

ADEDY	Civil Servants' Confederation
ATA	Automatic Indexation Mechanism
DEI	Public Power Corporation
DIKKI	Democratic-Social Movement
Drs.	Drachmas
EKAS	Pensioners Social Solidarity Supplement
GAD	Government Actuary's Department (UK)
GSEE	Confederation of Greek Workers

IKA	Social Insurance Organization
KEP	Free Citizens' Movement
KEPE	Center for Planning and Economic Research
KKE	Communist Party of Greece
LAEK	Special Account for Employment and Vocational Training
LAFKA	Solidarity Account for Social Security Funds
ND	New Democracy
OAED	Manpower Employment Organization
OAEE	Insurance Organization for the Liberal Professionals
OGA	Farmers' Insurance Agency
OTE	Telecommunications Organization
OTOE	Federation of Bank Sector Employees
PASOK	Pan-Hellenic Social Movement
POLAN	Political Spring
SEV	Federation of Greek Industries
SYN	Coalition of the Left
TAE	Storekeepers' Insurance Fund
TEADY	Fund for Civil Servants' Supplementary Insurance
TEAM	Wage Earners' Supplementary Insurance Fund
TEVE	Fund for Craftsmen and Small Entrepreneurs
TSA	Motorists' Fund

Notes

1. The Truman Doctrine had just been promulgated.
2. Before the 1986 revision of the Constitution the President of the Republic could veto legislation, dissolve Parliament and call for a direct vote of confidence in Parliament. From 1974 to 1986, no President used these powers.
3. Corruption scandals dominated the 1989 elections.
4. See for example Legislative Decree 2698/53, Art. 51.
5. Contributions for farmers were abolished in 1964.
6. In 1998, a new fund known as OAEE was created to include TEVE and two other funds of the self-employed (TAE and TSA).
7. Revenue from loans is not included (Ministry of Labor and Social Security 2002: 80).
8. The best five out of the last ten years for those employed by 31.12.1992 (Law 3029/02, Art. 2 para. 9).
9. http://www.ika.gr/gr/infopages/asf/insurance/milserv.cfm
10. However, mergers are more likely to occur not as a result of new legislation but out of necessity. Due to increasing financial imbalances, merger is the only option available for many small funds.
11. The minimum IKA pension rose from 40% of the average earnings of an industrial worker in 1979 to 66 percent in 1985 (OECD 1987: 47).
12. In May–June 1990, the increase was double the annual average (9–10 percent instead of 4–5 %) (Newspaper *To Vima* 24.06.1990).

13. If more than three children there was no retirement age linked to contribution records. If fewer, the pension would be paid after 15 years at 42 regardless of whether during the transition period the *children had reached adult age.*
14. PASOK considered the choice of this date a kind of political "revenge" against the policies enacted during its term in government.
15. The new calculation formula in these cases was used only for those who were employed after 01.01.1983.
16. This provision did not apply to funds where the ratio of employee—employer contribution was 1:2 (Law 1902/90, Art. 11, para. 4).
17. Although Manos was the chief negotiator, the reform was named after the Vice-Minister of Social Insurance, Dimitris Sioufas.
18. As noted, union leaders have strong links with political parties. It is not rare to see presidents and high-ranking members of the two biggest confederations becoming MPs after serving in unions.
19. Since 1999, the number of funds has been reduced by 68 (www.labor-minsitry.gr).
20. These are the provisions currently in force. A survivors' pension is paid to the surviving spouse for three years regardless of age. If the spouse was older than 40 at the time death occurred, the pension is paid even after the three years are over. If the spouse was younger than 40 at the time of death, the pension is paid for three years and is suspended until the surviving spouse is 65. If the surviving spouse is disabled (degree of disability exceeds 67 %) the pension is paid for as long as disability lasts.
21. Revising the list had been on the reform agenda of all governments from 1990 onwards. So far the list has not been substantially revised.
22. Calculation was previously based on the earnings of the 5 years preceding retirement for IKA pensioners. Civil servants' pensions were calculated on the basis of their earnings during the last month before retirement.
23. This reform, however, would only partly correct the financial imbalances of the system and a new reform would soon be necessary (Matsaganis 2001: 17).
24. The negative effect that the announcement of the reform proposals had among PASOK voters was the main reason that the party congress was rescheduled for October 2001 (five months early). In his speech, the Prime Minister asked party members to help the government create "a new welfare state" (Newspaper *Ta Nea* 12.10.2001).
25. The merger concerns funds insuring workers of the public sector (with strong unions) and it is not compulsory.
26. See http://www.parliament.gr/ergasies/nomosxedia/EisigisiEpitropon/M-KOINASF-eisig. pdf
27. See also Triantafillou (2003b).

Bibliography

Primary sources and government documents

Constitution of the Hellenic Republic.*
Regulation of the Hellenic Parliament.*
Law numbers are provided in the chapter text.

*Parliamentary proceedings**

Hellenic Parliament: Parliamentary proceedings, various sessions (numbers provided in text).

*Reports**

THE FAKIOLAS COMMITTEE (1992). *Report on the restructuring of the Social Insurance System in Greece*. Athens.
SPRAOS COMMITTEE (1997). *The Economy and Pensions: A Contribution to the Public Debate*. Athens: National Bank of Greece.
GOVERNMENT of GREECE (2001): *Review of the Retirement Pension System Report by the Government Actuary's Department (GAD), UK*. Athens.
MINISTRY OF NATIONAL ECONOMY and FINANCE, MINISTRY of LABOR and SOCIAL INSURANCE (2002): *The Greek Report on Pension Strategy: Appendices*. Athens.

Other sources

MINISTRY OF LABOR and SOCIAL SECURITY (2002)*. *Social Budget*.
MINISTRY OF LABOR and SOCIAL SECURITY (2002b)*. Interview with the Minister of Labor and Social Security and the Minister of National Economy and Finance (21/3/2002), http://www.labor-ministry.gr (Last access: April 2002).
IKA*: http://www.ika.gr/gr/infopages/asf/insurance/milserv.cfm (Last access: January 2005) http://www.ika.gr/gr/infopages/memos_search.cfm (Last access: January 2005).
MINISTRY OF LABOR and SOCIAL SECURITY: www.labor-minsitry.gr
Preamble to Law 3029/2002*: http://www.parliament.gr/ergasies/nomosxedia/EisigisiEpitropon/M-KOINASF-eisig.pdf (Last access: July 2003).
EUROPEAN FOUNDATION FOR THE IMPROVEMENT OF LIVING and WORKING CONDITIONS (2003): http://eurofound.eu.int/emire/GREECE/UNIONDENSITY-GR.html (Last access: December 2004).

*Newspapers**

Ta Nea: 11.9.1990, 12.9.1990, 17.09.1990, 12.10.2001
To Vima: 24.6.1990, 29.7.1990, 5.8.1990, 9.9.1990, 27.10.1991, 28.6.1992

Secondary sources

DIAMANTOPOULOS, THANASSIS (1997).* *Political Life in Greece: From the Pre-Venizelos to the Post-Papandreou era*. Athens: Papazisis.
DIAMANTOUROS, NIKIFOROS (1995). "Greece." In *The Encyclopedia of Democracy*, Vol. II. Washington: Congressional Quarterly Inc.
EUROPEAN COMMISSION, ECONOMIC POLICY COMMITTEE (2001). *Budgetary Challenges Posed by Aging Populations: The Impact on Public Spending on Pensions, Health and Long-term Care for the Elderly and Possible Indicators of the Long-term Sustainability of Public Finances*.
FEATHERSTONE, KEVIN, GEORGE KAZAMIAS and DIMITRIS PAPADIMITRIOU (2001). "The Limits of External Empowerment: EMU, Technocracy and Reform of the Greek Pension System." *Political Studies*, Vol. 49(3): 462–80.
FEATHERSTONE, KEVIN and PLATON, TINIOS (2003). "Facing up to the Gordian Knot: The Political Economy of Pension Reform". Manuscript.
FERRERA, MAURIZIO (1996). "The 'Southern' Model of Welfare in Social Europe." *Journal of European Social Policy*, 6(1), 17–37.
GUILLÉN, ANA and MANOS MATSAGANIS (2000). "Testing the 'Social Dumping' Thesis in Southern Europe: Welfare Policies in Greece and Spain during the last 20 years." *Journal of European Social Policy*, 10(2): 121–45.
IMF (2002). *Greece: Selected Issue: An Overview of Pension Reform*, Country report no. 02/58, Washington DC.
INE GSEE (1992)*. 'Bulletin' (Ενημερωτικό Δελτίο), no. 15, May 1992.

IOANNOU, CHRISTOS (1989).* *Wage Earners and Trade Unionism in Greece.* Athens: Idryma Mesogiakon Erevnon.

IOANNOU, CHRISTOS (1999). "Trade Unions in Greece: Development, Structures and Prospects." Electronic edition: FES library 2000. http://www.Fes.de/fulltext/bueros/athen/00740001.htm (Last Access: March 2003).

KATROUGALOS, GEORGE (1996). "The South European Welfare Model: The Greek Welfare State in search of an identity." *Journal of European Social Policy*, 6(1): 39–60.

KEPE -Center for Planning and Economic Research (1988)*. *Social Insurance*, Athens.

KIOUKIAS, DIMITRIS (1997) "Interest Representation and Modernisation Policies in Greece: Lessons Learned form the Study of Labour and Farmers." *Journal of Modern Greek Studies*, 15(2): 303–24.

LAVDAS, KOSTAS A. (1997). *The Europeanisation of Greece: Interest Politics and the Crises of Integration.* Basingstoke: Macmillan.

LYRINTZIS, CHRISTOS (1987). "The Power of Populism: The Greek Case." *European Journal of Political Research*, 15(6): 667–86.

MATSAGANIS, MANOS (2001). "Welfare State Reform and Modernization of Society." Working Paper 01–07. Rethymno: Department of Economics, University of Crete.

MAVROGORDATOS, GEORGE TH. (2001).* *Pressure Groups and Democracy.* Athens: Patakis.

MENDRINOU, MARIA (2000)*. *Electoral Politics in the Greek Political System.* Athens: Papazisis.

MOLINA, OSCAR and MARTIN RHODES (2002). "Corporatism: The Past, Present and Future of a Concept." *Annual Review of Political Science.* 2002(5): 305–31.

MOSCHONAS, GERASIMOS (1994).* "The Dividing Line Between Right and Anti-Right during and after the Transition to Democracy (1974–90). The Content of the Cleavage and some Aspects of the Strategy of the Political Parties of the 'Anti-Right' System." In Nikos Demertzis (ed.) *Greek Political Culture Today.* Athens: Odysseas.

MYLONAS, PAUL and CHRISTINE DE LA MAISONNEUVE (1999). "The Problems and Prospects Faced by Pay-As–You-Go Pension Systems: A Case Study of Greece." IMF Economics Department Working Paper no. 215. Washington, D.C.

NEW DEMOCRACY (2002). "Our Position on Social Security." *Political Texts* 2. (October).

O'DONNELL, OWEN and PLATON TINIOS (2003). "The Politics of Pension Reform: Lessons from Public Attitudes in Greece." *Political Studies*, 51(2): 262–81.

OECD (various years). *Economic Surveys: Greece.* Paris.

PAPADIMITRIOU, GIORGOS (1996).* "The Achilles Heel of Intra-party Democratic Deficit." In Spilios Papaspiliopoulos (ed.) *PASOK: Gaining and Exercising Power.* Athens: Sideris.

PAPPAS, TAKIS, S. (1999). *Making Party Democracy in Greece.* Basingstoke: Macmillan.

PETMESIDOU, MARIA (1991). "Statism, Social Policy and the Middle Classes in Greece." *Journal of European Social Policy*, 1(1): 31–48.

PETMESIDOU, MARIA (1992).* *Social Inequality and Social Policy.* Athens: Exantas.

PETRAS, JAMES et al. (1993). "Greek Socialism: The Patrimonial State Revisited." In Kurth, J. and Petras, J. (eds.), *Mediterranean Paradoxes: The Politics and Social Structure of Southern Europe*, Oxford: Berg Publishers.

PIERSON, PAUL (1994). *Dismantling the Welfare State? Reagan, Thatcher and the Politics of Retrenchment.* Cambridge: Cambridge University Press.

SCHLUDI, MARTIN (2001). "The Politics of Pensions in European Social Insurance Countries." Max Planck Institut für Gesellschaftsforschung Discussion Paper 01/11, December 2001. Cologne.

SPYROPOULOS, ANTONIS G. (1996).* *IKA Pensions: Transfer of Pension Rights; Legislation; Practice.* Athens: IKA.

TRIANTAFILLOU, POLYXENI (2003). "Reflections on where the Theory of Neo-corporatism in Greece has Stopped and where the Praxis (or the Absence?) of Neo-corporatism May Be Going." Paper presented at the 1st LSE Ph.D. Symposium on Modern Greece "Current Social Sciences Research on Greece," LSE, June 21, 2003.

—— (2003b). "Trade Unions, Veto Points, and European Pensions Reform: Pension Reform in Greece." Paper presented at the 15th Annual Meeting of the Society for the Advancement of Socio-Economics and LEST (Laboratoire d'Économie et de Sociologie du Travail) Aix-en-Provence, France, June 26–28, 2003.

TSAKALOTOS, EUKLID (1998). "The Political Economy of Social Democratic Economic Policies: The PASOK Experiment in Greece." *Oxford Review of Economic Policy*, 14: 114–38.

VENIERIS, DIMITRIS (1994). *The Development of Social Security in Greece, 1920–1990: Postponed Decisions*, Ph.D. Thesis. London: London School of Economics.

* Publications in Greek

CHAPTER 4

FRANCE: THE IMPORTANCE OF THE ELECTORAL CYCLE

EUGÉNIA DA CONCEIÇÃO-HELDT

I Introduction

ALTHOUGH the French political system is characterized by a strong executive, low number of veto points and fragmented interest groups, French governments' record on pension reform has been mixed. Even governments supported by a solid parliamentary majority had difficulty in moving pension reform from the political agenda into legislation, because pension reforms have been blocked by interest group protest.

The main issue in France was the financial sustainability of the pension system. The public pension system is generally popular, so there is no majority in favor of dismantling or privatization. The political game was about how to introduce cost-saving reforms that would preserve the basic structure of the public pension system. Serious discussion about pension reform began in the early 1980s and was marked by a multiplicity of reports, but few concrete measures until the mid-1990s. Even though there were several attempts to scale back the French welfare state, some important reforms to cut spending failed, such as the Juppé plan in 1995 (only partially implemented) and the Thomas Law in 1997. On the other hand, two major reforms were implemented by two Conservative governments: the 1993 Balladur and the 2003 Raffarin reforms. Do the different reform attempts suggest a *société bloquée* (Crozier 1970), that is to say a state of affairs where interest groups impede change by defending their acquired rights?

In order to explain why French governments are so reluctant in embarking on pension reforms introducing unpopular measures, this chapter argues that union mobilization and timing of the electoral cycle are the two determining factors that constrain and even impede policy change. First, in line with other scholars (Bonoli 2000; Marier 2002; Myles and Pierson 2001; Natali and Rhodes 2004; Schludi 2003) working on pension reform the first main argument is that "unions still matter." This chapter, however, goes one step further and tries to demonstrate how they matter and under what conditions they might cause governments to abstain from welfare cuts. Second, focusing on the informal veto power of unions alone does not seem plausible, since governments have been able to enact and implement pension reforms entailing cuts in benefits, both by strategic side-payments to dampen opposition and even by ignoring union protests. This is why one also needs to focus on the timing of the electoral cycle to explain the actions of French governments. It is expected that governments will be more successful in passing legislation that implements unpopular reforms in the first part of their mandates, because they enjoy greater freedom of political maneuver in the first two and half years of a legislature period, that is, during the "honeymoon period."[1]

II Political system

Constitutional history and nation-building

One of the keys to understanding the French political system is the nature of constitutional development in the aftermath of the 1789 French revolution. From 1789 until the beginning of the Fifth Republic, France has been governed by sixteen different constitutions, with government lifespan averaging only eleven months. The imperial period of Napoleon Bonaparte (1799–1815) was followed by a constitutional monarchy (1815–48), which for the first time introduced a parliamentary system in France, with a weak separation of powers. Although the Second Republic (1848–51) constituted a further attempt to establish a democratic system, it ended with a *coup d'état*. After the dissolution of the National Assembly, Louis-Napoleon Bonaparte established an authoritarian regime by retaining democratic institutions with the sole aim of reinforcing his personal power. After his capitulation at the Battle of Sedan, the Third Republic (1875–1940) was proclaimed. During this period, the President of the Republic elected by the Chamber of Deputies and by the Senate had the central executive functions (Crouzatier 2003: 7–9).

The short intermezzo of the Vichy regime (1940–44) was followed by the Fourth Republic (1946–58). In this parliamentary regime dominated by the National Assembly, the President of the Republic had a weak position, since he was elected by the parliament and his acts had to be countersigned by the Prime Minister and by a minister. Between 1946 and 1958 there were 29 governments, of which 12 were minority governments and the most durable lasted sixteen months (Huber 1996: 1). During this period, governments were rarely supported by stable majorities, so that the likelihood that deputies would override executive decisions was high. The French parliament was a critical veto point, in which the division of parliamentary factions often led to parliamentary stalemate (Immergut 1992: 80). The inability of the government to suppress an Algerian nationalist insurrection led to its collapse and the return to office of Charles de Gaulle in 1958.

After a national referendum in September 1958, the Constitution for the Fifth Republic was adopted and new institutional arrangements were set up with the aim of ensuring political stability and to strengthen the French government against the parliament.

Institutions of government

The Fifth Republic has been one of the most durable French political regimes since the 1789 French revolution. The drafters of the constitution of the Fifth Republic intended to remedy several perceived defects of French politics by strengthening the power of the executive in several ways. First, a directly-elected president was added to the parliamentary system, in order to provide stronger, and popularly-legitimate political leadership. Second, as unreliable parliamentary coalitions were viewed as the cause both of unstable governments and poor legislative records, institutional arrangements were settled to give the Prime Minister and his government tools to force the passage of legislation. Thus, although both houses of parliament, the National Assembly (*Assemblée Nationale*) and the Senate (*Sénat*), have legislative power, the Prime Minister may curtail the parliamentary discussion after a single reading in both chambers. Finally, the Constitutional Council (*Conseil Constitutionnel*) supervises the constitutionality of laws and in the last two decades it has often been the arbiter between the government and the parliamentary opposition.

The President of the Republic is directly elected for a five-year term by secret ballot with universal adult suffrage.[2] There is a second run-off between the two top candidates if none of the contenders receives a majority of the votes in the first round. The President is head of the Council of Ministers, commander-in-chief of the armed forces, promulgates laws, signs decrees and ordinances within fifteen days of their adoption. Furthermore, the President was given parliamentary power by his right to dissolve the National Assembly, by recourse to the Constitutional Council, by negotiating and ratifying treaties, and by calling or refusing to resort to a referendum (Duverger 1992: 144; Knapp and Wright 2001b: 83–4).

The Prime Minister, appointed by the President, heads and directs the government, controls the parliamentary agenda and is responsible to parliament (Huber 1996: 24). This dual executive arrangement, mixing parliamentary with presidential features, has been referred to as semi-presidential and semi-parliamentary system (Duverger 1980). When the President is backed by a parliamentary majority that belongs to the same political family, s/he may freely select the Prime Minister and also give general policy guidelines for the executive branch. Under cohabitation, when President and Prime Minister come from different parties, the latter exercises the key powers on domestic issues, so that the President's influence is confined to defense and external affairs (Thiébault 2000: 504). This distinction only plays an important role when studying "grey areas" such as the EU, as it is difficult to distinguish between domestic or external issues (Marier 2002: 73). In pension politics, however, the president does not matter much, because the Prime Minister is in charge of pension legislation, sets the legislative agenda and leads the decision-making process. Whether or not cohabitation occurs, it does not influence the policy outcome. Social security is a purely domestic issue where the intervention of the President does not occur in time of cohabitation. If governments are supported by stable majorities in parliament, they should be able to pass their proposals and the President is not expected to have a strong impact in the reform debate.

The French Constitution includes several rules strengthening the executive against the legislature: the Prime Minister can rely on the package vote (*vote bloquée*) and the confidence vote procedure, bypass the parliament entirely by issuing legislation through decrees, or even curtail the shuttle system between both houses of parliament after a single reading. The package vote procedure gives government the power at any time to select articles and amendments and exclude those it opposes (Arts. 44, 49 of the French Constitution). The National Assembly must then vote either to accept or to reject the government's policy package. Under the confidence vote procedure (in France commonly called *le 49.3*) there is no vote on the law itself, but instead all debate ceases immediately and if a motion of censure is not introduced and adopted within the next 24 hours, the law is considered passed in the form designated by the government. Due to the existing circumscription of parliamentary powers, Frears (1990) defines the National Assembly as a "loyal workhorse, poor watchdog," and Huber (1996) also considers it as a rather weak legislature. The same is valid for the Senate. Although it has the power of delaying legislation through its right to make amendments, it cannot be considered a veto player, since it cannot reject a bill. This is why some scholars (Kempf 2003; Tsebelis and Money 1997) assert that the Senate retains authority and influence without having power.

Finally, one of the most important functions of the Constitutional Council consists in supervising the constitutionality of general and constitutional laws and legislation by policing the executive-legislative boundary. The Constitutional Council defines not only the policy issues in which the parliament is entitled to legislate, while all other matters are governed by administrative enactments, but it also has to give

Table 4.1 Political institutions in France

Political arenas	Actors	Rules of investiture	Rules of decision-making	Veto potential
Executive	President (*Président*)	5-year term; directly elected; majoritarian electoral system in a two-round ballot (majority for first round, plurality for second round)	Must sign decrees and laws; before the promulgation of a law he can send laws back to parliament for reconsideration; can be given supplementary powers in times of emergency; can dissolve the National Assembly once a year; determines the agenda of the Council of Ministers	Not a veto point for laws; veto point for ordinances and decrees
	Prime Minister (*Premier Ministre*)	Selected and appointed by President, but requires confidence of National Assembly (i.e. majority of deputies)	Directs the government; controls the parliamentary agenda; initiates legislation; following instruments discipline parliament: Package vote (*vote bloquée*) i.e. the government can at any time exclude articles or amend a bill and ask the National Assembly to accept or reject the government's policy package; Confidence Vote (Guillotine) procedure: the government can cease all debates immediately; if a motion of censure is not introduced and adopted within the next twenty-four hours, the law is adopted	—
Legislative	National Assembly (*Assemblée Nationale*)	5-year term; 577 members; majoritarian electoral system in two-ballots; 577 constituencies;	Adopts legislation; decision by absolute majority of those deputies voting, can force government to	Not a veto point if a government has parliamentary absolute majority

		each department elects minimum of two deputies; one deputy represents approximately 100,000 inhabitants; can be dissolved by the President	resign by passing a motion of censure
	Senate (*Sénate*)	6-year term; 346 members; indirect election by electoral colleges	Participates in legislation; can amend legislation; decision by absolute majority, agreement of the Senate is required but after two rounds of conciliation (shuttle system), the government can denote an act to urgent and cut off this shuttle system	Not a veto point
Judicial	Constitutional Court (*Conseil Constitutionnel*)	9-year term; 10 members; President of the court is appointed by the President of the Republic; other members are appointed equally by the President of the Republic, by the President of the Senate and by the President of the National Assembly (three per institution)	When the President of the Republic decides to exercise emergency power, he must consult the Court; supervises referenda, elections and the constitutionality of laws	Veto point: has the power to invalidate any law, if it is considered to be unconstitutional
Electoral	Referendum	President can call for referenda (on the proposal of government or parliament) on general policy issues and on institutional arrangements	Used in three different situations: to approve a bill dealing with the organization of public authorities or institutions; to authorize the ratification of a treaty; to approve a bill to revise the constitution, if so requested by the President; since 1995, the President can call a referendum on a wider range of issues, e.g. economic and social policy and public service reform	Veto point, and firmly in control of President (rarely used by the President for these wider issues)

(Continued)

Table 4.1 (Continued)

Political arenas	Actors	Rules of investiture	Rules of decision-making	Veto potential
Territorial units	Departments (*départements*)	22 regions, 96 *départements* (divided into 320 administrative *arrondissements*, 555 electoral districts and 36,763 municipalities [each with its own mayor and municipal council])	Distribution of competencies between different tiers of local government: Regions: regional policy, culture, environment, rural development and urban policy	Not veto points
			Départments: social assistance, education, provision of subsidies and technical assistance to small rural communes	
	Communes (*arrondissements*)		Communes: economic assistance, town planning	

its assent to any proposed law and any new parliamentary standing order. Once petitioned, the Constitutional Council has the power to invalidate in part or in full any law, if the latter is considered to be unconstitutional (Knapp and Wright 2001a: 142). According to Tsebelis (2002: 226) when a rejection by a constitutional court is sufficient to abrogate legislation approved by the parliament, the judiciary can be considered a veto player. Since the Constitutional Council may invalidate a law on constitutional grounds, it acts as an additional chamber of parliament able to cancel whole pieces or parts of legislation.

The veto points and veto players approaches assert that the more institutional and partisan veto players there are, the more difficult it should be to pass legislation. Political systems with many veto players are more susceptible to be less successful in passing reforms than systems with few veto players (Tsebelis 1995; Immergut 1992). The French political system with a strong president, strong governments backed by stable majorities in parliament and a bicameral legislature is considered by Tsebelis (1995: 306) as a pure parliamentary system with one institutional veto player (the president) and two partisan veto players, usually the two parties in the governing coalition. The French case shows the limits of this approach, since a low number of veto players do not automatically imply that unpopular reforms can easily be passed. This is why one needs to take an alternative approach, in this case the timing of the electoral cycle and the role played by unions to explain the mixed record of French governments on pension reform.

Electoral system

In France, the presidential and legislative elections are decided by a mixed majority–plurality formula in single-member districts. On the first ballot an absolute majority is needed for election, but if no candidate wins a majority, a plurality suffices on the second ballot. In presidential elections, only the two top candidates may stand on the second round. In legislative elections, all parties receiving more than 12.5 percent of the registered electorate in the first ballot may participate in the second scrutiny. Given that the run-off takes place basically between the two principal parties, in fact, no big difference exists between the majority–plurality formula and the majority-run-off (Lijphart 1999: 146).

In legislative elections, the majority–plurality single-member district method has the effect that the party obtaining a nationwide majority is overrepresented in terms of parliamentary seats, while the others remain underrepresented (Lijphart 1999: 143). Since all parties need 12.5 percent of registered votes cast in the first round to be eligible to stand in the second round, some smaller parties may be eliminated in the first round (Mény 2002: 100). This was the intent of the drafters of the Constitution of the Fifth Republic, who aimed to strengthen governments and avoid parliamentary stalemate by stabilizing the party system.

Democracies seldom change from majority and plurality methods to proportional representation and vice versa (Lijphart 1999; Nohlen 2000). France, however, constitutes an exception to the rule: in 1979, proportional representation was introduced for the first direct elections to the European Parliament and in the 1986 legislative elections. The decision to elect deputies to the European Parliament with a different system from the existing electoral rules for presidential and legislative elections was based on the decision at the EC level that members of parliament should all be elected according to the proportional representation. The 1986 experiment with the proportional representation was replaced one year later with a single-member, two-round majority electoral system. For regional elections, in which the *départments* form the constituencies, however, proportional representation is still in place (Mény 2002: 101).

Although a majority electoral system produces clear parliamentary majorities, it also leads to a winner-take-all situation for the winning political party and automatically to a strong executive and to a high electoral and party competition. In democratic systems, parties compete for the people's vote (Downs 1957: 19; Schumpeter 1942: 269). Voters are able to change their electoral choice and thus punish or reward politicians, who usually wish to be re-elected. This is why the timing of the electoral cycle is a crucial variable to explain the failure or occurrence of policy change, and it is to be hoped that governments will have greater success in pushing through legislation implementing unpopular reforms in the first two-and-a-half years of their mandates, since voters will give the new government the benefit of the doubt and difficult decisions can be blamed as the legacy of the outgoing government.

The window of opportunity just after the elections offers new elected governments an ideal opportunity to introduce unpopular measures. Governments are aware that such policy windows come, but that they also very quickly pass and that they do not stay open long (Kingdon 1984). Missing an opened window means automatically losing an opportunity to solve a problem, in this case to reform the welfare state. On the one hand, the government can simply claim that is has just received the mandate to perform these changes. On the other hand, opposition parties are often weak and disorganized after an electoral defeat, as they may for example question their party leadership. Thus a weak and divided opposition can make the task of the government in initiating new programs or in bringing reforms to fruition easier.

Legislative process

The legislative process typically begins when a cabinet minister or a member of one of the Houses of Parliament submits a bill draft to the parliament. Members of parliament, however, have restricted competencies in financial matters: their legislative proposals and amendments are unacceptable if adoption will lead to an increase or decrease in public resources. In addition, government bills (*projets de loi*) have priority over Private Member's bills (*propositions de loi*). Both types of laws must be registered by the National Assembly or at the Senate, only financial matters

Party family affiliation	Abbreviation	Party name	Ideological orientation	Founding and merger details	Year established
Gaullist and Center-Right Parties	UMP	Union for a Popular Majority (*Union pour un mouvement populaire*)	Gaullist party	Succeeded the *Union des democrats pour la République* (1946) and de Gaulle's own Rassemblement du Peuple Français (RPF) (1951); since November 2002 UMP succeeded Rally for the Republic (*Rassemblement pour la République*) founded by Jacques Chirac	1976
	UDF	Union for French Democracy (*Union pour la Démocratie Française*)	Liberal Center-Right	Encompasses the following parties: *Force Démocrate*, the *Parti Populaire pour la démocratie Française*, the *Parti Radical* and the *Pôle républicain*, *Parti Républicain* (until 1998) and also direct supporters of the *UDF*; founded on the initiative of Valéry Giscard d'Estaing[a]	1978
Left parties Social democratic parties	PSF	Socialist Party (*Parti Socialiste Français*)	Social-democratic	Successor to the SFIO (French Section of the Workers International)	1905 (SFIO) 1969 (PSF)
	PCF	French Communist (*Parti Communiste Français*)	Leftist Party	Resulted from a split in the PSF; merged with the SFIC (French section of the Communist International)	1920 (SFIO) 1969 (PCF)
Greens	Les Verts	The Greens (*Les Verts*)	Militant, leftist movement	Merged after several failed attempts to unify the *Mouvement écologique* (1974) *Mouvement d'écologie politique* (1979) and *Les Verts* (1982)	1984
Liberal	DL	Liberal Democracy (*Démocratie Libérale*)	Conservative liberal party	Emerged from the Independent Republicans (1962) which became the Republican Party (1977); founded by Alain Madelin; left the UDF in 1998	1997
Right wing	FN	National Front (*Front National*)	Populist right wing party		1972
	MNR	National Republican Movement (*Mouvement national républicain*)	Populist right wing party	Split from the FN; founded by Mégret	1999

Fig. 4.1 Party system in France

[a] Until November 1998, the UDF was a confederation of parties, when its national party council decided to make it a unified party.

must be registered by the National Assembly. After its registration the text is sent for examination by a parliamentary committee, which prepares a report, in which the text of the bill is amended, rejected or adopted. In a further step, the text comes before the National Assembly. The discussion of a bill takes place in an open session and focuses on the government's proposal and not around that of the parliamentary committee. Furthermore, the government can oppose considering amendments not previously discussed at the committee level. Laws have to be approved by an absolute majority in the National Assembly and in the Senate. In case of disagreement, a shuttle system between the two houses of parliament starts: the legislation is passed back and forth between the two houses. After two readings, if the legislative text has not been adopted, the government calls a conference committee (the *commission mixte paritaire*), composed of seven deputies and senators until agreement can be reached. The government can, however, after a single reading in each house of parliament adopt the legislation and thus curtail the parliamentary discussion if it determines the law in question to be a matter of urgency. Although the National Assembly has the last word on legislation, about 90 percent of laws have been approved by both chambers (Bonnard 2003b: 58; Tsebelis and Money 1995: 104).

Passing legislation is also possible through ordinances and decrees. Whereas ordinances are primary legislation delegated to the government by parliament, decrees simply implement primary legislation. The French Constitution includes the attribution of exclusive jurisdiction to the government allowing it to rule by decrees. This means in practice that the government may ask parliament for special legislative authority in a specific policy area, for an explicitly limited period of time, to take measures normally within the legislative sphere, by ordinance or decree. Ordinances are enacted in meetings of the Council of Ministers and come into force upon publication. They become null and void, however, if the bill for their ratification is not submitted to parliament before the date set by the enabling act. To date 19 such requests have been made, authorized, and used. In other words, when exclusive jurisdiction is given to the government, all power is removed from the parliament, since the ratification process is reduced to the tabling of a bill that is never discussed.

After the final adoption of a bill, the President promulgates it within fifteen days. The President may, however, ask parliament to reconsider the bill or parts of it before the time limit expires. The President can only veto a government decree or an ordinance by refusing to sign it (Art. 13 of the French Constitution). Tsebelis' (2002: 81) assertion that the President has no veto power over legislation is only partially correct. The President has a veto power over ordinances and decrees (considered as legislative acts). In contrast, he has no veto power over laws, since he can only delay the legislation by asking Parliament to reconsider it. Before the promulgation of a bill, only the Constitutional Court has the jurisdictional power to veto it, if the Court considers a bill to be unconstitutional.

Parties and elections

The majority–plurality electoral system used in France led to a bipolarization of the party system, since it promotes coalition building among the Right and the Left parties. On the Left, the Social Democratic Party (the *Parti Socialiste Français*, PCF), has become clearly hegemonic. There is also the Communist Party (the *Parti Communiste Français*, PCF), and the Green Party (*Les Verts*). The former has steadily lost votes from 18.9 percent in 1958 to 4.8 percent of the votes in the 2002 parliamentary elections. The Green Party could only reach 3.4 percent in the 2002 elections. There are also extreme left parties, for example, *Lutte Ouvrière* (LO) or *Ligue Communiste Révolutionnaire* (LCR), but their political weight is rather slight.[3] The picture on the Right, however, is more complicated, with the Gaullist party *Rassemblement pour la République* (RPR), since November 2002 the *Union pour un mouvement populaire* (UMP), and the liberal center-right *Union pour la Démocratie Française* (UDF), which is an umbrella for several parties. These parties are in permanent competition and are both threatened by the rise of the *Front National* (FN). Furthermore, new parties of the Right have been established, including the *Démocratie Liberale* (DL), founded in 1997 by Alain Madelin. At the extreme Right, the *Front National* has recently split into two parties: the *Front National* directed by Le Pen and the *Mouvement National Républicain* (MNR) by Mégret in 1999 (Ysmal 2003: 108).[4]

Duverger even speaks of a *bipolar quadrille* characterized by two political families with two parties in each, the RPR and UDF on the Right and the PSF and the PCF on the Left. The composition of these two opposing electoral blocs (the Communists and the Socialists on the Left, the Gaullists and the moderate conservatives on the Right) facilitate both the formation, and also the maintenance, of governing majority coalitions (Thiébault 2000: 498). Since the beginning of the Fifth Republic two models of stable majority coalitions can be distinguished: a coalition system with a dominant party, and a system of bipolarization.

The system of coalitions with a dominant party was from 1962 to 1974 dominated by the Gaullist party (*Union pour la Nouvelle République*, UNR), in which the President Charles de Gaulle was backed by a parliamentary majority. In a second period (1981–86, 1988–93, 1997–2002), the Socialist Party was the dominant party of the Left. The presidential victory of François Mitterrand in May 1981 broke the domination of the Right, which had controlled the presidency, the government and the National Assembly since 1962. From 1981 to 1984 the PS had an electoral alliance with the Communist Party and in the legislature period 1988–93 it formed a minority government. Finally, from 1997 to 2002, the Socialists formed a coalition government with the so-called "plural left", which embraced the Communist Party and the Greens (Thiébault 2000, 500–501; Guyonnet 2003, 148).

The system of bipolarization in the French Parliamentary party system has three distinct periods: 1974–81, 1986–88, and 1993–95. From 1974 to 1981 it was characterized by a fierce rivalry between the Prime Minister, Jacques Chirac, and the President Valéry Giscard d'Estaing. Under Chirac's leadership the UDR became the RPR, and at the same time Giscard d'Estaing created the UDF, a smaller group made up of

Table 4.2 Governmental majorities in France

Date of change in political configuration	Election date: president	Start of presidency	President (party)	Presidential majority	Election date: Assemblée	Start of gov.	Head of gov. (party)	Governing parties	Gov. majority (% seats) Assemblée	Gov. electoral base (% votes) Assemblée	Gov. majority (% seats) Sénate	Institutional veto points	Number of veto players (partisan + institutional)
04.03.1978	05.19.1974	05.27.1974	Giscard d'Estaing (PR)	50.8%	03.12.1978	04.03.1978	Barre II (Ind)	RPR (154), UDF (123)	56.4%	38.2%	54.6%	Conseil Constitutionnel	2 + 1
05.21.1981	05.10.1981	05.21.1981	Mitterrand I (PS)	51.8%		05.21.1981	Mauroy I (PS)	PS (113)	23.0%	22.8%	35.5%	Conseil Constitutionnel	1 + 1
06.22.1981			Mitterrand I (PS)		06.14.1981	06.22.1981	Mauroy II (PS)	PS (285), PCF (44)	67.0%	52.5%	43.1%	Conseil Constitutionnel	2 + 1
03.22.1983			Mitterrand I (PS)			03.22.1983	Mauroy III (PS)	PS (285), PCF (44)	67.0%	52.5%	43.1%	Conseil Constitutionnel	2 + 1
07.17.1984			Mitterrand I (PS)			07.17.1984	Fabius (PS)	PS (285)	49.4%	36.3%	34.3%	Conseil Constitutionnel	1 + 1
03.20.1986			Mitterrand I (PS)		03.16.1986	03.20.1986	Chirac II (RPR)	RPR (155), UDF (131)	49.6%	40.9%	56.6%	Président, Conseil Constitutionnel	2 + 2
05.08.1988	05.08.1988		Mitterrand II (PS)	54.0%			Chirac II (RPR)	RPR (155), UDF (131)	49.6%	40.9%	63.0%	Président, Conseil Constitutionnel	2 + 2
05.10.1988			Mitterrand II (PS)			05.10.1988	Rocard I (PS)	PS (212)	36.7%	31.5%	31.0%	Conseil Constitutionnel	1 + 1
06.23.1988			Mitterrand II (PS)		06.05.1988	06.23.1988	Rocard II (PS)	PS (275)	47.7%	34.9%	31.0%	Conseil Constitutionnel	1 + 1

05.16.1991		05.16.1991	Mitterrand II (PS)	Cresson (PS)	PS (275)	47.7%	34.9%	20.6%	Conseil Constitutionnel	1 + 1
04.02.1992		04.02.1992	Mitterrand II (PS)	Bérégovoy (PS)	PS (275)	47.7%	34.9%	20.6%	Conseil Constitutionnel	1 + 1
03.29.1993	03.21.1993	03.29.1993	Mitterrand II (PS)	Balladur (RPR)	RPR (257), UDF (215)	81.8%	39.6%	63.2%	Président, Conseil Constitutionnel	2 + 2
05.17.1995	05.07.1995	05.17.1995	Chirac I (RPR)	Juppé I (RPR)	RPR (257), UDF (215)	81.8%	39.6%	63.2%	Conseil Constitutionnel	2 + 1
11.07.1995		11.07.1995	Chirac I (RPR)	Juppé II (RPR)	RPR (257), UDF (215)	81.8%	39.6%	62.0%	Conseil Constitutionnel	2 + 1
06.02.1997	05.25.1997	06.02.1997	Chirac I (RPR)	Jospin (PS)	PS (250), PCF (36), RCV (33)	55.3%	42.0%	28.0%	Président, Conseil Constitutionnel	3 + 2
05.05.2002	05.05.2002		Chirac II (RPR)	Jospin (PS)	PS (250), PCF (36), RCV (33)	55.3%	42.0%	33.0%	Président, Conseil Constitutionnel	3 + 2
07.03.2002		06.09.2002 06.25.2002	Chirac II (RPR)	Raffarin (DL)	UMP (365), UDF (29), DL (2)	68.6%	38.6%	58.9%	Conseil Constitutionnel	3 + 1

52.6%
82.2%

Sources: http://www.assemblee-nationale.fr/elections/historique-2.asp; http://www.assemblee-nationale.fr/connaissance/collection/conaissance-2-gouvernement.pdf (Guyonnet 2003).

centrist and moderate parties. From 1896 to 1988 for the first time in the history of the Fifth Republic there was a cohabitation between the socialist François Mitterrand and a narrow parliamentary majority of the RPR–UDF coalition led by Jacques Chirac (Bonnard 2003a: 29; Knapp and Wright 2001a: 203–5). The electoral victory of the center-right coalition RPR-UDF (486 of 577 seats) in the 1993 elections obliged the President to initiate a new period of cohabitation until 1995. With Jacques Chirac's presidential victory in 1995 the power came once more entirely into the hands of the right (Thiébault 2000: 504; Guyonnet 2003: 144).

Interest groups

The French state is considered to be strong enough to overrule interest groups in the pursuit of national interest. This power asymmetry between a strong centralized state and weak, highly fragmented interest groups constitutes the French basic pattern of policy-making and has been analyzed as the inheritance of the Jacobin and the Bonapartist tradition of a strong and plebiscitary state serving the general will by being independent of particular social interests.

This reading of French patterns of state–society relations underpinned Michel Crozier's (1970) thesis on France's *société bloquée*, Crozier explained the distinctive dynamics of crisis and protest in France as the result of hierarchical centralized forms of organization and leadership, in which demonstrations and protests constitute not only a challenge, but simultaneously reinforce the existing state–society patterns. Bozec and Mays (2001: 18) and Quittkat (2000: 8) underline that due to the absence of institutionalized or formally guaranteed access for interest groups to the policy-making process, trade unions have developed rather aggressive strategies, particularly demonstrations and strikes, as a way of protesting against proposed reforms in the different public policy sectors. Or, as Schmidt (1999: 141–2) puts it: "the state formulates policy largely without significant input from societal interests, but then accommodates them in the implementation, or risks confrontation."

As stressed by Merrien (1991), unions and other interest groups are only accepted into the decision-making process to the extent that they suit the logic of the state, under which they represent a sector of the national interest. Control, however, remains in the hands of the state, which decides who is representative of French society. Although there are several pensioners' associations, like the Pensioners' National Federation (*Fédération nationale des Associations de retraités*) with 500,000 members, the French Pensioners' Union (*Union Française de retraités*) with 50,000 members and the Office linking several pensioners organisations (*Bureau de liaison des organisations de retraités*) assembling eight different federations with two million members, the state only recognises unions as social partners and as the representatives of pensioners (Viriot Durandal 2003: 27). This explains why only the role played by trade unions in the legislative process will be taken into consideration.

The problem, however, is that unions have a low unionization rate and are fragmented around class and religion cleavages. From a total labor force of some

26.5 million, only approximately two million workers (8 percent of the working population in 1998) are union members. In contrast, public employees tend to dominate the labor movement as unionization rates are much higher, about 20 percent on average, than on the private sector. The high fragmentation around ideological, occupational and public and private sector cleavages leads to political rivalry between the different existent unions.

There are seven major national federations. The socialist-leaning *Confédération française démocratique du travail* (CFDT) has steadily increased its members from 655,000 in 1973 to 808,000 members in 2000. At the beginning of the 1980s it was allied with Mitterrand, but distanced itself from the PS in the end of the decade. It considers itself as a non-religious union and puts strong emphasis on seeking agreement with the employers and the government. In contrast, the *Confédération générale du travail* (CGT) with 1,870,000 members in 1973 has continuously lost members and had in 2000 merely 650,000 affiliations, falling behind the CFDT. The CGT is historically a Communist dominated labor union, though personal ties and ideology has been weakened through the disappearance of the real socialism. Although it has distanced itself from the PCF, many members of the CGT are also members of the Communist Party. The *Confédération générale du travail – Force ouvrière* (CGT-FO, thereafter simply called FO) is its runaway counterpart with about 300,000 members. It can be considered as an independent labor union, since it is not related to any party in particular. The FO sees itself as an anticommunist contesting union with the only aim of protecting the interests of workers. Most of FO and CGT members work in the public sector. The *Union nationale des syndicats autonomes* (UNSA) founded in 1994 assembles about 360,000 members and represents the civil servants; it unites the *Fédération de l'éducation nationale* (FEN) and the *Fédération générale autonome des fonctionnaires* (FGAF). School teachers are assembled on the *Fédération Syndicale Unitaire* (FSU). The *Confédération française des travailleurs chrétiens* (CFTC) with about 80,000 members is a Christian democratic union which advocates and actively promotes family and church values. Finally, white-collar workers (executives) are assembled at the *Confédération française de l'encadrement – Confédération générale des cadres* (CFE–CGC) (Knapp and Wright 2001b: 304–5; Mouriaux 2003: 116; Marier 2002: 74).

There are two main employer's organizations in the industrial sector: the French federation of industry *Mouvement des entreprises de France* (MEDEF), which until 1998 was called the *Conseil national du patronat français* (CNPF) and has about 750,000 companies as members (most of the big firms are represented in this main employers' organization); and the *Confédération générale du patronat des petites et moyennes Entreprises* (CGPME), which assembles small- and medium-sized enterprises in industry, commerce and service industries (Knapp and Wright 2001b: 305; Mouriaux 2003: 116). Employers' organizations are usually heard by right-wing governments. Concerning pension issues, they have been vocal on the reform of the public pension system as well as on settlement of private capital-funded pensions.

These major national federations compete for members, and for social elections, and the different French governments accord them the status of "social partners." In the same line of argumentation of scholars working on pension issues (Bonoli 2000; Marier 2002; Myles and Pierson 2001; Natali and Rhodes 2004; Pierson 1994; Schludi 2003), it is asserted that even if unions do not dispose of formal veto power to block government action, they are a central player in the reform process, because they are able to mobilize public support. This chapter, however, goes one step further and tries to demonstrate *how* they matter and under what conditions their demands are taken into account.

Union movements are still one of the largest mass organizations in modern industrial societies and so the mobilization of their membership to protest a government policy is a way of sending a major political signal (Boeri, Brugiavini, and Calmfors 2001: 184). It is expected that unions' ability to block pension reforms is based on two internal aspects of union structure: union fragmentation and the public sector unionization. Union structure is craft-based rather then industrial, so the railroad workers, subway workers, and others each has their own union. The special pension schemes largely follow this structure—each public sector occupation has its own special scheme, for instance, French railways *Société Nationale des Chemins de Fer* (SNPF) or Paris transport *Transports en Île de France* (RATP). This means that when governments try to reform the special schemes, the potential costs are concentrated and very visible. And since the unions are small, collective action is not difficult to organize. In his seminal book, *The Logic of Collective Action*, Olson (1965) argues that size is one of the determining factors in explaining whether organized interest groups are able to persuade governments to pursue their preferred course of action. Thereby, he argues that small special interests can be organized more easily and more effectively than larger general interest groups. One should expect that due to this high concentration of union membership in the public sector, unions representing this occupational cleavage are able to protect the earned rights of their members. Where pension issues are concerned, unions have a strong interest in keeping the present administration of the retirement system, in which together with employers and the state administration they are actively involved, since any change means losing power.

III Pension system

Historical overview

France set up a retirement system on a contributory basis as early as 1910, the "workers and peasants pension scheme" (*retraites ouvrières et paysannes*) covering manual workers. After the Second World War, a pay-as-you-go (PAYG) system, in French it is called *système de retraite par répartition*, was introduced. A new Social Security Plan introduced in 1945 aimed to guarantee all citizens a subsistence income whenever they were unable to obtain this through employment. At age 60, citizens with thirty years of contributions had the right to a pension of 20 percent of the reference salary. Those working until the age of 65 would obtain a pension of 40 percent of the reference salary. In 1956, an "old-age minimum" comprising several tiers of minimum income benefits and a national Fund for Old Age Solidarity (*Fonds de solidarité vieillesse*) were established; the latter funded the minimum pension for older retirees (Lautrette 1999: 27–31).

The Social Security Plan created a basic pension regime (the *régime general*) covering initially only private-sector employees. The government, however, did not manage to create a unified scheme covering the entire population. The already existing, more generous, separate schemes for the self employed, for agricultural workers and for civil servants (*régimes spéciaux*) were maintained. Public pension schemes for civil servants were established already in 1790. As Marier (2002: 68) underlines, the integration of these special schemes into the basic one was never really pursued, because pension schemes within the public service had been divided along socio-occupational lines, they have a longer history than the ones present in the private sectors, and contribution periods are defined differently in both sectors.

A compulsory supplementary scheme for executives (*Association générale des institutions de retraite des cadres*, AGIRC) and other schemes for self-employed were set up in 1947.[5] Finally, numerous compulsory supplementary schemes for blue-collar workers and employees of the private sector set up were federated in 1961 into a single institution (*Association générale des institutions de retraite des cadres*, AGIRC). Only in 1972 the supplementary tier of the first pillar was generalized and made compulsory for all employees (Bonoli 2000: 126; Observatoire des Retraites 2003a: 1–2).

In general, the 1970s were characterized by the progressive expansion of the generosity of the pension system. Three laws in particular improved the calculation of benefits in the basic pension scheme. First, the *Boulin* law of December 1971 stipulated that the calculation of the reference wage should be based on the best 10 years of wages, extended the contribution period for a full pension from 37.5 and raised the full pension from 40 percent to 50 percent of the reference wage. Second, in 1973 the minimum contribution period of 15 years was abolished for the basic pension. Today only a trimester contribution is needed to qualify for pension benefits, and inactive periods are also taken into account in the calculation of benefits. Finally, the December 24, 1974 reform made social security compulsory for all French citizens, and put in place a generalized compensation system among the pension schemes, with the aim of evening-out demographic disparities (Lautrette 1999: 33–4).

Description of the current pension system

Coverage

The French pension system is complex and highly fragmented, because of the coexistence of diverse schemes and the division across professional categories. Compulsory PAYG schemes predominate, however, and make up about 98 percent of total pension expenditure. The basic and the supplementary schemes in the first pillar are mandatory. Whereas the basic scheme is a PAYG defined-benefit system, supplementary pension schemes are PAYG-systems with defined-contributions (Bozec and Mays 2001: 12). The pension system is organized on three different levels:

1. *The general or basic scheme* offers benefits corresponding to wages below a social security ceiling; it covers about two-thirds of the working population and the greater part of salaried employees in the private sector;
2. *Supplementary schemes* organized on a socio-professional basis supplement the basic schemes and include salaried employees of the public sector; there is a large number of specific schemes federated in the AGIRC (67 funds) and in the ARRCO (34 funds);
3. *Optional supplementary occupational schemes* are offered within a professional framework and financed almost exclusively through funding; they are voluntary and can take the form of individual membership schemes in the public sector (*Caisse Nationale de Prévoyance de la Fonction Publique*, PREFON), or group insurance contracts ("Madelin arrangements") (Observatoire des Retraites 2003a: 6).

There is a socio-occupational division into the following four large categories:
1. *Employees in the private sector*: include executives of industry, commerce and services; workers and employees of industry, commerce and services; and civil aviation flight personnel. This socio-professional category has a relatively homogenous first and second tier scheme. Whereas the first tier consists of the basic scheme (*Caisse Nationale d'Assurance Vieillesse des Travailleurs Salariés*, CNAVTS), the second tier has two distinct complementary schemes: ARRCO for all workers and the AGIRC for executives only. This group makes up 65 percent of the labor force.
2. *Employees of the public and para-public sectors*: encompasses civil servants and soldiers, municipal workers, local authorities and hospital staff; miners, employees of power utilities (*Électricité de France – Gaz de France*, EDF–GDF), of the French railways, of Paris Transport, sailors, notary clerks, employees of Banque de France, and other schemes. Members of this group belong to the special schemes that are usually more generous than the system for employees of the private sector; they constitute about 20 percent of the active labor force.
3. *Farm sector employees*: farm workers and employees, who altogether make up 3 percent of the labor force.
4. *Non-salaried and self-employed*: cover farmers, industrialists and shopkeepers, craftsmen, liberal professionals, lawyers, and the clergy. These workers represent about 12 percent of the labor force, and have specific schemes that are less generous than the general scheme and ARRCO-AGIRC (Blanchet and Pelé 1997: 112–13; Bonoli 2000: 127; Observatoire des Retraites 2003a: 2).

The inability of political actors to negotiate a standard pension system for all wage earners after 1945 led to the entrenchment of the fragmented pension system. The three different pillars of the French pension system vary in terms of contribution rates, retirement ages and benefit formulae. In 2003, there were about 194 pension funds in the basic scheme and about 135 in the supplementary-earnings related (Observatoire des Retraites 2003a: 4). Employees are usually entitled to pensions from two or three pension schemes, depending on the sector of employment.

The special schemes for employees of the public sector are more generous than those in the private sector. First, the contribution period for full civil servants pension is lower, 37.5 and not 40 years of contribution as in the private sector. Second, the calculation of pension benefits is made with basis on the last six months salary and not on the best 25 years, as in the private sector. One of the central aims of the pension reforms in the last 25 years has been to remove these discrepancies between both occupational sectors.

Administration

The basic and the supplementary compulsory public pensions schemes are administered by different social insurance funds organized at the national, regional and local levels. The national social security office is divided into different offices corresponding to several types of social benefits, for example, pensions, health care, family, sickness. A central agency (*Agence centrale des organismes de securité sociale*, ACOSS) was created to recover social security contributions and has the legal status of public corporation. The basic pension scheme is managed by an administrative council including both employers and trade unions representatives. Regional and local insurance companies have their own directors appointed by the administrative council after consultation with the Ministry of Social Affairs. The directors of the national insurance companies are appointed by the government. The administration of the different supplementary schemes follows the general lines of the basic scheme, with the only difference that in the supplementary schemes individual employers and employees (i.e. not their representatives) sign the agreements and manage the finances without the involvement of the state (Palier 1999: 609; Marier 2002: 69; ARRCO 2001: 5).

The public pensions system is divided into different categories. At the national level, the health insurance funds for salaried employees (aggregated in the Caisse Nationale *d'Assurance Maladie des Travailleurs Salariés*, CNAMTS) are responsible for the national co-ordination of insurance covering health care, maternity, disability, death and widow's pensions, and occupational injury and diseases. At the regional level, the 16 health insurance funds (*Caisses Régionales d'Assurance Maladie*, CRAM) in charge of occupational safety also disburse pension benefits for employees. At the national level the National Office for the Old Age Security of Private Sector Wage Earners, the *Caisse Nationale d'Assurance Vieillesse des Travailleurs Salariés* (CNAVTS) manages and pays pension benefits to salaried workers, and is responsible for social assistance for aged persons. The national family allocation fund *Caisse Nationale d'Allocations Familiales* (CNAF) manages all family-related benefits for salaried and non-salaried employees of all occupational groups, with the exception of farmers. Finally, at the local level, 125 national pension funds (*Caisses*

First pillar	Second pillar	Third pillar
Third tier: none	Voluntary supplementary pension	Voluntary additional private pension: *plan partenarial d'épargne salariale volontaire pour la retraite* (PPESVR)
Second tier: earnings-related part of pensions/supplementary schemes: CRNPAC, IRCANTEC, CNAVPL, CNBF — Employees (ARRCO, AGRIC) / Self-employed (CANCAVA) / Farmers / Civil Servants (CNRACL, SNCF, RATP)	Government subsidized optional occupational schemes, mainly company schemes: Private sector: institutions for supplementary retirement; Madelin contracts for independent workers / Public sector: Mutual schemes for civil servants: PREFON and CGO, CREF / Farmers: 'Ex-coreva' type contracts; CREF	Government subsidized individual pension savings: housing savings and life insurance contracts (*plan d'épargne individuel pour la retraite* (PEIR))
First tier: basic pension — Employees of the private sector / Self-employed (farmers, shopkeepers, etc.) / Farm sector employees / Civil Servants	Mandatory occupational pension: none	Mandatory private pension: none
Social assistance: old age minimum (*minimum vieillesse*)		

Fig. 4.2 Pension system in France

Nationale d'Assurance Vieillesse, CNAF) manage and pay about 25 different types of pension benefits (Palier 1999: 609).

The pension system is monitored by the Ministry of Labour and Social Affairs, by parliament, by the Supervisory Council (*Conseil de Surveillance*) and by the Auditing Board of Social Security (*Commission des Comptes de la Sécurité Sociale*). Since 1996, Parliament votes annually on the law governing social security financing. This law sets the general conditions for social security's financial equilibrium by estimating total revenues and expenditures. The government controls the basic pension scheme by establishing the pension regulations and by concluding agreements valid for several years with the national pension fund concerning the objectives and management of the pension scheme (Palier 1999: 610).

In sum, the administration of the basic pension scheme is controlled by the state. The government has significant powers in the nomination and supervision of social security schemes, so that the managerial role of unions is limited. In contrast, the state has virtually no control over the management of the supplementary mandatory pension schemes. Different occupationally-based organizations, constituted by representatives of employers and employees, manage the benefit payments.

Financing

The earnings-related part of the pensions in France is financed by contributions on earned income. Contributions paid by employees and employers cover the major part of the cost of pension benefits. The remainder is financed by ear-marked taxes and duties, state subsidies, investment income and other contributions financed by the Social Security. Gross contribution rates for basic and supplementary schemes vary according to the different socio-occupational sectors. The employee contribution rate in the basic scheme for employees in the private sector can range from 6.55 percent up to 16.35 percent of occupational income within the limit of the social security ceiling (SSC). Employer contribution rates go from 8.20 percent up to 16.35 percent of income. In contrast, contribution rates in the main special schemes for the different groups of military and civil servants do not exceed 7.85 percent. Civil servants' contributions are paid directly from the state budget. In the supplementary mandatory schemes, contribution rates vary between 6 and 7.5 percent (ARRCO) and 16 to 20 percent (AGIRC), depending on the wage level and employee status (ARRCO 2001: 7; Observatoire des Retraites 2003b: 8).

Benefits

The complexity of the French system also extends to the calculation of the value of pensions for the basic and the supplementary schemes. The basic scheme provides contributory benefits based on the share of wages below the social security ceiling. The value of the pension takes into account the average annual salary received by the insured person within a certain limit. In 2002, the minimum pension benefit was €6,307.62 and the maximum €14,112 per year. The old age minimum is €131 for a person and €236 for a couple per week (Observatoire des Retraites 2004: 34).

Until 1993, the reference salary for a full pension was the average of the ten best years. The 1993 reform gradually increases the number of "best" years included in the reference salary to 25, to be completed by 2008 and the qualifying period for the full pension rate has been increased from 37.5 to 40 years (since 2003). The method used to calculate the pension amount is based on the following five elements: (i) the liquidation rate (T) equal to 50 percent; (ii) the abatement rate (t) equal to 1.25 percent per quarter of missing insurance; (iii) the number of missing quarters (n) from a maximum of 160; (iv) the insurance period under the general scheme (D) within a limit that has a ceiling of 150 quarters; (v) the annual average reference salary (SAM) calculated on the 10 best years indexed to prices. The pension formula is therefore:

$$P = (T - tn) \times (D/150) \times SAM$$

The maximum pension rate is 50 percent, depending on age and length of coverage. The claimant is entitled to the maximum rate if s/he is 60 or older and if s/he has a total of 150 quarters of contributions. A full pension at 60 is payable to war veterans or disabled people. Benefits are reduced if quarters are missing, but from the age of 65 one is entitled to the full pension, regardless of the contribution conditions. Additional qualifying periods are also granted, for instance, there is a bonus for each child (Observatoire des Retraites 2003a: 4–5).

Benefits from the supplementary scheme are almost fully based on contributions. Pensions are computed according to a system of "points." The method of calculating pension benefits is based on annual contributions received from employees and employers divided by the costs of acquiring a point (the "reference wage"). These points are then added to produce an annual number of points. The points acquired by an employee are aggregated and booked to a special account, along with any points obtained during periods in which the individual was unable to earn income (sickness, unemployment, war), or points earned during periods prior to the introduction of compulsory supplementary pensions in his/her profession or industry. When the employee retires, the total number of points is multiplied by the current value per point to determine the annual pension entitlement. Additional points are given to employees with three or more children, for every child a supplement of 5 percent is added to the total rights. The value of points varies: it is decided every year by the board of directors, depending on available resources and taking into account social considerations. The aim is that changes in the purchasing power of pensions are linked as closely as possible to changes in the level of wages (Observatoire des Retraites 2003b: 7; ARRCO 2001: 7).

The second pillar, constituted of voluntary occupational schemes, is composed of a few company schemes and a lot of collective insurance contracts, generally covering managers in small enterprises. The value of pensions acquired through voluntary supplementary schemes varies according to occupational category. For employees in the private sector, companies may add an optional funded pension to the basic and supplementary schemes in the form of company schemes, life insurance contracts and various group insurance contracts. For self-employed there are also collective insurance contracts ("Madelin Law" contracts).[6] Finally, employees of the public sector may contribute voluntarily to PREFON, a funded scheme managed by the PREFON association with a pool of insurers led by the *Caisse Nationale de Prévoyance* (CNP), a group insurance contract. For hospital personnel, there is a special optional scheme, the *Comité de Gestion des Oeuvres Sociales* (CGOS) (Observatoire des Retraites 2003b, 8, 24).

Since 2003, a third pillar pension funding was set up. There will be two new voluntary pensions saving schemes: the individual personal pensions saving plan (*plan d'épargne individuel pour la retraite*, PEIR) and the voluntary partnership employee pension savings scheme (*plan partenarial d'épargne salariale volontaire pour la retraite*, PPESVR). Both are insurance contracts enabling employees to accumulate entitlement to a life-long annuity, and must be based on an agreement with an insurance company through a not-for-profit personal saving fund-holding association.

In sum, in the basic pension scheme employees receive a pension proportional both to the number of contribution years and to their reference wage. The compulsory supplementary schemes are fully based on contributions and calculated using a system of points, providing pensions proportional to the cumulative contribution periods. Because the compulsory basic and supplementary pension schemes of the first pillar provide a high level of replacement, income voluntary schemes play a very minor role.

IV POLITICS OF PENSION REFORM SINCE 1980

Overview

The debate on the future of the French pensions system started in the early 1980s and has been marked by numerous reports and few measures until 1993. Altogether since 1980 there were three major reforms: the 1982 Mauroy reform, the 1993 Balladur reform, and the 2003 Raffarin reform. There were also two notable reform attempts that ended in failure: the 1995 Juppé Plan and the 1997 Thomas Law.

The 1982 Mauroy pension reform led to a decrease in the retirement age from 65 to 60. This was not really controversial, since it led to a further extension of the pension system benefits. The second reform wave started with the publication of the White Paper on Pensions in April 1991 and led to the 1993 Balladur reform that introduced

Table 4.3 Overview of proposed and enacted pension reforms in France

Year	Name of reform	Reform process (chronology)	Reform measures
1982	Mauroy Reform introduction of retirement age at sixty and settlement of a minimum contribution (*Ordinnance du 26 mars 1982; Ordinnance du 31 mars 1982*)	• 1981 Mitterrand campaign for president election: promise to reduce retirement age to 60 • January 6, 1982 framework law empowering the government to implement employment program and social reforms through decrees by 31 March 1982 • March 26, 1982 government issues decree on retirement age • 30 March 1982 president issues decree on taxes for working pensioners	• Reduction in retirement age from 65 to 60 for private sector employees with at least 37.5 years of contributions • limit on the accumulation of pension benefits and wage/work for a limited time (until 1990)
1993	Balladur Reform (RPR-UDF governing coalition) (*Loi relative aux pensions de retraite et à la sauvegarde de la protection sociale*)	• April 24, 1991 publication of the White Book on Pensions by Prime Minister Rocard • March 29, 1993 electoral victory of Balladur (start of cohabitation) • April 23, 1993 negotiations with unions • May 7, 1993 publication of the proposal • May 1993 CGT and FO call for a general strike • June 23, 1993 passage of the bill in the Senate • July 7, 1993 passage of the bill in the National Assembly	• Increase of reference period from best ten to best 25 years • extension of the qualifying period for full pension from 37.5 to 40 years • indexation of pensions to prices instead of wages • establishment of an "Old Age Solidarity Fund" (*Fonds de Solidarité Veillesse*) to finance non-contributory benefits • increase in contribution rate to the contribution social généralisée from 1.1 to 2.4%
1995	Juppé Plan (RPR-UDF governing coalition) (attempt to reform the special schemes)	• 1995 presidential elections; victory of Chirac; end of cohabitation • November 13, 1995 parliamentary debate on the Reform of Social Protection (Juppé Plan) • November 15, 1995 passage of the bill with large majority in the National Assembly • November 16, 1995 passage of the bill in Senate • November 17, to December 7, 1995 demonstrations and union protests; public transport strike • December 7, 1995 parliamentary debate on the attribution of exclusive jurisdiction to government; PS and PCF settled numerous amendments and tabled a censure motion • December 10, 1995 announcement of concessions to SNCF	

		- December 17, 1995 massive protests Further concessions i.e. abandonment of the proposed provisions in pension policy	- Proposed measures: increase in qualifying period for full civil servants' pensions from 37.5 to 40 years
- abolition of various special schemes e.g. retirement age of 50 for SNCF and RATP employees
- establishment of an autonomous pension office for civil servants
- change of the statutory composition of the managing boards of the social security schemes → reform failed
1997	Thomas Law (RPR–UDF governing coalition)	- May 30, 1996 reform proposal by Thomas and Millon
- November 22, 1996 passage of the Thomas Law in the National Assembly (only seven out of 577 deputies participated in the voting) Unions afraid that savings plans could replace existing supplementary schemes
- December 13, 1996 passage of the bill in Senate but with several amendments
- January 15, 1997 second reading and vote in National Assembly meeting of the conference committee
- February 20, 1997 adoption of the bill in National Assembly
- April 1997 early elections; Socialist victory; new Jospin government
- 1998 abrogation of the Thomas Law	- Introduction of optional retirement saving plans for all employees in the private sector (*plans d'épargne-retraite d'entreprise*)
2003	Raffarin Reform (*Loi n° 2003–775 du 21 août 2003 portant réforme des retraites*)	- 1999 Charpin report
- September 1999 Taddéi report
- 2000 Teulade report (Economic and Social Council)
- May/June 2002 presidential and parliamentary elections
- January 6, 2003 announcement of the Raffarin reform
- February 1, 2003 unions call for demonstration	- Increase in contribution period for a full pension to 42 years by 2020
- harmonization of public sector contribution rate with private sector from 2008 onwards
- introduction of indexation of pensions according to cost of living for the public sector
- introduction of a 3% pension supplement for each year worked beyond the age of 60

(*Continued*)

Table 4.3 (Continued)

Year	Name of reform	Reform process (chronology)	Reform measures
		• April 3, 2003 strikes organized by some trade unions (CGT, FO, UNSA, FEN) • May 2003 presentation of the Raffarin bill • May 13, 2003 nationwide protests and strikes • June 10, 2003 beginning of the parliamentary debate • July 3, 2003 passage of the bill in the National Assembly Senate suggests amendments • July 24, 2003 meeting of the conference committee of the houses • Passage of the bill in both houses of parliament • July 28, 2003 communists refer reform to the Constitutional Council • August 14, 2003 Constitutional Council rejects complaints • August 21, 2003 publication of the act	• replacement of 85% of the net national minimum wage for the lowest paid employees • establishment of a new voluntary scheme for civil servants and self-employed

some changes to the basic pension scheme for private sector employees. The 1995 Juppé Plan intended to abolish the special schemes for employees in the public sector and failed. A second attempt to reform the pension system still under the Juppé government (the 1997 Thomas Law, which established private capital-funded plans) passed in Parliament, but new elections in 1997 and a political change in the National Assembly led to the reversal of this law in 1998 by the Socialist government. Since then, numerous reports have proposed several measures to reform the French pension system. Only in August 2003, the newly-elected conservative Prime Minister Jean-Pierre Raffarin was successful in passing a pension reform that increased the contribution period for a full pension to 42 years in 2020, introduced a third pillar voluntary scheme, and established the indexation of pensions according to the cost of living for all schemes.

Before describing these five pension reforms in more detail, it is important to emphasize that none of these reforms introduced radical changes into the existing public retirement arrangements or involved drastic reductions in benefits or eligibility. Using a classification proposed by Legros (2002: v), reforms in the public pensions system can be included in two categories: *parametric reforms*, which redefine the rules of the pension schemes (e.g. by increasing the age of retirement) and *structural reforms*, which change the administration type and introduce a capitalized component into pension schemes. The 1993 Balladur reform can be considered a parametric reform, since the political actors tried primarily to avoid radical changes in the retirement system. The 2003 Raffarin reform is both a parametric and a structural reform: it not only changes the rules of the basic pension scheme, but also introduces a voluntary additional private pension.

The Mauroy Reform of 1982: retirement at age 60 and minimum contributions

France was not immune to the oil shocks and economic stagnation that affected Western Europe in the 1970s. Despite the unfavorable economic context, the parliamentary and presidential victory of the Socialists in 1981, led to a further expansion of social expenditure. Mitterrand promised a classic Keynesian policy to stimulate employment and economic growth, and he was in a strong position to carry this out.

The reduction of retirement age from 65 to 60 was favored by unions, especially by the CGT, at the time the largest union, and by employers, who were seeking to replace costly older workers. Faced with a high unemployment rate, the cost of maintaining workers on unemployment insurance was higher than putting them on retirement (Marier 2002: 70). Early retirement was part of Mitterrand's economic recovery strategy. This had more to do with the redefinition of employment policies than with improving pensions.

After the election of François Mitterrand, the Socialist and Communist governing majority coalition (PSF 285 deputies and PCF 44 deputies) led by Mauroy, used decree-laws to pass the reform. The ordinance of March 26, 1982 decreased the retirement age from 65 to 60 years for private sector employees in the basic scheme with at a least 37.5 years of contribution, the pension level was 50 percent of the ten best salary years, and "minimum contribution" was introduced in order to ensure that at the age of 60 employees would have the right to obtain a minimal pension from the basic scheme. The new legislation came into force on April 1, 1983. A further ordinance from March 30, 1982 stipulated that from April 1, 1983 until December 31, 1990, employees could only demand the basic scheme pension when they actually stopped working. People were allowed to resume work at a later date, but a solidarity contribution to the unemployment insurance was to be deducted from earned income. Employees were allowed to change, at the age of 55, from full- to part-time employment and as a compensation for the decrease in salary they obtained 80 percent of their previous salary if the employer had signed a solidarity agreement with the state. This solidarity agreement constituted an attempt by the French government to reduce the high unemployment rate and to integrate young people into the labor market (Blanchet and Legros 2002: 113; Buczko 1982: 324).

The central question here is why right-wing parties simply accepted all these changes and a further expansion of pension benefits. According to Article 34 of the French constitution, parliament must adopt all legislation concerning social security. This pension reform, however, was implemented through ordinances, since the Constitution of the Fifth Republic allows governments for a limited period to take measures by ordinances in areas normally within the legislative sphere. A law passed on January 6, 1982 authorized the socialist government to implement its employment program, as well as other social reforms (e.g. introduction of the 35-hour working week), through ordinances until March 31, 1982.

In such a situation, the hands of the parliamentary opposition are tied, because governance through decree-laws gives government the power to make a law without parliamentary discussion. The executive supremacy is strengthened and the available parliamentary initiative and control restricted.

The decrease of the retirement age from 65 to 60 led to a further improvement in pension benefits, but it also increased social security expenditure in the following years.

The Balladur Reform of 1993: the reform of private sector pensions

During the 1980s there was much debate about the long-term viability of the French pension system. Between 1985 and 1993 there were several government-mandated reports on pensions (the Tabah report in 1986, the Schofflin report in 1987 and the Teulade report in 1989) that emphasized the long-term unsustainability of current pension arrangements with the intention of increasing general public awareness of the financial difficulties of the public pension system (Bonoli 2000: 132; Bozec and Mays 2001: 31).

Although in 1991 a new tax was introduced on the social security contribution (*Contribution sociale généralisée*, CSG) levied on all sources of income including pensions at a flat rate of 1.1 percent, only in 1993 did the first reform of the basic pension scheme for private sector employees pass. Pressure to change the pension system can be explained by four factors. First, from the mid-1980s there was a general increase in the social security budget deficit, indeed, the basic pension scheme reached a deficit of 15.6 percent in 1986 and contribution rates had to be increased.[7] Secondly, the publication by the government of its long-term projections of pension expenditure in 1986 created additional pressure to reform the basic pension scheme. For the first time, these projections took into account the long-term impact of aging on pension expenditure (until 2025), and came to the bleak conclusion that by adhering to the current pension system, contributions would have to be increased by 170 percent by 2025, or benefits dramatically reduced (Bonoli 2000: 129). Thirdly, budgetary decisions at this time were also influenced by the desire to meet the 3 percent budget deficit criterion, one of the convergence criteria for Economic and Monetary Union (EMU). Finally, studies also began to emphasize that, on average, pensioners had a higher standard of living than people in the labor market (Marier 2002: 97).

The center-right parties obtained an overwhelming electoral victory at the end of March 1993 with more than 80 percent of all seats in the National Assembly: RPR 257, UDF 215 deputies (out of 577 possible deputies); in contrast, the PSF had only 57 and the PCF 23 deputies. This led to a significant strengthening of the governing RPR–UDF coalition disposing over an absolute majority in the National Assembly and in the Senate.

In the context of economic stagnation and high unemployment, there was a general consensus among Left- and Right-wing parties (with the exception of the Communist Party) that the French social security deficit should be reduced. The Balladur government did not waste time in addressing the issue of pension reform. One month after his electoral victory, Balladur acted quickly to discuss the reform content with union representatives on April 23, 1993, at the beginning of the legislative period, in which a majority of the population is typically in favor of the government. Despite several years of negotiation, the previous Socialist government had not been able to put a reform project on the table. Consequently, Balladur could easily blame the Socialist government for having done nothing to improve the financial situation of the basic pension scheme: this briefly opened policy window was used to pass an unpopular reform.

On May 7, 1993, Balladur presented his reform proposals for the basic scheme for private sector employees entitled *Pensions de retraite et sauvegarde de la protection sociale*, which included the following measures: gradual increase of the reference period from best 10 to best 25 years (by 2008); extension of the qualifying period for a full pension from 37.5 to 40 years; indexation of pensions to prices instead of wages; creation of the "Old Age Solidarity Fund" (*Fonds de solidarité vieillesse*) to finance non-contributory benefits and repay social security debt; increase in the contribution rate to the social security contribution from 1.1 percent to 2.4 percent of wages paid by all employees. In order to soften the reform proposal, Balladur formulated it as part of a more general effort to diminish social exclusion and stressed that in order to meet the EMU convergence criteria, public expenditure had to be decreased (Blanchet and Legros 2002: 114–15; Vail 1999: 320).

Although the Socialist and Communist deputies would have preferred to keep pensions indexed to wages, they were unable to block the government's reform proposal in the National Assembly. More generally, the PSF and the PCF opposed changing the retirement age of 60, because they considered it a *social acquis* that could not be questioned. So the government opted to reform the policy design less directly, by extending the qualifying period for a full pension from 37.5 to 40 years. Consequently, those wishing to retire earlier could do so, but would not receive full pensions. The opposition parties were also in a weak position, because in January 1993, before the legislative elections took place, the Socialist Prime Minister Bérégovoy had initiated the discussion on pension reform by suggesting the creation of a new pensions fund, and by opposing the extension of the contributions period. Beregovoy's reform proposal, however, was seen by the unions as suspect from the beginning, since it was presented at the end of the legislative period without any chance of being adopted (*Le Monde* 15.01.1993; 12.02.1993).

Social partners were divided on the government's reform proposal. On the one hand, the CFE–CGC, the CFDT and the CFTC took more conciliatory positions, and agreed that reform was necessary (*Le Monde* 08.05.1993). But the CFDT considered that increasing the social security contribution constituted a "blank check," dangerous to employment. The CNPF, the main employer's organization, even wished to have a higher increase in the contribution period to 42 years and to calculate pensions on the basis of the entire active labor life and not only on the last 10 years (*Le Monde* 15.01.1993: 1, 9). On the other hand, the CGT and the FO were against the reform, since in their view the government was questioning acquired rights, and called for a general strike. They were, however, not able to mobilize the rank-and-file. Due to low levels of unionization in the private sector, a public–private division could be exploited, since the special regimes for civil servants were not affected by the reforms (Vail 1999: 321).

There were no real hostile reactions to the government's proposals because Balladur successfully linked changes in the retirement system for the private sector with concessions to unions and the reform measures would be implemented progressively. This is clearly illustrated by the following elements of the reform. First, the option to increase the social security contribution instead of payroll taxes allowed the government to transfer much of the cost of the reform from beneficiaries to the entire working population. Secondly, the choice to implement the new policy design only gradually (the extension of the contribution period from 37.5 to 40 years beginning in 1994 and ending in 2003; the incremental change on the basis of the calculation of pension benefits from the 10 to the 25 best years will only be fully implemented in 2008), which, combined with the protection of the benefits of those already retired, created a division within the private sector itself. This, in turn, reduced the chances of mass mobilization. Thirdly, the government adopted parts of the Socialist Prime Minister Rocard's 1991 White Paper on Pensions with the aim of emphasizing that the pension reform was not going to put into question the basic pension scheme (Vail 1999, 321). Or as Simone Veil, the Social Minister at that time has put it:

> Such an important issue for the future social cohesion of our country, we should not entrench ourselves in ideological positions. We wish to keep the public PAYG pension system. In order to achieve this, we have to reform it. I do not envisage anyone denying this.
> (*Journal Officiel de la République Française* (1993: 3040) [Translation by the author])

This reference to the White Paper on Pensions, as well as the disarray of the Left after the elections, contributed to the weak position of the parliamentary opposition during the legislative process.

The Senate adopted the reform proposals on 23 June with an absolute majority (230 votes in favor and 89 against), and the National Assembly adopted them at the first reading on 7 July 1993 with an absolute majority (481 votes in favor—RPR–UDF and some of the independent deputies), and 90 against (PSF, PCF, and independent deputies). In less than seven hours of discussion the National Assembly examined all twelve articles and the 110 amendments introduced by the opposition and three by deputies from the governing coalition. All the amendments introduced by the opposition were refused and from the three from RPR and UDF deputies, two were accepted and one refused. Thus, military service is now taken into account in the pension calculation and a consultative commission was created with the aim of controlling pension revaluation. The refused amendment initiated by a UDF deputy, intended to reinforce family politics by including family allowances in the pensions calculation (*Le Monde* 09.07.1993).

Some authors (Bozec and Mays 2001; Vail 1999; Bonoli 2000) explain the success of the Balladur reform by referring to the consensual approach adopted by the government towards unions. Bonoli (2000: 132) goes one step further and explains the reform delay by referring to the time horizons of political decision-makers.[8] This also goes in line with the argument pursued in this chapter. Balladur used the policy window opened after his election and introduced the pension reform in the first part of his electoral mandate. Since France has a double electoral cycle, with parliamentary and presidential elections taking place every five years but staggered, the "windows of opportunity" (Kingdon 1984) for policy change for unpopular measures are rather short. The Balladur reform was successful because it took place in the first half of the electoral cycle, during the honeymoon period. The parliamentary opposition was weak after its recent electoral defeat. Moreover, controversial issues, like the special schemes were not part of the reform package. Furthermore, the government also adopted a quid pro quo strategy to gather the support of the unions by granting them specific requests, and the settlement of an old-age solidarity fund. In this way, unions were deprived of their focal points of resistance, and the reform could be passed almost unchanged into law.

The 1995 Juppé Plan: a first attempt to reform the special schemes

The presidential election of Jacques Chirac in May 1995 marked the end of cohabitation between the Left and the Right. During the electoral campaign, Chirac distanced himself from Balladur by promising to repair the apparent "social fracture" that France had been experiencing. After his election, Chirac replaced the Balladur government by that of one of his staunchest supporters, Alain Juppé (Bonoli 2000: 142), since the next important national election was not scheduled until 1998, and the right-center government coalition RPR–UDF, with an absolute majority in both houses of parliament, was well placed to pursue unpopular reforms.

During this period, France entered into economic recession, leading to speculative attacks on the Franc and public doubts that France would qualify for EMU. Since the 1993 pension reform, the media was increasingly focusing on the benefits (e.g. lower retirement age, a better indexation and a lower contribution period) granted to those covered by the special schemes which were perceived as being more generous than those received by the basic pension scheme for employees of the private sector. Before Juppé presented the social security reform in October 1995, President Chirac reassured the French population that the social security system, a part of French identity and French heritage would be kept, but that it needed radical changes (*Le Monde* 17.05.1997: 10).

On November 13, 1995, Alain Juppé presented his *Plan for the Reform of Social Protection* (thereafter called Juppé plan) at the National Assembly. The Juppé plan covered several changes in the health insurance scheme: the introduction of a new tax revenue to cover payment of the social security system debt; the harmonization of special schemes of the public sector employees with those of the private sector in the pension system; and a constitutional amendment allowing parliament to vote on the social security budget. Regarding pensions, four distinct measures were foreseen: (i) an increase in the contribution period for civil servants from 37.5 to 40 years; (ii) the abolition of various special schemes allowing SNCF and RATP employees to retire as early as 50; (iii) the creation of an autonomous pension office for the state civil servants to make the accounts of their system more transparent; (iv) change of the statutory composition of the managing boards of the social security schemes increasing state control and reducing the role of the unions (Bonoli 2000: 143–4; Juppé 1996: 221; Natali 2003: 28–9).

Two days after the presentation of the plan, the National Assembly approved it with an overwhelming majority: 463 voices in favor (RPR–UDF), 87 against (PSF and PCF). On November 16, 1995 the Senate also approved the Juppé Plan, with 218 votes in favor and 94 against. Unions were divided on the Juppé Plan. On the one hand, there were absolute opponents to the whole social security reform plan, especially those unions whose membership is composed mostly of civil servants, like the CGT, the FO, the FSU and the FEN (representing teachers' interests). For this group of unions, the government's attempt to change the code of the civil and military pensions was tantamount to denigrating the general stature of civil servants. On the other hand, the CFDT, the CFTC and the CFE-CGC accepted the increase in the contribution period for employees in the public sector, and agreed that the measures foreseen in the Juppé Plan were important steps in the reform of the pension system (*Liaisons Sociales* 1998: 272–3; *Le Monde* 12.11.1995).

November 17 marked the beginning of demonstrations against the Juppé Plan, with the unions of SNCF and RATP at the center of the protest. This, in turn, led to an almost total paralysis of public transport and the railways lasting three weeks. On December 7, there were between 700,000 and 1.3 million people on the streets of Paris. On the same day, Juppé submitted a bill to the National Assembly enabling the government to implement social security reform through ordinances. One of the consequences of the attribution of exclusive jurisdiction to government is that it allows governments to remove all power from parliament. Although the French constitution has numerous provisions limiting amendments prerogatives, in order to delay the passage of a bill at the National Assembly, one of the few instruments available to the opposition is the multiplication of amendments in order to gain time. So Socialist and Communist parties used this instrument of parliamentary obstruction by tabling together more than 4,500 amendments and 744 amendments of amendments. Furthermore, both parties also presented a censure motion, which was rejected, since only 94 deputies from the parliamentary opposition were in favor, and the bill on the ordinances was considered as adopted in the first reading by the National Assembly (*Liaisons Sociales* 1998: 273).

In the meanwhile, the Public Functions Minister met with representatives of the CFDT, UNSA, CFTC and CGC representing the interests of public servants and SNCF and RATP employees. Only the FO and the FSU refused to participate in the meeting and preferred to continue with the demonstrations until the government withdrew its plans. In subsequent days there were again demonstrations against the Juppé Plan involving more than a million people. Only after massive protests had taken place, on December 17, the government changed the reform plan by keeping the special schemes provisions as well as by allowing SNCF and RATF employees to keep retirement at the age of 50. The Juppé government made these concessions in the context of levels of social conflict not experienced since May 1968 (Bonoli 2000: 146; *Le Monde* 17.05.2003; *Liaisons Sociales* 1998: 276–7).

Although the government abandoned the proposals for the reform of pensions for public sector employees, some parts of the Juppé Plan passed, namely the constitutional amendment allowing parliament to vote on the social security budget, and also health-related measures. Given the government's strong position in the National Assembly and Senate, this reform failure is surprising.

Bonoli (1997) and Vail (1999) compare the Balladur with the Juppé reform and explain reform failure with the different governments' approaches chosen. Whereas the Balladur approach was based on a pattern of co-operation, Juppé relied on a confrontational approach. In 1993 the government had sweetened pension retrenchments with concessions on the management side of the social security schemes. In contrast, the Juppé government combined cuts with an attack on the trade unions within the system by reinforcing the state's control over the social security system. Lévy (2002: 18) underlines that French obsession with social order is one key feature of Gaullist parties. Jacques Chirac was junior government official in May 1968. This experience explains why Gaullist politicians are very reluctant to confront popular protests and respond to protests with policy concessions as Juppé also did.

The failure of the Juppé Plan illustrates very clearly that even governments with an absolute majority in the National Assembly are not necessarily able to pass their reforms. The reform failure can be explained with respect to two levels of policy-making: namely, the electoral and the corporatist arenas. First, the electoral arena (the timing of the electoral cycle) affected the policy preferences of governments, since these are embedded in a particular electoral system. Although Juppé was at the beginning of his mandate when he initiated the reform process, the parliamentary elections had taken place longer than two and half years ago. The reform took place already in the second part of the electoral mandate. The government had to face an election at the latest in two years, so it feared electoral punishment. The French majority electoral system leads to a high party competition, since voters very easily can reward or punish politicians. Second, in line with Palier (2003) and Bozec and Mays (2001) the high level of unionization in the public sector, and the privileges enjoyed by this socio-occupational category in the present pension system make reform difficult to achieve. Unions were able to ride a wave of public protest against what were perceived as attacks on the status of civil servants and in this way brought the country to a halt. Moreover, the unions' ability to get the government to back down demonstrates the tremendous mobilizing capacity of French unions, despite their small numbers. Confrontation between the state and labor unions through demonstrations remains an important political weapon in the hands of the unions, since public sector strikes can paralyze the country. In other words, well organized groups have informal veto power, because they can immobilize the economy.

The stillborn Thomas Law of 1997: the controversial establishment of private capital-funded plans

After the failed attempt at reforming the special schemes for civil servants, the Juppé government initiated a new reform proposal in May 1996 that resulted in the so-called Thomas Law of February 20, 1997. This new legislation was the result of a debate launched by insurance companies with the aim of providing private sector employees with an optional capital-funded third pillar and to strengthen the French financial market.

The establishment of retirement saving funds was not a new issue. In the late 1980s, private insurance companies, especially the French Federation of Insurance Companies (*Fédération française des sociétés d'assurance*, FFSA), had already started increasing pressure to include the pension issue in the public agenda, with the aim of building up their role in pension financing through the development of optional complementary funded schemes. In 1991, a *White Book of Insurers* asserted that the burden of the public pension scheme from 2005 to 2010 would lead to intergenerational inequity, and proposed to end pension revaluation and to create pension funds as additional pension schemes (Blanchet and Legros 2002: 117).

On May 30, 1996, two deputies (Thomas and Millon) of the governing party UDF presented a private member bill to establish firm retirement saving funds (*plans d'épargne-retraite d'entreprise*). The initial legislative proposal provided for optional retirement saving funds that could be created without the unions' agreement, would take the form of schemes to which employers should subscribe on behalf of their employees and should be managed by insurance agencies (*fonds d'épargne retraite*) especially set up to provide this service. The retirement saving fund was intended to provide an annuity from retirement age onwards, contributions should be optional and payments by both employees and employers would be counted as non-taxable income, up to a legally established ceiling (amounting to 10% of the gross annual salary, or 20% of the social security ceiling). Employers were also to be exempted from social security contributions up to a certain limit fixed by decree (Blanchet and Legros 2002: 117; Virard 1997: 42–3).

The debate began in earnest after the summer, and the National Assembly voted on the bill to establish retirement saving funds for the fourteen million employees in the private sector on November 22, 1996. Curiously, the debate on the law, which had only thirty articles, started on November 21, and went on until November 22, in a six hours debate. When the vote took place, only seven of the 577 deputies participated: five RPR–UDF and two from the parliamentary opposition (PSF, PCF). The law was adopted in the first reading by an absolute majority of the present deputies during the night (Philippon 1996: 60).

In the meantime, a letter signed by four main unions, the CGC, FO, CGT, and CFTC was sent to Prime Minister, Alain Juppé, in which they demanded a formal assurance that the retirement pension funds would not replace the existing supplementary schemes. If the Senate passed the bill, together with the CFDT, they would organize protest actions. Unions and the left-wing parliamentary opposition criticized the Thomas Law vehemently, because these proposals came from interest groups potentially interested in the development of such policy instruments. Moreover, the parliamentary opposition argued that far from strengthening the French pension system, the creation of pension funds would destabilize it without really addressing the problem of pension funding. The main critical point for the unions was that the tax exemption from the social contributions could undermine the basic pension scheme. The private capital-funded plans for the employees of the private sector would only be acceptable if the new system did not compete for funding with the PAYG system and if the unions were to control the management of the system through the introduction of funds managed with equal representation of social partners (*fonds à gestion paritaire*) (Blanchet and Legros 2002: 118). Only CFT and FO categorically refused retirement pension funds as a matter of principle, with the argument that capitalization undermines solidarity between generations, since today's workforce would now have to finance its own retirement (*Le Figaro* 14.01.1997).

On December 13, 1996, the majority of the RPR and UDF deputies in the Senate voted in favor of the Thomas Law, but introduced several amendments by restricting the tax exemption from the social contributions and by giving employees the right to ask for membership in an existing scheme. If the second house amends the legislation, it returns to the first house for a second reading thus initiating the shuttle system. Before the second reading of the law took place, the President of the Republic, Jacques Chirac reassured French citizens that the PAYG system would remain central to the French retirement system:

> The retirement savings scheme reform is socially and economically beneficial and modern. It was in preparation over a long period of time and will also serve us well for the future (…). The PAYG system is the basis for our pensions and we are not going to put it into jeopardy. (*Le Figaro* 16.01.1997 [Translation by the author])

On January 15, 1997 the National Assembly voted again on the retirement saving funds, accepting the amendments introduced by the Senate. However, there was no absolute majority on the second reading at the Senate. The RPR and UDF voted in favor, but the Republican and the Radicals Groups, both liberal center-right parties, together with the Socialists and the Communist Party rejected the bill. After the legislation had been reviewed twice by each house, the executive intervened in the shuttle system by calling the Conference Committee into play. The main point of dissent concerned the issue of the percentage of an enterprise's employees that could be affiliated to the same funds. Whereas the senators wished to have no more than 5 percent of an enterprise's employees in the same fund, the deputies preferred to have percent 10 (*Le Monde* 01.02.1997).

The law adopted by the National Assembly on February 20, 1997 allowed employees to choose between exit with interest or with a capital lump-sum. Generous fiscal incentives were foreseen, and internal management within the firm was allowed. The PSF and the PCF opposed the law. The last chance for the opposition to delay the implementation of the Thomas Law was to challenge its constitutionality by bringing this issue to the Constitutional Council. This is just what the Socialist senators did. Since the government had to wait for the response of the Constitutional Council, the bill could not come into effect until the autumn. The Socialist party committed itself to repealing the law if it returned to power.

In April 1997, the President, without any signs of political or institutional crisis, dissolved the National Assembly and called for new elections. The electorate, however, sanctioned the President by bringing the Left to power. Consequently, the third, and hitherto longest period of cohabitation (1997–2002) started, when Lionel Jospin became Prime Minister in June 1997. The Socialist Party obtained 250 seats and a multiparty coalition of the so-called plural left (*gauche plurielle*) was formed that brought together Socialists, Communists, the Greens and left-wing radicals (Guyonnet 2003: 148). Since the Juppé government did not sign the enacting decree for the Thomas

Law before the early parliamentary elections, it was never implemented. After winning the legislative elections, the Socialist Party simply revoked it.

The Thomas Law failed because of the timing of policy change. It had been already adopted in the second part of the government's electoral mandate, shortly before the President dissolved the National Assembly and called for new elections. The RPR–UDF governing coalition feared that the PSF and the PCF might use the recently passed reform to gain votes during the electoral campaign. Thus the government did not sign the enacting decrees. With regard to the corporatist arena, the government simply ignored unions' demands. Although unions felt that the government was seeking to marginalize them by excluding them from the management, they could not hinder policy change.

The 2003 Raffarin Reform: a further attempt to reform the special schemes

Under the Jospin government (1997–2002), the debate on the reform of the French pension system continued, but apart from a flurry of reports, very few concrete changes to the pension system were implemented. Among the most important reports during this period was the Charpin Report which proposed a gradual increase of the contribution period for public and private sector employees to 42.5 years by 2019, and supported the development of capital-funded plans as a complement to the basic and supplementary pension schemes. Other reports, like the Taddei and Teulade Reports, in contrast, rejected the extension of the contribution period and also opposed a change in the alignment of the special schemes with the rules of the private sector pension system (Bozec and Mays 2001: 54–5).

The victory of President Jacques Chirac's UMP party in parliamentary elections in June 2002 ended the Conservative–Socialist cohabitation that had lasted since 1997. On June 17, 2002, Chirac nominated Jean-Pierre Raffarin as Prime Minister of a governing coalition, with 396 out of 577 deputies. Before embarking on a new round of large scale reform, the government adopted some minor pension-related initiatives by incorporating unemployed people into the general employees' pension fund (CNAVTS) and by abolishing the "end of career leave" scheme for civil servants from 2003 on.[9]

The Raffarin Reform was officially initiated on January 6, 2003 by President Jacques Chirac, who guaranteed that the PAYG system would remain in place. Chirac also laid out the timetable, the outline, and the method to be adopted by Prime Minister Raffarin.

Even before the content of the proposal was known, unions called for a joint demonstration, in which between 250,000 and 500,000 people participated. Their principal aim was to pressure the government into incorporating union demands into its proposal. After this first demonstration, the government reassured the unions that they would not merely be spectators in the planned reform, stating that the principal aim of the reform was to ensure the financial sustainability of the basic scheme by gradually extending the length of contribution periods to retirement age. On April 3, the Communist dominated CGT, the more militant CGT–FO, and the two main unions representing civil servants UNSA and teachers FSU organized strikes and demonstrations to protest against the reform plan. From the beginning the unions were divided, the socialist-leaning CFDT, the Christian-democratic CFTC and the executive's union, the CFE–CGC, refused to participate, because the mobilization was unfounded before the government had presented the reform proposals (*Le Monde* May 17, 2003).

In May 2003, the Raffarin government issued a draft bill on pension reform that included concrete measures affecting the basic pension scheme and the special schemes of civil servants. The proposal included longer contribution periods (from 40 to 42 years to be phased-in between 2009 and 2020), calculation of pension benefits for public sector employees on the basis of the last three years of employment from 2008 onwards, indexation of public sector pensions to prices, introduction of a 3 percent pension supplement for each year worked beyond the age of 60, earlier retirement for workers who started work at the age of 14 or 15, a replacement rate of 75 percent of the net national minimum wage for low-paid workers, creation of a voluntary supplementary scheme for civil servants and for self-employed shopkeepers and industrialists, and the possibility of buying back periods of missed contributions for a maximum of 12 quarters. One of the most important innovations of the Raffarin reform is the introduction of a third pillar of pension funding with two new voluntary pensions saving schemes, an individual personal pensions saving plan (*plan d'épargne individuel pour la retraite*, PEIR) and a voluntary partnership employee pension savings scheme (*plan partenarial d'épargne salariale volontaire pour la retraite*, PPESVR) (Gouvernement Français 2003b; Jolivet 2003; *Le Monde* 29.05.2003).

After the government presented the draft bill, some unions (CGT, UNSA, and FSU) initiated a day of strikes and demonstrations on 13 May. Across the civil service, more than 50 percent of employees participated in the strikes. Altogether between one and two million people demonstrated across the country. Following this mobilization, the Minister of Social Affairs, François Fillon, accompanied by the Civil Service Minister, negotiated with all the main trade union confederations and employers' organizations. The CGT and the CGT–FO, however, wished to keep retirement at the age of 60, and refused to negotiate further with the government. At the end of the negotiations, only the more moderate CFDT and the CFE–CGC agreed to the government's proposals. The agreed deal contained 19 amendments, and it revised the draft bill, but the key issue of lengthening the contribution period was not challenged. The trade-off comprised a mix of cost-containment measures by extending the contribution periods from 40 to 42 years for all workers. In exchange, the existing benefits calculation for civil servants on the basis of the last six months salary was kept, and employers' old-age pensions were increased. On the employers' side, the MEDEF and the CGPME supported the government's draft, but were against these concessions. In response to union calls for greater equity, the pension guarantee for low-paid workers was raised from 75 percent of the minimum wage in the original draft to 85 percent in the final version of the bill. Furthermore, the new compulsory scheme will be managed jointly by the social partners as a public fund consolidating in this way the co-management role of unions (Jolivet 2003: 2; *Le Monde* 16.05.2003; 17.05.2003; Natali and Rhodes 2004: 18).

The integration of these amendments meeting the demands of the CFDT and of the CFE–CGC weakened the position of the CGT, CGT–FO, UNSA, FSU. The latter, however, continued to oppose the planned reform and demanded the opening of genuine talks and called more days of national action on May and June (*Le Monde* 03.06.2003). In contrast to the 1995 Juppé reform they could not argue that consultations had not taken place and that their demands were not considered. The government had initiated a dialogue with the unions wishing to cooperate. By treating the CFDT and the CFE–CGC as official partners and ignoring the others, the Raffarin government could play upon the divisions among unions by including the agreed deal with the CFDT and the CFE–CGC into the bill draft. This was a way of demobilizing opposition from unions, but also from the Left parties.

The Raffarin government could now initiate the phase of parliamentary discussion in both houses of parliament from a position of strength, since the bill incorporated the amendments based on the package deal supported by several unions. Scrutiny by the National Assembly began with a stormy debate on June 10. Not surprisingly, the ruling UMP and the UDF political parties supported the pensions reform proposal. In contrast, the PCF deputies tabled over 6,500 amendments to a government bill containing 81 articles. The PSF introduced more than 2,900 amendments. But their amendments had no impact, they were just symbolic. Both parties opposed above all the lengthening of the contribution period. Furthermore, the PS was not only very weak since its electoral defeat at the last presidential and legislative elections, there was also an internal division within the party with some deputies criticizing the party's obstructionist strategy. Some Socialist deputies, like Michel Rocard, Bernard Kouchner and Jacques Atali, even approved the government's reforms (Gouvernement Français 2003a; *Le Monde* 24.07.2003).

In such a situation of internal weakness of the main opposition party, with the government holding an absolute majority in the National Assembly, the reform could easily pass at the beginning of the legislature period. As in 1993, the Raffarin government used the window of opportunity just after the elections to pass a reform in the sensitive pension issue.

The debate in the National Assembly lasted 19 days, and the debate in the Senate 10 days. On July 3, the National Assembly approved the bill during the first reading. From the 521 expressed votes (an absolute majority of 261 deputies was needed to pass the law), 389 deputies voted in favor and 132 against the bill. The government can intervene in the shuttle system after a single reading if the executive determines that the legislation is "urgent." The Raffarin government called the conference committee of both houses of parliament into play. After the meeting of the Conference Committee on 24 July, the National Assembly and the Senate passed the law on the reform of the pensions system. In the National Assembly, from the 545 expressed votes, 393 deputies voted in favor and 152 against the law project. In the Senate the bill was adopted, with 204 of 317 votes in favor and 113 against. Thus, the law was published in its final form on 21 August 2003 (Le Sénat 2003; Assemblée Nationale 2003).

The new law has 116 articles. Parliament adopted a number of amendments: 23 from the National Assembly, 11 from the Senate and one from the Conference Committee. The most important ones concerned the financing of company early retirement schemes by contributions paid into the Old-Age Solidarity Fund, only missing annual pension contributions for years spent in education (up to a three-year ceiling) can be purchased and the sums paid for these purposes will be tax deductible.

Once more, Socialist and Communist deputies and senators brought the new legislation before the Constitutional Council on July 28, 2003. They argued that the new law violates the principle of equality, since it makes the issue of pension rights for those with arduous work a matter of collective bargaining, and because the same rights are not conferred on men and women. On August 14, the Constitutional Council validated the law by overturning the complaints. Following the Socialist position already assumed in the Thomas Law, François Hollande, the first secretary of the Socialist Party, emphasized that if the Left came to government the law would be reviewed.

V Conclusion

Summary of the magnitude of changes

The pension reform debate in France centered on the financial viability of the pension system, and the reform initiatives that were successfully adopted focused on the calculation of benefits in the basic pension scheme, the extension of the contribution period, and the setting up of capital-funded individual saving plans. The social impact of pension reforms will be incremental. The reforms were linked by a common concern for preserving the present system so that they do not solve the long-term financing problem of the French retirement system.

The 1993 Balladur reform of the basic scheme for the private sector is currently being implemented: the contribution period for a full pension was extended from 37.5 to 40 years; pensions are now indexed on prices instead of wages; increase of the reference period from the best ten to the best 25 years (from 2008 on); and an "Old-Age Solidarity Fund" was set up to finance non-contributory benefits and to repay social security debt.

Although Raffarin's draft proposal intended to increase the number of years public-sector employees must work to obtain a full pension and aligned it to the private sector, these changes were dropped after bargaining with some unions.

Accordingly, inequality between categories of employees in the pension schemes remains: employees affiliated to special schemes (mainly civil servants and employees of state-owned firms) still benefit from more favorable benefits, both in terms of replacement rates and of legal retirement age/minimum number of years to qualify for a full pension (for example, the calculation of pension benefits is made with basis on the last six months salary and not on the last ten or 25 years of contributions as in the private sector).

In sum, the overall pattern is one of parametric reforms and of strengthening the role of optional funded, supplementary schemes. It has proven difficult to reform special schemes. Governments have chosen a gradualist and not a big bang approach towards pension reforms. Whereas a big bang or shock therapy approach implements various reform measures in a concentrated time frame, a gradualist approach spreads various reform measures over an extended period. The advantage of using a gradualist approach is that it splits the resistance forces, since there is a sequential implementation of reform measures. In the presence of uncertainty about the distribution of gains and losses from reforms, a gradualist approach is politically better to push through.

Impact of the political system on pension politics

The French political system tends to produce strong governments backed by stable majorities in parliament. When the governing coalition holds an absolute majority in the National Assembly, opposition parties' role in changing law proposals is rather limited. Pension reform proposals were initiated by a center-right RPR–UDF coalition in 1993, 1995, 1997 and 2003 with an absolute majority at both houses of parliament. When discussing pension reform proposals retrenching the benefits of the retirement system, parties of the Left, which traditionally represent the positions of trade unions, were always opposed to change. Even when the Left was in office, it never really tried to reform the pension system. During the Jospin government (1997–2002) many consultations were made with the social partners, a flurry of reports was published, but very few concrete changes took place.

When a government enjoys a cohesive executive and a majority in both houses of parliament, there are very few mechanisms available for the opposition to block policy change. First, the parliamentary opposition can introduce as many amendments as possible in order to win time. This was done repeatedly in the analyzed reforms. During the 2003 Raffarin reform, it even allowed the opposition to lengthen the parliamentary debate in both houses of parliament. Second, the opposition parties also can refer a law to the Constitutional Council, so that this neutral actor can decide on the constitutionality of the law. This institutional mechanism was used continually by the opposition in order to delay the promulgation of laws. In 1997, the Socialist opposition was very successful with this strategy. The Socialist Party referred the Thomas Law on the creation of retirement saving funds to the Constitutional Council, obliging the government to wait for the decision before it could publish the legislative text. Since this occurred shortly before the early parliamentary elections took place, the government, already involved in the electoral campaign, did not have time to enact the decree. When the Socialist Party came to power in 1997, it simply revoked the Thomas Law. Thus the Constitutional Council plays a central role as mediator between the government and the parliamentary oppositions. A constitutionalization of the policy-making process has taken place, that is to say governmental legislation is examined by the Constitutional Council after it has been adopted by both Houses of Parliament.

The surprising thing about pension politics in France is that although governments have a lot of power with their stable majorities, they are reluctant to use this power. In this chapter, I have argued that the mobilization capacity of unions and the electoral competition between the Right and Left parties explains the reluctance of French governments to embark on reforms changing the very generous pension system. The government is afraid that parliamentary opposition can explore retrenchment for electoral purposes. This is why the variable timing of the electoral cycle has to be taken into consideration in explaining policy change.

The empirical evidence confirmed the thesis that governments are more successful in passing unpopular reforms in the first part of their mandates, during the so-called "honeymoon period," when the parliamentary opposition is weak and voters give the new government the benefit of the doubt, since difficult decisions can be blamed as the legacy of the outgoing government. Balladur in 1993 and Raffarin in 2003 used the policy window opened after their election and introduced pension reforms in the first half of their electoral mandate. In both situations, the PSF was weak and internally divided after the electoral defeat. Juppé's 1995 plan failed not only because he opted for a confrontational approach towards unions, but also because his unpopular reform abolishing special schemes for civil servants had already taken place in the second part of the electoral mandate. The government had to face an election at the latest in two years time, so it feared electoral punishment. The same is valid for the Thomas Law in 1997. Although the reform on the establishment of optional capital-funded individual saving plans was adopted in parliament it was reversed by the next government. The RPR-UDF governing coalition at the end of the electoral mandate feared that the opposition parties could exploit pension reform during the electoral campaign to gain votes, so the decrees were not enacted, making reform reversal very easy for the left-wing Jospin government.

Interest group influence

In France there is no institutional blockage, the problem starts when the reforms are announced to the unions and these start to demonstrate. The unions' ability to block reform can be explained with their mobilizing capacity. Despite their low membership numbers, unions are able to cause tremendous disruption very quickly, because union members are concentrated in sectors such as public transport. Mass demonstrations and strikes from the French railways and Paris transports as a reaction to the attempt of the Juppé government to change the very generous special schemes for civil servants illustrate very clearly the willingness of these unions to call strikes, and when they do, the impact is quick and dramatic: if for example, trains and public transport shut down, the economic costs are high, and the pressure on the government to end the strikes is intense. In this situation, union bargaining power is high. So membership numbers do not matter as much as mobilizing potential. Furthermore, the high rate of unionization in the public sector makes reforms in this sector strongly contested. So that when governments try to reform the special schemes, the potential costs are concentrated and very visible. Pension reforms in France clearly exemplify how difficult it is to change a certain policy design, when interest groups that would lose from a change in the status quo mobilize and put pressure on the government.

Furthermore, governments could not pass pension reforms without the support of some segments of the labor movement. The 1993 Balladur, and the 2003 Raffarin governments were more successful than the 1995 Juppé government, because they pursued a strategy of including unions early on in the negotiations about pension reform and then provided incentives for some unions to cooperate. The Balladur and Raffarin conservative governments show us that when package deals are tied up satisfying the demands of at least some unions, the other obstructionist unions have more difficulty in mobilizing. In such a situation, unions are ready to accept changes in the public pension system.

Union fragmentation and the fragmentation of the pension system itself facilitated this type of "divide and conquer" strategy. The Raffarin government took the demands of the socialist-leaning CFDT into the bill draft and weakened thus the other unions that had refused to bargain with government. The division of French unions allows the government to choose its preferred interlocutor.

Constraints of policy design

The current institutional features of the French pension system constitute a constraint on the different governments. First, limits are imposed by the sheer complexity of the pensions system, due to the existence of institutional arrangements consisting of a basic compulsory public scheme, numerous compulsory supplementary occupational schemes and a separate special scheme for the public sector. The second constraint on introducing a new policy design is the management of the French pension system. Whereas public pension schemes are managed according to a tripartite system constituted by trade unions, industry confederations and the government, complementary pension schemes are managed according to a bipartite arrangement involving trade unions and employers' representatives. This institutional structure is not unique in Europe, but changing the system can only be achieved by consensus. Finally, the various conceptual approaches to pensions make change rather difficult, for example, private-sector pension schemes are based on insurance principles, public-sector schemes on deferred income and finally self-employed or occupational schemes on wealth accumulation.

Pension reforms are particularly difficult to implement in France. Due to strong popular support for the existing generous institutional arrangements, with a high net replacement rate, any attempt to change the system leads to massive social protest.

Role of ideas and historical context

It has been difficult to reform the special schemes in the basic pension for civil servants. With the consequence that these special schemes have remained virtually unchanged. All attempts to significantly alter them were stopped by a huge public outcry. The difficulty of reforming these schemes has to do with the perception of pensions as a social right for civil servants.

Abbreviations

AGIRC	*Association générale des institutions de retraite des cadres*
ACOSS	*Agence centrale des organismes de la securité sociale*
ARRCO	*Association des régimes de retraite complémentaire*
CAF	*Caisse d'Assurance Vieillesse*
CFDT	*Confédération française démocratique du travail*
CFE-CGC	*Confédération française de l'encadrement – Confédération générale des cadres*
CFTC	*Confédération française des travailleurs chrétiens*
CGOS	*Comité de gestion des oeuvres sociales*
CGPME	*Confédération générale du patronat des petites et moyennes entreprises*
CGT	*Confédération générale du travail*
CGT-FO	*Confédération générale du travail – Force ouvrière*
CNAF	*Caisse Nationale d'Allocations Familiales*
CNAMTS	*Caisse Nationale d'Assurance Maladie des Travailleurs Salariés*
CNAVTS	*Caisse Nationale d'Assurance Vieillesse des Travailleurs Salariés*
CNP	*Caisse Nationale de Prévoyance*
CNPF	*Conseil national du patronat français*
CRAM	*Caisses Régionales d'Assurance Maladie*
CSG	*Contribution sociale généralisée*
DL	*Démocratie Libérale*
EDF-GDF	*Electricité de France–Gaz de France*
FEN	*Fédération de l'éducation nationale*
FFSA	*Fédération française des sociétés d'assurance*
FGAF	*Fédération générale autonome des fonctionnaires*
FN	*Front National*
FSU	*Fédération syndicale unitaire*
LCR	*Ligue Communiste Révolutionnaire*

LO	*Lutte Ouvrière*
MEDEF	*Mouvement des Entreprises de France*
MNR	*Mouvement National Républicain*
PEIR	*Plan d'épargne individuel pour la retraite*
PREFON	*Caisse Nationale de Prévoyance de la Fonction Publique*
PPESVR	*Plan partenarial d'épargne salariale volontaire pour la retraite*
PSF	*Parti Socialiste Français*
RATP	*Transports en Île-de-France*
RPR	*Rassemblement pour la République*
SAM	*Salaire annuel moyen*
SNCF	*Société Nationale des Chemins de Fer*
SSC	*Social security ceiling*
UDF	*Union pour la Démocratie Française*
UMP	*Union pour un Mouvement Populaire*
UNR	*Union pour la Nouvelle République*
UNSA	*Union nationale des syndicats autonomes*

Notes

1. To be sure, Bonoli also discusses the importance of the electoral cycle for French pension politics, but the following analysis goes further by specifying an exact and limited "honeymoon period."
2. Following a referendum in 2000, the presidential term was reduced from seven to five years.
3. For a more detailed overview of the different extreme-left parties see Ysmal 2003.
4. After some divergences between Le Pen and Mégret concerning an eventual alliance of the FN with the moderate right and the party leadership, Mégret decided to found a new right wing party which in contrast to the FN party should be able to form an alliance with the center right parties. Ysmal 2003: 108.
5. Other schemes for the self-employed come within an association of five broadly occupational categories: farmers, shopkeepers and industrialists, craftsmen, liberal professionals, lawyers, and the clergy.
6. For a general overview of how these different voluntary occupational schemes work see Observatoire des Retraites 2003b.
7. Since social security schemes are not part of the general government budget, they cannot incur debts to finance current expenditure. When there is a difference between receipts and outlays, government money can be used to cover it temporarily. The deficit, however, is transferred to the following year's budget.
8. For a broader overview of the role played by the time horizons of decision-makers, see Conceição-Heldt 2004 and Pierson 1996.
9. Established in 1996, this scheme enabled civil servants to retire as early as 56 on an income equivalent to their future pension, provided they had 40 years of contributions and 15 years of service in the Civil Service. The equivalent private sector, *Early Retirement for Jobs Scheme*, had already expired at the end of December 2001.

Bibliography

Primary sources and government documents

ASSEMBLÉE NATIONALE (2003). Analyse du Scrutin N° 313—Séance du 24 juillet 2003: Scrutin public sur l'ensemble du projet de loi portant réforme des retraites. [cited 26.09.2003]. Available from http://www.assemblee-nationale.fr/12/scrutins/j00313.asp

GOUVERNEMENT FRANÇAIS (2003a). Réforme des retraites: deuxième semaine du débat à l'Assemblée Nationale. [cited 26.09.2003]. Available from http://www.retraites.gouv.fr/article354.html

GOUVERNEMENT FRANÇAIS (2003b). Régime général et régimes alignés: ce que change la réforme. [cited 26.09.2003]. Available from http://www.retraites.gouv.fr/article296.html

JOURNAL OFFICIEL DE LA RÉPUBLIQUE FRANÇAISE (1993). Débats Parlementaires. Assemblée Nationale. Compte Rendu Intégral, 1ère séance du mercredi 7 juillet 1993.

LE SÉNAT (2003). Analyse politique du scrutin n° 228. [cited 07.12.2003]. Available from http://www.senat.fr/scrutin/s02-378.html

Newspapers

Le Figaro

14 January 1997. Épargne Retraite: le front commun des syndicats.

16 January 1997. Les fonds d'épargne-retraite adoptés par l'Assemblée.

Le Monde

15 January 1993. Le projet sur les retraites est rejeté par les socialistes.

12 February 1993. M. Bérégovoy dans le brouillard des retraites.

8 May 1993. La durée de cotisation des retraites serait progressivement allongée.

9 July 1993. Une concession aux retraités.

12 November 1995. Alain Juppé devrait consulter les syndicats sur le régime de retraite des fonctionnaires.

1 February 1997. Le Sénat refuse de céder sur les fonds de pension.

17 May 1997. Comment Alain Juppé, en voulant réformer la Sécurité sociale et les retraites, déclencha le mouvement de l'automne 1995.

16 May 2003. Retraites: le "non" des syndicats.

17 May 2003. La réforme des retraites divise le front syndical.

29 May 2003. Retraites: le gouvernement joue la fermeté face auy syndicats.

3 June 2003. Le mouvement contre la réforme des retraites relève les enjeux différents pour chaque organisation.

24 July 2003. Retraites: ce que la loi prévoit pour vous.

Secondary sources

ARRCO (2001). *Supplementary Pension Schemes for Workers in France.* Paris: ARRCO.

BLANCHET, DIDIER and FLORENCE LEGROS (2002). "France: The Difficult Path to Consensual Reforms." In Siebert, H. (ed), *Social Security Pension Reform in Europe.* Chicago: University of Chicago Press.

—— and LOUIS-PAUL PELÉ (1997). "Social Security and Retirement in France." [cited 03.08.2004]. Available from http://www.nber.org/papers/w6214.pdf

BOERI, TITO, AGAR, BRUGIAVINI, and LARS CALMFORS (eds.) (2001). *The Role of Unions in the Twenty-First Century. A Report for the Fondazione Rodolfo Debenedetti.* Oxford: Oxford University Press.

BONNARD, MARYVONNE (2003a). "Le Président de la République." In Parodi, J. -L. (ed.), *Institutions et vie politique: 3. édition mise à jour.* Paris: La documentation Française.

—— (2003b). "Le rôle du parlement." In Parodi, J. -L. (ed.), *Institutions et vie politique: 3. édition mise à jour*. Paris: La documentation Française.

BONOLI, GIULIANO (1997). "Pension Politics in France: Patterns of Co-operation and Conflict in Two Recent Reforms." *West European Politics* 20(4): 111–24.

—— 2000. *The Politics of Pension Reform: Institutions and Policy Change in Western Europe*. Cambridge: Cambridge University Press.

—— and BRUNO PALIER (1998). "Changing the Politics of Social Programmes: Innovative Change in British and French Welfare Reforms." *Journal of European Social Policy* 8(4): 317–30.

BOZEC, GÉRALDINE and CLAIRE MAYS (2001). Pension Reform in France. [cited 29.08.2004]. Available from http://www.iccr-international.org/pen-ref/report.html

BUCZKO, GERHARD (1982). Die Herabsetzung des Rentenalters in Frankreich. *Die Angestellten Versicherung* 29(9): 324–32.

CONCEIÇÃO-HELDT, EUGÉNIA DA (2004). *The Common Fisheries Policy in the European Union: a Study in Integrative and Distributive Bargaining*. London: Routledge.

CROUZATIER, JEAN-MARIE (2003). "Les constitutions françaises de 1789 à 1958." In Parodi, J. -L. (ed.), *Institutions et vie politique: 3. édition mise à jour*. Paris: La documentation Française.

CROZIER, MICHEL (1970). *La société bloquée*. Paris: Éditions du Seuil.

DOWNS, ANTHONY (1957). *An Economic Theory of Democracy*. New York: Harper & Brothers.

DUVERGER, MAURICE (1980). "A New Political System Model: Semi-Presidential Government." *European Journal of Political Research* 8(2): 165–87.

—— (1992). "A New Political System Model: Semi-Presidential Government." In Lijphart, A. (ed.), *Parliamentary Versus Presidential Government*. Oxford: Oxford University Press.

FREARS, JOHN (1990). "The French Parliament: Loyal Workhorse, Poor Watchdog." *West European Politics* 13(3): 32–51.

GUYONNET, PAUL (2003). "Les élections depuis 1958." In Parodi, J. -L. (ed.), *Institutions et vie politique: 3. édition mise à jour*. Paris: La documentation Française.

HUBER, JOHN, D (1996). *Rationalizing Parliament: Legislative Institutions and Party Politics in France*. Cambridge: Cambridge University Press.

IMMERGUT, ELLEN, M (1992). *Health Politics: Interests and Institutions in Western Europe*. Cambridge: Cambridge University Press.

JOLIVET, ANNIE (2003). "Pension reform adopted." [cited 06.12.2003]. Available from http://www.eiro.eurofound.eu.int/2003/09/feature/fr0309103f.html

JUPPÉ, ALAIN (1996). "Intervention du Premier Ministre Alain Juppé sur la Réforme de la Protection Sociale." *Droit Social* (3): 221–37.

KEMPF, UDO (2003). "Das politische System Frankreichs." In Ismayr, W. (ed.), *Die politischen Systeme Westeuropas*. Opladen: Leske + Budrich.

KINGDON, JOHN, W. (1984). *Agendas, Alternatives, and Public Policies*. Boston/Toronto: Little & Brown.

KNAPP, ANDREW and VINCENT WRIGHT (2001a). *The Government and Politics of France: Fourth Edition*. London/New York: Routledge.

—— and —— (2001b). "The State and the pressure groups." In Knapp, A. and Wright, V. (eds.), *The government and politics of France*. London/New York: Routledge.

LAUTRETTE, LAURENCE (1999). *Le droit de la retraite en France*. Paris: Presses Universitaires.

LEGROS, FLORENCE (2002). "La réforme des régimes de pension entre choix politiques et constraintes économiques." [cited 02.10.2003]. Available from http://www.cepii.fr/francgraph/publications/ecomond/dossierstrat/2002ch5.pdf

LEVY, JONAH, D. (2002). "Breaking Away? French Economic and Social Policy after Dirigisme." Paper presented at Discontinuity and Change at Köln, Max-Planck-Institut für Gesellschaftsforschung.

LIAISONS SOCIALES (1998). *Les Années Sociales 1986–1997*. Paris: Editions Liaisons.

LIJPHART, AREND (1999). *Patterns of Democracy: Government Forms and Performance in Thirty-Six Countries*. New Haven: Yale University Press.

MARIER, PATRIK (2002). Institutional Structure and Policy Change: Pension Reforms in Belgium, France, Sweden, and the United Kingdom, University of Pittsburgh, Pittsburgh.

MÉNY, YVES (2002). "France: The Institutionalization of Leadership." In Colomer, J. M. (ed.), *Political Institutions in Europe: Second Edition*. New York: Routledge.

MERRIEN, FRANÇOIS-XAVIER (1991). "L'État par défaut." In Durand, J. and Merrien, F.-X. (eds.), *Sortie de Siècle: La France en Mutation*. Paris: Editions Vigot.

MOURIAUX, RENÉ (2003). "Syndicats, organisations professionnelles et groupes d'intérêt." In Parodi, J.-L. (ed.), *Institutions et vie politique*. Paris: La documentation Française.

MYLES, JOHN and PAUL PIERSON (2001). "The Comparative Political Economy of Pension Reform." In Pierson, P. (ed.), *The New Politics of the Welfare State*. New York: Oxford University Press.

NATALI, DAVID (2003). "The Role of Trade Unions in the Pension Reforms in France and Italy in the 1990's: New Forms of Political Exchange?" In *EUI Working paper*. Florence: European University Institute.

—— and MARTIN RHODES (2004). "Trade-offs and veto Players: Reforming Pensions in France and Italy." *French Politics* 2: 1–23.

NOHLEN, DIETER (2000). *Wahlrecht und Parteiensystem* (3 edn) Opladen: Leske + Budrich.

OBSERVATOIRE DES RETRAITES (2003a). "The French System." [cited 15.08.2003]. Available from http://www.observatoire-retraites.org/versionanglaise/frenchsystem/Introduction.htm.

—— (2003b). *Retirement Pensions: A Statistical Analysis* (sp. edn) January 2003 N° 3 edn. Paris: Observatoire des Retraites.

—— (2004). *Les Retraites en Europe, en Amérique du Nord et au Japon*. February 2004 N° 4 edn *Les Chiffres de la retraite*. Paris: Observatoire des Retraites.

OLSON, MANCUR (1965). *The Logic of Collective Action: Public Goods and the Theory of Groups*. Cambridge Mass.: Harvard University Press.

PALIER, BRUNO (1999). "Réformer la sécurité sociale: Les interventions gouvernementales en matière de protection sociale depuis 1945, la France en perspective comparative." Dissertation. Paris: Institut d'études politiques de Paris.

—— (2003). *La réforme des retraites*. Paris: Presses Universitaires de France.

PHILIPPON, THIERRY (1996). "Fonds de Pension: pour qui?" *Le Nouvel Observateur* 28/11-4/12/1996, 60–1.

PIERSON, PAUL (1994). *Dismantling the Welfare State? Reagan, Thatcher and the Politics of Retrenchment*. Cambridge: Cambridge University Press.

—— (1996). "The Path to European Integration: A Historical Institutionalist Analysis." *Comparative Political Studies* 29(2): 123–63.

QUITTKAT, CHRISTINE (2000). "Strategies of Interest Intermediation in the European Union: French trade associations under pressure? Paper presented at "Clientelism, Informal Networks and Political Entrepreneurship in the European Union" at the 28th Joint Sessions of the European Consortium for Political Research," 14–19 April 2000 at University of Copenhagen, Denmark.

SCHLUDI, MARTIN (2003). "Politics of Pension Reform–The French Case in a Comparative Perspective." *French Politics* 1(2): 199–224.

SCHMIDT, VIVIEN, A. (1999). "The Changing Dynamics of State–Society Relations in the Fifth Republic." *West European Politics* 22(4): 141–65.

SCHUMPETER, JOSEPH, A. (1942). *Capitalism, Socialism and Democracy.* New York: Harper & Row.

THIÉBAULT, JEAN-LOUIS (2000). "Forming and Maintaining Government Coalitions in the Fifth Republic." In Müller, W. C. and Strøm, K. (eds.), *Coalition Governments in Western Europe.* Oxford: Oxford University Press.

TSEBELIS, GEORGE (1995). Decision Making in Political Systems: Veto Players in Presidentialism, Parliamentarism, Multicameralism and Multipartyism. *British Journal of Political Science* 25(3): 289–325.

—— (2002). *Veto Players: How Political Institutions Work.* Princeton: Princeton University Press.

—— and Jeannette Money (1995). "Bicameral Negotiations: The Navette System in France." *British Journal of Political Science* 25(1): 101–29.

—— and —— (1997). *Bicameralism.* Cambridge: Cambridge University Press.

VAIL, MARK (1999). "The Better Part of Valour: the Politics of French Welfare Reform." *Journal of European Social Policy* 9(4): 311–29.

VIRARD, MARIE-PAULE (1997). "Fonds de Pension: Tout n'est pas gagné." *Enjeux*, 42–5.

VIRIOT DURANDAL, JEAN-PHILIPPE (2003). *Le pouvoir gris: sociologie des groupes de pression de retraités.* Paris: Presses Universitaires de France.

YSMAL, COLETTE (2003). "Les partis politiques aujourd'hui." In Parodi, J.-L. (ed.), *Institutions et vie politique: 3. édition mise à jour.* Paris: La documentation Française.

PART II
MULTIPLE VETO POINTS

CHAPTER 5

SWITZERLAND: THE IMPACT OF DIRECT DEMOCRACY

GIULIANO BONOLI

I Introduction

THE Swiss pension system is often praised for its capacity to combine effective needs coverage with a solid financial basis. This combination of what are sometimes conflicting goals is achieved thanks to a system structured around three pillars of provision. The first pillar is universal and provides all retirees with a minimum income above the poverty line; the second pillar is compulsory for most employees, is fully funded, and provides earnings-related benefits. The third pillar is a voluntary top-up encouraged by generous tax concessions. The multi-pillar character of the system and the inclusion of both pay-as-you-go (PAYG) and funded financing are its key strengths.

Favorable evaluations of the Swiss pension system may surprise those who are well acquainted with Swiss political institutions and the hurdles inherent in policymaking. Swiss political institutions are extremely fragmented, and power is shared among a large number of actors. Switzerland is a federal country, it has a bicameral parliament, a fairly strict separation of powers between the executive and the legislative branches of government, and most notably, it allows legislation to be initiated and challenged directly by voters through referendums. In order to function properly, the Swiss political system requires extensive agreement, generally achieved through encompassing compromises and negotiation.

The result is that rational and goal-oriented policy-making is often difficult. Typically, legislation contains many potentially inconsistent elements because of the need to respond to the requests of the multiple actors involved in the policy-making process. This system allows the integration into decision-making of the many minorities that make up the country, but its key casualties are coherence, speed, and innovation in legislation. Viable compromises tend to deviate as little as possible from the status quo, but require lengthy negotiations. Yet, with regard to the establishment of a comprehensive pension system, an issue that caused much conflict in other European countries in the 1960s and 1970s, the Swiss political system did remarkably well.

Praise notwithstanding, the Swiss pension system is not immune from the effects of developments like population aging, or the transformation of labor markets putting pressure on pension systems throughout the industrial world. Expenditure on its PAYG first pillar is expected to increase over the next several decades at a much higher rate than receipts, and a key objective of current reform initiatives is to guarantee the medium and long term solvency of the scheme.

Population aging, however, does not affect the basic pension alone. Second pillar occupational pensions have to deal with the issue of higher life expectancy at retirement age. Longer life expectancy increases the cost of annuities, or put another way, with the same amount of accumulated capital, pensioners will obtain an increasingly lower annuity. This trend will make it difficult to achieve the target replacement rate of 60 percent of gross earnings unless contributions to second pillar pensions are increased. Occupational pension reform initiatives aimed at maintaining current benefits without imposing excessive burdens on pension funds—an effort complicated by the stock market crisis of early 2000.

In addition to preparing for population aging, policy-makers also faced pressure to change the exclusionary mechanisms built into the system. Within the basic pension, married women were generally not entitled to their own pension even when they had made substantial contributions. Within occupational pensions, employees earning less than 40 percent of the average wage were not compulsorily insured. Many part-time workers, in most cases women, failed to reach this threshold and were excluded from compulsory coverage. Recent reforms targeted these two issues, in conjunction with cost-containment measures.

The reforms discussed in this chapter span two decades of pension policy-making, and begin with the (late) completion of the multi-pillar system in 1982. More recent reforms aim to respond to the two types of pressure identified above. Both the basic pension and the occupational pension law have been modified in order to improve financial sustainability and to improve pension coverage for non-core workers, especially women.

The key independent variable shaping pension policy both in the establishment of the system and in the current adaptation process is the institutional structure of the Swiss political system. This finding is consistent with previous studies on Swiss social policy (see e.g. Immergut 1992; Obinger 1998). The case studies of individual reforms presented in this chapter show how political institutions, particularly referendums, have shaped the course of policy by determining the final outcome of the law-making process, but also by shaping actors' preferences and the definition of available options. Political institutions explain both the successful (if slow) development of a comprehensive and viable pension system, and the current stalemate on many crucial issues.

II Political system

Constitutional history and nation-building

Switzerland stands out in international comparisons for several reasons. Perhaps its most striking feature is the many cleavages that divide it. First, there are four national languages: German, spoken by about 65 percent of the population, French (20%) Italian (6%) and Rumanstch (0.5%). Second, Switzerland is also religiously divided, between roughly equal groups of Catholics and Protestants. A third important cleavage is the one between urban and rural areas. This cleavage emerged early in Swiss Politics and has been kept open by one of the most generous agricultural policies in the world. The current attempt at retrenchment in this field has revived this division. One important feature of Swiss society is that these three cleavages, along with the modern ones such as the class cleavage, do not overlap, but intersect. Communities and individuals thus tend to define their identity in relation to these numerous cleavages. This fragmentation and the absence of a hegemonic group are often taken as reasons for the peaceful cohabitation of the many different groups.

With regard to political institutions, Switzerland stands out for the weakness of its state. Until the mid-nineteenth century, Switzerland was a fairly loose federation of sovereign states, the Cantons. The modern state was established in 1848, after a short civil war pitted the more conservative Catholic cantons against the majority of Protestant, liberal states. The winners, the liberal cantons supported the creation of a centralized state, but were nevertheless willing to compromise with the Catholics, who were keener to retain features of cantonal independence. As a result, the Constitution adopted in 1848 allowed individual cantons substantial powers in all areas of government policy, and enshrined the principle of subsidiarity. Since its creation, the federal state was not meant to be the center of political power.

Moreover, the Swiss state, (the Civil Service, but especially Parliament), is very open to the influence of organized interests, particularly business associations. Many of these organizations are the descendants of the corporations that existed in pre-modern Switzerland, and were abolished by the 1848 Constitution. These re-emerged as interest groups, and in the mid-nineteenth century were considerably more developed than the new-born federal state. As a result the authorities had to co-operate with these associations in a range of economic and social policies, including vocational training, the collection of statistics, and the distribution of subsidies. The political role of interest organizations was further reinforced and institutionalized in more recent years, especially after World War II. For instance, the standard policy-making process includes consultation with relevant interest groups, and draft legislation is often prepared by "expert commissions," composed mainly of interest group representatives (Bonoli and Mach 2000; Mach 1999; Papadopoulos 1997).

The Swiss state, then, differs from most of its European counterparts because of its weakness. As Colin Crouch (1986) puts it, Switzerland has never completed the process of differentiation from civil society that other states experienced during the nineteenth and early twentieth centuries. A liberal state characterized by a limited range of competencies but with strong powers within that range, did not develop in Switzerland. Because of its weakness and its heavy reliance on organized interests, the Swiss state has never been able to assert its independence from particular interests. The result is "an indefinite boundary between state and society... [and a state that] is so weak that it invites organisational sharing of state functions" (Crouch 1986: 195).

The weakness of the Swiss state is further reinforced by the political institutions that are used to govern the country. The Swiss constitutional order includes a series of checks and balances aimed to reduce the potential for power concentration within the central government. These are discussed next.

Institutions of government

The Swiss political system is based on institutions that reduce the potential for power concentration and encourage the formation of large coalitions. The constitutional order is geared towards limiting the power of the federal government, and includes several mechanisms by which its authority can be challenged and its decisions overruled. The result is a political system in which the extent of agreement needed to legislate is particularly large. These institutional features, which are briefly reviewed here, are combined with a social structure characterized by multiple cleavages: socio-economic, religious, and linguistic, which further diminish the likelihood of power concentration in the hands of one group. This combination of institutional and socio-structural features has produced a political system based on the integration of dissent and on the inclusion of conflicting interests in the policy-making process, which has been termed consensus or consociational democracy (Lehmbruch 1993; Lijphart 1984; Linder 1997).

Formal institutions

There are at least three institutional features in the Swiss political system that contribute to reducing the concentration of central government power: de facto separation of powers between the executive and the legislative branches of government; federalism with minority representation at the parliamentary level; and a referendum system.

First, the relationship between the Swiss government (Federal Council, *Bundesrat*) and parliament has been described as a hybrid between European parliamentarism and US separation-of-powers (Lijphart 1984). As in parliamentary regimes, the Federal Council is elected by parliament, but as in a separation-of-powers system, the Federal Council cannot be brought down by the legislature during its four-year term. Parliamentarians are not under the same pressure to support government-sponsored legislation as in parliamentary systems. Conversely, the Federal Council cannot dissolve parliament. The result is a system in which the government has relatively little control over parliament. As in the US it has to negotiate policy with the legislature, as it cannot impose it.

The second element of power fragmentation is Federalism and the representation of the states (*Cantons*) in the upper chamber of parliament. Cantons have almost unlimited freedom regarding their internal political organization and are protected by the Constitution from central government interference. More crucially, cantons have powers in all areas of policy that are not explicitly attributed to the Federal state by the Constitution. As a result, before the Federal government can legislate in a new domain, it needs to modify the Constitution. Federalism also means that in many policy areas, substantial decision-making as well as managing powers are held by cantonal governments. This is the case, for instance, in education, fiscal policy, and some social programs, like social assistance and family benefits. This fragmentation creates co-ordination problems, which are dealt with by "inter-cantonal" co-ordination bodies, which may issue recommendations, or agree on common standards among cantons. The ability of these inter-cantonal bodies to create uniform and innovative policies is however rather limited (Kriesi 1995: ch. 3; Vatter 1999). Swiss federalism includes a bicameral parliament, inspired by the US model. The two chambers of parliament are symmetric: in the lower chamber (*Nationalrat*) territorial representation is proportional to the size of the population, and in the upper chamber (*Ständerat*) each canton is entitled to two representatives. The power of the numerous, but small, rural cantons is thus magnified.

Thirdly, and perhaps most notably, Switzerland has a referendum system which allows voters to bring various issues to the polls.[1] According to Neidhart (1970) referendums are the key factor behind the development of a consensus-based political system in Switzerland. Governments follow an inclusive policy-making strategy in order to reduce the vulnerability of their bills to the referendum challenge. By allowing the relevant actors to co-draft legislation, policy-makers have been able to diffuse the threat potential of referendums.

Of these constitutional features, direct democracy arguably has the largest impact on policy formulation. Referendum politics is substantially different from parliamentary politics because referendum politics favors the formation of "unholy" coalitions that are unlikely in parliament and stand good chances of defeating a bill. Typically, a government-sponsored bill is supported by the center of the political spectrum. However, it is not uncommon that both the far right and the far left oppose the bill, because it is seen as being "too little" for some and as "too much" for the others. A highly heterogeneous coalition is thus possible in a referendum, since it is a one-off event and does not require agreement on the alternative to the bill, as is normally the case in parliament.

Moreover, party discipline among voters is not as strong as it is among members of parliament. Typically, political parties issue voting recommendations for each referendum. However, on average, 12.5 percent of voters ignore party recommendations in referendums (Papadopoulos 1996: 30). This figure might suggest that lack of party discipline is rather innocuous behavior, given that the government coalition can count on the support of 80 percent of the electorate in general elections. However, many referendums are relatively uncontroversial, implying stronger compliance with party recommendations. On the other hand, in the case of controversial decisions, ignoring party guidelines is more widespread, with the result that voters sometimes reject policy proposals put forward by the government. Referendum politics, therefore, is characterized by a higher level of uncertainty than parliamentary politics, and this has caused governments to develop policy strategies intended to deal with this increased level of uncertainty.

Referendums are a key factor behind the development of an inclusive political system in Switzerland, and this results directly from governmental strategies aimed at improving the capacity to control and implement policy (Kriesi 1995: 90; Katzenstein 1984: 144; Neidhart 1970). For example, the participation of "unnecessary" parties in the ruling coalition began as a response to the obstructive use of referendums. Until 1891, in fact, the Liberal Democrats (FDP/PRD) were able to rule alone, but found it difficult to implement policy because of the obstructive strategy played by the Conservative Catholic Party (now CVP/PDC). Between 1871 and 1891 the Conservative Catholic Party called 20 referendums on acts passed by parliament and won 15. This created a situation of legislative impasse which was solved by the ruling FDP/PRD by incorporating the Conservatives in the ruling coalition (Kriesi 1995: 207–9). In short, referendums are a powerful force behind consensual politics. Typically, every effort is made to avoid a referendum since a defeat generally means a considerable waste of time and a loss of legitimacy for federal authorities, who as a result are unable to legislate in the relevant area for a number of years.

Government strategy is thus geared towards preventing a referendum from taking place by including groups that have the organizational capacity to call a referendum in policy decisions. Overall, the strategy has been rather successful, as only about 7 percent of all legislation passed by parliament is subjected to a referendum (Linder 1998: 5). If, however, the government cannot prevent a referendum, the risks are high because only about 50 percent of legislation subjected to a referendum eventually becomes law.[2] In addition, the government seems particularly vulnerable to the referendum threat in some specific policy areas, because it is unable to prevent a referendum call and has few chances of winning a referendum when it is called. This is the case for decisions concerning participation in international or supranational organizations (the EU or the UN), and in social policy, when legislation includes only expansion or retrenchment measures (Obinger 1998; Bonoli 1999).

More generally, it can be argued that the development of a model of democracy based on consensus is a result of both institutionally-based power fragmentation—of which the referendum system is only one element—and of the multicultural character of Swiss society, and requires some measure of power-sharing between groups in order to be cohesive (Lehmbruch 1993: 45).

Consociational practices

One of the most significant features of Swiss consociational democracy is an oversized coalition government. The Federal Council, which has had the same party composition since 1959, consists of a four-party coalition including the Christian Democrats, the Socialists, the Free Democrats and the Swiss People's Party (formerly the Farmers' Party).[3] Together, these parties account for more than 80 percent of seats in the lower chamber of parliament, and a government could rule with the support of any three of these four parties. Because Federal Councilors are elected individually, they need the votes of other parties, which encourages moderation. This facilitates the consensual character of the government's operations, but reduces government control over parliament and over the electorate in referendums. Overall, the Federal Council has less influence on policy-making than in most other parliamentary systems.

A second important consociational practice is a policy-making process in which interest groups play a substantial role in the definition of policy (Papadopoulos 1997). Typically, a lengthy and highly structured consultation process precedes legislative change, and this process can be more or less encompassing depending on the policy's potential for controversy. Legislation is often drafted by "expert commissions," which normally include representatives of all the relevant interest groups. Expert commissions usually produce a compromise that is acceptable to all parties concerned, as each group has de facto veto power which it can use by threatening a referendum challenge. During the golden age of the consensus model (the 1950s and 1960s) the agreements reached in this way were generally accepted by parliament with little change, thanks also to the existence of an informal core of policy-makers where most decisions were made (Kriesi 1982; 1995). In more recent years, as will be discussed later, parliament has become increasingly reluctant to ratify agreements reached by interest groups and, on various occasions, has imposed changes in a majoritarian way.

The Swiss consociational model guaranteed political inclusion to influential groups with the resources to exploit the veto points provided by the political system. Thus inclusion was not universal, however. Women did not have the right to vote until 1971, and foreigners, who make up about 20 percent of the population, do not have the right to vote at the federal level.

There are two chambers of parliament in the Swiss electoral system, which are elected according to different electoral laws. The National Council election is ruled by federal legislation requiring elections under a proportional representation system where the electoral districts correspond to the cantons. Each canton has a number of seats proportional to its population, ranging from 34 for the largest canton (Zurich) to one for small rural cantons. Elections to the upper chamber, which theoretically represents the interests of the cantons, is governed by cantonal law. Differences are

Table 5.1 Political institutions in Switzerland

Political arenas	Actors	Rules of investiture	Rules of decision-making	Veto potential
Executive	Federal Council (Bundesrat/Conseil fédéral)	4-year term; elected by parliament (both chambers combined – Bundesversammlung/Assemblée fédérale); each of the seven members are elected separately with absolute majority in several ballots if necessary; no possibility of vote of no confidence; minority representation is guaranteed; same partisan composition 1959–2003; Federal Council cannot dissolve parliament	Decision-making with simple majority; law-making process usually starts with establishment of expert commission; governmental draft (Botschaft/Message)	—
Legislative	National Council (Nationalrat/Conseil national)	4-year term; proportional representation; 200 seats in 26 electoral districts (= cantons) with 1 to 34 mandates; vote splitting, cumulating or panachage is possible; seat allocation following the Hagenbach-Bischoff method; Nationalrat/Conseil national cannot be dissolved by Federal Council	Bill shuttles between the two chambers until both agree; decision-making by simple majority	Traditionally not veto point because of government majority, although party discipline becoming less reliable, and hence legislative changes more frequent
	Council of the States (Ständerat/Conseil des États)	4-year term; 46 seats (2 for each of the 20 full cantons, 1 for each of the half-cantons); elected according to cantonal electoral system (mainly majority vote) on the same day as Nationalrat/Conseil national	Bill shuttles between the two chambers until both agree; decision-making by simple majority	Traditionally not veto point because of government majority, although party discipline becoming less reliable, and hence legislative changes more frequent, and incongruent bicameralism more important

Judicial	Federal Court (*Bundesgericht/ Tribunal fédéral*)	30 full-time and 30 part-time members elected by the two parliamentary chambers (*Bundesversammlung/Assemblée fédérale*)	No right to review constitutionality of federal law	Not a veto point
Electoral	Referendum (*Volksabstimmungen/Votations populaires*)	Compulsory referendum for: (a) constitutional changes (b) popular initiative for constitutional change (requiring 100,000 signatures) (c) Referendum challenging an act within 90 days after passage in parliament (50,000 signatures required)	Decision rule: (a) and (b) double majority required i.e. majority of voters and majority of cantons (c) simple majority of voters	Veto point
Territorial units	Regions (*Kantone/Canton*) Communities (*Gemeinden/Communes*)	20 full cantons (*Vollkantone/cantons*) and 6 half-cantons (*Halbkantone/demi-cantons*); autonomous political entities with constitutions and governments; 3,000 communities with high degree of autonomy	Cantons have the power to legislate in all areas of policy unless explicitly attributed to the federal state by constitution; communities have right to legislate on local level	Not a veto point although strong legislative powers

minimal, however, and most cantons elect their State Councilors with a two-round two-member constituency majority system. In the first round, an absolute majority is needed to obtain the office, whereas in the second round the two best-ranked candidates are elected.

Federal elections for both chambers take place simultaneously every four years, and, given the separation of powers system between government and parliament, there are no early elections. By-elections are held only for the Council of States. If a member of the National Council resigns, the best-ranked non-elected candidate of his or her party gets the office.

Legislative process

The legislative process is shaped by the political institutions already discussed. The Federal Council usually initiates the legislative process. If the new law is politically controversial, the government will normally begin by setting up a commission consisting of experts in the field, but more importantly of representatives of the various relevant interest groups. In the field of pensions, because policy change is so frequent, the government has established two permanent expert commissions: one for the basic pension (the AHV/AVS Federal Commission) and one for occupational pensions (the BVG/LPP Federal Commission). Their task is to elaborate reform proposals that are technically viable, and, especially, politically feasible. These Federal Commissions include representatives from different organizations that have a stake in pensions and can effectively oppose measures regarded as unsatisfactory. It is essentially an instrument for pre-testing the political feasibility of reform proposals and thus, ultimately, for consensus building. In the case of particularly controversial legislation, the government can also launch a consultation procedure that includes a wider range of social and institutional actors. Consultation procedures include cantonal governments. Pension reforms are always preceded by a consultation procedure.

Having collected evidence on the policy preferences of the various actors, the government produces a bill that is presented in parliament with a report defending the bill (*Botschaft/Message*). The bill is discussed by one of the two chambers of parliament, first by a smaller group of MPs within the relevant committee. Pension bills are always discussed in the Social Security Committee in both Chambers of Parliament. The Committee then submits the bill, possibly with modifications, to the whole chamber for approval or rejection. If the bill is approved it is transferred to the Second House of Parliament, where it follows the same procedure. The two chambers must pass the same version of a bill, so if changes are introduced, bills go back and forth several times between the two chambers before they are accepted. After the final parliamentary vote, the bill is published, and during the following 100 days citizens have the right to challenge the bill in a referendum.

As already mentioned, in the golden age of the Swiss consensus model (1950s and 1960s), government bills were generally approved without modification and

Party family affiliation	Abbreviation	Party name	Ideological orientation	Founding and merger details	Year established
Christian Parties	CVP/PDC	Christian-Democratic Party (*Christlich-demokratische Volkspartei der Schweiz/Parti Démocrate-Chrétien Suisse*)	Catholic social doctrine	Until 1912 "Conservative Catholic party"	1848
	EVP/PEV	Evangelic Party (*Evangelische Volkspartei/Parti Evangélique*)	Protestant		1919
Left parties — Social democratic parties	SPS/PSS	Socialist Party (*Sozialdemokratische Partei der Schweiz/Parti Socialiste Suisse*)	Social democracy		1888
Greens	GPS/PES	Green Party (*Föderation der Grünen Parteien der Schweiz/Fédération Suisse des Partis Écologistes*)	Environmentalist, left wing		1983
Liberal	FDP/PRD	Radical Party (*Freisinnig-Demokratische Partei der Schweiz/Parti Radical-Démocratique Suisse*)	Liberal, center-right		1848
	LPS/PLS	Liberal Party (*Liberale Partei der Schweiz/Parti Libéral Suisse*)	Liberal, conservative		1913
Right wing	SVP/UDC	Swiss People's Party (*Schweizerische Volkspartei/Union Démocratique du Centre*)	Right wing populist, national conservative	Until 1972 "Farmers', artisans' and self-employeds' party"	1936

Fig. 5.1 Party system in Switzerland

Note: Only parties with 3 seats or more in the National Council are included (2003 election).

sometimes even by unanimous vote in parliament (this was the case for some expansionist pensions reform). More recently, parliament has played a much bigger role in defining legislative content. As discussed below, this has been the case in pension policy too, as every important reform adopted between 1985 and 2002 has been thoroughly redrafted in parliament. This may be a result of increased political competition over the last few years as demonstrated by the electoral successes of the Swiss People's Party. Members of Parliament are, as a result, less sure of re-election and more likely to engage in high visibility law-making in parliament.

Parties and elections

Proportional representation has produced a multiparty system. The parliament elected in October 2003 includes members of 14 different parties. The big four in the ruling coalition account for most of the votes and political influence, however. Together the Socialists, the Free Democrats, the Christian Democrats and the Swiss People's Party obtained 81 percent of the votes in the last general election and control 86 percent of the seats in the lower house of parliament (in the upper house, they control all seats because of the smaller number of candidates per canton).

For most of the twentieth century, the Socialists (SPS/PSS) have been the largest party but they have never had a dominant position in government. The party has been a member of the ruling coalition since 1959, with two ministers.[4] In government it often finds itself in a minority position on social and economic policy issues, as the representatives of the three remaining parties tend to have a common view in these areas. That is why, in spite of being a government party, the SPS/PSS still periodically plays the role of an opposition party, campaigning against decisions taken by the government. The party has close links with the largest federation of trade unions (SGB/USS, see p. 217) and many of its leaders are recruited from the labor movement. In the 2003 election, the SPS/PSS obtained 22.47 percent of the votes cast for the lower house, winning 51 seats.

For most of the twentieth century, the second largest party was the Free Democrats (FDP/PRD), a liberal party, which because of its links with business and ability to build alliances, is arguably the most influential in Swiss politics (Kriesi 1980; 1982). On social and economic policy issues, the Free Democrats follow a traditional liberal orientation, favoring little state intervention in economic matters. Together with the Christian Democrats, the Free Democrats are considered to be a centrist party. In the 1999 election, the Free Democrats got 19.9 percent of the votes, giving them 43 seats in the lower house of parliament.

The Christian Democrats (CVP/PDC) have traditionally been strong, but their share of the vote has declined recently. The party has difficulty uniting its different wings, with the left–right cleavage being the main dimension of internal division. There are 35 Christian Democrats in the lower house, who were elected by 15.9 percent of voters. Because of its strength in several smaller rural cantons, the CVP/PDC has a much larger representation in the upper house, the Council of States, where it is the largest party.

Table 5.2 Governmental majorities in Switzerland

Election date	Start of gov.	Head of gov: Federal Council (7 seats, by party)	Governing parties	Gov. majority (% seats) National Council	Gov. electoral base (% votes) National Council	Gov. majority (% seats) States' Council	Institutional veto points	Number of veto players (partisan + institutional)
10.21.1979	12.27.1979	FDP/PRD: 2; CVP/PDC: 2; SPS/PSS: 2; SVP/UDC: 1	FDP/PRD (51), CVP/PDC (44), SPS/PSS (51), SVP/UDC (23)	84.5%	81.6%	93.5%	Referendum, National Council, States' Council	4 + 3
11.09.1983	12.19.1983	FDP/PRD: 2; CVP/PDC: 2; SPS/PSS: 2; SVP/UDC: 1	FDP/PRD (54), CVP/PDC (42), SPS/PSS (47), SVP/UDC (23)	83.0%	77.4%	93.5%	Referendum, National Council, States' Council	4 + 3
10.18.1987	12.09.1987	FDP/PRD: 2; CVP/PDC: 2; SPS/PSS: 2; SVP/UDC: 1	FDP/PRD (51), CVP/PDC (42), SPS/PSS (42), SVP/UDC (25)	80.0%	72.1%	91.3%	Referendum, National Council, States' Council	4 + 3
10.20.1991	12.04.1991	FDP/PRD: 2; CVP/PDC: 2; SPS/PSS: 2; SVP/UDC: 1	FDP/PRD (44), SPS/PSS (43), CVP/PDC (36), SVP/UDC (25)	74.0%	70.0%	89.1%	Referendum, National Council, States' Council	4 + 3
10.22.1995	12.13.1995	FDP/PRD: 2; CVP/PDC: 2; SPS/PSS: 2; SVP/UDC: 1	SPS/PSS (55), FDP/PRD (45), CVP/PDC (34), SVP/UDC (29)	81.0%	73.9%	93.5%	Referendum, National Council, States' Council	4 + 3
11.10.1999	12.15.1999	FDP/PRD: 2; CVP/PDC: 2; SPS/PSS: 2; SVP/UDC: 1	SPS/PSS (51), SVP/UDC (44), FDP/PRD (43), CVP/PDC (35)	86.5%	80.7%	100.0%	Referendum, National Council, States' Council	4 + 3
10.19.2003	12.10.2003	SVP/UDC: 2; SPS/PSS: 2; FDP/PRD: 2; CVP/PDC: 1	SVP/UDC (55), SPS/PSS (52), FDP/PRD (36), CVP/PDC (28)	85.5%	81.7%	100.0%	Referendum (National Council, States' Council)	4 + 1 (+2)

Finally, the Swiss People's Party (SVP/UDC), originally a farmers' party, has traditionally been the weakest of the big four, but has recently re-styled itself into a populist, anti-foreigner and anti-Europe party, becoming the largest party in the country in the 1999 election. In the 2003 election (*Nationalrat*) the party obtained 26.7 percent of the votes, resulting in 55 seats.

The party system reflects some of the key cleavages in Switzerland. The CVP/PDC is stronger, sometimes dominant, in the Catholic and religiously mixed cantons, but considerably weaker in Protestant ones. The CVP/PDC leadership still consists of Catholics only, whereas party elites of the three other main parties are predominantly Protestant (García 1991). There is no clear party political division across the linguistic cleavage, even though in recent years the electoral success of the SVP/UDC, built to a large extent on a new anti-Europe and anti-foreigner discourse, has been achieved almost exclusively thanks to electoral gains in the German-speaking parts of the country. It should be noted, however, that the SVP/UDC has so far avoided any hint at a divisive discourse. Rather, it has been intent on recruiting members and voters in the French-speaking part of Switzerland.

The French–German linguistic cleavage has become stronger in recent years, demonstrated by several referendums in which the two communities voted in opposite directions. This is generally the case with foreign policy decisions, which would have reduced the country's isolation, such as joining the UN or the EU. German speakers are generally more likely to oppose such moves than their French counterparts. The linguistic divide also operates in referendums on social policy issues, with French speakers usually more favorable to measures that expand the welfare state. The Italian-speaking minority tends to follow the Swiss-German lead in matters of foreign policy, but usually votes with the Swiss-French in social policy issues.

Interest groups

The Swiss system of organized interests is relatively fragmented. On the employers' side, there are five main peak associations.

1. Large, export-oriented employers are represented by the Swiss Business Federation, *Economiesuisse*,[5] and by
2. The Union of Swiss Employers (SAV/UPS). The former tends to deal with general economic policy matters, while the latter focuses on social policy and industrial relations.
3. Banks have a separate peak organization, the influential Swiss Association of Bankers.
4. Small business is represented by a distinct employers' organization, SGV/USAM, which is certainly less influential than its larger counterparts but tends to be more anti-statist.
5. Finally, agricultural employers and self-employed farmers are represented by the Swiss Farmers' Union (Mach 1999).

Recently, the strong cleavage between the export-oriented sectors of the economy and those producing mainly for the internal market has sharpened, with the former increasingly unsatisfied with rigidities and protectionist measures benefiting mainly domestic producers. Some sections of the export business were instrumental in many of the policy changes that took place in the 1990s, mainly in the areas of economic and fiscal policy, and much less, in spite of their attempts, in the area of social policy (Bonoli and Mach 2000).

On Labor's side, the key division is ideological. The SGB/USS, the largest peak association of workers, is close to the Socialist Party, and many trade unionists are also Socialist MPs in the federal or in cantonal parliaments. In addition, there is an association of white-collar workers (VSA/FSE) and a federation of Christian unions (CNG/CSC), which have recently merged into a new union confederation, *Travail Suisse*. At 25 percent, the unionization rate is rather low compared to most other European countries (Ebbinghaus and Visser 1999). Generally speaking Swiss unions are known for their moderation, and tend to use confrontation only as a last resort. Many of the collective agreements that they negotiate with employers (mostly at the branch level), moreover, include a so called "labor peace" clause, which forbids the signatories from taking industrial action. Especially in recent years, Labor has clearly emerged as the weakest of the social partners. Some of the more recent sectoral agreements include substantial elements of flexibility, allowing for example overtime work and salary adjustment at the plant level. In terms of political influence, however, the Labor movement has collected a few victories in the 1990s, when it successfully used referendums to challenge measures such as the deregulation of employment protection (which is not particularly developed anyway) and cuts in unemployment benefits (Bonoli and Mach 2000; Bonoli 1999).

Switzerland also has single-issue associations that can be rather influential in specific areas, such as the Swiss Touring Club, in matters of transport policy, or the Tenants' Association. In the broad area of social policy, however, the interests of the beneficiaries are generally a matter for the trade unions, more than for the relevant single-issue groups. Voluntary sector organizations, like Caritas or Pro Senectute, can be active players in referendum campaigns on relevant topics, and are generally consulted when new legislation is drafted, but they cannot match the level of power resources available to the trade unions.

III Pension system

Historical overview

The debate on the introduction of a pension scheme in Switzerland started in the late 1880s and 1890s, arguably prompted by developments in neighboring Germany. The

Federal Council was already engaged in setting up a health insurance scheme and declined to pick up the various proposals that were circulated at the time (Bernstein 1986; Binswanger 1987). It was only after 1918, when a general strike shattered the country's stability that the pension issue reached the political agenda. The introduction of a national basic pension scheme was one of the key demands of the strikers (Bernstein 1987: 23).

Over the next few years the debate turned around the technicalities of pension schemes, particularly the issue of which of the existing European models should be followed. In 1919, the Federal Council proposed adopting a Bismarckian contributory social insurance scheme rather than a means-tested tax-financed pension, as had been introduced in Sweden, Denmark and the United Kingdom (Baldwin 1990). In order to introduce a national scheme, the Constitution was changed in 1925 and this was later confirmed by the electorate in a referendum. The government's proposal from 1919 was fiercely opposed, mainly from conservative politicians, and Parliament finally adopted a much less generous version. Pensions were financed by flat-rate contribution (paid by employers and employees), and the flat-rate benefit was low: CHF 200 per year after age 65.

The bill, known as the *Schultess Bill*, after the Federal Councilor (FDP/PRD) responsible for pensions, was accepted by Parliament in June 1931 by a large majority (163 votes against 14 in the lower chamber; and 30 against 3 in the upper chamber). Despite broad parliamentary support, a referendum was launched, and 60.1 percent of voters rejected the pensions bill. A coalition of conservatives, anti-state liberals and clericalist-Catholics was behind the campaign to defeat the bill (Binswanger 1987: 21).

As a result, the proposals for a national pension scheme were shelved, and the Federal government continued to intervene in old-age policy by subsidizing voluntary organizations and cantons that provided financial support for poor elderly people. A similar development had occurred in the area of health care (Immergut 1992). At the same time, the gap in old-age provision provided room for the expansion of occupational pensions. In 1941 about 25 percent of employees had occupational pension coverage. This meant that a national pension scheme, when introduced, would have had to integrate existing occupational provision. The replacement of occupational by state pensions, in fact, was likely to be opposed by those who were already covered by an occupational pension. This explains the two-tiered character of the Swiss pension system (see pp. 220–3).

The pension issue emerged again at the end of World War II. By that time, a number of things had changed, which provided a more favorable context for the introduction of a national pension scheme. First, during the war, the government had introduced a system of compensation for lost earnings due to military service. Although Switzerland did not take part in the war, its army was permanently mobilized for the duration of the conflict. Those who were serving were entitled to income support through a scheme which resembled Bismarckian social insurance: while in-work employees paid contributions to the scheme (equally divided between themselves and their employer), and when serving in the army they were entitled to a benefit based on previous earnings and the number of dependants. The system was administered by a network of Cantonal and industry-based funds, known as compensation funds. The policy proved extremely popular among those who served. Those who favored the introduction of a pension scheme did not fail to spot an extremely favorable opportunity to reach their objective. The income replacement scheme could be converted into a pension scheme once the conflict was over.

Secondly, the experience of being surrounded by war strengthened social cohesion between social classes and between their political representatives. In 1943, for instance, the Socialists were invited for the first time to participate in government. This was a significant change in the political climate, which during the interwar period, had been characterized by confrontation between the left and the right, and by the exclusion of the left from executive power. As in other European countries (United Kingdom, France) the immediate post-war period provided a particularly favorable climate for the adoption of redistributive policies.

Work on a new pension bill started in 1944. It was clear that the existing system of compensation for lost earnings had to provide the basis for the new scheme. The compensation funds were to be used for the administration of the scheme. A bill was presented in parliament in 1946. Its main features were a universal pension scheme with earnings-related benefits and contributions, the latter being equally split between employers and employees. There was no contribution ceiling, whereas benefits varied between a 1 to 3 range (this was later reduced to 1 to 2). Parliament accepted the bill in December 1946. As on previous occasions, a referendum against the pension bill was called and the vote took place in 1947. Unlike in 1931, however, the pension bill was accepted by the electorate by an overwhelming majority of 80 percent. Turnout was also very high, at 80 percent.

In the following years, the basic pension was reformed several times (to date there have been 10 *revisions of the initial law*). Until the 1970s, reforms aimed at improving coverage and strengthening the finance of the scheme. An important expansionist reform was the adoption, in 1971, of a constitutional article establishing the principle of a three-pillar system with mandatory occupational coverage. The relevant legislation was not introduced until 1982 (in force since 1985) and will be discussed in more detail later.

Description of the current pension system

The Swiss pension system is best described as a three-pillar system (see Fig. 5.2 on 223. and in the Appendix, Table A5). The first pillar (*Alters- und Hinterlassenenversicherung/Assurance Vieillesse et Survivants*, AHV/AVS) covers the basic needs of retirees. It is moderately earnings-related and includes a means-tested pension supplement (*Prestations Complémentaires*, EL–PC). The second pillar provides retirees with a standard of living close to the one they experienced in employment and consists of mandatory occupational pensions. Finally, the third pillar allows people to tailor pension coverage to their individual needs, through non-compulsory personal pensions supported by tax-concessions. The functional division between three levels of pension provision is upheld by the federal Constitution, and is widely regarded as an important constraint to policy change in the area of pensions. Most pensioners receive income from a combination of these different pillars. On average, AHV/AVS contributes 60 percent of pensioners' income, and occupational pensions 22 percent (own calculations based on OFS 1998). The latter figure, however, will rise with occupational pension scheme maturation. In 2000, outlays of the basic pension accounted for 6.7 percent of GDP, and those of occupational pensions 7.5 percent of GDP (OFAS 2002).

The first pillar

The first pillar (AHV/AVS) provides universal coverage and is a fairly redistributive scheme because there is no contribution ceiling; but the amount of the benefit can vary between a floor and a ceiling that is twice as high as the floor. In 2005, the limits are set at CHF 1,075 and CHF 2,150 per month respectively, corresponding to approximately 20 percent and 40 percent of the average wage. Within these limits, the amount of the benefit is related to contributions paid during employment, with about a third of retirees receiving the maximum amount. Benefits are adjusted every two years according to a so-called "mixed index" derived from the arithmetic average between inflation and wage increases.

The scheme is universal, so that those who are not working (like students) are required to pay flat-rate contributions or, if providing informal care, are entitled to contribution credits. Unemployed people pay contributions based on their unemployment benefit, which is treated as a salary (the unemployment insurance fund contributes 4.2% of the unemployment benefit). In a way, the Swiss basic scheme is a compromise between the Bismarckian tradition of earnings-related contributory pensions and the Beveridgean flat-rate poverty prevention approach. Interestingly, in international comparisons the scheme is sometimes considered as a flat-rate pension scheme (Schmähl 1991: 48).

With regard to financing, the basic pension operates on a PAYG basis. As in Bismarckian systems, the AHV/AVS has a separate budget, and it has a fund roughly equal to one year's worth of outlays. The scheme is financed by contributions (4.2% of salary each for employees and employers; up to 7.8% for self employed), and receives a subsidy equal to 19 percent of outlays.[6] In addition, since 1999, one percentage point of VAT is assigned to AHV/AVS. The social partners participate in the management of the scheme by running some branch-related funds. The central fund, however, is managed by the federal administration. The rules governing entitlement, benefit and contribution levels are set by legislation. As a result, their modification can be subjected to a referendum challenge and must go through the lengthy law-making process.

The second pillar

The second pillar of the Swiss pension system, occupational pensions, were first granted tax concessions in 1916 and became compulsory in 1985 for all employees earning at least twice the minimum AHV/AVS pension.[7] In the 1990s, coverage was virtually universal among male employees but reached only about 80 percent of women (OFAS 1995: 10). A full occupational pension is granted to employees with a contribution record of 37 years for women and 40 for men (to be equalized over the next few years). When membership in an occupational pension scheme became compulsory, many employees were already covered by voluntary arrangements. Before the implementation of the new law, some 80 percent of employees already had access to occupational pension coverage. For a quarter of them, however, the level of provision was lower than the compulsory minimum introduced by the 1985 law (Conseil fédéral 2000b: 6). The situation was such that legislation needed to take into account the existence of a relatively developed system of occupational pension provision. As a result, it was decided to introduce a compulsory minimum level of provision (known as the *Obligatorium*) calculated on the basis of notional contributions,[8] leaving existing pension funds a relatively high level of autonomy over how to deliver and finance that minimum level of provision. Many pension funds (especially in the public sector, or those sponsored by large employers) still offer better conditions than the *Obligatorium* (Bonoli and Gay-des-Combes 2003; Vontobel 2000).

The objective of the new law was a combined (AHV/AVS + *Obligatorium*) replacement rate of 60 percent of gross earnings up to a ceiling equal to three times the maximum AHV/AVS benefit. For low wage workers, this goal could be achieved by the moderately earnings-related benefits provided by AHV/AVS. Those earning between one and three times the maximum AHV/AVS benefits (approx 40% and 120% of average earnings) were now guaranteed full coverage.

Minimum compulsory benefits are calculated on the basis of notional contributions. Depending on the employee's age, individual accounts must be credited with a percentage of insured earnings, ranging from 7 percent to 18 percent (rates are higher for older people). Pension funds are free to finance the specified amount as they wish, with the proviso that contributions must be split at least equally between workers and employers (the latter can contribute more than half of the contribution bill, if they so wish). For instance, a pension fund could decide to apply an age-neutral contribution rate of 12.5 percent, or alternatively to charge employees on the basis of their age, thus reflecting the pre-set notional contributions.[9] Because notional contribution rates are age-related, pension funds with an unfavorable demographic structure are disadvantaged. As a result, it was decided to introduce a demographic compensation mechanism whereby funds with more young employees subsidize those with a less favorable risk structure. Because of the way notional contributions are calculated and financed, the system is not a "pure" funded system but includes some intergenerational redistribution, or a PAYG element. The rationale for this was to guarantee adequate coverage to workers who were already employed before the 1985 law took effect and would not have a full contribution record. In theory, this PAYG element should disappear once, and if, every worker spends his/her whole working life in the system.

The occupational pension law also prescribes a government-set minimum nominal interest rate for second pillar pension funds. When the new law was introduced, this rate was 4 percent but was reduced to 3.25 percent in 2003 because of stock market losses. In 2004 the rate was further reduced to 2.25 percent, and for 2005 it has been set at 2.5 percent. The impact of these decisions depends on their duration. If limited in time, the effect will be negligible; otherwise, the 60 percent target replacement rate will be out of reach for many current workers.

When a worker reaches retirement age or takes early retirement (possible from the age of 62, but with an actuarially determined benefit reduction), the capital resulting from the notional contributions and the applicable minimum interest (compounded) is converted into a pension, on the basis of a conversion rate set by the government (currently 7.1%). The rate is used to convert the capital into an annual pension. There is no annuity market for (compulsory) occupational pensions, as the price of annuities is de facto determined by the government through the conversion rate which does not take into account sex-based differences in life expectancy. The result of this complex calculation represents the minimum occupational pension entitlement. In reality, many pension scheme members enjoy more favorable conditions than those guaranteed by the occupational pensions law. In 1996, for instance, about 29 percent of insured persons were covered by more generous defined-benefit plans, down from 33 percent in 1994 (OFS 1999).

The third pillar

The third pillar of the pension system, private provision, consists of payments made to personal pension schemes, supported by tax concessions. Employees who are already covered by an occupational pension can deduct contributions paid into a third-pillar pension from their taxable income, up to CHF 6,192 per year (in 2005). Tax concessions are more substantial for those not covered by an occupational pension, such as the self-employed, who can deduct up to 20 percent of their income. Personal pensions play a relatively small but fast-growing role in the Swiss pension system. The number of personal pensions doubled between 1995 and 2003 to approximately 2 million, but the assets held by third-pillar pension providers (banks and insurance companies) amounted to "only" CHF 30 billion in 1999, or 13 times less than those held by second pillar funds (OFAS 2004).

The Swiss pension system strongly resembles the structure recommended by international agencies like the World Bank. The origins of the present structure, however, go back to the late 1960s/early 1970s, long before the World Bank began to popularize the multi-pillar model. The adoption and implementation of the current arrangement in the mid-1980s was delayed by several obstacles, many originating in Switzerland's political institutions. The overall impact of the political system on the establishment of a multi-pillar pension system, however, has been bi-directional. The process that eventually lead to the adoption of a multi-pillar system was set off by initiatives sponsored by external, marginal groups, whose political influence was temporarily amplified by Switzerland's direct democracy institutions.

First pillar	Second pillar	Third pillar
Third tier: none	Additional occupational coverage (*überobligatorisch/ surobligatoire*)	Voluntary individual pension (no tax concession above ceiling)
Second tier: earnings-related part of pensions: none	Mandatory occupational pension (*BVG/LPP Obligatorium*): all employees earning CHF 19,350 per year or more —— Employees | Civil Servants | Self-employed	Voluntary individual pension: tax-subsidized (EET)
First tier: basic pension AHV/AVS: All residents aged 20 to 63—64 (partly earnings-related) EL–PC (means tested pension supplement) Social assistance		Mandatory private pension: none

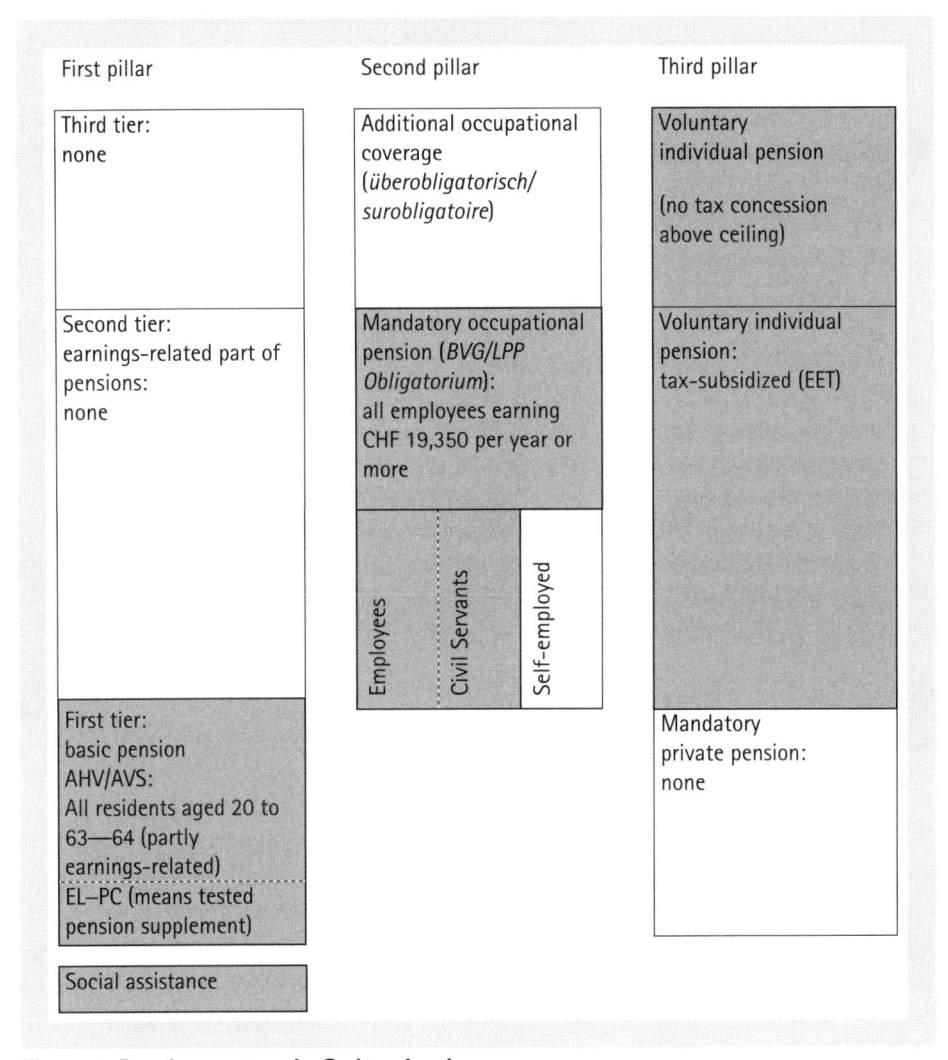

Fig. 5.2 Pension system in Switzerland

IV POLITICS OF PENSION REFORM SINCE 1980

Overview

The main changes in the Swiss pension system since 1980 have been the completion of the multi-pillar system. The 1982 Law on Occupational Pensions (BVG/LPP) adapted pensions to a changing social context; the 1995 basic pension reform (10th AHV/AVS revision) introduced gender equality and contribution credits for carers,

Table 5.3 Overview of proposed and enacted pension reforms in Switzerland

Year	Name of reform	Reform process (chronology)	Reform measures
1982	BVG–LPP	• 1966 popular initiative by unions for mandatory occupational pensions → unions withdrew their proposal • December 3, 1972 referendum on communist proposal (Bismarckian scheme) and government proposals (compulsory occupational pension) → gov. prevails • December 1975 submission of a bill to parliament • Fall 1977 passage of the bill in the *Nationalrat* • modification in the *Ständerat* • June 1982 passage of the bill in the *Nationalrat*	• coordination of basic and occupational pension: earnings insured by the basic pension are exempt from occupational pension coverage • notional contribution rates of 12.5% • pension funds had to set aside 1% of contributions to finance benefit improvements for older workers • no full indexation as envisioned in original proposal • no set-up of a central fund as envisioned in original proposal
1994	10th AHV/AVS Revision	• 1979 intention to introduce gender equality • 1982 commission draft to increase female pension age • 1990 pension reform bill • March 1991 passage of bill in *Ständerat* • April 1991 *Nationalrat* social security commission • March 1992 working group report • October 7, 1994 modified bill passed parliament • June 25, 1995 referendum → act accepted	• introduction of contribution-sharing and pension benefit-sharing • increase in female retirement age from 62 to 64
2003	11th AHV/AVS	• February 2, 2000 bill presented to parliament	• VAT increase for additional financing of basic pension

	Revision	• passage of the bill in *Nationalrat* with narrow majority • modifications in the *Ständerat* • October 3, 2003 agreement in conciliation committee; bill passes • socialists and trade unions announce referendum against the act • May 16, 2004 act is defeated in a referendum	• increase in female retirement age from 64 to 65 • abolition of widows' pension (with exceptions) • change in indexation timing • early retirement three years before standard retirement • no increase in self-employed contribution rate as envisioned in original proposal
2003	1st BVG/LPP Revision	• March 1, 2000 presentation of the proposal • April 2002 parliamentary debate • Social Security commission reduces threshold access • *Nationalrat* amends commission proposal • November 2002 *Ständerat* revoked the *Nationalrat* amendments • October 3, 2003 agreement between the two chambers; passage with large majorities	• reduction of the conversion rate from 7.2% to 6.8% • access threshold for compulsory occupational pensions lowered to CHF 18,990 • no increase in notional contribution rates as envisioned in original proposal

and later changes introduced some initial elements of retrenchment and adaptation to an aging society. Indeed, the 1995 basic pension reform represents an early reaction to demographic pressures because it increased women's retirement age. The 1st BVG/LPP revision, adopted in 2003, aimed explicitly at adapting the law on occupational pension to increasing life expectancy. This was done by lowering the conversion rate for the calculation of the *Obligatorium* from 7.2 percent to 6.8 percent. The reform also included a reduction in the access threshold to compulsory pension fund affiliation. Finally, the period under study also saw a failed attempt to adapt the basic pension to population aging. The 11th revision of the AHV/AVS, adopted by parliament in October 2003, included retrenchment measures (further increases in women's retirement age, cuts in widows' pensions, slower benefit adaptation, etc.) and extra financial resources, from VAT, but was rejected by voters in a referendum in May 2004.

The adoption of a law on occupational pensions 1982

The political origins of compulsory occupational pension coverage for employees date from the early 1960s. After World War II, Switzerland adopted a poverty prevention approach in pension policy. State intervention was not intended to provide income replacement to former workers, but was aimed at guaranteeing a minimum income level for everyone: hence the compressed benefit structure and universal character of the basic pension. The approach was similar to the one adopted by countries like the UK or Sweden, and can be considered Beveridgean in inspiration.

In all of these countries, the 1960s saw the emergence of new expectations among wage-earners concerning pension policy. Rapidly rising wages for blue-collar workers and the expansion of the middle classes made the original post-war settlement look increasingly inadequate. The security of a poverty-free retirement was to be supplemented by provisions guaranteeing retirees access to income levels allowing them to maintain their previous standard of living. The pressure on governments to include income replacement as a pension policy goal was exacerbated in all three countries by the existence of visible inequalities in pension coverage between those with access to occupational pension coverage, and those without. The issue, which in Britain became known as "superannuation," proved to be politically problematic in all three countries.

First, new legislation had to take into account the existence of a large number of pension funds that were popular with both employees and employers. This meant that politically, legislators were forced to develop a second pillar of pension provision in a way that permitted the survival of existing pension funds. This precluded a Bismarckian approach, where public schemes provide generous earnings-related benefits to all workers. Second, policy-makers had to overcome employers' resistance to compulsory occupational pension coverage. Employers have traditionally been willing to provide this kind of fringe benefit to highly-valued staff, but have always resented the imposition of rules that generate higher labor costs for low-skilled employees.

As a result, the expansion of second-pillar pensions remained a key political issue throughout the 1960s and the 1970s in countries which had initiated pension policy with a Beveridgean approach. Sweden was the first to settle the issue, with the introduction of the ATP scheme in 1959, which replaced existing pension funds. In Britain, the extension of second-pillar pension coverage had to wait until 1978 when the State Earnings Related Pension Scheme (SERPS) was introduced for workers without occupational pension coverage. In Switzerland, the settlement of the "superannuation" issue took somewhat longer, but, interestingly, the solutions adopted both by Britain and Sweden featured in the Swiss debate. Policy took a different course, however.

The first important step in establishing mandatory occupational pensions was a popular initiative sponsored by the Federation of Christian Unions in 1966, which, if approved in a referendum, would have required the government to make occupational pensions mandatory. The government was skeptical, however. In its official bulletin, the government argued that making occupational pensions compulsory would have been "extremely difficult, both legally and practically." In addition, the government maintained that such a measure was unnecessary, since voluntary occupational pension coverage had expanded rapidly in the previous two decades (FF 1968 I, 1: 682). In parallel, and possibly in partial response to the Christian unions' initiative, the government adopted a reform of the basic pension, which led to a 30 percent benefit increase. The unions were satisfied and withdrew their popular initiative before the referendum took place.

Things were to change in the following years. By the late 1960s/early 1970s the pension issue had regained momentum, and the left-wing parties were busy making policy proposals. Socialist Party policy at the time favored the Swedish solution, with the introduction of an ATP-style second-pillar pension, and a gradual abandonment of existing pension funds. The unions opposed this solution, however, and it was soon dropped (Binswanger 1987: 208–9). At the same time, the Communist Party, a marginal but vociferous actor, collected the 100,000 signatures needed for a popular initiative that would have changed the basic pension benefit structure in a Bismarckian direction. According to the proposal, AHV/AVS was to pay benefits equal to 60 percent of personal average gross earnings during the best five years.

A few months later, the Socialist Party also managed to obtain sufficient support for a popular initiative which essentially proposed the British solution to the superannuation problem: a state second pension with earnings-related benefits. Workers covered by occupational pensions, however, would be allowed to contract out of the state scheme and stay with their employer-sponsored plans. At the time, the saliency of the superannuation issue and the political climate by no means ruled out a successful referendum outcome for these two initiatives. As a result, the right-of-center parties joined forces in a third popular initiative that proposed a solution to the superannuation issue that was more acceptable to employers: making occupational pensions compulsory.

Faced with three different policy proposals that had a common goal, the government instructed an expert commission (AHV/AVS Federal Commission) to formulate a compromise. Rather than finding a compromise, however, the expert commission's work resulted in support for the proposal made by the right-of-center parties (with some minor changes): no direct state intervention as a provider of second-pillar pensions, but mandatory occupational coverage for all employees. This solution satisfied the Socialists, who withdrew their initiative, but not the Communists, who maintained theirs.

The government accepted the expert commission's reform plan and turned it into a proposal for constitutional change, automatically subject to a referendum. The proposal included mandatory occupational pension coverage for employees, but in the documentation accompanying the proposal (*Botschaft/Message*) there was no mention of the government's earlier opposition to mandating occupational pensions. The introduction of compulsory occupational pension coverage was justified on the basis of the large consensus that there seemed to be on this policy option (FF 1971 II, 2: 1624).

In the following year, on December 3, 1972, Swiss voters were asked in a national referendum to choose between the government-backed proposal and the Bismarckian scheme favored by the Communist Party. The outcome was unequivocal. The Communists' initiative was rejected by 83 percent of voters, whereas the government solution was accepted by a large majority (73%). The principle of compulsory occupational pensions was now enshrined in the federal Constitution: "the federal government requires employers to insure their staff with a pension fund... [and] establishes the minimal requirements that must be satisfied by such pension funds" (Swiss Constitution of 1874, Art. 34 as amended in 1971 [author's translation]). Under the pressure of more interventionist and radical solutions to the superannuation problem, key political actors, including employers' associations, agreed to mandatory occupational pension coverage. The details of how to achieve this goal, however, still needed to be worked out, and the process would prove to be difficult.

An occupational pensions bill embodying the spirit of the present legislation was submitted to parliament in December 1975. For example, the bill provided for a compulsory minimum, but allowed funds that offered better benefits to maintain them. The bill coordinated occupational and basic pension provision by exempting earnings insured by the basic pension from occupational pension coverage. The bill also contained the idea of notional contributions, although these were to be used only to calculate the transfer value of the pension, or to calculate benefits in defined contribution schemes. The bill allowed funds to decide whether to provide defined-benefit or defined-contribution benefits, and imposed different minimal conditions depending on the option chosen. In defined-benefit schemes, the benefit needed to equal at least 40 percent of average insured earnings over the three years prior to retirement. In defined-contribution schemes, the minimum requirements were based on notional contributions and a minimum interest rate. Like the present system, notional contributions were age-related, but set at a higher average rate.

In addition, the government would set up a central fund, jointly financed by pension schemes, to provide the funds needed to supplement the pensions for middle-aged workers who would not have enough time to accumulate capital sufficient to finance the prescribed benefits. This central fund would also finance the indexation of pensions after retirement. Funds for each task were to be provided by occupational schemes on a PAYG basis. Contribution rates earmarked for the central funds in order to offer older workers better retirement conditions were expected to increase gradually and peak in 1996 at 4.13 percent of insured earnings. The rate needed to finance inflation-proofing of pensions was expected to reach 2.5 percent of insured earnings by the year 2000 (FF 1976 I, 299–302).

The proposal was accepted with minor changes in the lower chamber, the National Council, and was subsequently debated in the more conservative Council of States. There, substantial criticism was expressed of what were perceived to be excessive levels of guaranteed benefits. In addition, a majority of right wing MPs attacked the introduction of a central fund because it would be too costly for employers (Pfitzmann-Boulaz 1981). As a result, the bill was substantially modified in the upper chamber. First, the minimum requirement (*Obligatorium*) would be established only on a notional defined-contribution basis. Funds providing defined-benefit pensions were subjected to the same minimum requirements as defined-contribution funds. Second, notional contribution rates were reduced from a career average of 14.625 percent of insured earnings to 12.5 percent. Finally, the revised bill did not include plans to establish a central fund, or to provide full benefit indexation. Older workers, who would be unable to accumulate sufficient capital to finance a full pension, were to be favored by the age-related structure of notional contributions. In addition, pension funds were required to set aside 1 percent of all contributions to finance measures to improve the benefits of older workers. Indexation was to be provided at the discretion of individual funds (BOAF CdE 1980: 241–301).

The National Council accepted the Upper Chamber's amendments with minor changes. Even though many, especially on the left, felt the new version of the Occupational Pensions Bill did not provide sufficient income protection for many workers, it was decided that it was not in their interest to further delay the adoption of this long awaited piece of legislation. In addition, there was a general agreement that the law did not completely fulfill the constitutional mandate, but that it was a first step towards a more generous occupational pension system such as the one put advocated by the Federal government in its 1975 bill. The law finally passed in June 1982. Despite these criticisms, there were no attempts to challenge the pension law with a referendum, and the new legislation took effect on January 1, 1985.

Of the Western European countries that were confronted by the superannuation problem in the 1960s, Switzerland was the only one to introduce mandatory occupational pensions. It is also one of very few OECD countries to have adopted this approach to pensions. The idea of mandating occupational pensions did of course surface in other countries, but was generally opposed by employers. Its adoption in a country like Switzerland, where employers are extremely influential political actors, is thus particularly striking, and can only be understood with reference to the country's peculiar political institutions, especially the popular initiative. It is very difficult to imagine that the government U-turn on mandatory pensions that took place between 1968 and 1971 would have occurred in the absence of the pressure exerted by the popular initiatives of the Communist and Socialist parties.

The 10th AHV/AVS Revision

The 10th AHV/AVS revision is a good example of the shift in the direction of social policy-making since the early 1990s, as well as Swiss political mechanisms for dealing with obstacles to policy change represented by institutional power fragmentation. Work on this reform started in 1979, with the intention of introducing gender equality in the basic pension scheme. The Federal government had asked the Federal Commission for the AHV/AVS to draft a reform proposal designed to improve the situation of women and eliminate discriminatory rules concerning contributions and benefit calculations. Previously the contribution record of married women was generally not taken into account in the calculation of the benefit. Instead, their husbands received a supplement in the shape of a couple pension.

The AHV/AVS Federal Commission drafted a reform proposal in 1982, which included some minor improvements for women. However, since the government had requested the reform to be cost-neutral, these measures had to be financed by an increase in women's retirement age from 62 to 63. The reaction to these proposals was lukewarm, and even within the Commission there was controversy about raising women's retirement age. The proposal was eventually dropped. According to Binswanger (1987: 250), it was the combination of cost-neutrality and the need to reach consensus that prevented the Commission from producing a more satisfactory proposal.

Towards the end of the 1980s, after Flavio Cotti (Christian Democrat) took office as Interior Minister,[10] the government decided to abandon the cost-neutrality requirement. In March 1990, the Federal Council was finally able to produce a bill for the reform of the AHV/AVS pension scheme (FF 1990II: 1–231). The centerpiece of the bill was the introduction of formal gender equality without abandoning couples' pensions. The bill provided for the removal of any reference to gender in the pension formula, but did not take any proactive action in favor of women (such as contribution credits or sharing between spouses) as was advocated by various actors. A few years earlier, a number of organizations and political parties had published reports in which they argued in favor of a system of individual pensions, granted regardless of gender and marital status, complemented by a contribution-sharing system between spouses. By the time the bill came to parliament, there was a relatively large consensus, most notably among the two largest parties (the Socialists and the Free Democrats) for a more proactive approach in this field.

Because it maintained couples' pensions, the 1990 Pension Reform Bill was seen by many with disappointment, especially by women's organizations and by women MPs in the Socialist and Liberal Democratic parties. The bill was nevertheless adopted by the Upper Chamber of Parliament in March 1991. According to the standard procedure, it was subsequently examined by the Social Security Committee of the Lower Chamber in April 1991. Some members of the Committee were unsatisfied with the bill, as it did not include provision for individual pensions regardless of marital status nor contribution-sharing between spouses. As a result, the Commission requested the Federal Office for Social Insurance (OFAS) to produce a report which would explore the technical issues involved in a contribution-sharing system. The report was to be based on the three proposals made by the Federal Commission for Women's issues (CFQF 1988), by the FDP/PRD (1988) and by the Socialist Party jointly with the unions (PSS/USS 1987). The report was followed by a working group with the task to elaborate a viable proposal for the introduction of a contribution-sharing system. The working group included MPs of the main political parties and convened seven times. It produced a final report that was published in March 1992 (*Groupe de travail "Splitting"* 1992).

By 1993, the bill had been significantly modified by parliament, precisely by adopting the measures suggested in the report published by the working group "Splitting." The bill, as amended by parliament, included the introduction of a contribution-sharing system between spouses and contribution credits for informal carers. Together with these measures, on which there was a relatively strong consensus, the new version of the bill also included the more controversial measure of raising the retirement age for women from 62 to 64 (men's retirement age is 65). This was imposed by the right-of-center parliamentary majority, against the Socialists, allegedly in order to comply with the constitutional requirement of gender equality as well as to achieve some savings in view of the predicted worsening of the ratio between pension scheme contributors and beneficiaries over the next few decades.

Outside parliament, the trade unions and some women's organizations attacked the proposed increase in women's retirement age and collected the 50,000 signatures needed to call a referendum. The referendum on the pension bill was held in June 1995. The decision to call a referendum was taken jointly by the main federation of Swiss Unions (SGB/USS) and by the Christian unions (CNG/CSC). For the SGB/USS, the increased retirement age for women was unacceptable. Indeed, the SGB/USS advocated a lower retirement age and had previously (with the SPS/PSS) collected signatures for an initiative which proposed, among other things, the introduction of a flexible retirement age for men and women between 62 and 65 with full benefits as long as retirees stopped working.[11] Thus it was not conceivable for the unions to accept an increase in women's retirement age. On the other hand, however, if the bill was to be defeated in a referendum, the improvements in the provision for women would have had to be rejected, and these had been long advocated by the unions. To avoid this dilemma, the SGB/USS and the CNG/CSC decided to collect the 50,000 signatures needed to call a referendum, but at the same time, to call a second referendum (initiative) with the aim of introducing, after the possible defeat of the pension bill in the referendum, what they regarded as the "good" elements of the 1995 pension reform, namely, contribution-sharing and credits.

The Socialist Party leadership faced a similar dilemma. They also opposed increasing the retirement age for women, but this was not the point any longer, since the referendum concerned the whole bill. As a result, the party was divided about whether the good elements of the reform outweighed the bad ones, or vice versa (PSS 1995). The SPS/PSS's dilemma was further complicated by the fact that the minister responsible for social security was now Ruth Dreyfuss, a Socialist, who had to comply with the majority view of the government, which favored the reform. Her own opinion on the issue was the following:

> It is most unfortunate that the issue of increasing women's retirement age has been tied to the improvements of the pension reform... I keep on thinking that this measure was not needed in this reform. Nevertheless, my support for the reform is based on a conviction that the positive elements of the reform outweigh the negative ones. (Dreyfuss, in TSR 1995 [author's translation])

The Socialist Party leadership decided to deal with the dilemma by consulting party members. Some 30 percent of members participated in a ballot, of whom 66 percent supported the reform (*Sécurité sociale* 2/1995: 59). On the basis of this result, the official recommendation of the SPS/PSS was to accept the 1995 Pension Reform.

For other parties and organizations, the decision about whether to support the referendum was more straightforward. All the other large parties had supported the reform in Parliament. Similarly, the main employers' associations favored the new pension bill. Women's organizations were divided, with more left-wing groups opposing the bill and their right-wing counterparts supporting the pension bill. The overall picture before the referendum was one in which the unions were largely alone in opposing the pension bill. Nevertheless, there was some concern among federal authorities that the bill could be defeated in the referendum. It was feared that conservative-Catholic voters might join the unions in rejecting the proposal, as the conception of the family on which the new law was based did not reflect traditional views on gender roles. Concern for the outcome of the referendum was also reflected by the important campaign launched by the Federal Office of Social Insurance through its periodical *Sécurité sociale*. Almost half of the 2/1995 issue addressed the pension reform, and included articles by Ruth Dreyfuss and Walter Seiler, then director of the office, in support of the bill. The vote took place on June 25, 1995. The turnout was 40.4 percent, which is fairly typical, and the result was a clear majority in favor of the bill (60.7%). There were cantonal variations though, as the bill was accepted in all German-speaking cantons but was rejected in four out of six French-speaking cantons and in the Italian-speaking canton. According to an opinion poll immediately after the vote, the best predictor of voters' behavior was not language but party preference. Among those who said they supported one of the three right-wing government parties (FDP/PRD, CVP/PDC and SVP/UDC), the proportion of "yes"-voters was 10 percentage points higher than the average (Vox 1995).

The same survey also asked voters why they voted as they did. The main division in the electorate was between those who believed that the positive aspects outweighed the negative ones on the "yes" side, and those who believed the opposite on the "no" side. A clear majority of "yes"-voters mentioned the expansive elements of the bill (e.g. contribution credits). According to the poll, not more than a quarter of voters would have supported the bill without these improvements. The bill would have encountered stronger opposition if it had not included elements which were widely regarded as improvements. Conversely, among "no" voters, the main reason for opposing the bill was, overwhelmingly, the increase in women's retirement age (59%, Vox 1995).

Survey data suggests that an increase in women's retirement age adopted independently of the improvements in the bill would have been at a much higher risk of being defeated in a referendum. Thus the bill's only element that involved retrenchment was possible only because it was combined with a series of improvements. This conclusion must be taken carefully, however, because of uncertainty about respondents' motives. Voters might have followed the recommendation of their party or reference group and subsequently rationalized their choice by backing it up with a plausible argument. However, the fact that (always according to the same opinion polls) some 30 percent of voters who said they identified with one of the three right-wing government parties voted against the bill, supports the hypothesis that an increase in women's retirement age would not have been accepted if it were not accompanied by improvements.

The 11th AHV/AVS Revision

Work on the 11th AHV/AVS revision had started before the adoption of the previous reform, the 10th AHV/AVS revision, was secured. Initially, the reform had two main objectives: to guarantee the solvency of the scheme until 2010–15, and to introduce more flexibility in the transition from work to retirement. The latter goal would be achieved by early-retirement, part-time pensions or delayed retirement, a set of measures that became known in Switzerland as *retraite à la carte*. These two objectives were to be pursued by a mix of expansion and retrenchment measures, in a way that very much reflected the result of the 10th revision, suggesting that the Federal administration now recognized the political robustness of such compromises.

A bill for the 11th AHV/AVS revision was presented in parliament on February 2, 2000 (*Conseil Fédéral* 2000a). The bill contained a catalogue of measures aimed at increasing revenues and containing expenditure. The most important element was the two-step increase in the VAT rate to bring additional revenue to the basic pension. The standard VAT rate was to be increased by 0.5 percentage points in 2003 and by 1 point in 2006 (approximately). The extra funds would be transferred to the basic pension scheme. The rest of the bill was a list of minor measures that either reduce outlays or increase receipts. These included the abolition of widows' pensions except for parents with at least one child younger than 18 (and some other cases); the change in the timing of benefit indexation from every two to every three years; the increase from 7.8 percent to 8.1 percent for the maximum contribution rate for the self-employed; a further increase in women's retirement age from 64 to 65; and the abolition of an AHV/AVS-contribution-free portion of income to which employed AHV/AVS beneficiaries were entitled.

Besides these measures, the bill presented in 2000 provided for a more flexible transition from work to retirement. Early retirement was to be made possible at the earliest three years before the standard retirement age, with favorable rules for low income earners. For example, low income earners would face a benefit reduction of 6.6 percent for retiring three years early. This reduction would then increase gradually for higher incomes up to the ceiling of 16.8 percent for someone with lifetime earnings exceeding CHF 72,360 per year, a reduction that would still be lower than the actuarially determined rate (18.6%). *Retraite à la carte* also included the chance to take part-time retirement as early as six years before the standard age of retirement, with more favorable conditions offered to low earners.

The reform aimed to guarantee the solvency of the basic pension until 2010. The task was facilitated by a previously adopted measure that increased the VAT by one percentage point (since 1999) and earmarked the revenue for the AHV/AVS pension scheme. After 2010, further measures will arguably be needed in order to guarantee the solvency of the scheme, because the proportion of the population over 65 is expected to continue to increase from the projected level of 17.5 percent for 2010 to 25 percent in 2040. This was to be the task of the 12th AHV/AVS Revision.

The reform bill presented in February 2000 contained many features that are typical of Swiss compromises. In particular, the bill included both savings measures and expansive elements (extra financial resources and improvements in provision). In the past, reforms that combined these two types of measures have been more successful in gaining the necessary support, both in parliament and in referendums (Bonoli 1999). As on other occasions, however, this carefully crafted compromise was to be overhauled by parliament.

The bill was first debated in the National Council. First the Social Security Committee and then the Council as a whole seemed to be strongly divided on a number of issues, essentially the abolition of widows' pensions and subsidized early retirement. In the end, the bill was accepted with some modifications. (1) The increase in the maximum contribution rate for the self-employed was abandoned; (2) widows' pensions were to be maintained for all women who have had children, regardless of their age. The government's proposal regarding early retirement remained unchanged.[12] However, most parliamentary groups expressed their dissatisfaction with the modified bill: according to the Left, subsidies for early retirement for low-income workers, at CHF 400 million per year, were insufficient, while the Right opposed the idea of subsidizing early retirement. A majority in the Council accepted the VAT increase. In the final vote, the reform was adopted by a very narrow margin: 62 votes in favor; 60 against and 63 abstentions. The Christian Democrats were the main supporters of the bill, the majority of the SVP/UDC and of the Free Democrats abstained, and the left rejected it.

The bill was then transferred to the Council of States in November 2002 and modified again. The National Council's decision to keep widows' pensions for all women with children was maintained, but the level of their pensions was to be lowered from 80 percent to 60 percent of a full pension. Most important, the Upper Chamber eliminated the subsidies for early retirement for low-income workers. Early retirement was thus to be compensated by actuarially determined benefit reductions. In addition, the VAT was not to be increased in order to bring additional finance to the pension scheme. The bill was accepted by all parties represented in the Council of States except the Socialists.

The bill was then sent back and forth between the two chambers in order to find a compromise. This was achieved only in October 2003 by a conciliation committee including members of both chambers. In the final version of the bill, adopted on October 3, 2003 in both chambers, early retirement was to be subsidized, but only for a limited period and only for women born between 1948 and 1952, at a cost of CHF 140 million. The VAT would increase, but only by 1 percent instead of the initially planned 1.5 percent. In the final vote in the lower chamber, the bill was accepted by 109 against 73 votes. The Free Democrats and SVP/UDC supported the bill, the Christian-Democrats were divided but mostly supported the bill, and the Socialists opposed it. A few days after the vote the Socialists announced they would challenge the bill in a referendum. They were quickly joined by the unions.

The vote on the 11th AHV/AVS revision was May 16, 2004, and was characterized by a clear Left–Right confrontation: all center-right parties and employers favored the bill, while the unions and the Left opposed it. For the first time an AHV/AVS revision was defeated in a referendum, by a staggering 68 percent of voters. In a way, the 11th AHV/AVS revision provided the counterfactual to the argument made concerning the previous reform (the 10th AHV/AVS revision). This time, the combination of retrenchment and expansion measures was undone by parliament, leaving only the cuts in the final version of the bill. This proved fatal to the bill's chances of referendum success. Voters with a Socialist identification rejected the bill (83% of them voted against) but so did SVP/UDC voters (59%) and Christian-Democrats (56%). Women, the main losers of the reform, were also more likely than men to oppose the bill (Vox 2004). After the May 2004 vote, it became clear that a unilateral pension policy strategy based on retrenchment is not feasible in Switzerland because of the country's direct democratic institutions.

The 1st BVG/LPP Revision

The original objective of the 1st BVG/LPP revision was to adapt the law on occupational pensions to increasing life expectancy and to improve coverage of atypical workers, especially part-time employees. Because of the access threshold to compulsory affiliation for second-pillar pensions, many part-time workers, mostly women with children, were excluded from compulsory occupational pension coverage. In a consultation procedure organized before the preparation for the bill, the idea of lowering or abolishing the access threshold to compulsory coverage (an option favored at the time by the unions and by the Socialists) was firmly rejected by employers. The government's assessment of the consultation procedure was that there was insufficient support for this particular measure so it was not included in the first version of the reform bill.

The bill was presented in Parliament on March 1, 2000. The bill dealt mostly with the issue of adapting the calculation method used by the minimum compulsory occupational pension (*Obligatorium*) to rising life expectancy. The reform's most important element was thus a reduction in the rate used for converting accumulated capital into an annuity. Because of longer life expectancy, the rate of 7.2 percent established in the early 1980s could no longer be sustained. As a result, the bill called for gradually reducing the conversion rate to 6.65 percent in 2016. In order to avoid benefit reductions, the notional contribution rates for determining the amount of capital available to employees were to be gradually increased. The result was expected to be neutral in terms of pension benefits, but during the transition period some male employees were expected to face a slight benefit reduction. Because the contribution rates to be increased are notional rates, this measure would not necessarily have resulted in higher actual contributions. Some pension schemes which achieved higher than expected returns on capital in recent years could have used these extra funds to finance higher notional contribution rates.

The main criticism against the government proposal was that it did not improve pension coverage for low paid, atypical, mainly part-time workers. The National Council discussed the bill in April 2002, and the Social Security Committee, which had examined the bill before, supported a modified version that included reducing the access threshold to compulsory occupational pension coverage by one half (from CHF 24,000 to CHF 12,000 p.a. approximately). The party composition of the Social Security Committee of the National Council reflects that of the Council as a whole. However, possibly because of self-selection, its members from center-right parties tend to have a more pro-welfare orientation, and the Committee often takes positions that are more expansionist than those defended by the government and by the National Council as a whole. It is thus not surprising that a majority in the Council rejected the Committee's proposal, but a more moderate reduction of the access threshold (to CHF 18,000 per year) obtained a fair majority (132 votes against 38), including the left, a majority of Christian-Democrats and Free Democrats and some SVP/UDC members. A further modification of the bill included a distinction between the access threshold and the amount of non-insured earnings. In the previous system these two parameters coincided, but in the modified version of the bill, non-insured earnings were to be defined as 40 percent of total earnings.[13] This solution was more favorable to part-time workers who would now see a larger proportion of their earnings insured. Finally, the reduction of the conversion rate was somewhat moderated: instead of 6.65 percent the new rate would be set at 6.8 percent. The effect of this reduction on benefits was expected to be compensated by the extension of insured earnings. As a result, the increase in notional contributions became unnecessary and was dropped.

In the spring of 2002, the National Council took an unusually pro-welfare line in the previously described pension reform but also on other issues (most notably subsidies for child-care centers). Clear majorities of two center-right parties, the

Christian-Democrats and the Free Democrats, supported these expansionist measures, and together with the Socialists they were able to push them through rather easily. This pro-welfare attitude of center-right MPs can probably be explained with reference to the overall encouraging economic and financial conditions at the time. Even though Switzerland was entering a recession, public finances were still reaping the delayed benefits of the late 1998–2000 boom. This situation would soon change.

The bill was transferred to the upper house and was debated in November 2002. By now, the economic outlook and the outlook for public finances had worsened, and the Council of States' Social Security Committee declared its intention to reverse the decision to lower the access threshold for compulsory occupational pension coverage and the amount of non-insured earnings. The Council accepted the Committee's proposals and the bill was returned to its original form, also with regard to the conversion rate and increased notional contribution rates. This time, center-right MPs voted consistently against improving provision for low-income and part-time workers.

As with the 11th AHV/AVS revision, the BVG/LPP bill went back and forth between the two chambers until October 2003 when majorities in both chambers agreed to a proposal that did include lower income workers in occupational pensions, but in a somewhat less generous way than in the proposal accepted by the National Council in spring 2002. The access threshold would be lowered to CHF 18,990 per year, and the amount of non-insured earnings to about CHF 22,155 per year. The conversion rate would be lowered to 6.8 percent and notional contributions would not increase. Given the more moderate increase in insured earnings than in the previous proposals, the reduction in the contribution rate will result in pension losses, especially for the transition generation for whom the new conversion rate will be applied, but who will not have sufficient contribution years with the higher insured earnings to compensate for the reduction.

Both chambers strongly supported this carefully crafted compromise. The Council of States accepted the bill unanimously, and in the National Council the bill received the approval of all political groups except a majority of SVP/UDC MPs. Similarly to the 10th AHV/AVS revision, the 1st BVG/LPP revision contained elements of both retrenchment and expansion. It was a strong compromise, since both the Left and Right had something to be satisfied with in the new law. The bill was not challenged by a referendum, which is rather unusual for an important social policy reform.

The stock market crisis of the early 2000s and occupational pensions

The difficult search for consensus on the 1st BVG/LPP was complicated by the stock market downturn in the early 2000s. The first casualty of this development in the Swiss pension system was the government mandated minimum interest rate. Since the adoption of the Occupational Pensions Law, this rate had been set at 4 percent (nominal). Even though it technically applies only to the notional contributions, the rate is often used as a benchmark by pension funds in attributing actual revenues in pension accounts. This benchmark was often exceeded in the 1990s, thanks to good stock market performance. As a result, branch- or company-based large pension funds had some room for maneuver when share prices started to fall. Since the 4 percent minimum interest is applied to the entire career, a few bad years can be compensated by good years.

The situation is different for employers who have contracted coverage with an insurance company or financial institution (usually smaller employers). Because of different legal regulations, the 4 percent minimum interest rate must be applied every year, which seemed unrealistic in the early 2000s. After intense lobbying by the insurance industry, a crucial sector in the Swiss economy which experienced dramatic losses in these years, the government reduced the rate first to 3 percent, and after a vehement reaction by the left and the trade unions, to 3.25 percent from 2003 onwards. The rate was subsequently reduced to 2.25 percent for 2004, and this time there was surprisingly less outcry, possibly because the unions (and the pension policy community) focused on developing an automatic rule for determining the minimum interest rate. In this case, the use of a referendum against the government's decision was not possible because according to the occupational pensions law the government can set the minimum interest rate by decree, without parliamentary involvement, and only acts passed by parliament can be challenged in a referendum

The impact of the change in the minimum interest rate on pension entitlements will depend on many factors. The most important factor is the number of years during which the lower minimum interest rate remains in force. For a complete career (40 years) the reduction in the minimum interest rate from 4 percent to 3.25 percent adopted in 2003 would result in a decrease of the pension benefit of around 10 percent. If the period is shorter, the reduction is lower. The impact of this decision will also depend on the decisions taken by individual pension funds, which may decide not to reduce their rates. If returns to capital are insufficient to achieve this, they can increase contributions rates.

The problem has been compounded by the disclosure made in early 2003 by the Federal Commission supervising the solvency of occupational pension schemes that about half of schemes failed to meet minimum funding regulations. The Ministry of Social Affairs has issued guidelines on how to restore compliance. The measures available to funds include increasing contributions and reducing benefits by freezing pensions rather than cutting nominal benefits.

The trade unions seem to favor a case by case approach to this problem. In fact, it seems that many of the schemes that are currently in breach of the minimum funding rules are those that in the late 1990s enjoyed contribution reductions, or even "contribution holidays." Under these circumstances, contribution increases are in their view justified. Even more problematic from the unions' perspective is the situation of pension funds managed by commercial insurance companies. In this case, the unions claim, the fabulous gains of the 1990s have neither resulted in contribution reductions nor in higher returns on scheme members' capital. The suspicion is that some of the gains have been swallowed by administrative expenses and fat profits. In these cases, the unions demand more transparency before agreeing to contribution increases. The improvement in stock market performance in 2003 has somewhat reduced the pressure on funds, as many have managed to re-build sufficient reserves.

In contrast to the larger reforms, decisions concerning the minimum interest rate and compliance with occupational pensions funding rules have generated little political debate and controversy. This is surprising because the potential effect of these decisions on benefits may be as large as, or even greater than that of higher profile reform initiatives. Three factors help explain why this has been the case. First, these are technical issues, the consequences of which are not entirely clear for many insured people. Second, it became widely accepted that pension fund losses required extra measures, either in the form of lower future benefits or higher current contributions. As a result, this was not a classical distributional issue with winners and losers, but simply a question of how and when the losers were going to pay. Finally, the fact that the relevant decisions did not require an act of parliament made it possible for the government to somewhat protect itself and the funds from public pressures. The government is not directly elected by voters and as a result is under less pressure to avoid unpopular policies than parliament.

V Conclusion

The recent history of pension policy in Switzerland has seen both success and failure. Switzerland has been successful in constructing a pension system that protects pensioners against poverty, guarantees a reasonable replacement income to the middle-classes, and is financially sustainable. Switzerland has also succeded in reforming the system several times, combining retrenchment and expansion measures. But there has been failure too. For the first time since the introduction of the basic pension scheme, in May 2004 a government-sponsored reform (the 11th AHV/AVS revision) was rejected by voters in a referendum.

These recent developments confirm the view that, given the country's political institutions, the only possible way to reform the Swiss welfare state is by combining retrenchment measures with improvements in provision (Bonoli 1999; Bonoli and Mach 2000; Bonoli 2001; Obinger 1999). A large scale, high visibility, social policy reform must be supported by at least the Socialists and the center-right if it is to survive a referendum challenge. This obviously creates strong pressures for compromise and for the inclusion of expansive elements in otherwise retrenchment-oriented reforms. Sometimes politicians of the center-right seem to forget this requirement of social policy-making in Switzerland and attempt to impose their preferences in a majoritarian way. Generally, however, voters reject such policies. Referendums, and more generally political institutions, are clearly the key to understanding developments in pension policy in Switzerland.

Summary of the magnitude of changes

The four reforms discussed in this chapter represent significant developments in pension policy, but they certainly differ in importance. The 1982 reform that introduced compulsory occupational pensions is by far the most important act discussed here because it shaped the Swiss pension system for decades. The significance of this legislation is further highlighted by international comparisons. The issue of obligatory occupational pension coverage arose in other countries but resulted in a political decision in very few cases. In Britain, for instance, the proposal makes it into the pension policy debate every now and then, but so far employers have successfully opposed such moves. The fact that this measure has been adopted in Switzerland, a country where employers are influential political actors can only be explained with reference to the country's particular political institutions.

A second important reform was the AHV/AVS 10th revision, which had a fundamental impact on provision for married women. Married women now profit from the contributions made by their husbands. The introduction of gender equality in pensions represents a profound change, especially in a country like Switzerland where advances in women's rights have been particularly slow.

Finally, the 1st BVG/LPP revision made some first-order changes in Peter Hall's (1993) terminology. Some of the settings of the system have been changed, with relatively moderate consequences. However, if the changes in the BVG/LPP are considered together with other changes, such as the possible temporary reduction from 4 percent to 2.25 percent–2.5 percent of the minimum interest rate for second-pillar pensions, then the impact may be more substantial. Together, these changes may result in some cohort's receiving pensions well below the constitutionally mandated 60 percent replacement rate.

Interest group influence

The reforms discussed in this chapter originated from the initiatives of party-political actors, the government most of the time and, on one occasion, of the Communist Party. Nonetheless interest groups played an important role in determining the current shape of the pension system, mainly because the extensive consultation procedures that provide the basis of government legislative proposals, interest group views are very influential. The law on occupational pensions, for example, was approved only ten years after the adoption of the constitutional article on compulsory second-pillar pensions. Much of the time that elapsed was needed to find solutions that would be acceptable for employers. Employers, and the unions, also directly influence policy through their presence in political representative bodies. Trade union leaders and representatives of employers' associations sit in parliament. Because being a member of parliament is a part-time job in Switzerland, these politicians remain employees of the relevant organizations, and openly defend their interests in parliament. In sum, even when decisions are taken by political actors, in Switzerland the influence of organized interest groups is strong.

More generally, interest groups play an important role during the whole policy-making process. Through their representatives in parliament, but also by reacting to developments made public by the relevant institutions, interest groups constantly signal their approval or disapproval of the measures that are being taken. Disapproval can be reinforced by a threat to call a referendum if the course of policy is not changed. Typically this happens several times in the preparation of a pension reform.

The referendum threat is used more frequently by the Left and by the unions. This is partly because the political composition of parliament means that the demands of the Left are often overruled. Other interest groups, essentially employers and the insurance industry, which play an important role in the provision of second- and third-pillar pensions, also have other threat means at their disposal. Employers typically emphasize the consequences on employment of, for example, contribution increases. The insurance industry sometimes threatens the use of the exit option, arguing that if a given measure is adopted, it may withdraw from the provision of occupational/private pensions. This threat has been used to obtain the reduction of the conversion rate needed to adapt to population aging (Müller 2003). In general, these threats produce the desired effects, so that parliament rarely adopts pension legislation that employers and the insurance industry do not support.

The unions' use of the referendum threat is also generally effective, as efforts are always made to avoid a referendum being called. However the referendum threat is not always sufficient to force through the desired changes in the legislation. This was the case with both the 10th and the 11th AHV/AVS revisions, and as a result the unions had to resort on both occasions to calling a referendum against the proposed legislation.

Impact of the political system on pension politics

The analysis in this chapter highlights the presence of three distinctive effects of political institutions on the shape of policy: (i) the development of new opportunities as a result of the use of the popular initiative; (ii) the centripetal effect of referendums; and (iii) the impact of the country's symmetrical incongruent bi-cameral parliament.

Popular initiatives are frequently used in Switzerland, but very seldom result in actual constitutional change, as fewer than 10 percent of popular initiatives are accepted by voters. Political scientists, however, have argued that the political significance of popular initiatives goes way beyond their low acceptance rate. Initiatives bring new issues onto the political agenda and can push the government to legislate in a new direction (Kriesi 1995: 107). The 1982 Occupational Pension Law is a case in point. Compulsory occupational pension coverage, a policy option which seemed politically unfeasible in the 1960s, suddenly became politically attractive when the

Communist Party was able, thanks to a popular initiative, to put on to the agenda the option of an even bigger role for the state in pension provision: a fully-fledged Bismarckian pension scheme. Without making reference to the existence of this instrument in the Swiss constitutional order, it is very difficult to explain why, in a country where employers are so influential and the state is weak, the government was able to impose compulsory occupational pension coverage.

Standard referendums, and perhaps even more so the threat to make use of them, have also played an important role in shaping pension policy over the last two decades. The most notable effect of the easy availability of referendums is the magnification of the power of otherwise rather weak political actors: essentially the unions and the Socialist Party. These groups would be much less able to see their own preferences included in the new policies if they were not able to effectively threaten to prevent the adoption of entire pieces of legislation. The inclusion of measures such as contribution credits, or contribution-sharing between spouses, or the reduction in the access threshold to compulsory occupational pension coverage, are all concessions that the right-wing majority has made to the Socialists (and to the unions) in order to dissuade them from making use of referendums against otherwise retrenchment-oriented reforms.

Finally, Swiss bicameralism has provoked delays in the adoption of legislation. The different political composition of the two chambers, but also the fact that the reforms were debated at different times, and as a result under different economic conditions, was responsible for the lack of agreement between the two councils. This resulted in the need to craft the sort of complex compromises that were eventually adopted.

Constraints of policy design

Swiss pension policy is certainly locked into the multi-pillar structure. The fact that this type of pension system design is generally considered as one of the best available suggests that this lock-in situation perhaps should not be considered so much as a constraint, but as a chance. Moves away from the current systems will be extremely difficult. In the early 1990s, a group of employers, inspired by neo-liberal economic thinking, put forward the idea of removing the compulsory requirement for occupational pensions, but this idea was barely noticed in political debates (Pury et al. 1995).

Role of ideas and historical context

Two sets of ideas seem to have played an important role in pension reform processes. First, the whole decision-making process in the context of the 10th AHV/AVS Revision was prompted and lead by the requirement to make the pension system compatible with prevailing gender equality norms. The actual result went way beyond the simple adaptation to the constitutional article on gender equality, and introduced elements that constitute de facto recognition of the unpaid role performed mostly by women in the family and household context. In this respect, the reform responded to claims coming from the feminist movement and women's organizations.

Second, policy is constantly influenced by the conception of adequate provision embodied in the Constitution: that the pension system should provide not only a subsistence income to retired people but also an income that allows them to enjoy a standard of living similar to the one they experienced while in work. To classify the impact of a constitutional article as an ideational effect may seem striking, but it is appropriate in Switzerland given the non-existence of a constitutional court. The government is free to interpret the Constitution when preparing legislation, and disagreements over its interpretation are fought out in a way that is akin to battles among competing ideas, without an official winner. One example of such disagreement concerns the constitutional mandate of AHV/AVS, which must provide a subsistence minimum pension to everyone. In the government's own interpretation of the Constitution, this mandate can be fulfilled by the AHV/AVS scheme together with the means tested EL–PC pension. Other actors, however, believe that AHV/AVS in its current shape is unconstitutional because in many cases it does not provide this subsistence minimum.

The influence on the course of pension policy of divergent views of how the pension system should be seems rather limited, if considered in comparison with the other determinants discussed above belonging to the realms of interests and institutions.

Abbreviations

AHV/AVS	Alters- und Hinterlassenenversicherung/Assurance vieillesse et survivants
BVG/LPP	Bundesgesetz über die berufliche Alters-, Hinterlassenen- und Invalidenvorsorge/Loi fédérale sur la prévoyance professionnelle
BSV/OFAS	Bundesamt für Sozialversicherung/Office federal des assurances sociales
CHF	Swiss francs
CNG/CSC	Christlichnationaler Gewerkschaftsbund/Confédération des syndicats chrétiens
CVP/PDC	Christlichdemokratische Volkspartei/Parti Démocrate-Chrétien Suisse
EET	Contributions are tax free, returns are tax free, benefits are taxed
EL/PC	Ergänzungsleistungen/Prestations complémentaires
EVP/PEV	Evangelische Volkspartei/Parti Évangélique
FDP/PRD	Freisinnig-Demokratische Partei der Schweiz/Parti Radical Suisse
GPS/PES	Föderation der Grünen Parteien der Schweiz/Fédération Suisse des Partis Écologistes
LPS/PLS	Liberale Partei der Schweiz/Parti Libéral Suisse
SAV/UPS	Schweizerische Arbeitgeberverband/Union patronale suisse
SGB/USS	Schweizerische Gewerkschaftsbund/Union syndicale suisse

SGV/USAM Schweizerischer Gewerbeverband SGV/Union suisse des arts et métiers
SPS/PSS Sozialdemokratische Partei der Schweiz/Parti Socialiste Suisse
SVP/UDC Schweizerische Volkspartei/Union Démocratique du Centre
VSA/FSE Vereinigung schweizerischer Angestelltenverbände/Fédération Suisse des Sociétés d'Employés

Notes

1. The Swiss constitution permits several types of referendums. Constitutional change and accession to a supranational organization is automatically subject to a referendum. Voters can also propose constitutional change by means of a "popular initiative," with the support of 100,000 signatures. For these referendums to succeed, a double majority of voters and Cantons is required. Voters can also use the referendum to challenge any act passed by Parliament, if there are 50,000 supporting signatures. In this case, a simple majority of voters is sufficient for the referendum to succeed (see Kobach 1993 for a comprehensive account).
2. This figure refers only to "optional referendums" (*référendum facultatif*). If compulsory referendums are included, then the government's rate of success is considerably higher.
3. The sharing of the seven ministerial posts was strictly regulated by the so-called "magic formula" (an unwritten agreement among the big four parties): the larger parties SP/PS, FDP/PRD, CVP/PDC had two councilors each, while the smaller SVP/UDC had one. In 2003, as a result of the electoral success of the SVP/UDC, this party was able to obtain two seats and the PDC/CVP only one.
4. The Socialist Party also held one ministerial post between 1943 and 1953.
5. *Economiesuisse* was created in 2000 when the Swiss Union of Commerce and Industry, known in Switzerland also as *Vorort*, merged with the Society for the development of the Swiss economy.
6. The Federal government subsidizes 17% of outlays, while the Cantons jointly provide an additional 2%.
7. The first BVG/LPP revision, adopted in 2003, lowered this threshold (see pp. 235–7).
8. The notional contribution concept usually refers to PAYG pension schemes (e.g. Italy or Sweden). In Switzerland pensions are funded, but the calculation method for the compulsory minimum is based on contributions determined by law that do not necessarily reflect actual payments. The use of the term "notional contributions/accounts" here is consistent with other English-language publications on Swiss second-pillar pensions (see e.g. Queisser and Vittas 2000).
9. In 1996, 36% of pension fund members paid fixed rate contribution; 58% paid age-related contribution, and for the rest some other method was used (OFS 1999: 28).
10. The Department of the Interior has responsibility for social insurance as well as for most social policy areas (including health care).
11. The vote on the USS/PSS initiative was the same day as the pension reform referendum (June 25, 1996). The proposal and was rejected by 72% of voters.
12. A small change was introduced that reduced the difference in the treatment of low and high incomes.
13. With a floor of CHF 15,450 per year and a ceiling of CHF 21,810 per year.

Bibliography
Primary sources and government documents
BOAF.CdE *Bulletin Officiel de l'Assemblée Fédérale. Conseil des Etats.* Various issues.

CFQF (Commission Fédérale Pour les Questions Féminines) (1988). "Propositions de la Commission fédérale pour les questions féminines en vue de la 10e révision de l'AVS", *Questions au féminin*, 1, 88. Berne.

CONSEIL FÉDÉRAL (2000a). *Message relatif à la révision de la loi fédérale sur l'assurance vieillesse et survivants (LAVS).* Berne.

—— (2000b). *Message relatif à la révision de la loi fédérale sur la prévoyance professionnelle (LPP).* Berne.

FF (*Feuille Fédérale*). Berne. Various issues.

GROUPE DE TRAVAIL "Splitting" (1992). *Rapport final du groupe de travail "splitting" de la Commission du Conseil national*, 92.149. Berne.

OFAS (Office Fédéral des Assurances Sociales) (1995). *Rapport du Département fédéral de l'intérieur concernant la structure actuelle et le développement futur de la conception helvétique des trois piliers de la prévoyance vieillesse, survivants et invalidité.* Berne: OFAS.

Secondary sources
BALDWIN, PETER (1990). *The Politics of Social Solidarity.* Cambridge: Cambridge University Press.

BBC RADIO 4 (1996). *Consequences: Personal Pensions*, broadcasted on 27/1/1996.

BERNSTEIN, ALEXANDER (1986). *L'assurance-vieillesse suisse, son élaboration et son évolution.* Lausanne: Réalités Sociales.

BINSWANGER, PETER (1987). *Histoire de l'AVS.* Zurich: Pro Senectute.

BONOLI, GIULIANO (1999). "La réforme de l'Etat social en Suisse. Contraintes institutionnelles et opporunités de changement." *Swiss Political Science Review*, 5(3): 57–78.

—— (2000). *The Politics of Pension Reform. Institutions and Policy Change in Western Europe.* Cambridge: Cambridge University Press.

—— (2004). "The Institutionalisation of the Swiss Multi-pillar Pension System." In Rein, M. and Schmähl, W. (eds.), *Rethinking the welfare state. The Political Economy of Pension Reform.* Cheltenham: Edward Elgar, 102–21.

—— (2001). "Political Institutions, Veto Points and the Process of Welfare State Adaptation". In Pierson, P. (ed.), *The New Politics of the Welfare State.* New York: Oxford University Press, 238–64.

—— and GAY-DES-COMBES, BENOÎT (2003). *L'évolution des prestations vieillesse dans le long terme: une simulation prospective de la couverture retraite à l'horizon 2040.* Berne: Office fédéral des assurances sociales, Aspects de la sécurité sociale, Rapport de recherche n° 3/03, mai 2003.

—— and MACH, ANDRÉ (2000). "Switzerland: Adjustment Politics within Institutional Constraints." In Scharpf, F. W. and Schmidt, V. (eds.), *From Vulnerability to Competitiveness: Welfare and Work in the Open Economy.* Oxford: Oxford University Press, 131–74.

CROUCH, COLIN (1986). "Sharing Public Space: States and Organized Interests in Western Europe". In Hall, J. A. (ed.), *States in History.* Oxford: Basil Blackwell, 177–210.

EBBINGHAUS, BERNHARD and VISSER, JELLE (1999). "When Institutions Matter: Union Growth and Decline in Western Europe, 1950–1995." *European Sociological Review*, 15(2): 135–58.

FDP/PRD (Parti Radical Démocratique) (1988). "Avenir de l'AVS. Rapport final d'un groupe de travail du Parti radical-démocratique suisse." *Revue Politique*, 67(2): 34–45.

García, Carlos (1991). "Identité sociale de l'élite partisanne suisse." In Ayberk, U.(ed.), *Les partis politiques à coeur ouvert.* Lausanne: L.E.P., 41–55.

Hall, Peter (1993). "Policy Paradigms, Social Learning, and the State. The Case of Economic Policymaking in Britain." *Comparative Politics,* 25(3): 275–96.

Immergut, Ellen (1992). *Health Politics. Interests and Institutions in Western Europe.* Cambridge: Cambridge University Press.

Katzenstein, Peter (1984). *Corporatism and Change. Austria, Switzerland and the Politics of Change.* Ithaca, NY: Cornell University Press.

Kobach, Kris (1993). *The Referendum. Direct Democracy in Switzerland.* Aldershot: Dartmouth.

Kriesi, Hanspeter (1980). *Entscheidungsstrukturen und Entscheidungsprozesse in der Schweiz.* Frankfurt: Campus.

—— (1982). "The Structure of the Swiss Political System." In Lehmbruch, G. and Schmitter, P. (eds.), *Patterns of Corporatist Policy Making.* London: Sage, 133–62.

—— (1995). *Le système politique suisse.* Paris: Economica.

Lehmbruch, Gerhardt (1993). "Consociational Democracy and Corporatism in Switzerland." *Publius: The Journal of Federalism,* 23: 43–60.

Lijphart, Arendt (1984). *Democracies. Pattern of Majoritarian and Consensus Government in Twenty-One Countries.* New Haven: Yale University Press.

Linder, Wolf (1997). *Swiss Democracy: Possible Solutions to Conflict in Multicultural Societies.* London: Palgrave.

—— (1998). *Licht und Schatten über der direkten Demokratie.* Bern: Schweizerische Akademie der Geistes- und Sozialwissenschaften, Heft 1.

Mach, André (1999). "Associations d'intérêt." In Klöti, U., Knoepfel, P., Kriesi, H., et al. (eds.), *Handbuch der Schweizer Politik.* Zurich: NZZ Verlag, 299–336.

Müller, Beat (2003). "Die Entzauberung des BVG-Umwandlungssatzes. Wie und warum die Lebensversicherer neu kalkulieren." *Neue Zürcher Zeitung,* 30 September 2003.

Neidhart, Leonhard (1970). *Plebiszit und pluralitäre Demokratie. Eine Analyse der Funktionen des schweizerischen Gesetzesreferendum.* Bern: Frank.

Obinger, Herbert (1998). *Federalism, Direct Democracy, and Welfare State Development in Switzerland.* ZeS-Arbeitspapier Nr. 8/98. Bremen: Zentrum für Sozialpolitik.

OFAS (Office Fédéral des Assurances Sociales) (2002). *Statistiques des assurances sociales.* Berne.

—— (2004). *Statistique des assurances sociales.* Berne.

OFS (Office fédéral de la statistique) (1998). *Enquête sur les revenus et la consommation,* Dataset. Neuchâtel.

—— (1999). *Statistiques des caisses de pensions 1998.* Neuchâtel.

Papadopoulos, Yannis (1996). "Les mécanismes du vote référendaire en Suisse: l'impact de l'offre politique." *Revue Française de Sociologie* 37: 5–35.

—— (1997). *Les processus de décision fédéraux en Suisse.* Paris: L'Harmattan.

Pfizmann-Boulaz, Hans (1981). "Le futur régime obligatoire de la prévoyance professionnelle." *Schweizerische Zeitschrift für Sozialversicherung,* 25: 81–93.

PSS (Parti Socialiste Suisse) (1995). *Presse Dienst. Sonderausgabe: 10. AHV-Revision,* No. 406/407. Berne.

PSS/USS (Parti Socialiste Suisse/Union Syndicale Suisse) (1987). *Droits égaux dans l'AVS. Propositions du Parti socialiste suisse et de l'Union syndicale suisse pour la révision de l'AVS,* PSS/USS. Berne.

Pury, de, David, Hauser, Heinz, and Schmid, Beat (eds.) (1995). *Mut zum Aufbruch. Eine wirtschaftspolitische Agenda für die Schweiz.* Zürich: Orell Füssli.

QUEISSER, MONIKA AND VITTAS, DIMITRI (2000). *The Swiss Multipillar Pension System. Triumph of Common Sense?* Washington: The World Bank, Development Research Group.

Sécurité sociale, various issues. Periodical publication of the Federal office of social insurance.

SCHMÄHL, WINFRIED. (ed.) (1991). *The Future of Basic and Supplementary Pensions Schemes in the European Community–1992 and beyond.* Baden-Baden: Nomos.

TSR (Télévision Suisse Romande) (10/6/95), *AVS 10e, 62 ou 64.*

VATTER, ADRIAN (1999). "Föderalismus." In Klöti, U., Knoepfel, P., Kriesi, H. et al. (eds.), *Handbuch der Schweizer Politik.* Zurich: NZZ Verlag, 77–108.

VONTOBEL, WERNER (2000). "Die Säulen-Scheinheiligen: Pech hat, wer in einem Kleinbetrieb arbeitet: Die Versicherung behält die Zinsen zurück". *CASH*, 01/12/2000: 44.

Vox (1995). *Analyse des votations fédérales du 25 juin 1996*, No. 57. Berne.

—— (2004). *Analyse des votations fédérales du 16 mai 2004*, No. 53, Berne.

CHAPTER 6

FINLAND: LABOR MARKETS AGAINST POLITICS

OLLI KANGAS

I INTRODUCTION

THE Finnish pension system defies standard classifications of pensions in terms of various tiers and pillars. Pensions are legislated and completely coordinated, and yet a great deal of corporatism is built into the decentralized system administered by the labor market partners. This system has its roots in the specific political and institutional context within which the Finnish welfare state was constructed. The Finnish institutional context has shaped the politics of reform not only in the expansion phases of Finnish social policy development, but even more so during the present period of austerity.

The Finnish legislative process combines both presidentialism and parliamentarism. This division of legislative power, together with extensive minority protections, provides several important veto points for social actors. To avoid parliamentary defeat, Finnish governments must be over-sized or ready to compromise, and parties must seek allies in order to form viable cabinets. Often this occurs across the political blocks—most often between the Center Party and the Social Democratic Party (SDP), sometimes among the bourgeois parties, and sometimes unifying the conservatives with the SDP and Left in "rainbow coalitions." Such an "unholy" or pragmatic pattern of policy-making has prevented strong inter-party confrontations, as is usual in two-party systems or in countries with a hegemonic party. This is why political pragmatism rather than ideological purity has colored policy-making. Pension policy design also shapes reforms patterns. In pension policy, the labor market partners administer the most important schemes, and this corporatist arrangement provides the social partners with opportunities to block governmental proposals. In such a context any government trying to cut pensions must seek to compromise with social partners.

According to Esping-Andersen (1985) social democracy is a political movement that uses national legislation to improve the lot of citizens. Politics is used "against markets." The Finnish experience confirms Esping-Andersen's analysis, but only partially. The Finnish case clearly shows that the SDP wanted to use national legislation to achieve its goals, but the SDP did not necessarily want publicly-organized insurance. Instead, the Finnish labor movement relied on a corporatist, labor market-based administrative structure.

The rationale for the Finnish "semi-public" solution is rooted in the state-party relationship. The Finnish Agrarian Party (ML) had long been a "natural party of government" and was able to use state machinery for its own purposes. Moreover, from the mid-1950s to the early 1980s, the President—who had the power to overrule bills proposed by Parliament—was from the ML and had a close relationship with party members (Hokkanen 2002). Therefore, the SDP and trade unions were willing to accept a decentralized, private, corporatist system (for a historical description see e.g. Ahtokari 1988; Niemelä 1988; Salminen 1987 and 1993). Markets were used against politics, to modify Esping-Andersen's adage. The Finnish case strongly supports a relational interpretation of interactions between the state and political parties: if some other political party controls the state, the Social Democrats may be willing to pursue their interests via the labor market and enter into coalitions with capitalists. This is precisely what happened in Finland, and the labor market-based, corporatist administration of pensions created an institutionally strong veto opportunity for the unions and employers against Parliament. Thus it is not surprising that the social partners have always been deeply involved in pension reform processes.

Although pension rights in Finland are modest by international standards, demographic and labor market developments will create challenges for the pension system. The Finnish population is graying faster than most other OECD countries. At the same time, early retirement has increased rapidly. These trends are forecast to increase pension contributions from less than 20 percent of wages in 1990 to 30–40 percent in 2040.

The economic crisis that hit Finland in the early 1990s raised fears about the sustainability of the existing social policy model. Bleak economic prospects formed the background for the policy discussions analyzed in this chapter, and economic difficulties doubtless led people to accept harsh retrenchment measures that would otherwise have been hard to implement, regardless of government ideology. The increasing sense of crisis and decreasing public confidence in the government's ability to finance social protection facilitated changes in pension design.

This chapter analyzes the politics of pension reforms in Finland in the 1990s and early 2000s. How was it possible to achieve consensus between the trade unions who wanted to preserve "their" pensions and the governments proposing cuts? How did political actors reach compromises in an institutional setting with multiple veto points? How were various institutional locks opened? The chapter begins with a discussion of the political decision-making procedures that shape policy-making and then reviews the development of national pensions and employment-related pension schemes. The chapter then discusses some of the most important pension reforms undertaken since 1980. These changes include, first, the introduction of employee contributions and second, reforms in the public sector pension schemes which abolished separate "tenured civil servant" benefits. The third change is the abolition of universalism from the national pensions system. This was perhaps the biggest policy change in terms of basic principles because the reform meant a shift from citizenship-based to more employment-based social rights. Fourth, the change in pension-carrying income was the first move toward a more extensive reform where career income is the basis for benefits. These piecemeal reforms paved the way for the fifth set of more substantial pension reforms that took place in 2002 in private sector pensions, and in 2004 in public sector pensions.

The final section tells the Finnish story at a more general level. The story is very much about labor's relational and strategic attitudes towards the state, but it is also about policy-making in a fragmented political structure where the legislative setting offers veto points to parliamentary minorities or to the President. However, various consociational devices were developed to avoid policy stalemates. Governments have tended to be over-sized, and as a rule important social policy reforms were carried through in a dialogue between Parliament and the largest interest organizations. The incentives favoring political consensus-seeking meant that parties have been much more inclined towards practical, non-ideological solutions, and less concerned about whether planned reforms were in line with their political mandates. The institutional framework of employment-related pensions meant that the government was dependent on trade union consent, so all major reforms were discussed in labor market negotiations. Only after employers and unions had agreed on reforms did the government prepare a bill and present it to Parliament.

The story is also very much about piecemeal reforms (see Hinrichs and Kangas 2003; Hinrichs 2004): the introduction of employee contributions was initially launched as a one-year austerity measure, the income base for pension purposes was first lengthened to ten years and then to lifetime income, public sector pensions were first harmonized with private pensions, and finally private pensions were completely reformed which provided the impetus to change other pensions as well. The reforms analyzed represent piecemeal solutions to large questions and in Finland the big issues were never really openly discussed: the political agenda consisted of small, non-radical or path-departing steps. In principle, none of these reforms was big enough to be called a system shift, but the processes initiated by those changes has led to major change in the foundations of the pension system. The story is also very much about "old politics": all the important decisions were made more or less in the same way as were the decisions that initiated the system in the early 1960s. Furthermore, the political constellations were replicated as well. The Finnish case follows "old politics" also in the total absence of representatives of social policy clients in the decision-making; when pension reforms were at stake, pensioners were neither seen nor heard. All in all, the Finnish case does not seem to lend much support to the theories of the "new politics" of the welfare state.

II Political system

Constitutional history and nation-building

Finland has only been independent since 1917. Until 1809, Finland was part of the Kingdom of Sweden, but with the end of the Napoleonic Wars, Finland was annexed to the Russian empire as a semi-independent Grand Duchy with its own Constitution, currency, legislature, Parliament (the Diet), and government called the Imperial Senate. However, the Russian Czar possessed ultimate power and all laws had to be promulgated by the Czar (see Jussila, Hentilä and Nevakivi 1999).

Political parties had already begun to form before independence from Russia in 1917. Both Finnish (*Fennomans*) and Swedish (*Svekomans*) linguistic parties had existed in some loose forms since the 1860s, but the first mass party was the Social Democratic Party (SDP), established in 1899. Even though Finland was still under Russian rule, the introduction of universal suffrage and the establishment of a parliament in 1906—perhaps the most radical electoral reform in Europe at that time—forced all political groupings to organize (Alapuro 1988). The peculiarity of the Finnish, or more generally the Nordic, political structure is that farmers have had their own political organizations, in the Finnish case called the Agrarian Party (ML), promoting the class-interests of farmers (Alestalo and Kuhnle 1987).

The 1907 elections, the first under universal suffrage, brought victory for the SDP with 80 seats out of 200, and in 1916 the SDP won an absolute majority with 105 seats. The desire for social reforms was high, but the socialists soon realized that their legislative initiatives would not lead to any improvements in the lot of the proletariat. The conservatives and agrarians usually opposed any reforms that would increase taxes and public spending, and these parties could appeal to the Czar to not promulgate social legislation (Kalela 1989: 39). From the social democratic point of view these attempts at social reform were disappointing and gradually they began to lose their faith in parliamentarianism and to look for alternatives (Kettunen 1986: 79–87).

The Russian Revolution gave inspiration to radical socialists and in the wake of the October Revolution a civil war broke out in Finland in 1918, just one year after the Declaration of Independence (for a fuller description see Alapuro 1988). The war was short, and ended in defeat for the socialists. The most prominent party leaders fled to

Russia, established the Finnish Communist Party and continued their revolutionary activities in exile. The majority of the SDP decided to follow the democratic route and, surprisingly, just nine years after the civil war the party formed a minority government. However, the civil war left its mark on the first Constitution of independent Finland. For the conservatives the war was evidence that democracy was not a reliable form of governance. Therefore, the country should have a King who would counterbalance the "unpredictable" Parliament. The Swedish People's Party (SFP) supported the Swedish type of royalism, whereas the SDP and the ML were strongly republican. Attitudes on the Constitution broke the Finnish Party. The royalist "Old Finns" formed the Conservative Coalition Party (KOK) and the republican fraction "Young Finns" established the Liberal Party (LKP).

The Constitution issue was resolved in favor of the republicans, but the monarch's political power was partially transferred to the President of the Republic. The Constitution Act of 1919 dictates that "Supreme executive power shall be vested in the President of the Republic." Thus the early Constitution established a semi-presidential regime that lasted eighty years.

Institutions of government

The 1919 Constitution states that all sovereign power belongs to the people, who are represented by the uni-cameral Parliament, but the Constitution also specified that Parliament share legislative power with the President (Pesonen and Riihinen 2002: 155). This division of legislative power reflects both radical republicanism and conservative royalism. The strong presidency was intended to bring stability and continuity, an idea supported by the electoral cycle: the President was elected for six years, whereas the parliamentary cycle was three years, and since 1954 four years. The President also had the right to nominate the Prime Minister and dissolve Parliament. This has occurred seven times, usually because of political tensions between coalition parties. In a fragmented multi-party system where no party is powerful enough to form a government alone, the President has acted as a general regulator to help parties out of political deadlock (Nousiainen 1998: 209).

The 1999 Constitution reduced the President's power. According to the new constitution, Parliament elects the Prime Minister, and the President can dissolve Parliament only on the basis of Prime Minister's initiative. In current Finnish policy-making, there is a clear tendency to strengthen the position of the Prime Minister.

If the President was supposed to counterbalance Parliament's power, the government "Council of State" was intended to check the power of President. All presidential decisions are made at meetings of the Council and each participating minister has political and judicial responsibility for the President's decision unless the minister's objection is recorded in the minutes of the meeting (Nousiainen 1998: 213). In principle, the President may act against the will of the whole Council—which has happened only twice (1924 and 1932)—but in practice all important issues are discussed and arbitrated in advance in presidential meetings.

The dyadic use of legislative and executive power seems to suit the Finnish political context with its fragmented party structure. There has been no dominant party and in such circumstances the President has been a conciliator in times of political tensions. This in turn has prompted the President to maintain distance from individual parties and to try to represent the public will and sometimes also act against his/her former party.

The Constitution does not mention political parties; it specifies only that each Member of Parliament (MP) must act "in line with justice and truth," observe the Constitution and "is not bound by any other instructions" (Pesonen and Riihinen 2002: 163). However, each party has weekly parliamentary strategy meetings, and this limits the freedom of individual MPs. Party discipline is strong, but still weaker than in England or the other Nordic countries (Lane and Ersson 2002: 261). The multi-party system means that Finnish parties regularly cooperate across the socialist–non-socialist divide, and this pattern of compromise makes it difficult to make ideological statements in advance on specific policy options that the party will adhere to at all costs.

The gradual shift towards parliamentarianism has strengthened the government's position vis-à-vis the President. The President still nominates and dismisses the cabinet and ministers, but decisive power lies with Parliament. Formally, the Prime Minister heads the Council of State, but in the Finnish decision-making process there are some features that diminish the Prime Minister's power. First, since Finnish governments are usually coalitions of parties belonging to different political camps, the Prime Minister is more a consensus builder than an independent leader. One such consensus-building device in cabinet is the so-called "evening schools" of the government. At these informal and confidential meetings the ministers can discuss difficult issues in advance and try to seek compromises. Often interest group representatives and experts from the ministries also participate (Nousiainen 1998: 228). Second, according to the so-called collegiality principle all ministers are, at least in principle, equally important, and as heads of their respective ministries have full sovereignty in their own areas. Furthermore, in order to reduce the Council's workload, a constitutional amendment in 1993 made it easier to transfer decision-making power from the government to individual ministers and further to bureaucrats in the ministries for some practical policy issues (Nousiainen 1998: 226). Interestingly enough, the reform strengthened the position of bureaucrats, and the deep recession of the 1990s continued the process. Senior bureaucrats, in the Ministry of Finance in particular, were used as messengers to convey news of unpopular welfare retrenchment measures. This was a more or less deliberate blame avoidance (Pierson 1994) or de-politicizing strategy used by the parties in government.

Electoral system

The electoral cycle for parliamentary and municipal elections is four years, with parliamentary elections held in March and municipal elections in October. Presidential elections are every sixth year, in two rounds. If none of the candidates gets

Table 6.1 Political institutions in Finland

Political arenas	Actors	Rules of investiture	Rules of decision-making	Veto potential
Executive	President	6-year term; directly elected; since 1994 candidate needs either absolute majority in first ballot or simple majority in a second ballot between the two best 1st-round candidates	Until 1999: decided whether governmental bills were forwarded to Parliament; ratified and promulgated laws (before 1986 suspensive veto for one term; 1987–1999 suspensive veto for one year); since 1999: no legislative function, only suspensive veto power; if government formation negotiations failed he could appoint a caretaker government; until 1991 right to dissolve Parliament, now only with prime ministerial consent.	Before 1999 veto point. Since 1999 not a veto point. Veto point is closed by presidential practice, then constitutional change
	Prime Minister	Until 2000 nominated by the President then elected by parliament; now appointment by the President after his election in Parliament; may be unseated by vote of no confidence	Right of initiative; can legislate in terms of decisions of the Council of State (*Valtioneuvoston päätös*); due to coalition governments often rather weak position and consensus builder	—

Legislative	Parliament (*Eduskunta*)	4-year term; 200 mandates; 14 multi-member electoral districts (between 33 and 6 mandates) and 1 single-member district; districts are provinces; proportional representation; voting for candidate not party; seat allocation according to d'Hondt can be dissolved by president upon prime minister's request	Right of initiative; 14 standing committees; decision by simple majority before 1992, minority rules: 1/3 could vote bill "dormant" until next elections; post 1992, rule only applies to constitutionally-relevant bills, unless 5/6 of parliament votes to allow simple majority for passage post-1999, can overrule President's veto immediately	Pre-1992 veto point when government enjoyed less than two-thirds majority; after 1992, 2/3rds majority relevant only for constitutional change
Judicial	No constitutional court!	Non-existent	No rights	Non-existent
Electoral	Referendum		No binding effect only consultative	Not a veto point
Territorial units	Previously 12 provinces (*lääni*); since 1997 only 6 provinces 432 Municipalities	Provincial governors (*maaherra*) are appointed by the President 4-year term elections	Conduct administration on regional level Some competencies in social affairs, education, health, construction and regional planning	Not a veto point

more than 50 percent of the votes in the first round in January, the second round between the two candidates with most votes takes place in February. The minimum voting age is 18 years.

The Finnish parliamentary electoral system has always been based on proportional representation (Lane and Ersson 2002: 248). For parliamentary elections there are 15 electoral districts and before each election, the seats for each district are allocated based on population. In the 2003 elections the biggest electoral district (*Uudenmaan lääni*) had 33 seats and the smallest one (Southern Savo) six. Semi-independent Åland is allocated one mandate (http://www.vaalit.fi/uploads/wqd56g48c2r.pdf). No vote threshold is used and seats are allocated using the d'Hondt method.

Finnish parliamentary elections offer much individual choice since the voter does not vote for a party list but for a single candidate. In addition to registered political parties, the so-called electoral associations can also nominate candidates for elections, providing that they have at least 100 members before the elections. Together with the absence of a vote threshold this contributes to the entry of minor groups, which of course increases the number of parliamentary parties.

Legislative process

The parliamentary agenda is strictly regulated. For important social policies like pensions, the government prepares bills and presents them to Parliament. Bills can also be initiated by individual MPs but the governmental route is more common.

To make the preparation of bills more effective, there are fourteen specialized standing committees that draft bills, which are then discussed and voted on by Parliament. Each party is proportionally represented within the committees (Pesonen and Riihinen 2004: 158). In addition, the so-called Grand Committee (GC) verifies the correctness of all laws and since recently has specialized in European Union issues. In principle, Parliament can still send any law to the GC for scrutiny but it has no formal veto right. Nevertheless, sending the bill to the GC gives MPs the chance to delay a bill they oppose. The same goes for the Constitutional Committee (CC) which handles all bills concerning the Constitution. It is not uncommon for MPs to argue that planned changes in social policy legislation violate the Constitution and therefore should be submitted to the CC. If the CC agrees, the bill falls under a more demanding procedure than normal legislation.

If a bill is uncontroversial and does not create tensions between the coalition partners, the government can present it to Parliament, but if the proposal is not unanimously supported and if there is a fear of interest group opposition, the situation demands some behind-the-scenes negotiations. Particularly for austerity measures the government usually prepares bills in consultation with the social partners. This consultation can take various forms. The experts and representatives of the social partners can be invited to participate in the "evening school" of the Council of State. For more difficult issues the government can set up an expert committee with representatives from all relevant organizations to investigate reform options (Lane and Ersson 2002).

If consensus is not reached, the opponents can express their objections in the final report. Such reports are consultative, but because they are prepared by experts, they often play a large role in subsequent political discussions.

If the government believes there is a consensus, it will prepare legislation. The committee and "evening school" phases are merely consultative and are not formal veto points, but they do provide reliable information about potential opposition. The government is free to act as it chooses, but ignoring the opinion of the central interest organizations can be risky.

When a bill comes to Parliament it is first discussed in a plenary sitting and then sent to the relevant committee (all pension policy issues are forwarded to the Committee on Social Affairs). The committee first gathers general information and consults with experts from the administration and interest organizations. On the basis of these discussions, the committee prepares its final draft, which need not be unanimous: members who are not satisfied with the result present their disagreements and their own bill proposals. In principle, the special committee has some scope for veto-playing: the committee can postpone or even prevent the proposal from going further. This fate often befalls the initiatives of individual MPs whose bills are buried under the committee's "extensive work load" and are never prepared.

Until 2000, bills went through three parliamentary readings, and since 2000 the first and second plenary discussions have been merged. Discussion in the first reading was intended to be general, whereas the second one was a detailed paragraph-by-paragraph scrutiny of the law. During this phase MPs could modify the bill. This stage offered possibilities for last minute negotiations and modifications aimed at avoiding defeat in the third reading when the bill could only be accepted or rejected as a whole.

If Parliament adopts the bill, it is sent to the President for promulgation. During the promulgation process the President has a so-called "suspensive" veto power. The President can refuse to sign the act, but Parliament can overrule the veto by adopting the bill again. Until 1986, the presidential veto could only be overruled after the next election; between 1987 and 1998 after one year; but according to the 1999 Constitution, Parliament can now re-adopt the bill without delay (Nousiainen 1998: 205–207; Pesonen and Riihinen 2002: 167–70).

Specific parliamentary procedures were designed to prevent legislative changes from being too radical and to protect minorities. One-third of the Members of Parliament (67 MPs) could prevent the adoption of a new law by voting it "dormant" until after the next election (Nousiainen 1998: 190). After that, the new Parliament could adopt the bill by simple majority. The one-third minority rule was abolished in 1992 and since then all bills except constitutional ammendments may be adopted by a simple majority. Changes to the Constitution, or laws considered to be closely related to the Constitution, can be adopted two different ways. One option is for Parliament to decide changes by simple majority and accept them by a two-thirds majority after the next parliamentary election. The other option is to declare the constitutional amendment "urgent," which demands a five-sixths majority, after which the bill can be accepted by the same Parliament if two-thirds of the MPs support it (Lane and Ersson 2002: 248).

Party family affiliation	Abbreviation	Party name	Ideological orientation	Founding and merging details	Year established
Left-wing parties	SKP	Finnish Communist Party	Radical revolutionary	Established in Moscow by red refugees; Finnish Socialist Party 1922–24; Workers and Smallholders Party 1924-30	1918 (forbidden by "communist laws" in 1930)
	SKDL	Finnish People's Democratic League	Combination of Moscow faithful and revisionist Euro-Communism	Established to unify communists and left-wing socialists	1944 (ceased in 1990)
	VAS	Left Alliance	"Red-green" socialist	Established on the ruins of SKDL	1990
	SDP	Social Democratic Party of Finland	Social democratic		1899
	TPSL	Social Democratic League	Socialist and rural orientation	A splinter group form SDP	1958 (ceased in 1970)
Green	Vihr	The Greens	Environmentalist		1988
Agrarian Center (Liberal)	ML / Kesk	Agrarian League / Center Party (1965–)	Agrarian conservative; since the 1960s universal centrist; in EU parliament included among Liberals		1906
Liberal	Lib	Liberal Party	Liberal	Republican "Finns"; "Young Finns"; Progressive Party 1918–50; People's Party 1951–65; Liberal Party 1966–	1918 (no MPs since 1970)
	SFP	Swedish Peoples Party	Liberal linguistic catch-all party		1906
Christian	KD	Christian Democrats	Christian conservative	Christian League (CD) 1959–2000	1958
Right wing	SMP / PS	Finland's Rural Party/ True Finns	Agrarian populist; since the 1980s right-wing populist	A populist splinter group from ML	1949
	Kok	National Coalition	Conservative	Monarchist "Old Finns"	1918
	IKL	Patriotic People's Movement	Radical nationalist anti-socialist, pro-Nazi	A right-wing splinter group from Kok	1932 (ceased in 1944)

Fig. 6.1 Party system in Finland

In sum, the legislative process in Finland includes several institutional veto points and many consociational practices. The previous one-third minority rule was an effective tool for the political opposition to diminish the power of the government. The presidential refusal to promulgate a law constituted another veto possibility. Changes in the constitution in the 1990s abolished these veto points. Partially due to the difficulties in gaining a sufficient majority for a bill, a number of consensus building devices—governmental "evening schools," presidential consultations, parliamentary and expert committees—were developed, and Finland, together with some other European countries, can be labeled a consociational democracy (Lijphart 1977).

Parties and elections

The Finnish party structure, with some modifications, follows the typical Scandinavian pattern of a tri-polar class-structure (Castles 1979; Esping-Andersen 1985; Alestalo and Kuhnle 1987; Baldwin 1990). Finnish class structure is tri-polar, with a politically strong and distinct class of independent farmers existing alongside labor and capital. This tri-polar class structure was more or less directly mirrored in the political spectrum. In addition to the left and right-wing parties, the relatively strong agrarian party came to play an important role.

Finnish party formation deviated from the other Nordic countries in several ways. First, in the middle of the political spectrum there is a linguistic catch-all party, the Swedish People's Party (SFP), representing Swedish-speaking Finns. Membership has fallen in recent years to about 4 percent in 2003 but the party's centrist nature means that it can enter into any possible coalition cabinet (see Table 6.2 on pp. 261–2).

Secondly, the strength of the Agrarian/Center Party clearly makes Finland a deviant case in the Nordic and European context. Peculiar to Finland is that an SDP-Agrarian red–green axis has continued with some interruptions up to the present. The Agrarian/Center Party participated in 27 out of 32 post-war political cabinets, and in 15 cabinets the party held the position of Prime Minister. The party name change in 1965 (from Agrarian to Center Party) indicated that the party wanted to transform itself into a universal centrist catch-all party that also appealed to urban Finns. In the short run, the shift was a catastrophe. In the 1970 elections, the party lost 13 mandates to the populist Finnish Rural Party (SMP) that campaigned exclusively for rural interests. Gradually the appeal of the SMP has faded, and the Center Party has regained its position and is successfully challenging the SDP to be the largest party. The Center has managed to expand its constituency beyond the farming population but it still has severe problems in attracting urban votes (see Nousiainen 1998: 55–7).

Thirdly, one decisive difference compared to the other Nordic countries has been the internal divide in the socialist bloc. After World War II, the previously forbidden Communist party (SKDL) made a phenomenal political comeback. It was the biggest party and provided the Prime Minister in the post-war "people's front" cabinet consisting of the SKDL, the SDP and the ML. Thereafter the SKDL had to wait twenty years to be included in the cabinet. Since the elections of 1966, which gave the socialist parties an absolute majority in Parliament, the SKDL (Left) has participated in nine governments. However, the once-powerful party, which in its heyday held as many as 50 seats in Parliament, is now down to 19 MPs. In the 1950s and 1960s the SKDL was a real challenge to the SDP, and as a result of this competition the SDP never obtained such a strong position in Finland as its sister parties did in Sweden and Norway.

The Finnish political map is highly fragmented. As a consequence, no party has maintained a dominant position. Since the legislative structure offered veto points to the political opposition, all effective cabinets had to be coalitions and preferably oversized ones with more than 133 mandates. This kind of institutional context was favorable to the ML/Center—as a party of the center it was able to build coalitions with the bourgeois or the socialist block (see Table 6.2 on pp. 261–2). This pattern continued until the 1980s and there were no coalitions across the Center. The collaboration between the ML and the SDP was long but turbulent. The average cabinet term was only 380 days in the 1950s–1970s. Interestingly enough, since the retirement of President Kekkonen (President 1956–81), governmental stability has improved. Since the early 1980s, cabinets have usually served the whole electoral period (average term 1,100 days).

As Table 6.2 shows, in 1987 the SDP and the KOK (assisted by the SFP and the SMP) formed a cabinet under conservative leadership for the first time in Finnish history. The cabinet turned out to be extremely stable, but in the 1991 elections the SDP lost the status of largest party and the victorious Center returned to power only to be immediately confronted with a deep economic recession. Unpopular cutbacks undermined the support for the Center, which lost 11 mandates in 1995, whereas the SDP achieved their best results since the 1930s with 63 seats. In the next two cabinets (1995–2003), led by Paavo Lipponen, the main partners were the SDP and the KOK, joined by the smaller parties SFP, the Greens and the Left Party (the Greens left the cabinet in 2000). Despite the odd ideological composition, Lipponen's over-sized "rainbow" coalitions functioned well.

The 2003 parliamentary elections were dramatic: by a margin of just two mandates the Center became the biggest party and the party leader, Anneli Jäätteenmäki, was nominated as the first female Prime Minister. Her choice of partners was the Center, the SDP and the SFP. However, within the SDP there was strong skepticism about the possibilities for collaborating with Jäätteenmäki who had obtained confidential material on discussions on the Iraq war between Lipponen and George W. Bush from the Council of President by questionable means. She then used this material in her electoral campaign against the SDP. After only 69 days in office Jäätteenmäki resigned due to the loss of parliamentary confidence. Only the Prime Minister changed, though: the rest of the cabinet remained the same.

Interest groups

Few countries can match Finland's high membership levels in various associations (Ingelhart 1997: 190). Labor market organizations are especially important. Union density in Finland is second highest (after Sweden) in the OECD. Over 80 percent of

Table 6.2 Governmental majorities in Finland

Date of change in political configuration	Presidential election date	President (party)	Presidential majority decisive round	Election date Eduskunta	Start of gov.	Head of gov. (party)	Governing parties	Gov. majority (% seats) Eduskunta	Gov. electoral base (% votes) Eduskunta	Institutional veto points*	Number of veto players (partisan + institutional)
05.26.1979		Kekkonen V (KESK)	86.7%	03.13.1979	05.26.1979	Koivisto II (SDP)	SDP(52), KESK (36), SKDL (35), SFP (10)	66.5%	63.6%	President, Eduskunta	4 + 2
10.27.1981		Koivisto I (SDP)				Koivisto II (SDP)	SDP(52), KESK (36), SKDL (35), SFP (10)	66.5%	63.6%	President, Eduskunta	4 + 2
02.19.1982		Koivisto I (SDP)			02.19.1982	Sorsa III (SDP)	SDP (52), KESK (36), SKDL (35), SFP (10)	66.5%	63.6%	President, Eduskunta	4 + 2
03.01.1982	02.26.1982	Koivisto II (SDP)	55.5%			Sorsa III (SDP)	SDP (52), KESK (36), SKDL (35), SFP (10)	66.5%	63.6%	President, Eduskunta	4 + 2
12.31.1982		Koivisto II (SDP)			12.31.1982	Sorsa IV (SDP)	SDP (52), KESK (36), SFP (10)	49.0%	45.7%	President, Eduskunta	3 + 2
05.06.1983		Koivisto II (SDP)		03.21.1983	05.06.1983	Sorsa V (SDP)	SDP (57), KESK (38), SMP (17), SFP (11)	61.5%	59.0%	President, Eduskunta	4 + 2
04.30.1987		Koivisto II (SDP)		03.16.1987	04.30.1987	Holkeri I (KOK)	SDP (56), KOK (53), SFP (13), SMP (9)	65.5%	53.7%	President, Eduskunta	4 + 2
03.01.1988	15.02.1988	Koivisto III (SDP)	62.8%			Holkeri I (KOK)	SDP (56), KOK (53), SFP (13), SMP (9)	65.5%	53.7%	President, Eduskunta	4 + 2
08.28.1990		Koivisto III (SDP)			08.28.1990	Holkeri II (KOK)	SDP (56), KOK (53), SFP (13)	61.0%	47.4%	President, Eduskunta	3 + 2
04.26.1991		Koivisto III (SDP)		03.17.1991	04.26.1991	Aho I (KESK)	KESK (55), KOK (40), SFP (12), SKL (8)	57.5%	53.0%	President, Eduskunta	4 + 2

(Continued)

Table 6.2 (Continued)

Date of change in political configuration	Presidential election date	President (party)	Presidential majority decisive round	Election date Eduskunta	Start of gov.	Head of gov. (party)	Governing parties	Gov. majority (% seats) Eduskunta	Gov. electoral base (% votes) Eduskunta	Institutional veto points	Number of veto players (partisan + institutional)
03.01.1994	02.06.1994	Ahtisaari (SDP)	53.9%			Aho I (KESK)	KESK (55), KOK (40), SFP (12), SKL (8)	57.5%	53.0%	President	4 + 1
06.28.1994		Ahtisaari (SDP)			06.28.1994	Aho II (KESK)	KESK (55), KOK (40), SFP (12)	53.5%	50.0%	President	3 + 1
04.13.1995		Ahtisaari (SDP)		03.21.1999	04.13.1995	Lipponen I (SDP)	SDP (63), KOK (39), VAS (22), SFP (12), VIHR (9)	72.5%	69.3%	President	5 + 1
04.15.1999		Ahtisaari (SDP)			04.15.1999	Lipponen II (SDP)	SDP (51), KOK (46), VAS (20), SFP (12), VIHR (11)	69.5%	67.5%	None	5 + 0
03.01.2000	02.06.2000	Halonen (SDP)	51.6%			Lipponen II (SDP)	SDP (51), KOK (46), VAS (20), SFP (12), VIHR (11)	69.5%	67.5%	None	5 + 0
04.17.2003		Halonen (SDP)		03.16.2003	04.17.2003	Jäätteenmäki (KESK)	KESK (55), SDP (53), SFP (8)	50.5%	53.8%	None	3 + 0
06.24.2003		Halonen (SDP)			06.24.2003	Vanhanen (KESK)	KESK (55), SDP (53), SFP (8)	50.5%	53.8%	None	3 + 0

Sources: www.tpk.fi & www.hallitus.fi/vn; Nousiainen 1998: 244–255; Nousiainen 2000; Auffermann 2003

the labor force is unionized, compared to about 30 percent in the UK and Germany and less than 10 percent in France (OECD 1997).

Labor movement history in Finland has been turbulent, marked by intense fighting between employers and employees, between the left-wing and bourgeois parties, and within the labor movement between communists and Social Democrats. The success of the 1905 General Strike prompted a wave of organization. In 1907 both employers and workers established their own central organizations, the Confederation of Finnish Employers (*Suomen Työnantajien Keskusliitto*, STK) and the Trade Union Organization of Finland (*Suomen Ammattijärjestö*, SAJ). Civil war slowed the growth of the nascent union movement. After 1918, membership picked up again, but in 1930 the Trade Union Organization and the Communist Party were banned. The Social Democrats immediately established their own organization, the Confederation of Finnish Trade Unions (SAK). After World War II, when communist activities were again accepted, an internal war broke out again and in 1960 a dissident fraction separated from SAK and at once established a new organization SAJ (Suomen Ammattijärjestö). However, the feuding partners gradually realized that the conflicts were detrimental to everybody and in 1969 the dissidents rejoined the SAK, which then began to grow rapidly in numbers and political importance. By 1980 the SAK commanded one million workers. Despite decreasing industrial employment, the SAK has maintained its membership. The unions with the highest membership are the Municipal Workers' and Employees' Union (KTV) with about 200,000 members, Service Unions with about 200,000 members, and the Metal Workers Unions (Metalliliitto) with 170,000 members. The SAK has a good relationship with the SDP and the Left.

The central organizations for salaried employees are more recent in origin. The Finnish Organization for Salaried Employees (STTK) was established in 1947. Until the 1970s, the STTK managed to organize less than 50,000 employees. In 2000 the membership was up to 630,000. Most of this increase is due to the annexation of members in 1992—mainly female lower level white-collar workers in the public sector—of the Central Organization of Salaried Employees (TVK, founded in 1957). Politically STTK is divided, as is the lower level white-collar class itself, between SDP, Conservatives and Center. The Central Organization of Academic Professionals (AKAVA, founded in 1950), with more than 400,000 members, represents higher level white-collar workers and tends to be politically conservative. In sum, just over two million Finnish employees are unionized in three central organizations, each with separate core membership groups and consequently different political orientations and political preferences.

Traditionally the Organization of Agricultural Producers (MTK) has had a strong position in Finnish politics, due to the sheer size of the agrarian sector and the MTK's direct links to the Agrarian party. The decline in the number of farmers and the effects of EU membership have undermined the MTK's importance, however.

Employer representation has also become more concentrated. In 1992 the oldest employers' federation the STK (representing heavy industry) merged with the smaller Confederation of Finnish Industries. The new Confederation of Finnish

Industry and Employers (TT later EK) represents the employers of approximately 550,000 employees. The concentration increased in 2004 when an employers' organization for the services (commanding 350,000 employees) joined the TT. In the public sector (with 550,000 employees) there are two separate employers' organizations: the Commission for Municipal Employers and the State Employer Office. Needless to say, the political orientation of the employers' organizations tends towards conservatism (Alestalo 1985: 194), and they actively pursue their interests in the political arena. In their social policy orientation, the employers' federations have had different orientations. For large-scale industry, indirect labor costs arising from social security contributions have not been as important as for small-scale industry and service-sector employers. However, global competition has changed the picture and perhaps the unification of the employers' federations is an indication that employers will strive for lower labor costs in greater unison.

The unification of the SAK inaugurated a new era of social corporatism in Finnish policy-making. Income policy negotiations were conducted on a tripartite basis. Employer and employee organizations bargained over wages while the government tried to promote agreements by using "sticks" and "carrots." Sticks were mainly increased taxes if wage increases were excessive, and carrots were typically promises of higher labor-related benefits. The first income-policy agreement was reached in 1968 and since then almost all wage negotiations have included "a social package" to which the government adhered as long as the labor market partners behaved themselves. The social package was used to provide longer holidays in 1971, introduce sick pay in 1972, lengthen the duration of maternity leave in 1980, and so on. Social package agreements could also include cuts in benefits (http://www.sak.fi/miksak.shtml/03?593). These agreements played a decisive role in parliamentary discussions when Parliament and government debated retrenchment bills in the 1990s. Because of their strength and strong role in the administration of employment-related pensions the government had to bargain with social partners with various sticks and carrots.

III PENSION SYSTEM

Historical overview

Since the 1890s, there have been attempts almost every decade—usually initiated by the Social Democrats—to reform the major social insurance laws, but most of them failed (Kangas 1991: 167). The struggle over social insurance was between the two main political forces, the SDP and the ML (Agrarian Party). The Social Democrats emphasized adequate earnings-related benefits and their strategy was aimed at insurance for wage earners but not necessarily for other socio-economic groups.

The Agrarians advocated universal coverage combined with flat-rate benefits. National insurance covering the entire population, including unpaid family workers in agriculture and housewives, and flat-rate pensions were more favorable for the rural population still living in a subsistence economy than for income-related benefits (Niemelä 1988; Kangas 1991; Salminen 1987, 1993). Due to the rural nature of Finnish society, the Finnish Agrarian party was much stronger than in any other Nordic country (Alestalo, Flora and Uusitalo 1985). Moreover, The ML line was often supported by the so-called back-woods rural communists (Allardt 1971). Through judicious tactical coalitions, sometimes with the communists, sometimes with the right-wing parties, the ML managed to use the minority rule veto options and block initiatives for workers' insurance unless the program covered the entire population. Thus the late introduction of the first laws and the rapid expansion of Finnish social insurance coverage can be explained by the postponed Social Democratic demands for income replacement, combined with the agrarian claims for extensive coverage (Niemelä 1988; Baldwin 1990; Salminen 1993; Kangas and Palme 2005). Had the SDP been more powerful, social insurance would have been adopted much earlier, and, with all probability, Finnish developments would have followed the Continental European pattern to a greater extent: first, coverage for industrial workers, and then a gradual expansion to other occupations (Mannio 1967).

The first National Pension (NP) Act in Finland came into effect in 1939—of the current OECD member countries only Switzerland and Japan were slower (Palme 1990). The pension design was a victory for the bourgeois parties, which wanted a funded pension scheme based on individual pension accounts and income-related contributions. The newly-established semi-public National Pension Institution (KELA) administered the scheme. In principle, the scheme had universal coverage, but due to the maturation period of 40 years, most of the elderly did not receive benefits, and pensions were meager (Niemelä 1988). The other problem was the low level of benefits: even with supplements, the full NP amounted to 15 percent of the average wage (Kangas 1988).

The scheme was totally reformed in 1957. The SPD-ML coalition agreed on a universal basic pension complemented by income-related pensions for employees. However, in the final vote, the ML abandoned the income-related part. Previous funds, accumulated mainly by employee and employer contributions, were distributed on a flat-rate basis to every citizen over 65 years of age. The general strike that took place when the bill was debated in Parliament distracted the SDP and trade unions, and the ML version of the bill passed. Employee organizations later criticized the 1957 law for confiscating employees' pension funds and distributing them to the agrarian elderly (Salminen 1987; Ahtokari 1988).

The 1956 Act established universalism: everybody older than 65 years became eligible for a national pension. The pension had two parts: a universal basic amount, contingent on five years residency, and an income-tested supplement. Compared to the other Nordic countries the universal basic amount was low (Palme 1990; Øverbye 1996). The principle of residualism and income-testing was applied until 1985, and since then the NP has only been tested against income from other legislated pensions.

The last major NP reform was carried out in 1996 when the basic amount was abolished. National pensions are indexed to a cost-of-living index.

Individual employers have long provided old age pensions to reward long service. Despite the rapid growth of occupational schemes towards the end of the 1950s, the actual coverage of these programs remained limited to as few as 20 percent of private sector employees, mainly white-collar workers in large companies. In order to guarantee portability and to extend the coverage to all blue-collar workers, the trade unions, supported by the SDP, insisted on legislated, compulsory schemes. In 1956, Fagerholm's (SDP) cabinet established a committee including all central partners to study the pension issue. Initially the employers rejected legislated pensions, but their attitudes gradually changed when they realized that such a reform was inevitable. The consultations between the STK and the Swedish employer organization SAF also contributed to this change in attitudes. SAF advised the STK to accept a legislated scheme if it was possible, to make it decentralized, with private insurance companies as insurance carriers and the administration of pension funds in the hands of the employers (see Salminen 1987).

For the employees, pension adequacy was more important than the question of organizational form. Moreover, the SAK and SDP were skeptical about a publicly-administrated scheme: they were afraid that once again the Agrarians would be able to "confiscate" employees' pensions if the scheme were to be publicly organized. A legislated scheme run by labor market partners offered employees the institutional veto opportunity to oppose Parliament. The proposal satisfied the SAK and STK. The former got statutory pensions financed by employer contributions, and the latter got a decentralized system, mainly organized through private pension insurance institutions (Salminen 1987, 1993). In a way, one can reformulate Esping-Andersen's (1985) famous adage and argue that in Finland "markets were used against politics."

In Parliament, the Agrarians and Communists opposed the committee proposal, while the SDP and the Conservatives backed it. The Agrarian minority government refused to introduce the bill and therefore, quite astonishingly, this major reform was adopted on the basis of a private member's bill (Salminen 1987). This SDP initiative was finally accepted in 1961, and private sector employees got their pension scheme (TEL). A separate scheme (LEL) was established for employees in short-term employment contracts. Later (in 1974) farmers and other self-employed persons got their own programs (MYEL and YEL, respectively). Thus a certain degree of corporatism is built into Finnish pension design, with coverage according to sectoral and occupational lines. The preliminary target pension level was 40 percent of the final wage after 40 years in employment. Pensions are indexed to the so-called TEL-index based on wages and the cost of living.

Existing arrangements for public sector employees were neither financially nor administratively merged with TEL. Pensions for state employees were somewhat standardized, but because of the independence of local administrations, there was a plethora of municipal arrangements. The introduction of the TEL-system accentuated the need to further codify and standardize the divergent public sector schemes. Again, special committees were established to study the issue and to formulate bills for the municipal and state employees. Just as the SAK and SDP feared putting employment-related pensions in public hands, the municipalities opposed joining the TEL-system. Municipalities—the majority of which were politically agrarian—feared that under TEL the labor market partners would get the upper hand. The municipalities therefore wanted to establish a separate scheme run by the local authorities. The act on local sector pensions (KVTEL) run by a special insurance body, the Municipal Pension Institution (KEVA), was adopted in 1964. A separate state pension scheme (VEL) became effective two years later (Blomster 2004).

Public sector benefits have traditionally been somewhat more generous than those in the private sector. Public sector pensions paid 66 percent of final salary after 30 years of employment and the pension age was 63 compared to 65 years in TEL. Thus the occupational "bonus" was built into the legislated schemes, and separate occupational arrangements which were commonplace in many other countries, were not developed.

The two main lines in developing pension policy, that is, the social democratic income-relatedness for the employees and the agrarian "equally to everyone" universalism, have frequently popped up in the political agenda. As early as 1966, the Center Party insisted on increasing the role national pensions in the overall pension design. Trade unions responded by informing the parliamentary groups that they would use "all labor market measures" to resist such plans (Varoma 1971: 60). The threat was effective and Parliament agreed to follow the course the trade unions recommended. Six years later the same situation emerged, but now the presidential veto was also involved (Salminen 1987: 127–38). In 1972, the Center Party presented to the SDP minority cabinet an interpellation on national pensions. Following its traditional line, the Center demanded that a higher flat-rate pension be adopted. The central labor market organizations resisted, fearing that a costly NP reform would block the further development of TEL-pensions. However, with elections rapidly approaching, the government did not dare refrain from proposing basic pension improvements. In search of credit, all parties accepted the bill and proposed their own improvements, and the reform passed in Parliament was three times more expensive than the original bill (Niemelä 1988). Both the employee and employer federations criticized the Cabinet and Parliament for neglecting the opinions of the social partners. After Parliament approved the bill, President Kekkonen consulted with the Minister of Social Affairs and representatives of the employers and employee organizations, after which he announced he would veto the law. Instead, Kekkonen asked the biggest labor market partners (SAK and STK) and the farmers' MTK to prepare a better proposal for the future development of the pension system and the coordination of NP and TEL. Following the recommendations of social partners, national pensions were increased only modestly, and the social package attached to the income-policy negotiations of 1974 increased the annual TEL accrual rate to 1.5 percent and the target level to 60 percent of income (Niemelä 1988). After this humiliating defeat the government resigned. The episode is revealing because it explains why subsequent governments have been willing to use consociational devices in order to avoid confrontations and save face.

Description of the current pension system

Coverage

Despite its corporatist traits and sectoral divisions, the Finnish pension system is compact and all pensions are coordinated with each other. Until 1996, all pensioners received the universal basic National Pension (NP). Earnings-related pension schemes paid supplemental benefits on top of the NP basic amount. For those with few or no employment-based benefits, the government paid an NP Supplement (Fig. 6.2; see also Fig. 6.3 and Appendix Table A6). In 1996, the basic amount was made subject to income-testing, and therefore abolished for most pensioners. Consequently, employment-related pensions started to play an even more decisive role. Put another way, employment began to trump citizenship and the Finnish pension design moved towards the Continental European type, with stronger emphasis on employment-based benefits.

In principle, the shift from the people's pension to basic security (see pp. 282–3) did not necessarily imply any deterioration in benefits. However, in Finland, there is a downward trend in the replacement rates of national pensions. In the 1970s, a full NP was 50 percent of the average wage. During the booming economy of the 1980s, basic pensions could not keep pace with increases in average income, and the replacement rate declined to 35 percent in the 1990s (Jäntti, Kangas and Ritakallio 1996). However, fewer pensioners depend solely on the NP; by 2000 the share of pensioners with only the NP was less than 10 percent.

As Figure 6.2 shows, there are no ceilings in Finnish earnings-related pensions. Until 1996, pension-carrying income was based on two median years for the four last years in employment—after 1996 according to the average income for the ten last years. This kind of pension calculation was beneficial for employees whose earnings increased with years in employment. Therefore, these groups had no incentives to demand alternative occupational pension schemes to compensate relative losses in income. That is one reason the second and third pillars are virtually non-existent in Finland.

Although existing occupational pensions were not merged with the TEL they were closely integrated with the legislated schemes when the TEL system was created in the early 1960s. First, the existing pension institutes could acquire responsibility for the running of the TEL scheme together with private insurance companies. Second, these institutes had the option of guaranteeing additional TEL benefits for those interim cohorts that, due to their age, had no chance to accumulate full pension "percentages." In principle, joining these schemes was voluntary, but after acceptance, benefits were regulated by TEL legislation. In practice this meant that portability, indexation, and target benefit levels in occupational schemes were the same as in TEL, but a full pension could be accumulated in less than 40 years. Thus, the coordination of first- second- and third-tier pensions in Finland follows the "difference" or "tie-in"[1] principle: the value of occupational benefits is determined by the difference between the target level of 60 percent and the actual TEL level. The closer the actual pension comes to the target level the less room there is for additional arrangements. Similarly,

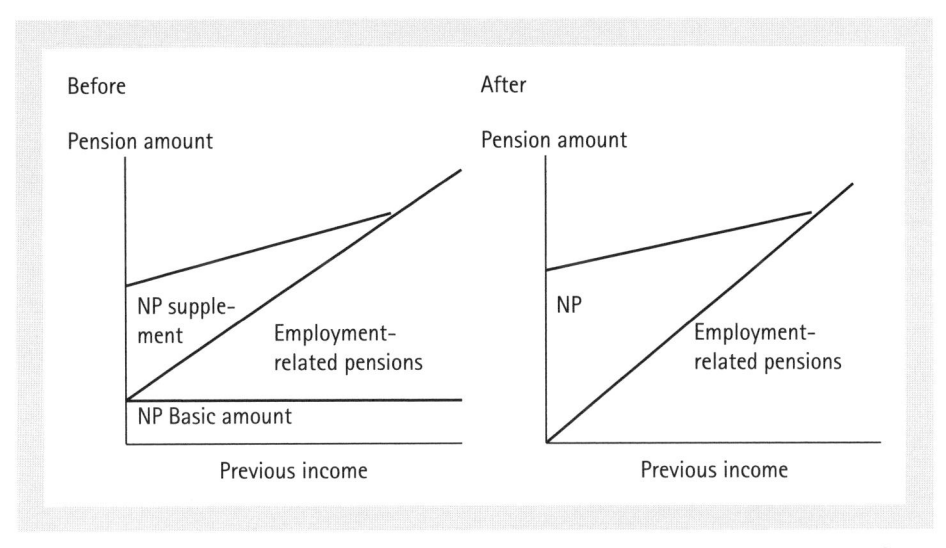

Fig. 6.2 The structure of Finnish pension schemes before and after the 1996 reform

the bigger the TEL/VEL/KVTEL pension the smaller the NP pension (see Table 6.3). The share of voluntary occupational schemes has declined from 6 percent in 1965 to 2 percent in 2000 and this declining trend is likely to continue since the in-flow of new members is gradually declining. In the mid-1970s about 20 percent of employees were covered by occupational schemes and in 2000 the share was close to 10 percent (Kangas and Palme 1996: 223; Hinrichs and Kangas 2003).

In Figure 6.3, Finnish pensions have been "pillarized" following the European Union categorization and the Finnish interpretation. The Finnish claim is that the first pillar should include both the national pension and all legislated (mandatory) employment-related pensions. As is evident on the basis of Figure 6.2, the Finnish employment pensions provide the equivalent of both basic (tier one) and supplemental pensions (tier two), and are compulsory and universal (first pillar). All additional or voluntary TEL-pensions are placed in the second pillar.

The coverage and importance of the second pillar voluntary occupational pension has been limited and it is further squeezed by the application of the "difference principle." In 2000, entry to the additional TEL pension was stopped which means that these pensions gradually will disappear (Härkönen and Laitinen-Kuikka 2003: 97). At present, the third pillar is not that well developed either. Until the early 1960s more than one million Finns had savings-based life insurance policies to compensate for the lack of proper pension security (Kangas 1988). The introduction of employment-related pensions changed this picture. By the mid-1980s there were hardly any private individual pensions left: the third pillar/tier was virtually non-existent. The stock market boom of the late 1980s and early 1990s caused a rapid increase in the popularity of individual pension policies. In a couple of years the number of policies increased by more than 200,000, aided by tax incentives. In the late 1990s, the

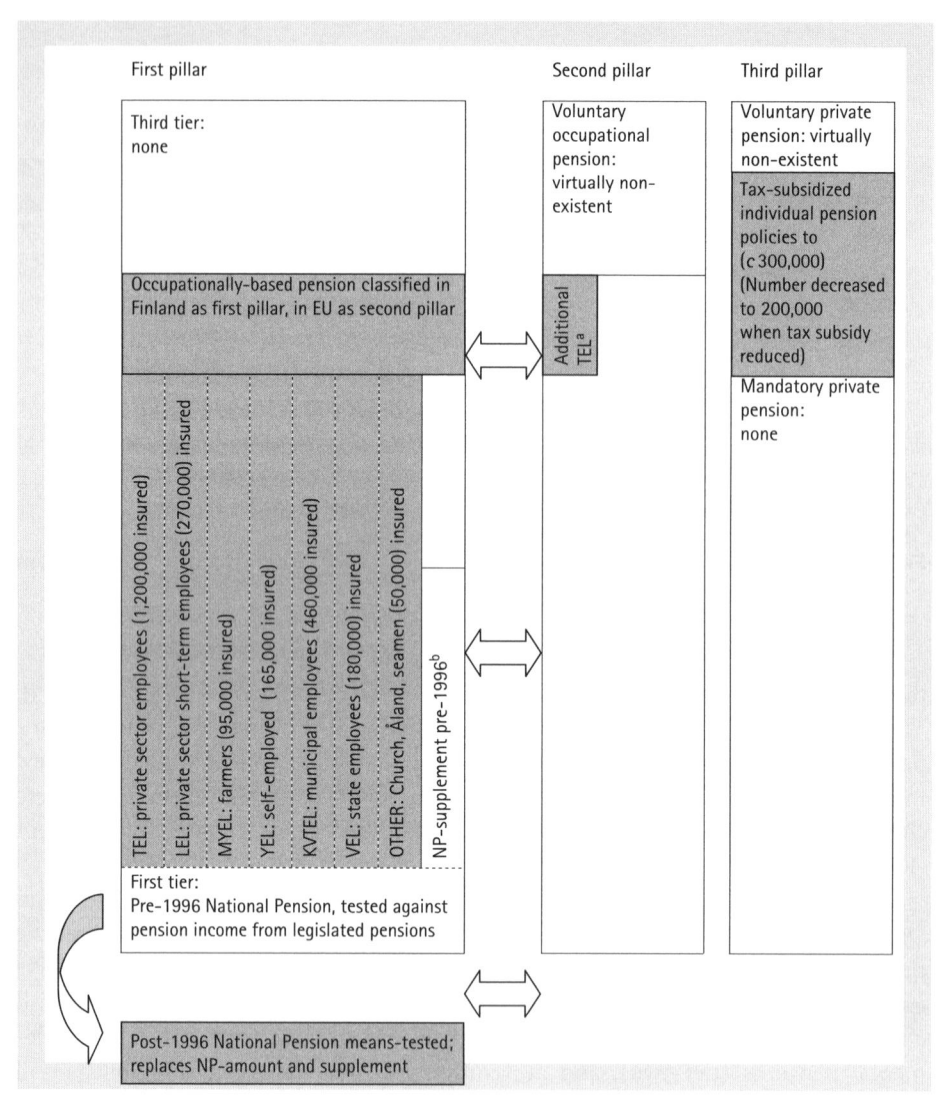

Fig. 6.3 Pension system in Finland

First pillar

Third tier: none

Occupationally-based pension classified in Finland as first pillar, in EU as second pillar

- TEL: private sector employees (1,200,000 insured)
- LEL: private sector short-term employees (270,000) insured
- MYEL: farmers (95,000 insured)
- YEL: self-employed (165,000 insured)
- KVTEL: municipal employees (460,000 insured)
- VEL: state employees (180,000) insured
- OTHER: Church, Åland, seamen (50,000) insured
- NP-supplement pre-1996[b]

First tier: Pre-1996 National Pension, tested against pension income from legislated pensions

Post-1996 National Pension means-tested; replaces NP-amount and supplement

Second pillar

Voluntary occupational pension: virtually non-existent

Additional TEL[a]

Third pillar

Voluntary private pension: virtually non-existent

Tax-subsidized individual pension policies to (c 300,000) (Number decreased to 200,000 when tax subsidy reduced)

Mandatory private pension: none

[a] Coverage less than 10% of employees.
[b] For pensioners without occupational pensions.
Source: http://www.etk.fi/Dynagen_attachments/Att20597/20597.pdf; Lattunen and Vidlund 2003: 27-29; http://www.etera.fi/finnish//Yritystiedot/lel_tyoelakekassa/index.html

government began to plan to abolish, or at least to limit, tax benefits, which immediately precipitated a decrease in the demand for individual pension.

Administration and financing

The NP system is administered by KELA, the national pensions administration body, which also administers all social benefits providing citizens' basic security.

Table 6.3 Proportional shares (%) of different pension schemes of total pension expenditure in Finland 1950–2000

Year	National pensions	Private sector	State pensions	Municipal pensions	Voluntary additional
1950	28.6	.0	69.0	1.5	2.4
1960	69.2	.0	27.0	3.0	5.3
1970	56.9	11.5	22.4	8.2	5.0
1980	42.1	29.3	18.5	8.7	4.5
1990	32.4	39.2	16.9	10.0	4.1
2000	19.6	48.8	17.8	13.8	2.1

Sources: KELA 2001: 38–39; KELA 1985: 28–29. Some minor pension schemes are excluded so the percentages do not sum up to 100%). "Private sector" includes TEL, LEL, YEL, MyeL and some minor schemes.

Parliament supervises KELA by electing 12 MPs to form KELA's supervisory board and by nominating the Managing Director and Deputy Directors (five persons). Because the NP has been PAYG since 1957, KELA no longer controls large funds. The employer contribution varies (2005) from between 1.4 percent to 4.5 percent of the payroll, whereas the employees do not pay national pension contribution.

In principle, a TEL pension provider can be a pension insurance company, a company pension fund, an industry-wide pension fund or an industry-specific pension provider. In 2000, there were 47 different insurance carriers (http://www.etk.fi). However, the majority of their activity is concentrated in the six pension insurance companies: almost 90 percent of TEL employees are insured in companies, with the two largest companies providing more than half of all insurance policies. Almost all TEL insurance polices (99%) are also run by TEL-companies. Thus, the system is nominally decentralized but in practice it is centralized in a handful of big companies.

The Finnish Centre for Pensions (*Eläketurvakeskus*, ETK) handles common tasks (e.g., employment and pension registers), and the Finnish Pension Alliance (TELA) promotes the common interests. Despite administrative decentralization, benefits are the same for all employee categories.

The representatives of the labor market partners participate in the administrative bodies of these institutions and at least half of the members of the supervisory board and board of directors are nominated by social partners (employees and employers have equal shares). The companies have collective responsibility: if one of the institutions goes bankrupt, the remaining ones must cover the costs. Activities are supervised by the Insurance Supervisory Authority (Hietaniemi and Vidlund 2003: 56). The other pension schemes (VEL, KVTEL, MYEL, and LEL) are "centralized" and each of them is run by a special pensions institution. The administration of the LEL follows the TEL's corporatist principles, whereas the employee's representation is less important in the other schemes.

Until 1993, employment-related pensions were financed entirely by employer contributions that equaled 17.4 percent of the payroll in 1990. Since 1993, financing has followed a more Bismarckian line with the introduction of employee contributions. By 2005, the average TEL contribution was 21.6 percent whereof the employee's contribution was 4.6 percent if the employee was younger than 53 years and 5.8 percent for older employees (http://www.etk.fi/Dynagen_attachments/Att21629/21629.pdf). Employment-related pensions are partially funded and part PAYG. In 2000, the assets in legislated pension funds corresponded to 60 percent of GDP. In the EU, only the Netherlands (120%), Sweden (85%), and the UK (80%) have a higher degree of funding.

Investment activity is loosely regulated in legislation: "the funds must be invested safely and productively." The Ministry of Social Affairs supervises the use of pension assets. In 2003, the lion's share (52%) of funds was invested in bonds and the rest in shares (23%), real estate (10%), loans (10%) and the remainder in market money investments (http://www.tela.fi/Avenglo1.nsf?OpenDatabase).

To summarize, Finnish pension funds have been used for two main purposes or "national projects." First, NP funds were used to build basic infrastructure such as power stations and electricity grids (Niemelä 1988; Kangas 1988). The shift to the PAYG principle halted this national project, but the maturing private-sector TEL scheme assumed the role of one of the main financiers of the Finnish economy. The second "national" project was industrial development. Until the 1980s most TEL fund investments were directed at Finnish industry and had two main forms. First, enterprises could borrow part of their pension contributions, and second, pension companies themselves could make investments. In the 1970s and 1980s about one-third of these investments went to industry with another 20 percent going to the construction section and 15 percent to the real estate sector (Kangas 1988: 42).

Economic integration means that the share of national investments has fallen markedly and lending to the Finnish enterprises has lost its importance. Also the role of domestic investments has decreased dramatically. In 2000, almost 60 percent of investments were domestic, but by 2004 the share was down to 34 percent, with another 40 percent going to the Eurozone and the remainder to non-European countries (http://www.tela.fi). In 2004, almost half of investments were in bonds, and half in shares (30% in foreign shares and about 30% in Finnish shares). The rest of the investments are divided between real estate and investment loans, about 10 percent in each (http://www.tela.fi).

Benefits

National pension benefits are payable to citizens at least 65 years old who have lived in Finland for at least at least 3 years after the age of 16, or non-citizen residents living in Finland for at least 5 years before retirement. Benefits are tested against other pensions income. The maximum benefit is about €495 per month, depending on place of residence and marital status. Forty years of residence is required for a full pension. Earnings-related pensions pay benefits based on accrual rates from age 18 to

68. From age 18 to 52, the accrual rate is 1.5 percent per year; between ages 53 and 62 the accrual rate is 4.5 percent; and from 63 to 68 the accrual rate is 4.5 percent (rules as of January 2005).

IV Politics of pension reform since 1980

Overview

The following section discusses the main pension reforms carried out in the 1990s: introduction of employee pension contributions; the harmonization (and reduction) of public sector pensions to the level of private sector pensions; the change in the calculation base for pension-carrying income; the abolition of the national pension basic amount; and the "big pension reforms" of 2003/2004. Besides these major reforms, several other changes were implemented: in 1985 means-testing was abolished from the NP, part-time pensions were introduced within the private sector pensions in 1987, the early retirement option was introduced to public sector pensions in 1989, the age limit for the eligibility for individual early-retirement was increased from 55 to 58 years in 1994 and so on. However, an analysis of a limited number of reforms in detail will give a sufficiently detailed picture of pension policy-making in Finland and illuminate how political actors and social partners have acted in the institutional settings described above.

The report of the 1990 Pension Committee (Komittebetänkande 1991: 41) formed the background for pension policy debates in the 1990s. This extensive report (almost 400 pages) included international comparisons on pensions, and analysis of demographic changes, financing, and the future challenges facing pension systems. The Committee noted that the old age dependency ratio would increase in Finland from 19 percent in 1990 to 39 percent in 2040. The 1990 figure was one of the lowest in Europe, while the 2040 forecast was among the highest. Pension expenditure was predicted to increase from less than 10 percent to 20 percent of GDP, and social spending from 25 to 35 percent of GDP, while employers' pension contributions were to reach 40 percent of payroll, up from less than 20 percent in 1990. These grim figures prompted discussion of rolling back pension entitlements and sharing costs. Based on these data the committee recommended several steps to make the Finnish pension system sustainable. First, the committee tried to find ways to increase the actual retirement age and reduce early retirement. It also made recommendations concerning pension-carrying income and the level of public pensions. The report proposed that pensions be based on the ten last years in employment. In order to reduce anticipated pension costs in the public sector, the VEL and KVTEL pension were to be cut to the level of TEL benefits, which would cut pension contributions by 5–6 percentage points in 2040.

Union representatives reacted negatively and proposed using the Swedish best-15-years principle for the benefit formula. Unions did not oppose cuts in public sector pensions, but they argued that such a dramatic policy change should be carefully discussed in a forum where public sector employees were properly represented. The employer representatives also expressed reservations, demanding that career income should be used for pension purposes.

When the Committee delivered its report in 1989, Finland was in the middle of an economic upturn. The situation changed rapidly in 1990, as the country fell into its deepest recession ever. GDP fell in three consecutive years. Unemployment rates skyrocketed, from less than 4 percent in 1990, to close to 18 percent in 1995, increasing public debt from virtually zero in 1990 to more than 60 percent of GDP in 1996. This was the national economic context in which all reform proposals were discussed, and this crisis-consciousness no doubt affected the perceptions of the public and political and labor market actors.

The introduction of employee contributions 1992

In the 1991 elections, the SDP lost its status as the largest party and the Center Party came to power. Center leader Esko Aho's bourgeois coalition government (Center, KOK, SFP, and Christian Democrats) was immediately hit by an economic avalanche. In early 1991, there was international speculation against various currencies including the Finnish Mark. The Director of the Bank of Finland tried to save the Mark from devaluation and the country from recession by negotiating an extensive crisis income-policy package including a wage freeze and a partial transfer of pension contributions from employers to employees. In this exceptional crisis situation the labor market actors accepted the "internal devaluation" package. However, the pressure against the currency was so strong that the agreement did not prevent devaluation. The incomes policy agreement remained valid, however, and it was against this background that Aho presented the bill on employee contributions to Parliament. The deep recession was the short-term factor that triggered the government to propose the bill, but the motivation for introducing employee contributions—as in all the other reforms discussed here—was based on long-term prognoses on demographic changes as well as the short-term need to combat the recession.

The bill called for the introduction of a 3 percent employee contribution for one year (HE 230/1991 vp). The bill had three motivations. First, the bill argued that the long-term demographic and expenditure trends indicated that the employee contribution would increase and be too high. Second, the bill was planned to produce short-term savings effects, calculated at FIM 3,700 million in 1993. Third, the measure was negotiated as part of the 1991 income-policy agreement. According to the

Table 6.4 Overview of proposed and enacted pension reforms in Finland

Year	Name of reform	Reform process (chronology)	Reform measures
1991	*Laki työntekijän eläkemaksusta*	• crisis income-policy package including wage freeze and a partial transfer of pension contributions from employers to employees • February 25, 1992 center, cons., Swedes, christian-democrats submit bill providing for employees' temporary participation in pension financing according to government, bill might affect Constitution; argument rejected • pension changes agreed as part of 1991 income-policy agreement • opposition from the left i.e. mainly SDP • April 24, 1991 report of the Constitutional Committee no major changes in Committee of Social Affairs • October 10, 1991 first reading • October 16, 1991 second reading • October 20, 1991 final reading • November 13, 1991 promulgation	• introduction of employees' pension contributions
1992	*Laki valtion eläkelain muuttamisesta (and Laki kunnallisten viranhaltijain ja työntekijäin eläkelain muuttamisesta)*	• Pension Committee 1990 suggested adjusting public sector to lower private sector pension system • July 1992 government bill to change state employees' pensions • September 15, 1992 general discussion in Parliament • October 1992 government bill for reform of the municipal pension scheme	• harmonization of public sector pension benefits with private sector pensions benefits

(Continued)

Table 6.4 (Continued)

Year	Name of reform	Reform process (chronology)	Reform measures
		• December 18, 1992 first and second parliamentary reading • December 21, 1992 third reading; bill passed with coalition majority (center, cons., SPP, and CD) • December 30, 1992 promulgation	
1995	*Laki kansaneläkelain muuttamisesta*	• September 29, 1995 submission of governmental bill to Parliament • October 6, 1995 parliamentary discussion • Constitutional Committee states that the abolishment of flat-rate basic pensions is not a constitutional issue • November 21, 1995 first and second reading • November 28, 1995 third reading; bill passed; some Social Democrats abstained • December 18, 1995 promulgation	• abolition of the basic universal pension and introduction of procedure of testing NP against other pension income
1995	*Laki työntekijäin eläkelain muuttamisesta*	• May 5, 1995 labor market agreement on changes in income for pension purposes • September 29, 1995 government proposal presented to Parliament and sent for preparation • November 9, 1995 Constitutional Committee accepts the proposal • November 11, 1995 Social Committee report given to Parliament • November 16, 1995 first reading • November 21, 1995 second reading	• pension amount is calculated on the basis of 10 last years in employment • previously two median years of the four last years in employment

		• November 28, 1995 third reading; dissidents from Left vote against
• December 18, 1995 promulgation
2002	*Laki työntekijäin eläkelain muuttamisesta*	• September 5, 2002 labor market organizations accept reform plan proposed by the Kari Puro expert committee
• November 6, 2002 government proposal presented to Parliament
• February 11, 2003 Social and Health Committee report to parliamentary plenum; objection of the Center party
• February 12, 2003 first reading
• February 17, 2003 second reading and vote
• June 27, 2003 promulgation	• change of accrual rate from 1.5% per insurance year between 23 and 64 with a maximum of 60% after 40 years in employment, to employment career between 18 and 69 with accrual rate of 1.5% between 17 and 52 and 1.9% between 53 and 62 and 4.5% beyond the age of 63
• taking into account study periods of five years and child rearing of three years
• abolishment of target replacement rate of 60%
• introduction of flexible retirement age between 63 and 68
• extension of the reference period from ten years to whole working career
• linking pension adjustment to increased life expectancy
• disincentives against early retirement
2004	*Laki kunnallisen eläkelain muuttamisesta* and *Laki valtion eläkelain muuttamisesta*	• April 16, 2004 submission of bill to change municipal and state public sector pension schemes
• June 17, 2004 Social Committee report
• June 17, 2004 first reading
• June 22, 2004 second reading and vote, accepted by clear majority
• July 30, 2004 promulgation	• Harmonization of the public sector with the private sector pension system

government, the bill might include constitutional issues, and so ought to be submitted to the Constitutional Committee (CC) for a decision about whether a simple majority would suffice for passage. In her presentation of the bill the Minister of Social Affairs strongly emphasized that the development of employment-related pensions was the domain of the labor market partners, who had given their consent to the reform. She also revealed that the employee contribution perhaps was going to be permanent, but in compensation, participation in financing would create opportunities for employee's organizations to participate more than previously in the administration of the pension funds (PTK 11/1991 vp).

The SDP and Left immediately criticized the bill. According to the SDP, the bill mirrored the old agrarian quest for flat-rate benefits, but the party did not explicitly oppose the bill. The Left rejected the bill, arguing that the tax-deductible contribution was highly regressive because low-income workers pay no taxes. With these comments the bill was sent to the Committee for Social Affairs for preparation.

A majority of the CC saw no reason why the law could not be passed with a simple majority. There were three objections (from the Left, the Rural Party and the SDP) demanding that the proposal be accepted according to constitutional procedure, that is, either to postpone it until the next parliament and accept it then by a two-thirds majority, or to declare the bill "urgent" with a five-sixths majority and then adopt it with a two-thirds majority of MPs. The minority argued that because of the employee contribution, the bill would conflict with property rights specified in the Constitution (PeVL 8/1992 vp).

The Social Affairs Committee made no major changes to the bill. In their objection, the Left Party MPs proposed that in order to avoid a regressive effect, the contribution should be only 1.5 percent of wages and not tax-deductible (StVM 27/1992 vp). In the first plenary debate (10 October 1992), the Social Democratic Chair of the Committee argued that pensions were a form of deferred pay, so that employees had always participated in the financing of their pensions. He also emphasized that the labor market partners had accepted the central principles of the reform: "In the SDP our starting point is that if the labor market organizations have agreed on this... the bill should go ahead in this format" (PTK 125/1992 vp: 3688). One negative issue that the Chair addressed was that the pension contribution would decrease pension-carrying income (PTK 125/1992 vp: 3688, 3692). The Left continued its criticism of the regressiveness of the proposal, citing the negative effects on pension-carrying income as well as qualifying income for other social benefits: "using this very simple legislative trick, that is, that the TEL-contribution will not be counted as part of the wage, the government can achieve large scale cuts in the whole area of social security..." (PTK 125/1992 vp: 3690). Thus the question was not just about a small percentage reduction, but a larger principle that would cut the level of social security in its entirety. The speaker from the Left Party emphasized that the trade unions had not accepted this point. The representative of the Rural Party argued: "The starting point of the Rural Party is that the trade unions have accepted this. We here in Parliament are not so good at changing the decisions made in Hakaniemi"[2] (PTK 125/1992 vp: 3691). But another speaker from the same party supported the Left, and insisted that pension contributions should be a part of pension-carrying income.

In the second reading (October 16) the Left Party continued to propose that the contribution should not be tax deductible and 1.5 percent wage. The proposal was defeated (138 to 31). Only the Left Party and some dissidents from the SDP voted for the changes proposed by the Left (PTK 128/1992 vp).

During the final plenary reading on October 20 (PTK 129/1992 vp), Rural Party MPs explained in their opening speeches why they would vote for the bill: because the social partners had agreed on it! They also lashed out against the Left and the SDP: Parliament could not vote against something the labor market partners had legally agreed on. By proposing this, the left-wing parties showed distrust in the ability of their own constituency to make reasonable decisions. The issue was delicate for the Left: "We cannot give the labor market partners an open mandate so open that even bad decisions will bind the hands of Parliament" (PTK 129/1992 vp: 3781). The Conservatives used irony against the leftist parties: "In the left they constantly insist that the Aho government has to negotiate with the labor market partners and prepare bills according to their will. Now we are handling a bill that the trade unions have agreed upon and the left are demanding that we reject the bill" (PTK 129/1992 vp: 3781). In the final ballot, the governmental proposal got 114 votes. In addition to the bourgeois parties, the majority of the SDP supported the government. Only the Left and a handful of left-wing Social Democrats voted against the bill.

The introduction of an employee contribution is a good example of the legislative process in Finland. Politically the situation was exceptional: for the first time since 1966 the country had a genuinely bourgeois cabinet that faced the most severe economic crisis in the history of independent Finland. However, the economic crisis also helped the cabinet. Crisis consciousness was already widespread and everybody understood that "extraordinary times demand extraordinary measures." The earlier attempts to avoid devaluation by carrying through "internal devaluation" had softened attitudes among the trade unions. Thus the window of opportunity was partially open for the government and it successfully jumped through. The impetus for the bill was the agreement between the labor market partners, which gave the impression that the government itself had no political ambitions but merely wanted to promote the will of the social partners. The government also maintained this low profile in the parliamentary discussions. A clever strategy, whether accidental or deliberate, was that the bill was limited to one year. This was politically easier to sell than a permanent law; although it appeared likely that the procedure would become permanent.

This governmental proposal included elements of obfuscation, compensation (Pierson 1994) and de-politicization. The impacts on pension rights were not addressed either in the proposal or in the very few speeches given by the governmental parties. There are some indications that the trade unions may not have been fully aware of the full consequences of the agreement (*Helsingin Sanomat* 14 December 2000). Employees were compensated for individual contributions with the promise to increase employee representation in pension administration. This issue was perhaps most important in the municipal KVTEL-scheme, where trade unions had a smaller role than in the TEL scheme (Blomster 2004: 137). The strategy of de-politicization was partially successful, and the parliamentary discussion centered on the question of what the labor market partners had or had not agreed on. This was particularly important for the bourgeois cabinet. On three other occasions when Aho's government unilaterally sent bills on curtailments in unemployment insurance, the trade unions threatened the cabinet with general strike and the cabinet had to retreat (Timonen 2003: 93–94). This reflects the central role of the labor market partners in Finnish retrenchment politics, and the need for the government to reach a deal with the trade unions.

The 1992 harmonization of private and public sector pensions

Aho's bourgeois cabinet continued its incremental approach to pension reform. In July 1992, the government presented a bill to harmonize VEL pensions with other occupational schemes. The government was motivated by majoritarian politics and fairness concerns. The government argued that there were no justifiable reasons for guaranteeing better benefits to minority groups that just happened to work in the public sector. Public sector pensions should thus be harmonized "downwards." In the crisis situation, an upwards harmonization of private sector pensions was hardly realistic. Thus in the name of equality the public sector employees had to refrain from their previous extra occupational benefits to save the national economy.

The 1990 calculations of the Pension Committee had shown that the public sector schemes had more severe problems than the TEL: for example, in 1990 the contribution rate was about 30 percent of payroll in VEL compared to 16 percent in TEL. The proposed reform did not promise short-term savings, but in the long run the savings on public sector pensions were predicted to be 19 percent of total costs by 2050 (HE 110/1992 vp: 3). Cuts would only apply to state employees whose work contracts began after 1 January 1993. The law was a so-called "grandpa/ma" reform (Pierson 1994), which hit only future beneficiaries and had no immediate effect on the state budget.

The general discussion of the bill took place on 15 September 1992 (PTK 97/1992 vp). On the same day, the Ministry of Finance published a list of austerity measures including cuts in all social benefits to reduce the accelerating budget deficit. The target replacement rate was to be cut to 50 percent for all pensions. The timing of the announcement was a clever move by the Treasury: the list overshadowed the parliamentary discussion on public sector pensions, and the acceptance of the government's austerity measures seemed to be a victory compared to the Treasury alternatives.

The Left (Vas) sharply criticized the bill, arguing that it foreshadowed more substantial cuts in all pension schemes and accusing the government of caving in to the Treasury. The speakers on the Left anticipated, correctly, that the municipal scheme would also be harmonized with the VEL. The Left demanded that instead of the proposed cuts, the pension reform should introduce an accumulation period of 35 years for all pensions, as well as a benefit ceiling. This would reduce the highest pensions, generate immediate savings and be socially more just. The speakers also demanded that the bill be returned to the social partners for better preparation. Some Social Democrats also argued that the bill should be sent back to the labor market actors, and agreed to the accumulation period of 35 years. However, the tone of their comments was rather lukewarm, and the bill was sent to the Committee of Social Affairs. The bill is exceptional in the sense that there was no explicit references to the negotiations with the labor market partners.

As some MPs expected, in October 1992, the government presented a bill to harmonize the municipal pension scheme with other schemes (HE 242/1992 vp). Long-term savings were also at stake: in 2004 the reformed KVTEL contribution would be 6 percentage points lower than under the status quo. The parliamentary discussion echoed the VEL debate a month earlier.

The Social Affairs Committee prepared the VEL and KVTEL bills simultaneously and consulted representatives of the major interest organizations and pension experts as usual (StVM 53/1992 vp). The majority accepted cuts in the VEL and KVTEL schemes with minor adjustments, while the Greens, the Left and the SDP rejected the cuts. The Greens criticized the grandma/pa dimension of the bill, arguing that "baby boomer" pensions would remain unchanged while younger generations would experience cutbacks. The Social Democratic Committee members criticized the bill for its Treasury bias, arguing that all pension bills should be dealt with simultaneously, not incrementally as the government was doing. The SPD members also called for more input from the labor market partners.

The first parliamentary reading of the bills was on 18 December 1992 and the discussion followed the lines discussed above (PTK 189/1992 vp). The Left emphasized that although the bills were supposed to cut the pensions of those with labor contracts beginning January 1, 1993, they would also reduce pensions for many academic employees who had worked for decades under renewable short-term contracts. The representatives of the government were unmoved by these criticisms and referred to the agreement between the labor market partners and expressed their wish that the non-socialist parties would be as "reasonable" as the social partners had been on the question. In the second reading (December 18, 1992; PTK 192/1992 vp), no changes were proposed, and the bills were sent unchanged to the third reading set for 21 December 1992. As the bills were not cutting existing benefits, the simplified legislative process could be applied that required only a simple majority. The parties in government (Center, Conservatives, SFP, and KD) voted for the bills, and the bill passed by a margin of 102 votes to 81 (PTK 193/1992 vp). The legislation took effect January 1, 1993.

The 1995 reform of the income base for calculating employment pensions

Unpopular cuts in social expenditure undermined support for the Center Party in the 1995 election, and the party lost eleven mandates. In contrast, the SDP achieved their best results since the 1930s, with 63 seats. The SDP, led by Paavo Lipponen, and the Conservatives, dominated the next two cabinets (1995–2003). The SFP was included in the governing coalition, but surprisingly so were the Greens and the Left (former SKDL). Despite the unconventional composition of the Cabinet, Lipponen's "rainbow" coalitions functioned well throughout both electoral periods. Both cabinets followed a very tight fiscal policy and adopted modest retrenchment measures. Compared to the previous cabinet, which had tried to navigate between the Scylla of the left-wing parliamentary opposition and the Charybdis of the trade unions, Lipponen had several advantages. First, his cabinet was over-sized, with 145 of 200 seats in Parliament which gave him extra room to maneuver. Second, the cabinet had better relationships with the unions and could contemplate reforms that were unthinkable for the previous bourgeois government.

One such reform was the change in the calculation basis for pension benefits. Previously, pensions had been calculated on the basis of income for the two median years of the last four years in employment. The Lipponen government lengthened the calculation period to the ten last years in employment. In its proposal, the government referred to practices in other countries that used much longer reference periods for calculating pensions. Moreover, the old calculation basis was argued to be out of sync with reality since many workers had short-term labor contracts and job mobility was increasing. The Finnish calculation procedure was beneficial for those with a single employer and disadvantageous for workers with several employers. Finally, the bill tried to establish a stronger actuarial link between contributions and benefits, which was predicted to produce savings of up to 4 percent in pension spending in 2030 compared to the status quo. This change was carefully prepared in negotiations between AKAVA, STTK, SAK and TT. On the basis of the agreement made on May 18, 1995, the government prepared a bill to Parliament on September 29, 1995 (HE 118/1995 vp). The bill did not generate much political heat; only the dissidents (former Moscow-oriented communists in SKDL) in the Left Party criticized the bill for damaging pension rights. The Center Party's critique was mild, and the bill passed easily, with effect in early 1996.

The 1995 reform of national pensions

At the same time, reform of the national pension had reached the political agenda. The previous Center-led cabinet had actively defended basic security and was reluctant to touch the national pensions. In its inaugural program the Lipponen government declared that pension security must be seen as a totality, and that the division of labor between employment-related pensions and the national pensions must be clarified. The government prepared a bill on the abolishment of NP basic amount (HE 119/1995 vp) and stated that the national pension as a form of basic security did not imply that flat-rate benefits should be paid to everyone, which was the traditional agrarian demand. Instead, basic security could be better achieved if the NP were tested against other legislated pensions. Pension-testing the

NP would cut national pension expenditure by €0.7 billion. The bill was intended to immediately generate savings to help relieve the budget crisis and, in the long run, dampen rising pension costs. The reform was planned so that those receiving only a national pension would not experience benefit reductions, whereas those with middle- and high-income total pensions would face cuts. Thus the reform reduced existing benefits, in contrast to previous reforms which only affected subsequent generations.

In practice, the "clarification" of the division of labor between the NP and employment-related pensions meant that the previously universal basic amount was abolished. In practice, the universal basic amount had lost importance, since its real value in 1995 was the same as it was in the mid-1960s. However, the change in government also seemed to change the orientation in austerity politics: the Center (together with SKDL/Communists) had favored its traditional flat-rate universalism, whereas SDP and KOK followed their former enthusiasm towards means- and income-testing to achieve more effective redistribution and controlling cost expansion (Salminen 1987: 157). This was also highly visible during the parliamentary discussions.

The bill on national pension reform was presented for preliminary plenary discussion on October 6, 1995. In her account of the motivations for the bill, the Minister of Social Affairs, Sinikka Mönkäre (SDP) argued that the proposal would not, in absolute terms, reduce existing pensions. Nor would the reform change the principle of universality (PTK 69/1995 vp). The Minister's introductory speech did not convince the audience, however, and the opposition and also some government parties—especially Left (following the traditional policy lines SKDL had had in the late 1950s and early 1960s)—heavily criticized the bill. The most vociferous criticism came from the Center, who accused the government of destroying universalism, which had been the overarching ideological motivation in the development of the Nordic welfare state model. The Social Democratic criticism dealt more with the fact that some pensioners would face income losses. Some MPs demanded that since the law would cut existing pensions and the level of basic security, the constitutional legislative process should be applied (PTK 69/1995 vp; PTK 70/1995 vp). If this option had been adopted, then the parties of the opposition would have been able to use their veto option. However, the CC concluded that the Constitutional guarantee of basic security for everyone did not imply that benefits had to be flat-rate. That is, the level of basic security is more important than the institutional form providing it (PeVL 12/1995 vp). Thus, the bill could be passed with a simple majority.

After consultations with the representatives of KELA, TELA, ETK, and the main labor market organizations, the Social Affairs Committee prepared a bill following the lines sketched by the government. The proposal (StVM 21/1995 vp), with dissents from the Left and Center, had its first reading on 21 November 1995. Representatives of the Center reiterated their opinion that the bill betrayed the principles of the Nordic model because of the departure from universalism (PTK 102/1995 vp). Left Party representatives expressed their fear that the pensioners would punish the party if its MPs supported the bill, but their loyalty to the Cabinet was stronger than their fear of voter punishment. Several Social Democrats were ambivalent. However, due to their commitment to the government, neither the Left nor the SDP dissidents voted against the bill. The Centrist alternative, in which the basic allowance would be preserved, lost the vote (83 to 36, the rest of the MPs were absent). Thus the bill prepared by the Social Affairs Committee was sent for a third and final vote. In this phase, the ambivalent Social Democrats chose to vote "no opinion," whereas the Left was divided between those voting for the governmental bill and those who favored the Centrist position (PTK 113/1995 vp). The bill passed by a margin of 104 votes to 51 and took effect in 1996.

The reform of the NP scheme was highly politicized and reflects the two social policy orientations followed by the two largest parties. As early as the bourgeois Aho cabinet, the Ministry of Finance (headed by a Conservative) had proposed the abolition of the basic NP, but strong opposition from the Center Party precluded reform. It was not until the Center lost its grip on power and the SDP and the Conservatives formed a government that it was possible to change the NP scheme. Both the KOK and the SDP had led the development of income-related pensions in Finland, and the NP had not been very important to their white-collar and blue-collar members. The social partners did not play a major role in NP reforms either, and on only a few occasions did the Social Democrats refer to decisions made in the labor market. For the labor market partners, the NP reform was not as crucial as changes in employment-related pensions. The institutional coordination of the NP and employment-related pensions contributed to this position. Since in Finland the coordination of pension schemes follows the so-called difference principle, namely, the target level of income replacement is 60 percent, when the NP disappeared the gap could be filled by other pensions. Therefore, the unions had no economic incentive to react, and solidarity towards the citizenship principle in the NP was not enough to bring trade unions to the barricades. The situation is very different for countries where occupational pension "float" on basic pensions, and employees see their total pension amounts circumscribed immediately if the national pension is cut.

Reforms of private sector pensions in 2002 and public sector pensions in 2004

In the 1990s, steps had already been taken to meet future demographic challenges. However, pension experts regarded these as inadequate, and pension reform reached the agenda again. The central labor market partners had initiated their own negotiations on pension reforms without the government, and even more interestingly, without a formal mandate from the government. Lipponen had given free hands to the organizations. The labor market partners called Kari Puro[3] to chair the negotiations and proposals began to take shape. When the group had agreed on the reform plan, it was presented to the Ministry of Social Affairs who began to prepare bills together with social partners and ETK experts. These bills were accepted by the labor market central organizations on September 5, 2002, whereafter they were ready to be presented to the Parliament.

Previously, each year in employment between the ages of 23 and 64 was counted at an accrual rate of 1.5 percent, so that the maximum pension of 60 percent was attained after 40 years of employment. Under the Puro plan, a new pension act for private sector employees with effect in 2005 would award pension credits for each year in employment between the ages of 18 and 69. A progressive accrual rate would discourage early retirement: between the ages of 18 and 52 the rate is 1.5 percent; between 53 and 62 years the accrual rate is 1.9 percent; and after the age of 63 it is 4.5 percent. A study period of up to five years and the care of children under three years of age will yield pension points based on a hypothetical income of €500 a month. The target level of 60 percent was abolished—so the pension could be 90 percent—for instance—and the retirement age would be flexible between 63 and 68 years of age. Tougher qualifying rules would make early retirement less attractive. A special formula adjusting pensions downward if life expectancy increased was also introduced. Finally, pension benefits are based on career income. That particular stipulation was heavily criticized by the academic union the AKAVA, whereas the blue-collar SAK welcomed it and STTK was ambivalent. Interestingly enough, this was the first occasion when there were apparent conflicts of interest between the trade union central organizations. Finally the AKAVA also accepted the agreement. The "super" accumulation percentage for older employees was seen to benefit the AKAVA members and to compensate for the abolition of the previous "final-salary-principle."

The Puro report was incorporated into the bill (HE 242/2002 vp) presented to Parliament by Lipponen's second rainbow cabinet on November 6, 2002. The government emphasized that the long-term pension system sustainability demanded that employees work longer. The government argued that the reform would increase the transparency of pensions and be socially more just because all workers would be treated the same. According to the government, the bill was a win-win proposal. It gave employees opportunities to earn better pensions than previously, yet at the same time, by postponing retirement, the bill would combat the need to increase pension contributions: if the reform was accepted, the pension contribution in relation to payroll would be about 4 percent points lower than in the status quo situation.

On the whole, the bill was received positively, not least because it took gender into account and because of the broad societal coalition supporting it (PTK 128/2002 vp). The latter aspect was recognized not only by the SDP and the conservatives, but also by the Center: "The labor market partners have agreed upon the pact and the government has taken the credit for that. If the government has not ruined the labor market agreement, it can proceed as it is." The major criticism was from the Center and Left, who complained that the flexible retirement age was only applicable for employment-related pensions and not for national pensions. The Constitutional Committee evaluated the bill and proposed that it be passed as an ordinary law (PeVL 60/2002 vp).

The Social and Health Committee submitted its work (StVM 58/2002 vp) to Parliament on February 11, 2003. In their objections, Center and Green MPs warned that national pensions were lagging behind and proposed increasing the hypothetical income for periods of education and child care to €840 a month. They maintained that periods of military and civil service should also earn pension points. In its objection, the Christian Democratic Party demanded that in the case of the care of children below school age the income for pension purposes should be €1,000 a month. National pensions should be increased and a pension ceiling introduced. The third objection came from the Left, repeating much of the Center's criticism.

In the first reading, many MPs expressed their satisfaction with the results, and they seemed to be aware of a "historical turning point" (PTK 201/2002 vp). Most MPs also realized that the bill was just the beginning: the corresponding legislation for the public sector schemes was still to come. MPs were generally happy with the issues that had been accepted by the labor market organizations. However, some representatives of the Center, the SDP and the Left were frustrated simply because they felt that once again the decision-making power had been given to the labor market partners. The loudest political debate involved the coordination between national pensions and employment-related pensions. The Center continuously referred to the Lipponen government's ideological decision to "ruin" the national pension system. Nevertheless the Center was ultimately ready to accept the main architecture of the bill.

In the plenary debate, the Social Democratic chair of the Social Committee remarked that it was easy to propose objections and improvements, but harder to evaluate if the changes would be sustainable. Therefore, it was hazardous to change proposals based on calculations of actuarial experts at the last minute. This comment captures an essential aspect of Finnish pension policy-making. Not only has the role of the social partners been crucial in Finnish pension policy reforms, but experts have also been more centrally involved than in many other countries. Interestingly enough pensioners' organizations were left out completely from the reform process—a finding that goes against the grain of prevailing assumptions of the "new politics" approach to the welfare state (Pierson 1994).

In the second and final plenary readings, the three objections outlined above formed the basis for a series of votes in which party discipline was not fully upheld (PTK 205/2002 vp). The representatives of the Left demanded that the "super-accumulation" and the life expectancy factor be abolished (both proposals were rejected, 181 against 10 and 180 against 13, respectively). The proposal to introduce flexible retirement in the national pensions was also rejected (118 against 75) as were the proposals by the Center and the KD to increase the hypothetical pension base for education and child-rearing. The Center's initiative to allow pension accumulation during military/civil service was also unsuccessful (116 votes against and 77 in favor). Thus Parliament adopted the government's bill, the President promulgated it on June 27, 2003, and the law became effective on January 1, 2005.

As in the preceding decade, the private sector pension reforms paved the way for changing public sector schemes. In fact, the labor market agreement of September 5, 2002 included a decision to reform the public sector schemes as well. The bill on changes in the municipal KVTEL (HE 45/2004 vp) and the state pension scheme VEL (HE 46/2004 vp) was submitted to Parliament on 21 April 2004. Now the bill was carried through by a new Center-SDP–SFP coalition. In describing the motivation for the bill the government simply referred to the private sector reforms carried out a year earlier and the labor market agreements on the reform. The bill was depicted as a logical and inevitable continuation of the process that had begun in the 1990s. The mood during the parliamentary discussions both in the first and second reading was one of resignation (PTK 45/2004 vp; PTK 78/2004 vp; PTK80/2004 vp; PTK 81/2004 vp). Here it seems that the continuous cuts create their own path dependency and a culture of reform acceptance (Timonen 2003).

Perhaps the most interesting thing about the public sector pension reforms was the change in political constellations within Parliament. The Conservatives and the Left—both in opposition—formulated their powerless objections and alternative proposals, and the previously most vociferous opposition party, Center, seemed to lose its previously eloquent vocabulary regarding the importance of national pensions. The bills were adopted on June 17, 2004 with minor changes made by the social committee (StVM 14/2004 vp) and the new legislation became effective simultaneously with the private sector reforms from early 2005. With these reforms, pensions for the cohorts born 1960 or later will be the same regardless of the sector of employment. This will strengthen the distinctiveness of Finnish pension design: partially private and decentralized insurance carriers guarantee standard pension rights for all employees.

V Conclusion

Summary of the magnitude of changes

Pension reforms in Finland have been incremental, but taken together, the changes introduced since the 1980s represent significant departures from existing policy. The introduction of individual employee contributions in 1992 broke the original pension contract made in 1961, and did so by introducing first a temporary change that soon after became permanent. A similar dynamic was present in the reform that changed the benefit formula from a final salary to a life-time income formula. This shift was not taken all at once, but in several steps. The same procedure was applied when reforming public sector pensions, and homogenizing (= reducing) them to correspond to private sector benefits. The abolition of universalism in the NP may be regarded as a change in the fundamental underpinnings of the pension system, but in monetary terms it was not that significant. There can be little doubt that the aggregate result of these many reforms was that the whole pension design was substantially altered (see Hinrichs and Kangas 2003; Hinrichs 2004), but the very fact that the reforms were presented in small steps prevented a thorough political debate on pension policy in the Finnish Parliament. To apply Peter Hall's (1993) classification, single reforms in Finland were of the first order adjustments, or at best second order changes; but in the end they resulted in third order changes, that is, in the long run the impact of these smaller adjustments is significant. Only the national pension reform of 1996 could be classified to change the underpinning ideology of the pension design, but interestingly enough the practical consequences of this "third order change" were probably much smaller than the impacts of those smaller "creeping" changes of the first or second degree. To summarize the paradox: small pension reforms produced big changes whereas fundamental reforms had no practical consequences.

Impact of the political system on pension politics

The history of the reforms of the Finnish pension system is one of consensus-seeking in an institutional and political context, where both political actors and social partners had various veto options. The legislative process guaranteed a "suspensive" veto to the President, minority rules made it possible for the parliamentary opposition to block reforms, and finally, the corporatist pension design provided the social partners with powerful tools against politics. Consociational negotiations were a way to try to close down these veto points and solve political deadlocks. Due to these factors Finnish parties have been much more inclined towards practical and de-ideologized solutions—the "rainbow coalitions" were excellent examples—and not so concerned whether the planned reforms are in line with the political mandate the electorate had given.

This de-politicizing strategy may be effective, but it undermines the political profiles of parties. Parliament has often been criticized for being a rubber stamp that simply qualifies the agreements negotiated by the social partners. On the other hand, consensual devices were effective, and at least in the pension policy reforms analyzed here political and labor market negotiation guaranteed that no actor needed to use their veto.[4] Interestingly enough, the President used his veto right only once in pension policy. In 1972, the President refused to promulgate a bill that Parliament and government had proposed. Ironically, the issue was submitted to the labor market partners for better preparation.

In all discussion on employment-related pensions, debates in Parliament revolved around what the labor market partners had negotiated. On the one hand, this reflects the central role of unions in Finnish politics, not least because of the administrative structure of the TEL, but on the other hand it was a good way to de-politicize cuts and avoid blame. In their blame-avoidance strategy, governments were reluctant to call attention to austerity measures and they willingly used experts and bureaucrats as message carriers. During the recession, the role of augurs relaying the bad news to the nation was given to, and willingly taken by, Treasury officials who have played a decisively political role.

Recent scholarship (Pierson 1994: 37) points to the minimal role played by bureaucrats and the dominant role of politicians in retrenchment strategies. In the

Finnish case, this does not hold at all, but it would be wrong to argue that politics does not matter. In the context of an economic crisis, the reforms carried through by different political constellations had different emphases. The Center leader Aho's bourgeois government was more eager to cut employment-related benefits, whereas Lipponen's SDP-led rainbow coalition also cut national pensions, which had been out of the question for the Center. Thus, recent social-political strategies reflect the old historical priorities and orientations of the major parties. In that sense, the Finnish pension reforms speak much more in favor of "old politics" (Korpi and Palme 2003) than "new politics" (Pierson 1994). The contents of politics and the ways of decision-making replicate the old legacies.

The ultimate decision-making power was, and is, in the hands of the politicians, but in some issues these hands are tied more tightly than in others. When the fate of national pensions was at stake the political parties had much more to say, and the NP reform was a political act. Trade unions were not very interested. Here again, we can refer to the impact of institutional design. In Finland, all pensions are coordinated with each other and the target replacement rate used to be 60 percent. The coordination follows the so-called difference principle, that is, for those with employment-related pensions the NP does not play any role, and when the universal basic amount was abolished, employment-related pensions automatically filled the gap. So the target level of 60 percent could also be reached without the NP. Thus, for the majority of trade union members the NP issue had no practical meaning, and the ideological meaning was not enough to arouse more than lukewarm reactions. The situation is radically different in countries applying the so-called "floating" principle. Cuts in basic pensions, on which occupational pensions "float", would reduce the overall pension level (unless pension schemes compensate for the reduction). Therefore, for instance, the Dutch trade unions are more interested in what is happening in the Dutch basic pension than Finnish unions are interested in the NP.

Interest group influence

Compared to Pierson's analysis, one additional peculiarity of Finnish retrenchment policy has been that pensioners' organizations were virtually non-existent in the reforms. They were neither heard nor seen. In that sense, the Finnish experience does not lend much support to the thesis stressing the importance of client organizations in the making of a "new politics" of welfare. Also on this point, the Finnish history is a history of "old politics" where the traditional interest organizations in tri-partite negotiations—usually led by a senior impartial pension expert—agreed on reforms that were then accepted by Parliament with minor modifications (Anderson 2001). Or, as a Center Party MP put it: "The tripartite negotiations are the foundation of the Finnish society today. The agreements achieved through that system represent in the best possible ways all partners." (PTK 128/2002vp: 39).

In many analyses of pension policy, the dilemma has been why powerful trade unions would have accepted retrenchment. Various explanations have been offered. One set of answers concentrates on the nature of retrenchment polices: it may be easier to get through reductions when only the benefits of future generations are cut. This grand-ma/pa (Pierson 1994) strategy was used in Finland. The other main set of explanations deals with the various compensations that are given in return for cuts (Pierson 1996). Most reforms discussed in this chapter included some compensatory elements: for example the participation in financing gave the employee organizations a more legitimate right to participate in the administration of the schemes and the move from final salary calculations to a life-time salary principle was compensated by ensuring academics would gain from the "super" accruals at the end of their working careers which softened critical attitudes of the academic unions towards the pension reform.

Under what circumstances do trade unions pursue interests more general than their immediate class-interests? Since the late 1960s, the income policies in Finland have been based on tri-partite negotiations in which governments have contributed through so-called social packages, including a wide variety of socio-political reforms. In response, the trade unions have promised to behave reasonably. Given the sheer size of the trade unions, they knew that every action they adopted would inevitably have ramifications for the national economy. This also encouraged reasonable behavior and consensus seeking (Przeworski 1985). And in fact, the reform process was initiated among the working group consisting of the representatives of labor market partners. Trade unions were somehow stakeholders or caretakers of the wider national interest—which in the longer run benefits them more than short-term profit seeking—which made them careful not to abuse their veto-power in the negotiations they participated in. Thus, the trade unions accepted reforms, or more interestingly they themselves sketched the reforms, because they realized that this was the only way to ensure the long-term sustainability of the pension system.

Constraints of policy design

A party system reflecting Finland's tri-polar class structure and fragmented political structures shaped the pension policy structures that policy-makers inherited at the beginning of the 1980s. The universal basic pension was mature in the sense that it already provided benefits to a generation of pensioners, but the development of mandated occupational pensions in the post-war period meant that occupational schemes began to provide more and more pension income as these schemes matured. This dual structure provided opportunities for policy-makers (mainly the SDP) to introduce changes that departed from the principle of universalism even though the national pension remained popular. Pensioners had nothing to lose because National Pension (NP) income had been subtracted from occupational schemes all along, and low income pensioners would continue to receive pension-tested benefits. The big loser here was the Center Party which had historically advocated generous flat-rate universal benefits.

Role of ideas and historical context

Ideas appear to have played only a marginal role in the episodes of reform analyzed in this chapter. To be sure, the Finnish pension system today looks very different than it did in 1980, but the changes introduced are more the product of political parties–(or, more correctly, social partners–bargaining to ensure that proposed changes did not overly affect their clienteles) than they are the product of elites pushing new grand ideas about how the pension system should be organized.

Abbreviations

AKAVA	Confederation of Unions for Academic Professionals in Finland (*Akateeminen alojen keskuslitto*)
CC	Constitutional Committee (*Perustuslakivaliokunta*)
Cen	Center Party (*Keskustapuolue*)
ED	National Progressive Party (*Kansallinen Edistyspuolue*)
EK	The Confederation of Finnish Industries (*Elinkeinoelämän keskusliitto*)
ETK	The Finnish Centre for Pensions (*Eläketurvakeskus*)
HE	Governmental Bill (*Hallituksen esitys*)
KELA	The Social Insurance Institution of Finland (*Kansaneläkelaitos*)
KESK	Party (*Keskustapuolue*)
KEVA	Municipal Pension Insurance Institution (*Kuntien Eläkevakuutus*)
KiEL	Pension Law for Church Employees (*Kirkon Eläkelaki*)
KOK	National Coalition Party (*Kansallinen Kokoomuspuolue*)
KVTEL	Pension Law for Municipal Employees (*Kunnallisten viranhaltijain ja työntekijäin eläkelaki*)
KTV	Municipal Workers' and Employees' Union (*Kunta-alan ammattiliitto*)
LEL	Pension law for the employees in short term employment contracts (*Lyhytaikaisissa työsuhteissa olevien työntekijöiden eläkelaki*)
LKP	Liberal Party (*Liberaalinen Kansanpuolue*)
MEL	Seamen's Pension Law (*Merimiesten Eläkelaki*)
ML	The Agrarian Party (*Maalaisliitto*)
MTK	Organization of Agricultural Producers (*Maataloustuottajien Keskusliitto*)
MYEL	Pension Law for Self-employed in Agriculture (*Maatalousyrittäjien Eläkelaki*)
NP	National Pension (*Kansaneläke*)
PeVL	Report of the Constitutional Committee (*Perustuslakivaliokunnan lausunto*)
PTK	Minutes of the Parliament (*Eduskunnan pöytäkirjat*)

SAK	Confederation of Finnish Trade Unions (*Suomen Ammattiyhdistysten Keskusliitto*)
SDP	Finnish Social Democratic Party (*Suomen Sosialidemokraattinen Puolue*)
SFP	Swedish People's Party (*Svenska Folkpartiet*)
SKDL	Finnish People's Democratic League (*Suomen Kansandemokraattinen Liitto*)
SKP	Communist Party of Finland (*Suomen Kommunistinen Puolue*)
SMP	Finnish Rural Party (*Suomen Maaseudun Puolue*)
SSTP	Finnish Socialist Workers' Party (*Suomen Sosialistinen Työväenpuolue*)
STK	Employers' Federation in Finland (*Suomen Työnantajien Keskusliitto*)
STTK	Finnish Confederation of Salaried Employees (*Suomen Toimihenkilökeskusjärjestö*)
StVM	Report of the Social Committee (*Sosiaalivaliokunnan mietintö*)
TaEL	Pension Law for Artists (*Taitelijoiden Eläkelaki*)
TEL	Pension Law for the Private Sector Employees (*Työntekijäin Eläkelaki*)
TELA	The Finnish Pension Alliance (*Työeläkevakuuttajat*)
TT	Confederation of Finnish Industry and Employers (*Teollisuuden työnantajien Keskusliitto*)
TVK	Central Organization of Salaried Employees (*Toimihenkilö-ja Virkamiesjärjestöjen Keskusliitto*)
VEL	Pension Law for the State Employees (*Valtion eläkelaki*)
ISA	The Insurance Supervisory Authority (*Vakuutusvalvontavirasto*)
Vp	Parliamentary Assembly (*Valtiopäivät*)
YEL	Pension Law for Self-Employed (*Yrittäjien Eläkelaki*)

Notes

1. In the other Nordic countries, occupational pensions follow a "floating" principle: occupational pensions are paid on top of other pensions regardless of the size of the other pension.
2. The headquarters of the SAK is on the Hakaniemi Square.
3. Puro was a former high-level civil servant in the Ministry of Social Affairs and he was later nominated to the Managing Director of a large pension insurance company and had been involved in all major pension reforms since the 1960s.
4. Unions did threaten a general strike when the government proposed cuts in the union-run unemployment insurance scheme (Timonen 2003: 94).

Bibliography

Primary sources and government documents

Bills by the Government

HE 230/1991 vp. Hallituksen esitys Eduskunnalle työntekijäin eläkemaksua koskevaksi lainsäädännöksi.

HE 110/1992 vp. Hallituksen esitys Eduskunnalle laiksi valtion eläkelain muuttamisesta.

HE 242/1992 vp. Hallituksen esitys Eduskunnalle laiksi kunnallisten viranhaltijain ja työntekijöiden eläkelain muuttamisesta.

HE 118/1995 vp. Hallituksen esitys Eduskunnalle yksityisalojen työeläkejärjestelmän uudistamista koskevaksi lainsäädännöksi.

HE 119/1995 vp. Hallituksen esitys Eduskunnalle kansaneläkejärjestelmän uudistamista koskevaksi lainsäädännöksi.

HE 242/2002 vp. Hallituksen esitys Eduskunnalle laiksi kunnallisten viranhaltijain ja työntekijöiden eläkelain muuttamisesta.

HE 45/2004 vp. Hallituksen esitys Eduskunnalle laiksi kunnallisen eläkelain muuttamisesta.

HE 46/2004 vp. Hallituksen esitys Eduskunnalle laeiksi valtion eläkelain ja eräiden siihen liittyvien lakien muuttamisesta.

Reports of the constitutional committee

PeVL 8/1992 vp.
PeVL 12/1995 vp.
PeVL 60/2002 vp.

Minutes of the Parliament

PTK 11/1991 vp.
PTK 125/1992 vp.
PTK 128/1992 vp.
PTK 129/1992 vp.
PTK 97/1992 vp.
PTK 189/1992 vp.
PTK 192/1992 vp.
PTK 193/1992 vp.
PTK 69/1995 vp.
PTK 70/1995 vp.
PTK 102/1995 vp.
PTK 113/1995 vp.
PTK 128/2002 vp.
PTK 201/2002 vp.
PTK 205/2002 vp.
PTK 45/2004 vp.
PTK 78/2004 vp.
PTK80/2004 vp.
PTK 81/2004 vp.

Reports of the social committee

StVM 27/1992 vp.
StVM 53/1992 vp.
StVM 21/1995 vp.
StVM 58/2002 vp.
StVM 14/2004 vp.

Internet sources

http://www.etera.fi/finnish/yritystiedot/lel_tyoelakekassa/index.html (08.01.2005)
http://www.etk.fi (08.01.2005)
http://www.etk.fi/page.asp?Section=11987 (16.09.2005)
http://www.etk.fi/Dynagen_attachments/Att20597/20597.pdf (08.01.2005)
http://www.etk.fi/Dynagen_attachments/Att21629/21629.pdf (16.09.2005)
http://www.hallitus.fi/vn/liston/print.lsp (07.06.2004)
http://www.sak.fi/miksak.shtml/03?593 (07.06.2004)
http://www.tela.fi/Avengl01.nsf?OpenDatabase (07.06.2004)
http://www.vaalit.fi/uploads/wqd56g48c2r.pdf (07.06.2004)

Secondary sources

AHTOKARI, REIJO (1988)."Tuntematon vaikuttaja: työeläkejärjestelmän isä Teivo Pentikäinen." Porvoo: WSOY.

ALAPURO, RISTO (1988). *State and Revolution in Finland*. Berkeley: University of California Press.

ALESTALO, MATTI (1985). "Yhteiskuntaluokat ja sosiaaliset kerrostumat toisen maailmansodan jälkeen". In Valkonen, T., Alapuro, R., Alestalo, M., Jallinoja, R., and Sandlund, T. (eds.), *Suomalaiset: Yhteiskunnan rakenne teollistumisen aikana*. Porvoo: WSOY, 101–200.

ALESTALO, MATTI., FLORA, PETER, and UUSITALO, HANNU. (1985). "Structure and politics in the making of the welfare state". In Alapuro, R., Alestal, M., Haavio-Mannila, E., and Väyrynen, R. (eds.), *Small States in Comparative Perspective*. Oslo: Norwegian University Press, 188–210.

—— and STEIN, KUHNLE (1987). "The Scandinavian Route: Economic, and Political Developments in Denmark, Finland, Norway, and Sweden." In Erikson, R., Hansen, E. J., Ringen, S., and Uusialo, H. (eds.), *The Scandinavian Model. Welfare States and Welfare Research.* Armonk, NY: Sharpe, 3–38.

ALLARDT, ERIK (1971). "The Radical Vote and the Social Context: Traditional and Emerging Radicalism." In Eisenstadt, S. N. (ed.), *Political Sociology.* New York: Basic Books, 490–7.

ANDERSON, KAREN, M. (2001). "The Politics of Retrenchment in a Social Democratic Welfare State. Reform of Swedish Pensions and Unemployment Insurance," *Comparative Political Studies*, 34, 9, (November): 1063–91.

AUFFERMANN, BRKHARD (2003). "Das politische System Finnlands." In Ismayr W., (ed.), *Die politischen Systeme Westeuropas*. Opladen: Leske + Budrich, 187–224.

BALDWIN, PETER (1990). *The Politics of Social Solidarity*. Cambridge: Cambridge University Press.

BLOMSTER, PETER (2004). *"Kunnallisen eläketurvan historia."* Helsinki: KEVA.

BONOLI, GUILIANO (2000). *The Politics of Pension Reform. Institutions and Policy Change in Western Europe*. Cambridge: Cambridge University Press.

BORG, OLAVI (1964). *Suomen puolueideologiat (Finnish party ideologies)*. Porvoo: WSOY.

CASTLES, FRANCIS (1979). *The Social Democratic Image of Society*. London: Routledge.

ESPING-ANDERSEN, GØSTA (1985). *Politics Against Markets: The Social Democratic Road to Power*. Princeton: Princeton University Press.

EVANS, PETER, RUESCHMEYER, DIETRICH., and SKOCPOL, THEDA. (1985). *Bringing the State Back In.* Cambridge: Cambridge University Press.

GAUTHIER, DAVID (1990). *Moral Dealing: Contract, Ethics, and Reasons*. Ithaca, NY: Cornell University Press.

HALL, PETER (1993). "Policy Paradigm, Social Learning and the State, the Case of Economic Policy in Britain." *Comparative Politics*, 25(3): 275–96.

HARDIN, RUSSELL (1988). *Morality Within the Limits of Reason.* Chicago: University of Chicago Press.

HÄRKÖNEN, TARJA and LAITINEN-KUIKKA, SINI (2003). "Työmarkkinoilla sovittu täydentävä eläketurva." In Hietaniemi, M., and Mika, V. (eds.), *Suomen eläkejärjestelmä.* Helsinki: ETK, 97–101.

Helsingin Sanomat 14 December 2000.

HIETANIEMI, MARJUKKA and VIDLUND, MIKA (2003): "Eläkejärjestelmän halinto." In Hietaniemi, M., and Mika, V. (eds.), *Suomen eläkejärjestelmä.* Helsinki: ETK, 51–5.

HINRICHS, KARL (2004): Active Citizens and Retirement Planning: Enlarged Freedom of Choice in the Course of Pension Reforms in Nordic Countries and Germany. Bremen: Zes Arbeitspapier Nr 11/2004.

HINRICHS, KARL and KANGAS, OLLI (2003). "When a change is big enough to be a system shift – small system-shifting adjustments in pension policy in Finland and Germany." *Social Policy and Administration,* 37(6): 573–91.

HOKKANEN, KARI (2002). *Kekkosen maalaisliitto 1950–1962.* Maalaisliitto-keskustan historia 4. Keuruu: Otava.

IMMERGUT, ELLEN (1992). *The Political Construction of Interests: National Health Insurance Politics in Switzerland, France, and Sweden, 1930–1970.* New York: Cambridge University Press.

—— (2002): "The Swedish Constitution and Social Democratic Power: Measuring the Mechanical Effect of a Political Institution." *Scandinavian Political Studies,* 25(3): 231–57.

INGLEHART, RONALD (1997). *Modernization and Postmodernization.* Princeton: Princeton University Press.

JUSSILA, OSMO, HENTILÄ, SEPPO, and NEVAKIVI, JUKKA (1999). *From Grand Duchy to a Modern State. A Political History of Finland since 1809.* London: Hurst & Company.

JÄNTTI, MARKUS, KANGAS, OLLI and RITAKALLIO, VELI-MATTI (1996). "From Marginalism to Institutionalism: The Transformation of the Finnish Pension Regime." *Journal of Income and Wealth,* 42(4): 473–91.

KALELA, JORMA (1989). *Työttömyys 1900-luvun suomalaisessa yhteiskuntapolitiikassa.* Helsinki: VAPK.

KANGAS, OLLI (1988). *Politik och ekonomi i pensionsförsäkringen: Det finska pensionssystemet i ett jämförande perspektiv.* Stockholm: Institutet för social forskning, Meddelande 5.

—— (1991). *Politics of Social Rights.* Stockholm: Akademitryck.

—— and JOAKIM PALME (1996). "The Development of Occupational Pensions in Finland and Sweden: Class Politics and Institutional Feed-backs." In Shalev, M. (ed.), *The Privatization of Social Policy? Occupational Welfare and the Welfare State in America, Scandinavia and Japan.* NewYork: Macmillan, 211–40.

—— —— (2000). "Does Social Policy Matter? Poverty Cycles in OECD Countries." *International Journal of Health Services,* 30(2): 335–52.

—— —— (2005). *Social Policy and Economic Development in the Nordic Countries.* London: Palgrave.

KELA (1985). *Statistical Yearbook of the Social Insurance Institution.* Helsinki: Kela.

KELA (2001). *Statistical Yearbook of the Social Insurance Institution.* Helsinki: Kela.

KETTUNEN, PAULI (1986). *Poliittinen liike ja sosiaalinen kollektiivisuus.* Helsinki: SHS.

KOMITTEBETÄNKANDE 1991:41 (Betänkande av pensionskommitten 1990). Helsingfors: VAPK-Förlaget.

KORPI, WALTER and PALME JOAKIM (1988). "The Paradox of Redistribution and Strategies of Equality: Welfare State Institutions, Inequality, and Poverty in the Western Countries." *American Sociological Review,* 63(5): 661–87.

KORPI, WALTER and PALME JOAKIM (2003): "New Politics and Class Politics in the Context of Austerity and Globalization: Welfare State Regress in 18 Countries, 1975–95." *American Political Science Review*, 97(3): 425–46.

LAATUNEN, REIJO and VIDLUND, MIKA (2003) "Eläkejärjestelmien kattavuus." In Hietaniemi, M. and Vidlund, M. (eds.), *Suomen eläkejärjestelmä*. Helsinki: ETK, 25–30.

LANE, JAN-ERIK and ERSSON, SVENTE (2002). "The Nordic Countries: Contention, Compromise and Corporatism." In Colomer, J. M. (ed.), *Political Institutions in Europe*. London: Routledge, 245–77.

LIJPHARDT, ARENT (1977). *Democracy in Plural Societies: A Comparative Exploration*. New Haven: Yale Univeristy Press.

LUNDBERG, URBAN (2003). *Juvelen i kronan. Socialdemokraterna och den allmänna pensionen*. Stockholm: Hjalmarson & Högberg.

MANNIO, NIILO (1967). *Sosiaalipoliitikon kokemuksia 50 itsenäisyysvuoden ajalta*. Porvoo: WSOY.

NIEMELÄ, HEIKKI (1988). *Kokonaiseläkejärjestelmän synty Suomessa*. Helsinki: Kela.

NOUSIAINEN, JAAKKO (1998). *Suomen poliittinen järjestelmä (Political System in Finland)*. Helsinki: WSOY.

NOUSIAINEN, JAAKKO (2000). Finland: "The Consolidation of Parliamentary Governance." In Müller W. C., and Strøm K. (eds.), *Coalition Governments in Western Europe*. Oxford: Oxford University Press, 264–99.

OECD (1997). *Employment Outlook*. Paris: OECD.

ORLOFF, ANN SHOLA and SKOCPOL, THEDA (1984). "Why not Equal Protection?: Explaining the Politics of Public Spending in Britain, 1900–11, and the United States, 1880s–1920." *American Sociological Review* 49(3): 726–50.

ØVERBYE, EINAR (1996). "Public and Occupational Pensions in the Mordic Countries." In Sheler, M. (ed.), *The Privatization of Social Policy? Occupational Welfare and the Welfare State in America, Scandinavia and Japan*, 159–86. New York: Macmillan.

PALME, JOAKIM (1990). *Pension Rights in Welfare Capitalism: the Development of Old Age Pensions in 18 OECD Countries*. Stockholm: Swedish Institute for Social Research.

PESONEN, PERTTI and RIIHINEN, OLAVI (2002). *Dynamic Finland: The Political System and the Welfare State*. Helsinki: Finnish Literature Society.

PIERSON, PAUL (1994). *Dismantling the Welfare State? Reagan, Thatcher and the Politics of Retrenchment*. Cambridge: Cambridge University Press.

PRZEWORSKI, ADAM (1985). *Capitalism and Social Democracy*. Cambridge: Cambridge University Press.

PUNTILA, LAURI (1971). *Suomen poliittinen historia (Political History of Finland)*. Helsinki: Otava.

SAARI, JUHO (2001). *Reforming Social Policy: A Study on Institutional Change in Finland during the 1990s*. Turku: Painosalama.

SALMINEN, KARI (1987). *Yhteiskunnan rakenne, politiikka ja eläketurva*. Helsinki: Central Pension Security Institution.

—— (1993). *Pension Schemes in the Making: A Comparative Study of the Scandinavian Countries*. Helsinki: Central Pension Security Institution.

SCHLUDI, MARTIN (2001). *The Politics of Pensions in European Social Insurance Countries*. MPIfG Discussion Paper 01/11. Köln: Max-Planck-Institut für Gesellschaftsforschung.

VAROMA, PEKKA (1971). *Työeläkekeskustelun rivejä ja välejä vuosikymmenen ajalta*. Helsinki: Eläketurvakeskus, Eläketurvakeskuksen tutkimuksia.

CHAPTER 7

BELGIUM: LINGUISTIC VETO PLAYERS AND PENSION REFORM

KAREN M. ANDERSON

SANNEKE KUIPERS

ISABELLE SCHULZE

WENDY VAN DEN NOULAND

I Introduction

Belgium is considered to be a "consensus" democracy in Lijphartian terms (Lijphart 1968), but this classification masks an important difference between Belgium and other consensus democracies. Consociational institutions have reinforced rather than ameliorated social—and especially language—cleavages. Moreover, a series of constitutional reforms that aimed to *reduce* the importance of institutional veto points has been compensated by an *increase* in the powers of linguistic veto players. Consequently, the Belgian political decision-making process is extremely time-consuming, incremental, and prone to inaction.

Two features of Belgian politics contribute to the incrementalist tendencies in pension policy. First, pensions are one of the few policy competencies remaining at the federal level, and there is a lot of pressure to keep it this way. Pension politics is not just about pensions per se, but it is also about conflicts concerning how the public pension pie is divided between the regions. Given that the linguistic/territorial cleavage dominates the ideological cleavage, pension politics is more about regional redistribution than about traditional Left–Right conflicts. Second, the central government budget constraint in Belgium is overwhelming: in 1993, the debt ratio reached its highest level ever, at 137.9 percent of GDP, leaving very little room for financial maneuver.[1] This constraint is particularly significant in the Belgian system since public pensions have not kept pace with wages and prices since the early 1980s, even though contribution rates have risen. Thus the federal nature of pension policy would seem to provide incentives for expansion (to keep the regions from fighting over the pension pie) at the same time that the budget constraint militates against expansion. So pension politics involves delicate negotiations and compromises about how to introduce marginal policy changes that will not provoke regional and hence, political conflict.

II Political system

Constitutional history and nation-building

Between 1831 and 1970, Belgium was a Constitutional Monarchy with a unitary state structure. The Constitutional Reform of 1970 introduced the first elements of a federal structure, and this process was completed in 1993. The Monarch, currently King Albert, is the Head of State and enjoys duties and powers beyond those typical of other European constitutional monarchies. The Monarch represents the nation abroad, appoints the prime minister, signs international treaties, and signs laws (countersignature by the minister, who is politically responsible). The monarch's most influential duty is the nomination of the *informateur* (mediator) and *formateur* (organizer) in the coalition-building process following national elections. The *informateur* explores possible coalition alternatives among the political parties, while the *formateur*, who usually becomes prime minister, nominates ministerial candidates and negotiates a government program between the parties involved (Keman 1996: 230).[2]

The Prime Minister is head of government. Following government formation, the Prime Minister asks parliament for confidence, requiring a simple majority (with a quorum of one half plus one) in the Chamber of Representatives (or "Second Chamber" in Dutch; *Tweede Kamer/Chambre de Representatives*). A 1993 reform introduced the constructive vote of no confidence. A simple vote of no confidence already existed. The 1993 reform means that parliament cannot force the government to resign unless a parliamentary majority supports an alternative government.

Parliament can still resort to a simple vote of no confidence, in which case the government is not legally required to resign, but in practice would have to step down. Neither option has been used since 1994 (Vande Lanotte et al. 2003).

Belgium has approximately 10 million inhabitants, encompassing three different ethnic groups: French-speaking Walloons, Dutch-speaking Flemish and a small German-speaking minority. Both Walloons and Flemish live in the Brussels area. Flanders has the largest population with 5.8 million inhabitants, compared to 3.2 million in Wallonia and 1 million in Brussels. The francophone south of the country, despite its smaller population, has dominated Belgium politically and linguistically for over a century (Woyke 1999: 365), but this has changed in recent decades.

The series of constitutional reforms that culminated in federation began in 1970 with the first decentralization of authority to the regions (see Hooghe 2003). The most far-reaching reform of the five constitutional reforms so far (reforms took place in 1970, 1980, 1988, 1993, and 2001) was the Fourth State Reform of 1993. Article 1 of the Belgian Constitution now reads "Belgium is a federal state, comprised of communities and regions" (whereas prior to this reform it said "Belgium is divided into provinces"). The Fourth State Reform expanded the competencies of the communities (*Gemeenschappen/Communautés*) and regions (*Gewesten/Régions*); provided for direct election to the regional parliaments, and abolished the "double mandate" that made it possible to simultaneously be a member of the Federal Parliament and of a regional parliament (*Vlaams Parlement* 2004: 10). Finally, the balance of power between the two Houses of Parliament changed. The Senate lost its legislative authority in all but a limited number of areas (such as constitutional reform, the organization of the judiciary, and matters relating to the monarchy) and is now mainly a chamber of "reflection." These reforms aimed to reduce institutional veto points by devolving decision-making powers, and thus lessen the burden on national political arenas. However, at the same time, minority veto rights at the national level were extended. Indeed, not only did institutional reconfiguration not eliminate policy blockages, the splitting of the party system along linguistic lines doubled the number of parties, and created what we call "linguistic veto players."

These political and administrative changes reflect Belgian cleavage structure. Increased competencies for the communities are designed to preserve regional ethnic culture, and include policies on language, education, culture, family support, and health care. There is a German, a Walloon, and a Flemish community. Because of geographically-based economic differences, the government also established autonomous regions. The Flemish, the Walloon and the Brussels regions, each with its own government and legislature, govern policy areas such as housing, employment, energy, infrastructure, environment, spatial planning, and transport. Because the Flemish community and region overlap, they are governed by the same public authority (Vande Lanotte et al. 2003). The federal government has authority over policy areas that affect the entire country, such as defense, justice, state finances and tax policy, social security, state-owned companies, and foreign policy.

Belgium is marked by three cross-cutting cleavages: between Catholics and anticlerical groups; between labor and capital; and between the Flemish and Walloons.

Political parties and societal organizations are organized along these lines, resulting in the strong "pillarization" of society and fragmented interest group structure. Pillarization has weakened in recent years, but continues to play a role as political parties and societal institutions conduct formal and informal relations based on their common religious, ideological, or linguistic perspective (Keman 1996; Jones 2002; Deschouwer 2002a; 2002b).

The decline of heavy industry following World War II affected the Walloon region more than Flanders, leading to much higher levels of unemployment in Wallonia than in Flanders. This economic imbalance gave rise to an ongoing political conflict known as the "transfer-problem:" the Flemish pay more taxes and social contributions than Walloons while the Walloons receive more benefits and subsidies than the other half of the population (see Deleeck 1991). Regionalist Flemish political parties therefore advocate a stricter separation between the regions. Despite the "transfer problem," social policy is exclusively a federal domain (Béland and Lecours 2005).

Institutions of government

The Belgian Parliament consists of two chambers: the Chamber of Representatives and the Senate. The 150 members of the Chamber of Representatives (henceforth: "the Chamber") are elected every four years by proportional representation. The 1993 constitutional reform had significant consequences for the organization of state institutions. Several competencies were decentralized to the regions and communities, and the size of the national government institutions was reduced. Before the 1993 reform, the Chamber was comprised of 212 members (Keman 1996: 213).

The number of mandates per electoral district depends on population density (see section on "electoral system"). Because of their larger population, Flemish members have a majority in the Chamber. Regardless of party affiliation, the members of the Chamber are organized into two linguistic groups. All legislation affecting the regions or the division of power between the regions and the federal government requires a quorum of 50 percent of both language groups and a two-thirds majority of all votes (Vande Lanotte et al. 2003). For legislation requiring a simple parliamentary majority, the special "alarm-procedure" is designed to prevent one linguistic group (read: the Flemish) from overruling the other (read: the Walloons) because of larger numbers. If this occurs, the minority (3/4 of a linguistic group) can invoke the "alarm bell" procedure, thereby temporarily halting the legislation, and consult the government. The government is required to provide its advice within 30 days, after which the Chamber again decides on the issue (Vande Lanotte 2000: 68). The rules turn both the cabinet and the parliamentary linguistic groups into institutional veto players (veto points). However, as the cabinet is based on surplus majority government in terms of both the overall parliamentary majority and a language group majority, as well (through the "linguistic" veto players), these institutional veto players can be considered as "absorbed" (see Tables 7.1 and 7.2).

Table 7.1 Political institutions in Belgium

Political arenas	Actors	Rules of investiture	Rules of decision-making	veto potential
Executive	King	Hereditary	Appoints prime minister; signs laws (countersignature by the minister)	not a veto point
	Prime Minister	Appointed by the king, confirmed by vote of confidence with (since 1995) a majority of all members of the Chamber of Representatives (before: majority of those voting and quorum of 50% in both chambers); cabinet consists of equal number of members from each language group	Right of initiative; Power to legislate "special power decrees" and royal decisions; both language groups must agree to cabinet decisions	qualified cabinet voting, but counterbalanced by parity representation $\Rightarrow$ absorbed veto point
Legislative	Chamber of Representatives (Tweede Kamer/ Chambre de Representatives)	4-year term; 150 members; compulsory voting; proportional representation in eleven multi-member districts (i.e. provinces); threshold 5% in a district; voters can issue list vote or preference vote; seat allocation according to d'Hondt; (before 1995 government could dissolve parliament at any time)	Right of initiative. Decision making by simple majority with quorum of 50%; legislation affecting regions or vertical distribution of power requires linguistic quorum of 50% of both language groups and 2/3 majority of all votes; 3/4 of a language group can invoke the alarm bell procedure that halts issue for 30 days	Qualified majority voting, but counterbalanced by governmental linguistic and partisan majorities $\Rightarrow$ absorbed veto point
	Senate (Senaat/ Sénat)	4-year term; 71 senators (41 Flemish, 29 Walloons, 1 German); 40 directly elected, 21 elected by the community councils, 10 elected by the Senate itself plus monarch's children	Right of initiative. Chamber of reflection; comments on legislative proposal within one month. (Before 1993 constitutional reform consent was mandatory and bills shuttled (navette) between both chambers until compromise was found).	No veto point (even before 1993 constitutional reform no veto point due to government majority)

(Continued)

Table 7.1 (Continued)

Political arenas	Actors	Rules of investiture	Rules of decision-making	veto potential
Judicial	Court of Arbitration (Arbitragehof/ Court d'arbitrage)	12 judges appointed for life by the crown.	Reviews the compliance of legislation with the constitutional articles on equality, non-discrimination and freedom of education; acts upon government or federal, regional or community bodies' initiative; decisions are binding	no veto point
Electoral	Referendum	Not possible on national level; can only be used at provincial and municipal level.	–	no veto point
Territorial units	Communities (Gemeenschappen/ Communautés) Regions (Gewesten/ Régions)	Directly elected legislatures; Flemish, Walloon and German communities; Flemish, Walloon and Brussels regions (Flemish region and community overlap)	Communities: legislation on language, education, culture, family support, health care Regions: legislation on housing, employment, energy, infrastructure, environment, spatial planning and transport	no veto point; due to veto power of language groups in cabinet, cabinet is veto point

The 1993 Constitutional Reform reduced the number of Senators from 184 to 71 (excluding the royal family). The Senate is now composed of 40 directly elected Senators (25 Flemish, 15 Walloons), and 21 Senators are elected by the community councils (10 Flemish, 10 Walloons, and 1 German-speaking). In addition, 10 Senators are selected by other members of the Senate (6 Flemish, 4 Walloons). The Monarch's children are automatically part of the Senate (King Albert has three children, which means there are currently 74 Senators). Like the Chamber, the legislative period for the Senate is four years (Vande Lanotte et al. 2003). Senators do not receive a salary (Woyke 1999: 370).

The Senate and Chamber had equal legislative competence before the 1993 constitutional reform. Now the Chamber enacts laws without the consent of the Senate, except for constitutional reforms, ratification of international treaties and legislation on the Courts of Justice. Constitutional reforms require a two-thirds majority in both the Chamber and Senate for passage. The Chamber, however, has full authority over legislation on budgetary policy. As noted, the Senate may still provide advice to the Chamber on other legislative proposals (Vande Lanotte et al. 2003).

Electoral system

The Chamber of Representatives is elected every four years. Voting is compulsory, and the electoral system is based on the d'Hondt method. The relatively low threshold required for parliamentary representation reduces the barriers to entry for new parties (Keman 1996: 213). Since proportional representation mirrors societal differences, the party political landscape in Belgium is highly fragmented. There are eleven electoral districts, which correspond to the eleven provinces. Each district has a threshold of 5 percent of the votes, and each district has a specific number of seats (for instance 24 mandates in the Antwerp district, which means that 24 out of 150 MPs are elected in Antwerp). Each political party is required to include an equal number of male and female candidates on its electoral list, and the sequencing of names on the party lists must alternate between male and female candidates (Vande Lanotte et al. 2003).

Parties and elections

Belgium is often described as a "party-ocracy," because parties are extremely strong, party discipline is high, and party chairs are very influential (De Wachter 2001; De Winter 1996). The three dominant party families in Belgium in the post-war period have been the Christian Democrats (CVP/PSC), the Socialists (SP/PS) and the Liberals (VLD/PRL). In the 1960s and 1970s the three large parties split into a Flemish branch and a francophone branch (see Alen 1995: 28). Today, according to de Winter et al. (2000: 301) "Belgium has two quasi-autonomous party systems, each with a

Party family affiliation	Abbreviation	Party name	Ideological orientation	Founding and merger details	Year established
Christian parties	CVP, later CD&V	Christian People's Party (*Christelijke Volks Partij*, later *Christen Democratische en Vlaamse Partij*)	Christian Democratic Party (Flemish)	Split in 1968	Successor of the Catholic Party, established in August 1945
Christian parties	PSC	Christian Social Party (*Parti Social Chrétien*)	Christian Democratic Party (Walloon)		
Left parties / Social democratic parties	SP, later SPa	Socialist Party (*Socialistische Partij*)	Social Democrats (Flemish)	Split in 1978	The Flemish Socialist party. Established in 1885 as the Belgian Workers Party
Left parties / Social democratic parties	PS	Socialist Party (*Parti Socialiste*)	Social Democrats (Walloon)		
Communists	KPB	Belgian Communist Party (*Kommunistische Partij België*)	Marxist Communist		Established September 1921
Communists	PVDA	Worker's Party of Belgium (*Partij van de Arbeid*)			
Greens	AGALEV	A different way of Living (*Anders Gaan Leven*)	Green (Flemish)		First participation in local elections in 1977, national party since 1981
Greens	ECOLO		Green (Walloon)		Cooperates with AGALEV. Established 1980
Liberal	PVV, later VLD	Flemish Liberals and Democrats (*Partij voor Vrijheid en Vooruitgang*, later *Vlaamse Liberalen en Democraten*)	Conservative liberal party (Flemish)		VLD since 1992

Fig. 7.1 Party system in Belgium

Liberal	PLP, later PRL, later MR	Liberal Reformation Party (*Parti Réformateur Liberal*); since 2003 Reformation Movement (*Movement Réformateur*)	Conservative liberal party (Walloon)	Split in 1972	PRL, MCC and FDF merged in 2002 into *Mouvement Réformateur* (MR) together with German-speaking PFF (*partei fur freiheit und Fortschritt*)	The former party leader of the PRL (Deprez) established a new party, *Mouvement des Citoyens pour le Changement* (MCC) in 2000
Regionalist Liberal	FDF	French-speaking Democratic Front (*Front Démocratique des Francophones*)	Regionalist Walloon Party			
	RW	Waloonian Rally (*Rassemblement Wallon*)	Regionalist Walloon Party		Established in 1968, partly merged into the *Parti Socialiste* in 1985. RW was dissolved in 1986	
	VU, later: NVA / Spirit	Peoples' Union (*Volksunie*)	Regionalist Flemish Party		*Volksunie* split into the more conservative NVA (*Nieuw Vlaamse Alliantie*) and more progressive Spirit in 2001. *Spirit* cooperated with the Flemish socialists (SP-A) in the 2003 elections.	
Right wing	Vlaams Blok	Flemish Block (*Vlaams Blok;* since 2004 *Vlaams Belang*)	Populist Flemish right wing party		Established 1978 by the right wing of the *Volksunie* who disagreed about cooperation between the VU and the Walloon regionalists in the 1977 Egmont Pact	
	FN	National Front (*Front National*)	Populist Walloon right wing party		Established in 1985	

Fig. 7.1 (*Continued*)

different balance of power between the main parties." Parties represent similar ideologies in each region, but the Christian Democrats are the major party in Flanders whereas the Socialist Party dominates Wallonian politics. Although the parties are grouped in party families, conflicts follow the north–south (Flemish–Walloon) dimension more frequently than ideological lines.

The Christian Democratic Party family CVP/PSC has often been pivotal in government coalition formation, and has served in most post-war governments. However, Christian Democratic influence has waned recently. The 1999 elections resulted in the formation of a "rainbow coalition," consisting of Liberals, Socialists, and Greens, and the 2003 election confirmed this trend. This electoral system and Belgian cleavage structure interact to produce multiparty coalition governments supported by oversized majorities in parliament.[3]

Cabinet formation is an unusually long process (usually several months), and results not only in the distribution of ministerial portfolios to government parties, but also in a detailed coalition agreement (often over 100 pages) outlining the policies that the cabinet will pursue. The coalition agreement is binding on the government parties and is referred to as the "bible." By specifying the policy agenda in advance, the coalition agreement reduces the uncertainties associated with multiparty coalitions and reduces potential conflict. Negotiating policy priorities in advance also means that most important decisions are "pre-cooked," in the sense that the coalition parties agree to them before forming the coalition. The cabinet is not supposed to depart from the coalition agreement unless the decision has been made by consensus. To sum up, most crucial political negotiations are part of the government formation process, and this process reflects the power of the political parties, at the expense of parliament and the executive.

Once in place, the cabinet functions according to the doctrine of collective cabinet responsibility. This means that the whole cabinet oversees decisions made by individual ministers. As de Winter et al. (2000: 308–9) put it, "... coalition parties have a large set of instruments giving them effective veto power over policies proposed by ministers of other parties." Cabinet formation is a delicate and time-consuming task because of the fragmentation of the party system and the informal requirement that governments include equal representation by the Flemish and Walloon branches of each party. This means, for example, that if the Christian Democratic Party participates in the government, both the Flemish and Walloon party are included.

Belgian political parties are deeply involved in the process of government formation and in monitoring subsequent policy-making. Party leaders are key players in cabinet negotiations, and ministers from any given party are generally subordinate to the party leader, who never occupies a ministerial post. Cabinet participation as well as the coalition agreement are ratified by party congresses before investiture. It is not uncommon for a party leader to intervene if government policy departs too much from the coalition agreement. Party organizations also ratify ministers and their high level assistants, so the parties have several opportunities to influence the cabinet. In sum, politicians in government and parliament are accountable to the party

Table 7.2 Governmental majorities in Belgium

Election date	Start of gov.	Head of gov. (party)	Governing parties	Gov majority (% seats) Kamer	Gov. electoral base (% votes) Kamer	Gov majority (% seats) Senaat	Institutional veto points[a]	Number of veto players[a] (partisan + institutional)
12.17.1978	04.03.1979	Martens I (CVP)	CVP (57), PS (32), PSC (26), SP (25), FDF (11)	71.2%	65.9%	74.6%	None	5 + 0
	01.23.1980	Martens II (CVP)	CVP (57), PS (32), SP (26), PSC (25)	66.0%	61.6%	69.6%	None	4 + 0
	05.18.1980	Martens III (CVP)	CVP (57), PS (32), SP (26), PSC (25), PVV (22), PRL (14)	83.0%	77.2%	84.5%	None	6 + 0
	10.22.1980	Martens IV (CVP)	CVP (57), PS (32), SP (26), PSC (25)	66.0%	61.6%	69.6%	None	4 + 0
	04.06.1981	Eyskens (CVP)	CVP (57), PS (32), SP (26), PSC (25)	66.0%	61.6%	69.6%	None	4 + 0
11.08.1981	12.17.1981	Martens V (CVP)	CVP (43), PVV (28), PRL (24), PSC (18)	53.3%	48.0%	54.7%	None	4 + 0
10.13.1985	11.28.1985	Martens VI (CVP)	CVP (49), PRL (24), PVV (22), PSC (20)	54.2%	50.2%	55.7%	None	4 + 0
	10.21.1987	Martens VII (CVP)	CVP (49), PRL (24), PVV (22), PSC (20)	54.2%	50.2%	55.7%	None	4 + 0
12.13.1987	05.09.1988	Martens VIII (CVP)	CVP (43), PS (40), SP (32), PSC (19), VU (16)	70.8%	66.0%	72.7%	None	5 + 0
	09.29.1991	Martens IX (CVP)	CVP (43), PS (40), SP (32), PSC (19)	63.2%	58.0%	65.6%	None	4 + 0

(Continued)

Table 7.2 (Continued)

Election date	Start of gov.	Head of gov. (party)	Governing parties	Gov majority (% seats) Kamer	Gov. electoral base (% votes) Kamer	Gov majority (% seats) Senaat	Institutional veto points[a]	Number of veto players (partisan + institutional)
11.24.1991	03.17.1992	Dehaene I (CVP)	CVP (39), PS (35), SP (28), PSC (18)	56.6%	50.0%	58.7%	None	4 + 0
05.21.1995	06.23.1995	Dehaene II (CVP)	CVP (29), PS (21), SP (20), PSC (12)	54.7%	49.3%	54.9%	None	4 + 0
06.13.1999	07.12.1999	Verhofstadt I (VLD)	VLD (23), PS (19), PRL-FDF (18), SP (14), ECOLO (11), Agalev (9)	62.7%	58.5%	66.2%	None	6 + 0
05.18.2003	07.15.2003	Verhofstadt II (VLD)	VLD (25), PS (25), MR (24), SP (23), ECOLO (4)	67.3%	57.7%	67.6%	None	5 + 0

[a]Qualified majority voting in Cabinet and Parliament absorbed by "linguistic veto players" in cabinet and "linguistic majorities" of governments.

organizations, increasing potential policy-making obstacles, and adding to the checks and balances inherent in the Belgian political system.

Legislative process

The government and both Houses of Parliament have the right to initiate legislation. The government usually introduces bills (*wetsontwerp/projet de loi*) via its own members of parliament. Proposals initiated by Members of Parliament (*wetsvoorstel/ proposition de loi*) have little chance of passage and "must be considered as kite-flying efforts to get an issue aired" (Fitzmaurice 1996: 110). Preliminary draft bills, decrees and ordinances require examination by the Council of State (*Raad van State/Conseil d'état*). The Council of State's opinion is not binding, but in practice government action nearly always is based on these recommendations (Vande Lanotte et al. 2003: 113).

Until the Fourth State Reform in 1993, the Chamber and the Senate possessed equal legislative competences, and each chamber had to approve identical versions of proposed legislation (Fitzmaurice 1996: 108). In cases of serious disagreement between the two chambers, a deliberation commission could be formed to resolve the conflict. A deliberation commission consists of 11 members of each house (Vande Lanotte et al. 2003: 53), and can make decisions by a two-thirds majority.

The 1993 Constitutional Reform introduced the legislative procedure which is now most commonly used, in which the Senate possesses only advisory functions. All legislative proposals are discussed by parliamentary committees, and committee members as well as government ministers can suggest amendments. When the relevant committee agrees on the text of a proposal, it is placed on the agenda of a plenary meeting of parliament. Amendments can also be proposed during the plenary session. The Senate may suggest amendments after the Chamber adopts legislation, and these amendments will then be accepted or rejected by the Chamber. In order for a vote to take place in either chamber, more than half of the total number of members of that house (>75 MPs or >37 Senators) must be present. Approval is by simple majority. Qualified majority voting[4] is used when the proposed legislation changes the division of competences between the federal state, the communities and the regions. As was the case in the pre-1993 period, a deliberation commission can be convened when there is a conflict between the Chamber and the Senate (Vande Lanotte et al. 2003: 53–67).

Before proposing legislation on social and economic policy, the government consults with representatives of unions and employers. In addition, representation by the trade unions and employers' organizations is institutionalized in important national negotiation forums. The bipartite National Labor Council (*Nationale Arbeidsraad/Conseil National du Travail*, NAR) advises government on social law and labor policy, the bipartite Central Council of Industry (*Centrale Raad voor het Bedrijfsleven/Conseil Central de l'Économie*) advises on economic and industrial policy (Vilrokx and Van Leemput 1997; Van Ruijsseveldt and Visser 1996).

The government has the authority to translate legislation already adopted by parliament into executive decrees. Executive decrees can be either a royal decree (this is always signed by the King) or a ministerial decree (this need not be signed by the King). A specific form of royal decrees are "special powers decrees," or decisions that governments can take in times of crisis in order to enact legislation without consulting parliament according to the normal rules. A special powers decree is based on a decision by parliament—"special powers law." In a special powers law, parliament gives the government extraordinary authority for a limited time for a specific purpose identified in the law. For instance, the Dehaene government used "special powers decrees" in the 1990s to pass legislation cutting public expenditures in order to meet the Maastricht criteria and qualify for the first stage of EMU. Special powers decrees are an exception to the rule that royal decrees may never alter or contradict the law they are based on. However, many special powers decrees are transformed into legislation by parliament after the fact (Vande Lanotte 2003: 89; see also Jones 2002).

Two features of the legislative process are crucial for understanding the politics of pensions in Belgium. First, as noted, all important proposals are "pre-cooked" in the sense that they negotiated as part of the coalition formation process. This will already reduce the potential for radical change since so many parties must agree to a reform project in advance. Moreover, consensus decision-making in the cabinet adds to the disincentives for radical reform. Second, governments have relied more and more on "special powers" procedures to pass difficult policies. The special powers periods equaled 87 months in total for the past 50 years (De Wachter 2001: 25). In other words, the government sidesteps Parliament, with Parliament's permission, in order to adopt the measures necessary to meet specific goals, such as meeting the EMU convergence criteria in the mid-1990s. However, given the "startup costs" of reaching cabinet agreement on reform proposals, resorting to "special powers" seems less dramatic because the party organizations are calling the shots anyway, both in the Cabinet and in Parliament. Particularly contentious issues that are not part of the coalition agreement are often referred to the social partners or "round table" discussions. If agreement is reached in these forums, it is likely that the Cabinet will reach consensus on the issue, and propose legislation that sails through Parliament (see Deschouwer 2002a; 2002b; De Winter et al. 2000).

To sum up, there are very high costs associated with substantial policy change in Belgium, and these costs are even greater in the area of pensions. Wallonia benefits disproportionately from the federal social security system, including pensions, so any proposal with the potential to reduce this advantage is bound to fail because of the linguistic parity rule in the Cabinet. Thus pension reforms aimed at reducing expenditure or improving financial balance are not likely to disturb this equilibrium; instead, the incentives point in the direction of incremental cuts, and even these are difficult for Belgian governments to agree on. As the discussion that follows demonstrates, the most radical (for Belgium) reforms were not radical at all in comparative terms, and they were only achieved in the context of acute economic pressures.

Interest groups

Pillarization and fragmentation are the hallmarks of Belgian politics and society. Interest groups are organized broadly along class lines, but unions and employers are further divided along religious, ideological and linguistic lines. This makes for a fragmented interest group structure; for example, despite high rates of unionization, the labor movement is ideologically divided as well as split along linguistic lines.

The 1944 "Social Pact" between unions and employers laid the foundations for post-war industrial relations and interest intermediation. This agreement set the stage for the development of a complex set of corporatist institutions, including works councils and the tripartite Central Economic Council (*Centrale Raad voor het Bedrijfsleven/Conseil Central de l'Économie*) that advises the government on economic and social legislation. The social partners play an important role in the administration of social security. Unions administer unemployment benefits and together with employers implement sectoral vocational training policies. Central agreements play an important role and unions have a strong presence at the firm level. In addition, the bipartite National Labor Council (*Nationale Arbeidsraad/ Conseil National du Travail*, NAR) advises the government and Parliament on general and social issues affecting all employees and employers. Since 1968, the NAR has also been used as a forum for economy-wide collective bargaining.[5]

Vilrokx and van Leemput (1997) divide the post-war development of industrial relations in Belgium into four phases. Between 1945 and 1959, the basic elements of the tripartite industrial relations system were institutionalized. Second, 1960–74 was a period of fairly stable bipartite negotiation with little state intervention. In the third period (1975–90), rising labor costs, declining competitiveness and economic stagnation led to conflictual bipartite negotiations that often ended in agreements that were costly for the state. In 1976, the state re-asserted its control over economic affairs, intervening directly in wage bargaining. Finally, the period 1990 to the present is a marked by flux: the government is trying to renegotiate its relationship with the social partners. In 1986, the state and social partners went back to two year central agreements, but these were less effective than those in the 1960s. Most of these were heavily influenced by state activity, such as the imposition of a wage norm.

The 1990s saw attempts to return to tripartite bargaining so that Belgium could qualify for EMU. An attempt at a social pact modeled on the 1944 pact failed, but was followed by a less ambitious agreement in 1993, the "Global Plan." Vilrokx and van Leemput interpret this as an attempt by the government to get the social partners, especially the unions, to "internalize" the implications of its strict budgetary policy of the past 15 years. The main idea was to try to limit wage increases and keep Belgium competitive in world markets.

The Confederation of Christian Trade Unions (*Algemeen Christelijk Vakverbond/ Confédération des Syndicats Chrétiens*, ACV/CSC) is the largest union federation in Belgium with 12 sectoral affiliates and 1.6 million members. The ACV/CSC is less confrontational and radical than the Belgian General Federation of Labor (*Algemeen Belgisch Vakverbond/Fédération Générale du Travail de Belgique*, ABVV/FGTB), the socialist union federation, with about 1 million members. The Federation of Liberal Trade Unions of Belgium (*Algemene Centrale der Liberale Vakbonden/Centrale Générale des Syndicats Libéraux de Belgique*, ACLV/CGSLB) follows a market liberal policy line, and has about 240,000 members.

Similar to the unions, employers are highly organized, but fragmented. The Federation of Belgian Enterprises (*Verbond van Belgische Ondernemingen/Fédération des Entreprises Belges*, VBO-FEB) is the main employers association, representing 50 sectoral associations. In addition, the National Christian Federation of Small Firms and Traders, Regional Flemish and Walloon associations (the *Vlaams Economisch Verbond* and the *Union Wallone des Entreprises*), and the Federation of Christian Employers represent various regional and sectoral interests.

In sum, the Belgian economy is highly organized, and corporatist institutions are important forums for wage bargaining and policy negotiations. However, Belgian cleavage structure results in a fragmented set of corporatist institutions within which linguistic or confessional minorities have ample opportunities to block compromise. This is especially true for unions. High levels of union membership mask the societal and linguistic cleavages that have led to the fragmentation of union structure along regional and ideological lines. The Christian ACV/CSC tends to be more accommodating while the Socialist ABVV/FGTB tends to resort more often to direct action such as strikes. The frequent inability of both union confederations to agree makes collective action difficult. As the discussion of reform processes later in this chapter shows, unified union opposition to reform proposals meant almost certain failure, while the implicit or explicit support of the more accommodationalist ACV/CSC was often a decisive factor in the government's capacity to adopt pension reform.

III PENSION SYSTEM

Historical overview

The earliest pension schemes in Belgium were civil service pensions and voluntary savings schemes for workers.[6] The separate scheme for civil servants was established in 1844 and has changed little since its origins. Direct government involvement in social security in Belgium began in 1891 during a period of Catholic Party dominance. Existing local insurance associations were unified into national associations, and occupational injury insurance became compulsory for employees in 1903. Pension insurance, survivor's benefits and mandatory vacations followed in the inter-war years. Catholic political ideas shaped the structure of the early pension system, influencing the division of pension schemes along class lines. Early attempts to legislate compulsory public pensions were postponed because of the outbreak of World War I, but miners pensions were legislated in 1911.

Following World War I, the Social Democratic government adopted a provisional pension scheme, but after the Social Democrats lost power, pension reform followed the lines proposed prior to World War I. This period culminated in the passage of the 1924 Manual Workers Act and the 1925 Salaried Employees Act, both heavily influenced by the Catholic Party. The schemes were similar and based on both capitalization and state subsidies. Social insurance for the self-employed, including pensions, was not compulsory until 1937. Finally, as noted, civil servant pensions were largely financed by the national government. In contrast to pensions for employees, civil servant pensions were explicitly seen as "deferred wages." A full civil servant pension paid benefits equal to 75 percent of earnings in the last five years of employment, and the formula was more generous for some categories of work.

The war years brought more fundamental changes to the pension system. Employers' associations, unions and the state agreed on the 1994 "Social Pact" that set the parameters for post-war industrial relations and reformed the social insurance system. The pact established the National Office for Social Security (*Rijksdienst voor Sociale Zekerheid van de provinciale en plaatselijke overheidsdiensten/Office National de Sécurité Sociale des administrations provinciales et locales*, RSZ/ONSS) as the central agency for collecting the social insurance contributions paid by employer and employee (one fee covered all of the insurances). The fund had a corporatist administration and disbursed funds to various branches of social insurance according to need. The emergence of the Social Pact marked the return to the basic structure of pre-war social insurance and marked the defeat of Social Democratic proposals based on the Beveridge report.

The Social Pact did not signal a complete victory for the non-socialists, however, since the pension system combined capitalization with solidaristic, publicly financed elements. This compromise was the result of competing Social Democratic and Catholic ideas about how to organize pensions. However, the provisional compromise turned to protracted stalemate as the two major political groups could not agree on a more permanent pension reform. In 1953, the Christian Democrats finally managed to pass more permanent legislation, but only for employees. This law abolished the capitalization in the system and established the corporatist (*Rijksdienst voor Arbeidspensioenen*, RAP) to administer employee pensions. This reform had a short life; in 1954 the Christian Democrats lost their absolute majority in Parliament and a Socialist Minister of Labor reversed the reform provisions concerning administration. The RAP was abolished and the National Fund for Retirement and Survivors' Pensions (*Rijkskas voor Rust en Overlevingspensioenen/Caisse National des Pensions de Retraite et de Survie*, RROP) was introduced to administer pension payments to retirees. The new system was based entirely on the pay-as-you-go (PAYG) principle and introduced a benefit formula that lasts to this day.

Legislation passed in 1957 reformed pensions for salaried employees. The new system was based on partial collective capitalization, a major shift from the existing system of individual capitalization. This scheme was also short-lived; a Christian Democratic majority government reversed it in 1958 and replaced it with a hybrid of individual and collective capitalization.[7]

By the 1960s, the Belgian system had evolved into a complicated and fragmented set of policies. Most people had some sort of coverage, but benefits varied widely according to occupation. In 1967, the Christian Democratic-Liberal government cooperated on a pension reform made possible by use of "special powers" in Parliament. The rationale for the reform was to promote economic recovery and simplify the various schemes. Some sectors (especially the miners' pension scheme) were running deficits, and the reserves in the salaried employees' pension funds could be used to finance the merger. The reform merged several schemes into a single scheme for salaried employees and abolished the principle of capitalization, despite loud protests from salaried employees' unions. The amalgamated scheme was jointly administered by the National Employees' Pensions Office (*Rijksdienst voor Werknemerspensioenen/Office National des Pensions pour Travailleurs Salariés*, RWP/ONPTS) and the RROP, and included manual workers, salaried employees, miners and seamen. Initially, the RWP was charged with the task of awarding pensions to those who were eligible, the RROP was responsible for the payment of pensions. The two organizations merged in 1987 and became the National Pensions Agency (*Rijksdienst voor Pensioenen/Office National des Pensions*, RVP/ONP). The RVP is responsible for the entire administration of Belgian employees' pensions, it collects contributions, grants claims and pays benefits (*Rijksdienst voor Pensioenen* 2004: 1).

The emergence of three separate schemes (for civil servants, self-employed, and private sector wage-earners) in the context of strong electoral competition between the Socialist and Christian Democratic Parties led to substantial improvements in pension provision in the two decades following World War II. As Marier (2002: 138) reports, benefits were increased 16 times between 1945 and 1962 as part of efforts by both parties to demonstrate "leadership" in public pension provision. The expansions of coverage and benefits adopted in the 1950s must be seen in this context.

Description of the current pension system

Coverage

The social security system is divided into three major schemes: one for dependent employees in the private sector; one for the self-employed; and one for civil servants. The current legal bases of the pension system are KB no. 50[8] (regulating workers' pensions), which took effect on October 24, 1967 and KB no. 72 (regulating pensions for self-employed persons), effective November 10, 1967.[9] These royal decrees are based on parent legislation that gives the Cabinet (the Crown) authority to amend the legislation as needed, within certain limits. The 1967 reform transformed the different sectoral pension schemes (except civil servant pensions) into a PAYG scheme for all wage earners (blue and white collar workers, seamen and miners used to have separate schemes). One important difference remained, however: a higher wage ceiling for contributions and pension rights for white collar workers. Aside from this, pensions were strictly related to average wages.

An employee's public pension is often topped up by sectoral or company pension schemes. Company pensions have traditionally been the most important supplementary arrangements. However, legislation regulating second-pillar pensions has been limited until recently. The most important regulation concerns the audit on insurance companies that provide supplementary arrangements to companies.[10] The so-called RSZ Law (*Rijksdienst voor Sociale Zekerheid/Office National Sécurité Sociale*, National Office for Social Security) made it illegal for employers to discriminate between their workers in the provision of second-pillar pensions.[11] Legislation adopted in 2001 creates greater incentives for the expansion of second-pillar schemes (see below).

Administration

The social partners administer the social security system, including pensions. The governing boards of organizations such as the National Pensions Agency (RVP), the National Employment Agency (RVA) and the National Agency for Sickness and Disability Insurance (Riziv) are composed of 50 percent union representatives and 50 percent employers' delegates. In most boards a government delegate takes part as well. The government monitors the work of these boards and can overrule their decisions if they are not in conformity with the law or the public interest (Deleeck 2001). Corporatist administration of social security arrangements in Belgium is partly a response to widespread distrust of state intervention (DeSwert and Janssen 1996). Social insurance programs used to be private mutual insurances, and they have been brought under state authority only as much as was necessary in order to guarantee financing or to make outcomes of bipartite negotiations binding by law.

Financing

The public pension system for employees in the private sector is a PAYG system based mainly on contributions and supplemented by government grants and other financial sources (e.g. a share of VAT revenue). Before 1995, contributions for the each social security branch were fixed separately and the National Office for Social Security distributed the respective amount to the quasi-state agency. Starting on January 1, 1995, the fixed percentages were phased out, and the general contribution (37.94% of gross wages) is now paid to the RSZ/ONSS. The RSZ/ONSS then distributes funds to each social security branch according to its requirements and needs (Jorens 1997). An alternative source of financing for pensions is the VAT. Twenty-one percent of VAT revenues are earmarked for the social security system. The goal of this arrangement is to reduce employers' contributions and relieve pressure on central government finances by limiting the size of the federal grant to the social security system.

The pension scheme for the self-employed is financed via contributions based on net income. Civil servants are exempt from contributions for most types of social insurance; they contribute only to the survivor's pension scheme and the health care insurance. The federal government pays the full cost of civil servant pensions.

	First pillar	Second pillar	Third pillar
Third tier	none	Voluntary occupational pension: none	Voluntary private pension
First and second tier combined	earnings-related pensions (Employees — *Régime des travailleurs salariés*; Self-employed — *Régime des travailleurs indépendants*; Civil Servants — *Régime des fonctionnaires*)	Subsidized occupational pension	Subsidized private pension: none
	Guaranteed minimum pension (*gewaarborgd minimumpensioen*)	Mandatory occupational pension: none	Mandatory private pension: none
	Social assistance at subsistence level (*bestaansminimum/ minimum d'existence*)		

Fig. 7.2 Pension system in Belgium

Benefits

Pensions are based on a "defined benefit" formula that is different for private sector employees and civil servants. Employee benefits are based on average gross wages, whereas civil servant pensions are calculated on income during the five last years of employment. Family situation also affects pension levels: the head of family receives 75 percent of average gross lifetime earnings while a single person receives 60 percent. Forty-five years of employment are required for a full employee pension.

Prior to 1997, the retirement age for women was 60 and the reference period for the pension benefit formula was 40 years. Because these rules differed from men's, the European Court of Justice declared them illegal. Women's and men's retirement ages and benefit formulas were standardized in 1996 to comply with European law. Women's retirement age is gradually increased every two years until it reaches 65 in 2009.

Pension contributions have been paid on the entire wage since 1982, but pension rights accrue on the income below a specific ceiling (€39,367 in 2004). There is also a guaranteed minimum pension for those with inadequate pension rights from employment. The minimum pension in 1996 was 56 percent of the average net wage (Pestieau and Stijns 1999: 47). In most cases, it is not possible to combine employment with the receipt of a pension.

Pensions are indexed to inflation, but governments have the freedom to adopt discretionary increases. This provision is seldom used, however; the last time was in 1991 (Pestieau and Stijns 1999: 47). Because wages usually rise faster than inflation, inflation indexing means that pensioners' incomes do not rise in step with wages. To deal with this, Parliament established the goal of indexing pensions to "welfare" (read: wages) in 1973 (*B.S.* March 30, 1973), but this goal was quickly abandoned. Instead of annual increases, Parliament has passed ad hoc increases when financial circumstances permitted. Many of these increases were not universal but instead were aimed at two groups: low income pensioners and older pensioners. For example, the minimum pension was increased in 1988 and 1989. The flexible pension age law also gave priority to older pensioners (Gieselink et al. n.d.).

Pensions for the self-employed are based on the number of years of contributions, but their pensions are not earnings-related. Depending on family situation, a self-employed person receives a flat rate pension (80% for single person households, 100% for breadwinners with a family). Until 1980, eligibility was means-tested. Civil servant pensions are indexed to civil servant pay scales. This indexing mechanism is called the *perekwatie/péréquation* and results in substantially higher pension increases than in the other two schemes (Pestieau and Stijns 1999: 48).

IV POLITICS OF PENSION REFORM SINCE 1980

Overview

Pension politics in Belgium since 1980 has been dominated by attempts to deal with recurring financing problems, adjust pension law to EU law, and expand the coverage of supplementary pensions. The economic crises of the 1970s caused a significant decline in employment that coincided with a trend toward increasing numbers of

Table 7.3 Overview of proposed and enacted pension reforms in Belgium

Year	Name of reform	Reform process (chronology)	Reform measures
1982	Reform of early retirement programs	• Royal decree Sept 28/29, 1982	• abolition of statutory bridge pension based on final salary; abolition of retirement for women at age 55 • introduction of bridge pensions, i.e. retirement at 60 without 5% reduction for every year of early retirement but benefits based on average wage
1984	Mainil Reform	• 1981 government decision to harmonize the fragmented pension system • bill introduced September 9, 1983 • May 15, 1984 passage	• introduction of family pensions for women and survivor's pension for men • introduction of proportional pension rights instead of flat rate • introduction of ceiling for income-related pension rights for self-employed • improvements for low-income self-employed persons' pensions • introduction of minimum pensions for civil servants with a minimum of 20 years of service • limitation of pension accumulation to 45 years of employment • limitation on accumulation of civil servant pensions
1986	St Anna Plan	• May 23, 1986 publication of St. Anna plan • union protests • Francophone Christian Democrats rejected proposal • after concessions Christian union accepts reform • July 16, 1986 enactment of St. Anna plan through Royal decrees	• increase of reference period for women from 40 to 45 years • no equalization of retirement age as originally intended

1990	Flexible pension age	- Legislation adopted July 20, 1990	- introduction of flexible pension age at 60 for both men and women - abolition of bridge pension and early retirement - benefits based on number of years actually worked
1992/93	Civil servant pension reform	- Round table discussions - public sector unions protest → reform failed	Proposed measures: - abolition of wage indexing for civil servant pensions - lower benefits for high-income civil servants - transfer of financing from the federal government to the regions and communities
1995	Comprehensive reform	- submission of issues to the National Labor Council to comment on by Minister Willockx - early 1993 round table discussions - January 1994 common statement by unions (ACV, ABVV) - resignation of social minister Willockx - reform failed - early 1995 passage in Second Chamber and Senate Committee	- reduction of vesting period to one year - increase in retirement age for women - weakening of wage indexing for civil servants - reduction of pension entitlements during unemployment
1995	Colla Law	- Early 1995 passage in Second Chamber and Senate Committee - Unions try to get the senate to veto law, but fail - Legislation adopted April 6, 1995	- improved provisions for occupational pensions
1996/97	Social Framework Law	- October commissioning of financial forecast for the civil servant pension scheme - Parliament grants government authority to take a wide range of measures until August 31, 1997 - April 18, 1996 cabinet decision - July 26, 1996 Framework law	- improvement of minimum pension - increase in minimum number of years for early retirement pension - extra revenues for social insurance from VAT income - improvement of federal subsidies to employee and self-employed pension schemes - improvement of federal subsidies to employee and self-employed pension schemes

(Continued)

Table 7.3 (Continued)

Year	Name of reform	Reform process (chronology)	Reform measures
1997	EU and Equal Treatment	• reform negotiated as part of Social Framework Law • June 19, 1996 passage	• increase of women's retirement age to 65 by 2009
2001	Silver Fund	• after 1999 election, new government announces measures to improve pension financing • legislation adopted 5 September 2001	• establishment of Silver Fund to accumulate reserves for future pension costs • revenues of the fund are non-tax revenues (sale of mobile phone licenses) or budget surpluses
2003	Vandenbroucke Law	• Early 2000 expert task force set up; no agreement • Pensions Minister negotiates with social partners in 2001; agreement reached • legislation introduced April 2001 • legislation adopted March 2003	• regulation of collective, funded supplementary pensions • option to make additional contributions to a collective fund

retirees with full pension rights. These trends led to substantial financing problems for the pension system, and Belgian governments responded with measures designed to reduce expenditures and broaden the financial support base for the system. The instability of governments in the 1980s hindered reform, although several incremental reforms were adopted. In the 1990s, governments were more stable, and the effort to qualify for EMU in the mid-1990s provided the necessary consensus for more far-reaching reform. In addition, European legal requirements concerning gender equality prompted a conflictual process of harmonizing men's and women's pension benefit formulae. Taken together, the reforms since the 1980s add up to a considerable weakening of the insurance principle, because reforms raised contributions for high income earners, at the same time that benefit levels decreased rapidly, particularly in relation to previous income. Most reforms were based on extensive consultation with employers and unions. Repeated attempts to reform civil servant pensions were notable failures.

Incremental reforms

The 1980s were to become a decade marked by repeated attempts to deal with recurring pension financing problems. In October 1980, the ruling Christian Democratic–Socialist coalition collapsed because of internal dissent, and Prime Minister Wilfried Martens formed a new government (Martens IV) without elections. The new government faced serious economic problems and managed to reach agreement on wage moderation by temporarily freezing wage indexation, introducing progressive solidarity contributions on civil service incomes, and absorbing the large debt of the pension scheme for the self-employed.[12] The same legislation also included several other changes pertaining to the rules of entitlement to a full pension or minimum pension, and the calculation of pension benefits.[13]

Despite opposition from the social partners to its policies, the government soon announced another austerity package, the "Disaster Plan" that included several public spending cuts including the capping of pensions. The pension freeze became a source of conflict for the Martens IV government, however. The employers had long advocated the abolition of the automatic price index, whereas indexation was sacred to the unions. The Christian Democratic parties both agreed to the Disaster Plan, but the Socialist ministers rejected it. The government fell because the coalition partners could not agree on the proposed wage freeze, and the "Disaster Plan" was abandoned. The Martens IV coalition was succeeded by the short-lived Eyskens cabinet, which also broke up (after only five months) because of internal conflicts between the Christian Democrats and the Socialists.

Financial imbalances in the pension scheme for the self-employed were also a problem, mainly because of unfavorable demographic trends; the ratio of retired self-employed persons to active self-employed persons was shifting in favor of the former, creating financing problems. A growing deficit, in spite of increasing state contributions, resulted in a rapidly increasing program deficits debt spiral. As already noted,

1981 legislation provided for the state's absorption of the pension debt of the self-employed. In separate legislation, the contribution of the self employed was raised considerably, as was the contribution ceiling.[14]

The 1981 election

In the fall of 1981, Parliament was dissolved and new elections took place. The Christian Democrats lost heavily (−7%), while the Liberal parties (PVV/PRL), and the Flemish Nationalists (*Volksunie*) made large gains. The Socialist parties kept the seats they had, and refused to join the Liberals in a coalition. Thus even though the Christian Democrats experienced defeat, a Christian Democratic–Liberal cabinet was formed with Wilfried Martens (CVP) as its "new" prime minister.

The new Martens V cabinet (CVP/PSC + VLD/PRL) requested special powers from Parliament in order to implement a "recovery" policy in the next year. In the next four years the government would (usually by decree) pursue a hard line budgetary policy and push through changes designed to restore health to the Belgian economy. The *Special Powers Act*[15] was formulated in terms of broad objectives (economic recovery; increasing economic competitiveness; restoration of financial balance in the social security system) and gave the government much freedom to achieve these goals. In addition, the government and the Central Bank decided to devalue the Belgian franc by 8.5 percent to stimulate the economy. This necessitated a strict budgetary policy in order to control inflation. Besides imposing wage moderation and freezing the automatic indexation mechanism, the government decided to impose extra levies, increased contributions to the pension system, and introduce savings in other social security sectors.

These changes aroused large-scale protest by the socialist labor union (ABVV/FGTB). With its political allies (the Socialist parties) in opposition, the Socialist union protested vehemently against the government decisions by decree. The Christian union ACV/CSC, by contrast, announced that even though it did not fully agree with all government decisions, it would not organize strikes against the Martens V government as long as it was convinced that the intervention was absolutely necessary for economic recovery. The absence of a united union front opposing the reforms facilitated the implementation of the measures included in the special powers legislation.

Differences between the two union camps had long-lasting effects: relations between the Christian and Socialist unions were tense throughout the 1980s. When the socialist ABVV does not have the support of the Christian unions, it is difficult to mobilize workers in Flanders, because the Christian union is much more strongly represented there. The strikes thus showed a regional profile, with large scale protests in Wallonia and acquiescence in Flanders. Although the employers' organization usually opposes government intervention in wage policy (the social partners prefer to retain control over wage setting) they agreed on the recovery policy by Martens V because of the economic recession and declining competitiveness.

Reform of early retirement 1982

In 1982, the bridge pension, or prepension, was introduced.[16] The bridge retirement pension allowed employees to retire at the age of 60, if their employers replaced them with a new employee (Masyn 1987: 550). If this condition was met, the retiring employee received a full pension based on the average wage (instead of a 5% reduction for each year of early retirement under the law at the time). This arrangement served both to stimulate employment (because of the worker replacement condition) and to reduce expenditures because another more generous early retirement scheme was abolished: the "statutory bridge pension." The latter was based on final wages instead of average wages (which are usually considerably lower). In addition, it had been possible for women to retire at the age of 55 in the statutory bridge pension scheme. The bridge retirement pension became popular among workers and their employers, but was later abolished with the introduction of the flexible pension age in 1990 (see below). The bridge pension was widely supported in Parliament.

The Mainil Reform of 1984

By the early 1980s, the development of the public pension system showed two contradictory tendencies. On the one hand, the Christian Democratic–Socialist government expanded coverage by introducing a minimum pension guarantee.[17] On other hand, growing financing problems prompted the government to reduce its own contribution to the public scheme and to widen the contribution base.[18] Both tendencies substantially weakened the insurance character of the pension system.

The Mainil Law, adopted in May 1984[19] was a first step in the harmonization of pension rights between men and women, as well as between wage-earners and the self-employed. In addition to the harmonization objective, budget deficits increased awareness of the need for reform. Government subsidies to the pension system had been decreased since 1975, and in 1981 a critical line was passed when the pension reserves amounted to no more than BEF 26 billion (€644 million; *De Standaard*, August 21, 1981).

The Pensions Minister, Mainil (PSC) presented a study (*De Problematiek van de pensioenen*—sent to the social partners in August 1982) in which he analyzed the problems of the pension system. In January 1981, Mainil had proposed limiting the pension rights of civil servants, reducing pension-carrying activities, and limiting the *perekwatie* for civil servants, but these attempts failed (*De Standaard*, January 27, 1981; January 8, 1981). Most of these plans had to be abandoned because of trade union opposition (De Baerdemaker 1987: 620). The proposed cutbacks on civil service pensions were defeated by the September strikes of 1983. (*De Standaard*, January 31, 1984).

After this initial round of failed reform, Mainil proposed legislation on September 9, 1983 designed to make the pension system financially sustainable for the coming decade and to harmonize existing schemes. The bill included retrenchment elements as well as expansionary provisions. First, the law promoted equal pension coverage for men and women because women would now be entitled to family pensions, and men were made eligible for survivors' pensions. These provisions also weakened the original rationale for different pension ages for men and women, which had originally been defended as a way to compensate for other inequalities. Second, the law introduced proportional pension rights (instead of flat-rate) and a ceiling for income-related pension rights for the self-employed. Third, benefits for the retired self-employed with low incomes were improved; from now on, those with pensions below a minimum threshold would receive an extra benefit in May each year (BEF 1200–1500). In May 1985, this yearly allowance was doubled. Fourth, the reform introduced a minimum pension for civil servants with low wages and at least 20 years of service, as well as a wage ceiling (as entitlement base) for civil service pensions at the level of three-quarters of the income of a secretary general. Fifth, the reform included limits on pension accumulation. Under the old rules it was possible to earn pension credits from several types of employment that added up to a combined pension benefit that exceeded the level of a full standard pension. The reform limited pension accumulation to the level of a full pension with 45 years of employment. Finally, the reform introduced similar limits on the accumulation of civil servant pensions.

The Mainil reform was a watered down version of the Commission Report that Pensions Minister Mainil discussed with the social partners, and the bargaining that resulted in the final reform followed a pattern typical of Belgian policy-making: the government proposes a reform based on an expert report, the social partners discuss it and voice their criticisms, and the government tries to adjust the proposal in order to quell some criticisms from the social partners, or it tries to bypass the social partners by enlisting the support of opposition parties, or persuading the coalition parties to stick to the reform despite opposition from the social partners. In this case, the government abandoned the reform measures that unions and civil servants opposed, especially the more retrenchment-oriented provisions such as cuts in civil servant pensions.

The 1985 election

The election of 1985 resulted in a modest victory for the Christian Democrats and the Socialist Party, at the expense of the Liberal PVV. The regionalist Flemish *Volksunie* experienced heavy losses. As they promised in their campaigns, the Liberals and the Christian Democrats continued their coalition, now in the sixth cabinet headed by Martens. In its government policy statement, the cabinet announced the continuation of its efforts to reduce unemployment and promote economic recovery. Parliament granted a new request for special powers for the unusually long period of 13 months.

With pension costs increasing and state finances continuing to deteriorate, pension reform remained on the political agenda. An academic advisory committee on the social security system presented its report in May 1985, proposing to simplify and harmonize existing legislation. At the same time, the draft law for special powers was adopted by the government in 1985 and by both houses of parliament in 1986.[20] The Council of State criticized the fact that another period of special powers was granted to the government, and for so many months. The Special Powers Law was, again, a broad framework for the passage of any kind of measure the government deemed necessary to stimulate competitiveness, employment and labor market flexibility. The law also contained a broad mandate to reduce public spending, but this was restricted to measures that would not affect the fundamentals of the social security system, or decrease the purchasing power of the minimum income programs.

The St Anna Plan 1986

In May 1986, the government (CVP/PSC and VLD/PRL) proposed a new budgetary operation, the "St Anna Plan," that aimed to cut expenditure by BEF 194.8 billion (approximately 5 billion euro). Major union protests were organized, but the government managed to push through many of its proposed measures anyway. The St Anna Plan, named after the negotiations at the St Anna parish, contained measures to reduce government expenditure by BEF 194.8 billion (approximately €5 billion). The reforms included heavy cuts in unemployment insurance, and a reform of pension rights. According to the first proposal, future pensions would be based on 45 years of contributions for men and women instead of 45 years for men and 40 years for women (as it used to be). The European Court of Justice had instructed the Belgian government to abolish different retirement ages for men and women, and the discussion focused on the question of whether men should retire earlier (at 60) or women later (at 65). In the early 1980s, the government had announced it would lower the statutory retirement age to 60 on a voluntary basis. Financing problems in the pension system prompted the government to reconsider this goal, however. Unions fiercely opposed the higher retirement age, and when the government consulted the social partners through the National Labor Council (NAR), they rejected it unanimously. The NAR argued that because of the high benefit dependency among workers older than 50, the later retirement age would lead to deficits in other social benefit schemes, which were more expensive than the pension scheme (*De Standaard*, January 14 and 19, 1987). The government then decided to let the social partners come up with an alternative plan, which led to a lingering disagreement among unions and employers.

The socialist trade union FGTB/ABVV organized massive protest actions as soon as the St Anna Plan became public (May 23, 1986). The Christian trade union ACV/CSC called the plan "unacceptable" and insisted that the government reconsider it and start negotiations with the social partners. The ACW (the umbrella organization of the Christian Labor Movement) also rejected the plan and pressured the CVP members of government to back down. When the government proposed minor adjustments to the St Anna Plan in June, the unions were not satisfied. Another round of negotiation led to more adjustments (such as postponing the decision on statutory retirement age) but there was still no consensus. Even though the ACV rejected the plan for the last time on July 2nd, it decided not to mobilize strikes after the summer. In August, the socialist FGTB/ABVV decided to abandon further protests; strikes were less effective because of ACV/CSC acquiescence.

On July 16, 1986, the government enacted the St Anna Plan in a series of royal decrees (see *B.S.* July 30, 1986), and these included incremental changes designed to achieve savings on several aspects of existing pension arrangements.[21] These measures included an indexation freeze, higher contributions, limits on the accumulation of benefits, decreased benefit levels for future pensions, and so on. The question of the equalization of retirement ages was not solved, however, and it would remain on the decision agenda for the next ten years. Early retirement for women was abolished by this royal decree, but the issue of different retirement ages for men and women remained open.

Thus there was unified union opposition to the proposed changes to the pension system included in the St. Anna Plan. Union opposition led the government to drop its plans for harmonizing retirement ages, but the St. Anna Plan nevertheless included several modest changes that would limit or decrease the level of future pensions for many retirees. Again it is worth noting that the eventual decision of the Christian trade unions to abandon their opposition to the St. Anna Plan was crucial for its successful implementation.

The government's victory had a price however. After the massive protests the St. Anna Plan provoked, the grass roots of the Christian Union (ACV) and labor movement (ACW) signaled to the government that no more cutbacks would be acceptable for the following year. The CVP leadership agreed to this, but the Liberal party PVV disagreed, stating that another round of savings would be required to fight the recession and eliminate the budget deficit. In order to balance their budget, the government decided to reduce expenditure on public administration, and to sell part of the gold stock of the Central Bank.

The leader of the Liberal PVV, Verhofstadt, launched a plan to reduce taxes financed by further cutbacks in public spending and by the privatization of state companies. All other coalition parties rejected the plan immediately. When the debates on the budget for 1988 started, Verhofstadt criticized the Minister of Social Affairs (Dehaene, CVP) for lagging behind in the implementation of the St. Anna Plan. The government had to find new ways to save on social expenses in order to control the budget deficit. Its proposal included smaller state grants to the Pension Administration Institute RWP, lower government contributions to finance the bridge pensions, and a shift in payment date (end of the month instead of first of the month) for future civil servant pensions. The coalition crisis in late 1987 delayed implementation of most of these measures.

The government fell in Autumn 1987, and most observers attribute this to the language/regionalization conflict. Others maintain that the fall of the Martens VII cabinet occurred because the Christian trade union pressured their Christian Democratic colleagues in government to break with the Liberals. The unions were allegedly fed up with the leader of the Flemish Liberals, Verhofstadt, who was inspired by Anglo-Saxon ideas on "new" public management. (De Wachter 2001).

The 1987 elections

In December 1987, parliamentary elections were held, resulting in a loss for the Christian Democrats (both CVP and PSC), and a victory for the Flemish Liberal PVV and the Walloon *Parti Socialiste*. A new coalition was formed in May 1988 that included both Walloon and Flemish socialists, Christian Democrats, and the regionalist Flemish *Volksunie*. In his presentation of the budgetary results of the previous year, ex-minister for the Budget, Verhofstadt (PVV), criticized the slow implementation of the planned cutbacks on social policy, stressing that the decisions were necessary for Belgian economic recovery.

By the end of the 1980s, the real value of pensions had declined further because of suspended indexing and other measures. Between 1983 and 1987 the annual growth rate of pensions was 1.3 percent, compared to 6 percent per year between 1970 and 1983 (OECD 1990: 76). Thus policy-makers were faced with conflicting priorities: on the one hand they wanted to improve the real value of pensions, but on the other hand there was little financial room for maneuver to accomplish this via the public system.

Flexible pension age and repackaging early retirement 1990

In 1990, the government introduced a flexible pension age, starting at age 60.[22] This set of rules also meant the abolition of reduced bridge retirement pensions and early pension with 5 percent reduction per year of early retirement. At the time, spending on early exit was higher in Belgium than in the rest of the EU, at 0.8 percent of GDP (OECD 1990: 75). The idea was to complement a flexible pension age with decreased incentives to use the existing early retirement schemes. Under the new rules, pensions would be based on the number of years actually worked. The law retained different calculation formulae for men's and women's pensions, however. Women's pensions would continue to be based on 40 years of contributions and men's on 45.

Like most other pension legislation, an oversized majority in Parliament supported this legislation, and the legislation fitted well with the coalition agreement's stipulation that the government take measures to guarantee the public pension system. Agreement on the pension age and formula was not unproblematic, however. Pensions Minister Mainil had previously proposed a formula based on 45 years of contributions for both men and women as part of the St. Anna Plan in 1986, but union opposition kept this idea off the bargaining table. The unions and the socialist parties vigorously opposed the change because of high unemployment levels among older workers. In this context, it seemed counterproductive to require women to work five years longer for a full pension. For most women, the change would simply result in a 12 percent reduction in their pension. In contrast, the unions and socialist parties accepted the flexible pension age because many workers had 45 years of contributions at age 60 anyway (if they started working at age 15, for example) so the new rules would allow them to draw a full pension from age 60 whereas the old rules required a deduction of 5 percent for each year of early retirement, even when the retiree had 45 years of contributions. Moreover, women's pensions would continue to be calculated on 40 years of contributions.

The social partners unanimously supported the flexible retirement provisions as well as the selective measures aimed at increasing lower pensions. As noted, the 1973 legislation allows pensions to be indexed to increases in wages (and not just inflation) but this provision has been used only a few times. As a result, the real value of pensions lags behind increases in living standards.

The introduction of unisex rules for a flexible retirement age was intended to head off a challenge by the European Court of Justice (ECJ) to Belgian pension law. An EC directive from 1978 required member states to remove discriminatory provisions (on the basis of sex) from their social security schemes, and the different contribution bases (40 for women, 45 for men) had aroused the attention of the ECJ. It was only a matter of time before the European Commission sued Belgium in the ECJ concerning these provisions. The Minister of Pensions insisted publicly that the 1990 legislation solved the problem, but there was much speculation in the press that Belgian pension law still violated the directive. A few years later, the issue reached the political agenda again.

The 1991 election

In October 1991, the government fell and new elections were called. The elections held on 24 November 1991 led to an unexpected outcome. Although the Martens VIII cabinet had accomplished most of its program, completed the constitutional reform of 1988 and reduced the state deficit, all government parties lost votes in the election (Fitzmaurice 1996: 179). VU (*Volksunie*), the party that left the government, and thereby provoked its collapse[23] was therefore seen as the cause for increased north–south conflict, and it lost heavily. Surprisingly, the Liberal Party family—the biggest group of opposition parties—also lost compared to the 1987 election. Both Green parties, the radical right *Vlaams Blok* (demanding independence for Flanders) and the libertarian Flemish *Rossem* picked up votes (Fitzmaurice 1996: 181).

More than three months after the election a Christian-Democratic/Socialist coalition took office headed by Jean-Luc Dehaene on March 7, 1992. Two issues affecting pensions played a major role in the election campaign: meeting the EMU criteria and the decentralization of the social security demanded by the Flemish parties (Fitzmaurice 1996: 181). According to *Le Soir,* one of the reasons for the Liberal Party's defeat was its support for pension retrenchment (*Le Soir,* January 15, 1995).

The new government inherited a dismal financial situation concerning pensions. In August 1991, the government forecast a deficit of BEF 16 billion in the social security sector for 1992, including pensions (*De Standaard,* August 3, 1991). The eroding real value of pensions was also a concern, and the government adopted measures to make it easier for pensioners to earn income in addition to receiving a pension. In March 1992, the government adopted a royal decree to allow pensioners to earn more income from employment than under then-current rules without losing pension benefits. The ceiling for pensionable income was also raised starting January 1, 1993 from BEF 245,000 gross to BEF 260,000 gross. Pensioners could now earn BEF 390,000 gross in addition to receiving their pension (*De Standaard*, July 9, 1992). Previous rules required pensioners to seek an exemption in order to earn extra income and draw a pension at the same time.[24]

The government invested much effort in trying to reduce social insurance expenditures and restore the competitive position of Belgian industry. In the second half of 1993, the government tried to orchestrate a pact with the social partners on employment, competitiveness and social security. The negotiations failed, and the government resorted to a less ambitious plan via legislation. Legislation adopted in 1994 continued the trend toward declining government share of financing and completed the shift to a "global" administration of social security, including pensions. The change in administration was part of a larger effort to restore financial balance to social security and decrease non-wage labor costs.[25]

Attempts at comprehensive reform

Pensions Minister Willockx (SP) quickly announced that he wanted to conduct "open discussions about pensions," and announced a series of roundtable discussions involving all societal groups. Based on projections that forecast serious problems by 2010, the Minister wanted to pass pension reform as soon as possible. In a policy note presented to the Social Affairs Committee in Parliament, Willockx emphasized the demographic and financial reasons for immediate reform, but did not make specific proposals (*De Standaard*, May 8, 1992). Willockx later attracted the anger of the civil servants unions by suggesting that the *perekwatie* (wage indexing) of civil servant pensions might be changed in order to reduce expenditures (*De Standaard*, June 17, 1992). Willockx's suggestions about civil servant pension reform prompted a discussion about the level of civil servant pensions relative to those of employees in the private sector. Unlike employee pensions, civil servant pensions were adjusted annually to wage developments for civil servants, so they rose more quickly than employee pensions.

For civil servants at all levels of government, the federal government paid the entire cost out of general revenues. In order to control spending, Willockx suggested (in addition to changing the *perekwatie*) other possible changes: lower benefits for high income civil servant pensioners and a transfer of financing from the federal government to the regions and communities. A shift in financing would not only save money, it would remove perverse incentives for local and regional government to hire more civil servants and increase their wages annually without regard to the effects of this on the civil servant pension system (*De Standaard*, August 8, 1992).

Willockx's attempts to rally support for his civil servant pension reform plans backfired. Given the consensual nature of Belgian policy-making and the sensitive nature of anything concerning the regions, civil servant reform had all the ingredients of failure: well-organized interests with close ties to parties and unions and the potential for regional conflict. As the following sections show, the government could only muster support for a few modest changes in the civil service pension system (see also Marier 2002).

Improving portability of supplementary pensions

Willockx also set out to improve the portability of supplementary pensions. In contrast to many other countries, Belgian legislation governing supplementary pensions was minimal in the early 1990s. Employers controlled most of the provisions of supplementary pensions, and many companies had rules that hindered portability. At the time, 600,000 employees participated in supplementary pension plans, with reserves of BEF 600 billion (*De Standaard*, October 1, 1992).

By early 1993, discussions on the reform of supplementary pensions were gathering momentum. The newspaper *De Standaard* called the issue of reform a "hot potato" that Minister Willockx dumped in the laps of the social partners (*De Standaard*, April 27, 1993). Ten years earlier, the Minister of Social Affairs Dehaene had attempted supplementary pension reform, but this attempt failed. Two issues caused discord: the rights of individual workers and the nature of collective pension rights. Individual rights mostly concerned portability while collective rights concerned the role of unions and employers in deciding the details of supplementary pension plans. At the time, there was very little regulation of supplementary pensions, and employers mainly controlled issues of portability and the details of pension regulations. To break the stalemate, Willockx submitted a list of issues for the social partners to comment on in the National Labor Council. Based on this advice, Willockx promised to present legislation to Parliament. Two issues created incentives for the government to reform supplementary pensions: the expansion of supplementary pensions during the previous two decades, and the declining real value of the public pension for employees. Reform of the second pillar provided the opportunity to expand coverage by guaranteeing portability and reforming membership rules. At the time, 10 percent of pensioners had supplementary pensions and 60 percent of active employees participated in such plans (*De Standaard*, June 23, 1993).

By early 1993, Willockx's round table discussions were in full swing, and Willockx promised to propose legislation in 1994 to guarantee the financial sustainability of the pension system. To cover deficits in 1993, Willockx dipped into the reserves in the RVP. Although Willockx promised to not change the *perekwatie* for civil servants, he managed to adopt a provision that cancelled the payment of the *perekwatie* for high income civil servant pensioners (*De Standaard*, April 1, 1993). In addition, the application of the *perekwatie* was delayed for one year for all pensioners, for a savings of BEF 500 million in 1993 and BEF 1 billion in 1994.

As the round-table discussions continued, Willockx tried to convey the message that public finances were in desperate need of reform. This was a response to statements from the socialist union ABVV that public finances were not "dramatic." The minister was probably trying to prepare people for possible pension cuts (*De Standaard*, May 7, 1993). In response to the declining real value of public pensions, Willockx also spoke out in favor of strengthening the supplementary pension pillar. A member of the SP, Willockx was careful to emphasize that such a development should not result in public pension retrenchment in favor of private pensions (*De Standaard*, June 14, 1993).

Meanwhile, Willockx's calls for substantial pension reform prompted criticism from pensioners groups and unions. In September, the Christian Pensioners Union (KBG) openly criticized Willockx's suggestions about changing civil servant pensions and public pensions for employees (*De Standaard*, September 9, 1993). As the round table discussion progressed, Willockx commissioned a study about the costs of civil servant pensions. Earlier rounds of talks had focused on employee pensions, but now Willockx wanted to call attention to the costs of civil servant pensions, especially for provisions (*perekwatie*) not enjoyed by employees in the private sector. A principal finding of the study was that salary increases for civil servants during the period 1988–94 had caused an increase in pension costs of BEF 23 billion.

By the end of 1993, the outlines of Willockx's reform plans were clear: a possible increase in retirement age, higher taxes/contributions for high pensions, and a weakening of the *perekwatie* for civil servants. The pension formula would be the same for men and women by 2006, and the "revaluation coefficient" for wages earned 1955–74 would be gradually abolished.[26] A less favorable formula would be used to calculate pension rights during unemployment. These measures were calculated to save BEF 4.7 billion (*De Standaard*, November 18, 1993). Predictably, Willockx's proposals drew criticism from many groups, including the Christian Pensioners Union (KBG) (*De Standaard*, December 15, 1993).

In December 1993, Willockx announced he would introduce several laws concerning pensions the following year, based on his round table discussions. First, Willockx had to satisfy the ECJ by making retirement ages equal for men and women. Second, the Minister wanted to raise the *actual* retirement age. Third, Willockx wanted to raise the lowest/oldest pensions, and finally, to change the *perekwatie* for civil servants (*De Standaard*, December 22, 1993). Willockx also hoped for a unanimous advice from the NAR on the issue of supplementary pension reform.

The following January (1994), the two largest unions, ACV and ABVV jointly criticized Willockx's reform plans. The unions rejected the cuts and called for improving the financing of the pension system in order to improve financial sustainability (*De Standaard*, January 22, 1994). Shortly thereafter, pensioners organizations joined the criticism of Willockx's plans, and women's groups criticized changes designed to comply with EC law that would reduce many women's pensions. In the meantime, individual legal actions by male pensioners demanding their right to a pension formula on the same basis as women's complicated Willockx's plans. The 1990 reform equalized pension ages for men and women in order to comply with European law, but left different benefit formulae in place. In 1994, a series of cases brought by men in Belgian courts upheld the principle that men's pensions could be calculated according to the more favorable formula for women. This development could continue indefinitely unless the government changed the law (*De Standaard*, January 26, 1994).

Willockx's resignation as Pensions Minister (to run for the European Parliament) brought the pension reform process to an abrupt halt. However, the crisis plan of the

Cabinet soon provided the rationale for the government to pursue some of Willockx's ideas. Instead of a comprehensive reform based on the round table discussions, the Cabinet approved a series of measures concerning pensions (among other things) in order to consolidate public finances. The main items passed as part of the crisis plan were a solidarity contribution for high income pensioners (*De Standaard*, July 15, 1994). The new Pensions Minister, Marcel Colla (SP), promised to tackle the problem of substantial reform. In particular, the issue of gender equality and European law could not be delayed much longer. Colla also emphasized his ambition to restore financial balance to the pension system without large cuts (*De Standaard*, November 2, 1994).

Despite Willockx's departure from the government, reform of supplementary pensions continued. Colla ran into one of his first challenges when both employers and unions tried to block and/or amend the supplementary pension legislation in the Senate in April 1995. The legislation had passed the Second Chamber and the Senate Committee. Neither the unions nor the employers were entirely satisfied with the compromise worked out in the legislation. The main issue was the decision rights of employees; unions claimed these were too weak and employers claimed they were too extensive. The unions tried to use the Senate vote as an opportunity to amend the bill and send it back to the Second Chamber (*De Standaard*, April 3, 1995). Employers also tried to force last minute changes to the legislation. Both efforts failed, and the Senate passed the "Wet-Colla" (Colla Law) on April 6, 1995 without amendments.[27]

In sum, the Dehaene I government took office with ambitious plans for pension reform but only managed to pass modest legislation concerning the regulation of supplementary pensions. Reform of civil servant pensions was an utter failure, as were attempts to harmonize men's and women's benefit formulae in order to satisfy EU law. In both cases, massive opposition from unions (especially public employee unions) and women's groups prompted the government to back down (see also Marier 2002). In the wake of these failed reforms, pensions figured prominently in the 1995 election campaign. The SP, despite its support for the expansion of the second pillar, positioned itself as the primary defender of the public system. The Liberals (VLD) accused the SP of letting the pension system go bankrupt and favored the introduction of some form of capitalization. The CVP occupied a position between these two extremes, but all three large parties advocated reducing the growth of pension spending (*De Standaard*, April 26, 1995).

The 1996 pension reform

The 1995 election

The Dehaene I Government (Christian Democrats and Socialists) scheduled early elections on May 21, 1995 "in the hope of strengthening political resolve for austere economic and monetary policies (Downs 1996: 169)." This was the first election after the constitutional reform. New laws such as those on the reduced size of Parliament, three new regional parliaments, and separate competences between federal and subnational levels of government had come into force right before the election. Downs (1996: 171) describes the new system as follows: "Designed in large part to pacify perennial conflicts between the country's ethnic–linguistic populations, the new federal system thus offers a dizzying array of structures, formulae and personalities.... so much so that citizens 'no longer know who is responsible for what' " (Downs 1996: 171).[28]

In spite of scandals surrounding the Socialist party family and budgetary problems, and conflicts on immigration, the three major parties secured over 72 percent of the votes in the 1995 election (Downs, 1996: 172). The radical right parties *Vlaams Blok* and *Front National* did not gain as much as feared. The Green parties lost considerably in the 1995 election. Prominent issues of the election campaign were unemployment and jobs (Downs 1996: 168–172).

Marcel Colla continued as Pensions Minister in the Dehaene II Cabinet and soon set out to prepare the ground for a reform of civil servant pensions. In October 1995, Colla commissioned a financial forecast for the civil servant pension scheme. Previous forecasts were carried out for 5–10 year intervals, but this one calculated projected expenditures until 2040. The study found that pension costs would increase by 2.6 times by 2040 (*De Standaard*, October 19, 1995). The study accompanied public announcements by Colla that the most urgent action was required in civil servant pensions in order to bring down expenditures (*Financieel Economische Tijd*, October 19, 1995). Again, the government targeted civil service pensions for major reform, but like previous attempts, the process would prove difficult (see also Marier 2002).

When the Dehaene II Cabinet took office, it promised to announce the main features of a social security reform by the end of 1995 and to make these plans more concrete in the first half of 1996. In addition, the cabinet wanted to pass a new law on competitiveness based on the advice of the social partners. Unrest in the public sector, especially a strike at the railways, slowed the plan down (Platel 1996). By now, Prime Minister Dehaene conceded that the pension system for employees was evolving into a system that could only deliver a basic benefit in the future. In order to fill the pension gap, employees and employers needed to improve supplementary pensions. At the same time, Dehaene announced the government's intention to decrease the differences between employee pensions and civil servant pensions (*De Standaard*, October 21, 1995). Thus the background to the 1996 pension reform was the government's renewed intention to reform civil service pensions, and to deal with declining benefit adequacy and financing problems in the public pension system. The run-up to EMU would provide the government with the political capital necessary to secure approval for some, but not all of its reform goals.

The pension reform discussion in 1995/1996 introduced important changes into the pension system. The framework law of July 1996 gave the government significant powers to enact a reform, after several years of failed reform attempts. The consensus about the desirability of a national social security system started to weaken after the publication of the *Club van Leuven* report in 1989 that noted that Wallonian incomes were higher than Flemish incomes despite the fact that Flemish wages were higher than Wallonian wages (Poirier and Vansteenkiste 2000: 347).

The main objective of the reform was to reduce long term pension expenditure. Civil servant pensions were considered to be one of the problems. In the 1970s the civil service was expanded to fight unemployment, creating a large group of future public pensioners. Due to the rapid growth of public sector pension benefits (wage indexed, last five years income) substantial costs were forecast for the future. As noted, an attempted reform by Willockx in 1994 was defeated by the municipality lobby (*Le Soir*, January 5, 1995).

The background to the pension reform consisted in plans to boost employment and reduce the government deficit so that Belgium could qualify for the first stage of EMU. In addition, employers were pleading for reforms that would improve the competitive position of Belgian industry, while the unions were pushing for negotiations about how to increase employment. In early 1996, the Prime Minister once again delayed social security reform by linking it to improving public finances, the budget for 1997, and discussions with the social partners about creating jobs. In early February 1996, the Cabinet invited the social partners to negotiate the broad outlines for a "Future Plan for Employment," inspired by the *German Bündnis für Arbeit*. The social partners reacted positively but as the negotiations began, news from the European Commission complicated the situation. The Commission gave the Belgian government only a few weeks to modify its "Maribel" program to the Commission's satisfaction. Maribel involved lower employer contributions and was introduced in 1981 for firms employing manual workers in order to maintain employment. Maribel was later extended to export firms, which the Commission argued was anti-competitive (de Weerdt 1997).

The Belgian social partners and government responded with a plan to try to keep wages in line with most important competitors (France, Germany, Netherlands). After marathon negotiations the deal was struck on April 18, 1996. The Cabinet approved the deal but the unions' grass roots membership was unhappy with the results and refused to ratify the package. After this rejection the Prime Minister announced that the government would implement similar measures rather than relying on the social partners. On May 2, 1996 the Chamber accepted the Cabinet's plans.

In late April 1996 the four majority parties in the Cabinet decided to ask for "special powers" in three areas, government finances; modernization of social security; and the "Future Plan for Employment." The government wanted to use program/framework laws instead of asking for a *volmacht* as the Martens government did in the 1980s. Ironically, the Socialists had opposed these methods in the 1980s but now insisted they were acting differently. The framework laws contained the broad outlines of policy, with the details to be specified in royal decrees. As such, the function of the framework laws was very similar to the special powers procedure. In concrete terms the government wanted to pass a framework law that gave them permission to take all necessary measures needed in order to reduce the deficit to 3 percent and to guarantee the financial balance of the social security system, including pensions.

The framework laws would allow the government to pass legislation on the 1997 budget, employment policy and social security reform, with only "post-factum" parliamentary control. As one analyst puts it, the "Socialists were willing to accept these special powers because they knew that the much feared social security talks would ultimately go their way without major cuts in benefits" (De Weerdt 1997). The opposition criticized the government's strategy to no avail, and discussion of the three laws in the lower chamber began on June 12. By the end of July, the Chamber had approved all three framework laws.

1. The EMU Law[29] gave the government until August 31, 1997 the authority to take a wide range of measures necessary to enable Belgium to join EMU. This included both taxing and spending measures. The main limitation was that the lowest incomes should be protected and the measures should not conflict with the framework law on the modernization of social security.
2. The Social Framework Law[30] was based explicitly on the coalition agreement. This law aimed to:
   - maintain the system of social security that combines social insurance with solidarity;
   - ensure a durable financial balance in the social insurance system;
   - confirm the importance of alternative means of financing in order to reduce labor costs;
   - modernize the administration of social insurance;
   - increase control and reduce fraud; and
   - maintain or improve living standards of those with minimum benefits.

The law also stated that equality between men and women in the social security system was a central goal. The right to the minimum pension was also expanded. Under the provisions of the framework law, the Cabinet was empowered to take any and all decisions it deemed necessary to reach these goals. In concrete terms, the law provided for extra revenues for the social insurance system from VAT income; at least BEF 104,490 from the VAT revenues would go to social insurance. In addition, the federal subsidies to employee and self-employed pension schemes would be improved. These measures were designed to reduce reliance on payroll taxes.

To summarize, the framework laws gave the government the breathing room to introduce several modest changes to the pension system that had proven so elusive in previous reform attempts: an increase in the reference period for women's pensions (from 40 to 45 years); an increase in the minimum number of years required for an early retirement pension (from 20 to 35); and the introduction of less advantageous rules for calculating pension rights on income earned between 1955–74. These modest cuts were compensated by long transition rules, the improvement of provisions for minimum pensions, and the introduction of pension points for child-rearing. The role of EMU membership was a crucial factor allowing the government to gain passage of social insurance and pension reform. As the Governor of the Central Bank, Fons Verplaetse, put it: "if Belgium misses the train for the European common currency, the unity of the country is endangered" (de Weerdt 1997).

No changes to civil service pensions were announced but the government said it wanted to pass a reform before April 30, 1997 when their special powers expired. Nothing came of these intentions.

The EU and equal treatment

These framework laws also finally introduced the changes to pension law necessary for compliance with EU law. As noted, Belgian governments had grappled with this issue since the late 1980s, with limited success. With the introduction of the flexible retirement age in July 1990, the retirement age for men and women was de facto equal. However, the benefit formula was still different for men and women (40 years of contributions for women and 45 years for men). In July 1993, the European Court ruled that Belgian pension rules did not comply with the principle of equal treatment in social security and instructed Belgium to change its law and practice (*Le Soir*, January 6, 1995).

Belgium's legal difficulties dated back to the adoption of a directive in 1979 that stated that a system could only have different pension benefit formulas if the retirement ages were also different. The Belgian law from June 20, 1990 introduced flexible retirement from age 60, but men were required to have 45 years of contributions and women 40. This was considered discriminatory. Belgium wanted to keep the lower number of contribution years for women, but financial concerns meant that Belgium could not afford to apply this rule to men. In 1993, the European Court found Belgium in violation of European Law.

The Law of June 19, 1996[31] introduced a temporary solution to the equal treatment issue in anticipation of a more permanent reform. The government agreed to gradually raise women's retirement age to 65 starting in 1997 so that by 2009 it is 65. Every three years it goes up by one year. In order to minimize negative effects, the rules for the minimum pension were relaxed somewhat. Whoever works for 15 years (including part-time) now had the right to a minimum pension.

The 1999 election

The elections held on 13 June 1999 can be seen as a turning point in the Belgian party system. Socialists and Christian Democrats lost votes, and for the first time since 1920 they did not form a parliamentary majority. In this new political landscape there is no single dominant party but rather four medium-size party families (Greens, Socialists, Liberals, and Christian Democrats). For the first time in 40 years the Christian Democrats were not part of the government. The new ruling coalition included Socialists, Liberals and Greens. The Flemish radical right, however—the *Vlaams Blok*—got 35 percent of the vote in Antwerp and good results in other cities. The Liberal Party family is now the largest party and their party leader, Verhofstadt, became prime minister. The Greens gained votes due to the Dioxin scandal that emerged during the election campaign (Fitzmaurice 2000: 177–9).

The new government's coalition agreement continued the policies of the Dehaene cabinet in emphasizing the importance of strict adherence to the EU's Stability and Growth Pact. There were several new policy elements in terms of pensions: promoting funded supplementary pensions and reforming social security to deal with "new" social risks. The coalition agreement also introduced the concept of the "active" welfare state into Belgian political discourse as the government promised to try to devote fewer resources to "passive" welfare state policies in favor of "active" ones that promote employment. As with previous governments, protecting public pensions also featured prominently in the coalition agreement. The government promised to improve the lowest pensions, and stated that the best way of promoting the sustainability of pensions was to decrease public debt (*Regeerakkoord*, July 7, 1999). Again, financial constraints loomed large in the government's pension policy. The element that broke with past policy was the intention to promote funded supplementary pensions as part of collective wage agreements.

The introduction of the "Silver Fund"

As part of the overall effort to ensure the future sustainability of public pensions, a savings fund was introduced by the Law of September 5, 2001.[32] The so-called "Silver Fund" (*Zilverfonds/Fonds de Vieillissement*) was proposed in response to EU rules concerning qualification for participation in EMU. The Silver Fund was designed to cover the increasing costs of an aging population without jeopardizing the EMU goal of sound public finances. The Silver Fund has been given the task of accumulating reserves to enable the Belgian state to bear the burden of aging without having to cut social benefits or raise taxes. The Silver Fund contains money intended for all public pensions, not just for employees. Income resulting from non-tax revenues (such as the sale of mobile phone licenses), budget surpluses, and other sources of income go in the fund. The government drafts an annual "Silver Nota" (*Zilvernota/Note sur le Vieillissement*) in which it outlines its financial policy with respect to aging and determines which resources will the allocated to the Silver Fund in the next budget. The first Silver Nota was prepared for the budgetary year 2003, and it determined that the Silver Fund would receive € 625 million (the same amount was allocated in 2001 and 2002), based on predictions of demographic changes and future employment policy, and of their consequences for long-term budgetary policy (*Belgische Kamer van volksvertegenwoordigers 2003*: 100–11).

Expanding supplementary pensions

According to Gieselink et al. (n.d.), the structure and development of the public pension schemes creates pressure for the expansion of supplementary pensions. For example, the pension for employees is calculated on average income throughout the career, so it does not maintain most employees' standard of living in retirement. The wage ceiling in place since 1982 also weakens the earnings replacement function of the employee pension system. Moreover, the earnings ceiling was only indexed to inflation until 1997 and not to wages. The result was that the number of people with income above the ceiling increased significantly between 1982 and 1997. This trend increased the pressure on supplementary pensions to fill the gap. The Royal Decree from December 23, 1997 indexed the earnings ceiling to wages, but not retroactively, so the problem has not been fully dealt with. Additionally, longer periods spent in education also decreased the number of people with a full pension and increases pressure on supplementary pensions.

Until the 1995 Colla Law (discussed in previous sections), there was no legislation that regulated the second pillar as a whole. Of the parties in the new governing coalition, the Liberal Parties together had the largest number of seats in Parliament, but the Minister of Pensions was Frank Vandenbroucke of the Flemish Socialist Party. With the Liberals playing a strong role in the cabinet, and given the limited options for expanding public pensions, the government settled on the strategy of expanding supplementary pensions. The government appointed a high level task force in early 2000 to investigate reform options, but the working group broke up in June following disagreements about the Liberals' preferences for supplementary pensions (www.ipe.com, 1 July, 2000) The Liberals pushed individual savings plans, which the other group members rejected. After this defeat, the Cabinet shifted its strategy.

After this failure, Minister Vandenbroucke initiated talks with unions and employers. The social partners were permitted to propose modifications to Vandenbroucke's proposal, resulting in an agreement in 2001. The Cabinet agreed to this blueprint, and legislation was introduced in April 2001. The law provides a unified framework for supplementary pensions and includes incentives to increase coverage beyond the then-current coverage rate of 40 percent. The legislation also aims to increase solidarity and democracy in supplementary pensions. Democracy would be achieved by extending coverage to as many workers as possible (via sectoral pensions), and solidarity would be achieved by also covering periods of non-insurance.[33]

The legislation passed in March 2003 and is know as the "Vandenbroucke Law" after the Minister of Pensions.[34] The law explicitly aims to relieve pressure on the public pension system by expanding the second pillar. The law allows workers in a sector to make minimum contributions (the rate is set by royal decree) to a collective fund with the option of increasing their contributions in return for a higher pension. Benefits are hybrid defined benefit/defined contribution, and there is a guaranteed rate of return (3.25%). The law also provides a framework for setting up sectoral or company level pension funds. Employers who already have a pension plan can opt out of sectoral plans as long as the relevant collective agreement permits this. Employees have the right to be consulted on the details of pension plans. Since the introduction of the law, coverage rates of second pillar pensions have increased significantly. Since the law went into effect, second-pillar coverage has increased by about one million workers (www.ipe.com, May 1, 2005).

V Conclusion

Summary of the magnitude of changes

The central tendency in Belgian pensions is the declining real value of the public pension for employees. Several policy changes during the past three decades have significantly weakened the insurance principle, and changes made since 1990 have accelerated these trends. Although public pensions have declined in real terms, civil servant pensions have largely remained intact, despite repeated reform attempts. In contrast to employee pensions, civil servant pensions retain their value relative to wages and prices.

In terms of policy changes, the main pattern is one of incremental cuts in order to promote financial balance in the pension system. These changes have been accompanied by attempts to improve benefits for lower income pensioners. A second trend concerns harmonization between the different pension schemes and between rules governing men's and women's pensions. European law played a crucial role in the latter process. A third trend is the failure to introduce significant changes in the civil servants' pension scheme, despite repeated attempts. A final trend concerns the expanded regulation and coverage of funded supplementary pensions. The declining real value of public pensions and the severe financial constraints on additional pension spending provided incentives for the expansion of the second pillar.

Belgian governments are caught between electoral incentives to increase pensions and the severe constraints posed by Belgium's very high level of accumulated debt and the requirements of the EU Stability and Growth Pact. The level of public debt in Belgium is a serious constraint on public pension spending. Until 2003, accumulated public debt exceeded 100 percent of GDP, leaving very little room for financial maneuver. Since the mid-1990s, public debt has decreased substantially (from more than 130% of GDP in 1993, to just below 100 percent of GDP in 2003), mainly because of government efforts to comply with the Stability and Growth Pact, and pension reform was an important component in this strategy. In particular, the drive to meet the criteria for the first stage of EMU in 1999 was a powerful motor for pension reform in 1996.

Impact of the political system on pension politics

The federal institutions that were created to deal with Belgian linguistic and regional cleavages make policy-making at the national level time-consuming, difficult and incremental. Regional and ideological cleavages mean fragmented party structure, government formation is a long and difficult process, and all important issues are discussed before parties agree to participate in government. Moreover, governments fall if the coalition parties do not agree on how specific policies are handled, and the coalition parties can veto policies anyway because of the consensus rule. Thus, although constitutional reform aimed to reduce policy blockages in Belgium, linguistic and partisan veto players impede radical reform. Policy-making is incremental, and the toughest decisions are usually made in the context of acute financial difficulties. All of the important pension policy changes made in the 1980s and 1990s that included retrenchment measures were negotiated as part of crisis programs (St. Anna Plan, the EMU laws). Moreover, governments used special powers laws, or framework laws, to facilitate parliamentary passage. Thus the role of Parliament was reduced, but the consensus rule in cabinet ensured that the proposals would not be radical in the first place. Clearly, the structure of Belgian political decision-making institutions is the single most important factor influencing the direction of pension policy.

Interest group influence

The social partners played a significant role in the construction of the Belgian pension system and the same is true for attempts at restructuring. Reform proposals are always discussed with the social partners in the NAR or in round table discussions before legislation is presented, so the social partners have an institutionalized seat at the bargaining table. However, the fragmentation of the unions provides opportunities for governments to pursue divide and conquer strategies or to just ignore union protests. This means that most reforms took place in the context of Socialist union opposition. When the Christian and Socialist unions jointly opposed reform, governments nearly always backed down. In sum, pension reforms were only possible when some segments of organized labor (the Christian union) implicitly or explicitly accepted reform. In contrast, the municipality lobby was almost always able to prevent substantial civil service pension reform.

Constraints of policy design

How did policy legacies influence pension politics in Belgium? First, the Belgian pension system is a fragmented, pay-as-you-go system that has been prone to financial imbalance for more than two decades. The state has gradually decreased its subsidy to the pension system since the 1980s and alternative forms of financing have failed to fill the gap. A series of policy decisions taken over many years has also greatly reduced the insurance principle in the public pension system. However, severe financial constraints at the federal level have limited the capacity of the state to find even more alternative forms of financing. The "Silver Fund" is a mild exception to this. The current government appears to prefer the policy of encouraging occupational pensions as the only viable method of topping up public pensions.

Second, the existing pension system was already mature so radical privatization was impossible. However, the declining real value of pensions and the expansion of supplementary pensions will probably have substantial long-term effects. The share of public pension income relative to supplementary pension income will no doubt decrease for most future pensions.

The role of ideas and historical context

The role of ideas in Belgian pension politics appears to be minimal. The desire to reduce public debt and to qualify for EMU were important reform motivations. But these were based less on neo-liberal ideas than on the importance of EU membership for Belgium, and the pragmatic desire to reduce state interest payments on public debt (because it crowded out other types of spending). To be sure, the expansion of supplementary pensions under the Liberal-led government can be attributed partly to liberal ideas about the desirability of funded pensions, but this was not a new Liberal Party idea. And the other coalition parties prevented the Liberals from prevailing in terms of individual versus collectively organized supplementary pensions. This appears to be simple party politics rather than a process influenced by the appearance of new and influential ideas about how pensions should be organized.

Abbreviations

ABVV	*Algemeen Belgisch Vakverbond* (General Belgian Trade Union Federation)
ACLVB	*Algemene Centrale der Liberale Vakbonden van België* (General Confederation of Liberal Trade Unions of Belgium)
ACV	*Algemeen Christelijk Vakverbond* (General Christian Trade Union Federation)
ACW	*Algemeen Christelijke Werkersbond* (General Christian Workers Federation)
Agalev	*Anders gaan leven* (Flemish Green Party)
ASLK	*Algemene Spaar-en Lijfrentekas* (General Savings and Annuity Fund)
BB	*Boerenbond* (Farmers Organization)
BEF	*Belgian franc*
CGSLB	*Centrale Générale des Syndicats Libéraux de Belgique,* French name for ACLVB
CNT	*Conseil National du Travail,* French name for NAR
CRB	*Centrale Raad voor het Bedrijfsleven* (Central Council of Industry)
CSC	*Confédération des Syndicats Chrétiens* (Confederation of Christian Trade Unions)
CVP	*Christelijke Volkspartij* (Christian Democratic Party, currently CdenV: *Christen Democratische en Vlaamse Partij* (Christian Democratic and Flemish Party))
EC	European Community
ECJ	European Court of Justice
EMU	European Monetary Union
EU	European Union
FEB	*Fédération des Entreprises Belges,* French name for VBO
FGTB	*Fédération Générale des Travailleurs de Belgique,* French name for ABVV
GDP	Gross Domestic Product
KBG	*Kristelijke Beweging van Gepensioneerden*
MP	Member of Parliament
NAR	*Nationale Arbeidsraad* (National Labor Council)
ONP	*Office National des Pensions,* French name for RVP

ONSS	*Office National de Sécurité Sociale des administrations provinciales et locales*, French name for RSZ
PRL	*Parti Reformateur Liberal* (Liberal Reform Party; Walloon Liberals)
PS	*Parti Socialiste* (Socialist Party)
PSC	*Parti Social Chrétien* (Christian Democratic Party)
PVV	*Partij voor Vrijheid en Vooruitgang* (Party for Freedom and Progress; Flemish Liberals). Currently VLD: *Vlaamse Liberalen en Democraten* (Flemish Liberals and Democrats)
RAP	*Rijksdienst voor Arbeidspensioenen*
Riziv	*Rijksinstituut voor ziekte-en invaliditeitsverzekering* (National Agency for Sickness and Disability Insurance)
RROP	*Rijkskas voor Rust en Overlevingspensioenen* (National Fund for Retirement and Survivors' Pensions)
RSZ	*Rijksdienst voor Sociale Zekerheid* (National Office for Social Security)
RVA	*Rijksdienst voor Arbeidsvoorziening* (National Employment Agency)
RVP	*Rijksdienst voor Pensioenen* (National Pensions Agency)
RWP	*Rijksdienst voor Werknemerspensioenen* (National Employees' Pensions Office)
SP	*Socialistische Partij* (Socialist Party)
UWE	*Union Wallonne des Entreprises* (Walloon Union of Enterprises)
VAT	Value Added Tax
VBO	*Verbond van Belgische Ondernemingen* (Federation of Belgian Enterprises)
VLD	*Vlaamse Liberalen en Democraten* (Flemish Liberal Party, formerly the PVV)

Notes

1. By the end of 2004, the public debt to GDP ratio had decreased by 40%, and in 2003 gross debt fell below 100% of GDP.
2. See also Vande Lanotte et al. 2003.
3. Constitutional amendments require a 2/3 majority in parliament, vastly increasing the incentive to have an oversized majority.
4. A bill passes when (a). a majority of members from each language group is present, (b). a majority of votes cast by each language group is in favor; and (c). two-thirds of the total number of votes cast is in favor.
5. See Marier 2002 for more background.
6. This section is based on Veldkamp 1978 and www.onprvp.fgov.be.
7. Of the total contribution of 10.25%, 3 % was individually capitalized and the rest went to a collectively capitalized fund.
8. "KB" refers to "*koninklijk besluit*" or royal decree. In this chapter we use the Dutch abbreviation and Dutch title when referring to royal decrees. We include the date in English, and where necessary, we shorten the title of the royal decree.

9. For the former, see *B.S.* October 27, 1967. For the latter, see *B.S.* November 14, 1967 and January 25, 1968.
10. The first legislation is the Law of June 30, 1930 (See *B.S.* July 18, 1930). (See also the KB of June 17, 1931; *B.S.* June 21, 1931; and the Law of July 9, 1975; *B.S.* July 29, 1975).
11. De wet van 27 juni, 1969 (*B.S.* July 25, 1969).
12. *De herstelwet inzake de middenstand van 10 februari 1981* (*B.S.* Feb. 14, 1981).
13. *De herstelwet inzake de pensioenen van de sociale sector van 10 februari 1981.* (*B.S.* Feb. 14, 1981).
14. KB no. 1 March 26, 1981, *houdende wijziging van het koninklijk besluit nr. 38 van 27 juli 1967* (See *B.S.* Apr. 3, 1981).
15. *De wet van 6 juli 1982 tot toekenning van bepaalde bijzondere machten aan de Koning* (See *B.S.* July 7, 1983).
16. KB no. 95, 28 September 1982 (B.S. Sept. 29, 1982).
17. In 1980, a guaranteed minimum pension was introduced for those with a full career (40–45 yrs of contribution) but whose wages had been below a certain level (*De wet van 8 augustus 1980 betreffende de budgettaire voorstellen 1979–1980* (See *B.S.* Aug. 15, 1980 and Sept. 9, 1980). One year later employees with 2/3 of a full career also gained the right to 2/3 of a minimum pension (*Herstelwet* Feb. 10, 1981, art. 33. See *B.S.* Feb. 14, 1981).
18. In 1982, the contribution ceiling was eliminated. (KB no. 96, September 28, 1982, which revised the Law of June 29, 1981. See *B.S.* September 30, 1982). This raised revenues but weakened the insurance principle in the pension system considerably. In addition, several "special contributions" were introduced to shore up pension financing. These included extra contributions on bridge pensions and disability pensions (KB no. 32, March 30, 1982. See *B.S.* Apr. 1, 1982) and an extra employer contribution on bridge pensions (Program Law art. 268–70, Dec. 22, 1989. See *B.S.* Dec. 30, 1989).
19. *Wet van 15 Mei 1984 houdende de maatregelen tot harmonisering der pensioensregelingen*, the so-called *Wet Mainil.* (*B.S.* May 22, 1984).
20. *De wet van 27 maart 1986 tot toekenning van bepaalde bijzondere machten aan de Koning.*
21. The third-pillar pension savings plan was also introduced (in legislation in December).
22. *De wet van 20 juli 1990 tot instelling van een flexibele pensioenleeftijd voor werknemers* (*B.S.* Aug. 15, 1990).
23. The government parties without VU still had the majority of seats in Parliament, but they did not reach the 2/3 majority required to complete the constitutional reform.
24. *Het koninklijk besluit van 30.10.1992 tot uitvoering van de artikelen 10, 25 en 39 van het koninklijk besluit no. 50* (*B.S.* 27 Nov. 1992).
25. *De wet van 30 maart 1994 houdende sociale bepalingen* (*B.S.* 31 March 1994).
26. This was basically a less favorable method of calculating pension rights for wages in this period.
27. *Wet betreffende de aanvullende pensioenen* (*B.S.* Apr. 29, 1995).
28. According to Downs "ballot papers the size of some newspapers had voters folding and unfolding in cramped booths, causing long queues at the busiest polling stations" (Downs 1996: 172).
29. *De wet van 26 juli 1996 "strekkende tot realisatie van de budgettaire voorwaarden tot deelname van België aan de Europese Economische en Monetaire Unie"* (*B.S.* Aug. 1, 1996).
30. *De wet van 26 juli, 1996 tot modernisering van de sociale zekerheid en tot vrijwaring van de leefbaarheid van de wettelijke pensioenstelsels* (*B.S.* Aug. 1, 1996). See also *De wet van 19 juni, 1996 tot interpretatie van de wet van 20 juli 1990* (*B.S. 1 augustus* 1996).
31. *De wet van 19 juni, 1996 tot interpretatie van de wet van 20 juli 1990* (*B.S.* 01.08.1996).

32. *Wet tot waarborging van een voortdurende vermindering van de overheidsschuld en tot oprichting van een Zilverfonds* (B.S. Nov. 14, 2001).
33. This paragraph is based on www.ipe.com, July 1, 2000; April 1, 2001 and Walthery 2004.
34. *Wet betreffende de aanvullende pensioenen en het belastingstelsel van die pensioenen en van sommige aanvullende voordelen inzake sociale zekerheid* (B.S. 15 May, 2003).

Bibliography
Primary sources and government documents
Acts and bills

BELGISCHE KAMER VAN VOLKSVERTEGENWOORDIGERS (2003). *Begrotingen van ontvangsten en uitgaven voor het begrotingsjaar 2003–Algemene toelichting.*

BELGISCHE SENAAT (2004) *Samenstelling en bevoegdheden van de Senaat.* www.senat.be/magazine/2003_10/n10-13.html, consulted 25 February 2004.

Regeerakkoord, July 7, 1999.

VLAAMS PARLEMENT (2004) *De Mijlpalen.* www.vlaamsparlement.bep3app/htmlpages/vp/HoeWerktHetVlaamsParlement, consulted 25 February 2004.

Parliamentary acts

DE WET VAN 30 juli 1930 (B.S. July 18, 1930)

DE WET VAN 27 juni 1969 (B.S. July 25, 1969)

DE WET VAN 9 juli 1975 (B.S. July 29, 1975)

DE WET VAN 29 december 1953 betreffende het arbeiderspensioen (B.S. van 31 december 1953)

DE WET VAN 8 augustus 1980 betreffende de budgettaire voorstellen 1979–1980

DE herstelwet inzake de middenstand van 10 februari 1981

DE herstelwet inzake de pensioenen van de sociale sector van 10 februari 1981 (B.S. February 14, 1981)

DE WET VAN 6 juli 1983 tot toekenning van bepaalde bijzondere machten aan de Koning (B.S. July 7, 1983)

DE WET VAN 15 mei 1984 houdende de maatregelen tot harmonisering der pensioensregelingen (B.S. May 22, 1984)

DE WET VAN 27 maart 1986 tot toekenning van bepaalde bijzondere machten aan de Koning

DE KADERWET VAN 22 december 1989 (B.S. December 30, 1989)

DE WET VAN 20 juli 1990 tot instelling van een flexibele pensioenleeftijd voor werknemers en tot aanpassing van de werknemerspensioenen (B.S. August 15, 1990)

DE WET VAN 30 maart 1994 houdend sociale bepalingen (B.S. 31 March 1994)

DE WET BETREFFENDE DE AANVULLENDE PENSIOENEN (B.S. April 29, 1995)

DE wet van 26 juli 1996 strekkende tot realisatie van de budgettaire voorwaarden tot deelname van Belgie aan de Europese Economische en Monetaire Unie (B.S. August 1, 1996)

DE wet van 26 juli tot modernisering van de sociale zekerheid en tot vrijwaring van de leefbaarheid van de wettelijke pensioenstelsels (B.S. August 1, 1996)

DE WET VAN 19 juni 1996 tot interpretatie van de wet van 20 juli 1990 (B.S. August 1, 1996)

WET tot waarborging van een voortdurende vermindering van de overheidsschuld en tot oprichting van een Zilverfonds (B.S. November 14, 2001)

WET betreffende de aanvullende pensioenen en het belastingstelsel van die pensioenen en van sommige aanvullende voordelen inzake sociale zekerheid (B.S. 15 May 2003)

Royal decrees

HET koninklijk besluit nr. 95 van 17 juni 1931 (B.S. June 21, 1931)

HET koninklijk besluit nr. 1 van 26 maart 1981, houdende wijziging van het koninklijk besluit nr. 38 van 27 juli 1967 (B.S. April 3, 1981)

Het koninklijk besluit nr. 32 van 30 maart 1982 (*B.S.* April 1, 1982)

Het koninklijk besluit nr. 95 betreffende het brugrustpensioen voor werknemers van 28 september 1982 (*B.S.* September 29, 1982)

Het koninklijk besluit nr. 96, September 28, 1982 (*B.S.* September 30, 1982)

Het koninklijk besluit nr. 205 van 29 augustus 1983 (*B.S.* September 9, 1983)

Het koninklijk besluit nr. 415 tot wijziging van sommige bepalingen betreffende de werknemerspensioenen van 16 juli 1986 (St Anna Plan)

Het koninklijk besluit van 30.10.1992 tot uitvoering van de artikelen 10, 25 en 39 van het koninklijk besluit no. 50. (*B.S.* November 27, 1992)

Het koninklijk besluit van 8 August 1997 houdende maatregelen met het oog op de uitbouw van het globaal beheer van de sociale zekerheid (*B.S.* August 29, 1997)

Newspapers

Le Soir

De Standaard

Financieel Economische Tijd

Secondary sources

Alen, André (1995). *Die Föderalstaat Belgien: Nationalismus, Föderalismus, Demokratie*. Baden-Baden: Nomos Verlagsgesellschaft.

Béland, D. and Lecours, A. (2005). "Nationalism, Public Policy and Institutional Development: Social Security in Belgium," *Journal of Public Policy*, 25, 2, 265–85.

Baerdemaker de, G. (1987). "Pensioenen Overheidssector". In van Langendonck, J. and Simoens, D. (eds.), *Ontwikkelingen van de sociale zekerheid 1980–1986*. Leuven: Die Keure: 593–607.

Deleeck, Herman (ed.) (1991). *Sociale zekerheid en federalisme*. Brugge: Die Keure.

—— (2001). *De architectuur van de welvaartsstaat opnieuw bekeken*. Leuven: Acco.

Deschouwer, Kris (2002a). "The Colour Purple. The End of Predictable Politics in the Low Countries". In Webb, P., Farrell, D. M., and Holliday, I. (eds.), *Political Parties in Advanced Industrial Democracies*. Oxford: Oxford University Press, 51–80.

—— (2002b). "Falling apart together: The changing nature of Belgian Consociationalism, 1961–2001." *Acta Politica*, 37: 68–85.

de Swert, G. and R. Janssen (1996). "De Hollandse kwiekte." *De gids op maatschappelijk gebied*, 87/12: 1027–38.

de Wachter, Wilfried (1994). "De Bestendigheid van de overlegeconomie in België." *Beleid en Maatschappij*, 3: 84–92.

—— (2001). *De mythe van de parlementaire democratie – Een Belgische analyse*. Leuven: Acco.

de Weerdt, Mark (1996). "Het Belgisch Politiek Gebeuren in 1995." *Res Publica*, 38, 2/3, 501–25.

—— (1997). "Het Belgisch politiek gebeuren in 1996." *Res Publica*, 39, 4: 468–521.

de Winter, Lieven (1996). "Party encroachment on the executive and legislative branch in the Belgian polity." *Res Publica*, 325–52.

—— Timmermans, A. and Dumont, P. (2000). "Belgium: On Government Agreements, Evangelists, Followers, and Heretics." In Müller, W. C. and Strom, K. (eds.), *Coalition Governments in Western Europe*. 300–55. Oxford: Oxford University Press.

Downs, William (1996). "Federalism Achieved: The Belgian Elections of 1995." *West European Politics* 19/1: 168–75

Fitzmaurice, John (1996, 2000). *The Politics of Belgium – A Unique Federalism*. London: Hurst and Company.

Gieselinck, G. Peeters, H., Van Gestel, V. et al. (n.d.). "Tweede tussentijds rapport – Het Belgisch pensioenlandschap sinds 1980."

Hooghe, Liesbet (2003). "Belgium. Hollowing the Center." In Amoretti, U. M. and Bermeo, N. (eds.), *Federalism and Territorial Cleavages.* Baltimore: The Johns Hopkins University Press, 55–92.

Huyse, Luc (1983). *Als in een Spiegel? Een Sociologische Kaart van België en Nederland.* Leuven: Kritak.

Jones, Erik (2002). "Consociationalism, Corporatism, and the Fate of Belgium," *Acta Politica* 37, Spring/Summer, 86–103.

Jorens, Yves (1997). "Das belgische Sozialversicherungssystem auf dem Prüfstand: Die Antworten auf die aktuellen Herausforderungen." *Sozialer Fortschritt,* 46/1–2: 8–12.

Keman, Hans (1996). "The Low Countries: Confrontation and Coalition in Segmented Societies". In Colomer, J. (ed.), *Political Institutions in Europe.* London: Routledge, 211–53.

Lijphart, Arend (1968). *The Politics of Accommodation: Pluralism and Democracy in The Netherlands.* Berkeley: University of California Press.

Marier, Patrik (2002). *Institutional Structure and Policy Change: Pension Reforms in Belgium, France, Sweden, and the United Kingdom.* D.Phil. thesis (University of Pittsburgh).

Masyn, R. (1987). "Pensioenen werknemers". In van Langendonck, J. and Simoens, D. (eds.), *Ontwikkelingen van de Sociale Zekerheid 1980–1986.* Leuven: Die Keure, 545–59.

OECD (1990). *Economic Surveys. Belgium.* Paris: OECD.

Pestieau, P. and Stijns, J.-P. (1999). "Social security and retirement in Belgium." In Gruber J. and Wise, D. A. (eds.), *Social Security and Retirement around the World.* Chicago University of Chicago Press, 37–71, 1999.

Poirier, J. and Vansteenkiste, S. (2000). "Le débat sur la fédéralisation de la sécurité sociale en Belgique." *Revue belge de sécurité sociale,* 2, 331–79.

Vande Lanotte, J., Bracke, S. and Goedertier, G. (2003). *België voor beginners – wegwijs in het Belgisch labyrint.* Brugge: Die Keure.

Van Ruijsseveldt, Joris (2000). *Het belang van overleg: CAO-onderhandelingen in België.* Leuven: Acco.

—— and Visser, J. (eds.) (1996). *Industrial Relations in Europe.* London: Sage.

Veldkamp, G. M. J. (1978). *Inleiding tot de sociale zekerheid en toepassing ervan in Nederland en België.* Deventer: Kluwer.

Vilrokx, J. and Van Leemput, J. (1997). "Belgium: The Great Transformation." In Ferner, A. and Hyman, R. (eds.), *Changing Industrial Relations in Europe.* Oxford: Blackwell Publishers, 315–47.

Walthery, Pierre (2004)."Belgium. Comparative study on occupational pensions," http://www.eiro.eurofound.eu.int/about/2004/04/study/tn0404101s.html

Woyke, Wichard (1999). "Das Politische System Belgiens." In Ismayr, W. (ed.), *Die Politischen Systeme Westeuropas.* Opladen: Leske and Budrich, 365–88.

PART III
MANY PARTISAN VETO PLAYERS

CHAPTER 8

SWEDEN: AFTER SOCIAL DEMOCRATIC HEGEMONY

KAREN M. ANDERSON

ELLEN M. IMMERGUT

1 INTRODUCTION

IN contrast to many of the other cases analyzed in this book, Sweden stands out for its single comprehensive reform, one of the most radical undertaken in the OECD in the last two decades. Rather than incremental cuts, Swedish policy-makers enacted a single reform explicitly designed to restore financial sustainability to the public pension system and obviate the need for incremental cuts in the future. The new system includes a "guarantee pension," an earnings-related "income pension," and unusual for the countries included in this book, an obligatory funded individual pension account, the "premium reserve." General revenues finance the guarantee pension, while contributions and investment income finance both the income pension and the premium pension. The revamped pension also includes automatic stabilizers that ensure that (notional) pension liabilities and notional and funded assets remain in balance.

A particularly striking feature of the reform process is the five-party coalition supporting it. The first phase of the reform was passed under a non-socialist minority government with Social Democratic support, and the subsequent provisions were passed by Social Democratic minority governments with non-socialist support. The five parties backing the agreement pre-committed to keeping the pension reform out of electoral competition, and they managed to stick to the agreement during nearly ten years of negotiations. Veto points and veto players analysis cannot account for this outcome. Large-scale reform should be exceedingly difficult under such circumstances.

In this chapter we argue that political competition was a crucial variable driving this outcome. Until recently, Sweden was home to the "Politics of Compromise" (Rustow 1955) or "Administered Politics" (Anton 1980). But, such conciliatory politics were made possible only because the hegemony of the Social Democratic Party (SAP) allowed the SAP to set the political agenda and dominate the legislative process. Consequently, given the choice between social democratic policies or no policies at all, the political opposition had been forced into cooperation.

Social democratic hegemony rested on both strategy (Svensson 1994) and the effects of the constitutional system in place until 1970 (Ruin 1988). Social democratic strategy broadened the electoral appeal of the party by using, first, at the beginning of the century, a "folk" strategy to appeal to the "popular" classes broadly understood, and later a "wage-earner" strategy to become an even broader "catch-all" party. As we shall see, pension politics were the centerpiece of both phases of this construction of a middle-class welfare state. The old Constitution was the linchpin of this strategy in the post-war period, because it gave the Social Democratic Party an institutional mechanism for controlling policy-making, and also made it almost impossible to dislodge the SAP from office—as we explain later in detail.

Constitutional reform changed all of this, and since then politics has been characterized by the loss of social democratic hegemony and intense electoral competition. During the 1970s and 1980s, the immediate impact of this new political framework was greatly weakened governments, as well as frequent changes in government. Moreover, the Social Democratic "lock" on government was eradicated. Consequently, the Social Democrats and the non-socialist parties outbid one another in expanding the welfare state and introduced a number of expensive reforms. The age of cooperation was over and despite occasional cross-bloc agreements, politics and policy-making in Sweden were now characterized by highly polarized political competition. The economic crisis of the early 1990s was just the final blow to a political pattern that was no longer working.

We explain the Social Democrats' cooperation in the 1994 Pension Reform as an attempt to restore its status as the "natural party of government." In the 1991 election the Social Democrats lost votes to the center and right, which jeopardized the party's position in Parliament as holder of the median or "pivotal" seat, which is connected to control of legislation. It also lost votes to the left, but these were not as important, because they did not affect the standing of the socialist bloc as a whole, and hence the Social Democratic Party's "office" (control of government) or "policy" (control of legislation) positions. The 1991 electoral loss—like the 1976 electoral loss—was caused by the Party's failure to move towards the political center along with the electorate. Indeed, caught up with internal political conflicts among more "liberal" versus more "traditional" union factions within the Party, the Social Democrats positioned themselves too far to the left, and lost the election. This created incentives for the Social Democrats to move to the right after 1991, and supporting the pension reform proposed by the non-socialist center was one way to try to do this. The Social Democratic Party could afford to withstand pressures from the left and the unions, because even if these constituencies defected, they would not hand the next election to the bourgeois coalition. More importantly, the 1991 election forced the SAP to come to terms with the loss of its hegemonic position and hence with its ability to dominate other parties. Political dominance after hegemony would require cooperation with other parties on far more equal terms, and hence a difficult balance in policy negotiations between greater policy concessions to political competitors, and defense of the interests of social democratic core constituencies. The loss of some votes was less important than the larger imperative of regaining cooperative relationships, and indeed the five parties backing the pension reform came to realize that entering a problem-solving mode required keeping pension politics out of the electoral arena.

II Political system

Constitutional history and nation-building

Sweden's history as an independent state stems from the peasant rebellion led by Gustav Vasa in 1521, and Swedish political development has been marked both by early and effective state-building, combined with late industrialization and democratization (Heclo & Madsen 1987). Indeed, the roots of Sweden's welfare state date to the expropriation of church lands and the establishment of a State church, which resulted in the State usurping the church in care for the poor and the aged, and in the provision of hospital services.[1]

The current constitution dates from 1974. It was the final step in a constitutional reform that began with the partial constitutional revision of 1968/1969, which took effect in 1970 and 1971. Despite the extension of the franchise and important changes in constitutional practice, such as the transition to parliamentarianism, the previous constitutional documents had remained untouched since the nineteenth century (Stjernquist 1996). The 1809 "Instrument of Government" (*Regeringsform*) and the "Parliament Act" (*Riksdagsordning*) had established a bicameral Parliament, whose chambers had equal weight but which were elected by different electoral methods. The difference in representation between the two chambers threatened to block political decision-making completely. In order to overcome these divisions,

Parliament and executive developed a practice of conciliation through parliamentary standing committees and the use of investigative expert commissions, as well as the associated *remiss* practice of submitting legislation to government agencies and interested parties for comment.

The Voting Reform Bill of 1907 (in force in 1909), established universal manhood suffrage for the Second Chamber and changed the property and income qualifications for the First Chamber. In 1918, the Riksdag extended the franchise to women, and eliminated plural voting. Equally important was an informal change in the interpretation of the Constitution in 1917 that ushered in the breakthrough of full parliamentarianism, under which government formation depended strictly upon the results of elections to the Second Chamber.

After World War II, the Social Democratic Party enjoyed an absolute majority in the indirectly-elected First Chamber. Not only did the indirect electoral method of the upper house advantage the Social Democrats as the largest party, the staggered elections (with only one-eighth of the representatives replaced every year) and the time lag (which based First Chamber elections on County Council election results as old as 12 years), allowed the Social Democrats to weather swings in electoral popularity and made it virtually impossible for the non-socialist opposition to unseat the Social Democratic Party. Furthermore, since each chamber needed to approve legislation, control of the First Chamber was sufficient to veto legislation. For votes on the budget, the two chambers met together. Here, the Social Democratic First Chamber majorities were sufficient to give the party a majority for these "common" votes. Not surprisingly, the non-socialist parties—led by the Liberals—demanded the elimination of the First Chamber entirely, as well as electoral reform. At first, progress was slow, but at the end of the 1960s, the Social Democrats agreed to eliminate the upper house, and surprised the non-socialist parties by outflanking them on the issue of proportionality: the Social Democrats proposed full proportionality based on compensatory seats. These were the most important changes introduced by the partial constitutional revision of 1968/1969. The full constitutional reform of 1973/74 (in effect since 1975) as well as subsequent partial reforms (1976, 1979, and 1994) cemented the practice of parliamentarism into law by officially removing the Monarch from government formation, guaranteeing civil rights, adding opportunities for binding referenda, and allowing Sweden to join the European Union in 1995.

Institutions of government

Sweden is a unitary state with centralized political institutions.[2] The Riksdag is unicameral, and neither judicial review nor popular referenda are binding. The Swedish Head of State is the Monarch, currently King Carl XVI Gustaf (since 1973). The constitutional reform has eliminated all remaining political functions of the Monarch.

Under the new constitution, Swedish governments rest on "negative parliamentarism," which means that the government remains in office as long as there is not a majority against it. Government formation is fairly straightforward. If the election result does not mean a change in government, the sitting cabinet remains in office. If the election results indicate that a new government should be formed, the Speaker of the Parliament consults party leaders about possible coalitions and then proposes a candidate for prime minister. As long as a simple majority does not vote against the candidate, he/she may form a government. Abstentions thus count for the government. Government formation is relatively rapid, as there is no complicated coalition agreement, and no positive vote requirement. As Bergman (2003: 607–8) puts it, "Swedish institutional arrangements... are such that they make it relatively easy to form a cabinet... and difficult to unseat a cabinet already in power." In order to unseat a government, an absolute majority is required for a vote of no confidence (*misstroendeförklaring*), which can be directed against an individual minister or against the prime minister, in which case, if successful, the entire cabinet must resign. If a new government cannot be formed on the basis of the same parliamentary distribution of seats, new elections may be held.[3] The cabinet may dissolve the Riksdag, but there is little incentive for this, because the next election must be held at its regularly-scheduled time nonetheless.

There is no Constitutional Court. Instead, a Law Council (*Lagrådet*) may scrutinize legislative proposals, but its opinion is advisory. The 1974 Constitution added the possibility of binding referenda for constitutional reforms, but none have been held to date. A Riksdag majority may also call for a consultative referendum, which has occurred six times—although the government has not always followed the popular mandate, as in the case of switching to right-hand traffic, which voters rejected in 1955 but the government introduced in 1968. One of the most important referendums did, however, concern pensions: the 1957 referendum concerning the introduction of earnings-related pensions (see p. 361).

Sweden has three types of sub-national territorial units: (i) provinces (*Län*); (ii) County Councils (*Landsting*); and (iii) municipalities (*Primärkommuner*). The provinces are administrative units of the national government, whereas the 20 County Councils are regionally-elected bodies with taxation powers that mainly provide health and hospital services. The municipal councils are also democratically elected, and charged with providing social services at the local level, such as elder and day care, schools, public transportation, as well as planning and construction. In order to improve the administrative efficiency of social service delivery, the number of municipalities was radically reduced from over 2,500 to 290 in the course of the "municipal" reforms of the late 1950s through early seventies, as well as some subsequent small shifts.

Electoral system

The Riksdag has 349 seats: 310 fixed seats and 39 "adjustment" seats (*utjämningsmandater*). Adjustment seats are used to increase the overall proportionality of the seat allocation. Parties must receive 4 percent of the national vote to win a seat in Parliament, unless a party wins at least 12 percent of the vote in one of the

Table 8.1 Political institutions in Sweden

Political arenas	Actors	Rules of investiture	Rules of decision-making	Veto potential
Executive	Monarch	Hereditary	Ceremonial functions, previous to 1975 Constitution initiated government formation	Not a veto point
	Prime Minister (*Statsminister*)	Speaker of Riksdag proposes PM candidate, Negative vote of investiture: lack of negative vote sufficient to form government; absolute majority needed for vote of no confidence; government may dissolve Riksdag, but next regularly-scheduled elections must be held	Government presents *propositioner* to Riksdag	————
Legislative	Parliament (*Riksdag*)	Mandates: 349 seats: 310 fixed seats and 39 "adjustment" seats (*utjämningsmandater*). Electoral threshhold: 4% of the national vote or 12% of the vote in one of the 29 multi-member electoral districts; electoral formula: modified St-Lagüe	MPs can propose *motioner*; Discussed by parliamentary standing committees; Legislation adopted by simple majority with no quorum	Veto point if minority government; Not a veto point if majority government
Judicial	Law Council (*Lagrådet*)	————	Non-binding	Not a veto point
Electoral	Referendum	Advisory referendum called by parliamentary majority; binding referendum on constitutional issues may be called by one-tenth of MPs (with approval of one-third), but only a negative vote of a majority of valid votes is binding (no binding referenda have been held)	Non-binding	Not a veto point
Territorial Units	County Councils (*Landsting*) Municipalities (*Kommuner*)	Elections to County Councils and Municipal Councils held on same day as parliamentary elections.	*Landsting*: hospitals and health care Municipalities: care for the elderly, day care, social assistance, schools, public transport, planning and construction	Not veto points

29 multi-member electoral districts. The electoral formula is the modified St-Laguë method, with 1.4 as the first divisor. Previously, Second Chamber elections had been based on the same electoral formula and districts, but without the adjustment seats to guarantee full proportionality. As a result of the change in electoral system, the Communists more than doubled their share of parliamentary seats. Similarly, the entry of the newer smaller parties into Parliament was aided by the change in formula—but one must note that the radical increase in the importance of the smaller parties took place more than 15 years after the constitutional reform.

Since 1998, voters may choose specific candidates from the party lists. If a candidate gets at least 8 percent of the party's vote, he/she moves to the top of the list. If two or more candidates meet this standard, the candidates move to the top of the list according to their number of votes. In the 1998 election, 12 of 349 MPs were elected on the basis of preference voting (Bergman 2003: 599).

Legislative process

The Riksdag appoints the Prime Minister, and the Prime Minister chooses his/her own ministers. The mandate period begins with the Prime Minister's statement of government policy (*regeringsförklaring*) at the opening of the Riksdag every September. Sixteen standing committees carry out the Riksdag's work and are often the forum for building legislative majorities. There are two types of legislative proposals, the Government Bill (*proposition*) and Private Member's Bill (*motion*). The legislative cycle begins when the government introduces a bill (*proposition*) to the Riksdag. For substantive proposals, the bill is usually based on the findings of an Official Commission of Inquiry that are published in an official government report (*Statens Offentliga Utredningar*). The Commissions are usually staffed by experts, public officials or parliamentarians, or any combination thereof. The Commission report is sent out for comment to interest groups, public agencies, local government, and other affected groups. This process is known as *remiss* and, while the government is not required to respond directly to objections, the *remiss* process does provide the government with important information about the extent of stakeholder support.

After the *remiss* period, the relevant ministry drafts a bill. The Legislative Council (*Lagrådet*), scrutinizes the bill if it contains elements that might conflict with the Consitution or existing law, but its opinion is not binding. The government then submits the bill to the Riksdag, where it is assigned to the relevant committee. MPs then have 15 days to introduce motions concerning the content of the bill. These can range from a motion to dismiss the bill to motions to modify the content of the bill. When the motion period is over, the relevant standing committee deals with the bill. All of the motions related to the bill are considered, and the Committee votes on a version of the bill to recommend to the full Riksdag. The Committee Report (*utskottsbetänkande*) contains the majority view, with dissenting views recorded at the end of the report. Committee reports are usually tabled twice before plenary

Party Family Affiliation	Abbreviation	Party name	Ideological orientation	Founding and merger details	Year established
Left	V	Left Party (Vänsterpartiet)	Left/ Communist	Sveriges kommunistiska parti; 1943 merger of various left splinter groups into Communist party; 1967 Vänsterpartiet kommunisterna (VPK); 1991 Vänsterpartiet	1921
Left	S	Social Democratic Workers' Party (Socialdemokratiska arbetarepartiet)	Social Democratic	1889	1889
Liberal	Fp	Liberal People's Party (Folkpartiet liberalerna)	Liberal	Frisinnade Landesförening; 1934 merger with Sveriges liberala Parti to form Folkpartiet; 1990 Folkpartiet liberalerna	1902
Agrarian	C	Centerparty (Centerpartiet)	Rural, Centrist	Bondeförbundet (Farmers' Party); 1943 Landsbygdspartiet-Bondeförbundet; 1958 Centerpartiet	1910
Conservative	M	Moderate Unity Party (Moderata samlingspartiet)	Conservative	Allmänna valmansförbundet; 1938 Högerns riksorganisation (Right); 1969 Moderata samlingspartiet	1904
Other	Kd	Christian Democratic Society Party (Kristdemokratiska samhällspartiet)	Christian Conservative	Kristdemokratiska sammling (Christian Democratic Unity); 1987 Kristdemokratiska samhällspartiet; First seat in parliament in 1985 through electoral alliance; first independently-won seats in 1988	1964
Other	MP	Environment Party The Greens (Miljöpartiet de gröna)	Green	First seat in 1988	1981
Other	NyD	New Democracy (Ny demokrati)	Populist right-wing	Only seats in 1991	1991

Fig. 8.1 Party system in Sweden

Source: Hadenius et al. 1991: 376–8.

debate and voting. Voting is by simple majority and there is no quorum rule. The legislation is then published in the Swedish Code of Statutes (*Svensk författningssamling*).

Parties and elections

The Swedish Party system was forged by struggles over voting rights and protectionism. Despite differences in ideology, Liberals and Social Democrats were united in their common struggle to achieve universal suffrage, free trade, and to introduce social legislation, whereas the Agrarians and the Conservatives promoted tariffs and resisted the extension of the franchise. Soon after the voting reform, the Social-Democratic Party emerged as the largest political party. But government formation and policy achievements were hampered by the fragmentation of the parties (which resulted in unstable minority governments), as well as the veto power of the Upper House. In the early 1930s, a sea-change occurred. Farmers fled the Conservatives for the new Farmers' Party (later Center), leaving the Conservatives as the representatives of business, and the Farmers as representatives of more popular, rural interests. This paved the way for the 1933 "Cow Trade" between the SAP and Agrarian Party, in which agricultural price supports were traded for unemployment benefits and active labor market policies for urban laborers. In 1934, competing liberal factions (previously split over free trade and temperance) fused into the new "Peoples Party" (*Folkpartiet*). In 1943, various left splinter parties merged into the Communist Party (later the Left Party; Rustow 1955: 3; Hadenius et al. 1991). Thus was born the "classic" Swedish five-party system, which remained stable until the late 1980s.

The Social Democratic-Farmers' Party crisis agreement also marked the beginning of social democratic "hegemony." From 1932 through 1976 every Swedish government was led by Social Democrats (other than a period of three months in 1936), and from 1951 to 1969, a single SAP Prime Minister held office (Tage Erlander). During this time, the SAP achieved a majority in the Second Chamber only twice. Instead, their control of the government was made possible by coalitions with the Farmers' Party (1936–9, 1951–7), and the passive support of the Communists, as well as all-party support during the war years. The narrow majorities in the Second Chamber, however, were compensated for by the Social Democrats' absolute majority in the First Chamber, which, as we shall see proved critical for pension politics in the late 1950s.

As Immergut and Jochem (2006) show, the Swedish political system has become more competitive since the constitutional reform in 1969. The elimination of the Upper House made changes in government more likely, and the increased proportionality of the electoral system reduced the advantages accruing to the largest party. Moreover, through the loss of the Upper House, the Social Democrats lost their ability to control policy-making unilaterally. Before 1971, the SAP could be assured of a majority in the bicameral Riksdag, and this created incentives for the opposition non-socialist parties to cooperate with the SAP, and it induced interest groups to

Table 8.2 Governmental majorities in Sweden

Date of change in political configuration	Election date	Start of gov.	Head of gov. (party)	Governing parties	Gov. majority (% seats)	Gov. electoral base (% votes)	Institutional veto points	Number of veto players (partisan + institutional)
10.11.1979	09.19.1979	10.11.1979	Fälldin II (C)	M (73), C (64), Fp (38)	50.1%	49.0%	None	3 + 0
05.19.1981		05.19.1981	Fälldin III (C)	C (64), Fp (38)	29.2%	28.7%	Riksdag	2 + 1
10.07.1982	09.19.1982	10.07.1982	Palme IV (S)	S (166)	47.6%	45.6%	Riksdag	1 + 1
10.04.1985	09.15.1985	10.04.1985	Palme V (S)	S (159)	45.6%	44.7%	Riksdag	1 + 1
03.12.1986		03.12.1986	Carlsson I (S)	S (159)	45.6%	44.7%	Riksdag	1 + 1
10.04.1988	09.18.1988	10.04.1988	Carlsson II (S)	S (156)	44.7%	43.2%	Riksdag	1 + 1
10.03.1991	09.15.1991	10.03.1991	Bildt (M)	M (80), Fp (33), C (31), Kd (26)	48.7%	46.7%	Riksdag	4 + 1
10.06.1994	09.19.1994	10.06.1994	Carlsson III (S)	S (161)	46.1%	45.3%	Riksdag	1 + 1
03.21.1996		03.21.1996	Persson I (S)	S (161)	46.1%	45.3%	Riksdag	1 + 1
10.06.1998	09.20.1998	10.06.1998	Persson II (S)	S (131)	37.5%	36.4%	Riksdag	1 + 1
10.01.2002	09.15.2002	10.01.2002	Persson III (S)	S (144)	41.3%	39.9%	Riksdag	1 + 1

Sources: http://www.const.sns.se/swedishpolitics/votes.htm; http://www.const.sns.se/swedishpolitics/seats.htm

cooperate with the SAP, especially employers (Immergut 2002: 241). Even previous to this reform, however, Swedish elections had become more competitive as the two blocs reached near parity in voter popularity during the 1960s. By the "bombshell" election of 1991, when the Social Democratic Party's electoral standing dropped to its lowest level since 1921, the SAP lost its position as the virtually inevitable party of government.

Until the 1970s, class-based voting was strong, and voter preferences were stable over time. Since the 1970s, however, volatility has increased; not only has class voting decreased, but voters switch parties more frequently and often decide their vote late in an election campaign (Bergman 2003: 597; Holmberg and Oscarsson 2004: 83 ff.). All in all, the more proportional electoral system, and the increase in voter volatility, resulted in a more fragmented party system and a stronger role for the smaller parties than in the heyday of social democratic hegemony.

Interest groups

Sweden is typically classified as a strong case of corporatism because interest organizations are centralized, they organize a large proportion of potential members, and they are deeply involved in wage bargaining, as well as public policy-making and implementation. In the golden age of Swedish corporatism, wage bargaining was centralized; unions and employers participated in the policy-making process formally as members of Official Commissions of Inquiry, and via the *remiss* process; and unions and employers were represented on the boards of state agencies. Since the 1980s, these corporatist institutions have become weaker. In the 1980s the employers (SAF) decided to leave the boards, centralized wage bargaining collapsed in 1982, and interest groups play a less important role in the Official Commissions of Inquiry. Nevertheless, in 2004 union density was as high as 80.1 percent, and employers remain highly organized. (See Lewin 1994; Rothstein and Bergström 1999; Pontusson 1992; Steinmo 2002; Swenson 2002.)

Swedish unions are industrial unions and are organized in three peak organizations.

1. The Swedish Trade Union Confederation (*Landsorganisationen*, LO) is the peak organization for blue-collar unions, with 16 affiliates. The 16 affiliates have about 1.9 million members, 46 percent of whom are women. The largest affiliate is the Municipal Workers' Union (*Kommunalförbundet*), followed by the Metalworkers' Union (*Metall*).
2. The Central Organization of Salaried Employees (*Tjänstemännens Centralorganisationen*, TCO) organized white collar workers, and has 7 affiliates and 1.3 million members.
3. The Swedish Confederation of Professional Organizations (*Sveriges Akademikers Centralorganisation*, SACO) counts 570,000 members in 25 unions for those with professional degrees such as lawyers, university lecturers, and others. About half of the members are women (www.saco.se). Neither TCO nor SACO is affiliated with a political party.

The Confederation of Swedish Enterprise (*Svenskt Näringsliv*) represents 55,000 firms in 51 branch associations. The Confederation resulted from the merger of the Swedish Employers' Confederation (*Sveriges Arbetsgivarförbundet*, SAF) and the Federation of Swedish Industries (*Industriförbundet*, IF) in 2001.

Anderson (2001) argues that unions are the primary defenders of pension interests in Sweden. To be sure, the emergence of a large public pension scheme has contributed to the rise of interest groups representing the interests of pensioners, the PRO with links to the SAP, and the non-socialist affiliated SPF. These organizsations have become increasingly active in monitoring pension-related legislation and lobbying the government and Riksdag. However, as this chapter documents, the influence of the LO and the TCO exceeded that of the pensioners' organizations.

III PENSION SYSTEM

Historical overview

Sweden was the first nation to introduce universal public pensions. Legislative efforts began in the late nineteenth century, but large-scale farmers in the Second Chamber blocked efforts to introduce a workers' pension along Bismarckian lines. A compromise solution was the introduction of a basic pension for all citizens financed by general taxes. The aristocratic First Chamber vetoed this plan, however, as well as a second effort in 1905. After the Liberal Karl Staaff demanded the dissolution of the First Chamber as a condition for his forming a government in 1912 (which substantially decreased the conservative majority), and extensive preparatory work in a government commission (which assured the Conservative support necessary for passage in the First Chamber), Staaff's government introduced a universal Old-Age and Invalidity Pension Scheme in 1913. The 1913 Law provided for a low pension (*avgiftspension*) based on contributions and investment growth, up to a maximum. Invalids could apply for a means-tested supplement (*pensionstillägg*). Total pensions were low, and in 1935 this "premium reserve system" (*premiereservsystemet*) was replaced by the flat rate basic pension (*folkpension*; Elmér, 1960: 50–1, 66 ff.). In 1948, as part of the Social Democratic "Harvest Period" during which the major programs of the post-war welfare state were introduced, the basic pension was raised significantly to cover basic living costs. By the early 1950s, the size of the pension equaled about 30 percent of average industrial wages (Ackerby 1992).

The 1950s were a period of intense conflict over earnings-related pensions. At the time, public employees and white collar workers enjoyed generous occupational pensions while the majority of households only had access to the basic pension. As early as 1938, the Metal Workers' Union had begun to demand the same pension rights as white collar employees, and in 1944 the LO began to push for a legislative solution to the problem of superannuated pensions, although the unions were not united behind the issue, and the SAP had to be pushed to adopt the LO line. At issue was whether supplementary or "superannuated" pensions should be introduced by law (the LO/SAP position), or by collective agreements (the Liberal and Conservative position). The Farmers' Party pushed for a more generous "*folkpension.*" After several years of contentious debate, and several government commissions to study the issue, a referendum and pre-term elections (after the break-up of the Farmer-Labor coalition on precisely this issue), the Riksdag approved an earnings-related pension scheme in 1959. At this time, the Social Democrats enjoyed an absolute majority of 79 out of 151 seats in the First Chamber, but only 111 out of 231 seats in the Second Chamber. Together with the Communists, the socialist bloc held 116 seats to the non-Socialist bloc's 115 seats. As the Speaker was not allowed to vote, the situation was a draw. After the government's proposal passed the First Chamber on May 13, 1959, the log-jam in the Second Chamber was broken by the abstention of a Liberal MP, so that the law passed by one vote. The SAP's lock on the First Chamber, and its continuation into the foreseeable future, meant that even with new elections, the SAP would be able to dominate the legislative process. Thus, the choice was accommodation or stalemate.[4]

The new national supplementary pension scheme (ATP) was designed to give all workers, not just white collar workers, an earnings-related pension. Collectively-negotiated white collar pensions were retained, and in 1971 LO members got their own collective pensions (Ståhlberg 1993: 13). Key to the negotiations, and to the SAP's new "wage-earner strategy," was the incorporation of the white-collar workers on favorable terms, the most important of which was basing benefits on the best 15 out of 30 years, which fitted the white-collar career pattern better than that for blue-collar workers (Svensson 1994).

The ATP Reform meant that the basic pension was supplemented with an obligatory earnings-related pension. Together with the basic pension, ATP was designed to provide 65 percent of previous income up to the ATP ceiling. According to the generous transition rules, the system would approach maturity by the early 1990s. The ATP system also included provisions for disability pensions (*förtidspensioner*) and family pensions (*familjpensioner*), which provided coverage to widows and orphans.

The political lessons of the ATP battle were not lost on any of the political parties—especially after both the Liberals and the Conservatives faced electoral losses for their opposition to pension expansion. Indeed, it provided an answer to the perennial question of Swedish Social Democracy, which was whether the introduction of the main pillars of the welfare state in the 1940s had eliminated the need for Social Democracy itself. The ATP victory showed that Social Democracy could go further in "reforming society," and would win inroads in new voter groups if it did so.

Consequently, in the 1960s and 1970s, SAP governments expanded and improved pensions with the support of the opposition. In 1969, the basic pension was complemented with the pension supplement (*pensionstillskott*) for those who were not included in ATP or who had few ATP points. This supplement was small at first, but by the early 1990s it equaled about half the basic pension. Between 1970 and 1972, eligibility rules were loosened for disability pensions so that this type of pension became available for so-called labor market reasons.[5] In 1974, sickness and unemployment insurance were made taxable and eligible for pension points. In 1976, the pension age was reduced from 67 to 65, and the partial pension (*delpension*) was introduced. Workers aged 60–64 who switched to part-time employment became eligible for the partial pension[6] until they reached retirement age. In 1982, the basis for ATP contributions was increased to include the entire wage sum even though only incomes up to a specified ceiling earned pension points. Since 1982, the care of small children has also been eligible for ATP pension points. Throughout the 1970s and 1980s, employer contributions to both the basic pension and ATP pension system were raised several times.

Debates about welfare state retrenchment reached the political agenda in the 1980s, but progress—as we shall see—was slow. In 1994, however, a four-party non-socialist coalition government negotiated a major reform with the opposition SAP. Detailed legislation came in 1998, and the reform has been implemented in steps between 1995 and 2001. The new system was fully operational starting in 2003.

Description of the current pension system

Coverage

The current pension system consists of three parts: the guarantee pension (*garantipension*), the income pension (*inkomstpension*), and the premium pension (*premiepension*). As in the past, contractual occupational pensions will continue to provide a top-up to public benefits.[7] This reformed system replaced the basic pension (introduced in 1913) and the ATP pension (adopted in 1959).[8] For low-income pensioners, means-tested allowances are available.

All residents are covered by the guarantee pension, but benefits are available only to those with insufficient earnings-related benefits. For those born before 1938, the old basic pension (*folkpension*) continued to pay a flat-rate benefit until 2003 when it was converted into the "transitional guarantee pension" (see section on "benefits" on p. 365). Those with income from employment (including the self-employed) are covered by the income pension and the premium pension. There is no separate scheme for civil servants or the self-employed.

Administration

The National Insurance Board (*Försäkringskassan*) adminsters the guarantee pension and the income pension.[9] The Premium Pension Authority (*Premiepensionsmyndigheten*, PPM), a state agency, administers the premium pension. The PPM was established in 1998 to administer contributions to the individual accounts (the premium reserve), and makes contracts with fund managers. In 2004, wage earners could choose between 600 investment funds, including a public default fund, the

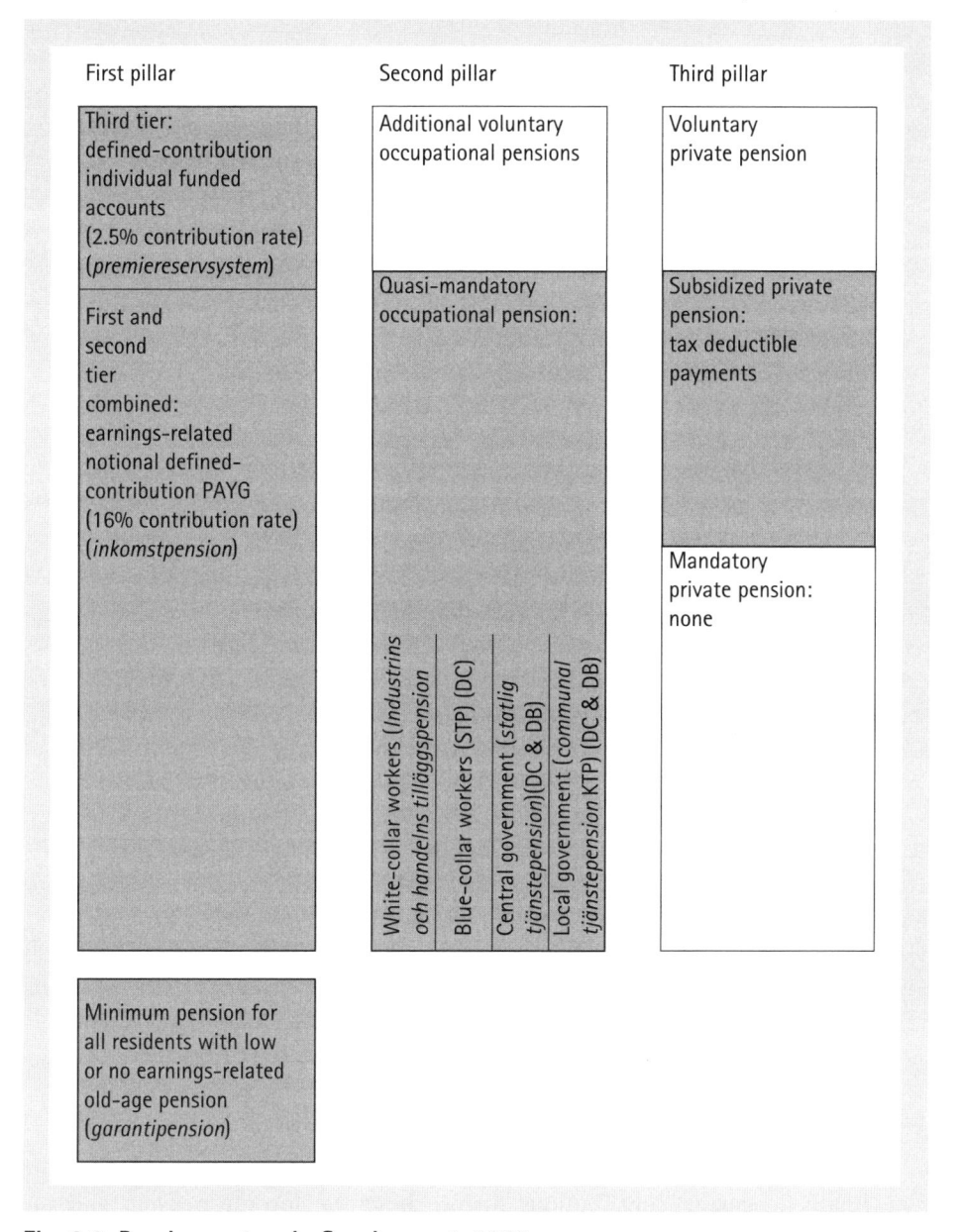

Fig. 8.2 Pension system in Sweden post-1998

First pillar

Third tier: defined-contribution individual funded accounts (2.5% contribution rate) (*premiereservsystem*)

First and second tier combined: earnings-related notional defined-contribution PAYG (16% contribution rate) (*inkomstpension*)

Minimum pension for all residents with low or no earnings-related old-age pension (*garantipension*)

Second pillar

Additional voluntary occupational pensions

Quasi-mandatory occupational pension:
- White-collar workers (*Industrins och handelns tilläggspension*)
- Blue-collar workers (STP) (DC)
- Central government (*statlig tjänstepension*) (DC & DB)
- Local government (*communal tjänstepension* KTP) (DC & DB)

Third pillar

Voluntary private pension

Subsidized private pension: tax deductible payments

Mandatory private pension: none

Premium Savings Fund (*Premiesparfonden*), for those who do not make an active fund choice.[10]

Financing

The state finances the guarantee pension out of general revenues. In the old system, employers paid an earmarked contribution (6.75%) that covered about 52 percent of basic pension costs in 1993. This contribution was eliminated in 1998.

364   SWEDEN

First pillar	Second pillar	Third pillar
Third tier: none	Additional voluntary occupational pensions	Voluntary private pension:
Second tier: earnings-related defined-benefit PAYG (*allmän tilläggspension* ATP)		Subsidized private pension: tax deductible payments
First tier: social insurance (*folkpension*)	Contractual defined-benefit occupational pension: White-collar workers (*Industrins och handelnst illäggspension*ITP) / Blue-collar workers (STP) / Central government (*statlig tjänstepension*) / Local government (*communal tjänstepension* KTP)	Mandatory private pension: none
Social Assistance		

Fig. 8.3 Pension system in Sweden pre-1994

Earmarked pension contributions finance both the income pension and the premium pension. The total contribution is 18.5 percent: 16 percent for the income pension and 2.5 percent for the premium pension. Wage-earners pay 7 percent of their eligible earnings up to a ceiling of 8.07 "income base amounts."[11] In 2004, the ceiling was SEK 42,300, and it is indexed to increases in average earnings. Employers pay 10.21 percent contribution to the earnings ceiling, and half of this for earnings above the ceiling. The latter is called a "tax" rather than a pension contribution.

The government pays the entire contribution for "child years"[12] and those in military service. For claimants of unemployment insurance or sickness benefit, the state pays the employer share of the contribution (10.21%), and the individual pays his/her contribution as if she were working. In 2002, 12 percent of pension contributions originate from state payments for those in receipt of social insurance benefits, or those not working (i.e. in military service or claiming "child years," RFV 2004: 32).

As with the old system, the new pension system operates largely on a Pay-As-You-Go (PAYG) basis, with "buffer" funds to even-out demographic peaks and valleys. In the new system, however, the size and function of the buffer funds in the new system is very different.[13] The old AP Funds functioned not only as a buffer but they also earned investment income and provided investment capital for public housing. At their peak, the old AP Funds contained about 40 percent of GDP in assets, or enough to cover pension payments for more than five years without contributions. The new buffer funds are smaller and play a smaller role in collective capital formation. Over time, the assets in the premium reserve will exceed those in the AP Funds.

One unique feature of the new Swedish pension system is that it contains automatic stabilizers designed to ensure the financial sustainability of the system. The "automatic balancing" mechanism requires the National Insurance Office to calculate the notional assets and liabilities of the system annually. Notional assets are 90 percent of total assets and are the sum of all future pension contributions (16% of qualifying income).[14] The remaining 10 percent is the financial assets in the AP Funds. Notional liabilities are the sum of pension promises to those still in employment and those already in retirement. If the ratio of assets to liabilities, the balance ratio (*balanstal*), falls below one, the balancing mechanism kicks in. Both pension rights and benefit payments are indexed at a lower rate until balance is restored.[15]

Benefits

Since the introduction of the ATP system in the 1960s, all social insurance benefits have been calculated on the basis of an accounting device called the base amount (*basbeloppet*). Since 1998 there have been three kinds of base amount: (i) the price base amount (*prisbasbelopp*); (ii) the increased price base amount (*förhöjda prisbasbeloppet*); and (iii) the income base amount (*inkomstbasbeloppet*). The old base amount was adjusted for price increases annually, and the new price base amount replaces it. The price base amount is used to calculate the guarantee pension and several other social insurance benefits. The increased price base amount is also indexed to inflation, but when it was introduced in 1998, its initial value was set higher than the price base amount. The increased price base amount is used to calculate supplementary pension rights for those born between 1938 and 1953 who are covered by the old ATP system and the new pension system. Finally, the income base amount is indexed to increases in pension-carrying income, and is used to determine the level of the income ceiling for income pensions (7.5 income base amounts) as well as the notional pension assets (*avgiftsunderlag*) in the new pension system. In 2006, the price base amount is SEK 39,700, the increased price base amount is SEK 40,500, and the income base amount is SEK 44,500.

The guarantee pension is payable at age 65 to those with insufficient pension income from the income pension system.[16] The guarantee pension replaces the basic pension, pension supplement and the special tax deduction for pensioners. Unlike the old basic pension, the guarantee pension is taxable. The guarantee pension is either a fixed amount or a supplement to the income pension. In 2006, the guaranteed minimum is 2.13 price base amounts, or SEK 86,149 annually. Married pensioners receive 1.9 price base amounts (SEK 76,820). The premium pension, private pension income and occupational pension income do not affect the guarantee pension. To qualify for the maximum benefit, 40 years of residence from age 25 are required. For those who do not meet this requirement (usually immigrants), there is a special maintenance allowance. Low-income pensioners are also eligible for the pensioners housing supplement (BTP). The guarantee pension is payable to those born 1938 or later.[17]

In the new income pension system, retirement is possible any time after age 61. The income pension is a "notional defined contribution" (NDC) pension based on lifetime earnings. This means that even though the new income pension system is not fully funded, the scheme emulates a funded defined-contribution scheme by estimating an internal rate of return for accumulated pension contributions. The new system counts all contributions, and the monthly benefit is calculated based on (gender-neutral) life expectancy at the time of retirement. All insured persons have an account with the National Insurance Office in which their contributions are entered. The notional balance in the account is indexed annually according to an "income index" (*inkomstindex*) based on changes in average pension-carrying income for wage-earners aged 16–64. At retirement, assets in the notional account are converted to an annuity using the "annuitization divisor" (*delningstal*) which is the expected remaining life expectancy for that cohort plus an internal rate of return of 1.6 percent. This means that later retirement increases the pension benefit significantly because the divisor decreases and pension assets increase. The reverse is true for earlier retirement. The notional assets of those who die are credited to the birth year cohort. Administrative costs are deducted annually. Benefit payouts are indexed to the adjustment index (*följsamhetsindex*) which is the income index minus 1.6%.[18]

In addition to the income pension, the new system contains a "premium reserve:" of the total 18.5 percent in pension contributions, 2.5 percent is placed in a defined contribution, individual investment account. To minimize administrative costs, pension contributions and fund choices are centrally managed by a government agency, the PPM, and individuals have a wide range of fund choices. All fund balances are annuitized at the time of retirement and can be paid out either as a fixed annuity with a minimum rate of return of 3 percent or as a variable annuity. Premium pensions cannot be inherited; and the individual bears all investment risk. The premium pension is payable from age 65.

Those born between 1938 and 1953 receive pensions according to the old and new systems.[19] Every person with pension rights in Sweden receives an annual pension statement from the National Insurance Office, the so-called "orange envelope," that contains estimates of future pension benefits (for both the income pension and premium pension) based on current individual employment and different economic growth scenarios.

IV Politics of pension reform since 1980

Overview

The mammoth reform leading to the current system just described is the main event of Swedish pension reform in the 1980s and 1990s. During the 1980s, incremental cuts and benefit freezes were made by both non-Socialist and Socialist governments, but pensions retained their role as a weapon in the battle for votes, and many cuts were rescinded after changes in government. The SAP refused to abandon its staunch defense of the ATP system—it's "jewel in the crown"—until 1994, after three years of non-Socialist rule. We interpret this about-face as a political strategy by the SAP to regain its role as the natural party of government.

The 1980s: political competition and policy stability

As in the rest of Western Europe, the oil crises of the 1970s caused a deep recession in Sweden. At the same time, the constitutional changes meant that Swedish politics became more competitive and changes in government easier. Indeed, younger Social Democrats—such as Olof Palme—were eager to leave the old model of compromise and moderation (a policy style sometimes described as a slow and steady "tortoise") behind, and to pursue a more radical ("harelike") politics of equality and social justice. Particularly the proposal for economic democracy through wage-earner funds proved unpopular with voters, however, and the SAP suffered a historic loss in the 1976 elections (as well as in 1979), bringing Sweden's first non-Socialist government in more than four decades to power.[20]

Despite their commitment to reducing the size of the public sector, however, these coalition governments were unsuccessful in this regard (Kato and Rothstein, 2006). By the end of the decade, high inflation was pushing pension costs up at the same time that budget deficits were ballooning. The Fälldin government finally cut pensions in 1981 by adjusting the index for pensions, and reduced benefit levels in the partial pension (*delpension*) from 65 percent to 50 percent in 1982. These changes provoked public outcry, and the SAP promised to restore the full value of pensions if elected in 1982. Indeed party leader Olof Palme stressed repeatedly in the campaign that the SAP was the party of "social security and ATP," (cited in Lundberg 2003: 35). The SAP won the election, and fulfilled this promise in 1983, although pensioners were not fully compensated for lost purchasing power as a result of the 1982 devaluation (Weaver and Pierson 1993: 137).

Table 8.3 Overview of proposed and enacted pension reforms in Sweden

Year	Name of reform	Reform process (chronology)	Reform measures
1981	Change in Indexing, cut in partial pension	• Introduced 1981 • introduced 1982	• indirect taxes, energy prices, food subsidies, and import duties, are removed from the pension index. • pension uprating only once per year rather than every three months if prices rose more than 3% over the level of the previous adjustment
1983	Restoration of pension indexing	• SAP restores full value of pensions after 1982 election	• full value of pensions is restored, although pensioners not fully compensated for lost purchasing power because of the 1982 devaluation
1987	Reform of widow's pension	• Pension Committee appointed 1984 Committee Report SOU 1987: 55 • law takes into effect January 1980	• widows' pension replaced by lower "adjustment pension" (omställningspension): 96% of the basic pension plus 20% of the deceased's ATP if children, 40% if not. Payable for 12 months. • Means-tested additional allowance (särskild efterlevandepension) payable after twelve months; widows married before 1990 still eligible for widow's pension, as well as women born before 1930; existing widows' pensioners grandfathered in. • child's pension: increased to 40% of the base amount and max benefit of 20% of the base amount plus 30% of the deceased's ATP, (slightly lower for siblings).
1992	"Crisis packages"	• November 1992 non-socialist government - SAP opposition agreement	• pensions are calculated at 98% of the already reduced base amount, this rule was extended in 1993, 1994, 1995, 1996, 1997, and 1998.
1994	Reformerat-pensionssystem	• 1990 The Pensions Commission (Pensionsberedningen) Report SOU 1990: 76 November 1991 non-socialist government appoints parliamentary working group to negotiate reform • January 1994 working group final report SOU 1994: 20	• 15/30 → lifetime earnings • Switch to defined contribution, life-time earnings benefit formula • Pension contributions 50:50 employers: employees. • 2.5% contribution to "premium reserve" (obligatory individual investment accounts). • guarantee pension replaced old basic pension (folkpension) and pension supplement (pensionstillskott) • recommendations: replace partial pension with flexible pension age from

	• TCO tries to pressure government to change some provisions and fails. • LO tacitly supportive. Metalworkers oppose; Municipal Workers support reform • Framework legislation adopted 8th June 1994	age 60; transfer disability pension scheme to sickness or work injury insurance system. • unresolved items: reduce guarantee pension for those with contractual occupational pensions?; construction of premium reserve; the swap in contributions; economic adjustment index; pension rights for students; automatic balancing
1998 Reformerat pensionssystem, implementation	• 1994 The parties behind the 1994 reform appoint an "implementation group" (*genomförandegruppen*) to work out remaining details • 1994–98 ongoing negotiations between five parties supporting agreement • January 1996 grass-roots opposition to reform at SAP Extra Party Congress. • January 1997 The parties behind the reform agree on the contribution swap and the structure of the premium reserve • 1997 grass roots opposition at SAP Regular Party Congress • January 1998 The parties behind the reform agree most remaining details • 2nd April 1998 The government propose two detailed bills one on the income pension and one on the guarantee pension • both bills passed easily the Riksdag on June 8, 1994	• income from the premium pension, private pensions and occupational pensions do not affect the level of the guarantee pension • increase in contribution to Premium Reserve from 2.0 to 2.5% of qualifying wages. • contribution to sickness insurance is transferred to pensions in order to achieve partity financing between employers and employees • Premium Pension Authority created • Default investment fund for those who do not choose a fund or who want the state to manage their premium pension account. • SEK 90 billion transferred from AP Funds to the state budget in 1999 and 2000 to cover tasks transferred to the government budget
2001 Buffer Funds	• 2001 The legislation passes	• SEK 170 billion transferred from AP Funds to state to cover transition costs. Total transfer is now SEK 258 billion.

Reform of the Widows' Pension

In the elections of 1985 and 1988, the future of the welfare state featured prominently, and the non-Socialist parties were repudiated at election time when they suggested modest cuts in pensions. Nevertheless, it was obvious that financial instability would threaten the ATP system in future, and the SAP government appointed a Pension Commission in 1984 to study comprehensive pension reform. The main legislation that resulted, however, was a reduction of the "widow's pension," which could be sold to the public as a necessary adjustment to societal change, and indeed change that had been produced by successful social-democratic policies, namely, the massive increase in women's employment (SOU 1987: 55).

The 1990s

The pension politics of the 1970s and 1980s—benefit expansion, followed by minor cuts—illustrate well the difficulties of welfare state retrenchment under severe political competition. Although Sweden's public household regained fiscal balance as a result of greater tax revenues during the economic upswing of the late 1980s, this overheated growth masked fundamental budgetary problems that came home to roost when the bubble burst (Svensson et al. 2006). The entire Swedish model was called into question, and in 1991 the SAP suffered its worst election defeat since 1921, falling to below the "magic" threshold of 40 percent of the vote (Gilljam and Holmberg 1993: 133–141). Moreover, the party lost its control of the pivotal seat in the legislature, which meant loss of control of policy-making (Bergman 1995: 71 ff.). Social Democratic hegemony had been lost through the constitutional reform; now the political dominance of the party was at stake, a major strategic imperative would be the re-capture of the political middle.

The non-Socialists, led by Carl Bildt (Conservative), formed a four-party minority coalition (Conservatives; Liberals; Center; and Christian Democrats) with the support of the populist New Democracy Party that had just entered the Riksdag. The new government promised to reform the welfare state along non-socialist lines and reform economic policy. The worsening budget situation soon became the government's overriding concern.

The Bildt government did not enjoy a parliamentary majority, but was dependent on New Democracy's support to pass its legislation. In other words, Parliament was a veto point. Furthermore, the government was comprised of four partisan veto players. Consequently, any policy decisions would require the agreement of all four governing parties, as well as an additional legislative ally. New Democracy soon proved to be an unreliable partner in the Riksdag, so the government pursued a two-track strategy: seeking New Democracy's support for incremental cuts and turning to the SAP for support for more fundamental reforms. The former strategy was important for passing several incremental cuts in pension provision, while the latter was crucial for the cost-cutting measures adopted as part of the 1992 "crisis packages" and the principles adopted in 1994 for a major pension reform.

Suspended indexing

When the economic crisis set in, adjustments in pension indexing were an important tool for budget consolidation.[21] Between 1991 and 1998 the base amount (*basbelopp*) which is used to calculate all transfer payments did not follow the CPI (consumer price index). Both the Bildt government (1991–94) and subsequent SAP governments pursued this strategy. Between 1991 and 1998, the base amount used to calculate benefits did not keep pace with inflation. During the November 1992 currency crisis, the non-Socialist government and SAP opposition agreed to calculate pensions at 98 percent of the already reduced base amount, and this rule was extended in 1993, 1994, 1995, 1996, 1997, and 1998. In 1995, the SAP government adopted an indexing rule in which the base amount was increased by 60 percent of the CPI as long as the budget deficit exceeded SEK 100 billion. This cut also applied to pension payments that had already been reduced by 2 percent. In 1997, the Ministry of Social Affairs estimated that these downward adjustments reduced the value of the base amount (and pensions) by 12 percent relative to prices (Dahlin 1997: 4). This decision was based on wide parliamentary support, so it remained in place until state finances improved.

Given the dire state of public finances, pension indexation adjustment was a quick way for politicians to achieve immediate budget savings. The 1992 index changes were made behind closed doors by party leaders during a period of acute economic crisis. Once in place, changed indexing rules could be relied on for yearly savings as long as deficits remained high. In a situation of electoral competition, these somewhat less visible cuts were the path of least resistance (and thus fit the Weaver-Pierson "obfuscation" thesis), but they did not solve the crisis in the pension system. More severe and more politically-sensitive measures would be needed.

Partial pension cuts

When the Bildt government took office in September 1991, one of its first actions was to propose the elimination of the partial pension—an expensive program, but one very important to working class constituents, as industrial workers' pay schemes and work conditions made this scheme particularly attractive. Not surprisingly, the Conservatives were especially opposed to this scheme, while Social Democrats, the Left and indeed, the right-wing populist party, (*Ny Demokrati*), with its working-class base fought the cuts. In its 1992 budget, the Bildt government proposed to eliminate the program in the spring of 1992. Earmarked employer contributions (0.5% of payroll) placed in a dedicated fund financed partial pensions. In 1992, the fund showed a surplus, so the Bildt government proposed to shift the contribution to the Work Injury Insurance Scheme, which was running a deficit. Thus the net effect would be the elimination of the partial pension but employer contributions would remain the same. The SAP and Left Party opposed the proposal, and the move backfired when New Democracy refused to support the proposal, arguing that eliminating the program would increase costs in long-term sick pay and disability pensions. The only thing the Bildt government could gain New Democracy's support for was a reduction in the partial pension fee from 0.5 percent to 0.2 percent with the difference going to work injury insurance.

Despite this initial failure, the Bildt government targeted partial pensions again the following year (1993), proposing to increase the qualifying age from 60 to 62 and cut benefits from 65 percent to 50 percent of qualifying income. These measures were projected to save SEK 200 million per year. Again, the government sought New Democracy's support, and again the SAP and Left Party opposed the proposal. New Democracy agreed to the cuts in committee but later reversed itself, and the proposal failed to gain a majority in the Riksdag vote. Despite this second victory against non-Socialist pension cuts, the SAP shifted course and by the spring of 1994, the SAP was prepared to support partial pension cuts. Two factors motivated the SAP's decision: the abysmal budget situation and the opportunity to influence the content of the reform. This marks a shift in Social-Democratic strategy, to regain the center by cooperating in solving the nation's economic problems.

The SAP agreed to accept an increase in the qualifying age to 61 years (rather than 62) as well as more modest reduction in benefits than the government wanted: from 65 percent to 55 percent of qualifying income rather than 50 percent. Thus, after three attempts, the Bildt government achieved only modest reductions in the partial pension program. At first, the savings would be small, but by 1999 they would have a more significant effect since the number of partial pensioners would be halved. Cuts in the partial pension were the first reductions in nominal benefits that the SAP supported. Although LO and TCO vigorously objected to partial pension cuts, the economic crisis supplied the rationale for the Bildt government's deal with the SAP, as by this time, the budget deficit had reached nearly 12 percent of GDP.

The 1994/98 reform

As noted, the SAP government had appointed a Pension Commission (*Pensionsberedningen*) in 1984 with explicit instructions to propose *parametric* reforms, while retaining the principles of basic security, earnings-replacement and PAYG financing. After five years of deliberations, the Pensions Commission released its final report in 1990 (SOU 1990: 76). The Commission could not agree on specific reform proposals, but recommended a number of general principles to guide future reform.[22] For a while the Commission seemed to have a majority in favor of swapping the 15/30 for a 20/40 rule, but TCO blocked this (Lundberg 2003: 157).

The Commission was largely in agreement about the ATP's weaknesses, especially the weak link between contributions and benefits. In the first place, with the basic pension/pension supplement combination paying nearly as much in pension benefits as the ATP pension of an industrial worker, the ATP's earnings replacement function was seriously endangered. In 1988, 8.1 percent of wage earners were at or above the ceiling (13.8% of men and 1.8% of women). The Commission did not explicitly recommend raising the ceiling but it did emphasize that the choice was between letting the ATP decline in value and letting private and contractual pensions fill the gap, or increasing the ceiling.

A second weakness highlighted was ATP's weakened financial basis: ATP contributions ceased to cover current expenditures in 1984, and since then AP Fund income covered the shortfall.

Moreover, the ATP system was particularly sensitive to demographic and productivity changes, especially reductions in working time. If work time decreases, wage-earners contribute less to the system so the revenue base for ATP decreases. Because of the generous 15–30 rules, many reductions in work time did not translate into reduced pension rights and led to a permanent deficit in the ATP system. The design of the earnings-related ATP system also assumed a stable annual economic growth rate of 3–4 percent and full employment in order to keep contribution rates stable. But in periods of stagnant or slow real GDP growth, the required level of pension contributions is much higher (Ståhlberg 1995).

Finally, Commission experts also pointed to the ATP's unintended redistributional effects, especially redistribution from lower income groups to higher income groups as a result of the best 15 of 30 years rule (Ståhlberg 1995: 90). Those with short career and uneven income benefited from the 15/30 benefit formula while those with longer careers and a flat-earnings curve were disadvantaged. The groups that benefited the most from the 15/30 rule were those with higher education and a rising career income curve; and women, who tend to work fewer years, rotate between full- and part-time work and have a more uneven wage profile.

Although there was little agreement on specific changes, the 1990 report marked a significant shift in thinking about the role of the pension system. Rather than focusing on the welfare of the elderly, the 1990 report emphasized the economic effects and the long-term stability of the pension system (Ackerby 1992: 15). Moreover, the Pensions Commission resulted in the accumulation of valuable expert knowledge about ATP's distributional and economic effects. The release of the Pension Commission report did much to advance the policy debate about pension reform, even if most subsequent analyses were far less sanguine than the Pension Commission report.

The release of the Pension Commission report meant that the ATP system's weaknesses were fairly well known, at least among experts and party leaders. The SAP took the first step by identifying pension reform as a priority in its 1991 budget. In particular, the SAP emphasized the need to increase long-term savings via the pension system and to strengthen the earnings-related aspect of the system. The SAP argued that the pension system should help to strengthen work incentives for the active population by increasing the total amount of income that forms the base for pension benefits (Ministry of Finance 1990). In the spring of 1991, the Social Democratic State Secretary in the Finance Ministry, Anna Hedborg, began to investigate reform options with (among others) Minister of Social Affairs, Ingela Thalén, and the State Secretary from the Prime Minister's Office (Lundberg 2003: 163–4). The elections scheduled for September interrupted the group's work, although the two main figures, Hedborg and Thalén, would later play key roles in the 1994 reform compromise.

Pension reform played little role in the 1991 election campaign, and the SAP's dramatic election loss in September 1991 meant that the initiative for reform now belonged to the non-Socialist coalition government headed by Carl Bildt. The Bildt government took office with an ambitious welfare state reform agenda, and one of its first steps (November 1991) was to appoint a parliamentary working group to negotiate a major pension reform. Bo Könberg (Liberal Party), the Minister of Health and Social Affairs, chaired the working group. The government instructed the working group to follow several principles: improving the pension system's financial sustainability; strengthening the link between contributions and benefits, and encouraging an increase in long-term savings. The working group's members agreed to try to achieve a compromise across the political blocs, if possible including all the parliamentary parties. Each party was allotted one representative, except for the SAP, which got two: Ingela Thalén and Anna Hedborg.

The working group's deliberations were atypical by Swedish standards. First, each party representative had a more or less free hand to negotiate on behalf of his/her party. Secondly, the working group members pre-committed to agree on guiding principles first and work out the details later. Finally, each member committed to not changing the content of the reform after the negotiations were complete. Interest groups and the media would be called in only for regular progress meetings and after the negotiations were finished.

Initially, the parliamentary working group included members of all Riksdag parties, but the representatives of the Left Party and New Democracy quickly left the group because of disagreements with the other five parties. The Left Party in particular has been highly critical of the "undemocratic" and "rushed" methods used within the group. The Left Party vigorously opposed changing the 15/30 rule, and its representative criticized the other parties for shutting them out. These criticisms seem to have had little impact.

The exclusion of interest groups from the working group prompted even more criticism. TCO in particular complained about the working group's closed door approach, but the government defended itself by portraying the working group as a continuation of the Pension Commission, in which interest groups had participated (Lundberg 2003: 170). Clearly, the working group intended to minimize the influence of the two most powerful potential opponents to pension reform, TCO and LO. Whereas TCO was highly critical of the eventual reform proposals, LO's reaction is best described as silent, reluctant support. It is fair to say that LO kept silent because it wanted a reform and was wary of having members' views stirred up, thus preventing a deal (see also Lundberg 2003).

The pension working group issued its first report (Ds 1992: 89) in August 1992, and it included a sketch of proposed reform principles: defined-contribution lifetime earnings benefit formula; and indexing pension rights and pension payouts to wages. The report outlined two possibilities for financing: full PAYG financing or a combination of PAYG and premium reserve. Thus the working group stuck to the principle of basic security topped up with earnings-related benefits, but the proposed principles would make the reformed system more insurance-like and insulate the system from future demographic and economic shocks. The working group rejected outright any type of reform that would transform the current PAYG into a fully-funded system because of the double payment problem involved (Ds 1992 89: 52).

The report echoed the pessimism of earlier studies, predicting that the ATP system would collapse in 20 or 30 years in its current form. On the financing side, slow economic growth and rising unemployment meant lower revenues. If contributions and benefits remained the same, the AP funds would be empty in 2025 with an average economic growth rate of 2 percent. If economic growth is slower, 1 percent or 0 percent, the AP Funds would be empty by 2015 or 2010 respectively (Ds 1992 89: 30). In order to prevent this, contributions would have to be raised to politically unacceptable levels in order to maintain the value of benefits.

Several of the changes proposed in the 1992 report have been suggested elsewhere. Jan Bröms, chief economist for the Swedish Federation of Professional Employees (SACO), argued for an obligatory system based on actual work performance in a book published in 1990 (Bröms 1990). In its annual survey of the Swedish economy in 1991, the Institute for Economic Studies (*Konjunkturrådet*) painted a picture of the ATP system "in crisis" and argued for a more actuarial system, in particular through the abolition of the 15–30 rule (Söderström 1991). Economist Assar Lindbeck also argued for a shift to a more actuarial system based on defined contributions rather than defined-benefits (Lindbeck 1992). The Economic Commission appointed in 1993 by the Bildt government to propose changes in Swedish institutions also argued for similar provisions (SOU 1993: 16). In sum, even before the working group issued its final report, the basic problems in the pension system had been identified, and the broad principles for pension reform had been made public.

Agreement on the final proposals for pension reform was still difficult. The final report was due in the summer of 1993, but was delayed until January 1994 because of remaining disagreements, particularly the premium reserve and whether contributions should be paid on incomes above the ceiling. The issue of contributions above the income ceiling resulted in tough last minute negotiations. The Liberals and Conservatives opposed contributions above the ceiling, because they did not earn pension rights. The SAP insisted that the system retain its redistributive character, and they pressed for keeping contributions above the ceiling. In January 1994, the group agreed that half of the ATP contribution would be paid on incomes above the ceiling. As a concession, the SAP agreed that this would be called a "tax" rather than a contribution, and the revenue from it would go to the state budget rather than to the pension system. As Bo Könberg put it, "the most important thing is to get the Social Democrats to agree. Then the proposal rests on a foundation that corresponds to 85 to 95 percent of the Parliament and the Swedish population." (*Svenska Dagbladet*, January 12, 1994).

On January 24, 1994, the working group presented its final report outlining the principles of the proposed reform (SOU 1994: 20). The legislation proposed to the Riksdag in late April 1994 conforms closely to these principles.

1. Benefits would be based on lifetime earnings rather than the best 15 years of 30.
2. Pension contributions would be divided evenly between employers and employees. The switch to employee payroll taxes was intended to increase public

awareness of the costs of retirement. Previously, employers paid the pension payroll tax, and it was not reported on wage-earners' paychecks. In addition, only one-half of pension contributions would be paid above the ceiling. Previously, pension contributions were calculated on the entire wage even though pension points were accumulated only up to a specified ceiling.

3. Benefits would be directly linked to the rate of real economic growth rather than inflation, as well as to changes in life expectancy. Consequently, the pension system would be more resistant to economic swings, and it would be be self-financing regardless of the state of the economy.

4. Spouses and partners could share pension rights, and pension points would be earned for military service, the care of small children, and higher education. These provisions were intended to compensate women and white-collar workers adversely affected by the switch to the lifetime earnings principle. The inclusion of pension points for education was a concession to TCO after it had vigorously protested the absence of pension rights for education in the working group's 1992 report. As in the old system, sickness and unemployment compensation earn pension points, but now the state or social insurance authority would pay the contributions for these benefits, resulting in increased costs for the government budget.

5. The new system would contain obligatory individual investment acounts: 2.0 percentage points (later increased to 2.5) would be placed in the so-called "premium reserve."[23] Wage-earners could choose from among different mutual funds or opt for the state to manage their accounts.

6. Finally, the pension system was designed to be transparent in that individuals would receive an annual statement about the size of their projected pension (from both the income pension and premium pension). For the non-Socialist parties, the annual pension statement was an ideological victory. The annual statement would increase public awareness about the pension system; as one participant put it, "households will get an annual statement where they can see which pension rights they have. They can also see that it is more expensive to retire at age 61 than at age 70."[24]

In addition, the old basic pension (*folkpension*) and pension supplement (*pensionstillskott*) would be replaced by a guarantee pension adjusted each year by the new type of index (this was later changed to inflation). The report also recommended replacing the partial pension with a flexible pension age from age 60 and transferring the disability pension scheme from the pension system to the sickness or work injury insurance system.[25] The working group proposed fairly generous transition rules: the new rules would apply to those born after 1954. Those born in 1934, or earlier, will be subject to the old ATP rules, and those born between 1935 and 1953 will receive benefits based on both systems.

The content of the proposed reform was necessarily a compromise between the five parties. The Christian Democrats and Center Party wanted shared pension rights for spouses, the SAP wanted to retain the obligatory system with high replacement rates, while the Liberals and Conservatives wanted a more explicit link between contributions and benefits, the premium reserve, and the elimination of contributions above the ceiling. All of the political parties favored the introduction of real wage indexing. Although the influence of the SAP in the reform process has been substantial, they acquiesced in three main areas: (i) contributions above the ATP ceiling; (ii) shared pension rights; and (iii) the premium reserve system. The switch to visible individual contributions was also a concession by the SAP. The Conservatives also compromised on several issues: contributions above the ceiling were not eliminated, and the premium reserve was probably smaller than they preferred. In the end, the pressure to compromise was intense because of the desire to prevent pensions from becoming an election issue. As SAP representative Anna Hedborg said, "the question is if we shall take the chance to get a broad agreement in the Riksdag or take the risk that something happens in the election campaign...one never knows if one or several parties will defect" (*Dagens Nyheter*, February 5, 1994). It certainly helped that the working group could promise that pensions would not be worse since the proposal assumed that the average wage earner who had worked 40 years would receive a pension equal to 60 percent of average earnings (*Dagens Nyheter*, January 25, 1994).

When the working group's final report was released, both the non-Socialist government and the SAP immediately claimed credit for the proposal, and each side emphasized the importance of the broad parliamentary coalition behind the proposal. The SAP stressed that the new pension system would be acceptable from a redistributive point of view, and the non-Socialist parties emphasized the significance of the fact that wage earners would now have better opportunities to plan for retirement (*Svenska Dagbladet*, January 25, 1994). In essence, the bourgeois government and the SAP had very different interpretations of the pension agreement. Prime Minister Carl Bildt (Conservative) said that the pension proposal "meant a historical departure from a system that no longer functions and that the foundation had now been laid for a new and stable pension system in Sweden." At the same time, the SAP's representatives saw the agreement as a way to "modernize and maintain the system for a long time to come... it means that one of the biggest and most important social reforms of our time will continue to play a decisive role for people's security and welfare" (*Svenska Dagbladet*, January 25, 1994).

If the political parties were satisfied with the proposal, many interest groups were not, especially TCO. TCO President, Björn Rosengren, charged that the switch to the lifetime earnings principle was unfriendly to women and opposed the method for calculating pension points for higher education (*Dagens Nyheter*, January 27, 1994). In April 1994, TCO announced that it was prepared to join forces with LO and SACO to defeat the proposal (*Dagens Nyheter*, April 25, 1994). As one federation leader put it, "it will be difficult for the Social-Democrats and the Liberal Party to push the proposal through in conflict with the entire wage earner collectivity" (*Svenska Dagbladet*, March 29, 1994). LO also publicly criticized several aspects of the reform, especially the change in contributions above the earnings ceiling and the fee swap, but its criticism was muted compared to that of the TCO.

Whereas the Labor organizations opposed many aspects of the proposal, business groups were more or less satisfied. The Employers' Organization (SAF) welcomed the proposal, saying that it would send a positive signal to the rest of the world, strengthen the currency, increase savings and increase work incentives (*Dagens Nyheter*, February 22, 1994). In particular, SAF praised the tighter link between contributions and benefits as well as the change in indexing and the lifetime earnings principle (*Svenska Dagbladet*, January 25, 1994). SAF called the proposal a step forward for Sweden, but complained that workers should still contribute more to their pensions.

In addition to opposition from the labor unions, the proposal also attracted the criticism of economists who pointed out that parts of the reform were not financed. Whereas the proposal largely solved the problem of future demographic shocks, it still did not fully address the system's financing problems. First, the new system required the state to pay the pension contributions for education, care of small children, and military service, necessitating additional state outlays and increased pressure on the budget. The working group proposed to use the AP Funds to cover these transition problems. Second, the AP Funds would have to finance disability pensions and partial pensions until these were reformed or phased out. Finally, the National Social Insurance Board (RFV) also criticized the financial aspects of the proposal, arguing that the reformed system would drain capital from the already diminishing AP Funds (Gauthier 1994a: 6).

Despite these criticisms, the working group members agreed that a parliamentary decision in the spring was absolutely necessary in order to preserve the compromise. According to Bo Könberg, "the longer we wait, the greater the pressure the agreement is exposed to" (*Dagens Nyheter*, February 5, 1994). A quick parliamentary decision required a shorter comment period, prompting severe criticism, in particular from LO and TCO. Working group chairman Bo Könberg answered this criticism by saying that "the pension issue had been investigated for ten years and already in the fall of 1992 the working group had presented a sketch of principles concerning the new system. It is primarily those who are against the reform who demand a longer comment period" (*Dagens Nyheter*, February 5, 1994).

Gaining the support for the party rank and file was a particularly difficult task for the SAP. The party conducted an internal comment process in March, and two-thirds of all responses advised that the reform should be postponed until after the election in September (*Svenska Dagbladet*, April 8, 1994). The SAP executive committee resisted this internal opposition and announced on April 8 that the Riksdag should make a decision on the principles for the reform but also postpone certain issues for further investigation. In particular, the SAP wanted more deliberation about the change in contributions and the administration of the new premium reserve (*Dagens Nyheter*, April 9, 1994). The decision to proceed with legislation met with massive criticism in the media and in the comment statements. Many organizations wanted a longer comment period, but this would have prevented a decision in the spring session of Parliament. The working group's strategy has been to work out the proposal and present it to the Parliament in the spring so that it would not become an election issue. But the pressure on the SAP to wait has been intense, especially from their youth organization and women's organizations (*Svenska Dagbladet*, April 8, 1994; see also Lundberg 2003).

By late March, the unified union front against the proposal began to collapse. The two dominant federations in LO, the Metal Workers Union (*Metallarbetareförbundet*) and the Municipal Workers Union (*Kommunalarbetarförbundet*), were divided. The Metal Workers opposed the proposal, while the Municipal Workers were in favor. The Municipal Workers Union is comprised mainly of women working in lower income jobs, so many members stood to gain from the reformed system. The Retail Workers' Union (*Handelsanställdas Förbund*) and the Paper Workers Union (*Pappers*) joined the Municipal Workers Union in its support. On the union "no" side, only TCO, Metall, and the Union of Municipal Salaried Workers (*Kommunaltjänstemannaförbundet*, SKTF) remained (*Svenska Dagbladet*, March 3, 1994).

Union disunity could have been explosive for LO. LO silently supported the proposed reform, for two reasons. First, the LO leadership wanted a solution to the ATP's problems, so a less redistributive but financially sustainable pension system was preferable to a more redistributive pension system with serious financial imbalances. Second, many LO members stood to gain from the switch to the lifetime earnings benefit formula, and this explains the support of the Municipal Workers Union, the Retail Workers Union and the Paper Workers Union.

In their official comments, the SAF and the Federation of Swedish Industries (*Industriförbundet*, IF) echoed their initial opinion about the proposal but also expressed their desire for a lower pension level and more in the premium reserve. SAF welcomed the proposal but added that the benefit level was still too high and that they could only accept the one-half contribution above the income ceiling as a transitional measure. LO, TCO, and SACO opposed the swap of employer contributions for individual contributions. The Metal Workers Union opposed the lifetime earnings principle and wanted a decrease in the retirement age to 60 or 61 since few of their members work until age 65. LO in particular voiced doubts that the employers would raise wages to compensate for the swap. SAF and IF fueled this disagreement when they issued a joint statement declaring that it was not the intention of the working group that workers would be fully compensated for the change in financing. SAF accused the unions of using their opposition to the fee swap as a back door method to get SAF to agree to the resumption of centralized wage bargaining. SAF agreed to the fee swap in principle, but would not promise anything. In particular, SAF pointed out that because of economic conditions or tax policies, there might not be room for wage increases equal to the decrease in employer contributions (*Svenska Dagbladet*, February 9, 1994). In response, Bo Könberg accused SAF of playing a high stakes game which could endanger the reform agreement (*Dagens Nyheter*, February 4, 1994).

Clearly, the parties backing the agreement did their utmost to preserve the compromise and prevent pension reform from becoming an election issue. Having overcome the parliamentary veto point through pre-parliamentary agreement, the last thing the working group wanted was a potential veto point in the electorate. Moreover, sealing the agreement in the spring would ensure that blame would be divided between five political parties. To the extent that pension reform was discussed in the September election campaign, it would be difficult for voters to punish any one particular party for pension reform.

The Riksdag approved the basic principles of the pension reform on June 8, 1994 by a vote of 279–19 (Proposition 1993/94: 250).[26] Several issues remained to be settled, so the parties behind the reform appointed an "implementation group" (*genomförandegruppen*) to work out remaining details. The items left unresolved were whether the new guarantee pension would be reduced for those who have contractual occupational pensions, the construction of the premium reserve, the swap in contributions, the economic adjustment index, the balancing mechanism, and the details of pension rights for students (Gauthier 1994b: 3).

Sticking to the agreement and working out the details

Since the adoption of principles for the new system in 1994, subsequent decisions were delayed several times. As expected, the SAP won the September 1994 election and formed a minority government with the support of the Left Party. Soon after taking office, the SAP passed legislation for a one-year delay in implementing the reform in order to gain more time to investigate the transition to the new eligibility rules (Proposition 1994/95: 100, bilaga 6). The SAP's intention was to present final legislation to the Riksdag in the spring of 1995. Despite this delay, the new financing rules of the pension system took effect in January 1995, including the one percent individual pension contribution and the contributions to the premium reserve system. The National Debt Office administered the premium reserve contributions until a new state agency was established.

The SAP could not agree on spring legislation, and events in late 1995 delayed matters further. SAP Prime Minister Ingvar Carlsson announced he would retire in early 1996, and this led to several months of speculation about his successor. The change in leadership required a special Social-Democratic Party Congress during which the pension reform could easily become a major issue. The four non-socialist parties agreed to wait until after the SAP Congress to negotiate the remaining provisions of the reform, but issued stern warnings in the media about a possible SAP defection.

To be sure, the SAP had consulted its membership already in 1992/93, but there was only lukewarm interest; the comment period was even extended by three months to increase the response rate (Lundberg 2003: 243–5). Whereas the party leadership had lined up in favor of reform by 1992, the membership had not. There was little awareness of the ATP's weaknesses or reform proposals among the party rank and file. Once the Riksdag had adopted the reform principles in 1994, however, opponents began to mobilize and the party leadership was forced repeatedly to defend the reform.

In January 1996, motions from the SAP rank and file began to flood into party headquarters in anticipation of the Party Congress in March. A total of 320 motions demanded that the pension reform be shelved and the previous system re-introduced

(*Svenska Dagbladet*, January 9, 1996).[27] As criticism swelled, one member of the working group stated that an SAP defection would be a "disaster for Sweden" and that the Conservatives would never make a cross-party agreement with the SAP again.[28] The SAP leadership managed to resist the pressure from below, but only by promising more consultation with members. Ingela Thalén (now Party Chairwoman) suggested taking the pension reform off the congress agenda, and conducting a separate internal consulation (*rådslag*), after which the party would make a final decision (*LO-tidningen*, March 22, 1996). This placated opponents but unsurprisingly angered the non-socialist parties behind the reform. The internal consultation (held in summer 1996) got a much higher response than earlier consultations, and the comments repeated earlier criticisms, especially concerning the premium reserve.[29] The party leadership was criticized for providing inadequate information to members about why the pension system required reform in the first place, and for not communicating what the party had "won" in terms of concessions from the bourgeois parties. Given that the reformed system would provide better benefits to most LO members than the old ATP system, it is surprising that this message was so poorly communicated (*Dagens Industri*, 30 November, 1996). The SAP member of the implementation group played down the issue, however, referring to the unfinished work of the committee established to propose the detailed structure of the premium pension (*LO-tidningen*, May 16, 1997).

Technical details also led to additional delays and gave opponents time to mobilize. In its budget bill presented in September 1996, the SAP proposed a one-year delay in the implementation of the eligibility rules of the new system, until January 1, 1999. The first pensions paid according to the new rules would also be moved up one year, to 2001 (Proposition 1996/97:1). The rationale for this second delay was the need to adapt the social insurance administrative apparatus to the new eligibility rules.

Despite massive grass roots criticism, the SAP leadership stuck to the deal. Clearly the leadership did not want to divide the party in the run-up to the 1998 election or damage the party's ability to make deals with the non-socialist parties. A regular party congress was scheduled for September 1997, so SAP leader and Prime Minister Göran Persson met with the leaders of the four non-socialist parties behind the agreement on January 17, 1997 to discuss the fee swap and the premium reserve. By now it was clear that the fee swap was unworkable, largely because employers would not guarantee that wage-earners would be compensated for the individual contributions. The one percent individual contribution was already in place, but the group had to identify a feasible method for increasing individual contributions to 9.25 percent of qualifying wages. The group decided to investigate three possibilities: transferring the individual contribution for sickness insurance to the pension system; having employers pay most of the contribution; and increasing the basic tax deduction to compensate wage earners for higher contributions. In addition, the group agreed on another expert report on the premium reserve (Lundberg 2003: 267) and to scrap shared pension rights for spouses in the income pension system but to allow this in the premium pension scheme (Dahlin 1997: 3; SOU 1997: 31).

The 1997 regular Party Congress was the scene of heated debate. Again, opponents generated motions extremely critical of the reform as well as the leadership's lack of internal democracy. After tough negotiations with the reform's opponents, the leadership won approval from the membership for the reform. Lundberg (2003: 272–3) reports that the critics faced intense pressure to drop their opposition, largely because of the potential repurcussions for the party's parliamentary cooperation with the Center Party. The pension reform was not the only thing at stake; the SAP's budget consolidation plans at that time rested on the support of the Center Party, and an SAP defection would jeopardize the government's legislative agenda. To get the Congress' support, the SAP leadership compromised with party opponents on several issues that the implementation group had not resolved (*LO-tidningen*, September 19, 1997). The SAP would push for a state agency to administer the premium pension as well as the introduction of a state-run default fund for those who do not choose a fund. Secondly, the SAP would push for the individual contribution in the sickness insurance scheme to be transferred to the pension system, thereby solving the problem of what to do about the fee swap. LO also supported some version of converting the sickness insurance contribution into the pension contribution.

The SAP now had to convince the four other parties behind the reform to accept these changes. The Liberals held fast to the fee swap principle, but an expert report published by the Ministry of Social Affairs (Ds 1997: 67) supported the SAP's position. The implementation group met for negotiations on January 9, 1998. The SAP accepted a somewhat larger individual account premium reserve (2.5% instead of 2%) in return for the non-socialist parties' acceptance of its model for individual contributions. The sickness insurance contribution would simply be renamed the pension contribution, while employers would take over the entire contribution for sickness insurance. Employees' pension contributions would also increase an additional one percentage point. The non-socialist parties also agreed to the introduction of a publicly administered fund to compete with private funds in the premium reserve, as well as a provision that those who do not choose a fund will have their money invested in a publicly-managed fund.[30]

In mid-January, the party leaders met to seal the agreement made by the implementation group and agreed to legislate the remaining details of the reform before the 1998 election. The main issue to be settled was the design of the premium reserve. Prime Minister Göran Persson (SAP) stuck to the agreement that the individual accounts would be obligatory but now had an irresitable incentive for the non-socialists to agree to state administration of the individual accounts. Since 1995, contributions to the individual accounts (11% of contributions) had been accumulating at the National Debt Office until the new scheme was up and running. By early 1998 there was SEK 20 billion in these accounts, which were counted as government assets for EMU accounting purposes. At the time, Sweden was trying to qualify for EMU, and Persson did not want to give up the advantage having premium pension capital count as a positive entry on government financial balance sheets (*Dagens Industri*, March 7, 1998).

The Persson government duly appointed an expert group to propose how to set up the new state agency, the Premium Pension Authority (PPM). By now the SAP had clearly conceded much ground. In 1996, the government had appointed an expert group to propose how to set up the premium reserve. In its instructions, the government recommended an insurance-like arrangement based on fund managers rather than individual choice (SOU 1996: 83). Expert Lennart Låftman (previously the head of the wage earner funds) recommended individual accounts instead. The January agreement with the non-socialist parties behind the reform made this a reality.

The expert group investigating the construction of the PPM moved quickly, releasing its report in June 1998 (SOU 1998: 87). The issue was fairly non-controversial, and the new agency was formally established on July 1, 1998. Contributions had been accumulating since 1995, but the first active fund choice did not take place until 2000.

The government proposed two detailed bills on April 2, 1998, one on the income pension (Proposition 1997/98: 150) and one on the guarantee pension (Proposition 1997/98: 152). The income pension bill dealt with the issues discussed above, while the guarantee pension bill included modifications negotiated by the implementation group in 1997 and 1998. The 1994 agreement called for guarantee pensions to be tested against all other pension income, including private and occupational pensions. The 1998 legislation changed this: income from the premium pension, private pensions and occupational pensions do not affect the level of the guarantee pension (see Ds 1997: 66). Both bills passed easily on June 8 (257 in favor, 17 against, and 16 abstentions). In the rush to pass the legislation before the September 1998 election, however, the government left several issues unresolved: the automatic balancing mechanism, the transfer of capital from the AP Funds to the state, and pension credits for higher education.

The buffer funds

The transfer of funds from the AP funds to the state was crucial in funding the transition to the new system. Because the reform involved higher costs for the government budget,[31] the working group recommended that the AP Funds pay the state SEK 300–350 billion. In 1997/98 capital in the AP Funds totalled SEK 715 billion. An expert report on the issue pointed out that SEK 475 billion would be required to meet the costs foreseen by the 1994 legislation, so the report recommended a transfer of SEK 300–350 billion from the AP Funds to the state in 1999 (Ds 1998: 7). The 1998 legislation called for two initial transfers in 1999 and 2000 of SEK 45 billion each (Proposition 1997/98: 151) and requested more investigation on the amount of the remaining transfer. The implementation group stuck to the recommendations of the expert report and decided on a third payment of SEK 155 billion in January 2001, bringing the total transfer to SEK 258 billion. This legislation passed easily in the Riksdag (Proposition 1999/2000: 46).

The transfers from the AP Funds to the state were projected to improve government finances dramatically. The state was expected to save about SEK 20 billion per year in interest payments alone. Between 1999 and 2001, accumulated public sector debt was projected to decrease by 23 percent of GDP, with one-third of the decrease coming from the AP Fund transfer (Norrbom 1998: 9). Several groups criticized the timing and magnitude of the measure, however. The National Social Insurance Board (RFV) recommended delaying the transfer, arguing that the intended amount was too high. The LO expressed its concern about transferring such a large amount, fearing that the depletion of the buffer funds would increase the likelihood of the automatic balancing mechanism kicking in. And the SPRF (pensioners' organization) opposed the transfer, arguing that the money belonged to pensioners. TCO was also skeptical, claiming the level of the transfer was higher than the costs for the state taking over the disability pension. These criticisms were not without effect; the implementation group agreed on a smaller amount than originally intended (SEK 258 billion instead of SEK 300–350 billion) and recommended that the government should wait until 2004 and then investigate whether additional transfers should be made (Proposition 1999/2000: 46). The group agreed on a rule stipulating that the amount of the transfer had to be small enough to ensure that the "automatic balancing" procedure would not have to be used before 2050. The issue still has not been settled: in June 2004 the implementation group decided to stick to the agreement, but ruled out a transfer for January 2005 because of the low level of the balance ratio (see below).

Automatic balancing

In May 2001, the Riksdag adopted legislation on the automatic balancing mechanism (Proposition 2000/01: 70). The issue had been studied in detail since 1997 (Ds 1997: 67) but techincal issues as well as the implementation group's negotiations on other items delayed legislation. One of the primary goals of the reform was to make the new pension system financially stable and sustainable, and several provisions promoted this: the switch to defined contributions; income indexing; and adjustments for changes in life expectancy. However, the reform's architects wanted to go further and introduce an automatic balancing mechanism to ensure that long-term pension liabilities did not exceed notional and real assets.

An expert group in the Ministry of Social Affairs worked with the implementation group to make recommendations for the structure of the automatic balancing mechanism, and the group issued its report in 1999 (Ds 1999: 43). The National Social Insurance Board also carried out an expert analysis (RFV 2000). The automatic balancing procedure is an explicit attempt to prioritize fairness between the generations over the rate of return on any one generations' pension level. The expert group settled on a method for calculating the ratio of notional pension liabilities to assets, the balance ratio (*balanstal*). Assets are the value of future contributions and the capital in the buffer funds, and this number is divided by the notional value of pension liabilities. If the balance ratio is 1.0 or more, the system has a surplus. If the ratio is below 1.0, the system has a deficit, and the automatic balancing procedure is activated. Pension credits and outgoing payments are indexed to the "balance index" (instead of the adjustment index for pension payments and the income index for pension rights). The "balance index" is wage growth multiplied by the balance ratio. Like all of the other legislation, this bill passed easily in 2001.

The issue of automatic balancing also raised the question of what to do with possible surpluses. The government appointed a Commission of Inquiry to study the issue, and it recommended using a balance ratio of 1.1 (assets equal to 110% of liabilities) as the threshold at which a surplus could be dedicated to both pension payments and notional pension assets (SOU 2004: 105). The SAP government announced in its budget for 2006 that it would consult with the four non-Socialist parties that backed the reform about the final legislation, expected in 2006 or 2007. However, given the low balance ratio of the AP Funds, the chances of an additional transfer in the next few years is unlikely.[32]

Effects of the reform

The new pension system is a major departure from existing policy, and identifying "winners" and "losers" is difficult. One thing is clear, however: the switch from defined benefits to defined contributions in the ATP system is a radical change, and this will mean that the new system will have much less potential for "decommodification" than the old system. A study conducted by the National Social Insurance Board (RFV) estimated that two-thirds of those studied would be losers in the new system, mainly TCO members and women (SOU 1994: 21. bilaga A). The biggest losers are those who work 20 to 40 years before retirement. The biggest winners are those who work less than 20 years and receive the new higher guarantee pension. In order to receive the same pension benefits under the new system as in the old, one must work at least 40 years. Still, this group, about 80 percent of the population, loses about 7–8 percent in pension value because of the new index rules. Women with little or no education fare the best, while women with higher education and fewer working years lose the most—about 17 percent. These calculations are based on a yearly economic growth rate of 1.5 percent. At higher rates of growth, pensions go up. Still, under the new system, at a yearly growth rate of 1.5 percent, pensions would be 12 percent lower. Only if growth is 2 percent will pensions remain about the same. In sum, the effects of the reform differ widely among social groups, but the overall impact is that of less decommodification. A later study found that the effects of the new system depend on economic growth. At 2 percent annual growth, the new system pays somewhat higher benefits than the ATP system. At zero growth, the opposite is true (Dudziuk et al. 1999).

These losses must be viewed in the context of the improvements introduced by the reform. Probably the most important improvement is the vastly enhanced long-term financial stability of the pension system. Secondly, the new income pension system pays benefits indexed to earnings rather than inflation, thereby halting the slow erosion of the value of ATP pensions as more and more wage-earners had earnings above the ATP ceiling for which they received no benefits. Finally, the new pension system stops the ATP system's unintended redistribution from low income groups to high income groups because of the 15/30 rule (Anderson and Meyer 2003).

In 1999, the first pensions were paid out according to the reformed system. In 2003, the basic pension was eliminated, and the first retirees covered by the premium pension reached the age of 65. Economic adjustment indexing has been in effect since

2002, for both the income pensions and those still covered by ATP. So far, the new index has meant higher cumulative uprating of benefits than under the old system, because real income growth was higher than the "norm" of 1.6 percent between 2001 and 2005 (RFV 2005: 5). Indeed, pensions increased by 0.5 percentage points more than would have been the case in the old system. However, the balance ratio has fallen to 1,0014 for 2006, dangerously close to the point when automatic balancing is activated. This negative trend is due to higher unemployment; average income has increased faster than the sum of contributions.

The premium reserve has been in operation since 2000 (although contributions have been in place since 1995). In the initial round of fund choice (2000), the PPM offered 462 funds, including the default fund, the Premium Savings Fund, and 4.4 participants chose funds worth SEK 56 billion (www.ppm.nu). About SEK 20 billion in contributions are added each year. The PPM estimates that by the end of 2005, 5.4 million participants had invested SEK 190 billion in their PPM accounts, about half in equities, and 31% in the Premium Savings Fund (PPM 2005). Seventy-eight percent of those with premium pension accounts have seen their account balances increase since the scheme was introduced, despite the stock market downturn in the early 2000s.[33] The number of active choosers has declined significantly, even as the number of fund choices has increased. Since the initial fund choice round, only 10–15 percent of new participants (110,000–120,000) have made an active choice; 688 funds were offered in 2005.

V Conclusion

Summary of the magnitude of changes

The 1994 reform is surprising for its radicalness and that it was adopted under adverse political circumstances. The non-socialist government included four parties, and as a minority government it had to seek the support of the opposition Social Democrats. The Social Democrats supported the reform and stuck to the agreement, despite union criticism and rank and file opposition, and even after the party won handily in the 1994 election. The reform process took ten years (1991–2001), and the cross-party coalition supporting the agreement has remained stable even through three election campaigns (1994, 1998, and 2001). No matter which parties were in government, representatives of the five parties behind the reform negotiated the details of legislation. In short, the five parties kept the pension issue out of electoral competition by negotiating reform content in small working groups and sticking to their agreement to not let the pension reform become an election issue. This was especially tricky for the SAP. Indeed, opposition from party rank and file nearly derailed the reform in 1996 and 1997.

The 1994/98 reform is a radical overhaul. An overarching objective of the pension reform is to separate "social insurance" (collective provision for risk) from "social policy" (objectives not based on shared risk), both in terms of program structure and financing. The new earnings-related scheme is autonomous and includes a notional defined-contribution scheme (income pension) and funded individual accounts (premium pension). Contributions are divided between employers and employees, retirement age is flexible starting at 61, and the system has built-in automatic stabilizers to ensure that long-term pension liabilities do not exceed notional assets. Disability pensions and widow's pensions have been transferred to the government budget. The state is also responsible for basic security via the guarantee pension.

In addition to this structural reform, Swedish governments adopted a number of incremental cuts in the early 1980s and the first half of the 1990s designed to reduce public spending in the context of acute budget imbalances. These reductions were eliminated after state finances improved, but pensioners have not been fully compensated for their losses.

Impact of the political system on pension politics

We argue in this chapter that the Social Democratic leadership's decision to cooperate with the non-socialist parties on the 1994/98 reform represents a sea change in party strategy. The reform contained several provisions that were unattractive to SAP voters (defined-contributions; premium reserve), and one might have expected the opposition SAP to have little incentive to cooperate. The SAP could simply have waited out the non-socialist government's term in office and adopted its own reform; indeed the financial reserves in the pension funds (AP Funds) were sufficient to finance several years of benefits even without contributions. Indeed, there was intense pressure on the SAP to defect from the agreement. Why did the SAP go along with the reform? According to Lundberg (2003: 166), the SAP leadership began to coalesce around the belief that reform was necessary, even if there was no consensus about what the reform should look like. The situation was very different at the grass roots level, however, where there was very little support for major reform—the pension issue was not even the topic of debate. Thus the SAP's role in the reform was very much top–down; it was a process in which a small number of party officials came up with a vision of how to reform the system, and then convinced the leadership that the SAP should cooperate with the non-socialists. SAP representatives then negotiated with the non-socialists without much input from the party. Then the party had huge problems convincing the rank and file to accept the reform, after it had finished the negotiations with the non-socialists.

We argue that this can only be explained by the leadership's coming to terms with the party's loss of hegemony. The 1991 election shattered all remaining hopes of outcompeting the opposition by "reforming" society and "going beyond" the welfare state. The psychological shock of being so roundly ousted from office (Könberg cited in Haag 2000: 51, 63) opened up SAP negotiators and policy experts to looking for new solutions, and leaving their routinized commitment to ATP behind. Permanent minority status meant that the party needed to rely on legislative coalitions, and hence credibility in policy bargaining was at a new premium, as the leadership stressed repeatedly in its arguments to its base.

Party leaders across the board did everything they could to keep pensions from being an election issue. Here, the working group—which in some ways resembles the old-style committee work and administrative expertise so stressed by Heclo (1974)—was helpful (Anderson and Weaver n.d.). But equally important was the long-term strategy of the party leadership: to adopt an elder statesmanlike attitude and problem-solving mode of policy-making. This meant sticking to political bargains, and achieving greater independence from interest groups, including the unions. Greater political competition thus forced the SAP to look for a new way to compete in changed circumstances: competent governance rather than welfare state expansion was now the winning ticket. But not just the Social Democrats, the three traditional non-socialist parties also recognized that to make progress in pension reform, the parties would have to keep the issue out of the electoral arena.

Interest group influence

The reform process was atypical by Swedish standards because interest groups were explicitly excluded from the negotiations. The five political parties behind the compromise agreed to conduct their negotiations in a closed, parliamentary working group. Interest groups had access to most of the working group's materials and had the opportunity to comment on the group's proposals, but they had few opportunities to influence the content of the reform or the direction of the negotiations. Additionally, the political parties backing the agreement gave their negotiators unprecedented authority to negotiate without interference from the party rank and file. The exclusion of interest groups was part of the working group's strategy to de-politicize the reform, and it was a strategy that hurt TCO the most. The LO silently supported the reform. This is not to say that LO and TCO were unimportant. It is worth noting, however, that they did not set the terms of the reform debate and could not block proposals contrary to their interests, something they often did in the 1980s.

Constraints of policy design

In Sweden, politicians faced a popular, universal, and nearly mature pension system. The "lock-in" effects of pension policy development dictated that reform would have to take place within the structure of the existing system. The non-socialist parties recognized this, but the large capital reserves in the AP Funds provided an opening for fundamental change. The role of the AP Funds in facilitating the transition to the new pension system can hardly be exaggerated. By 2004, the AP Funds had transferred SEK 350 billion (about €38 billion) to the government budget to compensate the state for increased costs resulting from the reform. This made it possible to devote a larger share of contributions to income pensions (16% as compared to 12% of qualifying income in the old system), and to devote 2.5 percentage points to the new funded accounts. Thus the reform means that more resources are going to earnings-related pensions while the state takes over the non-insurance functions of the old pension system (basic security, survivor's pensions, disability pensions). The financial cushion provided by the AP Funds gave reformers a degree of maneuvering room that simply does not exist in other public pension systems (Anderson and Meyer 2003).

The role of the AP funds is important for another reason as well: as assets accumulate in the new premium reserve, it will eventually replace the AP funds as a source of investment capital. Although this aspect of the reform would not affect the level of benefits, it was a major victory for the non-socialist parties because they succeeded in the partial privatization of very large publicly controlled pension funds.

Finally, Anderson and Meyer (2003) argue that the reform was an opportunity for political actors to pursue a strategy of "rationalizing redistribution" (Myles and Pierson 2001) because the existing benefit formula (the 15/30 rule) was considered unjust. (See also Palme 2003). This feature of the old system was repeatedly criticized by reformers, and given the very high levels of female labor force participation, the rationale behind the old rules was hard to justify.

Role of ideas and historical context

Ideas and history were important in two ways. First, the symbolic importance of the ATP scheme in Swedish labor politics both constrained and facilitated reform. Until their massive electoral loss in 1991, SAP party leaders were loath to touch their "jewel in the crown." Nevertheless, once the leadership decided to accept reform, its strong track record in defending the welfare state gave it the credibility to push through changes—particularly in order to correct the weaknesses that had emerged in the three decades since ATP was introduced. Chief among these was ATP's benefit formula that actually disadvantaged important SAP continuents: blue-collar workers with flat earnings profiles and well-paid blue collar workers with earnings above the ceiling.

Ideas were important in a second way as well. The working group agreed on a core set of principles to guide the pension reform process. This overarching vision of how the system should be reformed was shared by key experts and politicians. This included the shift to the notional defined-contribution system, the introduction of automatic stabilizers, the autonomy of the pension system from the rest of the government budget, and the separation of social policy and social insurance. Agreement on core principles allowed the working group to find common ground and compromise on content, like the premium reserve. Nevertheless, while technical expertise and policy ideas were important in shielding reform negotiations from political competition, some of the main changes echo previous policy debates. The premium reserve, after all, was the principle behind the 1913 Law; and eliminating the 15/30 rule simply meant a retraction of the concession made to white-collar workers in the 1959 reform.

Abbreviations

ATP	*Allmänna tilläggspensionssystem* (Supplementary Pension System)
IF	*Industriförbundet* (Federation of Swedish Industries)
LO	*Landsorganisationen i Sverige* (Swedish Trade Union Confederation)
PPM	*Premiepensionsmyndighet* (Premium Pension Authority)
RFV	*Riksförsäkringsverket* (National Social Insurance Board)
SACO	*Sveriges Akademikers Centralorganisation* (Confederation of Professional Associations)
SAF	*Svenska Arbetsgivareföreningen* (Swedish Employers Confederation)
SAP	*Sveriges Socialdemokratiska Arbetareparti* (Swedish Social Democratic Party)
TCO	*Tjänstemännens Centralorganisation* (Central Organization of Salaried Employees)

Notes

1. A legacy of these struggles was the Swedish tradition of administrative independence from both Monarch and Parliament in the form of independent agencies (*ämbetsverk*) governed by administrative boards (*styrelser*), often with corporatist representation. See Heclo & Madsen 1987; Anton 1980.
2. On Swedish political institutions, see Bergman 2003; Pettersson 1998; and Larsson 1993.
3. The Riksdag has to vote against the same candidate for PM four times before new elections are called.
4. For discussions of the ATP reform, see Heclo 1974 (ch. 5, esp. p. 246).
5. This change was intended to help wage-earners between the ages of 60 and 64 in poor health or with physically taxing jobs.
6. The partial pension paid 65 percent of lost income without reducing the amount of pension points earned until retirement age.
7. The collective agreement pensions provide pension benefits for income over the ceiling for earnings-related pensions, and four such systems today cover 90% of the labor market. See Palmer and Wadensjö 2004.
8. All citizens were entitled to the basic pension while ATP provided benefits based on previous income from work. In addition, the partial pension (*delpension*) and disability pension (*förtidspension*) provided benefits for early retirees.
9. The National Insurance Office (*Försäkringskassan*) took over this function from the National Social Insurance Board (*Riksförsäkringsverket*) in 2005.
10. On the premium pension see Weaver 2003/2004.

11. The pension contribution is not pension-carrying, so 93% of 8.07 income base amounts is 7.5 income base amounts (100% − 7% fee = 93%).
12. The amount of the pension credit is calculated according to the most favorable of three methods and goes to the mother unless the parents apply for the father to receive the credit. One of the calculation methods is to award the pension credit for income equivalent to one "base amount," or €4,500. Sixty percent of women are eligible for a higher credit. See *RFV redovisar* 1999: 12. Den nya allmänna pensionen.
13. In the new system, AP Funds 1–4, and 7 are the buffer funds. In the old system, AP Funds 1–4, 6, and 7 were the buffers.
14. Proposition 2005/06: 01. *Ålderspensionssystemet vid sidan av statsbudgeten*.
15. In 2004, the balance ratio was 1.0014. Notional assets were SEK 5,607 billion, and financial assets in the AP Funds were SEK 646 billion, for a total of SEK 6,263 billion in assets. Liabilities were SEK 6,244 billion.
16. The ceiling is 3.16 price base amounts for singles and 2.8275 price base amounts for spouses.
17. Those born earlier fall under the old system, so they received the old basic pension (and possibly supplements) until 2003, when a transitional guarantee pension was introduced for this particular group. The transitional guarantee pensions pays the same net amount as the old basic pension and pension supplements that the retired person was entitled to before 2003.
18. For example, if the income index is 2.0, the economic adjustment index is 2.0−1.6 = 0.4. 1.6% is deducted because the same percentage rate of return is applied to the notional annuity at retirement. Thus the annuity is front-loaded and this is compensated for afterwards by the construction of the economic adjustment index.
19. The calculation is proportional. For example, someone born in 1940 receives 13/16 of his/her pension from the old system and 3/16 from the new.
20. Thorbjörn Fälldin (Center Party) Oct. 1976–Oct. 1978; Ola Ullsten (Liberals) Oct. 1978–Oct. 1979; Thorbjörn Fälldin (Center Party) Oct. 1979–Oct. 1982.
21. The base amount is adjusted once per year for price increases. Because the base amount determines benefits in all pension programs (basic pension, ATP, disability pension, partial pension), a single adjustment would apply to all types of pension benefits. The non-Socialist government used the strategy in 1981, and even before the economic crisis hit, the SAP government secured support for an indexing rule (as part of the tax reform negotiated between the SAP and Liberal Party in 1990) that did not take into account all price increases for 1991 and 1992.
22. Unless otherwise noted, this section is based on Lundberg 2003, ch. 5; Anderson 2005; and Anderson and Weaver n.d.
23. This was later changed to 2.5%.
24. Margit Gennser (Conservative) in *Svenska Dagbladet*, January 25, 1994.
25. As part of the crisis packages between the Bildt government and the SAP in the fall of 1992, an Official Commission of Inquiry was set up to investigate the disability pension system.
26. Several minor changes were made in response to the *remiss* statements. The most important change concerned implementing the fee swap all at once rather than in steps.
27. Lundberg 2003: 257 reports a different number: 80 motions concerning the pension system, 42 of which proposed rescinding the reform.
28. Margit Gennser (Conservative) in *Svenska Dagbladet*, January 10, 1996.
29. The detailed results were never released. See Lundberg 2003: 267.
30. The individual contribution would be 8.47% of gross wages (9.25% of pension-carrying income), an increase in the total of existing individual contributions (the sickness

insurance contribution) of 1.5 percentage points. The standard income tax deduction would also be raised to compensate wage earners for higher contributions.
31. The government budget would not pay disability pensions, partial pensions, widow's pensions, and the guarantee pension. The disability pension alone was calculated to cost SEK 50 billion annually for several years.
32. Proposition 2005/06: 1. *Ålderspensionssystemet vid sidan av statsbudgeten*: 10.
33. Proposition 2005/06: 1. *Ålderspensionssystemet vid sidan av statsbudgeten*: 13. See Weaver 2003/2004 for further details.

Bibliography

Primary sources and government documents

Acts and bills

Proposition 1993/94: 250 *Reformering av det allmänna pensionssystemet*
Proposition 1994/95: 100 *Förslag till statsbudget för budgetåret 1995/96. Bilaga 6*
Proposition 1996/97: 1 *Förslag till statsbudget för budgetåret 1997, m.m*
Proposition 1997/98: 150 *1998 års ekonomiska vårproposition*
Proposition 1997/98: 151 *Inkomstgrundad ålderspension*
Proposition 1997/98: 152 *Garantipension m.m.*
Proposition 1997/98: 111 *Reformerad förtidspension*
Proposition 1999/2000: 46 *AP-fonden i det reformerade pensionssystemet*
Proposition 2000/2001: 70 *Automatisk balansering av ålderspensionssystemet*
Proposition 2005/06: 1 *Ålderspensionssystemet vid sidan av statsbudgeten*

Official government reports

Ds 1992: 89. *Ett reformerat pensionssystem- Bakgrund, principer och skiss. En promemoria av Pensionsarbetsgruppen*
Ds 1995: 29 *Vissa frågor avseende allmänna egenavgifter*
Ds 1995: 41. *Reformerat pensionssystem*
Ds 1995: 55 *Utvidgad avgiftsskyldighet vad avser ålderspension*
Ds 1997: 66. *Garantipension och samordningsfrågor*
Ds 1997: 67. *Inkomstgrundad ålderspension, finansiella frågor*
Ds 1998: 7 *AP-fonden i det reformerade pensionssystemet*
Ds 1998: 31 *Sammanställning av remissyttranden över betänkanden som legat till grund för propositionen om reformerat ålderspensionssystem*
Ds 1999: 43. *Automatisk balansering av ålderspensionssystemet*
SOU 1987: 55 *Efterlevandepension*
SOU 1990: 76. *Allmän pension*
SOU 1993: 16. *Nya villkor för ekonomi och politik*
SOU 1994: 20. *Reformerat pensionssystem*
SOU 1994: 21. *Reformerat pensionssystem. Kostnader och individeffekter. Bilaga A*
SOU 1996: 83. *Allmänt pensionssparande. Premiepension*
SOU 1997: 131. *Lag om premiepension*
SOU 1998: 87. *Betänkande av utredning om premiepensionsmyndigheten*
SOU 2000: 94. *Fördelningen av AP-fondens tillgångar*
SOU 2004: 105. *Utdelning av överskott i inkomstpensionssystemet*

Periodicals and newspapers

Dagens Industri
Dagens Nyheter

LO tidningen
RFV redovisar
RRV Anser
Svenska Dagbladet

Secondary sources

Ackerby, Stefan (1992). *Pensionsfrågan. Bilaga 12 till Långtidsutredningen 1992*. Stockholm: Ministry of Finance.

Anderson, Karen M. (2001). "The Politics of Retrenchment in a Social Democratic Welfare State. Reform of Swedish Pensions and Unemployment Insurance." *Comparative Political Studies*, 34 (9): 1063–91.

—— (2005). "Sweden: Radical Reform in a Mature Pension System." In Bonoli, G. and Shinkawa, T. (eds.), *Ageing and Pension Reform around the World*. Cheltenham: Edward Elgar.

—— and Meyer, Traute (2003). "Social Democracy, Unions, and Pension Politics in Germany and Sweden." *Journal of Public Policy*, 23, 1 (January): 23–54.

—— and Weaver, R. Kent (n.d.). "Pension Politics in Sweden: Fundamental Reforms in a Policy Cartel." Unpublished manuscript.

Anton, Thomas, J. (1980). *Administered Politics. Elite Political Culture in Sweden*. Boston: Martinus Nijhoff Publishing.

Bergman, Torbjörn (1995). *Constitutional Rules and Party Goals in Coalition Formation. An Analyis of Winning Minority Governments in Sweden*. Research Report 1995: 1. Umeå: Umeå University.

—— (2003). "Sweden: From Separation of Power to Parliamentary Supremacy—and Back Again?" In Strøm, K., Müller, W. C., and Bergman, T. (eds.), *Delegation and Accountability in Parliamentary Democracies*. Oxford: Oxford University Press, 594–619.

Bröms, Jan (1990). *Ur askan av ATP*. Stockholm: SACO, 1990.

Dahlin, Ann (1997). "Sänkt ålderspension betalar höjd garantipension." *Riksdag och departement*. 32, 3.

Dudziuk, Andrej, Ehnsoon, Gudrun E., Röstberg, Anna, and Westerberg, Anna. (1999). "Jämförelse av inkomsgrundad pension i den nya allmänna pensionen och i ATP-systemet." Bilaga till *RFV Redovisar* 1999: 12.

Elmér, Åke (1960). *Folkpensionieringen i Sverige*. Stockholm: Gleerups.

Folksam (various years). *Vår trygghet. Våra sociala rättigheter*. Stockholm: Folksam.

Gauthier, Kristina (1994a). "Pensionsförslagets financiering oroar remissinstanser." *Riksdag och department*. 14, 6–7.

—— (1994b). "Utan garantier ingen växling av egenavgifter." *Riksdag och departement*, 16.

Gilljam, Mikael, and Holmberg, Sören (1993). *Väljarna inför 90-talet*. Stockholm: Norstedts.

Haag, Dorothée (2000). *Die Schwedische Rentenreform 1998: Analyse eines Gesetzgebungsprozesses*. Diplomarbeit. Konstanz: University of Konstanz.

Hadenius, Stig, Molin, Björn and Wiesander, Hans, (1991). *Sverige efter 1900. En modern politisk historia*. 12th edn Stockholm: Bonniers.

Heclo, Hugh (1974). *Modern Social Politics in Britain and Sweden. From Relief to Income Maintenance*. New Haven: Yale University Press.

—— and Madsen, Henrik (1987). *Policy and Politics in Sweden: Principled Pragmatism*. Philadelphia: Temple University Press.

Holmberg, Sören and H. Oscarsson (2004). *Väljare, Svenskt väljarbeteende under 50 år*. Stockholm: Norstedts Juridik.

IMMERGUT, ELLEN M. (2002). "The Swedish Constitution and Social Democratic Power: Measuring the Mechanical Effect of a Political Institution." *Scandinavian Political Studies*, 25, (3): 231–57.

—— and JOCHEM, SVEN (2006). "The Political Frame for Negotiated Capitalism: Electoral Reform and the Politics of Crisis in Japan and Sweden." *Governance*, 19, 1 (January): 99–133.

KATO, JUNKO, and ROTHSTEIN, BO (2006). "Government Partisanship and Managing the Economy: Japan and Sweden in Comparative Perspective." *Governance*, 19, 1 (January): 75–97.

LARSSON, TORBJÖRN (1993). *Det svenska statsskicket*. Lund: Studentlitteratur, 1993.

LEWIN, LEIF (1994). "The Rise and Decline of Corporatism: The Case of Sweden." *European Journal of Political Research* 26: 59–79.

LINDBECK, ASSAR (1992). *Klarar vi pensionerna?* Stockholm: SNS Förlag, 1992.

LUNDBERG, URBAN (2003). *Juvelen i kronan. Socialdemokraterna och den allmänna pensionen.* Stockholm: Hjalmarson and Höberg.

MINISTRY of Finance (1990). *The Swedish Budget 1991*. Stockholm: Government Printing Office.

MYLES, JOHN, and P. PIERSON (2001). "Coping with permanent austerity: welfare state restructuring." In Pierson, P. (ed.), *The New Politics of the Welfare State*. Oxford: Oxford University Press.

NORRBOM, HANS (1998). "Pensionsreformen ger bättre finanser till staten." *Riksdag och departement.* 29, 9.

PALME, JOAKIM (2003). "Pension Reform in Sweden and the Changing Boundaries between Public and Private" In Clark, G. L. and Whiteside, N. (eds.), *Pension Security in the 21st Century. Redrawing the Public–Private Debate*. Oxford: Oxford University Press, 144–167.

PALMER, EDWARD and WADENSJÖ ESKIL (2004). "Public pension reform and contractual agreements in Sweden: from defined benefit to defined contributions." In Rein, M., and Schmähl, W. (eds.), *Rethinking the Welfare State*. Cheltenham: Edward Elgar, 226–50.

PETERSSON, OLOF (1998). *Svensk politik*. 3rd edn. Stockholm: Norstedts.

PONTUSSON, JONAS (1992). *The Limits of Social Democracy. Investment Politics in Sweden.* Ithaca, NY: Cornell University Press, 1992.

PREMIEPENSIONSMYNDIGHETEN (2005). *Pressmeddelande December 30 2005.*

RIKSFÖRSÄKRINGSVERKET (2004). *Pensionssystemets årsredovisning 2004*. Borås.

—— (2005). *Pensionssystemets årsredovisning 2005*. Borås.

—— (2000). "Automatisk balansering av ålderspensionssystemet–redovisning av regeringens beräkningsuppdrag." *RFV Analyserar* 2000:1.

ROTHSTEIN, BO and JONAS BERGSTRÖM (1999). *Korporatismens fall och den svenska modellens kris.* Stockholm: SNS förlag.

RUIN, OLOF (1988). "Sweden: The New Constitution (1974) and the Tradition of Consensual Politics." In Bogdanor, V. (ed.) *Constitutions in Democratic Politics*. Aldershot, UK: Gower, 309–27.

RUSTOW, D. (1955). *The Politics of Compromise*. Princeton: Princeton University Press.

STJERNQUIST, N. (1996). *Tvåkammartiden: Sveriges Riksdag 1867–1970*. Stockholm: Sveriges Riksdag.

SÖDERSTRÖM, HANS TSON (ed.) (1991). *Sverige vid vändpunkten. Konjunkturrådets rapport 1991.* Stockholm: SNS Förlag.

STEINMO, SVEN (2002). "Globalization and Taxation: Challenges to the Swedish Welfare State." *Comparative Political Studies*, 35, 7 (September): 839–62.

STÅHLBERG, ANN-CHARLOTTE (1995). *Våra pensionssystem*. Stockholm: SNS Förlag.

SVENSSON, TORSTEN (1994). *Socialdemokratins dominans. En studie av den svenska socialdemokratins partistrategi.* Uppsala: Acta Universitatis Upaliensis.

—— MABUCHI, M., and KAMIKAWA, R. (2006). "Managing the Bank-System Crisis in Coordinated Market Economies: Institutions and Blame Avoidance Strategies in Sweden and Japan." *Governance*, 19, 1 (January): 43–74.

SWENSON, PETER (2002). *Capitalists against Markets. The Making of Labor Markets and Welfare States in the United States and Sweden.* Oxford: Oxford University Press.

WEAVER, R. KENT (2003/2004). "Design and Implementation Issues in Swedish Individual Pension Accounts," *Social Security Bulletin* 65 (4): 38–56.

—— and PAUL PIERSON (1993). "Imposing Losses in Pension Policy." In Weaver, R. K. and Rockman, B. A. (eds.), *Do Institutions Matter? Government Capabilities in the US and Abroad.* Washington, D.C.: Brookings.

CHAPTER 9

ITALY: A NARROW GATE FOR PATH-SHIFT[1]

MAURIZIO FERRERA

MATTEO JESSOULA

I Introduction

BEGINNING in the 1970s, the Italian pension system came under political and scholarly scrutiny. Pension benefits were extremely generous—especially for civil servants—and created perverse incentives from the point of view of both equity and efficiency (Castellino 1976). Policy analysts and policy-makers also started to worry about the system's growing financial difficulties due to the maturation of the PAYG schemes, the rapid process of demographic aging, mounting unemployment and slow economic and wage growth (Ministero del Tesoro 1981). Nevertheless, during the 1980s, little political action was taken. Political actors began to recognize both demographic and pension expenditure problems, and issued some alarming reports. They established various commissions to tackle the problem, thus stoking the pension reform debate. But no important measures were adopted, and the decade was characterized by policy stalemate.

By contrast, the post-1980s period has witnessed several important reforms, within a wider effort to improve Italy's battered public finances. Five different governments have attempted pension reform; four of these (at least partly) succeeded, one failed.

The enacted reforms of 1992–3, 1995, 1997 and 2004–5 fundamentally altered the structure of the Italian public pension system, stabilizing old-age expenditure—which was projected to rise to almost 25 percent of GDP in four decades[2]—and introduced mechanisms to contain future costs. In addition, inequalities in pension benefits—especially concerning private versus public employees and civil servants—were reduced, and administration simplified.

The Italian sequence of pension reforms prompted a reconfiguration of the pension system resting on two fundamental ingredients: (i) the substantial reduction of the role of the first (public) pillar in old age provision; and (ii) the rapid development of funded supplementary pensions, at least in certain economic sectors. In other words, in a relatively short period Italy embarked on a delicate transition from a single-pillar pension system towards a multi-pillar configuration, thus departing from the path followed during the entire twentieth century. As we shall see, the transition is far from complete. But important steps have been taken to lay the foundations for a new institutional architecture.

The significance of these changes stands out if we consider the point of departure. The economic and policy situation of the early 1990s was not particularly conducive to switching to a multi-pillar pension system. Public debt was extremely high, as were contribution rates to the first pillar; demographic trends were very unfavorable, and supplementary funded schemes were virtually unknown. According to the expectations of both neo-institutionalists (Myles and Pierson 2001) and macroeconomists, the Italian system should have faced enormous difficulties in establishing a second pillar because of the notorious "double payment" problem.

Which factors allowed Italian governments during the 1990s to overcome the policy stalemate of the previous decade, prompting three reforms that significantly altered the structure of the public pillar? And which factors, in particular, facilitated the launch (and the first tangible steps) of an ambitious transition from a single-pillar to a multi-pillar configuration? We argue that the sequence of reforms was the result of a sudden change in the actor constellation—a change that had both a domestic and external source (Fig. 9.1).

The crumbling of the so-called First Republic (the political regime from 1948 through 1992) and the transition to the Second (1992 onwards) brought new actors to the scene, and at the same time transformed the rules of both political competition and policy-making. The exogenous pressures exerted by financial markets and the run-up to EMU significantly altered the costs and benefits of domestic policy options, and their distributive implications for national actors. In particular, external constraints prompted a process of political and social learning among key actors, and encouraged "concertation" between the government and the social partners, based on the assumption that a modification of the status quo was necessary.

Moreover, although proponents of path dependency, as well as pension experts, argue that the transformation of a Bismarckian pension scheme is very difficult, we contend that the transition towards a multi-pillar configuration was facilitated by the presence of a peculiar social policy institution—the so-called *Tfr* (*Trattamento di fine rapporto* explained on p. 417)—which operated as an "institutional gate" for policy

```
┌─────────────────────────────────┬─────────────────────────────────┐
│   INTERNAL DEVELOPMENTS         │   EXTERNAL DEVELOPMENTS         │
│   (crisis of the First Republic,│   (Maastricht process and       │
│   politico-institutional        │   internationalization dynamics)│
│   transition)                   │                                 │
└─────────────────────────────────┴─────────────────────────────────┘
                          ↓
              CHANGE OF THE ACTOR CONSTELLATION
                          ↓
              FAILURE-INDUCED LEARNING DYNAMICS
                    ↙              ↘
        Substantive learning     Political learning
                    ↘              ↙
              SEQUENCE OF REFORMS 1992–1997
```

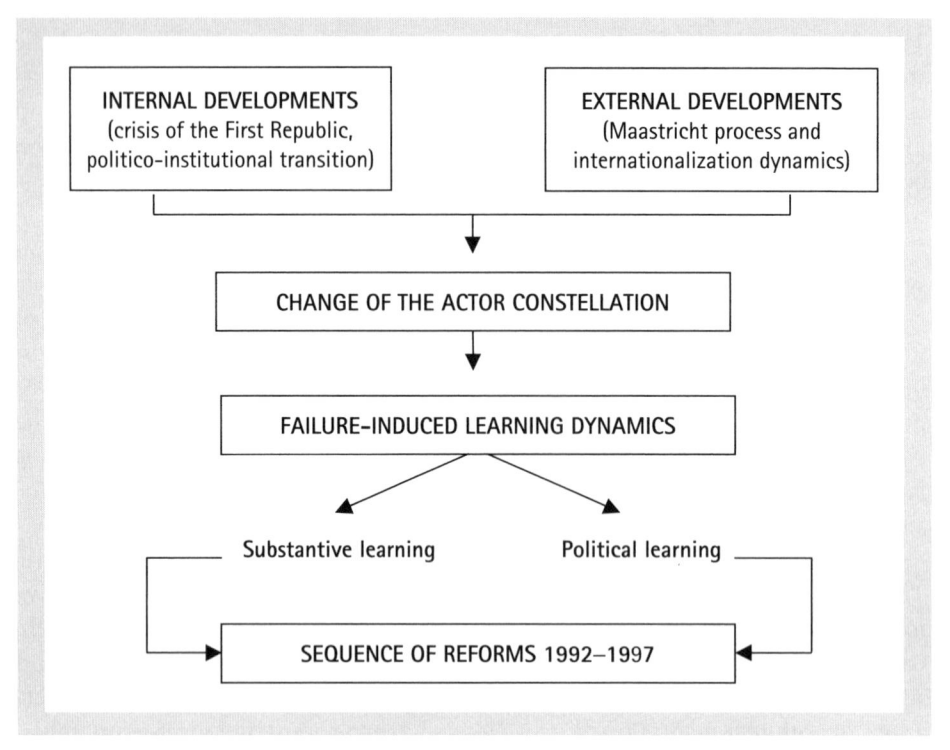

Fig. 9.1 Italy's reform sequence in the 1990s: the explanatory model

change. The transition could take off because policy actors recognized in the *Tfr* "a gate that could be opened" (Jessoula 2004), that is an institution that could be converted (Thelen and Streeck 2005), under appropriate conditions, into something like a second pillar.

II Political system

Constitutional history and nation-building

Although Italy as a geographical entity has been well known since the age of the Roman Empire, its history as a nation-state is relatively short, dating only from the nineteenth century. Italy was unified during the second part of the nineteenth century after three "wars of independence" in 1848, 1959–61 and 1866. In 1870, with the conquest of Rome, the Kingdom of Italy almost reached the territorial extension of the current Italian Republic.[3]

The Republican regime emerged from the ashes of the fascist dictatorship (1922–1943), restoring the centrality of Parliament and reintroducing free elections and political competition in a liberal-democratic system. At the end of the Second World War, Italians had to choose between a Republic or a Monarchy as the new form of state through a referendum in 1946, and they chose the Republic. The foundations of the Italian Republic lie in the Constitution which was elaborated after the referendum and has been in force since 1948.

The Constitution, that sketched the main features of a bi-cameral parliamentary system, was drafted under a grand coalition government composed of the Christian Democrats (*Democrazia Cristiana*), the Liberals (*Partito Liberale*) and a "Popular Front" including both Socialists (*Partito Socialista*) and Communists (*Partito Comunista*). It thus represents a carefully crafted compromise between the three major ideological sources that inspired it: the Catholic, the Socialist-Communist and the Liberal. Most important, from our point of view, is the third part of the text—on economic activity and relationships—that lays down the basic principles of the social protection system. According to Article 38, every *worker* must be protected against occupational injury, sickness, inability, old-age and involuntary unemployment, while Article 32 states that health care is a fundamental right of every *citizen*. In consequence, the Italian Welfare State follows the Southern European pattern of combining Bismarckian old age insurance with Beveridgean social services, in this case a Health Care System financed through general tax revenues and open to all residents.

Institutions of government

The Italian parliamentary regime has three central institutions: Parliament, the government and the President of the Republic. While legislative and executive powers are in the hands of the first two institutions respectively, the President of the Republic is the representative of the nation and guardian of the Constitution, although he/she does have some (very) limited legislative powers.

The Italian Parliament consists of two chambers: the Upper Chamber is called the *Senato della Repubblica* (315 members), and the Lower Chamber the *Camera dei Deputati* (630 members). However, Italian bicameralism was not conceived to give representation to sub-national or regional interests, as in some other bicameral systems, being on the contrary the result of an attempt to share legislative power between different institutions. Both chambers are elected every five years and MPs can sit in permanent as well as in ad hoc committees.

Executive power belongs to the government, which is formed by the Council of Ministers (*Consiglio dei Ministri*), led by the President of the Council (*Presidente del Consiglio*). The President of the Council is appointed by the President of the Republic after (in the past usually lengthy) consultations with party leaders. The relation of the executive to the legislative (and the parties represented in Parliament) is determined by specific rules concerning relations both between government and Parliament, and those between Parliament and the President. In particular,

Table 9.1 Political institutions in Italy

Political arenas	Actors	Rules of investiture	Rules of decision-making	Veto potential
Executive	President of the Republic (*Presidente della Rebubblica*)	7-year term; elected by a joint session of both chambers of parliament with a 2/3 majority in the first three ballots, or absolute majority in the fourth ballot	Can send laws back to parliamentary chambers, but the chambers can overrule the president by confirming the bill with simple majority	Not a veto point
	Prime Minister (*Presidente del Consiglio*)	Appointed by President; positive vote of confidence from both chambers (*voto di fiducia*)	Right of initiative (*disegno di legge*) Right of legislation by decree: • *decreto legge*: decree comes into force immediately but has to be approved and converted into ordinary law by Parliament within 60 days • *decreti legislativi*: Parliament delegates legislative power to the government for very complex issues (e.g. pensions) specifying limits of legislative power in a delegation law (*legge delega*)	—
Legislative	Chamber of Deputies (*Camera dei Deputati*)	5-year term, 630 members (475 single-member district seats and 155 proportional representation seats); Hare formula with 4% threshold; 26 constituencies magnitude between 1 and 11 seats; voters have two votes; chamber can be dissolved by President	Right of initiative (*proposta di legge*); decision taking by simple majority with quorum of 50% + 1 of MPs; may overrule the President with simple majority	Pre-1993: veto point due to unstable parliamentary coalitions post-1993: veto point only if minority government or defection from government coalition
	Senate (*Senato della Repubblica*)	5-year term, 315 directly elected members (238 single-member districts and 77 proportional representation seats; d'Hondt formula; voters have one vote; constituency magnitude between 1 and 12	Identical to lower house, and political composition generally similar	Veto point only when majority differs from that of Chamber of Deputies

Judicial		seats; chamber can be dissolved by President)	
	Constitutional Court (*Corte Costituzionale*)	9-year term; 15 members; 1/3 appointed by the President, 1/3 appointed by Parliament and 1/3 appointed by the highest administrative court	Tendency to take consensual decisions, finding a compromise between the different opinions; last resource: majority vote, with a quorum of 11 members.	Not a veto point: the court lacks the prerogative of judicial review. Only magistrates in ordinary courts—during a trial—may ask the Court to rule on the constitutional legitimacy of a law
Electoral	Referendum	Right to call referendum: 500,000 voters or five regions; promoting groups formulate referendum text	Different types of referenda: • referendum with annulling power (*referendum abrogativo*) or • referendum with suspending power (*referendum sospensivo*) decision by majority with quorum of 50% + 1 of voters	Formally: yes Actually: no
Territorial units	Regions (*Regioni*)	Different versions of majoritarian electoral system for regional and provincial governments and for municipal councils	Regions: shared responsibilities in supplementary pensions and exclusive responsibilities in employment policy and social assistance	Not a veto point
	Provinces (*Province*)		Provinces: competencies in employment and ALMP	
	Communes (*Comuni*)		Communes: competencies in assistance, employment and ALMP	

a newly-appointed government must obtain an explicit vote of confidence (*voto di fiducia*) from both chambers, and the maintenance of such a "trust-link" between the government and the majority in Parliament is necessary for the former to remain in power. On the other hand, the government cannot dismiss Parliament, this being a prerogative of the President, who is elected by the Chambers (see Table 9.1).

This set of relations, and in particular the lack of a direct (popular) investiture of the foremost executive in a polarized pluralist system (Sartori 1982), have determined a situation in which for a long period of time—between 1948 and the transition from the so-called "First" to the "Second Republic" in the 1990s, the Prime Minister had no effective control both over the Cabinet and the related majority in Parliament. This made it difficult for prime ministers to accomplish a governmental program because so much effort was devoted to reconciling the interests of the parties represented in government coalitions. The latter usually consisted of more than three parties, due to the high number of competing political formations and to the system of proportional representation. Political competition between the parties was typically not limited to specific situations (elections), but rather an everlasting and pervasive aspect of domestic politics. Institutional barriers to "insulate" government from the political struggle were weak, so that the former was continuously exposed to threats coming from the parties forming government coalitions. This penetration of political and administrative institutions by political parties (*partitocrazia*) was thus a typical feature of the Italian political system during the First Republic (Maranini 1967; Vassallo 1994), leading to very short cabinets and a high level of intra-government conflict. However, after the crisis of the traditional parties in the early-1990s and the modification of the electoral system in 1993, this has started to change, so that in recent years the President of the Council has acquired a more prominent and effective role.

The 1948 Constitution provides for a unitary state divided into 20 regions. The regions exercise the competencies listed in Art. 117, including health care and social assistance. The actual establishment of regions was very slow. Given their special geo-economic or geo-cultural situation, five autonomous regions were created in the 1950s and early 1960s, but the other 15 ordinary regions only became fully operative in the late 1970s.

The 1990s witnessed two new waves of regionalization and the launching of a thoroughgoing federalization process. In 2001, Title V of the Constitution was changed, devolving to the regions exclusive competencies in many fields—basically all those not explicitly listed as prerogatives of the state, or as shared national–regional competences.

The first wave of decentralization, in the 1970s, and even more so the two waves in the 1990s, also had important effects on the national social-protection system. More precisely, while social insurance *stricto sensu* is still controlled from the center, health and social care, active labor market policies, and, to some extent, supplementary pensions are increasingly sub-national competences.

Electoral system

During the two decades covered by this chapter, Italy experienced the transition from the so-called First Republic to the Second Republic. This was the consequence of a number of factors (see p. 407), including the modification of the electoral system in 1993.

From 1948, a fully proportional electoral system was in force for elections to both chambers. Parliamentary seats were assigned proportionally, and there were only slight differences between the calculation methods for the two chambers: in the Chamber of Deputies seats were assigned at the level of 32 electoral constituencies,[4] for the Senate they were distributed at regional level.[5] Party fragmentation was not entirely caused by the peculiar type of electoral system (Sartori 1982), although the system did not prevent the proliferation of political formations, and did not reduce the number of parties represented in Parliament, which was very high.

With the reconfiguration of the Italian political system, the electoral system was also drastically altered. In April 1993, the electoral rule for the Senate was modified through a referendum that introduced a first-past-the-post system.[6] A few months later, a law (L. 277/93) was passed to harmonize the electoral rules for the Chamber of Deputies with those for the Upper Chamber. Seats are currently assigned in both chambers on the basis of a mixed system—partly majoritarian, partly proportional. More precisely, about three quarters of MPs (475 in the Chamber of Deputies, 238 in the Senate) are elected in single-member districts with the first-past-the-post method, the remaining quarter (155 and 77 respectively) are elected by proportional representation in 26 constituencies (for the Chamber of Deputies) or at the regional level (for the Senate).[7] The main difference between the electoral rules for the two chambers is the 4 percent threshold required for participating in the allocation of the 155 seats assigned by proportional representation in the Chamber of Deputies. Despite this difference, the composition of the two chambers is quite similar in terms of the party groups represented. Elections are held every five years, but the President can call early elections by dismissing Parliament. Until the 1993 reform, voting was compulsory, but sanctions were weak and implementation lax. After the reform, voting is a citizen's *right* rather than an *obligation*.

The modification of the electoral rules brought some changes in the logic of party competition, moving the party system towards a bipolar configuration. Such developments will be illustrated in the section "Parties and Elections" (see p. 405).

Legislative process

In Italy, legislative initiative is not the exclusive prerogative of either the government or members of Parliament; indeed, other actors may propose legislation, including the National Council for Economy and Labor, the regional councils, and voters presenting a proposal supported by at least 50,000 signatures. In practice, however, the legislative process usually starts with the drafting of a government bill (*disegno di legge*) or a proposal by MPs (*proposta di legge*).

After the bill has been presented in one of the two chambers, the assembly transfers the bill to the pertinent committees for evaluation. The committees are asked to formulate an opinion on the proposal before returning it to the assembly. To become law, a bill must be approved—article by article—in the same form by the two chambers; if one of the chambers modifies the legislative text, it must be transferred to the other chamber for a further vote on the amended text. At the end of the legislative process, the bill must be signed by the President, who has the right to send the bill back to Parliament in the case of constitutional or formal irregularities. However, this may not be considered as actual veto power since Parliament can overrule this act by approving the bill again, even without changing the text.

In reality things are more complicated, and the legislative process can assume different forms, as legislative burdens on Parliament together with the complexity of many proposals make the transfer of bills to the committees a frequent practice, with the committee members playing various roles. Committees can perform three different tasks:

1. they may be asked to formulate an opinion about a government bill (*Commissione in sede referente*);
2. they can draft the final version of a bill and submit it to Parliament (*Commissione in sede redigente*).
   In these two cases the adoption of a bill follows the ordinary procedure once it returns to the assembly.
3. In the third case, however, the legislative process is substantially modified as committees can themselves adopt a bill (*Commissione in sede deliberante*), which does not need further Parliamentary approval.

A further note on the legislative power of the government is necessary because of its importance in recent pension reforms. The government can assume legislative authority in two cases. First, when urgent action is needed, the Cabinet may issue a decree (*decreto legge*) with immediate force, although it must be approved by Parliament within 60 days to become law. Second, Parliament may delegate legislative power to the government, especially for very complex issues (such as pension policy), specifying in the delegation law (so-called *legge delega*) the limits of the Cabinet's legislative power and the guidelines for the drafting of the subsequent legislative decrees (*decreti legislativi*). As we shall see below, both these procedures were used by governments in the last decade to pass pension legislation.

Apart from formal rules, the legislative process usually consists of interactions between members of the cabinet (ministers), their administrative bodies and the social groups involved in the proposed regulation. As illustrated on 410–15, in pension policy-making interaction between politico-institutional actors—members of Cabinet, heads of administrative departments, members of parliamentary committees—and social actors like the unions and other interest groups is common. Nevertheless, the number of actors involved in policy-making varies, as does the kind of relations between them. With respect to the latter, in the field of pensions, relationships with social actors varied a lot in recent decades, stretching from simple consultation to committed and institutionalized tripartite concertation.

Parties and elections

As noted already, an analysis of the period 1980–2004 in the Italian case requires us to consider two different phases marked by diverse political dynamics and equilibria: the last period of the First Republic (1980–92) and the first decade of the Second Republic (1993–2004).

During the First Republic, Italy was characterized by a highly fragmented and "polarized" party system with at least six parties ranging from the extreme left to the extreme right, and a high ideological distance between these extremes (Sartori 1982). The Christian Democratic Party (DC) occupied the center and was always the biggest party, gaining more than 30 percent of votes in most elections between 1948 and 1992. Next to the DC were two relatively small, non-confessional parties (*laici*): the Republican Party (PRI) and the Liberal Party (PLI). The left wing of the spectrum was occupied by the Communist Party—the second most important political group in terms of electoral results—and two parties with socialist roots, the Socialist Party (PSI) and the Social Democratic Party (PSDI). On the other side of the political spectrum the neo-Fascist party (MSI) occupied the extreme right. Finally, the Radical Party was an outsider in this representation, as its positions on many issues cut through the left–right dimension (see Fig. 9.2). Electoral results showed a very high, and relatively stable, share of votes for the three bigger parties (DC, PCI, PSI), which between them attracted more than 70 percent of votes in the period 1972–87.

In terms of overall configuration, the system showed at least three intersecting cleavages. The first cleavage concerned the acceptance of the democratic regime—as well as its allegiance to the Western foreign policy alliance—and was labeled the pro/anti system cleavage, with the extreme right and left wings (MSI and PCI) in the anti-system position—at least until the 1970s in the case of the Communist Party—and the center Christian Democratic Party playing the role of the "guardian" of the democratic system. The second cleavage separated confessional parties (DC, MSI) from non-confessional ones, while the third cleavage occupied the classical right–left dimension. The latter was dominated by the antagonism between two confronting subcultures. The Catholic subculture, which sustained the Christian Democratic Party because of the explicit support of the Church for the latter, had deep roots in the north-eastern part of the country and also prevailed in the South; on the other hand, the socialist subculture fuelled both the Communist and the Socialist Party and it had a strong grip in central regions. Despite such regional differences it is important to stress that a territorial cleavage was never activated until the late 1980s.

Against this background—and keeping in mind that the electoral system was a fully proportional one that transferred the complexity of the party system into Parliament—it is not difficult to understand that the formation of homogeneous and long-lasting parliamentary majorities was an extremely rare event in the Italian First Republic. In fact, coalitions were usually built around the pivotal center party (DC) and made up of four or five parties (DC, PSI, PSDI, PRI, PLI). Neither Communists nor neo-Fascists were ever allowed to take part in the coalitions led by the Christian Democrats, nor could they build a majority by themselves. The

Party family affiliation	Abbreviation	Party name	Ideological orientation	Founding and merger details	Year established
Communist parties	DP	Proletarian Democracy (*Democrazia Proletaria*)	Communist		1976
Communist parties	PCI	Italian Communist Party (*Partito Comunista Italiano*)	Communist	Separated from PSI	1921
Greens	GR	Greens (*Verdi*)	Green		1986
Left parties / Social democratic parties	PSI	Italian Socialist Party (*Partito Socialista Italiano*)	Socialist		1892
Left parties / Social democratic parties	PSDI	Italian Social Democratic Party (*Partito Socialdemocratico Italiano*)	Social democratic	Separated from PSI	1947
Radical parties	PR	Italian Radical Party (*Partito Radicale Italiano*)	Radical		1955
Christian Democratic parties	DC	Christian Democracy Party (*Democrazia Cristiana*)	Christian democratic		1942
Republican parties	PRI	Italian Republican Party (*Partito Repubblicano Italiano*)	Republican		1895
Liberal parties	PLI	Italian Liberal Party (*Partito Liberale Italiano*)	Liberal		1921
Neo-Fascist parties	MSI	Italian Social Movement (*Movimento Sociale Italiano*)	Neo-fascist		1947

Fig. 9.2 Party system in Italy (1980s)

Italian political system was thus often described as a sort of "blocked democracy," because alternation in government was effectively excluded. The DC and its minor pro-system allies were "condemned" to stick together to form a majority, which had no possible alternative. The spoils of government (ministerial jobs and other administrative positions) were assigned to each party (and to the various intra-party factions, especially within the DC) in strict accordance to their electoral strength, often with hidden agreements on temporary rotations among the various parties and factions. A Cabinet crisis always offered the chance of gaining more spoils, and general elections were opportunities for updating the vote count of each party. The high Cabinet instability and the frequent early elections of the First Republic responded to this competitive logic. The Christian Democrats remained in power for more than 40 years, and government crises usually resulted in limited reshuffling of coalitions and parliamentary majorities.

In the early 1990s, however, the move away from the "frozen landscape" of Italian democracy was prompted by different factors: (a) the repercussions for the domestic political arena of the collapse of the Berlin Wall; (b) the so-called *Tangentopoli* (Bribesville) scandal; and (c) the reform of the electoral system (already discussed). In particular, when the *Tangentopoli* scandal broke—revealing widespread corruption involving senior politicians and top businessmen—the traditional parties that had dominated politics for over 40 years fell in a deep crisis. The Christian Democratic Party and the Socialist Party were tainted by magistrates' investigations, and their electoral support shrank rapidly. In short, these changes led to both the transformation of the party system and the "unfreezing" of political games and competition dynamics.

The results were seen in the 1994 elections. First, completely new political formations appeared—the most important being *Forza Italia* (FI) founded by Silvio Berlusconi—while others transformed themselves, splitting in different parties (see Fig. 9.3). Second, responding to the requirements of the new—mostly majoritarian—electoral system, parties began to form pre-electoral alliances, leading to something like electoral cartels. In 1994, three cartels (left, center and right) competed in elections, but later in the 1990s parties aggregated into just two competing "poles" (center-right and center-left; see p. 409). Finally, the depolarization of the system, which had already started in the late 1970s, accelerated: in the mid-1990s both the former anti-system wings (MSI and PCI) had transformed themselves into fully democratic parties.

Although the transition from the First to the Second Republic is not complete, some relevant changes may be recorded. Most importantly, there is a clear bipolar tendency, and the party system has become more competitive. The overall process, from the presentation of candidates to the formation of the government, has completely changed. Whereas in the past elections only defined the parties' share of electoral power, some of which were later called to form a coalition after lengthy consultations between the President and party leaders, nowadays the process is much more straightforward. Before elections, parties build two competing electoral alliances and potential governmental majorities (center-left and center-right), each designating a prospective Prime Minister. Since 1996, such electoral alliances have

Party family affiliation	Abbreviation	Party name	Ideological orientation	Founding and merger details	Year established
Post-Communist parties	RC	Communist Refoundation (*Rifondazione Comunista*)	Neo-communist	Part of the former Communist Party (PCI), separated from DS	1991
Post-Communist parties	PDCI	Party of Italian Communists (*Partito dei Comunisti Italiani*)	Post-communist	Separated from RC	1998
Greens	GR	Greens (*Verdi*)	Green		1986
Left parties / Social democratic parties	DS	Left Democrats (*Democratici di Sinistra*)	Leftist	Transformation of the former Communist Part (PCI)	1991
Left parties / Social democratic parties	SDI	Italian Social Democrats (*Socialisti Democratici Italiani*)	Social democratic	Transformation of the former Socialist Party (PSI)	1998
Leftist Christian Democratic Parties	IV	*Italia dei Valori – Lista Di Pietro*		New party	2000
Leftist Christian Democratic Parties	DL	*Democrazia e libertà – La Margherita*	Social Christian	Formed from Democrazia e Libertà, Rinnovamento Italiano and a fraction of the former Popular Party (PPI)	2002
Christian Democratic parties	UDEUR	Democrats for Europe (*Unione Democratici per l'Europa*)	Christian democratic	Separated from CCD	1998
Christian Democratic parties	CDU	Christian Democratic Party (*Partito dei Cristiano Democratici*)	Christian democratic	Transformation of the former Popular Party (PPI), separated from CCD	1995
Christian Democratic parties	CCD	Christian Democratic Center (*Centro Cristiano Democratico*)	Christian democratic	Transformation of the former Christian Democratic Party (DC)	1994

Fig. 9.3 Party system in Italy (1990s)

Radical parties	PR	*Radicali*	Radical	Transformation of the former Radical Party (PR)	2002
Liberal parties	FI	*Forza Italia*	Conservative liberal	–	1994
	NPSI	New Italian Socialist Party (*Nuovo Partito Socialista Italiano*)	Liberal	Transformation of the former Socialist Party (PSI)	2001
Territorial parties	LN	Northern League (*Lega Nord*)	Federalist	Formed from Liga Veneta and Lega Lombarda	1991
Right wing parties	AN	National Alliance (*Alleanza Nazionale*)	Right wing	Transformation of the former post-fascist party (MSI)	1995
	MSI	*Movimento Sociale Italiano-Famma Tricolore*	Neo-fascist	Part of the former post-fascist party (MSI), separated from AN	1995

Fig. 9.3 (*Continued*)

been quite stable: at the center-left we find *L'Ulivo* or "The Olive Tree Alliance", formed by DS, La Margherita, Greens, PDCI, UDEUR and SDI; at the center-right the *Casa delle libertà* or "House of Freedoms" alliance composed of FI, AN, *Lega Nord*, CCD, CDU and new PSI. The winning coalition, which is usually clearly defined because of the mostly majoritarian electoral rule, forms the governmental majority, led by the already designated Prime Minister. Such developments give the electorate a greater role in choosing both the government and its leader, promoting government responsiveness and accountability.

Even more important, such changes were able to "unlock" the democratic process by permitting alternative majorities. While the need to create a "barrier against communism" slowly faded away, the option of a Left government became realistic as it would no longer imply a system change. Thus, the victory of the center-right coalition (*Polo della libertà* and *Polo del buon governo*, i.e. the predecessors of the *Casa delle Libertà*) in 1994 was followed by center-left (*Ulivo*) coalition in 1996; then, a center-right alliance (*Casa delle Libertà*) returned to power in 2001; and again, a centre-left coalition won the 2006 elections.

The new electoral rules also had implications for pension politics, mainly because single member districts favor parties with a territorially concentrated electoral basis. As we show later, in both the 1994 and 2004 pension reforms, *Lega Nord* assumed a peculiar position—even in contrast with the other political formations within governmental majorities—in order to protect the pension entitlements of its voters. In fact, *Lega Nord* proved unwilling to adopt changes that would tighten eligibility for seniority pensions (see pp. 435, 444) due to the concentration of such benefits in the north.

Interest groups

Interest group representation in Italy is relatively fragmented, dominated by several peak institutions and many less relevant groups. On the Labor side, three major organizations stand out: *Confederazione Generale Italiana del Lavoro* (CGIL), *Confederazione Italiana dei Sindacati dei Lavoratori* (CISL), and *Unione Italiana del Lavoro* (UIL). Traditionally, the main differences between these associations concerned ideological orientation and links with political parties. CGIL had a reputation for being the most radical, backing the former Communist and Socialist Parties, while CISL was linked to the Christian Democratic Party and the UIL had strong links with PSDI.

Union density has declined in Italy since the mid-1980s—from 39.7 percent in 1986 to 35.8 percent in 1997—but such figures, though not reaching the levels of Nordic countries, are remarkably high for continental Europe. More important, however, is the high mobilization potential of the main unions.

As for union size and composition, CGIL was, and still is, the largest association with more than five million members (5,542,677 in 2005, *c.* 25% of employed people), followed by CISL (4,287,551 associated, *c.* 19% of employed people) and UIL (1, 923, 885, *c.* 8%). What is significant here is that since the mid-1990s, most members of the CGIL were pensioners (53.7% in 1995), while CISL displayed a slight prevalence of active workers (54.1%), and these constituted a majority in UIL (75.2%). Thus pensioners' interests have always been protected by the unions. Some unions have even specific sections that promote pensioners' interests, for example SPI-CGIL; by contrast a separate "retirees' association" does not exist in Italy.

On the employers' and self-employed side, the picture is even more complex, with at least one interest group for each productive sector. The association *Confindustria* represents industrial employers; *Confcommercio* represents merchants in the commercial sector; *Confartigianato* supports the artisans; and finally *Confagricoltura*

Table 9.2 Governmental majorities in Italy

Election date: Camera & Senato	Start of gov.	Head of government (party)	Governing parties	Gov. majority (% seats) Camera	Gov. electoral base (% votes) Camera	Gov. majority (% seats) Senato	Institutional veto points	Number of veto players (partisan + institutional)
06.03.1979	08.04.1979	Cossiga I (DC)	DC (262), PSDI (20), PLI (9) + *PSI* (61) + *PRI* (16)[a]	46.2% (58.4%)[a]	44.1% (56.9%)[a]	47.9% (60.3%)[a]	Camera, Senato	3 + 2
	04.04.1980	Cossiga II (DC)	DC (262), PSI (61), PRI (16)	53.8%	51.1%	56.5%	None	3 + 0
	10.18.1980	Forlani (DC)	DC (262), PSI (61), PRI (16), PSDI (20)	57.0%	55.0%	59.7%	None	4 + 0
	06.28.1981	Spadolini I (PRI)	DC (262), PSI (61), PRI (16), PSDI (20), PLI (9)	58.4%	56.9%	60.3%	None	5 + 0
	08.23.1982	Spadolini II (PRI)	DC (262), PSI (61), PSDI (20), PRI (16), PLI (9)	58.4%	56.9%	60.3%	None	5 + 0
	12.01.1982	Fanfani V (DC)	DC (262), PSI (61), PSDI (20), PLI (9) + *PRI (16)*[a]	55.9% (58.4%)[a]	53.9% (56.9%)[a]	58.1% (60.3%)[a]	None	4 + 0
06.26.1983	08.04.1983	Craxi I (PSI)	DC (226), PSI (73), PRI (29), PSDI (22), PLI (16)	58.1%	56.4%	59.4%	None	5 + 0
	08.01.1986	Craxi II (PSI)	DC (226), PSI (73), PRI (29), PSDI (22), PLI (16)	58.1%	56.4%	59.4%	None	5 + 0
	04.17.1987	Fanfani VI (DC)	DC (226)	35.9%	32.9%	38.4%	Camera, Senato	1 + 2
06.14.1987	07.28.1987	Goria (DC)	DC (234), PSI (94), PSDI (17), PLI (11), PRI (21)	59.8%	57.3%	60.6%	None	5 + 0

(Continued)

Table 9.2 (Continued)

Election date: Camera & Senato	Start of gov.	Head of government (party)	Governing parties	Gov. majority (% seats) Camera	Gov. electoral base (% votes) Camera	Gov. majority (% seats) Senato	Institutional veto points	Number of veto players (partisan + institutional)
	04.13.1988	De Mita (DC)	DC (234), PLI (11), PRI (21), PSI (94), PSDI (17)	59.8%	57.3%	60.6%	None	5 + 0
	07.23.1989	Andreotti V (DC)	DC (234), PLI (11), PRI (21), PSI (94), PSDI (17)	59.8%	57.3%	60.6%	None	5 + 0
	04.12.1991	Andreotti VI (DC)	DC (234), PSI (94), PSDI (17), PLI (11)	56.5%	53.6%	57.8%	None	4 + 0
04.06.1992	06.28.1992	Amato I (PSI)	DC (206), PSI (92), PLI (17), PSDI (16)	52.5%	48.8%	54.3%	None	4 + 0
	04.28.1993	Ciampi I (Ind.)	DC (206), PSI (92), PLI (17), PSDI (16) + LN (55) + PRI (27) + DS (107)[a]	52.5% (65.6%)[a]	48.8% (61.9%)[a]	54.3% (87.0%)[a]	None	4 + 0
03.28.1994	05.10.1994	Berlusconi I (FI)	FI(112), LN (111), AN(109), CCD-CDU(27), other right (7)	58.1%	44.5%	49.5%	Senato	4 + 1
	01.17.1995	Dini (Ind.)	technocratic with support of Progressisti (162), LN (77), PPI (33), P-AD (21), SVP (3), others (6)	47.9%	46.1%	60.6%	Camera	6 + 1
04.21.1996	05.18.1996	Prodi (Komitees+PPI)	DS (172), PPI-Dem (67), RI (26), Verdi (14), Rete(5), SVP (3), PRI(2) + PRC(34)[b]	45.9% (51.3%)[b]	38.7% (43.0%)[b]	50.2% (53.7%)[b]	Camera	7 + 1

10.21.1998	D'Alema I (DS)	DS (177), PPI (66), UDR (27), PDCI (21), RI (19), Verdi (14), SDI (9)	52.9%	46.8%	55.9%	None	7 + 0
12.22.1999	D'Alema II (DS)	DS (177), PPI (46), Udeur (20), PDCI (21), Democratici (20), RI (19), Verdi (14)	50.3%	44.3%	53.3%	None	5 + 0
04.25.2000	Amato II (Ind.)	DS (177), PPI (46), Udeur (20), PDCI (21), Democratici (–), RI (19), Verdi (14), SDI (9)[c]	–	–	–	None	8 +0
06.11.2001	Berlusconi II (FI)	FI (177), AN (99), LN (30), CCD-CDU (41), NPSI (3), Others (17)	58.3%	47.4%	55.6%	None	5 + 0
05.13.2001							

[a] Parties indicated in italics provided passive support (a promise of abstention) for the government; hence, governmental parliamentary and electoral majorities are provided with and without this passive support. Passive support has not been included in the calculation of whether the parliament constitutes an institutional veto point.

[b] In this case, the party in italics provided external support for the government, rather than merely a promise of abstention.

[c] It is not possible to specify the exact number of MPs of the Democratici and the PPI in the Senato. In consequence there is no possibility to calculate the majorities and the veto points. Without the MPs of the Democratici and the PPI in the Camera the majority is 48.6%. Without the MPs of the Democratici and the PPI the majority in the Senato is 44.8%.

Sources: D'Alimonte & Bartolini (2002: 383 ff); *Deputati e senatori del IX parlamento repubblicano* (Rome: Editoriale Italiana, 1982); *Deputati e senatori del X parlamento repubblicano* (Rome: Editoriale Italiana, 1983); *Deputati e senatori del XI parlamento repubblicano* (Rome: Editoriale Italiana, 1987); *Deputati e senatori del XII parlamento repubblicano* (Rome: Editoriale Italiana, 1992); *Deputati e senatori del XIII parlamento repubblicano* (Rome: Editoriale Italiana, 1994); *Deputati e senatori del XIII parlamento repubblicano. Aggiornamenti: il governo Dini* (Rome: Editoriale Italiana, 1995); *Deputati e senatori del XIV parlamento repubblicano* (Rome: Editoriale Italiana, 2001); Thomas R. Cusack (personal communication).

represents agricultural entrepreneurs. Beside these major groups a number of minor associations exist, putting pressure on the former by challenging their representative authority.

In pension policy, other interest groups are also relevant, including administrative institutions such as INPS—the major national institution for public pensions—which is a powerful actor in pension policy-making and was managed, until the mid-1990s, by the social partners (unions). INPS thus brought to the pensions arena the perspective of state bureaucrats, but it also provided the unions with an institutionalized path to channel their requests into the policy-making process.

Italy is not usually considered a country where neo-corporatist practices are important, but some waves of corporatist bargaining have occurred. In 1975–76, 1983–84 and 1992–93 the government and the unions engaged in close and articulated negotiations on income policy and the revision of the automatic indexation for wages (*scala mobile*).

In the field of pensions, relations between government and interest groups took different forms in the last five decades (Regonini 1996). The role of workers' associations was marginal during the phase of occupational expansion of the old age protection system—from the mid-1950s to the mid-1960s—when the government introduced new pension schemes for farmers, artisans and merchants under pressure from the associations representing these groups, and because of the strong connections between the latter and some parties in governmental coalitions. However, during the 1960s, trade union influence grew, the first signs being visible in the participation of CNEL—the National Council for Economy and Labor (*Consiglio Nazionale dell'Economia e del Lavoro*)—in drafting the proposal for a broad reform of the pension system in 1963. After this plan failed, negotiations between the government and the unions were revived in the late 1960s, leading to reforms in 1968 and 1969 that increased the generosity of pension programs. The fundamental 1969 reform represented a turning point for pension policy. In the aftermath of the so-called "hot autumn" of 1969, characterized by clashes between the government and the union and student movements, the unions acquired an informal guarantee of involvement in social and economic policy-making, particularly pension policy.

In the mid-1970s, the agreement on indexing for pensions (and wages) was one of the results of negotiations between the unions and *Confindustria*; nonetheless things changed in the following decade, when such close cooperation in pension issues became less common, and the few important decisions were increasingly taken inside Parliament's legislative committees. The 1980s were in fact characterized by substantial stalemate in pension policy: informal consultations between policy-makers and the unions continued, but none of the plans prepared either by the cabinet or by ad hoc committees were ever enacted. Stalemate was finally overcome in the early 1990s in the wake of the resurgence of tripartite concertation between government, unions and the employers' association *Confindustria* (Regini and Regalia 1997). The cooperative attitude between the main political and social actors started in 1992 with bargaining on income policy, and it was later extended to pensions (partly) in 1992 and (fully) in 1995 (see pp. 432, 436). This period proved fundamental for the establishment of a more institutionalized pattern of negotiation between the government and interest groups on welfare and labor policy (Regini and Regalia 1997; Ferrera and Gualmini 2004), that lasted until the 2001 elections, when the newly elected Center-right government moved towards a less close consultation with social partners, usually defined as "social dialogue."

Finally, it is worth noting that, because of the weakness of national financial institutions and the predominantly single-pillar structure of the pension system, financial actors did not play a substantial role in pension politics until the 1990s. However, since the beginning of the reconfiguration of the pension system (1992–93), financial actors and other institutions have joined the debate. They have played a dual role: on the one hand financial markets demanded the Italian government (especially in 1992 and 1995) to commit to pension reform as part of a wider "obligation" to restore sound public finance; on the other hand, financial institutions,[8] together with the association of supplementary pension funds (*Assoprevidenza*), gradually increased their pressure for the development of supplementary funded pension pillars, which was likely to represent a sort of "megabusiness." Since the take-off of supplementary pension funds, the influence of financial institutions has increased, not least because of the support from the Berlusconi government.

III PENSION SYSTEM

Historical overview

Italy got off to an early start in pension provision, introducing in 1919 a compulsory funded scheme for all employees with earnings under a certain threshold. Such governmental intervention in the field of old-age protection was the consequence of the failed take-off of voluntary pension insurance, introduced in 1898 with the establishment of the National Fund for Disability and Old-Age (*Cassa Nazionale per l'Invalidità e la Vecchiaia*) for blue-collar workers. This first experiment failed mainly because the scheme was voluntary and blue-collar wages were low, so it was difficult for workers to afford to participate (Cherubini 1977).

After 1919, the system followed a Bismarckian path with separate occupational schemes. The original scheme was based on funded defined-contribution plans, and because contributions were low, benefits were extremely modest. However, after World War II, the PAYG principle was gradually introduced into the scheme to preserve the level of pensions, which had been drastically reduced by the erosion of reserves due to very high inflation. After 1947, pensions were thus financed through a mixed system—partly funded, partly PAYG.

The subsequent evolution of the Italian pension system resembled that of many Bismarckian countries, and had two major themes: (i) coverage extension to protect the various categories of workers by creating new schemes providing fixed benefits (in 1957 for farmers, in 1959 for artisans and in 1966 for merchants); and (ii) introduction of a basic means-tested scheme aimed at preventing poverty in old age (1969). Moreover, between 1968 (Law 238) and 1969 (Law 153) the old-age insurance shifted form a partly funded system providing contributions-related benefits, to a fully PAYG system where benefits were earnings-related. The year 1969 was also crucial for the level of old-age pensions, as benefit formula was modified, making it more generous: at that time benefits paid about 60 percent of reference earnings after 40 years of insurance, and this figure rose to 80 percent during the 1970s.

This expansion caused a rapid increase in pension expenditure relative to GDP, which passed from 4.5 percent in 1960, to 6.8 percent in 1970 and 10.8 percent in 1980 (Ministero del Tesoro 1981), and huge imbalances in the accounts of INPS and other autonomous funds. This was possible because INPS was allowed to run deficits that were compensated by annual transfers from the public budget.

The shift from a funded system to PAYG, the expansion of coverage and the increase in benefit generosity occurred in many developed nations during the post-war period, within a wider process that has been labeled "distributive slippage" (Ferrera 1998): social policies, originally crafted as re-distributive measures, turned into distributive policies, offering concentrated benefits to selected social groups while dispersing and obfuscating their costs. Consequently, such policies represented the main instruments for politicians to attract voters' support in a context where the diminished importance of "class politics" weakened the traditional ties between parties and interest groups. However, this process took on peculiar traits in Italy. First, it was supported by rapid economic growth and eased by the early and undisciplined conversion of policy-makers to deficit spending, which shifted the burden of welfare state financing onto public debt—and onto future generations (Ferrera and Gualmini 2004). Second, due to the occupational segmentation of the pension system, old-age (and disability) policies emerged as the typical currency of political exchanges. During the 1950s and the 1960s, pension policy became the realm of different interest groups exerting "micro-corporatist" pressures on either the government or individual parties in the governmental majority. Against the politico-institutional background sketched in the previous paragraphs, the best strategy of survival for weak and unstable Italian cabinets was thus to respond to all the inputs and micro-demands coming from social and political groups, by multiplying particularistic laws and regulations in order to distribute advantages and benefits to those social categories whose electoral support was particularly important.

The continuous and fiscally irresponsible response to particularistic claims had dramatic consequences on pension expenditure and public finances. Expansive reforms were rarely preceded by serious forecasts on their impacts, and virtually no pension expenditure projection was carried out until the late 1970s. A clear example of such developments was the introduction of very favorable "seniority pensions" for public sector employees (1956) who were allowed to retire after only 20 years regardless of age (so-called "baby pensions"), followed by "seniority pensions" provision for private sector employees (1965) and self-employed workers (1965) that permitted them to retire after 35 years, even prior to reaching retirement age.

From another perspective, social policies were a powerful way to enhance the legitimacy of the polarized Italian political system. Though highly combative in the electoral arena, since the early 1970s the PCI was de facto involved in most important domestic policy-making. Such involvement—aimed at constraining the potential anti-system orientation of the Communist Party—was manifest in pension policy, as most legislation was approved by very large parliamentary majorities (Cazzola 1995).

At the end of the golden age of the welfare state, the result of such political bargains was a bizarre pension system: generous, costly and extremely fragmented along occupational lines, with many different schemes for the various employment categories, each with peculiar regulations about eligibility conditions, contributions and benefits. Such a system was dominated by the public pension pillar, though another peculiar scheme existed—the so-called *Tfr* (*Trattamento di fine rapporto*, see below)—a quasi second-pillar pension. Proper second—(occupational) and third—(individual) pillar pensions were limited to high-income workers in specific sectors of the economy—especially the financial sector.

Expansions of the public pensions also conditioned the development of the whole Italian social protection system, orienting it towards the overprotection of old age: in the early-1990s pensions represented *c.* 60 percent of overall social expenditure.

Description of the current pension system

The old age protection system that has emerged from the reforms of the 1990s can be defined as a "single-pillar pension system in transition." The first pillar still plays a primary role, providing roughly 82 percent of the income of those aged 65 and over (Ministero del Welfare 2002), though its relevance is expected to decline in the coming decades. The public system consists of different schemes, organized along occupational lines, providing contributory benefits to retired workers. Underneath this tier, there is a social assistance scheme that provides means-tested, flat-rate "social pensions" to the elderly with no, or insufficient, contributory records.

Following the adoption of a legal framework for supplementary pensions (Legislative Decree 124/93) and subsequent revisions, both the second and the third funded pillars started to develop. Affiliation to supplementary pension funds is voluntary and state subsidized, as workers are encouraged to contribute to such funds through tax incentives.

Alongside the pension pillars, the above mentioned *Tfr* still exists, at least for those workers who entered the labor market before 1993 or those without supplementary pension coverage. The *Tfr* is severance pay that firms must pay their employees, either when they retire, or when they leave the company for any other reason. It is financed through payroll taxes (6.91% of gross wages) and operates as a defined-benefit scheme, though it can only be paid in a lump sum. It is basically a "deferred-wage" for all private employees: benefits are calculated as the sum of 1/13.5 of the annual earnings for each year of employment, revalued at a fixed interest rate of 1.5 percent plus 75 percent of the inflation rate.[9] As contributions are only "virtually" accumulated, the *Tfr* represents an important (and relatively cheap) source of finance for companies. The portability of the accumulated amount is not allowed if the worker changes company or if he/she is fired. Even if the *Tfr* has functioned for some as an unemployment subsidy in disguise, more often it performed old-age protection functions due to the dominant pattern of employment based on full-time, permanent contracts (i.e. "a job for life").

Coverage

All workers are covered by compulsory old-age insurance. The first pillar is still fragmented along professional lines, though most workers are members of one of the two major institutions: the National Institute for Social Insurance (*Istituto Nazionale della Previdenza Sociale*, INPS) provides coverage for over 18 million workers (2002) in the private sector, while the National Institute for Social Insurance of Civil Servants (*Istituto Nazionale di Previdenza per i Dipendenti dell'Amministrazione Pubblica*, INPDAP) insures over 3 million (2002) public employees. Workers covered by neither INPS nor INPDAP are compulsorily affiliated to the dedicated fund for their professional category: alternative regimes exist for journalists and show-business workers, while most free professionals have independent funds (e.g. for architects, psychologists, accountants, surveyors, agrarian experts and others). Individuals over 65 years old with no contributory record are covered by the social assistance scheme for the elderly (*assegno sociale*).

As for supplementary funded pillars, slightly fewer than 3 millions workers are members of "closed" and "open"[10] pension funds, or have subscribed to individual pension plans (not including pension provision through life insurance contracts, which is common). Since 1998, when the first fund was set up in accordance with the regulations adopted in 1993, coverage has been increasing. This development has been particularly intense for workers employed in private companies operating in the industrial sector. By contrast, the expansion of funded schemes for public employees and the self-employed has lagged behind.

Administration

The fragmentation of the system is revealed by its administrative structure. Both major pension institutions are internally fragmented, with diverse funds for different categories of workers. INPS is articulated into four major funds dedicated, respectively, to: private sector employees (*Fondo Pensioni Lavoratori Dipendenti* FPLD), farmers, artisans and merchants, and other smaller funds for narrow professional categories, working in telecommunications, energy, aviation, tax-advice, transport, members of the clergy and domestic workers. Similarly, INPDAP, which was created in 1994,[11] has two major funds for central government employees and local government employees, besides other regimes for law officers, doctors and teachers. After the 1995 pension reform a special committee—*Nucleo di Valutazione della Spesa Previdenziale*—was created to monitor public pension expenditure.

The supplementary pillars also look fragmented: at the end of 2004, 42 "closed" and 92 "open" pension funds existed. The main difference between the two types of

First pillar	Second pillar	Third pillar
Third tier: none	**Voluntary occupational pension:**	**Voluntary private pension:**
First and second tiers combined: earnings-related pensions (INPS and INPDAP are the two biggest institutions, but many more funds exist) — INPS, INPDAP; Self-employed: Employees (FPLD), Merchants, Farmers, Artisans, Local government, Central government	**Subsidized occupational pension:** "Closed" pension funds; "Open" pension funds in case of collective affiliation. Both tax subsidized (ETT)	**Subsidized personal pension:** "Open" pension funds in case of individual affiliation; PIP (*individual Pension Plans*)
Means-tested part (*Pensione sociale–Integrazione al minimo–Assegno Sociale*)	**Mandatory occupational pension:** none	**Mandatory personal pension:** none
Social assistance: none	**Mandatory severance payment/quasi-pension scheme** (private employees: *Trattamento di fine rapporto* (*TFR*); public employees: *Indennità di buonuscita*)	

Fig. 9.4 Pension system in Italy

supplementary funds is that the social partners play a role in both the establishment and management of the ("closed") funds, while "open" pension funds are directly managed by financial institutions. With regard to the former, 37 were for employees and 5 for the self-employed. Alongside these newly established institutions for retirement provision, we find 510 very small pension funds that pre-existed the introduction of the regulatory framework in 1993. The picture is completed by over

600,000 individual pension plans (*Polizze Individuali Pensionistiche*, PIP), which constitute the third pillar of the system. The activity of "closed" and "open" funds is supervised by an independent authority named *COVIP.*

Financing

The first pillar is financed on a PAYG basis, through workers' contributions. In accordance with the fragmentation of the system, contribution rates vary considerably between the different schemes. A complete account is well beyond the scope of this chapter, however we may note the most relevant regulations for workers affiliated to INPS. The contribution rate for private employees is high in a comparative perspective: 32.7 percent of gross wage, shared between workers (1/3) and employers (2/3). In the schemes for self-employed workers the contribution rate is lower: it ranges from 14.2 percent to 18.2 percent of gross income for artisans, from 14.59 percent to 18.59 percent for merchants and from 17.3 percent to 20.3 percent of the contribution base for farmers.[12] Since 1996, "atypical" workers are also covered by compulsory insurance, and the current contribution rate ranges from 10 percent to 18 percent of gross earnings.

If contributions are inadequate to cover the payment of benefits, the state fills the annual gap by transferring resources from the public budget. In 2001 this gap was about 0.8 percent of GDP. However, the financial relationship between the public budget and INPS is somewhat more complex: in fact, according to law 88/1989, social assistance benefits for the elderly (i.e. *pensione sociale, integrazione al minimo* and, after 1995, *assegno sociale*) should have been financed through general revenues, but such legal provision was never fully implemented. Consequently, social benefits are still partly financed through surpluses of INPS insurance funds, that is, through workers' contributions.

As for the second pillar "closed" pension funds, the legal framework envisages three sources of financing: workers' contributions, employers' contributions, and the *Tfr*. The state contributes through tax incentives, as workers' contributions to pension funds are deductible up to 12 percent of gross income and a maximum amount of €5,164 per year. The same tax exemption also applies to contributions paid into "open" funds and individual pension plans, which are usually financed by workers' contributions only.

Benefits

The first pillar of the Italian pension system provides diverse benefits to protect workers and individuals against different risks: old-age benefits, survivor benefits and disability benefits. As already observed, two major institutions are responsible for the payment of pensions: in 2002, INPS provided 15,186,189 benefits, of which 52.9 percent were old-age pensions, 24.9 percent survivors' benefits, 17.4 percent disability benefits, and 4.8 percent social assistance pensions—while INPDAP paid 2,397,250 pensions. Despite the extreme fragmentation of the system, six major funds (private employees, agricultural workers, artisans, merchants, employees of central and local governments) account for more than 90 percent of the overall pensions paid by INPS and INPDAP; in particular, the fund for private employees covers the lion's share with 9,856,898 pensions.

Taking into account old-age protection only, some crucial points must be noted. First, the Italian pension system provides both contributory benefits, such as: "old-age pensions" (*pensione di vecchiaia*) and "seniority pensions" (*pensione di anzianità*); and non-contributory benefits, including social pensions (*pensione sociale*) and a supplement for contributory pensions under a certain threshold (*integrazione al minimo*), both of which were replaced by a new benefit (*assegno sociale*) in 1995. Workers are entitled to old-age pensions when they reach the legal retirement age having fulfilled a minimum contributory period, while seniority pensions are paid to workers who have completed a longer period of contribution, regardless of age.

The 1995 and 2004 reforms made important changes to the rules concerning retirement age, contribution requirements for seniority pensions and the method for benefits calculation. Three groups of workers may be identified. (1) Those workers who in 1995 had more than 18 years of contribution may retire at 65 years of age (60 for women), after at least 20 years of regular employment, receiving earnings-related benefits. The reference period for the calculation of these benefits stretches over the last 10 years. (2) The same rules regarding pensionable age apply to those workers who in 1995 had less than 18 years of contributions. Unlike the first group, however, these workers will receive "mixed" benefits, in the sense that the latter will be partly earnings-related and partly contributions-related. (3) A third group is made up of those workers who entered the labor market after 1995. For such workers the legal retirement age is 65 years of age (60 for women), with at least 5 years of contributions, and benefits will be entirely calculated with the new contributions-related system. As we shall see, the value of benefits is expected to decline markedly in the next decades for the last group.

As for the regulation of seniority pensions, when the contributions-related system matures a minimum contributory period of 40 years will be requested. During the transition period the eligibility conditions for the first two groups of workers (already outlined) have been tightened by combining a contribution requirement (currently 35 years) with an age prerequisite (57 years).

As for social assistance measures, after 1995, every Italian citizen over 65 years old with an insufficient contribution record to be entitled to a contributory pension and with a very low income (below €4,783.61 per year), will receive a social allowance (*Assegno sociale*, the former *pensione sociale*) of €367.97 per month (for 13 months per year). Since 1995, retired workers receiving very modest contributory pensions, who in the past were granted a pension supplement up to a defined "pension minimum," are no longer entitled to such supplements, but they may apply for the new *Assegno sociale*.

Finally, a few words about the benefits delivered by supplementary pension funds. The legal framework of 1993 provides that both "closed" and "open" funds set up for employed workers must adopt the defined-contributions method of benefits calculation, while the defined-benefits method is allowed for the funds for the self-employed.

IV Politics of pension reform since 1980

Overview

Economic and demographic changes have had a tremendous impact on the Italian pension system, which already had deep internal imbalances. As we shall see, the critical situation of the national pension system was tackled differently in the 1980s and 1990s. The first phase was characterized by heated debate—some reform proposals were formulated but few changes were made. By contrast, the 1992 Amato reform was the first of several significant reforms. The most important reform was adopted in 1995 (Dini reform), and was followed by adjustments in 1997 and 2004–5.

The 1980s: "Much Ado About Nothing"

The first step in the recognition of the critical situation of the national pension system was made by the so-called *Castellino Commission* (named after the professor who presided over it) set up in 1981 by the Treasury Minister, Beniamino Andreatta. This committee provided the first comprehensive evaluation of the pension system since the 1960s, suggesting several ways to tackle the most evident problems. The Committee report (Ministero del Tesoro 1981) also contained one of the first projections on pension expenditure. Two different periods (1980–5 and 1980–2000), and two diverse scenarios for each period were considered. The situation was critical in both scenarios for both periods. Pension expenditure, which had grown from 4.5 percent of GDP in 1960 to 10.8 percent in 1980, was projected to rise to 11.7 percent of GDP in 1985 in the best scenario, and to 12.4 percent in the worst, while the transfers from the public budget were projected to grow from 4.2 percent to 6.1 percent of GDP. Thus, pension expenditure would be around 18–19 percent of GDP in 2000, and the equilibrium contribution rate for the seven major schemes would rise from 20 percent to an alarming 32–34 percent. Consequently, the committee proposed some reform measures, mainly aimed at restoring the financial viability of the system by promoting fairness:

(a) harmonizing contribution rates for public and private employees and raising the overall contribution rates for both employees and the self-employed;
(b) harmonizing eligibility conditions for seniority and old-age pensions between the different schemes and equalizing the retirement age for male (60 years of age) and female (55 years) private employees;
(c) gradually abolishing the privileged regulations of seniority pensions in the public sector;
(d) shifting indexation from real wages to inflation; and
(e) modifying the benefit formula to account the whole career rather than the last (and best) years.

Ever since, several ministers for Labor and Welfare proposed reforms (Table 9.3) which shared some objectives: harmonizing contribution rates, benefit formulas, eligibility conditions and retirement ages among the different schemes; or, alternatively, integrating the different schemes into a single public scheme. Other plans were more innovative and/or radical, proposing to raise retirement age and to reconfigure the system on different pillars. However, all these plans had the same fate: they rarely entered legislative assemblies and they were abandoned because of a change of government or early elections.

In fact, the Italian political system did not seem to be ready for pension reform, largely because it was still marked by high fragmentation and a polarized party system, with weak governments usually relying on broad coalitions. During the 1980s, five parties participated in governmental coalitions, with an average of 3.7 parties per coalition. These governments were "colorful" and heterogeneous, usually including both the center-right and center-left, with the pivotal Christian Democratic Party in the middle. Such coalitions were deeply divided, especially between the increasingly influential Socialist Party and the Christian Democrats, which affected governmental stability and often led to fierce confrontations between government and Parliament. Governments remained in power only 300 days on average—a formidable obstacle to comprehensive pension reform.

By the early 1990s, more than ten years had passed since the emergence of the pension reform debate and there were few results. The shift from the "credit claiming" distributive policies typical of the expansionary period to the retrenching policies required by the modified external and internal environment proved to be difficult, almost impossible, in Italy. Though the relation between power concentration (*majoritarianism*) and the likelihood of passing a pension reform is far from straightforward (see Immergut and Anderson, in the Editors' Introduction to this volume), the government in Italy had too little autonomy from the supporting coalition, and was therefore too often involved in struggles with Parliament to commit itself to a delicate exercise of "blame avoidance" and carefully work through the various stages of a pension reform.

On the contrary, the last government supported by the five-party coalition (*pentapartito*) of the First Republic passed a reform that followed the policy pattern of the "golden age." Despite population aging, rising unemployment, large public debt and increasing deficits, the earnings-related system was extended to self-employed workers, though maintaining the contribution rate at a low level. This represented another expansionary change—introduced without forecasting its impact on public expenditure—which further worsened the financial situation of the three schemes affected by the reform (Franco 2002), and created problems regarding the fairness of the system as the return on contributions was higher for the self-employed than the private employees. Both of these factors played a role in the reform of the system during the next decade.

By the early 1990s, however, Italy was on the verge of a new era, where the inefficiencies and the vices of its pension system were no longer acceptable because of the impact of both external and internal factors.

Table 9.3 Overview of proposed pension reforms in Italy 1980–1992

Year	Name of reform	Reform process (chronology)	Reform measures
1980	Scotti (DC) Reform Proposal (*Bill C1296*)	• January 23: presentation of the government bill • discussion at the Chamber of Deputies blocked in July 1982 • new elections in 1983 → no political action	• unification of the different regimes within the INPS (the National Social Insurance Institute) • harmonization of contribution rates between employees in the public and private sector • raising the retirement age: 65 years for men, 60 years for women → reform failed
1981	Castellino Committee	• Publication of the committee report → no political action	• harmonization of contribution rates for public and private sector employees • harmonization of eligibility conditions for seniority and old-age pensions between different schemes • equalization male and female retirement age • gradual phasing-out of seniority pensions in the public sector • change of indexation base from wages to inflation rate • lengthening of the period to assess reference earnings: entire working career
1983	De Michelis (PSI) plan	• October 1983 draft proposal of Minister for Labor and Welfare • August 1984 adoption by Council of Ministers → no political action	• Transition to a 3 pillars pension system: • ceilings on benefits in the first pillar • voluntary II and III funded pillars, public management • raising and equalizing retirement age: 65 years for men and women • disincentives for those who retire between 60 and 65 • lengthening of the period to assess reference earnings: from 5 to 10 years • lengthening of the contributory period for seniority pensions: 40 years • separation of social assistance (*assistenza sociale*) from social insurance (*previdenza*) • gradual phasing-in

1984	Cristofori (DC) commission's proposal (*Bill C1461 and others*)	• President of the parliamentary committee for pension reform Nino Cristofori (DC) presents competing proposal • 1985 De Michelis retracts his proposal • April 1985: Cristofori's proposal split in different parts; expansionary measures approved by parliament (L. 140/85 and 141/85): increase of minimum and social pensions • April 1986: Cristofori's proposal is strongly criticized by the Ministry of the Treasury Goria (DC) • November 1986: the Council of Ministers agrees on guidelines for reform proposal • Jan–Feb 1987: discussion in parliamentary committees • March 1987: crisis of government, new minister for Labor and Welfare • June 1987: new elections → reform failed	• extension of the general norms of the FPLD to all dependent employees in the public and private sector • extension of the earnings-related system to the schemes for self-employed • increasing minimum pensions for the self-employed (harmonization with private employees) • lengthening the minimum qualifying period for old-age pension from 15 to 20 years • gradual harmonization of the contributory period for seniority pensions: 35 years • institution of private pension funds supplementing the pension benefits paid by the state • gradual raising of retirement age for women: 60 years. Incentives for men who postpone retirement till 65

1987	Formica (PSI) plan	• September 1987: two commissions appointed to draft a reform proposal
		• December 1987: commissions deliver their plans
		• Critics by DC, unions, Confindustria
		• April 1988: change of government
			• Final proposal: ask parliament a delegation of power to reform pensions:
			  - raising and harmonizing retirement age: 65 years. Disincentives for those who retire between 60 and 65
			  - lengthening of the minimum contributory period for old-age pensions: from 15 to 20 years
			  - lengthening of the period to assess reference earnings: from 5 to 10 years
			  - gradual phasing-in

(*Continued*)

Table 9.3 (Continued)

Year	Name of reform	Reform process (chronology)	Reform measures
		• July 1988: final proposal • September 1988: critics by unions, Confindustria; no adoption by the Council of Ministers • 1989 crisis of government, new Minister of Labor and Welfare → reform failed	– foster the development of supplementary funded pillars through fiscal incentives and the (voluntary) use of the *Tfr*
1989	Donat Cattin (DC) plan	• 1989 formulation of an informal proposal • Spring 1991 death of Minister of Welfare and Labor Donat Cattin → no political action	• introduction of a compulsory second pillar pension financed by the *Tfr* • raising retirement age: 65 years • lengthening the qualifying period for seniority pensions to 40 years of contribution • increasing the period to assess reference earnings: from 5 to 10 years • reduction of the accrual rate
1991	Marini proposal	• June 1991: government draft • no consensus between coalition partners Socialist Party and Christian Democratic Party • August 1991: the Council of Ministers agrees on guidelines for reform proposal • September 1991: reform postponed due to contrasts within governmental majority • February 1992: end of legislature → no political action	• phasing-out of the seniority pensions for public sector employees i.e. introduction of 35 years as minimum qualifying period • raising retirement age: 65 • lengthening of period to assess reference earnings: from 5 to 10 years

Table 9.4 Overview of proposed and enacted pension reforms in Italy, 1992–2005

Year	Name of reform	Reform process (Chronology)	Reform measures
1992–3	Amato Reform • emergency measures: laws 359/92 and 438/92 • structural reform: delegation law 421/92, then implemented through D.Lgs. 503/92 (reform of public pillar), D.Lgs. 124/93 (framework for supplementary pensions)	• June 1992: technocratic government supported by a four-party coalition • nomination of a pension committee • July 1992: emergency measures: presented bill C1287 to convert D.L.333/92; approved 7.8.92: law 359/92; presented bill S463 for structural reform • September 1992: Union strikes and demonstrations; tripartite negotiations. bill S463 revised. Emergency measures: bill C1581 to convert D.L.384/92 • October 10, 1992: bill S463 approved by the Chamber of Deputies (vote of confidence). pro 303 (gov. parties) - con. 3 (Greens; RC; LN, Pds)– abst. 11 (Msi, Pri); October 22, 1992: Senate approves (vote of confidence): pro 158 (gov. parties) – con. 4 - abst. 7: Law 421/92 • 12 November 1992: bill C1581 approved by Senate (vote of confidence): Law 438/92 • December 1992: D.Lgs. 503/92 • April 1993: D.Lgs. 124/93	Law 421/92 – D.Lgs. 503/92 • retirement age raised from 55 to 60 for women and from 60 to 65 for men • extension of the period to assess reference earnings extended from last 5 years (for private sector) and last month (for public sector) to 10 years for those with at least 15 years of contributions and entire working career for new entrants in the labor market • phasing-out of seniority "baby pensions" for public employees: minimum qualifying period lengthened from 20 to 35 years • harmonization of the public sector seniority pension with private sector • lengthening of minimum qualifying period for standard old-age pension from 15 to 20 years • change of indexation base from wages to prices • limitation of compatibility of pensions and income from work • lengthening of minimum qualifying period for seniority pension from 35 to 36 years → proposed but not enacted • reduction of the accrual rate for workers with higher wages Law 438/92 • suspension of the option to retire with seniority pensions in 1993; reduction of pension indexation for 1993 D.Lgs. 124/93 • legal framework for open and closed pension funds in the second/third pillars. Possibility to use the *Tfr* to finance these funds

(Continued)

Table 9.4 (Continued)

Year	Name of reform	Reform process (Chronology)	Reform measures
1994	Berlusconi Reform	• 1994: pension reform crucial issue in electoral campaign for the elections • government coalition between Forza Italia, Alleanza Nazionale, Lega Nord, Ccd-Cdu • September 1994 submission of government bill • Oct/Nov 1994 general strike and union protests • December 1, 1994: agreement between unions and government on few and temporary measures → original reform proposal drastically smoothened • December 22, 1994: resignation of the Berlusconi government	• benefits reduction when retiring below standard retirement age of 60/65 years: 3% per each year below retirement age • reduction of the accrual rate from 2% to 1.75% for older workers • changing indexation from prices to projected inflation rate → reform failed (except for some minor changes: i.e. acceleration of the transition period to increase retirement age legislated in Amato reform)
1995	Dini Reform law 335/1995	• January 1995: Investiture of a technocratic government under Dini supported by PDS, Popular Party, Lega Nord and some smaller center parties • May 8, 1995: agreement between government and unions; *Confindustria* refuses to sign • Bill C2549 presented at the Chamber of Deputies • August 3, 1995: vote Senate: pro 175 (gov. parties) – con. 56 (AN, RC) – abst. 37 (FI, CCD) • August 4, 1995: vote Chamber of Deputies: pro 266 (gov. parties) – con. 92 (AN, RC) – abst. 125 (FI, CCD): Law 335/95	• change of pension calculation formula from earnings-related system to contributions-related system i.e. benefits depend on amount of contributions actually paid, indexed with mean GDP growth rate of the last five years; very gradual phasing-in. • flexible retirement age: 57–65 years • introduction of factors into the benefit formula to take account of the age of retirement, economic trends and demographic dynamics • seniority pensions: gradual increase of minimum qualifying period from 35 to 40 years • introduction of child rearing credits • increase in contribution rates • replacement of *pensione sociale* with a new means-tested benefit (*Assegno sociale*) • new scheme for workers with "atypical" contracts • extension of tax incentives for supplementary second pillar pensions (contributions are tax deductible up to 2% of annual income with an upper limit of €1,291)

1997	Prodi Reform Law 449/97	• 1996: Prodi government supported by Olive tree and the external support of *Rifondazione Comunista* • establishment of a committee (*Commissione Onofri*) • December 18, 1997: vote Chamber of Deputies: pro 305 (gov. parties) – con. 188 (opposition) – abst. 3 • December 23, 1997: vote Senate: pro 161(gov. parties) – con. 40 (opp.) – abst. 0: Law 449/97	Law 449/97 • tightening conditions for seniority pensions via harmonization between public and private sector • one-year freeze of pensions indexation • increase of basic pensions • restoration of partial compatibility of pensions and income from work Proposed but not enacted • unification of different pension regimes • acceleration of the introduction of the new pension formula of the Dini reform introduction of automatic revisions of the conversion coefficients
2000	D. Lgs. 47/2000	• May 1999: law 133/99, government presents a bill to ask parliament a delegation of power to issue a decree on supplementary pensions • February 2000: government decree D. Lgs. 47/00	• More generous tax incentives for supplementary pensions; contributions made deductible up to 12% of annual income with an upper limit of €5,164
2004–5	Berlusconi II Reform law 243/2004 D.Lgs. 252/2005	• 2001: Brambilla committee report • December 2001: government presents a bill (C2145) to ask parliament a delegation of power to reform pensions • 2002: debate and criticism by social partners and experts • Oct/Dec. 2003: general strike and a big demonstration • January 2004: original draft bill substantially modified to take into consideration social partners' requests	Law 243/2004 • introduction of bonus for deferred retirement despite eligibility to seniority pension • fixed and higher retirement age in the contributions-related system: 65 years for men, 60 for women • tightened conditions for seniority pensions in the transition period • compulsory transfer of *Tfr* into pension funds → Revised: transfer of the *Tfr* with the "silent assent" formula (to be confirmed by a government decree) • introduction of an extra 3% tax on very high pensions Proposed but not enacted: • reduction of contribution rate to 5% for newly hired workers

(*Continued*)

Table 9.4 (Continued)

Year	Name of reform	Reform process (Chronology)	Reform measures
		• May 13, 2004: vote Senate (vote of confidence): pro 153 (gov. parties) – con. 88 (opposition) – abst.0 • July 28, 2004: vote Chamber of Deputies (vote of confidence): pro 288 (gov. parties) –con.119 (opp.) – abst. 0: Law 243/04 • 2004–2005: debate starts on the new rules for the *Tfr* and supplementary pillars. Negotiations between the *Tfr* and the Ministry of Welfare and the unions; government divided. • November 24, 2005. Issued D.Lgs.252/2005	D.Lgs. 252/2005 (operative in 2008) • transfer of the *Tfr* with the "silent assent" formula • in the default option ("silence") the *Tfr* is automatically transferred to occupational funds; a residual fund, managed by INPS, is created to receive the *Tfr* if no pension funds are available. • compensatory measures for firms that "loose" the *Tfr* • revision of tax rules for supplementary pension funds

Over the course of the decade, three factors caused a decisive shift in the pattern of Italian pension politics. First, the downsizing of the public pillar (Table 9.4) was the result of a complex learning process, prompted by a sudden change of actor constellation in the early 1990s, in the wake of both internal and external developments (Fig. 9.1 on p. 398). Second, the formation of "technocratic" governments proved to be crucial in at least two respects: (i) they included social actors in the policy-making through a concertative approach, that eased the unfolding of the political and social learning process, (ii) being relatively more autonomous from their parliamentary majorities, and less exposed to electoral punishment, these cabinets had greater chances of successfully reforming pensions.

Finally, we suggest that the neo-institutionalist literature—though fruitful in highlighting the institutional resiliency that hampers public pension reform (see Immergut and Anderson, in the Editors' Introduction to this volume)—usually overstates the constraints posed by existing institutional configurations. Our contention is that within a complex policy architecture there may well be "institutional gates" which, if effectively exploited by policy-makers, can be "opened" thus facilitating institutional (policy) change. As we shall see, the presence of a peculiar institution such as the *Tfr* proved to be crucial for making the transition to a multi-pillar configuration (Jessoula 2004).

The 1992 Amato Reform

In the early 1990s the government's financial position was dramatic (public debt = 117.3% of GDP in 1992; public deficit = 10.5% in 1991) and Italy also suffered from a deep political and institutional crisis, after the *Tangentopoli* scandal broke in the spring of 1992.

In such a situation, Giuliano Amato—the Socialist Prime Minister who led the government after the 1992 elections—clearly perceived that the country needed firm guidance, otherwise the economic, financial and political-institutional challenges could have swept the whole democratic system away (Cazzola 1995). Amato put together a partly "technocratic" cabinet, supported by a four-party coalition (DC, PSI, PLI, PSDI), and then embarked on the so-called process of *risanamento*, that is, the restoring-to-health of the public finances. Central to this process, given the specific character of the Italian welfare state, was the reform of the pension system, then absorbing about two-thirds of social expenditure.

In 1991, a new consensus on the alarming trend of pension expenditure had emerged from the projections of both INPS and General Accounting Office. These estimates showed a gloomy future for the private employees' scheme, and the situation was no better in the schemes for public employees and the self-employed. Expenditure on public pensions had reached 12.8 percent of GDP in 1992, and projections were even more dramatic: it could reach 23.4 percent of GDP in 2040, according to General Accounting Office.

The government tackled the issue by following a two-fold strategy: reducing public expenditure in the short term through emergency measures, while nominating a committee to propose substantial reform. To achieve the first goal, the government's 1992 budget suspended pension indexation for one year. Concerning structural changes, the draft pension reform re-proposed most of the measures recommended during the 1980s: lengthening both the minimum contribution period from 15 to 20 years, and the minimum contribution period for seniority pensions from 35 to 36 years. The unions also adopted a two-fold strategy, protesting against the short-term measures in the budget, while proving their willingness to negotiate on the draft of an organic pension reform.

However, during the summer, external pressures increased. In September 1992, France was to hold a referendum on the Maastricht Treaty, and the prospect of a French "no" (which would have killed the EMU project) upset international financial markets, and this prompted a speculative attack against the Lira, and on other weaker currencies in the EMS. In late August, the Italian government could no longer defend the exchange rate. The Lira was first devalued and then Italy pulled out of the EMS. This put pressure on the government to restore credibility vis-à-vis financial markets, and one option was a more substantial pension reform. Yet the government did not abandon dialogue with the unions, even more relevant in a climate of strict austerity, and absolutely necessary in a situation in which the channel of inter-party negotiation was unavailable, because of the discredit into which the major parties had fallen (Natali 2001, see previous page). Some measures concerning pensions—the suspension of the option to retire with seniority pensions in 1993 and the neutralization of the indexation mechanism for the same year—were introduced in the 1993 Budget Bill (Decree 384/92, later converted with Law 438/92), which provoked union protests, including strikes and demonstrations in September and October 1992 that mobilized thousands of people. Nevertheless, the reform process was not blocked and the tripartite informal negotiation between the government, the unions and the employers' association (*Confindustria*) continued until the adoption of the bill, which delegated to the government the power to revise pensions by decree (October 1992–Law 421/92).

Although no formal agreement was signed, both *Confindustria* and the unions accepted the revised version of the structural pension reform. The unions did not reject the plan, which imposed a much deeper reform than expected only some months before, in part because they obtained some concessions in terms of smaller short-term cuts: the lengthening of the minimum contribution period for seniority pensions (from 35 to 36 years) was eliminated and pensions were indexed to inflation for 1993. Law 421/92 delegated the government to issue two legislative decrees aimed at moving the Italian pension system towards a multi-pillar configuration: the first decree (D. Lgs. 503/92) concerned the revision of the first public pillar, while the second (D. Lgs. 124/93) established a framework for supplementary occupational and private pensions.

The plan to reform the public pillar was informed by two basic principles: (1) stabilizing pension expenditure and, (2) harmonizing different regulations for private and public employees. The two goals were often pursued together. The first change modified the pension formula of the earnings-related system by lengthening the reference period from the last 5 years for private employees, or the last month for public employees, to 10 years for those with at least 15 years of contributions, and the whole career for new entrants in the labor market.[13] Likewise, modification of the retirement age was aimed at both (partially) harmonizing the rules and reducing the number of future pensions: the retirement age for private employees was raised from 55 to 60 for women and from 60 to 65 for men (public sector: already 65 for both men and women). Finally, eligibility conditions for seniority pensions were tightened: the minimum contributory period to be entitled to seniority pensions was to be gradually equalized at 35 years for public and private employees. Despite these important changes, the gradualist character of the reform stands out; there are long phase-in periods for all of these measures (INPS 1993). This was the price for union acceptance.

However, these were not the only measures adopted in 1992. Another important change that was expected to generate substantial savings affected not only future pensions but also current benefits. The previous, generous *indexation* mechanism that linked benefits to both prices and wages was replaced by a new index adjusting pensions to prices. Finally, in both the schemes for employees and those for the self-employed, the minimum contributory period for old age benefits was raised from 15 to 20 years, and the option of combining pensions with income from work was limited.

The Amato reform also created a legal framework for the development of supplementary pensions. As noted, two kinds of pension funds were envisaged: "open" and "closed" pension funds. However, the fundamental problem for the Amato government was how to promote the transition to a multi-pillar pension system in a situation characterized by both strong political constraints and the scarcity of resources for financing supplementary pillars because of high public pension contributions and budget constraints. The government tackled the issue by turning to the "institutional gate" represented by the *Tfr*. The compulsory transfer of *Tfr* funds to supplementary funds was ruled out in order to preserve the traditional control of social partners over the *Tfr*. But the option of voluntarily using the *Tfr* to finance pension funds was created—supported by tax incentives. However, for workers entering the labor market after 1993 the Amato reform prescribed that the *Tfr* must be transferred to a pension fund, *if* a worker subscribed to a supplementary pension plan. Pension funds for employees can only follow the defined-contributions principle.

The (projected) effects of the Amato reform were important for both harmonization and cost containment, but limited because of the introduction of transition periods—for the raising of the retirement age, the lengthening of the reference period, the phasing-out of "baby-pensions" for public employees. Projections showed that expenditure for pensions would be contained, with a sharp decrease in future unfunded liabilities (Beltrametti 1996). Moreover, the phasing-out of "baby pensions" would enhance the equity of the system, while the changes in the pension formula—reducing (or eliminating in the case of new entrants) the favorable treatment that the earlier system provided to workers with less "flat" careers—and the lengthening of the minimum contributory period for old age pensions would improve fairness at the individual level because of the stricter link between benefits and contributions.

On a negative note, the issue of the (comparatively) short minimum contributory period—35 years—for seniority pension entitlement and the persistent different regulations for the schemes for (public and private) employees and the self-employed had not been tackled.

The 1994 Berlusconi Reform

After the Amato reform, INPS released a report on the Italian pension system that showed that while the 1992 retrenchment measures had improved the system, some aspects still required further change. The projections soothed worries over the private employees' scheme, where the impact of the reform was significant, but made more alarming predictions regarding schemes for certain self-employed workers—artisans, merchants and farmers. These schemes had always shown a structural deficit and the situation had worsened dramatically after the 1990 reform, which had extended the earnings-related system (INPS 1993).

Therefore, the pensions debate remained lively: welfare and pension reform became crucial issues in the 1994 election campaign. The election—the first held with the new mostly majoritarian electoral system introduced in 1993—saw a partial restructuring of the party system, and the formation of a new Center-right majority that supported the first truly "political" government[14] after two "technocratic" cabinets (led by Amato and Ciampi). Silvio Berlusconi was appointed Prime Minister.

Determined to continue the austerity policy inaugurated by his predecessors, Berlusconi chose Lamberto Dini as Treasury Minister and Clemente Mastella as Minister of Labour and Welfare. Mastella soon started to work on a new pension reform, setting up a committee which included some experts appointed by social actors. However the Berlusconi government did not speak with a single voice in the pensions debate and it also threatened the unions with talk of radical interventions and the privatization of the Italian social security system (Natali 2001). Although this behavior made the unions suspicious, a very loose kind of negotiation between the government, the unions and *Confindustria* continued during the summer and early fall. A bill giving the government the power to reform pensions by decree was eventually submitted in late September. The proposal aimed at:

1. strongly discouraging early retirement through seniority pensions by lowering benefits by 3 percent for each year below the legal retirement age;
2. reducing the accrual factor from 2 percent to 1.75 percent for all workers with at least 15 years of contributions;

3. replacing the existing indexation to actual prices with a new mechanism linking pensions to projected inflation only.

Employers praised these measures, but the unions launched massive protests: on October 14, 1994, hundreds of thousands of workers went on a general strike. On November 12, one million people crowded Rome for one of the largest demonstrations in a decade, and a further general strike was threatened for December.

In the meantime, the parliamentary majority was becoming unstable because of conflict between the *Lega Nord* and the two other major parties, *Forza Italia* and *Alleanza Nazionale*. The *Lega Nord* was becoming increasingly lukewarm on the pension issue, as the planned changes in seniority benefits would negatively affect the pension prospects of its core voters, due to the high concentration of workers with such benefits in northern Italy. In early December, the government retreated, and the agreement signed on December 1, 1994 between the government and the unions retained only a few, mostly temporary measures, like the suspension of the right to retire with seniority pensions in 1995. The agreement also allowed the government to retain in its 1995 budget (Law 724/94) measures accelerating the transition period (introduced by the Amato reform) for raising the retirement age, and also stated that before June 1995 a structural reform had to be adopted, or else contribution rates would be increased by decree. On December 22, Silvio Berlusconi resigned, concluding his first political experience with a defeat in the field of pensions.

Imposing retrenchment measures against union protests proved to be impossible for a government that—though "directly" chosen by voters—rested on a heterogeneous parliamentary majority. This majority was in fact the "artificial" result of a double territorial alliance between the electoral cartel *Polo del Buon Governo* (basically including FI and AN) in the southern part of the country, and the *Polo della Libertà* (FI and *Lega Nord*) in the north.

This case supports our argument that commitment to a concertation process leading to a substantial consensus among political and social actors—especially between the government and the unions—seems to be a fundamental prerequisite for successful pension reform. The Cabinet led by Berlusconi, because it was obliged to deal with different preferences both within its heterogeneous majority, and within the government itself—as some differences emerged between the rigorous approach of the Treasury Minister (a technocratic ministry) and the Minister of Labour and Welfare (CCD), did not fully commit itself to negotiation with the unions. The government, backed by *Confindustria*, which was demanding a structural intervention (Natali 2001), decided to attack the very issues on which workers and their representatives were most sensitive: seniority pensions, the level of benefits for older workers (by changing the accrual rate) and the pensions of current retirees (via the indexation mechanism).[15] In short, the governmental plan failed because it aimed at achieving financial sustainability and expenditure cuts without providing any (compensatory) measures that might please the unions.

The 1995 Dini Reform

After Berlusconi's resignation no new elections were held—somewhat in contravention of the unwritten rules of a majoritarian democracy—and President Scalfaro worked to form a new government, led by Lamberto Dini and supported by a center-left coalition (PDS, Popular Party, *Lega Nord* and some smaller center parties). President Scalfaro's decision not to dissolve Parliament rested mainly on the urgent need for a government that could tackle the worsening financial situation in the face of pressures stemming from both financial markets and the run-up to EMU.

Even though the economic situation was improving (GDP growth was at 2.2% in 1994 and the deficit had decreased to 7.1% of GDP), a public debt at 125 percent of GDP and the political unrest that had upset international markets provoked a sharp decline in the value of the national currency, implying the need for austerity measures (Ferrera and Gualmini 2004). The hope was that the new Cabinet, which displayed an evident "technocratic" character and was thought to remain in power for a limited period, would prove to be successful in adopting the urgent measures clearly expressed in its program.

Pension reform, as stated in the previous agreement of December 1994, was central in this program and the Minister of Labor and Welfare soon launched a much more institutionalized tripartite concertation than in the past, paying particular attention to the unions' requests. On the other hand, the unions seemed to be convinced that a further pension reform was needed, and they supported the idea of rewriting the "social pact" by preparing a pension reform proposal (Cazzola 1995; Lapadula and Patriarca 1995; Natali 2001).

The talks focused on three major issues: the institutional and financial separation of social insurance and social assistance, the modification of the pension formula and the revision of seniority pensions. On May 8, 1995, the government signed a formal agreement with the unions, which later polled workers to get their approval of the reform draft. *Confindustria* refused to sign the pact, however, criticizing its cautious approach on seniority pensions. Despite this defection, the parliamentary process of the bill did not encounter insurmountable obstacles, and in early August, Law 335/95 was passed.

The unions' new cooperative approach, which proved to be a crucial variable for the success of the reform, can be explained by at least four factors. First, the trade unions had undergone an internal process of maturation: the reform-oriented components of the movement had grown stronger, supplying an articulated platform of proposals to the national leadership. The second factor was the consultative style of policy-making introduced by Dini (who was also technically supported in the Parliament by left parties), very different from the adversarial style adopted by Berlusconi. The third factor was the significant concessions granted to the trade unions by the Dini cabinet over the phasing-in of the pension reform. In fact, as we shall see, major changes are to be phased in very slowly, thus not affecting pension entitlements of older workers. Finally, the attacks of international speculators, which worsened the lira's exchange rate day after day, obliging the Bank of Italy to raise interest rates, with nasty consequences for the public budget, ultimately convinced the trade unions that the status quo was no longer sustainable. During the first three months of the Dini government (January–March 1995), the spread between interest rates on Italian and German state bonds (the "BTP" and the "Bund") reached a peak of almost seven base points, up from three base points only a year before; in the same months, the probability assigned by markets (e.g. JP Morgan's "EMU calculator") to Italy's admission into the EMU by 1999 was as low as 0.127 (Chiorazzo and Spaventa 2000). In this period Italian economic and social policy-making started to function as a sort of "Skinner box", where the international markets produced stimuli in terms of variations in the lira's value and of interest rates, and the logic of "operational conditioning" pushed the trade unions towards compromise. In other words, the lesson for the trade unions was: there is no status quo, only a declining trend that is rapidly leading to an abyss unless we agree on a credible pension reform capable of re-assuring the markets.

The Dini reform brought a substantial reconfiguration of the Italian pension system in the direction of financial sustainability and cost containment, intra-generational fairness, modernization and flexibilization. The main measure was the modification of the pension formula, with the shift from an earnings-related system to a contributions-related one for private/public employees and the self-employed. In the new system, which still rests on the PAYG principle, pensions not only reflect the length of the contributory period (as in the previous system), but also the amount of contributions actually paid. As will be suggested later, however, this shift per se would not have been so crucial without the introduction of some less visible provisions that link benefits to the age at retirement, economic trends and demographic dynamics. In fact pensions are calculated as follows: the contributions paid by the workers are "virtually" accumulated in a personal account and indexed to the mean GDP growth rate of the last five years. At retirement, this amount is converted into a pension through a conversion coefficient that varies in relation to the age of the worker. That is, to say, the reform introduced a flexible retirement age—between 57 and 65—with the maximum benefit obtained by retiring at 65. The Dini law established that these conversion coefficients must be revised every ten years to take into account changes in both economic and demographic factors.

To forestall union opposition, the reform largely protected the "acquired rights" of older workers by introducing long transition periods. The contributions-related system fully applies only to new entrants to the labor market, and the reform has different implications for workers depending on the length of the contribution period as of 1995. The old earnings-related system (as reformed by Amato) remains in force for those with at least 18 years of contributions. For those with fewer than 18 years the new system applies pro rata, that is, for working years *before* 1995, pensions will be calculated with the old rules as reformed by Amato, while the contributions-related method will apply to working years *after* 1995. In retirement, pensions will be indexed to prices alone.

The Dini reform included a similar protection of "acquired rights" in the new regulation of seniority pensions. The eligibility condition was tightened by lengthening the minimum contributory period from 35 to 40 years, but this measure will be implemented with a long transition period. In 2008, workers will be allowed to retire either at any age after 40 years spent in a regular job, or at age 57 with at least 35 years of contributions.[16] Other measures of the Dini reform included: the introduction of credits for periods of both child-rearing and care; the creation of a new scheme for workers hired under the new "atypical" contracts; an increase in contribution rates; specific rules for those employed in physically demanding jobs; the replacement of both the so-called *pensione sociale* and the supplement for lower pensions with a new means-tested benefit (*Assegno sociale*) for all citizens over 65 years of age with an income under a certain threshold; and the creation of a permanent body responsible for monitoring pension expenditure.

The introduction of the contributions-related system harmonized the rules regarding benefits calculation in the schemes for private employees, public employees and the self-employed and when the new scheme is fully operative, regulations on retirement age and seniority pensions will also be the same in the different schemes. In addition, the reformed system should induce workers to retire later because of the links between retirement age and pension value (via the conversion coefficients) (Lapadula and Patriarca 1995), and contribution evasion should diminish as benefits closely reflect the contributions actually paid.

Finally, the Dini reform revised the 1993 regulation for supplementary pensions, providing more generous tax incentives to develop the second pension pillar. Contributions to pension funds were made deductible up to 2 percent of annual income (up to €1,291).

The Dini reform brought fundamental change to the Italian pension system, which now rests on a more sound financial basis, and it reduced fragmentation and intragenerational unfairness. This seems to be the factor that played the crucial role in the negotiations between the government and the unions. Unlike Berlusconi, Dini and his Labor Minister paid real attention to the requests of workers' organizations; on their side, the unions played a "pro-active" role within the reform process by providing governmental policy-makers not only with original problem diagnoses and possible technical solutions, but also with delicate "local and relational" information (Culpepper 2002). After the political failure of the first Berlusconi government (1994), and under the pressure of financial markets, the Dini government desperately needed to find a solution to the pension crisis that was acceptable to the unions. Conditioned by the interest-rate punishments of the financial markets, the unions knew what the alternative was, and in the end supplied the government with precious information about the preferences of its members, as well as the distribution of costs and benefits of various reform proposals, thus allowing the government to balance technical soundness with political feasibility. In addition, the unions also mobilized all their dialogic capacity to secure grass-root acceptance—through the referendum—of the reform package negotiated with the government (Baccaro 2002). The specific content of the reform may in fact be considered the result of a successful political exchange between the government and the unions on this basis: substantial savings—especially in the long-run—in exchange for the protection of benefits of older workers and pensioners, and greater equity within the system. In particular, the adoption of the contributions-related system was perfectly in line with the interests of workers' associations because it put an end to: (a) the favorable treatment provided by the earnings-related system to those workers with the less flat careers, that is, high income workers; and (b) the privileged regulations for the self-employed introduced five years before. However, as we will illustrate, the reform provoked a "generational break," since the introduction of the contributions-related system and the long transition period implies the overburdening of younger generations, who will bear most of the costs of reforming pensions and restoring public finance to health.

The 1997 Prodi Reform

After the 1996 elections, won by a center-left coalition, a new government led by Romano Prodi was appointed, relying on the parliamentary support of the coalition formed by the "Olive Tree" and *Rifondazione Comunista*. The new government set up a commission (*Commissione Onofri*), charged with evaluating existing social and labor market policies, and formulating policy proposals. In the field of pensions the commission suggested:

1. quickly implementing the measures introduced by the Dini reform;
2. fully unifying the different regimes;
3. fully applying the contributions-related system, removing the existing exemptions;
4. introducing mechanisms for automatic revisions of the conversion coefficients; and
5. accelerating both the harmonization of transition periods for private employees and public employees, and the establishment of supplementary pension funds for the latter.

A heated debate arose over these proposals within the government itself, which had to confront the opposition of *Rifondazione Comunista* to the most important recommendation of the Onofri plan—the much faster phasing-in of the new pension formula introduced in 1995—which was finally withdrawn. The government did not manage to act unitarily because of both its heterogeneous nature, which was based on the electoral cartel between a proper center-left coalition and the left-wing party, RC, and the internal competition between the major party of the "Olive Tree" coalition, the DS, and the neo-Communist party, the RC. In spite of these conflicts, some measures were approved. These aimed at tightening the conditions for seniority pensions, and harmonizing the looser conditions for public employees with those for private employees. Moreover, a one-year freeze of indexation was introduced, a partial compatibility of pensions and income from work was restored, and basic pensions were increased.

A new multi-pillar architecture for Italian pensions

The three reforms of the 1990s prevented the collapse of the system by acting on different fronts: (i) financial sustainability and cost containment; (ii) normative fragmentation and inequity; and (iii) the move towards a multi-pillar configuration with the development of supplementary pension funds.

The financial impact of these reforms has been considerable. Projections of expenditure for the medium- to long-term are much more reassuring than they were fifteen years ago. Overall public pension expenditure as percent of GDP is projected to increase by roughly 2 percentage points in the next three decades, rising from 13.8 percent in 2001 to a peak of 16 percent in 2033 (Ministero del Welfare 2002). Pension expenditure is then expected to decrease due to the impact of the new contributions-related system (which will be fully operative, applying to all new pensions, only after 2035), and the forecast changes in the demographic situation. These figures are even more impressive if we consider that the projected economic dependency ratio is worrying in the Italian case, given that it is expected to grow from 48.8 percent in 2000 to 64.5 percent in 2020, 79.9 percent in 2030 and 97.8 percent in 2040 (Ministero del Welfare 2002).

These results will be made possible by the adoption of both the contributions-related system and two crucial mechanisms that link the value of future benefits to economic and demographic shifts: the revaluation of paid contributions according to the mean GDP growth rate of the last 5 years, and the compulsory revision of the conversion coefficients every 10 years to take into account demographic and economic trends.

With regard to the intra-generational fairness of the system, we have already noted that the Dini reform was quite incisive, putting an end to the privileged treatment of the self-employed, though with a transition period. The analysis of replacement rates reveals the magnitude of the reform: the expected reduction of the replacement rate for the self-employed is greater than for employees—34 percentage points in the period 2010–30 for the former against roughly 17 points for the latter. Similarly, the Amato and Prodi interventions in the field of seniority pensions for public employees also eliminated hard-to-justify favorable regulations and the most striking anomalies (entitlement with only 20 years of contributions and the very long period to phase-out seniority pensions after 1995). Moreover, both the Amato and the Dini reforms abolished the favorable treatment provided by the previous earnings-related system for those workers with the most dynamic careers.

Despite such positive results, some critical points may be identified. Due to the long period of transition for the implementation of several changes, it seems appropriate to distinguish the problems affecting the system in the short- to medium-term from those forecast for the long run, namely, around 2035, when the new contributions-related system will be fully operative.

As for financial sustainability, in the short term the slow phase-in does not contain the increase in the equilibrium contribution rates in the schemes for artisans and merchants. The situation is relatively better in the scheme for private employees, though in this case the level of the equilibrium contribution rate is already high. This will probably lead to more generous transfers from the public budget, as there seems to be little room to further raise the level of contributions. Moreover the system still in force for older workers continues to create disincentives to keep on working when the minimum condition for seniority pensions is met.

In the long run, the main problems concern inter-generational fairness, because intra-generational equity matters have already been tackled and solved by past reforms, and the contributions-related system is a strong device for maintaining the financial equilibrium. In terms of inter-generational fairness, the differential application of the contributions-related system will entail a drastic reduction of pension benefits for younger cohorts (Table 9.5), especially for those that entered the labor market after 1995 and are fully subject to the new system.

The reduction in the gross replacement rate provided by public pensions is substantial for the current "standard retiring" worker (i.e. an employee who leaves the labor market at the age of 60 with 35 years of contribution): in the period 2000–30 the replacement rate decreases by 17.5 percentage points dropping from 67.3 percent to 49.6 percent.[17] This reduction should be partly compensated by the growing replacement rate provided by supplementary funded pensions—from 0 percent in 2000 to 4.7 percent in 2010 up to 14.5 percent in 2030—so that the total replacement rate provided by compulsory public pensions plus supplementary pensions would decline only slightly: from 67.3 percent in 2010 to 64.1 percent in 2030. However, these figures provided by the government (Ministero del Welfare 2002) are somewhat misleading. In fact, the figures for supplementary occupational pensions are calculated assuming a contribution rate of 9.25 percent of gross wages—which is constituted by the whole *Tfr* (6.91%) plus further contributions paid by employers and employees. The replacement rate provided by supplementary pensions thus gradually absorbs the value of the *Tfr*, which, for a fair comparison, should be fully added to the total replacement rate reported for the year 2000. In fact, a worker who retired in 2000 received both the statutory public pension and the *Tfr* in a lump-sum.

Younger cohorts are actually twice disadvantaged, however. The Dini reform not only diminished the generosity of future pensions, but it also raised contribution rates. Consequently, younger workers have to pay higher contributions, and they will get lower pensions than previous generations.

Finally, some studies have also pointed at another problem: the possibility that the new indexation mechanism—linked only to prices—might create disparities in the future stock of pensions, thus generating demands for adjustment in real terms (Fornero and Castellino 2001; Ministero del Welfare 2002).

An "institutional gate" for the take-off of the second pension pillar

The issue of supplementary pensions development is crucial in the context of the retrenchment of the public pillar. The stepwise process of system reconfiguration (L. 124/93; Law 335/95 and recently D. Lgs. 47/2000) has created a legal framework to foster the take-off of supplementary schemes, with an emphasis on the second, occupational, pillar. The development of the second pension pillar has been rapid in Italy compared to the relatively static situation of second pillar schemes in other Southern European countries, most having only recently adopted legal frameworks to regulate this sector. In the short period between 1998 and 2001, roughly 1.5 million workers became members of a "closed" or "open" pension fund.[18]

These figures stand out if we consider that the starting conditions in the early 1990s in Italy appeared to be particularly adverse to a transition towards a multi-pillar configuration of the pension system, in at least four respects. First, Italy had basically no tradition in funded pension schemes, with roughly 5 percent of private employees covered by second pillar schemes in the early-1990s. Second, demographic aging is particularly intense in Italy, thus the time available for introducing/implementing changes in the pension system is reduced. Third, Italy presents the worst debt/GDP ratio in the EU (109.0%). And lastly, resources available to finance the second pillar were particularly limited because of the very high contribution rate in the first pillar (*c.* 33% for private and public employees).

In spite of such unfavorable conditions, second pillar funds have developed well, especially in the industrial sector. The take-up rate for "closed" pension funds in the industrial sector is slightly over 30 percent, and some funds have managed to attract between 60 percent and 80 percent of potential beneficiaries (*COVIP* 2005). Such figures reveal that, in the presence of an "institutional gate" as the *Tfr*, supplementary pension schemes may spread rapidly. More precisely, we may say that structural financial constraints that hamper the shift to a multi-pillar configuration were overcome under two conditions : (i) the "institutional gate" was available (for all private employees), and (ii) the social partners—especially the unions—exploited the "institutional gate," encouraging workers through informative and promotional campaigns to join supplementary funds.

In addition, the relevance of supplementary pensions for the income maintenance of future retirees stands out if we consider another positive element regarding the development of the second pillar: the comparatively high average contribution rate to occupational pension funds. In fact, for workers who entered the labor market after 1993, the contribution rate to "closed" funds is remarkably high at 9.25 percent of annual earnings, made up of the whole *Tfr* and additional contributions by employers and employees.

Alongside these positive notes, the development of supplementary pensions in Italy displays also some "gray areas." After the initial take-off, in the period 2001–4 membership numbers only increased moderately. However, this seems to be more the effect of the financial market crisis than the consequence of structural problems linked to the scarcity of financial resources (*COVIP* 2005). Moreover, in some sectors (e.g. commerce) coverage is still modest, implying the need for stronger initiatives by social partners and/or further legislative interventions directed at fully "opening the institutional gate." To this end, the current center-right government proposed in 2001 the compulsory devolution of the *Tfr* to pension funds for new labor market entrants. This measure would ensure a rapid shift to a multi-pillar configuration by mobilizing between €12 and €13 billion per year—around 1 percent of GDP (Ministero del Welfare 2002). However, as we will see in the next section, the issue is controversial.

The Berlusconi–Tremonti Reform: 2001–2005

In December 2001, the Berlusconi government asked Parliament to delegate the power to pass a new pension reform, suggesting some adjustments to the existing regulations for the three pension pillars with the aim of: (a) bolstering the development of supplementary funded pensions; and (b) gradually raising the average retirement age on a voluntary basis. The original proposal envisaged the abolition of the maximum retirement age (65 years), the provision of incentives (a tax free bonus equal to 50% of the amount of their pension contributions) for workers who attain the right to a seniority pension but continue in employment, the gradual restoration of the option of combining pensions and income from work, and a reduction in pension contributions (between 3% and 5%) for workers employed with non-temporary contracts—with no impact on the level of future benefits. Such measures were also accompanied by a proposal to promote funded schemes through the *compulsory transfer* of the *Tfr* to supplementary funds and the definition of a new legal framework to level the playing field between the different types of supplementary pension funds ("open" and "closed" funds, individual pension plans).

According to our interpretative framework, Berlusconi's project thus aimed at rapid institutional change through a redefinition of the respective importance of the PAYG and funded pillars, to be achieved by fully exploiting the "gate" represented by the *Tfr*. Despite fierce union opposition and the expert criticism, the proposal was approved by the Chamber of Deputies after lengthy debate in the spring of 2003. However, the *delega* had to be approved by the Senate so its final adoption was still far away. Between November 2001 and June 2004, the unions struggled against the reform, especially on: (a) reductions in pension contributions, which in their view would either violate the logic of the contributions-related system (if the projected level of future benefits was to be safeguarded, the state would likely have to fill the gap) or would worsen the pension prospects of younger cohorts; (b) the compulsory devolution of the *Tfr* to supplementary funds without a provision for a minimum guaranteed return. The unions accused the government of exposing workers to financial market risks—as supplementary benefits will be defined-contributions—in contrast to the modest but guaranteed return provided by the *Tfr*. Moreover, unions opposed the compulsory transfer of the *Tfr* to pension funds as this measure would threaten their control over this financial instrument.

Partly because of this opposition, the bill stalled in the Labor and Social Protection Committee of the Senate, but the reform process was reactivated during the summer of 2003 through a revision of the delegation law. Berlusconi's move re-started the expert debate within the governmental majority and between different ministries, and re-opened the negotiations between the government and the social partners. A highly controversial issue within the government was the modification of eligibility conditions for seniority pensions: the Minister of the Economy, Giulio Tremonti (*Forza Italia*) pushed for a rapid shift to a minimum contributory period of 40 years, while the Minister of Welfare, Roberto Maroni (*Lega Nord*), was favorable to a softer approach, not least to appease the unions. The Minister of Welfare also defended a partisan interest by supporting a "softer" approach to seniority pensions, as these benefits are disproportionately concentrated in Northern Italy, which is the traditional electoral constituency of the *Lega Nord*. The unions called a general strike in October 2003 and then a national demonstration in early December: they denounced the government's confrontational policy-making style and protested against the proposed reduction in pension contributions and the compulsory transfer of the *Tfr* to supplementary funds. By contrast, employers' reactions were basically favorable, but on the latter point.

Between late 2003 and May 2004, strong union opposition and disunity within the governmental majority induced the government to withdraw some basic elements of the reform proposal: the reduction in pension contributions for newly-hired workers with permanent contracts, and the compulsory devolution of the *Tfr* to supplementary funds. On the latter point the government, the unions and *Confindustria* compromised, agreeing to the transfer of the *Tfr* to pension funds with the "silent assent" formula. According to this mechanism, workers will have six months to decide if they want to keep the *Tfr*, or transfer it to supplementary pension funds. In the default option ("silence"), the *Tfr* will be automatically paid into supplementary schemes.

Concerning the revision of the first public pillar, the final version of the delegation law—submitted to Parliament with the 2004 budget—proposed a two-step reform process. During the first phase (until 2007), the main measure would be a set of incentives (tax bonus equal to 100% of pension contributions) to encourage later retirement, even if the entitlement to a seniority pension had been attained based on the transition rules in the Dini and Prodi reforms. The second phase will rest on "structural" changes: a higher, and fixed, retirement age for old age pensioners (65 years for men, 60 for women, with a minimum contributory period of 5 years) and tightened eligibility conditions for seniority pensions.

After the latest revision, during the summer of 2004, the *delega* had to pass through the legislative assemblies, where the government had to rely on a vote of confidence to secure the bill's adoption. In the Senate, the proposal was approved with a vote of 153 votes to 88, in the Chamber of Deputies 288 to 119 (Law 243/04). We may note that in the Treasury's projections, the reform will bring savings of about 1 percent of GDP per year, thus halving the projected increase in pension expenditure in the critical years between 2010 and 2035.

Law 243/04 directly reformed the first pillar, while prescriptions regarding the *Tfr* and supplementary pillars were to be confirmed and specified by a government decree. A lively and long-lasting debate started on this issue, focusing in particular on the mechanism for the transfer of the *Tfr* to pension funds in the default ("silence") option, the portability of employer's contribution when moving from an occupational to an "open" fund, and the definition of compensatory measures for firms in case of transfer of the *Tfr* to pension funds. With regard to the first two points, two different views emerged, cutting through the governmental majority and social partners. On the one hand, the Finance Ministry (*Forza Italia*) pushed for a bigger role of financial institutions, which in their turn lobbied for measures aimed at "leveling the playing field" between "open" and occupational pension funds. On the other hand, the Ministry of Welfare (*Lega Nord*), with the support of the unions, favored a more prominent role for occupational funds. The Employers' Association, in its turn, was very concerned about measures that might compensate the loss of an important source of financing such as the *Tfr*, especially because the difficult condition of public finances (expected deficit/GDP ratio in 2005: over 4.5%) seemed to leave the government little room to maneuver.

After more than one year of debate and negotiations, a final compromise was found: (a) in case of "silence" by workers, the *Tfr* is paid into occupational "closed" funds, (b) the portability of employer's contribution is not allowed when moving from an occupational to an "open" pension fund, (c) the reform of the supplementary pillar will become operative only in 2008, in order not to worsen the situation of public finance and to give some time to firms to find alternative sources of financing. The decree (D. Lgs. 252/2005) was finally issued on November 24, 2005.

The measures contained in the decree may represent an important step for the transition of the Italian pension system towards a fully-fledged multi-pillar configuration, though the procrastination till 2008 once more delays the definitive take-off of supplementary pension pillars and, above all, the final outcome on this front will ultimately depend on workers' choices on the transfer of the *Tfr* to pension funds.

V Conclusion

After the policy stalemate that had characterized the previous decade, the early 1990s marked a critical watershed: the actor constellation suddenly changed, thus offering fertile grounds for the rapid unfolding of learning dynamics and political exchanges that allowed two major reforms (1992, 1995) and subsequent fine-tuning (1997). Such sequence of reforms has deeply restructured the public pillar on the one hand, and moved the whole system towards a multi-pillar configuration on the other.

In the following paragraphs we will try to "unpack" the explanatory model that has guided our analysis (Fig. 9.1 on p. 398), summarizing both the major changes of the national pension system introduced by the three reforms and the main factors that have played a role in this transformation.

Summary of the magnitude of changes

The assessment of the magnitude of multi-dimensional interventions like pension reforms is always difficult. Nevertheless, we can briefly summarize the changes introduced by the three reforms of the 1990s along four fundamental dimensions:

(1) global architecture of the pension system; (2) financial sustainability of the public pillar; (3) adequacy and type of benefits; (4) homogeneity of rules.

Along the first dimension, Italy has departed from the traditional model of old-age protection based on a generous first public pillar. The 1992 and 1995 reforms initiated the transition from a single-pillar to a multi-pillar configuration. The compression of future first pillar pensions, together with the take-off of supplementary funded pensions, means that for younger generations income maintenance during old age will derive from a mix of public and private benefits relying on either the PAYG principle or pre-funding. This may lead to the emergence of novel political dynamics in old-age protection, rendering the "boundaries" of the pension space increasingly porous to new national, and especially non-national, actors, for example, financial institutions, foreign pension funds, and likely future pan-European IORPs.

In terms of financial sustainability, the three reforms of the 1990s have left some problems due to the slow phase-in of major measures, so that pension expenditure relative to GDP is expected to rise by 2 percentage points in the next two decades. However, comparing the figures of projected old-age expenditure before and after the reforms, the decrease is striking (i.e. *c.* 7 GDP points): before the reforms, pension expenditure was infact projected to rise up to 23.4 percent of GDP in 2040, after the Amato, Dini and Prodi reforms the peak was expected to be around 16 percent of GDP in 2035. Moreover, in the long run the introduction of the contributions-related system will both stabilize and control pension expenditure, substantially immunizing the system from adverse demographic and economic trends.

Concerning individual pension entitlements, the transition from a single, public, earnings-related pension system to a multi-pillar configuration that combines a public, contributions-related pillar with a second (and third) defined-contributions private pillar represents a sort of "Copernican revolution." While in the past pensions were generous, and defined-benefits, though financially unsustainable and consequently exposed to the so-called "political risk," in the future they will be significantly reduced. Their actual amount will depend on several (uncertain) factors, though they will rest on a sounder financial basis. In fact, both the contributions-related system and defined-contributions supplementary plans are powerful instruments for cost containment. This is at the expense of exposing future pensioners to risks of a different nature: the former, by providing automatic benefit adjustment according to economic and demographic trends, immunizes the system while placing on future generations the risks from such unfavorable developments; the latter charges future retirees with the financial risk linked to potential market failures. In a nutshell, such a system will provide no guarantee on the actual value of pensions. Moreover, as already noted, the long phasing-in of the contributions-related system entails a sharp reduction of benefits for workers who retire after 2020, thus burdening younger generations with the cost of restoring a financially sustainable pension system.

Finally, the public pillar that has emerged from the three reforms is much more homogeneous. Though still characterized by occupational fragmentation, the introduction of the contributions-related method has harmonized benefit calculation rules among the six major schemes, enhancing the fairness through the close link between contributions and benefits. Rules concerning eligibility conditions have also been substantially harmonized.

Impact of the political system on pension politics

The crumbling of the First Republic and the transition to the Second played a fundamental role in overcoming the policy stalemate of the 1980s and in prompting innovation. The internal political-institutional crisis had two main effects: it changed many of the actors, and it altered the rules of both political competition and policy-making. In particular, the disappearance of old parties loosened the ties between partisan actors and organized interests, removing some traditional obstacles for pension reform. Moreover, the formation of new parties and the participation (for the first time) in governmental majorities of some left-wing parties (PDS, Greens) eager to gain credibility in a situation of manifest national emergency on various fronts, facilitated the build-up of new relationships capable of pushing pension reform as an instrument to improve public finances. The establishment of these new links between governmental (and partisan) actors and the social partners was further eased by the presence—in the climate of emergency of the mid-1990s—of "technocratic cabinets" (Amato and Dini) that needed the support of social actors to compensate for their weak political legitimacy. By contrast, a truly "political cabinet" (the Berlusconi cabinet 1994), though with a direct electoral mandate, adopted a confrontational style of policy-making, and failed to reform pensions because of union opposition to both the low inclusiveness of the policy-making process and the content of the reform proposal.

More recently, a further reform has been adopted (2004) despite union opposition. This time the Berlusconi government relied upon its large parliamentary majority—a result of the new electoral system introduced in 1993—to push the reform through the legislative process. However, closer investigation reveals that, though sticking to an adversarial style of policy-making, at different stages of the long-lasting reform process (Nov. 2001–June 2004) the cabinet had to incorporate the demands of the social partners (unions) within the reform plan. The measures that had provoked union protest were ultimately withdrawn, confirming the difficulty even for a strong government of pushing through pension reforms despite the opposition of crucial social partners.

Interest group influence

From the analysis of the three reforms of the 1990s and the further intervention of 2004, the relevance of the unions in pension policy emerges clearly. The demands of social actors were taken into consideration by most governments that tried to intervene in the field of old age protection. When such interests were fully (Berlusconi Government 1994) or partly (Berlusconi Government 2001) disregarded, angry union reactions led to either the failure of the reform process—and, together with the weakness of governmental coalition, to the resignation of the Government (1994)—or the withdrawal of the most controversial elements of the reform (2001–4). Therefore, trade unions are definitely crucial actors in the Italian pension politics which, under certain conditions, may even act as veto players and block policy change. However, unions may also play a "pro-active" role in reforming pensions, especially if they are involved in the policy-making process under conditions of concertation. This dynamic was manifest in the major reform of 1995, when the unions not only took some steps towards compromise, abandoning their veto strategy, softening up their position and eventually converting themselves to a reformist path, under the stimuli of "operational conditioning," but they also provided governmental policy-makers with original problem diagnoses, possible technical solutions and with "local and relational" information (Culpepper 2002), and mobilized their aggregative and deliberative capacities to secure acceptance of the reform among their rank and file (Baccaro 2002). The channel of social concertation proved to be crucial for a "technocratic" cabinet that could not find the necessary political support among partisan actors, because of the way they had been discredited by the *Tangentopoli* scandal.

On the employer side, *Confindustria* was usually fully involved in the various stages of pension reform, though its influence proved to be much lower than that of the trade unions. Clear evidence of the power "gap" between these actors is represented by the fact that the agreement that led to the reform of 1995 was signed by the government and the unions only, without *Confindustria*'s consent.

Constraints of policy design

Developed public PAYG pension pillars are difficult to reform, especially if they are built according to the Bismarckian model, producing "pension clienteles" interested in defending their relative positions. Similarly, the transition from a single-pillar to a multi-pillar pension architecture is heavily constrained by the scarcity of resources related to the so-called "double payment problem."

Nonetheless, the Italian experience suggests that the Bismarckian status quo may prove to be less impervious to change than expected. First, the fragmentation of the public pillar allowed policy-makers to frame a public discourse centered on the issue of intra-generational fairness: this allowed the introduction of restrictive measures which were justified by the need to harmonize the rules for the different schemes, thus bringing about more "equity."

Secondly, Italy has embarked on a transition to a multi-pillar system with much more conviction than other countries presenting similar pension configurations (France, Germany, Portugal). This was facilitated by the presence of an "institutional gate" represented by the *Tfr*, which made available additional resources to finance funded pillars. However, we should not forget that institutional resilience may also emerge around "gates," as illustrated by the events that occurred during the

2001–04 reform process. In other words, the presence of an institutional gate may well increase the chances for policy change, but this gate must be actually "opened"—this remains a delicate and uncertain political operation.

Role of ideas and historical context

The historical context and the "critical juncture" represented by the establishment of EMU were crucial for getting political and social actors to commit to pension reform as part of the process of meeting the Maastricht criteria. Pension reform was facilitated by a change in the actor constellation that was prompted not only by an internal crisis but also by European developments. Italian pension reforms took place in a peculiar context characterized by the national financial crisis in the wake of EMS membership, the run-up to EMU and the pressures stemming from international financial markets.

These external developments significantly altered the costs and benefits of domestic policy options and their distributive implications for domestic actors. The Maastricht criteria and time schedules had to be treated as "givens" by domestic policy players, even when their unpleasant implications became clear, thus inducing learning-based policy change that altered the significance and cost of "failure." For a weak economy such as Italy's, as the 1999 deadline approached, it became clear that being denied entry into the new EMU club would bring high penalties on international financial markets. Thus, the real choice was no longer between adjusting to EMU or maintaining the status quo, it was between adjusting or losing ground.

The 1995 reform is a clear illustration of this choice configuration: the low (and actually declining) probability of EMU admission due to the political crisis and the stalling negotiations on pension reform resulted in high penalties on both the exchange and interest rates. Actors (especially the unions) thus learned that failure to reform would no longer mean maintaining the distributive status quo, but would mean suffering hitherto unexpected and unavoidable new losses. As the *vincolo esterno* (external constraint) was no longer negotiable, the only option for avoiding these losses was to go ahead with some credible reform.

If external pressures account for overcoming the policy stalemate, the role of ideas (together with the interests of the actors involved) must also be stressed, to help us interpret the choice to reconfigure the system on multiple pillars. All major actors, especially the Amato and Dini governments, believed that a more plural configuration was necessary for risk diversification. *Confindustria* and financial actors also believed that the take-off of supplementary funded pillars might be virtuous as regards both social protection, in terms of higher returns and more flexibility in the choices of retirement, and the prospects for economic growth, through an increase in national saving that would lead to more investment in productive activities. This common orientation was not opposed by the unions because they knew that in the next decades reduced public pensions will have to be supplemented by additional benefits provided by second-and third-pillar schemes.

Abbreviations

ABI	Associazione Bancaria Italiana
AN	Alleanza Nazionale
ANIA	Associazione Nazionale fra le Imprese Assicuratrici
CCD	Centro Cristiano Democratico
CDU	Partito dei Cristiano Democratici
CGIL	Confederazione Generale Italiana del Lavoro
CISL	Confederazione Italiana dei Sindacati dei Lavoratori
CNEL	Consiglio Nazionale dell'Economia e del Lavoro
COVIP	Commissione di Vigilanza sui Fondi Pensione
DC	Democrazia Cristiana
DL	Democrazia e Libertà—La Margherita
DS	Democratici di Sinistra
EMS	European Monetary System
FI	Forza Italia
FPLD	Fondo Pensioni Lavoratori Dipendenti
GR	Verdi (Partito dei)
INPDAP	Istituto Nazionale di Previdenza dell'Amministrazione Pubblica
INPS	Istituto Nazionale della Previdenza Sociale
IORPs	Institutions for Occupational Retirement Provision
IV	Italia dei Valori—Lista di Pietro
LN	Lega Nord
MSI-DN	Movimento Sociale Italiano—Destra Nazionale
NPSI	Nuovo Partito Socialista Italiano
PCI	Partito Comunista Italiano
PDCI	Partito dei Comunisti Italiani
PDS	Partito Democratico della Sinistra
PIP	Polizze Individuali Pensionistiche
PLI	Partito Liberale Italiano
PPI	Partito Popolare Italiano
PR	Partito Radicale
PRI	Partito Repubblicano Italiano
PSDI	Partito Socialista Democratico Italiano
PSI	Partito Socialista Italiano
RC	(Partito della) Rifondazione Comunista
RI	Rinnovamento Italiano
SDI	(Partito dei) Socialisti Democratici Italiani
SPI-CGIL	Sindacato Pensionati Italiani—CGIL
Tfr	Trattamento di Fine Rapporto
UDEUR	Unione Democratici per l'Europa
UIL	Unione Italiana dei Lavoratori

Notes

1. Maurizio Ferrera wrote sections I and V, Matteo Jessoula wrote sections II, III and IV.
2. See INPS (1993).
3. Further areas—basically Trentino, South Tyrol and Trieste with its surrounding area—were annexed after the First World War.
4. Within constituencies votes were assigned using a corrected electoral *quotient*, which indicated the number of votes required to gain one seat. The *quotient* was calculated as follows: number of valid votes / (number of seats + 2). This correction was meant to assign most seats at the constituency level. Remaining votes and seats at this level were then merged into a single national constituency, and assigned to those lists with the highest remainders from local constituencies.
5. The electoral system for the Senate was formally based on single member districts. Nevertheless, candidates very rarely reached the high vote threshold (65% of valid votes) required to be elected. The remainder thus merged at the regional level, where seats were assigned with a proportional system based on the d'Hondt formula.
6. This resulted from the abolition of the 65% threshold to be elected in single-seat districts (*collegi uninominali*). See note 5.
7. The methods to distribute the seats under proportional representation differ between the Chambers: for the Chamber of Deputies the *Hare* method is used, for the Senate the d'Hondt formula is applied. A slight difference also exists in the calculation of remaining votes for proportional assignation. However, these differences have not lead to very different party representation in the two Chambers.
8. Among these: *ABI* (Italian Banking Association), *ANIA* (National Association of Insurance Companies), and *Assogestioni* (Association of Investment Funds).
9. Public employees have traditionally a similar and more generous scheme called *Indennità di buonuscita*.
10. D. Lgs. 124/1993 envisaged two kinds of supplementary funds: "closed" occupational funds, emerging form collective agreements at different levels (firm, industrial sector) and "open" funds, mostly directed at individual workers, especially the self-employed. While "closed" funds are typical second-pillar pension institutions, the nature of "open" funds is somewhat ambiguous: in the case of individual affiliation they represent third-pillar pension funds, by contrast they resemble second-pillar institutions in the case of collective affiliation.
11. Before 1994, the Treasury Ministry was directly responsible for the pensions of public employees.
12. The income ceiling for contributions in the schemes for private employees, artisans and merchants: is €84,049 (2005).
13. For those with fewer than 15 contribution years the *reference earnings* would be calculated on the basis of the 5 last years, plus the period between January 1993 and the date of retirement.
14. The coalition was formed by Berlusconi's new party *Forza Italia*, the rehabilitated former neo-Fascist party *Alleanza Nazionale*, the *Lega Nord* and some smaller center parties.
15. It is particularly note worthy that in the mid-1990s, the majority of members of the major workers organization (CGIL) were retirees.
16. However, the age requirement at 57 years has been subsequently raised to 60 years by the Berlusconi reform; see pp. 443–5.
17. Those workers retiring at 65 with 40 years of contributions would face a slightly better situation, due to the incentives to postpone retirement incorporated in the new

contributions-related system, with a reduction of the gross replacement rate by 12.7 percentage points in the period 2010–40.
17. Though the regulatory framework dates back to 1993, no pension funds were established before 1998 due to the lack of specific regulations regarding procedural and financial matters, that were issued in the course of 1996 and 1997.

Bibliography

Primary sources and government documents

COVIP (2004). *Relazione Anno 2003*. Website: *www.covip.it*
COVIP (2005). *Relazione Anno 2004*. Website: *www.covip.it*
EUROPEAN COMMISSION and COUNCIL (2003). *Joint Report on Adequate and Sustainable Pensions*. Bruxelles.
INPS (1993). *Le Pensioni Domani: Primo Rapporto sulla Previdenza in Italia*. Bologna: Il Mulino.
MINISTERO DEL TESORO (1981). *La Spesa Previdenziale e i Suoi Effetti sulla Finanza Pubblica*. Roma: Istituto Poligrafico e Zecca dello Stato.
MINISTERO DEL TESORO (1998). *Convergenze dell'Italia Verso l'UEM*. Roma.
MINISTERO DEL WELFARE, BRAMBILLA COMMISSION (2001). *Verifica del Sistema Previdenziale ai Sensi della Legge 335/95 e Successivi Provvedimenti, nell'Ottica della Competitività, dello Sviluppo e dell'Equità*. Web site: *www.welfare.gov.it*
MINISTERO DEL WELFARE (2002). *Report on National Strategies for Future Pension Systems*. Website:*http://www.europa.eu.int/comm/employment_social/soc_protection/pensions_en.htm*

Secondary Sources

BACCARO, LUCIO (2002), "Negotiating the Italian Pension Reform with the Unions: Lessons for Corporatist Theory." *Industrial and Labor Relations Review*, 55(3): 413–31.
BELTRAMETTI, LUCA (1996). *Il debito pensionistico in Italia*. Bologna: Il Mulino.
CASTELINO, ONORATO (1976). *Il Labirinto delle pensione*. Bologna: Il Mulino.
CAZZOLA, GIULIANO (1995). *Le Nuove Pensioni degli Italiani*. Bologna: Il Mulino.
CHERUBINI, ARNALDO (1977). *Storia della previdenza sociale in Italia, 1860–1960*. Roma: Editori Riuniti.
CHIORAZZO, VINCENZO and SPAVENTA, LUIGI (2000). *Astuzia o virtù? Come accadde che l'Italia fu ammessa all'Unione monetaria*. Roma: Donzelli.
CULPEPPER, PEPPER D. (2002). "Powering, Puzzling, and 'Pacting': the Informational Logic of Negotiated Reforms." *Journal of European Public Policy*, 9(5): 774–90.
D'ALIMONTE, ROBERTO and BARTOLINI, STEFANO (eds.) (2002). "Maggioritario finalmente? La transizione elettorale 1994–2001." Bologna: Il Mulino.
FERRERA, MAURIZIO (1998). *Le Trappole del Welfare*. Bologna: Il Mulino.
—— and Gualmini, Elisabetta (2004). *Rescue by Europe? Social and Labour Market Reforms from Maastricht to Berlusconi*. Amsterdam: Amsterdam University Press.
FORNERO, ELSA and CASTELLINO, ONORATO (2001). *La Riforma del Sistema Previdenziale Italiano*. Bologna: Il Mulino.
FRANCO, DANIELE (2002), "Italy: a Never-Ending Pension Reform". In Feldstein, M. and Siebert, H. (eds.), *Social security pension reform in Europe*. Chicago: University of Chicago Press.
JESSOULA, MATTEO (2004). "La riconfigurazione del sistema pensionistico italiano tra vischiosità istituzionale, '*gates*' e processi di apprendimento." *Rivista Italiana di Politiche Pubbliche*, 2: 57–98.

Lapadula, Beniamino and Patriarca, Stefano (1995). *La Rivoluzione delle Pensioni*. Roma: Ediesse.
Maranini, Giuseppe (1967). *Storia del potere in Italia: 1848–1967*. Firenze: Vallecchi.
Myles, John and Pierson, Paul (2001). "The Comparative Political Economy of Pension Reform". In Pierson, P. (ed.), *The New Politics of the Welfare State*. New York: Oxford University Press, 303–33.
Natali, David (2001). "Là Ridefinizione del Welfare State Contemporaneo: la Riforma delle Pensioni in Francia e in Italia." Ph.D. Diss., EUI—Florence.
Pierson, Paul (1994). *Dismantling the Welfare State?: Reagan, Thatcher and the Politics of Retrenchment*. Cambridge: Cambridge University Press.
Rasner, Anika (2002), "Success and failure in public pension reform: the Italian experience," MA Thesis, University of Konstanz.
Regonini, Gloria (1996). "Partiti e pensioni: legami mancanti". In Cotta, M. and Isernia, P. (eds.), *Il gigante dai piedi d'argilla*. Bologna: Il Mulino.
Regini, Marino and Regalia, Ida (1997). "Employers, unions and the state: the resurgence of concertation in Italy?" In Bull, M. and Rhodes, M. (eds.), *Crisis and transition in Italian politics*. London: Frank Cass.
Sartori, Giovanni (1982). *Teoria dei partiti e caso italiano*. Milano: Sugar Co.
Thelen, Kathleen and Streeck, Wolfgang (2005). "Introduction: Institutional Change in Advanced Political Economies." In Thelen, K. and Streeck, W. (eds.), *Beyond Continuity: Institutional Change in Advanced Political Economies*. Oxford: Oxford University Press.
Vassallo, Salvatore (1994). *Il governo di partito in Italia*. Bologna: Il Mulino.

CHAPTER 10

DENMARK: A "WORLD BANK" PENSION SYSTEM

CHRISTOFFER
GREEN-PEDERSEN

I Introduction[1]

PENSION politics in Denmark has produced a pension system close to the multi-pillar ideal proposed by the World Bank. The Danish system is based on the national pension, which provides a fairly generous social safety net for retirees, combined with a network of occupational and private pensions that provide most wage earners with adequate pension coverage. Consequently, the logic of pension politics can be viewed as "dualistic," as the two main elements—the national pension and the system of occupational pensions—belong to different political arenas. The national pension is exclusively a matter for Parliament, whereas occupational pensions are the realm of the social partners, with the government acting as a regulator with regard to taxation, investments rules, and other framework conditions. The fact that occupational pensions are funded and based on the principle of defined contributions also implies that issues such as higher life-expectancy and falling interest rates are dealt with automatically. In Denmark, pension retrenchment, which has been such an important political issue in many other countries, has been limited to the national pension. Denmark has thus not seen the major pension reforms which have caused so much political debate and unrest in many other countries. Nevertheless, a discussion of the development of the national pension allows us to study the broader themes of this volume, relating to the link between political institutions and policy outcomes.

In this regard the message of this chapter is clear: The changes made to the national pension over the last few decades can only be understood by focusing on electoral competition. The national pension is popular with voters, and has been made more generous on several occasions since 1980, largely because of political parties' need to demonstrate a pro-welfare-state commitment. However, one important retrenchment measure was introduced by a Social Democratic-led government using an "obfuscation strategy."

The explanation for the emergence of this multi-pillar system is not to be found in the World Bank recommendation itself. The Danish pension system has never been deliberately designed and certainly not according to World Bank recommendations. The explanation lies in the political choices made in the 1950s and 1960s. Unlike many other countries, Denmark did not establish a major earnings related pay-as-you-go (PAYG) system during this period. This was due to the fragmentation of the Labor movement and the relative weakness of the Danish Social Democratic party. With craft-based unions, unskilled workers were represented separately, and their union representatives preferred higher wages to expanded social benefits. Moreover, a number of parties competed for the working class vote, ranging from the Communists to the Liberals, thus splitting the Left and weakening the basis for Social Democratic policy expansion—as for example, in neighboring Sweden. Due to this inability of the political system to provide pension coverage beyond the national pension, occupational and private pensions grew in importance.

By 1980, two-thirds of the Danish working population had access only to the national pension, which offered replacement rates of only one-third of wages for many groups. At the same time, however, about 20 percent of the employed were covered by funded, occupational pensions. Consequently, one could say that the window of opportunity for pension expansion in Denmark was still "open," but the path of public supplementary pensions was already "closed," given these widespread private occupational arrangements—together with the economic crisis of the 1980s. Pension politics in Denmark during the 1980s and 1990s thus became a debate mainly about the exact structure of occupational pensions and the question of government mandating and regulating the system of occupational pensions, such as taxation rules and the situation of those not covered by occupational pensions.

In looking at the wider Danish pension system, this chapter also offers several lessons for the literature on pensions systems and their development. First, path dependency and policy stability in pensions is not just due to the "double payment" problem when shifting from a PAYG solution to funded systems. Once countries have embarked on a funded path, shifting to a PAYG arrangement is also highly difficult. Second, the analysis shows how pension politics in pension systems without large earnings-related PAYG elements depends on the structure of the funded elements. In Denmark, the fact that occupational pensions are defined-contribution schemes under the control of the social partners has ensured that this issue has not been the scene of partisan conflict.

II Political system

Constitutional history and nation-building

Today Denmark is a democratic nation-state in which the Monarch, presently Queen Margrethe II, is the Head of State with only ceremonial functions. However, historically, Denmark was a monarchy covering several ethnic groups. The country gained its present status through democratization and the loss of territory, both events taking place mainly during the nineteenth century.

At the beginning of the nineteenth century, Denmark was an absolute monarchy ruling Denmark, Norway and Schleswig-Holstein (now a German federal state). As a result of Danish participation in the Napoleonic wars, Norway was ceded to Sweden in 1814 and Schleswig and Holstein were lost to Prussia in 1864. Thus, even though the northern part of Schleswig was returned to Denmark in 1920 as a result of a referendum in the aftermath of World War I, Denmark was transformed from a mid-sized European country at the beginning of the nineteenth century into the small country it is today, with just over 5 million inhabitants.

Absolutism ended with the peaceful introduction of the first democratic Constitution in 1849. However, the process of democratization dragged on for the rest of the century and into the next. This transformation was the result of a conflict between a party known as the Right, representing bourgeois interests in the cities, and a party known as the Left, representing independent farmers. The latter secured an absolute majority in the second chamber (*Folketinget*) and wanted to establish parliamentarism so that a government could not rule against the will of the majority of the Second Chamber. However, the Left did not achieve this until 1901. In the meantime, the King appointed governments from the Right, against the will of the Second Chamber but with the support of the First Chamber, which had a different electoral formula. By and large, democratization in Denmark was completed when women gained suffrage in 1915 and when parliamentarianism survived an attempt by the King to dismiss a government against the will of Parliament in 1920.[2]

In the period completing democratization, the basic structure of the Danish party system was also established. The two parties which had dominated the democratization process continued to be important actors. The Right changed its name to the Conservatives in 1915, whereas the Left has kept its original name, but is today best described as the Liberals. During the democratization process, the Social Democrats entered the political scene. The party gained representation as early as 1884, but first grew into a strong political force around the turn of the century. The conflict between the rural Left party and the city-based Right was thus gradually overtaken by a traditional Left–Right conflict, between the Social Democrats versus the "Left" and the Conservatives. In 1905, a splinter party from the Left called the Radical Left—but more properly described as the Social Liberals—was established, and it gained representation in 1906. The party represented the interests of small farmers and share-croppers and often cooperated with the Social Democrats. The basic structure of Danish party competition was thus established at this time. Danish party competition came to be mainly between the Social Democrats and Social Liberals on the one hand, and the Liberals and the Conservatives on the other (Elklit 2002).

Whereas the basic structure of party competition has remained almost the same for around 100 years, political institutions have seen some changes. The electoral system was changed from a first-past-the-post to a proportional system in 1920, and the new Constitution adopted in 1953 abolished the First Chamber.

Institutions of government

After the adoption of the new Constitution in 1953, the Danish *Folketing* with its 179 members—2 representing Greenland, and 2 The Faeroe Islands—became the only chamber in the Danish Parliament. The *Folketing* operates on the principle of negative parliamentarianism, that is, the government can survive as long as there is no majority against it. Hence, the Danish *Folketing* does not require a vote of investiture. Elections must be held every four years, but the Prime Minister can call an election at any time s/he wishes. Referendums can be called by one-third of the Members of Parliament, but laws regarding certain issues such as taxation cannot be decided by referendums. This mechanism of minority protection in the Danish Constitution plays a very limited role in Danish politics and it has not been used since 1963. Other issues such as changing the Constitution, changing the voting age, and the surrender of sovereignty require approval by a referendum. Advisory referendums are also possible. In practice, referendums have mainly been used with regard to the EU and lowering the voting age.[3]

Denmark is a unitary but decentralized state. The local governments, 5 regions and 98 municipalities, have the constitutional right to manage their own affairs subject to central government regulation. Municipalities have the right to levy taxes, and the governing bodies of both regions and municipalities are democratically elected for four years. Their main responsibility is the provision of welfare services. Hospitals, primary and secondary education, care of the elderly and day care are thus all the responsibilities of the local governments, under varying degrees of state regulation. Local governments are also responsible for public roads, environmental control, active labor market policies and a few cash benefit schemes, most importantly disability pensions and social assistance.[4]

Table 10.1 Political institutions in Denmark

Political Arenas	Actors	Rules of investiture	Rules of decision-making	Veto potential
Executive	Queen (*Dronningen*)	Hereditary	Ceremonial functions	Not a veto point
	Prime Minister (*Statsminister*)	Appointed by the Queen but choices are restricted by electoral outcomes; No investiture vote ("negative parliamentarism")	Right of initiative; right to dissolve Parliament and call early elections	—
Legislative	Parliament (*Folketing*)	4-year term; 175 seats in 17 multi-member districts; proportional list system; voters can vote for a party or an individual candidate on a party list; two-tier seat allocation based on the modified Saint-Laguë formula (1st tier: 135 multi-member constituency seats (*Kredsmandater*); 2nd tier: 40 compensatory seats (*Tillægsmandater*) for parties with at least 2% of national vote; 2 seats each for Greenland and the Faeroe Islands)[a]	Right of initiative; parliamentary work in committees; three readings with at least two days between readings; decisions by simple majority	Veto point if minority government; not a veto point if majority government
Judicial	Highest Court of Justice (*Højesteret*)	—	No constitutional court	Not a veto point
Electoral	Referendum	Facultative referendum called by 1/3 of the Members of Parliament; compulsory referendum for constitutional changes	Result is binding in both cases; several issues cannot be subject of a referendum e.g., tax laws, budget, citizenship, dispossession	Veto point (except for designated policy areas such as taxation), but mainly used for EU issues
Territorial units	Counties (*Amter*) municipalities (*Kommune*)	5 regions and 98 municipalities; elected governing bodies; right to levy taxes for municipalities.	Responsibilities: hospitals, primary and secondary education, care for the elderly, day care, public roads, environmental control, active labor market policies, disability pensions and social assistance	Not a veto point

Note: [a] As of January 1, 2007, electoral districts reduced to 10; formula changed to d'Hondt.

Electoral system

Denmark introduced a proportional electoral system based on party lists in 1920 after having first tried a mixed member proportional system. A number of subsequent minor changes have not changed the fundamental character of the system (Elklit 2002; 2005). Through 2006, the system functioned as follows: Each voter had one vote which could be cast either for a party, or for a specific candidate on the party list in the specific multi-member district where he or she resided. Denmark was divided into 17 multi-member districts. Seat allocation then took place in two steps. Of the 175 members elected in Denmark proper, 135 were distributed among the 17 multi-member districts, based mainly on the number of inhabitants. Within each multi-member district, seats were allocated to parties by the modified St. Laguë formula. The 40 compensatory seats were used to secure proportionality at the national level. In terms of threshold, the most important rule was that a party gaining 2.0 percent of the valid votes was entitled to take part in the allocation of the compensation seats, which meant that four seats in parliament was the usual minimum size of a party. Individual candidates were selected in each multi-member district based on the number of votes cast for them personally and the number of party votes to which they were personally entitled, according to the way the party decided to organize its candidate lists in the multi-member district in question. In most cases, the number of personal votes for each candidate was decisive for whether or not the specific candidate was elected. Voter registration was automatic and turnout averaged around 85 percent for national elections (Elklit 2002; 2005). Beginning on January 1, 2007, the number of electoral districts will be reduced to 10, and the electoral formula will be changed from modified St. Laguë to d'Hondt.

Legislative process

Both the government and individual members of the Danish Parliament can put forward bills, but the majority of these come from the government. A bill has to be read three times by Parliament to be adopted. Between the first and second reading, the bill is scrutinized by one of the 24 standing committees of the Danish Parliament, which sends its report to Parliament. Suggestions for amendments can be made during the second reading. Bills are adopted by a simple majority after the third reading. Parliament can also pass parliamentary resolutions, for instance instructing the government to put forward a bill. The procedure for parliamentary resolutions resembles that for bills, but they are only read twice in Parliament (Damgaard 2000).

Some bills are based on the work of committees, including experts, organized interests, and in some cases also representatives of the political parties. However, the number of such committees has decreased over the last 20 years. As Danish governments are nearly always minority governments, securing a parliamentary majority is typically the decisive factor for the passage of a bill; thus, the parliament is a veto point. In addition, as popular referenda can be called by only 1/3 of MPs and are binding, theoretically, the referendum should be considered a veto point—although this does not seem to be a frequently-used method of blocking legislation in Denmark, and it

Party family affiliation	Abbreviation	Party name	Ideological orientation	Founding and merger details	Year established
Left parties/Social democratic parties	SD	Social Democrats in Denmark (*Socialdemokratiet*)	Social Democratic		1871
		Communists (*Danmarks Kommunistiske Parti*)	Communist		1919
	SF	Socialist People's Party (*Socialistisk Folkeparti*)	Leftist	Splinter party from the Communists	1959
		Common Course (*Fælles Kurs*)	Leftist		1986
	VS	Left-Socialists (*Venstresocialisterne*)	Leftist	Splinter party from SF	1967
		Unity List (*Enhedslisten*)	Leftist	Merger of Left-Socialists, Communists and Socialist Workers Party	1989
Liberal	V	Liberals (*Venstre*)	Liberal/right wing	Originally agrarian party	1870
	RV	Social Liberals (*Det Radikale Venstre*)	Center	Splinter party from the Liberals	1905
		Justice Party (*Retsforbundet*)	Liberal	Based on Georgism/single tax movement	1919
Conservative-Rightwing	KF	Conservatives (*Konservative Folkeparti*)	Conservative		1883 (1915)
		Progress Party (*Fremskridtspartiet*)	Populist right wing		1972
		Danish People's Party (*Dansk Folkeparti*)	Populist right wing	Splinter party from the Progress Party	1995
Center parties	KRF	Christian People's Party (*Kristendemokraterne*)	Center		1970
	CD	Center Democrats (*Centrum-Demokraterne*)	Center	Splinter party from the Social Democrats	1973

Fig. 10.1 Party system in Denmark

cannot be used in all policy domains. In terms of veto players' theory, only the partisan veto players of Denmark's coalition government should be counted as veto players. But as we shall see, the main obstacle to the passage of a bill is whether minority governments can find support in Parliament, and indeed governments often refrain from putting forward bills when they do not expect to be able to assemble a supporting majority. Whether such a majority is forthcoming, however, depends mainly on the system of party competition, which I will now discuss.

Parties and elections

As mentioned above, the basic structure of the Danish party system was firmly established by the beginning of the twentieth century and the four "old" parties in Danish politics, the Social Democrats, Liberals, Conservatives, and Social Liberals are still crucial actors. However, a number of new parties have established themselves in the system during the last 40 years, making today's Danish party system a complicated version of the system founded a century ago.

The first major newcomer was the Socialist People's Party, which first gained representation in 1960. This party was a splinter party from the Communist party, which had been represented in Parliament since 1932 (except 1941 to 1945 when the party was prohibited), but had always been marginalized by the other parties. By launching itself as a moderate left-wing party, the Socialist People's Party was successful with the electorate, gaining around six to ten percent of the vote, and from 1966 to 1968 it was the main supporting party for the Social Democratic minority government known as the Red Cabinet. However, this was contentious within the party, and led to a splintering of the Socialist People's Party and the establishment of a new party, the Left Socialists. Since then, one or more parties to the left of the Socialist People's Party have been represented in the Danish Parliament most of the time. Today, the Unity List, formed by the merger of several left-wing parties, is represented in Parliament.

The 1973 election, known as the earthquake election, saw the entry of several new parties to the Danish Parliament. In the center, a splinter party from the Social Democrats, the Center Democrats, gained representation and remained in Parliament until the 2001 election. This small center party has tended to support the Liberals and the Conservatives with regard to government formation. Another centrist party, the Christian People's Party, also gained representation in 1973, and maintained representation until the 2005 election except for the period 1994 to 1998. However, the party has always been just above the 2 percent threshold. The party was founded as an anti-abortion and anti-pornography party and, like the Center Democrats, has generally supported the right-wing bloc.

The major newcomer at the 1973 election was the Progress Party, a radical right-wing party with a strong anti-tax profile. The party gained around 15 percent of the vote and became the second largest party in Parliament. The party kept its representation until the 2001 election with considerably fluctuating levels of support. This was not least due to internal conflicts, one of which led to the establishment of a splinter party in 1995: the Danish People's Party. This party is strongly focused on the immigration issue and was very successful in the 2005 election, gaining 13.3 percent of the vote (Pedersen 1987; Arter 1999).

Altogether, the Danish party system falls into five fairly cohesive segments: the parties to the left of the Social Democrats, the Social Democrats, the center parties, the two established bourgeois parties (Liberals and Conservatives) and the Danish People's Party. In terms of party competition and legislative coalitions, the Danish party system is best described as a "working bloc system" (Elklit and Pedersen 2003). For government formation, it works very much as a bloc system. The Social Democrats can normally rely on the support of the parties to the left, and the Liberal and Conservative parties can count on the support of the Danish People's Party to their right. Due to their small size, the center parties are in reality forced to choose between the two blocs. Therefore, minority governments can normally rely on a bloc majority, which will keep them in office because none of the parties constituting the bloc majority would prefer another government. However, the bloc majority will not automatically support bills put forward by the government. Here minority governments need to search for a different majority from bill to bill. Most laws in Denmark are passed with broad majorities, that is, including parties which do not form part of the government's bloc majority (Green-Pedersen and Thomsen 2005).

For the opposition parties, whether or not they support a bill will depend on how they weigh policy influence vs. electoral incentives. If the issue concerned is seen by the opposition as salient to electoral competition, the opposition will probably not be willing to support a bill since that would signal agreement with the government and thus make it more difficult to use the issue in electoral competition. For instance, the Social Democrats have often been very reluctant to support proposals for welfare retrenchment from a right-wing government, because the welfare state has been an area that the Social Democrats have tried to exploit with regard to electoral competition. However, if the opposition sees an issue as less important for electoral competition, it will focus on policy influence and thus probably be willing to strike a deal with the government. Thus right-wing parties have often been willing to support proposals for welfare retrenchment from Social Democratic governments, because the right wing parties have rarely seen the welfare state as an attractive area for electoral competition.

Interest groups

Danish employees are highly organized; approximately 75 percent of all Danish employees belong to trade unions, and the proportion is even higher for unskilled and blue-collar workers. Danish trade unions are craft-based and thus organized according to skills, not according to industry. The major trade unions is the Union Federation of Danish Workers, known as "3F" (*Fælles Fagligt Forbund*), which is the result of a merger in 2005 of the Union of the Unskilled Workers

Table 10.2 Governmental majorities in Denmark

Election date	Start of gov.	Head of gov. (party)	Governing parties	Gov. majority (% seats) Folketinget	Gov. electoral base (% votes)	Institutional veto points	Number of veto players (partisan + institutional)[a]
10.23.1979	10.26.1979	Jørgensen V (SD)	SD (68)	38.9%	38.3%	Folketinget (Referendum)	1 + 1
12.08.1981	12.30.1981	Jørgensen VI (SD)	SD (59)	33.7%	32.9%	Folketinget (Referendum)	1 + 1
	09.10.1982	Schlüter I (KF)	KF (26), V (21), CD (15), KRF (4)	37.1%	36.4%	Folketinget (Referendum)	4 + 1
01.10.1984	01.10.1984	Schlüter II (KF)	KF (42), V (22), CD (8), KRF (5)	44.0%	42.8%	Folketinget (Referendum)	4 + 1
09.08.1987	09.10.1987	Schlüter III (KF)	KF (38), V (19), CD (9), KRF (4)	40.0%	38.5%	Folketinget (Referendum)	4 + 1
05.10.1988	06.03.1988	Schlüter IV (KF)	KF (35), V (22), RV (10)	38.3%	36.7%	Folketinget (Referendum)	3 + 1
12.12.1990	12.18.1990	Schlüter V (KF)	KF (30), V (29)	33.7%	31.8%	Folketinget (Referendum)	2 + 1
	01.25.1993	Rasmussen, P.N. I (SD)	SD (69), CD (9), RV (7), KRF (4)	50.9%	48.3%	None (Referendum)	4 + 0
09.21.1994	09.27.1994	Rasmussen II (SD)	SD (62), RV (8), CD (5)	42.9%	42.0%	Folketinget (Referendum)	3 + 1
	12.30.1996	Rasmussen III (SD)	SD (62), RV (8)	40.0%	39.1%	Folketinget (Referendum)	2 + 1
03.11.1998	03.11.1998	Rasmussen IV (SD)	SD (63), RV (7)	40.0%	39.8%	Folketinget (Referendum)	2 + 1
11.20.2001	11.27.2001	Rasmussen, A.F. I (V)	V (56), KF (16)	41.1%	40.3%	Folketinget (Referendum)	2 + 1
02.08.2005	02.18.2005	Rasmussen, A.F. II (V)	V (52), KF (18)	40.0%	39.3%	Folketinget (Referendum)	2 + 1

[a] As referendum used mainly for Eu issues, we count only the parliament as a veto point (if government is minority, as explained in Table 10.1).

(*Specialarbejderforbundet i Danmark*, SID) and The Women Workers' Union (*Kvindeligt Arbejderforbund*). Other major unions are the Union of Commercial and Clerical Employees (*Handels- og Kontorfunktionærers forbund*, HK), the Union for Metal Workers (*Dansk Metal*) and the Union of Public Employees (*Forbundet af offentligt ansatte*, FOA). These unions are united in the Danish Confederation of Trade Unions (*Landsorganisationen i Danmark*, LO), which has approximately 1.5 million members. Other important trade unions, which are not LO members, are the Danish Confederation of Professional Associations (*Akademikernes centralorganisation*, AC) and the Salaried Employees' and Civil Servants' Confederation (*Funktionærernes og Tjenestemændenes Fællesråd*, FTF). Compared to Sweden, the Danish tradition of "macro-corporatism" is weaker, but LO in particular plays a very important role with regard to labor market policy, and there is a strong tradition in Denmark of involving interest groups in many policy areas. Furthermore, Denmark has a strong tradition of self-rule of the social partners, implying that issues such as the minimum wage are decided by the social partners and not by legislation. Governments are generally very reluctant to interfere in issues that are considered the domain of the social partners (Due et al. 1994).

With regard to pension politics, an interest organization by the name of the "elderly course" (*Ældresagen*) became particularly strong in the 1990s. This organization, which has around 450,000 members, is strictly non-partisan and has always been reluctant to negotiate directly with the government. It works largely through media contacts and lobbying for the interests of the elderly, mainly concerning national pensions, care for the elderly and other welfare benefits for the elderly.

III PENSION SYSTEM

Historical overview

The first public pension schemes were introduced in Denmark in 1891 with the introduction of old age assistance which provided limited means-tested benefits (Nørgaard 2000; Øverbye 1997). The same legislation modified existing civil service pensions (Vesterø-Jensen 1985: 60–3). In 1956, the old age assistance scheme was expanded considerably with the introduction of the national pension that was tax-financed and PAYG. All citizens aged 67 or over became entitled to a minimum pension, but the intention was to expand the system into a generous, flat-rate and universal pension scheme. This was achieved in 1964 when Parliament adopted a generous, flat-rate and universal pension scheme that was introduced gradually, and in place by 1970. At the same time, Parliament introduced the means-tested pension supplement for pensioners with limited income besides the national pension.

The Danish national pension has thus always contained an element of means-testing (Vesterø-Jensen 1985).

By the early 1960s around 20 percent of all Danish employees were covered by some form of occupational pension. However, whereas about half of white-collar workers had occupational pensions, the figure was less than 10 percent for blue-collar workers. In addition, more than half of white-collar workers with occupational pensions were civil servants with civil servant pensions (Vesterø-Jensen 1985: 175–6; Henriksen et al. 1988: 42–5). However, during the 1950s, other groups, such as public employees within the health care sector, had also gained access to occupational pensions. The attractiveness of such pensions had risen in connection with the political compromise concerning national pensions in 1956 that introduced generous tax incentives for private and occupational pensions (Due and Madsen 2003: 23–41).

In the early 1960s, the LO began to apply pressure for additional pension coverage for blue collar workers, most of whom only had access to the national pension. In 1964, a Danish supplementary pension scheme (ATP) was introduced, but it was a scheme of limited importance. Contributions were based on the number of hours worked rather than on income, and were thus flat-rate, equal to 1.5 percent of the average wage. Contributions were also nominally fixed and could only be increased as the result of collective agreements, something that did not happen until 1972 and then not again until 1982 (Vesterø-Jensen 1985: 56–9). Thus, ATP never came to provide a sufficient supplement to the national pension for the working class.

Nevertheless, trade union interest in the pension issue declined again after the introduction of the ATP. The debate about the "pension problem" continued during the 1960s and early 1970s, but the suggestions now came more from the Social Democratic Party than from the trade unions, and little progress was made (Larsen and Andersen 2004; Petersen 2002). The Labor movement (Social Democrats and LO) had linked the pension issue with the question of economic democracy. A fund with pension savings from all wage earners would quickly become a major actor on the Danish financial market. If the trade unions could get control of this fund, it would be a major step towards economic democracy (Vesterø-Jensen 1985: 56–9). The entire issue of economic democracy was, however, politically very controversial and the Social Democrats were isolated on the issue, since the other left-wing parties did not want a central fund. The issue of economic democracy and wage earner funds became a liability for the pension proposals of the Social Democrats. They did not have the political strength to introduce a reform on their own, and they could not attract support for change because of their insistence on the central fund (Green-Pedersen and van Kersbergen 2002).

Furthermore, Danish trade unions—as opposed to the trade union confederation, LO—and especially the trade union for unskilled workers, were not particularly interested in occupational pensions. This was already clear when the ATP was introduced. The trade unions feared that high contributions to the ATP would lead to lower ordinary wage increases (Petersen 2002) as can be seen, for instance, from the limited attention they paid to the issue of increasing ATP contributions. For unskilled workers, the national pension in combination with the ATP provided close to acceptable replacement rates. Thus, the relative weakness of the Social Democratic Party and the lack of union interest in earnings-related pensions seem to explain the lack of a definite answer to the pension question in Denmark (Petersen 2002; Øverbye 1996). The lack of union interest may also be related to the fact that the Danish trade unions are craft-based. This has led to diverse union interests with regard to the pension issue, with conflict between skilled and unskilled workers, and thus a constraining effect on their political power regarding this issue.

However, by the time the issue reached the agenda again in the 1980s, the Danish pension system had changed. Whereas in the early 1960s occupational pensions had primarily been for civil servants, other groups—especially the growing number of public employees who were not given the special civil servant status—had acquired occupational pensions during the 1960s and 1970s. Thus, the percentage of employees with occupational pensions had risen from around 20 percent in the early 1960s to around 35 percent in the early 1980s. Private pension savings had also grown considerably (Henriksen et al. 1988: 222). However, in 1981, 41 percent of Danish wage earners and 64 percent of the unskilled workers had no pension besides the national pension and the ATP (Vesterø-Jensen 1985: 172–5). One could thus speak of a "dual pension system" (Vesterø-Jensen 1985) where the majority of employees and most blue collar workers were left with only the national pension and the ATP, whereas occupational pensions were becoming widespread among white-collar workers. When the pension question had already been settled in many countries, the debate was still going on in Denmark as large groups of LO members, in particular, would face a considerable loss of income at the time of retirement.

However, the menu from which to choose answers to the pension question had become considerably more limited during the 1960s and 1970s. In the early 1960s, the civil servant pension, which is a PAYG, defined-benefits scheme, was the dominant form of occupational pension. In the early 1980s, funded, defined-contributions occupational pensions dominated. The percentage of wage earners covered by these pensions had risen from around 7 percent to around 20 percent (Henriksen et al. 1988: 42–6). In reality, Denmark had spent the 1960s and 1970s following a pension path dominated by funded, occupational pension schemes (Green-Pedersen and Lindbom 2006).

Description of current pension system

As discussed, the political debates and conflicts over the Danish pension system resulted in a system quite similar to the multi-pillar one advocated by the World Bank (1994). The first pillar consists of the national pension, ATP, the new SP (a compulsory pensions saving of 1% introduced in 1997), the SAP scheme (a voluntary pension scheme for disabled pensioners), and civil servant pensions. The second pillar consists of funded occupational pensions, and the third pillar consists of private pensions, which are still fairly widespread.

Coverage

The first pillar is dominated by the national pension. All Danish citizens residing in Denmark at the age of 65 who have spent a minimum of three years in the country are entitled to the national pension. Non-Danish citizens who have lived in Denmark for 10 years including the 5 last years before retirement are also entitled to the national pension, but benefits are reduced if a person has less than 40 years of residence. Danish citizens can also draw their pension abroad (Socialministeriet 2002; Økonomiministeriet 2003).[5]

The second tier of the first pillar has four elements:

1. The Danish ATP scheme is compulsory for all Danish employees working a minimum of nine hours per week. Wage earners receiving cash benefits such as unemployment benefits, sickness benefits, and maternity benefits pay a contribution twice the standard flat-rate, whereas self-employed people who had earlier paid contributions as employees, and people receiving early retirement benefits and disability pensions, can decide whether to pay the contribution or not.
2. Persons receiving work-related income pay 1 percent of income to the SP scheme.[6] This scheme thus automatically covers the self-employed and some recipients of cash benefits.
3. In 2003, a new pension scheme (SAP) was introduced for those on disability pensions, but paying contributions to this scheme is optional.
4. The final part of the second tier of the first pillar is the civil servants' pension scheme. Historically, this scheme covered many public employees but today few people are allowed to enter the scheme; only very privileged groups such as high-ranking civil servants and priests are eligible. However, a broader group of public employees such as teachers and railway workers were able to enter the scheme earlier and thus accumulate pension rights (Socialministeriet 2002; Økonomiministeriet 2003).

The coverage of occupational schemes in the second pillar is 93 percent. Contributions are tax deductible but benefits are taxed as normal income (Økonomiministeriet 2003: 43–6). The majority of contributors are covered as part of a collective agreement, but some are also covered through pension agreements agreed between individual firms and pension funds or insurance companies, as is typically the case when employees are not covered by collective agreements. The groups not covered by occupational pensions are young workers with a weak attachment to the labor market, and employees not covered by a collective agreement. The latter group comprises mainly professionals in well-paid jobs.

The third pillar still pays an important role, especially for people not covered by occupational pensions. Private pension savings plans in different forms are provided by banks, life insurance companies, and other financial institutions, and can pay out either a lump sum, known as capital pensions, or a monthly pension, in many cases for a limited number of years. Contributions are partly tax-deductible and pensions are taxed when paid out (Økonomiministeriet 2003: 46–8).

Administration

The national pension is administered by municipalities but under the supervision of the Ministry of Social Affairs, and the municipalities have no influence on benefits. The central government finances national pension expenditure (Socialministeriet 2002).

All contributions to the ATP scheme are paid into the ATP fund, which by law is a private institution, but under the control of the social partners. The fund invests the contributions in shares, bonds, or real estate, like any other professional investor. The ATP fund has also administered the SP scheme, but as of 2005 it will become possible to move contributions to private providers such as banks and life insurance companies. In the new SAP scheme, those on disability pensions can also choose between the ATP and private providers. The Ministry of Finance administers the civil servant pensions for those working for central government. Local governments have set up a special institution, *Kommunernes Pensionsforsikring*, which administers pensions for their employees.

Occupational pensions negotiated as part of collective agreements are administered by pension funds administered by the relevant trade union, and sometimes also by the employers' organization which was party to the collective agreement. However, in all funds, trade union representatives dominate. Firm-specific pension schemes are administered by pension companies, banks or life insurance companies. These providers also offer private pensions. All private providers, including occupational funds and the ATP, are monitored by the Danish Financial Supervisory Authority, which is under the jurisdiction of the Ministry of Economic and Business Affairs. This authority monitors whether pension funds can meet their liabilities, and ensures they do not violate the rules regarding the composition of investments.

Financing

The national pension is PAYG and is financed through general taxation, and the same is true for civil servant pensions. All other Danish pension schemes are fully funded. All pension funds are subject to the same government regulation with regard to the risk distribution of investments and other technical details. However, the ATP is subject to certain additional limitations. For instance, the fund is not allowed to acquire a controlling share of any individual company.

Contributions to the ATP depend on the number of hours worked. For full-time employees, (those who work 37 hours per week), the contribution was €358 per year in 2005. This is a fixed amount, which can be increased by a decision of the social partners. The contribution normally amounts to around 1 percent of average wages. In the SP scheme, contributions are 1 percent of work-related income, whereas in the new SAP scheme contributions are equal to 2.8 percent of the disability pension for a single pensioner. If a disability pensioner wants to participate in the scheme, the government pays two-thirds of the contribution.

Contributions to occupational pension schemes vary from around 3 percent to 17 percent of qualifying income. By 2004, the pension contributions of a majority of wage earners was 9 percent or more (Økonomiministeriet 2003).

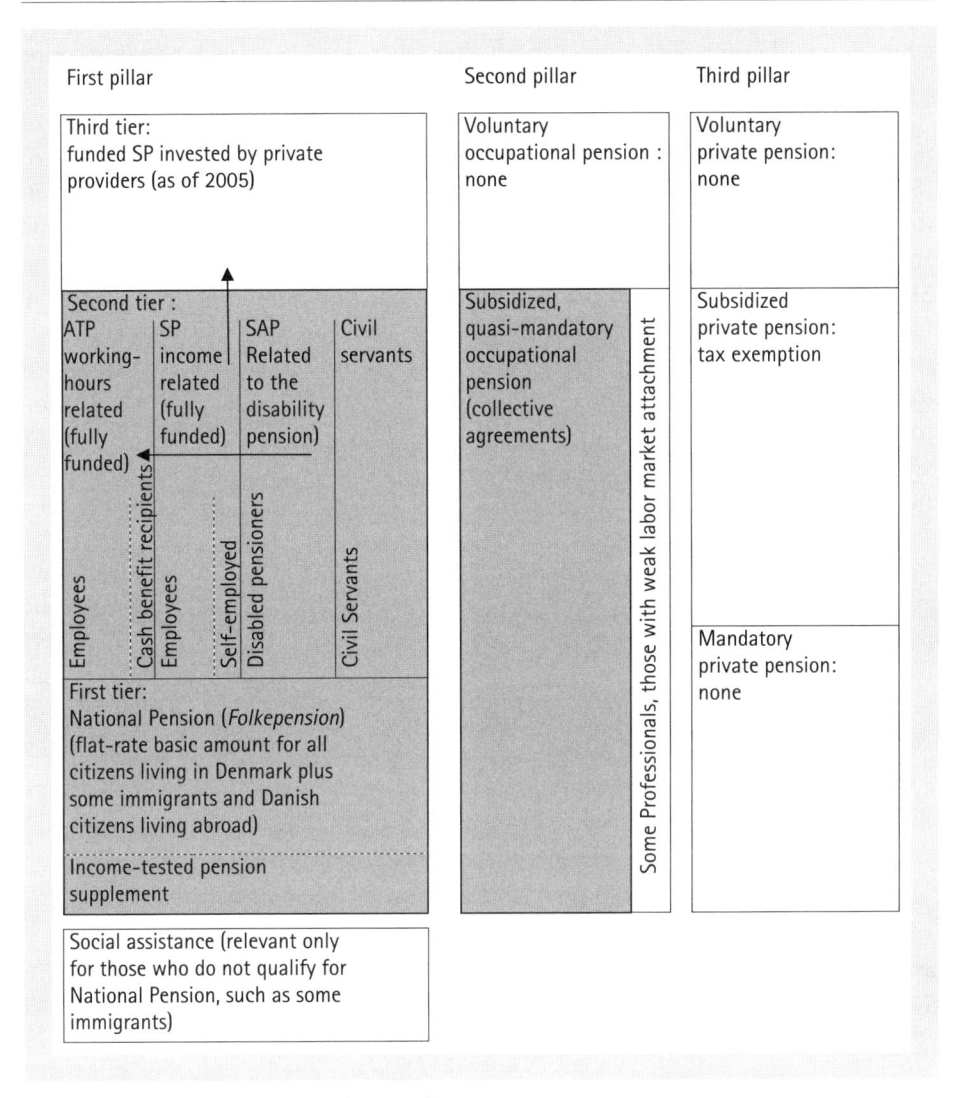

First pillar	Second pillar	Third pillar
Third tier: funded SP invested by private providers (as of 2005)	Voluntary occupational pension: none	Voluntary private pension: none
Second tier: ATP working-hours related (fully funded) / SP income related (fully funded) / SAP Related to the disability pension / Civil servants — applicable to: Employees, Cash benefit recipients, Employees, Self-employed, Disabled pensioners, Civil Servants	Subsidized, quasi-mandatory occupational pension (collective agreements) — Some Professionals, those with weak labor market attachment	Subsidized private pension: tax exemption / Mandatory private pension: none
First tier: National Pension (*Folkepension*) (flat-rate basic amount for all citizens living in Denmark plus some immigrants and Danish citizens living abroad) / Income-tested pension supplement		
Social assistance (relevant only for those who do not qualify for National Pension, such as some immigrants)		

Fig. 10.2 Pension system in Denmark

Benefits

The national pension consists of two main elements, the basic amount and the pension supplement. The basic amount is a flat-rate amount paid independently of other income, but it is reduced for those with high earnings. This exception affected around 1 percent of pensioners in 2002. The basic amount was €7,586 in 2005 and was taxable. The pension supplement, which for single pensioners was practically the same as the basic amount, but which was only €3,565 for married and cohabiting pensioners, was subject to an income test based on all other income including other pensions. In 2002, 64 percent of those above retirement age received the full pension supplement and a further 26 percent received a partial amount. Benefits are paid from the age of 65 for all pensioners born after July 1 1939.[7] For pensioners born prior to this, benefits are paid from the age of 67 (Socialministeriet 2002).[8]

In the ATP scheme, pensions are paid from the age of 67/65 (following the rules of the national pensions). As the scheme is based on defined-contributions, the value of the pension depends on the number of years and hours worked, and the return on investments. In 2004, the maximum pension for a person who had worked full time since 1964 was €2,990, but the average pension only €1206 (ATP 2004). Benefits in the SP scheme are paid for 10 years from the age of 67/65 (also following the rules for the national pension). The scheme is also based on the principle of defined-contributions, and since contributions are related to income from work, benefits depend on former earnings as well as on the return on investments. The scheme was only introduced in 1998, so the total value of pensions paid will be limited for many years. In the civil servants' scheme, pensions depend on previous wages and the number of years of employment as a civil servant. Pensions are typically equal to two-thirds of the final wage

The occupational pension schemes are also based on defined-contributions. However, the value of pensions also depends on average life expectancy for scheme participants. For example, if a person is a member of a pension fund whose members have a high average life expectancy, for example, one dominated by women, that person will receive a smaller pension. Private pensions depend solely on the value of contributions and returns on investments. In both types of scheme, benefits can be paid from the age of 60 and can be postponed until the age of 70. However, the earlier one starts to receive a pension, the smaller the pension will be.

IV Politics of pension reform since 1980

Overview

Danish pension politics since 1980 have been shaped by two main factors. First, the pension question was to some extent still open in Denmark in the early 1980s, whereas many other countries had answered the question decades earlier. Many Danish wage earners were only covered by the national pension and the ATP, and thus had insufficient pension coverage. Second, the economic situation in Denmark put questions of cost containment or revenue increases on the agenda relatively early. In the early 1980s, the issue was an acute economic crisis, whereas more recently the main problem appears to have been related to demographic changes. To provide an overview of the period, it is useful to divide it into three subparts, namely 1980 to 1984; 1984 to 1991; and 1991 to 2002.

Table 10.3 Overview of proposed and enacted pension reforms in Denmark

Year	Name of reform	Reform process (chronology)	Reform measures
1982	Tax on interest income of funded pension schemes	• 1981 Social Democratic government proposes taxes on interest income from pension savings; insufficient parliamentary support; government steps down • right-wing government suggests welfare state retrenchment → huge protests; pensions were spared • CD/Kons/KristFol/Ven-government suggests temporary tax on pension fund savings • Social-Democrats in opposition support tax but demand permanent tax • government concedes to the Social-Democrats	• interest income of private pensions with pension savings made after 1983 were taxed at a rate of 3.5% from 1984 onwards
1986	Lettelese af Samspilsproblemer	• Fall 1986 elderly report • 1986 publication of the bill • Spring 1987 unanimous passage in Parliament	• easing income testing for pension supplements i.e. more people became entitled to the full pension supplement and others receive a greater share of the maximum amount.
1987	Forhøjelse af pensionstillægget	• 1987 cross-party consensus and passage in Parliament	• increase in pension supplement
1990	Lov om satsreguleringsprocenter	• Alternative majority pressures the government to accept a new indexation system. New system passed by a broad majority.	• indexation changed from price increases to real wage increases; if annual increase exceeds 2% it is reduced by 0.3% which is used for the improvement of other cash benefits
1991	not applicable	• 1984 Metal Union demands occupational pensions through collective agreement • Fall 1985 union committee report	• introduction of occupational pensions through collective agreements

(Continued)

Table 10.3 (Continued)

Year	Name of reform	Reform process (chronology)	Reform measures
		• Spring 1986 opposition proposal to introduce occupational pensions with central fund • Fall 1987 tripartite negotiations: establishment of commission to investigate occupational pensions • intra-coalition conflict between Conservatives and Liberals with the Prime Minister leaning towards the Liberals who rejected any legislation on occupational pensions • Social Democrats' main interest was winning a parliamentary majority thus no interest in reaching agreement with government • failed negotiations → LO realizes that the only chance for occupational pensions is through collective agreement • 1991 most unions introduce occupational pensions	
1993	Konsekvenser af skattereform	• Majority government passes bill without negotiating with the opposition	• Compensation for single pensioners for the abolition of their special tax exemption through a temporary supplement which has gradually been transferred to the pension supplement, implies greater income testing in the long run • reduction of basic pension but compensation by higher supplement
1996	Dobbelt ATP for folk på overførselsindkomster	• 1989 ATP-board suggests introducing contributions for recipients of sickness, maternity and unemployment benefits • Dec 1991 governmental bill for revision of ATP but without contributions for unemployed etc. • Spring 1992 amendment of the Labor Market Committee change in government in 1993 (ditto) • budget agreement 1996: government suggests expanding ATP to include recipients of cash benefits	• recipients of sickness, maternity, and unemployment benefits to get twice the normal ATP contribution, recipients of social assistance get the normal ATP contribution • no introduction of indexation of the ATP contributions, contrary to original proposal

1998	Special Pension Scheme (SP) (særlig pensionsopsparing)	• Fall 1997 government proposes introducing 1% contribution of work-related income to ATP • March 1998 elections • passage in Parliament
2001	Førtidspensionsreform	• Spring 2001 passage in Parliament by broad majority • special pension scheme was made permanent and the benefit structure changed so that the value of the contributions would not matter for benefits as it did in the ATP scheme • introduction of ATP contributions for recipients of disability pensions financed 2/3 by the government and 1/3 by the recipient • establishment of voluntary pension scheme for disability pension recipients with contributions of 2% of average wage financed 2/3 by the government and 1/3 by the recipient.

The first period was dominated by the economic crisis in Denmark and different governments' attempts to improve public finances. Pension politics was therefore part of general economic policy-making, which was dominated by the logic of party competition. Due to popularity of the national pension it was spared from the cuts which governments made to other welfare benefits, but the broader pension system was affected because one of the major initiatives to improve public finances was a tax on the interest income of private and occupational pensions.

In the second period, the economy improved, and this facilitated a debate about how to increase income-related pension coverage. The already prominent role of funded occupational pensions ensured that this was the path that needed to be followed by the rest of the labor market. However, the government and the trade unions had different views on whether or not the rest of the labor market should be covered by one, or several, pension funds, and whether or not these funds should be introduced by law. Finally, the right-wing bourgeois government got it its way: a number of pension schemes were introduced through collective agreements without any legislation.

This answer to the pension question had consequences for pension politics in the third period. Large parts of the Danish pension system, namely occupational pensions and the ATP, have become the realm of the social partners and as such government interference is normally considered inappropriate. Thus, even if these schemes are affected by, for instance, falling interest rates, this does not become a partisan issue. With regard to pension politics, political parties have focused on the national pension, which was the subject of one cost containment reform during this period. The introduction of the SP scheme and some modest attempts to find a pension solution for the groups not covered by occupational pensions have attracted more limited political attention.

Tax on interest gains of funded pension scheme 1982

Denmark experienced economic difficulties in the 1970s, including high inflation and very large budget deficits, and the situation deteriorated further after the second oil crisis. The Social Democratic governments of the 1970s struggled in vain to find viable solutions to these problems. In 1979, the Social Democratic minister of Finance, Knud Heinesen, stepped down, declaring that the Danish economy was "at the brink of the abyss" (Nannestad and Green-Pedersen, forthcoming: 5). In the late 1970s and early 1980s, attention was drawn to the question of a tax on the interest income of private and occupational pensions. The tax advantage of the second- and third-pillar pension schemes had been an issue throughout the 1970s (Vesterø-Jensen 1985: 211–58). The left-wing parties had argued that these tax advantages pushed the system in the direction of a "dual pension system" where large groups had to make do on the national pension and the ATP, while others had generous occupational and private pensions supported by the tax system. The left-wing parties in the Danish Parliament thus made several proposals to limit the tax deductibility of contributions to private and occupational pensions. The right-wing parties opposed all of these proposals, arguing that they diminished the incentives for people to save for their own pensions. At first, the Social Democrats were not too enthusiastic either. They focused instead on making the pension funds and insurance companies invest in a way that would benefit employment, but without much success. However, after the national election in 1981, the economic troubles in Denmark continued to worsen, and the Social Democratic government started to pay attention to the idea of a tax on interest income from pension savings as a way to improve the budget. However, to build a majority in Parliament, the government needed support from either the center parties or one of the two right-wing parties. In opposition the right-wing parties saw no reason to support a Social Democratic government in raising taxes. In terms of electoral competition, it was attractive to be able to criticize the proposal, since taxation has traditionally been an issue "owned" by the right-wing parties. The failure to find parliamentary support for the tax caused the Social Democratic government to step down.

The new center-right government faced a dire economic situation involving high inflation, high unemployment, a very large balance of payments deficit and a large budget deficit. For the new government, getting the latter under control had high priority (Nannestad and Green-Pedersen (forthcoming)). Basically, there were two ways to achieve this: tax increases or cuts in public expenditure. The new government could draw on "crisis awareness" among the public, which implied some acceptance of otherwise unpopular measures. However, for a right-wing government welfare state retrenchment was risky, because it gave the Social Democratic opposition ample opportunity to criticize the government for being against the popular Danish welfare state.

The new government suggested some welfare state retrenchment measures, and was met with demonstrations and accusation that it was "bombing the Danish welfare state back to its 1930s level" (Green-Pedersen 2002: 113–16). Despite the extensive protests, the new government did introduce a number of cutbacks in welfare benefits, but the national pension was largely spared. Right from the beginning, Prime Minister Schlüter declared, "weak groups in society such as old age pensioners will be spared." The government did, however, introduce one minor retrenchment measure: the basic amount would be tested against income from employment (but not against pension income) for pensioners aged 67 to 69. Only considerable wage earnings would lead to a reduction of the basic amount, though, so the change affected only about 1 percent of pensioners (Green-Pedersen 2000). The Social Democrats had suggested the same change while in government, and could thus support the change (*Folketingets Forhandlinger* 1982–1983: 735–40). The national pension scheme was also simplified in 1983. The existing possibilities for receiving benefits before the age of 67 were abolished and instead a new and more generous disability pension scheme was set up (Green-Pedersen 2002).

Tax increases were just as unpopular as benefit, cuts, but a tax on the interest income of private pension was clearly attractive compared to all other alternatives. The revenues from such a tax were estimated at DKR 5 billion in 1983. In comparison, cuts in unemployment benefits, which caused huge protests, were expected to bring savings of DKR 3.5 billion. Furthermore, the tax would have no immediate negative effect on specific groups. In the long run, the pensions based on funding (i.e. the ATP, occupational pensions and private pensions) would be about 20 percent lower (Henriksen et al. 1988: 202–3), but this effect would occur far in the future. The tax is thus a good example of a government attempting to minimize protest by introducing a policy whose negative effects are difficult for people to understand (Green-Pedersen 1999). Even though the Conservative government had opposed this tax in opposition, it could also draw on a "Nixon goes to China logic," arguing that the economy was now in such dire straits that even a center-right government had to raise taxes.

The government had passed most of its new economic policy with support from the Social Liberals and the Progress Party, but with its anti-tax profile, the Progress Party could clearly not support the new tax. Therefore, the government would have to rely on the Social Democrats to get the proposal passed in Parliament. The Social Democrats had argued strongly for such a tax while in government and electorally had little to lose by supporting the tax. However, whereas the government proposed a temporary tax on the savings of the pension funds, the Social Democrats wanted a permanent tax on the annual interest income of the pension funds.[9] For the government, the revenue from the tax was essential and it had to accept the Social Democratic demand for a permanent tax on the real interest rate above 3.5 percent from 1984. However, only pension savings made after 1983 would be taxed. The revenue of the permanent tax was expected to rise to DKR 11–12 billion in 1986. For 1983, a tax on pension savings was introduced. In the end, the new taxes were passed with support from all parties in Parliament except the Progress Party (*Folketingstidende* 1982–1983: L81, L82; Vesterø-Jensen 1985: 254–8).

Improvements to the national pension 1986–1990

During 1984, the immediate economic crisis subsided, and this facilitated discussion of the more unfinished aspects of Danish pension policy. The question of improved earnings-related pension coverage was taken up again by both the government and the LO. Danish pension politics in the following period was thus clearly dualistic, as already suggested. On the one hand, the government and the LO discussed occupational pensions, whereas the development of the national pension was determined by the dynamics of party competition. Only a few changes to the national pension were related to the discussion of occupational pensions.

The center-right government had generally justified its retrenchment measures with reference to the need to get the Danish economy back on track. However, in the mid-1980s, the Prime Minister himself declared that things were going "incredibly well" and it was impossible to justify further retrenchment initiatives. The Social Democrats, in cooperation with the trade unions, had based their opposition strategy on a strong attack on the government for wanting to dismantle the welfare state and for implementing socially unfair retrenchment measures. A trade union leader had, for example, invented the image of "people sliding into social mass graves," (Green-Pedersen 2002: 113–18). When the economy improved, this strategy paid off as the government had to struggle with a negative social image (Andersen 1988). As the 1987 election approached, the government tried to improve its social image by reversing many of the retrenchment measures it had earlier implemented. The government also introduced a number of improvements to the welfare state (Green-Pedersen 1999; 2002). These included increases in the national pension, which was improved several times in mid- and late-1980s.

The government launched its first proposals for improvements in an "elderly report," submitted to Parliament in the fall of 1986 and followed by a bill. With regard to the national pension, the bill focused on "interaction problems" between the pension supplement and other pensions. Due to the income testing of the pension supplement, pensioners with small additional pensions would hardly benefit from these pensions, as they would simply lead to a smaller or no pension supplement. The government thus suggested easing the income testing of the pension supplement significantly over a four-year period starting in 1991. Part of the background for the proposal was the debate about occupational pensions, which was just beginning. One of the problems with getting occupational pensions introduced was that for low-wage earners, a considerable part of a future occupational pension would be lost again as the pensions supplement disappeared. A working group of civil servants had thus suggested an easing of the income test of the pension supplement as a way of encouraging trade unions to introduce occupational pensions through collective agreements. The Social Democrats declared that this promise of improvements in the future was a cheap way for the government to buy popularity during an election campaign, but in the Spring of 1987 the proposal was passed unanimously in the Danish Parliament (*Folketingets Forhandlinger* 1986–1987: L199; Green-Pedersen 2003b).

In the spring of 1987, the government also proposed an increase in the pension supplement. The national pension was indexed to prices not wages, and the government suggested improvements to the national pension to compensate pensioners for the wage increases in the 1987 collective agreements. Since the easing of income testing of the pension supplement would not benefit pensioners who already received the pension supplement, the government suggested that the improvement be made by raising the pension supplement, not the basic amount. The opposition considered the amount very small, but in the end the proposal was passed unanimously in Parliament (*Folketingets Forhandlinger* 1986–1987: L218).

The election in the fall of 1987, led to a significant deterioration of the government's parliamentary situation. Previously (after the 1984 election), the right-wing bourgeois government (KF-V-CD-KRF-coalition) had been able to rely solely on close cooperation with the Social Liberals for passing its economic policy. There were thus no parliamentary reasons for concessions to the Social Democrats. In the 1987 election, however, the government lost its majority with the Social Liberals and was forced back to the situation that prevailed from 1982 to 1984 when it had to gain support from either the Social Democrats or all the non-socialist opposition parties including both the Social Liberals and the Progress Party. The difficulty of the latter was already evident later in 1987 when the budget had to be passed. As a matter of principle, the Progress Party voted against the budget and the government had little choice but to try to get support from the Social Democrats, who were able to demand a high price for their support. Moreover, having lost the 1987 election, the government was under additional pressure to try to improve its social image. The image of implementing "unfair" cutbacks stuck to the government and was the major challenge to staying in power after the immediate economic crisis had subsided (Green-Pedersen 2002). The result was considerable improvements in a number of cash benefits, including the national pension. All benefits were increased, particularly the pension supplement. Income testing of the pension supplement was further eased with effect in 1988. The law thus meant an increase in expenditure on the national pension of around 6 percent (Green-Pedersen 2000), and the Social Democrats afterwards spoke of social democratic "footprints" on the budget. All parties but the Social Liberals supported the proposal when passed in Parliament. The Social Liberals found the general increase in pensions economically irresponsible and abstained (*Folketingets Forhandlinger* 1987–1988: L168).

After 1988, the Danish economy moved into recession again with rising unemployment and budget deficits (Nannestad and Green-Pedersen, forthcoming). Nevertheless retrenchment measures were not discussed, and in 1990 the national pension was improved again with the introduction of a new indexation system for cash benefits. Whereas the national pension had been linked to prices through the 1980s, the automatic indexation of benefits such as unemployment benefits and early retirement benefits was abolished in 1982. They were frozen until the beginning of 1986, after which they were indexed by an annual decision in Parliament. The new system that was introduced linked all benefits to real wages. However, if indexation exceeds 2 percent, 0.3 percent is deducted and used for other improvements in cash benefits. In connection with the introduction of this new system, the basic pension was also increased for married pensioners so that it was equal to that for singles.

To some extent, the new law was forced on the government. In 1989, the government tried to gain parliamentary support for limited indexation of cash benefits. However, the opposition parties joined forces and passed a resolution in Parliament demanding that the government propose a law ensuring automatic indexation of all cash benefits based on real wages. During the 1980s, a system of alternative majorities, that is to say, not including the government, had developed in the Danish Parliament. This majority was mainly active with regard to foreign policy and actually partly disappeared after the 1988 election, when the Social Liberals joined the government. However, on some social issues, the Center Democrats and the Christian People's Party, which had been more or less kicked out of the government in 1988, participated in an alternative majority that pressured the government to accept the new indexation system. The law was passed in 1990. For the national pension, this would most likely mean higher benefits in the long run, but the effect would of course depend on real wage development (*Folketingets Forhandlinger* 1989–1990: L223, 224).

Altogether, the period from 1986 to 1990 saw a number of improvements in the national pension in Denmark, the reasons for which can be found in the pressure on the government from the dynamics of party competition. First, because of the cutbacks it had implemented, the center-right government was under pressure to improve its social image and thus started making improvements between 1984 to 1987, when its parliamentary situation was favorable because of its majority with the Social Liberals. Second, after the 1987 election, the government was in a difficult parliamentary situation and was forced to make concessions to the opposition parties. Increases in the national pension were attractive both for a government wanting to improve its social image, and for an opposition needing visible concessions in return for parliamentary support, given that pensioners were considered deserving recipients after a long working life (Green-Pedersen 2002). The development of the national pension in this period was thus shaped by the interplay between electoral competition over a positive welfare image and the high popularity of the scheme.

The introduction of occupational pensions 1986–1991

When the economic crisis of the early 1980s disappeared, the pension question reappeared in Danish politics. However, by the early 1980s funded occupational pensions covered about one-fifth of the labor force so funded occupational pensions were the only realistic answer to the pension question. A PAYG solution for the rest of the labor market would be impossible to combine with these funded occupational pensions. The mainly public employees who had already saved for their pensions for years would not accept other groups being given a pension on a PAYG basis, since they would have had to contribute to such a scheme through the tax system. On the other hand, the funded schemes were so mature that it was impossible to dismantle them. The enormous sums of money from these funds could not be given back to those having paid contributions without overheating the economy. The funds are also privately organized which means that politically it would be very difficult just to tax the funds away. The contributors would see this as a government confiscation of their savings. Finally, the economic situation in Denmark also made the tax increases necessary to finance a PAYG solution very unattractive (Green-Pedersen and Lindbom 2006).

The pension question was not taken up again by the government until its budget in the spring of 1984 (Finansministeriet 1984). For the government, the introduction of occupational pensions had several advantages. First, if the contributions were part of normal wage increases, this would mean less immediate private consumption, which would help control Denmark's apparently permanent current account deficit. Second, if introduced in a decentralized way, occupational pensions would mean an acceptable end to the struggle over economic democracy and the establishment of a central wage-earner controlled fund. The trade unions and the Social Democrats had never been successful with their plan, but at times they had been close to successfully introducing a modified version of the proposal (Due and Madsen 2003: 63–92). The issue was not dead, obviously, and the government saw occupational pensions as a way to satisfy the demands of wage earners in a manner acceptable to employers. Thirdly, the government also considered the large number of people living on only the national pension and the ATP as a social problem, and as a factor that could force the government into raising the national pension (Green-Pedersen 2003b).

Occupational pensions were attractive for the government, but only if they were introduced through collective agreement and not through legislation. Introducing them through law could easily mean that wage earners would not view the contributions as part of wage increases, but as a type of social legislation on top of normal wage increases. The government wanted occupational pensions introduced by the social partners through collective agreements. The government declared that once this happened, it would be willing to consider legislation regarding two issues: pension schemes for wage earners not covered by collective agreements, and the interruption of pension contributions for those receiving unemployment, sickness and maternity benefits. The LO and the trade unions also had a strong interest in occupational pensions. It was mainly members of these organizations who lacked sufficient pension coverage. Furthermore, for the LO, occupational pensions were also an opportunity to introduce a system resembling economic democracy. However, the LO wanted a legislative solution. Only this would secure full coverage of all wage earners. Altogether, the issue of occupational pensions emerged because both the government and the LO had a stake in it, not because the groups with insufficient coverage put pressure on the government or the LO to find a solution.

The first initiative concerning occupational pensions came from the trade unions in the fall of 1984, when the Metal Workers Union demanded occupational pensions in the subsequent round of collective agreements. Other trade unions, especially those representing low-skill workers, were skeptical but LO responded by setting up a committee to work out a model for occupational pensions (LO 1985).

This committee issued its report in the fall of 1985, suggesting a system of legislatively mandated occupational pensions for all wage earners not already covered. The plan also called for one central pension fund under LO control as well as the doubling of the ATP contribution and additional income testing of the national pension. The latter two elements were designed to limit the increase in inequality between pensioners as a result of the introduction of earnings-related pensions (LO 1985). The social democratic parliamentary group was not enthusiastic about the income testing of the national pension, but in spring 1986, the Social Democrats put forward a proposal in Parliament for the introduction of occupational pensions with one central fund (Petersen 2002).

The Social Democrat's proposal was symbolic in the sense that the right-wing bourgeois government and the Social Liberals, which had a majority in the Danish parliament, were clearly against it. A legislative solution would not lead to lower immediate wage increases in collective agreements, and there was no way the government would accept one central pension fund under LO control. This was simply the reappearance of the economic democracy proposals from the 1970s.

Employers agreed with the government. They did not rule out occupational pensions, but they opposed a solution through legislation and a central fund as suggested by the LO (Green-Pedersen 2003b).

The situation in 1986 was, in other words, that both the government and the LO were interested in introducing occupational pensions, but not in the same way. The government wanted the LO to introduce occupational pensions through collective agreements, whereas the LO wanted the government to introduce them through legislation. There was, in other words, a stalemate of sorts. What the government could do was to make the introduction of occupational pensions more attractive—and indeed it did so, by easing the income testing of the pension supplement already mentioned.

During the collective bargaining rounds in 1987, occupational pensions played no role. The trade unions were still united around the LO proposal of occupational pensions introduced through legislation, and they also found the issue of reduced working hours more important (Due and Madsen 2003: 126–8). The collective agreements ended in a "wage feast" with damaging effects on Danish competitiveness (Nannestad and Green-Pedersen forthcoming). This, together with the changed parliamentary situation, to some extent broke the stalemate over occupational pensions. For the government, large wage increases had further increased the need for wage moderation. The changed political situation after the 1987 election meant that the government could not just rely on the Social Liberals to build a majority as it had done before, but it also needed the support of the Progress Party. This change in the parliamentary situation also made cooperation with the LO attractive for the right-wing government. If it could reach agreement with the LO, it would be impossible for the Social Democrats to oppose the agreements. The LO, for its part, had to recognize that the government had survived another election, and if the LO wanted political influence, cooperating with the government was one way to achieve this.

This new situation resulted in trilateral negotiations between the government, the LO and the Danish employers' association in the fall of 1987. These negotiations resulted in what became known as the "common declaration" signed by the social partners and the government. The declaration's main component content was union acceptance of wage moderation. In return, the trade union got acceptance of the appointment of a commission to investigate occupational pensions (Due and Madsen 2003: 126–62). This "Labor Market Pensions Committee" consisted of representatives from the social partners and civil servants. The government was thus not politically represented. There were no negotiations in the committee, but discussions of technical aspects of different models of occupational pensions. Indirectly, however, the Committee's report did indicate some movement on the LO side. For example, the report stated that pension contributions should be part of wage negotiations, and the LO also indicated that it could accept a decentralized solution (Arbejdsmarkedpensionsudvalget 1988).

The Committee issued its report just before Christmas 1988, and it was unclear what would happen. The LO hoped that the government would start serious negotiations on the issue, but was soon disappointed. In his New Year's Day speech to the Danish people, Conservative Prime Minister Schlüter instead suggested, with the round of collective agreements in early 1989 in mind, that workers accept wage cuts in return for tax relief. This was something which the unions saw as the exact opposite of an invitation to negotiate. The background for the Prime Minister's declaration was an ongoing internal conflict in the government. The Conservatives, represented by the Minister of Finance, were positive towards occupational pensions and were considering legislation that would ensure coverage for groups not covered by collective agreements. The Liberals, represented by the Minister of Taxation, opposed occupational pensions, at least if these were to involve any kind of legislation, preferring instead, the further expansion of private pensions. The Conservative Prime Minister had increasingly synchronized his political views with those of the Liberal Minister of Taxation, which was the background for the suggestion in his New Year's speech. At the time, it seemed that the negotiations over occupational pensions had come to an end. Yet the Prime Minister repeated that if occupational pensions were introduced through collective agreements, the government would be willing to consider accompanying legislation (Green-Pedersen 2003b).

In the negotiations over collective agreements on the private labor market in early 1989, occupational pensions played no role. The 1987 collective agreement was to expire in four years, but there was room for negotiations over limited wage increases in 1989. Thus, occupational pensions could not be included in the negotiations right away. Furthermore, the trade unions preferred a legislative solution and did not raise the issue. On the public sector labor market the situation was different. Here the unions representing the groups not already covered were interested in extending occupational pensions to their members, and here the collective agreement of 1987 only lasted for two years. Occupational pensions were thus extended to all public employees (Due and Madsen 2003: 177–81).

During the summer and early fall of 1989, the discussion over occupational pensions changed forum. The economic recession prompted the government and the Social Democrats to launch plans for reforms of the labor market and the tax system. The Social Democratic plan also included occupational pensions introduced through legislation, whereas the government plan simply expected occupational pensions to be introduced through collective agreements without any suggestion that legislation might be passed (Statsministeriet 1989; Socialdemokratiet 1989). In early fall of 1989, negotiations began. Internal government documents show that if a deal could have been reached, the government would have been prepared to commit itself to the introduction of occupational pensions during the 1991 collective bargaining round, by introducing a law including wage earners not covered by collective agreements (archive of the Prime Minister's Office). However, negotiations failed, to a large extent because the Social Democrats had no real interest in reaching an agreement with the government. The image the Social Democrats wished to portray was one of a tough opposition focused on winning a parliamentary majority with the Socialist People's Party.

After these negotiations, the LO realized that the only way to expand occupational pension coverage was through collective agreements. The Metal Workers Union now declared that they would give the issue top priority when negotiating the collective agreement of 1991. The metal workers were among the highest paid wage earners without an occupational pension, and they thus faced a strong decline in income on retirement. Moreover, the Metal Workers Union feared that if occupational pensions were not introduced, large Danish companies would introduce firm-based pension schemes, implying that the unions would have no influence on pension savings (Green-Pedersen 2003b). The LO still preferred some kind of legislation to solve two problems, namely the wage earners not covered by collective agreements and the interruption of of pension contributions when receiving unemployment, sickness and maternity benefits. However, for the LO, obtaining occupational pensions was now the most important issue, and the LO supported the attempts of the individual trade unions to establish occupational pensions in the 1991 collective bargaining round (LO 1990). The result was that most trade unions introduced occupational pensions. In subsequent rounds of collective agreements, occupational pensions have become part of all collective agreements, and contributions have gradually increased to around 9 percent of qualifying wages (Due and Madsen 2003).

With the introduction of occupational pensions in Denmark in 1991, the pension question in Denmark had finally been answered by funded occupational pensions introduced at the trade union (as opposed to the LO) level. There was, however, no legislation to secure pension coverage for wage earners not covered by a collective agreement, and no legislation to ensure that pension contributions were still made during periods of absence from the labor market.

The final shape of Denmark's pension settlement can be explained by focusing on two stages in the decision-making process. First, the fact that large groups on the labor market already had funded occupational pensions meant that the expansion of funded occupational pensions was the only feasible solution. Both the pension commission of the LO (LO 1985: 83–6) and the labor market pension committee (Arbejdsmarkedspensionsudvalget 1988: 2–3) briefly discussed PAYG solutions such as expanding national pensions, but concluded that such a solution was incompatible with existing occupational pensions (Green-Pedersen and Lindbom 2006).

Second, as we have seen, the government and the trade unions had different opinions with regard to the exact structure of occupational pensions. In the end, the government got its way. Occupational pensions were introduced through collective agreements, without any legislation, and the trade unions had to give up on their preference for one large scheme introduced through legislation. In fact, the unions never even got their accompanying legislation. The reason why the trade unions were not successful can be found in the organizational advantages for the trade unions concerning occupational pensions. For the trade unions, the fact that being covered by a collective agreement also means access to an occupational pension was seen as a way to increase membership, just as the control of the pension funds was attractive for the trade unions (Due and Madsen 2003). Furthermore, since the government was not willing to introduce occupational pensions through legislation, the alternative to the decentralized version of occupational pensions was further expansion of firm-based private pensions, which meant no union influence. Finally, it is debatable how important it was for the trade unions to get coverage for wage earners not covered by collective agreements, since this group was dominated by professionals who were not even union members. In other words, for the trade unions, the actual solution was far better than the only realistic alternative. For the government, on the other hand, one of the goals of introducing occupational pensions, namely that part of wage increases would be used for pension savings, would most likely not have been achieved if occupational pensions had been introduced through legislation, since wage earners would view the pensions as a social benefit on top of wage increases. Moreover, one of the governing parties, the Liberals, preferred the alternative solution: private pensions. Thus, the government could afford to be patient, whereas the unions could not.

Since the issue of occupational pensions was more or less settled in 1991, Danish pension policy has been a question of adapting the first pillar to take account of the role of occupational pensions. In particular, the absence of legislation requiring that pension contributions continue for those in receipt of unemployment, sickness and maternity benefits, has generated changes in some of the first-pillar schemes. Since occupational pensions are funded, defined-contribution schemes, the pressure arising from increased life expectancy and the graying of the population does not constitute the same problem in Denmark as in other countries. However, some of the public schemes, such as the national pension and the early retirement scheme, have come under pressure and have seen changes.[10] In addition, it is not just pension policy but also pension politics that has been shaped by the introduction of occupational pensions. The fact that occupational pensions, like the ATP, are administered by the social partners means that governments leave these schemes to the social partners. If the social partners reach an agreement, it is normally accepted by Parliament without further discussion. Thus, the political dynamics of the Danish parliamentary system applies mainly to the national pension, which has seen one important reform in the period since the introduction of occupational pensions, and the recently introduced SP scheme.

ATP for recipients of cash benefits

As mentioned above, the fact that an accompanying law was never passed when occupational pensions were introduced left two problems for the Danish pension system, namely a group of wage earners not covered by occupational pensions, and the loss of pension contributions during sickness, unemployment, and parental leave. These issues have attracted limited political attention since the introduction of occupational pensions. With regard to the wage earners not covered by occupational pensions, several government studies have concluded that the problem is not significant, for two reasons. First, some of the groups not covered are young people who will be covered later in their careers. Second, a significant proportion of those not covered are highly-paid professionals not covered by a collective agreement, but who will be able to pay into a private pension scheme (Økonomiministeriet 2003). Therefore, political attention has mainly been directed towards the lack of coverage during unemployment, sickness, and so forth.[11]

As early as 1989, the board of the ATP (i.e. the social partners) had suggested introducing ATP contributions for recipients of sickness, maternity and unemployment benefits as part of a modernized version of the ATP scheme. However, resistance from the Ministry of Finance meant that the proposal for a new ATP law, put forward in the spring of 1991, did not include contributions for recipients of sickness, unemployment and maternity benefits. However, with the opposition pressing for this change, the Labor Market Committee of Parliament asked the Ministry of Labor to sketch the necessary revisions of the ATP law. In December 1991, the government put forward a new version of the revisions of the ATP law, still without contributions for recipients of sickness, maternity and unemployment benefits, again because of continued resistance from the Ministry of Finance. However, in the spring of 1992, a majority in the Labor Market Committee, Social Democrats, SF, the Social Liberals and the Center Democrats introduced an amendment to the legislation that included contributions to the proposal, and in the end it was passed unanimously in Parliament, but with skepticism from the Liberals and Conservatives who feared increased government expenditure (*Folketingets Forhandlinger* 1990–1991: L86; 1991–1992: L152; archive of the Ministry of Finance).

The Social Democrat-led government that took office in 1993 was also not particularly interested in accompanying legislation, but in connection with the budget agreement for 1996 the government suggested expanding the pension systems, with ATP contributions for recipients of cash benefits. The recipients of sickness, maternity, and unemployment benefits would get double ATP contributions, recipients of social assistance would get normal ATP contributions and recipients of early retirement benefits and disability pensions would get the possibility of paying voluntary contributions. Finally, the government also suggested indexation of the ATP contributions. The right-wing parties in Parliament were quite critical of the proposal, but the Conservatives ended up making a budget agreement for 1996 with the government. The changes to the ATP scheme were then passed as part of this agreement. However, the proposal for pension indexation was removed from the final version (*Folketingets Forhandlinger* 1995–1996: L12).

The final initiative concerning the payment of contributions to labor market pensions for those on cash benefits came in connection with the new disability pension scheme passed in the Spring of 2001 by a broad majority in the Danish Parliament. Two aspects of the legislation are important. First, disability pension recipients would now pay normal ATP contributions, with the government financing two-thirds of the costs and the recipient paying the remaining one-third. Second, a voluntary pension scheme was set up for recipients of disability pensions so that they could join a voluntary pension savings system organized parallel to the ATP. Contributions are approximately 2 percent of average wages and are financed in the same way as the ATP contributions for those on disability pensions (*Folketingets Forhandlinger* 2000–2001: L137).

Just as the ATP is generally considered an area where Parliament does not interfere with the decisions of the social partners, civil servant pensions are generally regarded as an issue of negotiation between the Ministry of Finance and the trade unions of the civil servants. Once the Ministry and the civil servants' union agree, the necessary legislative changes are passed in Parliament with broad majorities, and changes are also made to the schemes for civil servants employed by local governments. The scheme has seen two noteworthy changes since 1980. First, reductions in the national pension for recipients of civil servant pensions have been abolished, resulting in higher overall pensions for civil servants. Further, in 1993 a new system of calculating benefits was introduced that links pensions more closely to previous wages. However, a transition phase lasting until 2022 has been agreed upon, compensating low-wage civil servants and involving higher costs for the government. Finally, it is also important to note that the number of people entitled to civil servant pensions has been cut by nearly one half. This is the result of a strategy of the Ministry of Finance to limit civil servant pensions to only a few groups, including high-ranking civil servants and pastors. Other groups of public employees are employed under collective agreements with funded occupational pensions. For instance, teachers in primary schools are no longer employed as civil servants.

As already discussed, the non-interference of Parliament and the government in the matters decided by the social partners also applies to occupational pensions. This became clear in 2002/2003 when the Liberal-Conservative government which had taken office in 2001 floated its ideas about introducing choice into funded occupational pension schemes, that is, allowing participants to transfer their savings to another pension fund. A government committee issued a report on the issue (Økonomiministeriet 2003), but it became clear that with regard to the occupational pension, introducing "free choice" would mean a major conflict with the social partners since they see these schemes as an issue to be dealt with through collective agreements. Consequently, the government gave up on the idea.[12]

The national pension and the SP scheme are considered within the authority of Parliament and the government. Since the introduction of occupational pensions, these areas have seen reforms that can best be explained by the logic of party competition in the Danish Parliament.

Increased means testing of the national pension 1993

In early 1993, a government consisting of the Social Democrats and the three small center parties, the Social Liberals, the Center Democrats and the Christian People's Party, formed a majority government; the only one in Denmark since 1971. At that time, the Danish economy had improved, especially public finances and the current account, but unemployment was still high. The new government introduced a tax reform that would provide a fiscal stimulus for a few years, but would thereafter mean tax increases. The aim was to kick-start the economy through tax relief—and the policy was successful (Nannestad and Green-Pedersen, forthcoming). Part of the tax reform involved transforming a number of existing net cash benefits into higher, taxable, gross benefits. The net amount would remain the same, but the effect would be make all cash benefits taxable, in line with existing policy for most other types of benefit. With regard to the national pension, this meant that the enhanced personal tax exemption for single pensioners would be abolished, as had already been proposed by an internal government commission in 1989 (Socialministeriet 1989). The government argued that such a change would also be necessary to ensure that the tax relief would also benefit pensioners (*Folketingets Forhandlinger* 1992–1993: L314).

The abolition of the special tax exemption of course meant that pensioners needed to be compensated with higher pensions. For a transitional period until 1999, all single pensioners would get a new supplement equal to the value of the special tax exemption, but after that the supplement would be transferred to the income-tested part of the pension supplement. Obviously not all pensioners would be entitled to this supplement. Finally, the basic amount was decreased slightly for all pensioners, but the pension supplement was raised by an equal amount. The government had designed the combined effect of the tax relief and the change in the national pension to ensure higher net income for all pensioners. However, in the long run the increased income-testing in the scheme also means savings for the government—not least because the number of people with pensions besides the national pension and the ATP will increase due to the expansion of occupational pensions.

Unlike the normal Danish minority governments, this government could use its majority to implement the changes without negotiating with the opposition, and it did just that. The right-wing opposition was critical of the tax reform and therefore voted against it and against the changes in the national pension as well. The opposition had nothing against the reform to make benefits part of gross income, but was critical of increased income testing, mainly because it diminished the incentives for pension saving. This had been a standard argument of the right-wing parties against income testing of the national pension for a long time (Green-Pedersen 2003a). In the long run, the consequences of increased income testing are significant, but nevertheless the reform did not create much public debate. Attention was focused on the tax reform in general and on labor market reforms passed at the same time. Furthermore, due to the complexity and the long-term effects of the changes, it was difficult to arouse much opposition. In other words, the changes are another good example of what Pierson (1994) calls strategies of obfuscation, where reform is structured in ways that make it hard for voters to comprehend negative effects. Furthermore, the fact that the change was made by a Social Democratic-led government also contributed to the "de-politicization" of the issue. The right-wing parties had little to gain from attacking the government on this retrenchment issue, and instead focused their opposition on other parts of the new government's policies, especially the tax reform.

With regard to the overall Danish pension system, the increased role of income testing is interesting since the policy direction in the 1980s had been the opposite.

Thus, while the governments of the 1980s had eased income testing to make occupational pensions more attractive for low earners, the government moved in the opposite direction once these occupational pensions had been introduced. Recently, the Danish national pension has been moved further in the income-tested direction, with the introduction of the so-called "elderly check," which was passed in connection with the budget for 2003. This check is paid only to pensioners who have no other income than the national pension. It was introduced as a concession to the Danish People's Party to obtain support for the budget. As before, improvements in the national pension were used by the political parties to shore up their social profile.

Introduction of the Special Pension scheme (SP)

The latest addition to the Danish pension system is the Special Pension scheme (SP). The scheme was initiated in the fall of 1997. The Danish economy was booming and the government wanted to curb private consumption (Nannestad and Green-Pedersen, forthcoming). Therefore, the government suggested that all wage earners and the self-employed should pay an extra contribution of 1 percent of work-related income to the ATP in 1998. With an election coming up, the government wanted to avoid being accused of raising taxes, and therefore launched this temporary increase in pension contributions. The government obtained support from the Liberals and the Conservatives for the proposal on condition of one change, namely that unlike the ATP scheme, benefits, in this case a lump sum, should depend on the size of the contribution paid. The parties argued that the original government suggestion, where the lump sum contribution would only depend on the number of hours worked, as in the ATP, was in reality a tax increase (*Folketingets Forhandlinger* 1997–1998: 1. samling, L31).

After the election in March 1998, the Social Democratic government wanted to introduce even more drastic measures to curb private consumption and it agreed on a tax reform with the left-wing parties in Parliament (Nannestad and Green-Pedersen, forthcoming). As part of this tax reform, the Special Pension scheme was made permanent and the benefit structure changed so that the value of contributions would not matter for benefits, as it did in the ATP scheme. However, the contributions paid for 1998 would be paid as originally agreed upon with the right-wing parties (*Folketingets Forhandlinger* 1997–1998: 2. samling, L108). This conflict over the connection between contributions and benefits was in fact a conflict over whether or not the scheme should have a redistributional function, and the struggle continued after the 2001 election. The new right-wing bourgeois government, with support from the Danish People's Party, changed the scheme again so that benefits are linked to contributions. The government also liberalized the investments in the scheme. From 2005, contributors can choose between different investment profiles within the SP or transfer the savings to other pension funds, banks, etc. This law was passed by the center-right majority in the Danish Parliament (*Folketingets Forhandlinger* 2002–2003: L195).[13]

The political dynamics around the SP scheme seem more like a traditional "politics matter" situation, where the Social Democrats argue for redistribution and the right-wing bourgeois parties argue against it. Thus, a "Nixon goes China logic" seems less important here. The reason is probably that the scheme receives limited political attention. Thus, the current Liberal government, for example, can pursue traditional center-right policies here, whereas in other areas with much more political salience, for instance health care, its policies have been very social democratic in the sense that they have brought further expansion of the welfare state.

V Conclusion

In many countries, pension politics over the last 20 years has been dominated by efforts to reduce the costs of earnings-related PAYG systems, where expenditure is threatening to rise dramatically in order to pay for benefits for graying populations. Furthermore, the "double payment" problem has made even modest moves in a funded direction politically difficult. Denmark does not have a large pay-as-you-go earnings-related pension scheme, and hence pension politics has followed a different path.

Summary of the magnitude of changes

Two decades ago, the pension question in Denmark was partly unanswered in the sense that around two-thirds of wage earners only had access to the national pension and the ATP, implying a significant drop in income following retirement. Today, Denmark has a multi-tiered pension system close to World Bank recommendations in which almost the entire work force is covered by occupational pensions. In this sense, the Danish pension system is more or less settled. The national pension still provides universal benefits and was actually expanded in the 1980s. The scheme did, however, see a significant retrenchment in 1993. New elements such as the SP and SAP have been added and the ATP scheme expanded to provide some coverage for recipients of cash benefits. In other words, the changes have been significant, but retrenchment has been very limited.

Impact of the political system on pension politics

The fact that occupational pensions in Denmark are the domain of the social partners means that the political system has mainly been relevant in connection with the national pension. This is a matter for the political parties and changes to the scheme are best understood through the logic of electoral competition. The national pension is one of the most popular welfare schemes in Denmark (Andersen 2003) and the political parties rarely, if ever, suggest retrenchment. Thus, it is hardly surprising that the scheme did not suffer retrenchment in the early 1980s, and that when the center-right government needed to improve its social image in the mid-1980s, improvements to the national pension played a significant role. Another example was the "elderly check" passed in connection with the budget agreement for 2003. The only important retrenchment in the national pension was the increase in income-testing introduced in 1993. This was passed by a Social Democratic government with a strong pro-welfare state image, and the change is a prime example of what Pierson (1994) calls the "politics of obfuscation." The retrenchment effects of the law are long-term and difficult to understand. The development of the national pension in Denmark thus shows the importance of the dynamics of electoral competition for public policy developments.

Interest group influence

Today occupational pensions and the ATP scheme are the domain of the social partners and they have been able to avoid government interference, as for example in connection with the "free choice" discussion after the change of government in 2001. This speaks for the strength of organized interests, but it is important to keep in mind that part of the reason why decentralized occupational pensions became so dominant in Danish pensions was the inability of the political system to agree upon a public earnings-related pension system. The disagreements at the parliamentary level thus left room for the social partners.

Constraints of policy design

The fact that around 20 percent of wage earners already had funded occupational pensions in 1980 meant that the only realistic answer to the remaining part of the pension question was funded occupational pension schemes. Thus, the Danish case shows that path dependence in pension systems is not just a question of the double payment problem, but it is also important with regard to funded systems, since a shift in the PAYG direction is also highly problematic (Green-Pedersen and Lindbom 2006). In reality, the funded part of the Danish pension system was a result of the many occupational pensions that had been introduced in the labor market during the 1960s and 1970s, when political agreement over other pension solutions could not be reached.

However, within this path, which all actors have recognized, there has been room for pension politics. In relation to occupational pensions, political conflict concerned the exact structure of occupational pensions. The LO wanted a centralized version through legislation, and the government wanted a decentralized solution introduced through collective agreements. In the end, the government won because unions had an obvious interest in the introduction of occupational pensions. Such a scheme maintains the importance of the system of collective bargaining, and gives the individual trade unions control over pension funds. The trade unions never got accompanying legislation covering wage earners not included in collective agreements and securing contributions during periods outside of the labor market due to unemployment, parenthood, and so on, but the system set up through collective agreements is still much more attractive for trade unions than the expansion of private pensions, which would have been the only realistic alternative.

The fact that the Danish pension system is structured as a multi-pillar system with funded, defined-contribution occupational pensions as the most important element also leads to a de-politicization of pension issues. Thus falling interest rates, and the stock market crash of 2001 and 2002, have not been transformed into political issues. They will lead to lower pensions from all the funded schemes in the future, but this is considered to be an automatic element of having these pension schemes. Political conflict with regard to the funded elements has centered on taxation issues. At the beginning of the period, private and occupational pension were indirectly subsidized through the tax system. This has changed significantly, due partly to the taxation of interest income, which also covers the ATP, the SP and the SAP, and partly due to the fact that three tax reforms passed in 1985, 1993 and 1998 have all reduced the tax deductibility of private and occupational pensions. Politically, the right-wing parties have opposed such changes in principle, but the taxation of interest gains on pension savings, for instance, was passed by a right-wing government due to the need to improve public budgets.

In general, this suggests that pension politics within pension schemes that do not have a major PAYG earnings-related component depends on the exact structure of the funded elements. The fact that the Danish pension system relies so strongly on funded, defined-contribution schemes, mostly controlled by the social partners, ensures that there is fairly little party political conflict with regard to the pension system, besides the national pension, even in the presence of pressures such as higher life expectancy and the retirement of the "baby boom" generation.

Role of ideas and historical context

The historical context played an important role for the final settlement of the Danish pensions system. The fact that the discussion came during the 1980s, in the context of economic problems and an ensuing reluctance to increase taxes, was an additional factor in the choice of funded occupation pensions, besides the fact that the already existing pension system would have made any other solution difficult. Thus, although Demark now has a pension system that seems to be modeled on the ideas of the World Bank, this pension system came about through a series of political compromises, in which both the need of minority governments to craft a legislative majority within the constraints of the logic of party competition, and accidents of sequence and timing placed Denmark's pension policy on the path to a multi-pillar system.

Abbreviations

AC	Akademikernes centralorganisation (Danish Confederation of Professional Associations)
ATP	Arbejdsmarkedets Tillaegspension (supplementary labor market pension)
CD	Centrum-Demokraterne (Centre Democrats)
DM	Dansk Metal (Union for Metal Workers)
FOA	Forbundet af offentligt ansatte (Union of Public Employees)
FTF	Funktionaer og tjenestemandsforbundet (the Salaried Employees' and Civil Servants' Confederation)
HK	Handels og kontorarbejderforbundet (the Union of Commercial and Clerical Employees)
KF	Konservative Folkeparti (Conservatives)
KRF	Kristendemokraterne (Christian democrats)
LO	Landsorganisationen i Danmark (Danish Confederation of Trade Unions)
RV	Det Radikale Venstre (Social Liberals)
SAP	Supplerende arbejdsmarkedspension for foertidspensionister (additional labor market pension for those on disability pensions)
SD	Socialdemoktratief (Social Democrats in Denmark)
SF	Socialistik Folkeparti (Socialist People's Party)
SID	Specialarbejderforbundet i Danmark (the Union of Unskilled Workers)
SP	Særlige Pensionsopsaring (special pension saving scheme)
V	Venstre (Liberals)
VS	Venstresocialisteme (Left-Socialists)
3F	Fælles Fagligt Forbund (Union Federation of Danish Workers)

Notes

1. Thanks are due to Trine Toftgaard Lund for excellent research assistance, Lone Winter for help with the manuscript and to Karen Anderson, Jørgen Elklit, Ellen Immergut and Isabelle Schulze for constructive criticism of earlier versions.
2. Jones (1986) provides a useful introduction to Danish political history.
3. Damgaard (2000) provides a useful introduction to Danish parliamentary politics.
4. This description of Danish local government refers to the situation after the local government reform effective of January 1, 2007.
5. The political parties have recently agreed to increase the age at which one can receive the national pension from 65 to 67, in the period 2024 to 2027. If life expectancy increases more rapidly than expected, however, the age from which one may receive the national pension will be further adjusted upwards. Please note that a previous reform of 1998 changed the retirement age for the national pension from 67 to 65, but only for people turning 60 after July 1, 1998.

6. Payments to the SP scheme have been suspended for the period 2004–7.
7. A change of the scheme in 2004 has made it possible to postpone receiving the national pensions and they have higher benefits later.
8. On top of the basic amount and pension supplement, each municipality has the opportunity to give personal supplements to elderly people with high costs, for instance for heating, glasses and medication. The central government pays half of the expenditure for the personal supplements, which equal approximately 3% of the overall expenditure for the national pension.
9. Most likely, the Social Democrats wanted the tax to be permanent because they wanted to avoid a new political debate on the issue when a temporary tax expired, maybe at a time when they were in government themselves and the pressure from the economic crisis was not there.
10. In comparative perspective, it is worth noting that the public schemes are financed out of general revenue not wage-related social contributions. The debate about pension expenditure causing high wage-costs is thus much less important in Denmark than in other countries. Thanks to Karen Anderson for pointing this out to me.
11. If you are entitled to normal pay during sickness, you are also entitled to pension contributions.
12. With regard to the ATP, the idea of free choice also had to be given up on since contributions are not individualized in a way that makes it possible to withdraw one's contributions. The only scheme affected by the free choice idea is thus the SP.
13. The same majority has suspended payments for the period 2004 to 2007.

Bibliography

Primary sources and government documents

Arbejdsmarkedspensionsudvalget (1988). *Redegørelse fra Arbejdsmarkedspensionsudvalget*. Copenhagen: The Ministry of Labor.
Archives of the Ministry of Finance.
Archives of the Prime Minister's Office.
Finansministeriet (1984). **Budgetredegørelse 1984**. Copenhagen: Finansministeriet.
Folketinget (various years). **Folketingets Forhandlinger**. Copenhagen: Folketinget.
Socialministeriet (2002). *National Strategirapport om det danske pensionssystem*. Copenhagen: Socialministeriet.
Statsministeriet (1989). *Planen*. Copenhagen: Statsministeriet.
Økonomiministeriet (2003). *Større valgfrihed i pensionsopsparingen*. Copenhagen: Økonomiministeriet.

Secondary sources

ANDERSEN, JØRGEN G. (1988). "Vælgernes holdning til den offentlige udgiftspolitik". In Bentzon, K. H. (ed.), *Fra vækst til omstilling*. Copenhagen: Nyt fra Samfundsvidenskaberne, 145–90.
—— (2003). "The Danish General Election 2001." *Electoral Studies*, 22(1): 186–93.
ARTER, DAVID (1999). *Scandinavian Politics Today*. Manchester: Manchester University Press.
DAMGAARD, ERIK (2000). "Denmark. The Life and Death of Government Coalitions". In Müller, W. and Strøm, K. (eds.), *Coalition Governments in Western Europe*. Oxford: Oxford University Press.
DUE, JESPER and MADSEN, JØRGEN S. (2003). *Fra magtkamp til konsensus*. Copenhagen: DJØFs forlag.
—— —— and PETERSEN, L. K. (1994). *The Survival of the Danish Model. A historical sociological analysis of the Danish system of collective bargaining*. Copenhagen: DJØFs Forlag.
ELKLIT, JØRGEN (2002). "The Politics of Electoral System Development and Change: The Danish Case." In Grofman B. and Lijphart A. (eds.), *The Evolution of Electoral and Party Systems in the Nordic Countries*. New York: Agathon Press, 15–66.

ELKLIT, JØRGEN (2005). "Denmark: Simplicity Embedded in Complexity (or is the other way around?)". In Gallagher, M. and Mitchell, P. (eds.), *The Politics of Electoral Systems*. Oxford: Oxford University Press, 453–71.

—— and PEDERSEN, MOGENS, N. (2003). "Decembervalget 1973: 30 år efter." *Politica*, 35(4): 365–76.

GREEN-PEDERSEN, CHRISTOFFER (1999). "The Danish Welfare State under Bourgeois Reign. The Dilemma of Popular Entrenchment and Economic Constraints." *Scandinavian Political Studies*, 22(3): 243–60.

—— (2000). *How Politics Still Matters. Retrenchment of old-age pensions, unemployment benefits, and disability pensions/early retirement benefits in Denmark and in the Netherlands from 1982 to 1998*. Ph.D. Dissertation. Århus: Department of Political Science, University of Aarhus.

—— (2002). *The Politics of Justification Party Competition and Welfare-State Retrenchment in Denmark and the Netherlands from 1982 to 1998*. Amsterdam: Amsterdam University Press.

—— (2003a). "Still There But For How Long. The Counter-intuitiveness of the Universal Welfare Model and the Development of the Universal Welfare State in Denmark." *Revue française des affaires sociales*, 57(4): 105–121.

—— (2003b). "Det danske pensionssystems endelige udformning. Kampen om pensionssystemet under Schlüterregeringerne." *Historisk Tidsskrift*, 103(2): 359–83.

—— and VAN KERSBERGEN, KEES (2002). "The Politics of the 'Third Way.' The Transformation of Social Democracy in Denmark and the Netherlands." *Party Politics*, 8(5): 507–24.

—— and THOMSEN, L. H. (2005). "Bloc Politics vs. Broad Cooperation. The Functioning of Danish Minority Parliamentarism." *The Journal of Legislative Studies*, 11(2): 153–69.

—— and LINDBOM, ANDERS (2006). "Politics within Paths. The Trajectories of Earnings-related pensions in Denmark and Sweden," *Journal of European Social Policy*, 16(3): 245–58.

HENRIKSEN, J. P., RASMUSSEN, JØRGEN and KAMPMANN, PER (1988). *Fordelingen af private pensioner*. Copenhagen: Institutionen Sociologi.

JONES, W. GLYN (1986). *Denmark. A Modern History*. New Hampshire: Croom Helm Ltd.

LARSEN, CHRISTIAN A. and ANDERSEN, JØRGEN G. (2004). *Magten på borgen*, Århus: Aarhus Universitets Forlag.

LO (1985). *Forslag til en samlet pensionsreform*. Copenhagen: LO.

LO (1990). *Arbejdsmarkedspensioner*. Copenhagen: LO.

MYLES, JOHN and PIERSON, PAUL (2001). "The Comparative Political Economy of Pension Reform." In Pierson, P. (ed.), *The New Politics of the Welfare State*. Oxford: Oxford University Press, 305–33.

NANNESTAD, PETER and GREEN-PEDERSEN, CHRISTOFFER (forthcoming). "Keep the Bumblebee Flying: Economic Policy in the Welfare State of Denmark, 1973–99". In Albæk, E., et al. (eds.), *Managing the Danish Welfare State under Pressure: Towards a Theory of the Dilemmas of the Welfare State*. Århus: Aarhus University Press.

NØRGAARD, ASBJØRN S. (2000). "Party Politics and the Organization of the Danish Welfare State, 1890–1920: The Bourgeois Roots of the Modern Welfare State." *Scandinavian Political Studies*, 23(3): 183–215.

ØVERBYE, EINAR (1996). "Pension Politics in the Nordic Countries. A Case Study." *International Political Science Review*, 17: 57–90.

—— (1997). "Mainstream Pattern, Deviant Cases: The New Zealand and Danish Pension Systems in an International Context." *Journal of European Social Policy*, 7(2): 101–17.

PEDERSEN, M. N. (1987). "The Danish 'Working Multiparty System': Breakdown or Adaptation". In Daalder, Hans (ed.), *Party Systems in Denmark, Austria, Switzerland, the Netherlands, and Belgium*. London: Frances Pinter, 1–60.

PETERSEN, KLAUS (2002). "Fordelingspolitik, samfundsøkonomi og organisationsinteresser. Den danske arbejderbevægelse og spørgsmålet om tillægspension 1963–1990." *Historisk Tidsskrift*, 102(1): 126–68.

PIERSON, PAUL (1994). *Dismantling the Welfare State. Reagan, Thatcher, and the Politics of Retrenchment*. Cambridge: Cambridge University Press.

SOCIALDEMOKRATIET (1989). *Gang i 90'erne*. Copenhagen: Socialdemokratiet.

VESTERØ-JENSEN, C. (1985). *Det tvedelte pensionssystem*. Roskilde: Forlaget Samfundsøkonomi.

WORLD BANK (1994). *Averting the Old Age Crisis – Policies to Protect the Old and Promote Growth*. Oxford: Oxford University Press.

PART IV

MODERATE VETO POINTS AND VETO PLAYERS

CHAPTER 11

SPAIN: BETWEEN MAJORITY RULE AND INCREMENTALISM

ELISA CHULIÁ

I INTRODUCTION

SPAIN faces dramatic demographic changes over the next fifty years. In spite of recent substantial immigration flows, in the twenty-first century Spain is expected to suffer one of the largest population decreases of all European countries, in parallel with a radical change of the age structure. The Population Division of the United Nations forecasts that people aged 65 and older, who in 1950 represented 7.3 percent and in 2000 around 17 percent of the Spanish population, will make up more than 34 percent by the end of 2050 (UNPD 2005).

In face of this data, national experts have been urging successive Spanish governments to introduce changes in the mandatory pay-as-you-go (PAYG) pension system, which may be financially unsustainable unless reformed. International organizations have also articulated similar misgivings. Thus, in its 2003 economic survey on Spain, the OECD regarded pension reform as the most important challenge facing the Spanish economy and deemed imperative the introduction of entitlement changes. In the same vein, the 2003 report of the International Monetary Fund (IMF) on the

Spanish economy emphasized the need to reform the public pension system, with the argument that the belated but rapid increase in the number of pensioners could provoke its bankruptcy.[1] In a volume published by the World Bank, Holzmann, Orenstein and Rutkowski (2003: 43) state that adverse demographics will probably ensure that by mid-century Spain will be spending more on public pensions, relative to GDP, than any other EU country.

The domestic and international pressure to cut pension costs notwithstanding, Spanish governments have in recent decades tended to implement only cautious and incremental reforms in this sphere. These choices must be interpreted in light of the fact that the Spanish welfare state is considerably smaller than that of neighboring countries, and registers lower pension expenditure than the European average. Therefore, if European governments are, by and large, worried about how to justify welfare cost-containment measures, in Spain this difficulty seems even greater, given that it can hardly be argued that the social protection system is oversized.

The institutional design of the Spanish political system favors the establishment of strong majority executives that can advance legislation without having to surmount effective veto points. Yet the government has only sanctioned unpopular pension reforms under adverse economic circumstances, and when very persuasive arguments regarding current developments of the pension system were available. This pattern of behavior has various plausible explanations. For one, the argument connecting the expansion of social rights with the transition to democracy in the 1970s is fairly deep-rooted in the Spanish political and academic discourse. Furthermore, opinion polls show an ample consensus among Spanish citizens as regards the maintenance of the welfare state, and even considerable support for social protection improvement, tax increases notwithstanding. Spanish political parties thus have very low incentives to put the issue of pension changes on their agenda, because it can be easily instrumentalized in electoral competition as a veiled intent to cut welfare spending.

Good arguments to justify pension reform were available in 1985, when the first Socialist government led by Felipe González passed a bill intending to put an end to the strategic behavior of many workers, who "manufactured" generous pensions by taking advantage of the system's design flaws. The 1985 reform restricted the eligibility criteria for contributory pensions and significantly cut benefits. The absolute majority of the González government was also crucial to passing legislation in 1987 on the establishment of private pension plans and funds, reforms which were not trusted by the political left or trade unions, and which the political right still considered inadequate. In contrast, the establishment of non-contributory means-tested Social Security pensions in 1990 was not so controversial, since there was consent about the inadequate protection level provided by existent social assistance benefits. Along with this reform process, Socialist governments effectively decreased the gap between the lowest and the highest pensions provided by the Social Security system.

Since the establishment and streamlining of the three-pillar pension system at the beginning of the 1990s, Spanish governments, opposition parties and social actors have aimed at consolidating this structure. Actually, the 1995 Toledo Pact stressed the political will to introduce incremental reforms intended not only to rationalize the system, but also to expand it. It can be argued that the Pact has transformed the pension policy area into a sort of multiple partisan veto player system: not only the opposition parties but also the trade unions would try to block any policy change not included in the agreement. But center-right governments between 1996 and 2004 used tax policy as an alternative channel to implement their policy preferences. Thus, while declaring their unconditional commitment to the public pension pillar, they greatly encouraged the development of pension plans managed by banks and insurance companies.

More recently, as the Spanish Socialist government keeps showing resilience to further Social Security reform, experts are increasingly putting forward new arguments to legitimize changes in the public pension system, among them "intergenerational equity". While according to some authors this principle implies working longer and retiring later (Garrido and Chuliá 2005), others postulate that intergenerational equity should lead workers to save more (García, Herce and Jimeno 2005). In both instances policy-makers are advised to act without much delay.

II Political system

Constitutional history and nation-building

Spain—which entered the twentieth century as a constitutional Monarchy and went through a military dictatorship (1923–31), a very unstable democratic Republic (1931–36), a civil war (1936–39) and a lengthy autocracy (1939–77)[2]—has begun the twenty-first century with its longest historical experience of a consolidated democracy. Appointed in 1969 by General Franco as his successor, King Juan Carlos I, whose grandfather had abdicated and gone into exile in 1931, encouraged the transition to democracy in the form of a parliamentary Monarchy after the dictator's death in November 1975 (Magone 2004: 1–26). The development of an incipient civil society during the latter period of the dictatorship helped political actors to lead a reform process which peacefully dismantled the Francoist institutional system (Maravall and Santamaría 1986; Pérez-Díaz 1993). The 1978 Constitution declared the Spanish people, which embodies the "indissoluble" nation integrated by "nationalities and regions," as sovereign. This constitutional text, overwhelmingly endorsed by the Spanish population in a referendum, remains the essential symbol of the democratic transition. So firm was the will of the main transition actors to establish consensually the institutional setting of a stable democracy, in contrast to the turbulent democratic experience of the Second Republic in the 1930s, that they agreed on a Constitution which includes very demanding reform mechanisms and is considered particularly resistant to change (Jiménez 2006).[3]

A very centralized country during Franco's dictatorship, Spain developed into a strongly decentralized state after 1978. The territory of Spain is divided into 17 autonomous communities (plus the two autonomous cities of Ceuta and Melilla in North Africa) which have political and administrative competencies. Like federal states, Spain has three levels of government: central, regional (*autonómico*) and municipal. In spite of this decentralized institutional design, nationalist conflicts represent the most persistent salient issue in the Spanish political debate. Neither the empowerment of the autonomous communities through the transfer of political competencies, nor the loss of the symbolic weight of the nation-state after the full integration of Spain into the European Economic Community (1986) and its outstandingly disciplined performance as a member of the European Union, have contributed to the solution of this fundamental political problem whose most ruthless manifestation is to be found in the attacks of the terrorist organization ETA.[4] Under persistent pressure from nationalist parties to increase the sovereign functions of the autonomous communities, especially in the Basque Country and Catalonia where these parties have been in government for decades, Spanish central governments have tended to stick to the 1978 Constitution as the institutional framework which sets the limits on changes in the territorial structure and organization of the state.

Institutions of government

As the head of the Spanish state and Commander-in-Chief of the Armed Forces, the King symbolizes the unity of the state and represents it in international relations. His main constitutional functions are to sanction laws, to convene and dissolve the parliamentary chambers, to call elections and referenda, and to propose to Congress the candidate for Prime Minister (*Presidente del Gobierno*) (after consultation with representatives of the political parties which have obtained parliamentary seats). Even though he has to be informed about affairs of state, he has in practice no capacity to intervene in the legislative process. The fact that all the acts of the Monarch have to be countersigned by the Prime Minister, the Ministers or the President of the Congress reveals his lack of political decision-making power during periods of normal democratic performance.[5]

As stated in the 1978 Constitution, popular sovereignty resides in the *Cortes Generales*, comprising the Congress of Deputies and the Senate. The Congress has 350 deputies and the Senate, defined in the Constitution as the chamber of territorial representation although in fact a chamber of secondary legislative approval, has 259 Senators. All deputies and around 80 percent of senators are directly elected in general elections, which normally take place every four years. According to the Constitution, Congress nominates the Prime Minister, who is then appointed by the King. In addition to this central investiture function, the Constitution ascribes to the *Cortes* the exercise of legislative power, the approval of the budget and the supervision of the government. The *Cortes* are also responsible for electing 8 of the

21 judges that make up the executive organ of the judiciary (*Consejo General del Poder Judicial*), and the ombudsman (*Defensor del Pueblo*) who is in charge of protecting the fundamental rights and liberties of citizens.

The Prime Minister, Deputy Prime Minister and the Ministers form the central government. Besides the central government, there are 17 governments of the autonomous communities. Each of these has a uni-cameral legislative assembly elected by universal suffrage. The assembly members elect a president who heads the autonomous council of government, and is the supreme representative of the autonomous community as well as the state's representative in the autonomous community. The election of the legislative assemblies is governed by rules for the distribution of seats very similar to those prevailing for the election of the members of Congress, whereas the structure of the autonomous councils of government is analogous to that of the central government (Magone 2004: 127–33).

Spain is one of the most decentralized European states with approximately 50 percent of public spending under the control of the autonomous communities and the local administrations (Colomer 1998). The relationship between these communities and central government depends to a great extent on the identity of the parties in power. Relations tend to be more conflictual when the autonomous communities are governed by nationalist parties backed by absolute majorities, which has often been the case in the Basque Country and Catalonia since the establishment of autonomous governments in the early 1980s. Whereas Basque governments persistently push for greater political and institutional independence from the central state, the Catalan autonomous governments have traditionally been more concerned with the imbalance between what the prosperous community of Catalonia contributes to the state's budget and what it gets in form of public spending.[6]

The state is represented in each autonomous community by the government deputy (*delegado del gobierno*, in the province where the capital of the autonomous community is located) or government sub-deputy (*subdelegado del gobierno*, in the rest of the provinces). The Constitutional Court (*Tribunal Constitucional*), defined as "the supreme interpreter of the Constitution" and independent from other constitutional organs, is responsible for resolving conflicts over competencies between the state and the autonomous communities.[7]

The autonomous communities can legislate on all issues within their defined areas of competence. During the last 20 years the central state has devolved substantial areas of government to these sub-national entities, including education, health care and social services. The Social Security Office, however, the institution responsible for the delivery of contributory and non-contributory pensions, remains a unitary body dependent on the Ministry of Work and Social Affairs (*Ministerio de Trabajo y Asuntos Sociales*) of the Spanish government. Thus, legislation on pensions is a competence of central government. Nevertheless, conflicts between the latter and autonomous governments have also arisen in this field, as will be shown later. Although autonomous governments do not act as institutional veto points in pension policy, with the backing of the Constitutional Court they have gained

Table 11.1 Political institutions in Spain

Political arenas	Actors	Rules of investiture	Rules of decision-making	Veto potential
Head of State	King (*Rey*)	Hereditary	With the countersignature of the Prime Minister, the Ministers or the President of Congress, sanctions and promulgates laws and decrees; calls elections and referenda; calls and dissolves parliament; appoints the Prime Minister elected by the Congress; appoints the Ministers proposed by the Prime Minister; manifests the consent of the state to international treaties	Not a veto point
Executive	Prime Minister (*Presidente del Gobierno*)	Appointed by the King after the Congress grants confidence to the candidate; investiture vote either absolute majority in a first vote or plurality in a second ballot 48 hours later	Right of initiative (*Proyecto de Ley*); may request the dissolution of parliament. Right to legislate in the following ways: • decree-Laws (*Decreto-Ley*) for cases of urgent need with provisional character until ratified by Congress within 30 days • legislative decrees (*Decreto Legislativo*), i.e. Congress delegates legislative power to the executive • decrees (*Decreto*) and ministerial orders (*Orden Ministerial*), i.e. legislation of lower status	—
Legislative	Congress (*Congreso de los Diputados*)	4-year term; 350 deputies; proportional representation based on closed, blocked party lists in 52 provinces (= electoral districts); minimum of 2 mandates per district (exception African cities of Ceuta and Melilla with one seat each); 3% entrance hurdle at district level; malapportionment due to low district magnitude in most districts to the benefit of small provinces; seat allocation according to d'Hondt formula	Right of initiative (*proposición de ley*); rules of decision-taking: • organic laws (*Ley Orgánica*): absolute majority in the Congress after approval by Senate • Ordinary laws (*Ley*): Simple majority of Congress and Senate • can overrule Senate's objection with an absolute majority or with simple majority after two months; right of vote of constructive no-confidence against Prime Minister	Not a veto point if government has majority; veto point when minority government

	Senate (*Senado*)	4-year term; 208 elected and 51 designated senators; 59 electoral districts; 4 elected senators per district (except for the Canary and Balearic islands, Ceuta and Melilla with 11, 5, 1 and 1 elected senators respectively); unblocked district lists; 3 votes per voter; seat allocation by majority system; rest of senators elected by the autonomous communities (one per community plus one for each million inhabitants)	May object to Congress' decisions; decisions by simple majority	Not a veto point due to Congressional override
Judicial	Supreme Court (*Tribunal Supremo*) as highest jurisdictional organ	Supreme Court President elected by General Council of the Judicial Power (*Consejo General del Poder Judicial*), governing body of judges. Its 20 members appointed by the King (thereof 8 proposed by 3/5 majority of Congress and 12 coopted); 5-year term; President of the General Council of the Judicial Power = President of the Supreme Court	Administration of justice; in case of penal liability members of government can only be convicted by Supreme Court	Not a veto point
Constitutional	Constitutional Court (*Tribunal Constitucional*)	Independent from other constitutional organs; twelve members appointed by the King (thereof 4 proposed by Congress by 3/5 majority, 4 by the Senate by 3/5 majority; 2 by the government and 2 by the General Council of the Judicial Power); 9-year term (1/3 of members change every 3 years)	Resolves appeals of unconstitutionality (presented by the Prime Minister, 50 Congress members, 50 Senate members, the ombudsman, a Court or a judge) against laws; appeals for protection against violation of fundamental rights and freedoms; and conflicts between the central government and the autonomous communities, the autonomous governments or different constitutional organs of the state	Post-hoc veto point

(*Continued*)

Table 11.1 (Continued)

Political arenas	Actors	Rules of investiture	Rules of decision-making	Veto potential
Electoral	Referendum	Types of referenda: • advisory referenda (proposed by Prime Minister and authorized by absolute majority in Congress) • referendum is one of two possible ways to initiate process leading to the creation of autonomous communities and approve/amend their basic laws (*Estatuto de Autonomía*) • Referenda on constitutional amendments	Government has the right to formulate the referendum to be called by the King; outcomes of advisory referenda are not binding for government or parliament	Veto point in case of constitutional amendments
Territorial units	17 regions/ autonomous communities (*Estado de las Autonomías*)	Each region has an autonomous council and an independent legislative assembly; representation of the central government in the autonomous community through government deputy (*delegado del gobierno*) and in the provinces through the government sub-deputy (*subdelegado del gobierno*); elections in 13 out of 17 communities are on the same day; Catalonia, Basque Country, Galicia and Andalusia have different electoral calendars	Assemblies of autonomous communities have the right to propose national legislation; they legislate on community level in wide range of policy areas such as education, health care and social services Indirect participation in national legislation through senate representatives	Veto point through Constitutional Court, but risky since the Prime Minister and the government can also use Constitutional Court to veto legislation by autonomous communities

some ground in being able to defy government decisions and make unconstrained choices regarding public pension supplements.

Electoral system

Elections to the *Cortes* take place every four years. All Congress deputies, as well as 208 of the senators, are elected by universal suffrage, but through different electoral methods. A proportional electoral system based on closed and blocked party lists is used to elect the members of Congress. Since constituencies are defined on a provincial basis, Spain is divided in 52 electoral districts. Each province has a minimum representation of two Congress seats, except for the provinces of Ceuta and Melilla on the North African coast with one seat each. The rest of the seats (up to 350) are assigned in proportion to the population. In the 2004 general elections, the district magnitude (number of seats per district) varied between one (Ceuta and Melilla) and 35 seats (Madrid). The average district magnitude (6.7) conceals great differences between districts: small provinces (with population below 200,000) regularly have between 3 and 4 seats; middle-size provinces (around 200,000 to 1 million inhabitants) between 5 and 10 seats; big provinces (up to 2 million inhabitants) between 11 and 16; the largest provinces, Barcelona and Madrid (with roughly 5 million inhabitants each), get more than 30 seats. The d'Hondt formula is applied to turn votes into seats. The exclusion barrier is established at 3 percent of the vote in each constituency.

As regards the Senate, each province elects four senators (except for the Islands, Ceuta and Melilla). The voter can vote for a maximum of three of the candidates who appear on a single ballot paper (each political party presents three candidates). Votes are translated into senators' seats basically through the rules of the majority system. The assemblies of the autonomous communities appoint the rest of the senators (one per community plus one for each million inhabitants).[8]

Elections to the legislatures of the autonomous communities are also held every four years. Thirteen autonomous communities hold elections on the same day, coinciding with the municipal elections in all the Spanish cities and towns. Catalonia, the Basque Country, Galicia and Andalusia have specific electoral calendars, a fact related to their own historic characteristics in the achievement of autonomy. Adding the elections to the European Parliament to the general, the autonomous and the municipal elections, it is not very surprising that there are few election-free years in Spain. Thus, the electoral cycle is very short. National executives seem vulnerable to this fact—as regards pensions, the recurrent decisions by the central government to increase the amount of benefits above the CPI can hardly be dissociated from the goal of furthering the electoral success of the government party not only at national, but also at sub-national elections.

The design of the Spanish electoral system, approved by a center-right government before the first democratic general elections took place, has since then remained practically unchanged. Formally a proportional system, but with strong correctives to preclude too much fragmentation of parliamentary representation, the electoral rules applied to Congress have been criticized for exhibiting a tendency towards bipartisanism as a consequence of the small size of constituencies and the minimum number of seats assigned to each of them, independently of their population. (Colomer 1997, 2004; Hopkin 2005). Certainly, the electoral system favors big parties in small electoral districts, but it also benefits parties with concentrated support in single provinces (regionalist and nationalist parties). The rules applied to elect senators reinforce the inconvenience for medium size national parties and, in general, enhance the reduction in the number of parties with parliamentary representation. Political actors recognize, nevertheless, that the electoral system has made the establishment of stable governments possible, averting some of the risks evidenced by the Second Republic (1931–36), which ultimately succumbed to overwhelming rightist or leftist electoral coalitions that, once in government, tended to exclude their ideological opponents from the political game (Aguilar 2002: 173–80).

Legislative process

The Spanish legal system consists of laws of different rank. "Organic" laws (*Ley Orgánica*) are those that affect the exercise of fundamental rights and public liberties, or endorse the Basic Laws of the autonomous communities (*Estatuto de Autonomía*) and the general electoral system. An absolute majority in Congress (i.e. 176 votes) is required to approve, modify or abolish these fundamental laws after approval by the Senate. Ordinary laws (*Ley*) are those whose subject matter is not covered by organic laws. They require a simple majority in Congress and in the Senate.

Although the right to initiate legislation is shared by the government, the *Cortes* and the assemblies of the autonomous communities, the central executive has the main initiating power in respect to producing law that affects the competencies of the state. It exercises this power through bills (*Proyecto de Ley*).[9] After approval by the council of ministers, the bill of ordinary or organic law is submitted to Congress. Permanent legislative commissions can approve bills by delegation of the plenary, except for those regarding constitutional reform, international questions, organic and basic laws and the state budget. Important bills are normally discussed and voted on in plenary sessions of Congress. Once approved by simple or absolute majority (depending on the type of law), the bill is delivered to the Senate, which may accept, veto or introduce amendments. Congress can nevertheless reject the veto of the Senate with an absolute majority, or with a simple majority after two months. It can also accept or reject the amendments by simple majority. Thus, ultimately the Senate cannot block a law and it remains subordinate to Congress in the production of law. At the conclusion of the parliamentary procedure, the King sanctions the laws approved by the *Cortes* within 15 days, so that they can be published in due course in the *Boletín Oficial del Estado* (BOE).

In addition to the legislative initiative, the government has the right to issue decree-laws (*Real Decreto-Ley*), legislative decrees (*Real Decreto Legislativo*), decrees (*Real*

Party family affiliation	Abbreviation	Party name	Ideological orientation	Founding and merger details	Year established
Christian Parties	PP	*Partido Popular*	Conservative, (economically) liberal	Before 1989 Alianza Popular (AP), party composed of 7 parties, some of them headed by former ministers of Franco	1977
Christian Parties	CiU	*Convergènciali Unió*	Nationalist	Coalition of CDC (*Convergència Democrática de Catalunya*) and UDC (*Unió Democrática de Catalunya*)	1978
Christian Parties	PNV	*Partido Nacionalista Vasco*	Nationalist	Founded by Sabino de Arana, main ideologist of Basque nationalism	1895
Left parties / Social democratic parties	PSOE	*Partido Socialista Obrero Español*	Social democratic	One of the first Socialist parties founded in Europe	1879
Left parties / Social democratic parties	IU	*Izquierda Unida*	Socialist	Party coalition originally headed by the Spanish Communist Party (*Partido Comunista de España*) founded in 1920	1986
Left parties / Social democratic parties	BNG	*Bloque Nacionalista Galego*	Nationalist	Origins in the 1960s when communist and socialist Galician political groups emerged clandestinely	1982
Left parties / Social democratic parties	ERC	*Esquerra Republicana de Catalunya*	Nationalist, pro-republican	Founded on the eve of the Second Republic (1931–1936)	1931
Left parties / Social democratic parties	Batasuna	*Batasuna*	Nationalist, separatist	Formerly *Herri Batasuna* and *Euskal Herritarrok*— party illegal since 2002	1978
Greens	Los Verdes	*Los Verdes*	Environmentalist	Confederation of small green parties without a central organ	1984

Fig. 11.1 Party system in Spain

Decreto) and ministerial orders (*Orden Ministerial*). Decree-laws are theoretically sanctioned in case of "extraordinary and urgent need" and have provisional character until the Congress ratifies them within 30 days. These rank as laws but can never concern the matters organic laws deal with. Legislative decrees are rules whose elaboration the Congress delegates to the executive according to certain criteria. Finally, decrees and ministerial orders are rules of a lower status, currently used to adopt resolutions and issue regulations with regard to areas under the competence of the government.

Parties and elections

It is a measure of their importance that parties *are* the political institution first mentioned in the 1978 Constitution: Article 6 acknowledges their role in the "formation and expression of the people's will" and defines them as "a fundamental instrument for political participation." Around 500 parties are currently registered in Spain, but no more than 15 have the minimum organizational capacity to compete in elections and obtain parliamentary representation. Candidates for Congress and the Senate have to be Spanish citizens in full use of their political rights[10] presented by a legally registered party. Because the drawing-up of electoral lists is conducted by party elites, the elected representatives have evident incentives to respect party discipline in their parliamentary behavior.[11] To vote differently from the party is commonly interpreted as a sign of internal conflict and party weakness.

At the general elections to the constitutive parliament of June 1977 (the first democratic vote since 1936), as well as at the 1979 general elections, the center party (*Unión de Centro Democrático*, UCD), which incorporated the reformers of the Franco regime, received the largest number of votes, although it did not achieve an absolute majority (176 seats in Congress) in either of these elections. The Socialist Party, (*Partido Socialista Obrero Español*, PSOE) was the main opposition group until 1982, when it obtained 202 seats with slightly less than 50 percent of the popular vote, and formed the first single majority government after the re-establishment of democracy. In the following years, the UCD vanished and was virtually replaced by the *Centro Democrático y Social*, CDS), but with little success. From 1982 to 1996 the Conservative party (*Alianza Popular*, AP), re-founded in 1989 as (*Partido Popular*, PP), developed into the main opposition party (Hopkin 1999). The PSOE, with Felipe González as general secretary, retained an absolute majority at the 1986 and 1989 elections, but lost it at the 1993 elections when it formed a minority government with the parliamentary backing of the Catalan Party CiU (*Convergència i Unió*). At the 1996 elections, the center-right PP obtained the majority of the votes, but lacked 20 seats to form a single majority government. It therefore had to look for the parliamentary support of nationalist parties to pass legislation. This was no longer necessary after the 2000 elections, in which the PP attained 183 seats with 45 percent of the popular vote.

The 2004 elections, held three days after the March 11 terrorist attacks in Madrid by radical Islamists, brought the Socialist Party back to power (Colomer 2005). Led by José Luis Rodríguez Zapatero, the PSOE has formed a minority government with the parliamentary support of parties to its left (*Izquierda Unida*, IU, and the Catalan nationalist and pro-republican *Esquerra Republicana de Catalunya*, ERC).

It has been argued that Spain is unique in Western Europe because its nationwide party system coexists with a number of regional party systems (Linz and Montero 1999). The nationwide multiparty system established in 1977 certainly does not evoke the very ideological and polarized party system of the Second Republic, even if tensions between the main parties have been growing in recent years vis-à-vis what is called "the national question" (*la cuestión nacional*), namely, the politics and policies to cope with nationalist demands. As in other democratic European countries, the expansion of the middle classes and the development of a consumer society in Spain during the 1960s and 1970s, on the one hand, and the recognition of the state's responsibility to fund parties in the first democratic law on political parties approved in December 1978, on the other, persuaded Spanish political leaders to concentrate on voters instead of on affiliates, and to adopt inclusive electoral strategies once the Franco dictatorship was over. This evolution, together with the electoral system, has fostered a tendency towards a national party system strongly dominated by two major parties. In fact, only the PSOE and the PP could currently hold the presidency of any government.

Due to the key roles of the government and Congress in the Spanish political system during the periods in which a party had an absolute majority (1982–93 and 2000–04), both institutions emerge as one and the same veto player. Hence there is no veto to government proposals. In contrast, minority governments are very vulnerable to the veto power of the minor parties backing them (Colomer 1997). Once passed by parliament, the Constitutional Court can veto legislation if it considers that it does not conform to the constitutional precepts. But this post-hoc veto power can only be exercised after presentation of an appeal of unconstitutionality (*recurso de inconstitucionalidad* or *cuestión de inconstitucionalidad* depending on who gives notice of it), an individual appeal for constitutional protection (*recurso de amparo constitucional*) or a request in the case of competence conflict between (a) the state and one or more autonomous communities, (b) various autonomous communities or (c) constitutional organs of the state.[12]

Interest groups

The 1978 Constitution mentions trade unions and employers' associations in a very prominent place, just after the political parties. Article 7 acknowledges their contribution to the defense and promotion of social and economic interests.

Trade unions played an important role in the demise of Franco's dictatorship and the peaceful transition to democracy (Fishman 1990). During the inaugural stage of

Table 11.2 Governmental majorities in Spain

Election date Congreso	Start of gov.	Head of gov. (party)	Governing parties	Gov. majority (% seats) Congreso	Gov. electoral base (% votes) Congreso	Gov. majority (% seats) Senado[a]	Institutional veto Points	Number of veto players (partisan + institutional)
03.01.1979	04.02.1979	Suárez II (UCD)	UCD (168)	48.0%	35.1%	55.1%	Congreso	1 + 1
	02.26.1981	Calvo-Sotelo (UCD)	UCD (168)	48.0%	35.1%	55.1%	Congreso	1 + 1
10.28.1982	12.02.1982	González I (PSOE)	PSOE (202)	57.7%	48.3%	61.4%	None	1 + 0
06.22.1986	07.24.1986	González II (PSOE)	PSOE (184)	52.6%	44.3%	58.3%	None	1 + 0
10.29.1989	12.07.1989	González III (PSOE)	PSOE (175)	50.0%	39.9%	50.2%	None	1 + 0
06.06.1993	07.14.1993	González IV (PSOE)	PSOE (159)	45.4%	39.1%	45.7%	Congreso	1 + 1
03.03.1996	05.06.1996	Aznar I (PP)	PP (156)	44.6%	39.2%	51.6%	Congreso	1 + 1
03.12.2000	04.27.2000	Aznar II (PP)	PP (183)	52.3%	45.2%	57.5%	None	1 + 0
03.14.2004	04.17.2004	Rodríguez Zapatero (PSOE)	PSOE (164)	46.9%	43.3%	43.2%	Congreso	1 + 1

[a]It is difficult to precisely ascertain this figure because of the fraction of senators appointed by the autonomous communities (51 in the 7th and 8th legislatures initiated in 2000 and 2004 respectively). These appointed senators may cease and be replaced by candidates of distinct party affiliation if new "autonomic" elections change the distribution of seats in the assemblies of the autonomous communities. The registered percentage of the Senate seats occupied by candidates of the national government party corresponds to the date of the constitution of the Senate in each legislature.

Sources: www.congreso.es/elecciones; www.senado.es; www.elecciones.mir.es/MIR/jsp/resultados/index.htm (retrieved 15 December 2005).

democracy they engaged in a process of social concertation in exchange for economic and institutional support, consensus-seeking behavior which contrasted with the polarization and radicalism of the social partners during the Second Republic (1931–36) and granted them a sort of democratic pedigree (Linz 1987).

The two most important trade unions, the General Workers' Union (*Unión General de Trabajadores*, UGT) and the Workers' Commissions (*Comisiones Obreras*, CCOO) represent something of a "duopoly at national level" (Mielke, Rütters and Tudyka 1994: 224–26). Although formally independent confederations, UGT and CCOO have been historically close to the Socialist (PSOE) and the Communist Party (PCE), respectively (Molíns and Casademunt 1999).[13] The traditionally good relationship between left governments and trade unions experienced a breach in the second half of the 1980s, when the PSOE adopted economic policy decisions oriented towards austerity and deregulation of the labor market (Gillespie 1989, 1990). Tensions dissipated in the early 1990s as the PSOE government decided to submit to important trade union demands, among them the establishment of the Economic and Social Council in 1992 (Lecher and Naumann 1994: 83–4; Mota 2002: 306–40).

It is estimated that both trade union confederations together count no more than one million members. But the low affiliation rate (around 10% of workers registered in Social Security) is not a good indicator of the trade unions' strength. Actually, CCOO and UGT do not compete for members, but for delegates elected to works councils (*comités de empresa*). These elections take place every four years and their results establish not only the bargaining power of unions in the workplace, but also their recognition as national social partners and consequently their political and economic resources (Mielke, Rütters, and Tudyka 1994: 226–9). CCOO and UGT have displayed considerable mobilizing capabilities in multiple demonstrations as well as in general strikes against employment deregulation and in favor of improvements in social protection in 1985, 1988, and 2000. Actually, the relative scarcity of interest associations in Spain ensures that trade unions are among the strongest non-governmental voices in the public space. Spanish policy-makers take them very seriously into consideration in order to avoid social conflict and strengthen the legitimacy of political decisions in the economic and social realms.

As regards the employers' organizations, the Spanish Confederation of Employers' Organizations (*Confederación Española de Organizaciones Empresariales* CEOE), founded in 1978, is the sole representative of business interests. Formally an association of roughly 200 employers' organizations, it also includes CEPYME, the organization of small- and middle-sized firms, which nevertheless also has an independent hierarchy. Involvement in several concertation pacts during the late 1970s and early 1980s turned CEOE and CEPYME into effective actors in the economic and labor policy arena (Molíns and Casademunt 1999).

Other Spanish interest groups have emerged or re-emerged since the establishment of democracy, taking advantage of the increase in the number of decision-making levels (local, regional, national, European). Although compared with other European countries they have a modest influence on public opinion, their networking with bureaucrats of the different ministries and their mobilization potential explain their leverage in the formulation of certain areas of public policy. In the domain of farming policy, agrarian organizations have developed considerable power. Some of the so-called professional colleges, like the ones for medical doctors or architects, also try to intervene in the process of decision-making in questions concerning their professions. Environmental associations have occasionally managed to become effective actors regarding policies affecting the ecosystem. Lastly, the Catholic Church—the only church explicitly mentioned in the 1978 Constitution, which nevertheless also states the a-confessional character of the Spanish state—has managed to maintain a significant voice in non-university education debates, and also tries to influence policies regarding ethical questions (notably abortion, homosexual rights and genetic engineering).

In contrast, pensioners' associations are scarcely present in the public debate. The main organization in this realm is the Democratic Union of Spanish Pensioners and Retirees (*Unión Democrática de Pensionistas y Jubilados de España*, UDP). Founded during the transition to democracy, it is composed of roughly 1,400 associations (for the most part operating in rural areas) encompassing about 850,000 members. The UDP acquired public saliency when in 1989 the PSOE government, in the face of difficulties in harmonizing its position on the indexation of public pensions for the coming year with the trade unions, signed an agreement on this issue with the pensioners' organization (Mota 2002: 322). Practically absent in the mass media, the UDP is nowadays a non-governmental organization primarily concentrating on the supply of services to improve the living standards of old people (care and domestic help, leisure, training of volunteers, etc.).

III PENSION SYSTEM

Historical overview

Two features of the history of the Spanish pension system deserve particular attention. First, the establishment of the PAYG pension system cannot be directly linked to the progress of left power resources (contrary to the hypothesis of Myles and Pierson (2001) based on Korpi). Second, even though initial concerns over social problems date from the end of the nineteenth century and state-subsidized social insurance for injured and retired workers started in the first decades of the twentieth century, the Spanish pension system in its current form developed approximately two decades later than in other European countries.

At the end of the nineteenth century, the Spanish government created the Commission of Social Reforms in charge of studying social questions. The Spanish state, encouraged by a philosophy of regeneration espoused by influential intellectuals after the loss of the last transatlantic colonies, tried to expand its limited intervention into social affairs in the first third of the twentieth century. Initially, as in most European countries, social insurance programs were established on a voluntary basis (Guillén 1990: 1–7); by 1919 the Obligatory Workers' Retirement program was launched, and ten years later Obligatory Maternity Insurance. In 1932, at the start of the Second Republic, the government asked the National Providence Institute (INP), created in 1908, to work out a proposal to set up a system of Unified Obligatory Insurance. The beginning of the civil war in 1936, however, hindered parliamentary approval of the bill.

One of the many manifestations of the institutional break provoked by General Franco's victory in 1939 evidenced itself in the social policy arena. The Francoist trade unions, divided by sectors, set up their own mutual funds, which delivered pensions on a funded basis, in addition to a flat-rate benefit provided by the state, to insured workers or their dependent survivors. Nevertheless, public expenditure in terms of GDP experienced a backlash during the first decades of the Franco dictatorship.[14]

Spain had to wait until the 1960s for the emergence of a comprehensive system of social security. The Social Security Law of 1963, enacted in 1967, laid the foundation for the unification and coordination of the existing organs of social insurance by the state (Comín 1996: 282–6). As regards pensions, it introduced a PAYG system financed by workers' contributions. A minimum contribution period of ten years was necessary in order to receive a pension. Contribution bases had a distant relationship with salaries and contribution quotas were initially established at 14 percent (10% paid by employer and 4% by the employee). Two parameters determined the pension amount: (1) the regulatory base, calculated on the basis of the highest salary during two uninterrupted contribution years (within the seven years prior to reaching the age of 65); and (2) a percentage of the regulatory base adjusted on a scale with an upper limit of 100 percent corresponding to 35 years of contributions. The scale favored those who had contributed for fewer years: 50 percent was applied after paying dues for only 10 years instead of 17.5 years.

The new Social Security system inherited to some extent the fragmentation of the former scheme of mutual funds. The working population was divided up into classes with different rights and obligations: alongside the general regime, which included the majority of employees, a variety of special regimes (more than 50) were established. The new scheme lacked, however, the actuarial characteristics of the mutual funds since benefits were not directly linked to the amount of contributions paid, but to the contribution base previous to retirement (Comín 1999: 18–21). In 1972, the Franco government approved a law whereby the contribution bases of workers ascribed to the general scheme were brought nearer to real salaries.

In the second half of the 1970s, during the transition to democracy, the center-right governments of the UCD rapidly increased social expenditure and introduced important changes concerning the institutional organization of Social Security.[15] But the structure of the pension system, and specifically the rules to calculate benefits, remained basically unchanged. The rapid expansion of benefits, especially unemployment subsidies in response to the economic crisis (2 million jobs were lost from the mid-1970s to the mid-1980s), as well as the reforms aiming to enhance the redistributive components of the system and universalize some services, form the basis for the argument that the development of the Spanish welfare state went hand-in-hand with the establishment of democracy (Comín 1999).[16] The main symbol of this new democratic regime, the 1978 Constitution, states the obligation of the state "to maintain a public Social Security regime for all citizens that warrants adequate assistance and social benefits in the face of situations of need, especially in the case of unemployment" (Art. 41).

Description of the current pension system

The Spanish pension system consists of state financed and administered pensions (first pillar) and private funded and managed pensions (second and third pillars). The first pillar consists of Social Security pensions as well as pensions of the so-called "passive classes of the state" (*clases pasivas del Estado*), which encompass the majority of civil servants of the central state and the members of the armed forces. Contributions to Social Security, or to the schemes for the passive classes, are compulsory for all workers and employees, whereas subscription to private pension plans is voluntary and mainly intended to supplement public pensions.

Social Security pensions can be contributory or non-contributory. The former have existed since the late 1960s, are earnings-related (defined-benefit pensions, as opposed to defined-contribution pensions, i.e. pensions calculated on the amount of contributions paid) and currently classified according to six different occupational regimes. In contrast, non-contributory pensions were introduced at the beginning of the 1990s, are flat-rate, means-tested, and exclusively for those elderly or disabled citizens who lack sufficient pension rights to get an earnings-related pension.

Coverage

The contributory pension system managed by Social Security covered 17,081,800 workers and 7,876,600 pensions in 2004: 59 percent of these were retirement pensions, 27 percent widow(er)s' pensions, 10 percent permanent invalidity pensions, 3 percent orphans' pensions and 1 percent pensions for dependent relatives other than spouses and children living with the deceased worker/pensioner. Workers as well as pensioners are split between the general scheme, which in 2003 embraced 75 percent of the former and 56 percent of the latter, and five special schemes (self-employed workers, coal miners, farmers, seamen and household employees).

The passive classes regime registers a lower employee/pensioner ratio than the Social Security. The number of civil servants paying contributions to the scheme amounted in 2001 to 883,100 and the number of pensioners to 494,800. Curiously enough, civil servants' pensions not directly run by Social Security do not for the moment represent a prominent issue in the Spanish pension policy debate. Therefore, in this chapter I will only make minor references to this aspect.

The non-contributory pension system of Social Security, established in 1991, granted around 490,000 pensions in 2004. Other social assistance public pensions provided by the central state stem from the time preceding the introduction of non-contributory pensions and nowadays constitute a residual class (less than 100,000 pensions in 2004).[17]

Administration

Economic benefits provided by Spanish Social Security are managed by the *Instituto Nacional de la Seguridad Social* (INSS), created in 1979. It is under the control of the General Secretary of Social Security, who works for the Ministry of Work and Social Affairs. The management of Social Security is efficient in comparative terms. Outlays on the administration of contributory pensions amounted in 2001 to no more than 4.2 percent of the value of benefits (Herce 2002).

Not only regionalist parties, but also the Catalan autonomous government, led since December 2003 by the Party of the Catalan Socialists (*Partit dels Socialistes de Catalunya*, PSC), which is integrated in the PSOE federal structure, demand competencies in the administration of Social Security benefits for their communities. However, PSOE and PP have consistently defended the central running of Social Security and the principle of the "single box" (*principio de caja única*).

The contributions and benefits of civil servants of the General State Administration are managed by the mutual fund *Muface*, dependent on the Ministry of Public Administration; likewise the civil servants working for the judiciary are ascribed to the the fund *Mugeju*, under the control of the Ministry of Justice; finally the military civil servants also have their own mutual fund, *Isfas*, run by the Ministry of Defense. The rest of the civil servants (working in municipalities, autonomous communities, management entities of Social Security and other public autonomous institutes) have been assigned to the Social Security general regime.

Financing

Social Security pensions are financed by contributions paid by both workers and employers. Contribution rates for "common contingencies" (covering situations of work inability due to illness and accidents—except for professional illness and work accidents—retirement, maternity and pregnancy risk) represented in 2004 some 28.3 percent of the contribution base of each worker in the general Social Security regime. Of this, 23.6 percent was paid by the employer and 4.7 percent by the employee.[18] This contribution rate has been stable since 1995 and is the lowest since the establishment of democracy.[19]

Each year the government determines maximum and minimum contribution bases for the various contribution groups. Workers are classified into these groups according to their professional status. Since 2002 all professional categories share one maximum contribution cap.[20] This has hindered the strategy of many firms of hiring certain employees, and paying them more than is appropriate to the professional category in which they are classed, in order to save on Social Security contributions.

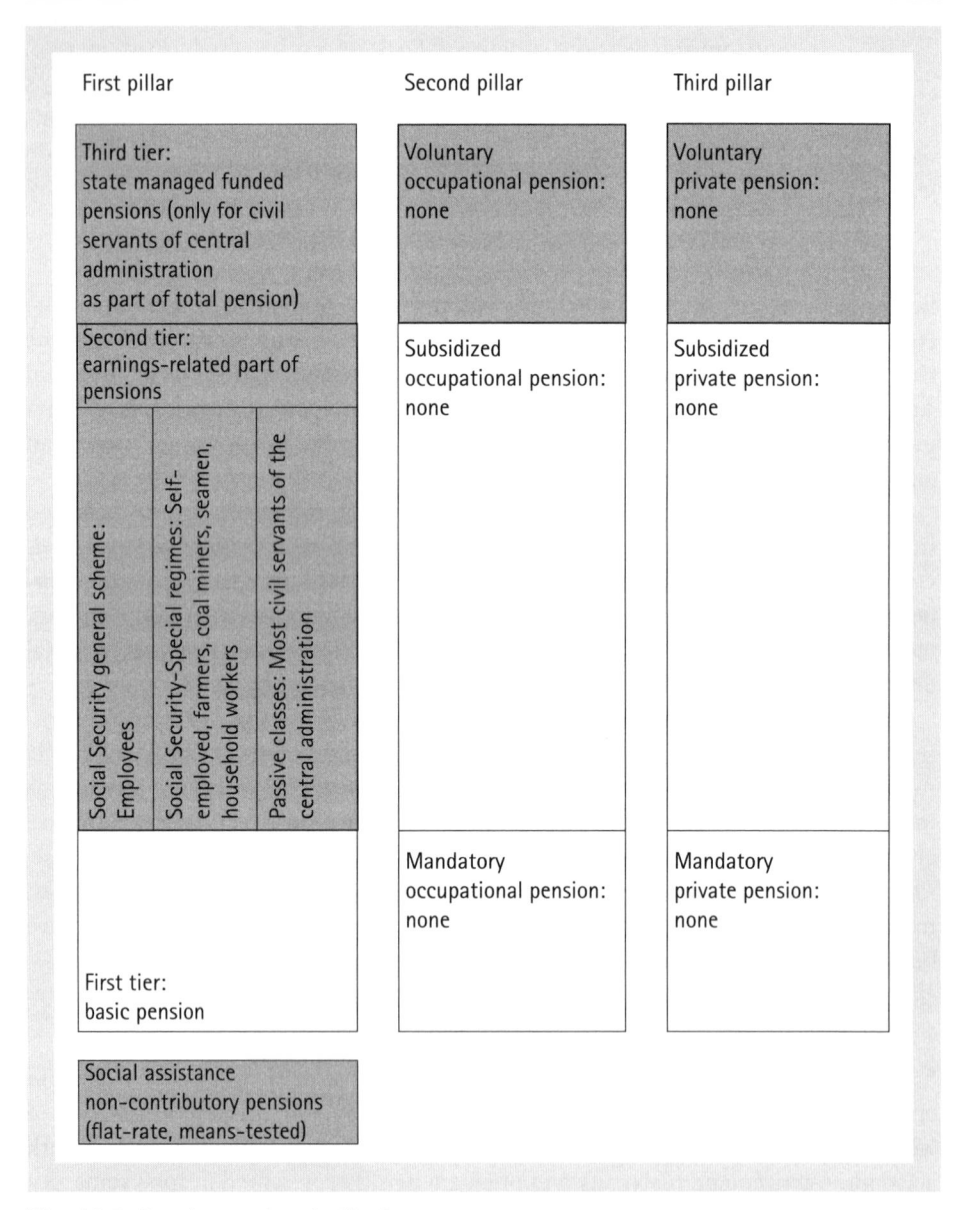

First pillar	Second pillar	Third pillar
Third tier: state managed funded pensions (only for civil servants of central administration as part of total pension)	Voluntary occupational pension: none	Voluntary private pension: none
Second tier: earnings-related part of pensions — Social Security general scheme: Employees; Social Security-Special regimes: Self-employed, farmers, coal miners, seamen, household workers; Passive classes: Most civil servants of the central administration	Subsidized occupational pension: none	Subsidized private pension: none
First tier: basic pension	Mandatory occupational pension: none	Mandatory private pension: none
Social assistance non-contributory pensions (flat-rate, means-tested)		

Fig. 11.2 Pension system in Spain

Workers included in the remaining regimes have specific contribution rules. Hence, in 2004, self-employed workers had to pay 29.8 percent of a contribution base which they could freely determine between a minimum of €755 and a maximum of €2,732 per month. The scheme for seamen applies correcting coefficients to the contribution base, so that the relationship between the latter and the wage is lower than for the workers affiliated in the general scheme (but benefits are calculated on the total contribution base, without taking into consideration the correcting coefficients). All workers included in the household employee scheme pay the same contribution since their contribution rate and their contribution base is established by the government (in 2004, 22% of €573 per month, 18.3% paid by the employer and 3.7% paid by the employee). The same is true of self-employed farmers (in 2004 18.75% of €597); finally, employed farmers pay 11.5 percent of contribution bases fixed yearly by the government according to their professional category.

Other contribution rules apply to civil servants. Thus, the members of *Muface* pay only 1.69 percent of their regulatory base (which is different depending on which of the five groups the civil servant belongs to) and the state contributes an additional 5.07 percent. Perhaps because civil servants' earnings are considered rather modest when compared with those offered by the private market, this evident positive discrimination of civil servants vis-à-vis workers of the private sector and bureaucrats not included in the passive classes regime does not provoke public criticism.

Since the emergence of Social Security the surplus in contributions was primarily used to build up and develop a public health care system. In accordance with the pact on pensions policy signed by all parliamentary parties in 1995 (Toledo Pact), the PP government has since 1998 been pushing for the progressive separation of financial sources of Social Security, which means that worker contributions to the Social Security pension system are going to finance only contributory pensions. In the year 2000, the government established a reserve fund with the remaining capital, which, at the end of 2005, amounted to nearly €27,200 million[21] (more than 5 months of contributory pension outlays).

Benefits

The age at which male and female workers can get a full pension is 65. However this legal retirement age has been voluntary since 2002. In that same year workers of the general regime retired on average at 62.5 years even though penalties for early retirement are comparatively high (up to 8% of the pension regulatory base for each year of anticipated retirement). In 2002, more than 40 percent of new pensioners in the general regime suffered penalties (Serrano, García and Bravo 2004: 78–80).

As of 2005, the pension regulatory base is calculated taking into consideration the contribution base during the 180 months preceding retirement. The percentage applied to the regulatory base is determined as follows: the first 15 contribution years needed to be eligible for a contributory pension, give the right to 50 percent of the regulatory base (thus, 3.3% per year); from the 16th to the 25th contribution year, each year adds 3 percent; from the 26th to the 35th contribution year, each year counts for an additional 2.5 percent.

If the calculated amount is below the minimum pension set by the government (according to the contingency covered, the age of the beneficiary and the existence of a dependent spouse), the pensioner gets a supplement (*complemento de mínimos*). On the other hand, the calculated amount cannot surpass the maximum amount established for a public pension. The amount of the minimum and maximum pensions has been revalued during the last decades so as to reduce the gap between the two. In 2005 the maximum pension was 4.3 times higher than the minimum retirement pension (for 65-year-old beneficiaries with a dependent spouse). This ratio was significantly higher in 1985, when it reached 6.48; it then fell progressively until 1990 (4.4) and experienced a minor drop in 2000 (4.3).

Since the early days of Social Security, most pensioners have been receiving 14 payments per year: 12 ordinary monthly payments and 2 extraordinary payments in July and December. Some pensioners on the special regimes (farmers, the self-employed and domestic employees) were nevertheless excluded from this right until the early 1990s.[22]

Furthermore, since 1998, the government is legally required to revalue pensions at the beginning of each year according to the expected inflation rate for that year. If the effective inflation rate exceeds the expected inflation rate, pensioners get post-hoc compensation for the suffered loss in the purchasing power of their benefits. More concretely, if the CPI between November of the last year and November of the current year goes above the expected CPI, according to which pensions have been indexed, pensioners get paid the difference in a unique payment by April 1, of the next year. Pensioners received this payment in 2000, 2001, 2002, 2003 and 2004.[23]

Contributory pensions differ notably in their amount depending on the contingency covered. The average Social Security contributory retirement pension amounted in 2004 to €649 per month and was more than €200 higher than the average widow(er)s' pension (€432), and €400 higher than the average orphans' pension.[24]

At the end of 2002, 60 percent of all Social Security contributory pensions were below the minimum salary established by the state (€442). This percentage was, however, 30 percentage points lower than in 1990, a development that results from the maturation of the pension system and from policy efforts to improve the lowest pension benefits during the last decades (Serrano, García and Bravo 2004: 70–7). Non-contributory pensions pay the same amount for all beneficiaries (retired and disabled people) and are much lower than contributory ones (€271 in 2004). Both contributory and non-contributory pensions are subject to the Income Tax of Physical Persons (IRPF).[25]

Table 11.3. summarizes the main data of the Spanish PAYG pension system during the last decades providing a useful background for the next sections.

IV POLITICS OF PENSION REFORM SINCE 1980

Overview

Although international organizations have portrayed Spain as having introduced only modest reform, the three pillars of the Spanish pension system experienced

Table 11.3 Indicators of the Social Security contributory pension system 1980–2003

	1980	1985	1990	1995	2000	2003
Workers paying social security contributions[a]	10,414,1	10,440,7	12,446,0	12,205,3	14,907,3	16,424,6
Contributory pensions[a]	4,308,1	5,326,3	6,109,7	6,971,4	7,605,6	7,822,9
Average contributory pension[b]	1,275,7	2,401,3	3,741,3	5,356,0	6,605,1	7,672,8
Average contribution[b]	857,0	1,394,9	2,140,7	3,105.7	3,854.3	4,116,9
Contributions as % of GDP	10.53	9.51	9.29	9.58	9.97	9.67
Contributory outlays as % of GDP	7.47	8.86	8.44	9.86	9.56	9.26
Surplus or deficit as % of GDP	3.06	0.65	0.85	-0.28	0.41	0.40

[a] In thousands.
[b] Annual amount in Euro.

Source: Garcia, Herce and Jimeno (2005: 35).

noteworthy changes between 1985 and 2002. As regards the first pillar, its first tier (non-contributory pensions) was only launched in 1991. Furthermore, the rules according to which second tier (earnings-related) pensions are granted were modified in 1985 and 1997 in the direction of improving proportionality between pensions and contributions. As regards the second and the third pillar, voluntary occupational pensions and voluntary individual pensions were initiated in 1987.

The most critical transformation in terms of cost containment was without doubt the 1985 reform, which was pushed forward by a PSOE government backed by an absolute majority in parliament. Although the center-conservative PP government formed in 1996 was suspected of having the aim of restricting welfare benefits and reinforcing the private components of the pension system, essentially it did not depart from the institutional path taken by former governments, even after it won 183 of the 350 parliamentary seats in the elections held in 2000. There are a number of ways of explaining this apparent inertia, some of them complementary. First, the PP could not deviate very much from the Toledo Pact, a consensus document approved in 1995 by all parties in parliament which stressed the political will to maintain the public pension system in its present form (i.e. contributory and PAYG) and to upgrade its lowest benefits. Dramatic cuts were made still more difficult by the fact that in 1996 the PP could only form a minority government, and was dependent on the CiU—the party which had initiated the Toledo Pact. Second, the government opted for a strategy of agreements with trade unions as a mechanism to deprive the PSOE of one of its fundamental critiques against the PP, namely its common interests with entrepreneurs and the wealthiest sectors of society. Third, the number of those affiliated to the Social Security pensions system began to increase rapid and unexpectedly as a consequence of economic growth, which alleviated the pressure to see through restrictive reforms. Last, but not least, public opinion polls show Spanish citizens giving substantial support to the current configuration of the social protection system in general, and the public pension system in particular.

At the beginning of 2000, 22 percent of a representative sample of Spaniards aged between 16 and 80 declared that the state should increase taxes and contributions in order to improve pensions and other social benefits, whereas 10 percent affirmed that it should cut tolls collected for that aim. The majority (38%) chose to maintain the fiscal burden (Rodríguez 2000). These results illustrate what other opinion polls have been proving: most Spanish people believe that the state has the obligation to provide the welfare benefits and services that citizens need for their well-being (Pino 2003: 63–70).

1985 Reform: Law of urgent measures for the rationalization of the structure and protective action of the Social Security system

In 1982, when the PSOE obtained the first absolute majority of the recently established democracy, the Spanish pension system had a single pillar embodied by Social

Table 11.4 Overview of proposed and enacted pension reforms in Spain

Year	Name of reform	Reform process (chronology)	Reform measures
1985	Law of urgent measures for the rationalization of the structure and protective action of the Social Security system	• October 1984 economic and social agreement establishes tripartite commission to propose guidelines for pension reform • March 1985 interruption of the tripartite commission as social partners do not agree to government proposals • June 18, 1985 bill passes Congress with Socialist absolute majority • July 23, 1985 Congress approves amendments by Senate and passes the bill; resistance from all opposition parties • June 1985 unions call for general strike; petition of unions to the ombudsman—unsuccessful	• increase in the minimum contribution period from 10 to 15 years • increase in reference period for assessment base from 2 to 8 years (6 of them revalued with consumer price index); new regulations applicable to new pensions only; increase in (non-contributory) social pensions; automatic indexation of new pensions to the expected inflation rate • suppression of the requirement to be affiliated at the moment of soliciting pension
1987	Law on regulation of pension plans and funds	• September 17, 1986 Socialist government submits bill to Congress • rejection by opposition parties; amendments by government party in Congress and in Senate • May 28, 1987 Congress approves amendments by Senate and passes the bill • November 29, 2002 the PP government approves a legislative decree that assembles dispersed rules in force and derogates the original law on regulation of pension plans and funds	• pension plans defined as institutions of voluntary and free protection • maximum contribution ESP 750,000 whereof 2/3 are tax-deductible • three types of pension plans: employment system, associated system and individual system

(Continued)

Table 11.4 (Continued)

Year	Name of reform	Reform process (chronology)	Reform measures
1990	Law on non-contributory pensions of the Social Security system	• December 1988 strikes against flexibilizing the labor market • November 29, 1990 Congress passes bill • March 15, 1991 Royal Decree developing the law on non-contributory pensions	• introduction of means-tested non-contributory benefits for elderly and disabled people (in 1991 benefits amounted to ca. €2,525 per year; in 2004 €3,868) • eligibility conditions: for retirement pension, 65 years old, minimum of 10 years residence in Spain including the last 2 prior to retirement and annual income below the annual sum of non-contributory pensions; for disability pensions, between 18 and 65 years old, at least 65% disability, minimum of 5 years residence in Spain including the last 2 prior to soliciting pension and annual income below the annual sum of non-contributory pensions
1995	Toledo Pact	September 1993 Catalan parliamentary group CiU presents proposal to create a working group to elaborate report on the economic reform of Social Security, including recommendations to the government February 15, 1994 Congress approves set up of commission to scrutinize Social Security April 6, 1995 Congress approves report known as Toledo Pact October 2, 2003 Congress approves report of parliamentary commission on the results obtained trough implementation of the Toledo Pact	Fifteen recommendations to be classified in four categories: • rationalization: separation of financing sources of contributory and non-contributory benefits; set up of reserve fund; simplification of special regimes and integration of management functions; • equity: greater parity between real wages and contributory bases; greater proportionality between contributions and benefits; avoiding positive discrimination of special regimes; improvement in mechanisms to collect contributions; improvement in mechanisms of benefit distribution; • incentivization: reduction of contributions for low-skilled workers; voluntary postponement of retirement; encouragement of private pension plans as supplement to public pensions; • improvement of benefits: automatic revaluation of all pensions, improvement of orphans' and widow(er)s' pensions

1997	Law on consolidation and rationalization of the Social Security system	October 9, 1996 Agreement on the Consolidation and Rationalization of the Social Security system between PP government and trade unions UGT and CCOO December 26, 1996 government submits bill to Congress June 26, 1997 Congress approves amendments by Senate and passes the bill July 4, 1997 passage of the bill	• keeping sources of financing of contributory and non-contributory benefits separate • establishment of a reserve fund with the surplus from social contributions • adjustment of the entitlement criteria and provisions of pensions for permanent disability • reduction in penalties for early retirement • automatic revaluation of pensions to the CPI • rise in age limit for orphans' pensions • increase in minimum widow(er)s' pension • increase in reference period for benefit calculation from 8 to 15 years • change in accrual rates: first 15 years 50% (instead of 60%) each additional contribution year from 16th to 25th 3% and 2.5% from 26th to 35th year
2002	Law on measures for the establishment of a system of gradual and flexible retirement	December 27, 2001 government sanctions a decree-law on measures for the establishment of a gradual and flexible retirement system February 5, 2002 ratification of Decree-Law by Congress February 15, 2002 government submits the bill on measures for the establishment of a gradual and flexible retirement system June 27, 2002 Congress approves amendments by Senate and passes the bill October 31, 2002 government passes new Decree to develop law	• compatibility of part-time work and partial retirement pension • workers postponing retirement after 65 increase their pension by 2 percentage points of the regulatory base per year if they have paid contributions for at least 35 years • 50% reduction in Social Security contributions for those 60 and older with at least 5 years of seniority in the firm • extension of early retirement from workers aged 60 with contributions before 1967 to workers aged 61 or older if they have been employment seekers at least during the 6 months previous to the retirement application with a minimum of 30 contribution years • punishment for retiring with between 31 and 40 contribution years 6 to 7.5% for each year anticipating retirement

Security: it offered public pensions calculated on earnings-related contribution bases and financed on a PAYG basis. Non-contributory social pensions had been introduced in the 1960s, but they were subject to very strict eligibility conditions and therefore rare. The majority of pensioners got a minimum pension which represented around 70 percent of the minimum salary, and there was no mechanism of automatic indexation. But among this group of pensioners were many who had made only a low contributory effort. In fact, around 50 percent of the pensioners of the special regime for the self-employed had contributed for only 10 or 11 years, whereas this applied to less than 5 percent of the pensioners belonging to the general regime (Mota 2002: 281). Thus, workers affiliated to some of the special regimes were "buying" pensions: if they contributed for a low contribution base and the calculated amount of their allowance was below the minimum pension, their benefit was supplemented. However they could also "buy" a high pension if they decided to contribute for a high contribution base. In both cases, they obtained pension benefits for fewer contributions than workers affiliated to the general regime.[26]

Additional incentives to fraudulent (but strictly not illegal) behavior were given by the short period on which the regulatory pension base was calculated. Some employees of the general regime agreed with their employers to make maximum contributions to Social Security during the two years prior to retirement so as to qualify for top retirement pensions. This modality of "pension buying" favored mainly those workers with privileged positions in the labor market, that is, workers with more negotiating power vis-à-vis their employers.

In short, the institutional design of the contributory pension system inherited from the Franco regime offered incentives to strategic behavior. Pensioners could obtain the same benefits on the basis of very different contributory efforts. Thus, the principle of proportionality between contributions and pension benefits was broken. Finally, a further problem of the pension system was to be found in the rapid increase in the practice of using invalidity pensions as a means for firms— with the tacit acquiescence of governmental authorities—to cover the increasing number of workers expelled from the labor market as a consequence of huge economic restructuring.

In late 1982, Felipe González formed the first left-wing government after the establishment of democracy in Spain. Although he immediately declared his desire to reform the pension system, his government was caught in a dilemma. On the one hand, it wanted to increase social expenditure and enhance redistribution, two objectives that marked the political identity of the PSOE and responded to the demands of its electoral base; on the other hand, Spain was facing a very deep economic crisis and the government was convinced that a sound and stable economy was only to be achieved through control of the public deficit and inflation, and without increasing contributions to Social Security. In the face of this dilemma the Socialist government decided to prioritize economic growth and employment, and only subsequently to pursue its goal of expanding social protection (Mota 2002: 257–66).

But the growing financial burden on Social Security put pressure on the government to introduce changes. According to the then Minister of Work, Joaquín Almunia, "... the situation was producing a fairly strong attack by rightist segments on the structure of the public pension system; the idea was gaining ground that Social Security was irremissibly bankrupt, that the only thing to do was to radically change the system" (Mota 2002: 278).

Backed by an absolute majority in both chambers of the Spanish parliament, the Socialist government decided to put an end to the "legal traps" allowed by the design of the pension system. Thus, in March 1983, the government hardened the means test to get a minimum pension; in 1984 it decreed that the maximum contribution base for workers older than 55 affiliated to the special regimes would be lower than the maximum contribution base for workers of the general regime (in order to prevent self-employed workers from strategically increasing their contributions during the years immediately preceding retirement). At the same time the government announced an increase in contribution rates to be paid by self-employed workers that should converge with the contribution rates of workers affiliated to the general regime. It also established a maximum pension, valid as of January 1984, to put an end to the rapid growth of the highest Social Security pensions. The same decree introduced a new category of minimum pensions for pensioners with a dependent spouse, the value of which was higher than other minimum pensions.

Simultaneously, González and his ministers initiated discussions with the trade unions. In October 1984, the government signed the Economic and Social Agreement, which created a tripartite commission to propose guidelines for pension reform. Based on the document that it presented to this commission, the Ministry of Work elaborated a first draft of a bill on pension reform without soliciting the consent of either trade unions or employers (Mota 2002: 272–5). One of the main aims of the bill was to eradicate "pension buying." The bill established an increase in the minimum contribution period to apply for a contributory pension from 10 to 15 years. The contribution period taken into consideration to calculate the pension regulatory base was also extended from 2 to 8 years prior to the claim (the first 6 should be revalued in accordance with the CPI). The new rules would only be applied to pensions which began after the publication of the law, and the recognition of a transition period was intended to alleviate inconvenience for people close to retirement. The bill also included some measures to balance the negative effects of these changes. Besides increasing (non-contributory) social assistance pensions, it incorporated the promise to automatically index "new" pensions at the beginning of each year according to the expected inflation rate. This meant a move towards a stable indexing policy that had a very fragile legal backing previous to that moment.[27] Furthermore the bill established a procedure to fill short contribution gaps in the calculation of the pension regulatory base.

The bill was approved by the Socialist absolute majority in Congress with two amendments proposed by the Socialist parliamentary group: a further increase in social assistance pensions and the commitment to compensate those pensioners getting pensions below the minimum wage, in cases where the real inflation rate would exceed the expected inflation rate.

The 1985 pension law provoked fierce resistance among all opposition parties. Four parliamentary groups presented amendments to the whole bill and requested that the government reconsider. Trade unions as well as employers' organizations had already expressed their misgivings in the tripartite commission whose working had been interrupted in March 1985. The CEOE maintained that the reform would not effectively contain the expansion of social expenditure. In contrast, trade unions argued that the reform reduced social protection (Mota 2002: 287–8). The Socialist UGT, two of whose main leaders were PSOE parliamentary deputies, was opposed to the bill but could not block it. The other major trade union confederation, CCOO, expressed a "frontal refusal" to the "counter-reform" proposed by the government and called for a general strike in June. UGT decided not to participate in the strike although it supported demonstrations against the law. CCOO and other organizations sent the Ombudsman (*Defensor del Pueblo*) a petition to present a demand to the Constitutional Court. The Ombudsman refused, but made a recommendation to the government.

Even if the majority of Spanish public opinion did not support the initiatives of the trade unions, the situation was very uncomfortable for the government. It had to confront not only the first general strike against its policy, but also the rupture of the historical unity and common political strategy with the Socialist trade union UGT (Gillespie 1989, 1990).[28] The PSOE government assumed this cost because it could publicly justify the cuts with a straightforward argument: the main losers would be those workers enjoying unfair advantages that granted them access to disproportionately high benefit levels, to the detriment of the financial capacities of the pension system.

The 1985 law can be considered the cornerstone of the pension policy of the first Socialist government. Mota (2002: 277) has emphasized that, strictly speaking, the law is not to be equated with a cost-containment reform since it introduced improvements in the protection provided by the pension system. Actually, while the expulsion effect produced by the enlargement of the minimum contribution period to get a pension has been estimated as small, the changes to the formula meant an average cut of 13 percent to all new pensions (Herce and Alonso 1998: 12). But the PSOE government combined these cutbacks with indexation measures furthering redistribution. Thus, whereas between 1984 and 1989 the amount of the maximum contributory pension (ESP187,950, roughly €1,130) was maintained unchanged, not even revalued in nominal terms, during this five-year period the lowest pensions were annually increased by between 4.5 percent (1989) and 8.3 percent (1986). These decisions had a direct impact on the gap between the maximum and the minimum pensions provided by the Social Security pension system. In 1985, the maximum retirement pension was more than six times higher than the minimum pension; five years later this ratio had fallen to 4.4. The government had achieved a significant reduction in income inequality among pensioners. Indexation was therefore conceived of as a mechanism to reduce intra-generational inequality (Mota 2002: 300–2).

1987 Reform: Law on regulation of pension plans and funds

The establishment of the Social Security pension system in the 1960s did not sweep away the system of social protection that mutual aid societies began to develop in the nineteenth century. Until the end of the 1980s, these non-profit *Mutualidades de Previsión Social* were practically the only instruments that people had to voluntarily supplement the Social Security benefits. In addition, certain large firms had established pension reserves to flesh out the public pensions of their employees, outstanding among them the banks and savings banks.

At the start of 1985, as the first Socialist government defined its position in the tripartite commission created to propose guidelines for pension reform, it declared its intention to create not only a non-contributory regime, but also supplementary schemes. The latter were envisaged as a sort of compensation for the unequal treatment that high pensions were suffering as a consequence of the selective indexation in favor of lower pensions. Private pensions should allow the better-off workers to maintain their income level after retirement (Mota 2002: 272–3).

In 1986, the second Socialist government submitted a bill to Congress with the declared aim of furthering the welfare of the retired population and strengthening the Spanish financial system by stimulating savings through pension plans and funds.[29] Pension plans were defined as "institutions of free and voluntary protection" that may cover risks derived from retirement, permanent inability and death. They were conceived of as a possible complement, "in no way" as an alternative, to the mandatory pension system of Social Security. The bill distinguished three pension fund systems depending on the type of promoter and participants: the employment system designed for pension funds set up by firms and enterprises and shared by employees; the associated system encompassing pension plans promoted by associations or trade unions whose members are the participants; finally the individual system incorporating the pension plans launched by financial entities and subscribed to by individual persons. Whereas pension plans classified under the employment and the associated systems could be defined-benefit, defined-contribution or mixed, individual pension plans were exclusively defined-contribution. As such, the amount of the benefits would depend on the contributions made and on the rate of return on the savings. Apart from regulating the institutions supervising pension plans, and the investment conditions that pension funds would have to observe, the law established the tax rates to be applied to pension plans. Contributions would be deducted from the taxable income of the participant in the pension fund with a maximum limit of 15 percent of net working profit, the maximum deduction being ESP500,000 per year and family unit. Additional contributions enjoyed a less attractive deduction rate (15% of their amount deductible from the tax return). Benefits, to be obtained in the form of annuities, as a lump sum, or as a combination of both, would be then taxed as income from work.

The government proposals on pensions plans and funds met great resistance inside and outside the *Cortes*. Whereas rightist parties criticized the meagerness of tax incentives to subscribe to pension plans and the excessive political and administrative controls upon the operation of the funds, parties to the left of the PSOE were suspicious of the overriding power given to the private financial sector. The former criticism coincided with the arguments of the employers' association CEOE, the banks and the insurance companies; the latter was widely shared by the trade unions.

The absolute majority held by the PSOE in Congress defeated the attempt by five opposition parties to return the bill to the government for reconsideration. However, the government had to take into account the amendments put forward by its own party, especially by the wing close to the trade unions. Thus, to prevent pension funds from being used strategically to reduce tax bills, the Socialist parliamentary group imposed a limit on the amount of annual contributions (either made by the participants or by the employer on behalf of employees). Each family unit could contribute a maximum of ESP750,000, only two-thirds of which could be deducted from the taxable income base. Other amendments aimed to increase the degree of control of parliamentary commissions and the Ministry of Economics and Finance over fund managers, and to guarantee the universal character of employment funds within a firm.[30] The discussions in the Senate were no less conflict-ridden. Again, the attempt by three conservative parties (AP, the Basque Nationalist Party, PNV, and the small Popular Democratic Party, PDP) to veto the whole bill was in vain, as were the nearly 300 amendments formulated by the opposition parties. But the 55 amendments presented by the Socialist group had to be discussed. The most significant ones were geared at scrapping requirements to invest in low profitability assets (including public debt) and at toughening the control by the government and the individual investors over the managing institutions. As regards already existing pension reserves—especially important in the case of banks and saving banks—another approved amendment established that only those institutions willing to externalize the accounts and to constitute a pension plan according to the new law (and thus subject to the control of the employees) would be able to benefit from the tax advantages designed for pension plans.[31]

The law on pension plans and funds was finally passed in June 1987, to the disgust of the business association CEOE and the financial sector, on the one hand, and the distrust of trade unions, on the other. The president of the Association of Institutions of Collective Investment and Pension Funds, INVERCO, bemoaned the loss of "an historical opportunity to endow our country with a supplementary pension system which it needs so much."[32] The trade unions on their part disliked the tax-deductibility of contributions to pension funds (which they deemed discriminatory with respect to Social Security contributions) suspecting that this tax incentive would reinforce the third pillar of the pension system to the detriment of the first. Their fear was that the more people covered by private pension plans, the less costly in terms of popular support it would be for a government to cut back public benefits. Furthermore they had misgivings about an additional clause included in the law according to which firms could, under specific circumstances, profit from the possibility of deducting from Corporate Income Tax contributions already made to pension reserves without adapting them to the new regulations for pension plans.[33] They could thus benefit from the tax advantages granted to pension plans without having to create control commissions with the participation of trade union representatives.[34]

Pension plans have indeed become an attractive financial product for adult Spaniards, so that the number of participants and the value of assets have grown rapidly in the last fifteen years. The employment system, whose take-off was fraught with conflicts between firms, trade unions and the administration that came up in the process of transforming the old pension reserves into new pension plans, has developed slower than expected. At the end of 2003 it included almost 700,000 subscribers and controlled about €23.5 billion in assets. In contrast, the individual system has drawn large numbers of subscribers: the number of participants, which in 1990 was about half a million, had increased to 6.6 million by the end of 2003. Its assets have gone from approximately €1 billion to €31.5 billion during the same period. Pension participants and the assets of the associated system have remained residual (less than 90,000 participants and €1 billion in December 2003). In fact, experts are optimistic about the progress of private pension funds in Spain. Expectations have been largely fulfilled: in 2004 it was estimated that assets, as of 2006, would be around 70 billion USD; at the end of March 2006 they were in fact nearly 95 billion USD.[35]

This evolution has been furthered by increases in the amount of deductible contributions to pension plans claimed from time to time by representatives of the financial and insurance sectors. Initially established at ESP 500,000 (c.€3,000) per family unit, this limit turned out to be only applicable to individual taxpayers when the Constitutional Court forced the *Cortes* in 1989 to reform the tax legislation in order to allow the members of a family unit to present separate income tax returns.[36] This apparent setback notwithstanding, the Socialist government raised the limit on contributions to private pension plans deductible from the income tax base to ESP 750,000 (c. €4,500) as of 1992.[37]

After the government change in 1996, the first PP government managed in 1998 to pass a bill rising the deductible amount to ESP1,100,000 (around €6,600) and one year later it introduced a series of gradual additional increases to this limit for people aged 53 and over, with a ceiling of ESP2,200,000 (around €13,220) for people aged 65 and over.[38] In 2002, two years after winning elections with an absolute majority, the PP voted for a reform of the personal income tax, which among other measures, included a substantial new rise in the tax exempted contributions to pension plans: starting in 2003 taxpayers can subtract €8,000 (per year) from their taxable base. To this sum people over 52 years can add €1,250 for each year that they are above this age (with a ceiling of €24,250 for people aged 65 and over).[39]

The incentives to subscribe to private pension plans have been improved by the PP governments through other legislative modifications. Since 1999, contributions to pension plans can be retrieved under the special circumstances of severe illness and long-term unemployment.[40] Since then it is also possible to subscribe to pension plans on behalf of handicapped relatives (with at least 65% disability), which enjoy identical fiscal advantages to standard pension plans.[41] Furthermore, the additional deductible amount a pension fund subscriber can contribute for his/her partner, provided that she/he earns less than €8,000 per year or is not employed, has been also increased to €2,000 as of 2003.[42]

Other changes affect the supply of new financial products which can be added on to pension plans (like the Guaranteed Protection Plans)[43] or the taxation of benefits. As regards this last issue, according to the 1987 law on Pension Plans and Funds, benefits obtained from contributions to pension plans had to be integrated in the income of beneficiaries subject to income tax. Since 2003, benefits of pension plans received in a lump sum enjoy a 40 percent reduction from the income tax taxable base, as long as the first contribution to the pension plan has been made more than two years before getting the benefits.

Still other initiatives reveal the encouragement of occupational private pensions. Thus the renewed text of the law on Pension Plans and Funds published in December 2002 seeks to promote the development of occupational pension schemes by allowing several companies to jointly constitute one pension scheme.[44] Moreover, in October 2003, the government negotiated with the trade unions the creation of collective pension plans for civil servants and employees of the central administration, so that half a percentage point of their contribution base would be compulsorily invested in private pension funds, in order to get supplementary retirement pensions.[45]

1990 Reform: Law on non-contributory pensions of the Social Security system

Pension policy, in general, and indexation in particular, remained in the years following the endorsement of the 1985 law a highly contentious issue in the relationship between the government and the trade unions. The Spanish economic recovery from 1986 prompted trade unions to call for a "social turn". They argued for the expansion of social expenditure in terms of GDP, while the government insisted on the need to control the public deficits and price increases. In December 1988 the trade unions organized a general strike. Despite these conflicts,[46] the incumbent party again won in the general elections in October 1989. Having exactly 50 percent of the seats in Congress (175), the PSOE enjoyed in practice its third consecutive absolute majority, since the elected deputies of the Basque separatist party *Herri Batasuna* refused to participate in the Spanish parliament.

At the end of 1990, Congress passed a law on non-contributory pensions, presented by the government as part of the move of the Spanish welfare system towards universalism.[47] Beneficiaries of these pensions were defined as handicapped or old persons who, lacking income above a legally established limit, did not satisfy the stipulated conditions to get a retirement or invalidity contributory pension. The Social Security pension system stopped being exclusively contributory and became hybrid.[48] Not that until then the Spanish state had not provided social assistance benefits: the central administration together with the autonomous communities and the city councils had offered means-tested economic aid to different collectives, among them old and handicapped people. But the provision of these benefits was discretional, inasmuch as it depended on the availability of public resources. Moreover, since these benefits were not based on specific rights their applicants could not appeal against their denial (Fernández 2002: 53–65).

In March 1991, the government published a decree developing the law on non-contributory pensions. The opposition, which had not contested the law during the legislative phase, criticized its slow implementation.[49] Only employers' associations voiced criticism, attacking the use of Social Security contributions paid by companies and workers to pay for non-contributory pensions.

The 1990 law on non-contributory pensions established strict eligibility conditions: thus, a person living alone is eligible for a retirement pension if h/she is 65 or older, has at least ten years of legal residence in Spain (including the two last years previous to retirement) and his/her annual income is below the annual sum of non-contributory pensions. If h/she lives with other family members, the aggregate income of all of them cannot exceed a specified limit. Although the fixed amount of non-contributory pensions is a bit higher than the amount of the previously existing social assistance pensions provided by the state, the number and rigorousness of the requirements that confer rights to the new pension may explain why many beneficiaries of the old social assistance benefits have preferred to keep their benefits (Fernández 2002: 60–2). Contrary to initial expectations, the non-contributory pensions have not absorbed the different social assistance benefits provided by the central state before the approval of the law.

The first non-contributory pensions were granted in the summer of 1991 and amounted to ESP364,000 (around €2,190) per year, distributed in 14 payments. Although the 1991 decree established strict eligibility conditions, the number of non-contributory pensions has increased year by year. In 2003, Social Security provided nearly 490,000 non-contributory pensions, 58 percent of which were retirement pensions. The benefit totaled up to €3,868 per year distributed in 14 payments. This sum represented approximately 57 percent of the minimum retirement contributory pension for a 65 year-old beneficiary with a dependent spouse.[50]

Non-contributory pensions have recently been the subject of conflicts between the central and the autonomous governments. Although this type of pension is fixed by the central government for all beneficiaries and paid by Social Security, the Andalusian autonomous government led by the PSOE decided in 1999 for the first time to use its own budget to supplement non-contributory pensions for beneficiaries living in its community.[51] The central PP government appealed this decision before the Constitutional Court, which in December 2002 decided for the Andalusian government, on the ground that supplements to non-contributory pensions are to be considered social assistance benefits and hence belong to the competencies that autonomous communities can assume according to the Constitution.[52] In the face of repeated supplements granted by the Andalusian and Catalonian autonomous governments since 1999, at the end of 2003 the PP government managed to pass legislation on the uniformity of Social Security pensions in all autonomous communities.[53] Yet one day after the parliamentary endorsement of the corresponding law the Andalusian government once again decreed supplementary allowances for the lowest Social Security pensions.

Excursus: the guidelines of Spanish pension policy since 1995 – The Toledo Pact

Although the 1985 pension reform attacked the two main factors contributing to the growth in expenditure on pensions, by means of the extension of the minimum contribution period to be eligible for a contributory pension, and the modification of the formula of calculation, the number of retirement pensions continued to grow rapidly. In 1985, there were 2,850,000; in 1991, 3,357,000. Likewise, while the changes to the formula meant an average cut of 13 percent to all new pensions, the net substitution rates of retirement pensions were still very high. An average employee who had worked all his/her life in manufacturing (with 35 years of Social Security contributions) and retired in 1990 would have received 98 percent of his salary of 1989. This percentage was significantly higher than that registered in other countries like Italy, France, (West) Germany and the United Kingdom, where it ranged from 89 percent down to 59 percent (Barrada 1999: 431, 554).

Hence, the financial pressure on the system, together with the problems of employment, which worsened from 1992 onwards, explain why the 1985 Law did not remove discussion of the future of the pension system from the public agenda. In the early 1990s, it was the subject of debate in a number of forums. On the one hand, the problem was analyzed by experts sponsored by bodies within the public administration, financial entities or business associations.[54] The main purpose of these studies was to draw up diagnoses by means of projecting the receipts and expenditures of the system. Given that all of these studies anticipated deficits of greater or lesser amounts before the end of the first decade of the coming century, they proposed a series of measures to deal with them. These ranged from slight alterations (MTSS 1995), to substantial changes in the operating regulations that did not, however, affect the structure of the system (Herce and Pérez-Díaz 1995; Barea, González-Páramo and Velarde 1996), to major reform that required the modification of the system of financing, specifically the transition towards a mixed or a pure model of capitalization (Herce, Sosvilla, Castillo and Duce 1996, Piñera 1996).[55]

On the other hand, in February 1994, the Congress set up a commission to study the problems of Social Security. The promoter of this commission was CiU, the center-right, Catalonian nationalist party which, after the 1993 elections, had become one of the parliamentary groups on which the minority Socialist government depended to pass legislation. As the party in the Catalan autonomous government since 1980, CiU had been generally arguing for liberal economic measures as well as lower tax contributions from the Catalonian region to the rest of Spain. However, it also stressed among its main policy goals the advancement of social justice and solidarity. The combination of these purposes helps to explain its will to play the lead in national pension policy geared to rationalizing and optimizing the Social Security system.

For one year the parliamentary commission consulted different experts (from academic circles and the public administration) as well as the leaders of trade unions and business organizations, and it drew up a report consisting of two parts. In the first part, it outlined the problem and the general principles that should govern the reform, while the second part made 15 recommendations. In April 1995, all the parties endorsed the document in the Congress; and because one of the most important meetings for concluding the agreement was held in Toledo, this city has given its name to the Pact.

As well as unanimous parliamentary approval, the Toledo Pact acquired additional legitimacy through the support of the main Spanish unions, UGT and CCOO, and the CEOE. Thus, it became a point of encounter between those who gave priority to the maintenance of a generous benefits system (and, therefore, oriented their main demands towards maintaining and, if possible, extending the present level of social expenditure), and those who were more preoccupied with the growing burden that this places on employment (and, therefore, oriented their main demands towards maintaining, and if possible reducing, the level of contributions).

Such broad support has several explanations. First, the proposals for reform included in the Pact are not of an executive, but a normative nature. They are desirable objectives whose conversion into political measures allows a wide margin for negotiation both in establishing priorities and in adjusting the intensity of the effects. Reaching an agreement on what is desirable may be easier than coming to a consensus on when and how to achieve it. Second, the Pact contains arguments in both its explanations and its recommendations that satisfy all the agents.

The fundamental characteristics of the Pact are, therefore, flexibility in the translation of objectives into concrete proposals and a balance between positions that reflect different priorities. But both characteristics are clearly limited by the declared purpose of the Pact: "To reinforce, consolidate and give future viability to the model of pensions that has taken shape in recent years...." The Pact explicitly excludes either "substituting the present system of PAYG and inter-generational solidarity for another based on the capitalization of the public pension system and on individual provision", or "limiting the present public pension system in Spain to the simple provision of minimum pensions."[56]

Within these margins, the balance between the positions of the leftist parties and the unions, on the one hand, and the liberal-conservative parties and employers' associations on the other, is demonstrated repeatedly. Thus, in the explanatory part, the Pact indicates that it would be desirable for Spain to approach the European average as regards the percentage of GDP that is allocated to social spending and pensions. This is an argument common in trade union discourse. In spite of the effort that Spain has made in this direction in recent years, in 1994, the current costs of social protection (excluding education) had reached 23.6 percent of GDP, still five points below the European average (Barrada 1999: 548). The Pact goes on to offer two observations central to the discourse of employers: (1) the importance of the cost of social contributions in the total salary of wage-earners (25.1% in 1993) and the inadvisability of increasing them, and (2) the asymmetry of 3 to 1 in the distribution of these contributions between employers and employees. In this way, it recognizes the causes of employers' discontent when they affirm that the high social contributions that they pay out for each worker (23.6% of the contributory base; the remaining 4.7% falling to the employee) are equivalent to a heavy tax on work.

In the recommendations, the tendency towards a balancing of positions is more easily appreciated if they are classified under four objectives: rationalization, equity, incentives and improved benefits. The recommendations oriented towards the rationalization of the system satisfy those who support maintaining high levels of benefits as well as those who put the criteria of financial health first. The recommendations aimed at achieving greater equity satisfy some more than others, depending on whether equity affects income or spending. The recommendations intended to encourage behavior that is directly or indirectly beneficial to the functioning of the system principally favor those who support containing expenditure, while the recommendations that involve the improvement of certain benefits satisfy those whose aim is the strengthening of the welfare state.

Among the recommendations for rationalization, what stands out is the importance that all the political and social actors attribute to the separation and clarification of the sources of financing (Recommendation 1). The objective is that "within the shortest period possible" social contributions should finance only contributory benefits instead of being allocated to cover part of universal social costs. The release of these funds would make it possible to implement Recommendation 2 for setting up reserves, the existence of which would permit to cushion the effects of economic cycles, avoiding the need to increase contributions in order to meet pension payments. Among employers, there is even hope that such reserves might allow for a reduction in contributions. Two further recommendations are aimed at rationalizing the pension system. First, the simplification and integration of the special regimes (Recommendation 6) and second, the integration of all the management functions relating to pensions (Recommendation 7), intended to increase the effectiveness and efficiency of the administration of the system.

Equity is the objective of five recommendations in the Pact, three of which affect income and the other two spending. Of the former, one particularly appreciated by the unions is the search for greater parity between real wages and contributory bases, putting an end to the practice of increasing remuneration by means of bonuses and allowances on which contributions are not paid to Social Security (Recommendation 3).

In relation to the above-mentioned recommendation to modify the structure of the 7special regimes, the Pact also advises remedying the inequity that derives from workers in these regimes paying lower contributions than workers in the general regime, yet later receiving the same benefits (Recommendation 4). The fifth recommendation, to improve the mechanisms for collecting contributions to avoid arrears of payment by businesses and the underground economy, is balanced by recommendation number 13 to improve benefit distribution mechanisms in order to fight against fraudulent pension claims for temporary or permanent disability. Also aiming to improve equity on the spending side is recommendation number 9, that "benefits should be in greater proportion to the contributory effort made."

The third group of recommendations underlines the convenience of rewarding behavior with positive consequences for the system or for its beneficiaries. These are the recommendations that most closely reflect the positions of employers. Thus, the reduction of social contributions for low-skilled workers (Recommendation 8) would provide an incentive to contract workers in labor-intensive sectors like construction. This recommendation would, however, be conditional "on the maintenance of the financial equilibrium of the system." Likewise, the reduction, or even the suppression, of social contributions would operate as incentives for voluntarily prolonging the working life of employees beyond the age of 65 (Recommendation 10). The benefits of voluntarily postponing the age of retirement would accrue to the employer (who would pay fewer contributions) as well as the worker (who could demand higher remuneration) and Social Security (which would be able to pay the worker's pension for fewer years). A different distribution of benefits would result from promoting private pension funds as a supplement to public pensions (Recommendation 14). In general, employers approve of improved tax incentives for subscribing to these funds, first of all because they would increase national savings, thus encouraging a fall in the cost of investment loans; but perhaps also because reinforcement of the supplementary system would make a hypothetical future cutback in public pensions less traumatic.

If the recommendations for incentives are those that best reflect the interests of employers, the unions find some of their principal demands reflected in the recommendations that affirm the need to avoid a deterioration of benefits and even to improve them. Consequently, maintaining the purchasing power of pensions through automatic revaluation (Recommendation 11) would at least guarantee the nominal growth of pensions. Moreover, the intention to extend the number of years for which orphans' pensions can be claimed and to increase the value of widow(er)s' pensions (Recommendation 12) would mean an increase in social spending in real terms.

The balance of influences reflected in the Toledo Pact has been one of the main keys to its institutional stability. Another is a commitment binding all the political parties which, however, was not recorded in the text of the Pact. Although they seemed to be embarrassed to write it down, the political parties have committed themselves not to use the question of pensions for electoral propaganda. In principle, this verbal agreement has the virtue of avoiding situations like the one that arose in the electoral campaign of 1993 when, in a TV debate, the PSOE candidate, Felipe

González, claimed that the candidate for the PP, José María Aznar, did not intend to revalue pensions. It appears that leaders of the PP are convinced that this allegation made a decisive contribution to their electoral defeat by the PSOE, over which they had an advantage according to many surveys.[57]

In a country in which citizens in some regions, or in the country as a whole, are frequently called to the polls to elect their political representatives at the different levels of government, to exclude a subject from electoral debate would amount to removing it from political debate. Thus, the danger highlighted by Rhodes (1997: 21) that corporate pacts sideline parliament and public opinion from the discussion of reforms of the welfare state became more real with this mechanism of self-protection. The risk of being accused of wanting to cut back pensions has led political leaders to downplay the problems of financing the pension system and to respect the content of the Pact. This risk has made the exit costs from the Pact extremely high for the political parties.

1997 Reform: Law on consolidation and rationalization of the Social Security system

Although the Toledo Pact meant that, during the electoral campaign prior to the general elections of 1996, the Popular Party was spared being the object of accusations such as those made by the PSOE in the 1993 campaign, in the eyes of many voters its conservative-liberal ideology placed it under suspicion of wanting to cut back welfare benefits. To banish this suspicion became one of the main objectives of the government that was formed at the beginning of May 1996. Six months later, its effort was rewarded by a result that not even the PSOE had managed to achieve in its thirteen years in government: on 9 October 1996, the Prime Minister, José María Aznar, signed the Agreement on the Consolidation and Rationalization of the Social Security system with the leaders of the trade unions UGT and CCOO. The formal, explicit objective of this agreement was to predetermine the legislative development of the Toledo Pact, an outcome sponsored by CiU, the party that supported Aznar's minority government. The implicit objective was to reinforce symbolically the strategic positions of the signatories in the political sphere.

The October Agreement, in force until the year 2000 (the end of the first PP legislature), consists of twelve points that develop certain recommendations from the Toledo Pact. In the brief explanation prior to the presentation of these points, the signatories declared "their *unequivocal* support for the consolidation and rationalization of the system of social protection" [my italics] and their desire that, in the future, "it should maintain and, economic progress permitting, improve its present share of Gross Domestic Product, bringing us closer to the (European) Community average."

On applying the analytical schema used above for an ordered exposition of the content of the Toledo Pact, what stands out is that the points developed in the

Agreement of October 1996 particularly affect the rationalization of the system and the improvement of benefits. Thus the recommendations for rationalization are visible in the demands for (1) separating the sources of financing of contributory and non-contributory benefits by the year 2000; (2) setting up a reserve fund with the surplus from social contributions; and (3) adjusting the criteria for the entitlement and provision of pensions for permanent disability. An improvement in benefits is the purpose of another four demands: (1) a reduction of the penalty for early retirement under the age of 65 in certain circumstances (like enforced retirement through job loss after contributing for 40 years); (2) the automatic revaluation of pensions in terms of the anticipated CPI; (3) a rise in the maximum age limit for entitlement to an orphan's pension from 18 to 21; and (4) an increase in the minimum widow(er)'s pension for those under the age of 60.

As regards the criterion of equity, which was also of core importance to the Toledo Pact, the 1996 Agreement extends the length of the period on which the regulatory base for pensions is calculated from the last 8 years to the last 15 years before retirement. It also modifies the percentage applicable to the regulatory base so that it is less favorable to workers who have only contributed for a short period. In particular, it establishes that the first 15 years give the right to 50 percent of the regulatory base (instead of 60%), and each year of additional contributions counts for 3 percent (from years 16 to 25) or 2.5 percent (from years 26 to 35). While this measure affects the equity of the benefits or costs of the system, another proposal affects the equity of income. The government committed to gradually eliminate the different maximum limits affecting the contributory bases until only one category remains, for the purpose of achieving parity between contributory bases and real wages.

The latter demand, together with the total absence in the Agreement of any reference to a reduction in social contributions, and the vague allusion to the advisability of establishing "adequate fiscal regulation" of pension funds, explain the irritation of employers and their decision not to endorse this document. Hence, although the Agreement did not deviate from the Toledo Pact backed by the employers' association CEOE, it did not include those items which entrepreneurs considered more relevant. This suggests that the trade unions managed to set the agenda of the negotiations. The government would probably have preferred a tripartite arrangement, but its rejection by employers provided a weapon with which to combat the idea that the PP was closer to employers than to unions. Besides the symbolic importance of the Agreement for the new government, this compromise with unions reduced the risk of demonstrations and strikes which would have destabilized the PP minority government.

On the basis of the Agreement of 1996, the government drew up a bill that became law in July 1997. Apart from the extension of the period to calculate the regulatory base and the modification of the percentage to be applied to that base, the 1997 bill included significant improvements for selected groups of pensioners (orphans, widow(er)s and the early-retired). It also implied further progress in pension indexing. Indeed the first PP government managed to set down in the 1997 pension law what the PSOE government had already been accomplishing in 1995 and 1996 without an explicit legal constraint: the law granted the right of pensioners to be compensated with a deferred extra payment when the expected CPI (according to which pensions are revalued at the beginning of each year) is lower than the real CPI of that year.[58] Since a pension reduction was not foreseen under inverse circumstances, in 1998 all Social Security pensions experienced a growth in real terms because the expected CPI (2.6%) according to which they had been revalued came out to be higher than the effective CPI.

As Herce and Alonso (1998) have shown, the effects of the 1997 law on the financial perspectives of the pension system have been moderate—less drastic than those of the reform of 1985. This time, the reform has attacked only one of the growth factors in pension spending, specifically, the differential between the amount paid out in new pensions and the corresponding amount of those that are terminated. But while the reform of 1985 led to a cutback in new pensions estimated at 13 percent, the analogous effect of the reform of 1997 is calculated at 3 percent. This will hardly lead to a reduction of this differential which, in 1997, one year before the reform was applied, had reached the following dimensions: depending on the regime, the average cost of new pensions was between 7.5 percent (the special regime for domestic employees) and 37.1 percent (the special regime for coal miners) higher than that of a corresponding pension that concluded.

The reform of 1997 did not tackle the second growth factor affecting spending: the increase in the differential between the number of new pensions and the number that are terminated. Even if we only take into account retirement pensions, in 1997 more than 225,000 new claims were made, while there were only 160,000 terminations.[59]

According to the financial projection set up by Herce and Alonso (1998), the pension law approved in 1997 will only manage to reduce the system deficit in the long term (from the year 2020), and by a very small amount. Meanwhile, in the short term, the measures that improve certain benefits will lead to an increase in pension expenditure, even if very moderate. It would therefore appear that none of the signatories achieved much of what they were supposed to have wanted. The government did not manage to relieve the financial pressure on the public pension system to a significant extent, nor did the unions manage to obtain significant improvements in benefits. Measured in these terms, the 1997 reform law hardly represented an effective instrument to any of the signatories of the 1996 Agreement.

In reality, by means of this arrangement, the government prevented the unions from organizing a social protest as they had in 1985 when the PSOE passed its first reform of the pension system. On the other hand, the unions offered the government and the PP the conditions necessary to counteract certain ideas that weighed negatively on their image. Apparently, the agreement with the unions allowed the government to initiate its mandate with a demonstration of sensitivity towards social matters and an aptitude for dialogue with workers' representatives that its political rivals had denied. Actually, the minority government of Aznar did not have much margin to act in a different way, because the PP had signed the Toledo Pact only two years earlier, a document sponsored by CiU whose votes the government needed to pass bills in Congress.

The first PP government publicly presented its understanding with the trade unions in pension policy as a great success. In the last days of 1999, only five months before the general elections, it approved a decree on pensions revaluation which pleased the trade unions. Minimum pensions would grow far beyond the expected 2 percent CPI increase for 2000: specifically between 5.37 percent and 15.95 percent depending on the type of benefit.[60]

2002 Reform: Law on measures for the establishment of a system of gradual and flexible retirement

After the 2000 parliamentary elections gave him the backing of an absolute majority, early during his second term of office, Aznar negotiated another pension reform with the trade unions. The final document, signed in April 2001 and valid until 2003, was rejected by UGT, but accepted by CCOO and the employers' associations CEOE and CEPYME. The Agreement for the Improvement and Development of the Social Protection System committed to completely separate, within a period of 12 years, the financing sources of contributory and non-contributory benefits, to consolidate the existing reserve fund (established in 2000), to recognize the right to an early retirement under certain conditions and to reduce penalties for retirement before the age of 65. But the main point of the agreement concerned the encouragement of late retirement and the incentives designed for this purpose.

Just a few days before the end 2001 the government sanctioned a decree establishing a new system of gradual and flexible retirement in force as of January 2002. The aim was to allow people to work after the retirement age either with the same or with less intensity than before. In the latter case the employment would be compatible with a partial retirement pension. Thus, if a worker decided to work only 60 percent of the previous working day, he would obtain 40 percent of his pension. To foster the postponement of retirement, the decree declared the exemption of the bulk of contributions to Social Security for workers aged 65 and older who could substantiate at least 35 contribution years.[61] The decree also established a 50 percent reduction (to be incremented by an additional 10% each year) from the Social Security contributions for those workers aged 60 and over with at least five years seniority in the firm. Nevertheless, not only employers but also workers could benefit from the incentives incorporated in the law to delay retirement. Workers opting for postponing retirement could increase their pension by 2 percentage points of the regulatory base per year provided that they were 65 years old or older and had paid contributions to Social Security for no less than 35 years.

As regards anticipated retirement, the former legislation granted this right to workers aged 60 or older who had contributed to Social Security before the first day of the year 1967. The new decree added that workers aged 61 or older who had contributed after that date could also anticipate retirement if they were registered as employment seekers at least during the 6 months previous to the retirement application, had contributed for at least 30 years to Social Security and had not voluntarily ceased to work. The pre-retirement penalties for all those workers having contributed no less than 30 years to Social Security were, furthermore, reduced. Previous to the release of the December 2001 decree, early retirement was penalized by 8 percent of the regulatory base independently of the number of years the worker had contributed to Social Security. After its publication the maximum penalty applied to workers having less than 30 contribution years, whereas workers verifying between 31 and 40 (or more) contribution years were penalized between 7.5 percent and 6 percent.

The content of this piece of legislation was reproduced with only small modifications in a law approved in July 2002, which formally repealed the former decree.[62] Three months later the government approved a new decree to develop the law. At the end of the same year the number of registered workers aged 65 or older amounted to 102,000; around 5,100 of them had resorted to the possibility of partial retirement opened by the new norms.[63] These figures nevertheless appear modest when contrasted with the estimated number of workers who in the same year left the labor market before retirement age: between 60,000 and 70,000 according to estimates of the Ministry of Work.[64]

The institutional solidity of the Toledo Pact

In May 2000, just a few weeks after the PP had obtained an absolute majority in the general elections, the parties represented in Congress agreed on the creation of the Non-permanent Parliamentary Commission to Assess the Results Obtained through the Implementation of the Recommendations of the Toledo Pact. This agreement followed from the last recommendation of the Toledo Pact, but the collective initiative underlying it demonstrated the political will of all parties to keep the Pact alive.

In October 2003, this parliamentary commission presented its report to Congress. It included a recommendation to further "the goal of achieving a greater proportionality between the pensions and the fulfilled contributory effort," but did not specify how and when to advance this objective. In fact the report strengthened the Toledo Pact as a compromise to maintain and enhance the PAYG pension system, emphasizing benefit improvements more than cutbacks. This conclusion can be drawn from the five new recommendations included in the revised version of the Toledo Pact: they refer to social problems that have to be solved more for the well-being of workers and pensioners than for the financial stability of the system. The extension of new forms of work (part-time, temporary), the equal protection of women, the dependence of people in need of care, disability and immigration are perceived as challenges, not as threats for the Spanish Social Security system.[65] After discussion in a plenary session of Congress on November 2, the document was approved by nearly all parliamentary deputies present. It should be mentioned that the particular amendments presented by all parliamentary groups, except for the one formed by the representatives of the PP, dealt mostly with the need to improve the extension or the level of some benefits, although the need to decentralize the administrative and even political competences of Social Security was also urged by all nationalist or regionalist parties.[66]

At the end of 2003, eight years after its parliamentary approval, the Toledo Pact in its revised version seemed as solid as ever. The new document was handed over to Prime Minister Aznar in a formal act, in which not only the deputies represented in the corresponding parliamentary commission took part, but also representatives of the trade union CCOO and of the employers' organization CEOE. The attendance of the European commissar of Social Affairs, Anna Diamantopoulos, at this event seemed remarkable given that at the beginning of 2003 the European Council had warned the Spanish government over "the risk of unsustainable public finances in terms of emerging budgetary imbalances in the long run" stemming "from the large projected increase in age-related spending on public pensions." It furthermore had urged "the Spanish authorities to agree a timetable for reaching policy conclusions and implementation of the envisaged reform of the pensions system to align contributions and benefits more closely" regretting that "no major review of the public pension system ha(d) yet been undertaken."[67]

Although in public discourse the PP governments had shown great respect for the opinions and recommendations of the European institutions, and repeatedly used them to back controversial political decisions, they apparently did not take them very seriously as regards pension policy. Instead of advancing reforms that reduce the financial pressure on the system forecast by national and international experts, the last government of Aznar adopted decisions that will certainly increase future public pension expenditure. The most important among these may be the ones affecting selective revaluation above the CPI, since the increase in real terms experienced by selected pensions has been consolidated. Thus, retirement pensions for beneficiaries below 65 years of age as well as widow(er)s' pensions were improved by the decree on revaluation of pensions to be paid in 2003.[68] Moreover, in the first days of 2004 the Official State Bulletin published a new decree on the revaluation of pensions involving an improvement of certain Social Security benefits: while all pensions would experience a 2 percent increase to maintain their purchasing power, minimum contributory pensions (among them for retired workers and widow(er)s under 65 years, as well as for orphans) would be revalued by between 4.8 percent and 11.4 percent and non-contributory pensions would be increased by 2.8 percent.[69] Both 2003 and 2004 were election years: in 2003 local elections and elections to the majority of autonomous communities took place in May; in 2004 national elections were held in March. The influence of the electoral cycle on the indexing decisions of the PP government is hardly to be denied. For a government party it may be too great a sacrifice to renounce such decisions when the number of contributing workers is increasing so much that the ratio of contributors/pensions is as good as it was twenty years ago. Actually, in 1980, when 10,512,000 workers financed slightly fewer than 5 million pensions, this ratio amounted to 2.4; in the following years it fell to its lowest level (1.8 in 1995); the rapid recovery of the Spanish economy as of 1997, coinciding with considerable immigration flows, pushed up the ratio to 2.1 in 2003, when nearly 16.5 million affiliated workers paid contributions to finance 7,823,000 pensions.[70] The upward tendency was still observable in 2005: the corresponding ratio at the end of this year was 2.24.[71]

V Conclusion

Summary of the magnitude of changes

Careful examination of Spanish pension policy since the 1980s allows us to distinguish two periods. The first one, encompassing the first three Socialist governments backed by absolute majorities, was decisive for the configuration of the pension system in its present shape. The contributory system was streamlined in order to avoid fraudulent strategies while significantly reducing the differences in the value of contributory benefits. Furthermore, the basis for the development of the second and third pillars was set up and non-contributory pensions were established to incorporate people into the Social Security pension system who did not fulfill the eligibility criteria for a contributory pension.

The second period, encompassing the last government led by Felipe González and the two governments headed by José María Aznar, stands out for the incrementalist pension policies adopted, with the only exception of the introduction of gradual and flexible retirement practices, the effects of which have as yet been very modest. During this second period, the structure of the Social Security pension system was strengthened through the Toledo Pact, while the private pillars of the pension system were also reinforced through substantial tax incentives. The renewal of the Toledo Pact at the end of this period has to be interpreted as an indicator of the stability of Spanish pension policy in the next years.

Impact of the political system on pension politics

At least two features of the Spanish political system deserve to be stressed when trying to explain pension policy over recent decades. The first one is the practical absence of institutional veto points when an absolute majority in Congress backs a government. The majoritarian bias of the Spanish political system, in spite of the formal establishment of a proportional electoral system, has often granted governments the capacity to pass legislation without needing the compliance of other political and social actors. In 1985, in the context of a very difficult economic situation and although pension reform was an issue of high public opinion interest around which society could be mobilized against the government, González used the Socialist parliamentary absolute majority to approve a very controversial pension reform.

When the PP became the party of government in 1996, Spanish pension policy was locked in the Toledo Pact, an arrangement which set the rules of the pension politics game for all players. To some extent the Pact had transformed this policy area into a sort of multiple partisan veto player system: not only the opposition parties, but also the trade unions would try to block any policy change not in the agreement. But instead of endeavoring to push reform to the limits established by the Pact, the first PP government showed itself eager to improve the coverage and benefits of the public pension system. Even before renowned Spanish economic experts anticipated the very positive employment trend that began in 1996, the PP refused to introduce some of the changes in the pension system that experts were pleading for and that the Toledo Pact permitted, such as the extension to the whole contributory career of the period on which the pension regulatory base is calculated.

Although backed by an absolute majority, during its second term in office the PP did not even attempt to introduce any change in the pension system involving future benefit cuts. The very favorable evolution of the labor market since 1996 and the slower rhythm of new Social Security pensioners due to the decline of birth rates during the Civil War (1936–39) combined to substantially improve the ratio between the number of pensions and of workers paying contributions. Furthermore, the reserve fund accumulated with the surplus in contributions after the disentanglement of the financing sources of Social Security benefits provided a cushion for the system. Under these conditions any cost-containment pension reform was certainly difficult to publicly justify, all the more so in a country that is at the lower end of the EU (15) in social protection spending and whose citizens appreciate (and probably reward in elections) government efforts to improve welfare benefits.

The second feature of the Spanish political system that has had a significant impact on pension policy is the decentralized structure of the state. Precisely because central governments have to counteract the centrifugal tendencies of the autonomous communities, not only to underpin the Spanish nation but also to preserve their own competencies, they are very interested in reinforcing nationwide institutions like Social Security. Initiatives to decentralize Social Security have therefore been strictly rejected by the parties which have had government responsibilities over the last decades. Strengthening Social Security implies legitimating an institution of the central state, and in some ways of the Spanish nation.

Interest group influence

The most important Spanish trade unions and employers' organizations gained considerable prestige during the transition to democracy, as elements of a consensus-seeking movement aiming at moderating the working class and adopting the necessary reforms of the labor market and the tax system, in order to revamp the battered economy. Since then their support has been crucial to legitimize difficult political decisions. Nevertheless, in 1985 the first Socialist government pushed forward pension reform against the frontal opposition of the CCOO and UGT.

Although the 1987 and 1988 legislation on private pension plans and funds was negotiated with trade unions, their participation was characterized by mistrust and critiques of the leverage acquired by the financial sector in these negotiations.

During the second period of pension policy the Toledo Pact transformed trade unions, as well as political parties, into powerful players in the pension politics game. The PP governments have easily obtained the consent of trade unions to sponsor incremental changes in the Social Security system. Aznar and his ministers have obtained symbolic benefits by exhibiting the capacity of a conservative party (time and again scorned as the heir of dictator Franco) to have satisfactory relationships with class-based trade unions.

Employers' organizations have not sanctioned all the pension policy decisions taken by the PP governments, but they have in general refrained from loudly criticizing the issues they most disliked. The governmental initiatives to lessen and exempt Social Security contributions for certain groups of workers on the one hand, and the incentives designed for the expansion of private pensions on the other, seem to have compensated for the entrepreneurs' unease with respect to specific measures (like the unification of the maximum contributory base for different workers' categories) or omissions (like the reduction of standard contribution rates to be paid by employers).

Constraints of policy design

After the institutionalization of private pension plans in the second half of the 1980s and of non-contributory Social Security pensions at the beginning of the 1990s, the structure of the Spanish pension system has remained stable. This structure has been sanctioned in the Toledo Pact, which currently represents the most important policy constraint in the Spanish pension reform process. Signed in 1995 and renewed in 2003, this agreement has definitely set a path in pension policy. The high symbolic value that political and social actors as well as mass media have attributed to the Toledo Pact ensures its stability, which seems only to be threatened by the attempts of nationalist parties to decentralize Social Security.

Role of ideas and historical context

Even though Spanish governments have pretended to be sensitive to the recommendations of international institutions and national experts, who have called for reforms that significantly reduce the future financial pressure on the public pension system, they have not actually paid heed to this advice. Like their Socialist forerunners, the PP governments since 1996 definitely improved the lower pensions.[72] They in fact followed an expansionary, even if moderate, pension policy. Their rather autonomous course of action cannot be explained in terms of ideological preferences since the most representative PP leaders probably supported the ideas displayed by the great international economic institutions like the OECD or the World Bank. This strategy has to be elucidated in the light of at least three circumstances: first, Spain ranks as one of the 15 countries of the "old" European Union with lowest pension spending, a fact that makes pension cutbacks more difficult to publicly legitimize; secondly, the financial position of Social Security has experienced a great improvement since the late 1990s, as a consequence of the powerful employment increase as well as of the progressively imposed use of contributions only to cover contributory benefits; thirdly, the PP was eager during its two terms in office to do away with its image as a rightist party, hostile to the workers and the welfare state, ally of well-off people and slave to big business interests.

Nonetheless, the argument that countries should develop a multi-pillar pension system, and bolster private provision, has not fallen on deaf ears in Spain. In fact, the PP governments reconciled policy stability in the first pillar with the creation of powerful fiscal incentives to promote fully-funded voluntary individual pension plans of the third pillar. Thus, they did not relinquish their pension policy preferences; rather they channeled them through the less publicly visible tax policy in order to avoid possible electoral losses, and above all to deactivate the main arguments against them in the discourse of their political opponents. Finally, it should also be stressed that neither the opposition parties nor the trade unions devoted noticeable energy to criticizing these initiatives.

Abbreviations

BNG	*Bloque Nacionalista Galego* / Galician Nationalist Bloc
BOCG	*Boletín Oficial de las Cortes Generales* / Official Bulletin of Congress and Senate
BOE	*Boletín Oficial del Estado* / Official State Bulletin
CCOO	*Comisiones Obreras* / Workers' Commissions
CEOE	*Confederación Española de Organizaciones Empresariales* / Spanish Confederation of Employers' Organizations
CEPYME	*Confederación Española de la Pequeña y Mediana Empresa* / Spanish Confederation of Small and Medium Enterprise
CGT	*Confederación General del Trabajo* / Spanish Confederation of Work
CiU	*Convergència i Unió* / Convergence and Unity
CSIF	*Confederación Sindical Independiente de Funcionarios* / Trade Union Independent Confederation of Civil Servants
ELA-STV	*Solidaridad de Trabajadores Vascos* / Solidarity of Basque Workers
ERC	*Esquerra Republicana de Catalunya* / Republican Left of Catalonia
ESP	Spanish Peseta
ETA	*Euskadi Ta Askatasuna* / Basque Country and Liberty
INP	*Instituto Nacional de Previsión* / National Providence Institute
INSS	*Instituto Nacional de la Seguridad Social* / National Institute of Social Security
INVERCO	*Asociación de Instituciones de Inversión Colectiva y Fondos de Pensiones* / Association of Institutions of Collective Investment and Pension Funds

IU	*Izquierda Unida* / United Left
IRPF	*Impuesto sobre la Renta de las Personas Físicas* / Income Tax of Physical Persons
PCE	*Partido Comunista de España* / Communist Party of Spain
PDP	*Partido Democrático Popular* / Popular Democratic Party
PNV	*Partido Nacionalista Vasco* / Basque Nationalist Party
PP	*Partido Popular* / Popular Party
PSOE	*Partido Socialista Obrero Español* / Spanish Socialist Workers' Party
UCD	*Unión de Centro Democrático* / Democratic Center Union
UDP	*Unión Democrática de Pensionistas y Jubilados de España* / Democratic Union of Pensioners and Retired People
UGT	*Unión General de Trabajadores* / General Union of Workers

Notes

1. The arguments of the OECD and the IMF have been described in the newspaper *El País* (Economía), 03.04.2003 and 27.02.2003.
2. Although the end of the Franco dictatorship is usually identified with the year 1975, I consider the dictatorial period only to have been concluded when the last non-democratic government called elections in April 1977.
3. Bills on constitutional amendments have to be approved by 3/5 of each of the two parliamentary chambers and, if at least 1/10 of parliamentary members of either chamber requires it, ratified by referendum. If the reform concerns the basic definition of the Spanish state and its attributes (language, flag, capital...), the fundamental rights and liberties or the Monarchy, it has to be approved by 2/3 of each of the two Chambers which immediately afterwards are to be dissolved. The newly elected Chambers have to ratify the reform again with a 2/3 majority vote and then submit it to national referendum. See Arts. 167 and 168 of the Spanish Constitution 1978.
4. ETA has been responsible for the deaths of more than 800 people since its creation in 1959.
5. The only really outstanding political intervention of King Juan Carlos since the establishment of democracy took place during the attempted military coup d'état in February 1981. After the Civil Guard (a traditional component of the Spanish State Security Forces) seized Congress and kidnapped the members of parliament present, the King publicly declared his lack of involvement in the coup attempt and ordered the insurgent civil guards and military to hand over their arms.
6. The Basque Country and Navarra enjoy a special financing system (*concierto económico*), according to which they collect taxes but transfer only a part (*cupo*) to the central state. Inversely, Catalonia and the rest of the autonomous communities get from the central state a part of the centrally collected taxes, in order to cover the costs of autonomous competencies.
7. See Organic Law 2/1979 of 3 October, Art. 1.
8. The demographic variable explains that the number of senators appointed by the 17 autonomous communities has varied since 1982 between 46 and 51.
9. In contrast, the Congress, the Senate and the autonomous communities present law proposals (*proposiciones de ley*). The Spanish Constitution also recognizes the popular initiative to present bills under certain circumstances when 500,000 signatures are gathered.

10. Political rights are acquired at the age of 18. Judges and attorneys as well as members of the armed forces and the police in active service are ineligible.
11. The PSOE celebrated primaries to choose the candidate to the presidency of government in the 1998 and 2000 party congresses, but the party executive board has maintained the grip in the writing of electoral lists.
12. For example, in 2003 the Constitutional Court resolved 31 appeals of unconstitutionality, 587 appeals for constitutional protection and 9 competence conflicts. For more details see www.tribunalconstitucional.es/MEMORIAS.htm.
13. The Spanish trade union system includes nonetheless other elements. Thus, the CGT (*Confederación General del Trabajo*) is a minor trade union linked traditionally with the anarchist movement; the (*Confederación Sindical Independiente de Funcionarios*, CSIF) is a sectoral trade union well established among civil servants; at regional level, ELA–STV *Solidaridad de Trabajadores Vascos* and *Intersindical Nacional de Trabajadores Gallegos*, related to nationalist parties of the Basque country and Galicia, have also gained influence in the last years.
14. By 1952, public outlays represented 7% of the national product, nearly five points lower than in 1935 (Comín 1999: 12).
15. The UCD governments implemented a fiscal reform to increase state revenues. This increase, together with the rise in contributions, made possible the expansion of social expenditure. According to data elaborated by Comín (1988: 96), the percentage of expenditure on social benefits in terms of GDP doubled between 1977 and 1982: from 6.8% to 13.8%. In this period Social Security expenditure increased by 8% in real terms (Mota 2002: 316).
16. This position is held by many scholars of Spanish social policy, although one may find critics, like Navarro (2002: 153–75), who link the lack of a fully developed Spanish welfare state to the power of the conservative decision-makers during the transition to democracy.
17. The data included in this paragraph stem from MTAS (2005a) (http://www.mtas.es/estadisticas/ANUARIO2004/index.htm, retrieved December 15, 2005) and INE (2003).
18. These contributions represent the bulk of the total contributions paid by employers and employees, which include other contingencies like unemployment and vocational training. Contributions intended for the coverage of work accidents and professional sickness and for the fund for guaranteeing salaries are only paid by the employer.
19. At the beginning of 1980, the contribution rate amounted to 34.3%. It then went progressively down to 28.8% before it was again increased to 29.3% in 1993. Governments have modified the contribution rates according not only to the financial pressure on the Social Security system, but also to the supposed potential of this parameter to impinge on employment creation.
20. As established in Art. 3 of Law 24/1997 of July 16, 1997.
21. See www.tt.mtas.es/periodico/seguridadsocial/200601/SS20040126.htm. According to the General Law of Budgetary Stability (Law 18/2001 of December 12, 2001) the surplus in the Social Security budget will be applied "with priority" to the Social Security Reserve Fund "with the aim of attending to the future needs of the system". The Law 28/2003 of September 29, 2003 regulating the Social Security Reserve Fund confirms this target.
22. See Royal Decree 2/1992 of January 10, 1992.
23. Although before the approval of the 1997 Law on the Consolidation and Rationalization of the Social Security system, governments did not have a legal mandate to compensate pensioners for such CPI deviations, the Socialist government did so anyway in 1995 and 1996.
24. See MTAS (2005a). It is interesting to note that at the end of 2001 the average retirement pension paid to beneficiaries of the passive classes regime encompassing many civil

servants was €1,117 (http://www.imsersomayores.csic.es/documentos/estadisticas/informe-mayores/2002/cap3/3–61tabla28.xls, retrieved December 15, 2005).
25. The majority of pensioners are nevertheless excluded from paying income tax since pensions under €500 per month (66.6% of all Social Security contributory pensions in 2003) are not taxable.
26. It was not uncommon that wives of middle- and upper-class workers who did not take part in the labor market affiliated to a special regime declaring a fictitious job (for instance household employee) in order to get a pension after ten years paying individual contributions.
27. In fact, Art. 92 of the General Law of Social Security inherited from the Franco regime established that pensions "would be periodically re-valued by the government... taking into account, among other indicative factors, the growth of average wages, the CPI and the general evolution of the economy, as well as the economic capacities of the Social Security system".
28. Approximately 60% of citizens, and a similar percentage of pensioners, were opposed to the conflictual behavior of trade unions (Mota 2002: 295–6). A more detailed description of this controversy can be read in Herce and Pérez-Díaz (1995: 70–1).
29. Law 8/1987 of June 8, 1987. The law distinguishes explicitly between pension plans and pension funds. The former refer to the conditions under which these private pensions are subscribed to, and the latter to the investment instrument of the savings.
30. See *El País* (Economía), 16.11.1986 and 27.11.1986.
31. See *El País* (Economía), 17.04.1987, 13.05.1987, 21.05.1987.
32. See the article by Mariano Rabadán in *El País* (Economía), 23.05.1987.
33. See the article by the CCOO leader José M. de la Parra in *El País* (Economía), 17.03.1988.
34. Amended several times since 1987, at the end of 2002 the second PP government approved a legislative decree (1/2002 of November 29, 2002) comprising all the regulation actually in force and derogating the 1987 law.
35. These data are extracted from www.inverco.es
36. Art. 4 of the Law 20/1989 of July 28, 1989.
37. Art. 71 of the Law 18/1991 of June 6, 1991.
38. Art. 46 of the Law 40/1998 of December 9, 1998 and Royal Decree 1589/1999 of October 15, 1999.
39. Second final disposition of the Law 46/2002 of December 18, 2002.
40. Art. 7 of the Royal Decree 215/1999 of February 5, 1999.
41. See the 17th additional disposition of the Law 40/1998 of December 9, 1998, Art. 7 of the Royal Decree 215/1999 of February 5, 1999, the fourth additional disposition of the Royal Legislative Decree 1/2002 of November 29, 2002 and Art. 61 of the Royal Legislative Decree 3/2004 of March 5, 2004.
42. Art. 60. 7 of the Royal Legislative Decree 3/2004 of March 5, 2004.
43. These plans (*Planes de Previsión Asegurada* or PPAs) have been institutionalized by Law 46/2002 of December 18, 2002. They offer warranted interest rates to their subscribers and are therefore especially designed for risk-averse people.
44. Royal Legislative Decree 1/2002 of November 29, 2002.
45. See *El País* (Economía), 15.10.2003.
46. In December 1988, UGT and CCOO had organized one of the largest strikes in Spanish history against a bill that aimed at making the labor market more flexible by introducing new types of work contracts. During the first months of 1989, negotiations between the government and the trade unions took place, but were finally broken off as the

government refused to accept the demands of trade unions, among them the immediate withdrawal of the bill presented to Congress.
47. Guillén (1999) and Mota (2002) attribute to the trade unions a significant role in the achievement of this incomplete universalization of the Spanish pension system.
48. Non-contributory pensions are paid by Social Security, but from their inception the management was decentralized to the social services institutions of the autonomous communities.
49. See for example *El País* (Economía), 19.06.1991.
50. Data calculated from the *Anuario de Estadísticas Laborales y Asuntos Sociales* 2001 (www.mtas.es).
51. To be paid as an annual extraordinary benefit of around €57.
52. Constitutional Court Sentence, December 11, 2002 (www.tribunalconstitucional.es/Stc2002/STC2002-239.html).
53. Law 52/2003 of December 10, 2003.
54. The studies carried out under the sponsorship of the Administration are MTSS (1995), as well as the first version of the work directed by Herce and Pérez-Díaz (1995). The latter study, published by one of the major Spanish savings banks, belongs in the category of studies sponsored by financial entities, together with the work of Barea, Velarde and González-Páramo (1996). Lastly, the financing of the study by Piñera (1996) was undertaken by an employers' organization.
55. Chuliá (2000) offers a comparison of the different data and arguments provided by these authors.
56. The text of the Pact is published in *Boletín Oficial de las Cortes Generales* (BOCG) E-134, April 12, 1995.
57. Aznar (2004: 76, 125) hints repeatedly at this issue in his memoirs.
58. For this purpose the effective CPI of the year t_1 is measured from November t_{-1} to November t_1.
59. Data calculated from MTAS (1998).
60. See Royal Decree 2064/1999 of December 30, 1999.
61. The exemption applies to contributions for "common contingencies" (except for temporary inability).
62. Law 35/2002 of July 12, 2002.
63. See *El País* (Negocios), 10.11.2002.
64. See *El País* (Negocios), 15.06.2003.
65. The report was published in BOCG, D, 596, October 2, 2003.
66. *Diario de Sesiones del Congreso de los Diputados*, 7th legislature, number 284.
67. See *Bulletin EU* 1/2, 2003; *El País*, 30.01.2003.
68. See Royal Decree 1425/2002 of December 27, 2002.
69. See Royal Decree 2/2004 of January 9, 2004.
70. See Table 11.3. Foreign people represented in 1992 0,9% (c 400.000 people) of the population living in Spain; at the beginning of 2005 the Municipal Register (*Padrón Municipal*) gave the figure of nearly 3,692,000 foreigners living in Spain, i.e. 8.5% of the population. By that time, the foreigners affiliated to Social Security amounted to around 1,112,000 (Garrido 2005).
71. Data calculated from MTAS (2005b) (http://www.mtas.es/estadisticas/BEL/index.htm, retrieved July 15, 2005). On July 13, 2006 the government of Rodríguez Zapatero signed the Agreement on Social Security Measures with the trade unions CCOO and UGT, and the employers' associations CEOE and CEPYME. The content of this Agreement on which the government is going to prepare a bill can be summarized in five points:

1) advance in separation of financing sources of contributory and non-contributory benefits; 2) amelioration of minimum supplements to pensions for permanent invalidity and widow (er)hood; 3) establishment of a minimum period of full 15 years (5.475days) to be eligible for an old age pension (previously 180 months which, taking into consideration 14 monthly payments per year, could be obtained with less than 13 full years); 4) new measures to incentivize postponement of retirement age, and 5) rationalization of special regimes for farmers. All these measures can be deemed as incrementalist and in line with the Toledo Pact.

72. Mainly re-valuing some benefits above the expected CPI, but also increasing the percentage to be applied to the regulatory base. The latter condition concerns widow(er)s, whose pensions have grown as a consequence of the increase in that percentage. Initially established at 45% of the regulatory base of the deceased worker (Decree 3158/1966 of December 23, 1966), it has been gradually increased since 2001 to 52% (see Royal Decrees 1465/2001, 1425/2002 and 1795/2003).

Bibliography

Primary sources and government documents

Boletín Oficial del Estado (BOE) (www.boe.es/iberlex) [legislation data base]

Boletín Oficial de las Cortes Generales (BOCG) (www.congreso.es) [parliamentary debates and other official publications of Congress]

Instituto Nacional de Estadística (INE) (2003). *Indicadores Sociales 2003*. Madrid: INE (http://www.ine.es/prodyser/pubweb/indisoc03/indisoc03.htm, retrieved 15 December 2005).

Ministerio de Trabajo y Asuntos Sociales (MTAS) (2005a). *Anuario de Estadísticas Laborales y Asuntos Sociales 2004*. Madrid: MTAS (http://www.mtas.es/estadisticas/ANUARIO2004/welcome.htm, retrieved 15 December 2005).

Ministerio de Trabajo y Asuntos Sociales (MTAS) (2005b). *Boletín de Estadísticas Laborales. Noviembre 2005*. Madrid: MTAS (http://www.mtas.es/estadisticas/BEL/index.htm, retrieved 15 December 2005).

Ministerio de Trabajo y Asuntos Sociales (MTAS) (1998). *Anuario de Estadísticas Laborales y Asuntos Sociales 1997*. Madrid: MTAS.

Secondary sources

AGUILAR, PALOMA (2002). *Memory and Amnesia. The Role of the Spanish Civil War in the Transition to Democracy*. Oxford: Berghahn Books.

AZNAR, JOSÉ MARÍA (2004). *Ocho años de gobierno. Una visión personal de España*. Barcelona: Planeta.

BAREA, JOSÉ, JOSÉ M. GONZÁLEZ-PÁRAMO and JUAN VELARDE (Dir.) (1996). *Pensiones y prestaciones por desempleo*. Bilbao: Fundación BBV.

BARRADA, ALFONSO (1999). *El gasto público de bienestar social en España de 1964 a 1995*, Bilbao: Fundación BBV.

CHULIÁ, ELISA (2000). *El Pacto de Toledo y la política de pensiones*. ASP Research Paper 33(a). Madrid: ASP, Gabinete de Estudios.

COLOMER, JOSEP M. (1997). "Las instituciones de la crispación política". *Claves de Razón Práctica*, 74: 44–7.

—— (1998). "The Spanish 'State of Autonomies': Non-institutional Federalism". In Heywood, P. (ed.), *Politics and Policy in Democratic Spain* 40–52. London: Frank Cass.

—— (2004). "Breve historia del sistema electoral en España". *Claves de Razón Práctica*, 140: 34–9.

—— (2005). "The general election in Spain, March 2004". *Electoral Studies* 24: 149–56.

Comín, Francisco (1996). *Historia de la Hacienda Pública, II. España (1808–1995)*. Barcelona: Grijalbo Mondadori.
Fernández Orrico, Francisco J. (2002). *Las pensiones no contributivas y la asistencia social en España*. Madrid: CES.
Fishman, Robert (1990). *Working-Class Organization and the Return to Democracy in Spain*. Ithaca, NY: Cornell University Press.
García, Emma, Herce, José Antonio and Jimeno, Juan Francisco (2005). *La reforma de las pensiones. El papel de los mercados financieros*. La Coruña: Fundación Caixa Galicia.
Garrido, Luis (2005). "La inmigración en España". In González, J. J., and Requena, M. (eds.), *Tres décadas de cambio social en España*. Madrid: Alianza Editorial, 127–64.
—— and Elisa Chuliá (2005). *Ocupación, formación y el futuro de la jubilación en España*. Madrid: Consejo Económico y Social.
Gillespie, Richard (1989). The Spanish Socialist Party: a History of Factionalism. Oxford: Oxford University Press.
—— (1990). "The break-up of the "socialist family": party–union relations in Spain, 1982–1989". *West European Politics*, 13: 47–62.
Guillén, Ana M. (1990). "The Emergence of the Spanish Welfare State 1876–1923: the Role of Ideas in the Policy Process". Working Paper 1990/10 of the Centro de Estudios Avanzados en Ciencias Sociales. Madrid: Instituto Juan March de Estudios e Investigaciones.
—— (1999). *Pension Reform in Spain (1975–1997): The Role of Organized Labour*. EUI Working Paper 99/6. Florence: European University Institute.
Herce, José Antonio and Victor Pérez-Díaz (eds.) (1995). *La reforma del sistema público de pensiones en España*. Barcelona: La Caixa.
—— and Alonso, Javier (1998). "Los efectos económicos de la Ley de Consolidación de la Seguridad Social. Perspectivas financieras del sistema de pensiones tras su entrada en vigor", *FEDEA, Documento de Trabajo 98–16*. Madrid.
—— (2002). "El sistema de pensiones en España. Situación y perspectivas". *Mercado de Valores*, May: 28–39.
—— Simón Sosvilla, Sonsoles Castillo, et al. (1996). *El futuro de las pensiones en España: hacia un sistema mixto*. Barcelona: La Caixa.
Holzmann, Robert, Orenstein, Mitchell and Rutkowski, Michael (eds.) (2003). *Pension Reform in Europe: Process and Progress*. Washington: IBRD/World Bank.
Hopkin, Jonathan (1999). *Party Formation and Democratic Transition in Spain: The Creation and Collapse of the Union of the Democratic Centre*. London/New York: Macmillan/St Martin's Press.
—— (2005). "Spain: Proportional Representation with Majoritarian Outcomes". In Gallagher, M. and Mitchell, P. (eds.), *The Politics of Electoral Systems*. Oxford: Oxford University Press, 375–94.
Jiménez, Fernando (2006). "El sistema político español contemporáneo". In Sodaro, M., Politica *ciencia política: una introducción*. Madrid: McGraw-Hill, 269–95.
Lecher, Wolfgang and Reinhard Naumann (1994). "The Current State of Trade Unions in the EU Member States". In Wolfgang Lecher, *Trade Unions in the European Union*, 3–126. London: Lawrence and Wishart.
Linz, Juan J. (1987). "Un siglo de política e intereses en España". In Giner S. and M. Pérez Yruela (eds.), *El corporatismo en España*. Barcelona: Ariel.
—— and José Ramón Montero (1999). *The Party Systems of Spain: Old Cleavages and New Challenges*. Estudio/Working Paper 139 of the Centro de Estudios Avanzados en Ciencias Sociales. Madrid: Instituto Juan March de Estudios e Investigaciones.
Magone, José M. (2004). *Contemporary Spanish Politics*, London: Routledge.

Maravall, José María, and Julián Santamaría (1986). "Political Change in Spain and the Prospects for Democracy". In O'Donnell, G., Schmitter, P. C., et al. (eds.), *Transition from Authoritarian Rule. Southern Europe*, 71–108. Baltimore: Johns Hopkins University Press.

Mielke, Siegfried, Rütters, Peter, and Tudyka, Kurt P. (1994). "Trade Union Organisation and Employee Representation". In Lecher, W. (ed.), *Trade Unions in the European Union*, 129–233. London: Lawrence and Wishart.

Ministerio de Trabajo y Seguridad Social (MTSS) (1996). *La Seguridad Social en el umbral del siglo XXI*. Madrid: MTSS.

Molíns, Joaquim M. and Alex Casademunt (1999). "Pressure groups and the articulation of interests". In Heywood, P. (ed.), *Politics and Policy in Democratic Spain*, 124–146. London: Frank Cass.

Mota, Rosalía (2002). *Regímenes, partidos y políticas de suficiencia en pensiones de jubilación. La experiencia española*. Madrid: Instituto Juan March de Estudios e Investigaciones/Centro de Estudios Avanzados en Ciencias Sociales.

Myles, John, and Paul Pierson (2001). "The Comparative Political Economy of Pension Reform", in Pierson, P. (ed.), *The New Politics of the Welfare State*, 305–333. Oxford: Oxford University Press.

Navarro, Vicenç (2002). *Bienestar insuficiente, democracia incompleta. Sobre lo que no se habla en nuestro país*. Barcelona: Anagrama.

Pérez-Díaz, Víctor (1993). *The Return of Civil Society. The Emergence of Democratic Spain*. Cambridge: Cambridge University Press.

Pino, Eloísa del (2003). "¿Qué esperan los ciudadanos del gobierno? Las expectativas sobre las políticas de bienestar en España". *Sistema* 172: 55–83.

Piñera, José (1996). *Una propuesta de reforma del sistema de pensiones en España*. Madrid: Círculo de Empresarios.

Rhodes, Martin (1997). *Globalization, Labour Markets and Welfare States: A Future of "Competitive Corporatis"?* EUI Working Paper 97/36. Florence: European University Institute.

Rodríguez, Juan Carlos (2000). "Pensiones y opinión pública española en febrero de 2000". *ASP Separatas* 8, Madrid: ASP, Gabinete de Estudios.

Serrano Pérez, Felipe, Miguel A. García Díaz, and Carlos Bravo Fernández (2004). *El sistema español de pensiones. Un proyecto viable desde un enfoque económico*. Barcelona: Ariel.

United Nations Population Division (2005). *World Population Prospects. The 2004 Revision. Volume II. Sex and Age Distribution of the World Population*. New York: UNO (http://www.un.org/esa/population/publications/WPP2004/wpp2004.htm, retrieved 15 December 2005).

CHAPTER 12

AUSTRIA: FROM ELECTORAL CARTELS TO COMPETITIVE COALITION-BUILDING

ISABELLE SCHULZE

MARTIN SCHLUDI

I INTRODUCTION[1]

ALTHOUGH pension policy was a central political issue in Austria throughout the 1980s and 1990s—as seen in debates over budget legislation, in electoral campaigns, and in protests on the streets—political discourse was not matched by far-reaching pension reforms. The impact of the reform efforts of the "grand coalition" governments of the traditional dominant parties—the Socialist SPÖ and the Catholic Conservative ÖVP—was limited, with very modest changes that did not fundamentally alter the overall structure of the public pension system (Schludi 2005: 166 ff.).

Whereas the classical grand coalition governments in Austria of the 1950s and 1960s had been based on a cartel-like division of the electorate among the parties, according to three traditional pre-war camps or "Lager"—socialist, catholic and national-liberal—pension politics in the 1980s and 1990s was conducted in the context of greatly increased party competition.

There were two causes for this increased competition: first, a changing and more fragmented party system, and second, a modified electoral system. The Austrian Freedom Party's decision to re-style itself as a right-wing populist party and to name the notorious Jörg Haider as leader was highly-successful in electoral terms, but this success had a price: until 2000, the Freedom Party was considered unfit for coalition government. Consequently, the dominant parties faced competition from the extreme right, but also jockeyed for position as the senior partner of their grand coalitions. This increased political competition was exacerbated by a change in the electoral system, which provided for a more personalized vote and smaller electoral districts. Finally, as in nearly all Western European nations, electoral volatility had increased.

Consequently, the SPÖ and ÖVP leaderships feared electoral punishment from their core constituencies. Suggested reforms for the private sector pension system were diluted and countervailed with cuts in civil servants' pension schemes. Intra-party conflicts within and between the Social Democrats and the People's Party and their affiliated unions, forced governments to make major concessions. Indeed, representatives of unions in parliament were in a position to veto reforms by voting against them—and did so. To make matters worse, state-level party politicians began to pressure their parliamentary peers to break with party discipline on retrenchment issues, because national pension politics were costing them votes at the state level. Thus, despite sustained efforts to introduce a series of consolidation measures, one by one each proposal was watered down to suit constituency interests.

The emergence of an ÖVP/FPÖ coalition in 2000 and the rapid decline in the union affiliation of parliamentary representatives greatly increased the tempo and severity of pension retrenchment and restructuring, although intra-party opposition in the context of regional electoral competition has slowed these efforts. At the same time the consensual policy-making that used to be typical for Austrian corporatism has declined in importance.

II Political system

Constitutional history and nation-building

The Austrian Constitution dates back to 1920. Colonial forces (*Heimwehren*) composed of rural armed bourgeoisie blamed parliamentarianism for the Austrian economic crisis of the late 1920s. The *Heimwehren* proclaimed in an oath (the *Kroneuburger Eid*) on May 18, 1930 their intention to take power, overthrow parliamentarianism, fight liberalism and establish a corporative state. A workers' uprising against the restrictions on unions and civil rights failed in February 1934. Chancellor Engelbert Dollfuß, attempting to combat threats from both sides of the political spectrum, proclaimed a corporative state (*Ständestaat*) on May 1, 1934 (Klenner and Pellar 1999: 272, 297). The idea was a system based on self-governing occupational ranks—a kind of "industrial democracy" (Maderthaner 1997: 166). This history constitutes the background for the strong democratic-corporatist ties between the social partners and Austrian governments, including the statutory occupational chambers, in the decades after World War II. Pension politics has long followed the path of tripartite policy-making, with emphasis on negotiated consensus. But in the 1990s corporatism eroded, especially after the advent of the ÖVP/FPÖ government in the year 2000.

Institutions of government

The Head of State is the President (*Bundespräsident*) who is directly elected for a 6-year term. Although the constitution provides the President with great powers (Arts. 29 I, 46, 70 and 80 B-VG), de facto, the President has abstained from using his power and restricts himself to representing the Republic internationally (Art. 65 B-VG; see also Pelinka and Rosenberger 2000: 116).

The President appoints the Head of the Government or Chancellor (*Bundeskanzler*, Art. 69 B-VG). The President generally nominates the leader of the party with the most seats in the Lower Chamber. If election outcomes are ambiguous, however, the *Bundespräsident* can exert considerable power in the government formation process and is free to nominate a *formateur* (mediator) of his choice.[2] There is no formal investiture vote but the chancellor or any minister can be displaced by a vote of no confidence in Parliament (Art. 74 B-VG). By custom the cabinet takes decisions unanimously (Müller 2000b: 90–1, 104; 1997b: 127).

Austria is a centralized federal state with nine states (*Bundesländer*), but the individual states do not have much power (Art. 2 I B-VG), since the states' legislative competences are restricted and national finances are the exclusive prerogative of the national government. Seven out of the nine states have a proportional government, which means that cabinet seats are allocated in proportion to their share of mandates in the state Parliament (*Landtag*). The consequences are long-term stability of state governments and the electorate's inability to punish state governments for unpopular policies (Pelinka 1999: 490; Fallend 1997: 23–5). However, the difficulty of establishing different policy profiles at the state-level has increasingly brought national political issues—including pension policy—into state election campaigns.

The *Nationalrat* and the *Bundesrat* are the two chambers of the national Parliament. Parliamentary work is predominantly done in standing committees that follow the structure of governmental departments. Only members of a party group or *Klub*,

Table 12.1 Political institutions in Austria

Political arenas	Actors	Rules of investiture	Rules of decision-making	Veto potential
Executive	President (Bundespräsident)	6-year term; directly elected by absolute majority of votes (if necessary two ballots)	Signs the legislative acts	Not a veto point
	Chancellor (Bundeskanzler)	Appointed by the President; no formal investiture vote but sometimes assuming office is linked to a vote of no confidence, requiring a majority of votes with a quorum of 50% of the members	Initiates legislation	—
Legislative	Chamber of Deputies (Nationalrat)	4-year term; proportional representation in three-tier constituencies (1 national, 9 state and 43 regional); can be dissolved by the President on chancellor's request or can dissolve itself by majority decision	Right of initiative; decision-making by majority of votes with quorum of 1/3; can overrule *Bundesrat*'s objection (*Beharrungsbeschluss*); constitutional amendments require a two-thirds majority with a quorum of 50%	Not a veto point due to majority governments and strong party discipline
	Senate (Bundesrat)	Terms dependent on state government terms; elected by the state parliaments according to party strength in the *Landtag*; at least one seat for the second largest party seats per state: Burgenland 3, Kärnten 5, Niederösterreich 12, Oberösterreich 11, Salzburg 4, Steiermark 10, Tirol 5, Vorarlberg 3, Wien 11	1/3 of members have right of initiative; can delay legislation for a maximum of 8 weeks	Not a veto point only suspensive objection
Judicial	Constitutional Court (Verfassungsgerichtshof)	Appointed by the *Bundespräsident* upon government recommendation; president, vice-president and 12 other members plus 6 backup members	Surveys constitutionality of legislation upon request; Parliament can deprive the court of its revision power by passing	Not a veto point if government has a 2/3 majority

		legislation with a 2/3 majority in the *Nationalrat*	post-legislative veto point if government has no 2/3 majority
Electoral	Referendum	Decision to call referendum by majority of *Nationalrat* members	Not a veto point
		Popular initiative – requiring signatures of 100,000 voters or of 1/3 of voters in 3 states – can also instigate referendum	
Territorial Units	States (*Länder*) communities (*Gemeinden*)	*Länder*: Proportional governments according to parties' share of mandates (*Proporzregierungen*) *Gemeinden*: parliamentary community councils; directly elected mayors in some states	*Länder*: indirect influence via *Bundesrat* *Gemeinden*: no formal influence on national legislation	Not a veto point

which requires a minimum of five members of parliament, may participate in committees (Pelinka 1999: 492–93; Pelinka and Rosenberger 2000: 98–99). The *Bundesländer* are represented in the second chamber, the *Bundesrat*. The composition of the *Bundesrat* changes often since members of the state parliaments elect their 62 members for the duration of the states' parliamentary term. The *Landtage* elect the delegates according to the share of seats of each party in the states' parliaments, with the prerequisite that the second strongest party of a *Landtag* receives at least one seat for the state in the *Bundesrat*. The *Bundesrat* members have a free mandate that is to say they are not bound to follow state orders and usually vote in the interest of their party (www.nationalrat.at/pd/doep/e-k3-2.htm).

An independent Constitutional Court (*Verfassungsgerichtshof*, VfGH) may verify the constitutionality of legislation and revoke laws (Arts. 89 II, 140 I B-VG). However, Parliament can circumvent the court's revision power by passing a law with a two-thirds majority, which grants the law constitutional significance. As we shall see, this was a strategy frequently used between 1987 and 1999, for example, in the reform of the female retirement age in 1992 (Obinger 2001: 12; Tálos and Kittel 2001: 60).

Electoral system

The 183 members of the *Nationalrat* are directly elected for a 4-year term by proportional representation (Arts. 26, 27 B-VG; see also NRWO 2001: §§1–3). The President may call an early election upon the Chancellor's request (Pelinka 1999: 494).

An electoral reform in 1992 established 43 regional districts and introduced preference votes (Fischer 1997: 102; Müller 1997a: 216). Both elements tightened the link between voters and candidates; politicians became more directly accountable to the voters. However, at the same time, the 1992 electoral reform established a three-level mechanism of mandate distribution. Every voter has one vote, but the ballot structure enables voters to select a specific candidate within the party of their choice—a so-called personalized electoral system (NRWO 2001: §36(32), §79; see also Pelinka 1999: 504). The distribution of mandates takes place on three levels: 43 regional districts (*Regionalwahlkreise*), 9 state districts (*Landeswahlkreise*) and one national district (Müller 1997a: 217). The number of mandates per electoral district depends on population size. Mandates on the regional and state levels are calculated using the Hare method; mandate distribution on the national level follows the d'Hondt method. Only parties that obtain at least 4 percent of the national votes or win one mandate on the regional level are entitled to take part in the third round of mandate distribution (NRWO 2001: §§100–101; Neuwirth 2003).

The national compensation of votes on the third level should guarantee the proportionality of votes to seats in the *Nationalrat*. Yet, parties can only take part in the third level distribution if they have won at least one regional district seat or 4 percent of the nationwide vote. Thus, the parties must do well at the regional level, and national level politicians cultivate their local roots. Consequently, the electoral system is ambivalent in that it creates incentives that foster both nationwide interests and local/regional interests. Moreover, the fact that Austrian parties are organized according to state constituencies in the national electoral system implies the strong attachment of politicians at the national level with their "home" constituencies. The elections of October 1994 were the first elections after the electoral reform of 1992. Not only the parties, but also candidates from the same party, ran against each other in 43 regional electoral districts on a first level, as well as in the old nine state districts. Voters now had the chance to use the so-called preference vote to rank politicians in a different order than on the party list. Politicians of all colors expected that the preference vote would increase the competition within parties' executive boards, and that the national parties' grip on candidates might loosen (*Profil* 03.01.1994). Further, the complexity of the new system—as well as the uncertainty associated with the first elections following the introduction of a new electoral law—increased the uncertainty of the dominant parties, and caused them to fight for every vote. The new electoral mechanism is complicated, and electoral outcomes are more difficult to predict. Thus, faced with great uncertainty over electoral outcomes, SPÖ and ÖVP took few risks in their fight for plurality and the Chancellorship in the mid-1990s.

Legislative process

There are four ways to initiate legislation: a bill can be introduced by a unanimous decision in cabinet, by a member of the *Nationalrat* with the support of a fraction, by at least one-third of the members of the *Bundesrat*, or by petition for a referendum, that is, the signatures of 100,000 voters or one-third of the voters in at least three states (Tálos and Kittel 2001: 37). Usually, a formalized pre-parliamentary process starts when the government sends out a proposal for comment by the ministries, federal offices, state governments, and the occupational chambers. Afterwards the cabinet takes a decision on the bill but there is no legal obligation to take into account the comments made during the appraisal process. Analysts have criticized this form of pre-parliamentary decision-making for its lack of transparency, and for taking decisions away from Parliament (Pelinka and Rosenberger 2000: 106).

Bills are first submitted to the *Nationalrat*. This house may consider the bill in a first reading but usually transfers it directly to the committee stage. The committees deliberate the specific clauses, may consult experts, modify and amend the bill, usually in non-public sessions. A *rapporteur* presents the committee's decisions to the *Nationalrat*. The second reading is a detailed debate and concludes with voting on the bill. A bill is adopted if it achieves a majority of the votes, if at least one-third of the members is present. Abstention is impossible but parliamentarians may leave the hall before the call for voting. The third reading of the bill deals with misspellings and stylistic defects (*Nationalrat* 2003). Members of parliament generally adhere to party discipline, although, more recently, it has been weakening (Pelinka and Rosenberger 2000: 109–10).

After the *Nationalrat* has passed a bill, the *Bundesrat* can object to the decision within eight weeks. If the *Bundesrat* takes a bill into deliberation, in most cases (98%) the *Bundesrat* decides explicitly "not to object." Decisions are taken by majority vote. The *Bundesrat*'s objection only has suspensive veto power; if the *Nationalrat* confirms the original decision with at least half of its members present the law is adopted (Art. 42 B-VG, see also Obinger 2001: 15–16). Thus, the Bundesrat is not a veto player or a veto point. Therefore the *Bundesrat*'s decision is not usually the focus of public interest, and is treated as being of minor importance in the literature (e.g. Pelinka and Rosenberger 2000: 110). However, as will be shown later in this chapter, in the 2003 pension reform, there were occasions when the *Bundesrat* used this symbolic

Party family affiliation	Abbreviation	Party name	Ideological orientation	Founding and merger details	Year established
Christian Parties	ÖVP	Austrian People's Party (*Österreichische Volkspartei*)	Conservative, center-right, catholic	Successor to the Christian-Social Party	(1889) 1945
Left Parties and Social-Democratic parties	SPÖ	Austrian Social-Democratic Party (*Sozialdemokratische Partei Österreichs*)	Center-left	Founded as Social-Democratic Labor Party in 1889, renamed Socialist Party in 1945, and renamed again 1991	1889
Greens	GA	Green Alternative (*Die Grüne Alternative*)	Ecological and peace-keeping ideology; social justice	Founded as lose electoral alliance in 1986 (merger of *Alternative Liste Österreichs* and *Vereinigte Grüne Österreichs*); party organization since 1992	1986
Liberal Parties	FPÖ	Freedom Party of Austria (*Freiheitliche Partei Österreichs*)	Since 1986 radical right, xenophobic, rejects EU-membership, pro-NATO membership	Founded as League of Independents (*Verband der Unabhängigen*) in 1949 renamed Austrian Freedom Party in 1955, renamed again in 1995	1955
	LIF	Liberal Forum (*Liberales Forum*)	Liberal	Founded by 5 FPÖ-dissidents because of FPÖ's anti-Europe policy	1993

Fig. 12.1 Party system in Austria

Sources: Müller (2000b); Day (2002); Jacobs (1989: 487); Munzinger (2003).

power and attracted media attention. The legislative process concludes with the President's signature and the promulgation of the act in the Federal Law Gazette (*Bundesgesetzblatt*).

Parties and elections

Three parties have dominated the Austrian party system since the end of World War II: the Social-Democrats (*Sozialdemokratische Partei Österreichs*, SPÖ), the People's Party (*Österreichische Volkspartei*, ÖVP) and the liberal Freedom Party (*Die Freiheitlichen*, FPÖ). Since 1987, the Greens, and from 1994 to 1999 the Liberal Forum were added to the parliamentary party spectrum. The two strongest parties combined, SPÖ and ÖVP, were able to win over 90 percent of votes and seats in parliamentary elections throughout the 1970s and early 1980s, so the party system resembled a two-party system. However, the SPÖ's and ÖVP's share of the vote dropped to 60 percent in 1999, but rebounded to 79 percent in 2002 (Pelinka and Rosenberger 2000: 135).

Traditionally, the ÖVP attracts voters from farmers, the self-employed, rural areas and Catholics. The SPÖ customarily recruits its electorate from blue collar workers and city dwellers, but the working class linkage is declining in importance (Pelinka 1999: 506; Jacobs 1989: 483–4, 489). The SPÖ dominates the Austrian Trade Union Federation (ÖGB). Growing numbers of young urban voters choose new parties or switch frequently between parties making them an important target group for electoral campaigns, both for SPÖ and ÖVP. Furthermore, both parties have shown tendencies towards inner-party federalism, in that *Länder*-party politicians have gained increasing power in policy decisions on the national level. As a consequence, national policy, including pension policy, has had a direct effect on party competition on the state level (Müller 1997a: 228, 231). The parties within the proportional state coalitions have little opportunity to distinguish themselves from their opponents as they strive for a relative majority in the *Länder*-governments. As the state election of Oberösterreich in 2003 demonstrated, electoral *Länder* campaigns are no less intense than national campaigns.

Neither socialist nor Catholic, the FPÖ has been called a party of the "third camp." It is characterized by a decentralized party structure with regional strongholds, low party membership and high voter volatility (Luther 1997: 286). After two decades of isolation following World War II the FPÖ strived for public acceptance and gained government participation between 1983 and 1986, as part of the SPÖ/FPÖ coalition that ended "the SPÖ and ÖVP's monopoly over government" (Luther 1987: 378). Conflict within the FPÖ culminated in the election of a new party leader in 1986, when Jörg Haider replaced Norbert Steger (Luther 1987: 395). Under Haider's leadership the party won a considerable share of the vote. But due to its populist right-wing ideology the SPÖ has not considered the FPÖ a viable coalition partner since 1986. After 13 years of a grand coalition, the FPÖ regained government participation in 2000. The FPÖ attracts nationalistic voters, unemployed blue-collar

Table 12.2 Governmental majorities in Austria

Election date Nationalrat	Start of gov.	Head of gov. (party)	Governing parties	Gov. majority (% seats) NR	Gov. electoral base (% votes) NR	Gov. majority (% seats) BR[a]	Institutional veto points	Number of veto players (partisan + institutional)
05.06.1979	06.05.1979	Kreisky (SPÖ)	SPÖ (95)	51.9%	51.0%	50.0%	VfGH[b]	1 + 1
		Kreisky (SPÖ)	SPÖ (95)	51.9%	51.0%	49.2%	VfGH	1 + 1
04.24.1983	05.24.1983	Sinowatz (SPÖ)	SPÖ (90), FPÖ (12)	55.7%	52.6%	49.2%	VfGH	2 + 1
	06.16.1986	Vranitzky I (SPÖ)	SPÖ (90), FPÖ (12)	55.7%	52.6%	47.6%	VfGH	2 + 1
11.23.1986	01.21.1987	Vranitzky II (SPÖ)	SPÖ (80), ÖVP (77)	85.8%	84.4%	100.0%	None	2 + 0
10.07.1990	12.17.1990	Vranitzky III (SPÖ)	SPÖ (80), ÖVP (60)	76.5%	74.8%	92.1%	None	2 + 0
10.09.1994	11.30.1994	Vranitzky IV (SPÖ)	SPÖ (65), ÖVP (52)	63.9%	62.6%	81.3%	VfGH	2 + 1
12.17.1995	03.12.1996	Vranitzky V (SPÖ)	SPÖ (71), ÖVP (53)	67.8%	66.4%	79.7%	None	2 + 0
[c]	01.28.1997	Klima (SPÖ)	SPÖ (71), ÖVP (52)	67.2%	66.3%	78.1%	None	2 + 0
10.03.1999	02.04.2000	Schüssel I (ÖVP)	ÖVP (52), FPÖ (52)	56.8%	53.8%	65.6%	VfGH	2 + 1
11.24.2002	02.28.2003	Schüssel II (ÖVP)	ÖVP (79), FPÖ (18)	53.0%	52.3%	64.5%	VfGH	2 + 1

[a] Includes changes in seat distribution in the Bundesrat (BR) following a state election when relevant for government majority in BR.
[b] Constitutional Court is a post-legislative veto point as government did not have a 2/3 majority.
[c] In some districts the elections in 1995 were successfully challenged and had to be re-run.

Sources: www.parlament.gv.at/portal/page?_pageid=886,81259&_dad=portal&_schema=PORTAL; www.bmi.gv.at/wahlen/nrw_history.asp http://sunsite.univie.ac.at/Austria/elections/

workers, and young male voters (Pelinka and Rosenberger 2000: 137–8; Hofinger and Ogris 1996: 6).

The origins of the Green party can be traced back to the protests against the nuclear power plant in Zwentendorf. The two movements *Alternative Liste Österreichs* (ALÖ) and *Vereinigte Grüne Österreichs* (VGÖ) merged into the *Grüne Alternative* and ran together for the national elections in 1986 (Pelinka and Rosenberger 2000: 137). The Liberal Forum (LIF) was founded by five FPÖ dissidents in 1993 who did not agree with the anti-EU and the xenophobic position of the FPÖ-leader Haider.

Interest groups

Interest group representation in Austria is based on two pillars: privately organized interest representation and statutory occupational chambers. The Austrian Trade Union Federation (*Österreichischer Gewerkschaftsbund*, ÖGB) is an umbrella organization of 13 individual trade unions, with the Federation controlling strike decisions, finances and personnel (Karlhofer 2001: 342). This legal foundation contributes to a very centralized unionism. The Union of Public Services GÖD is the only union with strong ties to the ÖVP; all other unions display rather strong ties to the SPÖ despite their formal independence. The League of Austrian Industrialists (*Vereinigung österreichischer Industrieller*, VÖI) represents the 2,000 most important employers in the industrial sector. Its political influence is based on its financial power rather than membership density.

Austria is known for its unique system of "occupational" chambers with mandatory membership. The chambers are public corporations and constitutionally anchored (Art. 10 B-VG; Pelinka and Rosenberger 2000: 168; *Profil* 13.07.1987). The three most important chambers are the Economic Chamber (*Wirtschaftskammer*, WK) unifying employers and self-employed, the Chamber of Labor (*Kammer für Arbeiter und Angestellte*, AK) and the Office of the Austrian Chambers of Agriculture (*Präsidentenkonferenz der Landwirtschaftskammern Österreichs*, Präko). The chambers' boards are elected by their members on a regular basis with choices between fractions that mirror the political parties (Pelinka and Rosenberger 2000: 168–71; Karlhofer 2001: 343).

Austria was long a model of traditional corporatism (Lehmbruch 1979: 157). The social partners have both formal and informal instruments to participate in political decisions: social partnership, institutionalized in the parity commission (*Paritätische Kommission*), deals mainly with voluntary price controls and wage negotiations (Pelinka and Rosenberger 2000: 173–74). The process of appraisal also gives the chambers a formal way of commenting on government policy. Moreover, corporate interests are often involved in commissions set up to sound out reform options. Due to office accumulation, the chairmen of interest organizations, who are also parliamentary deputies, may also affect the legislative debate directly (Tálos 1999: 282; Karlhofer 1999: 31). In 1987, about a quarter of all Austrian members of parliament, 17 percent of ÖVP deputies and more than 40 percent of SPÖ deputies, were trade union functionaries. As we shall see, this double representation was crucial for the promotion of union constituency interests in pension politics.

However, studies of Austrian policy-making in the 1990s show that both social partnership and corporatist structures are changing. Recent developments make cooperation between the government and the chambers more difficult, as conflicts are no longer exclusively organized along the cleavage between labor and capital (*Profil* 13.07.1987; Tálos and Kittel 1999: 156–7). Whereas some authors see continuation of the Austrian pattern of concertation and social partnership in spite of changes (Kittel 1998: 297), others perceive a decline in corporatism (Tálos 1999: 279). A strong indication for the declining influence of the social partners is the rapid decline of union representation in the *Nationalrat* in recent years. Within the SPÖ fraction the share of trade union functionaries fell by more than 50 percent between 1987 and 2000. At the same time trade union functionaries disappeared almost completely from the parliamentary group of the ÖVP (for details see Tálos and Kittel 2001: 73).

Other interest groups pale by comparison with the labor market partners. For instance, representation of pensioners is quite formalized with the Austrian Council of Senior Citizens (*österreichischer Seniorenrat*), with the right to participate in the process of appraisal since April 2000 (www.seniorenrat.at/history_p.html). However, since the parties' pensioners' sub-divisions (*Pensionistenverband*, SPÖ, *Seniorenbund*, ÖVP, *Seniorenring*, FPÖ) constitute the Council of Senior Citizens, partisan differences are transferred into the Council and the body cannot be counted as a strong independent actor in pension politics.

The main associations of financial institutions in Austria are the Association of Banks and Bankers (*Verband österreichischer Banken und Bankiers*, VOeBB) and the Association of Insurance Companies (*Verband der Versicherungsunternehmen Osterreichs*, VVO). However, these interest groups did not take a prominent role in pension politics in the 1980s and 1990s.

III Pension system

Historical overview

The first compulsory pension system was introduced in Austria for white-collar workers on December 16, 1906. It covered the risks of old age, disability and death. In 1926, pension insurance, together with health, unemployment and accident insurance, was divided along occupational lines, resulting in four separate insurance schemes: one each for civil servants, white-collar employees, blue-collar workers and agricultural workers. At the same time legislation provided for early retirement for men at age 60, and women at 55 (Hofmeister 1981: 620, 640–2).

In September 1955, the General Social Security Act (*Allgemeines Sozialversicherungsgesetz* or (ASVG)) combined the fragmented existing legislation on social security. Although organized in different schemes, eligibility criteria were harmonized for blue- and white-collar workers. Compulsory state pension coverage was introduced for the self-employed in 1957 and for farmers in 1969 (Bertuleit 1999: 5; Feher 2001: 2). One of the major changes was the Pension Adjustment Act (*Pensionsanpassungsgesetz*) of April 28, 1965, introducing annual revaluations of both pension entitlements and pensions, according to wage and price increases. The 1970s saw the following changes: introduction of substitute qualifying periods, that is, periods of unemployment, sickness and motherhood (1970), introduction of early retirement because of long-term service for the self-employed (1972), and farmers (1976), and an increase in widows' pensions (1972) (Wöss 2000: 1005; Hofmeister 1981: 677–80).

Description of the current pension system[3]

Coverage

The Austrian pension system mainly rests on the first pillar: the statutory, pay-as-you-go (PAYG) system covering 3.2 million directly insured persons and two million pensioners in 2004 (Hauptverband 2005: 12, 24). Compulsory insurance is linked to employment and follows occupational lines: a scheme for blue- and white-collar workers is regulated by the General Social Security Law (ASVG). Regulations for self-employed and farmers' pensions resemble the ASVG provisions, but are laid down in separate statutes: the Social Security Act for the Self-Employed in Trade and Commerce (*Gewerbliches Sozialversicherungsgesetz*, GSVG), the Social Security Act for Farmers (*Bauern-Sozialversicherungsgesetz*, BSVG), the Social Security Act for the Free Professions (*Freiberufliches Sozialversicherungsgesetz*, FSVG) and the Social Security Act for Notaries (*Notarversicherungsgesetz*, NVG).

Civil servants have a separate system of old-age provisions, administered and monitored by the Ministry of Finances. Although pension reforms in the 1990s aimed at greater harmonization between the private and the public sector, the majority of civil servants' pensions were still much more favorable until recently. With the *Pensionsharmonisierungsgesetz* that came into force on January 1, 2005, all occupations will be united in one general pension system, albeit with long transition periods.

Neither occupational nor private pensions are compulsory in Austria. Due to high replacement rates in the first pillar, demand for occupational or private pensions is fairly low. Occupational pensions cover approximately 11 percent of Austrian workers and equal 3 percent of pension benefits (Feher 2001: 6).

Administration

The pension system is administered by separate self-governing statutory pension insurance organizations for each scheme: blue- and white-collar workers'

(*Pensionsversicherungsanstalt*); miners (*Versicherungsanstalt des österreichischen Bergbaus*); railway workers (*Versicherunganstalt der österreichischen Einsenbahnen*); craftsmen (*Sozialversicherungsanstalt der gewerblichen Wirtschaft*); farmers (*Sozialversicherungsanstalt der Bauern*); and notaries (*Versicherungsanstalt des österreichischen Notariates*). The self-administrating pension boards consist of representatives of the economic chambers (§32 ASVG; Bertuleit 1999: 7–8).

The providers of pension, health and accident insurance are unified by law in the Association of Austrian Social Security Providers (*Hauptverband der österreichischen Sozialversicherungsträger*) (§31 ASVG). This peak association represents the interests of all social insurance schemes and is entitled to sign contracts in their names. The local offices of health insurance collect pension contributions and transfer the means to the responsible pension insurance provider, which, in turn, pays out pension benefits.

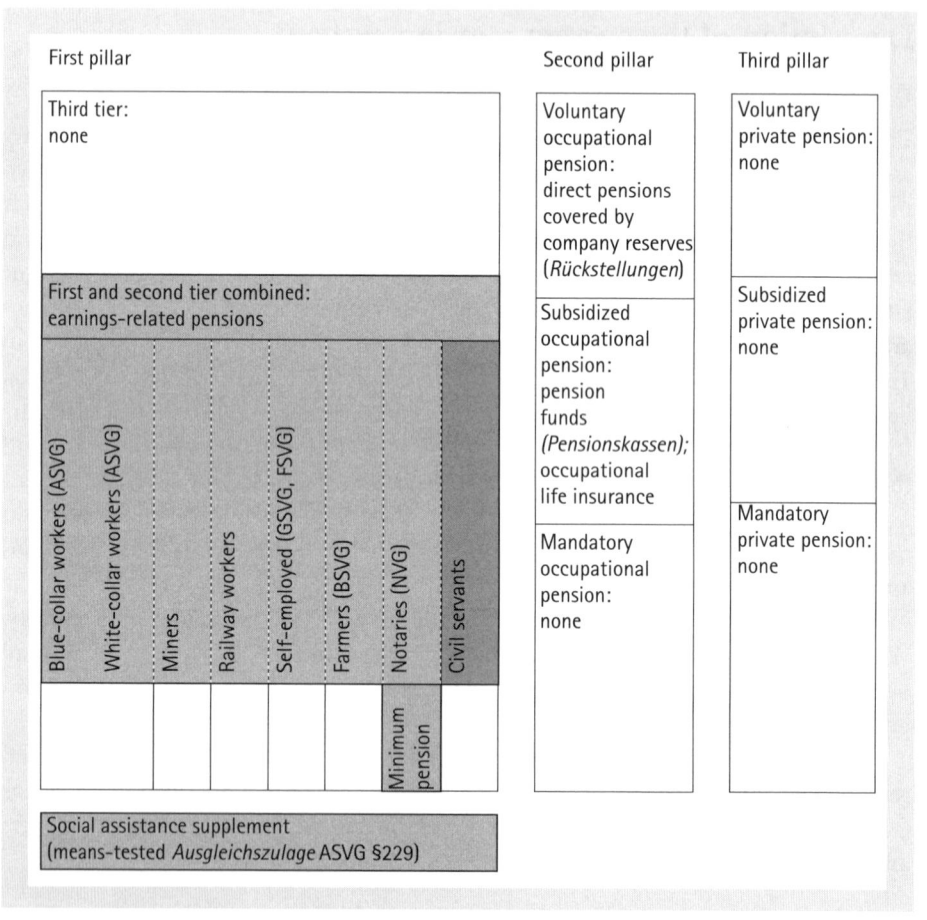

First pillar	Second pillar	Third pillar
Third tier: none	Voluntary occupational pension: direct pensions covered by company reserves (*Rückstellungen*)	Voluntary private pension: none
First and second tier combined: earnings-related pensions — Blue-collar workers (ASVG); White-collar workers (ASVG); Miners; Railway workers; Self-employed (GSVG, FSVG); Farmers (BSVG); Notaries (NVG); Civil servants; Minimum pension	Subsidized occupational pension: pension funds (*Pensionskassen*); occupational life insurance	Subsidized private pension: none
	Mandatory occupational pension: none	Mandatory private pension: none
Social assistance supplement (means-tested *Ausgleichszulage* ASVG §229)		

Fig. 12.2 Pension system in Austria

Note: With effect of the *Pensionsharmonisierungsgesetz* starting on January 1, 2005 all occupations will be united in one general system. Due to the long transition periods we still sketch the old system above.

Financing

The pension system is financed on a PAYG basis. Sources of revenue are earnings-related contributions as well as state subsidies (*Bundeszuschuss*). Contribution rates vary. Blue- and white-collar employees contribute 18.5 percent, split equally between the employee and the employer, and also a supplementary contribution to an equalization fund of 4.3 percent (3.3% from the employer and 1% from the employee). For low wage part-time employees (*geringfügig Beschäftigte*) employers pay a flat-rate contribution rate of 16.4 percent if their employees earn no more than 1.5 times the part-time employment income limit. The self-employed in the craftmen's scheme contribute 15 percent of their wages, whereas those in the one for the liberal professions (FSVG) pay 20 percent farmers pay 14.5 percent. Contributions are paid on gross monthly income up to €3,630 for dependent employees and €4,235 for the self-employed and farmers, as of 2005 (Hauptverband 2005: 7–8).

The government covers the costs of non-contributory benefits in all schemes (e.g. benefits for child-rearing periods). The level of additional government subsidies depends on the financial situation of the particular pension scheme. The state bridges the gap between contribution revenues and the expenditure of the scheme (§80 ASVG) up to a maximum of one-third of total pension expenditure. If the deficit rises above one-third of total expenditure the additional costs are equally shared between the general budget and the insured (§79a ASVG). Furthermore, the government transfers money from tax revenues to the pension schemes for the self-employed: in order to relieve the self-employed from paying both the employers' and employees' contribution rates, revenues from tax payments by the self-employed are used to double the contribution payments in the pension schemes for the self-employed and farmers. This mechanism of state subsidies leads to unequal shares of tax-financed benefits in the different schemes (Karl 2001: 166–7; Bertuleit 1999: 14).

Benefits

The current regular retirement age is 65 for men and 60 for women. Parliament adopted a harmonized retirement age of 65 in 1992, but this will only be phased-in between 2024 and 2033. The minimum qualifying period for old age retirement is 180 months of contributions, which guarantees *eternal eligibility* or 300 months of insurance that include credits for child-rearing periods, military service, and the like. Early retirement on the basis of long-service employment was abolished starting July 1, 2004, but due to a long transition period, it is still possible for certain age groups to retire at the age of 61.5 for men, or 56.5 for women until 2014 (Österreichische Bundesregierung 2003a). Early retirement requires a minimum insurance period of 420 months or 450 months with at least 240 insurance months within the last 360 months. Other types of pensions include those granted for early retirement because of unemployment, widow/widowers' pensions, orphans' pensions, invalidity pensions and partial pensions, the so-called sliding-scale pensions (*Gleitpension*). Periods of insurance are contribution periods plus periods of exemption (*Ersatzzeiten*). A contribution month entails that the insured contributes to the responsible pension scheme because of compulsory insurance due to employment or self-employed occupation. A maximum of 18 months per child are also counted as contribution months if child-rearing benefits (*Kinderbetreuungsgeld*) are drawn. Contribution months may also be acquired through voluntary insurance. Periods of higher education are only considered if annuities are purchased retroactively (for details see PV 2005a). Acceptable reasons for periods of exemption are periods of military or civilian service, periods of sickness benefits, of unemployment benefits, of maternity allowances and a maximum of 48 months of child-rearing per child (PV 2005e).

Pension benefits depend upon three components: the length of insurance periods, the earnings assessment base (*Bemessungsgrundlage*), and supplements for periods of child-rearing. The reference period for the assessment base (*Durchrechnungszeitraum*) for persons born before 1955 will increase from 15 years in 2004 to 40 years in 2028 (PV 2005d). The number of insurance years in the benefit formula is weighted with an accrual rate (*Steigerungsrate*) of 2 percent per 12 months, and results in the number of accrual points (*Steigerungspunkte*). The accrual rate will be reduced to 1.78 percent between 2004 and 2009. Pensions used to be net-wage indexed with the consumer price index as a lower limit. The Advisory Council for Pension Adjustment suggested an adjustment rate on the basis of the net-wage calculated adjustment target value, which the Minister of Social Affairs enacted by decree with approval by the cabinet and the *Nationalrat*'s main committees (Bertuleit 1999: 33–4). Pension adjustment will be changed to price indexing only from 2009 onwards (PV 2005c: 13–14).

Early retirement reduces the number of accrual points by 4.2 per year of early pension drawing (PVAng 2002: 12). Late retirement is rewarded by a 4.2 percent increase per extra year of suspended retirement up to 90 percent of the reference earnings.

To alleviate old-age poverty a minimum old-age income in the form of an old-age supplement is available. To qualify, total monthly income (gross pension plus net income from other sources) must be below €662.99 for singles and €1,030.23 for couples, as of 2005. The supplement is equal to the difference between the reference level and the sum of incomes the person receives (PV 2005b). Monthly pension benefits above €973.49 are subject to taxation and health insurance contributions (PV 2005f).

IV Politics of pension reform since 1980

Overview

No less than nine pension reforms were passed in Austria between 1980 and mid-2004. In 1984 the SPÖ/FPÖ coalition extended the reference period for the

Table 12.3 Overview of proposed and enacted pension reforms in Austria

Year	Name of reform	Reform process (chronology)	Reform measures
1984	40. ASVG Novelle	• November 7, 1983 pension commission established • Spring 1984 process of appraisal • May 1984 government draft • June 26, 1984 submission to Parliament • October 17, 1984 passage in *Nationalrat* • October 25, 1984 *Bundesrat* objection • November 27, 1984 *Nationalrat* overrules *Bundesrat* objection	• reference period increased from last 5 to last 10 years • abolishment of the basic minimum pension and progressive accrual rates • introduction of linear accrual rates • introduction of child supplements • introduction of eternal eligibility • reduction of deficit coverage • reduction of pension increase if unemployment rate above 2.5% • envisioned anti-accumulation rules for widows and widowers failed!
1987	44. ASVG Novelle	• 1985 commission established • September 1987 process of appraisal • November 5, 1987 submission to *Nationalrat* • November 25, 1987 passage in *Nationalrat* • December 3, 1987 passage in *Bundesrat*	• incremental periods for the assessment base relative to retirement age • reduction in credits gained for periods in higher education • anti-accumulation rules for widows and widowers • no decision on anti-accumulation for multiple pensions in general, contrary to first proposal
1992	*Constitutional Act on Unequal Retirement Age*	• December 6, 1990 Constitutional Court verdict: equalization regulation by December 31, 1992 • December 1, 1992 passage of constitutional act by 2/3 majority in *Nationalrat* • December 11, passage in *Bundesrat*	• maintenance of different retirement ages between men and women until 2019 • early retirement age for women increased from 55 to 60 between 2019 and 2028 • standard retirement age for women increased from 60 to 65 between 2024 and 2033
1993	51. ASVG Novelle	• January 1992 first government proposal • December 22, 1992 cabinet decision • February 1993 government amendments at committee stage • April 21, 1993 passage in *Nationalrat* • April 29, 1993 passage in *Bundesrat*	• net-wage instead of gross-wage indexation of pensions in private sector • introduction of pension securing contribution in public sector • increase in civil servants' contribution rate • assessment base in private sector changed from last 15 to best 15 years

(Continued)

Table 12.3 (Continued)

Year	Name of reform	Reform process (chronology)	Reform measures
1995	*Strukturanpas-sungsgesetz*	• December 1994 *Adventspaket*: retrenchment package affecting all sectors; trade unionist MPs announce they will vote against the bill • March 1995 submission of bill • April 5, 1995 passage in *Nationalrat* • April 20, 1995 passage in *Bundesrat*	• no bonus-malus-regulations, contrary to proposal • reduction of deficit coverage guarantee from 100.2% to 100% • increase in pension contributions for civil servants from 10.25% to 11.75% • no introduction of 5 year reference period for civil servants, contrary to proposal
1996	*Strukturanpas-sungsgesetz*	• Summer 1995 coalition negotiations on budget • October 1995 coalition breaks down • December 17, 1995 early elections • January 1996 coalition agreement SPÖ/ÖVP • April 15, 1996 submission of bill • April 19, 1996 passage in *Nationalrat* with 2/3 majority • April 25 passage in *Bundesrat*	• introduction of different accrual rates relative to age • increase in contribution rates for self-employed and farmers • reduction of governmental deficit guarantee • time in higher education no longer counted as qualifying period, unless purchased • increase in qualifying period for early retirement from 15 to 20 years, and retirement after long-term service from 35 to 37.5 years • no introduction of deductions for early retirement, contrary to proposal
1997	SRÄG 1997	• June 1997 Rürup Report, secret government meeting in Rust and proposal • October 10, 1997 cabinet decision • November 3, 1997 agreement in committees • November 5, 1997 passage in *Nationalrat* • December 17, 1997 passage in *Bundesrat*	• extension of reference period from 15 to 18 years for early retirement; limitation of losses to maximum of 7% • actuarial discounts of 2% for early retirement • limits on additional earnings in early retirement • extension of social security to marginal employment • introduction of reference period of 15 years for the public sector • no expansion of reference period for standard retirement, contrary to proposal
2000	SRÄG 2000	• November 1999–January 2000 SPÖ/ÖVP coalition negotiations and breakdown	• increase in early retirement age from 55 to 56.5 (women) and from 60 to 61.5 (men) • increase in child-rearing period from 24 to 36 months • increase in reduction for early retirement from 2 to 3% with losses limited to

		• February 2000 ÖVP/FPÖ coalition agreement • April 5, 2000 governmental draft • June 2000 public sector strike • July 5, 2000 passage in *Nationalrat* • July 19, 2000 passage in *Bundesrat*	• maximum of 15% • reduction in widows' pensions • increase in contribution rates for farmers and for crafts- and tradesmen
2003	*Budgetbegleit-gesetz 2003*	• February 2003 ÖVP/FPÖ government declaration • March 31, 2003 publication of ministerial draft • May 2003 protests, strikes and round table negotiations • June 11, 2003 passage in the *Nationalrat* • June 23, 2003 no decision in the *Bundesrat* → 8-week waiting period before passage	• extension of reference period from 15 to 40 years • increase in reduction for early retirement from 3% to 4.2% and, contrary to original proposal, limit on early retirement losses to 10% • increase in bonus for late retirement to 4.2% • reduction in accrual rate from 2% to 1.78%
2004	*Pensionsharmonisierungsgesetz*	• by October 8, 2004 appraisal process • October 13 submission to Parliament • November 18, 2004 passage in *Nationalrat* • December 2, 2004 passage in *Bundesrat*	• complete harmonization of pensions for all occupations, including civil servants and politicians • General Pensions Law (*Allgemeines Pensionsgesetz* (APG)) replaces ASVG, GSVG, BSVG, FSVG and BDG • introduction of individual pension accounts that register all contributions

[a] *Bundesverfassungsgesetz über unterschiedliche Altersgrenzen von männlichen und weiblichen Sozialversicherten* (BGBl. 832/1992a).

assessment base from the five last to the ten last years, abolished the basic minimum pension, and introduced progressive accrual rates. Due to controversies with women's groups the government decided not to enact new anti-accumulation rules.[4] In 1987 a SPÖ/ÖVP majority passed age-related accrual rates, abolished the substitute qualifying period for higher education and tightened requirements for widows' and widowers' pensions. The 1992 Constitutional Act on unequal retirement ages harmonized men's and women's pension ages. In 1993 the differences between the public and private sectors became an important issue for the first time: the response was a switch from gross wage to net wage indexing for the ASVG pension. The public sector scheme was also harmonized with that for the private sector. After the 1994 elections, a weakened SPÖ/ÖVP coalition tried to introduce penalties for early retirement and a reference period for civil servants. However, the *Strukturanpassungsgesetz 1995* failed to introduce anything more than cosmetic changes. In 1996, the reform brought about age-related accrual rates and increased contribution rates for the self-employed and farmers. The 1997 reform introduced a reference period for the assessment base for civil servants, and extended the reference period for early retirement in the private sector. In the year 2002, an ÖVP/FPÖ government coalition increased the early retirement age, increased the penalties for early retirement and tightened requirements for widows' and widowers' pensions. In 2003, the *Budgetbegleitgesetz* reduced the accrual rate, increased in the early retirement deduction, and extended the reference period to the entire career. Finally, in 2005, the four separate social security schemes were consolidated—albeit with a long transition period.

Thus, the 1980s and 1990s were characterized by piece-meal changes in Austrian pension policy. The SPÖ and ÖVP grand coalitions made some progress in harmonizing the private and the public sector pension systems. They also curbed pension benefit expenditure on the edges, but union members in the political parties managed to slow reform efforts. The ÖVP/FPÖ coalition, by contrast, implemented more substantial reforms in 2000, 2003 and 2005, but also had to make several concessions because of intra-coalition opposition.

Pension reform 1984: *40. ASVG Novelle*

Background

The 1970s were characterized by pension expansion. In the early 1980s, however, projections foresaw government transfers of over ATS 100 billion in 1990, indicating that a change in pension policy was necessary (*Profil* 04.01.1982: 11). The government's share in pension expenditure had grown from 19.6 percent in 1980 to 29.1 percent in 1984 (Hauptverband 1984: Table 95). Forecasts estimated that the tax-financed share in pension expenditure due to the government guarantee of deficit coverage would increase to 41.4 percent in 1990. Thus, the main goal for the

1984 pension reform was the reduction of government subsidies to the pension system (327 d.B. NR XVI. GP: 16).

After the national elections on April 24, 1983 and the formation of a SPÖ/FPÖ coalition, Minister of Social Affairs, Alfred Dallinger (SPÖ), established a commission to make suggestions for a pension reform (Tomandl 1984: 52). In the spring of 1984 the government released a draft bill for appraisal, which included the extension of the reference period to the ten last years of employment and the abolition of the basic minimum pension (*Grundbetrag*). The *Grundbetrag* meant that a pensioner received 30 percent of his or her assessment base irrespective of the number of insurance years. Previously, in combination with progressive accrual rates (6% of the calculation base for the first 10 years; 9% for the second ten years; 12% for the third 10 years and 1.5% for any further year), the *Grundbetrag* secured a minimum pension, especially for women and persons with gaps in their working careers. The abolition of the basic pension went hand in hand with a change from progressive to linear accrual rates. The new provisions were to credit 1.9 percent of the assessment base for each of the first 30 years (360 months) of insurance and 1.5 percent for any further insurance year up to a maximum of 45 years. Originally, the reform was supposed to include new anti-accumulation rules for widows' pensions. This idea was dropped because of disagreement (327 d.B. NR XVI. GP: 17–26). The reform included a number of additional provisions (see Table 12.3), but they were less controversial.

Reform process

During the appraisal process the main point of conflict was the abolition of the basic pension and the anti-accumulation rules for widows. According to the original plan, widows' pension benefits were to be limited to a total of ATS 6,000, or the widows' pension combined with a personal pension was to be restricted to ATS 10,200 (*OÖN* 20.01.1984). Common interests across-party lines led SPÖ and FPÖ women to build an alliance with opposition ÖVP women to fight the abolition of the *Grundbetrag* and the anti-accumulation limit (*OÖN* 23.01.1984; *KZ* 05.02.1984). Minister of Social Affairs Dallinger was able to silence SPÖ women's criticism by promising to credit child-rearing periods, and by not cutting widows' pensions (*OÖN* 20.01.1984; *WZ* 19.04.1989).

With respect to extending the reference period for pension calculation the unions and the Chamber of Labor favored the extension to a 10-year average. Thus, with unions' support the government proposal was submitted to Parliament on June 26, 1984 (NR XVI. GP, 52nd, 27.06.1984: 4438) and after deliberations in the relevant committee (Ausschuß für soziale Verwaltung 1984: 2) the bill passed the *Nationalrat* on October 17, 1984 with the support of the SPÖ/FPÖ majority (NR XVI. GP, 59th: 5061).

In the *Bundesrat*, however, the ÖVP had a majority (see Table 12.2) and this chamber voted against the bill. This was a good way to show female voters that the ÖVP championed the interests of women, but there was little risk, since the *Bundesrat* could not permanently block legislation anyway (BR 452nd: 18003–18009, 18052;

Sozialausschuß 1984). The SPÖ and FPÖ majority in the *Nationalrat* overruled the *Bundesrat* on November 27, 1984 (NR XVI. GP, 66th: 5698; Republik Österreich Parlamentsdirektion 2003; BGBl. 484/1984). Thus, the pension reform of 1984 contained some cutbacks, linear accrual rates and an extended reference period that mostly affected women with short working careers. Intra-party and intra-coalition resistance from female FPÖ and SPÖ members achieved some concessions in anti-accumulation rules for widows and child-rearing credits. Female representatives from the ÖVP opposition party were unable to block the changes, since the ÖVP-dominated second chamber lacked any veto power.

Pension reform 1987: *44. ASVG Novelle*

Background and pre-parliamentary stage

The outcome of the national election held on November 24, 1986 was surprising: in spite of, or maybe even due to, the FPÖ's shift from a liberal party to a populist right-wing party, it nearly doubled its share of the vote, from 4.98 percent to 9.73 percent. The SPÖ had its worst electoral result since 1966. A grand coalition of SPÖ and ÖVP came to office with the goal of enacting radical economic reforms, including a pension reform.

The discussions and negotiations on possible pension reform measures went on throughout the summer of 1987. In late September, a ministerial draft was circulated for appraisal. The three main provisions of the proposal were an age-related assessment base for pension calculation, the abolition of pension credits for higher education, and tighter anti-accumulation rules for widows' pensions. This last measure had also been proposed as part of the 1984 reform, but failed to pass (ÖAKT 1987: 5–10).

The reform proposal for the assessment base was to take into account the last 10 years if a person retired before 50 (e.g. invalidity). Between ages 50 to 55 years for women and 50 to 60 years for men the assessment period increase to the last 15 years and decrease again to 10 years at the age of 60 or 65 years, respectively (*Profil* 28.09.1987: 22). For higher education, the existing six years of pension credits would be abolished. Furthermore, periods of higher education that were retroactively purchased would not count as contribution periods for early retirement any longer. Concerning survivors' pensions, if a widow's or widower's pension was above ATS 6,878 and the person drew a second pension or income or if the sum of both pensions exceeded ATS 11,827, pension benefits would be reduced by 50 percent (*Tagblatt* 26.09.1987; ÖAKT 1987: 15, 19–20).

The ministerial draft met opposition from the unions. Although the Chamber of Labor supported an extension of the reference period for the assessment base in general, it objected to linking the reference period to the individual retirement age, because most employees could not choose their retirement age. The Chamber of Labor also rejected the changes in the treatment of periods in education because it would not only affect university graduates, who could be expected to compensate for the gap in insurance with higher incomes later in life, but it would also affect students of business schools and commercial colleges (ÖAKT 1987: 12–13, 22).

Even before the deadline for the appraisal process had passed the proposed rules for higher education were changed, and it was agreed that periods of high-school or technical college education would require lower contribution payments than university education, thereby satisfying union representatives (*Tagblatt* 23.10.1987).

The issue of anti-accumulation rules was most controversial and highlighted divergent positions within the SPÖ party. While the Minister of Social Affairs Dallinger (SPÖ) promoted the reform as mentioned above, the SPÖ women's organization accused Dallinger of irresponsible policy-making, scaring the public and attempting to ensure that women were relegated to the role of housewife and mother.[5] Women's groups of all parties criticized the fact that working women with high incomes would be affected more strongly by the reform. Minister Dallinger appeased these groups by signaling that neither the date of enforcement nor the income limit for earnings restrictions on retirees had yet been fixed, and that an increase in the maximum amount to ATS 13,000 was possible (*OÖTagblatt* 29.09.1987; *AZ* 30.09.1987; *KlZ* 30.09.1987). Four weeks later, the limit was even higher: ATS 14,000. All benefits above this limit would ensure that up to one-fourth of the widows/widower's pension would be cut, a solution which secured the agreement of women's interest groups (NR XVII. GP, 38th: 4371). However, by mid-October 1987, the government decided to postpone the section on the accumulation of multiple pensions, and to introduce it in 1988 as a separate constitutional law that would include the same regulations for civil servants (*Presse* 24.10.1987).

Parliamentary stage

The reform was negotiated mainly in the pre-parliamentary arena. When the bill was submitted to the *Nationalrat* on November 5, 1987, its content had been settled and the Social Affairs Committee had little impact on the legislation (NR XVII. GP, 34th: 3943; Tálos and Kittel 2001: 83). The social partners and the FPÖ criticized the rushed pension legislation, which they argued was driven by budgetary concerns (ÖAKT 1987). Moreover, the complicated and complex pension issue, with last-minute amendments, made it impossible for the majority of members of parliament to be well-informed when voting on the bill (see e.g. Manfred Srb (Grüne) in NR XVII. GP, 38th: 4339). The voting in Parliament took place on November 25, 1987, and the reform passed with the government majority (Republik Österreich Parlamentsdirektion 2003). The *Bundesrat* decided unanimously not to reject the bill on December 3, 1987 (BR 494th: 21361; BGBl. 609/1987).

Superficially, the *44. ASVG Novelle* looks like a successful pension reform. However, changes in the treatment of educational periods, accumulation of widows' pensions and incremental reference periods with a high of 15 years do not make for statutory pension system consolidation, nor can they be seen as a major shift in principles.

Pension reform 1993: 51. ASVG Novelle

Background: The early 1990s

When the 1987 reform passed the *Nationalrat*, it was clear that further reforms would soon be necessary. Although the FPÖ was the winner of the 1990-elections (with a gain of 15 seats), the SPÖ/ÖVP coalition remained in office. The government's main goal for the subsequent period term was to curb public expenditure and to stop th de facto decrease in the retirement age (BR 569th: 2607). In the governmental declaration, the coalition announced its intention to pass another private sector pension reform as well as a reform of civil servants' pensions (*Profil* 01.02.1993: 27; NR XVIII. GP, 114th: 13283).

The 1993 pension reform was developed mainly at the pre-parliamentary stage, where the initial proposal was significantly amended (Tálos and Kittel 2001: Table 4.1). The content of initial proposals was made public in January 1992. The government's reform draft foresaw net-wage instead of gross-wage indexation of pensions, harmonization of the assessment base in the private and public sectors, and the introduction of age-related accrual rates, child credits and partial pensions (NR XVIII. GP, 114th: 13283–13284; *Kurier* 25.01.1992). The ministerial draft envisaged limiting governmental subsidies to one-third of contribution revenues instead of one-third of total pension expenditures, implying a drastic reduction in financing through the general budget (ÖAKT 1992: 8). Early negotiations on the pension reform also covered increasing the female retirement age.

The Austrian Constitutional Court ruled on December 6, 1990 that different retirement ages for men and women were unconstitutional, and bound the legislator to resolve this issue by December 31, 1992 (Ausschuß für soziale Verwaltung 1992: 1). But the government pursued a devious strategy to avoid an immediate increase in the retirement age for its voters: it legislated the equalization of retirement ages in the context of a reform package of 14 separate laws affecting and improving gender equality in the labor market (735 d.B. NR XVIII. GP). The SPÖ/ÖVP coalition submitted a bill for constitutional amendment which maintened gender specific retirement ages until 2019: the early-retirement age for women would be increased from 55 to 60 in six month steps between 2019 and 2028, and the standard retirement age for women would be increased from 60 to 65 between 2024 and 2033 (737 d.B. NR XVIII. GP: 1).

Thus, even though it could blame the reform on the Constitutional Court, neither the SPÖ nor the ÖVP wanted to be held responsible by voters for raising their retirement age. Indeed, they chose to go for a constitutional act, which allowed the introduction of the equalization of the retirement age more slowly by ensuring that the Court would not be able to interfere. However, the act was very controversial since it was unclear whether its content justified constitutional status of the law (837 d.B. NR XVIII. GP). Nonetheless, it was adopted by a two-thirds majority in the *Nationalrat* (NR XVIII. GP, 90th: 9988, 10032) and supported by the *Bundesrat* (4384 d.B. BR; BR 562nd: 26980–26981, 26993; BGBl. 832/1992).

Pre-parliamentary stage of 51. ASVG Novelle

After the constitutional act on unequal pension ages had been passed, further pension talks concentrated on private/public sector harmonization, and indexation. On December 22, 1992 the Cabinet agreed on a reform package for the private sector, though this was made dependent on concurrent public sector pension reform (*Kurier* 23.12.1992).

The bill included an increase in the regular pension contribution rate for civil servants from 10 percent to 10.25 percent (*Kurier* 19.02.1993), and the goal of harmonizing the civil servants' system with ASVG was to be met by calculating ASVG benefits using the "best" 15 years (180 months) instead of the "last" 15 years. However, the effect of this regulation would be limited, as back-dated calculations were not based on appropriately adjusted contribution periods (932 d.B. NR XVIII. GP).

The negotiations with interest groups during the appraisal process were difficult and tedious (NR XVIII. GP, 114th: 13294). The private sector unions would only accept the bill if net wage indexation was also applied to civil servants' pensions, but the Union of Public Services (GÖD) and the Trade Union of Municipal Workers (GdG) opposed net wage indexation and threatened strikes (*Kurier* 17.02.1993). Differences within the coalition increased: regional and state ÖVP politicians alerted the government to the risks of cutting civil servants' pension rights in the context of upcoming state elections in Lower Austria (*Niederösterreich*) (*Profil* 01.02.1993).

In late February 1993, after the parliamentary committee sessions had already started, SPÖ/ÖVP introduced a motion for amendment (NR XVIII. GP, 114th: 13284). The amended bill incorporated the results of the pre-parliamentary negotiations and deviated from the original draft significantly. The compromise cancelled (in a concession to the GÖD) net-wage indexation for civil servants' pensions. Instead a different regulation was introduced that would have similar effects. Civil servants' pension adjustment would continue to be negotiated as part of wage negotiations as before. But, if the adjustment rate in the public sector was greater than that in the private sector ASVG scheme, the difference would be retained by the government as a "pension securing contribution" (*Pensionssicherungsbeitrag*) (*Profil* 22.02.1993). An advisory council with representatives of the unions and of the government was to calculate the *Pensionssicherungsbeitrag*. Based on the council's calculation the contribution rate would be fixed by decree, and approved by the main committee in Parliament (*Kurier* 26.03.1993). In other words, the unions secured some leeway to influence the pension securing contribution rate through their membership in the advisory council. In order to gain union approval for the reform, politicians had to juggle the interests of several unions, and both their sense of relative fairness and absolute gains. Consequently, a parliamentary majority of SPÖ, ÖVP and LIF votes passed the bill in the *Nationalrat* (Republik Österreich Parlamentsdirektion 2003), and the majority of the *Bundesrat* decided not to reject the bill on April 29, 1993 (BR 569th: 27637; BGBl. 335/1993). Once again, policy concessions had been necessary to avoid parliamentary blockage due to pressures from union members and state-level politicians worried about how national politics would play out locally.

Pension reforms 1995 and 1996: *Strukturanpassungsgesetze*

Background

Although polls and the regional elections had indicated difficult *Nationalrat* elections (*Profil* 15.03.1994: 17), the outcome was more dramatic than forecast and was described as an "earthquake in Austria" (Pulzer 1995). Expectations were that the new electoral system, with a 4 percent national hurdle, would favor the large parties, but the small Greens and Liberals were quite successful (Greens 13 and LIF 11 seats). Moreover, the FPÖ increased its vote share by almost six percentage points, up to 22.5 percent. Thus, Parliament became more fragmented and the governing coalition lost the two-thirds majority necessary to circumvent the Constitutional Court, as the 1992 reform has shown. Since the SPÖ and ÖVP had announced their intention to continue the grand coalition prior to the elections, coalition negotiations proceeded efficiently. The main goal of the coalition agreement was once again budget consolidation (Sebald 1998: 6).

Strukturanpassungsgesetz 1995

In the 1994 election campaign, politicians avoided discussions about welfare state reform. But, in the context of approaching EU membership and the necessity of budget consolidation, it was clear that further reform of the Austrian welfare state would be the most important topic after the elections. Facing a budget deficit which had increased from 2 percent to 5 percent of GDP between 1992 and 1994, the SPÖ/ÖVP government was under pressure to consolidate the budget in order to meet EMU criteria (OECD 2002; Schludi 2005: 168).

As part of the coalition agreement the government presented a broad consolidation package shortly before Christmas (*Adventspaket*). The coalition negotiations had been difficult because of the goal of submitting a single austerity package. The main incentive for a comprehensive package was that party leaders feared that voting on the different measures separately would have endangered coalition discipline (Sebald 1998: 13–14).

For the public sector, one of the measures discussed between SPÖ and ÖVP at the Ministry of Finance was the introduction of a reference period of five years as the assessment base for civil servants' pensions, instead of basing them on the final wage. Obviously, GdG chairman, Günter Weniger, and GÖD president, Fritz Neugebauer (ÖVP), representatives of the public sector unions, rejected this measure completely (*Kurier* 17.11.1994; 07.12.1994). The measures proposed by the ÖVP to reform private sector pensions included the introduction of penalties for early retirement, up to 15 percent actuarial reductions of pension benefit if a person retired before standard retirement age. The private sector ÖGB union, as well as the Minister of Social Affairs

Hesoun (SPÖ), rejected the proposed deductions for early retirement. Hesoun refused to cut private sector ASVG pensions if civil servants' pensions were left untouched (*Kurier* 21.10.1994). Again, relative gains and losses were as important as the costs themselves.

The unions (especially ÖGB) heavily criticized the package, causing great disputes between the ÖGB and the SPÖ. In protest against the reform measures envisaged, the chairman of the Metal Workers' Union and SPÖ MP, Rudolf Nürnberger, left the bargaining committee. But Chancellor Vranitzky (SPÖ) was determined to realize the savings even against union resistance (Sebald 1998: 7–9, 11; *Kurier* 16.11.1994; 05.02.1995). His position was weakened when the ÖGB threatened to go on strike, and even more so when some unionist parliamentary members announced their intention to reject the bill in parliamentary voting (Schludi 2005: 170). Eventually, the government abstained from most of its plans in pension policy.

When the SPÖ/ÖVP leadership submitted a budget bill to Parliament in March 1995, the content of the pension reform was watered down. Whereas the projected savings of the *Sparpaket* presented in late 1994 amounted to ATS 20 billion, the revised bill was expected to save only ATS 10 to 12 billion (Budgetausschuss 1995: 77). The bill did not include any early retirement penalties—a clear concession to the unions. Consequently, there were hardly any changes in the private sector pension system, except for a reduction of the deficit coverage guarantee. In negotiations with the government, the civil servants' unions had agreed on an increase in public sector pension contributions (from 10.25% to 11.75%) and an extension of the insurance period for eligibility to pension benefits (from 10 to 15 years; for full pensions 35 to 40 years) on February 5, 1995 (Budgetausschuss 1995: 5–7).

Shortly before the final parliamentary debate on the *Sparpaket*, Finance Minister Lacina (SPÖ) announced his retirement, citing (among other things) intra-party dissent and the fierce and unsuccessful negotiations with the unions over the last few months. Minister of Social Affairs, Hesoun (SPÖ), Minister for Women's Issues, Johanna Dohnal (SPÖ), and Minister of the Interior, Franz Löschnak (SPÖ), followed Lacina's example and retired the same week—showing the increasing disagreement within the party (*Kurier* 30.03.1995; 01.04.1995). Austrian corporatism was beginning to reach its limits, as unions demonstrated their veto powers in the economic domain and in parliament. Finally, however, the *Strukturanpassungsgesetz 1995* passed with SPÖ and ÖVP votes in the *Nationalrat* on April 5, 1995 and in the *Bundesrat* on April 20, 1995 (Sebald 1998: 18; NR XIX.GP, 32nd: 182).[6] Nevertheless, the pension reform of 1995 must be considered a failure. Although a legislative act was passed, it included none of the retrenchment measured originally envisaged.

Once again, electoral competition had precluded constructive political decision-making—this time escalating even more owing to the new preference-voting system and the uncertainties caused by the sudden resurgence of the smaller parties. Consequently, the SPÖ and the ÖVP were adamant not to appear to be abandoning their core constituents—and certainly not to be the first to do so. The SPÖ sought above all to cut back civil servants' pensions, while protecting the ASVG pensions in the private sector, while the ÖVP's priorities were exactly the reverse. Neither of the two governing parties were willing to be the first to abandon its clientele. Given this stand-off, the trade unionist members of parliament could pursue their policy interests uncompromisingly. By threatening to defect from the party line, they succeeded in blocking the introduction of early retirement penalties in the private sector, and of changes in the assessment base in the public sector.

Government breakdown and elections 1995

The cost-cutting measures of the 1995 budget legislation did not suffice to consolidate the budget, and the government asked the Economic and Social Council to make recommendations for further measures. The Chamber of Labor, the Economic Chamber, the Agricultural Chamber and the ÖGB negotiated and reached agreement on measures on several issues except for pensions. The social partners merely agreed on side-measures such as the reduction of credits available for periods in higher education (*Kurier* 07.09.1995).

Conflict within the government reflected this disagreement: The SPÖ favored budget consolidation by revenue-increasing reforms, such as raising the pension contribution rate, which had not been increased since 1985 (*Profil* 24.07.1995: 20). The ÖVP, however, preferred budget consolidation through structural reform and reduced expenditure such as through deductions for early retirement (*Profil* 03.07.1995; Plasser and Ulram 1996: 17–18). Neither side was willing to give in, especially regarding early pensions, a class-profiling political issue, as early retirement (like sickness pay) is much more important to blue-collar than white-collar workers (*Profil* 02.10.1995: 34; Sebald 1998: 60).

The controversial negotiations over the 1996 budget coincided with shifts of strength between the coalition partners. The SPÖ had to "stomach" the replacement of four ministers while the ÖVP was strengthened by Wolfgang Schüssel, the newly elected party leader, who took office in April 1995 with the aim of making the ÖVP the largest party (*Profil* 12.06.1995). Indeed, the polls showed increasing support for Schüssel and the ÖVP during the summer of 1995 (Sully 1996: 635). In September 1995 a majority of respondents said they trusted the ÖVP to do a better job of enacting retrenchment and consolidating the budget (Plasser and Ulram 1996: 18–19).

In October, Vice-Chancellor Schüssel (ÖVP) rejected the SPÖ proposal for the 1996 budget, which was tantamount to a coalition break-up (and indeed to a call for new elections). Against the background of the parties' opinion poll ratings, the non-agreement over the budget seems likely to have been a strategic move on the part of the ÖVP, which expected to improve its standing in early elections (*Die Zeit* 20.10.1995). Political strategy and especially the hope of becoming Chancellor took precedence over budgetary prudence.

Elections were scheduled for December 17, 1995. The main campaign issue was budget consolidation and both the SPÖ and the ÖVP sought to sharpen their policy profile at the expense of the coalition partner by avoiding loss-imposing reforms for their respective clientele (Schludi 2005: 171). Reforming pensions was one of the main measures to consolidate the budget and consequently a hot topic in the campaign. Opinion polls ranked pension policy the most important factor for voters' choice in the election (Plasser and Ulram 1996: 15, 38). But polls also found that 44 percent of voters were undecided two months prior to the elections (*Profil* 16.10.1995).

In this context of uncertainty the SPÖ did everything to attract elderly voters: the SPÖ promised not to touch pensions. Campaign posters guaranteed the safeguarding of the pensions of those who had already retired. Moreover, Chancellor Vranitzky mailed thousands of letters to pensioners and persons older than 53 years in early December 1995, promising that their pensions were safe and that they could rely on the SPÖ. The second main issue of the campaign was that the ÖVP was striving for the Chancellorship, but it did not make commitments to any specific coalition. The SPÖ used this non-commitment to campaign against a "black-blue experiment" (an ÖVP-FPÖ government), under the slogan "vote for Vranitzky, impede Haider!" (Kossdorff and Sickinger 1996: 58–60).

On election day the support for the ÖVP did not meet expectations: it won only one extra seat. Although a potential ÖVP and FPÖ coalition would have had a slender majority in the *Nationalrat*, the SPÖ was the clear winner (Sully 1996: 639).

The ÖVP's precondition for continuing the grand coalition was to include the main features of the budget 1996 and 1997 in the coalition agreement. Eventually, the SPÖ gave in, agreeing to tighter requirements and deductions for early retirement, and also accepting a focus on expenditure-reducing measures rather than revenue-generating ones. The ÖVP had to agree to a reduction of government subsidies for the pension schemes of farmers and the self-employed. Moreover, the agreement foresaw more linear accrual rates (Schludi 2005: 172; Sebald 1998: 60–1).

Strukturanpassungsgesetz 1996

In April 1996, the cabinet submitted a budget to the *Nationalrat* (72 d.B., NR XX. GP: 253-261). Projections calculated savings of ATS 66 billion (thereof ATS 19.4 billions in social policy) and ATS 33 billion of increased revenue (BR 612th: 61–62). In pension policy, the bill included an increase in contribution rates for the self-employed and for farmers, it reduced the government deficit guarantee, it abolished the practice of counting periods of higher education as qualifying periods (unless they had been retro-actively purchased), it increased the price for retroactive purchase, it restricted disability pensions to two years, it made accrual rates more linear (1.83% and 1.675% instead of 1.9% and 1.5%), it suspended pension adjustment for 1997 and it tightened the requirements for early retirement (increase from 15 to 20 years) (72 d.B. NR XX. GP: 253-261).

After the long pre-parliamentary process there were no significant changes in the pensions part of the *Strukturanpassungsgesetz 1996* at parliamentary stage (Tálos and Kittel 2001: Table 4.1; Sebald 1998: 85). The Act passed with the SPÖ and ÖVP votes, securing a two-thirds majority in the *Nationalrat* (NR XX. GP, 16th: 636), and the *Bundesrat* did not object (BR 612th: 108). This time, the coalition agreement held— although, as we shall see, it was the beginning of a pattern in which the ÖVP moved into a pivotal position by flirting with the FPÖ and thus could threaten the SPÖ to gain policy concessions.

Pension reform 1997: *ASRÄG* and *1. Budgetbegleitgesetz*

Background

The passage of the *Strukturanpassungsgesetz 1996*—which cut a key benefit for blue-collar workers—not surprisingly had a negative impact on the SPÖ's public standing (*Profil* 15.10.1996: 27). The results of elections to the European Parliament and the Vienna state Parliament on October 13, 1996 were disastrous. The elections to the European Parliament were a head-to-head race between the three big Austrian parties with ÖVP winning 29.65 percent, SPÖ 29.15 percent and FPÖ 27.53 percent of votes (www.bmi.gv.at/wahlen/). Chancellor Vranitzky (SPÖ) resigned from office and was succeeded by Victor Klima (SPÖ) (*Kurier* 20.01.1997; 21.01.1997). In pension policy, Klima announced incremental harmonization of the pension systems in his government declaration (NR XX. GP, 60th: 21).

The first step the government took was to ask the German pension expert, Bert Rürup, to make suggestions for a structural pension reform. The Rürup Report, published in June 1997, suggested equalizing the retirement age by 2015 (much faster than previously planned), calculating pensions on the basis of the entire working career, making the accrual rate more linear, introducing actuarial reductions for early retirement and using taxes to finance non-insurance benefits such as periods of sickness, unemployment, military service or child-rearing. Other proposals were the abolition of the state guarantee to cover pension schemes' deficits; the incorporation of a demographic factor in the calculation formula; the abolition of the price index as lower limit of pension adjustment and the introduction of incentives to join the second- or third-pension pillars (Rürup and Schroeter 1997: 223–5).

In contrast to the report, which dealt with private sector pensions only, the major topic in the media throughout the spring of 1997 was civil servants' pay and pensions. Civil servants received 80 percent of their last wage at retirement, and were not placed under any earnings restrictions while drawing their pensions (*Profil* 28.04.1997: 44). A study by Marin and Prinz showed that civil servants had higher life-time incomes at all levels of education than private sector employees (*Profil* 06.04.1996; Marin and Prinz 1999). Chancellor Klima (SPÖ) and Secretary of State for Finances Wolfgang Ruttenstorfer (SPÖ) were determined to abolish the privileges in the public sector and a majority of the general public welcomed this intention.

Fierce discussion on the pension reform started after a secret government meeting at Rust in June 1997. The government announced a pension reform with far-reaching retrenchment measures, though it was still more moderate than Rürup's proposal. The reference period for pension calculation was to be extended from the 15 best years to the 20 best years between 2000 and 2012. The proposal introduced actuarial discounts of 2 percent and the preclusion of partial employment for early retirement, an increase in the contribution rate for the self-employed, the extension of social security insurance to minor employees, an increase of the upper contribution limit and the first steps towards harmonization between civil servant pensions and private sector pensions (ASVG), that is, the introduction of a reference period for civil servants (*Profil* 28.07.1997: 22; Tálos and Wörister 1998: 261; Schludi 2005: 175).

The reaction to the reform proposal was intense. The most controversial measures were the extension of the reference period for private sector employees and the introduction of a reference period for civil servants. The GÖD, in particular, refused to accept any changes: the final wage as the assessment base was the "sacred cow" of the civil servants' pension system principles. The GÖD's resistance culminated in the threat of a general strike in June 1997 (*Kurier* 18.06.1997; *Profil* 16.06.1997: 22). The turmoil calmed down when Chancellor Klima pointed out that a reference period of 15 years for civil servants was still open to discussion (*Kurier* 29.06.1997). But union resistance persisted and spread to the general public when Klima observed that the average ASVG pension equaled ATS 11,000 while the average civil servant's pension was ATS 32,000 (*Kurier* 18.06.1997; 02.07.1997). The press saw a new kind of class conflict arising between civil servants and employees/self-employed. Once again, ASVG representatives and Social Minister Hostasch (SPÖ) demanded changes in the civil servants' pension scheme as prerequisites for any retrenchment in the private sector (Std 17.09.1997). Although the general public was split along the public/private sector dimension, the private sector unions backed the GÖD's protests. A *Profil* article presumed their strategy was to count on the resistance of the civil servants and thereby avert major changes in the ASVG (*Profil* 23.06.1997: 22–24, 28–29; 22.09.1997: 24).

The SPÖ also encountered opposition within its own ranks. Union members, representatives of the *Länder* and the chairman of the SPÖ youth organization refused to consent to the extension of the reference period. The SPÖ pensioners' group even threatened to defect to the FPÖ. The SPÖ- and ÖGB-leader of Lower-Austria, Ernst Höger, notified the government that union-members would openly resist in Parliament if Klima proceeded with unilateral actions in pension policy. There was also intra-party conflict within the ÖVP: some members, such as the leader of the ÖAAB, Werner Fasslabend, distanced themselves from their party leaders in government (*Kurier* 31.08.1997; *Std* 26.09.1997).

On October 9, 1997, the government offered a new proposal: the reference period for early retirement but not for standard retirement was to be extended to 20 years. The date for full implementation was open for discussion, but the Social Ministry suggested 2017 or 2020, instead of 2012 as suggested in June (*Std* 09.10.1997; 10.10.1997). The original proposal intended to stop people from earning income in early retirement, but the revised draft only limited additional earnings to a maximum of ATS 12,000 per month. Earnings above this limit would cut pension benefits by up to 50 percent (*SZ* 13.10.1997).

In spite of these concessions the political situation was difficult. It was expected that a defeat of the bill in Parliament, which was highly likely due to the number of opposed union members, both in SPÖ and ÖVP, would lead to the government's resignation and to new elections (*Std* 10.10.1997; Schludi 2005: 175–176; *SZ* 13.10.1997). As early as August 1997 Höger threatened that unilateral government action in the legislative process would severely damage the coherence of the SPÖ-parliamentary party (*Kurier* 31.08.1997, 20.09.1997). After another 14-hour session between the social partners, Klima (SPÖ) and Schüssel (ÖVP), the Cabinet[7] agreed on a common reference period of 15 years in all systems (ASVG, GSVG, BSVG and civil servants) at regular retirement age, and a reference period of 18 years for early retirement. The same day the government submitted the bill to the *Nationalrat* (NR XX. GP, 91st: 2).

Parliamentary stage

The strangest aspect of the 1997 reform occurred during the parliamentary proceedings. Although the pension bill for civil servants and the bill for private sector pension schemes had been negotiated simultaneously throughout the reform process, during the last two days of the committee stage, a peculiar state of affairs emerged. Neither the Finance Committee nor the Social Affairs Committee was prepared to vote on the bill first. Committee members argued that absolute simultaneity was necessary, in the introduction of the changes for civil servants (*Budgetbegleitgesetz*) and changes in the ASVG (*Sozialrechtsänderungsgesetz*). Yet, the convergence of different systems did not require debating and voting on the two acts on the very same day, let alone the very same hour. The importance of simultaneity rather mirrors the distrust between the coalition partners, which one member of parliament has described as a sign of no-confidence and inadequate political consensus (Volker Kier (LIF) in NR XX. GP, 93rd: 66). Their relationship was still strained by the government break-down of 1995. Given that the SPÖ had to deal with with the opposition of private sector ÖGB members, and that the ÖVP had to solve the conflict with the public sector GÖD, the simultaneity becomes more understandable. If only one of the two laws had passed the committee and parliamentary stages, one of the coalition parties would have had to face the defection of party members and criticisms from their most supportive union. The parties wanted to ensure that any loss in votes was equalized by a loss in votes of their main competitor.

The sessions of the Finance Committee and of the Social Affairs Committee on October 23, 1997 were interrupted and postponed to November 3, to give government and unions more time to reach an agreement, that is, "to soften the bill's hardness" (*Parlamentskorrespondenz* 23.10.1997: No 662). A SPÖ/ÖVP amendment modified the budgetary bill, limiting any pension losses caused by the introduction of the 15-year reference period for civil servants to 1 percent for pensions below ATS 10,000 and to a maximum of 7 percent for pensions up to ATS 28,000. The new regulations were to apply fully to pension benefits above the first ATS 28,000. The Finance Committee interrupted its session to await the unions' decision. The next day ÖVP and SPÖ members put down another amendment: the share of pension benefits which enjoyed loss limitation would be indexed each year after 2003. The Finance Committee approved the proposal. The Committee of Labor and Social Affairs was in session at the same time. In accordance with the changes in the civil servants' pension, union members in the Social Committee also demanded and received a loss limit in the private sector, which would be adjusted annually for the duration of the transition period (*Parlamentskorrespondenz* 03.11.1997: No 701; 04.11.1997: No 704, No 705).

The *Nationalrat* voted on both parts of the reform: private sector pensions (*Arbeits-und Sozialrechts-Änderungsgesetz*), and civil servant's pensions (1. *Budgetbegleitgesetz*), on November 5. Since the last committee session had only ended the night before, the committee report did not meet the minimum publication deadline of at least 24 hours prior to the plenary debate. Therefore, a two-thirds majority of the *Nationalrat* had first to suspend this requirement and then a ÖVP/SPÖ majority passed the reform (NR XX. GP, 93rd: 49–50). The *Bundesrat*'s majority (ÖVP/SPÖ) did not reject the bills (*Parlamentskorrespondenz* 05.11.1997: No 710; 17.12.1997: No 875).

To summarize, the reform proposed in 1997 was watered down massively: Rürup pointed out that the enacted reform achieved no more than 3 percent savings, compared to the 20 percent savings that he had considered necessary in his report on the Austrian pension system (cited from Schweitzer (FPÖ) in NR XX.GP, 93rd: 80). Thus, the reform would not suffice to stabilize the system. The reference period in the private sector was not extended to lifetime earnings or even to 20 years, but stayed at 15 years. An important change was the introduction of a reference period in the public sector, but the transition period would last longer than originally planned and benefit losses were limited (Bertuleit 1999: 38; Tálos and Wörister 1998: 261–3; *SZ* 13.10.1997). Balanced protection of constituency interests and an intense fear of defection and electoral profiteering made Rürup's plan for bold cuts politically impossible.

Pension reform 2000: *Sozialrechts-Änderungsgesetz* (SRÄG)

Background

The election results of 1999 made coalition formation difficult. For the first time in history the ÖVP fell to third place. The margin between the results for ÖVP and FPÖ was tight, with an FPÖ lead of just 415 votes nationwide. The SPÖ remained the strongest party in the *Nationalrat* but the electoral outcome was its worst result ever (Müller 2000a: 191, 198).

The SPÖ had committed itself in pre-election campaigning not to build a coalition with the FPÖ. After several weeks of exploratory talks, the ÖVP leadership was able to negotiate a coalition with the SPÖ, even though it had promised prior to the election to go into opposition if it ranked third in voters' preferences (Müller 2000a: 199). Several ÖVP state leaders did not approve of this change in strategy (*Std* 07.01.2000).

There were several topics on which SPÖ and ÖVP disagreed: most importantly on whether to pursue budget consolidation through changes in the pension system, such as increasing the early retirement age by two years by 2003 (57 for women and 62 for men) and the incremental privatization of pensions (*Kurier* 12.01.2000; *Parlamentskorrespondenz* 19.01.2000: No 15). After 108 days of consultation, the coalition agreement was a victory for the ÖVP. But, as SPÖ-affiliated ÖGB unions strongly objected to the increase in the retirement age (*Std* 12.01.2000; 20.01.2000), Chancellor Klima (SPÖ) was unable to guarantee the consent of parliamentary SPÖ trade unionists and, consequently, final negotiations with ÖVP failed on January 20, 2000. Not only had SPÖ parliamentarians threatened to defect, but an ÖVP representative had also previously announced that the members of the *Nationalrat* from the Steiermark would vote differently in plenum decisions if the party leadership opted for a coalition with the SPÖ (*Kurier* 21.01.2000). Thus, some of the ÖVP *Länder*-party organizations welcomed the breakdown of the coalition talks.

After the failure of coalition formation, President Klestil expressed his preference for a coalition without the FPÖ, by authorizing the SPÖ consider a minority government (*Std* 22.01.2000). But a minority government with FPÖ toleration was very controversial within the SPÖ. Consequently, ÖVP and FPÖ had the highest chances of successful coalition formation. The ÖVP/FPÖ government took office on February 4, 2000 (Obinger 2001: 19–20).

The new Chancellor, Wolfgang Schüssel (ÖVP), proclaimed the following goals for pension reform in his investiture speech: the establishment of an expert commission on pension reform, the creation of a three pillar system with stable public pensions, additional occupational pensions and private old age provisions, and several retrenching measures within the existing private and the public pension schemes (*Parlamentskorrespondenz* 09.02.2000: No 62).

In April 2000, the main features of the reform were fixed. The measures included an increase in the early retirement age of 18 months in 2-monthly steps, greater penalties for early retirement and the abolition of early retirement because of disability—all of which was to take effect as early as October 2000 (*Kurier* 03.04.2000). The coalition also presented a proposal for civil servant pension reform. The minimum age for early retirement of civil servants was to be raised to 61.5 years, penalties for early retirement would increase from two to three percentage points with a maximum limit of 18 percent, pension adjustment for civil servants would follow net wages, and pension contributions for active civil servants as well as for retired civil servants would increase by 0.8 percentage points (*Parlamentskorrespondenz* 30.06.2000: No 410).

The Cabinet agreed on a first draft on April 5, 2000. Opposition parties and unions rejected the proposal and announced that they would consult the constitutional court on whether the short transition period of the planned reform violated the principle of protection of confidence (*Parlamentskorrespondenz* 06.04.2000 No 175). On April 7, 2000 the government started negotiations with the social partners, but the unions rejected the reform measures and accused the government of pseudo-negotiations. On April 13, the first protest actions in the public sector took place. Although the negotiations with the GÖD had just begun, on April 24, 2000 the government issued a proposal and circulated it for appraisal. The ÖGB arranged a protest action day against the pension reform on May 16. On May 26, the negotiations between the GÖD and the Vice-Chancellor broke down, and the railway workers' union threatened to go on strike (Tálos and Kittel 2001: 90–91). By the time the *Ministerrat* decided to pursue pension reform on May 30, 2000 the Economic

Chamber was the only interest group to welcome the proposal (*Parlamentskorrespondenz* 31.05.2000: No 329).

Parliamentary stage

The parliamentary bill included more or less the same measures as the April draft. First, penalties for early retirement pensions would be calculated with three accrual points instead of two, but with a maximum of 10.5 accrual points or 15 percent of pension benefits. Secondly, the minimum age for early retirement was to be increased from 55 to 56.5 years for women and from 60 to 61.5 years for men, with the transition period starting October 1, 2000. Thirdly, widowers' and widows' pensions would range between 0 percent and 60 percent (previously 40% to 60%) of the insured's own pension, taking into account other sources of income and a new upper benefit limit (*Parlamentskorrespondenz* 06.06.2000: No 343). During the negotiations, the unions offered concessions over the increase in the early retirement age, but no consensus could be reached. The government refused to change its plans concerning implementation and the short transition period (Tálos and Kittel 2001: 92).

The opposition party SPÖ and the unions heavily criticized the government for the speed of the reform (*Kurier* 08.06.2000). The ÖGB organized another day of demonstrations against the pension plans on June 28, 2000. All railway workers went on strike for one hour, supported by bus and subway drivers, and teachers (Salzmann 2000). Nevertheless, the bill passed the *Nationalrat* with 100 to 76 votes on July 5, 2000 (NR XXI. GP, 32nd: 232) and the *Bundesrat* on July 19, 2000 without change (BR 667th: 72; BGBl. 101/2000).

Only half a year after taking office the FPÖ/ÖVP coalition had passed a pension reform that significantly overhauled the existing system (BR 667th: 71). During the 2000 reform process, the government made few efforts to come to terms with the social partners, pursuing a confrontational strategy instead. The ÖVP was now free to ignore at least the SPÖ-affiliated unions. In addition, although the FPÖ tended to make populist protests against pension cuts, now it was in government and could be pressured, as the ÖVP could always pivot to the SPÖ (although this would not always constrain the FPÖ as the 2003 *Bundesrat* vote will show). Moreover, a case can be made that the electoral risks associated with this reform were to a certain extent lowered by the sanctions that other EU member states had launched against Austria during that time (in response to the participation of the right wing extremist FPÖ in government). Clearly, this topic dominated other issues in Austrian politics in the spring of 2000. As a consequence, the issue of pension cuts was less salient in public discourse than it would have been otherwise. After the successful passage in Parliament the SPÖ opposition made use of the ultimate veto point and took legal action against the increase in the early retirement age in the Constitutional Court, but without success (Schludi 2005: 180; Obinger 2001: 32).[8] In the event, the 2000 pension reform brought much more significant retrenchment with shorter transition periods, than had any previous reform.

Pension reform 2003: *Budgetbegleitgesetz*

Background

A flood disaster in Austria burdened the government budget with the costs of financial support to the victims in the summer of 2002. The Minister of Finances, Karl-Heinz Grasser (FPÖ), suggested suspending the first stage of the tax reform, and the cabinet agreed. The state governor of Carinthia (*Kärnten*) and FPÖ shadow party leader, Jörg Haider, however, threatened to resign from all offices if the tax reform was not enacted in 2003. Haider's criticism of the national FPÖ leadership, reinforced by disagreements in other areas, led to open conflict between Haider and the vice-chancellor and party leader Susanne Riess-Passer (*SZ* 27.08.2002; 10.09.2002). The conflict resulted in the resignations of Riess-Passer, Grasser and Mathias Reichhold (Minister of Infrastructure). On September 8, 2002, Schüssel requested the dissolution of the *Nationalrat*.

The media coverage of the election campaign was dominated by poll results, debates over parties' competence to govern and by speculation over the outcome, rather than by policy issues (Plasser et al. 2003). The polls suggested that coalition formation was wide open: opinion polls ranked SPÖ and ÖVP about the same, and also predicted the FPÖ and the Greens would get about the same number of votes. As neither SPÖ nor ÖVP committed themselves to coalition partners, the press wrote that it had never been less transparent what the voters would achieve with their votes (*SZ* 22.10.2002, 22.11.2002).

Election day brought extraordinary results: the ÖVP achieved a landslide victory of 42.3 percent of votes and won 27 additional mandates, making it the strongest parliamentary party. The Social Democrats increased their share of the vote but lost the party's number one ranking in the *Nationalrat* after 36 years. The clear loser of the 2002 election was the FPÖ: its share of the vote fell from 26.9 percent to 10 percent. The coalition negotiations started slowly and were accompanied by chaos within the FPÖ (*SZ* 25.11.2002; 27.11.2002; 29.11.2002). Although the FPÖ had proved to be an unreliable partner riven by internal conflict, Schüssel (ÖVP) entered a new coalition with the *Freiheitliche*.

Pre-parliamentary stage

The main goal of the new ÖVP/FPÖ government was a balanced budget, to be achieved through national budget legislation. Although the Budget Act included 20 separate laws, the two most prominent issues were the pension reform and the purchase of the Eurofighter[9] (NR XXII. GP, 20th: 43). With an extraordinarily-strong position in the *Nationalrat*, the ÖVP leadership proposed changes in the pension system with expected savings of €2 billion. This would be an important step towards achieving the zero deficit goal, and allowing the first step in purchasing Eurofighters (BR 697th: 19, 23–4).

The FPÖ/ÖVP government declaration listed the following points for a pension reform: the harmonization of all pension systems, the establishment of contribution-based individual pension accounts and the development of the second and third pillars. The reference period for benefit calculation was to be extended from 15 to 40 years of age, the deduction and revaluation of pensions because of early or late retirement were to be increased to +/−4.2 percent, and any limits on deductions were abolished. The retirement age for public sector employees was to be increased. Child-rearing pension credits were to be extended from 18 to 24 months and, furthermore, three years per child were not to be taken into account for the calculation of the reference period. The yearly accrual rate was to be lowered from 2 percent to 1.78 percent, which would require an increase from 40 to 45 years of insurance to receive the full pension with an 80 percent replacement rate (Österreichische Bundesregierung 2003b: 18–20). The measures proposed in the ministerial draft (BMSG 2003) would have entailed a reduction of pension benefits by up to 40 percent (BR 697th: 11)—"the most severe pension retrenchment in Austrian history" (*Parlamentskorrespondenz* 06.03.2003: No 95: 93). Not surprisingly, there was strong opposition to these proposals.

The evidence is that although the Minister of Social Affairs, Herbert Haupt, was a member of the FPÖ, the original draft of the 2003 pension reform was dictated by the ÖVP. The FPÖ then demanded greater attention to the needs and rights of low-income earners and recipients of pensions below €1,000, and also promoted an increase in the "hardship funds,"[10] further restrictions on politicians' pensions, and the harmonization of the pension systems (*Profil online* 24/2003: 1). The FPÖ could claim credit for having made some improvements in the legislation, but not for having initiated it (*Parlamentskorrespondenz* 04.06.2003: No 394).

While the bill was being debated in the finance committee, there were large protests outside Parliament. A first peak was reached in a strike involving 10,000 companies and 500,000 employees on May 6, 2003 (BR 697th: 11). But it was not only representatives of the opposition parties and the unions that criticized the ministerial draft. ÖVP state governors also rejected the reform measures (*Parlamentskorrespondenz* 11.04.2003: No 208: 201). The pension reform looked like it would become an important issue in the state election Higher Austria (*Oberösterreich*) election campaign of September 2003. A survey conducted by the Institute for Social Research and Analysis showed that support for the ÖVP was only 23 percent, compared to 28 percent for the SPÖ and 37 percent undecided (SORA 2003). This already low level of ÖVP support coincided with the SPÖ's plan to initiate a referendum on pension matters. Higher Austria was also chosen as headquarter for the national strike (Pühringer 2003), and the SPÖ-candidate for the state elections, Erich Haider, threatened to revoke the pension reform in the case of SPÖ government participation on the national level.[11] In response to the electoral threat the state governor of Higher Austria, Josef Pühringer (ÖVP), demanded major changes in the pension reform bill (Strugl 2003d).[12] The state branch of the ÖVP party presented its own pension reform proposal at the national ÖVP party convention on April 24, 2003. The main demands were: no disadvantages for women because of child-rearing periods and the protection of confidence, which meant a rescheduling of the transition period for older active workers and the compensation of cases of hardship because of the extension of the reference period (Strugl 2003a, b). To alleviate hardship, a specific demand was the limitation of potential losses caused by the pension reform (Strugl 2003c).

Simultaneously, unions and employers suggested they might cooperate in a pension reform if the government would suspend the reform until September 2003. Schüssel rejected this unusual offer of social partner unity (*Parlamentskorrespondenz* 16.05.2003: No 327). Nevertheless, after further negotiations on the national level, including Higher Austria's Pühringer, the bill was modified. The transition period for the abolition of early retirement was extended until 2017, and the reduction of the accrual rate from 2 percent to 1.78 percent would be introduced within a five-year period. Additionally, deductions for earlier retirement were limited to a maximum of 10 percent. Women were granted a reduction of the reference period of three years per child, while four years per child were regarded as part of the qualifying period (*Ersatzzeit*). The revised bill foresaw the establishment of a hardship fund and *Hackler*-regulations for certain transition cohorts (Strugl 2003c).[13]

Parallel to the round table negotiations, public opposition to the governmental reform plans culminated in a demonstration on May 13, 2003 (*SZ* 13.05.2003): despite heavy rain and storms, 200,000 people protested in Vienna against the reform package. The union ÖGB threatened the legislators that voting results would be published, so all pensioners would know who was responsible for cutting their pensions (ÖGB 2003). Another one-day strike with one million participants took place on June 3, 2003 (BR 697th: 12).

Only a few days before the final parliamentary debate there was still disagreement within the coalition: eight FPÖ members of parliament threatened to vote against the reform. The FPÖ demanded a higher capital stock for the hardship fund: €20 million instead of €10 million (NR XXII. GP, 20th: 221, 34; BR 697th: 12). The media reported that the coalition was close to breakdown and that early elections were not completely out of the question. But the night before the final session in Parliament, it appeared that the FPÖ and ÖVP had come to an agreement (*Profil online* 24/2003: 3; 25/2003: 1) (though the tables were turned in the parliamentary voting).

Parliamentary voting

The *Nationalrat* adopted the amended bill on 11 June 2003 with the ÖVP and FPÖ majority (NR XXII. GP, 20th: 384–386). The pension reform 2003 was on the *Bundesrat*'s agenda for June 23, 2003. The result was spectacular: the opposition motion to object to the *Nationalrat*'s decision of June 11, was defeated by the ÖVP/FPÖ majority, as expected. But the routine motion not to object to the *Nationalrat*'s decision was declined when nine out of ten FPÖ representatives voted with the SPÖ and Green opposition (BR 697th: 199–200). For the first time in the history of the Austrian *Bundesrat*, no decision was taken on a bill that was debated. Consequently, an eight-week waiting period set in after which the bill automatically became law.

This procedural delay had highly problematic consequences: the pension reform was part of the Budgetary Act that also included a great number of other policy fields, among them the purchase of the Eurofighter. The contract between the Austrian government and Eurofighter-supplier EADS was signed July 1, 2003. As the *Bundesrat* had not passed the budget on June 25, and therefore the act would not come into force before August 7, the Minister of Defense had to spend money that he did not yet have (Die Grüne 2003).

The media considered the final content of the pension reform to be the realization of about one-third of the original proposal (*Profil* 25/2003), and both government parties, ÖVP and FPÖ, claimed credit for having improved the bill and pushed the legislation through (Mitterlehner (ÖVP) in NR XXII. GP, 20th: 74–75; FPÖ 2003).

Pension reform 2005: *Pensionsharmonisierungsgesetz*

Finally, in 2004, the Austrian government submitted a bill (653 d. B. NR XXII. GP) to the *Nationalrat* for complete harmonization of the pension systems in the private sector, the public sector and those for politicians, for people younger than 50 in 2005. This *Pensionsharmonisierungsgesetz*, passed on December 2, 2004, represents a fundamental overhaul of the Austrian pension system. A new General Pensions Law (*Allgemeines Pensionsgesetz*, APG) provides a single legal basis for the pensions of the self-employed, employees, farmers and civil servants (ASVG, GSVG, BSVG, FSVG, BDG). The reform introduced individual pension accounts for all insured persons that register all contributions and periods of exemptions per year. Transition regulations apply to persons who have acquired some pension entitlements before 2005. Thus, the pattern of more radical pension reform begun with the ÖVP/FPÖ coalition in 2000 culminated with this structural reform, although to be sure, the monolithic first pillar and PAYG nature of the Austrian pension system remained in full force.

V Conclusion

Summary of the magnitude of changes

The last 20 years of Austrian pension politics have been characterized by intense debate and controversy, but until recently there have only been limited reforms. Although governments have constantly strived for a consolidation of the general budget through a reduction of social security expenditure, government contributions to the pension system increased from ATS 16 billion (i.e. 1.57% of GDP) in 1980 to ATS 56.5 billion (i.e. 1.95% of GDP) in 2001[14] and to €5.8 billion in 2003 (Hauptverband 2004).

The sheer number of reforms and reform measures speaks for itself: the pension policy modifications of the 1980s and the 1990s did not suffice to consolidate the budget, which was the prime goal of all governments discussed in this chapter. If the reform outcomes are evaluated not in absolute terms but relative to the reform proposals, the result is even clearer: all governmental drafts were cut back, and concessions to various actors weakened the impact of the final pension acts. Even the radical reform proposals of the ÖVP/FPÖ coalition in 2000 and 2003 were watered down by including loss limitation measures.

None of the reforms introduced any measures that would make second- or third-pillar pension provisions more attractive, let alone mandatory. Nor did they work towards significant capital funding within the first pillar. Thus, in terms of structural change the Austrian pension reforms of the last two decades were limited. However, in terms of benefit cuts and restricting eligibility the last two reforms were much more incisive than their predecessors. Although the envisioned 40 percent cuts will not be enforced due to the loss limitation mechanisms, a 10 percent retrenchment in pension benefits is still remarkable (Wöss and Türk 2004). Moreover, in contrast to the previous pension reforms, these cutbacks will be enacted within a relatively short time period.

Impact of the political system on pension politics

Despite the existence of federalism, bicameralism and a constitutional court, the Austrian political system features few veto points. All of these institutional arenas either have no veto power over legislation or can be overridden by the two-third majorities typical of Austria's oversized coalition governments, which also render the parliament impotent as a veto point. Indeed, even proportional representation has not produced a high degree of parliamentary fragmentation—as one might expect—because of the stable patterns of electoral loyalties created by the traditional *Lager*.

Nevertheless, Austrian governments had great difficulty introducing the pension reforms that they themselves deemed were necessary to solve budgetary and economic problems, as well as to ensure the sustainability of the pension system. Although the veto players approach suggests that the policy distance within governments is also a critical factor in government's desire and likelihood of overturning the status quo, SPÖ-ÖVP cabinets nevertheless agreed on a series of reforms.

Instead, the problems of Austrian pension politics lay in the behavior of members of parliament. When faced with cuts to their constituents, MPs broke with party discipline and would not toe the line. Often, these defections were announced proactively, in the extended pre-parliamentary consultation procedures available in this consociational system. Indeed, the many trade unionists within the parliament played a dual role, being able to "voice" their objections through the trade unions and to "exit" from the party line in parliament.

We argue that the difficulties of Austrian pension politics can be best explained by changing patterns of political competition. The radical rightward move of the FPÖ placed the dominant parties into a position of extreme competition, which made it unattractive to pursue reform politics to the end. This intense competition was further exacerbated by the changed electoral system as well as the long-term decomposition of the social milieu.

Interest group influence

Trade union influence on the political decision-making process in Austria underwent a gradual transformation. We can distinguish three different phases in Austrian pension politics, which are marked by varying degrees of union influence (Schludi 2005: 183–5). Until the early 1990s, pension reforms were still largely developed within the traditional framework of social partnership. Typically, they were initiated and negotiated by the social partners, or at least worked out in close concertation between the government and the social partners. Trade unions were able to exert strong influence on the passage, content and timing of pension reforms. The unions participated in the formulation of policy proposals at a very early stage. This was based on a relatively strong political consensus that no major decision in social and economic policy was to be made without or against the social partners. This contributed to an extremely incremental reform process.

In the mid-1990s, this constellation changed. Faced with extraordinarily strong budgetary pressures the SPÖ/ÖVP coalition sought to get a tighter grip on the reform process. In particular, the government tried to determine the content as well as the timing of reforms (Tálos and Kittel 1999). Most importantly, it unilaterally established tight guidelines for the overall volume of expenditure cuts to be made in the pension system. In two cases (1994 and 1997) it proposed major changes to the pension system without prior consultation of the social partners. In striking contrast to the consensual tradition of social partnership, the government even considered the adoption of reforms against trade union resistance. Clearly, the unions had lost influence with respect to the formulation of policy proposals through corporatist bargaining. Instead, they increasingly tried to exert influence by way of lobbying, and sought to block unwanted legislative changes through their parliamentary representatives. Due to their strong numerical weight within the parliamentary group of the SPÖ and the increased intra-party competition because of the new preference vote, they were able to prevent the internally divided SPÖ/ÖVP government from putting through pension reform proposals against their resistance. Hence, until the late 1990s, Austrian pension policy still proceeded at a rather slow pace.

Since the year 2000, under the center-right ÖVP/FPÖ government, union influence on social and economic policy formulation (including pension reform) has eroded further. It appears that the current ÖVP/FPÖ government is less responsive to union demands than its predecessors. Remarkably, it is the first government that has openly rejected a joint initiative of the social partners in such an important matter of economic and social policy. This can be seen as a strong indication that the creeping erosion of the Austrian model of *Sozialpartnerschaft* has gained momentum under the incumbency of the Schüssel government. Perhaps the most important reason is that this government is less dependent on unions' institutional support. The current government constellation does not give the trade unions strong political bargaining power, mainly due to the much smaller number of trade unionists within the government fractions. In sum, the continuous decline in union representation in parliament over the last twenty years was critical to their dwindling influence on pension policy outcomes (Schludi 2005).

Constraints of policy design

The specific policy design of the private sector pension system (ASVG) has played a secondary role in Austrian pension reforms. Obviously, the Austrian pension system design constituted the context for the partisan and interest group actors to draft proposals and make demands, but it is not a sufficient explanation for the successful passage of major saving measures.

Although inequities within the system, the "vices" as Levy (1999) calls them, might have been used to justify cuts in privileges, this was not the case. The relatively low female retirement age, for example, was increased only after a Constitutional Court decision, and required an extremely long transition period. Under the guise of equalization, the government could have legitimized the benefit cuts and pension expenditure savings at the same time. The differences between the civil servants' pension scheme and the private sector blue- and white-collar schemes were more significant. The greater equity to be achieved by harmonizing the two systems was one of the main arguments used to legitimize changes in the 1990s. Although harmonization was important for the reforms under SPÖ/ÖVP grand coalitions, it cannot account for the deep retrenchment measures in ASVG in 2000 and 2003. The low number of years taken into account as the assessment base for pension calculation at the beginning of the research period (5 years) gave much greater scope for action than systems of other countries, where benefits have been calculated on the income base of the entire working career for a long time (e.g. Germany). However, it is not sufficient to explain the non-linear, erratic increases: whereas the SPÖ/ÖVP increased the base incrementally from 5 to 10 and from 10 to 15 years, the FPÖ/ÖVP government legislated an extension of the reference period from 15 to 40 years in one step.

Role of ideas and historical context

Austria is known for policy-making in concertation. For more than three decades legislation was enacted in consultation and agreement with the social partners in many policy sectors. With increasing party competition in the 1980s the consensual policy style changed. While the relationship between government and social partners became more distant, policy communities lost in importance. However, in pension policy the effect is not as far-reaching as in other policy areas: the highly technical and complicated matter of pension calculation and pension financing, in combination with a policy-making style of tripartite pre-parliamentary negotiations, only allowed a very small group of actuarial and pension experts to take full part in the discussions (see e.g. NR XVII. GP, 38th: 4339). This circle did not offer ground for the elaboration of fundamentally new ideas. Indeed, as we have seen, many of these reforms involved multiple attempts to introduce the very same policy ideas.

In none of the reforms described in this chapter are systemic overhauls negotiated, or even suggested. The smaller parties did have alternative concepts to the existing Austrian pension system: the Greens preferred a basic pension system and the FPÖ envisaged the establishment of a true 3-pillar-system. However, neither of these concepts was seriously debated during the reform processes. The conflicts that arose concerned trimming at the edges rather than fundamental change.

The only scientific study that apparently did influence the public debate, and consequently the issue dimension and development of the reform process, was the Marin and Prinz study in 1996 (*Profil* 06.04.1996). Their calculations showed that civil servants' life-time income exceeded private sector employee' income by far, which sensitized and mobilized the public. This research apparently had the potential to create a new cleavage between private sector employees and civil servants.

Abbreviations

AK	*Kammer für Arbeiter und Angestellte*
ASVG	*Allgemeines Sozialversicherungsgesetz*
ATS	*Österreichischer Schilling*
BDG	*Beamten-Dienstrechtsgesetz*
BMSG	*Bundesministerium für soziale Sicherheit und Generationen*
BR	*Bundesrat*
BSVG	*Bauern-Sozialversicherungsgesetz*
d.B.	*der Beilagen*
FPÖ	*Die Freiheitlichen*
FSVG	*Freiberufliches Sozialversicherungsgesetz*
GdG	*Gewerkschaft der Gemeindebediensteten*
GÖD	*Gewerkschaft Öffentlicher Dienst*
GP	*Gesetzgebungsperiode*
GSVG	*Gewerbliches Sozialversicherungsgesetz*
LIF	*Liberales Forum*
NR	*Nationalrat*
NVG	*Notarversicherungsgesetz*
ÖAAB	*Österreichischer Arbeiter und Angestelltenbund*
ÖAKT	*Österreichischer Arbeiterkammertag*
ÖGB	*Österreichische Gewerkschaftsbund*
ÖVP	*Österreichische Volkspartei*
PRÄKO	*Präsidentenkonferenz der Landwirtschaftskammer*
PVA	*Pensionsversicherungsanstalt*
SPÖ	*Sozialdemokratische Partei Österreichs*
SZ	*Süddeutsche Zeitung*

VOeBB *Verband österreichischer Banken und Bankiers*
VÖI *Vereinigung österreichischer Industrieller*
VVÖ *Verband der Versicherungsunternehmen Österreichs*

Notes

1. We thank the following persons for background interviews Richard Leutner (ÖGB General Secretary), Karl Öllinger (Grüne, Member of the Nationalrat), Werner Thum (ÖGB Pensioners); for research support Sieglinde Osiebe (Austrian Parliamentary Library), Michaela Mayer-Schulz (BMSG), Elena Bechberger; and for helpful discussions and comments Ellen Immergut, Sven Jochem and Emmerich Tálos. All remaining errors are our responsibility.
2. Government formation following the 1999 election constituted an unusual exception: although the SPÖ obtained the most parliamentary seats and the FPÖ more votes (1,244,087) than the ÖVP (1,243,672), President Thomas Klestil asked Wolfgang Schüssel of the ÖVP to form a government.
3. The following description refers to regulations in force in June 2004 unless otherwise noted.
4. These rules pertain to old-age and widows' pensions. Widows may not collect their own as well as a widows' pension if the combined benefit is above a certain limit. Old-age pensioners cannot earn income and collect a full old-age pension if the combined income is above a certain limit.
5. "Die scheidende SPÖ-Frauenchefin erinnerte daran ... Dallinger, der zugleich Obmann der Angestellten-Gewerkschaft ist, falle sogar den Frauen in der eigenen Gewerkschaft in den Rücken, weil er den gut ausgebildeten berufstätigen Frauen die Berufstätigkeit austreiben wolle: 'Sein Motto lautet: Zurück in die Küche'" (*KlZ* 27.09.1987; *Tagblatt* 26.09.1987).
6. Exact voting in the *Bundesrat* by name is not documented. According to unofficial statistical report on parliamentary voting the ÖVP did not support the bill unanimously on April 25, 1996. Nevertheless, the *Bundesrat* decided with SPÖ and some ÖVP votes not to object the *Strukturanpassungsgesetz 1996* (Republik Österreich Parlamentsdirektion 2003; BR 598th). Given that the *Strukturanpassungsgesetz 1996* affected 98 different laws the ÖVP's partial abstention may have had numerous reasons and cannot be linked to the pension reform.
7. The meeting was postponed until the negotiations with the social partners had come to an end (*Std* 11.10.1997).
8. The Constitutional Court considered the increase in the retirement age for early retirement, and the higher deductions for early retirement to be constitutional in its verdict of June 27, 2003. The changes in survivors' pensions, however, were considered unconstitutional (Präsidium des Verfassungsgerichtshofes 2003).
9. *Bundesgesetz über den Nachkauf von Luftraumüberwachungsflugzeugen.*
10. The establishment of a fund to alleviate hardship (*Härtefondausgleich*) was to enable pensioners with inadequate pensions to apply for supplements from the Ministry of Social Assistance. This fund was capital-funded for the first three years (BR 697th: 13).
11. Opinion polls in June 2003 showed that 71% of those interviewed believed that national policy topics played a role, and that the pension reform in particular would have negative

impact on ÖVP and FPÖ support at the state election (*Vorarlberg* Online 11.06.2003). Moreover, the SPÖ ran for elections with the explicit goal of becoming the strongest party in the state Parliament for the first time in 36 years (*OÖN* 23.06.2003b).

12. A survey among Higher Austrian *Nationalrat* deputies taken shortly after the publication of the governmental pension reform bill, displayed indecisiveness with respect to upcoming voting behavior on the pension issue: the deputies' intentions ranged from "no vote against the state party leader's objectives" to "confident that the bill will be changed" to "agreement if necessary" (*OÖN* 2003c, a). Considering that there were 13 ÖVP members from Higher Austria but the ÖVP/FPÖ had only an 11-seat lead in the *Nationalrat*, these "doubts" were important.

13. *Hackler* is Austrian for heavy workers. *Hacklerregelung* are regulations on early retirement. Women born before 1950 and men born before 1945 had been allowed to retire at 55/60 years if they had 480/540 months of insurance contributions. The pension reform of 2003 extended this regulation as a concession to intra-ÖVP disagreement to all women born before 1952 and all men born before 1947.

14. Data from personal e-mail from Michaela Mayer-Schulz, BMSG, 21.07.2003.

Bibliography
Primary sources and government documents
Acts

BGBl. 484/1984. *40. Novelle zum Allgemeinen Sozialversicherungsgesetz*. (27.11.1984).

BGBl. 609/1987. *44. Novelle zum Allgemeinen Sozialversicherungsgesetz, Änderung des Sonderunterstützungsgesetzes und des Nachtschicht-Schwerarbeitsgesetzes*. (25.11.1987).

BGBl. 832/1992. *Bundesverfassungsgesetz: Unterschiedliche Altersgrenzen von männlichen und weiblichen Sozialversicherten*. (29.12.1992).

BGBl. 335/1993. *Sozialrechts-Änderungsgesetz (SRÄG 1993)*. (26.05.1993).

BGBl. 101/2000. *Sozialrechts-Änderungsgesetz 2000 – SRÄG 2000*. (24.08.2000).

BGBl. Nr. 471 idF BGBl. I Nr. 98/2001. *Bundesgesetz über die Wahl des Nationalrates (Nationalrats-Wahlordnung 1992 – NRWO)*.

B-VG. *Bundes-Verfassungsgesetz*.

Bills and parliamentary documents

327 d.B. NR XVI. GP. *40. Novelle zum Allgemeinen Sozialversicherungsgesetz* (26.06.1984).

735 d.B. NR XVIII. GP. *Regierungsvorlage: Arbeitsrechtliches Begleitgesetz (ArbBG)* (27.11.1992).

737 d.B. NR XVIII. GP. *Regierungsvorlage: Bundesverfassungsgesetz über unterschiedliche Altersgrenzen von männlichen und weiblichen Sozialversicherten* (11.11.1992).

932 d.B. NR XVIII. GP. *Regierungsvorlage: Bundesgesetz, mit dem das Allgemeine Sozialversicherungsgesetz (51. Novelle zum ASVG), das Beamten-Kranken- und Unfallversicherungsgesetz (22. Novelle zum B-KUVG) und das Sonderunterstützungsgesetz geändert werden* (08.03.1993).

72 d.B. NR XX. GP. *Regierungsvorlage: Strukturanpassungsgesetz 1996* (15.04.1996).

653 d.B. NR XXII. GP. *Regierungsvorlage: Pensionsharmonisierunggesetz* (13.10.2004).

Ausschuß für soziale Verwaltung (1984). *Bericht des Ausschusses für soziale Verwaltung über die Regierungsvorlage (327 der Beilagen): 40. Novelle zum Allgemeinen Sozialversicherungsgesetz.* 390 d.B. NR XVI. GP.

Ausschuß für soziale Verwaltung (1992). *Bericht des Ausschusses für soziale Verwaltung über die Regierungsvorlage (737 der Beilagen): Bundesverfassungsgesetz über unterschiedliche Altersgrenzen von männlichen und weiblichen Sozialversicherten*. 837 d.B. NR XVIII. GP.

BMSG (2003). *Ministerialentwurf betreffend ein Bundesgesetz, mit dem das Allgemeine Sozialversicherungsgesetz, das Gewerbliche Sozialversicherungsgesetz, das Bauern-Sozialversicherungsgesetz*

und das Beamten-Kranken- und Unfallversicherungsgesetz im Rahmen des Budgetbegleitgesetzes 2003 geändert werden. 28/ME (NR XXII. GP).
BUDGETAUSSCHUSS (1995). Bericht des Budgetausschusses über die Regierungsvorlage (134 der Beilagen): Strukturanpassungsgesetz. 149 d.B. NR XIX. GP.
REPUBLIK ÖSTERREICH PARLAMENTSDIREKTION ABTEILUNG L3.4 Parlamentarische Dokumentation Archiv und Statistik. 2003: With reference to: *Abstimmungsverhalten im National- und Bundesrat XVI. bis XXI. GP.* Personal Correspondence, 14.07.2003.
SOZIALAUSSCHUSS (1984). Bericht des Sozialausschusses über den Gesetzesbeschluß des Nationalrates vom 17. Oktober 1984 betreffend 40. Novelle zum Allgemeinen Sozialversicherungsgesetz. 2874 d.B. des Bundesrates.
SOZIALAUSSCHUSS (1992). Bericht des Sozialausschusses über den Beschluß des Nationalrates vom 1. Dezember 1992 betreffend ein Bundesverfassungsgesetz über unterschiedliche Altersgrenzen von männlichen und weiblichen Sozialversicherten. 4384 d.B. des Bundesrates.

Parliamentary minutes
Nationalrat. *Stenographisches Protokoll*:
NR XVI. GP, 59th session, 17.10.1984: 4980:5061
NR XVI. GP, 66th session, 27.11.1984: 5672–5699
NR XVII. GP, 34th session, 05.11.1987: 3943
NR XVII. GP, 38th session, 25.11.1987: 4326–4401
NR XVIII. GP, 90th session, 30.11./01.12.1992: 9985–10033
NR XVIII. GP, 114th session, 21.04.1993: 13282–13383
NR XX. GP, 16th session, 18./19.04.1996: 360–636
NR XX. GP, 32nd session, 05.04.1995: 6–182
NR XX. GP, 60th session, 29.01.1997: 15–27
NR XX. GP, 91st session, 10.10.1997: 2
NR XX. GP, 93rd session, 05.11.1997: 15–50, 50–133
NR XXI. GP, 32nd session, 05.07.2000: 47–233
NR XXII. GP, 20th session, 10./11.06.2003: 12–392

Bundesrat. *Stenographisches Protokoll*:
BR 452nd session, 25.10.1984: 18002–18053
BR 494th session, 03.12.1987: 21333–21362
BR 562nd session, 11.12.1992: 26973–26994
BR 569th session, 29.04.1993: 27607–27638
BR 598th session, 20.04.1995
BR 612th session, 25.04.1996: 18–108
BR 667th session, 19./20.07.2000: 70–103
BR 697th session, 23.06.2003: 8–201

Newspapers and magazines (various issues)
AZ: *Abend Zeitung*
Die Zeit
KlZ: *Kleine Zeitung*
KZ: *Kronenzeitung*
Kurier
OÖN: *Oberösterreichische Nachrichten*
OÖTagblatt: *Oberösterreichisches Tagblatt*
Parlamentskorrespondenz

Presse: *Die Presse*
Profil
Profil online
Std: *Der Standard*
SZ: *Süddeutsche Zeitung*
Tagblatt
Vorarlberg Online
WZ: *Wiener Zeitung*

Secondary sources

BAWN, KATHLEEN and THIES, MICHAEL F. (2003). "A Comparative Theory of Electoral Incentives: Representing the Unorganized Under PR, Plurality and Mixed-Member Electoral Systems." *Journal of Theoretical Politics*, 15(1): 5–32.

BERTULEIT, ACHIM (1999). "Österreich." In Verband Deutscher Rentenversicherungsträger (ed.), *Rentenversicherung im internationalen Vergleich*. Frankfurt am Main: VDR, 5–41.

DAY, ALAN J. (ed.) (2002). *Political Parties of the World*. London: John Harper.

DIE GRÜNE (2003). *Eurofighter—Vertragsunterzeichnung nur "Absichtserklärung."* Österreichische Woche, [cited 03.02.2003]. Available from www.oe-journal.at/Aktuelles/0703/W1/30307Pplatter.htm.

FALLEND, FRANZ (1997). "Regierungsproporz in der Krise: Zur aktuellen politischen Debatte über die konkordanzdemokratische Regierungsform in Österreichs Bundesländern." *Österreichische Zeitschrift für Politikwissenschaft*, 26(1): 23–40.

FEHER, CSABA (2001). *The Austrian Old Age Pension System*. Prepared for "Learning from the Partners": World Bank/IIASA Conference. Vienna, April 6–7, 2001.

FISCHER, HEINZ (1997). "Das Parlament." In Dachs, H., et al. (eds.), *Handbuch des politischen Systems Österreichs: Die Zweite Republik*. Wien: Manzsche Verlags- und Universitätsbuchhandlung, 99–121.

FPÖ (2003). *Sichere Pensionen, Sichere Zukunft*. [cited 24.06.2003]. Available from www.fpoe.at/bundneu/folder/sichere_pensionen.pdf.

Hauptverband der österreichischen Sozialversicherungsträger (ed.) (1984). *Handbuch der österreichischen Sozialversicherung für das Jahr 1984 I. Teil*. Wien.

—— (2004). *Die österreichische Sozialversicherung in Zahlen*. [cited 10.06. 2004]. Available from www.sozialversicherung.at/mediaDB/21834.PDF.

—— (2005). *Die österreichische Sozialversicherung in Zahlen*. [cited 17.06.2005 2005]. Available from www.sozialversicherung.at/mediaDB/84792.PDF.

HOFINGER, CHRISTOPH and OGRIS, GÜNTHER (1996). "Achtung, gender gap! Geschlecht und Wahlverhalten 1979–1995." In Plasser, F., Ulram, P. A. and Ogris, G. (eds.), *Wahlkampf und Wählerentscheidung: Analysen zur Nationalratswahl 1995*. Wien: Signum, 211–32.

HOFMEISTER, HERBERT (1981). "Landesbericht Österreich." In Köhler, P. A. and Zacher, H. F. (eds.), *Ein Jahrhundert Sozialversicherung in der Bundesrepublik Deutschland, Frankreich, Großbritannien, Österreich und der Schweiz*. Berlin: Duncker & Humblot, 445–730.

JACOBS, FRANCIS (1989). "Austria." In Jacobs, F. (ed.), *Western European Political Parties: A Comprehensive Guide*. Harlow/Detroit: Longman Group, 478–99.

KARL, BEATRIX (2001). "Alterssicherung und demographische Entwicklung in Österreich." In Reinhard, H.-J. (ed.), *Demographischer Wandel und Alterssicherung: Rentenpolitik in neun europäischen Ländern und den USA im Vergleich*. Baden-Baden: Nomos Verlagsgesellschaft, 153–83.

KARLHOFER, FERDINAND (1999). "Verbände: Organisation, Mitgliederintegration, Regierbarkeit." In Karlhofer, F. and Tálos, E. (eds.), *Zukunft der Sozialpartnerschaft: Veränderungsdynamik und Reformbedarf*. Wien: Signum, 15–46.

KARLHOFER, FERDINAND (2001). "Österreich: Zwischen Korporatismus und Zivilgesellschaft." In Reutter, W. and Rütters, P. (eds.), *Verbände und Verbandssysteme in Westeuropa*. Opladen: Leske & Budrich, 335–54.

KITTEL, BERNHARD (1998). "Entaustrifizierung? Die Grenzen des Wandels des österreichischen Systems: Eine Literaturübersicht." *Neue Politische Literatur*, 43(2): 290–300.

KLENNER, FRITZ and PELLAR, BRIGITTE (1999). *Die österreichische Gewerkschaftsbewegung: Von den Anfängen bis 1999*. 2nd edn. Wien: Verlag des ÖGB.

KOSSDORFF, FELIX and SICKINGER, HUBERT (1996). "Wahlkampf und Wahlstrategien: Eine Biographie der Kampagnen 1995." In Plasser, F., Ulram, P. A., and Ogris, G. (eds.), *Wahlkampf und Wählerentscheidung: Analysen zur Nationalratswahl 1995*, Wien: Signum, 47–83.

LEHMBRUCH, GERHARD (1979). "Liberal Corporatism and Party Government." In Lehmbruch, G. and Schmitter, P. C. (eds.), *Trends Towards Corporatist Interest Intermediation*. Beverly Hills/London: Sage, 147–83.

LEVY, JONAH D. (1999). "Vice into Virtue? Progressive Politics and Welfare Reform in Continental Europe." *Politics and Society*, 27(2) (June): 239–73.

LUTHER, KURT R. (1987). "Austria's Future and Waldheim's Past: The Significance of the 1986 Elections." *West European Politics*, 16(3): 376–99.

—— (1997). "Die Freiheitlichen (F)." In Dachs, H., et al. (eds.), *Handbuch des politischen Systems Österreichs: Die Zweite Republik*, Wien: Manzsche Verlags- und Universitätsbuchhandlung, 286–303.

MADERTHANER, WOLFGANG (1997). "12. Februar 1934: Sozialdemokratie und Bürgerkrieg." In Steininger, R. and Gehler, M. (eds.), *Österreich im 20. Jahrhundert: Von der Monarchie bis zum Zweiten Weltkrieg*. Wien: Böhlau, 153–203.

MARIN, BERND and PRINZ, CHRISTOPHER (1999). "Arbeitnehmer oder Beamte: Wer hat höhere Lebenseinkommen? Eine 'profil'-Kolumne 1996 mit Folgen." In Prinz, C. and Marin, B. (eds.), *Pensionsreformen: Nachhaltiger Sozialumbau am Beispiel Österreichs*. Frankfurt am Main: Campus, 313–26.

MÜLLER, WOLFGANG C. (1997a). "Das Parteiensystem." In Dachs, H. et al. (eds.), *Handbuch des politischen Systems Österreichs: Die Zweite Republik*. Wien: Manzsche Verlags- und Universitätsbuchhandlung, 215–34.

—— (2000a). "The Austrian Election of October 1999: A Shift to the Right." *West European Politics*, 23(3): 191–200.

—— (1997b). "Regierung und Kabinettsystem." In Dachs, H. et al. (eds.), *Handbuch des politischen Systems Österreichs: Die Zweite Republik*. Wien: Manzsche Verlags- und Universitätsbuchhandlung, 122–38.

—— (2000b). "Austria: Tight Coalitions and Stable Government." In Müller, W. C. and Strøm, K. (eds.). *Coalition Governments in Western Europe*. Oxford: Oxford University Press, 86–125.

MUNZINGER (2003). *Österreich: Parteien und Verbände*. [cited 03.06. 2003]. Available from www.munzinger.de/

NATIONALRAT (2003). *Der Weg der Bundesgesetzgebung*. [cited 03.06. 2003]. Available from www.parlinkom.gv.at/pd/doep/d-k3-4.htm

NEUWIRTH, ERICH (2003). *Das Mandatsberechnungsverfahren der österreichischen Nationalratswahlordnung*. SunSITE Austria, University of Vienna. [cited 03.06. 2003]. Available from http://sunsite.univie.ac.at/Austria/elections/nrw95/nrw94man.html

OBINGER, HERBERT (2001). *Vetospieler und Staatstätigkeit in Österreich: Sozial- und wirtschaftspolitische Reformchancen für die neue Mitte-Rechts-Regierung*. Zes-Arbeitspapier 5/01. Bremen: Zentrum für Sozialpolitik/Centre for Social Policy Research.

OECD (2002). "General Government Financial Balances". *OECD Economic Outlook*, 71(1): 234 (Annex Table 228).

ÖGB (2003). *Pensionsklau geht weiter: Auch die PensionistInnen werden zur Kasse gebeten.* [cited 10.06. 2003]. Available from www.oegb.at/

ÖSTERREICHISCHER ARBEITERKAMMERTAG (1984). *Entwurf eines Bundesgesetzes, mit dem das Allgemeine Sozialversicherungsgesetz geändert wird (40. Novelle zum ASVG); Stellungnahme.* Wien: Arbeiterkammer.

—— (1987). *Ergänzungen zum Entwurf eines Bundesgesetzes, mit dem das Allgemeine Sozialversicherungsgesetz geändert wird (44. Novelle zum ASVG); Stellungnahme.* Wien: Arbeiterkammer.

—— (1992). *Entwurf eines Bundesgesetzes, mit dem das Allgemeine Sozialversicherungsgesetz geändert wird (51. Novelle zum ASVG); Stellungnahme.* Wien: Arbeiterkammer.

ÖSTERREICHISCHE BUNDESREGIERUNG (2003a). *Die Eckpunkte der Pensionssicherungsreform 2003.* Kanzleramt. [cited 17.07. 2003]. Available from www.austria.gv.at/eckpunkte.pdf

—— (2003b). *Regierungsprogramm der Österreichischen Bundesregierung für die XXII. Gesetzgebungsperiode.* [cited 10.06. 2003]. Available from www.austria.gv.at/regierungsprogramm.pdf

PELINKA, ANTON (1999). "Das politische System Österreichs." In Ismayr, W. (ed.), *Die politischen Systeme Westeuropas.* Opladen: Leske + Budrich, 489–517.

—— and ROSENBERGER, SIEGLINDE (2000). *Österreichische Politik: Grundlagen – Strukturen – Trends.* Wien: WUV.

PLASSER, FRITZ and ULRAM, PETER A. (1996). "Kampagnedynamik: Strategischer und thematischer Kontext der Wählerentscheidung." In Plasser, F., Ulram, P. A. and Ogris, G. (eds.), *Wahlkampf und Wählerentscheidung: Analysen zur Nationalratswahl 1995.* Wien: Signum, 13–46.

—— —— and SOMMER, FRANZ (2003). *Wahlverhalten in Bewegung: Analysen zur Nationalratswahl 2002: Ausgewählte Ergebnisse.* Zentrum für Angewandte Politikforschung. [cited 21.06. 2004]. Available from www.polimatrix.at/20102802.html

PRÄSIDIUM DES VERFASSUNGSGERICHTSHOFES (2003). *Pressemitteilung des Verfassungsgerichtshofes: Pensionsreform 2000: Erhöhung des Antrittsalters und Abschläge zulässig Regelung zur Hinterbliebenenpension verfassungswidrig.* VfGH. [cited 15.06. 2004]. Available from www.vfgh.gv.at/presse/PA_Pensionsrefom2000.html

PÜHRINGER, JOSEF (2003). *Pensionsreform auf dem Verhandlungstisch und nicht auf der Strasse lösen.* ÖVP Oberösterreich. [cited 03.02. 2004]. Available from www.ooevp.at/opencms/opencms/OEVP/FEATURE/News/News_Detail.html?id=1924

PULZER, PETER (1995). "Small Earthquake in Austria: The National Election of 9 October 1994." *West European Politics,* 18(2): 429–37.

PV (2005a). *Der Nachkauf von Schul-, Studien- und Ausbildungszeiten (Nachträgliche Selbstversicherung).* Pensionsversicherungsanstalt. [cited 17.06. 2005]. Available from www.pensionsversicherung.at/mediaDB/86590.PDF

PV (2005b). *Die Ausgleichszulage.* Pensionsversicherungsanstalt. [cited 17.06. 2005]. Available from www.pensionsversicherung.at/mediaDB/80663.PDF

—— (2005c). *Die Pensionsharmonisierung: ABC zum Nachschlagen.* Pensionsversicherungsanstalt [cited 17.06. 2005]. Available from www.pensionsversicherung.at/mediaDB/86710.PDF

—— (2005d). *Pensionen: Voraussetzungen—Berechnung.* Pensionsversicherungsanstalt [cited 17.06. 2005]. Available from www.pensionsversicherung.at/mediaDB/86691.PDF

—— (2005e). *Versicherungszeiten.* Pensionsversicherungsanstalt. [cited 17.06. 2005]. Available from www.pensionsversicherung.at/mediaDB/83713.PDF

—— (2005f). *Versteuerung von Pensionen.* Pensionsversicherungsanstalt. [cited 17.06. 2005]. Available from www.pensionsversicherung.at/mediaDB/90563.PDF

PVAng (ed.) (2002). *Pensionen: Voraussetzungen—Berechnung.* Wien: Pensionsversicherungsanstalt der Angestellten. Wien: Pensionsversicherungsanstalt der Angestellten.

Rürup, Bert and Schroeter, Ingo (1997). *Perspektiven der Pensionsversicherung in Österreich*. Gutachten. Darmstadt: Bundesminister für Arbeit, Gesundheit und Soziales.

Salzmann, Markus (2000). *Die Pensionsreform und das Ende der Sozialpartnerschaft*. World Socialist Web Site. [cited 02.10. 2002]. Available from www.wsws.org/de/2000/aug2000/oest-a18_prn.html

Schludi, Martin (2005). *The Reform of Bismarckian Pension Systems: A Comparison of Pension Politics in Austria, France, Germany, Italy and Sweden*. Amsterdam: Amsterdam University Press.

Sebald, Marisa (1998). "Die 'Sparpakete' Mitte der neunziger Jahre." In Tálos, E. and Kittel, B. (eds.), *Sozialpartnerschaft und Entscheidungsprozesse: Projektbereicht*. Wien: Hochschuljubiläumsstiftung der Stadt Wien, 5–106.

Sora (2003). *Aktuelle SORA-Umfrage: Gegenwind für Schwarz-Blau*. Institute for Social Research and Analysis. [cited 04.02. 2004]. Available from www.sora.at/objects/SORA%20Umfrage%20April%202003.pdf

Soziale Sicherheit (1984). "Amtliche Verlautbarungen Nr. 117/1984: Bundesministerium für soziale Verwaltung Gutachten des Beirates für die Renten- und Pensionsanpassung, betreffend die Festsetzung des Anpassungsfaktors für das Jahr 1985." *Soziale Sicherheit*, 1984 (12): 517–50.

Strugl, Michael (2003a). *Pensionsreform: ÖVP Oberösterreich mit eigenem Antrag beim Bundesparteitag*. ÖVP Oberösterreich. [cited 03.02. 2004]. Available from www.ooevp.at/opencms/opencms/OEVP/FEATURE/News/News_Detail.html?id=1886

—— (2003b). *Deutliche Verbesserungen gegenüber dem ursprünglichen Reformentwurf*. ÖVP Oberösterreich. [cited 03.02.2004]. Available from www.ooevp.at/opencms/opencms/OEVP/FEATURE/News/News_Detail.html?id=1887

—— (2003c). *Regierung greift Vorschlag von LH Ühringer auf: Deckelung von Verlusten bei Pensionsreform*. ÖVP Oberösterreich. [cited 03.02. 2004]. Available from www.ooevp.at/opencms/opencms/OEVP/FEATURE/News/News_Detail.html?id=1887

—— (2003d). *SPÖ macht mit Pensionsfrage Wahlkampf*. ÖVP Oberösterreich. [cited 03.02. 2004]. Available from www.ooevp.at/opencms/opencms/OEVP/FEATURE/News/News_Detail.html?id=1870

Sully, Melanie A. (1996). "The 1995 Austrian Election: Winter of Discontent." *West European Politics*, 19(3): 633–40.

Tálos, Emmerich (1999). "Sozialpartnerschaft: Zwischen Entmystifizierung und Anpassungsherausforderungen: Ein Resümee." In Karlhofer, F. and Tálos, E. (eds.), *Zukunft der Sozialpartnerschaft: Veränderungsdynamik und Reformbedarf*. Wien: Signum, 277–98.

Tálos, Emmerich and Kittel, Bernhard (1999). "Sozialpartnerschaft und Sozialpolitik." In Karlhofer, F. and Tálos, E. (eds.), *Zukunft der Sozialpartnerschaft: Veränderungsdynamik und Reformbedarf*, 137–64. Wien: Signum.

Tálos, Emmerich and Kittel, Bernhard (2001). *Gesetzgebung in Österreich: Netzwerke, Akteure und Interaktionen in politischen Entscheidungsprozessen*. Wien: WUV.

—— and Wörister, Karl (1998). "Soziale Sicherung in Österreich." In Tálos, E. (ed.), *Soziale Sicherung im Wandel: Österreich und seine Nachbarstaaten: Ein Vergleich*. Wien: Böhlau, 209–88.

Tomandl, Theodor (1984). "Enquete zur Pensionsreform: Grenzen, Ziele und Mittel der Reform." *Soziale Sicherheit*, 1984 (2): 52–60.

Wöss, Josef (2000). "Gesetzliche Pensionsversicherung: Rückblick auf die letzten 30 Jahre." *Soziale Sicherheit*, 2000 (12): 1000–08.

—— and Türk, Erik (2004). *Lügenkampagne zu den Pensionen?* Arbeit & Wirtschaft. [cited 15.06. 2004]. Available from www.arbeit-wirtschaft.at/aw_04_2004/art5.htm

CHAPTER 13

PORTUGAL: IN SEARCH OF A STABLE FRAMEWORK

ELISA CHULIÁ
MARÍA ASENSIO

I Introduction[1]

ALTHOUGH considered to be a Southern European latecomer to the European conservative welfare regime (Esping-Andersen 1999: 73–94), Portugal has made significant efforts to improve its welfare institutions since the establishment of democracy in the mid-1970s. Indeed, of all countries in the European Union (EU), Portugal experienced the highest increase in social protection expenditure between 1992 and 2001 (Guillén, Álvarez and Adão e Silva 2001; European Commission 2004: 14–17).

Established during the dictatorship, but only fully developed in the first decade of democracy, the Social Security pension system represents the core of the Portuguese welfare state. This mandatory pay-as-you-go (PAYG) pension system maintains a reserve fund, which at the end of 2004 amounted to around €5,800 million, the cost of approximately eight-and-a-half months of pension payments. High employment rates, especially among women and older workers, and below average levels of unemployment—combined with relatively low pension spending—largely explain the current favorable financial situation of the Portuguese Social Security pensions. Nevertheless, the maturation of the pension system, as demonstrated by the longer contribution periods of new pensioners, and the worsening of the old-age dependency ratio, which is predicted to double by 2050, are seen as challenges that may result in significant financial imbalances before 2020 (Holzmann, Orenstein, and Rutkowski 2003: 39; OECD 2003: 120–1). In addition to the persistent problem of contribution evasion, the recent difficulties of the Portuguese economy have intensified these fears. Beginning in 2002, Portugal fell into a deep recession, with both increasing unemployment and inflation. Many experts have interpreted this downturn as the logical outcome of the country's inability to adapt to the requirements of a globalized economy. Low productivity, high-energy dependence and low fertility rates are identified as the key structural problems of the Portuguese economy at the beginning of the twenty-first century.

However, without the consensus of the two major Portuguese parties, it is difficult in Portugal to bring structural change to the pension system, since any government wishing to do so has to surmount not only the opposition in parliament, but also the institutional veto power of the President of the Republic. The Portuguese Constitution endows the President with the power to refuse to sign legislation, and even to dissolve Parliament and call for early elections. This is what happened in December 2004, when the President Jorge Sampaio argued that the government of Prime Minister Pedro Santana Lopes was showing incompetence in coping with pending policy decisions, and was losing its legitimacy.

The kind of partisan consensus between the Social Democrats and the Socialists needed to allow substantial pension reform is to some extent impeded by competing definitions of the pension "problem." The Social Democrats have stressed growing Social Security outlays and financial difficulties, and as such have prioritized the enhancement of actuarial principles in the design of pension rules as well as of private funding. The Socialists, on the other hand, have focused on the need to control contribution fraud and on the severe economic conditions confronting many old-age pensioners.[2]

Consequently, pension politics since the mid-1980s, when the coalition government of the two main Portuguese parties managed to approve the first Social Security framework law after the transition to democracy, can be characterized as incrementalist. Policy has by and large been based on consensus among political elites, with the acquiescence of Social Security experts and bureaucrats. The reforms have been mostly parametric, with the emphasis on cost-containment and efficiency-enhancing measures. These have been combined with certain expansionary measures aimed at reinforcing the Social Security system, which most political and social actors associate with democratic values, such as social justice and solidarity.

Nevertheless, the debate on the role of funded pensions within the Social Security system has fueled the politicization of pension policy in recent years. Whereas the Social Security framework law, approved under the Socialist government in 2000, put supplementary schemes based on funding outside the Social Security structure, regarding them first and foremost as voluntary, two years later the right-leaning Social Democrats, in coalition with a smaller conservative party, changed the law and defined these schemes as one of the three Social Security systems. The 2002 Social Security Framework Law established that workers could opt to transfer their contributions above a specific wage ceiling to the public PAYG system or to the supplementary funded system. The goal of the reform was to promote mixed pensions consisting of a "first" defined-benefit (public) allowance and a "second" defined-contribution (public or private) pension. Yet the coalition government under which the new law was passed did not develop the concrete regulation of this new limited opting-out system.

II Political system

Constitutional history and nation-building

Portugal's century-long monarchy fell in 1910, under the pressure of a revolutionary process. The First Portuguese Republic was formally a democracy organized according to the principles of a parliamentary system, but it was beset by political factionalism, economic strife and social unrest. Frequent general strikes and monarchic upheavals led to extremely high governmental instability.

On the ground of this precarious situation the military staged a coup in 1926, and forced the President of the Republic to resign before establishing a dictatorship with the explicit aim of restoring social peace (Costa Pinto 2000: 8–9). The Minister of Finance, António de Oliveira Salazar, became Prime Minister in 1932. In the 1933 Constitution the military dictatorship was given the institutional design of a corporatist authoritarian regime. Fervently anti-communist, the New State (*Estado Novo*) declared itself neutral during the Second World War. The Cold War and the traditionally friendly relationship with Great Britain helped Portugal to get through the difficult post-war period. However, while Western Europe was experiencing what Huntington (1991) has called the second wave of democratization, Portugal and Spain remained the dictatorial exception in the Iberian Peninsula.

In the context of an expanding economy, bringing better living conditions for the Portuguese population in the 1960s, the outbreak of the colonial wars in Africa set off significant social changes, among them the rapid incorporation of women into the labor market.[3] Salazar ruled until 1968 when he was replaced by Marcelo Caetano, Professor of Law and former minister of the Colonies, known for his technocratic approach to policy. In spite of several efforts to legitimize the authoritarian regime by the "marcelist" elites, the frustration of Portuguese army officers with the colonial policies of the metropolis led them to organize around the Armed Forces Movement (*Movimento das Forças Armadas*, MFA) and stage a coup on April 25, 1974. The bloodless takeover, greeted with enthusiasm by many in Lisbon, entered into history with the name of the "Carnation Revolution" owing to the image of flowers inserted in the muzzles of tanks and rifles.

Between 1974 and 1976, the initial years of the Second Portuguese Republic, the platform of the MFA functioned as a sort of revolutionary constitution centered on decolonization, the nationalization of important industries and banks as well as of the mass media, land reform and the expansion of social rights. The provisional governments led by military officers depended on the Council of the Revolution, the highest political and judicial institution. Drafted at the climax of the revolutionary period, the 1976 Constitution brought together private property and economic freedom with state intervention in the economy, "irrevocable" nationalizations and a leading role for the working-class in the transformation to a "classless" society and the transition to socialism. Far from taking the constitutional design of contemporary European democracies as a model, the new political elites decided to write a Constitution reconciling pluralist representative democracy (under the supervision of the MFA-led Council of the Revolution, responsible for evaluating the conformity of legislation with the Constitution) and Marxist socialism. Yet the approval of the Constitution did not put a stop to political instability: between April 1974 and October 1979 Portuguese citizens witnessed no less than six provisional and five constitutional governments. The request for an IMF loan in 1977 revealed the grim economic situation during this first period of the political transition.

The 1982 Constitutional Reform, initiated by a center-right coalition government in the context of an atmosphere of national crisis, brought a serious reconsideration of the leftist course of the regime. The ideologically burdened rhetoric of the original text (especially of its economic section) was revised, and the constitutional obligations to state intervention in the economy reduced, even if the changes did not essentially alter the economic organization designed in the 1976 Constitution (Canotilho and Moreira 1993: 386–88). Furthermore, the Council of the Revolution was abolished. With the transfer of the Council's role to a Constitutional Court with civilian judges, the dominance of the military in the political system faded away.

In 1983, the Portuguese government had to apply for a new IMF loan. GDP per head in power purchasing parities was still lower than in the early 1970s (amounting to less than 55% of the European average) (INE 2004: 86). Nevertheless, the situation began to change in the mid-1980s. Accession to the EU in 1986 propelled economic liberalization and brought vast sums of new money through the European structural funds and foreign direct investment (FDI). As a consequence, Portugal experienced a huge socio-economic transformation. The Portuguese economy was becoming increasingly integrated and tertiarized, and in 1989 the two major parties signed an agreement to review the Constitution once again. The second Constitutional Reform introduced profound changes in the sections "Fundamental principles" (Arts. 1 to 11) and "Economic organization" (Arts. 80 to 110). The goals of constructing "a classless society" and abolishing "the exploitation and oppression of man by man" were removed. Their place was taken by commitments to realize "economic, social and cultural democracy", to deepen "participatory democracy" and to modernize economic and social structures.[4] Moreover, the principles of economic transformation that characterized the revolutionary period were abandoned: re-privatization of nationalized firms was allowed, the general principle of basing economic organization on social property was diluted, land reform disappeared as a constitutional goal and the socialist concept "plan" as the instrument of a state regulated economy was replaced by the reference to "plans of economic and social development" (Canotilho and Moreira 1993: 48–9, 388–90).

In the 1990s, the economic decisions preceding and following membership of the Exchange Rate Mechanism (ERM) from 1992, and of Economic Monetary Union (EMU) from 1999 (especially lower interest rates), prompted a consumer boom and a reduction of the public debt burden, both boosting economic expansion. Meanwhile, Portuguese governments embarked on a strategy of further reducing public ownership of banks and big enterprises (petrol, electricity, telecommunications, etc.), signaling a growing convergence with ideas of state retrenchment, as was popular in most other European countries (Syrett 2002: 18). Portugal managed to significantly reduce the shortfall between national GDP per head and the European average, and experienced a rise in living standards, albeit with important regional disparities remaining (*The Economist* 2000a and 2000b).

Although Portugal is traditionally a unitary state, the 1976 Constitution established three distinct levels of local government: parishes, municipalities and administrative regions. While the first two began to operate in that same year, nearly three decades later the regional tier of government has still not been implemented. Only the archipelagos of the Azores and Madeira have their own regional governments and regional assemblies. The legislation they approve is subject to preventive constitutional control by the Constitutional Court if the central government or the President of the Republic demands it. In contrast with the strong nationalist feelings that prevail in some Spanish regions not very far from the Portuguese borders, citizens in Portugal seem not at all interested in devolving power to territorial units. Actually, the creation of mainland regional administrations was rejected in a national referendum held in November 1998.[5] The process of administrative decentralization has made little progress and the central bureaucracy remains the locus of organizational power. Even if in recent years local governments have been gaining influence in the areas of environmental protection, social services and housing, the proportion of public outlays controlled by local administrations reveals the clear predominance of the central state: in the year 2000 municipalities spent less than 10 percent of public expenditure, well below the EU average (Nunes 2002: 198–214).

After several constitutional reviews Portugal has entered the twenty-first century as a consolidated liberal democracy which nonetheless still has remarkable structural problems. Political apathy seems to be growing, as the general tendency towards lower voter turnout suggests (Magone 1997: 87–8).[6] Strong regional inequalities, a bulky bureaucracy[7] providing unsatisfactory public services in education, health and justice, and the low competitiveness of the economy stand out as complaints voiced by citizens and experts. In the context of a slowing economy and marked difficulties to restrain the budget deficit, the consequences of the EU enlargement, in terms of decreasing funds and FDI, intensify the fears about Portugal's future in the global market.

Institutions of government

As regards the organization of political power the Constitution of the Portuguese Republic recognizes four "organs of supreme authority"; the President of the Republic, the Assembly (*Assembleia da República*), the government and the courts.

As in other semi-presidential systems, the President of the Republic is directly elected by universal suffrage. His mandate lasts five years and he is entitled to stand for re-election once. As the head of state he has to guarantee national unity and the normal functioning of state institutions. Although he does not share government functions with the Prime Minister, he has the power to dissolve the *Assembleia* (on his own initiative and without the agreement of the government, after hearing the parties with parliamentary representation and the State Council),[8] dismiss the government and call elections and referenda. Of fundamental importance is his exclusive competency to veto laws and decree-laws (that can only be overcome by an absolute or a qualified majority of the *Assembleia*, depending on the legislated issue) and ask the Constitutional Court for the preventive control of legislation produced either by the *Assembleia* or by the government and for the verification of unconstitutionality in case of omission. Additionally, the President has the constitutionally recognized right to be informed by the Prime Minister about governmental domestic and international performance, to address speeches to the *Assembleia* as well as to the regional parliaments of the Azores and Madeira, and to publicly manifest his opinions with regard to political questions.

It is also the President who appoints the Prime Minister, according to electoral results and after hearing the opinions of the political parties represented in the *Assembleia*. If no party or party coalition obtains an absolute majority of seats the President can encourage conversations between parties to negotiate a consensual proposal. But he nevertheless enjoys "a considerable scope to select the Prime Minister and nothing compels him to appoint the person indicated by the biggest party or party coalition" (Leite and Ferreira 2001: 39–49). Instead he can dissolve the *Assembleia* and call new elections.[9] Moreover, the 1976 Constitution confers on the President the power to remove the government "when it becomes necessary to guarantee the normal functioning of the democratic institutions" (Art. 195). Only three men—General Ramalho Eanes (1976–1985), Mário Soares (1986–1996) and Jorge Sampaio (1996–2006)—have held this post during the first three decades of Portuguese democracy.

The Constitution endows the uni-cameral *Assembleia* with extensive legislative and supervisory powers. Its 230 members, elected by universal suffrage, "represent the whole country and not the electoral circles in which they have been elected" (Art. 152),[10] but in fact party discipline restricts the freedom of representation.[11] The Constitution delimits a vast array of issues under the exclusive legislative competence of the *Assembleia*, only some of which can be delegated to the government through explicit authorization (among them the bases of the Social Security and health care systems). The wide legislative power of the *Assembleia* has been linked with the desire of the political parties that participated in the drafting of the Constitution to buttress the power of parliament, after four decades of dictatorship during which law-making was the exclusive preserve of the government (Leite and Ferreiro 2001: 54). In contrast to other democratic parliaments, the *Assembleia* plays a very active role in the production of legislation. It consistently presents many more projects than the government does for parliamentary discussion, even though the percentage of approved acts is higher in the case of governmental proposals (Freire et al. 2002: 64–8). This performance is almost certainly a result of institutional practice more than it is of constitutional design.

Besides legislating and electing some office-holders of state institutions (among them 10 of the judges of the Constitutional Court), the *Assembleia* controls the government through questions and requests that ministers participate in parliamentary debates, as well as through petitions to attend parliamentary commissions. If at least one-fifth of its members so decides, the *Assembleia* has also the right to ask the Constitutional Court for the preventive constitutional control of bills to be promulgated as organic laws. This Court also has to examine the constitutionality or legality of any norm in force if requested by the President of the *Assembleia* or by one-tenth of its members. The *Assembleia* can oust the government if an absolute majority of its members rejects a vote of confidence presented by the Prime Minister or approves a censure motion against the executive.[12] Finally, the competence of the President of the Republic to suspend constitutional rights and guarantees is limited by the necessary authorization of the *Assembleia*.

For all that its life cycle depends crucially on the President of the Republic, the government has autonomy to develop executive functions. As defined by the Constitution, the government of the Portuguese Republic is particularly broad. The Prime Minister, the Deputy Prime Minister (if there is one) and the Ministers form the Council of Ministers and share executive power with the holders of the State Secretariats and Under-Secretariats (the highest "political bureaucrats" of each Ministry who however lack political and legislative competencies and confine their functions to administrative questions). After his nomination by the President, the Prime Minister presents his agenda to the *Assembleia*, but explicit parliamentary approval is not necessary for investiture. In fact, if the *Assembleia* does not reject the Prime Minister's agenda by an absolute majority, the government achieves full executive power. Unlike the President, the Prime Minister lacks the right to ask the Constitutional Court for the preventive constitutional control of norms approved by the *Assembleia*, though once promulgated, he can claim a declaration of unconstitutionality or illegality. The members of the government do not formally belong to the *Assembleia*, but have the right to address plenary sessions and talk to the elected members, as well as to demand participation in the workings of parliamentary commissions.

The administration of justice falls to the courts of law, the administrative and fiscal courts, the military courts and the Court of Auditors (in charge of supervising the legality of public expenditure). Besides these, the Constitutional Court, created by the 1982 Constitutional Reform, enjoys specific powers: its 13 judges (10 of them elected by the *Assembleia* and the rest co-opted) are not only responsible for monitoring the conformity of legislation with the Constitution, but also for establishing the legality of political parties, electoral acts and referenda as well as the incapability of the President of the Republic to perform his constitutional functions. This Court can be asked by the President of the Republic, the Ministers, or one-fifth of the parliamentary deputies to check the constitutionality of legislative acts approved by the *Assembleia*. It consequently has the power to declare published laws null and void.

The distribution of power within the political system of the Second Portuguese Republic has often provoked tension between the three pivotal state institutions: the President, the government and the *Assembleia*. During the first years of the democratic system the political dominance of the presidency constrained the strength of prime ministers, whose parliamentary support was precarious. Even though the 1982 Constitutional Review substantially curtailed some of the President's competencies, conflicts between the head of state and the government have not been absent from Portuguese politics, especially when the posts have been held by representatives of different parties. The main instrument in the hands of the President against the government or the *Assembleia* is the preventive constitutional control (Magone 1997: 40–2; Braga da Cruz 2000: 115–24). However, the first three Portuguese presidents have made a fairly parsimonious use of this initiative: between 1983 and 1998 Eanes, Soares and Sampaio submitted less than 50 pieces of legislation of the *Assembleia* or of the government to the Constitutional Court. Analyzed by government periods, the highest frequency corresponds to the second presidential mandate of the former socialist leader Soares, whose tenure coincided with the absolute majority government of the center-right PSD. But even under cohabitation, the presidents have renounced the indiscriminate employment of preventive constitutional control as a form of political obstruction of parliamentary majorities or minority governments (Araújo and Coutinho 2000).

Whereas the presidency is generally perceived as an institution that gives stability to the political system (Magone 1997: 43; Corkill 2002: 221), a divided *Assembleia* and frequent changes of government during the first decade of the new regime conferred on both of these institutions an image of volatility. The autonomy of the executive power vis-à-vis the *Assembleia* and the President has increased since the mid-1980s, as a direct consequence of stable electoral majorities backing the governments. Nonetheless, since 1999, no government has been able to see out its full term.

Electoral system

Elections to the presidency of the Portuguese Republic are held every five years according to the majority principle. If one of the candidates fails to obtain an absolute majority on the first ballot, a run-off election is held within two weeks between the two candidates with the most votes. Presidential elections are typically

Table 13.1 Political institutions in Portugal

Political arenas	Actors	Rules of investiture	Rules of decision-making	Veto potential
Head of State	President of the Republic (*Presidente da República*)	5-year term; directly elected; if no candidate receives 50% of votes in first ballot then second ballot; only one consecutive reelection	Appoints Prime Minister; signs laws and decree-laws; power to dissolve *Assembleia* and remove government; absolute veto power over government legislation and relative veto power over legislation approved by *Assembleia* (presidential veto can be overcome by a qualified majority); can ask the Constitutional Court for preventive control of legislation	Veto point
Executive	Prime Minister (*Primeiro Ministro*)	Appointed by the President after legislative elections; has to inform the President regularly of government activities and can be held accountable by the *Assembleia* through vote of no confidence (*moções de censura*)	Right of initiative (*Propostas de Lei*); right to promulgate decree-laws that need not to be ratified by Parliament	—
Legislative	Parliament (*Assembleia da República*)	4-year term, but often not finished; 230 members elected on closed party lists in 22 multi-member electoral districts (between 2 and 49 mandates per district); proportional representation; seat allocation according to d'Hondt formula	Right of initiative (*Projectos de Lei*); voting decision rule: affirmative votes prevail over negative votes; organic laws (*Leis Orgânicas*) regulating matters exclusively dependent on the parliament, such as the election of certain office holders, referenda, the organization and functioning of the Constitutional Court, the organization of national defense, and the state of siege and emergency, require an absolute parliamentary majority for passage	Veto point if minority government

(*Continued*)

Table 13.1 (Continued)

Political arenas	Actors	Rules of investiture	Rules of decision-making	Veto potential
Judicial	Supreme Court of Justice (*Supremo Tribunal de Justiça*) as highest jurisdictional organ	Nomination, location, promotion and disciplinary control of judges is the competence of the High Council of the Magistrature (*Conselho Superior da Magistratura*) composed of 16 members: 2 designated by President, 7 elected by *Assembleia* and 7 elected by judges according to proportional representation	Administration of justice	Not a veto point
Constitutional	Constitutional Court (*Tribunal Constitucional*)	9-year term, 13 judges (10 of them elected by *Assembleia*; 3 co-opted)	Pre-emptive control of constitutionality upon President's request; monitors conformity of legislation with the Constitution; establishes the legality of political parties, electoral acts and referenda and the incapability of the President to fulfill his constitutional functions	Veto point
Electoral	Referendum	Called by President on proposal of the government or the *Assembleia* on issues of national interest (but not for constitutional amendments, budgetary or monetary policies)	Referendum outcome is binding if at least 50% of registered electors votes	Not a veto point
Territorial units	Autonomous regions municipalities	Madeira and Azores Islands 308 *municípios* and *freguesias*	Can legislate regional legislative decrees (*Decretos Legislativos Regionais*)	Not a veto point

highly personalized, but party-politics also plays a role since the candidates' biographies are usually linked to parties. Actually, although parties do not present candidates for the presidency and the President is formally independent from any party, he can be a party member.

Elections to the *Assembleia* are constitutionally scheduled every four years. Nevertheless, governmental instability has frequently led to short legislatures and anticipated elections (in 1979, 1983, 1985, 1987, 2002 and 2005). In each electoral district parties present closed lists of candidates to the voters. Seats are allocated according to the d'Hondt method of proportional representation, which favors larger parties, but since no minimum percentage of votes is required in order for a party to enter parliament and because of the large size of some electoral districts, small parties have access to the *Assembleia*. Thus, the electoral system does not provide incentives for parties to arrange electoral coalitions, while at the same time impeding the creation of absolute majorities (Braga da Cruz 2000: 109–10; Freire et al. 2002: 101). As of 2005, the 230 parliamentary deputies are elected in 22 multi-member constituencies, 18 from the continent, two from Portugal's two autonomous archipelagos, the Azores and Madeira, and two by emigrants in Europe and beyond. The electoral districts may be classified in three groups according to their magnitude: Lisbon and Porto form the first group and send 49 and 37 representatives to the *Assembleia* respectively; the second group encompasses eight districts with between 8 and 17 mandates; the majority of districts, 12, belong to the third group ranging from 2 to 7 mandates.

The electoral system was established in 1976, but it is not a settled issue in Portugal. Discussions on electoral reform have focused on the likely advantages of mixed member systems, the reduction of the magnitude of the big districts and the creation of a national district. The major parties perceive electoral reform as a way of bringing political representatives nearer to voters and improving the public image of politicians, and to a lesser extent as a mechanism that could help create absolute majorities of one party (Robinson 2002: 188–9; Freire et al. 2002: 86–92). The 1997 Constitutional Review enabled electoral reform, but it has not hitherto been carried out.

Local elections are held every four years in 308 municipalities. They generally have lower participation rates than national elections and are often used as opportunities to voice disapproval with national politics (Nunes 2002: 201). Finally, elections to the European Parliament (with still lower turnouts) are organized in a single constituency (24 seats) so that each party presents a single list of candidates for the whole country. The seats are distributed among the parties according to the d'Hondt method.

Legislative process

According to the Portuguese Constitution, legislative power is shared between the *Assembleia*, the government and the Regional Legislative Assemblies. The

Assembleia produces laws (*Leis*), and the government can promulgate decree-laws (*Decretos-Lei*).[13] Finally, regional legislative decrees (*Decretos Legislativos Regionais*) are those approved by the parliaments of the Azores and Madeira on matters of their specific interest which are not reserved to the *Assembleia*. Laws, decree-laws and regional legislative decrees are the constitutionally established legislative acts.

Legislative initiatives in the form of *Propostas de Lei* (presented by the government or the regional assemblies) or *Projectos de Lei* (presented by the parliamentary groups or by individual members) are subject to a two-fold discussion and a three-fold approval. Bills are first approved by the plenary of the *Assembleia* after a general discussion; the second approval takes place after a specialized discussion within the corresponding parliamentary commissions; finally, drafted in their final version, the bills have to be endorsed again in Parliament, either by a simple majority, an absolute majority (organic laws) or a qualified majority (particularly constitutional reform and changes in electoral legislation).

The government can also legislate by using decree-laws, an option especially valuable for minority governments because it allows them to circumvent the *Assembleia*. It cannot, however, legislate on matters exclusively reserved to the *Assembleia*, like electoral norms, constitutional reform, national defense, the armed forces and the police, parties and associations, state symbols and states of siege and emergency. Nor can decree-laws lay down the principles or bases on which issues concerning the political and administrative organization of the state are to be decided. These general principles have to be formulated and passed in the form of framework laws (*Lei de Bases* or *Lei Quadro*) before the government is authorized to develop them. In any case, all decree-laws, except for those that relate to the exclusive competence of the government (that is, the organization and functioning of the executive power), can be discussed in the *Assembleia* and rejected or modified by a majority of its members. Still, not only quantitatively but also from the perspective of the content relevance, decree-laws tend to outstrip laws, a trend that has been connected with the stronger parliamentary support that Portuguese governments have enjoyed since 1987 (Leite and Ferreira 2001: 59).

Based on laws and decree-laws the government issues regulations, which can take the form of *Decretos Regulamentares, Portarias* or *Despachos Normativos*. The *Decretos Regulamentares* (frequently published as *Resoluçoes*) have to be approved by the Council of Ministers and are subject to the presidential veto, whereas the rest are endorsed by the individual ministers or state secretaries.

Laws, decree-laws and *Decretos Regulamentares* are promulgated by the President of the Republic, but need the formal countersignature of the government. This provision can be interpreted as a symbolic manifestation of the collective responsibility of the government and the President in running state affairs.

Finally, legislative inflation and lack of legislative stability are perceived as nuisances of Portuguese policy-making, which harm the efficacy and transparence of the legal system. Critics also disapprove of the occasional misuse of decree-laws and regulations, specifically when the former concern merely administrative questions and the latter cover spaces left by the legislator (Leite and Ferreira 2001: 53–4).

Party family affiliation	Abbreviation	Party name	Ideological orientation	Founding and merger details	Year established
Christian/Right Parties	CDS-PP	*Centro Democrático Social-Partido Popular*	Right-of-center	Formed out of the CDS (*Partido do Centro Democrático Social*), created by members of the semi-legal opposition to dictatorship. Changed its name after breakdown of Democratic Alliance in 1985	1974
Christian/Right Parties	PSD (former PPD)	*Partido Social Democrata*	Center-right, moderate conservative	Emerged as semi-legal opposition to dictatorship	1974
Left parties	PS	*Partido Socialista*	Social democratic	Founded in West-Germany before the collapse of dictatorship and supported by German SPD	1973
Left parties	PCP	*Partido Comunista Português*	Communist	Illegal between 1926 and April 1974. Strong allies of MFA (*Movimento das Forças Armadas*) during transition to democracy	1921
Left parties	BE	*Bloco de Esquerda*	Radical left	Coalition of *Partido Socialista Revolucionário*, *União Democrática Portuguesa* and *Política XXI*	1999
Greens		*Os Verdes*	Environmental		1982

Fig. 13.1 Party system in Portugal

Parties and elections

The first two years of Portugal's transition to democracy were extremely volatile. In the context of intense conflict between the MFA and radical left nationally-oriented organizations on the one hand, and moderate political parties predominantly oriented towards the representative West-European democracies on the other hand, six provisional governments tried to establish the foundations of a new regime. This turbulent period ended in 1976 when two important elections were held in the country, for the *Assembleia* in April and for the presidency in June.

One year earlier, on April 25, 1975, the newly-established regime had celebrated the first elections in Portugal's history based on the principle of universal suffrage. With a 92 percent turnout, these elections to the Constituent Assembly gave birth to a fairly stable party system. By 1976, four main parties represented nearly 91 percent of the electorate. The *Partido Socialista* (PS, Socialist Party) represented the center-left. The *Partido Popular Democrático* (PPD, Popular Democratic Party—but since 1976 known as the *Partido Social Demócrata*, PSD, Social Democratic Party) represented the center-right. The *Centro Democrático e Social* (CDS, Democratic and Social Center; *Centro Democrático e Social–Partido Popular* (CDS–PP) since 1992), was a right-of-center party. Finally, the *Partido Comunista Português* (PCP, Portuguese Communist Party) attracted the more radical leftist votes. Having contributed much to reversing the revolutionary process, the first three parties garnered more than 70 percent of the total vote in the 1975 elections. Although this four-party format has remained fairly stable during subsequent decades, the increasing share of votes obtained by the PS and PSD since the late 1980s has been interpreted as a tendency towards an imperfect two-party system, with the consequent tendency to bipolarization of politics (Magone 1997: 90–1).[14]

In the second regular parliamentary elections of 1976, the Socialist Party under Mário Soares won a majority and formed the first constitutional cabinet. Internal divisions provoked the fall of Soares' single party minority government, initiating a period of governmental instability until the general elections of 1979.

The Democratic Alliance (AD) between the PSD, the CDS and the small *Partido Popular Monárquico* (PPM) in the 1979 elections produced right-of-center governments backed by parliamentary majorities for the next two years. The electoral victory of the rightist coalition led to conflict in the relationship between the President of the Republic (Ramalho Eanes) and the Council of the Revolution on the one hand, and the Prime Ministers (Sá Carneiro, until he died in an air crash in December 1980, and subsequently Pinto Balsemão) and the *Assembleia*, on the other. Though the Portuguese system clearly remained divided between right and left, the 1979 elections revealed the leaning of the majority of Portuguese society towards moderate political positions.

After adjusting the PS platform towards social democratic ideology, Soares won the 1983 elections and formed a grand coalition government with the PSD. The so-called *Bloco Central* had to face a period of severe economic problems and high unemployment. This period only lasted two years, during which time accession to the European Community was also negotiated. The breakdown of the coalition led to early elections in October 1985. In retrospect, these elections mark the beginning of a slow but steady decline of the PCP, which was vehemently opposed to Portugal's membership of the EC and stuck to the revolutionary legacy of the first transition years (Álvarez-Miranda 1996: 123–212). The PS, which led an electoral coalition called *Frente Republicana e Socialista*, received its worst results in 1985. The *Partido Renovador Democrático* (PRD), a new party inspired by the President, Ramalho Eanes, became the main beneficiary of the Socialists' electoral setback.

The PSD formed a minority government between 1985 and 1987. The vigorous parliamentary opposition it faced during these years reached a climax when it lost a motion of censure called by the PRD and the *Assembleia* had to be dissolved. In the 1987 elections, the electorate punished the conflictual stance of the opposition parties and gave the PSD, led by the charismatic neo-liberal Aníbal Cavaco Silva, the absolute majority of seats and votes.

The PSD was able to form a majority government for the second time after the 1991 elections, but four years later, after having been present in Portuguese governments for 16 years, it had to give up executive power. No longer led by Cavaco Silva, the party appeared internally divided. The PS, under the leadership of António Guterres, profited from the electorate's weariness of an ineffective and allegedly corrupt executive. Although Guterres lacked three seats to form a majority government, he managed to lead a rather stable and efficient cabinet. The PS again won elections in 1999, but failed to reach the absolute majority by one seat, leaving the *Assembleia* evenly balanced between the Socialists and the combined opposition. Thus the new PS government was again forced to seek the support or abstention of other parliamentary groups in order to pass legislation. The 1999 election also gave access to the *Assembleia* to a challenger of the PCP, the *Bloco de Esquerda*, an alliance of communist and extreme-left parties fighting against globalization and for social justice and equality (Robinson 2002: 184–92).

The poor results obtained by the PS in the 2001 local elections, after some scandals that concerned the government, induced Guterres to resign. In the 2002 parliamentary elections the PSD re-emerged as the largest party, but fell short of an overall majority in the *Assembleia*. Its leader, José Manuel Durão Barroso, negotiated the formation of a post-electoral coalition with the CDS-PP, incorporating some of the members of this party in his government. The PS, under its new leader Eduardo Ferro Rodrigues, performed better than expected: it retained 96 seats, only nine less than the PSD. The elections brought another poor result for the Communists of the PCP, which saw its percentage share of the vote and its presence in the *Assembleia* reduced to the lowest levels since the establishment of democracy. Divided between the PCP and the *Bloco de Esquerda*, the Portuguese extreme left obtained the support of less than 10 percent of the electorate.

After the election of Durão Barroso as President of the European Commission in 2004, the President of the Portuguese Republic, Jorge Sampaio, named a conservative coalition government led by Santana Lopes. In the first few months of his leadership, the new Prime Minister made several ministerial changes, and a number of decisions, that irritated public opinion. Sampaio's decision to dissolve the *Assembleia* and call new elections to be held in February 2005 made evident a conflict which is latent in the Portuguese constitutional design: the President exercises a major control on the

Table 13.2 Governmental majorities in Portugal

Date of change in political configuration	Presidential election date	President (party)	Presidential majority	Election date Assembleia	Start of gov.	Head of gov. (party)	Governing parties	Gov. majority (% seats)	Gov. electoral base (% votes)	Institutional veto points	Number of veto players (partisan + institutional)
07.27.1976	27.07.1976	António Ramalho Eanes (Ind)		04.25.1976	07.23.1976	Soares I (PS)	PS (107)	40.7%	36.6%	President[a] (PRES) Parliament (PARL)	1 + 2
01.23.1978		António Ramalho Eanes (Ind)			01.23.1978	Soares II (PS)	PS (107), CDS (42)	56.7%	53.4%	PRES	2 + 1
08.29.1978		António Ramalho Eanes (Ind)			08.29.978	Nobre da Costa (Ind)	Presidential appointment; non-partisan[b]	–	–	PARL[a]	0 + 1
11.22.1978		António Ramalho Eanes (Ind)			11.22.1978	Mota Pinto (Ind)	Presidential appointment; non-partisan[b]	–	–	PARL	0 + 1
07.07.1979		António Ramalho Eanes (Ind)			07.07.1979	Lourdes Pintassilgo (Ind)	Presidential appointment; non-partisan[b]	–	–	PARL	0 + 1
03.01.1980		António Ramalho Eanes (Ind)		12.02.1979	01.03.1980	Sá Carneiro I (PSD)	AD (coalition of CDS, PSD and PPM) (128)	51.2%	46.5%	PRES, PARL	3 + 2
05.10.1980		António Ramalho Eanes (Ind)		10.05.1980	10.05.1980	Sá Carneiro II (PSD)	AD (134)	53.6%	48.7%	PRES	3 + 1
07.12.1980	12.07.1980	António Ramalho Eanes (Ind)	55.9%			Sá Carneiro II (PSD)	AD (134)	53.6%	48.7%	PRES	3 + 1

01.09.1981	António Ramalho Eanes (Ind)		01.09.1981	Pinto Balsemão I (PSD)	AD (134)	53.6%	48.7%	PRES	3 + 1
09.04.1981	António Ramalho Eanes (Ind)		09.04.1981	Pinto Balsemão II (PSD)	AD (134)	53.6%	48.7%	PRES	3 + 1
06.09.1983	António Ramalho Eanes (Ind)		04.25.1983 06.09.1983	Soares III (PS)	PS (101), PSD (75)	70.4%	65.0%	PRES	2 + 1
11.06.1985	António Ramalho Eanes (Ind)		10.06.1985 11.06.1985	Cavaco Silva I (PSD)	PSD (88)	35.2%	30.6%	PRES, PARL	1 + 2
03.09.1986	Mário Soares (PS)	50.7%		Cavaco Silva I (PSD)	PSD (88)	35.2%	30.6%	PRES, PARL Constitutional Court (CC)	1 + 3
08.17.1987	Mário Soares (PS)		07.19.1987 08.17.1987	Cavaco Silva II (PSD)	PSD (148)	59.2%	51.3%	PRES, CC	1 + 2
01.13.1991	Mário Soares (PS)	67.9%		Cavaco Silva II (PSD)	PSD (148)	59.2%	51.3%	PRES, CC	1 + 2
10.31.1991	Mário Soares (PS)		10.06.1991 10.31.1991	Cavaco Silva III (PSD)	PSD (135)	58.7%	51.6%	PRES, CC	1 + 2
10.28.1995	Mário Soares (PS)		10.01.1995 10.28.1995	Guterres (PS)	PS (112)	48.7%	44.6%	PARL, CC	1 + 2
01.14.1996	Jorge Sampaio (PS)	52.7%		Guterres (PS)	PS (112)	48.7%	44.6%	PARL, CC	1 + 2
10.25.1999	Jorge Sampaio (PS)		10.10.1999 10.25.1999	Guterres (PS)	PS (115)	50.0%	45.0%	CC	1 + 1
01.14.2001	Jorge Sampaio (PS)	54.0%		Guterres (PS)	PS (115)	50.0%	45.0%	CC	1 + 1
04.06.2002	Jorge Sampaio (PS)		03.17.2002 04.06.2002	Durão Barroso (PSD)	PSD (105), CDS-PP (14)	51.7%	49.9%	PRES, CC	2 + 3
03.12.2005	Jorge Sampaio (PS)		02.20.2005 03.12.2005	Sócrates (PS)	PS (121)	52.6%	46.4%	CC	1 + 2

[a]President was coded as a veto point only under conditions of cohabitation.
[b]Government replaced as Program not approved by Parliament.

Source: Comissão Nacional de Eleições (CNE) (www.cne.pt/index.cfm, retrieved January 6, 2006).

government, particularly when the latter is not backed by an absolute parliamentary majority.

In sum, although the two major parties (PS and PSD) have been criticized for scandals and ineffectiveness, they continue to dominate Portuguese governments. These parties compete for the center of the political spectrum, with the PSD showing a more favorable stance to the market and private institutions and the PS stressing the need to cope with social problems. Nonetheless, given that the electoral support of both parties has declined, the other three parliamentary parties have become crucial for governmental stability, either backing minority governments or entering into government coalitions.

The Portuguese political system has been criticized for being "the captive of political parties" and suffering a "partisan monopoly" (Leite and Ferreira 2001: 69–71). In fact, as a reaction to the legacy of dictatorship, the 1976 Constitution stressed the relevance of national parties in the new system by declaring them the exclusive channels to present candidates to national, regional and local elections (except for the elections to the Presidency of the Republic). Perhaps because of this unquestionable protagonism, parties have made little effort to enhance citizens' participation in the political system. Low party affiliation, scarce involvement in civil society associations and political apathy are interpreted as symptoms of public detachment vis-à-vis politicians and office-holders, and are taken to illustrate the unsatisfactory quality of Portuguese democracy.

Interest groups

Portuguese trade unions enjoy a constitutionally recognized role in policy-making. The Permanent Council for Social Concertation (*Conselho Permanente de Concertação Social*) was created in March 1984, after a period of bitter conflict between workers and employers, under the coalition government formed by the PS and PSD. This consultation and consensus-producing organ in the realm of economic and social policies, composed of representatives of the government, the trade union organizations and employers' associations, was replaced in 1991 by the Economic and Social Council (*Conselho Economico e Social*, CES).[15] The CES has a much broader composition than its forerunner, including the government, the trade unions and the employers' organizations as well as representatives of the autonomous regions and local authorities, economic interests, the liberal professions, environmental organizations, family and consumers' associations and universities. One of the central organs of the CES is the Permanent Commission for Social Concertation (*Comissão Permanente de Concertação Social*, CPCS), which replicates in its composition and functions the former Permanent Council. The CPCS examines and discusses policies concerning socio-economic development, elaborates proposals addressing the performance of the economy and evaluates political decisions affecting the labor market. In spite of the existence of this neo-corporatist instrument, labor organizations in

Portugal are considered weak and only moderately influential in public policy other than labor legislation.[16]

The Portuguese labor movement became more organized from the beginning of the twentieth century. The General Confederation of Labor (*Confederação Geral dos Trabalhadores*, CGT) was founded in 1917, only four years before the Communists set up the PCP, which rapidly became influential within the labor movement. Although the Salazarist dictatorship was defined as corporatist, the intervention of social partners in public policy was merely symbolic. The Labor organizations operating during the First Republic had been smashed in the initial years of the *Estado Novo*, and employers' associations were in practice treated like state institutions. Nonetheless, the clandestine PCP managed to organize the "class trade union," *Intersindical*, in the final phase of the dictatorship, becoming a critical element in the revolutionary period after 1974. Under the new denomination, CGTP-In, the confederation encompassed a vast array of professional trade unions and between 1975 and 1976 it was the only legal labor organization. After modifications in 1977 in the law on trade unions, which guaranteed trade union pluralism, the influence of CGTP-In on governmental decision-making declined and it began to face opposition from the General Union of Workers (*União Geral dos Trabalhadores*, UGT), founded in 1978. With the backing of party leaders of the PS and PSD, the new trade union confederation displayed from the beginning a more reformist, pro-European and less conflictual attitude than the CGT-In.[17]

Both big Portuguese trade unions have furthered pensioners' associations. During the 1990s, the CGTP-In supported the public presence and influence of the *Inter-Reformados*, the organization of its retired members, and cultivated close relationships with a pensioners' pressure group, the *Movimento Unitário de Reformados, Pensionistas e Idosos* (MURPI). The analogous association close to the UGT is called the *Movimento Democrático da Reformados e Pensionistas*. These efforts notwithstanding, the ability of the trade unions to mobilize elderly people in the context of the fairly loose Portuguese civil society has been very limited.

The representation and advancement of employers' interests in Portugal is dominated by three sectoral organizations. The Confederation of Portuguese Industry (*Confederação da Indústria Portuguesa*, CIP) was created after the fall of the dictatorship in reaction to the progress of several initiatives against the private sector.[18] Business in the trade and agricultural sectors is represented through the Confederation of Portuguese Trade (*Confederaçao do Comercio Português*, CCP) and the Confederation of Portuguese Peasants (*Confederaçao dos Agricultores Portugueses*, CAP), respectively.[19] Although the CPCS has provided employers' organizations an institutional space to advance their positions and exert influence on decision-makers, the fragmentation and rather low membership of these associations undermine their power to negotiate vis-à-vis other social partners and the government (Magone 1997: 125).

III Pension system

Historical overview

The term "Social Security" only entered Portuguese official language in 1973, one year prior to the fall of Salazar's dictatorship. Nevertheless, more than one century before this date, concerns about the need to cover social risks derived from sickness, work injuries, disability, old age and the survival of a spouse had led to the organization of mutual aid associations, cooperatives and assistance funds managed by employers. These private institutions, created in the first half of the nineteenth century and under the supervision of the Ministry of Public Works—named Trade and Industry since 1852—were already referred to with the expression "*previdência*" (literally, foresight) before the start of the twentieth century. In 1916, the recently established Portuguese Republic created a Ministry of Work and Social Foresight, and few years later legislation was passed with the intention of establishing obligatory social insurance for workers under a certain income limit not covered by a pension fund or a mutual aid association. However, this effort to establish the foundations of "a new social state" ended up in "almost absolute failure". Mutualism represented the basic feature of this first phase in the history of Portuguese social protection (Medina 1996: 387; Silva 1998: 95–117).

The institutional involvement of the Portuguese state in social insurance is therefore usually dated back to the mid-1930s, during the first phase of Salazar's dictatorship. As in Spain, the structure of the Portuguese welfare system was constructed by an authoritarian regime, without the direct involvement of civil society struggling to get better working and life conditions. The societal contribution was circumscribed to what Santos (1990) has called the "secondary civil society," that is, to the organizations that the Salazarist *Estado Novo* allowed to participate in decision-making.

According to the tenets of exclusionary corporatism, each professional group was responsible for the protection of its members against social risks, and consequently each profession had to establish its own scheme. In 1935, the government issued a law which defined the general principles to organize the *previdência social*, a mandatory social insurance scheme for employees in the industrial, trade and service sectors financed by funded contributions of employers and employees and managed by the corporatist organizations. This social protection program, excluding the self-employed as well as agricultural workers and fishermen, covered sickness, disability, old age and survival.[20] In addition to the system of *previdência social*, the government created in the 1940s the system of *assistência social* (social assistance), with the explicit aim of "improving the moral, economic and health conditions of individuals under circumstances of severe trouble" (Medina 1996: 385–6). In this latter realm, the Portuguese state under Salazar, and his successor Caetano, never ceased to conceive of its role as subsidiary in relation to private or individual initiative.

The development of social insurance was rather sluggish until the 1960s. In 1940, around 6 percent of workers in industry, trade and services were covered by the *previdência social*; twenty years later the number of beneficiaries was more than seven times higher. Despite this substantial increase in coverage, the system still only covered around half of employees in these sectors (Medina 1996: 395). It suffered from great fragmentation and important coverage gaps: domestic and most self-employed workers were left out, small peasants under-represented, and salaried employees in agriculture rarely incorporated. Furthermore, the system of *previdência social* did not protect against risks derived from maternity, widow(er)hood, being an orphan, unemployment, work injuries or professional sickness.

These evident shortcomings, together with problems derived from inefficient management, persuaded the government elite of the need to redesign the program of social insurance. In 1962, a law created a unified state-managed social insurance system integrating pensions, health care and social assistance, setting off the break with the concept of corporatist *previdência* (Silva 1998: 114–15). Although funded financing was not fully abandoned for deferred benefits, current pensions were to be financed on a PAYG basis. Coverage for maternity was recognized, but professional sickness and industrial accidents remained uncovered until 1965. In that same year a unique nationwide institution was created to assign disability, old-age and survivors' benefits, the *Caixa Nacional de Pensões*.

In the hope of legitimizing the regime inherited from Salazar, Caetano also pushed forward measures favoring workers (Marques 1997: 23–4). Thus, in 1973, the required period to get an old-age pension was reduced from 60 to 24 contribution months. While eliminating the upper limit under which the wage was subject to contributions, the retirement age for women was dropped from 65 to 62 years and the benefit formula improved. Instead of taking into account the average salary of the whole contributory career to calculate the reference wage, the amount of the pension was now determined by the average wage over the best five years within the ten last contributory years (Medina 1996: 393). Although domestic employees were not fully incorporated in the social insurance program, they were granted some benefits. It was also at the end of 1973 that the expression "Social Security" (*Segurança Social*) began to be commonly used in political discourse, as a consequence of a change in the name of the corresponding Ministry.[21]

The last years of the dictatorship witnessed a rapid increase in the number of pensioners. At the beginning of the 1970s, salaried employees were practically fully covered by social insurance. Yet benefits were very low and important coverage gaps persisted.

The Carnation Revolution of April 1974 that toppled the long-lasting authoritarian dictatorship gave a significant impulse to the recognition of social rights.[22] The evolution from the corporatist *prêvidencia* to the *segurança social*, that had begun in the 1960s, was accelerated. In May 1974, the first provisional government established a national minimum wage and imposed a temporary freeze on prices, housing rents and the highest wages. It furthermore doubled the value of the minimum statutory pension, establishing that it could not amount to less than 50 percent of the minimum salary guaranteed to employed workers. In addition, it raised the number of monthly pension annuities to 13, the additional benefit being paid at Christmas. The initial steps leading to a means-tested non-contributory system were also taken with the creation of "social pensions" for those elderly or disabled people not satisfying the eligibility criteria for a contributory pension.

In the spring of 1975, unemployment protection was launched (though on a non-contributory basis) and risk coverage for agricultural workers improved. The welfare system continued to be dominated by income maintenance instruments, but with a growing importance for measures oriented towards universalism and redistribution. In fact, Article 63 of the 1976 Portuguese Constitution credited a universal right to Social Security ("Everyone is entitled to Social Security") and established the state's responsibility "to organize, coordinate and subsidize a unified and decentralized Social Security system with the participation of trade unions, other representative organizations of workers and representative associations of the remaining beneficiaries." The same article recognized the support and control by the state of the activity and functioning of non-profit institutions, thus acknowledging the relevance of private organizations in the achievement of social solidarity with a special focus on childhood, youth, disability and old age.

Between 1977 and 1979 self-employed workers, domestic employees and even workers without a work contract were incorporated into Social Security. In the early 1980s, coverage was again enlarged by including artists as well as citizens who voluntarily decided to pay contributions to the system. This expansion of social rights, accompanying the political and social mobilization in the aftermath of the Carnation Revolution, coincided with a severe economic crisis, which in 1977 and 1983 forced the Portuguese governments to ask for IMF support. Consequently, expansionary social protection measures had to be combined with restrictive ones. In 1977, the contributory tax increased three percentage points to 26.5 percent (19% paid by employers and 7.5% by employees) and the eligibility period for an old-age pension was raised to 60 months (36 months for disability pensions) beginning in 1980. One year later the contribution tax was raised once again to 28.5 percent (8% paid by employers and 20.5% by employees).

At the end of the 1970s, the Portuguese Social Security system suffered a deep financial crisis. The reserve funds had practically disappeared as a consequence of high inflation and the nationalization of the companies in which the governments had invested. Moreover, the governments of the time were not able to successfully cope with the problem of contribution arrears. Under growing financial pressure the eligibility period was again raised in 1982: beginning in 1987 a contributory old-age pension required at least 120 contribution months whereas a disability pension could be only claimed after having contributed for at least 60 months.

Curiously enough, the changes made during the first decade, after the fall of the dictatorship, to reinforce the public social protection system were not geared to undermining the activities of private non-profit institutions. In 1979 and 1981, laws were passed to regulate these institutions, which recognized their contribution to the achievement of social solidarity. The Revolution did not sweep away the long philanthropic and mutualist tradition based on private initiative that had emerged at the beginning of the nineteenth century.

Description of the current pension system

The Social Security pension system grants contributory disability, old-age and survival defined-benefit pensions, as well as non-contributory disability and old-age pensions.[23] The general contributory scheme (*Regime Geral*) includes three different regimes: the mandatory regimes for employed and self-employed workers, and the voluntary regime which covers the risks of disability, old age and death of people not compulsorily covered by the Portuguese social protection scheme (for example, seamen working for foreign countries and volunteers of non-profit organizations). Agricultural workers are integrated in a special contributory regime (*Regime Regulamentar Rural*).[24]

The non-contributory scheme (*Regime não contributivo o equiparado*, RNCE), includes social pensions, and means-tested flat benefits for disabled and elderly people whose monthly gross incomes do not exceed 30 percent of the statutory minimum wage, and who have not paid (enough) contributions to Social Security. Beneficiaries of social pensions can also apply for the non-contributory supplements of dependence and of solidarity.

Public sector workers are not covered by Social Security, but by the *Caixa Geral de Aposentações* (CGA). Bank employees, only partially integrated in Social Security, enjoy private occupational pensions financed on a funded basis.[25]

Coverage

As of January 2003, the *Regime Geral* covered slightly more than two million pensioners, approximately three-quarters of all Portuguese pensioners (Table 13.3). Old-age pensioners represented 60 percent of the pension beneficiaries of the general regime. The eligibility criteria for contributory pensions changed significantly between the 1970s and the 1990s (Table 13.4). Since 1994, workers with 15 or more (continuous or non-continuous) contribution years with at least 120 contribution days per year qualify for an old-age pension.[26] Old-age pensions are compatible with work income. Under these circumstances, the monthly pension benefit is slightly increased (1/14 of 2% of the earnings registered the previous year).

The statutory retirement age is 65 years for both men and women, but recent years have witnessed significant efforts to promote delayed retirement, under the slogan "flexibilization of retirement age." Since April 1999, early retirement is possible if the beneficiary has contributed for at least 30 years to Social Security and is older than 54.[27] Workers nevertheless lose 4.5 percent of the pension base for each anticipated year before age 65. The penalty is reduced if the worker's contributory career is longer than 30 years: every three additional contribution years do away with one year of penalty.

Workers can also improve the amount of their pension if they decide to retire after 65. If they have made contributions to the general regime for at least 40 years, the percentage to be applied to the pension base is raised by 10 percent for each year up to the age of 70.

As of the end of 2002, the CGA covered about 121,000 pensioners. CGA pension rules applying to civil servants who began working before 1993 are more favorable than Social Security pension rules. The eligibility period is much shorter (5 years instead of 15) and the statutory retirement age lower (60 instead 65 year old). Higher wages and a more advantageous pension formula mean that civil servants' pensions are far more generous than pensions of the Social Security general regime. In 2003, around 2.5 percent of the Social Security disability and old-age pensions were higher than €999. The corresponding percentage of pensions for state employees was about 50 percent (Table 13.5).

Legislation passed in 1993 eliminated the differences in pension rules between the beneficiaries of the *Regime Geral* and the CGA. The pensions of people who

Table 13.3 Number of Portuguese pensioners by scheme and regime (September 2002)

	Pensioners	%
Social Security: Regime Geral	2,030,468	76.1
Social Security: Regime Regulamentar Rural	413,416	15.5
Social Security: RNCE – Regime de Pensão Social	80,183	3.0
Social Security: RNCE – Regime Rural Transitório	21,616	–
Caixa Geral de Aposentações[a]	121,192	4.5
Total	2,666,875	100

[a]The figure is from 31 December 2002.
Sources: Segurança Social (2002) and Caixa Geral de Aposentações (2003).

Table 13.4 Changes in the eligibility criteria for old-age pensions

Up to 31.12.1973	10 years (at least 60 contribution months)
Up to 31.12.1979	3 years (at least 24 contribution months)
Up to 30.09.1987	60 months
Up to 31.12.1993	120 months
Since 1994	15 years (with at least 120 contribution days per year)

Source: Own elaboration based on Portuguese pension legislation.

Table 13.5 Differences in the amount of pensions between private sector employees and state employees 2003

Amount in euros	Disability and old-age pensioners of the Social Security general regime		Disability and retirement pensioners of the CGA	
	Number	%	Number	%
≤ 249	957,043	61.1	52,327	14.7
> 249 and ≤ 999	570,069	36.4	159,111	44.8
> 999	38,166	2.5	143,659	50.5
Total	1,565,278	100	355,097	100

Source: Instituto Nacional de Estatística (www.ine.pt/prodserv/quadros/quadro.asp retrieved 15 May, 2006).

entered the civil service after that year will be subject to the conditions applicable to contributory Social Security pensions.

Administration

The Ministry responsible for Social Security has had different names throughout the democratic period. During the PSD/CDS–PP coalition government (2002–05) it has been called successively *Ministério da Segurança Social e do Trabalho* and *Ministério da Segurança Social, da Família e da Criança*. The management of Social Security pensions is carried out by the *Centro Nacional de Pensões*, subordinated to the *Secretária de Estado da Segurança Social*. These central institutions supervise the work of the five regional Social Security centers, which have administrative autonomy. The management of civil servants' pensions falls to the Ministry of Finance.

The social partners participate in Social Security councils established at the regional level, embracing representatives of local authorities, trade unions and employers' organizations. They have consultative functions, but lack the power to veto decisions adopted by the central Social Security institutions.

Financing

Contributory benefits in the Social Security scheme are PAYG-financed, except for those covering professional sickness. The contribution, *Taxa Social Única* (TSU), covers all contingencies protected by the general regime and is high in comparative terms. Moreover, in contrast to the majority of European countries, salaries subject to contributions are not capped. The contributory rate in 2004 came to 34.75 percent of registered earnings: 11 percent paid by workers and the rest by employers. In that year, self-employed workers paid 25.4 percent of their contribution base for compulsory coverage (maternity, disability, old age and survival) to which they could add 6.6

percent in order to ameliorate risk coverage.[28] During the 1990s, the number of workers paying Social Security contributions fluctuated around 4 million. Their contributions outweigh the pension outlays, the surplus being added to the capitalized savings of the Social Security reserve fund (*Fundo de Estabilizaçao Financeira da Segurança Social*, FEFSS).[29]

Having a considerably worse affiliated workers/pensioners ratio than Social Security, in spite of the significant increase in affiliation during the 1990s, the CGA pension system needs a growing proportion of state subsidies in order to finance pension expenditure. Given that the quota paid by civil servants covered less than 30 percent of CGA pension outlays, the government decided in December 2002 to create a special reserve fund to relieve the rising financial pressure on this scheme (Caixa Geral de Aposentações 2003: 31).

Non-contributory pensions, as well as the supplements to contributory old-age pensions below the minimum pension, are financed by state revenues. The resources for social outlays were increased in 1995 with a 1 percent increase in the value added tax, known as the Social VAT.

Fraud, and arrears in the payment of contributions, have been structural problems for the Portuguese Social Security system. At the end of 2001, the debt amounted to more than €2,500 million.[30] The evolution of the amount overdue has been to some extent dependent on the economic cycle, evasion tending to increase in periods of recession.

Although contributions continue to be the predominant financing source of Social Security benefits, there have been widespread demands to diversify resources. In fact, a tendency towards the growing importance of the state budget is already observable (Comissão do Livro Branco 1998: 18–19).

Benefits

As of 1999, a complete contributory career amounts to 40 years. Until 2002, every contribution year implied a flat accrual rate of 2 percent, so that the maximum pension amounted to 80 percent of the reference wage. However, the effective substitution rate for a full pension (that is the relation between the first pension benefit and the last salary) is considerably higher due to the fiscal advantages granted to pensioners as well as the suspension of contribution payments to Social Security.[31] In contrast, since the qualifying period to get an old-age pension is 15 years, the minimum contributory pension equals 30 percent of the reference wage. Workers affiliated as of January 1, 2002 get a 2 percent flat accrual rate if they have 20 or fewer contribution years. Workers who have contributed at least 21 years, achieve accrual rates between 2.3 percent and 2 percent depending on the reference wage: the lower the wage, the higher the percentage to be applied.

The pension base or reference wage of pensioners entering the system after 1993 used to be calculated on the 10 best years' monthly wages (indexed according to inflation) out of the last 15 years of contributions. Thus, the benefit formula was formulated as follows:

$$0.02 \times N \times R,$$

where N is the number of contribution years, and R the average salary of the ten best years within the last 15 contribution years (the sum of all wages obtained divided by the number of payments, that is 140). This formula is only applicable to workers affiliated to the Social Security system before 2002 who will become pensioners before 2017 (or later if they had already covered the eligibility period by 2002). Those workers can nevertheless also calculate their pensions according to the new rules based on the Decree-Law 35/2002, which increased the period on which the pension base was to be calculated from ten years to the whole contributory career.[32] Its full application has been deferred to 2017.

Low wages and short contributory careers explain the typically low value of Portuguese pensions. The average contributory career of all old-age pensioners in 2001 was 21 years (Ministério da Segurança Social e do Trabalho 2002). It is therefore no surprise that the average old-age pension represents less than 50 percent of the average after-tax salary (Holzmann, Orenstein and Rutkowski 2003: 38). Since nearly half of all contributory pensions fall below the minimum pension, they have to be supplemented. The repeatedly stated aim of matching the amount of the minimum contributory pensions with the amount of the minimum salary had not been achieved at the beginning of 2005.

Without a formal compromise as regards periodicity, indexation of pensions has remained discretionary. In spite of this lack of formal indexation mechanisms, many pensions (especially non-contributory ones, but also a considerable share of those integrated in the contributory subsystem of Social Security) have increased in real terms as a consequence of the widely-accepted need to increase them from their very low level. The selective indexation has damaged higher pensions, which have experienced lower increases than the rest (Medina 1996: 393; Correia de Campos 2000: 195–6; Pereira and Rodrígues 2001: 12).

Civil servants' pensions stand out for their high replacement rate and fixed indexation rules. The Portuguese working civil servants (more than 700,000) tend to earn higher wages than private sector employees and to have longer contribution careers. This, combined with a more advantageous pension formula, explains why average pension benefits for retired civil servants were, as of 2001, four times higher than in the Social Security scheme, with replacement rates that exceed 100 percent (Pereira and Rodrigues 2001: 6–8). In the long run, this difference is going to fade away because civil servants who started work since 1993 are subject to the same pension formula as private sector workers.

As will be discussed in more detail below, the most controversial issue in Portuguese pension politics are proposals to create mandatory, funded, defined-contribution second- and third-pillar pensions. Conflicts regarding the income ceiling for this mandatory second- or third-pillar pension—as well as the extent to which the public sector should retain its dominant role in Social Security—have

First pillar	Second pillar	Third pillar
Third tier: state-managed funded pensions (foreseen in the 2002 Framework Law of Social Security as an option for workers paying contributions above X (to be determined) minimum salaries)	**Voluntary occupational pension:**	**Voluntary private pension** (*Planos de poupança-reforma, planos de pensões*)
Second tier: earnings-related part of pensions *Regime Geral* Employees, Self-employed and contributors of voluntary regime | Special regime for agricultural activities | Civil servants (CGA) **First tier:** basic pension	Subsidized occupational pension Mandatory occupational pension: (foreseen in the 2002 Framework Law of Social Security as an option for workers paying contributions above X (to be determined) minimum salaries)	Subsidized private pension Mandatory private pension: (foreseen in the 2002 Framework Law of Social Security as an option for workers paying contributions above X (to be determined) minimum salaries)
Non-contributory pensions (means-tested) (RNCE)		

Fig. 13.2 Pension system in Portugal

precluded the introduction of such a scheme thus far. These conflicts will most probably be resolved in the near future, however, and hence, this component of the Portuguese pension system has been included in Figure 13.2.

IV POLITICS OF PENSION REFORM SINCE 1980

Towards comprehensive Social Security: The creation of the non-contributory regime in 1980 and the Social Security Framework Law of 1984

As described above, since the Carnation Revolution, Portuguese governments have made significant efforts to improve the social protection system inherited from the dictatorship.[33] Social Security was seen as the main instrument to accomplish social justice, a fundamental element in the construction of a strong democracy (Magone 1997: 130). Universalization of Social Security benefits was the goal of a decree-law published in December 1979, according to which citizens who had not paid contributions were given access to certain cash benefits. But the deficiencies observed in the implementation of this piece of legislation convinced the conservative government of the Democratic Alliance (PSD in coalition with CDS and PPM) of the need to focus on those people most in need. Thus, Decree-Law 160/80 established a system of non-contributory benefits to be granted after means-testing, including disability and old-age social pensions.

The creation of this new type of pension allowed the government (sustained by the same party coalition and headed by Francisco Pinto Balsemão of the PSD) to pass a decree in 1982 extending the eligibility period for contributory disability pensions from 36 to 60 contribution months, and for old-age pensions from 60 to 120 contribution months.[34] The need to clarify the goals and principles of Social Security and rearrange the different elements encompassed by the system led to the approval of the first Social Security Framework Law in August 1984, roughly one year after the formation of the grand coalition government of the *Bloco Central* (1983–85). The starting point of this law was a *projecto de lei* presented by the CDS parliamentary group and discussed in the *Assembleia* on November 17, 1983.[35] António Bagão Félix, the CDS deputy who defended the project, spoke of the unfair discrimination suffered by "millions of Portuguese people," the main responsibility for this "drama that nowadays prevails on Portuguese social life" falling on the state, "which causes distortions, creates inefficiencies and hinders equity in the distribution of national resources."[36] Departing from the system of two different Social Security regimes, the contributory and the non-contributory, the CDS project stated the need to separate financing sources, in order to avoid the payment of non-contributory benefits with contributory revenues. Furthermore, it included a commitment to index benefits and salaries considered in the calculation of the pension base. The importance of private institutions of social solidarity in the design of the social protection system was also stressed in the project. As Bagão Félix proclaimed, the project rejected the exaggerated insurance bias as well as the predisposition towards full publicly-guaranteed protection, which would inhibit individual responsibility and initiative.[37]

The Minister of Work and Social Security demanded the postponement of the parliamentary discussion of this opposition project until the government presented its own proposal. Although the majority of the *Assembleia* members, including those of the PS and PSD parties backing the government, decided to continue the debate, the CDS did not achieve approval of its project. Some months later, the government presented a new proposal that, together with the former CDS document, was discussed by the parliamentary Commission of Health and Social Security. This Commission elaborated the final text of the law, which the *Assembleia* approved on June 7, 1984, with the votes of all parties except for the Communists of the PCP (who voted against it) and the leftist *Movimento Democrático Português* (MDP) (who abstained).

The imprint of the CDS on the approved framework law was quite evident, not only because this conservative party had taken the legislative initiative, but also because Bagão Félix was the President of the Commission of Health and Social Security. In his speech on the day on which the law was approved, Bagão Félix underlined that the Commission had managed to eliminate some of the more controversial aspects of the governmental proposal concerning the state's intervention in the functioning of private non-profit solidarity institutions, which were explicitly allowed to operate separate social welfare programs in conformity with the goals of Social Security. In addition, he emphasized the "unequivocal" support for the establishment of supplementary schemes provided by mutual societies, insurance companies and other collective entities. The Framework Law was therefore not to be interpreted as legislation exclusively affecting the public Social Security system, but as a text defining the context in which this institution should operate.[38]

In accordance with the 1976 Constitution, this law put universality foremost among the general principles underlying Social Security. But in fact, the prevailing principle was that of covering citizens according to their contributory efforts or to their needs. Integrated by the general (contributory) regime and the non-contributory regime, Social Security was also responsible for "social action," the main aims of which were defined as the prevention of social dysfunction and marginalization, and the encouragement of community integration. The law introduced several innovations concerning the value of pensions. Thus, general regime pensions could not be lower than the minimum statutory pension, or the the non-contributory pension—both fixed by law. Moreover, the salaries considered to calculate the pension base were to be indexed "in concert with the criteria established by legislation." Although it did not sanction automatic pension indexation, the new law provided for the "periodical" review of Social Security pensions, under consideration of the "available financial means and the significant variations in the general level of wages and other forms of income from work as well as of the cost of living" (Art. 12).

With regard to the financing of the system, the Framework Law clearly distinguished between three types of benefits:

Table 13.6 Overview of proposed and enacted pension reforms in Portugal

Year	Name of reform	Reform process (chronology)	Reform measures
1980	Decree-Law 160/80		• establishment of a system of non-contributory benefits to be granted after means-testing, among them disability and old age "social pensions"
1984	First Social Security Framework Law	• November 17, 1983 discussion in plenary session of bill presented by the opposition party CDS • January 13, 1984 government bill presented in the *Assembleia* • June 7, 1984 parliamentary approval of the law; final version elaborated the Commission on Health and Social Security	• components of the Social Security system: (1) Social Security regimes (general regime and non-contributory regime); and (2) social action programs (prevention of social exclusion) • separation of financing of contributory and non-contributory benefits: contribution-financed general regime, state-financed non-contributory benefits and social action programs • private social solidarity institutions entitled to offer social action programs • possibility to establish supplementary pension schemes • "periodical" revision of contributory and non-contributory pensions' amount
1985 1986 1989 1991 1999	Decree-Law 323/85 Decree-Law 396/86 Decree-Law 225/89 Decree-Law 415/91 Decree-Law 475/99		• introduction and regulation of occupational pension plans and funds under the supervision of the *Instituto de Seguros de Portugal* • definition of supplementary professional regimes providing "supplementary" cash benefits to the benefits guaranteed by the Social Security general regime" • introduction and regulation of individual pension plans ("open" pension funds in contrast to "closed" occupational pension funds)
1993	Decree-Law 329/1993		• increase in minimum qualifying period from 10 years to 15 years • introduction of minimum contribution density of 120 days per year • harmonization of male and female retirement ages at 65 • no pre-retirement before 60 • change of calculation of the assessment base: best 10 years out of last 15 instead of best 5 years out of last 10 • introduction of 14 instead of 12 salaries to calculate the average • reduction of accrual rate from 2.2% to 2% per contribution year

(Continued)

Table 13.6 (Continued)

Year	Name of reform	Reform process (chronology)	Reform measures
			• increase in qualifying period for full pension from 37 to 40 years
• permission to accumulate pension benefits with income from work
• introduction of the *complemento social* to supplement pensions lower than the minimum pension
1998	White Paper on Social Security	• October 1995 election of PS minority government
• Resolution of the Council of Ministers 22/96 to create expert commission to prepare a white paper on Social Security and explore reform options
• January 1998 publication of the Commission's White Paper | Recommendations:
• exclusive responsibility of the state to finance non-contributory benefits
• introduction of flexible retirement age
• consider in the establishment of the minimum pension amount the number of contribution years so as to privilege pensioners with longer contributory careers
• improvement in process of pursuing Social Security arrears
• strengthening of the Social Security Reserve Fund
• revision of the self-employed scheme to make it financially sustainable
• reduction of the maximum percentage to be applied to the pension base from 80 to 75% of pension base

no agreement on the following recommendations:
• the *plafonamento*, i.e. establishment of a second obligatory funded defined-contribution pension
• increase in the reference period for the calculation of the pension base
• fiscal reform so as to progressively tax pensions according to their amount |
| 1999 | Decree-Law 9/99 | • June 1993 European Council resolution on the flexible retirement age
• January 8, 1999 approval of Decree-Law on flexible retirement age | • introduction of flexible retirement age between 55 and 70 (minimum of 30 contribution years for early retirement)
• introduction of bonuses for late retirement, i.e. increase of benefits by 10% per year of deferment
• deductions for early retirement, i.e. reduction of benefits by 4.5% per year of early retirement; but for every three contribution years above 30, the penalty is reduced by one year
• introduction of pensions for long-term unemployed at 55 with minimum contribution period of 20 years |

2000	Solidarity and Social Security Framework Law	• June 3, 1998 CDS/PP presents *projecto de lei* • June 24, 1998 PS government presents *proposta de lei*, not approved because end of legislature • November 3, 1999 CDS/PP presents new *projecto de lei* • November 11, 1999 PCP presents new *projecto de lei* • November 25, 1999 PSD presents new *projecto de lei* and PS government presents new *proposta de lei* • March 2, 2000 BE presents *projecto de lei* • June 6, 2000 passage of the final text of the bill with the votes of PS and the abstention of BE, PCP and OS Verdes • November 2001 government commission to prepare legal implementation of the Framework Law • November 2001 unions and employers sign agreement on the modernization of social protection • April 2002 early elections	• structuring of Social Security into three subsystems: a) social protection for citizens, 2) family protection and 3) social insurance • reform goals: improve social protection levels and reinforce equity; enhance efficacy and efficiency, financial sustainability of the system • old-age pensions shall progressively be based on indexed work income get during the complete working career • possible introduction of the *plafonamento* under two conditions: (1) report demonstrating that this measure safeguards the rights of present pensioners and workers while contributing to the financial sustainability of the public pension system, and (2) agreement of National Council of Solidarity and Social Security (composed of social partners and government) • consolidation of Fund of Financial Stabilization of the Social Security: contributory surplus + additional 2%–4% of contributions until fund guarantees at least 2 years of pension payments
2002	Decree-Law 35/2002		• new benefit calculation formula: total amount of annual indexed wages of the entire working career divided by the number of contribution years with maximum of 40, multiplied by 14 • change in accrual rates: first 20 years 2% per year; above 20 years accrual rates between 2% and 2.3% per contribution year depending on the amount of the pension base

(Continued)

Table 13.6 (Continued)

Year	Name of reform	Reform process (chronology)	Reform measures
2002	Framework Law on Social Security	• July 2, 2002 PSD government presents *proposta de lei* • October 17, 2002 Commission on Work and Social Affairs approves the final text • November 17, 2002 passage of the bill with the votes of PSD and CDS/PP	• structuring of Social Security into public Social Security system, social action system and supplementary system • reform goals: guarantee the right to Social Security, improve social protection levels and reinforce equity; enhance efficacy and management, efficiency as well as financial sustainability of the system • minimum disability and old-age contributory pensions shall be linked to the length of contributory careers and achieve the net minimum income guaranteed to all workers • minimum disability and old-age non-contributory pensions shall not be lower than 50% of net minimum income guaranteed to all workers • introduction of a maximum contributory limit to be fixed by law • below maximum contributory limit the law can establish a wage ceiling above which contributions can be either put in the public Social Security system, or in the supplementary system (*plafonamento*) • supplementary system divided into legal regimes (funded by Social Security contributions above wage ceiling), contractual regimes (occupational and voluntary) and optional regimes (individual and voluntary)

1. Contributions of workers and employers should exclusively finance the *Regime Geral*.
2. Non-contributory benefits and social action programs were to be financed by general state revenues.
3. Article 76 of the framework law stated nonetheless that the financing of non-contributory and other social benefits through state revenues would "progressively materialize in accordance with the economic and financial conditions", allowing for slow change.[39] And in fact, governments continued for the next ten years to resort to contributions in order to pay all types of benefits.

In brief, the 1984 Social Security Framework Law was the result of a wide parliamentary consensus which comprised the parties that dominated the ideological spectrum from the right to the moderate left. It thus represented a solid basis for the government to develop specific legislation through decree-laws. In fact, during the following years the PS and PSD governments endorsed a variety of regulations aimed at reducing regime fragmentation,[40] expanding the coverage of the general regime (by means of incorporating unemployment protection)[41] and launching the second and third pillars of the pension system on a voluntary basis.

The creation of the second and third pillars of the Portuguese pension system in the second half of the 1980s

The sixth chapter of the 1984 Framework Law, with the title "On individual initiatives," made it possible to establish supplementary schemes, though how these were to be articulated with Social Security remained unclear. In the summer of 1985, the minority PS government led by Mário Soares approved a decree-law legalizing pension funds. Only companies offering life insurance were allowed to manage pension funds to cover risks derived from retirement, old age, disability and death, while the task of monitoring pension fund managers rested with a public agency, the Insurance Institute of Portugal (*Instituto de Seguros de Portugal*). The initiative to establish these programs was to come from "firms or groups of firms, or combined efforts of interested persons, specifically in the socio-professional realm, or to result from agreements between employers' associations and trade unions." Consequently, pension funds were implicitly defined as resources of the second pillar of the pension system.[42]

After the November 1985 legislative elections, Cavaco Silva became the Prime Minister of a center-right minority government, the agenda of which referred unambiguously to incentives for the creation of private supplementary Social Security schemes. In November 1986, he signed a new decree-law which described the creation of pension funds as "one of the varieties of private Social Security that better responds to the protection needs of citizens," and extended pension fund management to societies founded for this specific purpose (*sociedades gestoras*) and authorized by the Ministry of Finance. Pension schemes created by firms after January 1,

1987 had to be constituted as pension funds and "could take on the nature of supplementary schemes of Social Security."[43]

The fiscal incentives introduced to encourage companies to launch pension funds were very enticing. In 1987 and 1988, firms could deduct from taxes twice the value of their contributions to pension funds with a maximum limit of 30 percent of wage outlays. Since then, deductible contributions to pension funds have been limited to 15 percent of wage outlays. As a result of these incentives, the early legislation on pension funds favored the rise of pension plans which offered second-pillar defined-benefit pensions but lacked a clear system for articulation with the Social Security regimes (Oliveira 1987: 72–3).

Finally, a 1989 decree-law outlined the rules according to which supplementary professional regimes could be created. Apart from insurance companies and management societies of pension funds, it was decided that mutual associations and social solidarity foundations, under the supervision of the Ministry of Work and Solidarity, could manage these supplementary professional schemes.[44] Without clear advantages with respect to the traditional pension plans, the majority of firms have stuck to the latter, so that this type of second-pillar pension has developed very slowly.

The third pillar of the pension scheme also arose in 1989, with the approval of a decree-law establishing individual saving funds for retirement (*Planos Poupança Reforma*, PPR) with attractive fiscal incentives.[45] The option to subscribe to a pension plan was only established in 1991. In the last days of his first majority government, Cavaco Silva signed a decree-law allowing individual or collective subscription to pension plans by participants not necessarily linked to each other. In contrast to "closed" (second-pillar) pension funds, the new regulation determined that "open" (third-pillar) pension funds could only provide defined-contribution benefits to individual participants.[46]

On the basis of this legislation, pension funds have become a moderately widespread financial product among employees of big firms and more affluent citizens. In 2002, nearly 282,000 people were covered by pension funds: 62 percent of them were participants in occupational pension funds, which controlled *c*. 95 percent of all assets and for the most part provided defined-benefit pensions (Instituto de Seguros de Portugal 2002).

To sum up, in line with its ideological preferences to promote private funding, the PSD governments between 1986 and 1992 made significant efforts to expand the second and third pillars of the Portuguese pension system. But there is no strong evidence suggesting that the PS disliked this strategy. Actually, the Socialist minority government of Guterres passed a decree-law in 1999 to refine "the management and the financial reliability" of pension funds, in which these were defined as a "privileged vehicle of private and supplementary financing for the coverage of social risks linked to retirement".[47] Basically, the Socialists of the PS share with the Social Democrats of the PSD a favorable stance towards the development of the private pension pillars. Yet, as will be shown later, they disagree over the question of whether this development should be furthered with contributory revenues originally assigned to the first pillar.

1993: cutting the costs of pensions and preventing strategic behavior by pensioners-to-be

During the period of PSD center-right governments backed by absolute majorities in the *Assembleia* (1987–95), the structure of Social Security as defined in 1984 stayed stable. Social Security expenditure in terms of GDP fell in 1988 and 1989 (mainly because of rapid GDP growth), but saw a substantial increase during the following years (Comissão do Livro Branco 1998: 18). In 1990, the right to a 14th Social Security pension annuity, to be paid in July, was recognized.

This expansion notwithstanding, concerns about the sustainability of the system were gaining ground. Facing economic recession and increasing arrears in the Social Security contributions payable by employers, as well as pressure to fulfill the Maastricht criteria, in 1993 the PSD government introduced several cost-containment reform measures (Marques 1997: 32–5). With the explicit aim of eliminating any "incongruence" and "anachronism" in the method of calculating pensions, which were causing "distortions and relative injustice" towards beneficiaries with longer contribution careers, the government approved a decree-law that introduced changes in the eligibility criteria, the retirement age, and the benefit formula concerning old-age and disability pensions of the general regime.

First, the government increased the minimum contribution period to obtain an old-age pension from 10 to 15 years, and established a minimum yearly contribution density of 120 days. This meant that at least this number of contribution days were necessary to get a contribution year recognized, where time caring for young children was to be certified as counting to the contribution period. Second, the statutory retirement age for men and women was unified at 65 as of 1999, excluding retirement before 60. Third, the benefit formula was changed: the reference wage should now be calculated taking into consideration average wages over the 10 best of the 15 last years before retirement (instead of the 5 best out of the 10 last contribution years), introducing as a novelty the consideration of 14 (instead of 12) monthly salaries to calculate the average annual wage, as well as the indexation of the wages included in the formula.[48] The extension of the period on which the pension reference base was calculated was intended to hinder the strategic behavior of people paying higher contributions during the five years previous to retirement in order to achieve a higher pension base. Furthermore, the accrual rate was established at 2 percent (instead of 2.2%) for each contribution year. Since the decree-law determined that the maximum percentage of the pension base a pensioner retiring at 65 could obtain was 80 percent, the number of years to get a full pension was indirectly set at 40 (previously 37). To compensate for this income drop, old-age pensioners were allowed to accumulate benefits with income from work. Finally, the decree-law created the "social supplement" (*complemento social*), a non-contributory benefit to supplement pensions under the guaranteed minimum amount set by law. This supplement was not means-tested and it could not be higher than that established for the non-contributory "social pension."[49]

Although according to the preamble of this decree-law all changes were intended to advance "the objective interests" of Social Security beneficiaries, most of them were clearly geared to reducing the growing financial pressure on the pension system. As regards the sensitive question of indexation, the governmental commitment was rather loose. Without going further than the text of the 1984 Framework Law, the 1993 decree-law only conceded that benefits would be "periodically" indexed, taking into account the available financial means and the evolution of consumer prices.

The White Paper Commission 1996–1998

At the end of the eight-year period of PSD majority government (1987–95), fears of mushrooming financial problems for Social Security were more and more present in the public debate. The PSD had not been able to implement all the measures provided for in the 1984 Framework Law, first and foremost the clear separation of the financing sources of contributory and non-contributory benefits (Marques 1997: 28–9). In spite of the anticipated financial difficulties, employers managed to get a 0.75 percent reduction in Social Security contributions in 1995. At the same time, in line with the principle of diversifying the financial sources of Social Security, VAT was increased by one percentage point to expand state revenues for social protection policies (Social VAT) (Pereira and Rodrigues 2001: 3).

In October 1995, the PS won general elections with a relative majority. In his government agenda António Guterres recognized that "being a basic value to preserve, the Social Security system needs reform to guarantee its future viability" (Comissão do Livro Blanco 1998: 9). In the following months, the new minority government made two important decisions regarding Social Security: first, it decided to relieve the contributory system of its role in paying non-contributory benefits; secondly, it sanctioned the creation of a Commission entrusted with the job of elaborating a White Paper on Social Security and formulating recommendations. In March 1996 the Minister of Work, Ferro Rodrígues, summoned 17 experts (former ministers, academics, civil servants and a pension fund manager), who should spend the next 18 months studying the evolution and current situation of Social Security in its demographic, political and financial dimensions, as well as devising reform proposals based on the principles of sustainability, sufficiency and equity. As the Minister stated, "he who wants to preserve the public system of Social Security must try to reform it. The best way to kill the public system is to leave it like it is."[50]

In January 1998, the Commission delivered the White Paper to the government, consisting of an extensive report and several final declarations of the commissioners. The report focused on the current problems of Social Security, particularly its financial overload due to the inclusion of non-contributory benefits and social action programs, on top of professional regimes making low contributory efforts (mostly self-employed, agricultural workers, domestic employees and people affiliated to the voluntary regime), as well as the huge debt provoked by contribution arrears. These difficulties increased the vulnerability of a pension system already struggling to remain true to the commitment to provide increasingly higher pensions to more and longer-living pensioners. But apart from these specific problems, the Commission acknowledged that a pure PAYG pension system as the one prevalent in Portugal generated inequities, inefficiencies and potential intergenerational conflicts. Well-off people tended to live longer than poorer people, thus enjoying pensions for longer periods. Furthermore, workers with better access to information were inclined to behave strategically, making higher contributions in the years prior to retirement. The relatively short period on which the pension base was calculated (at that time 15 years for an old-age pension) discriminated against women, who typically have lower salaries than men and also see lower wage increases in their final working years (Comissão do Livro Blanco 1998: 96–100).

On the grounds of both this diagnosis and the demographic and financial estimates predicting growing Social Security deficits as of 2010 (which could result in accumulated debts of more than 50% of GDP by 2040), the Commission suggested the introduction of mandatory funded pensions for high-salary workers. Since parametric reforms (such as reducing the maximum percentage to be applied to the pension base from 80% to 70%, enlarging the period to calculate the pension base from 15 to 25 years or postponing legal retirement age to 68 years) could only postpone the crisis by 5 or 10 years, the White Paper claimed that "restructuring Social Security is indispensable to guarantee the sustainability of the system," (Comissão do Livro Blanco 1998: 116). In fact, the keyword "plafonamento," referring to the establishment of a wage ceiling (for instance, four times the minimum salary) above which contributions would be obligatorily invested in pension funds, divided the Commission between a majority of supporters and a minority of opponents (Correia de Campos 2000: 178).

This division became evident in the final recommendations of the Commission. Among the proposals to ensure the sustainability of Social Security, the Commissioners agreed on the need to:

(i) stress the exclusive responsibility of the state for the financing of non-contributory benefits;
(ii) promote the flexible retirement age by offering incentives to those workers willing to postpone retirement;
(iii) ensure the receipt of Social Security arrears;
(iv) strengthen the Social Security reserve fund created in 1989; and
(v) revise the scheme for self-employed workers in order to make it self-financing.

No general consensus was attained with respect to the "plafonamento."

As regards equity, the Commission also acknowledged the existence of dissenting opinions. On the one hand, it unanimously recommended a gradual increase in the minimum pension in order to privilege long working careers. On the other hand, the proposal to increase the number of contribution years on which the reference wage of pensions should be calculated, so as to include the entire contributory period, did not find consensus. The Commission did consent to improve control over access to universal benefits, and to review the fiscal privileges associated with the subscription to savings funds for retirement. Measures to advance the efficiency of Social Security were also agreed upon, such as the dis-aggregation of social contributions according to different contingencies, and the need to legally fix the criteria underlying previously discretionary measures, such as the indexing of pensions (Comissão do Livro Branco 1998: 229–32).

The White Paper can be seen as a technical instrument to legitimize changes in the pension system. The Commission had fulfilled the purpose of catalyzing public debate on the future of Social Security, and the circumstances seemed to be ripe for substantial reforms. But even though the opposition parties on the right would have favored these reforms, the minority PS government decided to proceed very cautiously. It probably thought that by endorsing the reforms proposed by the Commission and espoused by the opposition, the PS risked diluting its ideological differences vis-à-vis the PSD and losing further votes in the coming elections.

The 1999 measures to introduce a flexible retirement age, and to improve the benefits for dependent pensioners

One year after delivery of the White Paper, the PS government, having signed with the trade unions in January 1999, approved a decree-law which would encourage people to work longer.[51] The new regulation included penalties for retiring early and bonuses for delaying.

Whereas the 1993 decree-law had ruled out retirement before 60, the new legislation allowed workers to retire at 55 if they had completed a contributory career of at least 30 years. Early retirement was nevertheless penalized, with pensioners losing 4.5 percent of the pension base for each year before 65, although the penalty was reduced by one year for every three contribution years above 30. But the incentives to postpone retirement were higher than the disincentives to retire early. Workers with 40 registered contribution years who deferred retirement would obtain a supplement of 10 percent of the pension base for each year between 65 and 70. A worker retiring at 70 could thus obtain a maximum of 130 percent of his pension base (80% + 50%). The decree-law also included incentives for hiring elderly workers, in the form of a reduction of contributions to be paid for workers with a full contributory career.

Although the main aim of this reform was to encourage later retirement, the new rules, combined with those approved by another decree-law on unemployment passed some months later, could be strategically applied to attain the opposite outcome. Actually, Decree-Law 199/99 on unemployment offered the opportunity to long-term unemployed to retire at 55 if they had a contributory career of at least 20 years. In addition, unemployed workers were counted as making contributions to Social Security during the period in which they obtained unemployment benefits: unemployment years were considered as contribution years. Thus, in contradiction to Decree-Law 9/99 many workers could retire at 55 with less than 30 contribution years if they were registered as long-term unemployed, and many others could escape the penalties applied to pre-retirement by being declared unemployed before asking for an old-age pension.[52]

A third decree-law approved in 1999 affected pensioners and Social Security outlays. The Socialist government created a supplement for dependence (*complemento por dependencia*), in place of a subsidy limited to pensioners of the Social Security general regime.[53] The new supplement for dependence covered disability, old-age and survival pensioners of the contributory and non-contributory regimes in a situation of dependency, those unable to autonomously satisfy basic needs concerning domestic care, mobility and hygiene. Depending on the circumstances of the dependent pensioner, the amount of the supplement was to range between 45 percent and 80 percent of the social pension. In contrast to the previous subsidy, the benefit was compatible with the institutionalization of the pensioner.

Restructuring Social Security: the 2000 and 2002 Social Security Framework Laws and the issue of the "plafonamento"

Several months after the presentation of the White Paper on Social Security in January 1998, the government and the main opposition parties (PSD, PCP, and CDS–PP) put forward different bill proposals for a new Social Security Framework Law. All parties advocated increasing the minimum contributory pension to the level of the net minimum salary. The "plafonamento", the plan to set upper limits to the contribution base of workers and invest the remaining contributions in pension funds in order to get a second defined-contribution pension, obtained the support of the CDS-PP and the PSD. The PS agreed to the establishment of this second pension on a voluntary basis, as did the PCP, albeit more ambiguously. As regards indexation, the proposals of the conservative CDS-PP were even more generous than those of the PSD and the PS: the former proposed the indexation of pensions to salaries, whereas the Social Democrats and the Socialists favored indexation to inflation. The Communists of the PCP, for their part, wanted pensions to be indexed to inflation and to GDP evolution. Contrary to expectations, the PCP accepted the strengthening of proportionality between contributions and benefits and was not opposed to more capitalization within the Social Security system, so long as the management of the funds remained in the hands of the state. As Correia de Campos (2000: 176) writes, these different proposals "don't confirm the traditional stances on socioeconomic matters. Parties located on the right of the political spectrum showed extraordinary social generosity, and the parties on the left demonstrated attitudes of economic modernity."

Although approved in a first general vote by the plenary of the *Assembleia*, these proposals could not go through the entire legislative process before the end of the legislature in 1999. At the beginning of 2000, the minority government, led again by

Guterres of the PS, presented a new proposal that, according to its preamble, took into consideration the parliamentary discussions interrupted by the last elections. The proposal divided Social Security into a citizen social protection subsystem (*Subsistema de Protecção Social de Cidadania*), a family protection subsystem (*Subsistema de Protecção a Família*) and a social insurance subsystem (*Subsistema Previdencial*). The goals of the citizenship social protection subsystem were to be attained through the "solidarity and social action regime," financed exclusively by state revenues. This regime covered primarily the minimum guaranteed income, old-age, invalidity and survivors' social pensions, supplements to minimum contributory pensions and economic support for programs to fight against poverty and social exclusion. The family protection subsystem, also primarily financed by general revenues, included family allowances and benefits covering care for dependent family members. Finally, the social insurance subsystem encompassed employed and self-employed workers, as well as those persons who might voluntarily adhere to it, and were to be exclusively financed through contributions.[54]

Thus, the Socialist government left private supplementary pension plans outside the Social Security structure. This was not a formal decision, as the PSD proposal made clear. Relying on the argument that funding would increase the value of pensions because of higher return rates, the PSD argued that every worker should have the option of either allotting his/her contributions to the PAYG-financed pension system, or investing them in funded pensions. In accordance with the tenet of "a state producing less and contracting more", the PSD envisaged a structural modification of the Social Security system, which would result in a social insurance subsystem (mandatory for all workers, but offering them the opportunity to choose the pension provider) and a social solidarity subsystem.[55] The CDS–PP also supported a structural reform, but through different mechanisms. For this conservative party the goal of reform was not only to ensure the sustainability of the Social Security system, but also to foster personal responsibility. The party insisted on defining a wage ceiling for contributions, above which workers should be free to decide what to do with their money. The Social Security system envisaged by the CDS–PP comprised a public obligatory system (consisting of a social insurance subsystem and a social solidarity subsystem) and a private supplementary system.[56] Finally, the PCP and the *Bloco de Esquerda* presented two projects stressing the comparatively low levels of social protection in Portugal and the need to "revitalize the public Social Security system," while disapproving of structural pension reform, seeing it as triggered by a campaign of "national and international grand financial capital."[57]

Even though all these documents illustrate the commitment of the parties to improving the existent levels of social protection, the differences between their positions on how to organize Social Security were greater than at the end of the previous legislature. After the discussion of all proposals, the Parliamentary Commission on Work, Solidarity and Social Security worked out a text that came close to the government stance. In July 2000, the final text was approved by the *Assembleia* with the votes of the Socialists (PS) and the abstention of the Communists (PCP), the Greens (*Los Verdes*), the *Bloco de Esquerda* and three PS representatives. The PSD and the CDS–PP voted against the bill and the representatives of the latter party showed their disgust by stamping on the floor. The 2000 Framework Law relied more heavily on the standpoint of the dissenting minority of the White Paper Commission, than on the positions maintained by the majority of its members. This peculiarity, together with the fierce opposition of the parties to the right of the PS, increased the vulnerability of the new arrangement.

In fact, this Framework Law on Social Security, which revoked the one endorsed in 1984, did not discard the "plafonamento" as a possible reform strategy. True, the law did not explicitly mention the possibility of a second defined-contribution pension being financed with contributions on earnings above a certain wage ceiling, but Article 63 left the adoption of this critical measure to be decided by further legislation. The government assumed responsibility for presenting a proposal on the basis of: (1) a report demonstrating that the "plafonamento" safeguarded the rights of present pensioners and workers and contributed to the financial sustainability of the public pension system, and (2) the agreement of the National Council of Solidarity and Social Security (*Conselho Nacional de Solidariedade e Segurança Social*, CNSSS), to be formed from the employers' organizations, the trade unions and government representatives.

In November 2001, the government created a new commission composed of representatives of the Ministry of Work and Solidarity, the Ministry of Finance and the Ministry of State and Administration Reform, in order to prepare the implementation of the Framework Law. According to the government resolution setting up the commission, this working group had to take into consideration the stance of the social partners as manifested in the CPCS. Within this neo-corporatist institution, agreement was reached that the government, the trade union confederations UGT and CGTP-IN and the employers' associations CCP and CAP would subscribe to an "Agreement on the Modernization of Social Protection."[58] This bargain focused on six points to modernize the Social Security system from the perspective of its financial sustainability and social efficacy:

(1) the financing of the system, stressing the need to include revenues other than earnings-based contributions;
(2) the complementary nature of PAYG and funded financial mechanisms within Social Security, a first goal being to fund 2 percent of workers' contributions in order to guarantee the equivalent amount of at least two years of pension payments;
(3) the development of (occupational and individual) supplementary regimes under cautious consideration of the fiscal costs of incentives and the repercussions in terms of solidarity distortion;
(4) the progress towards efficient management of the system;
(5) the fight against fraud in the payment of contributions and the claiming of benefits; and
(6) the progress in collecting statistical information concerning the evolution of Social Security.

Furthermore, the agreement made the commitment to stronger involvement of the social partners in the definition, planning, organization and running of the Social Security system as an answer to the trade unions' criticism of "governmentalized" management (Almeida and Cristovam 2000). The CNSSS, the creation of which was laid down by the 2000 Framework Law, was to act as the main instrument of this participation.

The fragility of the 2001 Agreement on the Modernization of Social Protection became evident some months later, after the PS lost the 2002 general elections. But in the last weeks of 2001, the Guterres government approved several decree-laws on the basis of this arrangement, two of which stand out for their importance for the financial sustainability of the system.

Decree-Law 331/2001 describes the different financing sources of the Solidarity and Social Security System on the principle of selective adequacy. This principle implies that financial resources have to reflect the nature and aims of the different types of social protection benefits. Decree-Law 35/2002 contains rules for calculating pensions for newly-affiliated workers, and for beneficiaries getting their first pension after December 31, 2016, according to the principles established in the 2000 Framework Law.[59] As of January 1, 2002, the pension base includes the total value of annually indexed wages over the entire contributory career. The maximum percentage to be applied to the pension base (80%) corresponds to 40 years with registered earnings.[60] The new rules imply a substantial reduction of the estimated replacement rate of pensions whenever wage increases exceed the inflation rate. Thus, on the assumption of a yearly 2 percent real wage increase, Watson Wyatt has forecast that a full pension calculated according to the old rules would entail 73 percent of the final wage, and a pension calculated according to the new rules only 64 percent.[61]

As regards the determination of the contributory ceiling, above which workers could decide on the means of funding their contributions, the Agreement on the Introduction of Optional Limits to Contributions to the PAYG system, signed on November 20, 2001 by the government and the social partners (except for the CGTP-In and the CIP), saw a compromise: the relevant proposal would be submitted to the executive committee of the CNSSS within the next year.[62] Under the premise of a technical report showing the lack of negative effects for the financial viability of the public pension system, the proposal would be to grant workers with income above 12 times the minimum salary the right to assign extra contributions to the PAYG pension system, to a public- or a private-funded system.

This proposal never materialized. Elections in April 2002 brought the PSD, in coalition with the CDS-PP, back into government. The CDS-PP member Bagão Félix, Secretary of State for Social Security under the conservative coalition governments between 1980 and 1983, and professionally linked to the banking and insurance sectors, was appointed minister for Work and Social Security in the new government of Durão Barroso. The 2000 Framework Law on Social Security was one of the first pieces of legislation to be reviewed.

In July 2002, the new government put forward a proposal which represented a sort of negotiated combination of the PSD and CDS-PP positions, as expressed in the projects both parties had formulated two years earlier. The "culture of sharing social risks," also dubbed "social subsidiarity," and a "flexible Social Security" were the principles inspiring this proposal. To substantiate those principles the government proposed a new Social Security structure, integrating the supplementary regimes and encouraging funded pensions. The supplementary regimes could take three forms:

(i) legal regimes, obligatory for some groups of workers and types of risks;
(ii) contractual regimes granting supplementary benefits to workers with salaries above the contributions limit for the PAYG pension system; and
(iii) optional regimes covering those people who wanted to subscribe to pension funds or other funded insurance products.

Altogether these supplementary regimes constituted the third Social Security system (*Sistema Complementar*), alongside the public system (*Sistema Público de Segurança Social*, involving contributory and non-contributory benefits), and the social action system intended to combat social exclusion (*Sistema de Acção Social*, in which the institutions of private social solidarity should play a prominent role). In accordance with the preferences of the CDS-PP the proposal backed the introduction of a maximum contributory limit. Below this limit there would be contributory echelons (*patamares*), not all of them subject to contributions to the public PAYG system. This design should allow high salaried workers aged 35 or older and with a contributory career of ten years or less to divert part of their mandatory contributions to (public or private) pension funds.[63]

Only the representatives of the left parties PCP and *Bloco de Esquerda* submitted alternatives to the government proposal, both rejecting further privatization of Social Security and demanding more resources to finance social protection through new taxes on capital and on the wealthiest. Neither proposal obtained enough votes to be discussed in detail within the respective parliamentary Commission.[64]

In a very tense parliamentary debate Bagão Félix assured the *Assembleia* that although the new law aimed at the convergence of old-age and disability contributory pensions with the net national minimum wage, thus expanding pension expenditure, the simultaneous but gradual introduction of the "plafonamento" would not impair the financial balance of Social Security, resulting on the contrary in medium and long-term financial gains. He argued that the "plafonamento" was not the "essential goal" of the reform.[65] But he could not convince the opposition on both of these issues. The government proposal was finally endorsed with the votes of the PSD and CDS-PP members and went to the parliamentary Commission of Work and Social Affairs. This commission approved a final document based on an "integration text" elaborated by the PSD and CDS-PP parliamentary groups. Against all the votes of the opposition parties, except for one PS representative who abstained, in October 2002 the *Assembleia* passed the 2002 Framework Law on Social Security (the word "Solidarity" disappeared from the title). In contrast to the longevity of the 1984 Framework Law on Social Security, the 2000 Framework Law had been in force for scarcely two years before it was replaced.

Although the mass media anticipated that the "plafonamento" would be in force by the beginning of 2004, the PSD coalition government failed to publish the decree-laws implementing this system before the 2005 general elections.[66] The immediate loss of income from contributions that the "plafonamento" would imply probably dissuaded the government, and explains the alleged resistance of Social Security civil servants to assist the government in this implementation process (Ferreira 2003).[67] But technical problems seem not to be the most important explanatory factor for this failure. The 2002 Framework Law was even more fragile than its forerunner. Opposed by all opposition parties as well as by trade unions, from its very inception it was seen as an attack on the public universal Social Security system introduced by the democratic regime.[68] Such political and social isolation reduced the government's ability to drive the reform forward, not least because the President of the Republic, a former leader of the PS, seemed unlikely to make any substantial effort to neutralize this animosity, and would perhaps even veto the highly controversial measures.

V Conclusion

Summary of the magnitude of changes

During the first decade of Portugal's transition to democracy, governments and political elites agreed on the need to expand and improve the social protection system inherited from the Salazarist dictatorship. But since the beginning of the 1990s policy-makers have been concerned by the growing financial pressure on Social Security, and especially on its core element, the contributory pension system. The views of experts on the worrying evolution of pension expenditure, as a combined effect of the maturation of the system and demographic aging, have put pension reform on the agendas of all political parties. All the same, most experts think that the political reaction has been too slow and the measures adopted too timid.

Significant changes in pension rules were introduced in 1993 under the center-right majority government headed by Cavaco Silva. The extension of the eligibility period for contributory pensions and the increase in the number of years considered to calculate the reference wage, and the change in the statutory retirement age for women, were without doubt important measures to reduce pension costs in the medium and long term. The decision to apply the pension rules of the Social Security general regime to civil servants hired as of 1993, and consequently to put an end to the extensive privileges enjoyed by state employees, also represented a substantial cost-containment reform measure. By the same token, when the PS minority government resolved in 2001 to include wages drawn during the whole contributory career in the pension base, it signaled a clear political will to adjust pension costs, too.

All these changes have been generally seen as necessary, and as such provoked little opposition. But they have not removed the impression among decision-makers of the main parties that structural changes are indispensable.

Despite this awareness, the center-left Socialists and the center-right Social Democrats, who in 1984 agreed on a framework law on Social Security that stayed in force for 16 years, now have less in common as regards the design of Social Security, and were unable to reach an understanding on this issue. The most contentious question affects the "plafonamento", the setting of a wage ceiling above which contributions could (or would have to) be saved in funds to finance a second defined-contribution pension. This provision was included in the 2002 Social Security Framework Law, but the conservative coalition government which pushed forward this reform did not succeed to pass the corresponding decree-law to implement it.

Impact of the political system on pension politics

The features of the legislative process tend to reinforce the consensual character of Portuguese laws setting the foundations of action in a policy area. Bills, presented by the government or by parliamentary groups and approved in general by the plenary of the *Assembleia*, have to be jointly discussed in detail in specific parliamentary commissions. The latter are responsible for presenting a final text which again requires the approval of the chamber. This time-consuming, consensus-seeking procedure explains why the main instruments of Portuguese policy-making are not laws but decree-laws. The *Assembleia* decides on the principles according to which policy-making has to be designed, leaving the implementation details to the government.

This is exactly what has happened in the realm of Social Security. The basic principles have been laid down in framework laws passed in the *Assembleia*, and their implementation has been controlled by governments. Nonetheless, executives do not have boundless autonomy to pass decree-laws. First, the members of the *Assembleia* can demand their discussion and vote in Parliament; secondly, the President can veto laws and decree-laws. These constraints help to explain why the PSD governments headed by Durão Barroso (2002–04) and later by Santana Lopes (2004–05) have failed to publish the norms developing the 2002 Framework Law on Social Security. The likely mobilization of the parties of the left and the trade unions against the implementation of the 2002 Framework Law have been strong disincentives for a government scrutinized by a President who was once leader of an opposition party.

A structural reform of the Portuguese pension system seems difficult to put into practice without consensus between the two major parties. But the tendency towards bipartite politics and party polarization definitely shapes electoral competition, inducing Socialists and Social Democrats to focus their attention on distinctive aspects of political problems and thus hampering attempts to reach understandings between them. For attempts to bridge their ideological distance would entail the risk of losing electoral support to rivals on both the left and the right.

Interest group influence

The social partners are in principle important institutional actors in the Portuguese political system. The Constitution not only recognizes the need to consult them in the policy-making process, but also establishes the organs in which they have to be represented. In spite of this constitutional recognition, and of the symbolic power achieved by trade unions because of their prominent role in the demise of the dictatorship and the construction of the democratic system, Portuguese trade unions do not have enough mobilization power to obstruct pension reform on their own.

Hostile to changes that may weaken the public pension system and intergenerational solidarity, the trade unions, first and foremost the Communist CGTP-In, have repeatedly denounced the failure of PS and PSD governments to fulfill their commitments regarding Social Security and pensioners. The Socialist minority government, under which the 2000 Framework Law was passed, tried to incorporate social partners in the implementation process so as to legitimize changes in the pension system. But it seems there is little hope of persuading the Communist trade union to support any reform introducing the "plafonamento". Governments seeking the consent of trade unions on significant policy changes have to rely on the UGT, a fact that may increase the leverage of this organization in the ongoing discussion of pension reform.

Constraints of policy design

The Portuguese Social Security system has a complex identity as a result of the legacies of the dictatorial period and the revolutionary phase. Initially designed as a public professional insurance system, leaving space for the development of private initiatives, the system was changed in the aftermath of the revolution that toppled the dictatorship, which stressed universalism as the ideal to be pursued by the state. The need to revise the generous system established by the last dictatorial governments, as well as by the first revolutionary and constitutional governments, became evident when recession hit the Portuguese economy. These reforms have in fact reinforced the mixed legacies of the Social Security system. Thus, in parallel with several efforts to adjust pensions to contributory efforts (in line with the social insurance principle), a number of measures expanding non-contributory coverage have been adopted (in accordance with universalism). Moreover, even the parties on the extreme left acknowledge the role of private solidarity institutions in the fulfillment of specific social protection goals, although conservative parties are even keener on this type of welfare provision, which began to develop in Portugal almost two centuries ago.

Role of ideas and historical context

Since the extension and consolidation of Social Security are relatively recent phenomena linked with the establishment of democracy, the public justification of retrenchment policies in this area has been a sensitive issue for governments. The creation of the White Paper Commission in 1997 represented a clear effort to spread ideas and arguments concerning the need to reform the pension system. The members of this Commission were well acquainted with the arguments of international institutions promoting pension reforms. Being a small country with a relatively small academic community, it seems that Portugal's experts look eagerly to the debates other countries are conducting, and the policies they are proposing and implementing. Approaches favoring the development of pension systems with stronger funded pillars have penetrated both academic and political circles.

In fact, although the Socialists and the Social Democrats seem to have very different ideas as regards the structure of Social Security, they share the will to enhance pension funding. The Socialists try to circumvent the integration of private pension pillars in the structure of Social Security, whereas the Social Democrats defend a more comprehensive Social Security concept. But in truth, the main difference is over the value of the wage ceiling above which workers would freely decide to continue paying contributions to the Social Security PAYG pension system, or invest them in private or public funds. If the ceiling is very high (as proposed by the PS: roughly 12 minimum salaries), the effective enhancement of the funded pension pillars would be very small. In contrast, if the ceiling is significantly lower (as proposed by the PSD and CDS-PP: around 5 minimum salaries) the second and the third pillars would experience a significant boost, and Social Security would see much lower contributions. This dilemma is blocking the implementation of a controversial pension reform, which, in one form or another, will be probably enacted in the coming years.[69]

Abbreviations

CAP	*Confederaçao dos Agricultores Portugueses* / Confederation of Portuguese Peasants
CCP	*Confederaçao do Comercio Português* / Confederation of Portuguese Trade
CDS-PP	*Centro Democrático e Social–Partido Popular* / Social and Democratic Center–Popular Party
CES	*Conselho Económico e Social* / Economic and Social Council
CGA	*Caixa Geral de Aposentações* / General Retirement Savings-bank
CGT/CGTP-In	*Confederação Geral dos Trabalhadores/ Confederação Geral dos Trabalhadores-Intersindical* / General Workers' Confederation
CIP	*Confederação da Indústria Portuguesa* / Portuguese Confederation of Industry
CNP	*Centro Nacional de Pensões* / National Pensions' Center
CNSSS	*Conselho Nacional de Solidariedade e Segurança Social* / National Council for Solidarity and Social Security
CPCS	*Comissão Permanente de Concertação Social* / Permanent Commission of Social Concertation
FDI	*Foreign Direct Investment*

FEFSS	*Fundo de Estabilizaçao Financeira da Segurança Social* / Financial Stabilization Fund of Social Security
INE	*Instituto Nacional de Estatística* / National Statistic Institute
MDP	*Movimento Democrático Português* / Portuguese Democratic Movement
MFA	*Movimento das Forças Armadas* / Armed Forces Movement
MURPI	*Movimento Unitário de Reformados, Pensionistas e Idosos*/ Unified Movement of Retired and Old-aged
PCP	*Partido Comunista Português* / Portuguese Communist Parties
PRD	*Partido Renovador Democrático* / Democratic Renovative Party
PS	*Partido Socialista* / Socialist Party
PSD	*Partido Social Democrata* / Social Democratic Party
PTE	Portuguese Escudos
RG	*Regime Geral* / General Regime
RNCE	*Regimes não contributivo o equiparado* / Non-contributory and equivalent regimes
TSU	*Taxa Social Única* / Unique Social Contribution Rate

Notes

1. The authors wish to thank António Correia de Campos for his useful comments on a previous draft of this chapter.
2. See the 2005 party platforms of the PSD (2005: 51–3) and the PS (2005: 66–74).
3. In the 1960s, Portugal still controlled some of the territories occupied by Portuguese settlers in the 15th and 16th centuries. Besides the Azores and Madeira in the North Atlantic Ocean, which were not inhabited at the time of their conquest, and got some governmental competencies in the 19th century, Portugal ruled over the "overseas provinces" of Angola, Mozambique, Portuguese Guinea (present-day Guinea-Bissao) and several islands off the African west coast, as well as Macao and Timor in Asia.
4. See Art. 2 of the Constitution of the Portuguese Republic. Since 1989 three further constitutional reviews have been endorsed without having much impinged on the structure of the political system. The 1992 Constitutional Review brought about the adjustments required by the Treaty of Maastricht in order to permit residents from other EU countries to vote in local elections. This amendment was followed by a new revision in 1997 allowing national referenda to take place (a proposal responding to the perceived disillusionment of citizens with politics, according to Robinson 2002: 185–7). The fifth Constitutional Review was approved in December 2001, after the September 11 attacks, to enhance the methods to fight against terrorism in Europe.
5. Since less than 50% of the electorate participated in this referendum, its result was not binding. However, nearly two-thirds of voters were opposed to the establishment of administrative regions on the mainland (Robinson 2002: 189–90).
6. In the 1970s, around 90% of the electorate participated in parliamentary elections. The figure has dropped steadily since 1979 and reached its lowest point in the 1999 elections with 61% of the people entitled to vote. Turnout experienced a slight increase in the 2002

(62.3%) and 2005 (65%) elections. Participation in other types of elections also shows the same trend towards greater abstention (See www.idea.int/vt/region_view.cfm?Country Code=PT, retrieved 25 April 2004; INE 2004: 106).

7. In 2002, nearly 779,000 public employees, approximately 15% of the employed population, were contributing to the specific social protection regime for civil servants (Caixa Geral de Aposentações 2003: 14).
8. The State Council (*Conselho de Estado*) is the consultative body of the President of the Portuguese Republic. It is composed of the highest representatives of the *Assembleia*, the government, the Constitutional Court and the regional governments, as well as the ex-Presidents and ten citizens elected by the President and the *Assembleia*.
9. As President Eanes did in 1983 when he refused to appoint the candidate proposed by a party coalition that had an absolute majority in the *Assembleia*.
10. Because administrative districts do not coincide with electoral districts, the Constitution and the electoral laws speak of "electoral circles" (*círculos eleitorais*).
11. Until 1991, the *Assembleia* was made up of 250 deputies.
12. The minority government of Cavaco Silva fell in 1987 as a consequence of the censure motion presented by the PRD (*Partido Renovador Democrático*) and supported by the Socialists and the Communists. The President of the Republic, Mário Soares, could have entrusted the PS (*Partido Socialista*) with the formation of a new government, but he decided to dissolve the *Assembleia* and call for elections.
13. At the top of the hierarchy of legislative acts are the organic laws concerning matters exclusively dependent on the *Assembleia*. These must be approved by an absolute parliamentary majority.
14. Regional parties as well as racist or fascist parties are prohibited by the 1976 Constitution.
15. The CES was incorporated in the Portuguese Constitution through the 1992 Constitutional Review.
16. According to a survey cited by Magone (1997: 114), in 1990 42% of workers in the formal economy were unionized.
17. Besides the CGTP-In and the UGT, there are also independent trade unions representing specific professional groups. At the beginning of the 1990s, they covered an estimated 10% of all unionized workers (Lecher 1994: 77–8, 220–1; Magone 1997: 120–1).
18. The Portuguese Industrial Association (*Associação Industrial Portuguesa*) encompassing around 3,000 enterprises, mainly in the public sector, is the main national competitor of the CIP. Less influential is the Movement of Small and Medium-Size Traders and Entrepreneurs (*Movimento dos Pequenos e Médios Comerciantes e Industriais*) which is in the orbit of the Communist Party.
19. The CAP coexists with other farming associations, among them the *Confederação Nacional de Agricultores* (CAN, National Confederation of Farmers) which is close to the Communist Party.
20. In fact, agricultural workers and fishermen, integrated in specific institutions (the *Casas do Povo* and the *Casas dos Pescadores*, respectively) could basically claim sickness and survival benefits depending on the availability of financial resources.
21. The *Ministério das Corporaçoes e Previdência Social* was in 1973 renamed as *Ministério das Corporaçoes e Segurança Social*.
22. Medina (1996: 394) does not interpret the political change that took place in 1974 as a break in social policy. He tends to stress continuity with the policies adopted by the last dictatorial governments rather than a path shift, even though he recognizes that between 1974 and 1975 the system of obligatory social insurance developed into a system of social security. Actually, he links the discontinuities in the evolution of social security policies more clearly with changes in the financing capacity of the state.

23. Portugal stands out for having an important proportion of disabled pensioners. Thousands of Portuguese workers affected by the deep industrial restructuring of the 1980s got a disability pension before the age of 65. The conditions for getting disability pensions were toughened in the 1990s (Correia de Campos 2000: 190).
24. The former occupational scheme for agricultural workers, which has been closed to new contributors since 1986 and is therefore expected to disappear around 2025, has been renamed *Regime Rural Transitório*.
25. Bank employees nevertheless have access to Social Security family allowances, unemployment subsidies and professional sickness benefits.
26. Disability benefits can be obtained after five contribution years and survivor benefits after three contribution years. Contributors to the voluntary Social Security regime need 144 contribution months to qualify for an old-age pension and 72 months for a disability pension.
27. Workers may also pre-retire under different conditions if they are long-term unemployed or work in specific occupations, like miners, fishermen, seamen, dockers, aircraft pilots, customs officers, etc.
28. These are the contribution rates for "standard" employed and self-employed workers. The Social Security system, however, distinguishes many specific professional groups within both regimes with special contribution rates (church members, farmers, football and basketball players, etc.). The website of Portuguese Social Security (www.seg-soc.pt) details the range of contribution rates within each regime.
29. This fund was created in 1989 and is managed by the *Instituto de Gestão de Fundos de Capitalização*. At least 50% of its assets have to be invested in Portuguese public debt.
30. Press release of the CGTP-In of 24 January 2003 (www.cgtp.pt/temas/segsocial/030124finance.htm).
31. Between 90% and 106% according to the data of the White Paper on Social Security (Comissão do Livro Branco 1998: 99–100). See also Correia de Campos (2000: 191). As regards fiscal treatment, the income ceiling below which pensioners do not need to pay taxes is higher than the one established for salaried workers.
32. Pensioners affiliated to the Social Security system before 2002 also have the right to claim the proportional application of the old and the new rules if this gives a higher pension benefit.
33. Interviews with experts have been a very important source of information in the elaboration of this paragraph. The authors wish to thank António Correia de Campos, Henrique Medina Carreira, Diogo Lucena and Fernando Ribeiro Mendes for kindly talking with us about the Portuguese pension system in the second week of March 2004. Press articles were also very useful in the process of composing our text. We therefore are thankful to GESCO, Edimpresa and *Expresso* for facilitating access to their databases.
34. See the *Decreto Regulamentar* 60/82, 15 September 1982.
35. See the *Projecto de Lei* n° 93/III (CDS).
36. See *Diário da Assembleia da República*, III Legislatura, 1a sessão legislativa (1983–4): 2024.
37. See page 2028.
38. See *Diário da Assembleia da República*, III Legislatura, 1a sessão legislativa (1983–4): 5137–8.
39. See the Law n° 28/84 of August 14, 1984.
40. Among them the Decree-Law 401/86 of December 2, 1986 establishing the incorporation of agricultural workers in the Social Security general regime, and 143/88 of April 22, 1988 introducing a unified pension for workers having contributed to Social Security as well as to the civil servants program (*Caixa Geral de Aposentações*).
41. See the Decree-Law 20/85 of January 17, 1985 which set up an unemployment insurance scheme integrated in the Social Security general regime and the Decree-Law 140-D/86 which created a unified social contribution, thus integrating the financial resources to cover unemployment in the general regime.

42. See the Decree-Law 323/85 of August 6, 1985.
43. Our italics in the quotation. See the Decree-Law 396/86 of November 25, 1986.
44. See the Decree-Law 225/89 of July 6, 1989.
45. According to the Decree-Law 215/89 of July 1, 1989 the invested amount in a savings plan for retirement was deductible from the personal income taxable base with the maximum limit of the lowest of following rates: 20% of total income or PTE 500,000. Like pension plans, saving plans for retirement can be administered either by management societies or by insurance companies.
46. See the Decree-Law 415/91 of October 25, 1991.
47. See Decree-Law 475/99 of November 9, 1999.
48. The effect of including the two extraordinary payments was probably that of reducing the average wages since the latter are often lower than ordinary monthly salaries. In contrast, the indexation of earnings used to calculate the reference base achieved the opposite effect.
49. See the Decree-Law 329/93 developed by the *Portaria* 96/94.
50. See the interview with Ferro Rodrígues in the Portuguese magazin *Já*, May 16, 1996.
51. See the *Decree-Law* 9/99 of January 8, 1999.
52. See *Expresso* June 17, 2000 ("*O 'truque' das pré-pensões*").
53. See the Decree-Law 265/99 of July 14, 1999.
54. See the *Proposta de Lei* n° 2/VIII.
55. See the *Projecto de Lei* n° 24/VIII (PSD).
56. See the *Projecto de Lei* n° 7/VIII (CDS-PP).
57. See the *Projectos de Lei* n°10/VIII (PCP) and 116/VIII (*Bloco de Esquerda*).
58. The business organization CIP refused to adhere to the agreement, the text of which can be read in *Acordo sobre a modernização da proteccão social*, November 20, 2001 (www.ces.pt/html/p_main.htm, retrieved 5 May 2004).
59. Affiliated workers who had contributed for at least 15 years up to December 31, 2001, and those getting their first pension before December 31, 2016, have the right to get pensions calculated according to the old rules if the resulting amount is higher.
60. The indexation criterion to be applied to earnings registered before January 1, 2002 is the CPI, excluding housing costs. A more favorable index combining CPI without housing costs (75%) and wage increases (25%) will be used to revalue wages earned after that date. With reference to the accrual rate on the pension base, the Decree-Law determined its variation according to several criteria. Thus, workers with 20 or fewer contribution years were to accumulate 2% of the pension base per contribution year. However, workers with 21 or more contribution years should get between 2% and 2.3% per contribution year, depending on the value of the individual pension base (the lower the pension base the higher the accrual rate).
61. See www.watsonwyatt.com/europe/portugal/research/assuntos2.asp, retrieved 20 December 2004.
62. The text of the agreement can be read in *Acordo sobre a introdução de limites opcionais às contribuições para o sistema de repartição*, November 20, 2001 (www.ces.pt/html/p_main.htm, retrieved 5 May 2004).
63. See the *Proposta de Lei* n° 20/IX.
64. See the *Projectos de Lei* n° 64/IX and n° 89/IX.
65. See *Diário da Assembleia da República*, IX Legislatura, 1a sessão legislativa (2002–03), 33: 1326 and 1332.
66. See, e.g., *Diário de Notícias* May 29, 2003 ("Jovens optam nas pensões"), 5 and 7 June 2003 ("Pensões de invalidez completas..." and "Desconfiança brinda abertura ao privado").
67. Social Security bureaucrats are studying how to design the corresponding rules. According to Ferreira (2003), one should not dismiss their power to block this implementation process.

68. See, e.g., the CGTP_IN press release number 40 (2002) (www.cgtp.pt/imprensa/comunica/2002/ci001-40.html, retrieved 20 July 2004).
69. During the first months of his government, José Sócrates, the PS leader appointed Prime Minister in February 2005, has constrained conditions for pre-retirement and established an increase in contributions for self-employed workers. By the end of 2005 the new government seemed to have set aside the issue of "plafonamento". According to the Secretary of State for Social Security, Pedro Marques, "the 'plafonamento' not only does not solve the problems of the Social Security systems, but aggravates them. Fortunately this obsession is going out-of-date..." (*Diário Económico* October 18, 2005).

Biliography
Primary sources and government documents

CAIXA GERAL DE APOSENTAÇÕES (2003). *Relatório e Contas*. Lisbon: CGA.

COMISSÃO DO LIVRO BRANCO DA SEGURANÇA SOCIAL (1998). *Livro Branco da Segurança Social*. Versão final. Lisbon: INA/IGFSS.

DIRECÇÃO-GERAL DOS REGIMES DE SEGURANÇA SOCIAL (1999). *Portuguese Social Security System. Social Security Schemes*. Lisbon: International Relations Division.

EUROPEAN COMMISSION (2004). *European Social Statistics. Social protection. Expenditure and Receipts*. Data 1992–2001. Luxemburg: Office for Official Publications of the European Union.

INSTITUTO DE SEGUROS DE PORTUGAL (2002). *Estadísticas de Fundos de Pensões*. Lisbon.

INSTITUTO NACIONAL de Estadística (2004). *30 anos de 25 de abril. Un retrato estadístico*. Lisbon.

MINISTÉRIO DA SEGURANÇA SOCIAL E DO TRABALHO (2002). *Relatório Nacional de Estratégia sobre o Futuro dos Sistemas de Pensões* (National Strategy Reports: Adequate and Sustainable Pension Systems) Lisbon.

PPD/PSD (2005). *Um contrato con os Portugueses. Manifesto Eleitoral Legislativas 2005*. Lisbon.

PS (2005). *Compromisso de Governo 2005–2009. Voltar a acreditar. Bases programaticas. Legislativas 2005*. Lisbon.

SEGURANÇA SOCIAL (Instituto de Informática e Estatística da Solidariedade) (2002). *Boletim Estatístico. Invalidez, Velhice e Sobrevivência*. Lisbon.

Secondary sources

ALMEIDA, ANA ISABEL, and CRISTOVAM, MARIA LUISA (2000). "A Lei de Bases da Segurança Social reforça a participaçao dos parceiros sociais nas instituiçoes da Segurança Social." *European Industrial Relations Observatory on-line*, July 2000; www.eiro.eurofound.eu.int/2000/07/word/pt0007100fpt.doc, retrieved 1 February 2004.

ÁLVAREZ-MIRANDA, BERTA (1996). *El sur de Europa y la adhesión a la Comunidad. Los debates políticos*. Madrid: CIS.

ARAÚJO, ANTÓNIO DE, and COUTINHO MAGALHÃES, PEDRO (2000). "A justiça constitucional: una instituição contra as maiorias?" *Análise Social*, 154–5, XXXV, 207–46.

BRAGA DA CRUZ, MANUEL (2000). "El desarrollo de la democracia portuguesa." In Costa Pinto, A. (ed.), Portugal Contemporáneo. Madrid: Sequitur, 108–25.

CANOTILHO, JOSÉ JOAQUIM and MOREIRA, VITAL (1993). *Constituiçao da República Portuguesa Anotada*. Coimbra: Coimbra Editora.

CORKILL, DAVID (2002). "Challenge and Change: Prospects for the 21st Century." In Syrett, S. (ed.) *Contemporary Portugal: Dimensions of Economic and Political Change*. Aldershot: Ashgate, 221–30.

CORREIA DE CAMPOS, ANTÓNIO (2000). *Solidariedade Sustentada. Reformar a Segurança Social*. Lisbon: Gradiva.

Costa Pinto, António (2000). "Portugal en el siglo XX: una introducción." In Costa Pinto, A. (ed.), *Portugal Contemporáneo*. Madrid: Sequitur, 1–36.

The Economist (2000a). "In the Club. EU Membership Has Brought Increased Prosperity—as well as a Few Problems," November 30.

—— (2000b) "Half-way There: In Only 15 Years, Portugal Has Halved the Big Gap in Living Standards Between Itself and the Rest of Europe," November 30.

Esping-Andersen, Gøsta (1999). *Social Foundations of Postindustrial Economies*. Oxford: Oxford University Press.

Ferreira, Silvia (2003). "The Past in the Present Portuguese Social Security Reform." Paper presented at the Inaugural ESPAnet Conference. Copenhagen, 13–15 November 2003.

Freire, André, de Araújo, António, Leston-Bandeira, Cristina. et al. (2002). *O Parlamento Português: uma reforma necessária*. Lisbon: Instituto de Ciências Sociais da Universidade de Lisboa.

Guillén, Ana, Álvarez, Santiago and Adão e Silva, Pedro (2001). "Redesigning the Spanish and Portuguese Welfare States: The Impact of Accession into the European Union." *Center for European Studies Working Paper* 85. Harvard University, Minda de Gunzburg Center for European Studies.

Holzmann, Robert, Orenstein, Mitchell and Rutkowski, Michael (2003) (eds). *Pension Reform in Europe*: Process and Progress. Washington: World Bank.

Huntington, Samuel (1991). *The Third Wave: Democratization in the Late Twentieth Century*. Norman: University of Oklahoma Press.

Lecher, Wolfgang (ed.) (1994). *Trade Unions in the European Union. A Handbook*. London: Lawrence & Wishart.

Leite Pinto, Ricardo and Ferreira de Almeida, José Mário (2001). *O Sistema Político-Administrativo Português*. Oeiras: INA.

Magone, José M. (1997). *European Portugal: The Difficult Road to Sustainable Democracy*. Houndmills, Basingstoke: Macmillan Press.

Marques, Fernando (1997). *Evoluçao e problemas da Segurança Social em Portugal no após 25 de abril*. Lisbon: Cosmos.

Maxwell, Kenneth (1999). *A Construçao da democracia em Portugal*. Lisbon: Presença.

Medina Carreira, H. (1996). "A Segurança Social." In Barreto, A. (ed.), *A situação Social em Portugal, 1960–1995*. ICS: Lisbon, 385–408.

Nunes Silva, C. (2002). "Local and Regional Government: Continuity and Innovation in Local Government." In Syrett, S. (ed.), *Contemporary Portugal: Dimensions of Economic and Political Change*. Aldershot: Ashgate, 197–220.

OECD (2003). *Economic surveys: Portugal*. Paris: OECD.

Oliveira Guimarães, Maria Leonor (1987). "Esquemas complementares de Segurança Social". *Cadernos Sindicais*, 9: 67–74.

Pereira, Alfredo M. and Rodrigues, Pedro G. (2001). "Ageing and Public Pensions in Portugal: A Snapshot before the Reform," *European Economy—Reports and Studies* 4.

Robinson, Richard A. H. (2002). "National Political Change in Portugal, 1976–99." In Syrett, S. (ed.) *Contemporary Portugal: Dimensions of Economic and Political Change*. Aldershot: Ashgate, 179–96.

Santos, Boaventura S. (1990). *O Estado e a Sociedade em Portugal (1974–1998)*. Porto: Afrontamento, 193–266.

Silva Leal, António da (1998). *Temas de Segurança Social (Coordenaçao e prefácio de Ilídio das Neves)*. Lisbon: União das Mutualidades Portuguesas.

Syrett, Stephen (2002). "Portugal Transformed." In Syrett, S. (ed.), *Contemporary Portugal: Dimensions of Economic and Political Change*. Aldershot: Ashgate, 1–23.

CHAPTER 14

GERMANY: BEYOND POLICY GRIDLOCK

ISABELLE SCHULZE

SVEN JOCHEM

1 Introduction

EVER since Germany introduced the first social insurance-based pension system in 1889, the nation has been esteemed as the "mother" of statutory social insurance. Currently, however, the German model is in crisis, and the pension system in particular is the subject of intense reform deliberations. For many commentators, *Reformstau*—or reform gridlock—resulting from institutional obstacles to reform in a fragmented political system is responsible for mounting costs and the decline of the German model, including the generous public pension system (Alber 1998; Czada 2004; Kitschelt and Streeck 2003). Focusing on this one aspect of the German political economy—namely the pension system—we argue instead that problems in pension reform politics are not caused by policy blockage, but instead by new patterns of political competition.

Since the 1980s, Germany has faced problems similar to those of other continental European countries: demographic change, rising pension costs, budgetary pressure, declining rates of return in the pay-as-you-go (PAYG) systems, high unemployment (and comparatively modest labor market participation rates), globalization, and

Europeanization. Crucially, however, Germany had to face the challenge of national unification and the expansion of the existing social security systems to an additional population of 17 million people. This unique aspect of German (pension) politics not only exacerbated the problems of the pension system, but also had an impact on the political logic of reform.

The German political system is characterized by high political obstacles to reform, with a highly effective veto point in the bicameral parliament, a strong role for judicial review, federalism and constitutionally-protected corporatist procedures for interest-intermediation (Immergut 1992; Saalfeld 2003). These institutional levers enable different interests to block legislation and, thus, to influence reform content. Hence, policy-making is embedded in a dense network of negotiations between the government (*Bundesregierung*), the lower house of Parliament (*Bundestag*) and the *Bundesrat*, in which the executives of the federal states (*Bundesländer*) are represented. Additionally, this constitutional power distribution is embedded in a specific mode of party competition. Intense competition is to be observed between the two *Volksparteien* in the middle of the party spectrum, the CDU/CSU and the SPD. These catch-all parties are complemented on each side by (potential) junior partners in coalition governments: the liberal FDP on the right and the Green Party on the left. After 1990, a new party entered the party system—the communist PDS—and the pattern of coalition building in the *Länder* became more heterogeneous than ever before. Recently, the PDS merged with left wing dissenters from the SPD and the trade unions (WASG) and formed the new party *Die Linke.PDS* (Left Party), which successfully entered the *Bundestag* in the federal elections 2005. Finally, the policy-making process is affected by formal and informal channels of influence, institutionalized through traditions of policy negotiations between government actors and interest groups involved in pension politics. These negotiations are located on a sectoral level or are institutionally fixed to one policy field, creating rather closed "epistemic policy communities" (Döhler and Manow 1997; Czada 2003), which hampers concertation over different policy domains.

We argue that in order to understand the (sometimes) erratic reform processes in German pension politics, one has to take into account the specific institutional design of the German negotiation democracy. Hence, institutions do matter in German pension politics. But our argument is that despite the constraining institutional framework for reform measures, pension reforms are rarely blocked in Germany. Indeed quite the opposite is true: the frequency of reform and the scope of retrenchment in German pension politics seems to be quite high, and certainly not below a "European average." This challenges many influential accounts of German reform politics that emphasize institutional obstacles. The formal veto point and the multitude of informal channels of influence allow access for "interests" to influence reform content, tending to lead to incoherent policy solutions, and reforms biased towards the status quo. But they do not block policy-making. Instead, the hesitation of politicians to introduce large scale reform is a product of highly intensified political competition.

II POLITICAL SYSTEM

Constitutional history and nation-building

After the Nazi dictatorship, the division of Germany into the *Deutsche Demokratische Republik* and the *Bundesrepublik Deutschland* led to competition between East and West quickly becoming an institutionally embedded imperative in politics on both sides of the Iron Curtain (Winkler 2000).

At the time of the unexpected unification of these two states in 1989, the Eastern part of the nation was plagued by an inefficient and out-dated industrial sector with an over-supply of labor, while the West German model was at its peak of international admiration. From this point of view it seemed rational to transfer the "successful" political institutions of the West to the new federal states (*Neue Bundesländer*), hence the "institutional transfer" from West to East (Lehmbruch 1991; Wiesenthal 2003). One of the most challenging enterprises in German history, the integration of a communist society and economy into an already existing democratic and capitalist system, was at first seen by almost all political actors as a manageable task. However, since about 1993, the problems and the misguided expectations on both sides of the former divide have become increasingly obvious. As we will show in detail below, unification contributed to the problems in the pension system and significantly influenced the logic of subsequent policy-making.

Institutions of government

The German polity is shaped by institutions that reduce power concentration and enforce policy negotiations and compromises. In this section we review the major pillars of this fragmented system of governance, focusing on formal institutions (Table 14.1).

The President (*Bundespräsident*) is the official head of the state, and is indirectly elected for a five year term by an electoral college (*Bundesversammlung*) composed of the members of the Lower Chamber—the *Bundestag*—and an equal number of members chosen by the State Parliaments (*Landtage*). The *Bundespräsident*'s functions are mainly representative. He signs and promulgates legislative acts (Art. 58 GG) but holds no more than a formal function in the legislative process.

Executive power resides with the Chancellor (*Bundeskanzler*). The *Bundestag* elects the nominated candidate with an absolute majority of its members (Art. 63 GG). The *Bundestag* has the right to call a constructive vote of no-confidence (Art. 67 GG), and the Chancellor may call for a vote of confidence. If he does not receive the majority of votes, the President may dissolve the *Bundestag* (Art. 68 GG). The Chancellor plays a leading role within the Cabinet in determining the general guidelines of policy (*Richtlinienkompetenz*) (Art. 65 GG).

Table 14.1 Political institutions in Germany

Political arenas	Actors	Rules of investiture	Rules of decision-making	Veto potential
Executive	President (*Bundespräsident*)	5-year term; elected by combination of *Bundestag* members and an electoral college chosen by the state parliaments (*Landtage*)	Signs and promulgates legislative acts	A formal veto point with practically no impact
	Chancellor (*Bundeskanzler*)	Elected by majority of *Bundestag*'s members on President's proposal; then appointed by the President; may be subject to vote of no-confidence requiring the majority of members in the Bundestag; prominent role within cabinet (*Richtlinienkompetenz*)	Cabinet proposes most legislation; possibility to legislate by decree with *Bundesrat*'s consent	—
Legislative	Chamber of Deputies (*Bundestag*)	4-year term; proportional representation with 5% threshold; 299 direct mandates and 299 state list mandates plus excess mandates; President can dissolve *Bundestag* upon chancellor's request after a lost vote of confidence	Fractions have right of initiative (5% of members); decision making by majority of votes; right to overrule *Bundesrat*'s objection for non-mandatory legislation	Not a veto point due to majority governments and strong party discipline
	Senate (*Bundesrat*)	Term dependent on how long state government retains power; 69 members; state governments delegate representatives; number of delegates related to population size (between 3 to 6)	Right of initiative (decision by majority of members): • differentiation between mandatory consent and non-mandatory consent legislation; • majority agreement needed for mandatory consent legislation; voting by states (unified votes); • agreement needed for governmental decrees	Veto point in mandatory consent legislation; usage of veto power dependent on political constellations of government coalition and states

(Continued)

Table 14.1 (Continued)

Political arenas	Actors	Rules of investiture	Rules of decision-making	Veto potential
Judicial	Constitutional Court (*Bundesverfassungsgericht*)	12-year term (only once); *Bundestag* and *Bundesrat* each elect half of the judges by 2/3-majority; 2 senates of 8 judges	Surveys the constitutionality of legislation upon appeal	Only post-legislative veto point; fairly strong influence
Electoral	Referendum	De facto non-existent; only allowed for territorial restructuring of the federal states (*Volksentscheid zur Neugliederung des Bundesgebietes*) and in single *Bundesländer*, such as in Bavaria	None	Not a veto point
Territorial units	States (*Länder*) Communities (*Gemeinden*)	State electoral laws (different terms and electoral formulas)	*Länder*: influence via *Bundesrat* – see above; almost all national administration is delegated to the states → de facto influence through administration *Gemeinden*: no formal influence on national legislation	See above, *Bundesrat*

Germany is a federal country divided into 16 states that have their own constitutions, executives and legislative bodies. The states are responsible for legislation in all policy areas that are not explicitly reserved for the federal government in the Constitution (Art. 70 GG). The areas in which the federal government retains exclusive legislative jurisdiction (Art. 71 GG) include external affairs, citizenship, tariffs, currency etc. (Art. 73 GG). Some areas are subject to "competitive legislative jurisdiction" (*konkurrierende Gesetzgebung*), meaning that the states may enact legislation as long as the federal legislators do not claim competency (Art. 72 I GG). The federal government can claim this competency if it can establish that this is essential for the provision of consistent standards of living, or for ensuring the economic and juridical unity of the country (Art. 72 II GG). Pension policy is a field of national legislation. However, if administrative matters or tax issues are involved, the *Bundesrat* has the right to co-determine policy reforms.

Parliament is divided into two chambers. The first chamber—the *Bundestag*—has 598 members and relies heavily on the work of standing committees that correspond to the competencies of government ministries. The state governments (*Länderregierungen*) appoint representatives to the second parliamentary chamber—the *Bundesrat*, which is thus indirectly elected. The number of delegates per state depends on population size and varies from three to six (Art. 51 II GG), thus privileging the smaller states. The *Bundesrat* (currently 69 members) decides by majority, but each state must cast its votes unanimously, that is to say the delegates are bound by the instructions of the state governments (Art. 51 III GG). The *Bundesrat* must also agree to executive legislation such as decrees and regulations.

The Supreme Court (*Bundesverfassungsgericht*) has the power to survey the constitutionality of legislation upon appeal (Art. 93 GG). As we shall show in detail later, some reform initiatives originate from the Court's decisions, either as it rejects laws passed because they contradict the imperatives of the Constitution, or when the Constitutional Court explicitly demands a change in policy. This was the case with the survivors' pension reform in 1975, and the verdict on the taxation of pension benefits in 2002.

Electoral system

The members of the *Bundestag* are elected via a mixed electoral system for a four-year term (Art. 39 I GG). Every voter has two votes. With the first votes (*Erststimmen*), one candidate is directly elected to Parliament in each of the 299 constituencies with a relative majority; before 2002, there were 328 constituencies. With the second vote (*Zweitstimme*), the voter chooses a party that distributes seats according to state party lists (*Landeslisten*) following the Hare-Niemeyer method. If a party wins more direct mandates than it would deserve from the party's share of second votes, it receives excess mandates (*Überhangsmandate*) which means the standard size of Parliament of 598 seats is exceeded. A 5 percent hurdle hinders entry to Parliament for small parties. But regionally concentrated parties can bypass the entrance barrier if they win at least three direct mandates (Schick and Feldkamp 2005).

Legislative process

Beyond the autonomy of *Länder*-legislation in some policy fields, there are two kinds of federal laws in Germany: those for which the consent of the *Bundesrat* is mandatory (*zustimmungspflichtig*), and those for which its consent is not mandatory (*nicht-zustimmungspflichtig*). We will refer to these two types as *mandatory consent* and *non-mandatory consent* legislation. In most cases, the legislative process starts with a governmental bill (Art. 76 I GG).[1] Usually, the ministry in charge invites experts, associations, unions, sub-national bodies and other national departments to comment on a first draft. Then, the proposal is amended—if necessary—and forwarded to the cabinet, which takes a resolution. Government bills must be submitted to the *Bundesrat*, which may pass comment within six weeks (Art. 76 II GG). Next, the proposal, the comment and a government statement on this comment are presented to the *Bundestag*.

After a first reading the bill is transmitted to the committee stage. The assigned committee may amend the bill, and concludes its work by drafting a report and issuing a recommendation that is presented to the plenum. The second and third readings—which take place in immediate sequence—provide another opportunity for debating the individual articles and amendments, and finish with the final vote. After the *Bundestag*'s vote, the *Bundesrat* receives the bill and can ask, by majority decision, for the Mediation Committee (*Vermittlungsausschuss*) to be set up, which consists of 16 members of the *Bundesrat* and an equal number from the *Bundestag*.[2] In contrast to voting in the *Bundesrat* plenum, the states' delegates in the Mediation Committee are not bound by instructions (Art. 77 II GG). For *mandatory* legislation, the bill fails if the mediation committee, which decides by simple majority, does not come up with any suggestion, or if the committee's compromise is blocked by one of the houses. With *non-mandatory* legislation, the *Bundestag* can vote down a *Bundesrat* objection with an absolute majority.[3] Finally the law is signed by the President and published in the Federal Law Gazette (*Bundesgesetzblatt*) (Art. 82 GG).

Until the late 1980s, German pension legislation was prepared and negotiated in a rather closed policy community, with the consequence that most major pension reforms were passed with opposition support (Hinrichs 1998). After unification, however, political competition increased and even made consensual policy-making in pension politics rare (Hinrichs 2004; Nullmeier 2003).

Parties and elections

In the golden age of the German model, the party system was dominated by two *Volksparteien* in the middle of the party spectrum, that is the Christian Democratic Union (CDU) in collaboration with her Bavarian "sister party" the Christian Social Union (CSU),[4] and the Social Democratic Party of Germany (SPD). The CDU/CSU and the SPD are big, traditional "omnibus" parties with somewhat heterogeneous electorates. The Liberal party (FDP) long served as the "King maker" of the coalition governments, which are typical forms of government in Germany. In fact, the FDP

Party family affiliation	Abbreviation	Party name	Ideological orientation	Founding and merger details	Year established
Christian parties	CDU	Christian Democratic Union (*Christlich Demokratische Union*)	Inter-denominational, Christian center-right party	Predecessor *Deutsche Zentrumspartei* of 1871	1945
	CSU	Christian Social Union in Bavaria (*Chrstilich-Soziale Union in Bayern*)	Bavarian conservative, social party	Predecessor *Bayerische Volkspartei*	1946
Left parties/ Social democratic parties	SPD	Social Democratic Party (*Sozialdemokatische Partei Deutschland*)	Center-left	Predecessor *Sozialdemokratische Arbeiterpartei* in 1869	1945
Greens	Grüne	Alliance 90/ The Greens (*Bündnis 90/ Die Grünen*)	Ecological, peace oriented, champion of women's rights and New Social Movements	Merger of ecological and peace movement initiatives	1980
Liberal	FDP	Free Democratic Party (*Freie Demokratische Partei*)	Liberal	Sucessor to two liberal parties from 1918: the *Deutsche Demokratische Partei* and the *Deutsche Volkspartei*	1948
Left	PDS	*Partei des Demokratischen Sozialismus*	Socialist party; representative of East German interests	Predecessor *Sozialistische Einheitspartei Deutschlands* (SED)	1990
	Linke	*Die Linke* (PDS)	Socialist party; defender of the welfare status quo	Merger of PDS and WSAG, a grass-root movement opposing the SPD reform strategy	2005

Fig. 14.1 Party system in Germany

Sources: Schmidt (2003), Sturm (1989).

managed to stay in government for most of the time between 1960 and 1998. The FDP draws its electorate from the middle class, but the core electorate is rather small and the party relies to a high degree on swing voters (Vorländer 1990: 273–5).

Table 14.2. Governmental majorities in Germany

Date of change in political configuration[a]	Election date (Bundestag)	Start of gov.	Head of gov. (party)	Governing parties	Gov. majority (% seats) BT	Gov. electoral base (% votes) BT	Gov. majority (% seats) BR[b]	Institutional veto points	Number of veto players (partisan + institutional)
12.15.1976	10.30.1976	12.15.1976	Schmidt II (SPD)	SPD (214), FDP (39)	51.0%	50.5%	36.6%	BR	2 + 1
11.05.1980	10.09.1980	11.05.1980	Schmidt III (SPD)	SPD (218), FDP (53)	54.5%	53.5%	36.6%	BR	2 + 1
10.01.1982		10.01.1982[c]	Kohl I (CDU)	CDU/CSU (226), FDP (53)	56.1%	55.2%	63.4%	None	2 + 0
03.29.1983	03.06.1983	03.29.1983	Kohl II (CDU)	CDU/CSU (244), FDP (34)	55.8%	55.7%	63.4%	None	2 + 0
03.11.1987	01.25.1987	03.11.1987	Kohl III (CDU)	CDU/CSU (223), FDP (46)	54.1%	53.4%	56.1%	None	2 + 0
06.21.1990			Kohl III (CDU)	CDU/CSU (223), FDP (46)	54.1%	53.4%	43.2%	BR	2 + 1
10.03.1990[d]			Kohl III (CDU)	CDU/CSU (223), FDP (46)	54.1%	53.4%	39.6%	BR	2 + 1
11.09.1990[e]			Kohl III (CDU)	CDU/CSU (223), FDP (46)	54.1%	53.4%	54.7%	None	2 + 0
01.17.1991	12.02.1990	01.17.1991	Kohl IV (CDU)	CDU/CSU (319), FDP (79)	60.1%	54.9%	51.5%	None	2 + 0
04.05.1991			Kohl IV (CDU)	CDU/CSU (319), FDP (79)	60.1%	54.9%	45.6%	BR	2 + 1
11.17.1994	10.16.1994	11.17.1994	Kohl V (CDU)	CDU/CSU (294), FDP (47)	50.7%	48.4%	25.0%	BR	2 + 1
10.27.1998	09.27.1998	10.27.1998	Schröder I (SPD)	SPD (298), Grüne (47)	51.6%	47.6%	50.7%	None	2 + 0
04.07.1999			Schröder I (SPD)	SPD (298), Grüne (47)	51.6%	47.6%	43.5%	BR	2 + 1
10.22.2002	09.22.2002	10.22.2002	Schröder II (SPD)	SPD (251), Grüne (55)	50.7%	47.1%	23.2%	BR	2 + 1
11.22.2005	09.17.2005	11.22.2005	Merkel (CDU)	CDU/CSU (226), SPD (222)	73.0%	69.4%	52.2%	None	2 + 0

[a] We consider a "change in political configuration" the change in party composition of a state government that leads to a change in government share of seats (column government majority) in the *Bundesrat* or a change in seat distribution in the *Bundestag*. Dates correspond to day of swearing-in of state prime minister or chancellor.
[b] We count Länder as part of government majority if the parties in the state coalition matches exactly one or all parties in the federal government. Berlin is not included until 3 October 1990 as voting rights for Berlin in Bundesrat were restricted in the old FRG.
[c] A constructive vote of no confidence resulted in the change in Chancellor.
[d] October 3, 1990 is the date of the German reunification. From that date on, the BR representatives for Berlin received voting rights such that the total number of seats increased and the majority was affected.
[e] Seats in the Bundesrat are granted to the "new" *Länder* according to their population size.

Sources: www.bundeswahlleiter.de; Parliamentary Minutes of State Parliaments: various issues; Seemann (2005), Andersen and Woyke (2003).

In 1982, the entry of the Green Party, which had its roots in various citizens' initiatives for environmental protection and peace movements, into the *Bundestag* changed the party system at the federal level for the first time since the 1960s. The entry of a fifth party into the *Bundestag* was a consequence of German unification: the PDS (*Partei des Demokratischen Sozialismus*) was a successor to the former communist East German political party (it was the only party allowed)—the *Sozialistische Einheitspartei Deutschlands* (SED). The PDS relies on electoral support from the Eastern *Bundesländer* and has played the role of a (sometimes populist) defender of the welfare state against reform measures undertaken by the government. However, it could not overcome the 5 percent threshold in 2002 and was only represented in the *Bundestag* by two members, who entered Parliament on first-vote tickets. Shortly before the 2005 parliamentary election (which was called prematurely as the result of a vote of no-confidence orchestrated by the then chancellor, Gerhard Schröder), however, the PDS fused with the West German Left Alternate List (WASG), mainly dissenters from the SPD and dissatisfied union members, to form a new party, *Die Linke.PDS* or the Left Party, which received nearly 9 percent of both votes and Lower House seats.

The party systems in the new *Bundesländer* differ notably from the systems in the Western states. Until the emergence of the Left Party, the socialist PDS was not represented in the legislatures of the old states, but received more than 20 percent in state elections on East German territory, sometimes surpassing even the CDU/CSU or the SPD. At the same time, the FDP and the Green Party play no significant role in East Germany (Pulzer 1999: 247). Hence, through the 2002 federal election campaign, party competition in unified Germany was divided. It became obvious that the catch-all parties cannot win elections in the East, but that they can certainly lose them there. This compels the CDU/CSU as well as the SPD to balance reform ambitions—highly appreciated in the western part of the country—with the defense of social rights, as prioritized by the electorate in the East. With the emergence of the Left party, the future for cuts and reforms is even more unclear.

Interest groups

The landscape of interest group organization in Germany is dominated by a few important interest groups, at least so far as pension politics is concerned. At least until the 1990s, pension politics were dominated by a highly segmented epistemic policy community, in which traditionally secure interest groups dominated: the trade unions, the employers' organizations and the *Sozialbeirat*. During the past decade, however, the VDK (*Verband der Kriegsbeschädigten, Kriegshinterbliebenen und Sozialrentner Deutschlands*) moved more and more into the inner circle of pension politics. After its renaming in 1994—*Sozialverband VdK Deutschland*—the *Sozialverband* took up the interests of pensioners more aggressively in the public debate. It is noteworthy that after internal conflicts in the CDU/CSU about the future course of the party in social policies during 2004, the former Health Minister, Horst Seehofer, was nominated as leader of the Bavarian branch of the VDK and future director of the federal VDK. In 2005, Horst Seehofer left the VDK and became Minister for Agriculture in the Grand Coalition.

German trade unionism is marked by a concentrated, fairly centralized structure. The main umbrella organization, *Deutscher Gewerkschaftsbund* (DGB), represents eight individual unions. Despite formal neutrality in party politics, the trade unions historically foster close relationships with the SPD. Tensions between the wings of the labor movement increased tremendously as the Red–Green government decided to push through painful reforms, after 2003, with the implementation of "Agenda 2010."

With respect to policy reforms, unions are regularly perceived as blocking actors and obstacles for modernizing the welfare state (Schroeder and Weßels 2003: 12). From a comparative perspective, German trade unions do not pursue particularly militant strategies in interest mediation. In the first years of the new millennium, however, internal tensions in the trade union movement became apparent, as the programmatic hegemony of the *IG Metall* was challenged on the one side by the newly-created public sector union *ver.di*, and on the other side by intra-*IG Metall* competition between "reformers" and "traditionalists" with respect to programatic re-adjustment and leadership choice.

The main employers' and business associations are the German Industry Association (*Bundesverband der Deutschen Industrie*, BDI), and the Confederation of German Employers' Associations (*Bundesvereinigung der Deutschen Arbeitgeberverbände*, BDA). Both are umbrella organizations: as of 2004 the BDA united 54 federal associations and the BDI 36 associations from various sectors. German employers, especially the BDA, were seen as important pillars of the German welfare state model. In contrast to other European employers' associations, the BDA opted for a partnership with organized labor and the defense of the structure of the German welfare state. In the 1990s, the BDI forcefully challenged this programatic position and revealed an internal split in the employers' camp, thereby reducing the capacity of the employers to act as unified actors in reform policies. As some observers have put it, the internal cohesion in both camps is still eroding: "Disarray and lack of unity on the employer side, so prominently on display in the late 1990s, have lately been overshadowed by an even more dramatic collapse of unity on the union side" (Thelen and Kume 2006: 26).

With respect to financial markets, there are several groups with strong interests in pension policy as it affects private and occupational pensions. The Federation of the German Insurance Industry (*Gesamtverband der Deutschen Versicherungswirtschaft*, GDV) is the umbrella organization of private insurers of all branches, including private old-age pension providers. The Consortium for Occupational Pensions (*Arbeitsgemeinschaft für betriebliche Altersversorgung*, aba) represents 1,300 companies, unions and employers' associations, and speaks on their behalf in the field of supplementary pensions. Both GDV and aba usually take part in the discussions around the preparations of government bills, and they are sometimes invited to public hearings of *Bundestag* committees.

A last noteworthy feature of German social policy is the Social Council (*Sozialbeirat*). The Federal Cabinet nominates the 12 members of the Council for a period of four years (§156(2) SGB VI). These must include representatives of the scientific community, of labor and capital and of the Central Bank (*Bundesbank*). The Social Council comments on the yearly government report on the pension system (*Rentenversicherungsbericht*) and advises the relevant ministry and the cabinet on pension policy issues (§§155–156 SGB VI). The *Sozialbeirat* serves as a clearing position between labor, capital and the scientific community. Above all, though, it surveys the available data on pensions and provides the most sophisticated reform proposals to the specific ministries. Hence, the *Sozialbeirat* influences pension policies behind closed doors and at an early stage of the reform process. To date no systematic research on the impact of this complex actor has been conducted.

III PENSION SYSTEM

Historical overview

Together with the *Accident Insurance Act* of 1884 and the *Health Insurance Act* of 1883, the *Disability and Old Age Insurance Act* of 1889 (*Invaliditäts- und Altersversicherungsgesetz*) marked the beginning of a compulsory public social insurance system (Frerich and Frey 1993b: 95–101). The *Disability and Old Age Insurance Act* introduced mandatory insurance for blue-collar workers. Insured persons were entitled to benefits at the age of 70 after a minimum of 30 years of contributions, and they were also entitled to invalidity benefits. Contribution rates depended on wage groups—the average across these groups was 1.7 percent (Frerich and Frey 1993b: 100–1).

At the beginning of the twentieth century, the government established a separate insurance scheme for white-collar workers in order to avoid the federal grant that was already in force for the blue-collar system (*Versicherungsgesetz für Angestellte* of December 20, 1911). The act foresaw contribution-financed benefits at the age of 65, after 10 years of contribution for men and 6 years for women, and disability benefits (Frerich and Frey 1993b: 115). After World War II, the administrative separation of blue- and white-collar employees was re-established. As the calculation of pension benefits did not take into account inflation or wage increases, the level of benefits in the early 1950s was inadequate. Deliberations on a comprehensive pension reform throughout the 1950s resulted in the pension reform of 1957 (see Frerich and Frey 1993a: 43–6). In 1956, both the CDU/CSU/DP/FVP government coalition and the SPD opposition submitted pension reform bills that envisioned gross wage indexation—a reform rejected both by the FDP and the employers' associations. Despite some intra-party resistance within the CDU/CSU, Chancellor Konrad Adenauer pushed this "dynamic pension" (*dynamische Rente*) through the *Bundestag* on January 21, 1957 (BGBl. I 45/1957b; BGBl. I 88/1957a). The short-term effect of the reform was an average 65 percent increase in pensions (Frerich and Frey 1993a: 48).

After their accession to power in 1969, the new SPD/FDP coalition submitted a bill for a major pension reform in the early 1970s. The core element of the bill was the extension of voluntary insurance coverage to the self-employed (Ney 2001: 15). The circumstances leading to the passage of the Pension Reform Act of 1972 in Parliament were most unusual. Voting took place between the request for a vote of confidence and the actual vote of confidence.[5] Within these two days the CDU/CSU opposition gained a majority and replaced the pension reform bill with their own plan. Nevertheless, the SPD/FDP coalition and the CDU/CSU opposition agreed on the proposal and passed the Pension Reform Act "in consensus" on October 16, 1972 (Hockerts 1992).

In the field of occupational pensions, the 1974 *Occupational Old-Age Protection Act*[6] is the most important piece of legislation, setting the context for second-pillar pensions. The act regulated the vesting of pension entitlements for employees who switched employers, and safeguarded pension benefits against the risk of inflation and employer insolvency (Schmähl and Böhm 1996: 8). It is of note that as a kind of a "functional conversion" (Thelen 2000), the existing early retirement schemes since the 1970s were used by labor and capital more and more as "normal exit-pathways" for employees. Employers were able to retire less productive workers, shifting labor market problems to the pension system.

Description of the current pension system

Coverage

The German pension system is divided into the compulsory statutory pension insurance for blue- and white-collar employees (*Arbeiter- und Angestelltenversicherung*), the pension scheme for the agricultural sector (*Altershilfe für Landwirte*), coverage of civil servants and judges through the *Beamtenversorgung* (§5 SGB VI) and several professional schemes. Statutory pension insurance (*Gesetzliche Rentenversicherung*, GRV) in Germany is compulsory for all private sector employees (§1 SGB VI) and is based on the wage-based contribution principle. GRV covers approximately 82 percent of the employed population (Council of the European Union 2003: 118).

Germany stands out for not having compulsory insurance for all types of self-employed. The self-employed may join the state pension system voluntarily (Reinhard 2001: 22, 41).[7] Liberal professions who are members of occupational chambers are compulsorily covered through occupational provision institutes (*berufsständische Versorgungswerke*). As occupational and private pensions are not mandatory, the importance of the second- and third-pension pillars is moderate. Although 54 percent of private sector employees were covered by an occupational old-age pension in 2003, occupational and private pensions are not major sources of old-age income (BfA 2003: 16; Ruppert 2000: 24).

Administration

Administrative responsibility for the statutory pension system (GRV) is divided into three institutional branches: first, the 23 regional insurance funds (*Landesversicherungsanstalten*, LVA) plus the federal railway insurance fund (*Bundesbahnversicherungsanstalt*) and the seamen insurance fund (*Seekasse*) administer all blue-collar workers and compulsory insured self-employed such as craftsmen. Second, the Federal Insurance Fund for Salaried Employees (*Bundesversicherungsanstalt für Angestellte*, BfA) administer the insurance records and pension payments for white-collar employees, and the Federal Insurance Fund for Miners (*Knappschaftliche Rentenversicherung*) is responsible for pension insurance for miners (§125 SGB VI).

These pension insurance carriers were united in the Federation of German Pension Insurance Institutes (*Verband Deutscher Rentenversicherungsträger*, VDR). The VDR was an institution of self-administration with a board of directors composed of an equal number of employers' and labor representatives. One of the main tasks of the VDR was consultation and the provision of expert reports during the legislative process (§146 SGB VI). Hence, in Germany, data collection on pension politics is more or less in the hands of the VDR, and the government relies to a great extent on this data base (Nullmeier and Rüb 1993). Organizational reforms passed in late 2004[8] going into effect on October 1, 2005 fused the VDR and BfA into a new *Deutsche Rentenversicherung Bund*. The number of LVAs is reduced through regional fusions.

Employers have five different options for offering occupational pensions. They may either promise and administer the occupational pensions themselves (*Direktzusage*), or make use of insurance institutions (*Unterstützungskasse, Pensionskasse* or *Pensionsfond*) or they may take out a direct insurance with an insurance company in favor of their employee (*Direktversicherung*) (BfA 2003). Private pension insurance companies are subject to monitoring by the Federal Institute for Financial Services Supervision (*Bundesanstalt für Finanzdienstleistungsaufsicht*, BAFin) under supervision of the finance ministry.

Financing

The pension system is financed on the PAYG principle (§153 SGB VI). The German pension system has a contingency reserve (*Nachhaltigkeitsrücklage*) of between a minimum of 0.2 and a maximum of 1.7 times monthly expenditure (§158 SGB VI). Employees pay contributions as a fixed share of their gross income (19.5% in 2005) up to a contribution limit of €5,200 (in the West) and €4,400 (in the East) per month. The government, or more precisely, the Ministry of Labor and Social Affairs with approval of the *Bundesrat*, sets the contribution rate by decree every year (§160 SGB VI). Contribution payments are shared equally between the employee and the employer. The employer pays the entire contribution for employees still in apprenticeship and employees who earn less than €400 per month. Low-income earners with monthly wages between €400 and €800 pay reduced but progressively increasing contributions (VDR 2004: 16).

674 GERMANY

First pillar	Second pillar	Third pillar
Third tier: none	Voluntary occupational pension	Voluntary private pension
First and second tier combined: earnings-related pension	Subsidized voluntary occupational pension: state-regulated; reduced tax rate; compulsion for employer to offer at least one type of occupational pension (*Entgeltumwandlung*)	Subsidized private pension: *riester-rente*
GRV / Self-employed — Miners (*knappschaftliche Vers.*); White-collar (BfA); Blue-collar and self-employed craftsmen (23LVAs); Other self-employed; Liberal proffessions (*Berufsständische Versorgungswerke*); Farmers; Civil service	Mandatory occupational pension: none	Mandatory private pension: none
Social assistance (*bedarfsorientierte Grundsicherung*)		

Fig. 14.2 Pension system in Germany

The German pension system is partly tax-financed, as the federal government subsidizes pension insurance with a grant (*Bundeszuschuss*). Since April 1, 1998 there is a supplementary federal subsidy to cover non-contribution benefits. This lump-sum payment is financed by having increased VAT by one percentage point and, since 2000, by the revenues from an "ecology" tax on energy (§213 SGB VI). To guarantee a revenue/expense balance in the budgets of the pension carriers, the contribution rate must be increased if expenses grow. However, the pensions schemes receive a short-term solvency assurance (*Liquiditätssicherung*) from the government, which has to be paid back without interest the following year (§214 SGB VI).

Civil servants' pensions are tax-financed. The pension schemes of liberal professions are mainly capital-funded and partially PAYG with revenues from members' contributions only (BfA 2001: 25–6).

Occupational and private pensions are generally capital-funded, with different forms of capital investment. In order to protect employees' occupational pension entitlements in case of insolvency of their employers, all occupational pension schemes are members of the Pension Safeguarding Association (*Pensions-Sicherungs-Verein*, PSVaG). If an employer is insolvent the PSVaG pays current pension benefits and guarantees vested entitlements (BfA 2003: 14).

Benefits

Pensions are paid if the insured person reaches the standard retirement age of 65, meets the requirements for long service pensions (*langjährige Versicherte*), is incapacitated for work (disability), or dies leaving his/her spouse eligible for a survivor's pension (§§ 33–46 SGB VI).

The minimum qualifying period (*Wartezeit*) to be eligible for pension benefits for old age, disability and death of a spouse is five years (§50 SGB VI). Fifteen years are necessary to qualify for old-age pensions for the unemployed, for partial retirement and for women over 60. Periods that are counted as qualifying periods include periods of compulsory and voluntary contributions, contribution-free periods (*Anrechnungszeiten*, i.e. periods of illness, unemployment or maternity leave), child-rearing periods of three years (*Kindererziehungszeiten*), and other credited periods (*Berücksichtigungszeiten*, i.e. up to ten years of credit for child-rearing or home-nursing care).

The value of pension benefits depends mainly on the contributions paid throughout the working career, and therefore on the level of income from employment. Contributions paid are converted into personal earnings points (*Entgeltpunkte*): contributions in line with the average income of people who are insured earn one *Entgeltpunkt* per year (§63 II SGB VI). *Entgeltpunkte* can also be earned in child-rearing periods, military service or, until 2004, higher education. The total of *Entgeltpunkte* is multiplied by a pension type factor (*Rentenartfaktor*; i.e. 1 for old-age pension and 0.6 for widow/widower's pension) by the pension accrual factor (*Zugangsfaktor* i.e. 1 reduced by 0.003 per month prior to standard retirement age or increased by 0.005 per month of deferred retirement beyond 65 years) and by the current pension value (*Rentenwert*)[9] at the time of retirement.

Pensions are adjusted yearly by government decree: so far, the new pension value (*Rentenwert*) has been calculated by multiplying the current pension value with the changes in the average gross wage (of the real contribution base since 2005) between the previous year and the year before that, and with the changes in pension contribution rates including the private pension contribution rate of 4 percent in 2009.[10] Since January 2005, the indexation formula further includes a demographic factor known as the *Nachhaltigkeitsfaktor* that reflects the ratio of pensioners relative to contributors. This ratio is weighted by a factor α (= 0.25 in 2005) (for the exact formula and explanation see Hain et al. 2004: 340). The minor widows' or widowers' pension equals 25 percent of the full pension payment. Survivors are eligible to the major widow/widowers' pension that amounts to 60 percent (55% after 2026) of full pension payment if the widow/widower is rearing a child under 18, is older than 45 years, or has reduced earning capacity.

The income limit for pensioners drawing an old-age pension is €340 (since April 1, 2003). Only the profit share of pension benefits used to be taxable. Between 2005 and 2040, pension benefits will become fully liable to taxation but contributions will become tax-free. Pensioners are also included in the mandatory health and, since April 2004, long-term care insurance in Germany.

With respect to benefits from the second- and third-pension pillars, the distribution of income shows that occupational pensions have been the least important pillar in Germany (Bruno-Latocha and Tippelmann 2003: 13): the main share of old-age income, that is, 78 percent, stems from state pensions. Only 7 percent of old-age income comes from occupational pensions and 10 percent from private pensions, mainly life insurance schemes (Council of the European Union 2003: 119). Occupational pensions may be defined-benefit or defined-contribution with minimum benefits, that is the employer guarantees to repay at least the paid-in contributions (BfA 2003: 26).

IV POLITICS OF PENSION REFORM SINCE 1980

Overview

Since the 1980s, there have been a number of attempts made to reform the pension system in Germany. Apart from the major reform projects we shall discuss in detail (see Table 14.3), pension politics in the 1980s was dominated by consolidation measures, by the reform of the survivors' pensions and by the expansion of early retirement. Immediately after the change in government in 1982, the CDU/CSU and FDP coalition consolidated social insurance schemes with two legislative "emergency-brakes" (Zohlnhöfer 2001), that is, the *Haushaltsbegleitgesetz 1983* and the *Haushaltsbegleitgesetz 1984*. These reforms aimed at consolidating social security and especially the pension schemes by deferring pension adjustments, by increasing the contribution rate and through other technical measures.

The reform of survivors' pensions was induced by the *Witwenrentenurteil* of the Constitutional Court in 1975.[11] After lengthy negotiations within the coalition, and against the opposition of the SPD, the government agreed upon the *Anrechnungsmodell mit Freibetrag*. This reform was intended to be cost neutral. For the first time in German history, survivors' pensions were made dependent on the income of the

Table 14.3 Overview of proposed and enacted pension reforms in Germany

Year	Name of Reform	Reform Process (Chronology)	Reform Measures
1989	Blüm I Reform: Pension Reform Act 1992	• February 1989 four-party agreement (CDU/CSU, FDP and SPD) • March 7, 1989 cross-party bill submitted to Bundestag • November 9, 1989 passage in Bundestag • December 1, passage in Bundesrat	• change from gross- to net-wage indexation; • increase in retirement age for women, unemployed, disabled; • introduction of deductions for early retirement; • increase in child rearing period from one to three years
1997	Blüm II Reform: Pension Reform Act 1999	• May 1996 Blüm Commission • June 26, 1997 submission to Parliament • October 7, 1997 submission of separate finance bill • October 10, 1997 passage of RRG 1999 in BT • October 31, 1997 passage of finance bill in BT • November 7 and 28, 1997 initiation of Mediation Committee • November 28, 1997 Bundesrat objection • December 11, 1997 Bundestag overrules BR-objection of RRG 1999	• introduction of demographic factor in the pension indexation formula; • increase of child credits from 75% to 100% of average wage; • reduction in disability benefits of 0.3% per month of early retirement, limited to total of 10% of benefits; • increase in retirement age for disability pensions from 60 to 63; • increase in federal subsidy to pension system through 1 percentage point increase of VAT
2001	Riester Reform: AVmG and AVmEG	• December 19, 1997 passage of finance bill in Bundesrat • June 1999 Riester proposal • September 2000 ministerial draft (major changes compared to proposal of June 1999) • November 14, 2000 separation of private pension act (AVmG) from other reform measures (AVmEG) • January 26, 2001 passage of AVmEG in Bundestag • February 16, 2001 passage of AVmEG in Bundesrat • March 2001 Mediation Committee on AVmG • May 11, 2001 passage of AVmG in Bundestag • May 11, 2001 passage of AVmG in Bundesrat	• introduction of voluntary, subsidized private pensions; • reduction of replacement rate of statutory pension system benefits from 70% to 64%; • fixation of upper contribution rate limit (20% up to 2020); • introduction of means-tested social assistance minimum pension; • reduction of survivor's pension from 60% to 55% of deceased's benefits

(Continued)

Table 14.3 (Continued)

Year	Name of Reform	Reform Process (Chronology)	Reform Measures
2004	Rürup Reform RV-Nachhaltigkeitsgesetz	• November 2002 establishment of Rürup Commission • August 28, 2003 Rürup Commission report • September 30, 2003 Herzog Commission report • March 11, 2004 passage in Bundestag • April 2, 2004 objection in Bundesrat and call of Mediation Committee • June 16, 2004 Bundestag overrules of Bundesrat's objection	• introduction of Nachhaltigkeitsfaktor with loss limitation to 46% of one's former average wage; • change of assessment base for pension indexation to real contributory base; • suspension of pension adjustment for 2004; • abolition of credit points for periods of higher education; • increase in retirement age for unemployed and partial pension from 60 to 63; • change in lower limit of contingency reserve from 0.5 to 0.2 times monthly expenditure (Nachhaltigkeitsrücklage); • increase in retirement age from 65 to 67 → failed!
2004	Alterseinkünftegesetz	• March 6, 2002 BVerfG verdict on taxation • May 28, 2004 passage in Bundestag • June 11, 2004 passage in Bundesrat	• introduction of taxation of pension benefits; • introduction of gender-neutral benefits in Riester-Rente (Unisextarife); • streamlining of criteria for certification of Riester-Rente products

widow/widower (Nullmeier and Rüb 1993). The government simultaneously introduced pension credits for child-rearing in the calculation of pension benefits, which may be interpreted as a concession the government had to make to internal opposition in the CDU/CSU, and especially to appease the labor wing as well as women's organizations in the party.

The government decided to expand the early retirement schemes as early as 1984. In order to dampen the pressure on the labor market—and to counteract the ambitions of *IG Metall* to reduce the working week to 35 hours—the government eased the conditions for the retirement of those above the age of 58. This reform, and other reforms in labor market policies, expressed the political will to cushion labor market fluctuations by enabling older workers to withdraw from the labor market early—a policy decision that had dramatic consequences after German unification and put tremendous pressure on social security budgets.

The Growth and Employment Promotion Act—which covered all social policy schemes—adopted in 1996, was crucial for pension politics for two reasons. First, when the negotiations on this reform failed, the strategy of a concerted reform, institutionalized in the first *Alliance for Jobs*, broke down. The subsequent reform was implemented unilaterally, which opened the way for an intensification of party competition and was the starting signal for the SPD to veto many reform measures of the government with its majority in the *Bundesrat*. Second, the reform accelerated the increase of the retirement age. Hence, in this respect the reform meant a significant programatic shift of the incumbent parties and especially the CDU/CSU. This reform marked the breakdown of consensus in pension politics, it became even more obvious in the process of the pension reform of 1997 (See pp. 682–6).

Pension politics under the Red–Green government, the so-called *Riester-Rente*, brought about a "paradigm-shift" in German pension policy by introducing a (non-mandatory) private insurance pillar and readjusting the overall goals of pension policies (Schmähl 2003; Hinrichs 2004). Finally we discuss the latest reform undertaken in 2004, which marked retrenchment in Red–Green pension policies.

Blüm I reform 1989: Pension Reform Act 1992

Pre-parliamentary stage

There were several reasons why a structural pension reform was necessary in the early 1980s. First, the great number of early retirements, the reduction in working hours and mounting unemployment had fuelled pension expenditure in comparison to contribution receipts (VDR 2000: 220–1). The contingency reserve was used up and the statutory pension system had to take government loans to cover pension expenditure in 1985. The problems were aggravated by low economic growth and moderate wage increases. Thus, all major parties agreed on the necessity of consolidating the pension system and, in reaction to projections that estimated the overall contribution rate would rise to 36.4 percent in 2040 (Frerich and Frey 1993a: 249), policy-makers attempted to stabilize pension contribution rates.

The reform process started with two expert Commissions in the early 1980s: the *Transfer-Enquête-Kommission* and the *Sachverständigenkommission "Alterssicherungssystem."* Both Commissions suggested net wage indexation and the harmonization of the public and private sectors. The Ministry for Labor and Social Affairs in the SPD/FDP government had drafted a proposal in 1982 for a *Pension Reform Act of 1984*, but it was abandoned because of the costs of the new provisions in survivors' pensions. The 1984 *Pension Reform Bill* provided for an extension of minimum income pension after 1972, a re-valuation of non-contribution periods (in particular education periods were to be shortened), the tightening of eligibility criteria for disability pensions and the introduction of the participation model in the survivors' pensions scheme (Nullmeier and Rüb 1993: 128–31). Although the proposed *Pension Reform Bill* of 1984 never left the Ministry, the SPD confirmed the core features of the proposal a couple of years later. During the parliamentary debate on survivors' pensions reform the SPD submitted a proposal for a *Pension Reform Bill* of 1985 to the *Bundestag* (BT-Drs. 10/2608; Nullmeier and Rüb 1993: 139).

In contrast to the two precise and comprehensive proposals of the SPD, the government did not come up with an encompassing reform proposal. However, outside the ministerial arena the Christian-Democratic camp was quite active in mapping new ideas for a revised pension system. The CDU party leader in Nordrhein-Westfalen, Kurt Biedenkopf, advocated a three-pillar old-age pension with a basic pension for all citizens, supplementary compulsory insurance and voluntary private pensions (Biedenkopf 1985: 404–9). The association representing small- and medium-sized firms in the CDU/CSU (*Mittelstandsvereinigung*) rejected both the minimum pension as well as the machine tax, but suggested reducing pension benefits from a replacement rate of 70 percent to a level of 63–68 percent through incrementally reduced pension indexation and concurrent reinforcement of private old-age insurance to compensate for the lower replacement rate in the statutory scheme (Schwarz-Schilling 1988: 25–7). In contrast, another CDU/CSU subgroup—the party wing connected to the Christian churches—advanced the concept of linking the contribution level to the number of children (Frerich and Frey 1993a: 251).

The VDR published guidelines in June 1987, which suggested maintaining all basic principles of the pension system and its organization (Frerich and Frey 1993a: 252). Only a modified minimum income pension, available only to insured persons with at least 35 to 40 years of insurance, was considered acceptable. Furthermore the VDR Commission suggested indexing pensions to net wages and to harmonize the taxation of employees' and civil servants' pensions. The federal grant was to be increased to 20 percent of pension expenditure. Revaluations of non-contribution periods were to be harmonized. On the issue of retirement age, the Commission decided that the labor market did not allow for changes before the year 2000 (Doetsch 1987: 512–18).

The Parliamentary stage

Following the 1987 national elections, in which both *Volksparteien* (the CDU and the CSU) lost votes and the FDP and the Green Party increased their shares of seats, Chancellor Helmut Kohl (CDU) announced in his investiture speech that he would set up a coalition working group to work out the main features of a new pension law (Pabst 1999: 7; Nullmeier and Rüb 1993: 187–8). One point of conflict within the Kohl government was the increase of the federal grant to the pension system. Social Minister Norbert Blüm (CDU), as well as the FDP, demanded the coverage of non-contributory benefits through the general budget (BT-PlPr 11/5: 207C-D). But the Minister of Finance, Gerhard Stoltenberg (CDU), was most interested in the tax reform under way and was not willing to spare extra money for the pension system (Spiegel 03.02.1986).

The coalition working group's final session in August 1988, at which Stoltenberg was not present, overturned an earlier compromise between Blüm and Stoltenberg to increase the federal grant by DM 300 million, and demanded DM 2.3 billion (Nullmeier and Rüb 1993: 193).

The ministerial draft was presented to the public on November 14, 1988. The proposal adopted in large part the measures suggested by the VDR Commission in June 1987. Immediately thereafter, the government initiated consensus meetings with the opposition, which ran between November 1988 and February 1989. The coalition was especially interested in a broad party consensus in pension policy after the Berlin state election showed losses for the Christian-Democratic and the Liberal parties. At an early point of the reform process, the SPD opposition announced its willingness to cooperate. When government and opposition negotiated on the timetable for the pension reform process, they agreed to keep the pension reform out of the 1990 election campaign (Pabst 1999: 14; Ney 2001: 24).

The main point of dispute—especially between SPD and FDP—was the retirement age for women, the long-term insured and the unemployed. At first, the SPD opposition rejected any increase in the retirement age. Blüm's offer formally acquiesced to the SPD demands without departing too much from the government's goals. As the SPD wanted to make the rise in retirement age dependent on the labor market situation, Blüm extended the transition period to 2001 instead of 1995 (*Der Spiegel* 21.11.1988).

Another issue of conflict was the size of the federal grant. Previously, the federal budget had refunded the costs of the credits for child-rearing to the pension insurance carriers. From 1992 on, this was to be changed to a lump-sum allowance of DM 4.8 billion which should be indexed dynamically (Heine 1989: 151). Consequently, the federal grant would equal 20 percent of expenditure and it would thus provide the illusion of complying with SPD claims (Nullmeier and Rüb 1993: 210). Moreover, the SPD considered entitlements of 75 percent of the final gross wage to be too low for the unemployed. The coalition was willing to increase the benefits up to 85 percent of the gross wage. Although Blüm rejected the Social-Democratic idea of a minimum pension, he extended the regulations for a quasi-minimum pension.

Previously, if employees had paid contributions for 25 years but had a low income, their pension entitlements had been increased as if they had earned 75 percent of average wages all along. This regulation was only an option for incomes before 1972. Blüm then proposed to expand it to cover incomes up until 1991, but at the same time the employee had to have 35 years of contributions (Heine 1989: 154–5). Finally, the Coalition was ready to pass some changes in the civil servants' old-age scheme (*Der Spiegel* 21.11.1988).

The negotiating parties—CDU/CSU, SPD and FDP—agreed on a proposal in early February 1989 which was presented to the *Bundestag* on March 7, 1989 as a CDU/CSU, SPD and FDP Bill (BT-Drs. 11/4124). As the SPD declared it would make its vote on the pension reform act dependent on the partial harmonization of the public and private sector pension systems, the CDU/CSU, SPD and FDP parties decided to link the pension reform act to a revision of the civil servants' pension scheme. The work in the parliamentary committee of the *Bundestag* was more or less symbolic, as consensus between the three main parties had been reached at the pre-parliamentary stage (Frerich and Frey 1993a: 254, 258).

The *Pension Reform Act of 1992* passed the *Bundestag* with cross-party agreement on November 9, 1989, on the very day that the GDR-government opened the Berlin Wall (BT-PlPr 11/174: 13182D–13188A). The *Bundesrat* agreed unanimously on the act on December 1, 1989 (BR-PlPr 607/1989: 522A).

The *Pension Reform Act of 1992* reveals broad political consensus on the eve of German unification. Although it introduced major changes, the reform nevertheless maintained the key characteristics of the German social insurance paradigm. In other words, the reform enabled huge savings without changing the overall rules of the system. The political consensus was not institutionally induced, as the SPD was not in a situation to block legislation in the *Bundesrat* (as Table 14.2 indicates). As the SPD tried to enhance the party profile in opposition, the Federal Government reacted to losses of votes in *Länder* elections and tried to prevent the pensions issue from playing a role in the federal election campaign of 1990. Hence, the political consensus was not caused by institutional obstacles, but was induced by party strategies that referred to the imperatives of party competition.

Blüm II reform 1997: Pension Reform Act 1999

Pre-parliamentary stage

German unification and the "institutional transfer" (Lehmbruch 1991) from West to East, changed German politics in several ways. First, the problem pressure increased as a consequence of the economic transformation strategy in the East. Unemployment soared and, partly because of comparatively long working careers of Eastern women, pension spending increased while at the same time the inflow of contributions was declining. Second, in the East, the major party in government, the CDU/CSU, could strengthen her power position. Despite electoral decline in the West, and internal rebellions against the party leader and Chancellor, the electoral stronghold in

East Germany at least strengthened the party. Thirdly, with the PDS, a new party entered party competition, not only articulating the interests of the East German population, but emphasizing foremost the defense of the welfare status quo. Because of the party's Communist history, no major party of the West dared to cooperate with this party at that time (despite some attempts of the SPD in the East, which were in turn heavily criticized in the public). Hence, the third major party in the East was defined as an anti-system party and relegated to the role of critic of existing policies, not as decision-maker.

The problems of unification became apparent at least as early as 1993, as the employment crisis in the East showed no sign of reversal, and the labor relations between trade unions and employers' associations revealed the first signs of tension. As regards pension policies, the goal of stabilizing the pension budget became imperative. As the FPD increased its share of votes in different elections, the policy stance of the coalition government became more liberal. One telling point is that the first initiative to install an *Alliance for Jobs* in 1995/1996, which was to function as a tripartite body to discuss and frame reform packages, collapsed because the FDP pushed through some programatic reforms that were not negotiable for trade unions—in particular, sick pay reductions. Hence, the resulting reform package, the *Growth and Employment Promotion Act* of 1996, realized cutbacks in all social policy fields and provoked vehement protests from the opposition. Nevertheless, for pension policy more reform steps and cutbacks were deemed necessary. One major political goal was still to secure global competitiveness and to promote the creation of new employment by reducing social insurance contributions.

The Blüm Commission—a group of experts, scientists and politicians—was designated to elaborate on proposals about how to maintain the statutory pension system in the context of demographic change in May 1996. The Commission recommended in its January 1997 report that compulsory social insurance coverage should be extended to include marginal employment and "quasi" self-employment. A demographic factor was to be introduced into the pension indexation formula. The demographic factor multiplied by the current pension value (*Rentenwert*) would slow down pension adjustment and, consequently, would reduce the replacement rate from 70 percent to 64 percent for a standard pensioner by 2030 (Richter 1999: 62).

The Commission further suggested adding child credits to pension entitlements if the child rearing periods coincidence with contributions/entitlements through employment and child credits were to be assessed with 100 percent instead of 75 percent of average wage (BT-Drs. 13/8671: 3).[12] In disability pensions, the retirement age was envisioned to be increased from 60 to 65, and deductions of 0.3 percent per month with an upper limit of 18 percent reduced pension benefits if disability pension was drawn before the set age limit. Occupational disability was to be abolished completely and disability pensions were to be granted according to health only and not according to the labor market situation.

The FDP considered the CDU/CSU proposal to be too moderate and established its own commission. The FDP Commission strongly objected to extending compulsory insurance coverage to the marginally-employed, and demanded an even more rapid reduction in the replacement rate in order to keep contribution rates below 20 percent. The FDP rejected the demographic factor as an instrument to reduce the replacement rate because this instrument was too precarious to forecast future pension spending (*SZ* 07.03.1997).

An SPD Commission presented a third alternative proposal on May 5, 1997 (BT-Drs. 13/8032). As with the CDU, the SPD demanded the extension of coverage to marginal employment, self-employment and quasi-self-employment. The Social-Democratic proposal guaranteed full disability pensions for all those unable to work more than four hours a day for health reasons.

Although Social Minister Blüm offered to negotiate with the SPD opposition, SPD Party Chairman, Oscar Lafontaine, refused the invitation for negotiations. SPD-led states had had a relative majority in the *Bundesrat* since May 1991, and the strategy of the party leadership was—since the breakdown of the first *Alliance for Jobs*—to veto reform measures induced by the government instead of changing them (*SZ* 13.05.1997). The CDU/CSU/FDP bill was formulated on May 28, 1997. The Cabinet approved the bill, which was mainly the unchanged Blüm-commission proposal, on June 18, 1997 (Richter 1999: 64).

The parliamentary stage

After the first reading in the *Bundestag* on June 24, 1997, the Labor and Social Affairs Committee conducted public hearings. The Committee Report of October 1, 1997 included the following changes: (a) the increase in retirement age for reduced-earning-capacity pensions was made less drastic (increase from 60 to 63 instead of 60 to 65); and (b) the pension benefit reductions for early claiming of these benefits were limited to 10.8 percent instead of 18 percent (BT-Drs. 13/8671: 20, 79, 114–15).

After it had become clear during the Committee negotiations that a consensus with the opposition was out of range, the government separated the financial part of the reform, which required the SPD-led *Bundesrat*'s agreement, from the rest of the *Pension Reform Act 1999*. The *Bundestag* plenum approved the non-mandatory consent part—the *Pension Reform Act 1999*—on October 10, 1997 with the reservation that the law to finance the changes, that is, the additional federal grant, be enacted as well. The *Bundestag* overruled the *Bundesrat*'s objection on December 11, 1997 (BT-PlPr 13/210: 19140–19143).[13]

In the meantime, the two parliamentary chambers were preoccupied with the mandatory part of the law, for which the Finance Committee was in charge. The party negotiations were deadlocked. The government tried urgently to avoid an increase in the contribution rate to 21 percent in 1998. But in order to stabilize the contribution rate, it had to increase the federal subsidy to the pension insurance system and the coalition needed money to do so. The options were an increase in VAT, a rise in petrol tax, or the introduction of compulsory insurance for marginal employment. The CDU, as leading party in the Cabinet, could have boosted the petrol tax but the coalition partners—CSU and FDP—rejected this option. Consequently, the alternative was to increase the VAT. Although employers may pass VAT costs on to consumers, the FDP opposed an increase unless it went into force simultaneously with the structural pension reform (*StZ* 10.11.1997). Moreover, the VAT increase required the consent of the SPD-led *Bundesrat*.

In sum, the FDP demanded the introduction of the demographic factor in January 1998, while the CSU insisted on delaying until January 1999 the date of effect of the new indexation formula. The forecast of low increases in pensions, combined with the reduced adjustment formula, was not an attractive prospect for the CSU, since it had to compete in Bavarian state elections in 1998. Consequently, the CSU's idea was to delay both the increase in VAT and the structural reform until 1999 (*StZ* 11.11.1997).

The CDU/CSU parliamentary group offered a compromise to the FDP: pension adjustment would be reduced and the improvement in child-rearing periods would be suspended for one more year. In return, the FDP would agree to the expansion of compulsory insurance for DM 610/520-jobs—the third option for increasing the pension insurance carriers' revenues. But the FDP blocked any change that would extend the compulsory social insurance to marginal employment. As in the Social-Liberal coalition in 1981, the FDP blocked any reforms in this issue area (*StZ* 04.11.1997).

The SPD—in particular the SPD social policy expert Rudolf Dreßler—clung to the inclusion of marginal employment in the pension system as a prerequisite for agreement to the VAT increase (*SZ* 08.11.1997)—if a petrol tax increase was impossible in the first place. But when Dreßler was abroad for one week in November 1997, SPD State Prime Minister of Lower-Saxony, and later Chancellor Gerhard Schröder, offered a compromise to the government coalition: they suggested that the SPD-led states would agree on the VAT increase, but with the proviso that it would take effect in April 1998 instead of January 1999 (*SZ* 11.11.1997).

In the end, the CDU/CSU/FDP Bill (BT-Drs. 13/8704) issued on October 7, 1997 provided for an increase of one percentage point in VAT, that is from 15 percent to 16 percent. This extra revenue would accrue entirely to the federal budget[14] and would be used to subsidize the statutory pension system. The Finance Committee adopted the coalition proposal. The voting results were quite interesting and illustrate the clash of interests within the coalition: CDU/CSU members agreed on the bill against the votes of SPD, the PDS abstained and representatives of the Green Party and of the FDP were absent (BT-Drs. 13/8869: 4). The Financial Bill passed the *Bundestag* plenum on October 31, 1997[15] and was transferred to the *Bundesrat* for approval.

The *Bundesrat* called in the Mediation Committee on November 28, 1997 (BR-PlPr 719/1997: 548C), which affirmed the financing of the extra federal grant through an increase in VAT from 15 percent to 16 percent and, additionally, lowering the income limit for marginal employment not subject to compulsory insurance to DM 200 (BT-Drs. 13/9419). The *Bundestag* did not agree on Part Two of the Mediation Committee proposal—that is, on the inclusion of marginal employment—but accepted Part One.[16] Eventually, the *Bundesrat* accepted the Finance Bill on December 19, 1997 (BGBl. I 1997: Nr. 86).

All in all, the pension reform of 1997 reveals a significant departure from traditional German pension policy-making. First, the consensus between both *Volksparteien* abruptly eroded and opened up the way for intense confrontation and policy stalemate (Hinrichs 1998) that was circumvented only by splitting the reform package and making programatic concessions to the opposition. Second, the introduction of the demographic factor (and the induced (de facto) reduction of the replacement rate in the years to come) may also be seen as a programatic shift in pension policies. One traditional goal of pension policies in Germany—the goal that pension benefits should assure the living standard of the pensioners—was thus (implicitly) abandoned. Third, the political process of the 1997 pension reform was without doubt influenced by institutional obstacles and negotiation imperatives built into the German polity. The veto power of the SPD, which was made possible by and only by the party's strength in the *Bundesrat,* was decisive. However, in contrast to previous cross-party compromises, such as the so-called *Lahnstein* compromise in health politics in 1992 when the CDU/CSU cooperated with the SPD opposition (Lehmbruch 2000), the FDP now blocked such a compromise in pension politics. Indeed, the FDP could profile itself as pivotal actor in this reform process that efficiently blocked the inclusion of marginal employment and quasi-self-employment into pension insurance schemes. Hence, beyond institutional constraints, party competition and the negotiations in the federal government influenced the design of the 1997 pension reform.

The Riester Reform 2001

During the 1998 election campaign, the SPD successfully exploited the pension reform negotiated in 1997. The SPD announced a partial reversal of the Pension Reform Act 1999 as soon as possible if the party came to power. Although the CDU/CSU/FDP government coalition tried to keep the pensions off the agenda, the reform became an important election issue in 1998.

The SPD had led the opinion polls since the victory of Gerhard Schröder in the Lower-Saxony state elections and was the clear winner of the *Bundestag* elections on September 27, 1998. With 6 percent points ahead of CDU/CSU, the SPD exceeded all expectations and won 46 extra seats. A Red–Green coalition was able to build a majority government (Pulzer 1999: 241). As SPD-led *Länder* were in the majority in the *Bundesrat* (Table 14.2), the Red–Green coalition began its term in office under very favorable institutional conditions.

Nevertheless, the first two years of the SPD/Green government were characterized by preparatory legislation for a more substantial pension reform. One of their first actions in office was the passage of the Pension Correction Law (*Rentenkorrekturgesetz*) in December 1998, which suspended major parts of the 1997 reform and abolished the demographic factor. At the same time, a new regulation that the revenues from the eco-tax would flow to the pension system, was intended to stabilize the contribution rate at 19.3 percent (Ney 2001: 28). As an instrument to avoid the "flight from social insurance compulsion" (Reinhard 2001: 39), the government introduced compulsory social insurance coverage for marginal employment[17] and pseudo self-employment, that is, persons who work mainly for a single client (Ney 2001: 28; BGBl. I 14/1999: 388–95). The government's plan for the inclusion of atypical employment in social security was to substitute the previous flat-rate tax with a 12 percent contribution to pension insurance and 10 percent contribution to health insurance. The SPD and Bündnis 90/Die Grünen agreed in early 1999 that the employers' contributions for marginal employment would establish exclusively old-age pension rights, but not survivors' or disability pension rights. The acquired pension rights during minor employment would equal 60 percent of full contribution entitlements; but periods of minor employment would not count as contribution time. The proposal was adopted by a *Bundestag* majority[18] and the *Bundesrat* approved on March 19, 1999 (BR-PlPr 736/1999: 92C-D). The inclusion of marginal employment was—after the blocked legislation due to the FDP veto in 1997—an important change in the German social security system.

The pre-parliamentary stage

Intensive work on the pension reform 2001 started in February 1999. Social Minister, Walter Riester (SPD), nominated a team of seven experts for consultations. The introduction of private pensions was the most important and innovative component in the pension reform 2001. The set-up of a private old-age pension provision was to start in 2003, according to Riester's plans, presented in June 1999. A yearly increase of 0.5 percent of gross wage (up to the contribution ceiling) to a private pension fund would establish a permanent contribution of 2.5 percent by 2007. As the compulsory private pension would reduce net income, the relative pension benefits would shrink as a side effect. The contribution to private pensions was to be compulsory for all employees, but they would be free to choose the types of investment.

The CSU rejected the obligation to insure oneself privately. Instead, a CDU/CSU inner-party commission proposed a "Bavarian optional model" which would use tax deduction as an incentive for opting-out of the state PAYG system. Combined state and private pensions were to reach a certain level, namely, the higher the share in private provision the lower the contribution rate to the state pension scheme. In order to ensure that families were able to take part in the private pension model, the CSU suggested introducing a monthly child allowance (Berliner Bericht, February 2000: 46).

When Riester first presented his concept for the pension reform in summer 1999, the CDU/CSU, the union of white-collar employees, the Metal Workers' Union, employers' associations and several state governments objected to the proposal. The Social Ministry encountered protest and criticism not only from the opposition but even from within the coalition parties: the Greens as well as some SPD members expressed their opposition to obligatory private insurance (*SZ* 18.06.1999). The states with CDU-led governments in Hessen, Saxony, and Baden-Württemberg, but also the Social-Democratic-led Saarland, announced they would vote against the suspension of net wage adjustment in 2000 and 2001 in the *Bundesrat* (Bonner Bericht,

Aug. 1999: 208). In the context of state elections on September 5, 1999, the SPD state government of Saarland even started a campaign against the pension plans of the national government (*SZ* 06.07.1999). The unions perceived the reduction of state pension contribution in combination with the compulsory contribution rate to private pensions without employer's share as an unjust redistribution. The government quickly dropped the compulsory element in private pensions when the SPD and the Greens repudiated coercion (*SZ* 18.06.1999). In response, Riester scaled back his proposal by presenting a voluntary model for private pensions in the next round of pension talks.

The CDU/CSU, Greens and FDP considered a supplementary private pension contribution of 2.5 percent far too low to guarantee a decent old-age income. They suggested 4 percent (Berliner Bericht, June 2000: 158). The FDP also favored a model where 4 percent of gross wage could be voluntarily invested in private pensions and an extra 2 percent would be compulsory (Berliner Bericht, Oct. 2000: 264).

Riester also proposed a new tax-financed means-tested minimum pension. The controversy on minimum pensions that had already started during the election campaign in 1998 revived in March 1999. The SPD and Bündnis 90/Die Grünen had laid down a means-tested, tax-financed minimum pension in their coalition agreement (Berliner Bericht, Mar. 2000: 75). The Employers' Association rebuffed Riester's means-tested minimum pension and demanded the freezing of the contribution ceiling as well as the assessment of income for survivors' pensions in order to curb pension expenditure. The unions were in favor of the minimum pension but wanted to amend the stipulation that a minimum pension must not be dependent on family members. The means tests ought to take into account solely the spouse's income (Bonner Bericht, May 1999: 126–7).

When it became clear that a new pension law could not be passed before 2000, the Red–Green coalition had to come up with an interim solution to avoid a step back to the demographic factor in pension adjustment. Riester planned to increase pensions with inflation rate instead of with wage increase in 2000 and 2001. While Riester found allies in the Social Council (for example the influential policy advisor Winfried Schmähl), the VDR, the CDU/CSU and the FDP, the leader of the Employers' Association BDA and the coalition partner—the Greens—rejected the idea (*SZ* 16.02.1999). There was also considerable discord in the SPD itself. After a party meeting, the leader of the SPD parliamentary party—Peter Struck—pointed out that the SPD would maintain the net wage indexation (*SZ* 09.03.1999). However, Riester announced that there would be no adjustment of pensions for inflation in 2000 and 2001. This implied an expected reduction of the replacement rate from 70.1 percent to 66.3 percent by 2002 (Bonner Bericht, Aug. 1999: 206). In other words: this suspension of wage-indexation implied a much faster reduction in replacement rates than had any other previous reform proposals. Riester forecast a contribution rate of below 20 percent up to 2020, and of 22 percent after that (*SZ* 16.06.1999).

In August 1999, Riester completed his pension reform proposal by announcing new provisions for survivors' pensions. The proposal of summer 1999 left three models to choose from for couples who married after the reform. Furthermore,

Riester planned to upgrade pension entitlements for parents by 50 percent for children up to ten years (*SZ* 02.08.1999). Although the CDU/CSU was in favor of greater consideration being given to child-relevant pension rules, their concept was different to that of the coalition parties. The CDU/CSU supported the idea of linking benefits in the survivors' pension system to the number of children. A widow or widower received 60 percent of the beneficiary's pension if he/she had one child, 70 percent with more than two children and 50 percent with no children (*SZ* 14.04.2000).

Despite broad opposition, Riester prevailed on the issue of indexation. The *Bundesrat* majority agreed on the decree for pension adjustment to inflation of 0.6 percent against strong protests from the CDU/CSU. However, Bremen, Berlin and Brandenburg—states led by grand coalitions of SPD and CDU—did *not* abstain from the final vote, as it is common for those coalitions, but *supported* the governmental decree. In contrast, the SPD state government of Saarland fulfilled its promise and rejected the suspension of pension adjustment.[19] The suspension of the net wage indexation for two years was included in the *Haushaltssanierungsgesetz* in 1999 and fixed in the *Pension Adjustment Decree 2000* (*Rentenanpassungsverordnung 2000 – RAV 2000*).[20]

The Riester draft of May 2000 also contained the first criteria for types of investment to be eligible to federal allowances: the investment had to be paid out as a life-long pension and the minimum return had to equal the deposited value at least. The Minister of Finance, Hans Eichel (SPD), also accepted investment funds as a type of investment for private pensions. Yet, in the Green Party's opinion this did not go far enough. Bündnis 90/Die Grünen demanded the acceptance of shares, life insurances or purchase of real estate as types of investment that qualified for federal grants (Berliner Bericht, Dec. 2000: 317).

The CDU/CSU party leaders Angela Merkel and Edmund Stoiber tied further negotiations with the coalition to three demands. First, the coalition had to abandon the idea of a minimum pension. Second, pensions were to return to net wage adjustment. Third, the CDU/CSU demanded that the private pensions were to be subsidized with DM 30 per child to make the development of a third pillar more attractive, and to honor the societal task of child rearing (Berliner Bericht, Sept. 2000: 238).

At the beginning of the negotiations on subsidizing private pensions, SPD and Bündnis 90/Die Grünen intended to subsidize low-income earners (i.e. maximum yearly income of DM 60,000 maximum) with up to DM 250 a year (*SZ* 13.01.2000). In the May 2000 version of the draft, Walter Riester had already significantly extended the spectrum of potential beneficiaries of government subsidies. The federal grant would account for half of the contribution payments with an upper limit of DM 400 a year. The CDU criticized this allowance as still too low. The CDU/CSU counted on DM 500 a year, a monthly allowance per child of DM 30 and tax deductibility (Berliner Bericht, July 2000: 189).

Chancellor Gerhard Schröder took the opposition by surprise when he fulfilled these demands. Schröder's offer for subsidizing the private pensions even exceeded the claims. The coalition promised to make available DM 19 billions by 2008 and offered as a compromise allowances for low-income employees and tax deductibility for higher incomes. Starting in 2001, 0.5 percent of private pension contributions would be deductible; then the rate would rise by 0.5 percentage points a year up to 4 percent in 2008 (*SZ* 15.06.2000). Yet, the level of allowances changed even further. The grant that would subsidize private pensions amounted to DM 300 for singles and DM 600 for married persons. High-income earners may deduct the sum of DM 4,000 for singles or DM 8,000 for married persons from tax (Berliner Bericht, Nov. 2000: 296). The total sum provided by the government would reach about DM 21 billion in 2008 (*SZ* 12.05.2001).

The Schröder government also moved towards the CDU/CSU position concerning the survivor's pension. When Riester presented the survivors' pension draft again during the pension consensus talks, only two of the original three models remained: the partner's model and the alimony replacement model. For couples younger than 40 years, the survivors' pension benefit should be 50 percent of the insured. Later this was modified to 55 percent. The income limit when pensions were deducted was to be frozen in West Germany and index-linked in East Germany. Women without children and under the age of 45 years would get survivors' pension for two years only. A transition period would be 25 years (Berliner Bericht, Feb. 2001: 49). Interestingly, the CDU/CSU was divided now on whether to cooperate in pension policy or not. Bavaria's Prime Minister, Edmund Stoiber (CSU), still rejected any pension consensus while CDU-party leader, Angela Merkel, strived for compromise.

The accommodation to CDU/CSU demands did not help to find support among Labor representatives. Metal Union Chairmen, Zwickel, considered the reform proposal as unacceptable (Berliner Bericht, Aug. 2000: 208). Throughout the entire legislative and pre-legislative process, the unions demanded a further bipartite financing of the private pension contributions and higher replacement rates. The unions signaled to protest against the pension reform plans. But Schröder replied that he was not worried about the protests. Nevertheless, the trade unions eagerly tried to fuel intra-party opposition in the SPD, not without success.

The parliamentary stage

As mentioned above, the Red-Green coalition emerged victorious from the elections in 1998 and had a government majority of 345 seats (SPD 298, Greens 47) against an opposition of CDU/CSU (245), FDP (43) and PDS (36). But in contrast to the beginning of the legislative term, SPD-led states lost the clear *Bundesrat* majority after March 1999. From October 1999 to October 2001 SPD-led states occupied 26 seats, CDU/CSU-led states 32 seats and 11 votes belonged to grand coalition governments.

Riester presented his final draft for a pension reform in September 2000 and the Federal Cabinet approved the bill in November 2000. The legislative proposal was submitted to the *Bundestag* as a SPD/Green Party bill on November 14, 2000. The bill provided for the following change: to keep pension contribution rates below 22 percent until 2030 with a simultaneous replacement rate of 64 percent.[21]

The proposal introduced an adjustment factor (*Ausgleichsfaktor*) into the indexation formula. The adjustment factor would be first applied in 2011 with a reducing effect of 0.3 percent. The factor would rise by 0.3 percent per year until 2030 and would remain at 6 percent afterwards (BT-Drs. 14/4595: 1–3, 39).

The main innovation was the set-up of a capital-funded supplementary private pension pillar that would be subsidized through tax-deductible contributions as already discussed. The private pension was to compensate for the reduced replacement rate in state pensions. The occupational pensions were to be strengthened in granting employees the right to convert part of their wage into pension contribution payments to occupational pension schemes (*Entgeltumwandlung*). Furthermore, the government's draft promised a revaluation of contribution times of a parent during the first ten years of life of a child. Earning points (e.g. from part-time work) during the first ten years of child-rearing were to be increased by 50 percent of the individual income to a maximum of 100 percent of average wage if the insured person had at least 25 years of qualifying period. The same would apply to non-working parents with two or more children: they receive an equivalent to the highest possible revaluation of individual income, that is 0.3 earning points a year until the child turns ten.

When the bills were examined by the parliamentary Committee of Labor and Social Affairs, the Committee eliminated the controversial adjustment factor and replaced it with the VDR proposal to reduce gross-wage increase by changes in pension contribution rates (BT-Drs. 14/5146 2001: 3–4). Furthermore, the Committee separated the minimum pension from the rest of the pension reform and drafted an independent act (BGBl. I 2001: 1310; Dünn and Fasshauer 2001: 274). Most importantly, the Committee recommended dividing the pension reform into a part with mandatory *Bundesrat* agreement, namely, the *Altersvermögensgesetz* that regulated the promotion and subsidizing of private old-age provisions and improvements in occupational pensions, and a non-mandatory part, that is the *Altervermögensergänzungsgesetz* that regulated the pension indexation formula, survivors' pension and pension splitting for married couples (BT-Drs. 14/5146: 9).

The *Bundestag* passed the bills *Altersvermögensergänzungsgesetz*[22] and *Altersvermögensgesetz*[23] on January 26, 2001. The *Bundesrat* agreed on the *Altersvermögensergänzungsgesetz* on February 16, 2001. The new regulations on minimum old-age pension and on subsidizing private pensions (*Altersvermögensgesetz*), however, did not pass the *Bundesrat* during the same session. Not only states led by grand coalitions of SPD and CDU defeated the proposal but also states with SPD as senior partner in coalitions did not agree on parts of the reform package. Schleswig-Holstein's Prime Minister, Heide Simonis (SPD), requested a Mediation Committee because the pressure on state and municipal budgets had to be relieved and the administration costs for private pensions had to be reduced by creating a federal institute (BR-PlPr 759/2001: 6D). When it came to the *Bundesrat* decision on whether to call for the Mediation Committee, or to agree to the proposal, neither proposal got a majority. Even the voting on single paragraphs did not find a majority. Unfortunately, the voting behavior by states is not reported in the minutes, but *Bundesrat* president,

Kurt Beck, pointed out that this constellation of voting behavior had never occurred before (BR-PlPr 759/2001: 16A). Consequently, as the *Bundesrat* was unable to take any decision; it was the Cabinet that had to call the Mediation Committee (BT-Drs. 14/5367).

Although Riester did not envisage subsidizing real-estate as investment for private old-age security, the issue became more prominent in December 2001. The opposition parties, the Greens and even several SPD-*Länder* favored the inclusion of real-estate. Riester's first move towards the inclusion of real-estate foresaw as a precondition that these contracts should also comply with the criteria for other private old-age provisions such as life-long pensions with minimum return of deposited value. Furthermore, private pensions were to be taxed at the time of pay-out. These requirements were almost impossible to apply to real-estate, however, as it cannot be "used up" and is in any case not taxable in Germany. Rhineland-Palatinate—the German state with the second highest rate of owner-occupied real estate[24]—suggested solving the problem of taxation by inventing an artificial rent that would be taxed in old age (BR-PlPr 763/2001: 227C). The government of Rhineland-Palatinate and the housing industry also suggested that private pension funds could be used to purchase houses or apartments without losing the subsidy. To guarantee that the grants were paid back when estates were sold, the private pension component had to be enlisted in the cadastral registry (Berliner Bericht, Feb. 2001: 49).

The Mediation Committee amended the proposal on private pensions by including the purchase of real-estate into the types eligible for federal grants. Insured persons could take between €10,000 and €50,000 out of their private pension fund and had to start paying back one year later at steady rates (Berliner Bericht, July 2001: 183). Other changes referred to the foundation of a federal institute responsible for calculation and payment of government allowances on private pensions (BR-PlPr 763/2001: 221A-B).

When the *Altersvermögensgesetz* was debated in the Mediation Committee, the *Altersvermögensergänzungsgesetz* that had already been passed in February, was changed again. The retrenchment affecting survivors' pensions was alleviated through an amendment law. Widows and widowers would get two instead of one earnings points for their first child and one additional *Entgeltpunkt* for every further child. Additionally, the coalition cancelled the freezing of the income limit for widows and widowers. The consequences were that the savings in survivors' pensions would be smaller than expected (BR-PlPr 763/2001: 221C, 226A-B; BGBl I 2001: 1589).

Eventually, *Bundestag* and *Bundesrat* agreed on the mandatory BR-consent part of the reform—the version of the *Altersvermögensgesetz*, negotiated in the Mediation Committee.[25] In the *Bundesrat*, the SPD/Green governed states with the help of the two grand coalition states of Berlin and Brandenburg, the red-red (SPD/PDS) coalition in Mecklenburg-Western Pomerania and the SPD/FDP coalition in Rhineland-Palatinate supported the proposal in the *Bundesrat*. As Bremen's abstention counted as a "no"-vote, the final result on May 11, 2001 was 38 "yes" and 28 "no" plus three abstentions (BR-PlPr 763/2001: 232). In other words, the government coalition achieved the smallest majority possible in the *Bundesrat*.

The Schröder government then faced the accusation of "having bought" the support of some states. Berlin and Brandenburg profited from the choice of location for the federal institute for private pension subsidy administration, which would provide approximately 1,000 jobs to the region (*SZ* 03.04.2001). Rhineland-Palatinate's agreement became possible after the federal government met some of the state's demands and the purchase of real-estate had become a subsidized type of investment in private pension (*SZ* 07.05.2001). The coalition contract between SPD and PDS in Mecklenburg-Western Pommerania required the state to abstain from voting in the *Bundesrat* if the coalition partners could not agree on a common stance. Although the PDS did not support the content of the *Altersvermögensgesetz*, State Prime Minister Harald Ringstorff voted in favor of the bill in *Bundesrat*, which caused a major conflict in the Red–Red coalition (*SZ* 12.05.2001).

The pension reforms of 2001 marked a clear change in the contours of the German pension system. The discussion demonstrates how highly interwoven negotiations occurred not only between the incumbent parties, but also between the government and the parties in opposition, between parties and interest groups and even— importantly—between different wings of the SPD. Thus, the empirical picture of the German "negotiation" democracy is far more complex than a simple "Federalism" or "intergovernmental power relations perspective would suggest. As a result, a specific pension mixture occurred. This mixture can be explained by the configuration of institutional veto points, the dynamic of party competition and the imponderable nature of intra-party politics in catch-all parties that together opened up the reform process to various interests. The fact that the private pension known as *Riester-Rente* is non-compulsory can be attributed to criticism from the opposition as well as from within the government. It is an irony of pension politics and a sign of the somehow erratic reform process in Germany that some politicians in the Red–Green camp, as well as some politicians in the CDU/CSU, publicly consider making this pension scheme compulsory.

The Rürup reform 2004 (*RV-Nachhaltigkeitsgesetz*)

The SPD/Green coalition was confirmed in office only with a very slight margin in the 2002 elections. In his government declaration, Chancellor Gerhard Schröder announced structural reforms in the labor market as well as in the health and the pensions system (Schröder 2002: 10). It is noteworthy, that the *Alliance for Jobs* was not effective as a forum for negotiating welfare reforms. After some disappointments, Schröder changed the reform strategy even before the election by appointing the so-called Hartz Commission (named after the leader of the Commission, who is director of the staff management at the Volkswagen AG). The Commission was staffed not by the elites of the German social partners but by personally-selected representatives of some trade unions and employers' associations, and academics. In November 2002, the government established another commission under the leadership of Bert Rürup, an influential economist and long-term adviser to several German governments, to make suggestions for reforming the social security systems (*Rürup-Kommission*). With these commissions, the government signaled new reform ambitions and at the same time side-stepped the social partners. These commissions were mainly introduced to enhance the reform pressure through commission reports that were intensively debated in public (Trampusch 2005). Or as two social scientists involved in the Hartz Commission put it: the Commissions worked as "icebreaker" in the German reform debate (Jann and Schmid 2003). The Rürup Commission advocated increasing the standard retirement age from 65 to 67 years, with full effect for all insured born in 1969 or younger. Another recommendation was the introduction of a sustainability factor (*Nachhaltigkeitsfaktor*), taking into account changes in the ratio between pensioners and insured (Rürup Kommission 2003: 8–9).

The SPD/Green government did not adopt the proposal regarding the increase of the retirement age but guaranteed the maintenance of the pension age of 65 until 2010. Other than that, the Cabinet decided to introduce the sustainability factor into the indexation formula. The *Nachhaltigkeitsfaktor* reflects the ratio of pensioners relative to contributors adjusted to pensioners with 45 years of full contribution employment (Hain et al. 2004: 338). It affects both current pensioners (although with modifications during transition period) as well as future pensioners. The *Nachhaltigkeitsfaktor* is weighted by a certain parameter α that was fixed to 0.25 in 2004 but provides easy access for future political retrenchment. The assessment base of wage increases for pension indexation is reduced from all employees to the real contribution base, that is civil servants' wages, and wages above the contribution limit, are excluded. As higher incomes have increased considerably in recent years, this change in the assessment base will also have a reducing effect on the level of pension benefits (Hain et al. 2004).

Furthermore, the reform bill included the suspension of pension adjustment for 2004, and the deferment of pension payments until the end of the month, starting in April 2004. Additionally, the Cabinet resolution included the abolition of credit points for periods of higher education for pensions after 2008, a reduction of the contingency reserve from 0.5 to 0.2 times monthly expenditure (*Nachhaltigkeitsrücklage*), and the imposition of the full (instead of half) long-term care contribution rate on pensioners. Additionally, the road to early retirement was partially blocked as the government increased the age for early retirement for unemployed and partial pensioners from 60 to 63 years (Dünn et al. 2004; Brall et al. 2004; Reimann 2004; BT-Drs. 15/2149).

Reacting to the intra-party complaints of SPD-left wing members, Social Minister, Ulla Schmidt (SPD), limited the losses caused by the *Nachhaltigkeitsfaktor* to 46 percent of the former average wage (*SZ* 09.03.2004). The *Bundestag* approved the bill on March 11, 2004. The *Bundesrat* with CDU/CSU majority called the Mediation Committee in early April 2004. However, as this reform was a piece of non-mandatory consent legislation, the *Bundestag* could overrule the veto of the *Bundesrat* (albeit with the smallest majority possible, i.e. with one vote difference). As the SPD was confronted with intense opposition from the left-wing members (backed by the trade unions), the party leadership decided to let an extra party meeting in 2004 decide about the 2010 agenda and the pension reform. The majority of the party backed Chancellor Schröder, and eventually, only one prominent left-wing politician (Ottmar Schreiner) abstained from voting in the *Bundestag*.

Trade unions, as well as the CDU/CSU and FDP, opposed the reform. The trade unions criticized the reduction of the pension benefits, while the employers demanded an increase in the retirement age instead of "half-hearted" reductions, as they put it, of the benefit level. The CDU/CSU questioned the political goal of stabilizing the contribution rate and at the same time reducing the benefit level to 46 percent of the former gross wage. Instead, the overall message should be to increase the retirement age from 65 to 67 years. This position was, by and large, shared by the FDP.

After the *Nachhaltigkeitsgesetz* was decided, the government, following a verdict of the *Bundesverfassungsgericht* of March 6, 2002, switched taxing rules in the pension system. Until 2005, the taxation of the pension contributions was the rule. With the reform passed on June 11, 2004 (*Alterseinkünftegesetz*), pension benefits shall be taxed instead of pension contributions. Before, only the returns of pensions with a yearly amount of exemption of €7,664 were taxable, but not the pension itself (BfA 2004). Pension contributions were mostly subject to taxation. The new regulations entail tax-free contributions but taxable pension benefits at the time of payment (*nachgelagerte Besteuerung*). The government decided to introduce the new taxation rules gradually; a full system shift should be finished in 2040. At the same time, the *Alterseinkünftegesetz* changed elements of the *Riester-Rente*, and simplified the application for Riester grants, streamlining the criteria for private pension certification, and improving the information service. Most importantly, the act stipulated that benefits for men and women must be equal in the *Riester-Rente*, if equal contributions had been paid (Bruno-Latocha and Tippelmann 2004: 394).

V Conclusion

Summary of the magnitude of changes

The magnitude of pension reforms in general is difficult to assess (Immergut and Anderson in the Editors' Introduction to this Handbook; Leitner and Lessenich 2003; Hinrichs and Kangas 2003; Clegg and Clasen 2003; Clasen and Siegel 2006). For example, the 1989 pension reform is estimated to save DM 100.7 billion of expected expenditure by 2010 (BT-Drs. 11/4124). In contrast, the *Pension Reform Act* 1999, passed in 1997, had only been expected to reduce estimated expenditure by DM 65.3 billions in the same period of time, that is, 20 years (own calculation based on BT-Drs. 13/8671: 5). An alternative measure to compare the "savings" of the reform is to estimate the magnitude of anticipated contribution rate changes. The *Pension*

Reform Act of 1992 (passed in 1989) ranks highest in curbing potential pension contribution rate increases. Hence, this indicator suggests that the reform passed by a broad issue coalition between the government parties CDU/CSU and FDP, and the major party in opposition, the SPD was the most far-reaching pension reform in Germany during the past twenty years.[26]

Beyond monetary criteria, the 1989 pension reform is judged neither as an "innovative" change nor a "system shift". Changes were implemented more or less within the old programatic structures (Hinrichs 1998; Nullmeier and Rüb 1993). To be sure, the *Pension Act 1992* is by all means assessed to be one of the major pieces of pension legislation of the past 20 years, but when considering the time of preparation of the act and the innovative proposals, the outcome is somewhat unspectacular. Features, already suggested in the SPD/FDP and SPD proposals of the *Pension Reform Bill of 1984* and *Pension Reform Bill of 1985*, were realized. But none of the more innovative ideas being bandied around throughout the 1980s, such as minimum or basic pension, capital funding, reduction of replacement rate or pension contributions rates relative to number of children, prevailed.

The core element of the pension reform passed in 1997 was the introduction of a demographic factor in the pension indexation formula with the effect of reducing the replacement rate from 70 percent (1999) to 64 percent (2030). Model calculations estimated a reduction of pension expenditure of DM 137.3 billion by 2030 or a reduced increase in contribution rate of 2.9 percentage points (Hain and Müller 1998). However, due to the change in government in 1998 and the "corrective" measures of the Red–Green government, this pension reform could not develop its impact. Nevertheless, the introduction of a demographic factor may be seen as an erosion of the principle of *Lebensstandardsicherung*. After some more bungling of pension politics, the Red–Green government reinstated the demographic factor under the heading of a *Nachhaltigkeitsfaktor* in 2004, with even more severe effects.

The introduction of a private pension as an additional, capital-funded pillar of the system in 2001 is often considered to be an important structural improvement. Some observers argue that a system change or even "a paradigm shift" in German pension policies occurred (Schmähl 2003). For the first time since 1957, the statutory pensions system does not rely completely on PAYG financing anymore. This reform can also be considered as a step towards World Bank's and experts' recommendations that favor multi-pillar pension systems. But the private pension is still not compulsory. Considering that there has always been a substantial amount of voluntary private pension provision, for example, voluntary life insurance, and that the *Altersvorsorgegesetz* generated high costs in terms of subsidies and tax deductions, it is still open to discussion whether this reform measure is really an element of retrenchment. Much more important is the significant reduction of the replacement rate in statutory first-pillar pension benefits. In all, its effect is to quasi-privatize the risk of old age and to use private pensions as partial substitutes for the public pension system in retreat (Hering 2002). But until today, the German population does not overwhelmingly draw on the subsidies provided. At the end of 2002—one year after the *Riester-Rente* came into effect—only 3.5 million out of 31 million of eligible persons had taken out a private pension contract (Dünn and Fasshauer 2003: 6–8; Leinert 2002). Nevertheless, the statement of the government that private provision is necessary in order to achieve pension benefits that secure the standard of living in the future, points up to a new policy paradigm in German pension politics (Hinrichs 2004).

All in all, the German pension system *is* changing—the German pension "elephant" has started to move speedily during the past decade. What is open for discussion, however, is the question of whether German pension policies departed from their previous developmental path. On the one hand, most of the old system is still intact. On the other hand, new elements have been introduced that have supplemented the existing system and might change the system logic more than can be readily assessed simply by looking at single discrete changes.

What we have detailed here is that cost containment in the German public pension scheme is far from witnessing a politically induced *Reformstau*. Despite the institutional power distribution and the veto points, reforms were enacted during the past decade, and they were quite successful in containing pension costs.

Impact of the political system on pension politics

The analysis of pension reforms during the past two decades has shown that institutions of German "negotiation democracy" influence the legislative process, enforce interwoven negotiations and open the way for societal and partisan interests to shape the timing, and especially the content, of pension reforms. We argue that the institutional design of the German polity does not automatically produce reform gridlock. More decisive seems to be the interdependence of the institutional framework with party competition in a unified country that still has a divided electorate, and where specific mechanisms of intra-party politics of "old-fashioned" catch-all parties prevail. Moreover, the imponderables of intra-party politics are to a great extent responsible for sometimes erratic or inconsistent reform patterns and reform results.

We argue that the position of the Constitutional Court in German pension politics is important. As already shown, the *Bundesverfassungsgericht* intervenes in pension politics as it does in the widowers' pension or the taxation of pension benefits. In part, it vetoes *ex-post* reform measures undertaken by parliament, and partly it frames reforms that have to be implemented by the executive. The *Bundesverfassungsgericht* is by no means dependent on the strategies of political actors, as it cannot autonomously judge certain features of the pension system, and very often it is in fact the parliamentary opposition that brings the Court into the political game. Nevertheless, the Constitutional Court stands outside politics when it formulates concrete norms that influence the strategies of the political actors, in government as well as in opposition.

Further, the German political system provides for intense policy deliberations in different commissions. In the parliamentary committees, in particular, last-step changes of reforms are no exception. In part, interest groups (see p. 700) can lobby different party factions in order to bring to bear their specific interests in the last round of reform decisions, and in part, in these commissions internal dissenters of incumbent parties may be compensated.

One additional peculiarity of the German pension system is the prominent role of the Social Council. Until very recently, the Social Council was the "natural" inner circle of the pension policy "epistemic community," who used the Council to both provide data to the Ministries, and press for particular reform trajectories. With the advent of the Rürup-Kommission, however, the role of the Social Council seems to have been be effectively reduced. Certainly, the most prominent policy adviser—not only on pension issues—of the current Red–Green government, Bert Rürup, is President of the Social Council. But with the Rürup-Kommission, the government successfully opened the epistemic community to voices on the periphery of the advisory mainstream in Germany. As the CDU also investigated reform possibilities of the German welfare state in a commission under the leadership of the former *Bundespräsident*, Roman Herzog (*Herzog-Kommission*), it seems to be the case that both *Volksparteien* try to break up former closed-policy communities, break up segmented interest mediation, and fuel the public debate with new reform trajectories.

Finally, reform politics are embedded in the logic of party competition in a federal state, and political negotiations under the frame of—as Lijphart (1984; 1999) calls it—"incongruent" bi-cameralism (Lehmbruch 2000; Schmidt 2003). Especially in the case of mandatory consent legislation, the hurdles to consensus between the majority in the *Bundestag* and the majority in the *Bundesrat* are high. After 1990, for much of the time, majorities in both chambers differed, and the opposition could push through their interests via the *Bundesrat*. This *Politikverflechtung* (Scharpf 1985) has been made responsible for consensual reform imperatives and the hidden Grand Coalition in German reform politics (Schmidt 2003; Trampusch 2005) that, in consequence, fosters immobility in reform politics (Darnstädt 2004), as critics emphasize.

Incongruent bi-cameralism (as is the case with the German *Bundesrat* and *Bundestag*), and the imperative of negotiation between both chambers (in the case of mandatory consent legislation), present a formal veto power for the parties in majority in the Second Chamber. Nevertheless, during the 1980s, the Kohl government could more or less rely on stable majorities in both chambers. After German unification, however, this situation changed. Partly because of new actors and coalition patterns, partly because of the declining popularity of the CDU/CSU and the FDP in the West, negotiations between both chambers became complicated and sometimes unpredictable. As it could be shown with the pension reform of 1997 as well as with the pension reform of 2001, this veto point opens up access to different societal and special interests that influence policy reforms. As was the case with the SPD government of Rhineland-Palatinate in 2001, even the "own" government at the federal level was vetoed in drafting the concrete content of the reform: interests of real estate-owners were pushed through and made the final solution much more complicated (and expensive) than was the case before the intervention.

The same can be seen, in hindsight, as regards the interests that entered the political arena via the CDU/CSU and their veto power in the *Bundesrat* in 2001. The degree to which the state should subsidize low-income earners was expanded gradually, due to party pressures. While CDU/CSU rejected (at least in 2000/2001) an obligatory private pension pillar, the government was forced to spend more money for subsidies (and even for middle-income earners), thereby undermining the cost-saving effects of the reform. In effect, the opposition successfully counteracted the cost containment ambitions of the Red–Green government at the first step; and after the reform was implemented the government could be criticized at the second step, because the *Riester-Rente* was not a success. This is a classic case of the diffusion of responsibility inbuilt in the German polity under conditions of divided government.

The CDU/CSU and SPD dominate party competition in Germany. However, both "*Volksparteien*" in the middle of the party-spectrum have to manage internal party compliance, and it became more and more difficult during the last decade. Obviously, the left wing of the SPD (with support from the trade unions) influenced decision-making in the SDP during the first incumbency of the Red–Green government, and especially in the case of subsidizing low-income earners during the negotiations of the pension reform of 2001 (Schludi 2001: 36). Hence, intra-party politics and the need of the party leadership to foster compliance over centrifugal party factions open up further channels of influence for societal interests. This observation applies especially for large omnibus parties with a multitude of factions (Wiesendahl 2004; Saalfeld 2003).

Party competition in the bi-cameral polity changed in part because of the effects of German unification not only because a "new" *Volkspartei* (i.e. the PDS) entered the political space in East Germany. German unification rearranged the traditional pattern of bloc-competition at the state-level. After unification, the number of states in the *Bundesrat* increased significantly, leading to an increase in elections and in succession to a quasi perpetual electoral campaign in Germany. Furthermore, the party system in unified Germany is to a great extent divided:

> The two party systems in reunified Germany mirror a divided German electorate with a far greater proportion of non-aligned voters in the east, and an east–west division in the political culture. The latter manifests itself most visibly in a much stronger demand of the East German electorate for a powerful role of the state vis-à-vis the market and in a significantly higher dissatisfaction in the east with the way democracy works (Schmidt 2003: 138).

Hence, reform measures in Germany are so difficult to agree upon, because both truly national parties, that is, the CDU as well as the SPD, are torn up in this electoral split. Politicians are not able to win elections alone in the East, but they can loose them there.

All in all, reform politics in Germany are no doubt influenced and shaped by institutions. However, as the institutional chain of decision-making since German unification is formally unchanged, we observe rather a "functional conversion" in the German polity. It is the division of the electorate in unified Germany, the division of mobilization patterns, political behavior and party competition that undermines the efficiency of the policy-making process. Despite these obstacles, however, reforms are indeed possible. But they are half-hearted, sometimes contradictory and altogether reveal a high degree of ineptness, or of political learning in small steps. The reform politics of the Red–Green government at least in pension policies therefore have to be evaluated carefully. Beyond a certain amount of bungling, the Red–Green government enabled a partial paradigm-shift in pension politics in Germany. As we could show, the government had to make many concessions that made the reform in 2001 expensive and partially contradictory. Nevertheless, despite the critique from within the SPD, from the opposition in a powerful position, and from trade unions, the *Riester-Rente* marks one example that path-breaking reforms "beyond incrementalism" are possible in Germany.

Interest group influence

Unions indirectly influenced pension policy in Germany through their participation in government commissions and their statements in committee hearings. In a more direct way the unions lobbied with the government or the incumbent party factions in parliament and negotiated with the chancellors and the ministers of social affairs in non-public meetings. On the one side, interest group influence was limited. For example, in the Riester reform of 2001, the main objection of the unions was the abandonment of the principle of bipartite financing of pensions. Schröder repeated several times that he was not afraid of union protests and would proceed with his reform paths even without the unions' agreement. On the other side, trade unions (and other interest groups) successfully pushed through their interest via lobbying party factions. The case of loss limitation in the 2004 pension reform has already been discussed.

Recently, the role of interest groups in pension policy-making—and the role of German trade unions in public policy-making especially—was confined. As we have already shown, the move to post-corporatist agencies, such as the *Rürup-Kommission*, in which social interests were included but carefully selected by the executive, in the end diminishes the influence of the main interest organization, or at least makes the decision about which interests may enter the inner circle of the political decision-making process a decision of the executive. These commissions served not as a means to organize policy consensus, nor to filter out the best policy solution from a cornucopia of different possibilities. These commissions in contrast effectively influence the public debate along the guiding lines of the executive and they partly serve as a whip against party defectors.

With the development from segmented corporatism towards neo-pluralism the influence of interest groups on pension decisions becomes more difficult to predict. While the pension reform decided in 1989 was by and large managed by a closed epistemic community, the pension reform of 2001 as well as more recent adjustments reveal that policy deliberation has moved into the public sphere.

Constraints of policy design

Social insurance institution in itself may impose constraints for reform. Our empirical results reveal an impressive leeway for reform—even in a Bismarckian PAYG system. Hence, this institutional design of the pension schemes may be only a limited explanation for reform gridlock or reform success. The German Constitutional Court, for example, considered vested pension entitlements to be property rights, but the preservation of the entitlements did not preclude dampening pension benefit increases, reducing replacement rates, or introducing compulsory private pensions for young persons entering the labor market.

Compared to other countries there have been fairly few obvious privileges that might serve as a catalyst for reform in the German pension system, even at the beginning of the period under research. The contribution-benefit link has already been tight due to working life-long reference periods. Privileges for certain occupational groups were restricted to the self-employed, farmers and civil servants. For all dependent employees, pension calculation was standardized. However, the harmonization of the public and the private sector would give great leeway for action and savings under the label of "equalization." But none of the governments in the 1980s and 1990s has seriously considered the inclusion of civil servants in the statutory pension system.

Conversely, other constraints of policy design became obvious. Because of the dominance of social insurance schemes, the way new policy goals are framed becomes to a certain extent predestined. Here we are not able to discuss the interesting story of the multiple switchyards between different pillars of the German social insurance state (Trampusch 2003), but emphasize that family policy goals are to a certain extent, implemented and publicly exploited in public pension insurance schemes. This policy reaction by governments of different composition—and partly backed by the Constitutional Court—burdens the pension insurance schemes with additional tasks, instead of lowering problem pressures (Jochem 2001).

The role of ideas and historical context

To understand the development of pension politics during the past two decades is not possible without acknowledging the historical uniqueness and the tremendous impact of unification on German politics. With unification, the problem pressure increased and the political basis for consensual pension politics eroded. On the one hand, the unemployment crisis in the east undermined, and still undermines, the financial basis of (comparatively) generous pension benefits. This implied judge transfer flows from the West to the East, increasing the financial burden and—other things being equal—increasing the overall pension contribution rate. On the other hand, new political actors and new political patterns of consensus building and conflict resulted from unification.

Additionally, the ideas behind the German social insurance state are on retreat. Partly combined with changing career patterns of the decision-makers in social policies, in the SPD as well as in the CDU/CSU (Trampusch 2005), classical ideas of the social insurance state vanished. With the move from segmented corporatism to neo-pluralism in pension politics, the Red–Green government further opened up the ideational space for new and hitherto "foreign" ideas. It goes beyond our ambition here to judge whether these new ideas reflect aggressive neo-liberalism (Rieger and Leibfried 2004). However, we can state that currently many new ideas influence the debate on pension reforms in Germany. But because of the start made by the Grand Coalition government in 2006, not only are power relations in Germany highly uncertain, but also the multitude of different reform proposals in the public debate make it impossible to forecast possible developments of the German pension system.

Abbreviations

Art.	*Artikel*
AVmEG	*Altersvermögensergänzungsgesetz*
AVmG	*Altersvermögensgesetz*
BaFin	*Bundesanstalt für Finanzdienstleistungsaufsicht*
BDA	*Bundesvereinigung der Deutschen Arbeitgeberverbände*
BDI	*Bundesverband der Deutschen Industrie*
BfA	*Bundesversicherungsanstalt für Angestellte*
BR	*Bundesrat*
BT	*Bundestag*
BVerfG	*Bundesverfassungsgericht*
CDU	*Christlich Demokratische Union*
CSU	*Christlich-Soziale Union*
DGB	*Deutscher Gewerkschaftsbund*
DM	*Deutsche Mark*
DP	*Deutsche Partei*
Drs.	*Drucksache*
FDP	*Freie Demokratische Partei*
FVP	*Freie Volkspartei*
GDR	*German Democratic Republic*
GDV	*Gesamtverband der Deutschen Versicherungswirtschaft*
GG	*Grundgesetz*
GRV	*Gesetzliche Rentenversicherung*
IG	*Industriegewerkschaft*
LVA	*Landesversicherungsanstalten*
PDS	*Partei des Demokratischen Sozialismus*

PlPr   *Plenarprotokoll*
PSVaG   *Pensions-Sicherungs-Verein*
RAV   *Rentenanpassungsverordnung*
SED   *Sozialistische Einheitspartei Deutschlands*
SGB   *Sozialgesetzbuch*
SPD   *Sozialdemokratische Partei Deutschlands*
VDK   *Verband der Kriegsbeschädigten, Kriegshinterbliebenen und Sozialrentner Deutschlands*
VDR   *Verband Deutscher Rentenversicherungsträger*
ver.di   *Vereinte Dienstleistungsgewerkschaft*
WASG   *Wahlalternative Arbeit und Soziale Gerechtigkeit*

Notes

1. Federal Constitution or Basic Law.
2. One representative for each of the 16 states and 16 *Bundestag* members, distributed among the parties relative to their shares of seats in the chamber (Bauer 1998).
3. If a two-thirds majority in the *Bundesrat* objects, the *Bundestag* also needs a two-thirds majority to overturn (Art. 77 IV GG).
4. In the literature, the treatment of CDU and CSU as one or two parties is controversial. While currently the tensions between both parts of the Christian Democratic movement are obvious, in most parliamentary decisions the leaderships in both factions enable common voting patterns. However, while we therefore argue that one should count both parts as *one* party, we would also like to emphasize that intra-party politics in the CDU/CSU is highly complex, volatile and the final strategy decision of the CDU/CSU is an empirical question, the researcher has to detect and not to deduce.
5. Strong criticism on Chancellor Brandt's *Ostpolitik* led to a vote of no-confidence requested by the CDU/CSU in April 1972. Willy Brandt won the vote, but due to continuing disapproval and a growing number of dissenters in the government coalition he called for a vote of confidence on September 20, 1972 with the intention of calling new elections (Hockerts 1992).
6. *Gesetz zur Verbesserung der betrieblichen Altersversorgung, BetrAVG.*
7. There are several types of self-employment that have compulsory coverage. Self-employed teachers, nursing staff, midwives, artists and members of the publishing professions, craftsmen and longshoremen are obliged to pay into the statutory pension scheme (§2 SGB VI).
8. *Gesetz zur Organisationsreform in der gesetzlichen Rentenversicherung (RVOrgG).*
9. The pension value is the same for all pensioners. The pension value since July 1, 2003 is €26.13 for the *Alte Bundesländer* and €22.97 for the *Neue Bundesländer* (www.bfa.de).
10. The pension contribution in this context is composed of the contribution rate to the statutory pension system, plus the rate to (voluntary) private pension provisions that equals a maximum of 4% from 2009 on. Before 2009, the rules for the transition period apply, as regulated by §255e SGB VI.

11. *Witwerrentenurteil* on March 12, 1975 (BVerfGE 39, S. 169ff.): the court ruled that the unequal treatment of men and women in survivor's pension was constitutional, but recommended changing pension law by 1984 (Frerich and Frey 1993a: 232).
12. The change in child-care credits was a reaction to the Constitutional Courts verdict to improve the value of child-rearing periods for working women. The *Bundesverfassungsgericht* required that contributions from employment and notional credits for child-rearing should be added (Richter 1999: 81).
13. The *Bundesrat* had called the Mediation Committee by majority decision on November 7, 1997 (BR-PlPr 718/1997: 503C). The Mediation Committee—with relative SPD majority—proclaimed its decision on November 13, 1997: the committee dismissed the CDU/FDP bill (BT-Drs. 13/9065, 1997b). The *Bundestag* majority rejected the Mediation Committee proposal on November 25, 1997 (BT-PlPr 13/205: 18561A). Consequently, the *Bundesrat* objected on November 28, 1997 (BR-PlPr 719/1997: 548C); this was overturned by the *Bundestag* on December 11, 1997 (BT-PlPr 13/210: 19140–19142).
14. VAT revenue is usually shared between the *Länder* and the federal budget.
15. Voting: 592 votes; 311 yes (CDU/CSU/FDP); 280 no (SPD/Grüne/PDS); 1 abstention (SPD) (BT-PlPr 13/201: 18286A).
16. Voting: 641 votes; 286 yes (SPD, Grüne, PDS), 336 no (CDU, CSU, FDP), 19 abstentions (PDS) (BT-PlPr 13/210: 19154C).
17. *Geringfügig Beschäftigte* were employees who work less than 15 hours per week and earn a maximum of DM 630 (in 1999) per month.
18. Voting on 4 March 1999. Outcome: 564 total votes, 308 yes (SPD, Greens), 256 no (CDU/CSU, FDP, PDS) (BT-PlPr 14/25: 2010–2012).
19. The Saarland government had filed a motion not to suspend pension adjustment in the middle of a state election campaign in July 1999. By the time of the *Bundesrat* debate and voting the SPD had already lost the state elections and four days after the *Bundesrat*'s voting on the *Haushaltssanierungsgesetz* the new CDU state government took office (BR-Drs 417/99).
20. It was the first time in history that a pension adjustment decree was debated in the second chamber and not adopted by consensus. The decree passed by majority voting (BR-PlPr 751/2000: 202A).
21. Before the pension reform 2001, the replacement rate of pensions was at 70% of average net wages. In June 1999, Riester calculated that his reform measurements would lead to a replacement rate of 65%. Employers and the FDP demanded a much faster decrease of the replacement rate (*SZ* 15.07.2000). Left-wing SPD party members, however, considered 68% in the short run and 65.5% by 2030 as the minimum replacement rate. Ottmar Schreiner as representative of the left-wing of the SPD suggested a higher contribution rate in order to finance these margins for the replacement rate (*SZ* 03.07.2000; 05.07.2000). Unions—in particular the Metal Workers' Union—strived for the maintenance of the current replacement rate of 70% with the adequate contribution rate. The reform act entailed that the replacement rate was supposed to drop to 67% by 2020 and to 64% in the long-run (§154 III 2 AVmEG).
22. Voting results: 580 votes; 319 yes (SPD, Greens), 258 no (CDU/CSU, FDP, PDS), 4 abstentions (Greens) (BT-PlPr 14/147: 14444D).
23. Voting results: 576 votes; 316 yes (SPD, Greens), 256 no (CDU/CSU, FDP, PDS), 4 abstentions (Greens) (BT-PlPr 14/147: 14452–14453).
24. Saarland had an owner-occupied real estate ratio of 58.1%, Rhineland-Palatinate of 55% in 1998, the German average was at 40.9% (Statistisches Bundesamt 2003: 246 Table 10.8).

25. In the *Bundestag* 294 (SPD, Greens) members of parliament out of 548 voted "yes", 250 (CDU/CSU, FDP, PDS) voted "no", 4 (3 Greens, 1 CDU/CSU) abstained from voting (BT-PlPr 14/168: 16449–16452).
26. The estimated reduction in contribution rate by the *Pension Reform Act 1992* was 2.5 percentage points after 10 years and 3.5 percentage points after 20 years. The *Pension Reform Act 1999* would have reduced the contribution rate by 2 percentage points after 10 years and 2.6 percentage points after 20 years. The *AVmG* of 2001 was expected to save 1 percentage points after 10 years and 1 percentage point after 20 years (own calculations based on Müller 1989b: 852, column 5–8 (medium employment version); Hain and Müller 1998: 120 (Übersicht 6); BT-Drs. 14/5146: 6).

Bibliography

Primary Sources and Government Documents

Acts

BGBl. I 1957. *Gesetz zur Neuregelung der knappschaftlichen Rentenversicherung.* (21.05.1957): 533.

BGBl. I 1957. *Gesetz zur Neuregelung des Rechts der Rentenversicherung der Angestellten (Angestelltenversicherungs-Neuregelungsgesetz (AnVNG)).* (23.02.1957): 88.

BGBl. I 1957. *Gesetz zur Neuregelung des Rechts der Rentenversicherung der Arbeiter (Arbeiterrentenversicherungs-Neuregelungsgesetz (ArVNG)).* (23.02.1957): 45.

BGBl. I 1989 Nr. 60. *Gesetz zur Reform der gesetzlichen Rentenversicherung (Rentenreformgesetz 1992 – RRG 1992).* (18.12.1989): 2261.

BGBl. I 1997 Nr. 86. *Gesetz zur Finanzierung eines zusätzlichen Bundeszuschusses zur gesetzlichen Rentenversicherung.* (19.12.1997): 3121.

BGBl. I 1997 Nr. 85. *Gesetz zur Reform der gesetzlichen Rentenversicherung (Rentenreformgesetz 1999 – RRG 1999).* (16.12.1997): 2998.

BGBl. I Nr. 14. *Gesetz zur Neuregelung der geringfügigen Beschäftigungsverhältnisse.* (24.03.1999): 388–95.

BGBl. I 2000 Nr. 25. *Verordnung zur Anpassung der Renten im Jahre 2000 (Rentenanpassungsverordnung 2000 – RAV 2000).* (31.05.2000): 788–9.

BGBl. I 2001 Nr. 31. *Gesetz über eine bedarfsorientierte Grundsicherung im Alter und bei Erwerbsminderung (GSiG).* (26.06.2001): 1310–1343.

BGBl. I 2001 Nr. 13. *Gesetz zur Ergänzung des Gesetzes zur Reform der gesetzlichen Rentenversicherung und zur Förderung eines kapitalgedeckten Altersvorsorgevermögens (Altersvermögensergänzungsgesetz – AVmEG).* (21.03.2001): 403–18.

BGBl. I 2001 Nr. 31. *Gesetz zur Reform der gesetzlichen Rentenversicherung und zur Förderung eines kapitalgedeckten Altersvorsorgevermögens (Altersvermögensgesetz – AVmG).* (26.06.2001): 1310–43.

BGBl. I 2001 Nr. 36. *Gesetz zur Verbesserung des Hinterbliebenenrentenrechts.* (17.07.2001): 1589–99.

BGBl. I 2004 Nr. 38. *Gesetz zur Sicherung der nachhaltigen Finanzierungsgrundlagen der gesetzlichen Rentenversicherung (RV-Nachhaltigkeitsgesetz).* (21.07.2004): 1791–1805.

Bills and parliamentary documents

BR-Drs. 417/99. *Entschließung des Bundesrates zur langfristigen Sicherung der Altersvorsorge. Antrag des Saarlandes.* (07.07.1999).

BT-Drs. 10/2608. *Entwurf eines Gesetzes zur Reform der gesetzlichen Rentenversicherung (Rentenreformgesetz 1985 – RRG 1985),* 10. Wahlperiode, (12.12.1984).

BT-Drs. 11/4124. *Gesetzentwurf der Fraktionen der CDU/CSU, SPD und FDP: Entwurf eines Gesetzes zur Reform der gesetzlichen Rentenversicherung (Rentenreformgesetz 1992 – RRG 1992)*, 11. Wahlperiode, (07.03.1989).

BT-Drs. 13/8704. *Entwurf eines Gesetzes zur Finanzierung eines zusätzlichen Bundeszuschusses zur gesetzlichen Rentenversicherung*, 13. Wahlperiode, (07.10.1997).

BT-Drs. 13/8032. *Strukturreform statt Leistungskürzungen in der Alterssicherung*, 13. Wahlperiode, 13. Wahlperiode, (24.06.1997).

BT-Drs. 13/8671. *Entwurf eines Gesetzes zur Reform der gesetzlichen Rentenversicherung (Rentenreformgesetz 1999 – RRG 1999). Beschlußempfehlung und Bericht des Ausschuss für Arbeit und Sozialordnung*, 13. Wahlperiode, (02.10.1997).

BT-Drs. 13/8869. *Entwurf eines Gesetzes zur Finanzierung eines zusätzlichen Bundeszuschusses zur gesetzlichen Rentenversicherung. Beschlußempfehlung und Bericht des Finanzausschusses zu dem Gesetzentwurf der Fraktionen der CDU/CSU und F.D.P.*, 13. Wahlperiode, (29.10.1997).

BT-Drs. 13/9065. *Gesetz zur Reform der gesetzlichen Rentenversicherung (Rentenreformgesetz 1999 – RRG 1999). Beschlußempfehlung des Ausschusses nach Artikel 77 des Grundgesetzes (Vermittlungsausschuß)*, 13. Wahlperiode, (13.11.1997).

BT-Drs. 13/9419. *Gesetz zur Finanzierung eines zusätzlichen Bundeszuschusses zur gesetzlichen Rentenversicherung. Beschlußempfehlung des Ausschusses nach Artikel 77 des Grundgesetzes (Vermittlungsausschuß)*, 13. Wahlperiode, (10.12.1997).

BT-Drs. 14/4595. *Entwurf eines Gesetzes zur Reform der gesetzlichen Rentenversicherung und zur Förderung eines kapitalgedeckten Altersvorsorgevermögens (Altersvermögensgesetz – AVmG)*, 14. Wahlperiode, (14.11.2000).

BT-Drs. 14/5146. *Entwurf eines Gesetzes zur Reform der gesetzlichen Rentenversicherung und zur Förderung eines kapitalgedeckten Altersvorsorgevermögens (Altersvermögensgesetz – AVmG). Beschlußempfehlung und Bericht des Ausschusses für Arbeit und Sozialordnung*, 14. Wahlperiode, (24.01.2001).

BT-Drs. 14/5367. *Gesetz zur Reform der gesetzlichen Rentenversicherung und zur Förderung eines kapitalgedeckten Altersvorsorgevermögens (Altersvermögensgesetz - AVmG). Unterrichtung durch die Bundesregierung*, 14. Wahlperiode, (19.02.2001).

BT-Drs. 15/2149. *Entwurf eines Gesetzes zur Sicherung der nachhaltigen Finanzierungsgrundlagen der gesetzlichen Rentenversicherung (RV-Nachhaltigkeitsgesetz)*, 15. Wahlperiode, (09.12.2003).

Parliamentary minutes

Bundestag. *Stenographischer Bericht*, Legislative term/Sessions:
BT-PlPr 11/5, 19.03.1987: 137B-251C
BT-PlPr 11/174, 09.11.1989: 13100C-13186D
BT-PlPr 13/205, 25.11.1997: 18560D-18561D
BT-PlPr 13/201, 31.10.1997: 18182C, 18186A-18188B
BT-PlPr 13/210, 11.12.1997: 19140–19143
BT-PlPr 14/25, 04.03.1999: 1982C-2007C, 2071C-2072D/Anl.
BT-PlPr 14/168, 11.05.2001: 16446D-16447A, 16449D-16452A
BT-PlPr 14/147, 26.01.2001: 14403–14459

Bundesrat. *Stenographischer Bericht*, Sessions:
BR-PlPr 607, 01.12.1989: 518–522
BR-PlPr 718, 07.11.1997: 493C-503C
BR-PlPr 719, 28.11.1997: 545C-548C
BR-PlPr 736, 19.03.1999: 84–92

BR-PlPr 751, 19.05.2000: 198A-202A
BR-PlPr 759, 16.02.2001: 3–38
BR-PlPr 763, 11.05.2001: 220D-232B

Newspapers and Magazines (various issues)
Bonner/Berliner Bericht in *Die Sozialversicherung*
Spiegel: *Der Spiegel*
StZ: *Stuttgarter Zeitung*
SZ: *Süddeutsche Zeitung*

Secondary Sources

ALBER, JENS (1998). "Der deutsche Sozialstaat im Licht international vergleichender Daten." *Leviathan*, 26(2): 199–227.

ANDERSEN, UWE and WOYKE, WICHARD (eds.) (2003). *Handwörterbuch des politischen Systems der Bundesrepublik Deutschland*. Opladen: Leske + Budrich.

BAUER, THOMAS (1998). *Der Vermittlungsausschuß: Politik zwischen Konkurrenz und Konsens*. Bremen: Universität Bremen.

BFA (ed.) (2001). *Altersvorsorge: Gesetzliche Rentenversicherung, Betriebliche Altersversorgung, Private Altersvorsorge*. Berlin: Bundesversicherungsanstalt für Angestellte.

—— (2003). *Betriebliche Altersversorgung*. Berlin: Bundesversicherungsanstalt für Angestellte.

—— (2004). *Neues Steuerrecht für Versicherte und Rentner*. Frankfurt: VDR.

BIEDENKOPF, KURT H. (1985). *Die neue Sicht der Dinge: Plädoyer für eine freiheitliche Wirtschafts- und Sozialordnung*. München: Piper.

BRALL, NATALIE, FASSHAUER, STEPHAN, LÜBKE, ECKHARD, et al. (2004). "Neuregelungen im Bereich der Altersgrenzen." *Deutsche Rentenversicherung*, 2004 (6–7): 350–63.

BRUNO-LATOCHA, GESA and TIPPELMANN, ORTRUN (2003). "Betriebliche Altersversorgung im Umbruch: Aktuelle Entwicklungen durch das AVmG." *Deutsche Rentenversicherung*, 58 (1–2): 13–29.

—— and —— (2004). "Änderungen bei betrieblicher und privater Altersvorsoge durch das Alterseinkünftegesetz." *Deutsche Rentenversicherung*, 2004 (6–7): 393–408.

CLASEN, JOCHEN and SIEGEL, NICO A. (eds.) (2006). *Exploring the Dynamics of Reform: The Dependent Variable Problem in Comparative Welfare State Analysis*. Cheltenham: Edward Elgar.

CLEGG, DANIEL and CLASEN, JOCHEN (2003). *Conceptualising and Measuring the Changing Principles of Social Security in Europe: Reflections from a Five-country Study*. Prepared for ESPAnet Annual Conference Changing European Societies: The Role of Social Policy, Session: Comparative Methodology. Copenhagen, Nov. 13–15, 2003.

COUNCIL OF THE EUROPEAN UNION (2003). *Joint report by the Commission and the Council on Adequate and Sustainable Pensions*. Report 6527/2/03. Brussels: EU.

CZADA, ROLAND (2003). "Konzertierung in verhandlungsdemokratischen Politikstrukturen." In Jochem, S. and Siegel, N. A (eds), *Konzertierung, Verhandlungsdemokratie und Reformpolitik im Wohlfahrtsstaat: Das Modell Deutschland im Vergleich*. Opladen: Leske + Budrich, 35–69.

—— (2004). *The End of a Model? Crisis and Transformation of the German Welfare State*. Working Paper WP 1/04. Osnabrück: University of Osnabrück.

DARNSTÄDT, THOMAS (2004). *Die Konsensfalle: Wie das Grundgesetz Reformen blockiert*. München: Deutsche Verlagsanstalt.

DOETSCH, WERNER (1987). "Maßnahmen zur Anpassung der gesetzlichen Rentenversicherung an die sich verändernden Rahmenbedingungen." *Deutsche Rentenversicherung*, 1987 (7a): 509–19.

DÖHLER, MARIAN and MANOW, PHILIP (1997). *Strukturbildung von Politikfeldern: Das Beispiel bundesdeutscher Gesundheitspolitik seit den fünfziger Jahren*. Opladen: Leske + Budrich.

DÜNN, SYLVIA and FASSHAUER, STEPHAN (2001). "Die Rentenreform 2000/2001: Ein Rückblick." *Deutsche Rentenversicherung*, 2001 (5): 266–75.
—— —— (2003). "Ein Jahr Riesterrente: Eine Übersicht aus Sicht der gesetzlichen Rentenversicherung." *Deutsche Rentenversicherung*, 2003 (1–2): 1–12.
DÜNN, SYLVIA and LOHMANN, ALBERT, STAHL, HELMUT et al. (2004). "Die Neuregelung zur Bewertung schulischer und beruflicher Ausbildungszeiten." *Deutsche Rentenversicherung*, 2004 (6–7): 364–83.
FRERICH, JOHANNES and FREY, MARTIN (1993a). *Handbuch der Geschichte der Sozialpolitik in Deutschland bis zur Herstellung der Deutschen Einheit*. München: Oldenbourg.
—— —— (1993b). *Handbuch der Geschichte der Sozialpolitik in Deutschland: Von der vorindustriellen Zeit bis zum Ende des Dritten Reiches*. München: Oldenbourg.
HAIN, WINFRIED, LOHMANN, ALBERT and LÜBKE, ECKHARD (2004). "Veränderungen bei der Rentenanpassung durch das 'RV-Nachhaltigkeitsgesetz.'" *Deutsche Rentenversicherung*, 2004 (6–7): 333–49.
—— and MÜLLER, HORST-WOLF (1998). "Demographische Komponente, zusätzlicher Bundeszuschuß, Verstetigung des Beitragssatzes und finanzielle Auswirkungen des RRG 1999." *Deutsche Rentenversicherung*, 1998 (1–2): 105–24.
HEINE, WOLFGANG (1989). "Rentenreformgesetz 1992–Kontinuitäten, Kompromisse, Konsequenzen (Teil I)." *Arbeit und Sozialpolitik* (6): 146–56.
HERING, MARTIN (2002). *The Politics of Privatizing Public Pensions: Lessons from a Frozen Welfare State*. Prepared for American Political Science Association 98th Annual Meeting. Boston, August 29–Sept 1, 2002.
HINRICHS, KARL (1998). *Reforming the Public Pension Scheme in Germany: The End of the Traditional Consensus?* ZeS-Arbeitspapier 11/98. Bremen: Centre for Social Policy Research.
—— (2004). "Alterssicherungspolitik in Deutschland: Zwischen Kontinuität und Paradigmenwechsel," In Stykow, P., and Beyer, J. (eds.), *Gesellschaft mit beschränkter Hoffnung: Reformfähigkeit und die Möglichkeit rationaler Politik*. Wiesbaden: VSVerlag, 266–86.
—— and KANGAS, OLLI (2003). "When Is a Change Big Enough to Be a System Shift? Small System-shifting Changes in German and Finnish Pension Policies." *Social Policy and Administration*, 37(6): 573–91.
HOCKERTS, HANS GÜNTER (1992). "Vom Nutzen und Nachteil parlamentarischer Parteienkonkurrenz: Die Rentenreform 1972–ein Lehrstück." In Bracher, K. D., et al. (eds.), *Staat und Parteien. Festschrift für Rudolf Morsey zum 65. Geburtstag*. Berlin: Duncker & Humblot, 903–34.
IMMERGUT, ELLEN M. (1992). *Health Politics: Interests and Institutions in Western Europe*. Cambridge: Cambridge University Press.
JANN, WERNER and SCHMID, GÜNTHER (2003). *Ein Jahr Hartz-Reform: Eine zukunftsfähige Strategie?* Pressemitteilung vom 02.10.2003. Berlin: Wissenschaftszentrum Berlin.
JOCHEM, SVEN (2001). "Reformpolitik im deutschen Sozialversicherungsstaat." In Schmidt, M. G. (ed.), *Wohlfahrtsstaatliche Politik. Institutionen, politischer Prozess und Leistungsprofil*. Opladen: Leske & Budrich, 193–226.
KITSCHELT, HERBERT and STREECK, WOLFGANG (eds.) (2003). "Germany: Beyond the Stable State." Special issue of *West European Politics*, 26(4). London: Frank Cass.
LEHMBRUCH, GERHARD (1991). "Die deutsche Vereinigung: Strukturen und Strategien." *Politischer Vierteljahresschrift*, 32: 585–604.
—— (2000). *Parteienwettbewerb im Bundesstaat: Regelsysteme und Spannungslagen im politischen System der Bundesrepublik Deutschland*. 3rd edn. Wiesbaden: Westdeutscher Verlag.
LEINERT, JOHANNES (2002). *Die Riester-Rente: Wer hat sie, wer will sie: Vorabauswertung einer repräsentativen Umfrage zum Vorsorgeverhalten der 30- bis 50-Jährigen*. Bertelsmann Stiftung, [cited 31.03. 2005]. Available from http://www.bertelsmann-stiftung.de/cps/rde/xbcr/SID-0A000F0A-00F1A92B/stiftung/BST-VS-14.pdf

LEITNER, SIGRID and LESSENICH, STEPHAN (2003). "Assessing Welfare State Change: The German Social Insurance State between Reciprocity and Solidarity." *Journal of Public Policy*, 23(3): 325–47.

LIJPHART, AREND (1984). *Democracies: Patterns of Majoritarian and Consensus Government in Twenty-one Countries.* New Haven: Yale University Press.

—— (1999). *Patterns of Democracy: Government Forms and Performance in Thirty-Six Countries.* New Haven: Yale University Press.

MÜLLER, HORST-WOLF (1989b). "Finanzierungsvorschriften und finanzielle Auswirkungen des Rentenreformgesetzes 1992." *Deutsche Rentenversicherung*, 1989 (12): 841–59.

NEY, STEVEN (2001). *Pension Reform in Germany.* The Interdisciplinary Centre for Comparative Research in the Social Sciences, [cited 07.06.2001]. Available from ftp://ftp.iccr.co.at/spa/penref-d2country-de.pdf

NULLMEIER, FRANK (2003). "Alterssicherungspolitik im Zeichen der 'Riester Rente' " In Gohr, A. and Seeleib-Kaiser, M. (eds.), *Sozial- und Wirtschaftspolitik unter Rot-Grün.* Opladen: Westdeutscher Verlag, 167–87.

—— and RÜB, FRIEDBERT W. (1993). *Die Transformation der Sozialpolitik: Vom Sozialstaat zum Sicherungsstaat.* Frankfurt am Main: Campus.

PABST, STEFAN (1999). *Sozialpolitische Entscheidungsprozesse in der Bundesrepublik Deutschland zwischen 1982 und 1989: Eine Literaturübersicht.* ZeS-Arbeitspapier 8/99. Bremen: Zentrum für Sozialpolitik.

PULZER, PETER (1999). "The German Federal Election of 1998." *West European Politics*, 22(3): 241–49.

REIMANN, AXEL (2004). "Das RV-Nachhaltigkeitsgesetz: Gesamtwirkungen und Bewertung." *Deutsche Rentenversicherung*, 2004 (6–7): 318–32.

REINHARD, HANS-JOACHIM (2001). "Demographischer Wandel und Alterssicherung in Deutschland." In Reinhard, H.-J. (ed.), *Demographischer Wandel und Alterssicherung: Rentenpolitik in neun europäischen Ländern und den USA im Vergleich.* Baden-Baden: Nomos Verlag, 15–55.

RICHTER, SASKIA (1999). *Ideen, Interessen, Institutionen: Was bestimmt den rentenpolitischen Entscheidungsprozeß in Deutschland? Literaturkritik und empirische Überprüfung anhand des Rentenreformgesetzes 1999.* Konstanz: Universität Konstanz.

RIEGER, ELMAR and LEIBFRIED, STEPHAN (2004). *Kultur versus Globalisierung: Sozialpolitische Theologie in Konfuzianismus und Christentum.* Frankfurt am Main: Suhrkamp.

RUPPERT, WOLFGANG (2000). *Betriebliche Altersversorgung.* Achtes Forschungsvorhaben zur Situation und Entwicklung der betrieblichen Altersversorgung. München: ifo Institut für Wirtschaftsforschung.

RÜRUP KOMMISSION (2003). *Gesamtkonzept zur Reform der staatlichen Alterssicherung: Beschluss der Kommission für die Nachhaltigkeit in der Finanzierung der Sozialen Sicherungssysteme.* Arbeitnehmerkammer, [cited 22.04. 2004]. Available from http://www.arbeitnehmerkammer.de/sozialpolitik/doku/1_politik/sv_ruerup_2003_06_27_rente.pdf

SAALFELD, THOMAS (2003). "Germany: Multiple Veto Points, Informal Coordination, and Problems of Hidden Action." In Bergman, Torbjörn (ed.), *Delegation and Accountability in Parliamentary Democracies.* Oxford: Oxford University Press, 347–75.

SCHARPF, FRITZ W. (1985). "Die Politikverflechtungs-Falle: Europäische Integration und deutscher Föderalismus im Vergleich." *Politische Vierteljahresschrift*, 26(4): 323–56.

SCHICK, RUPERT and FELDKAMP, MICHAEL F. (2005). *Wahlen.* Deutscher Bundestag, [cited 07.07. 2005]. Available from http://www.bundestag.de/interakt/info_mat/download/stichwort/stichwort_wahlen.pdf

SCHLUDI, MARTIN (2001). *The Politics of Pensions in European Social Insurance Countries.* Discussion Paper 01/11. Köln: Max-Planck-Institut für Gesellschaftsforschung.

SCHMÄHL, WINFRIED (2003). *Dismantling the Earnings-Related Social Pension Scheme: Germany Beyond a Crossroad*. ZeS-Arbeitspapier 9/03. Bremen: Zentrum für Sozialpolitik, Universität Bremen.

SCHMÄHL, WINFRIED and BÖHM, STEFAN (1996). "Supplementary Pensions in the Federal Republic of Germany." In Reynaud, E. et al. (eds.), *International Perspectives on Supplementary Pensions: Actors and Issues*. Westport: Quorum Books, 7–15.

SCHMIDT, MANFRED (2003). *Political Institutions in the Federal Republic of Germany*. Oxford: Oxford University Press.

SCHRÖDER, GERHARD (2002). *Gerechtigkeit im Zeitalter der Globalisierung schaffen – für eine Partnerschaft in Verantwortung*. Regierungserklärung, Pressemitteilung 559/02. Berlin: Presse- und Informationsamt der Bundesregierung.

SCHROEDER, WOLFGANG and WEßELS, B. (2003). "Das deutsche Gewerkschaftsmodell im Transformationsprozess: Die neue deutsche Gewerkschaftslandschaft." In Schroeder, W. and Weßels, B. (eds.), *Die Gewerkschaften in Politik und Gesellschaft der Bundesrepublik Deutschland: Ein Handbuch*. Wiesbaden: Westdeutscher Verlag, 11–37.

Schwarz-Schilling, Christian (1988). *Langfristig sichere Rente: Ein Weg zur Erfüllung des Generationen-Vertrages*. Bonn: Economica.

SEEMANN, WENKE (2005). *Der Einfluss von Landtagswahlen auf die Regierungspolitik im Bund: Eine empirische Untersuchung anhand der Bundesgesetzgebungstätigkeit 1976–2004*. Berlin: Humboldt Universität.

STATISTISCHES BUNDESAMT (ed.) (2003). *Statistisches Jahrbuch 2003*. Wiesbaden: Statistisches Bundesamt.

STURM, ROLAND (1989). "West Germany." In Jacobs, F. (ed.), *Western European Political Parties: A Comprehensive Guide*. Harlow: Longman Group, 441–75.

THELEN, KATHLEEN (2000). "Why German Employers Cannot Bring Themselves to Dismantle the German Model." In Soskice, D. (ed.), *Unions, Employers, and Central Banks: Macroeconomic Coordination and Institutional Change in Social Market Economies*. Cambridge: Cambridge University Press.

—— and KUME, IKUO (2006). "Coordination as a Political Problem in Coordinated Market Economies." *Governance*, 19 (1) (sp. iss.): 11–42.

TRAMPUSCH, CHRISTINE (2003). *Ein Bündnis für die nachhaltige Finanzierung der Sozialversicherungssysteme: Interessenvermittlung in der Bundesdeutschen Arbeitsmarkt- und Rentenpolitik*. Discussion Paper. Köln: Max-Planck-Institut für Gesellschaftsforschung.

—— (2005). "From Interest Groups to Parties: The Change in the Career Patterns of the Legislative Elite in German Social Policy." *German Politics*, 14(1): 14–32.

VDR (ed.) (2000). *Rentenversicherung in Zeitreihen*. Frankfurt am Main: Verband Deutscher Rentenversicherungsträger.

—— (2004). *Rund um die Rente: Die deutsche gesetzliche Rentenversicherung im Überblick*. Frankfurt am Main: Verband Deutscher Rentenversicherungsträger.

VORLÄNDER, HANS (1990). "Die FDP zwischen Erfolg und Existenzgefährdung." In Oberreuter, H. and Mintzel, A. (eds.), *Parteien in der Bundesrepublik Deutschland*. München: Olzog, 237–75.

WIESENDAHL, ELMAR (2004). "Parteien und die Politik der Zumutungen." *Aus Politik und Zeitgeschichte*, 40: 19–24.

WIESENTHAL, HELMUT (2003). "German Unification and 'Model Germany:' An Adventure in Institutional Conservatism." *West European Politics*, 26(4): 37–58.

WINKLER, HEINRICHZ August (2000). *Der lange Weg nach Westen: Deutsche Geschichte vom Dritten Reich bis zur Wiedervereinigung*. München: C. H. Beck.

Zohlnhöfer, RAIMUT (2001). *Die Wirtschaftspolitik der Ära Kohl: Eine Analyse der Schlüsselentscheidungen in den Politikfeldern Finanzen, Arbeit und Entstaatlichung, 1982–1998*. Opladen: Leske + Budrich.

PART V

CLOSED VETO POINTS, MODERATE VETO PLAYERS, UNUSUAL ELECTORAL SYSTEMS

CHAPTER 15

THE NETHERLANDS: POLITICAL COMPETITION IN A PROPORTIONAL SYSTEM

KAREN M. ANDERSON

I Introduction

THE Dutch pension system is often regarded as one of the most financially stable, effective pension systems in Europe because it combines a fairly generous flat-rate national pension (AOW) with quasi-mandatory, funded occupational pensions.[1] The basic pension protects against poverty in old age while occupational pensions provide supplemental benefits related to previous income. This combined public–private approach to pension provision is considered to be fairly resistant to the kinds of demographic and financial shocks that affect public pension systems elsewhere in Europe because the risk of old age is shared between the state and the social partners (Haverland 2001; van Riel et al. 2003).

Dutch consociational politics and industrial relations practices have substantially influenced the development of this multi-pillar system. More recently, increasing political competition has had a substantial influence on pension politics, leaving its mark more on the political bargaining about how to reform the public AOW scheme than on the reform of occupational pensions. The reform of occupational pensions has followed more of a neo-corporatist wage bargaining logic than a political logic. Unions and employers negotiate the details of occupational pensions as part of collective wage bargains, but they do so in the context of government regulation. Because of the tough funding requirements for pension funds, investment losses often translate directly into immediate pressure for change, with contribution hikes and benefit cuts unthinkable in the context of strong political competition. Indeed, recent stock market losses have led to serious deteriorations in pension arrangements, and dealing with this crisis has led to a tense tug of war between the government and the social partners about how to reform pension regulation. On the one hand, the social partners do not want to give up their autonomy in this area, and government is only too happy to let other actors take the blame for occupational pension cuts. On the other hand, Dutch governments have used their regulatory powers to push the social partners in specific directions concerning occupational pensions, with variable success.

Dutch pension politics has proceeded along two tracks. First, reforming the public AOW scheme is a story of incremental cuts that have led to several years of deteriorating real benefits. When the Christian Democrats had the temerity to announce benefit freezes in the 1994 election campaign, voters handed the party a spectacular defeat, and two pensioners parties entered Parliament for the first time. With the pensioners' lobby flexing its muscles, and the electoral risks of additional public pension benefit cuts abundantly clear, subsequent governments have adopted reforms to improve the financial sustainability of the AOW system and maintain its current structure. Second, reform of occupational pensions is a story of tripartite bargaining, with the government using its authority to grant or withdraw tax deductibility for occupational pension contributions to push the social partners in its preferred policy direction.

II Political system

Constitutional history and nation-building

The Netherlands is a country of provinces and minorities, and the religious cleavage has played a major role in Dutch history and politics. The northern provinces have historically been Protestant and the southern provinces Catholic.[2] The revolutions of 1848 in Europe inspired a Catholic emancipation movement in the Netherlands and Catholics soon began to expand their own organizations, forming unions, employers' organizations, etc. Fundamentalist Calvinists soon followed suit (van Waarden

2002). This religious cleavage is enormously significant for Dutch politics: Catholics and Protestants formed their own "pillars," each with its own political parties, schools, unions, employer organizations, newspapers, and radio stations. The secular working class and middles classes followed suit, also forming their own subcultures.

Institutions of government

The Dutch government (*de regering*) dominates political decision-making in the Netherlands.[3] The Cabinet (*ministerraad*) is headed by the Prime Minister and consists of ministers as well as state secretaries (although only ministers can vote in cabinet meetings). Unlike most other constitutional monarchies, the Dutch Monarch is formally part of the government. The prime minister is weak compared to other parliamentary systems, performing a policy-coordinating role, acting as spokesperson for the government, but without significant agenda-forming powers common in other parliamentary systems. The principle of ministerial responsibility applies, and important ministries have a state secretary in addition to a minister. The state secretary is usually from a different party than the minister, and is usually responsible for a specific policy area within the ministry. For example, it is not uncommon for the Ministry of Education and Research to have a State Secretary for Higher Education and the Ministry of Social Affairs and Employment to have a State Secretary responsible for pensions. Ministers and State Secretaries may not be members of Parliament.

There are two houses of parliament, the Second Chamber (*Tweede Kamer*)[4] with 150 members elected by proportional representation for a four-year term, and the First Chamber (*Eerste Kamer*, Senate) with 75 members chosen by the provincial councils. The First Chamber only has the power to approve or reject bills; it may not initiate or amend them (see the next section). Elections for both chambers take place every four years, but at different times. Since 1983, the entire First Chamber is selected at one time by the provincial councils (shortly after provincial elections).

As noted, the Monarch, currently Queen Beatrix, is not entirely without political power. The Monarch plays an active role in the process of cabinet formation, and her other important duty is to the deliver the Annual Speech from the Throne (*troonrede*). The speech outlines the government's legislative agenda and is part of the opening of the Parliamentary session, or *Prinsjesdag*.

The Council of State (*Raad van State*) is the main advisory organ for the government. The government must consult the Council of State on all proposed legislation. The Court of Audit (*Algemene rekenkamer*) oversees the government's financial activities and those of the public sector. The Supreme Court (*de Hoge Raad*) ensures that the law is applied correctly and uniformly, but it does not have the power of judicial review.

The Netherlands is a centralized state, but the provincial and municipal levels of government play important roles in policy implementation, and they have some autonomy to set their own regulations as long as these do not conflict with national legislation, or with provincial regulations in the case of the municipalities. The twelve

Table 15.1 Political institutions in the Netherlands

Political arenas	Actors	Rules of investiture	Rules of decision-making	Veto potential
Executive	Monarch	Hereditary	Role in cabinet formation; annual royal address	Not a veto point
	Prime Minister (*Ministerpresident*)	Norm of majority government; Queen invites formateur or informateur; no formal vote of investiture; Ministers named by decree signed by Queen and PM; government can dissolve Parliament by Royal Decree; no formal vote of no confidence	Detailed coalition agreement between government parties; cabinet prepares bills (*wetvoorstel*)	
Legislative	Second Chamber (*Tweede Kamer*)	4-year term, 150 members, 12 electoral districts combined into 1 national district for distribution of seats via d'Hondt method	Votes on government bills, may propose or amend legislation; majority rule with quorum of 50% plus 1.	Veto point only if government lacks Second Chamber majority $\Rightarrow$ absorbed veto point
	Senate (*Eerste Kamer*)	75 members appointed by the provincial councils	May approve or reject but not initiate or amend bills	Veto point if government lacks Senate majority $\Rightarrow$ absorbed veto point, or if party discipline is weak
Judicial	Supreme Court (*de Hoge Raad*)	president, six vice-presidents, and 35 justices; lifetime appointment, but mandatory retirement at 70	No judicial review	Not a veto point
Electoral	Referendum		The Interim Referendum Act passed in 2001 allows advisory referendums until 2005	Not a veto point
Territorial units	Provinces (*provincies*)	Direct elections to the 504 municipal councils are held on the same day, every four years.	Policy implementation provinces: environmental management, spatial planning, social work	Not veto points
	municipalities (*gemeenten*)	provincial council elections are held every four years	municipalities: education, housing, water supply	

provinces are responsible for policies such as environmental management, spatial planning and social work. The 478 municipalities are responsible for policies such as education, housing, and water supply. Neither the provinces nor the municipalities has much impact on pension policy.

Electoral system

Proportional representation was introduced for the Second Chamber in 1917. A distinctive feature of proportional representation in the Netherlands is that the entire country forms a single constituency, and the Second Chamber is elected by the d'Hondt system. There is no predetermined threshold that parties must meet in order to gain representation; the de facto threshold is the number of votes divided by the number of seats in the Second Chamber. Depending on voter turnout, a party needs about 60,000 votes to win a seat in the Second Chamber. This corresponds to an electoral threshold of less than 1 percent, about 0.66 percent. Members of the First Chamber, as noted, are indirectly elected in that they are appointed by the 12 provincial governments.

One consequence of this system is the perceived "distance" between elected policians and voters. It is very difficult for geographically-based groups to push their interests because the entire country is a single electoral constituency. A second consequence is the fragmentation of the party system since the electoral threshold is so low (see below).

Legislative process

Ministers and members of both the First and Second Chamber may initiate legislation, but most bills are introduced by cabinet ministers. Amendments to bills is permitted by simple majority, and when the bill has passed the Second Chamber, it moves to the First Chamber for approval/rejection. After approval by the First Chamber, the monarch and a minister sign the bill, and it becomes law. The Second Chamber plays a much more important role in decision-making than the First Chamber, but the role of the First Chamber should not be underestimated. As noted, members of the First Chamber are elected by the provincial councils, so the composition of the First Chamber can be different from the Second Chamber's. Party discipline is not as strong in the First Chamber as in the Second Chamber. Morever, the First Chamber has the right to veto legislation, even if it may not initiate or amend legislation. If a majority in the First Chamber objects to specific aspects of a bill, it can request the government to change the bill by adding new elements (*novelle*) before it approves the bill or it can simply reject a bill outright. Between 1945 and 1995, the First Chamber rejected 37 bills (Andeweg and Irwin 2002: 124). In this sense, bicameralism plays an important role in Dutch policy-making, even if the directly elected Second Chamber is more important.

The legislative cycle typically begins with the government's release of a white paper (*nota*) on a specific policy problem. For pensions, this *nota* can either be a specific one, or pensions can be discussed in the yearly social policy chapter in the budget, the *sociale nota*. The *sociale nota* contains the Minister of Social Affairs' assessment of social welfare problems that need to be addressed as well as proposals for dealing with these. The relevant ministry then draws up a bill, and the cabinet votes, usually by consensus, to present the bill to the Second Chamber.

The formal legislative cycle begins when the cabinet (or a member of the Second Chamber) sends a bill (*wetsvoorstel*) to the Council of State for examination on legal and constitutional grounds. The bill then passes to the monarch, who attaches a royal message, and then the bill, including the Council of State's recommentation and the monarch's signature, is presented to the Second Chamber. An explanatory memorandum (*memorie van toelichting*) by the relevant minister is also part of the bill. The bill is then sent to the relevant standing committee in the Second Chamber. The committee may choose to consult interested parties and/or experts, and then the committee issues a report expressing their views of the bill. The committee report is distributed to all MPs, and the bill is scheduled for the plenary agenda. At this point, MPs may propose amendments. Once the bill has been accepted by a majority, it is sent to the First Chamber for consideration.

Covenants are often used instead of legislation. This is common in the area of occupational pensions where the government provides the regulatory framework and the social partners decide the details of pension schemes. The idea here is that the government and social partners agree to achieve specific goals, and if the social partners fail to do this, the government can intervene with legislation. Since occupational pension contributions are tax deductible, this is a powerful weapon in the hands of the government.

Consociational practices

The Netherlands is known for its strong form of consociationalism, at least until recently. According to Lijphart (1968), leaders of the different pillars tried to prevent political conflict between the pillars by practicing a "politics of accommodation." At least until the 1960s, Dutch politics followed this pattern, with representatives of the pillars working out political compromises at peak level in a context of low conflict.

According to van Waarden (2002), Dutch consociationalism rested on a thorough organization of society; collegial government; the autonomy of pillars; and the goal of consensus. Elites representing the pillars agreed to tolerate each other and to use a depoliticized decision-making process in order to achieve distributional outcomes that were considered to be fair by all the pillars. Distributional issues were often solved technocratically.

Political power is centralized, but power-sharing is institutionalized in several practices: multiparty majority governments and extensive consultation norms. A good example of this consultation is the Autumn and Spring negotiations on social and economic policy between the unions, employers and the government in the

Party family affiliation	Abbreviation	Party name	Ideological orientation/ cleavages	Founding and merger details	Year established
Christian Parties	CDA	Christian Democratic Appeal (*Christen Democratisch Appèl*)	Religious Christian party	Formed from ARP (protestant, Gereformeerd), CHU (protestant, Dutch reformed) and KVP (catholic)	1980
	SGP	Political Reformed Party (*Staatkundig Gereformeerde Partij*)	Calvinist party		1918
	CU	Christian Union (*Christen Unie*)	Calvinist party	Formed from two smaller Calvinist parties	2000
Left parties Social democratic parties	PvdA	Labor Party (*Partij van de Arbeid*)	Secular working-class party	Formed from Sociaal-Democratische Arbeiders Partij (SDAP), the Vrijzinnig-Democratische Bond(VDB) and the Christelijk-Democratische Unie (CDU)	1946
	SP	Socialist Party (*Socialistische Partij*)	Leftist party		1972
Greens	GL	Green Left (*GroenLinks*)	Green party, environmentalist	Formed from several small parties	1989
Liberal	VVD	Liberal Party (*Volkspartij voor Vrijheid en Democratie*)	Conservative, secular liberal party for middle-class	Formed from the LSP (Liberale Staatspartij) and the PvdV (Partij van de Vrijheid)	1948
	D66	Democrats 66	Progressive liberal party		1966
Right wing	LN	Livable Netherlands (*Leefbaar Nederland*)	Populist right-wing party		1999
	LPF	List Pim Fortuyn (*Lijst Pim Fortuyn*)	Populist right-wing party		2002

Fig. 15.1 Party system in the Netherlands

Labor Foundation (STAR; see pp. 733–4). These negotiations usually form the basis for government legislation.

The far-reaching secularization of Dutch society and the weakening of the pillars has resulted in a decline in consociational practices. The 1970s were particularly difficult; tripartite bargaining failed to deliver wage restraint and economic growth. The 1980s saw the re-emergence of Dutch consociationalism with the 1982 Wassenaar Accord. Unions promised wage restraint in return for increased emphasis on boosting employment. The Wassenaar Accord facilitated a period of sustained economic growth and welfare state reform that Visser and Hemerijck (1997) call the "Dutch Miracle" (see also Hemerijck and van Kersbergen 1997 and Cox 2001).

Parties and elections

The religious and class cleavages in the Netherlands, as well as the highly-proportional electoral system, make it difficult for any single party to achieve a majority in Parliament.[5] Five main political parties emerged to represent the members of these social groups: the KVP (Catholic People's Party) represented Catholics; ARP (Anti-Revolutionary Party) and CHU (Christian Historical Union) represented Protestants;[6] the PvdA (Labor) represented the working class; and the VVD (Liberals) represented the middle class. Figure 15.1 shows the main political parties and their ideological stances, as well as how cleavages affect party affiliation. The "pillarization" of Dutch politics and society has not led to political instability; on the contrary, until recently Dutch politics was remarkably stable and based on the ability of political elites to cooperate (Lijphart 1968).

As noted, majority coalition governments are the norm in the Netherlands, and the process of coalition formation is relatively long.[7] It usually takes several months for the coalition parties to work out the details of their governing accord and to form a government. The monarch consults with the political parties and on their advice appoints an *informateur* (mediator) or *formateur* (organizer) if the political situation is sufficiently clear-cut, who conducts the negotiations between the political parties about government formation. The monarch then appoints a *formateur*, usually the leader of the largest potential coalition party and designated Prime Minister, to form a government. According to Andeweg and Irwin (2002), Dutch coalition agreements are among the most detailed and lengthy for countries that usually have coalition governments.

The extreme proportionality of the electoral system and the effects of pillarization produce a fragmented, multiparty system in which no single party is likely to gain a majority. Between 8 and 10 parties are usually represented in Parliament, and 2 or 3 parties typically form the majority coalition government. The Christian Democratic Party (CDA) generally plays the role of "pivot party" as the largest party located in the center of the party system. On the left, the Labor Party (PvdA) is the largest party, and on the right, the Liberal Party (VVD) is largest. Until 1994, majority coalitions including

Table 15.2 Governmental majorities in the Netherlands

Date of change in political configuration	Election date Tweede Kamer	Start of gov.	Head of gov. (party)	Governing parties	Gov. majority (% seats) Tweede Kamer	Gov. electoral Base (% votes) Tweede Kamer	Gov majority (% seats) Eerste Kamer	Institutional veto points	Number of veto players (partisan + institutional)
12.19.1977	05.25.1977	12.19.1977	van Agt I (CDA)	CDA (49), VV (28)	51.3%	49.8%	52.0%	None	2 + 0
09.11.1981	05.26.1981	09.11.1981	van Agt II (CDA)	CDA (48), PVDA (44), D66 (17)	72.7%	70.2%	73.3%	None	3 + 0
05.29.1982		05.29.1982	van Agt III (CDA)	CDA (48), D66 (17)	43.3%	41.9%	42.7%	Eerste Kamer, Tweede Kamer	2 + 2
11.04.1982	09.08.1982	11.04.1982	Lubbers I (CDA)	CDA (45), VV (36)	54.0%	52.5%	53.3%	None	2 + 0
07.14.1986	05.21.1986	07.14.1986	Lubbers II (CDA)	CDA (54), VV (27)	54.0%	52.0%	57.3%	None	2 + 0
11.07.1989	09.06.1989	11.07.1989	Lubbers III (CDA)	CDA (54), PVDA (49)	68.7%	67.2%	69.3%	None	2 + 0
08.22.1994	05.03.1994	08.22.1994	Kok I (PvdA)	PVDA (37), VV (31), D66 (24)	61.3%	59.4%	53.3%	None	3 + 0
08.03.1998	05.06.1998	08.03.1998	Kok II (PvdA)	PVDA (45), VV (38), D66 (14)	65.3%	62.7%	58.7%	None	3 + 0
07.22.2002	05.15.2002	07.22.2002	Balkenende I (CDA)	CDA (43), List PimFortuyn (26), VVD (24)	62.0%	60.4%	52.0%	None	3 + 0
05.27.2003	01.22.2003	05.27.2003	Balkenende II (CDA)	CDA (44), VV (28), D66 (6)	52.0%	50.6%	57.3%	None	3 + 0

Sources: www.eerstekamer.nl; www.tweede-kamer.nl; Timmermans/Andeweg in Müller/Strom p. 371 and Lepzsy in Ismayr p. 339.

the CDA, one of the other two larger parties, and one or more of the smaller parties, have governed.

The 1994 "earthquake" election broke this pattern. The CDA fell from 54 seats to 34 seats (35.3% to 22.2%), a historic low. The PvdA also lost heavily, falling from 49 to 37 seats (31.9% to 24%). The liberal parties D66 and VVD scored spectacular victories; D66 doubled its vote share from 7.9 percent in 1989 to 15.5 percent and the VVD went from 14.6 percent in 1989 to 20 percent in 1994. The most surprising development was the success of two parties representing pensioners: the Elderly Alliance (AOV) entered Parliament with 3.6 percent and 6 seats, and the PU +55 got just under one percent of the vote, enough for one seat (see Hippe, Lucardie and Voerman 1995). From 1994 to 2002, a Labor-led "purple coalition" including the VVD and D66 governed. This new constellation lasted only two electoral cycles; the 2002 election saw the spectacular rise of the populist List Pim Fortuyn (LPF) and the formation of a center-right government led by the CDA and including the VVD and LPF.[8] Conflict within the LPF caused the coalition to collapse in less than a year, and after new elections in 2003 the CDA formed a majority coalition with the VVD and D66. Early elections are scheduled for November 2006 because D66 withdrew from the coalition after conflict with the VVD.

Consensus decision-making practices in the Netherlands have weakened considerably, the party system has become more polarized, and political competition has increased significantly. A depoliticized elite politics no longer characterizes Dutch politics; instead, Parliament has become more adversarial, voters more volatile, and politics more unpredictable. This is not to say that consensus democracy has disappeared; it does suggest, however, that the electoral risks associated with unpopular policies have increased significantly since the heyday of consociationalism.

Interest groups

Dutch society is highly organized, and interest groups are important actors in the policy-making process. Despite the recent secularization of Dutch society, pillarization has left a strong imprint on economic organizations. The Federation of Dutch Trade Unions (FNV) was formed in 1976 after the merger of the Netherlands Trade Union Federation (NVV) and the Netherlands Catholic Trade Union Federation (NKV). Today the FNV has 18 affiliates and about one million members. The Dutch Christian Trade Union (CNV) remains separate, with 16 affiliates and 320,000 members. The Federation of Managerial and Professional Staff Unions (MHP) was formed in 1974 and has two affiliates and 160,000 members. In total, about 30 percent of Dutch wage earners belong to unions. Union influence exceeds this membership number because of the binding extension of collective agreements to entire sectors.[9] Unions negotiate wages and working conditions for about 80–90 percent of all wage earners.

Employers are also well organized. The Confederation of Dutch Industry and Employers (VNO/NCW) formed from the merger of the Federation of Dutch Industry (VNO) and the Dutch Christian Employers' Association (NCW). The VNO/NCW represents about 150 sectoral employers associations and 65,000 member firms.

The legislative process unfolds in the context of strong corporatism. Interest groups are highly organized and have a privileged role in the policy-making process. The tripartite Social Economic Council (SER), established in 1950, plays an important advisory role in the legislative process; in nearly all important matters, the government asks the SER for an advisory opinion before initiating legislation. The SER has 33 members; 11 each from unions, employers and the Crown. The SER's influence has declined in recent years, but its advisory opinions are still important. According to van Waarden (2002: 56), the SER "forces the social partners to engage in scientific discourse to justify their demands."

The bipartite Labor Foundation (STAR), established in 1947, also advises on policy issues, but its function is more of a negotiating forum for organized labor and business. The STAR has been the scene of some important accords in recent decades: the 1982 Wassenaar Accord, the 1993 deal on a "New Course" in wage formation, and the 1997 covenant on the modernization of occupational pensions (discussed later in this chapter).

SER and STAR are the main bargaining institutions and are located at the top of an extensive array of subsidiary organizations and associations. The state facilitated the development of corporatist organizations by permitting cartels or by extending collective agreements (including pensions) to entire sectors. Corporatism stalled in the 1970s but was revived in the 1980s with the Wassenaar Agreement. In recent years corporatist consultation practices have been criticized, especially from Liberal quarters for being too slow to react to economic and social changes and for leading to toothless compromises. Union influence has also been criticized because of declining membership (Visser and Hemerijck 1997).

The occupational pension sector is well-organized, with two peak organizations. The Dutch Association of Industry-wide Pension Funds (VB) was established in 1985 with 88 member funds representing about 75 percent of all participants. The Association of Company Pension Funds (Opf) represents 365 funds with 900,000 participants. Together with the social partners, these two pension fund associations are a formidable lobby, usually favoring the status quo and social partner autonomy in occupational pension issues.

Pillarization and the Dutch penchant for organization means that pensioners are well-organized. Elderly organizations have long been part of the Catholic and Protestant pillars, and even elderly immigrants have their own organization. An umbrella organization, the Association of Elderly Organizations (CSO) has five member organizations: the Dutch Association of Senior Citizens (ANBO), the Dutch Association for Older Migrants (NISBO) the Dutch Confederation of Pensioners' Organizations (NVOG), the Protestant Association of Senior Citizens (PCOB), and the Catholic Elderly Association (KBO).

The density of interest groups representing both occupational and public pension stakeholders means that governments face formidable opposition if they attempt to change the pension status quo. This means that for the AOW pension, politicians face several influential elderly organizations. The fragmentation of these organizations sometimes hinders collective action, but the sheer number of organized elderly also provides a strong constraint on public pension retrenchment. In the area of occupational pensions governments face a well-organized, effective pension lobby led by the social partners and the pension fund organizations.

III Pension system

Historical overview[10]

The early involvement of the state in public pension provision, and the regulation and promotion of occupational pensions are perhaps the most important features of pension policy development in the Netherlands, and pillarization has substantially influenced both processes. The adoption of a universal basic scheme in 1956 represented the victory of Labor over conservative confessional groups who favored corporatist (read: pillarized) implementation, while the occupational system emerged in tandem with corporatist wage bargaining practices.

The first pension law was adopted in 1913 and provided benefits only to workers and their families. The Labor Party (PvdA) and Liberals (VVD) advocated universal coverage, but the influence of the confessional parties favoring employment-related benefits was too strong. Confessional parties and interest groups, including unions, wanted to limit the role of the state in pension provision so they successfully pushed for pensions to be administered by industrial insurance boards (corporatist bodies with representatives of employers and unions) and the National Insurance Bank (NIB). In keeping with their general distrust of state interference in the private sphere, confessional groups preferred public tasks to be carried out by private bodies. This type of administrative arrangement would set a strong precedent for all subsequent social welfare legislation.

World War II marked a turning point in Dutch welfare state development, not least in the area of pensions. The Dutch government in exile set up a commission to plan for future reforms, headed by the Social Democrat, A. van Rijn. Mindful of the earlier rejection of universal public pensions, the commission recommended universal pension insurance. The distinction between universal state pensions à la Beveridge and the Dutch model of universal pension insurance is important: reformers wanted universal, equal benefits for all, but these would be "earned" via residence and the payment of "premiums" by those considered most capable of financing the system, wage earners. This financing structure was also meant to promote solidarity between wage earners and non-wage earners. The contribution ceiling was set fairly low, about equal to average earnings, so as not to discourage the development of occupational pensions. Employer contributions were never seriously considered.

In 1946, the PvdA Minister of Social Affairs managed to convince the Catholic Party to support an Emergency Pensions Act until a permanent system could be negotiated. The Emergency Act provided benefits to all persons over 65, including those with occupational pensions which the 1919 legislation had excluded. Despite the cooperation of the Catholic Party, corporatist interests were divided, especially on the issue of administration. However, the Emergency Act set in motion a process in which all citizens were entitled to a public pension, and the Act established a new administrative structure that left little room for the corporatist industrial insurance boards favored by conservative confessional groups.

Disagreement about administration led to a ten-year policy stalemate. Confessional groups opposed the centralized bureaucratic structure created for the emergency pensions and wanted to return to corporatist administration in the permanent legislation. The PvdA-controlled Ministry of Social Affairs managed to get Liberals and moderate Catholics to support the new legislation (with state administration), and the reform was adopted by Parliament in 1956. The new law, the AOW (*Algemene Ouderdoms Wet*) went into effect on January 1, 1957.

Occupational pensions also have a long history. The first occupational pension scheme covered railroad workers and was established in the mid-1800s. Employers started pension schemes to reward employees for loyal service, but growth was slow. At the start of World War II there were only a few dozen, but by 1938 there were more than 750 schemes with more than 50 members each. Regulation began fairly early with the first legislation in 1908. Among the first items subject to regulation was the requirement that assets be held outside the firm and not be included in the calculation of company assets. In addition, workers were represented on the administrative boards. The first sectoral pension fund was established in 1917, and 1937 legislation introduced the option for the Minister of Social Affairs to require participation in sectoral pension schemes (Tulfer 1997: 12–16).

Although occupational pensions are organized as part of collective wage bargaining, several features promote social solidarity. Coverage is nearly universal; unions and employers are equally represented on pension fund governing boards; and risks are pooled within entire sectors (Clark 2003: ch. 6). Occupational pensions are viewed as the collective responsibility of unions and employers.

The pillarization of Dutch society has significantly influenced the shape and development of occupational pensions. Confessional groups opposed statist arrangements because they wanted to retain confessional influence on social policies. The introduction of a public occupational pension system has never been seriously considered in the Netherlands. First, funded occupational pensions have a long history, and occupational pensions are explicitly seen as an instrument of wage policy. Occupational pensions are negotiated as part of wage contracts so transferring them to the public sector would deprive unions and employers of important bargaining tools. The state provides a regulatory framework for occupational pensions, but the social partners have considerable freedom to negotiate the details of occupational pensions, and they jealously guard this prerogative. Second, the initially uneven coverage of occupational pensions meant that "lock-in" effects generated a powerful coalition in favor of extending the existing system to new groups rather than transforming it into one public scheme. The unions and employers that negotiated the first occupational schemes did not want to relinquish this tool of wage bargaining, so workers without occupational pension coverage had every incentive to try to achieve coverage through collective bargaining. As the popularity of occupational pensions increased, the state stepped in to provide incentives for extending coverage to new groups (see below).

Description of the current pension system

The Dutch pension system is a multi-pillar system combining public flat-rate pensions (AOW) for all residents over 65, and publicly regulated occupational pensions provide earnings-related benefits to more than 90 percent of wage earners. Until recently, the Dutch system represented a strong case of "the male breadwinner model" because the pension system provided benefits to the (usually male) breadwinner as the head of the household. When the AOW was introduced, benefits were fairly low, but have been progressively increased. Since 1970 the AOW has been defined as 70 percent of the net minimum wage. Thus it serves both as a basic minimum during retirement and as the floor above which supplementary pensions are paid.

Coverage

In 2004, AOW spending was almost 5 percent of GDP and provided benefits to 2.4 million pensioners, or about 13 percent of the population. All Dutch residents accrue AOW pension rights for each year they live in the Netherlands between the age of 15 and 65. Fifty years is required for a full pension.

Administration

The Social Insurance Bank (SVB) administers the AOW, as well as other social benefits such as survivor pensions and child allowances.

Financing

The AOW is financed by wage-earner contributions (17.9% of income in 2005 up to a ceiling of €30,357). AOW is constructed as a pay-as-you-go (PAYG) system, and until recently financing was designed to be self-regulating in that the level of pension contribution is set every year so that revenues cover expenditures. Since the late 1990s, there is an upper limit on contributions (18.25%) and financing shortfalls are financed from general revenues. The recently established AOW Reserve Fund will help to finance benefits starting in 2020 out of its forecast €126 billion reserves. Reserves are financed by annual government deposits.

Benefits

Fifty years of residence are required for a full pension.[11] In January 2005, the net pension benefit for a single person was 70 percent of the net minimum wage, or €866.63 per month including vacation supplements (gross is €930.17 plus €46.20

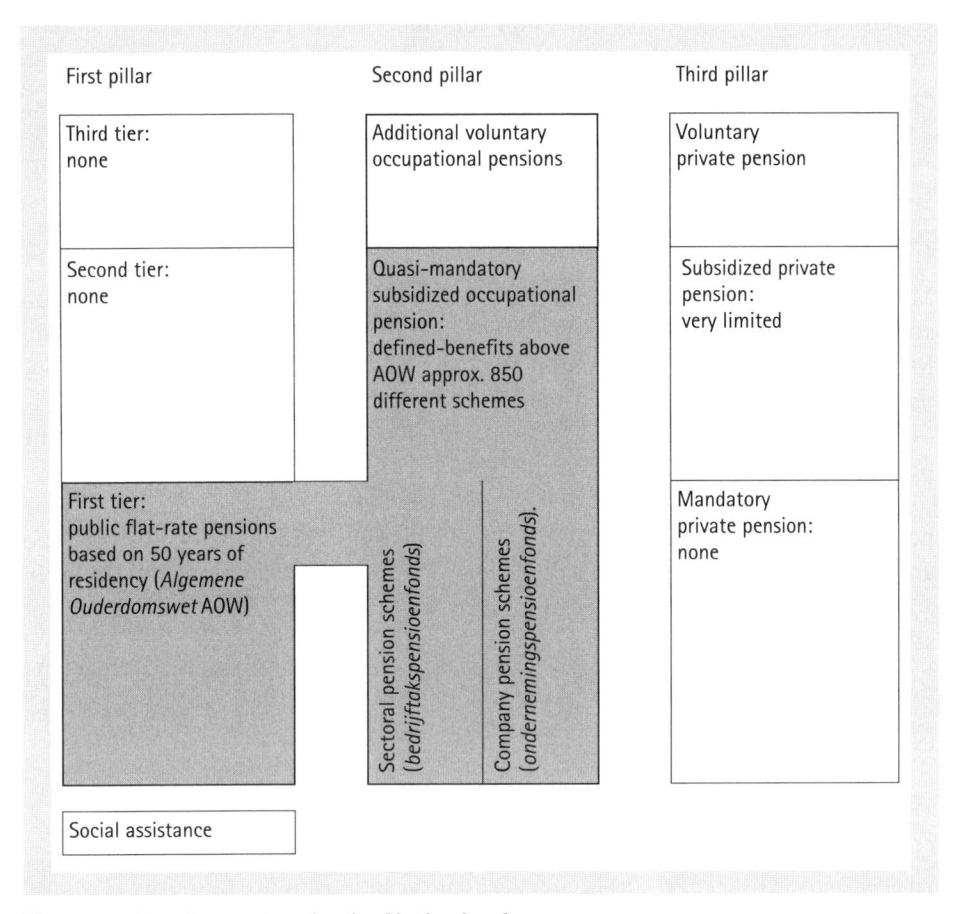

Fig. 15.2 Pension system in the Netherlands

First pillar	Second pillar	Third pillar
Third tier: none	Additional voluntary occupational pensions	Voluntary private pension
Second tier: none	Quasi-mandatory subsidized occupational pension: defined-benefits above AOW approx. 850 different schemes	Subsidized private pension: very limited
First tier: public flat-rate pensions based on 50 years of residency (*Algemene Ouderdomswet* AOW)	Sectoral pension schemes (*bedrijftakspensioenfonds*) / Company pension schemes (*ondernemingspensioenfonds*)	Mandatory private pension: none
Social assistance		

vacation payment). This is about 55 percent of average wages. For married pensioners, the net pension is 50 percent of the net minimum wage, or €608.03 including vacation payment (gross is €631.81 plus €30.53 vacation payment) for each spouse. The pension amount is indexed to "net minimum wages."[12] The Indexing Conditions Suspension Act (WKA) permits Parliament to suspend indexation if the ratio of inactive to active persons of employable age is below 82.6:100. Since 1996, the AOW (and other social insurance schemes) has been fully indexed.

Occupational pensions

Occupational pensions have a long history in the Netherlands, and in the last several decades they have grown significantly. The state provides the regulatory framework and generous tax deductions: in 2003 the size of the deduction for pension and annuity contributions was €9.6 billion or 2.1 percent of GDP (Caminada and

Goudswaard 2004). Since 1999, pension contributions are tax deductible to a maximum of 2 percent accrual rate per year for a final pay scheme and 2.25 percent for an average pay scheme (lowered to 1.75% in 2003).

There are two types of pension scheme: sectoral pension schemes (*bedrijftakspensioenfonds*) and company pension schemes (*ondernemingspensioenfonds*). There are currently about 850 different pension schemes.

Coverage

More than 90 percent of wage earners are covered by an occupational pension scheme (SER 2001). Supplementary pensions are quasi-mandatory. The law on Mandatory Participation in Sectoral Pension Funds (*Wet betreffende de verplichte deelneming in een bedrijfspensioenfonds, Bpf*) dates from 1949 and permits the Ministry of Social Affairs to require an entire sector to participate in the same pension fund if a formal request is made.

In 2005, there are 829 different pension funds, including industry-wide pension schemes, company pension schemes, pension funds for the self-employed and other schemes, such as the ABP system covering civil servants (DNB 2005). In addition to normal retirement benefits, most workers have access to early retirement schemes negotiated in the same way as supplementary pensions. The so-called "VUT" schemes, or Pre-Retirement schemes were introduced in the early 1980s. At first, these were designed primarily for persons aged 63 or 64 but have since been expanded to include persons aged 60 and above.

Administration

Occupational pensions are regulated by the state in the Pension Savings Act (*Pensioen en Sparfondsen Wet, PSF*). Until 2004, the Pension and Insurance Authority (*Pensioen en Verzekeringskamer, PVK*) was the supervisory body charged with oversight. In 2004, the PVK merged with the Dutch Central Bank and is now called the Pension Chamber (*Pensioenkamer*). Because the PSW provides only the institutional framework for second tier pensions, the social partners have considerable freedom to negotiate the details of their pension arrangements, and they are negotiated as part of collective wage agreements (CAOs).

The PSW regulates issues such as the coverage ratio of pension funds, measures to correct deficits, investment rules, pension portability, representation on administrative boards, and so forth. One distinctive feature of the Dutch occupational pension sector is the requirement that funds be held outside of pension schemes and may not be considered company assets.

Financing

Occupational pension contributions are set in collective wage bargaining negotiations, and are typically shared between employers and wage-earners with employers usually paying a higher share. In 1998, employers paid 6.7 percent of their wage bill into second-pillar schemes, while employees paid 2.3 percent of their wages (Ministry of Social Affairs and Employment 2000: 6). Today pension contributions are much higher. Occupational pension contributions are paid only on the salary above the level of the AOW. This accounting construction is called the "franchise."

Benefits

Pension schemes are overwhelmingly defined-benefit (DB), and until recently most schemes used a final salary benefit formula in which a benefit equal to 70 percent of the final wage (including the AOW) could be accumulated over 35 (or more) years, with a limit of 100 percent of the final wage (Caminada and Goudswaard 2004: 4). In 1998, 66.5 percent of active participants (current workers covered by pension schemes) participated in final pay schemes; by 2005 the number had fallen to 10.5% (*Pensioenkamer* 2005). More than 90 percent are still covered by DB schemes.

The majority of pensioners do not achieve the target of 70 percent of the final wage including the AOW, for several reasons. First, supplementary pension benefits are tightly linked with AOW benefits through the use of a "franchise" that represents the level of the AOW benefit. Occupational pension rights accrue only on the amount above the franchise. Until recently the franchise was usually equal to the AOW couple benefit, which for obvious reasons is too high for both singles and dual-earner couples. Since many pension schemes have been slow to lower the franchise, wage earners (especially dual earners and singles) face a gap in coverage. Second, many wage earners do not work the number of years required for a full pension (usually 35 or 40). Getting the social partners to use an individualized franchise has been one of the top priorities of Dutch governments since the late 1980s. In 1998 30.4 percent of participants were covered by a franchise based on the couple benefit, and this had fallen to 22.3 percent by 2005. About 60 percent of active participants are now covered by some sort of fixed franchise (DNB 2005).

The indexation of accrued rights and benefits is not legally required, and the various schemes use different rules. Until recently, most pensions were indexed to wages, but most pension funds decided to cancel indexation in 2002 and 2003 in the wake of heavy stock market losses. More than 80 percent of schemes have indexing conditional on pension fund performance, and if indexing is awarded, about 60 percent use some form of contract wages (sectoral or economy-wide), about 20 percent use inflation, and 20 percent use some other formula (DNB 2005).

IV POLITICS OF PENSION REFORM SINCE 1980

Overview

Although the overall structure of both public and occupational pensions has remained fairly stable, both systems have undergone substantial changes since the

Table 15.3 Overview of proposed and enacted pension reforms in the Netherlands

Year	Name of reform	Reform process (chronology)	Reform measures
1985	Cost containment of the AOW in the 1980s	• Indexing of AOW pensions suspended in 1983–1988 as part of annual budget consolidation measures	
1985	Adapting to European Equal Treatment Law	• 1979 EC issued directive on equal treatment in statutory social security. Transposition deadline was December 23, 1984 • July 1981 Government asked the Social Economic Council (SER) for an advisory opinion on how to legislate changes in the AOW to conform to European law. The SER agreed with the cabinet that legislative changes must not increase expenditures • late 1983: cabinet introduced its draft legislation • February 1985 the CDA and PvdA cooperated on an amendment to the bill • March 1, 1985 the Second Chamber adopted the CDA-PvdA version of the bill • Senate threatens to veto because of provisions concerning younger spouses, but finally passes the bill with 38 to 30 votes in the Senate	• AOW benefit for spouses individualized • supplement available to AOW pensioners with spouse younger than 65
1987	Enhancing portability of occupational pensions	• 1987 Labor Foundation (STAR) urged legislation to guarantee portability of occupational pensions	• improvement of portability and protection of accumulated pension rights in occupational pensions • introduction of the SDS (Stichting Dienstverlening Samenwerkingsverband) and other similar organizations for coordinating the transfer of pension reserves for employees between pension schemes
1992	Wet koppeling met afwijkingsmogelijkheid (WKA; Conditional Indexation Act)		• indexation made conditional on moderate wage increases and increased labor market participation; indexing suspended 1993, 1994, and 1995

1994	Improving Coverage of Supplementary Pensions	• 1991 cabinet issued green paper on supplementary pensions • May 1993 cabinet introduced draft legislation. • late 1993 the first bill passed the second chamber • February 1994 first bill passed the Senate	• no indexation if there are more than 82 inactive for every 100 active • change in regulatory framework for supplementary pensions (PSF), introduction of the right to transfer pension rights • inclusion of part-time workers in pension schemes
1997	AOW Reserve Fund	• September 1996 cabinet releases green paper "Working for Security" ("Werken aan zekerheid") • September 1996 budget bill providing a grant to AOW from general revenues • AOW Savings Fund was proposed in the Second Chamber at the initiative of the PvdA	• establishment of AOW Reserve Fund to help finance future pensions • upper limit on the AOW contribution of 16.5% (later 18.25%).
2002–2004	Premium increases and shift to average salary benefit formulae in occupational pensions	• September 1996 green paper "Working for Security" ("Werken aan zekerheid") proposes switch from final salary to average salary formulae in occupational pensions • December 1997 the social partners concluded a covenant for occupational pensions, agreeing to control costs; introduce mobility-enhancing measures: reduce the breadwinner bias; and increase coverage • 2000/2001 Stock market downturn • 2002 ABP (civil servant pension fund) and other pension funds raised premiums substantially and announced a switch from final salary benefit formula to average career earnings formula starting in 2004.	
2004–present	Legislative revision of the PSF (process is not yet complete)	• November 2004 a draft of the bill was sent to stakeholders for comment • legislative adoption expected in 2006	• increase transparency in pension fund governance • clarify roles of the social partners in pension fund governance • modernize rules for pension fund solvency

1980s in terms of the basis of entitlement, the structure of benefits, and the structure of financing (cf. Haverland 2001; van Riel, Hemerijck, and Visser 2003). First, both systems have been individualized; the breadwinner basis of the AOW was changed to individual entitlement in 1985, whereas occupational pensions have been slower to change. In both cases, EU law was a major force driving change. Second, the value of the AOW has decreased in real terms: benefit indexing was suspended for several years, and these cuts have not been fully restored. Third, general revenues now finance a larger share of AOW costs, and a reserve fund has been established to help cover future expenditures. Fourth, there is a massive shift from final salary to average salary benefit formulae in occupational pensions, and coverage has improved for part-time workers and other atypical workers.

Cost containment of the AOW in the 1980s

AOW costs and the premiums that finance them have increased steadily since 1957. The contribution rate has increased from 6.75 percent of income (up to a ceiling) in 1957 to 17.9 percent in 2001. By the early 1980s, policy-makers began to raise concerns about the future sustainability of the system. When the AOW was introduced in 1957 with a contribution rate of 6.75 percent, the legislation forecast a premium for 1981 of 8 percent. By 1983, however, the contribution had been raised to 12.0 percent, prompting concerns about future premium increases beyond levels envisioned by policy-makers (van den Bosch, van Eekelen, and Petersen 1983). At the time, the number of AOW recipients was predicted to double by 2030, prompting arguments that AOW premiums would have to increase to 23 percent in 2030 or benefits would have to be reduced by 50 percent.

These statistics alarmed policy-makers, especially in the context of sluggish economic growth and rising employment. Thus by the early 1980s the debate about the future sustainability of the AOW had begun. One of the government's responses was to establish a commission to investigate the financial sustainability of the AOW. In 1986, the Commission on the Financing of Old Age Provision was established, led by Willem Drees. The "Drees Commission" produced a report with less dramatic conclusions than other expert studies, concluding that the current system was financially sustainable and predicted increases in premiums to 15–17.5 percent of qualifying income by 2030 (*Commissiee Financiering Oudedagsvoorziening* 1987). The Commission offered several proposals:

- introduce contributions for pensioners;
- increase or abolish the contribution ceiling;
- increase the retirement age; and/or
- decrease the benefit for unmarried pensioners to 50 percent of the minimum wage.

FNV and CNV opposed the latter, and the FNV opposed raising the retirement age. The elderly organization ANBO with 170,000 members joined the chorus of opposing voices (*Financiële Dagblad,* October 3 and 6, 1987).

Other studies were less optimistic; for example, one expert study predicted that the combined cost of AOW premiums and supplementary pension premiums would reach 35 percent of gross wages by 2030 (see Kune 1988; C. Petersen 1988: 264–6). A study by the Central Bank concluded that contributions would have to rise to 20 percent by 2025 if policy did not change (*Financiële Dagblad*, February 27, 1986). The Drees Commission report was the first step in a long debate about how to deal with the demographic and financial challenges faced by the AOW. In the short term, there were periodic increases in the contribution rate in order to cover expenditures, but there were no changes in the structure of the AOW scheme.

At the same time that experts began to debate the future financial sustainability of the AOW, central government budget constraints provided the rationale for governments to suspend AOW indexing. Nominal benefits stayed the same, but lost some of their real value and their value in relation to wage growth. What began in 1980 as an ad hoc measure to control costs, and to prevent rapidly rising wages from causing substantial social insurance benefit increases, gradually turned into a more or less permanent feature of the annual budget negotiations.

By the mid-1980s, the elderly had begun to make their voices heard, and they sharply criticized the suspension of AOW indexing. The elderly organization Cosbo was particularly vocal, emphasizing that the AOW had lost 13 percent of its value between 1980 and 1984 (*Financiële Dagblad*, May 22, 1986). The freezing of benefits in the 1980s set the stage for additional cost-cutting measures in the early 1990s and a showdown between the electorate, especially the organized elderly, and the government about the future of the AOW. This issue is addressed later in the chapter.

Supplementary pensions

Portability

The main reform concerning supplementary pensions in the 1980s concerned portability and the protection of accumulated pension rights. This reform followed the corporatist consensus decision-making process typical in the area of occupational pensions. In 1987, the Labor Foundation (STAR) urged the introduction of legislation to guarantee portability by allowing wage earners who changed jobs to transfer pension assets to the pension scheme of their new employer. Regulations forbid the cashing out of pension assets, and when workers changed jobs they usually could not take their pensions with them. The pension rights from their previous employment remained with the pension scheme of the previous employer and the worker began to accumulate new pension rights in the new place of employment. Inflation, however, was always a threat that could erode the value of accumulated pension rights. This was no problem for wage earners with final salary pensions, but it could have negative consequences for those whose pension rights were not indexed yearly to wage increases and/or inflation.

When the indexing of pension rights was introduced, this applied only to the pension rights of active participants, not those who still had pension rights in one scheme but had changed employers and now participated in another scheme. For workers who changed employers, indexing usually stopped when employment ended. This often resulted in significant losses in pension rights relative to active participants.

The STAR's call for portability came after more than a decade of discussion about how to deal with these challenges. Since 1969, the STAR sought to remedy the situation by introducing mandatory pensions for all employees, but this effort failed. By 1985, the STAR recommended that its members make specific changes to protect pension rights of workers who changed jobs or had career interruptions (Nouwen 1987). The STAR promised to evaluate the results of these recommendations in three years.

To facilitate the portability of pension reserves, the SDS (*Stichting Dienstverlening Samenwerkingsverband*) was set up in 1986, and other similar organizations soon afterwards. These organization coordinated the transfer of pension reserves for employees between pension schemes with similar benefit regulations.

The legislation proposed to deal with these problems was largely in line with the SER's advisory opinion and the STAR's opinion, but it stopped short of guaranteeing full portability (TK 19 638). This was only an interim solution, in anticipation of more comprehensive changes in the PSW. In 1987, some stronger form of *obligatorium* for supplementary pensions was on the agenda again as part of the overhaul of the PSW. In November 1987, State Secretary De Graaf (Liberal Party) asked the SER for an opinion concerning the "pension problematic" including whether the state should play a larger role in mandating supplementary pensions. The background to this move was the previously discussed problem of pension portability and the protection of pension rights, as well as gaps in pension coverage. Among the proposals the SER was asked to consider were: improving the rights of "sleepers" (non-active participants in pension schemes); and mandating and/or improving pension scheme participation to sectors and employers not covered by collective agreements, including atypical workers (as discussed in later sections).

The end of the 1980s also saw the first of the so-called "pension surveys" of the Netherlands. This was the first comprehensive attempt to gather data on all of the supplementary pension schemes in the Netherlands, the number of workers covered by which types of schemes, the structure of financing, and so on. The 1983 law establishing the Pension Chamber requires periodic evaluations of the extent and type of supplementary coverage in order to provide the factual basis for policy-making in this area. The first survey, published in 1987, found that 20 percent of workers over the age of 25 had no supplementary pension coverage. So the 80 percent coverage rate was higher than anticipated (*Pensioenskamer* 1988).

Adapting to European equal treatment law

EU law provided the impetus for the only significant reform of the AOW system in the 1980s, prompting substantial modifications in the structure of AOW benefit entitlement and financing. Since its establishment in 1957, the AOW was based on the breadwinner principle. Non-working spouses (overwhelmingly women) did not receive an individual benefit; instead, the breadwinner received a benefit intended for both spouses. Unmarried breadwinners over 65 did receive an individual benefit. Similarly, the structure of AOW financing was based on the breadwinner principle; only the breadwinner paid contributions, even if the spouse was employed. These provisions directly conflicted with European law concerning equal treatment. Starting in 1979, all Dutch social security schemes were adjusted to the EC equal treatment directive.[13] For the AOW system, this required the modification of existing rules excluding dependent spouses from individual eligibility.

Before the EU directive, there was little political pressure to modify the AOW system in order to provide dependent spouses with individual benefits. Because the AOW system provided married breadwinners with a benefit that "included" a benefit for the dependent spouse, the system was not perceived by most to be unfair. However, when the EU issued its directive, Dutch policy-makers changed the existing rules without protest, but the process took five years. Unlike other parts of the social insurance system that violated EU equality law (such as unemployment insurance), modifications to the AOW system to conform to EU rules did not require additional AOW pension spending and did not result in *direct* benefit cuts. However, some pensioners experienced a decline in income because of the indirect effects of the changes.

The basic solution that the Lubbers I government (CDA and VVD) settled on was to simply divide the AOW benefit for spouses in half and pay an individual benefit to both spouses. For married couples over 65, the financial effect was neutral, and the state was not required to spend additional money on pension benefits. However, the issue of how to treat a situation in which one spouse received an AOW benefit, and the other was younger than 65, raised several difficulties.

The EC gave member states until December 23, 1984 to comply with the directive. In July 1981, the State Secretary for Social Affairs and Employment asked the Social Economic Council (SER) for an advisory opinion on how to legislate changes in the AOW to conform to European law. The Cabinet had already expressed its preference for a new AOW benefit structure that gave single pensioners 70 percent of the current benefit for married pensioners and that divided the current benefit level in two for married pensioners. For married pensioners with a spouse younger than 65, a supplement would be awarded. In its advisory opinion, the SER largely agreed with the Cabinet and emphasized that legislative changes should not increase expenditures, and the function of AOW as a universal basic pension providing a minimum income in old age should be retained (SER 1984).

The Cabinet introduced its draft legislation in late 1983 (TK 18 515). There was substantial agreement on the main provisions of the legislation (dividing the AOW benefit in two for couples, etc.) but the issue of AOW pensioners with a spouse younger than 65 led to difficult negotiations in Parliament. Under the existing rules, an AOW pensioner received a full couple's pension even if the spouse was younger than 65. The difficult issue was how to treat spouses younger than 65, who also had earned income. If the younger spouse was not the breadwinner, then s/he paid no AOW premiums and her/his husband/wife received the full AOW couple's pension. The original bill provided a 50 percent income-dependent supplement for AOW pensioners supporting a spouse younger than 65. After opposition, the income test was suspended for three years (*Financiële Dagblad*, January 19, 1985).

The source of most opposition was that the supplement would violate the insurance principle. For example, this was the argument used by the NCW (Christian Employers' Organization). The VVD (one of the government parties) opposed income testing of the supplement for similar reasons, suggesting instead to award the full AOW pension (equal to the amount for a couple) to those with younger spouses, regardless of the spouse's income. The PvdA also had some reservations about the bill because it discouraged employment for the younger spouse. As a short-term solution the PvdA proposed a longer transition period (five years) during which AOW pensioners with spouses under 65 would receive the full couple's benefit (*Financiële Dagblad*, January 31, 1985).

In February, the CDA and PvdA cooperated on an amendment to the bill to deal with these issues, mainly by increasing the amount of income of the younger spouse not subject to the income test. The VVD responded with an amendment to exempt AOW spouses younger than 57 from the income test, but this attempt failed (*Financiële Dagblad*, February 1, 5, and 7, 1985). On March 1, the Second Chamber adopted the CDA-PvdA version of the bill.[14]

The Senate nearly derailed the Second Chamber's compromise. By now, minorities in both the CDA and PvdA fractions in the Senate opposed the legislation because of the negative financial effects for AOW households with a spouse younger than 65 (*Financiële Dagblad*, March 21, 1985). As a result of the final compromise, the married AOW pensioner receives 70 percent of the old couple benefit and a 30 percent supplement for the younger partner. Again the NCW criticized the "social assistance" character of the AOW supplement.[15] The bill was passed with 38 to 30 votes in the Senate.

This episode demonstrates the significance of the First Chamber in Dutch politics, since it very nearly blocked the compromise worked out in the Second Chamber. As noted at the beginning of this chapter, party discipline in the First Chamber is not as strong as in the Second, since senators are not full-time politicians and view themselves as guardians of the constitution and other important principles. Enough senators deemed the AOW's "insurance" principle important enough to pressure the Second Chamber to make last-minute changes in the legislation.

The EU and occupational pensions

EU legislation in the field of equal treatment also had substantial influence on the structure of occupational pensions. Until the early 1990s, many occupational pension schemes excluded married women from participation. Again, this was a legacy of the "male breadwinner" principles on which the Dutch pension systems were constructed. As a result, occupational pension schemes have had to modify their eligibility rules to comply with recent interpretations of EU law.

Until the 1980s/1990s, discrimination against women was prevalent in second tier pension schemes. The most common types of discrimination were different participation ages for men and women, the exclusion of married women, and the exclusion of part-time workers. The Barber[16] decision by the ECJ in 1990 would have cost the second-tier pension schemes in the Netherlands an estimated NLG 400 billion if pension rights were to be made retroactive for women who had previously been excluded from occupational pension schemes (Kraamwinkel 1995). Because of the substantial costs involved, the Dutch government (pushed by the pension funds and employers) lobbied successfully in Brussels (along with the UK) for a protocol to the Treaty of Amsterdam that would limit the retroactivity of the Barber decision. In other words, the new interpretation of EU law would only take effect in 1990.

Kraamwinkel (1995) argues that these changes in the Dutch pension system were driven largely by legal actors, especially the ECJ. Domestic actors had little to do with pushing these changes, although they did exert substantial impact on the way that the rulings were implemented. There has been some reparation of pension rights for previously excluded women, but as Kraamwinkel notes, because supplementary pensions are built up over 40 years, it will take at least until 2035 before the first Dutch woman is entitled to a full pension.

Supplementary pensions: improving coverage

The early 1990s saw the first of several attempts to adjust supplementary pensions to changing demographic and labor market trends. Corporatist bargaining "in the shadow of hierarchy" (van Riel et al. 2003) has marked this process. As noted, the government took the initiative in 1987 by asking the SER to investigate the "pension problematic," including gaps in coverage and portability. The SER issued its advisory report in 1990 (SER 1990) focusing on the need for further modernization, expansion of coverage, and cost control. This recommendation confirmed the responsibility of the social partners for supplementary pension provision, with the government playing a supervisory/regulatory role.

Now it was the Cabinet's turn, and it duly issued a green paper (TK 22 167) on supplementary pensions in 1991, outlining its view of how the supplementary pension scheme should develop in the following decades. The Cabinet confirmed the central role and responsibility of the social partners in the area of supplementary pensions and ruled out compulsory pension coverage for employees without pension provision. More controversially, the cabinet expressed its preference for a switch from final salary benefit formulae to average salary formulae, both for reasons of cost containment and in order to accommodate atypical employment biographies.[17] To achieve these goals, the Cabinet announced it would negotiate with the STAR to secure voluntary compliance. The Cabinet also agreed with the SER's view of how to deal with gaps in pension coverage caused by the lack of portability:

the introduction of a legal right to transfer pension reserves when changing employers. In addition, the Cabinet pushed for equal rights for unmarried couples (for occupational survivor pensions) and improved coverage for part-time workers. The use of the AOW franchise meant that many part-time workers did not earn enough to qualify for occupational pension coverage. The Cabinet also emphasized that the franchise was a problem because it resulted in gaps in coverage.

The 1991 Green Paper included a call for negotiations with the social partners in the STAR, and these began in October 1991. The social partners agreed on most issues, except the switch to average earnings schemes. This line of conflict would turn out to be the main source of conflict between the government and social partners, and it would not be settled until the stock market downturn in 2001/2002 (see pp. 746–8).

By 1993, the negotiations between the Cabinet and social partners began to produce results. In May 1993, the Cabinet presented its draft legislation to change the regulatory framework for supplementary pensions (PSF), in particular the introduction of the right to transfer pension rights. This draft was the first of several based on the SER and STAR opinions as well as the Cabinet's Green Paper. The bill would also make it illegal to exclude part-time workers from pension schemes. It was hoped that the next round of legislation would include increased obligations for pension schemes to provide information to their members and introduce additional measures concerning modernization and flexibilization (TK 23 123). The first bill passed the Second Chamber easily in late 1993 and the Senate in February 1994.

Several points of disagreement remained between the social partners and the Cabinet, however, particularly the issue of cost containment. The government and social partners disagreed fundamentally about the necessity of switching to an average-pay-benefit formulae, and the pension funds were still slow to move from an AOW franchise based on the couple benefit to an individualized franchise. I shall return to these issues later in this chapter.

AOW cost-containment in the 1990s

The 1990s saw another round of expert reports about the future financial sustainability of the AOW system, as well as the adoption of several important changes. In 1991, there were 18.7 persons over the age of 65 for every 100 persons between the ages 15 and 64. In 2035, the number of persons over 65 (per 100 of working age) was forecast to rise to between 32.6 and 42.9 (WRR 1992: 25). The, by now, common practice of freezing AOW pension benefits had substantial repercussions on national politics, and the CDA's promise to continue the practice led to its worst election defeat ever.

By the end of the 1980s, there was significant political support for restoring wage indexation to the AOW and other social benefits. In the 1989 election campaign, the indexing of the AOW and other social benefits was a major issue. In March 1989, the VVD published its election manifesto, including more money for AOW pensioners. By now, a majority in the Second Chamber favored a return to full indexing to contract wages. The PvdA, for example, announced it advocated full indexing except in emergency situations. As discussed, indexing was suspended or reduced from 1983–1988, and 1990 saw a temporary return to full indexation.

The 1989 election resulted in moderate losses for the Liberals (VVD) and Labor (PvdA), with the CDA holding steady, and the two small parties, Green Left and D66 picking up significant gains.[18] The CDA turned to the PvdA to form the government instead of the VVD, and the new Cabinet quickly adopted additional welfare state reform measures, including a freeze on AOW benefits. The Cabinet made indexation conditional on moderate wage increases and increased labor market participation. This informal rule was later transformed into legislation with the Law on Conditional Indexation in 1992 (WKA). The WKA stipulates that if there are more than 82 inactive for every 100 active persons, there will be no indexation. Indexing was suspended in 1993, 1994, and 1995 (Alber 1998, 28; Visser and Hemerijck 1997).

With the AOW in what seemed like a permanently frozen condition, the influential WRR released a report in 1992 that added to the voices calling for more fundamental AOW reform. The report, *Ouderen voor ouderen*, forecast a rapid increase in the number of people over 65 and urged the government to take steps immediately, even though the effects would not be felt for several decades. The WRR proposed limiting early retirement, as well as requiring well-off pensioners to pay AOW contributions (WRR 1992).

Elderly organizations criticized the report's findings, especially given the context of AOW freezes. The AOW had not been fully indexed to contract wages since 1980 and between 1980 and 1992 had lost 10 percent of its value (*Financiële Dagblad*, June 4, 1993). The CSO, an elderly organization, publicly called for the restoration of indexing. For retirees relying only on the AOW, the suspension of indexing led to relative income loss, but the cancellation of indexing also had repercussions for occupational pensions. Since occupational pensions are linked to AOW benefits, the pension schemes have to compensate for the decline in the AOW. This was generally not a problem for the pension funds since the 1980s were advantageous: the real rate of return was higher than real wage increases and the growing number of participants meant that pension funds had extra cash that could be used to improve benefits and make up for lower AOW benefits. However, the pension funds and their spokespeople began to join the elderly in calling for a return to full AOW indexing.

By the early 1990s, the AOW contribution rate had risen to 14.30 percent of qualifying wages, even in the context of declining real benefits.[19] Several influential actors now joined the WRR's call for affluent pensioners to pay AOW contributions. Retirees paid a lower income tax rate, even on their occupational pension income.[20] Not only did the Central Planning Bureau (an influential independent government agency) support the WRR, but the SER, NCW, and FNV also expressed their support. The basic idea was to increase taxes on more affluent pensioners in order to strengthen the AOW's financing. The FNV later modified its stance after conflict among member unions, arguing that levying AOW contributions in the second income tax bracket was also an option (*Financiële Dagblad*, February 17, 1994).

The 1994 election

Campaigning for the 1994 Second Chamber elections started in late summer 1993 at the same time that the future of the AOW was high on the political agenda. The government budget deficit was forecast to be between 3 and 4 percent, and both unemployment and the active–inactive ratios were persistently high. In January, the CDA announced that the AOW would have to be frozen for the next four years. The other parties did not rule out continued freezes, but they did not specifically promise them either. In early March, the municipal elections provided a hint of things to come: the CDA lost heavily, falling from 33 percent to 25 percent of the vote. In the wake of this disaster, the CDA membership began to revolt against the savings measures announced in the manifesto for the national election (*Financiële Dagblad*, March 8, 1994). As many as 75 percent of CDA members polled said they opposed the freeze, prompting the party chairman, Van Velzen, to resign. Elco Brinkman remained as Fraction Leader and Party Leader. By mid-March the CDA had backpedaled and qualified its plans for freezing the AOW.

The PvdA now capitalized on the situation, announcing it would consider indexation the following year. Predictably, the CDA lost heavily in the national election, scoring its worst result ever. The PvdA also lost heavily, while the two liberal parties, VVD and D66, picked up votes. The real surprise, however, was the success of two parties representing the elderly. The AOV (*Algemeen Ouderen Verbond*) received 3.6 percent of the votes, enough for 6 seats, and the *Unie 55+* got 1 seat.[21] The freezing of the AOW, as well as government plans to reform care for the elderly, provided enough electoral material for the two parties, especially the AOV to succeed. Eighty percent of AOV voters were older than 55 (van Stipdonk and van Holsteyn 1996: 140).

For the first time since 1918, the CDA did not participate in government. Instead, the PvdA, VVD and D66 formed a "purple coalition." The coalition agreement between the VVD, PvdA and D66 explicitly promised to take measures to improve the financial sustainability of the AOW in order to maintain the AOW as an adequate basic pension. Despite this promise, the coalition agreement contained several cost-cutting measures, including the abolition of the AOW supplement for spouses/partners younger than 65. This would deliver savings of NLG 450 in 1998. Since 1986, the breadwinner had been entitled to a benefit equal to the individual benefit (70% of the minimum wage) and a 30 percent supplement for a partner younger than 65.[22] The new Cabinet proposed to make the supplement dependent on the combined income of the couple and not just on the income of the younger spouse.

The proposal prompted widespread opposition. The VB (Association of Industry Pension Funds) and the elderly organizations complained that the proposal was not fair, and according to one estimate, one-third of AOW pensioners currently entitled to the supplement would lose it (*Financiële Dagblad*, August 25, 1994). The NCW (Christian Employers) also rejected the Cabinet's plan to cut the AOW supplement because it opposed the introduction of additional income-testing in social insurance, and feared the cut would create pressures for the social partners to "repair" the damage in wage agreements (*Financiële Dagblad*, September 8, 1994). The VNO (employers) also criticized the proposal, citing the long term deterioration in AOW benefits, and the Opf complained about the pressure that the proposal would place on supplementary pensions to fill the gap left by the decreased supplement.

The three coalition parties were not united behind the measure; indeed only the PvdA solidly backed it, and the VVD and D66 advocated trying to find other cost-saving measures. In early 1995, the government scrapped the proposal, thus ending one of the few concrete attempts to reduce nominal benefits in the AOW scheme. Most political actors agreed that the AOW's financial problems were far from solved, but politicians were caught between the electoral risks of additional benefit freezes and their perceived need to improve the financial sustainability of the AOW. And as noted, by this time the WKA (law on conditional benefit indexation) was in place, and it allowed for automatic benefit freezes if the active–inactive ratio was not in line with the accepted definition. In 1995, AOW benefits were frozen because of the WKA, but this had no impact on AOW pensioners because of the introduction of a new tax deduction for pensioners.

The punishment of the CDA in the 1994 election and the failure of the Purple Coalition to enact even a small reduction in AOW benefits appear to have convinced politicians that further cuts in the AOW were too risky. Indeed, so present was the fear of additional AOW-related electoral backlashes, that in early 1994 the VVD and D66 began to push for the AOW to be excluded from the WKA law. The PvdA initially opposed this, but later backed down. Luckily the active–inactive ratio for the next few years benefited from rising employment associated with the "Dutch miracle," but the long-term problem of the AOW's financial sustainability remained.

With AOW cuts off the agenda, the PvdA started a debate in the spring of 1994 about the future of the AOW, stating its intention to find some sort of solution before the end of the mandate period. One of the PvdA's most prominent ideas was the introduction of higher AOW contributions for higher income earners. This proposal met with the predictable opposition of the CDA (one of the opposition parties) because it would introduce an element of income-testing into the financing structure and violate the insurance principle. Thus the PvdA's initiative rekindled a conflictual debate, but even the cabinet was divided about how to go forward: the PvdA advocated increased contributions from higher income workers, D66 pushed for higher income taxes for pensioners, and the VVD favored a higher retirement age.

In late May 1995, the PvdA published its proposals for reforming the AOW, including an income-linked contribution for both wage earners and pensioners; the introduction of a reserve fund, and an increase in the retirement age. By now the AOW debate was in full swing and the FNV also announced its ideas: introducing pension contributions for well-off pensioners and requiring wage earners to pay contributions on their entire salary. The Elderly Party, AOV (with six seats in Parliament) adamantly opposed additional cuts; the establishment of a reserve fund was one of the only measures it supported.

Based on broad internal discussions, the PvdA fraction presented a more detailed plan in November. It required well-off pensioners to pay a contribution to an AOW reserve fund starting in 2004, as well as a small contribution increase for wage-earners: 0.5 percent per year for a total of 2 percent.[23] Contributions for pensioners would be phased-in at 1.5 percent and rise to 17.7 percent in 2015 (the AOW premium was 14.6% at the time; *Financiële Dagblad*, November 28, 1995). Public opinion was against AOW contributions for pensioners, however. In a poll taken in early December, 72 percent opposed the introduction of AOW contributions for pensioners (*Financiële Dagblad*, December 5, 1995).

The introduction of the AOW reserve fund

By early 1996, a broad consensus in favor of strengthening AOW financing had emerged, but actors differed in terms of where they thought the extra resources should come from. The staunchest defenders of the status quo were the pensioners' organizations, who rejected any moves toward "fiscalization" (tax financing), preferring instead increased wage earner contributions and the introduction of a reserve fund. The FNV and CNV also supported the reserve fund, although the FNV was flexible on the issue of pensioner contributions. The PvdA was the strongest proponent of increased tax financing and pensioner contributions, as well as the introduction of the reserve fund. The VVD and CDA were willing to accept the reserve fund, but rejected far-reaching attempts at fiscalization.

By early 1996, D66 had joined the PvdA in pushing the idea of the reserve fund and AOW contributions for well-off pensioners.[24] This was essentially a response to the erosion of the AOW contribution base because of the recent tax reform, the freezing of the first income tax bracket (within which AOW contributions are paid), and the increase in the standard deduction (Stoekenbroek 1996). Despite the erosion of the contribution base, AOW costs had been held down because the AOW did not increase in line with contract wages.

The elderly people's organizations KBO and Anbo criticized the government's plans to finance future AOW deficits out of general revenues, proposing instead to increase contributions for high-income wage earners. Both organizations warned that the "fiscalization" of the AOW would increase the future likelihood that pensioners would be required to pay the costs of the AOW. As noted, AOW contributions are levied as part of the first income tax bracket for wage earners (37% in 1996). Because pensioners do not pay AOW contributions, their tax rate in the first bracket was 15 percent in 1996 (*Financiële Dagblad*, July 10, 1996).

The Cabinet's release of an important Green Paper, "Working for Security," (*Werken aan zekerheid*, TK 25 010) in September 1996 summarized the government's position on both the AOW and occupational pensions and outlined plans for a modern, flexible, and financially sustainable welfare state. This Green Paper would set the boundaries for continued debate on pension reform for the next several years. For the AOW, the Cabinet emphasized its intention to maintain the AOW as an adequate basic pension and to improve the financing structure so that the system would able to deal with the increased number of AOW pensioners forecast for the period until 2035. The Cabinet also repeated its calls for general revenue financing and contributions for well-off wage earners and/or pensioners. More controversially, but in line with previous policy statements, the cabinet called on the social partners to switch to average pay occupational pensions in order to hold down non-wage labor costs and tax expenditures. I shall return to this issue in later sections.

The employers soon joined the AOW debate, publishing their own discussion paper. Employers emphasized two things: supplementary pensions must remain the domain of the social partners, and any plans to reform the AOW must take macroeconomic conditions into account. This seemed to be a clear signal to the government concerning its ideas about switching to average salary schemes. Employers also criticized the AOW fund idea, and argued for decoupling the AOW from occupational pensions. Thus employers wanted to de-emphasize the "supplementary" nature of occupational pensions and their tight link to AOW benefits. The tight coupling of the AOW and occupational pensions created expectations for employers to guarantee the combined pension result (AOW plus occupational pension), and with the AOW continuing to lose value, pension funds often had to compensate workers for this gap, increasing non-wage labor costs. De-coupling the AOW and occupational pensions would reverse this dynamic and create incentives for individuals to take steps to compensate for a lower AOW benefit rather than pushing employers to make up the loss. By now the decreasing value of the AOW had introduced an element of uncertainty into occupational pension schemes because of their defined benefit structure, and pension funds wanted to avoid this uncertainty (*Financiële Dagblad*, July 10 and 11, 1996).

The Budget Bill presented in September 1996 temporarily solved the AOW's financing shortfall by providing a grant from general revenues. This would not solve the AOW's long-term financing problem, but the Cabinet was divided on the issue of contributions for well-off pensioners and higher contributions for high income earners. The Cabinet finally settled on a combination of contribution increases combined with the introduction of a maximum contribution rate, increased general revenue financing and the establishment of a reserve fund to finance future benefits (*Financiële Dagblad*, August 22, 1996).

The elderly organizations were quick to criticize general revenue financing. OVGO (Occupational Pensioners' Group) warned against the "fiscalization of the AOW" (*Financiële Dagblad*, September 10, 1996). OVGO offered to accept inflation indexing as long as there was no fiscalization and that the estimated 7 percent loss in purchasing power was repaired.

One benefit of the reserve fund was that the government could use the AOW fund to reduce its public debt in order to qualify for the final stage of EMU, but the EU Commission stated that this was only possible if the funds were invested in government bonds and not shares. The Cabinet briefly discussed the option of investing reserve fund assets in equities, but this option was much less attractive because of the EU's requirements, and the Cabinet soon dropped it. At the time, the AOW contribution was 15.4 percent, and the government subsidy to the AOW was NLG 1.3 billion in 1997 and 5.5 billion in 1998 (*Financiële Dagblad*, November 16, 1996).

The AOW Reserve Fund was proposed in the Second Chamber at the initiative of the PvdA (TK 25 699). The Cabinet could count on easy passage since a majority in the Second Chamber had already signaled its support when the Social Affairs Committee discussed the Green Paper, "Working for Security (TK 24 328)." The legislation established the AOW Reserve Fund and set an upper limit on the AOW contribution of 16.5 percent. Thus the Cabinet wanted to hold contributions down so that the first income tax bracket would not increase, and at the same time would finance a fully-indexed AOW benefit. The Reserve Fund would be invested in government bonds, and would start to help finance AOW pensions in 2020. Indeed, the number of AOW pensioners was projected to double by 2035, increasing from 13 percent of the population in 1995 to 24 percent in 2045.

The legislation specifically rules out both increasing the AOW retirement age and introducing contributions for high income pensioners. The Cabinet argued that the establishment of the Reserve Fund did not violate the insurance principle. The state contribution was calculated at NLG 350 million in 1997 and a one time deposit of NLG 2.1 billion. In 1998, the deposit would be NLG 3.15 billion. In early October 1997, the Cabinet agreed to the AOW Fund. In 1997, tax revenues were higher than expected so the government put 2.8 billion NLG into the AOW Reserve Fund (*Financiele Dagblad*, February 21, 1998).

The introduction of the AOW Reserve Fund and a maximum contribution level thus concluded nearly 15 years of intense debate and frequent conflict about how to finance current and future AOW pension commitments. Governments opted for the short-term solution of benefit freezes to hold costs down, but the spectacular defeat of the CDA in the 1994 election revealed the limitations of this strategy. It is fair to say that all of the mainstream political parties concluded that retrenchment in the AOW pension was a losing electoral strategy. After the disastrous 1994 election, the Purple Coalition settled on a strategy of contribution hikes and the establishment of a reserve fund financed by annual state subsidies. In the context of the mobilization of retirees (via political parties and several pensioners' organizations), the PvdA backed away from its proposal to shift part of AOW financing onto well-off pensioners. The final compromise adheres closely to what the Dutch consider to be the "insurance character" of the AOW: contributions are higher, but they are not income-dependent, and pensioners do not contribute to AOW financing. The deeply-held principle of the AOW as a social insurance financed by wage-earner contributions was vigorously defended by pensioners' groups as well as the VVD and opposition parties.

Reforming occupational pensions

As politicians grappled with AOW reform, the process of reforming occupational pensions, begun in the late 1980s, continued. Corporatist decision-making was its typically slow self, and two thorny issues had yet to be settled: the reduction of occupational pension costs and the continued "modernization" of occupational pension schemes. The Cabinet wanted to contain rising government financing (in the form of tax expenditures) on occupational pensions and it wanted to prevent pension costs from contributing to non-wage labor costs. On the other hand, additional modernization measures, such as lowering the franchise, would increase the cost of occupational pensions. Achieving cost control and modernization was not just about occupational pensions, it also concerned the issue of authority. The social partners strenuously opposed all government proposals to intervene directly in occupational pensions, and they jealously guarded their authority to negotiate the details of occupational pension schemes. The government's ultimate resource was its authority to decide the details of tax deductability, and it used this "stick" to try to push the social partners in its desired direction.

The Purple Coalition's Green Paper, "Working on Security" from 1994 restarted the debate on occupational pension reform. As noted, the Green Paper explicitly called on the social partners to switch from final pay schemes to average salary schemes, largely to reduce costs. The Cabinet backed up its proposal with the threat of limiting the tax deductability of contributions to final pay schemes. This was not a new proposal; the 1991 Green Paper (under the CDA-PvdA government) had already advocated this. The Cabinet could even claim public support for its proposal: a poll taken for the influential *Social and Cultural Report* in September showed that 69 percent of those polled favored the average wage formula (*Financiële Dagblad*, September 11, 1996).

The Cabinet faced unified opposition to its proposals from the social partners and pension funds. FNV came out strongly against the switch to average benefit formulas; the FNV president called the idea "fundamentally wrong" given the fact that many wage earners do not accumulate a full pension (*Financiële Dagblad*, September 18, 1996). Prime Minister Wim Kok countered that the final salary formula represented "the wrong kind of solidarity" because mainly white-collar workers with above-average incomes benefited from the rule. Moreover, the government continued to warn about expected increases in occupational pension costs in the absence of change. Indeed, according to the Central Planning Bureau (CPB), occupational pension contributions were expected to double within ten years, from 7 percent of payroll in 1995 to 13 percent in 2010 and 25 percent in 2025. The CPB also calculated that an average wage formula would be 20 percent cheaper than final pay formulas. State Secretary for Pensions, De Grave (VVD) also defended the government's proposal, arguing that the savings could be used to finance the expansion of coverage, including the switch to the lower (and costlier) individual AOW franchise (*Financiële Dagblad*, November 13, 1996). The Association of Insurers came out against the Cabinet's plans to pare down occupational pensions as did the Association of Sectoral Pension Funds and the Association of Company Pension Funds (*Financiële Dagblad*, December 17, 1996).

By late 1996, the government began to back away from its plans to limit tax breaks in order to get the social partners to switch to cheaper occupational pension plans. Significant numbers of backbenchers in all three coalition parties signaled their opposition, as did the opposition CDA. The Cabinet agreed to refrain from legislation if the social partners could agree on an alternative plan on their own, and on March 20, 1997 the social partners struck an agreement in the bipartite Labor Foundation (STAR 1997). State Secretary De Grave responded that the agreement was insufficient because it did not address the problem of "back service," which accounts for much of the higher costs of final salary pension plans. Again the Cabinet called for more far-reaching measures, arguing that final salary schemes hamper mobility and make it harder to retain older workers.

Insurers, pension funds, and social partners maintained their pressure on the government to back down, with little effect. State Secretary De Grave made the government's threat more explicit: if the social partners did not introduce changes on their own within two years, the government would withdraw tax deductability for final pay pension contributions (*Financiële Dagblad*, November 13, 1997). The pressure produced results. In December 1997, the social partners concluded a covenant for occupational pensions agreeing to:

- control costs;
- introduce mobility-enhancing measures;
- reduce the breadwinner bias; and
- increase coverage (Stichting van de Arbeid 1997).

In particular, the social partners agreed to reduce reliance on final pay benefit schemes and to expand coverage of part-time and flexible workers.

The stock market downturn

The results of the covenant have been evaluated positively (SER 2001) but the 2001/2002 stock market downturn has led to widespread cuts in pension schemes and tense discussions about the regulations governing the coverage rate of supplementary pensions. Most pension funds have significant investments in stocks (30–40% of assets), and the bear market has led to heavy losses. The reserves of many pension funds fell below the required 100 percent coverage rate for the first time in 2002. The drastic deterioration of the financial position of many funds prompted the pensions regulator, PVK, to introduce tougher rules governing pension fund solvency. For most funds, restoring solvency means increasing premiums, suspending pension indexation, or both.

The recent difficulties experienced by occupational pension schemes are surprising given that only a few years ago, many funds had such large surpluses that employers and workers were offered premium rebates or so-called "premium holidays," periods during which no contributions were paid. For example, Unilever Corporation enjoyed contribution holidays for 8 years in the 1990s. The social partners used some of the reserves to lower contributions or finance the restructuring of costly early retirement schemes.

Pension fund surpluses also sparked conflict about whom the money belonged to. Pensioners claimed that the money (or some of it) belonged to them. Indeed, the Dutch Association of Pensioners' Organizations (NVOG) announced it would legally challenge Shell and Unilever about their use of pension surpluses, claiming that pensioners should have a share of the profits. Estimates are that about NLG 1.5 billion was returned to firms in 1999 (van het Kaar 2001). Pension fund surpluses also sparked an upsurge in pensioner organizing: 12 firm-specific pensioner organizations were formed between 1998 and 2000.[25]

In 2001, pension funds lost an average of −2.8 percent after averaging gains of 10 percent per year for a decade. In 2002, in the wake of substantial stock market losses, the social partners and pension funds joined together in order to pressure government to relax rules about the coverage ratio (the ratio between assets and liabilities). The coverage ratio was 120 percent at the end of 2001, down from 151 percent in 1999.

Two factors exacerbated the effects of the stock market downturn. First, the method for estimating liabilities (until 2002) produced overly optimistic estimates of the coverage ratio. In the 1990s, pension funds probably also had coverage problems, but this was masked by the fact that a fictional interest rate (4%) was used to estimate liabilities, so pension funds basically underestimated their liabilities. This, combined with good investment returns, meant funds could lower premiums, or even suspend them altogether, and the social partners could use the extra capital to finance benefit improvements. A CPB report estimated that the underfunding rate is about 30 percent (Westerhout et al. 2004: 14). As interest rates fell, this fictional rate of return was out of sync with the market. Since 2002, the fictional rate of return has been replaced by a fair market rate. Second, funds had increased their investments in shares to about 50 percent, so when share prices fell, pension funds were much more exposed to risk than in the past.

In September 2002, the PVK issued tougher rules for pension scheme solvency. The new rules required funds in danger of falling below the 100 percent coverage requirement to notify the PVK and devise a recovery plan that could be accomplished within one year. The PVK also raised the coverage requirement to 105 percent. At the same time, however, the social partners were pressing the government for more latitude for pension funds to restore solvency. In 2002, about one-third of funds were in the danger zone. The OPF and VB immediately criticized the PVK's move, saying that the new requirements were unnecessarily stringent and would have negative macroeconomic effects because pension funds would have to raise contributions, suspend indexing, or both. Employers and unions echoed these criticisms, but the PVK stuck to its tough stance. The planned revision of the regulatory legislation for occupational pension funds (PSF) provided an opportunity for the pension fund organizations and the social partners to press their case (see below).

The heavy losses in 2001 and 2002 also led to collective bargaining conflict in 2003 as employers tried to introduce changes into pension schemes to cut costs. Many schemes adopted a mix of measures to restore solvency: suspended benefit indexation; non-indexation of accrual; contribution increases; and switching to average career formulas. At the end of 2002, 60 percent of company funds were in the danger zone. Unions signalled their willingness to compromise, as long as de-indexation was temporary (Gruenell 2003). The experience of the Netherlands' largest pension fund, ABP (for civil servants) is instructive: assets fell by 7.2 percent to €135.5 billion at the end of 2002. To restore adequate coverage, the ABP has raised premiums substantially and announced a switch from a final salary benefit formula to average career earnings starting in 2004. The ABP pension contribution (employers and employees combined) was 11.6 percent of wages above the franchise in 1996 and has risen to 21.4 percent in 2005 (ABP 2005).

The move by ABP illustrates a wider trend among pension schemes: the massive shift from final benefit schemes to average salary schemes. Only 10 percent of active participants are in final salary plans in 2004, down from 50 percent in 2003 and 66 percent in 1998. About 75 percent now participate in average salary schemes and indexation is overwhelmingly conditional on fund solvency (DNB 2005).

Revision of the PSF

In the wake of massive pension fund losses, regulators focused on two issues: updating rules for calculating the coverage ratio and clarifying the "ownership" of both pension fund deficits and surpluses. The boom years of the 1990s led to conflict about which groups were entitled to pension fund surpluses, and the stock market downturn of 2001/2002 led to conflict about which groups should bear the burden of correcting shortfalls. As noted, the initiative belonged to the pensions regulator, PVK, rather than with the government or social partners. At the same time, reform of the PSF was considered incomplete, and with the change of government in 2002, the initiative rested with the CDA-led center-right coalition (CDA, VVD, and LPF). What the social partners and pension fund organizations could not get from the pensions regulator (that is, more flexibility for restoring the coverage rate), they now tried to achieve within the reform of the PSF.

One of the priorities of the new CDA-led government was to increase labor market participation, especially of older workers, so the coalition agreement called for a decrease in the accrual rate from 2.0 percent annually to 1.7 percent in order to increase work incentives. This technical change means that people have to work longer to achieve the goal of 70 percent of the final salary (*NRC Handelsblad*, July 5, 2002). With AOW cuts and pensioner AOW contributions off the agenda, limiting early retirement was also a way to broaden the contribution base because longer working lives translate into more AOW contributions.

As already mentioned, reform of the PSF has been discussed since the early 1990s, but the legislative process is not yet complete. The legislative proposal is currently (December 2005) in the final stages of parliamentary consideration, and indications are that the legislation will be passed in the first half of 2006. The legislative proposal has three goals: (i) to increase transparency; (ii) to clarify the roles of the social partners, pension fund/insurance company, and pensioners; and (iii) to modernize the rules governing pension fund solvency. Pension funds will be required to inform participants about their pension accrual, and issues such as what to do in cases of under- or over-funding will be clarified. The proposal also introduces a "minimum test," and a solvency test. The minimum test is essentially the coverage rate (the ratio of assets to liabilities: 105%) while the solvency test is a complicated buffer arrangement.[26] Finally, the proposal changes how the present value of pension liabilities are calculated. Rather than discounting the liabilities at a fixed rate of 4 percent, funds will use a market rate. If interest rates go up, the present value of liabilities decreases.[27]

The legislative process has been time-consuming and marked by delay. The SER provided its opinion in May 2001 (SER 2001), and the CDA-led government proposed the main lines of the bill to the Second Chamber in March 2002. In November 2004, a draft of the bill was sent to stakeholders for comment. Predictably, the pension fund organizations, backed by the social partners, pleaded for more flexible rules governing solvency, but the Cabinet (backed by the pensions regulator) refused to budge. Specifically, fund managers argued that the rule that 105 percent coverage be restored within one year was too stringent. Coverage rates dropped substantially in 2002 and 2003, and pension funds were still experiencing the negative repercussions of this. In 1997, the coverage rate was 126 percent of liabilities and in 2003 it had fallen to 104 percent (DNB 2005).

V CONCLUSION

Summary of the magnitude of changes

Pension politics in the Netherlands is notable for the absence of large scale reform. Reform of the public pension scheme has been incremental and largely driven by ad hoc cost-cutting efforts. The suspension of benefit indexing brought major savings in the 1980s and 1990s, but the CDA's dramatic loss in the 1994 election demonstrates the limits of this strategy. Recent policy innovations have involved broadening the AOW's financial base, most importantly by the introduction of the AOW Reserve Fund. Concerns about financial sustainability have also driven policy change in occupational pensions. The most significant change is arguably the shift from final salary benefit formulae to average salary formulae and the large contribution increases in the wake of the stock market downturn in 2001/2002. In 2005, nearly 75 percent of workers are covered by average wage DB schemes, whereas in 1980 more than 75 percent were covered by final pay schemes. There is no serious discussion of replacing defined-benefit schemes with defined-contribution schemes, however. Reform has not only involved cost-cutting measures. In both the AOW, and occupational pensions, individual entitlement has replaced the breadwinner model, largely in response to the requirements of European law. Occupational pension reform has also involved expanding coverage to part-time and flexible workers, as well as improving portability.

In the area of occupational pensions, governments across the political spectrum have relied on covenants (binding agreements made with the social partners) to bring about policy change. This is consistent with the logic of policy change in the second pillar: the state provides the regulatory framework and tax concessions for qualifying pension schemes, and the social partners negotiate the details of pension arrangements at the sector or firm level. There have only been two substantial revisions of the regulatory framework for occupational pensions, in 1994 and 2006. The first reform enhanced portability and the rights of inactive pension scheme participants, while the second reform introduced major changes in the rules governing pension fund solvency. Both of these reforms are the result of rather slow, corporatist consensual decision-making routines, although the latter reform has been anything but de-politicized.

Impact of the political system on pension politics

This chapter argues that political competition is an important factor in explaining the absence of large-scale pension reform in the Netherlands since 1980 (cf. van Riel et al., 2003). The Dutch political system has become much more competitive since the 1970s. The CDA is no longer the natural party of (multiparty) government; several new parties have entered parliament, and voters have become much more volatile. Before the 1994 election, the CDA (or the parties that formed it) participated in all cabinets since 1918. Thus since 1994, there is a viable alternative to CDA-led cabinets, and the spectacular success of the List Pim Fortuyn in 2002 demonstrated that all the established parties risked losing votes to new parties. The frequency of elections has not increased, but the de facto importance of local elections has. The Dutch political system is centralized, but municipal and provincial elections increasingly function as barometers for voter satisfaction with the national government.

Despite numerous expert commissions and the explicit recommendations of influential agencies like the WRR, no Dutch government has been able to introduce changes in the overall structure of the AOW pension scheme. Indeed, the only substantial change—the individualization of benefits in 1986—was prompted by EU law. Despite the rising cost of AOW pensions, politicians could achieve nothing more than annual benefit freezes. And this strategy had disastrous consequences for the CDA in the 1994 election. After the CDA announced additional freezes, the party experienced a historic defeat, and two pensioner parties entered Parliament for the first time. Since then, politicians have focused on finding additional sources of financing; additional benefit freezes are off the agenda. Clearly, politicians are unwilling to take the electoral risks associated with AOW benefit freezes or cuts, and the parties compete far more with each other on pension-related issues. Thus, while political competition makes cuts difficult, it also causes rapid response to new problems and new issues—even if politicians prefer to refer difficult issues to corporatist institutions.

Despite recent stock market losses, occupational pensions in the Netherlands will continue to grow in importance. Assets are forecast to increase from 131 percent of GDP in 2001 to 172 percent in 2020 and 195 percent in 2040 (Westerhout et al. 2004: 30). However, the importance of occupational pensions relative to the AOW will shift substantially in the next few decades. Dutch spending on supplementary pension benefits (about 4% of GDP) is nearly equal to AOW spending (4.3% of GDP). Today, more than 90 percent of wage earners participate in a supplementary pension plan, but only 50 percent of current pensioners receive supplementary pension income (Carey: 2002). As the number of retirees with supplementary pension income increases, income distribution among retirees is likely to more closely resemble the income distribution among wage earners than is currently the case.

Interest group influence

Interest groups have been major players in all of the reforms discussed in this chapter. Certainly the "traditional" interest groups, unions and employers, have played important roles, largely because they have a privileged status in decision-making affecting both the AOW and occupational pensions. The social partners no longer have a monopoly on interest group influence, however, since they now have to compete with pensioner organizations whose interests are often at odds with those of the social partners.

The Dutch political system is centralized, but multiparty cabinets and consociational practices ensure that the social partners are consulted on matters of importance to them, including public and occupational pensions. So political decision-making is centralized but subject to predictable patterns of social partner influence. Only the unions and employers have an institutionalized seat at the corporatist bargaining table, but the extreme proportionality of the electoral system means that new parties frequently enter Parliament, providing opportunities for single issue groups (like pensioners) to achieve representation in Parliament.

What is striking about the politics of AOW reform is the emergence of elderly people's organizations as important political actors. These organizations have a long history in the Netherlands, and they found their *cris de coeur* in the AOW benefit freezes of the 1980s and 1990s. What is even more striking is the way that the debate over the distribution of pension fund surpluses in the 1990s, and deficits in the 2000s, sparked a wave of pensioner-organizing. Pensioners receiving company pensions organized in order to try to influence the distribution of surpluses, and these same organizations have tried to limit the damage experienced by pensioners as part of the stock market downturn of 2001/2002.

Pension fund associations have also been important players in occupational pension politics. Their interests often run parallel to those of the social partners, whose representatives sit on the pension fund boards.

Constraints of policy design

As noted, Dutch pension politics follows two tracks: the highly politicized, electorally risky track of the AOW, and the corporatist bargaining track of occupational pensions. The AOW is a universal, fairly generous, flat-rate pension available to all

Dutch residents over 65. This unified structure creates widespread support for the AOW. Moreover, the AOW is mature, and occupational pensions are tightly linked with AOW benefits. This means that not only have citizens planned their retirement on the basis of the AOW, but pension funds have calculated occupational benefits on the basis of the AOW. This creates a powerful coalition in favor of the status quo: retirees who do not want to see their benefits cut or frozen, and pension funds run by the social partners who do not want AOW reductions or freezes to result in higher occupational pension costs.

The tight coupling of AOW and occupational pension schemes also creates incentives for cost-shifting between the AOW and occupational pensions. When AOW indexing was suspended in the 1980s and early 1990s, occupational pension funds bore a significant part of these costs since they were obligated (in most cases) to maintain a specific benefit level that included the AOW. Thus the occupational pension funds became some of the most vocal proponents for improving the financial sustainability of the AOW, since declining real AOW benefits created higher costs for them.

Role of ideas and historical context

Ideas and principles closely connected to the origins and structure of the AOW played an important role in all attempts to reform the scheme. The AOW is commonly viewed as an insurance since wage earners pay contributions for benefits "earned" by residence. The supposedly insurance-like character of the AOW creates a powerful argument in the hands of those who oppose the introduction of pension contributions for pensioners, claiming that this would be tantamount to making pensioners pay twice for the AOW. The PvdA has tried for at least a decade to introduce some form of AOW contribution for affluent pensioners, and has always failed. Instead, the PvdA and other parties have introduced pensioner financing through the back door, by increasing general revenue financing of the AOW.

The perceived insurance character of the AOW is rooted partly in principles advocated by the Dutch confessional parties of the 1940s and 1950s, and this principle has survived the secularization of Dutch society. Confessional principles, especially the Catholic notion of subsidiarity, continue to shape Dutch pension politics, especially in the second pillar. The state provides the regulatory framework for occupational pensions, but the social partners negotiate plan details as part of wage agreements, and there is a lot of pressure to maintain this arrangement. The social partners have repeatedly resisted government attempts to interfere in occupational pension provisions, preferring instead to conclude agreements with the government on policy changes in order to avoid legislation.

Abbreviations

ABP   *Algemene Ouderdomswet* (General Old-Age Pensions Act)
AOW   *Algemeen Burgerlijk Pensioenfonds* (General Civil Pension Fund)

AOV	*Algemeen Ouderen Verbond* (National Elderly Association)
ARP	*Anti-Revolutionaire Partij* (Anti-Revolutionary Party)
CDA	*Christen Democratisch Appèl* (Christian Democratic Appeal)
CHU	*Christelijk Historische Unie* (Christian Historical Union)
CNV	*Christelijk Nationaal Vakverbond* (Christian Trade Union Federation)
D66	*Democraten 66* (Democrats 66)
FNV	*Federatie Nederlandse Vakbeweging* (Dutch Trade Union Federation)
KVP	*Katholieke Volkspartij* (Catholic People's Party)
LPF	*Lijst Pim Fortuyn* (List Pim Fortuyn)
MHP	*Vakcentrale voor middengroepen en hoger personeel* (Union for Academic and White Collar Employees)
NCW	*Nederlands Christelijk Werkgeversverbond* (Dutch Christian Federation of Employers)
NKV	*Nederlands Katholiek Vakverbond* (Catholic Federation of Dutch Trade Unions)
NVV	*Nederlands Verbond van Vakverenigingen* (Dutch Federation of Trade Unions)
OPF	*Vereniging van Ondernemingspensioenfondsen* (Association of Company Pension Funds)
OVGO	*Overlegorgaan Vereinigingen van gepensioneerden van ondernemingen* (Association of Company Pensioners)
PCOB	*Protestants Christelijke Ouderen Bond* (Protestant Christain Seniors Association)
PVDA	*Partij van de Arbeid* (Labor Party)
SER	*Sociaal-Economische Raad* (Social and Economic Council)
SP	*Socialistische Partij* (Socialist Party)
VB	*Vereniging van Bedrijfstakpensioenfondsen* (Dutch Association of Industry-wide Pension Funds)
VNO	*Vereniging van Nederlandse Ondernemingen* (Federation of Dutch Enterprises)
VNO-NCW	*Vereniging van Nederlandse Ondernemingen-Nederlands Christelijk Werkgeversverbond* (Confederation of Netherlands Industry and Employers)
VVD	*Volkspartij voor Vrijheid en Democratie* (Liberal Party)
WKA	*Wet koppeling met afwijkingsmogelijkheid* (Conditional Indexation Act)

Notes

1. The Dutch refer to their second-pillar pensions as "supplementary" (*aanvullend*) pensions. I use the terms supplementary and occupational pensions synonymously in this chapter.
2. For example, the House of Orange (the Royal Family) is Protestant.

3. This section is based on Andeweg and Irwin 2004 and Keman 2002.
4. Breaking with convention, the Dutch name for the Lower House is "Second Chamber;" that of the Upper House is "First Chamber."
5. Unless otherwise noted, this section is based on Keman 2002; Andeweg and Irwin 2002; Deschouwer 2002; and Timmermans and Andeweg 2005.
6. Most of the religious parties merged in the 1970s to form the CDA (Christian Democratic Appeal).
7. The Constitution contains few rules concerning cabinet formation. The longest formation took 208 days 1977 and the shortest was 10 days in 1958. More typical is 60–80 days.
8. Pim Fortuyn, LPF party leader, was assassinated a few weeks before the election. The LPF got 17% (26 seats). After the in-fighting that plagued the party in government, voters repudiated the LPF in the January 2003 election, and the LPF recieved only 8 seats.
9. The Minister of Social Affairs and Employment can declare a collective agreement binding for an entire sector.
10. This section is based on Anderson 2004; Cox 2001; Jaspers et al. 2001, Veldkamp 1978, and Rigter et al. 1995.
11. For those with fewer than 50 years residence, 2% of the benefit is substracted for each missing year.
12. Parliament sets the level of the net minimum wage twice per year.
13. 79/7/EEC.
14. *Financiële Dagblad*, March 2, 1985. The final version awarded the full couple's AOW pension to the pensioner over 65 with a spouse under 65 without her own income. If the younger spouse had her own income, the supplement for the spouse was proportionally reduced.
15. This was later changed to 70% for the married AOW pensioner with a younger spouse, with a 30% supplement (TK 87/88 20384). Legislation in 1996 introduces the rule that the partner supplement will disappear in 2015 (TK 94/95 24258). In 1986, non-married cohabiting couples were given rights equal to married pensioners (TK 85/86 19258).
16. The *Barber* decision extended the meaning of Art. 119 to include age requirements in occupational pension schemes. This includes both the age of entrance into a scheme and the age of retirement.
17. In 1987, 72% of participants were in final salary schemes.
18. Green-Left was elected to the Second Chamber for the first time in 1989. The previous government was a CDA-VVD coalition.
19. Between 1980 and 1997, net minimum wages (and the value of pensions) decreased 22% in real terms (Alber 1998, 38).
20. The 1994 tax reform integrated social insurance contributions (including AOW) into the first income tax bracket, and retirees paid a much lower rate because they did not pay AOW contributions.
21. The two elderly parties soon descended into internal conflict and quickly ceased to have much influence on Dutch politics. Neither party made it into the Second Chamber in the 1998 election. See van Stipdonk and van Holsteyn 1996.
22. In February 1994, this was changed by the caretaker cabinet to 50%–50% so that age was not the decisive factor.
23. The increase would be compensated by contribution reductions to other social insurance schemes.
24. The Minister for Social Affairs and Employment was from the PvdA, but the state secretary responsible for pensions was from the VVD.

25. As noted, only unions and employers are represented on pension fund boards, although nothing prevents a retired worker from occupying one of the union slots. Pensioners had long pushed for representation on the boards of the pension schemes, backed by D66. The social partners agreed to increase pension representation on the boards, but there has been little progress.
26. The solvency test is a way of assessing whether pension funds can withstand financial shocks and remain at 105% coverage after one year of market movements. There should be more than 97.5% probability that a fund can meet all its obligations in one year (using a standard risk model). Experts estimate that a funding ratio of 130% is required to meet the solvency test.
27. The solvency test and minimum funding test are part of the "Financial Assessment Framework" (*Financiële Toetsingkader*, FTK) that is embedded in the new pension legislation.

Bibliography

Primary sources

Green Papers

Ministerie van Sociale Zaken en Werkgelegenheid (1991). *Pensioennota*. Tweede kamer 1990–1991, nr. 22167.

Second Chamber legislative dossiers

TK 18 515
TK 19 258
TK 19 638
TK 20 384
TK 23 123
TK 24 258
TK 25 010
TK 25 699

Publications from interest groups and state agencies

Commissie Financiering Oudedagsvoorziening. 1987. *Gespiegeld in de tijd, de AOW in de toekomst*, Ministerie van Sociale Zaken en Werkgelegenheid, Den Haag.
DNB (Den nederlandsche bank) (2005) *Pensioensmonitor*. www.dnb.nl.
Ministry of Social Affairs and Employment (2000). *The old age pension system in the Netherlands*. The Hague: Ministry of Social Affairs and Employment.
Pensioenkamer (1987). *Witte vlekken op pensioengsgebied*. The Hague.
SER (Sociaal Economische Raad) (1984). *Advies gelijke behandeling in de AOW*. Advies 84/02.
—— (1990). *Pensioenproblematiek*. Advies 90/23.
—— (2001). *Rapport evaluatieonderzoek convenant arbeidspensioenen*. Den Haag: SER.
—— (2001). *Pensioenskaart van Nederland*. SER: Leiden.
SCP (Sociaal en Cultureel Planbureau) (1998). *Sociaal en Cultureel Rapport 1998, 25 jaar sociale verandering*. Rijswijk: SCP.
STAR (Stichting van de Arbeid) (1997). Overwegingen en aanbevelingen gericht op vernieuwing van pensioenregelingen. Den Haag.
—— (1997). "Covenant inzake de arbeidspensioen. Overeengekomen tussen het Kabinet en de Stichting van de Arbeid op 9 december 1997."

Verzekeringskamer (1999). *Pensioensmonitor, niet financiële gegevens pensioenfondsen. Stand van zaken 1 januari 1998.* Apeldoorn: Stichting Verzekeringskamer.

WRR (Wetenschappelijke Raad voor het Regeringsbeleid) (1992). *Ouderen voor ouderen; Demografische ontwikkeling en beleid 1993*, rapport nr. 43, The Hague: Sdu Uitgeverij.

Newspapers
Financiële Dagblad
NRC Handelsblad

Secondary sources

ALBER, JENS (1998). "Recent developments in continental European welfare states: Do Austria, Germany, and the Netherlands prove to be birds of a feather?" Paper presented at the 14th World Congress of Sociology, Montreal, 29 July.

ANDERSON, KAREN M. (2004). "Pension Politics in Three Small States: Denmark, Sweden, and the Netherlands," *Canadian Journal of Sociology*, 29 (2): 289–312.

ANDEWEG, RUDY B. and IRWIN, GALEN A. (2002). *Governance and Politics of the Netherlands.* Houndsmills, Basingstoke: Palgrave Macmillan.

ANDEWEG, RUDY B. and TIMMERMANS, ARCO (2005). "Conflict Management in Coalition Government." In Strøm, K. and Müller, W. C. (eds.), *Coalition Governance in Parliamentary Democracies.* Oxford, Oxford University Press.

CAMINADA K. and GOUDSWAARD, K. P. (2004). "The fiscal subsidy on pension savings in the Netherlands," *Tax Notes International*, March 29.

CAREY, DAVID (2002). "Coping with Population Ageing in the Netherlands." Economics Department Working Papers no. 325. OECD: Paris.

CLARK, GORDON L. (2003). *European Pensions and Global Finance.* Oxford: Oxford University Press.

COX, ROBERT H. (1993). *The Development of the Dutch Welfare State.* Pittsburgh: University of Pittsburgh Press.

—— (2001). "The Social Construction of an Imperative: Why Welfare Reform Happened in Denmark and The Netherlands, but not in Germany," *World Politics*, 53 (3): 463–98.

DESCHOUWER, KRIS (2002). "The Colour Purple. The End of Predictable Politics in the Low Countries." In Webb, P., Farrell, D. M., and Holliday, I. (eds.), *Political Parties in Advanced Industrial Democracies.* Oxford: Oxford University Press.

GRUENELL, MARIANNE (2003). "Deadlock on occupational pensions in company bargaining," www.eiro.org.

HAVERLAND, MARKUS (2001). "Another Dutch miracle? Explaining Dutch and German pension trajectories," *Journal of European Social Policy*, 11 (4): 308–23.

HEMERIJCK, ANTON and VAN KERSBERGEN, KEES (1997). "A miraculous model? Explaining the new politics of the welfare state in the Netherlands," *Acta Politica*, 32 (3): 258–301.

HIPPE, JOOP; LUCARDIE, PAUL and VOERMAN, GERRIT (1995). "Kroniek 1994. Overzicht ven de partijpolitieke gebeurtenissen van het jaar 1994." In *Jaarboek 1994.* Documentatiecentrum Nederlandse Politieke Partijen. Groningen: DNPP.

JASPERS, A. et al. (2001). *"De gemeenschap is aansprakelijk"... Honderd jaar sociale verzekering 1901–2001.* Den Haag: Koninklijke vermande.

KEMAN, HANS (2002). "The Low Countries: Confrontation and Coalition in Segmented Societies." In Colomer, J. (ed.), *Political Institutions in Europe.* London: Routledge, 211–53.

KRAAMWINKEL, MARGRIET (1995). *Pensioen, emancipatie en gelijke behandeling.* Deventer: Fed.

KUNE, J. B. (1988). "De kosten van pensioenvoorzieningen in de 21e eeuw," *Tijdschrift voor Arbeidsvraagstukken*, 4 (2): 27–33.

LIJPHART, AREND (1968). *The Politics of Accommodation: Pluralism and Democracy in The Netherlands*. Berkeley: University of California Press.

NELISSEN, JAN (1994). *Towards a payable pension system*. Tilburg: TISSER.

NOUWEN, P. A. (1987). "Pensioenverlies door pensioenbreuk. Oplossing mogelijk en willicht nabij!." *Tijdschrift voor pensioenvraagstukken*. January: 3–5.

PETERSEN, C. (1988). "De AOW in de toekomst," *Economisch-statistische berichten*, 73: 264–66.

RIGTER, D. et al. (1995). *Tussen sociale wil en werkelijkheid*. Den Haag: VUGA.

STOEKENBROEK, B. (1996). "Misverstanden over the AOW," *Economisch-statistische berichten*, 2 October.

TULFER, P. M. (1997). *Pensioenen, fondsen en verzekeraars*. Deventer: Kluwer.

VAN DEN BOSCH, F. A. J, VAN EEKELEN, P. J. C and PETERSEN, C. (1983). "De toekomst van de AOW: verdubbeling van de premies of halvering van de uitkeringen?" *Economisch-statistische berichten*, 16 November.

VAN HET KAAR, ROBBERT (2001). "Occupational pension fund issues still controversial." www.eiro.org.

VAN KERSBERGEN, KEES (1995). *Social Capitalism*. London: Routledge.

VAN RIEL, BART, HEMERIJCK, ANTON and VISSER, JELLE (2003). "Is there a Dutch way to Pension Reform?" In Clark, G. L., and Whiteside, N. (eds.), *Pension Security in the 21st Century. Redrawing the Public–Private Debate*. Oxford: Oxford University Press.

VAN RUIJSSEVELDT, JORIS and VISSER, JELLE (eds.) (1996). *Industrial Relations in Europe, Traditions and Transitions*. London: Sage Publications.

VAN STIPDONK, V. P. and VAN HOLSTEYN, J. J. M. (1996). "Wat ouderen verbond. Verklaringen van het ontstaan en succes van een nieuwe partij." In Voerman, G. (ed.), *Jaarboek Documentatiecentrum Nederlandse Politieke Partijen 1995*. Groningen: Documentatiecentrum Nederlandse Politieke Partijen, 127–48.

VAN WAARDEN, FRANS (2002). "Dutch Consociationalism and Corporatism. A Case of Institutional Persistence," *Acta Politica*, 37 (1/2): 44–67.

VARKEVISSER, J. (1988). "Gespiegeld in de tijd. De ontwikkeling van de AOW," *socialisme en democratie*, 7/8.

VELDKAMP, G. (1978). *Inleiding tot de sociale zekerheid en de toepassingen in Nederland en België; Deel I, Karakter en geschiedenis*. Deventer: Kluwer.

VISSER, JELLE and HEMERIJCK, ANTON (1997). *A Dutch miracle. Job growth, welfare reform and corporatism in the Netherlands*. Amsterdam: Amsterdam University Press.

WESTERHOUT, Ed; VAN DE VEN, MARTIJN; VAN EWIJK, CASPER and DRAPER, NICK (2004). *Naar een schokbestending pensioenstelsel. Verkenning van enkele beleidsopties op pensioengebied*. CPB report no. 67.

CHAPTER 16

IRELAND: PENSIONING THE "CELTIC TIGER"

ISABELLE SCHULZE

MICHAEL MORAN

I Introduction

IRELAND is different! The difference can be simply expressed: the outlook for the pension system is fairly benign. The demographic circumstances are much more favorable than in other European Union countries: Ireland has the highest fertility rate and the lowest share of people older than 64 years (Eurostat 2004: 48, 62). The flat-rate state pension provides for low replacement rates; consequently, the burden on the national budget is only moderate. Moreover, Ireland's economic performance since the mid-1990s has been excellent, producing national budget surpluses that allowed the introduction of partial pre-funding of future state pension expenditure. The country has a well-developed net of voluntary occupational and private pension schemes from which over half of the working population profits. Legislative changes in the 1990s contributed to further increases in coverage of occupational and private pensions: statutory regulations make private supplementary pensions easier to access and benefit rights more secure.

The main problem in pension policy has been less the financial sustainability of the system than the inadequacy of state pension benefits, and inequality in coverage rates of supplementary pensions. But political competition in Ireland has not placed pensions at the center of the political agenda. Elections do not turn on pension politics; and unions have not made pensions a mobilizing issue. Moreover, some of the key social interests that powerfully shaped Irish politics for much of the history of the state, saw a great transformation in their fortunes from the 1990s onwards. Two of particular significance are the Church, which suffered a catastrophic decline in its popularity, and farming interests which, while remaining important, had to compete now in a society that was industrializing and urbanizing on a historically unprecedented scale. To anticipate our argument, Ireland seems to support the proposition of some scholars: that pension policy is a highly technical matter, insulated from public interest, and the scope and effect of pension legislation is very long term. Therefore, the issue is suitable for cross-party consensus and not suited to electoral party competition. Irish pension reforms indeed have been negotiated quietly in commissions and have received little press coverage. Although public pensions are extremely low by international standards, and inequalities in occupational and private pensions extremely large, pensions are not a hot topic on the political agenda.[1] Unions' demands for compulsory occupational pension coverage are feeble measured by the kind of mass protests on the streets found in other Western European nations.

In contrast to other countries, the historical legacies in Ireland did not allow serious pension retrenchment measures in times when the government needed to economize, because with state pension benefits of less than 30 percent of industrial average wage there was no scope for cutting; thus a reduction of pensions was not even considered. Available options were to increase the revenue base and to provide incentives for employers to set up occupational pension schemes.[2]

The greatest achievement of the last twenty years has been the establishment of the Pensions Board assigned to monitor and penalize if necessary the private pension industry, in other words to guarantee its compliance to funding standards, and to inform and educate pension scheme trustees and members. Through the union of representatives of the Ministry, pension insurance funds, employers, unions, lawyers and actuaries, the Pensions Board constitutes a form of institutionalized partnership. With hands-on observation of current developments in the private pension sector it is fit to advise the Social Minister and Parliament on legislation in related matters. The use of such semi-state boards is a well-established Irish method of "depoliticizing" issues. This context makes pronounced future conflicts in Irish pension politics unlikely.

II Political system

Constitutional history and nation-building

Ireland was under British rule from the twelfth century until 1921. The War of Independence (1916–21) and the resulting civil war (1921–23) between those who supported the agreement with the British Commonwealth and those who desired full independence of a united Ireland laid the foundation of the Irish party system (Mitchell 2003: 418).

Ninety-one percent of the Irish population is Catholic and the devout, traditional culture was reflected in the very late liberalization of abortion, divorce and homosexuality (1992, 1995 and 1993). This culture of Catholic devotion has weakened considerably in the last couple of decades, notably in the capital, Dublin. Rapid secularization, coupled with numerous scandals affecting the Church, have provided an important backdrop to both the wider struggles of Irish politics and to the detailed workings of the more esoteric parts of the policy-making system. The weakening of the Church also helps explain the innovations in pensions in recent decades, for the Church was not only a powerful institution in Irish society, it was socially reactionary in character, an obstacle to the development of welfare entitlements in many policy domains.

The Irish economy has boomed in the last 15 years. EU subsidies and a targeted tax and economic policy have contributed to economic growth, low unemployment rates and comparatively low inflation. Following Luxembourg, Ireland ranks second in GDP per capita in the EU (Eurostat 2004: 118). The boost from a country of traditional livestock farming to a modern nation with an expanding IT sector led to the coining of the label "Celtic Tiger."

Institutions of government

The Head of State of Ireland is the President (*Uachtarán na hÉireann*) (Art. 12 I Constitution). The president is also part of the parliament (*Oireachtas*) and has mainly representational functions. S/he monitors the law-making process and may call the Supreme Court if s/he questions the constitutionality of a bill. Upon request of the Senate and one-third of the lower house (*Dáil*) she can deny her signature on a bill. Then the bill either requires passage by referendum or affirmation by a newly elected parliament (Mitchell 2003: 420). The president is directly elected by the people in a system of proportional representation by means of single transferable vote for a term of seven years (Art. 12 II 3, III 1 Constitution). The Irish executive is headed by the Prime Minister (*Taoiseach*) but the cabinet shares collective authority and collective responsibility (Art. 28 IV 2 Constitution). All other cabinet members have to be members of the parliament (Art. 28 VII 1, 2 Constitution), which in combination with the candidate-centered electoral system, can easily lead to turnover of ministers after elections. Government formation does not follow a structured process. No specific party leads the negotiations but government formation follows a "freestyle bargaining." In the vote of investiture, the government requires the majority of those voting with a quorum of 20. Minority governments are possible and have frequently been the case under Fianna Fáil rule (Table 16.2). The electoral system gives incentives to pre-election coalition commitment as parties recommend possible coalition partners for transfer votes to their electorate (Mitchell 2003: 429; 2000: 131–3).

The Irish parliament (*Oireachtas*) consists of two chambers. The House of Representatives (*Dáil*) is composed of 166 members (*Teachtaí Dála*) to which the government is responsible. Decisions are taken by majority vote of the members present. The speaker of the house (*Ceann Comhairle*) has no right to vote but if there is a tie in voting, the chairman has the final decision (Art. 15 Constitution). Groups of at least seven members may build a parliamentary fraction. The opposition in parliament mirrors the government front bench with a shadow cabinet.

One of the most striking features of the *Dáil* bears closely on the character of pension politics. Its institutional capacity to either develop or scrutinize in detail policies of any technical complexity has been very limited. For instance, a system of specialized committees has only been established in the last decade. Before 1993, the only regular committee was the Public Accounts Committee. Between 1993 and 1999 the Committee system was re-structured: a system of standing, select, joint and special committees has been established. Today, the third stage of legislation usually takes place in specialized Select Committees of each house (Houses of the Oireachtas 2003; Gallagher 1999: 188). The weakness of the Committee system means that parliamentarians are at a clear disadvantage in making sense of policy domains, like pensions, where there is a premium on grasping the details of proposals.

The Senate (*Seanad*) is made up of 60 members whereof eleven are nominated by the Prime Minister and 49 represent corporate bodies: three representatives for the National University of Ireland, three seats for the Dublin Trinity College, 11 seats each for the agricultural sector and employees, nine seats for industry and trade, seven seats for public administration and five representatives of the cultural and educational sector. Each corporation has the right to decide its own electoral system (Art. 18 Constitution). The idea of guaranteeing representation of universities was that these candidates, who are independent most of the time, would counterbalance partisan composition. The electorate for the university seats are university graduates (Gallagher 1999: 199).

Senate elections take place within 90 days after the *Dáil* has been dissolved. Because of this timely proximity, *Seanad* elections are overshadowed by the *Dáil* elections. Candidates for senate have to be appointed either by a corporation or by at least four members of the Lower Chamber (*Dáil*). The electorate of the corporation candidates are elected by councilors at local level, thus, local election outcomes may affect senate election results (Coakley 1990: 148–150). One could assume that this would produce unequal majorities in *Dáil* and *Seanad*, but the eleven nominees of the prime minister make such a distribution of seats unlikely.[3] It should be noted that many of the local councilors are members of the *Dáil* or *Seanad* at the same time. Originally the Upper Chamber was introduced as a "vocational" chamber in 1937, but party politics have since superimposed themselves upon occupational interests. Therefore, also "regional considerations are of limited concern" (Coakley 1990: 156). The Senate's legislative role is restricted to commenting on, and amending, bills. In 1997 a committee was assigned to examine the *Seanad*'s functions leading to a comprehensive report in 2004 (Seanad 2004). But legislative changes have not yet been undertaken.

Table 16.1 Political institutions in Ireland

Political arenas	Actors	Rules of investiture	Rules of decision-making	Veto potential
Executive	President (*Uachtarán na hÉireann*)	7-year term; directly elected by the people in system of proportional representation with single-transferable vote	Upon request of the *Seanad* and one third of the *Dáil* he can deny his signature on a bill leading to a referendum or affirmation by new *Dáil*	Not a veto point
	Prime Minister (*Taoiseach*)	"Freestyle bargaining" in government formation confirmed with an investiture vote by majority of those voting with a quorum of 20	Initiates legislation	—
Legislative	Chamber of Deputies (*Dáil*)	5-year term; 166 seats in 41 multi-member districts (3 to 5 mandates); system of proportional representation with single-transferable vote; seat allocation according to Droop-Quota formula; frequently pre-election coalition commitments; can be dissolved by president upon Prime Minister's request	Right of initiative; decision-making by majority of votes; quorum for voting is 20 members; fairly new and weak committee structure	Veto point if minority governments (occurs frequently); not a veto point if majority government
	Senate (*Seanad*)	5-year term; out of 60 members 11 are nominated by the Prime Minister and 49 are chosen by panel elections i.e. universities and corporations	Right of initiative (groups of 3–6 senators); can comment on and amend bills; decision-making by majority of votes; quorum for voting is 12 members	Not a veto point; only suspensive right for 90 days
Judicial	Supreme Court (*Chúirt Uachtarach*)	Court of Final Appeal consists of Chief Justice and seven ordinary judges	Power to decide whether an Act is unconstitutional	Only post-legislative veto point
Electoral	Referendum	Compulsory referendum for constitutional amendments; majority of *Dáil* decides on wording of the amendment Popular initiative	Constitutional amendments require approval of 50% of valid votes	Veto point if government has no majority in the *Seanad* and no 2/3 majority in *Dáil* combined (also important in moral issues i.e. abortion, divorce, etc.)
Territorial units	Counties	27 county boroughs and county councils with county parliaments; 6-year terms	Financially dependent on central government	Not a veto point
	Communities	Communities		

As the above description shows, the Irish parliament (*Oireachtas*) is heavily dominated by the government. Gallagher points out that the legislative role of the parliament is further undermined by social pacts such as the *Programme for Competitiveness and Work* and the *Partnership 2000*. These conclude agreements between the government and the major interest groups leaving the parliament to rubber-stamp measures negotiated in the pre-parliamentary arena (Gallagher 1999: 201). In this sense, the Irish system marks the strength of functional over territorial representation, a dominance made more marked by the way the behavior of members of the *Dáil* is governed by local clientelism.

Referendums are mandatory for constitutional amendment and have frequently been used since the late 1960s in moral and in institutional (EU) issues. The wording of the referendum is decided by the majority of the *Dáil* and the referendum passes with a simple majority of votes (Mitchell 2003: 421).

Electoral system

The electoral system for the *Dáil* is a system of proportional representation with single-transferable vote (Art. 16 II 5 Constitution). The basic system has been in force since 1919 and attempts to change its basic structure have failed twice. Fianna Fáil initiated referendums in 1959 and in 1968 to change the electoral system into a first-past-the-post system with the goal of making governments more stable, but both failed (Radio Telefís Éireann 2003; Jacobs 1989: 143; Nohlen 2000: 346). The legislative term is 5 years but early elections are possible—an instrument that has been frequently used by governments of the 1980s and early 1990s. Election campaigns are very short compared by other countries i.e. only between three to four weeks (Mitchell 2003: 421–2).

The *Dáil* is composed of 166 members elected in 41 multi-member districts. The number of seats per district depends on the population size, that is, three-to-five mandates, and the constituencies usually comply with county borders. (Art. 16 II 2, 4 Constitution). Although there is no formal entrance barrier the system's small district magnitude favor large parties or geographically concentrated interests and imply a de facto hurdle of on average 17.2 percent (Lijphart 1994: 31). The distribution of seats predominantly depends not on the votes of first preference but the transfer of votes that is, the second, third, fourth, and so on preferences often determines the outcome of an election.

Each voter has one single vote and votes for individual candidates. It is possible to express preferences on the ballot sheet in ranking the candidates within or across parties. The candidate with first preference will receive the vote unless the candidate has no chance of winning a seat or he has already a secure seat. If either is the case, the candidate marked with second preference will receive the vote. In detail, mandates are distributed according to the Droop-Quota formula. The total valid votes in a constituency are divided by the sum of the number of mandates of that constituency plus one; the result is augmented by one and leads to the quota. Each candidate who achieved as many votes as the quota, receives a mandate. If no candidate reaches the quota after the first round, the candidate with the lowest number of votes is eliminated and the calculation is re-done (Nohlen 2000: 339, 343).

One important consequence of this electoral system is that it sets up a system of virtually perpetual competition not only between parties, but between deputies of the same party (see also Mitchell 2003: 424–5). This gives to the daily life of the average member of parliament an intense preoccupation with the cultivation of local reputation and local interests. What issues are focused on then depends on how far they can be turned to local advantage. The difficulty of using pensions in this manner is one important reasons for their low salience in electoral competition.

Legislative process

Legislation in Ireland is a 5-step process. The right of initiative belongs to Parliament. Usually ministers and state secretaries in their positions as members of the *Dáil* initiate bills; private members' bills initiated by the opposition have hardly any chance of being passed. In the First Stage, the government submits the bill to Parliament and distributes copies to all members of the house. The Second Stage starts with the presentation of the bill by the responsible minister, a response by the opposition spokesperson (Gallagher 1999: 186) and a general discussion that terminates with a vote on the basic principles of the bill. The necessary quorum for business and voting in the *Dáil* is 20 members, and 12 members in the *Seanad* (Mitchell 2003). The Third Stage is a deliberation of each paragraph of the bill. Although the Third Stage took place in the plenary until 1993, it is called "Committee Stage" because procedural rules of the committees are applied to circumvent the stricter regulations of the Plenary. The bill may be amended and changed as long as the basic principles are not touched. Each amendment is voted on separately.

At the Fourth Stage of the law-making process (the Report Stage), another reading of the bill takes place and the fifth step—the Final Stage—is the transfer of the bill to the other house. After a bill has passed in one house it enters automatically in Second Stage of the other house. If a bill was initiated in the *Dáil* and the *Seanad* rejects the bill, or if the *Seanad* initiated a bill but does not accept *Dáil*'s amendments, or if the *Seanad* takes no decision at all, the law will pass automatically after 90 days (Art. 23 I 1 Constitution).

The government party or government coalition dominates the entire law-making process. The Irish Second Stage debate sets the framework of the act before the committee deals with the bill, and consequently the committee has much less scope for action than continental style committees (Gallagher 1999: 188). Even more important, the "public" phases of pension policy in Ireland are more important for the way they contribute to the wider parliamentary battle, rather than for the way to contribute to the substantive shaping of policy—a natural consequence of the weakness of parliamentarians in coming to the terms with the details of policy proposals.

Party family affiliation	Abbreviation	Party name	Ideological orientation	Founding and merger details	Year established
Left parties	WP	Workers' Party (*Pairti na nOiri*)	Left-wing socialist; expansionary economic policies; large role of the state in economy	Split from the Sinn Féin parties in the 1970s, renamed in 1982; transformed into Democratic Left	1982
	LP	Labour Party (*Páirti Lucht Oibre*)	Left-wing, support within farm workers and rural white collar workers	Merger with Democratic Left in 1999	(1912) 1922
	DL	Democratic Left	Left-wing	Split from Workers' Party	1992
Center-right parties	FG	Family of the Irish (*Fine Gael*)	Center-right party; emphasis on economic austerity; support among upper-middle class and middle-size and large farmers,	"pro-Treaty" split of Sinn Féin, namely Cumann na nGaedheals, merged with several small parties into Fine Gael in 1937	1933
	PD	Progressive Democrats (*Páirtí Daonlathach*)	Liberal party; emphasis on economic austerity	Split from Fianna Fáil	1985
	FF	Soldiers of Fortune (*Fianna Fáil*)	Traditional supporters of united, independent Ireland	"Anti-Treaty" split of Sinn Féin	1926
Extremist parties	SF	We Ourselves (*Sinn Féin*)	Originally revolutionary, nationalist party; reemergence of political significance in 1960s as radical political wing of the Irish Republican Army (IRA); possibly left-wing and dedicated to Irish reunification	Party spit in FF and FG in 1921 over the issue of treaty of independence with Great Britain; re-gain of seat in *Dáil* in 1997 after 40 years	1905
Green parties	GP	Green Party (*Comhaontas Glas*)	Environmental party; decentralization of power	Established as Ecology Party of Ireland in 1981, renamed in Green Alliance 1983 and renamed in 1987	1981

Fig. 16.1 Party system in Ireland

Sources: Mair (1987; 1997; 1999), Jacobs (1989).

Parties and elections

The party system in Ireland does not follow the division between labor and capital, as has been the case in many other countries. Because of the struggle for independence from Britain described above, the historical cleavage between the main parties was between supporters of the treaty with Britain (semi-independent dominion) and the opponents who wanted a fully independent, united Ireland. Additionally, the general historical conservatism in Irish society due to the strength of the Catholic Church hinders a classification of the party system into left and right (Jacobs 1989: 143).

Another reason why Ireland is difficult to classify is its exceptionally strong center-right bias with 80 percent of voters choosing center-right parties and an extremely weak Irish Left. Until the 1980s and the rise of the Progressive Democrats, Ireland featured no Right party that expressed any anticlerical views. Moreover, the party system has been characterized by the dominance of Fianna Fáil (Mair 1999: 129–35; 1992, 1987) providing only two alternatives for governments: Fianna Fáil single party government; or coalition governments of all non-Fianna Fáil parties between 1948 and 1989. The 1989 elections and subsequent government building marked a significant change in the Irish party system. For the first time Fianna Fáil agreed to enter into a coalition with the Progressive Democrats. Contrary to the two-block system—Fianna Fáil versus "the rest"—the political spectrum now offered various alternatives for governments. Although Fianna Fáil was pressured into coalition governments, due to decreasing electoral support, it actually increased its bargaining power: maintaining the largest share of seats in the *Dáil* it had more options for building majority coalitions than all other parties. Fianna Fáil is a conservative party which, historically, has put stress on the cultural and linguistic unity of the country. However, in the last generation it has also been associated with policies of economic modernization, and in the last couple of decades has abandoned much of the traditional stress on cultural and linguistic traditionalism. Fianna Fáil is the party for small farmers in the West of Ireland and of the middle class. But unlike other European conservative parties, Fianna Fáil also has strong ties to the working class and trade unions and "claims to represent the interests of the poor and the underprivileged" (Mair 1999: 129–30, 144–5; 1992, 1997).

Fine Gael classifies itself as a party of the progressive center (FG 2003). Its policy program concentrates on social justice and free market-economy, and it has tended to advocate policies of economic austerity (Elvert 1999: 269). It has also tended to be the party of the (relatively small) Dublin intelligentsia. The Labour Party was established in 1922 and tried to maintain a neutral position in the civil war issue, which might be one explanation for its historical weakness. Labour's electorate are farm workers, working class and some trade unionists (Mair 1999: 133). In urban areas the Labour Party has lost voters to the Workers' Party, a small left-wing socialist party with strongholds in Dublin. The Progressive Democrats started as a splinter group from Fianna Fáil in the mid-1980s. It originated partly in the ambitions of competing members of the party elite, and partly as a reaction to the perceived

Table 16.2 Governmental majorities in Ireland

Election date *Dáil*	Start of gov.	Head of gov. (party)	Governing parties	Gov. majority (% seats) *Dáil*	Gov. electoral base (% votes) *Dáil*[a]	Gov. majority (% seats) *Seanad*	Institutional veto points	Number of veto players (partisan + institutional)
06.16.1977	07.05.1977	Lynch III (FF)	FF (84)	56.8%	50.6%	45.0%	Referendum[b]	1 + 1
	12.12.1979	Haughey I (FF)	FF (84)	56.8%	50.6%	45.0%	Referendum	1 + 1
06.11.1981	06.30.1981	FitzGerald I (FG)	FG (65), LP (15)	48.2%	46.3%	60.0%	Dáil	2 + 1
02.18.1982	03.09.1982	Haughey II (FF)	FF (81)	48.8%	47.3%	46.7%	Dáil, Referendum	1 + 2
11.24.1982	12.14.1982	FitzGerald II (FG)	FG (70), LP (16)	51.8%	48.6%	58.3%	None	2 + 0
02.17.1987	03.10.1987	Haughey III (FF)	FF (81)	48.8%	44.1%	50.0%	Dáil	1 + 1
06.15.1989	07.12.1989	Haughey IV (FF)	FF (77), PD (6)	50.0%	49.6%	58.3%	None[c]	2 + 0
	02.11.1992	Reynolds I (FF)	FF (77), PD (6)	50.0%	49.6%	58.3%	None[c]	2 + 0
11.25.1992	01.12.1993	Reynolds II (FF)	FF (68), LP (33)	60.8%	58.4%	56.7%	None	2 + 0
	12.15.1994	Bruton (FG)	FG (46), LP (32), DL (6)	50.6%	46.6%	43.3%	Dáil, Referendum	3 + 2
06.06.1997	06.26.1997	Ahern I (FF)	FF (77), PD (4)	48.8%	44.0%	45.0%	Dáil, Referendum	2 + 2
05.17.2002	06.06.2002	Ahern II (FF)	FF (81)	48.8%	41.5%	50.0%	Dáil	1 + 1

[a] Refers to first preference votes.
[b] Referendum is a veto point if the government has less than 2/3 majority in the *Dáil* and no majority in *Seanad* at the same time, then the president may decide not to sign a bill but submit it to referendum (Art. 27 Constitution).
[c] Although the government has only 50% of seats straight we do not count the *Dáil* as veto point in this case as "there is a strong convention that the *Ceann Comhairle* (Speaker) will vote with the government" (Mitchell 2003: 420).

Sources: http://www.oireachtas.ie/; Coakley (1987; 1990; 1993; 1999), Gallagher (1990); Gallagher and Weeks (2003), Manning (1978).

corruption of the party, notably as led by Charles Haughey. However, standing for liberal values and economic austerity it has drawn more voters from Fine Gael than from Fianna Fáil. With vote shares of only 5 to 10 percent the Progressive Democrats have managed to participate in four government coalitions since 1989. Sinn Féin the oldest Irish party was insignificant to *Dáil* elections for decades. It re-emerged as the radical political wing of the Irish Republican Army (IRA) in Northern Ireland. It won one parliamentary seat in the Republic of Ireland parliament in 1997 and enlarged its representation in the last election in 2002. It may well be the fastest growing party in Ireland, and has the distinction of fighting elections on both sides of the border. The Irish Green party has had *Dáil* representation since 1989.

In summary, perhaps the most significant feature of the Irish party system is the historical weakness of parties of the left. This is partly a result of the way the division over the terms of independence shaped party cleavages at the birth of the state, "freezing" those cleavages for over 60 years; and partly to the way a socially onservative Catholic church dominated society for much of the history of the state.

Interest groups

The *Irish Congress of Trade Unions* (ICTU) as an umbrella organization for unions comprises 64 unions in 2001 (ICTU 2003a). The largest single union within the ICTU is the *Services, Industry, Professional, Technical Union* (SIPTU) with approximately 200,000 members. The *Irish Municipal Public, and Civil Trade Union* (IMPACT) unites the majority of public sector employees with a total membership of 37,000. On the employers' side the *Irish Business and Employers' Confederation* (IBEC) represents approximately 7,000 companies from all economic sectors. A merger of the *Confederation of Irish Industry* (CII) and *Federal Union of Employers* (FUE) in 1993 founded IBEC (Elvert 2001: 205, 209; Murphy 1999).

The agricultural sector is declining in Ireland as in other European countries, but the agricultural interest group is significant, nevertheless. The main representative body is the *Irish Farmers' Association* (IFA) with approximately 85,000 members in 2003 (IFA 2003). IFA has taken part in the tripartite negotiations between the social partners and the government such as *Programme of National Recovery* in 1987.

Although interest group representation is multiple and displays "a relatively weak level of centralization" (Taylor 2003: 201) "macro-political bargaining has formed the cornerstone of government policy for over a decade" (191). Successive Irish governments achieved an economic upswing by reducing the national debt from 94 percent to 33.7 percent of GDP, and an unemployment rate of 16.8 percent in 1987 to quasi full employment at the turn of the century, by means of comprehensive tripartite agreements (www.oecd.org). The Programme for National Recovery (1987 to 1990), the Programme for Economic and Social Progress (1990 to 1993), the Programme for Competitiveness and Work (1994 to 1996), the Partnership 2000 (1997 to 2000), the Programme for Prosperity and Fairness (2000 to 2003), and the Sustaining Progress

Programme (2003 to 2005) have been at the center of the policy-making system, and in some accounts are the root cause of the transformation of the Irish economy in the last fifteen years (ICTU 2003b).

In the pension sector the *Irish Association of Pension Funds* (IAPF), founded in 1973, is the non-profit, non-commercial, representative body of the pensions industry. Occupational pension schemes, employers and providers of services to pension schemes constitute IAPF's membership. There are 370 schemes in the IAPF with approximately 200,000 members and 70,000 pensioners (*Irish Times* 29.06.2001). The Association's goal is—apart from providing information services to its members—to participate in, and influence, Irish and European pension policy-making (IAPF 2003). The Society of Actuaries in Ireland represents actuaries in public and issues position papers on current pension policy issues (Society of Actuaries in Ireland 2005). A further actor at the intersection of the pension sector and the financial market is the Irish Association of Investment Managers (IAIM).

Ireland has a number of senior citizens' and pensioners' organizations, for example, *Age & Opportunity, Age Action Ireland, Irish Association of Older People, Federation of Active Retirement Associations*, or *National Federation of Pensioner's Associations*. Moreover the federation of unions has its own pensioners section—the *ICTU Retired Workers' Committee*. However, these organizations have played but a negligible role in pension policy processes of the last two decades. A representative of consumer (i.e. pensioner's) interests was only nominated to the Pensions Board June 1, 2002 for the first time (Pensions Board 2003b: 6).

III Pension system

Historical overview

The first Irish pension institutions go back to British legacies that were carried on after the independence of Ireland in 1922. A means-tested, tax-financed old-age pension was set up in 1908, followed by widows and orphans contributory pensions in 1935. After World War II, compulsory social security insurance was re-established for blue-collar workers and for white-collar workers below a certain income ceiling. In 1961, the non-contributory means-tested pension was complemented by a contribution-financed old-age pension. A minimum qualifying period of 15 insurance years was required for flat-rate benefits at an age of 70 years. In 1970, a flat-rate and contribution-financed Retirement pension and invalidity pension was introduced. In 1973 (going into effect in 1974) the coverage was extended to all white-collar employees, and between 1973 and 1977, the standard retirement age was lowered to 66 years. In the early 1970s, the Fine Gael/Labour government suggested the introduction of an earnings-related supplementary pension scheme but after the change in government back to Fianna Fáil in 1976 the idea sank into oblivion (Maguire 1986: 244; Rechmann 2001: 72; Department of Social Welfare 1976).

Occupational pensions in the public sector have existed in Ireland since 1921. Occupational pensions in the private sector have been based on the Trustee Act 1893, but fund management, investment strategies and preservation of entitlements were unregulated until 1990 (Rechmann 2001: 167; see also Bristow and Ryan 1985).

Description of the current pension system

Coverage

The Irish pension system is composed of three pillars: state, occupational and private pensions. The state pension—Social Welfare Pensions—is a low flat rate pension linked to employment. On top of this basic pension the state provides no other mandatory, supplementary earnings-related or individual pensions, but voluntary, occupational pensions are widely spread to complement the statutory pension benefits. Since 2002, private retirement savings accounts have been more attractive and more secure.

The first tier, first pillar Irish statutory pension system (*Social Welfare Pensions*) covers everybody between 16 and 66 years who makes *Pay-Related Social Insurance* (PRSI) contributions. Social Insurance features two co-existing types of pensions that differ in the required retirement age and qualifying period:[4] the Old Age Pension and the Retirement Pension. The entire active workforce with income above €38 per week is covered (Department of Social and Family Affairs 2005a). Voluntary coverage after previously compulsory insurance is possible (Rechmann 2001: 134).

Non-contributory means-tested old-age pensions are available to all citizens who fail to qualify for the Social Insurance Pension. The *Non-contributory Old Age Pensions* are paid under social assistance, and income from capital assets is taken into account.

Although occupational and private pensions are voluntary, the rate of coverage is considerable and has increased at least in absolute numbers in the last decade (Connell and Stewart 2004: Table 7.1). In 2002, employers offered 105,863 occupational pension schemes insuring 709,332 members (Pensions Board 2003b: 21). Recent statistics on supplementary pensions coverage by the Irish Central Statistical Office showed that the non-state pension coverage of persons in employment aged 20 to 69 with supplementary pensions is 50.7 percent, with 35.2 percent covered by an occupational pension scheme, 12.6 percent covered by a personal pension, and 2.9 percent enjoying both occupational and personal pension coverage. The probability of coverage increased with employment in the banking sector, with age, with income, with male gender, with marital status, with company size, with full-time employment and with regional location of the workplace. With respect to the regional differentiation, Dublin has the highest coverage with 55.8 percent of the workforce, and the West the lowest coverage with 41.5 percent. In matters of occupation pensions, catering and agriculture have the lowest rate of coverage with 12.5 percent and 15.8 percent, while the public sector enjoys a rate of 87.7 percent. Forty-four percent of members of personal pensions are self-employed and assisting relatives (CSO 2002: 1–2; Hughes and Whelan 1996).

It is reasonable to assume that private pension coverage, that is the third pillar of the pension system, will increase within the next years because of the establishment of *Personal Retirement Savings Accounts* (PRSA) aimed at the target coverage rate of 70 percent for the population 30 years or older. In short, full-time, older employees in the financing or public sector where employers provide defined-benefit occupational pensions are the ones best protected by the Irish private–public pension mix.

Administration

The Department of Social and Family Affairs is responsible for the administration of state pensions. Ireland has neither a separate agency nor separate contributions for the state pension insurance, but all social security benefits are covered by an overall contribution rate (PRSI) paid to the Social Insurance Fund. The Revenue Commissioners, as representatives of the Department of Finances, collect PRSI on behalf of the Department of Social, Community and Family Affairs. Pension benefits are administered and distributed by the Department of Social and Family Affairs' Pension Services Office which pays pensions directly to a bank account, or issues "payable orders" to be cashed at the local post office (Department of Social and Family Affairs 2002a: 11–12).

All regulations concerning occupational pensions and the newly established PRSA (*Personal Retirement Saving Accounts*) are monitored by the *Pensions Board* (*An Bord Pinsean*). Established by the *Pensions Act 1990*, under the umbrella of the Department of Social and Family Affairs, the Pensions Board supervises the implementation of *Pensions Act 1990* and advises the Minister on pension matters (Section 10 Pensions Act 1990). Its main purpose is to "protect the interests of Irish scheme members and to spread information on pensions" (Pensions Board 2003a: 6). The Pensions Board grants certificates to the registered pension schemes that fulfill the funding standards. The Pensions Board's 16 members are appointed by the Minister for Social, Community and Family Affairs for terms of five years. The membership includes representatives of trade unions, the employers, the pension industry, trustees and the departments of Finances and Social Affairs. Financial companies, insurances or employers may be providers of occupational pension schemes and PRSA.

Financing

The Irish Social Welfare pensions (i.e. the Contributory Old-Age Pension and Retirement Pension as well as Non-Contributory Old Age Pension), have been financed solely on the PAYG principle until recently. *Pay-Related Social Insurance* (PRSI) contributions are paid to the Social Insurance Fund according to the insurance class on a weekly basis. Employees with weekly earnings above €38 belong to Class A. Employers of Class A employees paid in 2005 a contribution rate of

First pillar	Second pillar	Third pillar
Third tier: none	Additional voluntary contributions (AVCs) (only open to members of occupational pension schemes)	Voluntary private pension: virtually not existent
Second tier: none	Subsidized and regulated voluntary occupational pensions: Defined-benefit schemes (1,901 schemes with 471,841 members) / Defined contribution schemes (105,863 schemes with 237,491 members)	PRSA subsidized private pension: mandatory in terms of employer has to provide access but no insurance compulsion for employee
First tier: *Contributory Old Age Pension* and *Retirement Pension* — Employees, Self-employed, Farmers, Civil servants / Minimum contributory old age pension with yearly average of 10 weeks of contributions	Mandatory occupational pension: none	
Means-tested *Non-Contributory Old age Pension* Plus Social Assistance Free Schemes		

Fig. 16.2 Pension system in Ireland

8.5 percent up to €356 and a rate of 10.75 percent for all income above that level. Employees with income below €287 per week are exempt from the payment of their share of contribution. Persons with earnings above €287 pay 4 percent of all weekly income above €127, and with earnings above €400, 2 percent for the first €127, and 6 percent for earnings above. Self-employed in Class S contribute 3 percent of income to PRSI up to €400 and 5 percent for income above. Currently, the Social Insurance Fund produces a surplus (Department of Social and Family Affairs 2005a; 2004: Table A7), but the state granted a deficit coverage from general taxation most of the time in the past and—according to projections—will be covering shortfalls in the future. In order to reduce the future financial burden on the state budget caused by demographic developments the *National Reserve Fund Act 2000* introduced a funded component into the Irish state pension system: the National Pension Reserve Fund (NPRF) is to accumulate reserves of 1 percent of GDP per year between 2001 and 2055 which will be used to reduce pension costs from 2025 onwards (Section 18 Bill 36 of 2000).

Occupational pension schemes are predominantly funded systems. An exception is the public sector supplementary pension scheme that functions on the basis of PAYG (National Pensions Policy Initiative 1998: 4). The funded schemes of the private sector must meet minimum financing standards as fixed in the *Pensions Act 1990* and its amendments. The funding standards imply a capacity to 100 percent of present liabilities in case of winding-up a pension scheme. However, not only a minimum standard is imposed on occupational and private pension schemes; there is also a maximum of reserves. If the reserves exceed coverage of all liabilities by more than 5 percent the pension scheme managers either have to return the excess amount to the employer, which has to pay regular corporation tax for these gains, or the pension scheme takes "contribution holidays," that is contribution payments are suspended for a time period until the reserves and liabilities match again.

Benefits

Ireland has three types of state pensions: (i) the contribution-related *Contributory Old-Age Pension*; (ii) the *Retirement Pensions*; and (iii) the *Non-Contributory Old-Age Pension* for persons without sufficient insurance periods. The contributory old-age, and retirement, pensions hardly differ from each other: benefits are the same but eligibility conditions vary slightly. To be entitled to a Contributory Old-Age Pension a person must have reached the retirement age of 66 years and requires entrance to insurance at an age younger than 56 years. Retirement Pension is available at the age of 65 and requires insurance entrance at an age younger than 55, a minimum of 260 weeks (5 years) of contribution payments, and no further earnings for one year (*retirement condition*). The minimum qualifying condition for a retirement pension is currently in transition. Before 2002, 156 weeks were required; between 2002 and 2012, 260 weeks are necessary; thereafter, 520 weeks of compulsory insurance periods qualify for a Retirement Pension. In order to be eligible for full first-tier pensions a person needs an average of 48 weeks of full-rate contributions per year over his/her entire working career; the minimum rate for an Old-age Contributory Pension is available with a yearly average of 10 weeks of contributions (Department of Social and Family Affairs 2002b: 28–32; 2002a: 4). Credited contributions are provided for periods of unemployment, sickness and maternity leave. Up to 12 years of child-rearing are disregarded in calculating the yearly average (since April 1995). Benefits in the state pension system are flat-rate. The full weekly benefit rate in 2005 for a retirement and contributory old-age pension is €179.30; the minimum for a contributory old-age pension with a yearly average of 10 contribution weeks is €89.70. Additionally, the pensioner may draw supplements for dependants, for example €119.50 per adult 65 years or younger and €19.30 per child. The social welfare Non-contributory Old-age Pension is means-tested but may amount to the maximum of €166.00 with social assistance free schemes on top (Department of Social and Family Affairs 2005b: 12–14). These schemes cover fuel allowances, free travel, free electricity, free bottled gas, free natural gas, free television license and free telephone rental.

Benefits from occupational pensions accounted for approximately 23.5 percent in 2000 of total old age income for the 65- to 74-year olds.[5] As the Pensions Board points out in one of its information leaflets: "Occupational Pension Schemes come in all shapes and sizes—no two are exactly the same" (Pensions Board 2001: 2). It is therefore difficult to generalize about the supplementary benefits. The retirement age ranges from 60 to 70 years; usually the occupational pension schemes follow the standard state retirement age of 65 years. Contribution rates are fixed individually for each scheme in the contract between employee and employer. Apart from old-age benefits occupational schemes usually provide a lump-sum payment to survivors in case of pre-retirement death. Pension rights in occupational pensions are preserved in case of change of employment or leaving service with a minimum vesting period of two years for persons leaving service after June 1, 2002 (*Irish Times* 08.03.2002). Previously, occupational pension entitlements required a minimum of five years in order to be revalued and transferred to another employer.

Occupational pension benefits stem either from defined-benefit or from defined-contribution schemes. Benefit calculation differs considerably. Defined-benefit schemes calculate pensions on the employee's (last) salary—most common is 40/60ths (Hogan and O'Sullivan 2002). Benefits in defined-benefit schemes are very often integrated into the Irish Social Welfare pension; that is, the occupational scheme promises a certain percentage of the employee's income, but the estimated amount is reduced by the amount received through the Social Welfare pension. More precisely, the actual salary is reduced by the fictional salary that would be equivalent to the Social Welfare pension benefit. For instance: if the salary was Ir£ 18,000 and the yearly Social Welfare benefit Ir£ 4,628 the pensionable salary for occupational pensions would only be Ir£ 11,058, which means the employer would have to pay a pension of Ir£ 7,372 instead of Ir£ 12,000 (example taken from Pensions Board 2001: 7).

Benefits in defined-contribution or money-purchase schemes depend on the contributions paid and the rate of return that was achieved through investment. Defined-contribution pension holders are required to buy a personal annuity at the time of retirement. The annuity fund guarantees a life-time pension income but when the person dies any remaining assets are lost (Pensions Board 2000).

Personal pension benefits in terms of Pay-Related Savings Accounts may be drawn from the age of 60 but retirement age is flexible. At the time of retirement, the retiree may take out 25 percent of the personal fund as a tax-free lump sum which can be invested in an Approved Minimum Retirement Fund or Approved Retirement Fund. After the insured person dies, the remaining assets are handed down to descendants (*Irish Times* 08.03.2002).

IV POLITICS OF PENSION REFORM SINCE 1980

Overview

At the beginning of the 1980s, the Irish pension system "promised" poverty in old age for many people. Full Social Insurance Pensions were only about 15 percent higher than social assistance pensions, disregarding further social assistance free schemes. The self-employed and farmers were totally excluded from Social Welfare Insurance. Voluntary, supplementary occupational pension coverage was widespread among male white-collar workers in large companies and in the public sector. But women with interrupted working careers, low-income earners and employees of the service industries hardly enjoyed any occupational pension coverage. With increasing numbers of people frequently changing employment, occupational pension coverage decreased: when transfer and revaluation of benefits was not practised, employees who left service before retirement (early-leavers) cashed-in their contributions and were left with inadequate pensions. Private pensions, completely unregulated, were risky investments and often too expensive for low-income earners.

The *Social Welfare Act 1988* made state Social Insurance compulsory for the self-employed and farmers. The main act in Irish pensions law—the *Pensions Act 1990*—guaranteed that pension schemes would be adequately funded and administered and that pension entitlements were not lost or cashed-in if a worker changed his/her employer. As the self-employed, farmers, housewives or students could not benefit from occupational pension schemes, the *Pensions Act 2002* introduced flexible Personal *Retirement Savings* Accounts (PRSAs) to close this gap in coverage.

Table 16.3 Overview of proposed and enacted pension reforms in Ireland

Year	Name of reform	Reform process (chronology)	Reform measures
1988	Social Welfare Act	• 1976 Green Paper on the introduction of an income-related pension scheme including self-employed and farmers • 1978 Green Paper on PRSI insurance for self-employed • 1986 set up the National Pensions Board • January 1987 First Report of the National Pensions Board • March 3, 1988 publication of the bill • March 10, 1988 passage in *Dáil* • March 29, 1988 passage in *Seanad*	• introduction of compulsory PRSI for self-employed and farmers • introduction of a Pre-Retirement Allowance for people over 60 years who had been unemployed and receiving benefits for at least 15 months • *pro rata* pensions for pre-1974 insurance
1990	Pensions Act	• March 30, 1990 submission of the bill • July 10, 1990 passage in *Dáil* • July 17, 1990 passage in *Seanad*	• regulation of occupational pensions • guarantee of adequate funding and administration of occupational pension schemes • vesting of occupational pension entitlements after 5 years
1996	Pensions (Amendment) Act	• December 13, 1995 publication of the bill • June 12, 1996 passage in *Dáil* • June 26, 1996 passage in *Seanad*	• increase in fines for offences from Ir£1,000 to Ir£ 1,500 • introduction of a "whistle blowing" section requiring to report fraud and misappropriation of funds • two more members for the Pensions Board

2000	Pensions Reserve Fund Act	• October 30, 1996 establishment of the National Pensions Policy Initiative • May 1998 report of the Pensions Policy Initiative • June 12, 2000 presentation of the bill • November 21, 2000 passage in *Dáil* • November 29, 2000 passage in *Seanad*	• establishment of a pensions fund financed by 1% of GNP per year between 2001 and 2055 • set-up of a National Pensions Reserve Fund Commission • appointment of a National Treasury Management Agency
2002	Pensions Act	• July 25, 2001 publication of the bill • February 28, 2002 passage in *Seanad* • March 27, 2002 passage in *Dáil* • March 28, 2002 passage of amended bill in *Seanad*	• introduction of personal pension accounts (PRSAs) • regulation of PRSA: maximum administrative charges of 5% of contributions or 1% of annual value assets; compulsory provision of access by employers; guarantee of transferability between different providers • reduction of minimum vesting period from 5 to 2 years • guarantee of revaluation of entitlements with inflation up to 4% • establishment of a pension ombudsman

Social Welfare Act 1988: PRSI for the self-employed and farmers

Prelude to the Celtic Tiger

Mandatory social insurance for the self-employed had been part of social policy discussions since the late 1970s. The Government published a Green Paper on the introduction of an income-related pension scheme that highlighted the shortcomings of the pension system and presented three possible models of a national pension system in 1976. The paper stated: "One of the shortcomings of the present pensions arrangements arises from the fact that self-employed persons as such are not covered by the present insurance system either for pensions or for any other benefit" (Department of Social Welfare 1976: 61). Another Green Paper (*Social Insurance for the Self-Employed: A Discussion Paper*) published in 1978, provided a first proposal for the extension of PRSI contributions to self-employed to cover for old age, survivors and invalidity (National Pensions Board 1988: 9). However, the fast-changing governments of the early 1980s took no action.

In January 1987, the Fine Gael/Labour government dissolved on conflicts over budget and retrenchment measures. Both Fine Gael and the Progressive Democrats, the latter running for election for the first time, fought for economic orthodoxy and dismissed tax cuts as unaffordable in the election campaign. On election day, February 17, 1987, the right-wing Progressive Democrats won 11.8% of votes, further benefited from transfer votes from Fianna Fáil as well as Fine Gael voters, and became the third strongest party in the *Dáil* (O'Leary 1987: 455–7). Fianna Fáil ran for single-party government although it slightly missed an absolute majority in the *Dáil* (81 out of 166 seats) leading to a tight Prime Minister investiture vote decided by the Speaker's vote (Dáil, Vol. 371, 10.03.1987: 48–50).

Ireland was in a national crisis in the second half of the 1980s with respect to unemployment, national debt and emigration rates. In order to deal with the critical economic situation Fianna Fáil was determined to start a *Programme for National Recovery*. Negotiations with unions and employers led to centralized wage bargaining. In exchange for modest wage increases over a three year period in line with inflation and a reduction in working hours, unions had to accept major cuts in the public sector, especially in the health service. Unions thus exchanged limits on bargaining freedom for some income guarantees and the prospect of a long-term recovery in the fortunes of the economy—which was realized. Although the pact started out in the public sector it became the model for the private sector agreement (EMIRE 2003a). Against the background of the economic state of the country it is quite obvious that the government tried to increase revenues in areas where it was unable to enact cuts—such as the Social Welfare Pensions system. Indeed, perhaps the single most important source of the crisis which produced the first phase of the Programme for National Recovery was the deep crisis in the state's finances by the late 1980s. And the Programme for National Recovery can therefore be legitimately identified as the prelude to the birth of the Celtic Tiger—and to the relatively benign fiscal conditions of the last decade and a half.

Expansion of pay-related social insurance

Already in 1986 the Minister for Health and Social Welfare, Barry Desmond (LP), had set up the National Pensions Board which included members of the Department of Social Welfare, the pension industry, employers and unions. The Board was assigned to report on occupational pensions and to make recommendations for pensions policy in general (Dáil, Vol. 399, 29.05.1990: 603). On July 29, 1987 the Fianna Fáil government announced the inclusion of the self-employed in social insurance, and the National Pensions Board was charged with reviewing and commenting on the proposal of inclusion of the self-employed.

The National Pensions Board proposed extending coverage to the self-employed for three reasons: to "provide the self-employed with basic pension cover;" to "improve the equity in the financing of social welfare by providing for the self-employed to make a direct contribution towards financing their own social insurance cover;" and to "bring Ireland into line in this regard with most other EEC countries" (National Pensions Board 1988: 7–8). Previously, the self-employed were eligible for means-tested social assistance pensions although they had not contributed to the system. Differences between employees and self-employed remained inasmuch as the new contributions did not provide cover for disability or invalidity pensions for self-employed (Dáil, Vol. 378, 09.03.1988: 2049, 2245).

Although the National Pensions Board was in favor of equal flat-rate benefits for employees and the self-employed, it considered the option of restricting the benefits of the self-employed to a maximum level of non-contributory pensions if financial consequences of full extension of insurance coverage to the self-employed could not be borne. The Board did not reach consensus on the question of whether self-employed Old Age Contributory Pension benefits required retirement, but deferred the decision until later (National Pensions Board 1988: 10).

Although the First Report of the National Pensions Board, published in January 1987, had recommended a comprehensive Pensions Act not only to deal with pension coverage of the self-employed but also to establish a broad framework for occupational pensions, the ministerial draft for legislation in 1988 was part of the yearly Social Welfare Act and included only the former.

The then Minister for Social Welfare, Michael Woods (FF), initiated a bill on March 3, 1988. The Bill proposed to increase social assistance, occupational injuries and unemployment assistance benefits and to increase the earnings limit for social insurance contributions. Another change was known as *pro rata* pensions for pre-1974 insurance. Some employees did not meet the minimum qualifying period due to the fact that social insurance excluded non-manual workers above a certain income prior to 1974. In other words, if their income rose above the limit at some point during their working career before 1974, it caused gaps in their social insurance account. The *Social Welfare Act 1988* empowered the Minister of Social Welfare to offset this drawback and to grant reduced pension benefits by regulations (Dáil, Vol. 378, 09.03.1988: 2048, 2070). Furthermore, the bill envisioned the introduction of a Pre-Retirement Allowance that would allow the retirement of people over 60 years who had been unemployed and receiving benefits for at least 15 months (Bill 8 of 1988: Expl. Memo. 2).

The most relevant section of the 1988 *Social Welfare Bill* was the introduction of compulsory social insurance for self-employed and farmers which would entitle them to old–age benefit and, after a minimum qualifying period of four years, to widows' and orphans' benefits in case of death (Bill 8 of 1988 Expl. Memo. 1, 5). The self-employed who paid income tax under Schedule D, persons under Schedule E (e.g. proprietary directors of companies) and employees that had been excluded so far such as clergy, coroners, doctors and dentists would be required to make PRSI contributions.

An innovation was that the self-employed, unlike employees, would be liable for contributions on their non-earned income from rent or investment. Opposition parties (FG, PD) protested in parliamentary debate against this unequal treatment of employees and self-employed, since for employees unearned income would remain PRSI-free. Contrary to earlier indications, the bill did not allow the self-employed to opt out from the state contributions, in order to avoid the Exchequer forgoing the contributions of the higher income self-employed (Dáil, Vol. 378, 09.03.1988: 2050–2054, 2277–2278). However, the Fine Gael and Progressive Democrats opposition must be regarded more as a strategy of political positioning and differentiating from the government (as part of party competition) than as a critique of policy content. As the parliamentary voting results on the *Social Welfare Act 1988* show (see p. 798 n. 7) their policy interests concerning social insurance for self-employed and farmers were not so much different from the government's stance.

The National Pensions Board had recommended a PRSI contribution rate for the self-employed of 6.6 percent. The bill, however, envisioned a lower contribution rate of 5 percent. The contribution rate for self-employed would be phased-in incrementally starting with 3 percent from April 6, 1988 up to 5 percent from April 6, 1990 on with a minimum annual contribution of Ir£208 (Bill 8 of 1988 Expl. Memo. 1, 5).

The introduction of compulsory coverage for the self-employed also brought changes for employees. Prior to the *Social Welfare Act 1988*, insured persons who did not meet the minimum qualifying period for the Contributory Old-age Pension of ten years received a refund of their contribution payments regardless of their entitlement to a Non-contributory Old-age Pension. As self-employed, they would no longer enjoy the privilege of Non-contributory Old-age Pensions without prior PRSI contributions; there was no longer any justification for refunding the contributions of employees if they received means-tested benefits. Self-employed people who reached the standard retirement age in less than ten years, and were therefore unable to qualify for the Contributory Old-Age Pension, were not included in the new regulation. In other words, the system would profit from ten years of revenue inflow before it had to pay any additional pension benefits to self-employed or farmers.[6] According to government projections, the Social Insurance Fund would profit from around Ir£ 360 million from self-employed contributions until 2000 which would reduce the governmental subsidy, that is deficit coverage, during this period (Dáil, Vol. 378, 09.03.1988: 2058–2063, 2245).

At the time of the Second Stage parliamentary debate, self-employed and farmers beyond parliament united to campaign against the proposal. They pledged in favor of the possibility to opt out of the state system. In the context of the protests of the self-employed, trade unions warned the Minister for Social Welfare not to back down on compulsory social insurance for self-employed as the unions would regard such a retreat as "a serious breach of the Programme for National Recovery" (*Irish Independent* 11.03.1988).

Parliamentary process

Several of the changes in the *Social Welfare Bill 1988* received unanimous support, such as the pre-1974 pro rata pensions and the increases in social welfare benefits. There was also cross-party consensus in the *Dáil* for the introduction of some kind of pension insurance for self-employed and farmers. But Labor was the only opposition party that unreservedly welcomed the inclusion of self-employed in the social insurance system (Dáil, Vol. 378, 09.03.1988: 2103, 2107).

Criticism alluded to the fact that the self-employed did not have to retire to qualify for old-age pensions: it would decrease incentives for older farmers to hand over their businesses. Previously, retirement and transfer of the farm to a son or daughter was a pre-condition for the means-tested Non-Contributory Old-Age Pension. The later hand-over in farming could not only have negative effects on the economy but was likely to affect the insurance system negatively itself: if the farmers' sons waited for 20 to 30 years to become owner of the farm they would be working as assisting relatives and would not be liable to PRSI contributions, thus not earning any pension entitlements (Dáil, Vol. 378, 09.03.1988: 2074, 2261–2262).

The major opposition party, Fine Gael, advocated the idea of requiring the self-employed to prove their membership annually in a private pension scheme, in order to secure old-age income for the self-employed and reduce government pension expenditure. The Progressive Democrats agreed with the government that non-contributory pensions for the self-employed should be abolished, but, like Fine Gael, they stood for the idea of establishing social insurance for self-employed through private schemes. They rejected the extension of the state system and instead recommended negotiations between insurance companies, self-employed, farmers and the government (Dáil, Vol. 378, 09.03.1988: 2237).

The bill did not specify how surpluses during the first ten years of self-employed coverage should be used. Therefore the Progressive Democrats blamed the Fianna Fáil government for extending the insurance coverage to the self-employed to relieve the state budget in the short-run. To counter this argument, the government committed itself to a review of the pension scheme for the self-employed by December 1990 (Section 17C (e) of the *Social Welfare Act 1988*). But while the surplus in the short run ameliorated the situation of the budget, the Progressive Democrats suspected that self-employed compulsory PRSI insurance was irresponsibly financed in the long-term under the new regulations: there were too few contribution payers and the cost estimations for extending the insurance coverage was based on a collection rate of 100 percent to keep the extended system cost-neutral, which was considered unrealistic

(Dáil, Vol. 378, 09.03.1988: 2094–2095, 2272). The Progressive Democrats tried to clear up the misperception that the extension of insurance coverage to the self-employed was not an additional tax to the self-employed but rather the "greatest bonanza they will ever get from any Government" as they became entitled to a state pension for a contribution rate as low as 3 percent in the first year and with a maximum of 5 percent after the transition period, whereas the combined employers' and employees' PRSI contribution rate for social insurance was 16.8 percent in 1988 (Department of Social Welfare 1988: Table A10). Even the Labour Party was concerned that the system might become under-funded in the future (Dáil, Vol. 379, 22.03.1988: 583–586). Further support for the claim that the extension of insurance is beneficial to farmers and the self-employed stems from the accident that—according to deputy Carey (FG)—the farmers' president agreed to PRSI coverage within the *Programme for National Recovery* without knowing the exact contribution rate. Carey (FG) argued in his parliamentary address that the farmer's president would have never done so if the PRSI coverage was not valuable for the agricultural sector all together.

The very special place of farmers in these reforms is part of a more general pattern to the system of pension politics which developed, especially out of the Programme for National Recovery. The patterns of institutional incorporation and exclusion clearly privileged certain groups in the policy process, such as farmers, and conversely marginalized others, such as consumers.

PD amendments at Committee Stage were defeated (*Irish Independent* 23.03.1988) and consequently, the *Dáil* adopted the bill with 74 to 17 votes.[7] The senate debate brought no significant changes and the bill was finally passed on March 29, 1988 (Seanad, Vol. 119, 29.03.1988: 475).

The Pensions Act 1990

Background

Prime Minister Charles Haughey (FF) called early elections in May 1989 after the polls had displayed favorable support for the government after two years in office (Marsh and Sinnott 1990: 126; Mitchell 2000: 153). However, two-thirds of the voters considered the early election to be unnecessary. This had a negative impact on the government's popularity and turned the election itself into a campaign issue (FG 1989: 1). Polls showed that the most important issues in the election were unemployment and health cuts. Welfare and pensions ranged on rank seven following unemployment, health, emigration, tax cuts, prices and economy (Marsh and Sinnott 1990: 108).

Fine Gael, which had been in opposition for two years, promised to reform the tax system, the social welfare system, economic structures and the criminal law if elected into government. With respect to reducing poverty, Fine Gael proposed to replace all different means tests with a single eligibility test. The number one goal was to reduce the national debt and to stabilize public expenditure. Furthermore, the Fine Gael election program envisioned reducing Pay-Related Social Insurance (PRSI) and income tax to provide greater incentives to work and to create jobs. The employee PRSI and self-employed PRSI contributions were even to be abolished altogether, being replaced by a 5 percent levy. Income tax rates were to be reduced in several steps to 40 percent and 25 percent. The minimum age for pre-retirement was to be lowered to 55 years with the restriction of concurrent employment to 18 hours per week (FG 1989: 2, 5–7, 51).

The voting on June 15, 1989 brought the following results: Fianna Fáil was able to maintain its share of votes but lost four seats. Nevertheless, it remained the biggest party in the *Dáil* with 77 out of 166 seats. It made improvements in better-off constituencies attracting middle-class former PD voters, but at the same time it lost among the working class electorate. The Progressive Democrats were the losers of the election: the party lost half of the votes of 1987 (a drop from 11.85% to 5.49%) and of its 14 deputies only six representatives remained in the *Dáil*. The votes transfer pattern was different in 1989 from that in previous elections. Whereas the three-party-system of the 1980s featured vote transfers between Fine Gael and the Labour Party, the 1989 ballot displayed the greatest transfers between Fine Gael and the Progressive Democrats, but also strong transfers between Labour and the Workers' Party. The election results showed that Ireland in 1989 had 19 marginal constituencies: that is, a swing vote of less than 3 percent would change the distribution of seats (Gallagher 1990: 73–4; 78–9; 90–1).

Even though Fianna Fáil and the Progressive Democrats were the only two parties which lost seats, these electoral losers formed the new government. For the first time in history, Fianna Fáil entered into a coalition government. This was a momentous event. It marked not only a great historical shift in Fianna Fáil strategy, but also marked a great shift in the terms of party competition, since it introduced into the very heart of policy-making a significant new institutional actor in the party system. After the rise of the Progressive Democrats, the whole character of party competition necessarily changed, notably as far as Fianna Fáil was concerned, since the new party was essentially a breakaway from Fianna Fáil. The Senate election resulted in a Fianna Fáil majority although the party did not win any of the university constituencies. Moreover, three of the eleven prime minister nominees were members of the Progressive Democrats. The *Taoiseach* was constrained to make these nominations as part of the coalition agreement (Coakley 1990: 154).

Shortly after the government took office another tripartite agreement was signed. As the *Programme for National Recovery* of 1987 expired, and the economy was still at a low, social partnership was renewed in the *Programme for Economic and Social Progress* (PESP). The main goal was a ten-year strategy to reduce the national debt as percentage of GDP, to balance the budget, to decrease unemployment and to create new employment (EMIRE 2003c).

The bill

Occupational pensions had existed since the nineteenth century but the *Pensions Act 1990* "marks a milestone in the history of the development of an overall system to provide for adequate and secure pension cover for our citizens" and was "the most important piece of legislation concerning occupational pensions to come before this House since the foundation of the State" (Minister Woods (FF) in Dáil, Vol. 399, 29.05.1990: 596–597). Until then, occupational pension schemes were based on the *Trustee Act 1893* which was not intended to regulate pension schemes but rather charity organizations. This single example emphasizes the importance of policy legacies—including British originated policy legacies—in shaping the Irish system. The collapse of several firms in the mid-1980s drew attention to the vulnerability of members' old age benefits if an employer's pension scheme dissolved during the winding-up of the company (e.g. H. Williams Group, Castlecomer, and Roscrea Meats; see Dáil, Vol. 399, 31.05.1990). When the media uncovered more cases of under-funded pension schemes in the mid-1980s, the public became aware of the need to provide for monitoring employers' operation of pension schemes (Dáil, Vol. 399, 29.05.1990: 649).

The general revision of the pension system had started with the establishment of the National Pensions Board in 1986 as describe above. Although the First Report of the National Pensions Board was published in 1987 no immediate action followed (National Pensions Board 1987). When the social insurance coverage was extended to the self-employed in 1988, the Progressive Democrats accused the government of not following the Board's recommendations to enact a comprehensive pensions act (Dáil, Vol. 378, 09.03.1988: 2091–2092). The Minister for Social Welfare, Michael Woods (FF), submitted a pensions bill on March 30, 1990.

The major parts of the bill were the establishment of a Pensions Board, the definition of the responsibilities of the occupational pension schemes' trustees, the protection and revaluation of entitlements, the provision of minimum funding standards and the realization of equal treatment of men and women in occupational pensions. The Pensions Board was set up to ensure that occupational pension providers followed all other regulations of the 1990 pension reform. The Pensions Board comprised 12 members and a chairperson, each appointed by the Minister for Social Welfare: four representatives of the Department for Social Welfare, one for the Department of Finances, two for the pension industry, one member for actuaries, pension lawyers, accountants, employers and unions each (Pensions Board 1993: 23). As decisions were to be taken by the majority (*Pensions Act 1990*, First Schedule, 21) the composition of the Board over-represented the pensions industry as well as the social welfare ministry, while completely excluding consumers', pensioners' or women's interests. The Board was entitled to employ staff to support the exercise of its functions and to levy fees from member schemes for its own financing.

The former trust law had required the trustees to manage the pension schemes in the interest of its members. As this vague definition of duties often necessitated court trials if a member suspected a trustee of mismanagement, the Pensions Bill regulated the responsibilities of the trustees which included sensible investment of assets, supervising benefit payments and guaranteeing correct records of membership and finances (Dáil, Vol. 399, 29.05.1990: 621). Compulsory disclosure of information to scheme members was among the duties. If a trustee was found guilty of an offence of breach of duties the Pensions Board could impose fines.

One of the most important measures was the statutory preservation of pension entitlements if a worker changed employment. In the past, 90 percent of all early-leavers claimed a refund of their contributions from the old employer (Dáil, Vol. 399, 31.05.1990: 1006). But this refund included neither the employer's contributions nor a revaluation of entitlements with inflation. Thus many reached retirement age without adequate protection, or left widows and orphans behind who were not provided for. The Pensions Bill improved the conditions for transferability of pension rights. Regulations in this matter were also proposed to ameliorate mobility and flexibility in the labor market. Concerning the revaluation of pension entitlements, the National Pensions Board suggested adjusting entitlements where the inflation rate was up to 4 percent, and where inflation was between 4 percent and 10 percent suggested increasing the entitlements further with half the excess over 4 percent. There was to be a maximum indexation rate of 7 percent. After opposition from the insurance industry, on the grounds that it was unable to offer contracts with flexible revaluation, and due to the possibility of very high revaluation, the bill just provided for benefits adjustment up to 4 percent. But the bill did not require employers to preserve and revalue pension rights that were acquired before the passage of the *Pensions Act*, (i.e. all entitlements from pre-1991 service). The new funding standards compelled the occupational pension schemes to cover 100 percent of liabilities. All schemes were compelled under the bill to have the minimum funding standards of the scheme certified by an actuary every three and a half years.

As retirement age in the majority of occupational pension schemes for men and women was already equal, there was not much justification for action to implement equal treatment by January 1, 1993. Moreover, the EC Directive permitted inequality in this respect for the time being. As the EC Directive also allowed deferment of equalization of survivors' pensions for men and women, the Minister for Social Welfare deferred this aspect as he wanted to avoid overburdening the schemes that already had to bear the financial burden of the other Pensions Bill measures (Dáil, Vol. 399, 29.05.1990: 605, 609–14, 623–5).

Parliamentary process

The *Pensions Bill 1990* was positively received across parties in the *Dáil*. All spokesmen welcomed the bill for its goal of protecting pension scheme members' interests (Flatherty (FG), Byrne (WP) in Dáil, Vol. 399, 29.05.1990: 627, 655; McCormack (FG), Kirk (FF), Wyse (PD) in Dáil, Vol. 399, 31.05.1990: 1023, 1033, 1051).

Except for reservations on the section on composition of the boards of trustees, even the trade unions supported the bill. Disagreement remained on details. All parties criticized the government for not exactly following the National Pensions Board's recommendations, but for different reasons. The Labour party criticized the government for not regulating supplementary old-age provision for the self-employed and farmers, and for not making the supply of occupational pension schemes compulsory for all employers. Promoting the idea of universal pension coverage the Labour party recognized the Pensions Bill as a first step of the Government taking greater responsibility in caring for the elderly.

The Left in Parliament, in line with the Irish Congress of Trade Unions, demanded that employers should be required to have members' representatives on the boards of trustees. Labour claimed one-third of the trustees should be representatives of the scheme members and the Workers' Party promised to submit an amendment on Committee Stage to alleviate this major flaw in the bill (Dáil, Vol. 399, 29.05.1990: 656; Vol. 400, 19.06.1990: 214).

After the Second Stage had shown the importance of the issue of member representation on the Board of Trustees, the Minister negotiated with the ICTU and the employers. As a consequence the Minister proposed to amend the bill on Committee stage in the following way: that the Pensions Board should encourage voluntary trustee appointment by members for three years after the act coming into effect. With effect from January 1994 the Minister "may" enact regulations requiring the employers to provide for appropriate members' representation. Although the National Pensions Board had proposed to allow members participation only in pensions schemes, with at least 50 members, the Ministers' amendment applied the new regulations to all funded schemes (Dáil, Vol. 400, 19.06.1990: 210–11).

The ICTU had also complained that the fines introduced were too low to effectively punish the violation of responsibilities by trustees. Another ministerial amendment raised "conviction on indictment" to Ir£ 10,000 or two years' imprisonment while the maximum limit for "summary conviction" remained at Ir£ 1,000 as before. In presenting this amendment, the Minister followed the demands of the Labour and Workers' Party more closely than Fine Gael. However, the Workers' Party's demands went even further: they asked for the fines indexed to be (Dáil, Vol. 400, 19.06.1990: 233–7).

The ICTU and (on their behalf) the Workers' Party and Fine Gael demanded the incorporation in the legislation of rules to cover election proceedings for trustee appointments and the management of committees in matters such as the regulating of frequency of meetings. The main reason for this was if the Board was responsible for the Code of Practice, it would be "outside the Minister's competence to be answerable to this House in regard to them" (Dáil, Vol. 400, 20.06.1990: 335). The Labour Party proposed an amendment more in line with the Minister's bill: that while the Board should outline the Code of Practice, it should obtain the consent of the Minister, thus leaving responsibility with the government and its accountability to Parliament rather than with an independent board. The question was put to vote on the Labour amendment. The vote on the amendment was lost resulting in 76 votes by Fianna Fáil and Progressive Democrat members, and 69 votes uniting Fine Gael, Labour, and the Workers' Party (Dáil, Vol. 400, 20.06.1990: 348–50).

At Committee Stage the minister added a new section. The original Bill provided that disputes (between members and their schemes) were to be resolved by the Pensions Board through its standing orders. By the time of the Committee Stage, the Minister had decided to legislate these procedures establishing a quasi-judicial appeals body with instruments such as holding oral hearings. This change was also in accordance with the opposition parties and the ICTU who criticized the omission of regulating this matter (Dáil, Vol. 400, 20.06.1990: 366–8).

Furthermore, the Workers' Party accused the government of not following the National Pensions Board's recommendation in another matter: which was, whereas the Board had suggested five years for members younger than 25, and an incremental reduction to two years thereafter, the government bill envisaged five years to qualify for preserved benefits, with at least two years acquired after the enactment of the *Pensions Act 1990* (Dáil, Vol. 399, 31.05.1990: 1000). But the Minister's watered down version prevailed (Dáil, Vol. 401, 10.07.1990: 770, 777).

The Pensions Bill was subject to government guillotine[8] at the third day of the Committee Stage in the *Dáil* because the government wanted to pass the bill in both houses before the parliamentary summer recess. Due to the guillotine, there was not enough time to discuss at any length the important parts of the bill on disclosure of information, and equal treatment, in the *Dáil*. The bill as amended by the Committee was adopted by a majority of 72 to 40 votes supported by Fianna Fáil and the Progressive Democrats. Fine Gael rejected the bill while Labour abstained from voting (Dáil, Vol. 401, 10.07.1990: 818, 822–5).

The bill was debated in *Seanad* on July 17, 1990. Members of the *Seanad*, like the deputies in the *Dáil* received the bill in a generally positive way: "I do not regard this as a very controversial Bill; in fact, I contend it should be welcomed by all sides of the House" (Harte (LP) in Seanad, Vol. 126, 17.07.1990: 618). Regarding disagreement, the opposition parties in the *Seanad* repeated the main arguments of the *Dáil* session. Fine Gael was especially concerned about the additional burden for employers of providing information and training. Fine Gael and Labour also blamed the Minister for leaving out self-employed and farmers from the bill (*Seanad*, Vol. 126, 17.07.1990: 603–604, 625). In short, the second chamber stage was of minor importance.

The *Pensions Bill 1990* went through the Committee Stage with no further amendments. Due to the government's guillotine and four failed opposition amendments to change the order of business—namely, not to enact the guillotine—the debate was ended the same day with the passage of the act (*Irish Times* 18.07.1990; Seanad, Vol. 126, 17.07.1990: 705).

The Pensions Amendment Act 1996

Background

On November 4, 1992, the Progressive Democrats left the government coalition over personal conflicts with the Prime Minister, Albert Reynolds, in a beef industry tribunal (O'Leary 1993: 401; Mitchell 2000: 153).[9] Fianna Fáil lost a subsequent vote of confidence and new elections were held November 26, 1992. The main winner in the election was the Labour Party that campaigned against the politics of austerity of the government. Labour more than doubled its number of *Dáil* seats. After a long government formation process, Fianna Fáil and Labour reached an agreement: Against intra-party resistance the Labour Party leadership entered the coalition when Fianna Fáil compromised on Labour demands concerning legislation on homosexuality, abortion, and ethics.

In February 1994, the Government, the Irish Congress of Trade Unions, the Irish Business and Employers' Confederation and the Irish Farmers' Association started negotiations on another tripartite agreement that was to succeed the *Programme for Economic and Social Progress*. By then, the economy was starting to grow rapidly. The new *Programme for Competitiveness and Work* provided for pay increases of 8 percent in the private and public sector over the period 1994 to 1996 (EMIRE 2003b).

The Fianna Fáil/Labour coalition fell in November 1994. A scandal over a pedophile priest was the immediate cause for coalition conflict. The scandal and its setting provides important background to the changing character of pensions policy, for the scandal was a symptom of the rapid decline in the importance and power of what had historically been the central institution in post-Independence Irish society—the Catholic Church. By the 1990s, therefore, one of the great obstacles to any modernization of the pension system was being marginalized in a rapidly secularizing society. Although Prime Minister Reynolds (FF), resigned, Labour left the Cabinet and government broke down. Without new elections Fine Gael and Labour started negotiations and after they had agreed they invited the Democratic Left to join their coalition (O'Duffy 1998: 178; Mitchell 2000: 137). The rainbow coalition set out for a "renewal" of the country including reforms of the political institutions, measurements to meet the Maastricht criteria of national debt and deficit, development of the economy and a reform of the tax system (FG, LP, DC 1994; European Commission 2003).

National Pensions Board—Final Report

The National Pensions Board had published its Final Report in December 1993. It mainly dealt with the relationship between Social Welfare Pensions and occupational pensions. The majority of the Board advocated the maintenance of the existing Social Insurance pension system with additional means-tested social assistance, whereas the trade unions supported a universal pension scheme. With respect to income-related pensions trade union representatives on the Board demanded mandatory minimum contributions on top of PRSI. However, the employer confederation IBEC rejected any proposal to make such an earnings-related pension coverage compulsory (National Pensions Board 1993: 8–9, 22–23). Consequently, by majority decision the National Pensions Board abstained from recommending any compulsory measures.

The National Pensions Board and the Pensions Board are forums where the competing interests negotiate and solve differences. Although formally decisions are taken by majority, the Board tries to achieve consensus among its members. To make disputes and non-unanimous decisions public is rather unusual.

Parliamentary process

The purpose of the *Pensions Amendment Bill 1995*, published December 13, 1995, was to "[reinforce] the safeguards already in place in relation to occupational pensions" (Dáil, Vol. 463, 13.03.1996: 253). After the *Pensions Act 1990* had been in force for five years irregularities were identified and removed.

Not only the Minister for Social Welfare, Proinsias De Rossa (DL), himself but also Fianna Fáil as the major opposition party confessed that the bill was mostly technical. Most amendments were of a clarifying or corrective nature. One of the more significant changes was to grant the Pensions Board the right to provide guidelines in occupational pensions in general instead of guidelines for trustees only. Investigations by the Pensions Board were facilitated in that the Board was allowed to designate people outside the Board to conduct such an investigation and fines for offences were increased from Ir£ 1,000 to Ir£ 1,500—still a fairly low charge considering the possible consequences of an offence (Dáil, Vol. 463, 13.03.1996: 255; 27.03.1996: 1187). Against the opposition of the insurance industry, a so-called "whistle blowing" section was introduced which required the "relevant persons" in the pension industry, that is to say, actuaries, lawyers and trustees, to report any fraud or misappropriation of funds. Failure to report irregularities could be punished with fines of up to Ir£ 10,000 or two years' imprisonment. Additionally, two new members were added to the Pensions Board, namely trustees of pension schemes, one nominated by the ICTU the other one by the IBEC. Yet, a representative of pensioners was still not included on the Board. Other issues that had already been relevant during the 1990 reform process were deferred, to be dealt by the Pensions Board in consecutive years: for example, the preservation of pension entitlements earned before 1991; the creation of a compensation fund; and the establishment of a pensions Ombudsman (Bill 95 of 1995: Expl. Memo. 3, Section 34; *Irish Times* 23.08.1996; Dáil, Vol. 463 02.04.1996: 1761; 27.03.1996: 1187–1188).

All parties welcomed the bill in the Second Stage speeches. The Pensions Amendment Bill as a whole passed the House of Representatives (*Dáil*) on June 12, 1996 (Dáil, Vol. 466, 12.06.1996: 1799). The *Seanad* agreed on the bill on June 26, 1996 (Seanad, Vol. 148, 26.06.1996: 288).

The Pensions Reserve Fund Act 2000

Background

The rainbow coalition entered the 1997 *Dáil* elections in a favorable economic situation. Decreasing unemployment and high economic growth should have provided a positive context for the re-election of the government. The senior coalition partner Fine Gael, indeed, won eleven extra seats but it could not make up for 16 lost Labour seats. The big parties, Fine Gael and Fianna Fáil, were the winners at the polls. In explaining this trend O'Duffy (1998: 186) argues that "within the current bubble of economic prosperity, the national question (concerning negotiations over the future of Northern Ireland) remains a significant, if usually latent, cleavage in Irish politics." Another sign of the timeliness of the Northern Ireland issue was the electoral success of Sinn Féin: it won its first seat since World War II. A Fianna Fáil and Progressive Democrats government took office on June 26, 1997 dependent on two independent votes for a majority in the House of Representatives.

The new coalition had to continue the broad economic framework the rainbow coalition had set with the tripartite agreement in the fall of 1996—the *Partnership 2000*. The main purpose of the *Partnership 2000* was to manage the rapid economic growth Ireland experienced in the mid-1990s and to use the economic gains to reduce social inequalities (Department of the Taoiseach 2000: 4).

National Pensions Policy Initiative

A survey of occupational and private pension coverage by Hughes and Whelan in 1995 showed that only 46.4 percent of those at work were covered by an occupational or personal pension. The employees' coverage rate amounted to 52 percent, but only 27.2 percent of farmers and self-employed had private pension insurance (Hughes and Whelan 1996: 42 Table 44.13; see also National Pensions Policy Initiative 1998: 4–5). Supplementary pension coverage had even declined as the economic rise of the Celtic Tiger had created many jobs without pension provision (Seanad, Vol. 168, 04.10.2001: 146). Considering that the state flat-rate pension was inadequate for maintaining the standard of living in old age, politicians regarded the uptake as alarmingly low. Consequently, the Department for Social Welfare launched the National Pensions Policy Initiative on October 30, 1996. The Initiative was assigned to sound out the options for a "fully developed", comprehensive, national pension system (National Pensions Policy Initiative 1998: v). As the members of the Initiative were recruited mainly from the Pensions Board, the Departments for Social Welfare and Finances, unions, employers and the pension industry were—once again—present in the Initiative's deliberations.

The National Pensions Policy Initiative presented a first Consultation Document on February 13, 1997 and requested interested groups to comment on the issue of a national pension system. After the evaluation of 143 submissions, and a National Pensions Conference on July 2, 1997, the Pensions Policy Initiative published its report *Securing Retirement Income* in May 1998.

The ultimate goal was to achieve supplementary pension coverage of 70 percent of the workforce in three steps, that is, a coverage rate of 62 percent within five years, 66 percent within ten years, and 70 percent thereafter. As an instrument to achieve this target rate the Initiative recommended introducing *Personal Retirement Savings Accounts* (PRSA)—a new pension type to facilitate continuous pension insurance even if the working career contains both periods of employment and self-employment or non-employment. Employers who did not offer an occupational pension scheme open to all groups of employees were to be required to provide access to such individual schemes. Employers had to deduct the PRSA contributions from payroll for their employees but they were not obliged to contribute. Possibly, compulsion for contribution payments would have to follow at a later point of time if the coverage targets were not met (National Pensions Policy Initiative 1998: 11, 18).

With respect to adequacy of pension benefits the report recommended a target minimum pension of 34 percent[10] of average industrial earnings with a transition period of five-to-ten years, incurring estimated costs of around Ir£ 440 million. Although all members of the Pensions Board signed the Pension Policy Initiative's

Final Report, employers had reservations concerning the fixing of a target pension benefit. Yet, an interesting effect of such an increase in Social Welfare Pensions would have been as follows: occupational pension schemes that were integrated into the Social Welfare pension would have less expenditure while maintaining the promised benefit level (National Pensions Policy Initiative 1998: 10–12, 27).

With respect to Social Welfare Pensions financing, the Initiative envisaged establishing funding in the first pillar "that would minimize the additional burden on future generations of taxpayers" (National Pensions Policy Initiative 1998: 13). The fund was to be financed from the realization of assets and was to amount to Ir£ 30 billon, that is 26 percent of GNP by 2031.

Additionally, the Initiative proposed to decrease the minimum qualifying period for the preservation of occupational pension entitlements in case of change in employment from five years to two years starting January 1, 2001. Furthermore, pre-1991 pension rights were to be preserved from 2001 on, revalued after 2006, and the funding standards for occupational pension schemes would include pre-1991 pension rights from 2011 onwards (National Pensions Policy Initiative 1998: 26).

Parliamentary process

The Government started to enact partial pre-funding with the announcement of two separate funds in 1999—one for Social Welfare Pensions and one for public service pensions. A provisional law in December 1999 created the *Temporary Holding Fund for Superannuation Liabilities*. Revenues from the sale of *Telecom Éireann* (renamed *Eircom*) shares plus 1 percent of GNP were paid resulting in a fund of Ir£4.8 billion in 2000 (Dáil, Vol. 523, 03.10.2000: 82).

The bill, presented by the FF/PD-government on June 12, 2000, foresaw a transformation of the temporary fund into a permanent fund, the set-up of an independent National Pensions Reserve Fund Commission to oversee the fund, and the appointment of a National Treasury Management Agency manager who would manage investments and act on behalf of the Commission. The Commission was accountable to the Minister for Finance and to the *Dáil* (Bill 36 of 2000: 1–2).

The main goal was to build up a fund by contributing 1 percent of GNP each year between 2001 and 2055. From 2025 onwards these assets would be used to reduce the Exchequer expenditure for Social Welfare pensions and public service pensions. The usage of the fund was to stretch over a minimum period of 30 years, and the drawing of financial resources from the fund was to follow the projected demographic changes (Section 18 and Section 20, Bill 36 of 2000). Investment of the fund had to follow solely economic goals: the fund should not be used as Government securities. The Commissioners had to maximize the rate of return in investing in Ireland as well as abroad.

The *Pensions Reserve Fund Act* was a significant departure from traditional financing of Social Welfare. Minister for Finance, Charlie McCreevy, pointed out that the idea of the fund was to take advantage of the favorable age structure of the Irish population and the prospering economy at the beginning of the twenty-first century to provide for future generations (Dáil, Vol. 523, 03.10.2000: 79).

During the parliamentary debate the opposition accused the government of asking the present taxpayers to pay twice for their pensions: on the one hand, to continue to contribute to the PAYG pension system; on the other hand to pay taxes that are used to build up a fund. The main concern was that such a bill could only be proposed in times of surpluses, but the opposition drew attention to the fact that if the general budget went back to deficits, it would be very hard to afford contributions of 1 percent of GNP.[11] Another point of criticism for the Fine Gael Party was that the bill required commercial investment which would result in investing most of the fund's assets abroad. Thus, neither the Irish economy nor the Irish infrastructure would be able to profit from the establishment of a pensions fund (Dáil, Vol. 523, 03.10.2000: 84–85).

The bill passed both chambers without major amendments—Final Stage in the *Dáil* took place on November 21, 2000 and *Seanad* decided one week later (Dáil, Vol. 526, 21.11.2000: 538; Seanad, Vol. 164, 29.11.2000: 1136).

The Pensions (Amendment) Act 2002

The bill

A draft of the long-awaited pension reform to boost supplementary pension coverage took shape in the spring of 2001. The *Pensions (Amendment) Bill*, initiated on July 25, 2001, was to increase private pension coverage. The bill was incorporated into the broader framework of the social partnership agreement of late 1999—*Programme for Prosperity and Fairness*—which had promised in its pension section to implement the National Pension Policy Initiative's recommendations (Department of the Taoiseach 1997: 13).

The act introduced individual investment accounts, known as Personal Retirement Savings Accounts (PRSAs), open to all persons irrespective of their status of employment. The self-employed, homemakers, unemployed people, students and part-time workers were able to profit from supplementary private old-age pensions. PRSA were more attractive than pre-existing private pensions in several ways. First, access for economically active persons was easier as all employers who did not provide an occupational pension scheme had to offer PRSA. Although employers were not forced to contribute to PRSA, they were required to deduct the employees' contributions from the payroll if they decided to join a scheme. After controversial debate, whether second-pillar and/or third-pillar pension provisions should be mandatory, the National Pension Policy Initiative had recommended maintaining the voluntary status with the option of compulsion after a first review (Seanad, Vol. 168, 04.10.2001: 119). Second, providers of PRSA had to express charges in terms of percentage of contributions or of percentage of assets but not in terms of cash amounts. Maximum charges were either 5 percent of contributions or 1 percent of annual value assets. Third, the insured person could make contribution payments on an irregular basis and could transfer assets to a different PRSA provider any time without loss. Fourth, contributions were exempt from taxation up to a certain, age-dependent share of income.[12] Furthermore, the bill established a pensions Ombudsman financed by the *Oireachtas* with the duty to investigate complaints of mismanagement in occupational or PRSA schemes (*Irish Times* 16.03.2001). The bill also amended regulations on indexation of pensions, handling of entitlements of early-leavers and dealing with surpluses. An important measure which had been part of the debate in 1990 and 1996 was the reduction of the qualifying period for preserved benefits in occupational pensions from five-to-two years for persons leaving service after January 1, 2002 (Bill 45 of 2001a: Expl. Memo. 1–3, 5). Additionally, preserved rights of pension benefits of pre-1991 service will be revaluated with inflation up to 4 percent (Seanad, Vol. 168, 04.10.2001: 121).

Parliamentary process

The *Pensions (Amendment) Bill 2001* was first debated in the *Seanad* on October 4, 2001. Unsurprisingly, after a lengthy negotiation process of five years and tripartite agreement the principles of the bill, and especially the establishment of a pensions Ombudsman, were welcomed across the party spectrum (Seanad, Vol. 168, 04.10.2001: 123–133; Vol. 169, 13.02.2002: 203).

Committee Stage in the senate was ordered for October 10, 2001 but the drafting of amendments took such a long time that the Committee Stage session took place four months later—on February 13, 2002. Even at the Committee Stage, participants of the debate were aware of the fact that further major changes were ahead and would be submitted at Report Stage. The government was under time pressure: it aimed to pass the Pensions Bill within the current legislative term, but new elections had to be called in June 2002 at the latest. This hurried course of action did have some problematic implications on the procedures on Committee Stage: the senators had to vote on the deletion of sections with nothing but a promise that the amendments on Report Stage would substitute those sections (Seanad, Vol. 169, 13.02.2002: 203, 210).

As regards content, heavy criticism came from independent senator Shane Ross, representative of Trinity College, who asked for truly independent consumer representation on the Pensions Board—free of party politics—that is to say, appointed by the *Consumers' Association of Ireland* (CAI) and not by the Minister for Social, Community and Family Affairs (Seanad, Vol. 168, 04.10.2001: 131–133). The voting result was 30:15 in favor of the bill (i.e. against Ross). The *Seanad* passed the bill on February 28, 2002 (Seanad, Vol. 169, 13.02.2002: 256–66; 28.02.2002: 666).

There are two amendments made at Committee Stage of the *Dáil* that are worth mentioning. The country's largest union—the Services, Industrial Professional and Technical Union (SIPTU)—did not welcome the PRSA enthusiastically, as they feared that the establishment of PRSA would undermine any concurrent efforts to increase participation in occupational pension schemes. Concurrently, *Dáil* legislators were afraid that employees would use the establishment of PRSAs to transfer their existing occupational pensions to PRSA. Consequently, the government introduced restrictions on transfers: employees who had been in occupational pension schemes for more than 15 years could not transfer to PRSA.[13] The second important amendment eased the requirements for PRSA providers: contrary to the original bill, where providers had to set up a separate company, the changed bill foresaw that existing insurance companies, credit institutions and investment managers would be allowed to provide PRSA themselves (*Irish Times* 17.02.2001; 08.03.2002).

After the *Dáil* had again amended the bill and passed it on March 27, 2002 (Dáil, Vol. 551, 27.03.2002) the *Seanad* had to vote on the bill as amended by the *Dáil* again on March 28, 2002 (Seanad, Vol. 169, 28.03.2002: 1504).

V Conclusion

Summary of the magnitude of changes

The Irish state pensions system has changed in two significant ways. First, Pay-Related Social Insurance has been extended to the self-employed and farmers, that is, increasing coverage to an extra 20 percent of the workforce (Dáil, Vol. 378, 09.03.1988: 2045). Second, the government established a National Pension Reserve Fund to partially pre-fund the PAYG system. Minor, piecemeal changes have increased benefit rates, augmented contribution limits or modified the qualifying period for Old-Age and Retirement Pensions. But there were no further structural or even systemic changes. With respect to pension expansion, plans to introduce an earnings-related national pension system have never gone further than Commission consultation level throughout the post-World War II period. Consequently, retrenchment of generous state old-age provisions could not arise as a political issue.

The voluntary supplementary occupational and private pensions experienced greatly increased regulation both in scheme administration and in benefit transferability. From complete lack of pension entitlement preservation requirements, legislation has changed to full preservation, revaluation and transferability of accrued pension entitlements after only two years of service with one employer. Furthermore, policy amendments ruled out the delivery of unpleasant surprises for employees and pensioners when a company is wound up, namely, that their benefit claims cannot be met. First, every pension scheme must register with the Pensions Board and renew its adequate funding certificate on a regular basis. Second, to help deter speculation in funds, there is power to punish mismanagement or fraud in pension fund investment, as well as the obligation to report any such deception by "whistle blowing." Third, according to the *Pensions (Amendment) Act 2002*, employees with less than 15 years membership in an occupational pension scheme may transfer their pension rights to a Personal Retirement Savings Account (PRSA), which might increase competition between PRSA and occupational schemes to the members' advantage. Eventually, access to private pension schemes will be easier for employees, as employers have to guarantee either an occupational pension scheme or, upon request of the employee, pay deduction to a PRSA. Pension coverage became more affordable for low-income earners and for persons with irregular working careers or periods of child-rearing as administrative costs for PRSA are limited, and contribution payments can be interrupted or stopped without loss.

The magnitude of the reforms are difficult to assess. The qualitative changes have just been described. But one has to bear in mind that all second-and third-pillar pensions are completely voluntary. Nevertheless, quantitative indicators also point to a much greater awareness and relevance of supplementary occupational pensions: the number of schemes registered with the Pensions Board more than tripled between 1992 and 2002[14] and members covered by these schemes rose from 438,000 to 709,332 (Pensions Board 1993: 9; 2003: 21). As PRSA was only enacted in 2002 it is too early to assess whether the new regulations will result in higher coverage and meet the political target of 70 percent in the long-run.

Impact of the political system on pension politics

The procedures of Irish law-making ensure government dominance throughout the legislative process. The government party or coalition—provided it can muster a majority—has no problem getting proposals passed as it faces neither a powerful president, nor a senate, able to block a bill. In practice, a non-committal objection of the Upper Chamber is unlikely because even minority governments have similar majorities in the Senate due to eleven prime ministerial nominees.

Pensions have not been a hot issue in electoral campaigns in Ireland in the 1980s or 1990s. On the one hand, the electoral system with single-transferable votes, where individual candidates compete not only against candidates of other parties but also against members of the same party, puts a strong emphasis on local issues and personal characteristics—two areas where pension politics are hard to turn to advantage.[15] On the other hand, Irish parties do not compete much for the votes of retired persons although they are a sizeable group of voters with the highest turnout.[16] The electorate of voters 65 years or older are over-represented both in Fianna Fáil and Fine Gael but under-represented with Progressive Democrats and Labour. However, the most marginal *Dáil* seats are in the Dublin area where the parties compete for a younger, urban electorate (Garry et al. 2003: 131, 141).

The role of the party system and its cleavages in pension politics does not stand out. The key acts—*Social Welfare Act 1988*, *Pensions Act 1990*, *National Pensions Reserve Act 2000* and *Pensions (Amendment) Act 2002*—passed the *Oireachtas* under Fianna Fáil controlled governments. But as Fine Gael-headed governments initiated the Commissions, the National Pensions Board and the National Pensions Policy Initiative that led to those major reforms, and also passed the *Pensions (Amendment) Act 1996*, there is no evidence that the improvement of occupational pensions was solely attributable to Fianna Fáil. It is striking that the early 1980s did not see significant pension changes. The process of reform set in right after the Progressive Democrats—a right-wing party with a young urban electorate—entered the *Dáil* with their first startling impact. It is thus hard to correlate features of the party system, or party system change, with the process of pension reform.

As is elaborated on p. 797, the existing pension system has influenced the option development in pension policy throughout the 1980s and 1990s. Possibly, party politics and electoral competition played a more hidden role in Irish pension politics. Although it is out of range of the time period scrutinized in this case study, further research should concentrate on the causes for such a "backward" first-pillar pension. Whereas party competition on welfare between Social-Democratic and Christian-Democratic parties in continental Europe has built up credit-claiming for generous expansion of statutory pension benefits, the number one cleavage in Ireland has been the traditional pro-Treaty/anti-Treaty issue between Fianna Fáil and Fine Gael. Consequently, the exceptionally weak political Left[17] was unable to improve social services because no other party campaigned for the same potentially benefiting electorate.[18]

Interest group influence

According to Rhodes (2001: 184), who refers to various social partnership agreements in Ireland, since 1987 these pacts have been accompanied by a centralization of the process of wage bargaining and policy negotiation; that is, in his eyes, Ireland developed corporatist structures. Against such a background one might tend to attribute the successful pension reforms to social partnership as well. The 20-year period researched here was dominated by two Commissions—the National Pensions Board and the National Pensions Policy Initiative—that provided suggestions for all legislative changes between 1988 and 2002. The government and pensions industry were well represented in these Commissions, and unions and employers were also fixed constituents of the membership. Hence, the proposition that general corporatist tendencies helped to pass consensual pension acts cannot be ruled out as explanation for the successful reforms. Yet, the partnership did not extend to pensioners' or scheme members' interest groups. In June 2002, consumers were first represented in Pensions Board's membership. Pensioners' interest groups did not influence the reform processes in any significant way. In short, what the corporatist system, designed to cope with economic crisis, ensured was that some well organized interests, notably in the business community and in trade unions, were securely incorporated into the institutional system of policy-making, but others were "organized out."

Constraints of policy design

The pension policy design of low state pension benefits and a long tradition of an independent occupational pension sector set the framework for the changes in the last two decades. On the one hand the system displayed "vices" (Levy 1999) that allowed "legitimate" changes. The exclusion of the self-employed, prior to 1988, offered a way to increase revenue under the labels "equality" and "security": equality because after 1988 both employees and self-employed would be treated equally with respect to Non-Contributory Old-Age-Pensions; security because the compulsory PRSI contributions would safeguard a non-means-tested minimum of old-age income to farmers and self-employed. The "vices" in the occupational pension sector were the inadequacy of the *Trustee Act 1893* and the lack of other regulations. On the other hand, the low flat-rate first-pillar pensions did not even provide scope for retrenchment, and the well-established pension industry could keep its stakes in as long as the occupational pensions remained the main income source to maintain the standard of living in old age.

Role of ideas and historical context

The Pensions Board, its predecessor the National Pensions Board, and associated Commissions, that is the National Pensions Policy Initiative, form a sort of institutionalized policy community. This has perhaps been the single greatest change in the character of pension politics over recent decades. When combined with the institutional weaknesses of the *Dáil* as a scrutinizer of technical policy detail, it has ensured that the policy community is dominated by a "low" politics in which pension professionals exercise great influence over the shaping of policy. The cohesiveness of this policy community is further assisted by an important feature of Irish policy structures generally namely, their small scale—partly a product of governing a small country, and partly a product of the marked degree to which policy institutions are centralized on the capital city.

This institutionalized policy community is, however, hardly a recipe for great policy innovation. The membership on the Board is above all representative of department, union, or interest association; thus its relevance as a location for revolutionary, system-changing ideas is doubtful. Moreover, its business area is occupational pensions only, although it can advise the Minister on pensions legislation in general. Throughout the 1990s, the Board has rather proven to be a place where compromises could develop remote, from public, attention. Ideas, concepts or actuarial models did not dominate or even determine reform outcomes.

Scientific work that did initiate policy action came in the form of the seminal study on occupational pension coverage by Hughes and Whelan (1996). Only after the figures were published did the government commission the National Pensions Policy Initiative to prepare what resulted in the establishing of the Personal Retirement Savings Accounts.

Abbreviations

CAI	Consumers' Association of Ireland
CII	Confederation of Irish Industry
DL	Democratic Left

FF   Fianna Fáil
FG   Fine Gael (former Cumann na nGaedheals)
FUE   Federal Union of Employers
IAIM   Irish Association of Investment Managers
IAPF   Irish Association of Pension Funds
IBEC   Irish Business and Employers Confederation
ICTU   Irish Congress of Trade Unions
IFA   Irish Farmers' Association
Ir£   Irish Pound
LP   Labour Party
NPRF   National Pension Reserve Fund
PD   Progressive Democrats
PESP   Programme for Economic and Social Progress (1990)
PRSA   Personal Retirement Savings Account
PRSI   Pay-Related Social Insurance
SIPTU   Services, Industrial, Professional and Technical Union

Notes

1. The average expenditure per old age pension recipient amounted to €698.70 per month in 2003 (own calculation based on Statistical Information on Social Welfare Services (Department of Social and Family Affairs 2004: Table B2 and B3)). For comparison average monthly gross wages in 2003: female industrial worker €1,693; male industrial worker €2,430; earnings in banking sector €3,002 (www.cso.ie/statistics/earnings.htm). Differences between pensioners' income and net income is less pronounced see Connell and Stewart (2004: Table 7.4). The occupational pension coverage varied between 9.1% of female employees in the service sector and 92.3% for male public administration employees (CSO 2002: Table 2a).
2. These developments are, as so often, inseparable from the wider features of a clientelist system of politics which greatly empowered particular sectional groups, like farmers.
3. An exception is the period 1994–1997: government changed without new elections after the Labour party left the Finna Fáil/Labour coalition. The new Labour/Fine Gael/Democratic Left coalition commanded only a minority of deputies in the senate (Gallagher 1999: 200; Mitchell 2000: 152–3).
4. For details see section on benefits pp. 773–5.
5. For comparison: 47.9% stem from state welfare sources, the rest from other sources (Connell and Stewart 2004: Table 7.7).
6. Minor expenditures would set in after four years when the minimum qualifying period for widows' and orphans' pensions was met (Dáil, Vol. 378, 09.03.1988: 2074).
7. The bill was supported by Fianna Fáil, the bill was rejected by the Workers' Party, the Labour Party, the Democratic Socialist and one Independent. The parliamentary minutes do not mention members of the Fine Gael nor the Progressive Democrats party. It must be assumed Fine Gael and PD abstained from voting (Dáil, Vol. 378, 10.03.1988: 2530–2532).
8. The parliamentary majority—thus, in effect, the government—decides on the allocation of time in parliamentary debates. The purpose of the instrument known as *guillotine* is to prevent opposition filibustering. But de facto the government can deprive parliament from the possibility of debating a bill in detail by restricting the time for deliberation.

Guillotining pension policy is delicate because the complexity of the pension policy already challenges the parliamentarians' laymen capacities to assess the consequences of highly technical changed regulations.
9. Scandals in the processing of beef, and in the awards of contracts, were one of many to be the subject of investigation by tribunals of inquiry in Irish politics throughout the 1990s.
10. State pension benefits were at 28.5% of average industrial earnings in 1998 (National Pensions Policy Initiative 1998: 10).
11. It is open to discussion whether the creation of the fund also served another purpose—namely, to remove money from the market to slow down the economic boom (see e.g. *Irish Times* 15.06.2000).
12. For insured persons under 30 years PRSA contributions of 15% of earnings were tax-deductible, from 30 to 39 years this percentage increased to 25% and to 30% for those over 40 years (*Irish Times* 20.04.2001).
13. Officially, this change came about in discussions between the Department of Finance, the Department for Social, Community and Family Affairs and the Revenue. According to the press, rumors uttered the possibility that large occupational funds who were afraid of losing significant parts of their funds lobbied for the amendment (*Irish Times* 01.04.2002).
14. Raise from 30,746 in 1992 to 107,764 schemes in 2002 (Pensions Board 1993: 9; 2003: 21).
15. Polls show that voters think it matters more which candidate wins a seat than which party wins a seat (CSO 2003: Table 6a,b).
16. Polls illustrate that 87% of retired persons who were eligible to vote, did vote in the 2002 elections (CSO 2003: Table 1). Total turnout was at 62.5%.
17. According to Gallagher, Laver and Mair (1995: 206 cited in Mair 1999: 129) combined forces of Labour Party, Workers' Party and Democratic Left received only an average of 14% of votes in national elections compared to a European average of 40% in the 1980s and 1990s. Ireland was most similar to Switzerland with respect to the weak left.
18. For a description of social politics in the 1950 see Maguire (1986: 246–7).

Bibliography

Primary sources and government documents

Acts and bills

Bill No. 8 of 1988. *Bill (as initiated) entitled An Act to amend and extend the Social Welfare Acts, 1981 to 1987, and the Employers' Employment Contribution Scheme Act, 1981 (Social Welfare Bill, 1988)*, (03.03.1988).

Bill No. 95 of 1995. *Bill (as initiated) entitled An Act to amend and extend the Pensions Act, 1990: Explanatory Memorandum*, (13.12.1995).

Bill No. 36 of 2000. *Bill entitled an Act to provide for the establishment of a fund to be known as the National Pensions Reserve Fund and a body to be known as the National Pensions Reserve Fund Commission to control and manage the fund, to dissolve the Temporary Holding Fund for Superannuation Liabilities, to amend the Taxes Consolidation Act, 1997, and to provide for connected matters: National Pensions Reserve Fund Bill: Explanatory Memorandum*, (12.06.2000).

Bill No. 45 of 2001. *Bill entitled an Act to amend and extend the Pensions Act, 1990, and to provide for related matters: Pensions (Amendment) Bill, 2001*, (25.07.2001).

Parliamentary minutes

Dáil Debates Official Report:
25th Dáil, Vol. 371, (10.03.1987): 20–52.
25th Dáil, Vol. 378, (09.03.1988): 2045–2107, 2219–2279.

25th Dáil, Vol. 378, (10.03.1988): 2368–2435.
25th Dáil, Vol. 379, (22.03.1988): 571–625.
26th Dáil, Vol. 399, (29.05.1990): 596–660.
26th Dáil, Vol. 399, (31.05.1990): 998–1062.
26th Dáil, Vol. 400, (19.06.1990): 209–252.
26th Dáil, Vol. 400, (20.06.1990): 328–371.
26th Dáil, Vol. 401, (10.07.1990): 769–824.
27th Dáil, Vol. 466, (12.06.1996): 1756–1799.
27th Dáil, Vol. 463, (13.03.1996): 249–257.
27th Dáil, Vol. 463, (27.03.1996): 1183–1210.
27th Dáil, Vol. 463, (02.04.1996): 1760–1768.
28th Dáil, Vol. 523, (03.10.2000): 77–87.
28th Dáil, Vol. 526, (21.11.2000): 512–538.
28th Dáil, Vol. 551, (27.03.2002): 646–690.
Seanad Debates Official Report:
18th Seanad, Vol. 119, (29.06.1988): 419–476.
19th Seanad, Vol. 126, (17.07.1990): 567–661, 662–705.
20th Seanad, Vol. 148, (26.06.1996): 248–288.
21st Seanad, Vol. 164, (29.11.2000): 1125–1136.
21st Seanad, Vol. 168, (04.10.2001): 117–148.
21st Seanad, Vol. 169, (13.02.2002): 203–271.
21st Seanad, Vol. 169, (28.02.2002): 603–666.
21st Seanad, Vol. 169, (28.03.2002): 1499–1504.

Other government documents

DEPARTMENT OF SOCIAL WELFARE (1976). *A National Income Related Pension Scheme: A Discussion Paper*. Green Paper Prl: 5737. Dublin: Stationery Office.

DEPARTMENT OF THE TAOISEACH (1997). *Partnership 2000*. Dublin: Department of the Taoiseach.

DEPARTMENT OF THE TAOISEACH (2000). *Programme for Prosperity and Fairness*. Dublin: Department of the Taoiseach.

NATIONAL PENSIONS BOARD (1987). *First Report*. Commission Report Pl. 4776. Dublin: Stationery Office.

NATIONAL PENSIONS BOARD (1988). *Report on the Extension of Social Insurance to the Self-Employed*. Commission Report Pl. 5411. Dublin: Stationery Office.

NATIONAL PENSIONS BOARD (1993). *Final Report*. Commission Report Pl. 9979. Dublin: Stationery Office.

NATIONAL PENSIONS POLICY INITIATIVE (1998). *Securing Retirement Income*. Report. Dublin: The Pensions Board.

Newspapers (various issues)
Irish Times
Irish Independent

Secondary sources

BRISTOW, JOHN and RYAN, TERENCE (1985). *Irish Occupational Pension Schemes*. Dublin: Trinity College.

COAKLEY, JOHN (1987). "The Senate Election." In Penniman, H. R. and Farrell, B. (eds.), *Ireland at the Polls 1981, 1982, and 1987: A Study of Four General Elections*. Duke: Duke University Press, 192–205.

—— (1990). "The Senate Election." In Gallagher, M. and Sinnott, R. (eds.), *How Ireland voted 1989*. Galway: Centre for the Study of Irish Elections in association with PSAI Press, University College Galway, 148–61.

—— (1993). "The Seanad Elections." In Gallagher, M. and Laver, M. (eds.) *How Ireland voted 1992*. Dublin: PSAI Press, University of Limerick, 135–45.

—— and MANNING, MAURICE (1999). "The Senate Elections." In Marsh, M. and Mitchell, P. (eds.), *How Ireland voted 1997*. Boulder: Westview Press, 195–214.

CONNELL, PETER and STEWART, JIM (2004). "Income of Retired Persons in Ireland: Some Evidence from Household Budget Surveys." In Hughes, G. and Stewart, J. (eds.), *Reforming Pensions in Europe: Evolution of Pension Financing and Sources of Retirement Income*. Cheltenham: Edward Elgar, 139–62.

CSO (2002). *Quarterly National Household Survey: Pensions*. Central Statistics Office, [cited 14.12.2005]. Available from http://www.cso.ie/qnhs/spe_mod_qnhs.htm

—— (2003). *Quarterly National Household Survey: Voter Participation and Abstention*. Central Statistics Office. [cited 25.10.2003]. Available from http://www.cso.ie/publications/labour/qnhsvoterparticipationandabstention.pdf

DEPARTMENT OF SOCIAL AND FAMILY AFFAIRS (2002a). *Retirement and Old Age (Contributory) Pension*. [cited 05.08.2003]. Available from http://retired.welfare.ie/publications/sw18.pdf

—— (2002b). *Sustainable and Adequate Pension Provision for an Ageing Population*. European Commission. [cited 03.08.2003]. Available from http://europa.eu.int/comm/employment_social/soc-prot/pensions/irl_pensionreport_en.pdf

—— (ed.) (2004). *Statistical Information on Social Welfare Services*. Dublin: Stationery Office.

—— (2005a). *PRSI Contribution Rates and User Guide for the Period 1st January 2005 to 31st December 2005.* [cited 14.07.2005]. Available from http://www.welfare.ie/publications/sw14.pdf

—— (2005b). *Rates of Payment, applicable as from January 2005.* [cited 14.07. 2005]. Available from http://www.welfare.ie/publications/sw19/sw19.pdf

DEPARTMENT OF SOCIAL WELFARE (1988). *Rates of Payment from the Department of Social Welfare, Rates of PRSI Contributions under Pay-Related Social Insurance, Rates of Payment from Health Boards, Rates applicable as and from mid-July 1988.* Dublin: Department of Social Welfare.

ELVERT, JÜRGEN (1999). "Das politische System Irlands." In Ismayr, W. (ed.), *Die politischen Systeme Westeuropas*. Opladen: Leske + Budrich, 255–87.

—— (2001). "Irland: Korporativismus aus Tradition." In Reutter, W. and Rütters, P. (eds.), *Verbände und Verbandssysteme in Westeuropa*, Opladen: Leske & Budrich, 197–220.

EMIRE (2003a). *Programme for National Recovery (PNR)*. European Foundation for the Improvement of Living and Working Conditions. [cited 27.10.2003]. Available from http://www.eurofound.eu.int/emire/IRELAND/PROGRAMMEFORNATIONALRECOVERYPNR-IR.html

—— (2003b). *Programme for Competitiveness and Work*. European Foundation for the Improvement of Living and Working Conditions. [cited 27.10.2003]. Available from http://www.eurofound.ie/emire/IRELAND/PROGRAMMEFORCOMPETITIVENESSANDWORK-IR.html

—— (2003c). *Programme for Economic and Social Progress*. European Foundation for the Improvement of Living and Working Conditions. [cited 27.10.2003]. Available from http://www.eurofound.ie/emire/IRELAND/PROGRAMMEFORECONOMICANDSOCIALPROGRESS-IR.html

EUROPEAN COMMISSION (2003). *National Labour Market Policies: Basic Information Reports: 3.1.1. IRL-i.1 A Government of Renewal, 1993 to 1999*. European Commission. [cited 27.10.2003]. Available from http://www.eu-employment-observatory.net/ersep/irl_uk/00802858.asp.

EUROSTAT (ed.) (2004). *Eurostat Jahrbuch 2004: Der statistische Wegweiser durch Europa: Daten aus den Jahren 1992–2002.* Luxemburg: Europäische Kommission.

FG (1989). *Putting the Country First: Election Programme 1989.* Election Programme 1989: Fine Gael.

—— (2003). *Fine Gael's Core Beliefs.* Fine Gael. [cited 20.10.2003]. Available from http://www.finegael.ie//index.cfm/level/page/aID/188/Content_Key/571/type/Category/CatName/Our_Values.html

FG, LP, DL (1994). *A Government of Renewal: A Policy Agreement between Fine Gael, The Labour Party and Democratic Left.* Government Programme.

GALLAGHER, MICHAEL (1990). "The Election Results and the New Dáil." In Gallagher, M. and Sinnott, R. (eds.), *How Ireland voted 1989.* Galway: Centre for the Study of Irish Elections in association with PSAI Press, University College Galway, 68–93.

—— (1999). "Parliament." In Coakley, J. and Gallagher, M. (eds.), *Politics in the Republic of Ireland.* New York: Routledge, 177–205.

—— and WEEKS, LIAM (2003). "The Subterranean Election of the Seanad." In Gallagher, M. Marsh, M., and Mitchell, P. (eds.), *How Ireland voted 2002.* New York: Palgrave Macmillan, 197–213.

GARRY, JOHN, KENNEDY, FIACHRA and MARSH, MICHAEL et al. (2003). "What Decided the Election?" In Gallagher, M., Marsh, M., and Mitchell, P. (eds.), *How Ireland voted 2002.* New York: Palgrave Macmillan, 119–42.

HOGAN, VINCENT and O'SULLIVAN, PATRICK (2002). *Implications of the Shift from Defined Benefit to Defined Contributions for Pensions.* Prepared for Dublin Economic Workshop. Kenmare, 11–13 October 2002.

HOUSES OF THE OIREACHTAS (2003). *Legislation.* Parliament of Ireland, [cited 21.10. 2003]. Available from http://www.irlgov.ie/oireachtas/frame.htm

HUGHES, GERARD and WHELAN, BRENDAN J. (1996). *Occupational and Personal Pension Coverage 1995.* Dublin: Economic and Social Research Institute (ESRI).

IAPF (2003). *About Us, Mission Statement, Goals.* Irish Association of Pension Funds. [cited 24.10. 2003]. Available from www.iapf.ie

ICTU (2003). *About Congress.* Irish Congress of Trade Unions. [cited 24.10.2003]. Available from www.ictu.ie/html/aboutcon/about.html

—— *Social Partnership in Ireland.* Irish Congress of Trade Unions. [cited 24.10.2003]. Available from http://www.ictu.ie/html/publications/pubagr.html

IFA (2003). *Membership.* Irish Farmers' Association. [cited 24.10. 2003]. Available from www.ifa.ie

JACOBS, FRANCIS (1989). "Ireland." In Jacobs, F., (ed.), *Western European Political Parties: A Comprehensive Guide,* Harlow/Detroit: Longman, 141–67.

LEVY, JOHNAH, D. (1999). "Vice into Virtue? Progressive Politics and Welfare Reform in Continental Europe." *Politics and Society,* 27(2): 239–73.

LIJPHART, AREND (1994). *Electoral Systems and Party Systems: A Study of Twenty-Seven Democracies 1945–1990.* New York: Oxford University Press.

MAGUIRE, MARIA (1986). "Ireland." In Flora, P. (ed.), *Growth to Limits: The Western European Welfare States Since World War II. Volume 2: Germany, United Kingdom, Ireland, Italy.* Berlin: Walter de Gruyter, 241–384.

MAIR, PETER (1987). *The Changing Irish Party System: Organisation, Ideology and Electoral Competition.* London: Frances Pinter.

—— (1992). "Explaining the Absence of Class Politics in Ireland." In Goldthorpe, J. H. and Whelan, C. T. (eds.), *The Development of Industrial Society in Ireland.* Oxford: Oxford University Press, 383–410.

—— (1997). *Party System Change: Approaches and Interpretations.* Oxford: Clarendon Press.

—— (1999). "Party Competition and the Changing Party System." In Coakley, J. and Gallagher, M. (eds.), *Politics in the Republic of Ireland*. New York: Routledge, 126–51.

MANNING, MAURICE (1978). "The Senate Election." In Penniman, H. R. (ed.), *Ireland at the Polls: The Dáil Elections of 1977*. Washington DC: American Enterprise Institute for Public Policy Research, 165–73.

MARSH, MICHAEL and SINNOTT, RICHARD (1990). "How the Voters Decided." In Gallagher, M. and Sinnott, R. (eds.), *How Ireland voted 1989*. Galway: Centre for the Study of Irish Elections in association with PSAI Press, University College Galway, 94–130.

MITCHELL, PAUL (2000). "Ireland: From Single-Party to Coalition Rule." In Müller, W. C. and Strøm, K. (eds.), *Coalition Governments in Western Europe*. Oxford: Oxford University Press, 126–57.

—— (2003). "Ireland: 'O What a Tangled Web ...': Delegation, Accountability, and Executive Power." In Strøm, K. Müller, W. C. and Bergman, T. (eds.), *Delegation and Accountability in Parliamentary Democracies*. Oxford: Oxford University Press, 418–44.

MURPHY, GARY (1999). "The Role of Interest Groups in the Policy Making Process." In Coakley, J. and Gallagher, M. (eds.), *Politics in the Republic of Ireland*. New York: Routledge, 271–93.

NOHLEN, DIETER (2000). *Wahlrecht und Parteiensystem*. 3rd edn., Opladen: Leske + Budrich.

O'DUFFY, BRENDAN (1998). "Swapping the Reins of the Emerald Tiger: The Irish General Election of June 1997." *West European Politics*, 21(2): 178–86.

O'LEARY, BRENDAN (1987). "Towards Europeanisation and Realignment? The Irish General Election, February 1987." *West European Politics*, 10(3): 455–65.

—— (1993). "Affairs, Partner-Swapping, and Spring Tides: The Irish General Election of November 1992." *West European Politics*, 16(3): 401–12.

PENSIONS BOARD (1993). *Annual Report and Accounts 1992*. Annual Report. Dublin: The Pensions Board.

—— (2000). *A Brief Guide to Annuities: A Guide to Annuities and How They Work*. Booklet. Dublin: The Pensions Board.

—— (2001). *A Brief Guide to Pensions: A Guide to Help You Understand Your Pension Scheme and its Benefits*. Booklet. Dublin: The Pensions Board.

—— (2003a). *About us*. The Pensions Board. [cited 24.09.2003]. Available from http://www.pensionsboard.ie/about.asp

—— (2003b). *Annual Report and Accounts 2002*. Annual Report. Dublin: The Pensions Board.

RADIO TELEFÍS ÉIREANN (2003). *The Irish Electoral System – PR-STV*. Irish National Public Service Broadcasting Organisation. [cited 11.08.2003]. Available from http://www.rte.ie/news/election2002/site_files//bg-structure_electsys.html

RECHMANN, SUSANNE (2001). *Alterssicherung in Großbritannien und Irland: Eine institutionelle und empirische Analyse*. Berlin: Duncker & Humblot.

RHODES, MARTIN (2001). "The Political Economy of Social Pacts: 'Competitive Corporatism' and European Welfare Reform." In Pierson, P. (ed.), *The New Politics of the Welfare State*. New York: Oxford University Press, 165–94.

SEANAD (2004). *Report on Seanad Reform*. Report. Dublin: Seanad Éireann Committee on Procedure and Privileges, Sub-Committee on Seanad Reform.

SOCIETY OF ACTUARIES IN IRELAND (2005). *Briefing Statements*. Society of actuaries in Ireland, [cited 14.07.2005]. Available from http://www.actuaries.ie/Press%20Office/BriefingStatementsListing.htm

TAYLOR, GEORGE (2003). " 'Bargaining Celtic Style': The Global Economy and Negotiated Governance in Ireland." In Van Waarden, F. and Lehmbruch, G. (eds.), *Renegotiating the Welfare State: Flexible Adjustment Through Corporatist Concertation*. London/New York: Routledge, 191–224.

CHAPTER 17

LUXEMBOURG: AN ELECTORAL SYSTEM WITH PANACHE

ISABELLE SCHULZE

I INTRODUCTION[1]

LUXEMBOURG´s electoral system has decisively shaped the pension politics of the 1980s and 1990s. With only four electoral districts, a parliament composed of less than 100 representatives, and rules allowing for vote accumulation and vote splitting (*panachage*), electoral disproportionalities encourage politicians to tailor pension policies to particular constituencies. At the same time, however, this system allowed the emergence of a new pension reform party (ADR), which, over the course of more than 15 years, kept pension policy at the top of the political agenda for as many as three elections, and created competitive pressures for significant benefit expansions for particular groups.

In the early 1980s, financial consolidation and structural reforms were undertaken, which converted the previously-funded system (with notional debt guarantees by the government) into a pay-as-you-go (PAYG) system. As this reform used the large reserves of the private sector white-collar scheme to shore-up the failing finances of the schemes for blue-collar workers, farmers and the self-employed—without, however, touching the more generous public sector scheme—it both placed the pension system as a whole on a sound financial footing, and gave electoral imperatives the priority. In order to avoid the electoral arena, a Christian Socialist–Liberal coalition government introduced this reform in two steps: a minimal financial fusion previous to the 1984 election, followed by more significant benefit restructuring after the election. Among those disadvantaged by the reforms were many cross-boarder workers who were not eligible to vote, and hence did not constitute an electoral threat. Over the course of the 1980s, however, these cuts and consolidation measures led to voter discontent with the large inequities remaining between the public and the private sectors. Indeed, this gave rise to a new party—the Action Committee for Democracy and Pension Justice (ADR), which promoted the need for harmonization during the 1989, 1994 and 1999 elections.

Consequently, Christian Democratic governments in 1991 and—against ILO advice—in 2002 expanded pension benefits in the private sector significantly, increasing age-related accrual rates in benefit calculation, adjusting benefits and introducing extra components such as end-of-year bonuses and lump sum mothers' pensions. At the same time, these governments successively reduced the privileges of the public sector scheme, and finally eliminated the public sector system entirely for newly-employed civil servants and public-sector workers.

Thus, contrary to what one might have expected, Luxembourg pension politics consolidated pension finances by converting from capital funding to PAYG; then later, used reserves to increase the defined-benefits components of pensions. At each step, as shall be shown, benefit expansions and the redistribution of financial burdens reflected the exigencies of political competition within the electoral system.

Nevertheless, unlike other continental pension regimes, Luxembourg's pension system is not threatened by demographic and labor market developments, nor are its government budgets under stress. First, this is because economic performance has been extremely good for the last two decades: the national budget features a surplus and GDP per head is the highest in the EU.[2] Second, because the pension system relies on high capital reserves, generous and costly pension benefit expansion has been possible. Instead, Luxembourg faces pressures of a different kind. A very high share of cross-border workers (35%; STATEC 2002: 10) and a small and open economy relying on a limited number of sectors, mainly the banking sector, imply great uncertainties. Consequently, the Luxembourgian pension system is vulnerable to external shocks and therefore international pension experts recommended abstaining from benefit expansions that would be difficult to retract.

II Political system

Constitutional history and nation-building

The Grand Duchy of Luxembourg is a parliamentary democracy in the form of a constitutional monarchy. The population of 451,600 inhabitants (2004) is composed of a large share of foreigners, namely 38.5 percent, with the Portuguese as the biggest minority group.[3] As it borders with Belgium, France, and Germany, the country's languages are Lëtzeburgish, French, and German.

Luxembourg's constitution goes back to 1868, when it achieved full independence from Belgium. More recent constitutional changes include fixing the size of the parliamentary assembly to 60 seats in 1988, and changes in the Council of the State in 1989 and in 1996.[4] Nestled among a series of great powers, the Duchy of Luxembourg made the transition from a constitutional monarchy to parliamentarianism, and then to democracy, peacefully—more the result of international treaties than domestic revolution. Consequently, the role of the Monarch has been gradually reduced, while ancient parliamentary checks on royal power—in particular the Council of State—were maintained, but with reduced veto powers, in order to facilitate decision-making.

Historically, the strong economy was based on iron ore deposits and mining. The mining company ARBED (*Aciéries Réunies de Burbach-Eich-Dudelange*), founded in 1911, was the biggest non-state employer for decades. In the mid-1970s ARBED faced serious difficulties due to low world steel market prices and outdated production plants. The restructuring of the sector, a reduction of the workforce from 24,000 to 7,000 employees and the cessation of mining all helped to diminish the sector's economic importance. The focal point of the Luxembourgian economy has shifted towards the banking sector. The country hosts 189 national and foreign banks with around 24,000 employees or 8.5 percent of the workforce in 2001 (STATEC 2002: 23, 10).

Institutions of government

The Luxembourg Head of State is the Grand Duke Henri of the Nassau family. His office is hereditary, and his duties are mainly representative (Art. 3; 37 Const.). Although the Grand Duke has the right to appoint the Prime Minister (Art. 33; 77 Const.), de facto he is bound by electoral outcomes and nominates the leader of the biggest parliamentary party to form a government coalition. He signs and promulgates laws but every act needs the counter-signature of the relevant minister (Art. 34; 45 Const.).

The leader of the current government is Prime Minister Jean-Claude Juncker. The Constitution does not require a formal investiture vote, nevertheless Parliament votes on the government after the inaugural speech. Furthermore, voting on the annual budget is usually linked to a vote of confidence (Dumont and de Winter 2000). The ministers are autonomous in their departments; but, the Prime Minister sets the strategic direction of the Cabinet. The Prime Minister may ask the Grand Duke to dissolve Parliament and call early elections (Art. 74 Const.).

The Council of State (*Conseil d'État*)[5] is a constitutional body whose participation in the law-making process is mandatory. The 21 members of the council are appointed by the Duke on suggestion of the Parliament and of the Council of State itself. Common practices are that the members of the Council roughly reflect party composition in the chamber. However, only four parties—CSV, LSAP, DP,

Table 17.1 Political institutions in Luxembourg

Political arenas	Actors	Rules of investiture	Rules of decision-making	Veto potential
Executive	Grand Duke	Hereditary office	Counter-signature on final act	Not a veto point
	Prime Minister	Leader of the strongest party in national elections is appointed by the Grand Duke to form a government. No mandatory investiture vote but usually PM is elected by simple majority of the *Chambre des Députés* with a quorum of 50% of members of parliament being present. Yearly budget is linked to vote of no confidence	Initiates legislation	
	Council of State (*Conseil d'État*)	15 year term or maximum age of 72; Appointed by the Grand Duke upon recommendation of the *Chambre des Députés* and the Council of State itself	Issues legal opinion on constitutionality of bills (*avis*) on bills within three months (before 1996 opinion was mandatory precondition for passage of the act)	Post-1996, not a veto point (previously, not highly significant, due to similar party composition as chamber)
Legislative	Chamber of Deputies (*Chambre des Députés*)	5-year term; 60 mandates in 4 multi-member districts (South 23, Center 21, North 9, East 7), proportional representation with vote splitting (*vote panaché*) and vote accumulation; compulsory voting; can be dissolved by the Grand Duke upon Prime Minister's demand	Right of initiative; decision making by majority of votes; without consent of the Council of State waiting period of three months before second vote and passage of a bill; constitutional amendments require new elections between first and second vote on bill	Not a veto point

(*Continued*)

Table 17.1 (Continued)

Power arenas	Actors	Rules of investiture	Rules of decision-making	Veto potential
Judicial	Constitutional Court (*Court d'appel*)	Composed of the President of the Superior Court of Justice, the President of the Administrative Court, two counsellors of the *Cour de Cassation* and five magistrates nominated by the Grand Duke		Not a veto point
Electoral	Referendum	May be called at the request of Parliament	Non-binding (although controversial); not used since 1937	Not a veto point
Territorial units	12 cantons 118 communities	Cantons: not political entities; communities: directly elected mayors and jurymen (*Schöffen*)	Communities: power to enact decrees concerning school organization and local planning	No veto potential on national level

Déi Gréng—have representatives in the Council. As of yet, the fourth strongest party—ADR—which occupies more seats than the Greens, has not been granted a seat.[6]

The Council of State is required to issue a legal opinion (*avis*) on the constitutionality of every bill (Art. 83 Const.). In the past, there was no time limit on the Council, which allowed it to slow down the policy-making process significantly or—de facto—even block the bill entirely by refusing to issue an opinion shortly before national elections (Schroen 1999). With the entry into effect of the constitutional reform of January 1, 1997,[7] the Council's legislative activity is subject to a time limit of three months after the first vote on a bill in Parliament. If the Council has not issued its comment within this period, Parliament has the right to pass the bill with a second vote. Thus, the Council's agreement is only necessary in order to shorten the legislative process, that is, to release Parliament from a second vote (Service Information et Presse de l'État & Conseil d'État 2002).

The Parliament is uni-cameral and composed of only 60 representatives (*Chambre des Députés*; Art. 46–48 Const.). Most work is done in standing committees (*commissions*) that are organized along the lines of the government departments. Committees have the right to consult non-parliamentary bodies and experts. A minimum number of five members of parliament may build a parliamentary fraction. Party discipline is not especially strict and, according to Schroen (1999: 392–3), decision outcomes frequently cross-cut government and opposition parties. As the Constitution allows local office holders such as mayors to become members of parliament, there is a close relationship between local and national politics, and local lobbying is significant.

According to Article 51 of the Constitution, referendums are possible and may be called by Parliament. Their non-binding character is controversial. The fact that the last referendum was held in 1937 shows the insignificance of this (Dumont and de Winter 2003: 492).

Luxembourg is a central, unitary state geographically divided into 12 cantons but with communities as the only political subdivision below the national level. The 118 communities are governed by directly elected councils headed by a mayor, and two-to-five jurymen (*Schöffen*). The communities have the power to enact decrees concerning education and local planning. Sources of income for the communities are energy, water, land and business taxes as well as transfers from the national budget (Schroen 1999: 410).

Electoral system

The legislative term is five years (Art. 56 Const.). Owing to stable government coalitions, early elections are rare. National elections determine the 60 members of parliament who are elected through a system of proportional representation in four districts (North, South, East and Center; Art. 51 (3), (5) Const.). Voting is compulsory

(Dumont and de Winter 2000). Prerequisites for the right to vote are: age 18, and Luxembourg nationality. The four electoral districts are represented in the chamber relative to their population size (Art. 51(6) Const.) causing distortions due to high immigrant ratios[8] and over-representation of the East and North districts due to their small size.[9] There is no legal entry hurdle, but the multi-member districts create de facto hurdles ranging from between 5 percent in the South and 10 percent in the East (Schroen 1999: 399).

Every voter has as many votes as there are mandates in his district. As the electoral system allows vote splitting, the voter may either vote for a party list, for individual candidates on one party list or for individual candidates on several party lists. In the context of a small nation, the split vote (*vote panaché*) in Luxembourg often expresses a personal relationship between candidates and voters (Poirier and Fehlen 2000: 136). The voter may also cast up to two votes for a single candidate (Art. 114, 119 Loi électorale). Vote counting and the distribution of mandates follows the Hagenbach-Bischoff method (Nohlen 2000; Art. 136–137 Loi électorale). The seats are distributed to the candidates on each list with the highest numbers of votes.[10]

Legislative process[11]

The government (*projet de loi*), or a member of parliament with the support of a minimum of five colleagues, (*proposition de loi*) have the right to initiate a bill. Usually legislative projects are prepared and drafted in the responsible department. After customary consultations with the social partners and the subsequent cabinet decision, the bill is forwarded to the Council of State. The Council comments on the bill; subsequently, the assigned parliamentary committee starts its sessions. In urgent cases, Parliament may start with the debate and the parliamentary negotiations before the Council has issued its comment, as long as the statement is published before the final parliamentary vote (Service Information et Presse de l'État & Conseil d'État 2002). The Committee examines the bill and reports to Parliament. In cases where the Committee changes and amends the original proposal or accommodates the Council's suggestions, the Council makes a second comment (*avis complémentaire*). Furthermore, the government must consult the occupational chambers (see p. 815), however, their comments are not binding. According to Article 59 of the Constitution, Parliament is required to vote twice on every bill with three months between votes. Decisions are taken by absolute majority with a quorum of 50 percent of the members of parliament plus one. However, the *Chambre des Députés* can file an application with the Council of State to discharge the chamber from the second vote. The bill must then be signed by the Grand Duke and the respective minister, and the law is published in the official, law journal—the *Mémorial*. Constitutional changes require the dissolution of Parliament and the support of two-thirds of a new Parliament with a three-quarter quorum (Dumont and de Winter 2003: 476).

Party family affiliation	Abbreviation	Party name	Ideological orientation	Founding and merger details	Year established
Christian Democratic	CSV	Christian Social People's Party (*Chrëschtlëch Sozial Vollekspartei*)	Center-right; religious with strong Catholic wing	Founded as Right Party (*Partei der Rechten*), renamed in 1944	1914
Social Democratic	LSAP (POSL)	Socialist Workers' Party (*Lëtzebuerger Sozialistesch Arbechterpartei*)	Left-wing, social-democratic	Founded as Social Democratic Party (*Sozialdemokratische Partei Luxembourgs*); renamed in 1944	1902/03
Social Democratic	SDP	Social Democratic Party	Social-democratic	Right-wing dissidents of the Socialist Workers' Party	1971
Liberal	DP	Democratic Party (*Demokratesch Partei*)	Liberal; main clientele self-employed and civil servants	Founded as Liberal League; renamed in 1947 (*Groupement Patriotique et Démocratique*), 1952 (*Groupement Démocratique*) and 1955 (*Demokratesch Partei*)	1904
Greens	GAP	Green Alternative (*Di Gréng Alternativ*)	Left-wing of Green movement		1983
Greens	GLEI	Green Left Ecological Initiative (*Gréng Lëscht Ekologesch Initiativ*)	Pragmatic greens	Dissidents of the GAP after conflict over party organization	(1984) 1986
Greens	Déi Gréng (GLEI-GAP)	Greens (*Déi Gréng*)	Environmental policy issues	Merger of GLEI and GAP	1992
Communist	KPL	Communist Party (*Kommunistesch Partei vu Lëtzebuerg*)	Far-left	Financially dependent on the East German Socialist Party (SED) until 1990	1921
Communist	Déi Lénk	The Left (*Déi Lénk*)	Far-left	Federation supported by the KPL	1999

Fig. 17.1 Party system in Luxembourg (*Continued*)

Special Interest	ADR	Action Committee for Democracy and Justice (*Aktiounskomitee fir Demokratie a Rentegerechteg keet*)	Conservative, one-issue party (pensions), protest party	Founded as *Aktiounskomitee 5/6 Pensioun fir jiddfereen* renamed in 1992	1987
	EDF	Party of Forced Recruits in the German Army (*Enrôlés de Force/Zwangsre krutierte*)	Protest party of those forcibly conscripted into the German army during World War II		1979

Fig. 17.1 (*Continued*)

Sources: Budge et al. (2001: 53 Appendix I); Schroen (1999: 400–404); Jacobs (1989); www.munzinger.de; www.polisci.com/almanac/nations/nation/LU.htm

Parties and elections

The Christian-Socialists (CSV), the Socialist Worker's Party (LSAP) and the Democratic Party (DP) have dominated the party system since 1945. The Christian-Socialists are the "natural" party of government. The party has continuously been in government since World War II, except for a short period from 1974 to 1979. The CSV typically gets the highest electoral support in three of the four electoral districts, with over-proportional results in rural areas in the North and the East. CSV voters are rather diverse. With respect to age structure, voters over 65 are over-represented and the CSV gets below average results within the age group 18 to 34. The Socialist Worker's Party recruits its voters mainly in the Southern district where the steel industry and many blue-collar workers are located. Just like the CSV, the LSAP is supported by a big share of voters over 65 years old (Poirier and Fehlen 2000: 318–9). The liberal stronghold is Luxembourg City in the Central electoral district: among DP voters are predominantly civil servants, the self-employed (Schroen 1999: 402) and high-income individuals. The liberal party has a greater appeal for male than female voters (Poirier and Fehlen 2000: 318–20). The Communist Party (KPL) was able to win between one and five seats between 1948 and 1989, mainly with blue-collar votes in the Southern district, but lost its parliamentary representation in the 1994 elections. In 1999, the radical left *Déi Lénk* party regained one seat. Representatives of green political movements (GLEI and GAP) have entered candidates in national elections since the early 1980s. After their amalgamation in *Déi Gréng* in 1992, they received nearly 10 percent of the vote, and became the fourth strongest partisan force in the chamber (Schroen 1999: 403). The Action Committee for Democracy and Pension Justice (ADR) had a most successful start in its first elections in 1989.

Table 17.2 Governmental majorities in Luxembourg

Election date	Start of gov.	Head of gov. (party)	Governing parties	Gov. majority (% seats)	Gov. electoral base (% votes)[a]	Institutional veto points	Number of veto players (partisan + institutional)
06.10.1979	07.16.1979	Werner IV (CSV)	CSV (24), DP (15)	66.1%	58.2%	None	2 + 0
06.17.1984	07.20.1984	Santer I (CSV)	CSV (25), LSAP (21)	71.9%	68.4%	None	2 + 0
06.18.1989	07.14.1989	Santer II (CSV)	CSV (22), LSAP (18)	66.7%	58.6%	None	2 + 0
06.12.1994	07.13.1994	Santer III (CSV)	CSV (21), LSAP (17)	63.3%	55.7%	None	2 + 0
01.26.1995		Juncker I (CSV)	CSV (21), LSAP (17)	63.3%	55.7%	None	2 + 0
06.13.1999	08.07.1999	Juncker II (CSV)	CSV (19), DP (15)	56.7%	52.4%	None	2 + 0
06.13.2004	07.31.2004	Juncker III (CSV)	CSV (24), LSAP (14)	63.3%	59.6%	None	2 + 0

[a] As the number of ballots per voter is different across districts, the governmental electoral base cannot be calculated as in other countries (i.e. total votes for the governmental parties divided by total valid votes). Thus, the share of votes by party in each district were weighted according to the relative size of the electorate (calculated as the number of valid votes in the district divided by total valid votes in the country). The weighted percentages of votes by party per district were then summed so as to estimate the national share of votes by party.

Sources:
www.elections.public.lu/legislatives/2004/resultats/index.html (Access 12.05.2005);
www.wahlen-99.lu/CIE/wahlen/ftp/nat_s_total.htm (Access 11.03.2003);
www.elections.public.lu/legislatives/1999/resultats/index.html (Access 10.01.2005);
www.gouvernement.lu/gouvernement/gouvernements_precedents/index.html (Access 10.05.2005);
Dumont and de Winter (2000).

The ADR was founded in reaction to the pension reform in 1987 and campaigned on a single issue: pension harmonization between the private and the public sector (www.adr.lu). Throughout the 1990s the ADR was able to improve its electoral results, and it expanded its parliamentary representation to 7 seats (= 11% of all seats) in 1999. Although the pension issue drew voters from all other parties, the ADR was strongly represented among farmers and wine-growers in the North and the East districts and among the self-employed. Thirty-five percent of ADR voters were between 50 and 64 years old and more than 50 percent of its voters were male in 1999. The ADR owes the favorable election results of 1999 to 17 percent of its voters who had previously (i.e. 1994) voted for CSV and 13 percent who had previously voted for LSAP. Moreover, 14 percent of its supporters were recruited from non-voters (Poirier and Fehlen 2000: 318–21, 326). There were several other splinter parties (Social Democratic Party and Socialist Independents) or special interest parties (e.g. Party of Forced Recruits, *Enrôlés de Force*) in the 1970s but they relapsed to unimportance.

Pensions dominated the election campaigns of 1989, 1994 and 1999 (LW 28.07.1998). Even previously, in 1984, the proposed pension reform had to be divided into an immediate financial reform and a deferred structural reform because of the closeness of the election date. The 1989 campaign was led by the ADR party manifesto with claims in pension policy only. In the 1994 elections, the call for pension harmonization between public and private sector was renewed; and the 1999 campaign was dominated by the liberal party's announcement to undo the 1998 changes in the public sector pension system. Especially in the 1999 election, the liberal party counted heavily on winning the election with the votes of the civil servants and public sector employees. An election analysis ascertained via opinion polls that voters considered pension equity to be one of the five most important issues influencing the national election in 1999.[12] Asked for the three issues determining, rather than influencing, the elections, 54 percent respondents named pension equity followed by education (24% of respondents), reform of public sector pensions (23%) and unemployment (20%) (Poirier and Fehlen 2000: 348). After most of the ADR's original demands had been carried out, the last election campaign—in 2004—concentrated on different topics (e.g. unemployment and education) for the first time in over a decade (*d'Lëtzebuerger Land* 21.05.2004).

Interest groups

Despite its small size and low number of inhabitants, Luxembourg features a pluralism of interest representation. The biggest union was first founded in 1919 and was a merger of earlier mining and metal workers' unions; it was re-established as *Lëtzeburger Arbechterverband* (LAV) in 1945 and transformed into the OGB-L (*Onofhängege Gewerkschafts-Bond Lëtzebuerg*) in 1979. The independent but LSAP-leaning union with 48,500 members (in 2000) strives for a long-term unification of the Labor movement.

The second biggest union—the *Lëtzebuerger Chrëschtleche Gewerkschafts-Bond* (LCGB)—founded in 1921—has tight links to the Christian-Socialist Party. A third general union is the *Neutral Gewerkschaft Lëtzebuerg*—a small union with mainly craftsmen membership. It was established in 1984 and has been the interest representation behind the ADR.

More specialized unions include the white-collar workers' union (*Fédération des Employés Privés*, FEP),[13] the union of employees and managers (*Fédération Indépendante des Travailleurs et Cadres* FITC), the Farmer's Union (*Central Paysanne*, C.P.), the union for the banking sector (ALEBA), and the union of teachers (APESS). The largest public sector union is the *Confédération Générale de la Fonction Publique* (CGFP) with approximately 20,700 members, of whom 30 percent are already retired or survivors. The CGFP does not allow its board of directors to also hold a parliamentary mandate (Schroen 2001). But it is not only the private sector that displays a wide variety of unions; the public sector also has specialized unions, for example, the union for community civil servants, the union for railway workers (*Fédération Nationale des Cheminots, Travailleurs du Transport, Fonctionnaires et Employés Luxembourgeois*, FNCTTFEL) or the Trade Union Federation of Luxembourg Postal Delivery Staff (*Fédération syndicaliste des facteurs Luxembourgeois*, FSFL).

The occupational chambers are elected public bodies. There are six occupational chambers respectively for blue-collar workers, white-collar workers, trade, craftsmen, farmers and employees of the public sector. The chambers represent their occupational sectors in public decision-making and have the right to comment on the government budget proposal and on bills. For each chamber, the number of representatives per specific sub-sector is fixed. The union's electoral lists for the occupational chambers must correspond to this balanced representation. The electoral term for the chambers is five years (Schroen 2001).

The *Fédération des Industriels Luxembourgeois* (FEDIL) and the *Union des Entreprises Luxembourgeoises* (UEL) represent private sector employers. Financial actors are united in the *Association des Banques et Banquiers Luxembourg* (ABBL; Schroen 2001: 247).

With respect to pensioners, the *Lëtzebuerger Rentner- an Invalide-Verband* (LRIV) lobbies for the interests of retirees. The LRIV was one of the founding members of the pension party ADR, and was previously close to the communists.

III Pension system

Historical overview[14]

The first state pension system in Luxembourg was established in 1911 (Loi du 6 mai 1911). It covered blue-collar workers and white-collar workers with incomes below a certain limit. The act on Social Insurances of 1925 united old age, health and accident insurance into a "social security code" (Loi du 17 décembre 1925). The structure of pension benefits was fundamentally changed in 1929. While the system enacted in 1911 granted a basic pension, pension benefits after 1929 were composed of a government-financed basic part (*part fixe*), and a variable part based on earnings and length of insurance. In the course of the past century, pension insurance coverage was extended to different occupational groups: white-collar workers in 1931 (Loi du 29 janvier 1931); craftsmen and independent professions in 1951 (Loi du 21 mai 1951); farmers in 1956 (Loi du 3 septembre 1956); and the industrial self-employed in 1960 (Loi du 30 juillet 1960).[15]

The pension reform of 1964 was a major step towards the harmonization of the different pension schemes, as benefit calculations and financing principles were aligned. At the same time, the act introduced pension adjustment to the standard of living for dependent employees (Loi du 13 mai 1964). The indexation principle was extended to craftsmen in 1967, to the industrial self-employed in 1970 and to farmers in 1974 (IGSS 2002a: 15). Additionally, intellectual/professional self-employed were allowed to join the pension scheme for white-collar workers from 1964 (Loi du 23 mai 1964). Further important changes in pension policy took place in 1969 when the retroactive purchase of pension entitlements was permitted (Loi du 28 juillet 1969) and in 1974 when a minimum pension of 5/6ths of the minimum social wage was introduced under the condition of having made at least 35 years of contributions (Loi du 14 mai 1974; Projet de loi No 2602: 31).

Demographic developments in the different schemes have been quite unequal: due to a displacement from the industrial and mining sector towards the service and banking sector, the blue-collar workers' scheme as well as the craftsmen's scheme displayed an unfavorable ratio of active employees to pensioners. The scheme for white-collar workers enjoyed positive finances. A report of 1968 suggested unifying all pension funds in a national risk community that would counterbalance adverse demographic trends (Projet de loi No 2602: 32). One of the major reasons for the financial burden was the adjustment of pension entitlements. As a complete unification of the different pension funds was not to be realized within the short-term, a risk community for financing pension adjustments to wage increase was built as a first step in the 1970s (IGSS 2002a: 16).

In the public sector a statutory pension system guaranteeing 5/6th pensions (i.e. pension benefits equal to 5/6ths of last salary) was introduced at a time when wages in the public sector did not meet the level of wages in the steel industry. As compensation, civil servants were granted a maximum share of the income as old-age income. However, over the next decades, wage increases in the public sector led to income levels converging to the private sector, thus creating injustice with respect to the pension regulations (ChD, 48e séance, 05.06.2002: 1721).

Description of the current pension system

Coverage

The entire working population is covered by a statutory pension system (IGSS 2002a: 22).[16] The pension system provides insurance against the risks of old age, invalidity and death. Until 1998 there was a major distinction between the private sector contributory pensions system and the public sector non-contributory system. Today, the private sector pension principles also apply to all civil servants who started work after January 1, 1999.

The private sector pension system is divided into four schemes and covers the workforce along occupational lines: the blue-collar workers are insured with the *Établissement d'Assurance contre la Vieillesse et L'invalidité* (AVI); white-collar employees with the *Caisse de Pension des Employés Privés* (CPEP); the pension scheme for craftsmen and the self-employed is administered under the *Caisse de Pension des Artisans, des Commerçants et Industriels* (CPACI); the *Caisse de Pension Agricole* (CPA) covers farmers (MSS 2001b).

The four schemes together covered 278,237 active insured persons and paid 115,326 pensions in 2003.[17] The pension scheme for white-collar workers covers approximately 50 percent of all insured in the private sector, followed by the blue-collar worker's scheme with 45 percent and CPACI with 3.4 percent and CPA with 1.2 percent. The ratios for pensioners per scheme to total pensioners are quite different: the blue-collar workers' scheme comprehends 65 percent of all pensioners, the CPEP 20 percent, CPACI 7.6 percent and the farmers' scheme 5 percent of all pensioners.[18]

In addition to compulsory pension insurance there are three ways of joining these schemes voluntarily. First, if a person can account for at least twelve months of compulsory insurance within the last three years, he or she can voluntarily remain insured (*l'assurance continuée* and *l'assurance complémentaire*). Second, persons who give up their employment for family reasons and who have at least twelve months of compulsory insurance, who are Luxembourg residents and who are not older than 60 years can also be insured voluntarily (*l'assurance facultative*, Art. 173 C.A.S. III). Third, persons who gave up employment for family reasons, or persons with pension rights from countries without bi- or multilateral social security contracts with Luxembourg may complete their pension periods through the retroactive purchase of pension rights (*forfait de rachat*). Preconditions for the so-called *forfait de rachat* are the same as for *l'assurance facultative* (Art. 174 C.A.S. III; IGSS 2002a: 25).

Due to generous benefits and comprehensive coverage by the state pension system, occupational pensions have consistently played a subordinate role in Luxembourgian pension politics. Voluntary occupational pensions were regulated in 1999. The issues regulated were the vesting of acquired rights, funding requirements and statistical assessment of occupational pension coverage (Loi du 8 juin 1999).

Administration

The administration of the private sector pension system is shared between the four schemes—AVI, CPEP, CPACI, CPA—and the *Centre Commun de la Sécurité Sociale* (CCSS). The CCSS is a central agency located in Luxembourg City that handles pension contributions from employers, employees and the general government budget for the entire country (Art. 320 seq. C.A.S. VI). After collection, these revenues are transferred to the relevant pension fund. The four funds—mentioned here—invest the reserves, calculate, and pay out benefits. Together they have built a financial unity since the 1984 pension reform.

The CCSS and these schemes are independent public bodies controlled by the Ministry of Social Security through its *Inspection Générale de la Sécurité Social* (IGSS, Art. 320, 328 C.A.S. VI and Art. 268–272 C.A.S. III). The schemes are headed by pension boards (*comité-directeur*) consisting of an equal number of representatives of employers and employees (Art. 259, 260 C.A.S. III).

Occupational pension funds can be organized as a corporate structure (*société d'épargne-pension à capital variable*, sepcav) or as partnership structure (*association d'épargne-pension*, assep). The *Commission de Surveillance du Secteur Financier* (CSSF) registers occupational funds and monitors second-pillar pension schemes (Courtois 1999: 305–6).

Financing

The financing method of the statutory pension system is PAYG with large reserves based on seven-year-coverage periods (*système de la répartition des charges par périodes de couverture de sept ans*, Art. 238 C.A.S. III). The contribution rate is determined at the beginning of each period by an act of parliament, and remains constant for the seven years. Currently, employers, employees and the state each pay 8 percent. The capital reserves of the pension funds are allowed to range between 1.5 and 2.5 times the yearly expenditure, which gives scope to balance out temporary crises. If the balance sheets indicate that the reserves will fall short of one and one-half times annual expenditure for two years in a row, the contribution rate must be raised by government decree (*réglement grand-ducal*) even within the seven-year-period, as the state does not guarantee deficits or provide other kinds of tax revenues. However, the contribution rate of 24 percent has remained constant since the introduction of the financing system in 1984 as actual reserves have always exceeded the legally required minimum by far.[19] Contributions are paid on gross wages (including supplements and special payments) with a lower and an upper contribution limit.

There are three different ways of financing occupational pensions: book reserves, insurance schemes or pension funds. Luxembourgian occupational pension funds joined the German Pension Safeguard Association (*Pensions-Sicherungs-Verein*, PSVaG) in 2002. This association insures occupational pension funds against employer insolvency.

Benefits

The standard retirement age for men and women in Luxembourg is 65 years (Art. 183 C.A.S. III). But in practice, the timing is quite flexible. Early retirement is possible at 57 or 60 with special qualifying periods. The pension system differentiates between several types of insurance periods: effective insurance periods (*périodes effectives*, Art. 171 C.A.S. III) include periods of professional activity, maternity and parental leave, periods of war, military or peace-keeping service, time spent as the spouse of a farmer, apprenticeships, and time covered by wage-replacement benefits such as

First pillar	Second pillar	Third pillar
Third tier: none	Voluntary occupational pension	Voluntary private pension
Earnings-related pension (*Majoration proportionelle*) — White-collar (CPEP), Blue-collar (AVI), Self-employed (CPACI), Farmers (CPA), Public sector (*régimes spéciaux*)	Subsidized voluntary occupational pension: state-regulated; reduced tax rate	Subsidized private pension: none
Basic pension (*Majoration for faitaire*) — White-collar (CPEP), Blue-collar (AVI), Self-employed (CPACI), Farmers (CPA), Public sector (*régimes spéciaux*); Minimum pension with 20–40 years of insurance	Mandatory occupational pension: none	Mandatory occupational pension: none
Social assistance: cost of living bonus (*allocation de vie chère*, AVC)		

Fig. 17.2 Pension system in Luxembourg

sickness or unemployment benefits (IGSS 2002a: 141–42). Assimilated periods (Art. 172 C.A.S. III) are periods of disability, of higher education (ages 18 to 27), youth unemployment and child-rearing periods during the first six years of a child's life (minimum of eight years for two children and minimum of ten years for three children). There is also special treatment of periods of voluntary insurance, and scope for the retroactive purchase of insurance periods (Art. 173–174 C.A.S. III).

The qualifying period (*stages*) for old-age pension eligibility is 10 years of effective or voluntary insurance (Art. 183 C.A.S. III). To be entitled to a pension at the age of

60 (*pension de vieillesse anticipée*) the insured person has to account for 40 years of effective, assimilated or voluntary insurance periods, of which at least ten have to be effective or voluntary insurance. Retirement at the age of 57 years is possible only if the insured possesses 480 months of exclusively effective insurance periods (Art. 184 C.A.S. III).

Pension benefits are composed of four parts.[20] The basic, flat-rate pension depends on the number of insurance years only. The so-called *majoration forfaitaire* equals 23.5 percent of the minimum wage, weighted by the number of years of insurance (maximum of 40 years). The *majoration proportionelle* is the second and earnings-related part. Yearly benefits equal 1.85 percent of the sum of all working/career earnings. The *majorations proportionnelles échélonnées* is an incremental factor to increase the accrual rate and depends on the person's age at retirement and the total number of years of insurance. Based on an initial assumption of 55 years of age and 38 years of insurance contributions—a total of 93 years—each year surpassing 93 increases the accrual rate of 1.85 percent by 0.01 percent points, up to a limit of 2.05 percent (Art. 214 C.A.S. III). The fourth part of pension benefits is a flat-rate end-of-year bonus depending on the duration of insurance. The maximum bonus amounted to €564 in 2005 (MSS 2005). In total, benefits are generous, with a monthly minimum pension of 90 percent of the reference social wage.

The statutory pension system provides for two methods of pension adjustment. Pension entitlements as well as benefits are automatically adjusted to price inflation (*adaption au coût de la vie*). Additionally, the government scrutinizes wage developments every two years; based on these figures the government submits a *projet de loi* which contains an adjustment to the rise in the standard of living (*ajustement au niveau de vie*, Art. 224–225 C.A.S. III).

IV POLITICS OF PENSION REFORM SINCE 1980

Overview

The top issue in pension policy is pension justice. After pressing financial problems were eliminated by restructuring pension finance in 1984, conflict over pension policy throughout the 1980s and 1990s concentrated on the differences between public and private sector benefits. The discrepancy between the two systems, both in contributions and in benefit calculation rules, nurtured private sector demands for convergence towards public sector pensions. There were sharp differences in the monetary values of pensions in the two sectors. The ADR stated that in 1994, 90 percent of all public sector pensions were above LUF 90,000, while 90 percent of all private sector pensions were below this margin (ADR 1994).

Table 17.3 Overview of proposed and enacted pension reforms in Luxembourg

Year	Name of reform	Reform process (chronology)	Reform measures
1984	Loi du 23 mai 1984	• 1971 ILO report on building financial risk community • 1977 Economic and Social Council report • June 24, 1982 CSV/DP submission of government bill • March 13, 1983 Thullen report • April 5, 1984 Conseil d'État comment • May 10, 1984 passage of the bill	• replacement of capital funded system with PAYG (*Kapitalabschnittsdeckungsverfahren*) • introduction of state pension contributions (8%) • introduction of a financial risk community • reform measures concerning benefits failed!
1987	Loi du 27 juillet 1987	• February 27 and March 13, 1987 cabinet agreement • March 19, 1987 submission to Parliament • March 27, 1987 cabinet revision of the bill • March 28, 1987 union protests but low participation • May 26, 1987 parliamentary debate • June 5, 1987 cabinet revision of the bill • July 16, 1987 passage with cross-party consensus	• additional pension adjustment of 7% which would be reimbursed 1% per year • substitution of the *part fixe* by *majoration forfaitaire* • introduction of a tax-financed baby-year as contribution year based on average last 12 months' income before birth of child • increase of the qualifying period from 5 to 10 years for standard pensions • increase of qualifying period to 40 years for early retirement • increase of minimum insurance period from 15 years of residence to 40 years of insurance (in CPEP) • introduction of widowers' pensions and anti-accumulation rules • introduction of adjustment for supplemental pension
1991	Loi du 24 avril 1991	• October 1990 submission of bill • 28 March 1991 passage of bill	• guarantee of the 1987 7% increase • normal pension adjusted by 5% • additional pension increased by 5% • increase in basic pension from 20% to 22% of minimum wage • increase in accrual rate from 1.6 to 1.78 • increase in upper contribution ceiling

(Continued)

Table 17.3 (Continued)

Year	Name of reform	Reform process (chronology)	Reform measures
1996	Loi du 8 janvier 1996	• October 27, 1995 submission of government proposal • November 27, 1995 government amendments • October 24, 1995 CGFP protest manifestations • December 15, 1995 public sector strike • December 19, 1995 passage of the bill	• augmentation of widows' pension from 66.6% to 75% of deceased's pension rights • introduction of early retirement after 40 years of contributions and an age of 57 (instead of 60) • increase in child rearing period from 12 to 24 months
1998	Loi(s) du 3 août 1998	• Nov 11, 1996 presentation of government proposal • August 1997 submission of bill • March to May 1998 conciliation commission • July 14, 1998 and July 21, 1998 protests and strike in public sector • July 21, 1998 passage of bill	• Abolishment of *péréquation* in the public sector • introduction and incremental augmentation of public sector contributions from 3% to 8% by 1999 • introduction of equal adjustment rules in public and private sector starting in 1999 • Introduction of equal retirement and pension regulations for public sector employees entering job after 1 January 1999 but without contribution limit • transition scheme for public sector employees employed before 1999: reduction of replacement rate from 5/6 i.e. 83.33% to 72%
2002	Loi du 28 juin 2002	• May 10, 2000 establishment of *Rentendësch* • July 16, 2001 *Rentendësch* consensus • December 13, 2001 submission of bill • June 5, 2002 passage of bill in cross-party consensus	• Increase in linear pensions of 3.9% • increase in basic pension of 11.6% • increase in minimum pension of 7% • increase in widows' pension of 33.8% • introduction of end-of-year bonus • introduction of a "mothers' pension" i.e. *forfait d'éducation*

The establishment of a financial risk community within the private sector neutralized the pernicious demographic development of some schemes, and reduced the projected future financial burden for the public budget. The last benefit-reducing changes in the private sector pension were made in 1987 and established a link between the basic pension and the duration of contribution payments, and transferred financial liability for the basic pension from general tax revenues to the pension funds. After the mode of financing issue had been settled, private sector pensions were increased in 1991 and 2002 to reach the public sector replacement rate of 5/6ths of active income. The claims of the protest party ADR contributed to the abolition of the public sector pension system, to the application of private sector rules to new civil servants and to the increases in private sector pensions.

The 1984 reform

Background

Preparatory work for the pension reform of 1984 started in the early 1970s. Changes in the overall employment structure caused different demographic developments and consequently different future financial burdens in the existing schemes. An ILO report demanded an equalization of the financial risk between blue- and white-collar workers and suggested integrating the reorganization of financing into a global pension reform (Projet de loi No 2602: 33). The ILO report gave the government the impetus to assign several groups of experts with the task of drafting guidelines for a structural pension reform (e.g. Economic and Social Council report 1977; Thullen 1983: 2).

The years 1974 to 1979 were the first term of government not to have included the Christian-Socialists since 1919. The Liberal-Socialist government (DP/LSAP) were faced with the crisis in the iron and steel sector. At the same time, the socialist trade union LAV (*Lëtzebuerger Arbechterverbond*) attempted to unify the unions. According to Hirsch (1980: 250) the "plans for a unified trade-union organization, constituted a threat to the privileged position of employees and civil servants." During the electoral campaign for the 1979 elections the CSV "played on the fears of employees and civil servants: that the 'crisis argument' was just a pretext to reinforce the influence of the Socialists in state and society" (Hirsch 1980: 251). The Socialists were further challenged from within the left block of the party system by the Independent Socialists and by *Enrôlés de Force*. The LSAP lost over four percentage points of the vote, and the CSV and DP formed a new government coalition. The CSV/DP government "was determined to modernize Luxembourg society and embark on a far-reaching program of social reform" (Hirsch 1980: 250). But, contrary to the recommendation of the Economic and Social Council, the CSV/DP coalition in its inaugural address announced that the legislative changes in the pension sector would be restricted to the private sector (Projet de loi No 2602: 34). On the basis of the Economic and Social Council report the Minister of Social Security, Jacques Santer (CSV), drafted a first governmental proposal in 1982 (see also Thullen 1983: 2).

The demographic developments in three of the four pension schemes were the main reason why reform of the financial structure of the pension system became necessary. The pension schemes for blue-collar workers, for craftsmen and for farmers displayed very high ratios of pensioners to the active workforce.[21] These ratios indicated that the capital-funded system with separate funds for each branch was not sustainable. As the financial system provided for government guarantees to cover the lack of reserves for full capital funding, the burden on the general budget had increased and would have increased even more in the future. The establishment of financial equalization between the funds was suggested, as this would make the schemes financially more sustainable without the necessity of increasing contribution rates (LW 10.05.1984). At the same time, the government's involvement in the pension system was to be changed from a virtual benefit guarantor to a real engagement on the contribution side.

Project de loi No 2602

Social Minister Santer submitted a reform bill on June 24, 1982 (Projet de loi No 2602). The main provisions of the bill can be divided into a financial part and a structural benefit part. Most important was the reform of the financing structure of the pension system. Prior to the 1984 reform, the system was a modified capital-funded system with governmental debt certificates. That is, as the pension funds could not fully cover the implicit pension debt, the state guaranteed that it would cover the difference between contribution revenues and the reserves required for full funding. However, the governmental deficit guarantees were not actual payments, but rather notional guarantees in terms of debt certificates, on which the state paid a fairly low interest rate of 4.25 percent per year to compensate for forgone interest on the capital market.[22] If the state had transferred actual monetary payments, the pension regimes would have been able to invest theses reserves at a much higher interest rate in the late 1970s and early 1980s. In other words, the mode of financing had a negative impact on the rate of return of the schemes (Thullen 1983: 17). As contribution payments did not cover reserves and expenses, the notional government debt in the pension system rose to LUF 28 billion in late 1983 (IGSS 1984: 9; see also LW 14.04.1984). Although the system was capital-funded, de facto it operated on a PAYG basis with high reserves. The reform proposal envisioned making a formal transition from capital funding to PAYG where the contribution rate would be fixed for 7-year periods. The notional government debt certificates were to be phased-out, and the state was to participate instead in contribution payments. The state was to pay one-third of the contribution rate of 24 percent, that is to say, 8 percent. According to the first proposal, reserves were to be kept between 2.5 percent and 3.5 percent of yearly pension expenditure. If the reserves were in danger of falling below the 2.5 percent mark, the contribution rate was to be increased (Projet de loi No 2602: 41; Chambre des Employés privés 1983: 59).

The second part of the reform plan envisioned changes in benefits. More precisely, it entailed the abolishment of the fixed basic pension (*part fixe*) and its replacement with a flat-rate percentage of the minimum social wage (*majoration forfaitaire*).

Contrary to the former practice of using the absolute value of the tax-financed *part fixe*, the new contribution-financed *majoration forfaitaire* would depend on the number of years of insurance and would reach the maximum after 40 years of insurance (Thullen 1983: 10; Projet de loi No 2602: 34–35).

The bill also touched a variety of issues: the coverage of handicapped persons, the equal recognition of voluntary contributions and retro actively purchased entitlements, the introduction of an occupational disability pension as a second stage of invalidity, changes in qualifying conditions for invalidity pensions, the rise from 35 to 40 years of insurance to be entitled to minimum pension of at least 5/6ths of the minimum wage, change in indexation from gross wage to modified gross wage, introduction of widowers' pensions, new anti-accumulation rules, the introduction of a child credit, and the splitting of pension entitlements in cases of divorce.

The pre-parliamentary stage and parliamentary process

The Economic and Social Council assigned an external expert Peter Thullen—a Swiss professor working for the ILO and author of the 1971-ILO study on Luxembourg—to comment on the governmental proposal of 1982 (LW 21.05.1983). Thullen welcomed the restructuring of the financing of the pension system: that is, the introduction of a PAYG system with time-segments. However, he criticized the fact that the proposal did not foresee the inclusion of the public sector pension scheme into a unitary pension system (Thullen 1983: 3, 16; LW 21.05.1983). As for the structural pension reform, Thullen (1983: 5–15) suggested minor modifications of several articles, for example, concerning voluntary contributions, retroactive purchase, disability pensions, widows' and widowers' pensions, and anti-accumulation. But, he did not criticize the core elements of the bill.

In October 1983, the government met with the social partners to negotiate the pension reform project. All participating actors agreed on the necessity of a pension reform and on the transition to a PAYG system. Difficulties and disagreements remained with the details of the financial union of the pension funds and with the structural reform measures.

The bill met opposition from various sides (ChD, 60e séance, 09.05.1984: 3107). The Occupational Chamber for White-Collar Workers vehemently rejected the financial union. It accused the government of trying to get rid of over LUF 20 billions of debt certificates, and argued that the proposal fully relied on the financial means of the pension fund for white-collar employees—the CPEP. The chamber argued that the CPEP reserves would not suffice to keep the system stable in the long-term. In order to gain time for the elaboration of a more sustainable reform plan, the Chamber for White-Collar Workers recommended a short-run increase in the interest rate on debt certificates that would be close to real market rates and thus would provide adequate rates of return. Furthermore, the Chamber criticized the extension of the qualifying period from 15 to 40 years, the abolition of widows' pensions for persons younger than 43, the requirement to find part-time work when benefiting from an occupational disability pension, and the abolishment of the female white-collar workers' retirement age of 55. Otherwise the *Chambre des*

Employés privés welcomed the introduction of voluntary insurance for housewives, the introduction of the baby year, the inclusion of the handicapped, the adjustment of the basic pension (*majoration fortfaitaire*), and the increase in the survivor's pension to two-thirds of the deceased's pension. Most importantly, for obvious reasons, the *Chambre des Employés Privés* objected to the loss of the financial autonomy of the CPEP. The white-collar workers did not accept "solidarity between occupations" as justification for the reform, as the public sector was not included in this "occupational solidarity" (Chambre des Employés privés 1983: 59–62). The government was criticized for reducing its obligations at the expense of the CPEP reserves (OGB-L actualités 3/1984: 10).

The Chamber of Labor also refused its consent to the bill, though its objections related to the benefit measures. Moreover, the chamber considered itself unable to estimate the financial implications of the reform measures due to its limited resources, and asked for a "round table" with the political parties and the social partners to renegotiate the reform plans (Chambre de Travail 1983: 72). In accordance with the other private sector pension schemes the pension fund for craftsmen and the self-employed regretted the neglect of the public sector in the reform proposal (CPACI 1983).

The farmers' union criticized the government proposal especially because of the anti-accumulation regulations. Farmers were hit harder by these regulations than other occupational groups since farmers were frequently forced to work beyond the age of 65, either for financial reasons or because no other manpower was available to cultivate the land. The *Centrale Paysanne* (1983: 75–6, 85–6) argued against the distribution of excess contribution revenues according to the extent to which each pension fund has generated surpluses. The reason expressed in their comment on the bill was that the proportional redistribution of revenues would endanger the idea of a unitary pension system in the contributory sector. Concerning the pension contribution rate for farmers, the *Centrale Paysanne* objected because the payments were based on the total agricultural revenue a farmer achieved, but at least 50 percent was attained through remuneration of the capital assets. Salaried employees and their employers paid together 16 percent of wages as a contribution to the pension system, but employers did not pay extra contributions on the revenues achieved though capital assets. Therefore, farmers argued for a reduction in their 16 percent contribution rate (Centrale Paysanne 1983: 77, 96; see also LW 25.05.1983).

These hostile comments are just a few examples of the fierce opposition that the proposed reform measures drew from all sides (ChD, 60e séance, 09.05.1984: 3106). There was consistent repudiation of the structural reform—the weighting of the basic pension and the new anti-accumulation rules—across all unions. Nevertheless the government aimed at passing the bill before the next parliamentary election, which was scheduled for June 17, 1984 (LW 15.10.1983). But agreement on a structural reform appeared to be unfeasible before that date. Consequently, a fiscal law restructuring the financing of pensions was separated from the overall pension reform project. Santer submitted a new bill to Parliament on financing reform on February 15, 1984—the Projet de loi No 2781; all other parts of a comprehensive structural pension reform were dropped (LW 13.04.1984; 05.05.1984). Compared to the 1982 proposal, the restructuring of pension financing differed in two ways: the financial compensation between the different pension funds was restricted to the necessary minimum, and the funds were to maintain their administrative autonomy with respect to investment (Commission des affaires sociales 1984: 8).

The Council of State issued its legal opinion on April 5, 1984 to say that it considered the establishment of a risk community between the four pension funds as an adequate measure to sustain financing in the long-run. However, the Council pointed to the necessity of changes in pension benefits at a later point in time (LW 14.04.1984). The parliamentary Committee for Social Affairs under chairwoman Vivian Redding (CSV) debated the proposal and the Council's opinion in various sessions, but decided not to amend the bill (LW 06.05.1984).

The OGB-L union organized a demonstration against the government proposal on April 15, 1984, but its call found little response. The protest was criticized for being a left-wing electoral campaign event to win non-left voters (LW 16.04.1984; 17.04.1984). The rather CSV-oriented newspaper *Luxemburger Wort* criticized the LSAP for using the pension issue for electoral campaign (LW 19.04.1984). On May 9, 1984, the pension section of OGB-L and the FEP submitted petitions to Parliament. Both petitions called for the rejection of the bill. The OGB-L and FEP demanded a global pension reform including the public sector and the structural changes (LW 10.05.1984). But the CSV-affiliated union—the LCGB—supported the reform (LW 17.04. 1984). Parliament debated and passed the act on 9 and 10 May 1984 (Loi du 23 mai 1984).[23]

To summarize, the pension reform proposal of 1982 failed, after two years of negotiation, to introduce structural measures affecting benefit calculations. However, the financial reform was successful in getting through Parliament, and had important implications for the public finances. The transition from capital funding to PAYG with government responsibility on the contribution side has—at first sight—increased state contributions from 27.4 percent (1975–84) of pension spending to 30.2 percent (1985–90) and to an average of about 32 percent in the 1990s.[24] But the interest payments of 4.25 percent on debt certificates and some other pension costs that were covered through the state (such as administration costs and the basic pension benefits, *part fixe*) were the only items that appeared in the general government budget. The accumulated debt certificates were not listed. But if the debt certificates for each year were added to the interest payments and the other state costs, the share of the state reached 39.6 percent of total pension expenditure. And, as there was no ceiling on state guarantees, it is reasonable to expect that the share would have increased further due to the unequal demographic development in the different pension schemes. Put into figures, the financial impact of the 1984 reform was a decrease in public pension financing of about 9.4 percentage points.[25]

The impact of the reform on the various pension schemes, however, was considerable. The white-collar scheme's surpluses were used to solve the financial problems of the schemes of the blue-collar, self-employed (including craftsmen) and farmers' schemes, without touching those of public sector workers and civil servants.

In addition, the social insurance contributions of non-Luxembourgian citizens—cross-border workers and immigrants—would provide additional financing in the PAYG system. Having taken back its dominant position in the 1979 election, now the CSV was more concerned about the fiscal sustainability of the pension system as a whole, and about its core electorate: the self-employed and farmers in the Northern and Eastern electoral districts.

The 1987 reform

1984 Election

Following the national elections in 1984, a new CSV/LSAP government coalition took office on July 20. The main issue of the electoral campaign had been crisis management in the steel sector. The previous CSV/DP government had attained the financial means for the restructuring of heavy industry through a suspension of automatic wage increases indexed to inflation, through tax increases and through immense job cuts in the steel industry. Prior to the elections, the main opposition party LSAP promised to re-establish wage indexation if it came to power. As the LSAP campaign concentrated on income policy and steel policy only, and made limited use of ideological slogans, there was a danger of the party becoming appealing to members of the Christian union LCGB. However, the CSV was able to maintain its share of the vote in 1984. The LSAP won seven extra seats. Most notably the Liberals (DP) were held accountable for the hardship of the economic reforms and lost votes even in their electoral stronghold—the Center district (Hirsch 1985: 116–17). The logical consequence was the formation of a CSV/LSAP government, which had the support of 71 percent of the seats in Parliament.

Pre-parliamentary stage

The 1987 pension reform[26] did not rest solely upon the government's inaugural speech of July 23, 1984,[27] but also on the reform proposal made in 1982, and the Thullen report of 1983 (Projet de loi No 3039: 35). The 1987 reform goals were stabilization of pension expenditures, and selective improvements in pension benefits (LW 17.07.1987). The main idea was to draft a unified pension regime with equal rights for the insured of all occupations. In other words, the provisions of the four private sector pension schemes were to be completely harmonized. Social Minister Benny Berg justified the exclusion of the public sector from the envisioned pension reform by referring to the terms of the coalition agreement.

In February 1987, Berg mapped a pension reform bill. The proposal contained many of the measures suggested in the 1982 bill, such as: the substitution of the *part fixe* by the *majoration forfaitaire*; the introduction of a baby-year; an increase in the qualifying period from 5 to 10 years for regular old-age pensions; and an increase in the qualifying period to 40 years for early retirement and for full basic pension (Projet de loi No 3093).[28]

Several reform features were to ameliorate pension benefits. Minister Berg announced pension increases of 3 percent to 5 percent. But as the structural changes in the system would require time for administrative adaptation, Berg did not envision pension increases until January 1988 (LW 25.02.1987). However, the new qualifying periods made it more difficult to qualify for a pension, and linked the basic pension, as well as the right to retirement at the age of 60, more closely to employment.

While the small Neutral Luxembourgian Union (NGL) strongly rejected the proposal, and immediately called for protests against the bill (LW 10.03.1987), the criticism of the Christian union LCGB was more moderate. Although the LCGB welcomed several reform measures such as the baby-year, occupational disability and widowers' pensions, it demanded a steep increase in basic pensions (from LUF 15,000 to LUF 24,000) over the course of 1987 (LW 25.02.1987).

Cabinet meetings on February 27, 1987 and March 13, 1987 led to agreement on the main features of the bill (LW 28.02.1987; see also LW 14.03.1987). Expected costs of the reform measures amounted to LUF 3.6 billions up to 1991, and were to be financed through a reduction of capital reserves from 2.42 times to 1.9 times yearly pension expenditures. Afterwards, that is for the next 7-year time segment, an increase in contribution rates of 2–3 percent was expected (LW 14.03.1987). Although Minister Berg had planned to defer any pension increases until 1988, the March proposal foresaw a preliminary rise in pensions of 6 percent instead of 3–5 percent, to be put into force in mid-1987 (LW 19.03.1987). The bill (Projet de loi No 3093) was submitted to Parliament on March 19, 1987.

The 1987 bill envisioned taking into account certain periods other than compulsory insurance periods for the fulfillment of the qualifying periods for early retirement, the minimum pension and the basic pension (*majorations forfaitaires*), and also continued voluntary and purchased insurance periods. For example, periods of child-rearing up to an age of six years and higher education were recognized as non-contributory insurance periods, eligible as qualifying periods for basic pensions and early pensions. The introduction of a tax-financed baby-year created pension entitlements and counted as a regular insurance period (Projet de loi No 3093: 38). Retirement at 60 with a minimum of 40 years of compulsory and assimilated insurance periods was extended to all occupations. The introduction of differentiation between disability and occupational disability was also envisioned; thus the possibility of drawing a partial disability pension up to an upper limit of 80 percent of the average income over the best five years of the individual's employment history.

The formula for pension benefit calculation was also changed in 1987: the *part fondamentale* was replaced by the *majoration forfaitaire*. The basic pension was to be split into 40/40, which implied a minimum insurance period for full basic pension of 40 years compared to 15 years of residence prior to reform (Projet de loi No 3093: 38; LW 14.03.1987). Elections to the pension fund boards were to be abolished; instead, a delegation of occupational representatives by the occupational chambers would be part of the pension funds. The bill introduced a widowers' pension, made up of the full basic pension plus two-thirds of earnings-related pension. These were to be financed through the concurrent introduction of anti-accumulation regulations (LW 26.05.1987). Pension adjustment was to be applied to the entire pension, not only for the earnings-related part as had been the case prior to reform; under the status quo ante, the supplementary (earnings-related) pensions were adjusted, but the basic pension was not. As for low-income earners, the share of the basic pension was higher than the supplementary benefits, the former rule penalized low pensions. The proposed anti-accumulation rules resembled the ones suggested in 1982. Survivors' pensions would be reduced by 45 percent if the income of the household exceeded 60 percent of household's income before death (Projet de loi No 3093: 43; LW 26.05.1987). Spouses of the self-employed (*aidants*) were forced to take out insurance (LW 16.07.1987). The most important, or at least the most controversial, aspect of the reform process was the increase in pension benefits.

The OGB-L proclaimed that the union considered an increase in pensions of 6 percent to be too low, and would only be a very first step in the equalization of all insured (LW 18.03.1987). The NGL called for protests and demonstrations as the structural reform would not bring about pension harmonization between the public and the private sector, which would entail a guaranteed replacement rate of 5/6ths of final income in the private sector. On March 27, 1987, the Cabinet revised the part of the bill on the pre-increase in pensions—one day before the scheduled protests against the pension reform. The Cabinet decided to increase pensions by 7 percent instead of 6 percent on July 1, 1987 instead of January 1, 1988. The expected additional cost of LUF 210 million was to be covered by reducing reserves (LW 28.03.1987).

Although all private sector unions had supported the idea of a 5/6th pension for all those insured under the contributory pension system, that is, the complete harmonization of pension benefits between the private and public sectors (LW 16.03.1987), the two major private-sector unions—OGB-L and LCGB—did not participate in the protests on March 28, 1987. A fairly small crowd of 800 people representing three interest groups—the NGL, the *Union des Journalistes Luxembourg* (UJL) and the *Lëtzebuerger Rentner – an Invalideverband* (LRIV)—requested "pension justice for everybody." The protest participation exposed the non-uniform and fragmented interests within private sector unions and associations (LW 30.03.1987).

Although it did not support the protests, the CSV-affiliated union LCGB criticized the pension reform proposal because—according to the union's predictions—the provisions would increase the differences between the private and the public sector instead of reducing them. Those insured under the contributory system would be negatively affected by the anti-accumulation regulations, the weighting of basic pension by number of years of insurance, and stricter requirements for early retirement (LW 16.05.1987, 21.05.1987). The LCGB requested a suspension of the structural features of the bill to permit more time for further negotiations between unions and government, but insisted on an immediate increase in pensions by 7 percent and the introduction of occupational disability (LW 16.05.1987, 21.05.1987). Minister Berg ruled out the splitting of the reform act into two sequential parts (LW 30.05.1987).

The OGB-L accused the other unions of irresponsibility: the NGL-claim for 5/6th pensions was unrealistic and the LCGB demands of an immediate pension increase, but deferred structural cuts, would endanger the realization of improvements for many pensioners. The OGB-L itself also rejected several features, namely the weighing of basic pensions by years of insurance, the abolition of pension funds' board elections, and the anti-accumulation rules (LW 21.05.1987).

Parliamentary stage

The parliamentary committee debated the reform on May 26, 1987. The controversial issue was that pensioners who also received social assistance would not profit from the full 7 percent increase (*ajustement*) in pensions as the social assistance sponsored cost of living bonus (*allocation de vie chère*, AVC)[29] would be reduced by the increase in pension benefits (LW 27.05.1987). The number of pensioners affected in this way, would have been 7,632. As pension benefits were subject to taxation and social security contributions, but social assistance was not, the result would be that pensioners with social assistance would have been receiving less after the reform (LW 02.06.1987). After another meeting between LCGB representatives and members of the Cabinet, the government agreed to reconsider changes with respect to cost of living bonuses (LW 04.06.1987). The OGB-L was split: on the one hand it welcomed the 7 percent increase, but on the other hand it still rejected the more restrictive measures of the pension system. The union took a "wait-and-see" stance on the reform, pending the government's presentation of its amendments (LW 04.06.1987).

The Cabinet decided to review the bill on June 5, 1987. It agreed to increase the cost of living bonuses for pensioners by 7 rather than 6 percent. The cabinet also rescinded the abolition of social insurance elections. To soften the impact of the increase in the qualifying period from 15 to 40 years, the government amendments allowed a transition period, that is, all white-collar workers above the age of 45 years were guaranteed the right to retire early, at the ages of 60 for men and 55 for women, with only 15 years of insurance contributions. The revaluation of pensions was pulled forward to July 1, 1987. The article on the baby-year was also changed: the public budget was to pay contributions on the personal average wage of the 12 months prior to birth, instead of on the social minimum wages as envisioned in the first draft (Projet de loi No 3093/1: 5, 7–8; LW 06.06.1987).

The white-collar workers' union and the union for the banking sector (FEP and ALEBA) rejected the reform proposal altogether: the main reason was that foreigners and cross-boarder workers were disadvantaged because they were hardly able to fulfill the 40 qualifying years compared to the previous 15 years of residence for the fixed part of the pension benefit (FEP/ALEBA 1987: 39). Although the reform did not accomplish a unitary pension system for the public and private sectors, the two big unions—LCGB and OGB-L—deemed the reform to have more positive than negative aspects by early July, and accepted the reform proposal (LW 02.07.1987, 08.07.1987). The *Aktionskomittee 5/6 fir jidfereen*—founded in connection with the protests in March 1987—asked all parliamentary representatives together to pass the 1987 pension reform: a declaration of intent that the next step in pension policy would be a single public pension system with pensions of 5/6ths for everybody (LW 10.07.1987).

The governmental reform proposal was accepted by an overwhelming majority of 60 "yes"-votes on July 16, 1987—with the support of the two government parties CSV, LSAP and of the major opposition party DP.[30] Parliament also passed a motion to consider the application of the reform features to the public sector pension system (LW 17.07.1987, 18.07.1987), which the liberal party did not support (ChD, 84e séance 16.07.1987: 4645–4647). Once again, the CSV used its pivotal position to push through reform, allowing it to place the priorities of its "stronghold-district" voters first.

The 1991 reform

1989 Elections

A side-effect of the 1987 reform was the establishment of the *Aktionskomitee 5/6-Pensioun*—an action committee that emerged from the protests in March 1987. The action committee was founded on May 12, 1987 with the aim of achieving the equalization of pension legislation for all citizens (LW 28.07.1987). Although the founding members did not initially intend to form a party, the action committee threatened to stand for election if the 7 percent increase in pensions enacted through the 1987 reform were used as advancement on future pension adjustments. The final act as enacted, however, did indeed envision reducing future wage increases by 1 percent until the 7 percent were re-couped (Loi du 27 juillet 1987: 1122 Art. 225). In response, the committee made good on its threat and ran for election in 1989 as the *Aktiounskomitee fir Demokratie a Rentegerechtegkeet* (ADR).

In its party manifesto, the ADR presented a list of claims for pension reform which included a legal guarantee that the 7 percent pension increase enacted on July 27, 1987 was defined as a pension increase, and not as anticipated future pension adjustment. The ADR also requested a structural pension increase of 5 percent on top of the adjustment to wage inflation, an increase of small widows' pensions from 2/3 to 75 percent of the deceased's pension rights, and a relaxation of anti-accumulation rules, especially in cases of households with one minimum pension (ADR 1999).

The three major parties CSV, LSAP and DP all lost seats in the national elections on June 18, 1989.[31] The two Green parties and ADR profited from the election. The ADR had an extremely successful start and won 7.9 percent of the votes and four parliamentary seats. Key to its victory was its use of local notables to take advantage of the *panachage* system, thus directly threatening the dominant position of the CSV, particularly in the North and East districts.

Reform process

In response to the ADR's demands, the CSV/LSAP government announced already in its inaugural speech of July 24, 1989 that it would propose legislation to harmonize the public and the private sector pension schemes.[32] In October 1990, the Minister of Social Security, Johny Lahure (LSAP), presented a proposal. The bill envisioned the convergence of the two systems through extensive pension increases in the private sector, but did not foresee touching the public sector provisions. The main points of the reform proposal were (Projet de Loi No 3447):

- the transformation of the 7 percent advance on pension adjustment of 1987 into a structural and guaranteed pension rise,
- an additional structural pension increase of a total of 5 percent realized through an increase of the *majorations forfaitaires* by 10 percent, and
- an increase of the *majorations proportionelles* by 4 percent.

The share of the minimum wage in the basic pension was augmented from 20 percent to 22 percent, and the accrual rate in the earnings-related part of pension benefits was raised from 1.6 to 1.78 percent. The reform of the adjustment method implied the income of insured people younger than 25 or older than 59 were not taken into account to estimate average wage increase. Furthermore, raising the upper contribution ceiling from 4 to 5 times the minimum wage secured a more adequate replacement rate for high-income earners. Another improvement of the reform was the more flexible retirement age, that is, early retirement at age 57, if certain preconditions were fulfilled. The reform rendered part-time employment possible during early retirement, raised the threshold value for anti-accumulation rules from LUF 26,639 to LUF 41,556 and introduced a second baby-year (for a total of 24 months). The expected costs of the reform amounted to LUF 3.7 billion per year, which was equal to an increase in expenditure of 12.3 percent. Higher revenues, due to the increased upper contribution limit, and due to contribution payments for the second baby-year, were to partially compensate the extra costs. Additionally, the bill projected a reduction of the reserves from 2.51 times annual expenditure in 1990 to 1.84 times in 1998. However, it is important to note that the general government budget was burdened with contribution payments of the second baby-year and higher payments for contributions up to the new ceiling (Projet de loi No 3447: 19–21).

Despite the significant amelioration of pension benefits, in retrospect most politicians considered the 1991-pension reform as a technical change, rather than a major reform. The bill was adopted on March 28, 1991 with 43 "yes"-votes and 13 abstentions.[33] Nevertheless, the ADR had succeeded in its main goal: it had used its entry into the political arena to put pressure on the pre-existing parties to reduce the inequities between the public and the private pension schemes.

Public sector reform 1995–1998

The 1994 Election

The pension reform of 1998 created a contributory pension system in the public sector that calculated pension benefits on the same principles as in the private sector. The introduction of this new pension regime was not realized in a single shot. The following description of the 1998 reform will thus be divided into two parts: the changes enacted in 1995/1996, and the main reform of 1998.

In 1994, the ADR once again succeeded in making pension justice the number one electoral campaign. In its party manifesto of 1994, the ADR presented a list of claims for pension policy, which mainly tackled the public sector system. It included the abolition of the 3 percent *péréquation*,[34] the introduction of an 8 percent contribution rate for the public sector, equal pension adjustment mechanisms in the private and the public sectors, the harmonization of a single reference base for all private and public sector pensions, based on contributions made and the assessment of child-rearing years for children born before January 1, 1988 (ADR 1999).

Though not as spectacularly as in the 1989 election, the ADR improved its share of the vote from 7.9 percent to 9 percent, while both the CSV and LSAP lost several percentage points (Smart 1995). Although the damage was minimal in terms of seats (each party lost only one seat such that the coalition maintained control of the government), the national election held on June 12, 1994 put pressure on the sitting government to act on the ADR's policy demands.

Changes in 1995/1996

The government bill submitted on October 27, 1995 (Projet de loi No 4092) dealt with wage increases and pensions in the public sector. After long negotiations with representatives of the main public sector union, the CGFP, which involved the appointment of a mediator who made several propositions of his own as well as conveying those of the government, the government finally complied with the mediator's proposal in order to secure social peace. The bill envisioned a change in the mechanisms of pension adjustment, the abolition of the life-long career principle (*péréquation*), and the incremental introduction of pension contribution rates for employees (8%) in the public sector (Projet de loi No 4092: 7). As civil servants and public sector employees had paid a 3 percent share of income to finance the *péréquation*, the introduction of the contribution rate burdened the civil servants with the difference of an extra five percentage points. However, this income loss was compensated through wage increases of 1.1 percent per year (1995–99; *augmentation de la valeur du point*) and an increase in the end-of-year bonus. After a five-year transition period, the full contribution rate of 8 percent would be in effect for all public sector employees (LW 06.12.1995, 15.12.1995). As civil servants were more than compensated for the changeover to a contributory pension, the projected costs of the reform amounted to LUF 3,307 million by 1999.[35]

On November 27, 1995, the government introduced two amendments to the reform. After negotiations with unions the government granted an extra leave day and bound itself to review the effects of the reform after January 1, 1997 (on request of the CGFP) and, if needed, to modify earnings-related measures (Projet de loi No 4092/1; LW 06.12.1995). The Council of State agreed in its comment to the most important feature of the bill—the abolition of the *péréquation* and its replacement with the contribution payments and adjustment mechanisms used in the private sector. However, the Council of State did not approve the retroactive legislation with effect from January 1, 1995 (Conseil d'État 1995; LW 06.12.1995).

Even before the Cabinet had submitted the bill to Parliament the public sector union CGFP had called for protests on October 24, 1995, which saw a turnout of 40,000 participants. Resistance increased as the legislative process proceeded. After a ballot among its members, the CGFP announced a strike to be held on December 15, 1995 (FP 10/1995, 12/1995). The union of the community employees' (FGFC), the railway workers' union (FNCTTFEL) and the OGB-L's public sector section demanded polls of their members to determine whether the union base supported participation in the strike. The railway workers' and Post Office Workers' unions (FNCTTFEL, FSFL, FCPT-Syprolux) chose not to participate in any strike action. As more than 50 percent of OGB-L union members abstained from voting and over 70 percent of those voting supported the governmental proposal, the OGB-L leadership decided not to take part in any strike actions either. The Christian union LCGB left the decision to take part in the strike up to its individual members.[36] The indecisiveness of the general unions OGB-L and LCGB gave CGFP reason to criticize the lack of private sector union support in the strike actions (LW 14.12.1995, 06.12.1995, 16.12.1995).

The Chamber of Public Functionaries and Employees rejected the bill for several reasons: first, it claimed the unions were not consulted, secondly, it criticized the way wages and pensions were intermingled in the bill, and thirdly, it argued that the bill was a break with the traditional concept of the pension system in the public sector. The Chamber supported the CGFP instead (LW 11.12.1995). The CGFP justified its rejection of the private sector pension adjustment instead of *péréquation* with the general principles of the public function and with the negligible financial effects on the budget (LW 14.12.1995). CGFP general secretary, Jos Daleiden, accused the government of working hand in hand with " 'its secret coalition partner ADR' "[37] (LW 14.12.1995).

On December 14, 1995 the responsible committee (*Commission de la fonction publique*) accepted the bill by CSV and LSAP votes. The DP and Déi Gréng rejected the bill while ADR abstained from voting (LW 15.12.1995). The *Chambre des Députés* debated bill No 4092 on December 19, 1995. The CSV and the LSAP considered the changes to be a first step towards pension harmonization. The DP and Déi Gréng, however, regarded the bill as a violation of government employees' status, and vehemently rejected the abolition of the *péréquation* (LW 27.11.1996). In contrast, ADR complimented the government parties for their reform proposal that proved the parties' independence from public sector unions' (LW 19.12.1995, 20.12.1995). The bill was adopted the same day with the votes of CSV, LSAP and ADR (LW 21.12.1995).[38]

To summarize, the abolition of the *péréquation*, the introduction of an 8 percent contribution rate for all public sector employees and civil servants, and the equalization of pension adjustment in the private and public sectors meant that this reform realized the three main ADR electoral campaign points of 1994.

The 1998 reform

The introduction of contributions in the public sector was only a first step in the process of merging the two pension systems. In November 1996, the government submitted a new proposal, which foresaw the final abolition of the public sector pension regime. All future public employees would participate in a new pension scheme with harmonized terms to the private sector system. The Minister for Public Functions, Michel Wolter (CSV), asked all seven public sector unions to comment on the proposal by December 2, 1996, giving them three weeks to draft a statement, before the government would enter into negotiations. Although the government coalition tried to prevent strong union resistance, the CGFP saw the measures as a violation of the existing public sector pension system. The FGFC refused to take any stance on the pension bill before consultations with its membership had been conducted (LW 13.11.1996). The private sector white-collar employee unions (FEP and FIT) expressed their solidarity with the public sector (LW 20.12.1996).

The liberal opposition party was hesitant in commenting on the government's reform plans. The CSV-leaning newspaper *Luxemburger Wort* accused the DP of not taking a position in the reform debate because it preferred to "wait until public opinion becomes obvious"[39] (LW 23./24.11.1996). The CGFP also pointed out that a pension reform in the public sector was not necessary except for political and electoral reasons. The civil servants' union blamed the governing parties for striving to prevent the ADR from gaining ground among the electorate. The CGFP was especially concerned about members of parliament with a public sector background who voted for the governmental changes (LW 18.12.1996).

The government negotiated with the public sector unions for several months, but agreement with the CGFP appeared impossible. Consequently, the government submitted a bill to Parliament in August 1997 (Projet de loi No 4339). The new pension regime was applicable to all civil servants and employees of the public administration (*Function Public*) taking office after January 1, 1999. The reference period for benefit calculation was to be the entire working career instead of the final wage. There would, however, be no upper contribution limit and consequently the civil servants' scheme would still differ slightly from the private sector. Additionally, the governing coalition introduced a second proposal concerning the transition regime (Projet de loi No 4338).

The CGFP expressed broad agreement with the new pension system for all civil servants who entered the public sector in the future (*régime de pension spéciaux*). But the union opposed the transition regime. The CGFP drafted an alternative proposal that implied benefit calculations based on final incomes. A conciliation commission tried to mediate between the two positions. The mediator's proposition was to reduce the replacement rate of final income during the transition period to 72 percent (retirement age of 60 years), with the possibility of increasing that replacement rate to 5/6ths through further employment up to the age of 65. Following a referendum of its members, the CGFP rejected the mediation proposal (LW 02.07.1998). Nevertheless, the government decided to amend Projet de loi No 4338 in line with the Conciliation Commission's suggestions (Projet de loi No 4338/4).

The main point of controversy was the acquired rights that were supposedly touched by the cuts in the transition regime. The DP backed the public sector and argued that the rights of current civil servants could not be retrenched. Moreover, the DP rejected a unitary pension system (LW 14.07.1998). But the Council of state concluded that there were no acquired pension rights in the public sector, as the civil servants had not paid contributions, and thus the argument *pacta sunt servanda* was not applicable (Conseil d'État 1998: 6).

The legislative reform process was accompanied by union turmoil and protests on the streets. The three public sector unions FNCTTFEL, FCPT-Syprolux and FSFL agreed on concerted strike action (LW 07.07.1998). CGFP and FGFC also joined the protest action on July 14, 1998 (LW 11.07.1998). Furthermore, the CGFP scheduled a 24-hour strike in the public sector for July 21, 1998—the very same day when the parliamentary chamber was to discuss the bill (LW 14.07.1998). The teachers' union APESS pledged respect to all parliamentary members of the coalition parties who intended to resist party discipline and would reject the bill on the day of voting (LW 17.07.1998). The CGFP pursued a similar idea. The union's monthly paper *Fonction Publique* left a blank page in several issues[40] for the names of parliamentarians who would "kill" the public sector pension system with their vote in the final parliamentary voting (LW 20.07.1998).

The OGB-L accused the government of disguising cuts in public sector pensions under plans for the convergence of the public and private sectors, which would still not bring real harmonization of the systems. Thus, the OGB-L repeated its claim for an increase in the accrual rate to 1.9 percent for the private sector to achieve sectoral equity from a different angle (LW 18.07.1998). As scheduled by the CGFP leadership the strike in the public sector took place on July 21, 1998. The unprecedented number of twenty thousand[41] civil servants and employees of the public sector participated in the walkout, and 15,000 took part in demonstrations in front of the parliamentary building (FP 12/1998).[42]

In the final plenary decision on July 21, 1998 42 CVS, LSAP and ADR deputies supported the new pension regime. DP and *Déi Gréng* voted "no" and one CSV-member abstained from voting. The transition regime won only the votes of CSV and LSAP (37 votes) against a 23-vote opposition composed of DP, ADR, *Déi Gréng* and one CSV member (ChD, 21.07.1998: 3735–3738).[43] The ADR did not support the transition regime, as it was not curbing expenditure effectively enough. The ADR accused the coalition of electoral tactics with respect to the transition provisions (LW 22.07.1998).

Looking back at the reform process, it can be recognized that the legislation constituted an enormous victory for the ADR. The demands of this small protest party had been at the center of the reform process throughout—so much so that the public sector unions accused the ADR of being the secret coalition partner of the government (see e.g. FP 12/1998, 12/1996, 12/1997, 3/1997). The proposal for equitable pension calculations—that is, that contribution payments be made throughout the entire working career for both public and private sector employees—was put forward by the ADR in its election campaign manifesto in 1994. Although Projet de loi No 4339 was a CSV/LSAP bill, the passage of the 1998 reform can be considered a realization of ADR goals. A *Luxemburger Wort* commentary summarized that the liberal party was the true loser of the 2.5-year long pension reform process in the public sector. In defending civil servants' acquired pension rights the DP had not only followed overly blatant tactical and electoral strategies, but had also chased away its core electorate, namely white-collar employees (LW 18.07.1998).

The 1998 reform moved approximately 20,000 public sector employees from the pre-existing public sector scheme to a new special regime within the private sector scheme. For public sector employees, it meant a reduction in the wage replacement rate of old-age benefits. Although the aggregated financial consequences of the reform will take effect only in the long-term future, and so are difficult to assess, the symbolic value of the external pension harmonization should not be underestimated. Together the reforms of 1995 and 1998 constituted an increase in the coverage of the employed population with contribution-financed pensions by about 9 percent.[44]

Thus, the ADR had not only placed the issue of pension justice on the political agenda, but was also able to convince the parliamentary majority to introduce almost all of its demands into law. Nevertheless, the abolition of the public sector pension scheme did not make the ADR party redundant, as some political actors had expected, and indeed, hoped.[45]

The 2002 reform (*Rentendësch* 2001)

The 1999 Election

The *régime speciaux*, introduced in the public sector by the 1998 pension reform, was a great success in terms of harmonization. But the transition regime would enshrine unequal pension benefits between the private and public sectors for another 30 to 40 years. As the ADR did not consent to this extensive conversion period, it had refused its approval in parliamentary voting on the transition act (Project de loi No 4338). Parties and unions still demanded improvements in private sector pensions.[46] Right after the passage of the pension reform in the public sector the ADR-affiliated union NGL called for a manifestation on October 13, 1998 to remind parliamentarians of the deficiencies in the private sector (LW 24.07.1998).

In the national elections of June 1999, pensions were an important campaign issue once again. In its manifesto for the 1999 national election, the ADR presented a list of demands for further reforms. The first demand was an increase in contributory pension benefits to make them comparable to public sector pensions. Second, a minimum pension equal to the minimum social wage should be introduced. Third, the transition regime for the public sector should be harmonized with the private sector pension regimes, as benefits in the transition scheme were still calculated on the final wage instead of lifetime contribution payments. The ADR proposed that pension benefits for all working years served before January 1, 1999 would be calculated on the 5/6ths system; all subsequent years served would be calculated according to the contributory system's formula. Furthermore, the pension party called for the establishment of a pension fund for the public sector, and the build-up of reserves to guarantee the long-term financial safety of pensions, as well as more flexible regulation of the investment of pension fund reserves. As the enactment of pension-splitting in the case of divorce had failed in every reform since 1982, the ADR now renewed this demand. The party further pledged to fight for the recognition of 12 years of child-rearing per child, for tax-financed contributions based on the social minimum wage, and for the extension of periods of higher education that are recognized in basic pension calculation. Last but not least, the ADR requested the establishment of a legal framework for occupational supplementary pensions, such as a guarantee of entitlement transfer if employees changed workplaces (ADR 1999). Contrary to the expectations that ADR had lost its right to exist, it used the achievements in pension policy as a proof of its political impact and for legitimating its aim to complete the fight for pension justice.

The Liberal Party also used pensions in its electoral campaign and emphasized the loss of acquired rights in the public sector. It announced plans to revoke the 1998 pension reform if it gained office.

On June 13, 1999, the DP and the ADR were the winners of the election. The ADR gained two extra seats (for a total of 7) and even beat the LSAP in the Northern district, in terms of votes as well as seats.[47] The DP won three more seats and became the second largest party in Parliament. Both government parties lost seats: the CSV two and the LSAP four seats. As the CSV remained the strongest over-all party, it entered into coalition negotiations with the relative winner—the DP. These negotiations led to the formation of a CSV/DP coalition government, which entered into office on August 7, 1999.

Background of the reform

The CSV/DP coalition agreement of 1999 stated that the two coalition parties were unable to reconcile their policy positions with respect to the public sector: the DP wanted to revoke the public sector pension reform which, obviously, was impossible for the CSV. The partners agreed not to touch the public special regime during the legislative term to come. However, the coalition did commit to commissioning an expert study to compare the new public pension regime enacted in 1998 with the private sector regime (DP 1999: 70–1). As regards the private sector, the coalition agreement argued that the middle- and long-term financial viability of the system did not allow a structural pension reform financed with a reduction in reserves. Yet, the government promised the maintenance of the price and wage increase adaptations. In order to improve the lowest pensions (*Hongerrenten*) within the narrow limits of financial viability, the coalition parties planned to release the insurance system from these costs; the public budget was to finance future minimum pensions (DP 1999: 88–9). As part of his inaugural speech on August 12, 1999, Prime Minister Juncker announced he would commission another actuarial study of the pension system from the ILO and form a round-table (Projet de loi No 4887: 2).[48]

ILO study and Rentendësch

In mid-February 2001, the ILO report attested to the sound financial situation of the Luxembourgian pension system until 2050, on the assumption that the legal framework in force in 2001 was maintained and economic growth averaged 4 percent. The ILO study drew attention to the hidden demographic problem: the group of cross-border workers that would start to retire around 2020. In order to demonstrate the sensibility of the system to the development of cross-border employment rates, the ILO projections were carried out under an optimistic and a pessimistic setting—that is, a growth rate of 4 percent versus a growth rate of 2 percent. The optimistic scenario estimated that the number of cross-border workers would treble. The ILO recommended refraining from the introduction of any structural pension improvements that were difficult to revoke (ILO 2001; Projet de loi No 4887; ChD, 48e séance, 05.06.2002: 1756).

Despite the government's promise to take action in the private sector pension system, the first year in government was characterized by inactivity. The unions continued to campaign for fair redistribution in the pension system throughout 2000/2001, and OGB-L and LCGB threatened a general strike (OGB-L 2002; LW 25.10.2000). On May 10, 2000, Prime Minister Jean-Claude Juncker initiated a round-table (*Rentendësch*).[49] Members of the *Rentendësch* represented five of the six parliamentary parties (CSV, DP, LSAP, ADR, *Déi Gréng*), the main unions and employers' association (OGB-L, LCGB, CGFP, UEL) and the government, represented by the Minister of Social Security, Carlo Wagner (DP), and the Finance Minister, Luc Frieden (CSV). All participants forwarded their goals and demands for a comprehensive structural pension reform. The ADR repeated the items the party had already presented in the electoral campaign (ADR 2001). The LSAP requested an end-of-year bonus if 40 years of insurance were fulfilled, the CSV promoted the idea of a child-rearing lump-sum benefit for non-working women, and the DP advocated age- and insurance-related increase in the accrual rate (LSAP 2001: Tableau Comparatif).

At the final meeting on July 16, 2001, all members of the *Rentendësch*, except for the Employer's Association, agreed on the following measures (MSS 2001a: 13–14):

- basic pensions (*majorations forfaitaires*) were to be increased by 11.9 percent;
- a price- and wage-indexed end-of-year bonus of LUF 500 was to be introduced; and
- the accrual rate for earnings-related pension benefits (*majorations proportionnelles*) was to be increased from 1.78 percent to 1.85 percent.

The round-table agreement also foresaw the introduction of an incremental accrual rate, depending on age and length of working career: the sum of age of 55 plus a career of 38 years provided the reference point of 93; for each year above 93 the accrual rate was increased by 0.01 percentage points up to an upper limit of 2.05 percent. Moreover, minimum pensions were to be increased to the semi-net level of the minimum social wage. The baby-year pension rights ought to be extended to all children born before January 1, 1988,[50] and the reference base was augmented to 1.5 times minimum wage (Andrich-Duval 10.12.2002). The most unusual reform measure was the introduction of a child-rearing lump-sum allowance of LUF 3,000 per month and per child, granted to women who could not profit from the baby-year, that is, mothers who had no individual pension entitlements (MSS 2001a: 14–15). Persons without insurance prior to childbirth, and consequently not eligible for baby-years, were to be rewarded for their social task of child-rearing. For technical reasons it was impossible to extend the baby-year to those mothers already in retirement. As compensation, pensioners who had children could apply for the child-rearing lump sum (*forfait d'éducation*). The lump sum was equal to €76.13 per child per month in 2001 and was financed by the national solidarity fund (CSV Divers 21.06.2002; CSV 21.06.2002).[51] The total costs of the measures envisioned by the *Rentendësch* amount to LUF 5.2 billion per year (CSV 25.07.2001).[52] Based on this *Rentendësch* consensus the government submitted a pension reform bill to Parliament on December 13, 2001 (Projet de loi No 4887; ChD, 19e séance, 13.12.2001: 649).

Parliamentary process

As the *Rentendësch* had already resulted in compromises between the unions and parties, not very many conflict issues were left for parliamentary stage. The chambers of white- and blue-collar workers, the chamber of public sector employees and the chamber of agriculture gave their general consent to the reform. The only fundamental opposition towards the entire reform project stemmed from the Chamber of Commerce and Chamber of Trade. Representing the employers, who had already refused their consent to the *Rentendësch* agreement, these chambers considered the reform measures as an immense extra burden on the pension system, which was in complete opposition to the ILO recommendations (Commission de la santé et de la sécurité sociale 2002b: 9–10).

Although the child-rearing lump sum was a benefit improvement, it was not uncontroversial. The farmers' occupational chamber had strong reservations at the beginning, because it saw the *forfait d'éducation* as a disadvantage for mothers in agriculture. As farmer's wives were compulsorily-insured for pensions, they were entitled to the baby-year but could not profit from the child-rearing lump sum (Chambre d'Agriculture 2002: 2). The bill was changed to ensure that women with individual pension rights, but with less entitlements arising from the baby-year than they would get through the *forfait d'éducation*, were granted the difference between the two benefit types. The parliamentary Commission for Social Security also modified the regulations on the child-rearing lump sum. The age at which women would be able to profit from the lump sum was lowered from 65 to 60.[53] Another controversial aspect of the *forfait d'éducation* was that the benefit was linked to Luxembourgian residents. In other words, thousands of cross-border workers would be excluded from the new rights (*Territorialklausel*; déi Lénk in ChD, 05.06.2002: 1752).

Parliament voted on the reform bill on June 5, 2002. The proposal was adopted and the law was issued on June 28, 2002. Most remarkable about the reform—especially from a European comparative perspective—was that none of the changes enacted in 2002 implied benefit losses, either in absolute or in relative terms.[54]

V Conclusion

Summary of the magnitude of changes

Any measure of the impact of reforms on Luxembourgian pension policy over the last 20 years must consider the extremely favorable economic situation of the country in the late 1980s and throughout the 1990s. The public budget surplus, the low unemployment rate, and the positive demographic structure within the active workforce due to cross-border workers ensured that the problems facing the system in Luxembourg in the 1990s were much less severe than in most other European countries. On top of this, the enormous pension fund reserves allowed broad scope for political action.

Nevertheless, the pension policy expansions introduced in Luxembourg are not simply explained by the budget surpluses of the pension schemes—for three reasons. First, the positive situation of the pension funds was only established after the fundamental financial reform of the pension system in 1984, and is thus a result and not a cause of pension politics in Luxembourg. Second, although the country did not suffer from the same tremendous economic and demographic problems as its neighbors, there was no reason to expect benefit expansion to the extent that they were legislated in 1991 and in 2002. Indeed, Luxembourg faces a different kind of problem pressure than most other EU countries: its high share of cross-border workers and immigrants increases uncertainties for future pension projections, and makes the pension system more vulnerable to external shocks. Its positive economic and budgetary situation relies predominantly on the success of the strong banking sector. The low degree of economic diversification holds great risk. Both factors lead international pension experts, including those of the ILO, to recommend restrictive policies in order to guarantee the long-term financial sustainability of the pension system in the context of such risks and sources of economic fluctuation. Thirdly, the lack of severe problem pressure cannot explain why new civil servants should not receive the same privileged pension benefits as their predecessors. Rather issues of justice and equity that translated into party politics can account for this trend.

Taken together, these pension reforms entail an initial shift of resources from the white-collar pension funds to those for farmers, the self-employed and blue-collar workers, followed by relative gains for private sector workers and employees, coupled with relative losses for public-sector employees. In terms of actual benefit losses, the conversion from final salary (5/6th rule) to life time contribution benefit calculations implies a benefit loss for newly-hired public sector employees and civil servants. In terms of structural reform, these pieces of pension legislation did introduce harmonization, but not for the purposes of budgetary consolidation, and indeed the changes in private sector pensions greatly increased the projected costs of the Luxembourgian pension system.

The impact of the political system on pension politics

Pension politics in Luxembourg have been shaped by the pattern of political competition and not by the existence of veto points and veto players. There are no veto points, and with a dominant party in government, the CSV can dominate the partisan veto player in its coalition government. Instead, the most important feature in its political framework for understanding the dynamics of pension policy is its electoral system, with its unusual combination of proportional and disproportional features. With only four electoral districts, winning districts takes precedence over winning votes—as in a single-member district system—and with population disproportionalities among the districts, this places some voters—in particular the craftsmen, wine-growers and farmers in the rural North and East districts in a position to swing a district. Moreover, with less than 100 legislators, the overall impact of the electoral formula is less proportional than in larger legislatures, and the possibilities for vote-splitting and cumulation makes politicians individually accountable for their actions, and increases competition even within parties. As Luxembourg is a very small country where the elites accumulate national and local political and societal offices, this accountability aspect might be reinforced by personal contacts with voters, which reduces incentives to obey party discipline (Dumont and de Winter 2003: 479).[55]

At the same time that the electoral system makes politicians hypersensitive to some electoral demands, it is also necessary to pay attention to the great divergence between those who had the right to vote and those who were affected by the policy. Only nationals are allowed to vote for Parliament, but 8.7 percent of the insured in 1980 were cross-border workers (EURES 2003). In 1988, already 16 percent of all wage earners were cross-border workers and an additional 25 percent of the employed were non-Luxembourgian nationals, so that in total 41 percent of the workforce in Luxembourg was not allowed to vote in national elections.[56] This huge percentage of non-nationals varies between the four different pension regimes: while the schemes for farmers and for self-employed craftsmen enclosed hardly any foreigners, the blue-collar and white-collar worker' scheme featured high shares of foreign pensioners: 42 percent and 16.8 percent respectively in 1985 (own calculation based on IGSS 1986: 161).

The consequences of this pattern of political responsiveness for pension reform saw great improvements in the financial situation of the pension funds for farmers, craftsmen and the self-employed. The funds for blue-collar workers also experienced some financial relief through the 1984 and the 1987 pension reforms. But these improvements came at the cost of the scheme for white-collar employees. Later—after the rise of the ADR—the pattern of beneficiaries shifted, with continual improvements in the private sector schemes, in general, but with some glaring exceptions that affected the non-enfranchised, namely cross-border workers. This pattern is also visible in the most recent reform, of 2002: the lump sum child-rearing supplement (*forfait d'éducation*) is linked to Luxembourgian residence, thus again disadvantaging cross-border workers.

Constraints of policy design

The Luxembourg pension system had a tremendous advantage when the country was hit by the economic crisis of the late 1970s and early 1980s. The system was officially still a capital-funded system and one of the pension schemes possessed large reserves. The transformation of the system into a PAYG system increased the scope for political action in this area in the 1990s. But the high reserves did not only allow benefit improvements in order to solve problems of injustice. The fact that the reserves were invested in rather unprofitable ways also neutralized possible resistance to reducing the reserves in order to fund expansion of the system.

Interest group influence

The consent of the social partners to pension reforms cannot be identified as a necessary condition for the passage of reforms. The fragmented nature of trade unionism in Luxembourg makes pacts between the government and the workforce as a whole very unlikely. The public sector pension reform of 1998 was violently opposed by the relevant union, the CGFP; nevertheless the bill passed in Parliament. Unions did not initially welcome the 1987 reform, but after minor modifications the government won the support of the Christian union LCGB. The 2002 reform found consensus among the round-table participants except for employers. Although the agreement of the LCGB, or at least the toleration of changes, seems to have been important for the governments of the last two decades, this factor was not in itself decisive. As the LCGB is neither the only unionist participant in pension administration, nor the biggest union membership-wise, it only becomes an important actor in constellation with other political variables.

Even opposition from the occupational chambers during the mandatory consultation process does not necessarily lead to the revision or the blockage of reform acts. The 1984 and the 1987 reforms showed that the government was able to pass legislation without conceding to the criticism from the white-collar employee chamber.

The need to elect the boards of occupational chambers turns different unions into competitors and might account for the configuration, that is, the fragmentation and diversity of unionism. The diverse, split and even contradictory interests of unions in pension policy (LW 04.08.1998), in combination with a party system that has been dominated by the pivotal party the CSV, created strange interest coalitions in Luxembourg (LW 28.07.1998).

Role of ideas and historical context

The statutory pension system in Luxembourg is a generous system with broad coverage, a fairly low retirement age and high absolute pension entitlements but also high wage replacement rates (see e.g. Bouchet 2003: 24–5). Therefore occupational pensions and private old-age provision have been neither economically necessary nor politically enforced. Except for some regulations passed in 1999 on voluntary occupational pensions, the second and third pillars are hardly regulated by law, and employers and insurance companies are relatively free in their decisions over private and occupation pension eligibility.

Abbreviations

ABBL	*Association des Banques et Banquiers Luxembourg*
ADR	*Aktiounskomitee fir Demokratie a Rentegerechtegkeet*
ALEBA	*Association Luxembourgeoise des Employés de Banque et Assurance*
APESS	*Association des Professeurs de l'Enseignement Secondaire et Supérieur du Grand-Duché de Luxembourg a.s.b.l.*
ARBED	*Aciéries Réunies de Burbach-Eich-Dudelange*
assep	*Association d'épargne-pension*
C.A.S.	*Code d'assurance sociale (Livre III: Assurance pension)*
C.P.	*Central Paysanne*
CCSS	*Centre Commun de la Sécurité Sociale*
ChD	*Chambre des Députés*
CGFP	*Confédération Générale de la Fonction Publique*
CPA	*Caisse de Pension Agricole*
CPACI	*Caisse de Pension des Artisans, des Commerçants et Industriels*
CPEP	*Caisse de Pension des Employés Privés*
CSSF	*Commission de Surveillance du Secteur Financier*
CSV	*Chrëschtlech-Sozial Vollekspartei*
DP	*Demokratesch Partei*
FCPT-Syprolux	*Fédération Chrétienne du Personnel du Transport*
FEDIL	*Fédération des Industriels Luxembourgeois*
FEP-FIT	*Fédération des Employés Privés – Fédération Indépendante des Travailleurs et Cadres*
FGFC	*Fédération Générale des Fonctionnaires Communaux*
FNCTTFEL	*Fédération Nationale des Cheminots, Travailleurs du Transport, Fonctionnaires et Employés Luxembourgeois*
FSFL	*Fédération Syndicaliste des Facteurs Luxembourgeois*
GAP	*Déi Gréng Alternative*
GLEI	*Gréng Lëscht Ekologesch Initiativ*
IGSS	*Inspection Générale de la Sécurité Sociale*
ILO	*International Labour Organization*
KPL	*Kommunistesch Partei vu Lëtzebuerg*
LCGB	*Lëtzebuerger Chrëschtlech Gewerkschaftsbond*
LRIV	*Lëtzebuerger Rentner- an Invalideverband*
LSAP	*Lëtzebuerger Sozialistesch Aarbechterpartei*
LUF	*Luxembourgian Francs*

LW   Luxemburger Wort
Mém.   Mémorial
MSS   Ministère de la Sécurité Sociale
NGL   Neutral Gewerkschaft Lëtzebuerg
OGB-L   Onafhängege Gewerkschaftsbond–Lëtzebuerg
SDP   Sozialdemokratesch Partei
sepcav   Société d'épargne-pension à capital variable
STATEC   Service Central de la Statistique et des Études Économiques
UEL   Union des Entreprises Luxembourgeoises
UJL   Union des Journalistes Luxembourg

Notes

1. My thanks to Ellen Immergut for comments on earlier versions of this chapter. My thanks also to the following persons for background interviews on pension policy in Luxembourg: Romain Ewert (MSS), Gast Gibéryen (ADR), Mady Kries (IGSS), Marcel Mersch (LCGB), Paul-Henri Meyer (CSV), Myriam Wagener-Schanck (LSAP), Vic Thome (CPEP); and Aiko Wagner and Hannah Heist for research assistance. All errors are my responsibility.
2. www.innovation.public.lu/html/publication/publication_detail.jsp?idUrl=377&publicationLanguage=EN Access on 12.05.2005.
3. www.statistiques.public.lu/stat/tableviewer/document.aspx?FileId=84 Access on 10.05.2005.
4. For details see sub-ch. "Institutions of government" paragraph on Council of the State.
5. The following section draws on www.ce.etat.lu/ Access on 10.05.2005.
6. www.ce.etat.lu/htm/Dep1945.htm Access on 01.07.2005.
7. *Loi portant réforme du Conseil d'État* (1996).
8. The electoral system has been under discussed for several years because of the biased representation of interests in politics due to the fact that 36.6 percent of Luxembourg residents and 60.9 percent of Luxembourg employees (27.7 percent foreigners and 33.2 percent cross-boarder workers) are not allowed to vote in national elections (LW 29.09.2000).
9. In the 1999 national election, on average 66,445 votes were required to win one mandate in the South district, 24,467 in the East, 47,305 in the Centre and 28,673 in the North (own calculations based on STATEC 2001: W6).
10. See also www.chd.lu/docs/Elections.doc
11. The following section draws on Schroen (1999).
12. Other issues were education, social policy, unemployment and the environment (Poirier and Fehlen 2000: 345).
13. FEP membership is very heterogeneous. The union consequently faces disagreements between banking sector employees and white-collar employees of the steel industry (Schroen 2001).
14. The following section draws on IGSS (2002: Ch. 2).
15. The scheme for the industrial self-employed and that for craftsmen merged into a single scheme in 1979 (Loi du 23 décembre 1976).

16. See also www.mss.etat.lu/publications/Apercu/Apercu2004.pdf Access on 10.05.2005.
17. See www.mss.etat.lu/publications/rg/RG_2003.pdf (Table 1.1; Table 2.1a) Access on 10.05.2005. In 2003 the public sector pension scheme covered 23,443 employees and civil servants (www.mss.etat.lu/publications/rg/RG_2003.pdf (Table 1.8, page 215) Access on 10.05.2005).
18. My own calculation based on IGSS (2002: 217).
19. At the end of 2003 reserves equaled three years of pension expenditures (www.mss.etat.lu/publications/rg/RG_2003.pdf (Table 18), Access on 10.05.2005).
20. For further details see Appendix Table A17.
21. In 1980 the ratios of pensioners to active workforce were 53.2 in the blue-collar workers' scheme AVI, 77.8 for craftsmen's scheme CPACI and 99.7 for the farmers' scheme CPA. Only the white-collar workers' scheme had a more favorable ratio of 23.7. These ratios have not changed much for the individual regimes since the early 1980s, but because of the financial union of the four systems it is necessary to look at the total dependency ratio, which was 41.8 in 2001 (IGSS 2002b: 217).
22. When the interest rate was fixed by law in 1964, the interest rate corresponded to market rates, but, due to developments on financial markets this rate was inadequate in the early 1980s.
23. The vote was 41 to 17 votes (LW 11.05.1984). The CSV, DP, EdF, and SDP voted for the reform; the KPL, and LSAP against (ChD, 62e séance, 10.05.1984: 3230).
24. My own calculations based on Commission des affaires sociales (1984: 5) and IGSS Rapport générale (various issues).
25. My own calculations.
26. Parallel to the structural reform of old-age pensions a bill on interim pensions (*préretraite*) was under debate. This type of early retirement benefit was open to workers at the age of 57 and was partly financed by unemployment insurance. However, the following chapter will concentrate on the structural reform only, as the goal of the *préretraite* act was of labor market nature (reduction of unemployment, securing companies and employment) rather than motivated by social intensions (see e.g. LW 23.03.1987, 16.03.1987).
27. ChD, 1e séance, (23.07.1984: 32).
28. This was considered a big change for the white-collar worker's regime where the qualifying period was at 10 years. In the other three pension regimes there was no early retirement and therefore they were not affected negatively by this change.
29. Pensioners with benefits below a monthly limit of LUF 27,593 were eligible for social assistance cost of living bonus (LW 02.06.1987).
30. The two representatives of the Communist Party (KPL) and the two members of the Greens (GAP) abstained from voting (ChD, 84e séance, 16.07.1987: 4639–4640).
31. Electoral outcomes: CSV 32.4%/22 seats, LSAP 26.2%/18 seats, DP 17.2%/11 seats, GL 3.7%/2 seats, GA 3.6%/2 seats, ADR 7.9%/4 seats.
32. ChD, 3e séance extraordinaire, (24.07.1989: 52–53).
33. Yes votes: CSV, LSAP, GAP (Green Alternative); No votes: none; Abstentions: DP, ADR, GLEI (Green List) (ChD, 49e séance, 28.03.1991: 2690–2691). The abstention of the opposition parties shows that none of the parties dared to oppose pension benefit improvements but that the opposition also refused to openly support the government coalition.
34. Civil servants and public sector employees paid no contributions. But they forfeited 3% of their income to secure the financing of the principle that salary and pension rose with the course of a career—so-called *péréquation*.
35. See table "Impact budgétaire du projet de loi (montants annuel cumulés)", Projet de loi No 4092: 12.

36. Note that only civil servants and white-collar workers in the public sector have the right to go on strike. Blue-collar workers in the public sector have no freedom of strike (LW 06.12.1995).
37. Translated by the author.
38. Final voting: 43:17. DP and Déi Gréng members of parliament voted "no" (ChD, 18e séance, 19.12.1995: 1059; see also LW 21.12.1995).
39. Translated by the author.
40. E.g. *Fonction Publique* (FP 06/1998: 3; 07/1998: 6).
41. These figures were reported by the public sector union itself, and should be handled with care.
42. This was one of the biggest and most violent strikes in Luxembourg. Due to tripartite concertation mechanisms strikes are a rather unusual political instrument in policy-making. Therefore the strike and the demonstration attained tremendous attention.
43. Alphonse Theis, CSV representative of the South district, was the CSV member who rejected the bill (Le Greffe de la Chambre des Députés 1994).
44. My own calculations based on IGSS (2002), STATEC (2000; 2001).
45. An article in the CGFP magazine *Fonction Publique* predicted that the ADR party would be superfluous and dissolve itself after 95% of its party program was accomplished (FP 12/1997).
46. OGB-L, for example, maintained throughout its claim for an increase in the accrual rate from 1.78% to 1.90% and a raise in upper contribution limit from 5 times to 7 times minimum wage (LW 24.07.1998).
47. A narrow slide of 522 votes i.e. 0.2 percentage points brought a return of two seats to ADR, leaving LSAP with only one mandate in the Northern district (STATEC 2001: W6).
48. Before the ILO study had been finished and before the round-table met, the government promoted a legal framework for voluntary occupational pensions. The DP drafted a bill regulating the legal framework for supplementary pensions (LW 17.12.1996). The new act was designed to bind employers who had at some point promised supplementary pensions to their obligations. The provisions guaranteed the perpetuity of pension entitlements in cases of employer bankruptcy and regulated the transfer of entitlements for job changes (LW 17.12.1996).
49. The following paragraph draws on (MSS 2001a: 13).
50. A baby-year is a feature of continued insurance. One precondition for the granting of a baby-year is that the mother worked for at least 12 months within the last three years before the child was born. For the first and second child the baby-year equals 24 months of insurance, and for any further child 48 months are taken into account. However, baby-year credits and regular pension entitlements from employment cannot accumulate. The national budget covers contributions based on the average wage during the last 12 months prior to birth, with a minimum of 1.5 times minimum wage (CSV 21.06.2002).
51. The CSV proclaimed in its party newspaper that it was able to prevail with its demand for a baby-year for children born prior to 1988, and child raising lump sum allowance (CSV Profil 18.12.2001). The question was: against whom or which party did the CSV prevail? The ADR has already made the same demands for higher recognition of child-rearing in the early 1990s. But the major opposition party—the LSAP—has presented a *proposition de loi* sponsored by Lucien Lux which foresaw a *forfait d'éducation* for all mothers or fathers irrespective of gender or prior employment (Projet de loi No 4879).
52. The magnitude of costs was roughly confirmed by the report of the parliamentary Committee of Social Security later on: their estimation of May 2002 accounted for additional costs of €133.7 million per year (Commission de la santé et de la sécurité sociale 2002b: 11).

53. The reason for this change was that policy-makers felt that women without personal pension rights had to wait till 65 to benefit from the payments. Women who had worked and thus were able to draw an anticipated pension at an age of 60 profited from the *forfait d'éducation* five years earlier (Commission de la santé et de la sécurité sociale 2002a: 2).
54. A table published by the Ministry of Social Security shows that all income brackets profited from the benefit improvements, and even those retiring early or with a low number of insured years end up with 5% increases (Wagner 2002).
55. According to Dumont and de Winter "those parties (DP and CSV) that presented well-known candidates benefited most from panachage" in the past (Dumont and Winter 2003: 480). But recently, another party took advantage of this system feature: the ADR has used the recruitment of notables (e.g. innkeeper Jean-Pierre Koepp in Northern district) to boost its electoral success.
56. In 2001, 38% of those insured in the private sector pension regimes were cross-boarder workers and only 52% of the pensioners drawing pensions from the statutory system possessed Luxembourgian citizenship (own calculations based on IGSS 2002b: 183–4, 225).

Bibliography
Primary sources and government documents
Parliamentary acts
Constitution du Grand-Duché de Luxembourg (22.10.1868), Révision de 19.11.2004: 220.
Loi du 6 mai 1911 sur l'assurance vieillesse et invalidité (Mém. 1911).
Loi du 17 décembre 1925 concernant le code des assurances sociales (Mém. 1925: 877).
Loi du 29 janvier 1931 ayant pour objet la création d'une caisse de pension des employés privés (Mém. 1931: 243).
Loi du 21 mai 1951 ayant pour objet la création d'une caisse de pension des artisans (Mém. 1951: 809).
Loi du 3 septembre 1956 ayant pour objet la création d'une caisse de pension agricole (Mém. 1956: 1047).
Loi du 30 juillet 1960 concernant la création d'un fonds national de solidarité (Mém. 1960: 1199).
Loi du 13 mai 1964 unique ayant pour objet l'amélioration et l'harmonisation des régimes de pension contributifs (Mém. A 1964: 830).
Loi du 23 mai 1964 concernant l'admission des travailleurs intellectuels indépendants à la caisse de pension des employés privés (Mém. A 1964: 952).
Loi du 28 juillet 1969 relative à l'achat rétroactif de périodes d'assurance auprès des différents régimes de pension contributifs (Mém. A 1969: 934).
Loi du 14 mai 1974 qui a introduit une pension minimum de 5/6 du salaire social minimum en cas de stage d'assurance de 35 années et a mis à charge de l'État le complément à fournir le cas échéant (Mém. A 1974: 798).
Loi du 23 décembre 1976 portant fusion des régimes de pension des artisans et des commerçants et industriels (Mém. A 1976: 1508).
Loi du 23 mai 1984 portant réforme du système de financement des régimes de pension contributifs (Mém. A 1984: 696).
Loi du 27 juillet 1987 concernant l'assurance pension en cas de vieillesse, d'invalidité et de survie (Mém. A 1987: 1102).
Loi du 24 avril 1991 ayant pour objet l'amélioration des pensions du régime contributif (Mém. A 1991, p. 505).
Loi du 8 janvier 1996 fixant le régime des traitements des fonctionnaires de l'Etat (Mém. A 1996: 2)
Loi portant réforme du Conseil d'État (Mém. A 1996: 1319).

Loi(s) du 3 août 1998 portant modification 1. de la loi modifiée du 26 mai 1954 réglant les pensions des fonctionnaires de l'Etat (Mém. A 1998: 1378).
Loi du 8 juin 1999 créant les fonds de pension sous forme de société d'épargne-pension à capital variable (sepcav) et d'association d'épargne-pension (assep) (Mém. A 1999: 1476).
Loi du 28 juin 2002 1. adaptant le régime général et les régimes spéciaux de pension; 2. portant création d'un forfait d'éducation; 3. modifiant la loi modifiée du 29 avril 1999 portant création d'un droit à un revenu minimum garanti (Mém. A 2002: 1587).
Loi électorale. (31.07.1927), Révision de 25.03.1999: 741.

Parliamentary minutes
ChD. Compte Rendu de la Chambre des Députés (www.chd.lu/archives/ArchivesPortlet)
60e séance, (09.05.1984): 3104–3152.
62e séance, (10.05.1984): 3225–3230.
1e séance, (23.07.1984): 23–49.
84e séance, (16.07.1987): 4601–4647.
3e séance, (24.07.1989): 46–79.
49e séance, (28.03.1991): 2581–2694.
18e séance, (19.12.1995): 915–1060.
63e séance, (21.07.1998): 3644–3739.
19e séance, (13.12.2001): 649.
48e séance, (05.06.2002): 1705–1784.

Parliamentary bills: Chambre des Députés, Luxembourg:
Projet de Loi No 2602. (24.06.1982).
Projet de Loi No 3093. (19.03.1987).
Projet de Loi No 3093/1: Amendements gouvernementaux. (10.06.1987).
Projet de Loi No 3447. (16.10.1990).
Projet de Loi No 4092. (27.10.1995).
Projet de Loi No 4092/1: Amendements gouvernementaux. (27.11.1995).
Projet de Loi No 4338. (05.08.1997).
Projet de Loi No 4339. (05.08.1997).
Projet de Loi No 4338/4: Amendements gouvernementaux. (01.07.1998).
Projet de Loi No 4887. (13.12.2001).
Proposition de Loi No 4879. (04.12.2001).

Other parliamentary documents: Chambre des Députés, Luxembourg:
Centrale Paysanne Luxembourgeoise (1983). Projet de Loi No 2602/3: Avis.
Chambre d'Agriculture (2002). Projet de Loi No 4887: Avis.
Chambre de Travail (1983). Projet de Loi No 2602/3: Avis.
Chambre des Employés privés (1983). Projet de Loi No 2602/3: Avis.
Comité Directeur de la Caisse de Pension des Artisans des Commerçants et Industriels (1983). Projet de Loi No 2602/3: Avis.
Commission de la santé et de la sécurité sociale (2002a). Projet de Loi No 4887/7: Amendements.
Commission de la santé et de la sécurité sociale (2002b). Projet de Loi No 4887/9 1: Rapport.
Commission des affaires sociales (1984). Projet de Loi 2781/4: Rapport.
Conseil d'État (1995). Projet de Loi No 4092/2: Avis.
Conseil d'État (1998). Projet de Loi No 4338/5, No 4339/3: Avis.

FEP/ALEBA (1987). *Projet de Loi No 3093/4: Avis minoritaire.*
IGSS (1984). *Projet de Loi No 2781/1: Avis.*
Le Greffe de la Chambre des Députés Conseil d'état (1994). *Compte Rendu des Travaux de la Chambre des Députés: Les résultats des élections législatives du 12 juin 1994.* Luxembourg: Chambre des Députés.
Thullen, Pierre (1983). *Project de Loi 2602/4: Rapport a l'intention du Conseil économique et social.*

Government documents:
IGSS (1986). *Rapport général sur la sécurité sociale.* Luxembourg: Ministère de la Sécurité Sociale.
IGSS (2002a). *Droit de la Sécurité Sociale Luxembourg.* Luxembourg: Ministère de la Sécurité Sociale.
IGSS (2002b). *Rapport général sur la sécurité sociale 2001.* Luxembourg: Ministère de la Sécurité Sociale.
MSS (2001a). *Rapport d'activité 2001.* Luxembourg: Ministère de la Sécurité Sociale.
MSS (2001b). *Les différents organismes de l'assurance pension.* [web-site]. Ministère de la Sécurité Sociale [cited 28.05. 2003]. Available from www.etat.lu/MSS/pension/orgpens.htm.
MSS (2005). *Parametres sociaux.* [web-site]. Ministère de la Sécurité Sociale 2005 [cited 10.05. 2005]. Available from www.etat.lu/MSS/paramsoc.htm

Newspapers and magazines
Luxemburger Wort (LW). (various issues).
Fonction Publique (FP). (various issues).
d'Lëtzebuerger Land [web-site]. Available from www.land.lu/ (various issues).

Secondary Sources

ADR (1994). *E Programm fir Letzebuerg: 20 Reformpunkte für unser Land.* Luxembourg.
—— (1999). *E Programm fir Lëtzebuerg: 1. Rentengerechtigkeit: Schluss mit den Hungerrenten.* [web-site]. Aktiounskomitee fir Demokratie a Rentegerechtegkeet [cited 29.05. 2003]. Available from www.adr.lu/wahlprogramm.htm#1.
—— (2001). *Position de l'ADR: Table ronde sur les pensions.* [web-site]. Aktiounskomitee fir Demokratie a Rentegerechtegkeet. [cited 27.05. 2003]. Available from www.adr.lu/Renten2001.pdf
Andrich-Duval, Sylvie (10.12.2002). *Die Pensionsreform: eine zukunftsweisende Frauenreform.* [web-site]. CSV Divers. [cited 17.03. 2003]. Available from www.csv.lu/text/news.-php?id=1005&highlight=pension
Bouchet, Muriel (2003). *The Sustainability of the Private Sector Pension System From A Long-term Perspective: The Case of Luxembourg.* Luxembourg: Banque centrale du Luxembourg.
Budge, Ian, Klingemann, Hans-Dieter, Volkens, Andrea, et al. (2001). *Mapping Policy Preferences: Estimates for Parties, Electors and Governments 1945–1998.* Oxford: Oxford University Press.
CCSS (2003). *Demande d'admission à l'assurance pension continuée/compementaire/facultative.* [web-site]. Centre Commun de la Sécurité Sociale. [cited 28.05. 2003]. Available from www.ccss.lu/pdfligne/VP031F.pdf
Courtois, Luc (1999). "Legislative Developments and Case Reviews: Adoption of the Luxembourg Pension Fund Law." *Journal of International Banking Law* 14(9): 305–310.
CSV (25.07.2001). *Conclusions de la Table ronde sur les pensions.* [web-site]. CSV. [cited 17.03. 2003]. Available from www.csv.lu/text/news.php?id=625&highlight=pension

CSV (21.06.2002). *Pensionsverbesserungen und Erziehungspauschale im Mittelpunkt.* [web-site]. CSV. [cited 17.03.2003]. Available from www.csv.lu/text/news.php?id=625&highlight=pension

—— Divers (21.06.2002). *Nützliche Informationen zur Erziehungspauschale.* [web-site]. CSV [cited 17.03. 2003]. Available from www.csv.lu/text/news.php?id=11&highlight=rente

—— Profil (18.12.2001). *3000 Franken und Babyjahre: CSV hat sich durchgesetzt.* [web-site]. CSV [cited 17.03. 2003]. Available from www.csv.lu/text/news.php?id=556&highlight=pension.

DP (1999). *Le programme gouvernemental: Accord de coalition PCS/PDL du 12 août 1999* [website]. DP. [cited 17.03.2003]. Available from www.dp.lu/mirror/www.dp.lu/pdf/accord_de_coalition.pdf

Dumont, Patrick, and de Winter, Lieven (2000). "Luxembourg: Stable Coalitions in a Pivotal Party System." In Müller, W. C., and Strøm, K. (eds.), *Coalition Governments in Western Europe*. Oxford: Oxford University Press, 399–432.

—— (2003). "Luxembourg: A Case of More 'Direct' Delegation and Accountability." In Strøm, K., Müller, W. C., and Bergman, T. (eds.), *Delegation and Accountability in Parliamentary Democracies*. Oxford: Oxford University Press, 474–97.

Eures (2003). *Marché du travail au Grand-Duché de Luxembourg.* [website]. European Employment Services. [cited 05.07.2004]. Available from www.eureslux.org/eures.taf?Idnav=46

Hirsch, Mario (1980). "European Elections: Luxembourg." *West European Politics* 3(1): 250–2.

—— (1985). "The 1984 Luxembourg Election." *West European Politics*, 8(1): 116–18.

ILO (2001). *Évaluation actuarielle et financière du régime général d'assurance pension du Grand-Duché de Luxembourg*. Genève: ILO.

Jacobs, Francis (1989). "Luxembourg." In Jacobs, Francis (ed.) *Western European Political Parties: A Comprehensive Guide*, 232–50. Harlow: Longman.

LSAP (2001). *Revendications du POSL au sujet du régime général d'assurance pension: Table ronde sur les pensions "Rentendësch".* Luxembourg: LSAP.

Nohlen, Dieter (2000). *Wahlrecht und Parteiensystem*. 3rd edn. Opladen: Leske & Budrich.

OGB-L (2002). "Das neue Rentengesetz: Endlich mehr Rentengerechtigkeit!" *OGB-L aktuell: Monatszeitschrift des OGB-L*, 2002 (Juni): 7.

—— actualités (3/1984). "Prise de position de la fraction OGB-L au sein de la Chambre du Travail. *OGB-L actualités*, 1984 (3): 9–10.

Poirier, Philippe and Fehlen, Fernand (2000). *Les élections au Grand-Duché de Luxembourg, Rapport sur les élections législatives du 13 juin 1999*. CRP-Gabriel Lippmann; Étude réalisée pour la Chambre des Députés du Grand-Duché, Grand-Duché de Luxembourg. [cited 15.05. 2003]. Available from www.chd.lu/docs/pdf/0_e.pdf

Schroen, Michael (1999). "Das politische System Luxemburgs." In Ismayr, W. (ed.), *Die politischen Systeme Westeuropas*. Opladen: Leske + Budrich, 389–414.

—— (2001). "Luxemburg: Interessensvermittlung in einem Kleinstaat." In Reutter, W., and Rütters, P. (eds.), *Verbände und Verbandssysteme in Westeuropa*. Opladen: Leske & Budrich, 241–62.

Service Information et Presse de l'État & Conseil d'État (2002). *Der Staatsrat des Großherzogtums Luxemburg*. [web-site]. Le Gouvernement du Grand-Duché de Luxembourg. [cited 16.05. 2003]. Available from www.gouvernement.lu/publications/download/viepolAL2.pdf

Smart, Michael (1995). "Luxembourg: European Parliament and National Elections of 1994." *West European Politics*, 18(1): 194–6.

STATEC (ed.) (2000). *Annuaire statistique/Statistisches Jahrbuch 2000: Saar, Lor, Lux, Rheinland-Pfalz, Wallonie.* Luxembourg: Service central de la statistique et des études économiques.

—— (2001). *Annuaire statistique 2001.* Luxembourg: Service central de la statistique et des études économiques.

—— (2002). *Le Luxembourg en chiffres.* Luxembourg: Service central de la statistique et des études économiques.

WAGNER, CARLO (2002). *Pensionsversicherung – "Rentendësch".* Luxemburg: Ministerium für Gesundheit und soziale Sicherheit.

CHAPTER 18

DATA APPENDIX: PENSION SYSTEMS IN WESTERN EUROPE

Table A1 Demographic, fiscal, and labour market indicators for Western Europe

Country	Public social expenditure for old-age and survivors in percentage of GDP 1980	1990	2000	Labour market participation rate 55-64 year-olds 1980	1990	2000	Net reproduction rate 1980	1990	2000	Elderly (60+) as percentage of total population 1980	1990	2000	General government balance in percent of GDP 1980	1990	2000
Austria	11,7	12,5	13,2	n.a.	29,5%	29,7%	0,79	0,70	0,66	19,1%	20,1%	20,6%	−1,7	−2,4	−1,6
Belgium	9,2	10,5	11,2	30,6%	22,2%	25,9%	0,81	0,78	0,77	18,2%	20,5%	21,9%	−9,5	−6,8	0,2
Denmark	8,3	8,6	8,3	54,0%	57,1%	56,9%	0,74	0,80	0,85	19,5%	20,4%	19,8%	−3,2	−1,0	2,5
Finland	6,1	8,1	8,6	49,5%	43,8%	46,6%	0,78	0,85	0,83	16,4%	18,5%	19,9%	3,9	5,5	7,1
France	9,7	11,1	12,1	53,6%	38,1%	37,3%	0,93	0,85	0,91	17,2%	19,1%	20,6%	0,0	−2,0	−1,5
Germany	10,9	10,5	11,9	44,5%	43,7%	42,9%	0,74	0,64	0,67	19,3%	20,4%	23,3%	−2,8	−2,0	1,3
Greece	6,0	11,5	12,7	47,5%	41,5%	40,6%	1,02	0,67	0,62	17,5%	19,9%	22,5%	−2,6	−15,9	−4,1
Ireland	5,7	5,4	3,4	48,7%	42,1%	46,3%	1,52	1,01	0,91	14,8%	15,2%	15,1%	−11,8	−2,9	4,3
Italy	9,1	12,1	13,8	24,5%	33,4%	29,0%	0,80	0,64	0,60	17,0%	20,7%	24,3%	−8,5	−11,8	−0,8
Luxembourg	10,6	9,3	7,8	25,3%	28,3%	27,6%	0,71	0,77	0,85	17,8%	19,0%	18,8%	−0,3	4,8	6,0
Netherlands	8,2	9,0	7,2	37,5%	30,8%	38,9%	0,76	0,77	0,83	15,7%	17,3%	18,2%	−4,0	−5,3	2,2
Portugal	4,1	5,4	9,0	51,7%	48,0%	52,5%	1,03	0,72	0,75	15,6%	18,8%	21,6%	−6,7	−4,9	−2,9
Spain	6,4	8,3	9,1	46,8%	40,1%	40,9%	1,08	0,64	0,60	15,3%	19,0%	21,6%	−1,7	−3,5	−0,9
Sweden	8,5	9,4	9,9	66,7%	70,5%	67,4%	0,80	1,01	0,75	21,9%	22,8%	22,2%	−5,8	3,4	5,1
Switzerland	6,2	9,3	12,9	n.a.	63,8%	65,1%	0,74	0,76	0,72	18,3%	19,4%	20,2%	n.a.	−0,2	2,2
UK	7,3	7,9	8,9	52,4%	53,0%	52,7%	0,91	0,89	0,79	20,0%	21,0%	20,7%	−3,2	−1,6	3,9

Sources: OECD (2004), Social Expenditure Database (SOCX, www.oecd.org/els/social/expenditure) (20.01.2006)
OECD (2004) Labour Market Statistic Data http://www1.oecd.org/scripts/cde/queryScreen.asp?DSET=CDELFS_C1T02_3D&
SETNAME=LFS++by+sex+and++age&DBASE=LFS_DATA&EMAIL=&DBNAME=Labour+Market+Statistics+%2D+DATA (20.01.2006)
http://www.imf.org/external/pubs/ft/weo/2005/02/data/dbcoutm.cfm?SD=1980&ED=2000&R1=1&R2=1&CS=3&SS=2&OS=C&DD=0&OUT=1&C=122-124-137-138-128-172-182-132-134-184-174-144-146-178-112-136&S=GGB_NGDP&CMP=0&x=128&y=7 (20.01.2006)

Table A2 Current pension system in the United Kingdom

	1st pillar	2nd pillar	3rd pillar
Coverage	First tier: • employed persons between 16 and 65 (60 for women) with weekly income above £94 • self-employed persons with income above £4,895 per year • state pension recipients: 11.4 million. • three categories of pensions: category A: basic pension category B: husband and wife pension category D: non-contributory pension (over 80) • insured persons are differentiated according to classes (see financing) • voluntary insurance is possible for low income employees, non-employed and self-employed persons with low profits Second tier: • SSP (introduced in April 2002 replaced SERPS) covers all employees that are not members of a contracted-out occupational or private pension scheme	• Quasi-mandatory as alternative to SSP/SERPS • possibility of contracting-out from SSP to choose an occupational pension • types of contracted-out occupational pension schemes: COSRS (DB); COMPS (DC); COMBS; COHS • types of voluntary occupational contracted-in schemes: CISRS (DB); CIMPS (DC) • approximate coverage 8.3 million persons	• Quasi-mandatory as alternative to SSP/SERPS and contracted-out occupational pensions if the insurance can guarantee the same benefits as SERPS/SSP • types of contracted-out private pension: Personal Pensions Scheme (PPS) Appropriate Personal Pension Schemes (APPS) Group Personal Pension Scheme (GPPS) Stakeholder Pension Scheme (SPS) (since April 2001; since Oct. 2001 most employers with 5 or more employees must offer access to a SPS if they do not offer suitable pension arrangements); 840,000 members • additional voluntary insurance possible
Financing	First tier and second tier: • PAYG • contribution financed; contributions based on working hours • contributions for first and second tier are combined and collected by the Inland Revenue • employers' contribution rate (basic pension	• Fully funded schemes (except for public sector) • Pension Protection Fund since April 2005 for compensation payment to members of defined-benefit schemes if their employers become insolvent; funded through mandatory levies on managers of defined-benefit schemes • contribution financed by employer and	• Fully funded schemes • contribution rate depends on individual scheme • Stakeholder Pension Schemes must accept small contributions (£20 per month) • contracted-out Appropriate Personal Pension Schemes receive payments that

and SSP/SERPS): 12.8% on earnings above £94 a week (no upper earnings limit); contracted-out rebate: 3.5% (salary-related) or 1% (money-purchase)

- employees' contribution rate:
  class 1: 2% of income below the lower earnings limit; 11% of £94 to £630 a week i.e. for income between the primary threshold and Upper Earnings Limit, 1% of income above UEL; entitlements to contributory benefits start at the LEL (£82 a week); contracted-out rebate: 1.6%

  class 2 (self-employed): flat-rate of £2.10 a week; small earnings exception: £4,345 p.a.
  class 3: £7.35 a week
  class 4 (self-employed): 8% of net profits between Lower and Upper Profits Limit (LPL: £4,895 p.a./UPL: £32,760 p.a.)
- contribution base: gross pay up to income UEL
- for late retirement employer has to pay contributions, employees pay no contributions
- inland revenue is not allowed to have more than 105% of surplus

employee (exception: in 14% of all schemes employers pay total contribution rate)
- contribution rate must not be below national insurance contribution rebate

- investment in assets such as company shares, government securities and property both in the UK and abroad
- employee contributions are tax exempt
- employers' contribution are personnel costs and are subtracted from profit before tax
- investment return is tax exempt

correspond to the reduced contribution rate from the Inland Revenue National Insurance Contributions Office at the end of each year

Administration
- Inland revenue collects social security contributions via regional and local National Insurance Contributions Offices
- payment of pension benefits via Social Security Benefits Agency and since April 2002 the Pension Service, which is an executive agency of the DWP

- Administration of occupational pensions by private organizations
- the governing body of these organizations is the NAPF
- representation in occupational pension funds' board: since 1995 reform at least 2 employee representatives up to 1/3 of the board

- Monitored by the Financial Services Authority (FSA), the statutory regulator for financial services since 2001

(Continued)

Table A2 (Continued)

1st pillar	2nd pillar	3rd pillar
	• monitoring of the occupational pension sector by Pensions Regulator since April 2005 (previously OPRA)	

Benefits First tier:
- retirement age 65 (men)/60 (women; will rise to 65 between 2010 and 2020) (basic and SSP)
- full contribution period: 44 years (m)/39 (f); minimum qualifying period 25% of 90% of the working-life (=10 years)
- maximum basic pension benefits: £79.60 per week.
- no early retirement possible
- late retirement age 70 (m)/65 (f); between 42 days and 5 years later retirement increases basic pension benefits by +10.4% per year
- benefits indexed annually in line with prices
- pension credits available for unemployment, sickness, disability, maternity, home responsibilities protection and starting credits (persons between 16 and 18)
- since 2003 Pension Credit guaranteeing minimum of £105.45 a week for singles or £160.95 for couples (before 2003 MIG)

Second tier:
- calculation of SERPS: 20% of average income of total working career
- SSP/SERPS benefits are fully indexed to inflation beyond 2.5%

2nd pillar:
- Most of the Occupational Pension Schemes are Contracted-out Salary-related Schemes (COSR); benefit calculation is up to the individual schemes as long as they provide at least SERPS/SSP level benefits; common calculation: pensions are calculated by taking a minimum of 1/80th of the average salary over the three years prior to retirement for each year of service in the scheme up to a maximum of 40 years service
- in Contracted-out Salary-related Scheme (COSRS): benefits are indexed to inflation up to a maximum of 2.5% per year since April (previously up to 5% per year)

3rd pillar:
- Eligibility criteria and benefit calculation is up to the individual schemes as long as they provide benefits at least equal to SERPS/SSP level;
- PPS and SPS: benefits may be drawn from the age of 50;
- 25% of the value of the pension fund can be taken as a tax free lump sum

- the SSP uses different accrual rates for lower income bands during a transition period; persons with income between the LEL and the LET (Band 1) are treated as if they earned the LET, i.e. the accrual rate will be twice the SERPS rate (i.e. 40%); band 2 reaches from the LET plus £1 to three times the LET minus two times the LEL i.e. £27,800 in 2005 and is multiplied with half the SERPS rate i.e. 10%; from the top of the second band plus £1 to the Upper Earnings Limit (Band 3) accrual rate correspond with SERPS rates (i.e. 20%) (The Pension Service 2004: 37); after the transition period SSP will be flat-rate benefits, calculated as if everybody had earned the Lower Earnings Threshold (Bill HC 9/1999: EN Part II 211.-212.)
- income tax applies to basic pension and SERPS; but there are different free amounts depending on age and marital status

Benefit
Examples
- State pension £79.60 per week
- State pension over 80 addition £79.85

Table A3 Current pension system in Greece

	1st pillar	2nd pillar	3rd pillar
Coverage	• Compulsory coverage for wage-earners, farmers, self-employed, civil servants • covers the risks of old-age, invalidity and death of spouse (survivors' pension)	• Voluntary occupational pensions (created for in 2002; cover only a limited number of workers)	• Voluntary private pensions
Financing	• PAYG • contribution-financed • contribution rate for: • main pension is 20% of gross wage (employee 13.33%; employer 6.67%) • supplementary pension (TEAM) is 6% equally shared between employer and employee • additional revenues through social taxes and assets and government subsidies; government subsidy to IKA 1% of GDP • if a fund merges with IKA the general budget covers existing deficits • revenues of the supplementary funds are frequently used to cover the deficits of the main schemes	• Fully funded occupational pension schemes • tax breaks apply	• Fully funded schemes
Administration	• Fragmented state pension system with 170 funds, some covering only small occupational groups • IKA is the main scheme with 34% of all pensioners; it covers wage-earners • other schemes are e.g. OGA, which covers farmers or TEVE, which covers self-employed; there are also supplementary funds such as TEAM • the IKA Managing Board is composed of six representatives of employees, three employers' representatives, two pensioners and 13 IKA bureaucrats, and is headed by a government appointed scheme governor • all schemes are monitored by the Ministry of Labor	• Administration by the social partners with state supervision	• Administration by private insurance companies

| Benefits | - Retirement age: 65 (men), 60 (women)
- minimum qualifying period: 15 years
- minimum contribution period for full pension: 35 years
- indexation rules: pensions are indexed according to increases in public sector wages
- benefits consist of two parts: the basic amount and the supplement
- basic amount

Old system:
- basic amount is calculated on the number of contribution years and the reference income i.e. average daily wage of the last five years before retirement up to a ceiling (excluding holiday allowances and bonuses); the imputed daily wage is multiplied by 25 and by the coefficient corresponding to each insurance class
- supplement available for non-working spouses, or for mothers of young children
- benefit bonus of 1% for every 300 days of contribution payments over the minimum qualifying period of 15 years
- if the calculated pension is below a certain limit a minimum pension is paid; IKA minimum pensions consist of contribution-linked part, a top-up welfare part and the income-tested Social Solidarity Supplement |

(Continued)

Table A3 (Continued)

	1st pillar	2nd pillar	3rd pillar
	New system (post-1993 entrants): • benefit calculation: monthly imputed salary is multiplied by the number of contribution years and the accrual rate of 1.714% (after 35 years replacement rate of 60%) • calculation of supplementary pension • OGA-benefits to farmers or uninsured population		
Benefit example[a]	Basic pension • monthly wage: 1000 Euros (income of last 5 years divided by days of contributions and multiplied by 25) • days of contributions: 11000 • benefit = 1,714 × 11000/300 = 62,84% 62,84 × 1000 = 628, 4 Euros Supplementary pension: • monthly wage: 1000 Euros (income of last 5 years divided by days of contributions and multiplied by 25) • days of contributions: 11000 • benefit = 0,571 × 11000/300 = 20,94 20,94 × 1000 = 209,4	n.a	n.a

[a] Post-1993 workers

Table A4 Current pension system in France

	1st pillar	2nd pillar	3rd pillar
Coverage	• Compulsory social security for all French citizens • basic scheme covers 2/3 of working population; especially private sector employees • supplementary scheme covers both private and public sector	Voluntary occupational schemes coverage via individual membership in the public sector (PREFON) or group insurance (*Madelin arrangements*)	Voluntary private pension schemes: individual personal saving plans (*plan d'épargne retraite individual pour la retraite[PEIR]*); *plan partenarial d'épargne salariale volontaire pour la retraite* [PPESVR])
Financing	Basic scheme: • PAYG system (PAYG) • mixed financing of contributions and state subsidies • contribution rates vary between 6.55% and 16.35% of gross wage between FRF 8,404 and social security ceiling per year Supplementary scheme: • PAYG system (PAYG) • contribution rates vary between 6–7.5% for ARRCO and 16–20% for AGIRC • compensation between pension schemes to balance demographic disparities (*compensation généralisée*)	Funded: defined-contributions	Funded: defined-contributions
Administration	• Highly fragmented system (194 funds for basic pensions; 135 funds for supplementary pensions) • pension insurance funds are public bodies • funds' boards consist of representatives of employers	Organization for public sector occupational pensions: PREFON pool of insurers: *Caisse Nationale de Prévoyance* (CNP)	Private insurance contracts enabling employees to accumulate entitlement to an annuity

(Continued)

Table A4 (Continued)

	1st pillar	2nd pillar	3rd pillar
	and employees;; in basic pension scheme boards' directors are appointed by the government; supplementary schemes' boards are without state participation • organization of pension system (régimes legaux) along four socio-professional categories • *Caisse Nationale d'Assurance Vieillesse des Travailleurs Salariés* (CNAVTS) administers the basic pensions of the employees of the private sector; AGIRC (67 funds) and ARRCO (34 funds) administrate the supplementary pensions of the private sector (*régime general*) • *Régime spéciaux* administers the public and para-public sector (20% of workforce) • *Régime agricole* administers pensions of farmers • *Régimes autonomes* administer pensions of self-employed	Special scheme for hospital personnel: *Comité de Gestion des Oeuvres Sociales* (CGOS)	
Benefits	• Retirement age 65 but retirement possible at 60 • minimum qualifying period 3 months (= one quarter) • minimum qualifying period for full pension 40 years i.e. 160 quarters Basic scheme: • benefit calculation based on the average annual salary of the insured person and the number of years of insurance • reference period for the assessment base was the 10 best years until 1993 but has increased since and will be 25 years in 2008	Benefit calculation depends on scheme and on contributions	Benefit calculation depends on individual scheme and on contributions

- benefit formula: {50%–1.25% * (160 quarters – real number of contribution quarters)} * (real number of contribution quarters /150) * average yearly wage of best ten years

Supplementary scheme:
- defined-contribution
- benefit calculation on insurance "points" (points are calculated by annual contributions divided by a "reference wage") multiplied by the current value per point
- contribution-free pension points are available for periods of sickness, unemployment disability or more than three children
- increase in pension entitlements by 5% per child

Benefit example
- Average pension in the different socio-occupational categories: shopkeepers and industrialists: €488, per month in 2002
- farmers: €528
- craftsmen: €648
- salaried employees: €1,590
- employees of the public sector: €2,058
- liberal professions: €2,085

Table A5 Current pension system in Switzerland

	1st pillar	2nd pillar	3rd pillar
Coverage	• All residents (except diplomats, asylum-seekers)	• compulsory coverage for employees earning at least twice the amount of minimum basic pension (CHF 24,720 per year); • 80–90% of employed	• voluntary coverage encouraged by modest tax deductions (premiums are tax deductible up to CHF 6,077) • 60% of employed
Financing	• PAYG with buffer fund equal to one year's benefits • contribution rate is 8.4% (employers and employees pay 50% each; 7.8% for self-employed) of qualifying income with no ceiling • for residents without earnings from work (*sans activité lucrative*), the amount of the contribution is calculated on the basis of assets • federal subsidy equal to 17% of outlays plus 2% from the cantons • 1% point of VAT	• fully funded; for short periods funds are allowed to have lower coverage ratios • 30% of funds can be invested in company shares • contributions are tax deductible • funds may chose any contribution rate they want but revenues (and investment income) must cover the costs of government mandated notional contribution rates based on age and gender notional contribution rates: Men / Women Age — Rate — Age — Rate 25-34 — 7 — 25-31 — 7 35-44 — 10 — 32-41 — 10 45-54 — 15 — 42-51 — 15 55-64 — 18 — 52-62 — 18	• fully funded • contributions depend on individual pension plans
Administration	• joint administration by 100 compensation funds (*Ausgleichskassen/Caisses de compensation*) at the federal and cantonal level; large employers and economic sectors administer their own compensation funds; people working in other sectors are insured with one of the 26 cantonal compensation funds; administrative structure varies	• there are 8,550 (2001) mandatory occupational funds governed by trusts consisting of equal numbers of representatives of employers and employees; small employers can insure employees in branch or inter-branch funds or with foundations set up by insurance companies or banks • at the federal level, the guarantee fund	• private insurers, financial services providers

- parity representation of employers and union in branch and company funds; retirees not represented

(Sicherheitsfonds BVG) insures against bankruptcy, and is financed by a contribution paid by all funds
- the federal default fund (Auffangeinrichtung/institution supplétive) insures people who are not covered but should be (for example if the employer fails to insure its employees)
- cantons have supervisory authorities for pension funds
- trustees decide fund rules, benefits above legal minimum, benefit indexation, investment policy; some tasks can be delegated to financial service providers

Benefits
- Retirement age 65 (men)/63 (women); (64 after 2006))
- minimum qualifying period 1 year for Swiss nationals
- early retirement possible with reductions of 6.8% per year
- pension adjustment to average increase in prices and wages
- insures earnings up to approx. CHF 3,500 per month; combined replacement rate with 2nd pillar approx. 60%
- benefit calculation: if indexed annual average earnings are lower than CHF 37,080 (1.5 times the maximum AHV benefit of 2002), then:

- Retirement age 65 years (men)/63 years (women); (64 after 2006))
- reference period: 40 years (men)/38 years (women)
- indexation not compulsory
- insures earnings between CHF 2,060 and CHF 6,180 per month; combined replacement rate with 1st pillar is around 60%; exact benefit calculation depends on fund
- benefits are subject to social insurance contributions
- if the recipient has not reached the AHV/AVS retirement age; lump sum payments taxed at a lower rate (varies between cantons)

- Retirement age flexible, but no earlier than 5 years before AHV-AVS retirement age
- generally paid as lump sum

(Continued)

Table A5 *(Continued)*

1st pillar	2nd pillar	3rd pillar
P = 74/100 *mP + 13/600 * iae if indexed annual average earnings are higher than CHF 37,080), then: P = 104/100*mP+8/600*iae if the result is lower than mP or higher than MP, mp and MP are applied instead where: P = monthly pension benefit mP = minimum AHV pension (CHF 1,030/month in 2002) MP = maximum AHV pension (CHF 2,060/month in 2002) iae = indexed annual average earnings		

	1st pillar	2nd pillar	3rd pillar
Coverage	National pension: • all residents • earnings-related pension: • compulsory for working population; different schemes for the private sector employees (TEL & LEL), municipal employees (KVTEL), state employees (VEL), self-employed (YEL), seamen (MEL) self-employed in agriculture (MYEL); in addition some small groups – church employees(KiEL), artists (TaEL) etc have their own pension schemes. From 1.1. 2007, TEL, LEL and TaEL will be merged together into "Employee's pension" (TyEL).	• Voluntary supplementary occupational pensions (e.g. additional TEL-pensions) • coverage rate: 10% of employees	• Voluntary private pensions • coverage rate: less than 10% of working population
Financing	National pension: • PAYG • mixed financing of contributions from employers, state subsidies, VAT revenues (only up to 1.1. 2006) and capital funding (National Pension Insurance Fund functioning as buffer fund) • minimum liquidity requirements: the National Pension Insurance Fund must equal at least 40% of yearly expenditure; if a fund is still short of the required minimum level after transfers between schemes, the state will cover the deficits by "guarantee payments" • employers' contribution rate varies between 1.4% and 4.5% of the payroll; the insured do not pay national pension contributions. Earnings-related pension (as of 2005): • employees scheme: mixed PAYG and funded system; about one fourth of the contribution revenue is funded for payment of future pensions • self-employed and farmers' schemes are purely PAYG • contribution rates: • TEL: if less than 50 employees the contribution is 21.9%; more than 50 employees 19.75%–23.3% depending on the age and gender of the employee; the average contribution 21.6%. LEL: 22.7%; TaEL: 19.6% (in TEL, LEL & TaEL the employee's contribution is 4.6% for 18–53 years of age and 5.8% for older than 53 years of age); MEL: 22 % (shared equally between the employer and employee); VEL: 23.5 % (employee: 4.6%); KVTEL: 28.3% (employee: 4.6%); KiEL: 31.7% (employee: 4.6%); self-employed rates: YEL: 21.4% for 18–53 years of age and 22.6% for older than 53 years of age; MYEL: 10.5% for younger than 53 years of age and 11.1% for older than 53 years of age. (Source: http://www.etk.fi/page.asp?Section=11987)		• Savings-based life insurance • limited tax-deductibility of contributions (contributions are deductible up to 10% of earned income; maximum deducible amount: €500 per year (2005 rules)

(Continued)

Table A6 (Continued)

	1st pillar	2nd pillar	3rd pillar

Administration	• no contribution ceiling
	• emergency safety net in case of fund's bankruptcy
	• National pension
	  • combined administration of pensions, sickness insurance, unemployment, housing and study allowances by a semi-public body KELA monitored by Parliament; the KELA administrative board consists of 12 trustees appointed by Parliament and 8 auditors chosen by the trustees
	• Earnings-related schemes:
	  • fragmentation according to occupational lines; there are 54 "pension funds" (6 pension insurance companies, 37 pension foundations, 11 insurance funds)
	  • main different schemes that account for over 92.5% of pensioners:
	  • for private sector employees: TEL
	  • for temporary employees: LEL (e.g. employees in forestry, logging, civil engineering, housing construction, dock work, work on board vessels in domestic traffic, agriculture and gardening)
	  • for performing artists and journalists: TaEL (also applies to employment contracts in TEL branches of shorter duration than one month and employment contracts lasting for at least one month with earnings below the TEL limit)
	  • for seamen: MEL
	  • for self-employed and their family members: YEL
	  • for farmers and fishermen: MYEL administered by the Farmers' Social Insurance Institution MELA
	  • for public-sector scheme: KVTL (local government employees) and VEL (state employees) administered by the State Treasury and the KVTEL pensions by the Local Government Pensions Institution (KEVA).
	  • for the Evangelical-Lutheran Church scheme: KiEL administered by the church council
	• the Ministry of Social Affairs and Health is in charge of the general supervision of the earnings-related schemes and the specific supervision is in the Insurance Supervisory Authority (Vakuutusvalvontavirasto)
	• the Finnish Centre for Pensions (ETK) is a statutory central body for the statutory earnings-related pension scheme that e.g. keeps records on work histories of the insured and centrally keeps records on the insured's pension rights.
		• the Finnish Pension Alliance TELA represents the private sector pension providers, which are supervised by the Ministry of Social Affairs and Health, and the Insurance Supervisory Authority	

- most private sector insurance (67%) is TEL- and LEL- insurance
- collection of contributions and payment of pensions is handled by private pension institutions e.g. a pension insurance company, an industry-wide pension fund or a company pension fund; most employers and self-employed persons may choose their own pension institution; in addition, there are also some pension institutions for special branches of industry; the pension insurance companies administer TEL pensions for employees and YEL pensions for self-employed persons; employers and the self-employed may establish a joint industry-wide pension fund to operate TEL and YEL pensions; a company pension fund operates TEL pensions of one single employer; some branches of industry have their own pension institutions, the functions of which have been prescribed by special acts; the LEL Employment Pensions Fund operates pension provision for employees in construction, dock work, forestry and agriculture; furthermore, there is a special pension fund operating TaEL pensions for performing artists and certain other employee groups

Benefits
- National Pension:
  - standard retirement age: 65 years; early retirement age: 60 years
  - minimum qualifying period for Finns (and employees from EU member countries) 3 years after reaching age 16; citizens of other countries: residence in Finland for an uninterrupted period of at least 5 years; for full benefits 40 years of residence between 16 and 64 years of age.
  - benefits are tested against income from legislated pensions
  - minimum pension benefit: single recipient (class 1. municipality): €505.24 a month; married recipient (class 1. municipality): €445.38 a month
  - supplementary amount for those with no or few employment-based benefits
  - indexation: yearly adjustment of both pensions and entitlements to changes in cost of living

- Earnings-related pension (as in 2005):
  - no ceiling on benefits in absolute nor proportional terms, i.e. the amount of pension can be even higher than previous wage
  - no minimum qualifying period
  - reference period: life time income, beginning from the age of 18, income for those years when the claimant has taken care of children or studied is fixed at €538.27 per month

- For registered supplementary pensions same rules apply as in TEL with respect to portability, indexation and target benefit levels
- minimum qualifying period for full pension may be less than 40 years
- benefit calculation follows the difference principle i.e. occupational benefits are determined as difference between the targeted 60% replacement rate and the actual TEL level

(Continued)

Table A6 (Continued)

	1st pillar	2nd pillar	3rd pillar
	• flexible retirement age 63 to 68 years of age • benefit reduction for early retirement at the age of 62; reduction by 0.6% for each month of early retirement (maximum reduction if retiring at the age of 7.2%) • postponement of retirement beyond the age of 68 increases pension by 0.4% for every month of postponement • indexation: the index for persons of working age is used for adjusting pensionable wages, earnings from self-employment, and pensions until the end of the year during which the person reaches the age of 65; the same index is also used when adjusting the Euro limits for the earnings-related pensions; changes in prices and wages affect the index for persons of working age equally • pensions and pension-carrying incomes are indexed. In the index changes in the price level are weighted by 20% and changes in the wage level by 80% • the accrual rate varies according to age: 1.5% for 18 to 52 years of age; 1.9% for 53 to 62; and 4.5% for 53 to 68 • in 2010 a "longevity" formula will be used to take demographic changes in to consideration (long-living cohorts will get their pension reduced) • assessment base (pensionable wage) is calculated as average of earnings of the working career.		
Benefit example	Old system up to 2004: private sectors average monthly wage in basic metal industries: €2,526/month (year 2001) • in Finland only possible pension age of 58 is through disability pension or part time pension. • ...employees covered by the old Employees' Pensions Act (TEL): the accrual rate for persons younger than 60 who are working is 1.5% for each year of employment; the accrual rate increases to 2.5% from the beginning of the year when the person reaches the age of 60; the earnings for different years are made comparable by using the index under the Employees' Pensions Act (TEL-index); when calculating the pensionable monthly wage the employees' pension contribution is first deducted from the annual earnings (in Finland employees have paid contributions since 1996).		

The annual, TEL-indexed earnings are then added together (the maximum number of included years was 10 years; in our example nine years), the sum is divided by the total number of days for the included income years (360 * the number of income years included in the calculation; in our example 360 * 9 = 3 240 days) and the quotient is multiplied by the average number of days a month (30).

30 * (24912+24912+25077+25235+25662+26268+26760+27917+28978) / 3240 = €2182, 60/month (average wage used for pension calculation)

The person has began his/her work career at the age of 24 and takes out pension when filled 64 in the beginning of 2008.

Old rules: The pension accumulation has been 1,5% for the 24–59 years of age (1,5 % * 36 years) = 54.0%. Accumulation up to the year 2008 in the age bracket 60–63 is 2,5% (2,5% * 4 = 9%); thus the total pension percentage is 63%.

During the transition period the claimant's pension is calculated both according to the new and old rules and the best one is applied.

The new 2005 system: According to the new rules the worker would get 1,5% for the age years 24–52; 1,9% for 53–62 years of age and 4,5% for 63 years of age. Thus the total pension percentage would be 67% (1,5% * 29 + 1,9% * 10 + 4,5% * 1) and since the latter one is better for the claimant, s/he will get pension at that rate; which would yield a monthly pension of €1462.34 (67% * €2182.60) which would be 58% of the claimants income in 2001.

Table A7 Current pension system in Belgium

	1st pillar	2nd pillar	3rd pillar
Coverage	Three separate schemes for: • wage earners • self-employed • civil servants	• Voluntary occupational pensions • about 50% of workers covered	• Voluntary occupational insurance or life insurance

Financing	• PAYG system
	• contribution financed and VAT-tax-financed
	• contribution rates:
	  • employees' combined contribution rate for all branches of social security since 1995 37.94% of gross wages
	  • self-employed pay contributions based on net income
	  • civil servants are exempt from social security contributions except for survivor's pension and health care insurance
	• 21% of VAT revenues are earmarked for the social security system
	• no ceiling on contributions
		• joint employee/employer financing
		• funded accounts
		• contribution are tax deductable	

Administration	• Total social security contributions are collected by the National Office for Social Security (RSZ/ONSS) • responsible body: National Pensions Agency (RVP) • pension boards are composed of 50% of representatives of employers and employees each • monitoring by the Ministry of Social Affairs	• sectoral or firm pension funds • both employees and employers represented on boards	
Benefits	• Retirement age for 65 (female retirement age is still in transition from 60 to 65 and will be achieved in 2009)	• varies according to scheme	

- full pension after 45 years of contributions
- early retirement is possible with reductions of 5% per year of early retirement
- pensions cannot be combined with income from employment above a certain level
- pensions indexed to inflation
- benefit calculation: 60% of average lifetime gross wages for single persons and 75% of average gross wage for heads of family
- benefits for self-employed are not related to earnings but flat-rate pensions depend on marital status (100% for breadwinners; 80% for single person households)
- guaranteed minimum pension for employees with full qualifying period (€9,991 for singles and €12,485 for heads of family in 2004)

Benefit example

- 60% or 75% × $\dfrac{\text{gross salary} \times \text{number of career years}}{45}$

Table A8 Current pension system in Sweden

	1st pillar	2nd pillar	3rd pillar
Coverage	Guarantee pension (*garantipension*): • residents with low or no earnings-related old-age pension Earnings-related pension (*inkomstpension*): • those with income from employment, including self-employed Premium pensions (*premiereservsystem*): • those with income from employment, including self-employed	• Quasi-mandatory occupational pension negotiated in collective agreements • coverage rate: 90% of employees.	• Voluntary private pensions • coverage rate: 35% of those aged 20 to 64 had individual pension schemes in 1999.
Financing	Guarantee pension (*garantipension*): • general revenue financing Earnings-related pension (*inkomstpension*): • pay-as-you-go with buffer funds • notional defined-contribution • 16% contribution rate contribution is shared between wage-earners and employers • wage-earners pay 7% of their eligible earnings up to a ceiling of 8.07 "income base amounts;" (2004 ceiling was SEK 42,300); ceiling is indexed to increases in average earnings • employers pay 10.21% contribution up to the earnings ceiling, and half of this for earnings above the ceiling • the government pays the entire contribution for "child years" and those in military service; for claimants of unemployment insurance or sickeness benefit, the state pays the employer share of the contribution (10.21%), and the individual pays his/her contribution as if/she were working • the "automatic balancing" mechanism requires the National Insurance Office to calculate the notional assets and liabilities of the system annually; if the ratio of assets to liabilities, the balance ratio (*balanstal*), falls below one, the balancing mechanism kicks in; both pension rights and benefit payments are indexed at a lower rate until balance is restored Premium pensions (*premiereservsystem*): • defined-contribution individual funded accounts • 2.5% contribution rate	• Contribution rate is usually between 2 and 5% of wages.	

Administration	• The National Insurance Board (*Försäkringskassan*) adminsters the guarantee pension and the income pension	
	• the Premium Pension Authority (*Premiepensionmyndigheten*, PPM), a state agency, administers the premium pension; in 2004 wage earners could choose between 600 investment funds, including a public default fund, the Premium Savings Fund, (*Premiesparfonden*) for those who do not make an active fund choice	
Benefits	Guarantee pension:	• Occupational pensions typically add 10% to the public benefit below the income ceiling, and 65% of final salary above the ceiling
	• the guarantee pension is payable at age 65 to those with insufficient pension income from the income pension system	
	• the guarantee pension replaces the basic pension, pension supplement and the special tax deduction for pensioners; unlike the old basic pension, the guarantee pension is taxable	
	• the guarantee pension is either a fixed amount or a supplement to the income pension; in 2006 the guaranteed minimum is 2.13 price base amounts, or SEK 86,149; married pensioners receive 1.9 price base amounts (SEK 76,820); the premium pension, private pension income and occupational pension income do not affect the guarantee pension	
	• 40 years of residence from age 25 are required; for those who do not meet this requirement (usually immigrants), there is a special maintenance allowance; low-income pensioners are also eligible for the pensioners housing supplement (BTP)	
	• the guarantee pension is payable to those born 1938 or later	
	Earnings-related pension (*inkomstpension*):	• defined-benefit and defined-contribution
	• retirement is possible any time after age 61	
	• the income pension is a "notional defined contribution" (NDC) pension based on lifetime earnings; the monthly benefit is calculated based on (gender-neutral) life expectancy at the time of retirement; all insured persons have an account with the National Insurance Office in which their contributions are entered; the notional balance in the account is indexed annually according to an "income index" (*inkomstindex*) based on changes in average pension-carrying income for wage-earners aged 16–64; at retirement assets in the notional account are converted to an annuity using the "annuitization divisor" (*delningstal*) which is the expected remaining life expectancy for that cohort plus an internal rate of return of 1.6%	

(*Continued*)

Table A8 (*Continued*)

	1st pillar	2nd pillar	3rd pillar
	• benefit payouts are indexed to the adjustment index (*följsamhetsindex*) which is the income index minus 1.6 Premium pensions (*premiereservsystem*): • all fund balances are annuitized at the time of retirement and can be paid out either as a fixed annuity with a minimum rate of return of 3% or as a variable annuity • the premium pension is payable from age 65 • those born between 1938 and 1953 receive pensions according to the old and new systems		
Benefit example	Income pension and premium pension: benefits are defined contribution so they depend on the number of years of contributions, the level of contributions, and the rate of return; the individual bears all risk, and benefits cannot be defined in advance		

Table A9 Current pension system in Italy

	1st pillar	2nd pillar	3rd pillar
Coverage	• All dependent employees (public and private sector) • self-employed and farmers • unemployed people receiving unemployment benefit • voluntary coverage of housewives	• Voluntary supplementary occupational pensions • "closed" (occupational) pension funds • "open" pension funds in the case of *collective* affiliation • coverage of approximately 2 million people. Take up rate for closed funds in the industrial sector: 30%. • Compulsory severance payment for all private employees (*Trattamento di fine rapporto – Tfr*)	• Voluntary supplementary private pensions • c. 700.000 *PIP* (individual pension) contracts subscribed plus life-insurance contracts (widespread) • "open" pension funds in the case of *individual* affiliation
Financing	• Contribution financed • PAYG system with individual notional accounts. Contributions are "virtually" accumulated in a personal account and indexed to the mean GDP growth rate of the last five years. At retirement, this amount is converted into a pension through a conversion coefficient that varies in relation to the age of the worker. • No government reserves. Transfers form the public budget to balance deficits and finance non-contributory benefits; social allowance for retirees (*assegno sociale*), social pension (*pensione sociale*), pension supplement (*integrazione al minimo*). • contribution rate for employees in the private sector: 32.7% of gross wage (employee: 8.89%; employer: 23.81%; public sector employees: 32.35% (employee: 8.75%; employer: 24.20%)	• capital funded • strict quantitative regulation on funds' investment. • tax-deductibility of contributions up to 12% of income or a maximum of €5,165 • transfer of the *Tfr* with the "silent assent" formula; *Tfr*: payroll-tax-financed by 6.91% of gross wage; companies use the virtually accumulated revenues as cheap source of company finance	• Capital funded • strict quantitative regulation on funds' investment. • tax-deductibility of contributions up to 12% of income or a maximum of €5,165 • *Tfr* through the "voice" option

(Continued)

Table A9 (Continued)

	1st pillar	2nd pillar	3rd pillar
Administration	• National body for the private sector: *Istituto Nazionale della Previdenza Sociale* (INPS) articulated in four major pension schemes: employees: *Fondo Pensioni Lavoratori Dipendenti* (FPLD) farmers: *Gestione coltivatori diretti, mezzadri e coloni* artisans: *Gestione degli artigiani* merchants: *Gestione degli esercenti attività commerciali* • national body for the public sector: *Istituto Nazionale di Previdenza per i Dipendenti dell'Amministrazione Pubblica* • plus various special schemes for small occupational groups • pension fund board appointed by the government and approved by parliament; since 1994 no participation of representatives of employees and employers in pension fund boards	In 2005: • 43 closed occupational pension funds: managed by social partners (employees and employers representative) • 89 open pension funds, directly managed by financial institutions	• Directly managed by financial institution
Benefits	• Contributory pensions (second tier) • Standard retirement age 60 for women and 65 for men • benefit calculation differs between different cohorts of workers: Old system: for workers with more than 18 years of contributions in 1995: earnings-related minimum qualifying period: for old-age pension: 20 years for full old-age pension: 40 years for seniority pension: 35 years, gradually raising to 40 by 2008, alternatively 35 years of contributions and 57 years of age (35+60 in 2008, 35+62 in 2010) reference period for benefits calculation: 10 years; benefit calculation: accrual rate of 2% multiplied by the number of years of insurance, then multiplied by the average wage of the last ten years of employment (reference earnings);	• Pension funds: for dependent workers: only defined-contributions. for the self-employed: also defined-benefits • retirement age: same of 1st pillar with a minimum qualifying period of 5 years • seniority pensions: no earlier than 10 years before standard retirement age with 15 years of contributions • *Tfr*: compulsory severance pay that employers pay their employees when they leave the company or retire; Benefits	• Mostly defined-contributions • possibility to have minimum guaranteed returns • retirement age: same of 2nd pillar • seniority pensions: same of 2nd pillar

example: worker that retires after 40 years of contributions (full pension): pension = 2% * 40 * RE = 80% RE (RE: reference earnings)
- New system:

for new entrants in labor market after 1.1.1996: contributions-related

minimum qualifying period: 5 years;

reference period: –

benefit calculation: the accumulated sum of contributions (*montante contributivo*) indexed yearly to the mean GDP growth of the last five years is multiplied by a conversion coefficient (0,06136)
- Transition system:

for workers with less than 18 years of contributions in 1995: mixed system *pro rata*
- all systems: pensions indexed to prices
- Non contributory pensions (first tier):
  - Before 1996: means-tested, flat-rate social pension (*pensione sociale*); means-tested pension supplement (*integrazione al minimo*) up to 5358 Euros per year (in 2004), for contributory pensions under the threshold
  - After 1996: means-tested (eligibility with income under 4783 Euros per year) old-age social allowance (*Assegno sociale*), flat-rate (367 Euros in 2004)
  - Eligibility conditions: 65 years of age for social pension and old-age social allowance; entitlement to a contributory pension for pension supplement

calculated as the sum of 1/13.5 of the annual earnings for each year of employment, revalued at a fixed interest rate of 1.5% plus 75% of the inflation rate
- for public sector employees: *Indennità di buonuscita*

Table A10 Current pension system in Denmark

	1st pillar	2nd pillar	3rd pillar
Coverage	First tier (*Folkepension*) • all Danish citizens, immigrants (if they have lived 10 years in Denmark, including the five years before retirement) Second tier: • ATP: all employees between 16 and 67 if working time exceeds 9 hours a week • SP: contributions of 1% of income for employees and self-employed • special earnings-related pensions for some groups of civil servants (*tjenestemænd*) (but today very restricted entrance into this pension scheme (e.g. for high-ranking civil servants and priests) • as of 2003, a special and voluntary pension scheme (SAP) for disabled pensioners has been introduced	• No compulsory occupational pension but high coverage rate: 93% of wage-earners aged from 30 to 60 • unemployed, sick persons and certain groups of wage earners (particularly young people and highly paid professionals) are NOT covered	• No mandatory private pensions • approximately 1 million people paying contributions
Financing	First tier: • basic pension is PAYG, tax-financed from general budget revenues (i.e. the central government fully reimburses municipalities for pension expenditure) Second tier: • ATP and SP are capital funded • investment regulation for ATP: no more than 70% of investment in risky assets or shares and no control over any company • contributions to ATP depend on hours worked (e.g. for a full time employee with 37 hours per week contribution was DKR 2,683 (approx 1% of average wage)) Recipients of unemployment or sickness benefits pay double ATP contributions • contribution rate: SP: 1% of work-related income. SAP contributions, which are voluntary, equal 2.8% of the disability pension whereof 2/3 are paid by the government • civil servants PAYG financed (as contributions to ATP and SP are tiny, de facto the only group that has substantial first pillar second tier pension coverage is civil servants)	• Fully funded; 100% of liabilities must be funded • regulation of their investment • contribution financed; the contribution rate varies from scheme to scheme between 3% and 17% • contributions are tax-deductible	• Fully funded • investment policies regulated • contributions are partly tax-deductible

Administration	First tier: • administered by the municipalities, but completely regulated and monitored by the Ministry of Social Affairs Second tier: • ATP and SP are administered by ATP, i.e. a private organization set up by law, governed by the social partners and monitored by the Ministry of Labor • the new SAP for recipients of disability pensions can either be administered by the ATP or a private provider such as a bank or life-insurance company with effect as of 2005, contributions to SP can be invested with private insurance companies, so the scheme will partly become a first pillar, third tier scheme. The same is the case for the new SAP scheme • civil servant pensions administered by the Ministry of Finance and a special body (*Kommunernes Pensionsforsikring*) set up by local authorities	• Usually, there is a pension fund set up in connection with each collective agreement • the funds are monitored by the Danish Financial Supervisory Authority (*Finanstilsynet*) under the Ministry of Industrial Affairs • all funds' boards are composed of either wage-earner representatives only, or the seats on the boards are shared between representatives of the employers and employees; in general, employees' representatives have a majority	• The system of private pensions is quite fragmented: banks and insurance companies offer private pension schemes of various kinds • there are two associations for private insurers: one covering insurance companies (*Forsikring og pension*) and one covering banks (*Finansrådet*) • private pension funds are monitored by the Danish Financial Supervisory Authority (Finanstilsynet) under the Ministry of Industrial Affairs
Benefits	First tier: • retirement age 65 for men and women born after 1 July 1939, 67 for men and women born earlier • minimum qualifying period for Danish citizens: 3 years of residence between the age of 15 and 65/67; for non-Danish citizens 10 years of residence including the last 5 years before retirement • basic amount = €7,586 a year in 2005, pension supplement = €7,636 for single pensioners, €3,565 for married or cohabiting pensioners; the basic amount is subject to an income test based on income from work only (other pensions are not taken into account) • pension supplement subject to income test. It is reduced by DKR 30 for each DKR 100 of additional income from work, pension, rents or capital interest if income is above €7,107 a year for single pensioners and €14,280 for a married or cohabiting couple	• Same as standard state retirement age i.e. 67/65, but possibilities to retire from the age of 60 • no indexation of occupational pension benefits or entitlements; level of benefits depends on investments only, but the law specifies a minimum interest rate of 2% • benefits are calculated based on pure actuarial principles i.e. the value of	• 60 to 65/67 • benefits depend on contributions and investments • no indexation; benefits depend on the rate of return from investment only, but legal minimum interest rate of 2% in schemes paying monthly benefits • pension benefits are taxed at the time of payment; the tax rates

(*Continued*)

Table A10 (Continued)

	1st pillar	2nd pillar	3rd pillar
	• indexation: adjustment to average wage increase but if increase exceeds 2%, 0.3% is put into a special fund that is used for the improvement of cash benefit schemes which the political parties find need improvements Second tier: • no minimum qualifying period for ATP and SP; small pensions are paid as lump sum; • ATP benefit calculation based on number of contribution years and returns on investments; Average ATP pensions in 2004 were €1,206 per year • SP benefit calculation based on the value of contributions and returns on investments, and paid out over a 10 year period; if the person is entitled to less than DKR 15,000 in total, it is paid as a lump sum • no indexation of ATP and SP entitlements or benefits; benefits depend on rate of return on investments only, but funds have to guarantee a minimum annual return of 2% • late retirement in ATP and SP, until the age of 70, increases the pension by 7% per year • civil servants: Minimum qualifying period 3 years; reference period to calculate assessment base total number of years employed (maximum 37 years) plus wage at retirement indexation with civil servants' wages benefit calculation: 57% of last wage if the person has 37 years of employment (special supplement for low-wage civil servants during transition period until 2022 to compensate for a decline in pensions as a result of new calculation system) reduced pensions if early retirement with less than 37 years of employment after the age of 25 all pensions are taxed as income from work	the contributions paid, the interest rate, average life-expectancy and the risk profile of the people in the fund • pension benefits are subject to income tax at the time of payment and annual interest gains are taxed during the contribution period	depend on the type of pension; the annual interest gains are taxed
Benefit examples	Example is based on the first tier only. The SP benefits are still so tiny that they will be paid as lump sum. As SP matures, benefits will of course grow, but due to the limited contributions, they will never dramatically exceed the ATP for an average worker. "blue-collar man" (single person, working life of 40 years, insurance paid for 40 years, earning average production worker's income) would be entitled to the national pensions = €7,586 + €7,646 = 15,222 + ATP = €16		

Table A11 Current pension system in Spain

	1st pillar	2nd pillar	3rd pillar
Coverage	• In 2004 17m workers and 7.9m pensions (7.3 pensioners of whom c. 63% old age pensioners) covered under one general and five special schemes for self-employed, coal miners, farmers/agricultural workers, seamen and household employees; a considerable number of civil servants ascribed to the "passive classes regime" and not covered by Social Security but by various mutual schemes; 488,000 pensioners in non-contributory system	• Voluntary occupational private pension plans	• Voluntary individual private pension plans
Financing	• Social Security contributory pensions financed with contributions; • non-contributory pensions financed with general revenues; • as of 2004 Social Security contribution rate in the general scheme: 28.3% of contribution base (23.6% by employer; 4.7% by employee); self-employed scheme: 29.8% of a self-determined contribution rate between €755 and €2,732; household employees: 22% of €573; farmers: 18.75% of €597; agricultural workers 11.5%; civil servants integrated in passive classes regime: 1.69% of the regulatory base plus 5.07% by the state; reserve fund since 2000 equaling approx. 4 months of contributory pension outlays.	Privately funded defined-benefit, defined-contribution or hybrid pensions (almost all new pension plans are established on defined contribution basis): generally financed by the plan's promoter (employer); as of 2004 annual contributions cannot exceed €8,000; limit may be increased for participants over 52 years old (additional €1,250 for each year over 52) up to €24,250	Privately funded-defined-contribution pensions: as of 2004 annual contributions cannot exceed €8,000; limit may be increased for participants over 52 years old (€1,250 for each year over 52) up to €24,250
Administration	• The *Instituto Nacional de la Seguridad Social* (INSS) administers the general scheme and the five special schemes under control of the Ministry of Work and Social Affairs; pensions of civil servants not covered	• Management companies and insurance companies run pension funds which are supervised by Ministry of Finance (*Dirección General de Seguros y Planes de Pensiones*) and supervisory commission	• Management companies and insurance companies run pension funds which are supervised by Ministry of Finance

(Continued)

Table A11 (Continued)

	1st pillar	2nd pillar	3rd pillar
	by Social Security administered by mutual funds depending on different ministries	(Comisión de Control) with representatives of promoter, participants and beneficiaries; pension funds are not subject to any restrictions in equities or foreign investments; at least 75% of assets have to be invested in financial securities dealt on regulated market, banking deposits, credits with mortgage guarantees and properties	(Dirección General de Seguros y Planes de Pensiones) and Ombudsman (Defensor del Partícipe) appointed by promoter; pension funds are not subject to any restrictions in equities or foreign investments; at least 75% of assets have to be invested in financial securities dealt on regulated market, banking deposits, credits with mortgage guarantees and properties
Benefits	• Contributory and non-contributory benefits; as of 2004 retirement age 65; reference period 180 months previous to retirement; accrual rates: 50% for the first 15 years; 3% per year between 16th and 25th year; 2.5% from 26th to 35th year; 35 years = 100% of regulatory base; no bonus for additional contribution years if retiring at 65; supplements (complemento de mínimos) if benefits are below minimum pension established by government; yearly pension benefit adjustment to inflation	• Annuities or lump-sum for retirement, total or permanent disability and death of beneficiary; benefits must be included in the beneficiaries' taxable base as regular salary income (40% tax free if received as lump-sum)	• Annuities or lump-sum for retirement, total or permanent disability and death of beneficiary; benefits must be included in the beneficiaries' taxable base as regular salary income (40% tax free if received as lump-sum)
Benefit example	* Pension regulatory base: €1,200; 35 contribution years (=100% of regulatory base); retirement at 65; pension amount = €1,200 * pension regulatory base: €1,200; 40 contribution years (=100% of regulatory base); penalty for retiring at 63 (100%–12%=88%); pension amount = €1,056 *pension regulatory base: €1,200; 20 contribution years (= 65% of regulatory base); penalty for retiring at 64 (65%–8% = 57%); pension amount = €684		

Table A12 Current pension system in Austria

	1st pillar	2nd pillar	3rd pillar
Coverage	• Entire working population • private sector: 3.2 million active insured persons and 2 million pensioners in 2004 • tax-financed system for public sector • voluntary insurance after termination of employment with compulsory insurance possible	• No mandatory occupational pension	• No mandatory private pension
Financing	• PAYG financing • government subsidies; deficit coverage guarantee • total contribution rate for employees 18.5% of gross wage (split equally between employer and employee, plus contribution to an equalization fund of 4.3% (3.3% from the employer and 1% from the employee); contribution rate for self-employed 15%, professionals 20% and farmers 14.25% • upper contribution limit in 2005: €3,630 for employees; €4,235 for self-employed and farmers • government tax transfers from tax payments by self-employed to double the contribution payments for self-employed and farmers	• Capital funded	• Capital funded
Administration	• 6 self-governing pension funds • legal basis: ASVG, GSVG, BSVG • peak association represents common interests of all social insurance schemes • monitoring through the ministry of social security • funds are headed by pension boards consisting of representatives of employers and employees i.e. in the blue- and white-collar pension fund 1/3 of board's members are representatives of the employer and 2/3 of the employees	• Private organizations	• Private organizations
Benefits	Retirement age for men 65; for women 60 (65 from 2033 onwards (transition period starting in 2024)): • minimum qualifying period for standard old age retirement 180 months of contributions, or 300 months of insurance including child credits or military service	• No general rules; dependent on individual scheme	• No general rules; dependent on individual scheme

(Continued)

Table A12 (Continued)

	1st pillar	2nd pillar	3rd pillar
	• early retirement abolished since 1 July 2004 but transition period until 2014 at an age of 61.5 for men and 56.5 for women with a minimum of 420 months of insurance; reduction of benefits of 4.2% per year of early retirement • 18 months of child-rearing benefits and 48 months of periods of exemption for child-rearing • other periods of for which contributions credited: periods of sickness benefits, unemployment benefits, maternity leave, military or civilian service • reference period for the assessment base for persons born before 1955 increases from 15 years in 2004 to 40 years in 2028 • accrual rate 2% per 12 months; will be reduced to 1.78% by 2009 • pension indexation used to be net-wage and price-index adjusted; will be transformed to price-indexing only by 2009 • compensation supplement for persons with net income below €662.99 (singles) or €1,303.23 (couples) • pensions are subject to income tax and health insurance contributions		
Benefit example	Benefits = accrual rate * years of insurance * assessment base (best 40 yrs) accrual rate 1.78% retirement at 65 40 years of insurance 1.78% * 40 yrs * average wage = 71.2% of average wage		

Table A13 Current pension system in Portugal

	1st pillar	2nd pillar	3rd pillar
Coverage	• Entire workforce	• Voluntary occupational private pension plans, which in 2002 covered c. 175,000 workers	• Voluntary individual private pension plans, which in 2002 covered c. 107,000 citizens
Financing	• PAYG system • Social Security is contribution financed with a unified total rate of 34.75% in 2004 (employees' rate 11%; employers' rate 23.75%) (special contribution rates for specific professional groups) • contribution rate for self-employed was 25.4% in 2004 • reserve fund: *Fundo de Estabilizaçao Financeira da Segurança Social* (FEFSS) established through contribution surpluses • special reserve fund for CGA pension outlays: INDEP; government subsidies • non-contributory benefits: since 1998 financed from general taxes • additional source of financing: revenues from 1% VAT increase	• Privately funded defined benefit or defined contribution pensions (almost all pension plans provide defined-benefit pensions): firms can tax-deduct contributions with the limit of 15% of total wage outlays	• Savings plans for retirement (*Planes Poupança-Reforma*) and closed pension plans providing defined contribution pensions; invested amount in a savings plan for retirement deductible from the personal income taxable base with the limit of 20% of total income
Administration	• Ministry responsible for Social Security: *Ministerio da Segurança Social e do Trabalho* (until September 2004) • pensions are administered by the *Centro Nacional de Pensões* depending on the ministry • general contributory scheme: *Regime Geral* • non-contributory scheme organized in the *Regime não contributivo e equiparado* (RNCE) • public sector workers: organized in the *Caixa Geral de Aposentações* (CGA)	• Fund managers and insurance companies under the supervision of the *Instituto de Seguros de Portugal*	• Fund managers and insurance companies under the supervision of the *Instituto de Seguros de Portugal*

(Continued)

Table A13 (Continued)

	1st pillar	2nd pillar	3rd pillar
Benefits	• Standard retirement age 65 years (flexible retirement between 55 and 70) • minimum qualifying period: 15 contribution years with at least 120 contribution days per year • qualifying period for full pension: 40 years • early retirement possible with at least 30 contribution years and a minimum age of 55; benefit reduction for early retirement of 4.5% of the benefits per year of early retirement; if more than 30 contribution years, every three extra years neutralize one year of benefit reduction in early retirement • late retirement between 65 and 70 with at least 40 contribution years increases accrual rate by 10% per year • accrual rate 2% per contribution year if 20 or fewer contribution years; if 21 or more contribution years accrual rates between 2.3% and 2% depending on the reference wage • reference wage/assessment base: sum of wages for which contributions have been paid during the whole contributory career divided by the number of payments (14 per year) • benefit calculation: accrual rate * number of contribution years * assessment base • pension indexation is discretionary • pension benefits are tax-free up to a certain limit • civil servants employed before 1993: minimum qualifying period 5 years, retirement age 60; civil servants employed after 1993: same regulations as private sector	• Annuities for retirement, disability and death of beneficiary; benefits must be included in the beneficiaries' taxable base as regular salary income	• Annuities for retirement, disability and death of beneficiary; benefits must be included in the beneficiaries' taxable base as regular salary income
Benefit example	Pension regulatory base: €1,000; 42 contribution years (= 80% of regulatory base); retirement at 65; pension amount = €800 * pension regulatory base: €1,000; 40 contribution years (= 80% of regulatory base); no penalty for retiring at 62 because more than 9 contribution years above 30; pension amount = €800 pension regulatory base: €1,000; 20 contribution years (=40% of regulatory base); penalty for retiring at 64 (40%–4,5% = 35,5%); pension amount = €355		

Table A14 Current pension system in Germany

	1st pillar	2nd pillar	3rd pillar
Coverage	• In GRV: all private sector employees, certain groups of self-employed including persons with minor employment and quasi-self-employed • coverage of GRV: 82% of the employed population • separate system for farmers (*Altershilfe für Landwirte*) • liberal professions are compulsorily covered through occupational provision institutes (*berufsständische Versorgungswerke*) • separate system for civil servants and judges (*Beamtenversorgung*)	• No mandatory occupational pension • coverage of voluntary occupational pension: 54% of private sector employees in 2003	• No mandatory private pension • coverage of voluntary subsidized *Riester-Rente* approximately 9% of eligible persons in 2002
Financing	• PAYG principle • contingency reserve (*Nachhaltigkeitsrücklage*) of between a minimum of 0.2 and a maximum of 1.7 of monthly expenditure • contribution financed: 19.5% up to contribution limit of €5,200 (*Alte Bundesländer*) and €4,400 (*Neue Bundesländer*) per month in 2005; equally shared between employer and employee • tax-financed governmental subsidies to cover non-contributory benefits; supplementary subsidy financed through one percentage point of VAT and revenues of eco-tax • civil servants' pensions are tax-financed • pension of liberal professions are mainly capital-funded and contribution financed	• Dependent on individual scheme but usually capital funded. • types of capital investment: • pensions as a source of company financing in terms of reserves (*Rückstellungen*) • pension funds (*Pensionsfonds*) • protection against insolvency of employers: Pension Safeguard Association (*Pensions-Sicherungs-Verein* (PSVaG)). Types of occupational pensions • *Direktzusage* • *Unterstützungskasse* • *Pensionskasse* • *Pensionsfond* • *Direktversicherung*	
Administration	Until 2005 the GRV has been divided into: • 23 regional insurance funds (LVAs) for blue-collar workers • Federal Insurance Fund for Salaried Employees (BfA) • Federal Insurance Fund for Miners → umbrella organization: VDR With effect of 1 October 2005: • BfA and VDR merge into the new *Deutsche Rentenversicherung Bund* • number of LVAs will be reduced through mergers		• Private insurances, banks and other financial actors monitored by the Federal Institute for Financial Services Supervision (BAFin)

(Continued)

Table A14 (Continued)

	1st pillar	2nd pillar	3rd pillar
Benefits	• Standard retirement age: 65 years • minimum qualifying period: 5 years • periods that count as qualifying periods: times of contributions, non-contribution periods (3 years of child raising), *Berücksichtigungszeiten* (e.g. caring for elderly or disabled) and *Anrechnungszeiten* (e.g. periods of illness, unemployment, maternity leave) • contributions paid convert into personal earning points: average income of all insured earns one *Entgeltpunkt* per year • calculation formula: total of *Entgeltpunkte* multiplied by pension type factor (*Rentenartfaktor*; i.e. 1 for old age pension and 0.6 for widow/widower's pension), by the pension accrual factor (*Zugangsfaktor* i.e. 1 reduced by 0.003 per month prior to standard retirement age or increased by 0.005 per month of deferred retirement beyond 65 years) and by the current pension value (*Rentenwert*; €26.13 (West)/€22.97 (East) in 2005) • pension indexation with wage increase of contribution-paying work force reduced by changes of the ratio pensioners/contribution-paying workforce	• Dependent on individual scheme	• Dependent on individual scheme • *Riester-Rente*: gender-neutral benefits
Benefit example	Pensioner (in *Alte Länder*) with 45 years of contribution retiring at 65 years with average wage income through his working career benefits = *Entgeltpunkte* * *Rentenartfaktor* * *Zugangsfaktor* * *Rentenwert* = 45 * 1 * 1 * €26.13 = €1,175.85		

Table A15 Current pension system in the Netherlands

	1st pillar	2nd pillar	3rd pillar
Coverage	• all Dutch residents accrue AOW pension rights for each year they live in the Netherlands between the age of 15 and 65. 50 years is required for a full pension	• More than 90% of wage earners are covered by an occupational pension scheme • supplementary pensions are quasi-mandatory; the law on Mandatory Participation in Sectoral Pension Funds (*Wet betreffende de verplichte deelneming in een bedrijfspensioenfonds, Bpf*) permits the Ministry of Social Affairs to grant requests to require an entire sector to participate in the same pension fund • 829 different pension funds in 2005 (industry-wide pension schemes, company pension schemes, and pension funds for the self-employed) most workers also have access to various provisions for early retirement.	• 10% of pension income comes from the third pillar.
Financing	• The AOW is financed by wage-earner contributions (17.9% of income in 2005 up to a ceiling of €30,357) • PAYG financing with government grant to cover deficits since the late 1990s there is an upper limit on contributions (18.25%) and financing shortfalls are financed from general revenues • the recently established AOW Reserve Fund will help to finance benefits starting in 2020 out of its forecast €126 billion reserves. Reserves are financed by annual government deposits	• Occupational pension contributions are set in collective wage bargaining negotiations, and are typically shared between employers and wage-earners with employers usually paying a higher share • in 1998, employers paid 6.7% of their wage bill into second pillar schemes, while employees paid 2.3% of their wages • Occupational pension contributions are paid only on the salary above the level of the AOW.	• eligible contributions are tax deductible

(Continued)

Table A15 (*Continued*)

	1st pillar	2nd pillar	3rd pillar
Administration	• The Social Insurance Bank (SVB) administers the AOW.	• Occupational pensions are regulated by the Pension Savings Act (*Pensioen en Sparfondsen Wet (PSF)*) • until 2004, the Pension and Insurance Authority (PVK, *Pensioen en Verzekeringskamer*) was the supervisory body charged with oversight • in 2004 the PVK merged with the Dutch Central Bank and is now called the Pension Chamber (*Pensioenkamer*) • details of pension plans are negotiated in collective agreements (CAOs) • the PSW regulates issues such as the coverage ratio of pension funds, measures to correct deficits, investment rules, pension portability, and representation on administrative boards, etc. The PSW requires that funds be held outside of pension schemes and may not be considered company assets	
Benefits	• 50 years of residence are required for a full pension. • in 2005, the net benefit for a single person was 70% of the net minimum wage, or €866.63 per month including vacation supplements (gross is €930.17 plus €46.20 vacation payment). This is about 55% of average wages • for married pensioners the net pension is 50% of the net minimum wage, or €608.03 including vacation payment (gross is €631.81 plus €30.53 vacation payment) for each spouse	• Pension schemes are overwhelmingly defined benefit (DB), and until recently most schemes used a final salary benefit formula in which a benefit equal to 70% of the final wage (including the AOW) could be accumulated over 35 (or more) years, with a limit of 100% of the final wage • in 1998, 66.5% of active participants participated in final pay schemes; by 2005 the number had fallen to 10.5% (DNB 2005). More than 90% are	• most third-pillar pensions are individual life insurance policies.

- the pension amount is indexed to "net minimum wages." The Indexing Conditions Suspension Act (WKA) permits Parliament to suspend indexation if the ratio of inactive to active persons of employable age is below 82.6:100. Since 1996 the AOW has been fully indexed

- still covered by DB schemes
- the majority of pensioners do not achieve the target of 70% of the final wage including the AOW, because supplementary pension benefits are tightly linked with AOW benefits and many wage earners do not work the number of years required for a full pension (usually 35 or 40)
- the indexation of accrued rights and benefits is not legally required, and the various schemes use different rules. Until recently most pensions were indexed to wages, but most pension funds to cancel indexation in 2002 and 2003 in the wake of heavy stock market losses. More than 80% of schemes have indexing conditional on pension fund performance, and if indexing is awarded, about 60% use some form of contract wages (sectoral or economy-wide) and about 20% inflation, and 20% some other formula (DNB 2005)

Benefit example: See above; 2% deducted for each year not resident in the Netherlands between the ages of 16 and 64

Most schemes are defined benefit; AOW + occupational pension = 70% of final salary. Recently many funds have switched to 70% of average career earnings.

Table A16 Current pension system in Ireland

	1st pillar	2nd pillar	3rd pillar
Coverage	Social Welfare Pensions: • entire workforce between 16 and 66 years with incomes above €38 per week (January 2005) • voluntary coverage as continuation to prior employment is possible	• No mandatory occupational pensions • voluntary coverage approximately 38.1% of persons in employment aged 20 to 69 (CSO 2002: 1) • members of occupational pension schemes in 2002 709,332 (Pensions Board 2003: 21)	• Private pension coverage, is expected to increase within the next years because of the establishment of Private Retirement Saving Accounts (PRSA) aimed at the target coverage rate of 70% for the population 30 years or older
Financing	• PAYG principle • contribution financed (Pay-Related Social Insurance (PRSI)) • contribution rate according to the insurance class on a weekly basis. Employees with weekly earnings > €38 belong to Class A. Employers of Class A employees paid in 2005 8.5% up to €356 and a rate of 10.75% for all income above employees with income < €287 per week are exempt from the contribution payment; with earnings above €287 pay 4% of all weekly income above €127; with earnings above €400 2% for the first €127 and 6% for earnings above self-employed in Class S: 3% of income up to €400 and 5% for income above • National Reserve Fund Act 2000 accumulates reserves of 1% of GDP per year between 2001 and 2055 to be used to reduce pension costs from 2025 onwards	• Predominantly funded systems except for the public sector supplementary pension scheme • minimum financing standards as fixed in Pensions Act 1990 and its Amendments: 100% funding of present liabilities in case of winding-up a pension scheme maximum of reserves: 105% of liabilities (possibilities if reserves are higher: return of excess amount to the employer or "contribution holidays" i.e. contribution payments are suspended for a time period until the reserves and liabilities match again	• Funded systems

Administration	• Responsibility of the Department of Social and Family Affairs (Pension Services Office in Sligo) • no separate agency for the state pension insurance, but all social security contributions are paid to the Social Insurance Fund • revenue Commissioners collect PRSI on behalf of the Department of Social, Community and Family Affairs	• Providers: financial companies, insurances or employers • monitoring by the Pensions Board • certification and registration of schemes by the Pensions Board if funding standards are fulfilled • Pensions Board consists of 16 members appointed by the Minister for Social, Community and Family Affairs including representatives of trade unions, the employers, the pension industry, trustees and the Departments of Finances and Social Affairs for five-year terms	• Providers: financial companies, insurances or employers
Benefits	• Types of state pensions: Contributory Old Age Pension, Retirement Pensions and Non-Contributory Old Age Pensions • contributory Old Age Pension and Retirement Pensions Social Welfare Pension: flat-rate pension benefits linked to employment • Non-Contributory Old Age Pensions: means-tested and paid under social assistance • entitlement criteria: Contributory Old Age Pension: retirement age 66 years; requiring entrance to insurance at an age younger than 56 years Retirement Pension: retirement age of 65 years with insurance entrance younger than 55, a minimum of 260[a] (5 years) weeks of contribution payments and no further earnings for one year (retirement condition) • definition of contribution year: average of 48 weeks of full rate contributions per year over her entire working career • credited periods of unemployment, sickness and maternity leave • periods for up to 12 years of child rearing are disregarded in calculating the yearly average (since April 1995)	• Benefits depend on scheme • retirement age: between 60 and 70 years; usually 65 years • contribution rates are fixed individually for each scheme in the contract between employee and employer • usually provision of a lump-sum payment to survivors in case of pre-retirement death vesting period: two years • defined-benefit schemes: most common formula is 40/60ths. Benefits are often integrated into the Irish Social Welfare pension i.e. the occupational scheme promises a certain percentage of the employee's income but the estimated amount is reduced by the amount received through Social Welfare pension. • benefits in defined-contribution or money purchase schemes depend on the contributions paid and the rate of return that was achieved through investment	• Individual benefits in terms of Pay-Related Savings Accounts • minimum retirement age 60 years (flexible) • at the time of retirement the retiree may take out 25% of the personal fund as a tax-free lump sum, which can be invested in an Approved Minimum Retirement Fund or Approved Retirement Fund. • heritage of remaining assets to descendants in case of death

(Continued)

Table A16 (Continued)

	1st pillar	2nd pillar	3rd pillar
Benefit example	• Retirement and Contributory Old Age Pension benefit rate in 2005: €179.30 per week • minimum for Contributory Old Age Pension with a yearly average of 10 contribution weeks was €89.70 • supplements for dependents e.g. €119.50 per adult younger than 65 years or €19.30 per child • non-contributory Old Age Pensions amounted to €166.00 with social assistance free schemes on top		

[a] The minimum qualifying condition for Retirement Pension is currently in transition. Before 2002, 156 weeks were required, between 2002 and 2012, 260 weeks are necessary and thereafter 520 weeks of compulsory insurance periods qualify for Retirement Pension (Department of Social and Family Affairs 2002a).

Table A17 Current pension system in Luxembourg

	1st pillar	2nd pillar	3rd pillar
Coverage	• Entire working population, except for self-employed with an income of less than 1/3 of minimum social wage and dependent employment of three months or less per year • private sector: 278,237 active insured persons and 115,326 pensions in payment in 2003 • public sector: 23,443 covered employees and civil servants in 2003 • voluntary insurance possible: l'assurance continuée and l'assurance complémentaire; l'assurance facultative or forfait de rachat (IGSS 2002a: 25).	• No mandatory occupational pension	• No mandatory private pension
Financing	Private sector: • PAYG financing with 7-year reserve periods (système de la répartition des charges par périodes de couverture) • total contribution rate 24% of gross wage (employer, employee and the state 8% each) • self-employed pay contributions of 16% of their income • lower contribution limit: income below 1/3 of minimum social wage is exempt from contribution payments • upper contribution limit in 2005: €7,333.85 (=5 times minimum social wage) (MSS 2005) • voluntarily insured may chose between four different reference bases for their contribution payments: social minimum wage, twice social minimum wage, personal maximum wage (average out of 5 best years), or anything between social minimum wage and personal maximum wage (CCSS 2003) • capital reserves: de jure 1.5 to 2.5 times yearly expenditure (de facto reserves 3 times yearly expenditure)	• Three types of financing: Book reserves, Insurance funds or Pension funds • protection of entitlements in case of insolvency of an employer through membership of funds in the German Pension Safeguard Association (PSVaG)	• Capital funded

(Continued)

Table A17 (Continued)

	1st pillar	2nd pillar	3rd pillar
Administration	Public sector: • until 1996 *péréquation* i.e. reimbursement of 3% of civil servants' income to secure the financing of salary and pension adjustments in public sector • since 1999: same rules for new civil servants as for private sector, but no upper contribution limit • Pension funds: AVI, CPEP, CPACI, CPA and *régimes spéciaux* • central agency: *Centre Commun de la Sécurité Sociale* (CCSS) • monitoring through the ministry of social security and its IGSS • funds are controlled by pension boards (*comité-directeur*) consisting of an equal number of representatives of employers and employees	• Two types of funds: corporate structure (SEPCAV) or partnership structure (ASSEP) • registration of occupational funds and monitoring through *Commission de Surveillance du Secteur Financier* (CSSF)	• Private organizations
Benefits	• Minimum qualifying period (*stages*) for standard retirement at age 65: 120 months of effective insurance • qualifying period for early retirement at 60 (*pension de vieillesse anticipée*): 480 months, i.e. 40 years, of effective, assimilated or voluntary insurance periods whereof at least ten years have to be covered by effective or voluntary insurance • qualifying period for early retirement at 57: 480 months of exclusively effective insurance periods • qualifying period is the sum of all months of insurance. If the insured registered professional activity below the		

minimum limit of working hours these working hours are transferred to the following month. For any two months "combined" working hours above 64, one month of effective insurance is credited to the person's pension insurance account (C.A.S. III Art. 175).

- state contribution payments for baby-years i.e. 24 months of child rearing

benefit calculation (4 parts)

- formula for *majoration forfaitaire*:

$$= \frac{\text{number of years of insurance}}{40} \bullet 0.235 \bullet \text{minimum social wage}$$

note: the number of years of insurance may not be greater than 40!
Minimum social wage in 2003: €344.75 per months (MSS 2005)

- formula for *majoration proportionelle*

$$= \frac{(0.0185 + \text{maj.prop.echelonnees}) \bullet \text{total income of entire working career}}{12}$$

- formula for *majorations proportionnelles échélonnés*:
= age + number of years of insurance − 93
- end of year bonus: maximum yearly bonus in 2005: €564 (MSS 2005).

$$= \frac{\text{no. of years of insurance}}{40} \bullet \frac{€564}{12}$$

- indexation: entitlements and pension benefits are adjusted to inflation (*adaption au coût de la vie*) indexed on basis year 1984 i.e. 620.75 in 2004. Additionally, every two years governmental review of wage development and subsequent adjustment (*ajustement au niveau de vie*): coeffient of 01.01.2004: 1.301 (www.avi.lu Access on 13.07.2004).

(Continued)

Table A17 (Continued)

	1st pillar	2nd pillar	3rd pillar
	• minimum pension after 40 years of insurance: 90% of reference wage (€2,085) per year = €1,876.50 indexed with factor 620.75 and adjusted with 1.301 → €1,262.88 per month (in 2004); with a minimum of 20 years of insurance the minimum pension is reduced by 1/40 per absent/missing insurance year (www.avi.lu Access on 13.07.2004).		
Benefit example [a]	Fictional biography: • male industrial worker; personal working career age 19 to 58 • months of insurance: 480 • average monthly industrial wage for men in 2003:[b] €4,310 • indexed and adjusted to basis year 1984 (adjustment rate 1.301; index 620.75): €533.68 • total income during working life: = €533.68 * 480 = €266,167.77 *Majorations forfaitaires:* reference amount €2,085; accrual rate: 23.5% = (40/40) * 0.235 * €2,085 = €489.98 per year → €40.83 per month *Majorations proportionnelles échelonnées:* = (age (>55) + years of insurance (>38) − 93) * 0.0001 = (58 + 40 − 93) * 0.0001 = 5 * 0.0001 = 0.0005		

Majorations proportionnelles:
accrual rate: 1.85% + *Majorations proportionnelles échelonnées*
= accrual rate ∗ total working career income
= (0.0185 + 0.0005) ∗ €266,167.77 = 5,057.19 per year
→ 421.43 per month
indexed and adjusted (adjustment rate 1.301; index 620.75):
€3,403.45
Allocation de fin d'année:
= (40/40) ∗ €564 per year
→ €47 per month
total pension benefit: €40.83 + €3,403.45 + €47 = €3,491.28

[a] For more examples see also www.avi.lu; Access on 13.07.2004.
[b] www.statistiques.public.lu/stat/tableviewer/document.aspx?FileId=525; Access on 11.05.2005.

Index

1990 Pension Committee [Finland] 273
3F 462, 492
ABI [Italy] 450, 451
ABI [UK] 58, 87
ABP 728, 731747, 748, 752
ABVV 311, 312, 319, 322, 325, 326, 330, 331, 341
AC 464, 492
ACA 80, 87, 93
Aciéries Réunies de Burbach–Eich–Dudelange. See ARBED.
ACLVB 341
ACOSS 169, 194
ACV 311, 312, 319, 322, 325, 326, 331, 341
ACW 325, 326, 341
Adenauer, Konrad 671
ADR 36, 804, 805, 809, 812, 814, 815, 820, 823, 832–840, 843, 845–849, 851
Ældresagen 464
Agalev 304, 308, 341
Agence centrale des organismes de la sécurité sociale. See ACOSS.
AGIRC 167, 168, 171, 194
AHV/AVS 212, 219, 220, 221, 223, 224, 225, 226, 227, 228, 230, 233, 234, 235, 237, 239, 240, 241, 242, 243, 246
AK 565, 597
Akademikernes centralorganisation. See AC.
AKAVA 263, 282, 285, 291
Aktionskomitee 5/6–Pensioun 832
Aktiounskomitee fir Demokratie a Rentegerechtegkeet. See ADR.
ALEBA 815, 831, 845, 851
Algemeen Belgisch Vakverbond. See ABVV.
Algemeen Burgerlijk Pensioenfonds. See ABP.
Algemeen Christelijk Vakverbond. See ACV.

Algemeen Christelijke Werkersbond. See ACW
Algemeen Ouderen Verbond. See AOV.
Algemene Centrale der Liberale Vakbonden van België. See ACLVB.
Algemene Ouderdomswet. See AOW.
Algemene Spaar–en Lijfrentekas. See ASLK.
Alleanza Nazionale. See AN.
Allgemeines Sozialversicherungsgesetz. See ASVG.
Allmänna tilläggspensionssystem. See ATP.
Almunia, Joaquín 527
Alonso, Javier 528, 540, 553
Alters–und Hinterlassenenversicherung/ Assurance Vieillesse et Survivants. See AHV/AVS.
Alterseinkünftegesetz 678, 695
Altersvermögensergänzungsgesetz. See AvmEG.
Altersvermögensgesetz. See AvmG.
Amato reform 29, 30, 422, 427, 428, 431–434, 440, 446
Amato, Giuliano 412, 431–434, 437, 440, 446, 447, 449
AN 409, 412, 413, 428, 435, 450
Anders gaan leven. See Agalev.
Anderson, Karen M. 13, 28, 29
Andeweg, Rudy B. 720, 754
Andreatta, Beniamino 422
ANIA 450, 451
Anti–Revolutionaire Partij. See ARP.
AOV 722, 740, 741, 753
AOW 713, 714, 723, 725–727, 729–736, 738–745, 748–752, 754
APESS 815, 837, 845
APEX 87
ARBED 806, 845

Arbejdsmarkedets Tillaegspension. See ATP.
ARP 719, 720, 753
ARRCO 168–172, 194, 196
ASLK 341
Asociación de Instituciones de Inversión Colectiva y Fondos de Pensiones. See INVERCO.
Assemblée Nationale 152–164
ASSEP 818, 845, 850
Association d'épargne–pension. See ASSEP.
Association des Professeurs de l'Enseignement secondaire et supérieur du Grand–Duché de Luxembourg a.s.b.l. See APESS.
Association des régimes de retraite complémentaire. See ARRCO.
Association générale des institutions de retraite des cadres. See AGIRC.
Association luxembourgeoise des employés de banque et assurance. See ALEBA.
Association of British Insurers. See ABI.
Association of Consulting Actuaries. See ACA.
Association of Professional, Executive, Clerical and Computer Staffs [UK]. See APEX.
Associazione Bancaria Italiana. See ABI.
Associazione Nazionale fra le Imprese Assicuratrici. See ANIA.
ASVG 567–569, 571, 573, 576–579, 581, 585, 586, 593, 596, 597, 599, 602, 603
ASVG Novelle 571, 574–580
ATP [Denmark] 465–470, 472–474, 476, 480, 484–493
ATP [Sweden] 361, 362, 364, 365, 367, 368, 370, 372, 373, 375–377, 379–381, 385, 386, 388–391, 393
Austria 31–33, 39, 41, 44, 555 ff.
  Austrian People's Party 555, 556, 561–564, 574, 597
  Austrian Social–Democratic Party 32, 555, 556, 561–566, 570, 572, 574–592, 594–599, 604
  corporatism 556, 557, 565, 566, 581, 602
  electoral system 560, 561

  employers' organizations 565, 566, 592
  Freedom Party of Austria 556, 557, 562–566, 570, 573–578, 580, 583–585, 587–599, 601
  Green Alternative 562, 563, 565, 580, 590, 592, 597
  Liberal Forum 562, 565, 579, 580, 586, 597
  occupational pensions 567, 568, 588
  parliament 557–563; role in pension politics 594, 595
  party system 556, 562, 563
  pension reform 1984: *40. ASVG Novelle*, 574–576
  pension reform 1987: *44. ASVG Novelle*, 576, 577
  pension reform 1993: *51. ASVG Novelle*, 578–580
  pension reform 1997: *ASRÄG* and *1. Budgetbegleitgesetz* 584–587
  pension reform 2000: *Sozialrechts–Änderungsgesetz* (SRÄG), 587–589
  pension reform 2003: *Budgetbegleitgesetz*, 590–593
  pension reform 2005: *Pensionsharmonisierungsgesetz* 593
  pension reforms 1995 and 1996: *Strukturanpassungsgesetze* 580–583
  pension system 566–570, 889–890; history 566, 567
  political institutions 557–563
  political system, 556–566
  politics of pension reform 1980 to present 570–593
  private pensions 567, 568
  unions 565, 566; membership 565, 566, 579; role in pension politics 595, 596
  veto players 562, 564, 594
  veto points 558, 559, 562, 564, 589, 594
AVmEG 677, 691, 692, 702
AVmG 691–693, 702, 705,
Aznar, José María 512, 538, 540, 541, 543, 544, 546, 551, 552

BaFin 673, 702
Bagão Félix, António 633, 634, 648, 649
Balladur reform 151, 173, 174, 177–183, 190, 192, 193
Balladur, Édouard 26, 163, 177–183, 190, 192, 193
base amount [Sweden] 364–366, 368, 371, 391
basic pension reform (10th AHV/AVS revision) 223, 224, 230, 233, 235, 237, 242
Bauern–Sozialversicherungsgesetz. See BSVG.
BB 341
BBA 59, 87, 88
BDA 670, 688, 702
BDG 573, 593, 597
BDI 670, 702
Beamten–Dienstrechtsgesetz. See BDG.
Beck, Kurt 692
Belgium 5, 15, 20, 28, 297 ff.
  1996 pension reform 332–338
  Attempts at comprehensive reform 329–332
  Christian Democratic Party (PSC) 303, 304, 306–308, 322, 323, 325, 327, 341, 342
  Christian Democratic Party/Christian Democratic and Flemish Party (CVP/CdenV) 303, 304, 306–308, 322, 325–327, 332, 341
  electoral system 303–309
  employers' organizations 309
  Flemish Green Party (Agalev) 304, 308, 341
  flexible pension age and repackaging early retirement 1990 327–329
  Liberal Reform Party (Walloon Liberals, PRL) 305, 307, 322, 325, 342
  Mainil reform of 1984 323–325
  occupational pensions 319, 340
  parliament 28, 300–310; role in pension politics 339–340
  Party for Freedom and Progress/Flemish Liberals and Democrats (PVV/VLD) 303, 304, 308, 322, 324, 325, 326, 327, 332, 342

  party system 299, 304, 305, 336
  pension system 312–317, 874–875; history 312–314
  political institutions of 300–309
  political system 298–312
  politics of pension reform since 1980 317–338
  private pensions 331
  reform of early retirement 1982 323
  Socialist Party (PS) 303, 304, 305, 307, 308, 327, 342
  Socialist Party (SP) 303–305, 307, 308, 329, 330, 332, 342
  St. Anna plan 1986 318
  unions 311–312; membership 312, 334; role in pension politics 340
  veto players 297, 299, 300, 307, 308, 339
  veto points 297, 299, 300, 307, 308
Béregovoy, Pierre 180
Berg, Benny 828–830, 852
Bergman, Torbjörn 353
Berlusconi reform 428, 434–436
Berlusconi, Silvio 29, 407, 412, 413, 415, 428, 429, 434–436, 438, 443, 447, 451
Berlusconi–Tremonti reform 443–445
BfA 672–676, 695, 702, 703, 707
Biedenkopf, Kurt 680, 707
Binswanger, Peter 230
Blair
Blair, Tony 25, 50, 55, 57, 78, 79, 84, 89, 93
blame avoidance 11–13, 253, 288, 423
Bloque Nacionalista Galego. See BNG.
Blüm Commission [Germany] 677, 683, 684
Blüm, Norbert 681, 682, 684
BMA 87
BMSG 591, 597–599
BNG 509, 547
BOCG 547, 551, 552
BOE 508, 547, 552
Boerenbond. See BB.
Boletín Oficial de las Cortes Generales. See BOCG.
Boletín Oficial del Estado. See BOE.
Bonoli, Giuliano 10, 26, 71

Botschaft/Message 210, 212, 228
Boulin law 167
Bozec, Géraldine 164, 168, 179, 181, 184, 187, 197
Bridgen, Paul 9
Brinkman, Elco 740
British Bankers' Association. *See* BBA.
British Medical Association. *See* BMA.
Brooks, Sarah 9, 38, 40
BSV/OFAS 243
BSVG 567, 568, 573, 586, 593, 597
Budgetbegleitgesetz 573, 574, 584, 586, 587, 590, 600
Buffer funds [Sweden] 18
Bundesamt für Sozialversicherung/Office federal des assurances sociales. *See* BSV/OFAS
Bundesanstalt für Finanzdienstleistungsaufsicht. *See* BaFin.
Bundesgesetz über die berufliche Alters–, Hinterlassenen–und Invalidenvorsorge/ Loi fédérale sur la prévoyance professionnelle. *See* BVG/LPP.
Bundesministerium für soziale Sicherheit und Generationen. *See* BMSG.
Bundesrat [Germany] 7, 33
Bundesrat [Switzerland] 207, 210
Bundesverband der Deutschen Industrie. *See* BDI.
Bundesvereinigung der Deutschen Arbeitgeberverbände. *See* BDA.
Bundesverfassungsgericht. *See* BverfG.
Bundesversicherungsanstalt für Angestellte. *See* BfA.
Bureau de liaison des organisations de retraités 164
BVerfG 664, 665, 678, 695, 697, 702, 703
BVG/LPP 212, 223, 224, 225, 226, 235, 237, 240, 243, 244, 246

C 50, 55–59, 67, 70–76, 80, 84, 85, 87, 89–91
C.A.S. 817–820, 845
C.P. 815, 826, 845, 850
Caetano, Marcello 607, 624, 625
CAI 793, 797
Caisse de pension agricole. *See* CPA.
Caisse de pension des artisans, des commerçants et industriels. *See* CPACI.
Caisse de pension des employés privés. *See* CPEP.
Caisse Nationale d'Allocations Familiales. *See* CNAF.
Caisse Nationale d'Assurance Maladie des Travailleurs Salariés. *See* CNAMTS.
Caisse Nationale d'Assurance Vielleisse des Travailleurs Salariés. *See* CNAVTS.
Caisse Nationale de Prévoyance de la Fonction Publique. *See* PREFON.
Caisse Nationale de Prévoyance. *See* CNP.
Caisses Régionales d'Assurance Maladie. *See* CRAM.
Caixa Geral de Aposentações. *See* CGA.
Camera dei Deputati 29
CAP 623, 647, 653, 655
capitalism, varieties of, *See* VoC
Carey, Pat 782
Carnation Revolution [Portugal] 608, 625, 626, 633
Casa delle libertà 409, 410
Castellino Commission 422
Castle, Baronesse Barbara 81
Catholic Church 35, 514, 766, 768, 788
Cavaco Silva, Aníbal 619, 621, 639, 640, 650, 655
CBI 58, 70, 73, 86, 87, 89, 91
CC 256, 278, 283, 291
CCD 408, 410, 412, 413, 428, 435, 450
CCOO 513, 525, 528, 535, 538, 541, 543, 545, 547, 550
CCP 623, 647, 653
CCSS 817, 818, 845, 851
CD 460, 463, 471, 477, 492
CDA 34, 719–722, 730, 735, 736, 738–742, 744, 745, 748–750, 753, 754
CDS–PP 617–619, 621, 629, 645–649, 653, 657
CDU [Germany] 661, 666–669, 671, 672, 676, 679–691, 693–696, 698, 699, 702–706

CDU [Italy] 408, 410, 412, 413, 428, 450
ceilings, earnings 19, 364, 377, 876
Centrale Paysanne. See C.P.
Centrale Raad voor het Bedrijfsleven. See CRB.
Centre Commun de la Sécurité Sociale. See CCSS.
Centro Cristiano Democratico. See CCD.
Centro Democrático e Social– Partido Popular. See CDS–PP.
Centro Nacional de Pensões. See CNP.
Centrum–Demokraterne. See CD.
CEOE 513, 528, 530, 535, 539, 541, 543, 547
CEPYME 514, 539, 541, 547
CES 622, 653, 655, 657
CFDT 165, 180, 183, 185, 188, 189, 193, 194
CFE–CGC 165, 180, 183, 188, 189, 194
CFTC 165, 180, 183, 188, 194
CGA 627–630, 632, 653, 658
CGIL 410, 450, 451
CGOS 173, 194
CGPME 165, 188, 194
CGT [France] 165, 174, 176, 177, 180, 182, 185, 188, 189, 194
CGT [Spain] 547, 549
CGT/CGTP–In 623, 653
CGT–FO 165, 188, 189, 194
Chambre des Députés. See ChD [Luxembourg].
ChD [Luxembourg] 807, 809, 810, 824–826, 835, 841, 845, 848, 850, 851
checks–and–balances 5
Child Support, Pensions and Social Security Act 61, 67, 69, 79, 83, 91
Chirac, Jacques 159, 161–164, 174, 182, 184, 186, 187
Chrëschtlech–Sozial Vollekspartei. See CSV.
Christelijk Historische Unie. See CHU.
Christelijk Nationaal Vakverbond. See CNV.
Christelijke Volkspartij/Christen Democratische en Vlaamse Partij. See CVP/CdenV
Christen Democratisch Appèl. See CDA.
ChristenUnie. See CU.
Christlich Demokratische Union. See CDU.
Christlichdemokratische Volkspartei/Parti Démocrate–Chrétien. See CVP/PDC.
Christlichnationaler Gewerkschaftsbund/ Confédération des sysndicats Chrétiens. See CNG/CSG.
Christlich–Soziale Union. See CSU.
CHU 719, 720, 753
Chuliá, Elisa 31, 32
CII 768, 797
CIMPS 63, 87, 89
CIP 623, 648, 653, 655, 657
CISL 410, 450
CISRS 63, 87, 89
CiU 31, 509, 510, 522, 524, 534, 535, 538, 539, 547
civil servants 17, 20–22, 32, 36, 38
closed party lists 30, 613
Club van Leuven 333
CNAF 169, 171, 194
CNAMTS 169, 194
CNAVTS 168, 169, 187, 194
CNEL 414, 450
CNG/CSC 217, 231, 243
CNP [France] 173, 194
CNP [Portugal] 653
CNPF 165, 180, 194
CNSSS 647, 648, 653
CNV 722, 732, 742, 753
Coalition of the Left [Greece]. *See* SYN.
Code d'assurance sociale (Livre III: Assurance pension). See C.A.S.
COHS 61, 63, 87
Colla, Marcel 319, 332, 333, 338
COMBS 61, 63, 87
Comisiones Obreras. See CCOO.
Comissão Permanente de Concertação Social. See CPCS.
Comité de gestion des œuvres sociales. See CGOS.
Commission de la fonction publique 835
Commission de Surveillance du Secteur Financier. See CSSF.
Commission des comptes de la sécurité sociale 171
commission mixte paritaire 160

Commissione di Vigilanza sui Fondi Pensione. See COVIP.
Commissione Onofri 429, 439
Communist Party of Greece [Greece]. See KKE.
competition; electoral 10, 15, 25, 26, 28, 29, 32–34; party 37; political 3, 4, 10, 12, 24, 26, 27–38
COMPS 61, 63, 87
Conceição–Heldt, Eugénia da 26
Confederação da Indústria Portuguesa. See CIP.
Confederaçao do Comercio Português. See CCP.
Confederaçao dos Agricultores Portugueses. See CAP.
Confederação Geral dos Trabalhadores/ Confederação Geral dos Trabalhadores–Intersindical. See CGT/CGTP–In.
Confederación Española de la Pequeña y Mediana Empresa. See CEPMYE.
Confederación Española de Organizaciones Empresariales. See CEOE.
Confederación Nacional de Trabajo. See CGT.
Confederación Sindical Independiente de Funcionarios. See CSIF.
Confédération des Syndicats Chrétiens. See CSC.
Confédération française de l'encadrement – Confédération générale des cadres. See CFE–CGC.
Confédération française démocratique du travail. See CFDT.
Confédération française des travailleurs chrétiens. See CFTC.
Confédération générale du patronat des petites et moyennes entreprises. See CGPME.
Confédération générale du travail – Force ouvrière. See CGF–FO.
Confédération générale du travail. See CGT.
Confederation of British Industry. See CBI.
Confederation of Greek Workers. See GSEE.
Confederation of Irish Industry. See CII.
Confederazione Generale Italiana del Lavoro. See CGIL.
Confederazione Italiana dei Sindacati dei Lavoratori. See CISL.
Confindustria 425, 426, 428
Conseil Constitutionnel 152, 155, 162, 163
Conseil de Surveillance 171
Conseil national du patronat français. See CNPF.
Conselho Economico and Social. See CES.
Conselho Nacional de Solidariedade e Segurança Social. See CNSSS.
Conselho Permanente de Concertação Social 622
consensus democracy 4–6, 12
Conservative Party [UK]. See C.
Consiglio Nazionale dell'Economia e del Lavoro. See CNEL.
constitution(s) 3, 5–9, 24, 25, 27, 28, 31, 32
constitutional court(s) 7, 31, 32
constitutional structures 6, 8, 9
Consumers' Association of Ireland. See CAI.
Contracted–in Money Purchase Schemes. See CIMPS.
Contracted–in Salary–related Schemes. See CISRS.
Contracted–out Hybrid Schemes. See COHS.
Contracted–out mixed benefit schemes. See COMBS.
Contracted–out money–purchase Schemes. See COMPS.
Contracted–out Salary–related Schemes. See COSRS.
Contribution sociale généralisée. See CSG.
contributions 12, 18–23, 26–28, 30, 32, 36, 38 [See also individual country entries]
Contributions are tax free, returns are tax free, benefits are taxed. See EET.
Convergencia i Unió. See CiU.
corporatism 13 [See also individual country entries]
Correia de Campos, António 631, 643, 645, 654, 656, 658

Cortes Generales 502, 547, 551
COSRS 61, 63, 66, 87
Cotti, Flavio 230
coverage 2, 18, 21, 24, 27, 33–35 [*See* also individual country entries]
COVIP 420, 442, 450, 452
CPA 817, 819, 845, 847
CPACI 817, 819, 826, 845, 847
CPCS 622, 623, 647, 653
CPEP 817, 819, 825, 826, 845
CRAM 169, 194
CRB 309, 311, 341
Crewe, Ivor 84
cross–border workers [Luxembourg] 36, 805, 828, 840–843
Crouch, Colin 206, 245
Crozier, Michel 151, 164, 197
CSC 311, 312, 322, 325, 326, 341
CSG 179, 194
CSIF 547, 549
CSSF 818, 845
CSU 661, 666–669, 671, 672, 676, 677, 679, 690, 696, 698, 699, 702–706
CSV 36, 807, 811–814, 821, 823, 827, 828, 830, 832, 834–837, 839–841, 843–849, 851, 852
CU 719
CVP/CdenV 303, 304, 306–308, 322, 325–327, 332, 341
CVP/PDC 208, 213, 214, 215, 216, 232, 243, 244
Czar 27, 251

D66 719, 721, 722, 739–742, 753, 755
Dallinger, Alfred 575, 577, 598
Dansk Metal. *See* DM.
DC 405–408, 411, 412, 424–426, 431, 450
De Grave, Frank 745, 746
De Rossa, Proinsias 789
De Winter, Lieven 303, 306
Defined–benefit 18–20, 28
Defined–contribution 18–20, 23, 28, 30
Dehaene, Jean–Luc 308, 310, 326, 327, 330, 332, 333, 336
Déi Gréng Alternative. *See* GAP.

Democraten 66. *See* D66.
Democratic Left. *See* DL.
Democratic Unionist Party [UK]. *See* DUP.
Democratici di Sinistra. *See* DS.
Democratic–Social Movement [Greece]. *See* DIKKI.
Démocratie Libérale. *See* DL.
Democrazia Cristiana. *See* DC.
Democrazia e Libertà – La Margherita. *See* DL.
demographic(s) 2, 3, 8, 16, 17, 19, 21, 27, 30, 31, 33, 35
Demokratesch Partei. *See* DP.
Denmark 9, 22, 30, 454 ff.
  ATP for recipients of cash benefits 484–486
  Centre Democrats 460, 463, 471, 477, 492
  Christian People's Party 460, 461, 463, 477, 478, 486, 492
  Conservatives 457, 460–463, 472, 477, 482, 485, 488, 492
  corporatism 464
  electoral system 457, 459
  employers' organizations 468, 481, 490
  improvements to the national pension 1986 to 1990 476–479
  increased means testing of the national pension 1993 486–488
  introduction of occupational pensions 1986–1991 479–484
  introduction of the Special Pension scheme (SP) 488, 489
  Left–Socialists 460, 492
  Liberals 460–463, 472, 477, 482, 484, 485, 488, 492
  occupational pensions 454, 455, 465–472, 474–477, 479–484, 486–491
  parliament 457–462; role in pension politics 489, 490
  party system 456, 460–462
  pension system 464–470, 883–886; history 464–466
  pensioner organizations 464
  political institutions 457–461
  political system 456–464

politics of pension reform 1980 to
    present 470–489
private pensions 454, 455, 466–471,
    474–476, 482, 484, 485, 491
Social Democrats in Denmark 455–457,
    460–463, 465, 466, 471, 472, 474–482,
    485–490, 492, 493
Social Liberals 457, 460, 461, 463,
    476–481, 485, 486, 492
Socialist People's Party 460, 485, 492
tax on interest gains of funded pension
    schemes 1982 474–476
unions 462, 464, 465, 472, 474, 476, 477,
    479–484, 486, 491, 492; role in pension
    politics 490
veto players 461, 463
veto points 458, 459, 463
Department for Health and Social Services
    [UK]. See DHSS.
Department for Work and Pensions [UK].
    See DWP.
Department of Social Security [UK]. See
    DSS.
Det Radikale Venstre. See RV.
Deutsche Partei. See DP.
Deutscher Gewerkschaftsbund. See DGB.
DGB 670, 702
DHSS 70–73, 87, 91
Diamantopoulos, Anna 543
Diamantopoulos, Thanassis 105, 106, 147
Diamantouros, Nikiforos 105, 147
DIKKI 104, 106, 144
Dini reform 29, 30, 422, 428, 429, 436–441,
    444
Dini, Lamberto 412, 413, 428, 434,
    447, 449
Disaster Plan 321
discourse 3, 17, 33, 38
DL [France] 159, 161, 163, 194
DL [Ireland] 765, 767, 789, 797, 802
DL [Italy] 408, 450
DM 464, 492
Dohnal, Johanna 581
Downs, William 343
DP [Germany] 671, 702

DP [Luxembourg] 806, 811–813, 821, 823,
    828, 832, 835–840, 845–847, 852
Drees Commission [Netherlands] 732, 733
Drees, Willem 732
Dreßler, Rudolf 685
Dreyfuss, Ruth 232
DS 408, 409, 412, 413, 439, 450
DSS 61, 76, 87, 92, 96
DUP 55, 58, 87
Durão Barroso, José Manuel 619, 621, 648,
    651
DWP 61, 62, 65, 82, 87–90, 92
dynamische Rente 671

Eanes, Ramalho 610, 612, 618–621, 655
early retirement 21, 27, 32
ED 291
EDF–GDF 168, 194
EET 223, 243
Eichel, Hans 689
EK 264, 291
EL/PC 219, 223, 243
Eläketurvakeskus. See ETK.
ELA–STV 547, 549
electoral districts 6, 8, 24, 36
electoral system, electoral law 3, 5, 6, 10, 12,
    24, 25, 29–31, 33–37 [*See* also individual
    country entries]
Electricité de France– Gaz de France. See
    EDF–GDF.
Elinkeinoelämän keskusliitto. See EK.
employees 20, 22, 27, 36
EMU 25, 28, 29
equities 2, 15
ERC 509, 511, 547
*Ergänzungsleistungen/Prestations
    complémentaires. See* EL/PC
Esping–Andersen, Gøsta 11, 66, 94, 249, 266
Esquerra Republicana de Catalunya. See
    ERC.
Estado Novo 607, 623, 624
ETA 502, 547, 548
ETK 270–272, 283, 285, 291, 294
European Court of Justice 20, 317, 325,
    328, 341

European Observatory on Aging 17
European Union (EU) 16, 83, 256, 269, 352, 502, 547, 605, 758
Euskadi Ta Askatasuna. See ETA.
Evangelische Volkspartei/Parti évangélique. See EVP/PEV.
EVP/PEV 213, 243

Fælles Fagligt Forbund. See 3F.
Fagerholm, Karl–August 266
Fakiolas Committee and law 119, 130, 131, 147
Fakiolas, Rossetos 119, 130–132, 135, 140
farmers 22, 27, 32, 35, 36
Fasslabend, Werner 585
FCPT–Syprolux 835, 837, 845
FDP 661, 666–669, 671, 672, 676, 677, 680–688, 690, 692, 695, 696, 698, 702, 704, 705
FDP/PRD 208, 213, 214, 215, 218, 231, 232, 244, 245
Federal Union of Employers. *See* FUE.
federalism 5, 8, 206, 207, 563, 594, 661, 693
Federatie Nederlandse Vakbeweging. See FNV.
Fédération Chrétienne du Personnel du Transport. *See* FCPT–Syprolux.
Fédération de l'éducation nationale. See FEN.
Fédération des Employés Privés – Fédération Indépendante des Travailleurs et Cadres. *See*
Fédération des Industriels Luxembourgeois. *See* FEDIL.
Fédération française des sociétés d'assurance. See FFSA.
Fédération générale autonome des fonctionnaires. See FGAF.
Fédération Générale des Fonctionnaires Communaux. *See* FGFC.
Fédération Générale des Travailleurs de Belgique. See FGTB.
Fédération nationale des associations de retraités 164
Fédération Nationale des Cheminots, Travailleurs du Transport, Fonctionnaires et Employés Luxembourgeois. *See* FNCTTFEL.
Fédération syndicale unitaire. See FSU.
Fédération syndicaliste des facteurs luxembourgeois. *See* FSFK.
FEDIL 815, 845
FEFSS 630, 654
FEN 165, 176, 182, 194
FEP–FIT 815, 827, 831, 836, 845, 846, 851
Ferrera, Maurizio 13, 29
Ferro Rodrigues, Eduardo 619
FF 760, 763, 765–768, 770, 778, 779, 782–789, 791, 795, 796, 798
FFSA 184, 194
FG 765–769, 778, 780–783, 785–789, 792, 795, 796, 798, 802
FGAF 165, 194
FGFC 835–837, 845
FGTB 311, 312, 322, 325, 326, 341
FI 407, 409, 412, 413, 428, 435, 443, 444, 450, 451
Fianna Fáil. See FF.
Fifth Republic [France] 25, 151, 152, 157, 161, 164, 178
Fillon, François 188
Finance Act 60
Financial Services Authority [UK]. *See* FSA.
Fine Gael (former *Cumann na nGaedheals*). *See* FG.
Finland
  1992 harmonization of private and public sector pensions 280, 281
  1995 reform of national pensions 282–284
  1995 reform of the income base for calculating employment pensions 281, 282
  Center Party (Kesk) 258, 261, 291
  Communist Party of Finland (SKP) 258, 292
  corporatism 248, 264, 266
  electoral system 253–256
  employers' organizations 263, 264, 289, 290

Finland
  Finnish People's Democratic League (SKDL) 258–261, 282, 283, 292
  Finnish Rural Party (SMP) 258–261, 292
  Finnish Social Democratic Party (SDP) 248, 249, 251, 252, 258–267, 274, 275, 278, 279, 281, 283–287, 289, 290, 292
  Finnish Socialist Workers' Party (SSTP) 292
  introduction of employee contributions 1992 274–280
  Liberal Party (LKP) 252, 291
  National Progressive Party (ED) 291
  occupational pensions 268–270, 284, 289, 290, 292
  parliament 252–260; role in pension politics 288, 289
  party system 249, 252, 253, 258, 259, 260
  pension system 264–273, 869–873; history 264–267
  pensioner organizations 268, 289
  political institutions of 252–259
  political system 251–264
  politics of pension reform 1980 to present 273–287
  private pensions 250, 266, 270
  reforms of private sector pensions in 2002 and public sector pensions in 2004 284–287
  Swedish People's Party (SFP) 259–262, 274, 281, 282, 287, 292
  The Agrarian Party (ML) 249, 251, 252, 258–260, 264, 265, 291
  unions 263, 264; membership 260, 263; role in pension politics 289, 290
  veto players 261, 262
  veto points 248, 250, 254, 255, 257, 259–262, 288
flate-rate 22, 276, 469, 518, 727, 857, 859, 875, 881, 899
Flora, Peter 9
FN 159, 161, 194, 195
FNCTTFEL 815, 835, 837, 845
FNV 722, 732, 739, 741, 742, 745, 753

FOA 464, 492
Föderation der GrünenParteien der Schweiz/ Fédération Suisse des Partis Écologistes).
  See France 2, 10, 13, 15, 24–26, 39, 42–44, 150 ff.
  Balladur reform of 1993, 151, 173, 174, 177–183, 190, 192, 193
  class interests 164–166, 192, 193
  corporatism 184, 187
  electoral system 157, 158, 161, 184
  employers' organizations 164–166, 188
  French Communist (PCF) 159, 161–163, 165, 174, 178–182, 185–187, 189
  Greens, the 159, 161, 186
  Juppé plan of 1995, 151, 173, 174, 177, 182–186, 189, 192, 193, 196, 197
  Liberal Democracy (DL) 159, 161, 163, 194
  Mauroy reform of 1982, 173, 174, 177, 178
  National Front (FN) 159, 161, 194, 195
  National Republican Movement (MNR) 159, 161, 195
  occupational pensions 168, 170, 172, 193–195
  parliament 152–164; role in pension politics 191, 192
  party system 159
  pension system, 166–173, 863–865; history 166, 167
  pensioner organizations 164, 165
  political institutions 152–158
  political system, 151–166
  politics of pension reform 1980 to present, 173–190
  private pensions 165, 170, 177, 184–187
  Raffarin reform of 2003, 175, 176
  Socialist Party (PSF) 159, 161–163, 165, 174, 178–182, 185–187, 189, 192, 195
  Thomas law of 1997, 184–187
  Union for a Popular Majority (UMP) 159, 161, 163, 189, 195
  Union for French Democracy (UDF) 159, 161–164, 174, 175, 179, 181, 182, 185–187, 189, 194, 192, 195
  unions 151, 157, 164–166, 169, 171, 174–177, 180, 181; membership 166, 182,

192, 193; role in pension politics 192, 193
veto players 153, 157, 162, 198, 199
veto points 150, 152, 154–157, 162, 163
Folkpartiet liberalerna. See Fp.
Fondo Pensioni Lavoratori Dipendenti. See FPLD.
Fonds à gestion paritaire 185
Fonds d'épargne retraite 185, 196
Fonds de solidarité viellesse 167, 174, 179
Forbundet af offentligt ansatte. See FOA.
forfait d'éducation 822, 841, 843, 848, 850
Forza Italia. See FI.
Fourth Republic [France] 25, 152
Fowler, Norman 71
Fp 352, 356–358, 361, 370, 375, 376, 382, 391
FPLD 418, 419, 425, 450
FPÖ 32, 556, 557, 562–566, 570, 573–578, 580, 583–585, 587–599, 601
Franco 501, 502, 509–511, 515, 526, 546, 548, 550
Freiberufliches Sozialversicherungsgesetz. See FSVG.
Freie Demokratische Partei. See FDP.
Freie Volkspartei. See FVP.
Freiheitliche Partei Österreichs. See FPÖ.
Freisinnig–demokratische Partei der Schweiz/ Parti Radical Suisse. See FDP/PRD.
Front National. See FN.
FSA 62, 87
FSFL 815, 835, 837, 845
FSU 165, 182, 183, 188, 189, 194
FSVG 567–569, 573, 593, 597
FTF 464, 492
FUE 768, 774, 798
funded, funding 19, 21, 22, 28, 33–35
Fundo de Estabilizaçao Financeira da Segurança Social. See FEFFS.
Funktionaer og tjenestemandsforbundet. See FTF.
FVP 671, 702

GAP 811, 812, 832, 845, 847
Gaulle, Charles de 152, 157, 161
GdG 579, 580, 597

GDR 682, 702
GDV 670, 702
gender 3, 20, 34, 70, 223, 224, 230–232, 240, 242, 243, 285, 321, 332, 366, 578, 678, 770, 848, 866, 869, 877, 894
General and Municipal Workers' Union [UK]. See GMWU.
German Democratic Republic. See GDR.
Germany 2, 13, 16, 33, 34, 39, 660 ff.
  Alliance 90/The Greens 33, 661, 667, 669, 670, 679, 681, 685–690, 692–694, 696, 698–700, 702, 704
  Blüm I: Pension reform act 1992 679–682
  Blüm II reform 1997: Pension reform act 1999 682–686
  Christian Democratic Union 661, 666–669, 671, 672, 676, 679–691, 693–696, 698, 699, 702–706
  Christian Social Union in Bavaria 661, 666–669, 671, 672, 676, 677, 679, 690, 696, 698, 699, 702–706
  corporatism 661, 700, 702
  electoral system 665
  employers' organizations 669–671, 688, 702
  Free Democratic Party 661, 666–669, 671, 672, 676, 677, 680–688, 690, 692, 695, 696, 698, 702, 704, 705
  occupational pensions 670, 672–676, 691
  parliament 662–669; role in pension politics 697–700
  party system 661, 666–669, 699
  pension system 671–676, 893–894; history 671, 672
  pensioner organizations 669–671
  political institutions 662, 663
  political system 662–671
  politics of pension reform 1980 to present 676–695
  private pensions 672–677, 680, 687–693, 695–697, 699, 701, 703
  Riester reform 2001 686–693
  Rürup reform 2004 (*RV–Nachhaltigkeitsgesetz*) 693–695

Germany
  Social Democratic Party 661, 666–670, 672, 676, 677, 679–696, 698–700, 702–704
  Socialist party 661, 667, 669, 683, 685, 690, 692, 693, 699, 702, 704
  unions 669–671, 702; role in pension politics 700, 701
  veto players 668
  veto points 661, 663, 664, 668, 693, 697, 698
Gesamtverband der deutschen Versicherungswirtschaft. See GDV.
Gesetzliche Rentenversicherung. See GRV.
Gewerbliches Sozialversicherungsgesetz. See GSVG.
Gewerkschaft der Gemeindebediensteten. See GdG.
Gewerkschaft Öffentlicher Dienst. See GÖD.
GG 662, 665, 666, 702, 703
Giannitsis proposals 120, 137–139, 142
Giannitsis, Anastasios 120, 137–139, 142
Gieselink, Gerhard 337
Giscard d'Estaing, Valéry 159, 161, 162
GLEI 811, 812, 832, 845, 847
GMWU 70, 87, 92
GÖD 579, 580, 585, 586, 588
González, Felipe 500, 510, 512, 526, 527, 538, 544
government subsidies 22, 170, 244, 323, 575, 583, 674, 689, 743, 860, 889, 891
governments; single–party 24, 31; majority 27, 30, 31; minority 28, 30
GPS/PES 213, 243
GR 406, 408, 450
grand coalition 31–33, 399, 555, 556, 563, 574, 576, 580, 583, 596, 618, 633, 670, 689–692, 698, 702
Grasser, Karl–Heinz 590
Greece 17, 24–26, 97 ff.
  Coalition of the Left 104, 107, 133, 144
  Communist Party of Greece 98, 104, 145
  corporatism PPP
  Democratic–Social Movement, 104, 106, 144
  electoral system 100–102
  employers' organizations 108, 109
  Fakiolas Committee and law 1976/91, 119, 130, 131, 147
  Giannitsis proposals, 120, 137–139, 142
  New Democracy 97, 98, 102–107, 119, 123, 127, 128, 130–133, 135, 142, 145
  occupational pensions 113
  Pan–Hellenic Social Movement 98, 102, 104–108, 122, 127, 133, 135–139, 142, 145, 146, 148, 149
  parliament 98–107; role in pension politics 141–142
  party system 104–107
  pension system 109–117, 860–862; history 109–111
  pensioner organizations 108, 109
  political institutions 99–104
  political system, 98–109
  politics of pension reform 1980 to present, 117–140
  private pensions 113
  Reppas Reform (Law 3029/02) 121, 139, 140, 142
  Souflias Reform 1990 (Law 1902/90) 120, 123–130
  Souflias Reform 1992 (Law 2084/92) 120, 131–135
  Spraos report and the 'Mini Reform Package' (Law 2676/99), 135–137
  Unions 108, 109; role in pension politics 143, 143
  veto players 107
  veto points 103, 107, 194
Green–Pedersen, Christoffer 10, 30
Gréng Lëscht Ekologesch Initiativ. See GLEI.
Grundgesetz. See GG.
GRV 672–674, 702
GSEE 108, 109, 126, 131, 132, 138, 139, 144, 147
GSVG 567, 568, 573, 586, 593, 597
Guarantee Pension [Sweden] 22, 876–878
guaranteed minimum pension 28
guillotine 26, 53, 54, 154, 787, 798
Gustav Vasa 351
Guterres, António 619, 621, 640, 642, 646, 648

Haider, Erich 591
Haider, Jörg 556, 563, 565, 583, 590
Hall, Peter 240, 288
Handels og kontorarbejderforbundet. See HK.
Hartz Commission [Germany] 693, 694
Haughey, Charles 767, 768, 782
Haupt, Herbert 591
Heclo, Hugh 17
Heinesen, Knud 474
Hemerijck, Anton 720
Her Majesty's Stationery Office [UK]. *See*
   HMSO.
Herce, José Antonio 528, 540, 553
Herri Batasuna 509, 532
Herzog Commission [Germany] 678
Herzog, Roman 698
Hirsch, Mario 823, 828, 852
HK 464, 492
HMSO 88, 95
Höger, Ernst 585
Hollande, François 190
Hongerrenten 839
Hostasch, Eleonora 585
House of Lords 24, 25 [*See* also UK entries]
Huber, Evelyne 8
Huber, John D. 153
Hughes, Gerard 790, 797

IAIM 769, 798
IAPF 769, 802, 798
IBEC 768, 788, 789, 798
ICPR 76, 88, 94
ICTU 768, 769, 786, 789, 798, 802
IFA 768, 798, 802
IG Metall 670, 679
IGSS 816–820, 824, 843, 845–849, 851
ILO 805, 821, 823, 825, 839–842, 845, 848, 852
Immergut, Ellen M. 29, 357
immigrants 36, 111, 122, 124, 366, 469, 723, 828, 842, 877, 883
Impuesto sobre la Renta de las Personas Físicas. See IRPF.
index, indexing 12, 19, 20, 26, 34
INE 608, 654, 655

Inland Revenue National Insurance Office
   [UK]. *See* NICO.
INP 515, 547
INPDAP 417–421, 450
INPS 414, 416, 418–420, 424, 430, 431, 433, 434, 450–452
Inspection générale de la sécurité sociale. See
   IGSS.
INSS 517, 547
Institute of Directors [UK]. *See* IoD.
institutionalism 4–10
Institutions for Occupational Retirement Provision. See IORPs.
Instituto Nacional de Estatística. See INE.
Instituto Nacional de la Seguridad Social. See
   INSS.
Instituto Nacional de Previsión. See INP.
interest groups 3, 7, 11, 13–15, 23, 26, 27 [*See* also individual country entries]
International Center For Pension Reform [UK]. *See* ICPR.
International Labour Organization. *See*
   ILO.
INVERCO 530, 531, 547, 550
IoD 58, 88
IORPs 446, 450
Ireland 16, 35, 36, 758 ff.
   Democratic Left 765, 767, 789, 797, 802
   electoral system 760, 761, 763, 764, 795
   employers' organizations 768, 769, 796
   Family of the Irish (*Fine Gael*) 765–769, 778, 780–783, 785–789, 792, 795, 796, 798, 802
   Green Party 765, 768, 776, 778
   Labour Party 765–767, 769, 778, 779, 782, 783, 785–790, 795, 798, 799, 802
   occupational pensions 759, 769–776, 779, 783–785, 788–798, 800
   parliament 760–768; role in pension politics 795, 796
   party system 760, 765–768, 783, 795, 796
   pension system 769–775, 898–900; history 769, 770;
   pensioner organizations 769, 796
   pensions (amendment) act 2002 792–794

Ireland (*cont.*)
  pensions act 1990 771, 773, 782–787, 795
  pensions amendment act 1996 787–789, 795
  pensions reserve fund act 2000 773, 789–792, 795
  political institutions 760–768
  political system 759–769
  politics of pension reform 1980 to present 775–794
  private pensions 758, 759, 770–773, 775, 781, 790, 792, 794
  Progressive Democrats 765, 767, 780, 782, 783, 785, 791, 798
  Social welfare act 1988: PRSI for self–employed and farmers 775, 778–782, 795
  Soldiers of Fortune (*Fianna Fáil*) 760, 763, 765–768, 770, 778, 779, 782–789, 791, 795, 796, 798
  unions 768, 769; membership 768, 769, 796; role in pension politics 796
  veto players 767
  veto points 762, 767
  We Ourselves (*Sinn Féin*) 765, 768
  Workers' Party 765, 766, 783, 785, 786, 787, 798, 799
Irish Association of Investment Managers. *See* IAIM.
Irish Association of Pension Funds. *See* IAPF.
Irish Business and Employers Confederation. *See* IBEC.
Irish Congress of Trade Unions. *See* ICTU.
Irish Farmers' Association. *See* IFA.
Iron and Steel Trades Confederation [UK]. *See* ISTC.
IRPF 520, 548
Irwin, Galen A. 720
ISA 292
ISTC 70, 88, 92
Istituto Nazionale della Previdenza Sociale. See INPS.

Istituto Nazionale di Previdenza dell'Amministrazione Pubblica. See INPDAP.
Italia dei Valori – Lista di Pietro. See IV.
Italy 16, 17, 28, 29, 396 ff.
  1992 Amato reform, 422, 427, 428, 431–434, 440, 446
  1994 Berlusconi reform 428, 434–436
  1995 Dini reform 422, 428, 429, 436–441, 444
  1997 Prodi reform 429, 439, 444, 446
  Berlusconi–Tremonti reform: 2001–2005 443–445
  Christian Democratic Center 408, 410, 412, 413, 428, 435, 450
  Christian Democratic Party 405–408, 411, 412, 424–426, 431, 450
  Communist Refoundation 408, 427, 428, 439, 450
  corporatism 414, 416
  Democrats for Europe 408, 409, 413, 450
  Democrazia e libertà – La Margherita 408, 450
  electoral system 401–403, 405, 407, 434, 447, 451
  employers' organizations 410, 414, 432, 445, 447, 448
  Forza Italia 407, 409, 412, 413, 428, 435, 443, 444, 450, 451
  Green Party 406, 408, 450
  Italia dei Valori – Lista Di Pietro 408, 450
  Italian Communist Party 405–408, 417, 450
  Italian Socialists 408, 409, 413, 450
  Left Democrats 408, 409, 412, 413, 439, 450
  National Alliance 409, 412, 413, 428, 435, 450
  New Italian Socialist Party 409, 413, 450
  new multi–pillar architecture for Italian pensions 440–442
  Northern League 409, 410, 412, 413, 427, 428, 435, 436, 443–445, 450, 451
  occupational pensions 419, 441, 442, 444

parliament 399–410; role in pension
  politics 447, 448
Party of Christian Democrats 408, 410,
  412, 413, 428, 450
Party of Italian Communists 408, 409,
  413, 450
party system 405–410
pension system 415–421, 879–882;
  history 415–417
pension system, 697
pensioner organizations 410
political institutions 399–404
political system 398–415
politics of pension reform 1980 to
  present 422–445
private pensions 419, 425, 432
Radicali 406, 409, 450
unions 410, 414, 415; role in pension
  politics 447, 448
veto players 411–413, 448
veto points 400, 401, 411–413
IU 509, 511, 548
IV 408, 450
Izquierda Unida. See IU.

Jäätteenmäki, Anneli 260, 262
Jochem, Sven 357, 394
Jospin, Lionel 163, 175, 186, 187, 191, 192
Juan Carlos I 501, 548
Juncker, Jean–Claude 806, 813, 839, 840
Juppé plan 151, 173, 174, 177, 182–186, 189,
  192, 193, 196, 197
Juppé, Alain 26, 151, 163, 173, 174, 177,
  182–186, 189, 192, 193, 196, 197

Kammer für Arbeiter und Angestellte. See AK.
Kangas, Olli 27
Kansallinen Edistyspuolue. See ED.
Kansallinen Kokoomuspuolue. See KOK.
Kansaneläkelaitos. See KELA.
Karamanlís, Konstantínos 98, 107
Katholieke Volkspartij. See KVP.
Katrougalos, George 111, 117, 148
Kay, Stephen J. 10
KBG 331, 341

Kekkonen, Urho 260, 261, 267
KELA 265, 270, 271, 283, 291, 295
KESK 258, 261, 291
Keskustapuolue. See KESK.
KEVA 267, 291
KF 457, 460–463, 472, 477, 482, 485, 488, 492
KiEL 291
King, Anthony 84, 85, 89, 91, 93, 94
Kirkon Eläkelaki. See KiEL.
Kitschelt, Herbert 10
Kittel, Bernhard 9
KKE 98, 104, 145
Klestil, Thomas 588, 598
Klima, Victor 564, 584
Kohl, Helmut 668, 681, 698
KOK 252, 258, 260–262, 274, 283, 284, 291
Kommunernes Pensionsforsikring 468
Kommunistesch Partei vu Lëtzebuerg. See
  KPL.
Konservative Folkeparti. See KF.
KPL 811, 812, 845, 847
KRF 460, 461, 463, 477, 478, 486, 492
Kristeligt Folkeparti. See KRF.
*Kristelijke Beweging van Gepensioneerden.
  See* KBG.
KTV 263, 291
*Kunnallisten viranhaltijain ja työntekijäin
  eläkelaki. See* KVTEL.
Kunta–alan ammattiliitto. See KTV.
Kuntien Eläkevakuutus. See KEVA.
KVP 719, 720, 753
KVTEL 267, 269–271, 273, 279, 281, 287, 291

L 50, 55, 56, 70, 88
L'Ulivo 409, 410, 429, 439
Lab 50, 55–60, 68, 70, 72, 75–80, 83–85, 88,
  89, 91, 96
labor market, labour market 12, 27, 28, 31,
  35
Labour Party [Ireland]. *See* LP
Labour Party [UK]. *See* Lab.
Lacina, Ferdinand 581
Lafontaine, Oskar 684
Lahure, Johny 832
Landesversicherungsanstalten. See LVA.

Landsorganisationen i Danmark. See LO [Denmark].
Landsorganisationen i Sverige. See LO [Sweden].
Law Council [Sweden] 353, 354
Law on Occupational Pensions 223, 226, 235, 240
LCGB 815, 827–831, 835, 840, 844, 845
LCR 161, 194
LDP 55, 58, 85, 88
Leemput, Jim van 309, 311, 346
Lega Nord. See LN.
Legros, Florence 177, 178, 180, 185, 196, 197
Lehmbruch, Gerhard 37
LEL 266, 270, 271, 291
Lëtzebuerger Chrëschtlech Gewerkschaftsbond. See LCGB.
Lëtzebuerger Rentner– an Invalideverband. See LRIV.
Lëtzebuerger Sozialistesch Aarbechterpartei. See LSAP.
Levy, Jonah D. 10, 184, 198, 596, 602
Liberaalinen Kansanpuolue. See LKP.
Liberal Democratic Party [UK]. *See* LDP.
Liberal Party [UK]. *See* L.
Liberale Partei der Schweiz/Parti Libéral Suisse. See LPS/PLS
Liberales Forum. See LIF.
LIF 562, 565, 579, 580, 586, 597
Life Offices Association [UK]. *See* LOA.
Ligue Communiste Révolutionnaire. See LCR.
Lijphart, Arend 4, 5, 36, 37, 297, 346, 698, 709, 718, 720, 757
Lijst Pim Fortuyn. See LPF.
Lipponen, Paavo 260, 262, 281, 282, 284–286, 289
LKP 252, 291
LN 29, 409, 410, 412, 413, 427, 428, 435, 436, 443–445, 450, 451
LO [Denmark] 464–466, 472, 476, 480, 481, 483, 490, 492, 494
LO [Sweden] 359–361, 369, 372, 374, 377–379, 381, 382, 384, 388, 390
LO [France] 161, 195

LOA 59, 70, 88, 92
Löschnak, Franz 581
Low–income earners 20, 22, 50, 60, 61, 67, 69, 76, 77, 79, 80, 673, 689, 699, 775, 795, 830
LP 765–767, 769, 778, 779, 782, 783, 785–790, 795, 798, 799, 802
LPF 719, 722, 748, 753, 754
LPS/PLS 213, 243
LRIV 815, 830, 845
LSAP 806, 811–814, 823, 827, 828, 832, 834, 835, 837, 839, 840, 845–848, 852
Lutte Ouvriére. See LO [France].
Luxembourg 15, 36, 39, 804 ff.
  1984 reform 823–828
  1987 reform 828–832
  1991 reform 832, 833
  2002 reform (*Rentendësch* 2001) 838–841
  Action Committee for Democracy and Justice 804, 805, 809, 812, 814, 815, 820, 823, 832–840, 843, 845–849, 851
  Christian Social People's Party 807, 811–814, 821, 823, 827, 828, 830, 832, 834–837, 839–841, 843–849, 851, 852
  Communist Party 811, 812, 845, 847
  Democratic Party 806, 811–813, 821, 823, 828, 832, 835–840, 845–847, 852
  electoral system 804, 805, 809, 810, 843, 846
  employers' organizations 814, 815, 844
  Greens 809, 811, 812, 832, 845, 847
  occupational pensions 817–819, 845, 848
  parliament 806–814; role in pension politics 843
  party system 811, 812–814, 823, 844
  pension system 815–820, 901–905; history 815, 816
  pensioner organizations 814, 815
  political institutions 806–810
  political system 805–815
  politics of pension reform 1980 to present 820–841
  private pensions 819, 833
  public sector reform (1995–1998) 833–838

Social Democratic Party 811, 846, 847
Socialist Workers' Party 806, 811–814, 823, 827, 828, 832, 834, 835, 837, 839, 840, 845–848, 852
The Left 811
unions 814, 815; membership 844, 846; role in pension politics 844
veto players 813, 843
veto points 807, 808, 813, 843
LVA 673, 674, 702
Lyhytaikaisissa työsuhteissa olevien työntekijöiden eläkelaki. See LEL.

M [Sweden] 356, 357, 361, 370, 371, 375–377, 381, 391
Maalaisliitto. See ML.
Maataloustuottajien Keskusliitto. See MTK.
Maatalousyrittäjien Eläkelaki. See MYEL.
Madelin Law 168, 170, 173
Madelin, Alain 159, 161, 168, 170, 173
Mainil Reform 318, 323, 234
Mainil, Pierre 323, 324, 327, 343
Major, John 57, 74, 85
majoration forfaitaire 820, 824, 825, 829
majoration proportionelle 819, 820
majorations proportionnelles échélonnées 820
majoritarian 4, 5, 12, 24, 29–31
Manos, Stefanos 131, 146
Marier, Patrik 167, 314
Marin, Bernd 584, 597, 602
Maroni, Roberto 443
Martens, Wilfried 307, 321, 322, 324, 326, 328, 334
Martin, Ron 62, 85, 93, 95
Mastella, Clemente 434
Mauroy reform 173, 174, 177, 178
Mavrogordatos, George Th. 108, 148
Maxwell, Robert 74, 75, 83
Mays, Claire 164, 184
McCreevy, Charlie 791
MDP 634, 654
means–tested 22, 27
MEDEF 165, 188, 195
MEL 291

Merimiesten Eläkelaki. See MEL.
Merkel, Angela 668–690
Merrien, François–Xavier 164, 198
Metropolitan Pensions Association [UK]. *See* MPA.
Meyer, Traute 9
MFA 607, 608, 617, 654
MHP 722, 753
MIG 63, 65, 88
Minimum Income Guarantee. *See* MIG.
Minns, Richard 60, 62, 85, 94
Mitterand, François 174
ML 249, 251, 252, 258–260, 264, 265, 291
MNR 159, 161, 195
Moderata samlingspartiet. See M.
Mönkäre, Sinikka 283
Moran, Michael 25, 35
Mota, Rosalía 528
Mouvement des entreprises de France. See MEDEF.
Mouvement National Républicain. See MNR.
Movimento das Forças Armadas. See MFA.
Movimento Democrático Português. See MDP.
Movimento Sociale Italiano – Destra Nazionale. See MSI–DN.
Movimento Unitário de Reformados, Pensionistas e Idosos. See MURPI.
MPA 88
MSI–DN 405–407, 409, 427, 450
MTK 263, 267, 291
Multi–pillar 30, 33
MURPI 623, 654
Mutualidades de Previsión Social 529
MYEL 267, 271, 272, 291
Myles, John 514, 554

Nachhaltigkeitsfaktor 675, 678, 694, 696
NAPF 59, 70, 72, 73, 86, 88, 92
NAR 309, 311, 325, 331, 340, 341
National Association of Pension Funds [UK]. *See* NAPF.
National Federation of Self–Employed [UK]. *See* NFSE.
National Insurance Act 59

National Insurance Board [Sweden]. *See* RFV.
National Insurance Contributions [UK]. *See* NICs.
National Insurance Fund [UK]. *See* NIF.
National Insurance Scheme [UK]. *See* NI.
National Pension Reserve Fund. *See* NRPF.
National Pensioners Convention [UK]. *See* NCP.
National Pensions Policy Initiative. *See* NPPI.
National Pensions Reserve Fund Commission [Ireland] 777, 791, 799
Nationale Arbeidsraad. See NAR.
Nationalrat 207, 210, 216, 224, 225
NCW 722, 736, 738, 740, 753
ND 97, 98, 102–107, 119, 123, 127, 128, 130–133, 135, 142, 145
Nederlands Christelijk Werkgeversverbond. See NCW.
Nederlands Katholiek Vakverbond. See NKV.
Nederlands Verbond van Vakverenigingen. See NVV.
Neidhart, Leonhard 207
Netherlands 20, 34–36, 713 ff.
　1994 election 714, 740–742, 744, 749, 750
　adapting to European equal treatment law 730, 734–736
　Anti–Revolutionary Party 719, 720, 753
　AOW cost containment in the 1990s 738, 739
　Catholic People's Party 34, 719, 720, 753
　Christian Democratic Appeal 34, 719–722, 730, 735, 736, 738–742, 744, 745, 748–750, 753, 754
　Christian Union 719
　corporatism 714, 723–735, 733, 737, 744, 746, 750, 751
　cost containment of the AOW in the 1980s 730, 732, 733
　Democrats 66 719, 721, 722, 739–742, 753, 755
　electoral system 717, 720, 751
　employers' organizations 722–724, 751
　EU and occupational pensions 736, 737
　Green Left 719, 739, 754
　introduction of the AOW reserve fund 742–744
　Labor Party 34, 719–722, 724, 725, 730, 731, 736, 793, 742, 744, 745, 752–754
　Liberal Party 719, 722, 724, 735, 736, 738–742, 744, 745, 748, 753, 754
　List Pim Fortuyn 719, 722, 748, 753, 754
　occupational pensions 713, 714, 718, 723–733, 736–739, 742–747, 749–754
　parliament 715–722; role in pension politics 750, 751
　party system 717, 719–722
　pension system 724–729, 895–897; history 724–726
　pensioner organizations 722–724, 751
　political institutions 715–720
　political system 714–724
　politics of pension reform 1980 to present 729–749
　private pensions 727
　reforming occupational pensions 744–746
　revision of the PSF 748, 749
　Socialist Party 719, 753
　stock market downturn 746–748
　supplementary pensions 726, 728, 729, 731, 733, 734, 737, 738, 741, 743, 746, 750 751
　unions 722–724; membership PPP; role in pension politics 751
　veto players 717, 721
　veto points 716, 717, 721
Neutral Gewerkschaft Lëtzebuerg. See NGL.
New Democracy [Greece]. *See* ND.
new politics 10–14, 251, 286, 289
NFSE 70, 88, 92
NGL 829, 830, 838, 846
NI 61–66, 71–73, 75, 76, 78–82, 88, 94
NICO 61, 64, 88, 94
NICs 61, 62, 64–66, 71, 73, 76, 78, 81, 88, 94
NIF 62, 64, 75, 82
NKV 722, 753
Notarversicherungsgesetz. See NVG.
NPC 58, 73, 88

NPPI 773, 777, 790, 791, 795–797, 799, 800
NPRF 773, 794, 798
NPSI 409, 413, 450
Nucleo di Valutazione della Spesa Previdenziale 418
Nuovo Partito Socialista Italiano. See NPSI.
NVG 567, 568, 597
NVV 722, 753

O'Duffy, Brendan 789, 803
ÖAAB 585, 597
ÖAKT 576–578, 597
Obinger, Herbert 9
Obligatorium 221, 223, 226, 229, 236
Occupational Pensions Regulatory Authority [UK]. *See* OPRA.
OECD 16, 18, 31, 229, 249, 260, 265, 349, 499, 548
ÖGB 563, 565, 580–582, 585–589, 592, 597, 598, 602
OGB–L 814, 826, 827, 830, 831, 835, 837, 840, 846, 848, 852
Old Age and Widows' Pensions Act 59
old–age poverty 1, 18, 21, 141, 570
Olson, Mancur 166, 198
Onafhängege Gewerkschaftsbond Lëtzebuerg. See OGB–L.
OPF 723, 741, 747, 753
OPRA 62, 69, 81, 88, 89
Österreichische Gewerkschaftsbund. See ÖGB.
Österreichische Volkspartei. See ÖVP.
Österreichischer Arbeiter und Angestelltenbund. See ÖAAB.
Österreichischer Arbeiterkammertag. See ÖAKT.
Overlegorgaan Vereinigingen van gepensioneerden van ondernemingen. See OVGO.
OVGO 743, 753
ÖVP 32, 555, 556, 562, 563, 597

Palier, Bruno 184
panachage 36, 210, 804, 832, 849

Pan–Hellenic Social Movement [Greece]. *See* PASOK.
Pappas, Takis S. 99, 106, 148
parliamentary regimes 6, 152, 207, 399
Partei des Demokratischen Sozialismus. See PDS.
Parti Communiste Français. See PCF.
Parti Reformateur Liberal. See PRL.
Parti Social Chrétien. See PSC.
Parti Socialiste [Belgium]. *See* PS.
Parti Socialiste Français. See PSF
Partido Comunista de España. See PCE.
Partido Comunista Português. See PCP.
Partido Democrático Popular. See PDP.
Partido Nacionalista Vasco. See PNV.
Partido Popular. See PP.
Partido Renovador Democrático. See PRD.
Partido Social Democrata. See PSD.
Partido Socialista Obrero Español. See PSOE.
Partido Socialista. See PS [Portugal].
Partij van de Arbeid. See PVDA.
Partij voor Vrijheid en Vooruitgang/Vlaamse Liberalen en Democraten. See PVV/VLD.
Partito Comunista Italiano. See PCI.
Partito dei Comunisti Italiani. See PDCI.
Partito dei Cristiano Democratici. See CDU.
Partito dei Socialisti Democratici Italiani. See SDI.
Partito della Rifondazione Comunista. See RC.
Partito Democratico della Sinistra. See PDS.
Partito Liberale Italiano. See PLI.
Partito Popolare Italiano. See PPI.
Partito Radicale. See PR.
Partito Repubblicano Italiano. See PRI.
Partito Socialista Democratico Italiano. See PSDI.
Partito Socialista Italiano. See PSI.
partitocrazia 402
PASOK 25, 98, 102, 104–108, 122, 127, 133, 135–139, 142, 145, 146, 148, 149
pay–as–you–go, *See* PAYG
PAYG 2, 18–21, 28, 36
Pay–Related Social Insurance. *See* PRSI.

payroll tax(es) 21, 180, 271–273, 280, 285, 371, 375, 376, 417, 745, 790, 792, 879, 882
PC 55, 88
PCE 513, 548
PCF 159, 161–163, 165, 174, 178–182, 185–187, 189
PCI 405–408, 417, 450
PCOB 723, 753
PCP 617–619, 623, 634, 637, 645, 646, 649, 654, 657
PD 765, 767, 780, 782, 783, 785, 791, 798
PDCI 408, 409, 413, 450
PDP 530, 548
PDS [Germany] 33, 661, 667, 669, 683, 685, 690, 692, 693, 699, 702, 704
PDS [Italy] 427, 428, 436, 447, 450
PEIR 170, 173, 188, 195
Pensioen en Sparfondsen Wet. See PSF.
Pensioenkamer
pension costs 20
Pension Law Review Committee 68, 74, 92
Pension Protection Fund [UK]. See PPF.
Pensions Act 1995 62, 65, 67, 68, 74–76, 83
Pensions Act 2004 62, 65, 69, 81, 82, 92
Pensions Board 759, 769–771, 774–776, 778–780, 784–790, 793–797, 799, 800, 803
Pensions de retraite et sauvegarde de la protection sociale 179
Pensions Reserve Fund Act 777, 789, 791
pensions, occupational 9, 22, 27, 30, 34, 35, 39 [See also individual country entries]
pensions, private 11, 18, 20, 22, 36 [See also individual country entries]
pensions, public 1–3, 6, 11, 15, 17, 18, 20, 21, 24, 26, 34–38
Pensionsharmonisierungsgesetz 567, 568, 573, 593
Pensionssicherungsbeitrag 579
Pensions–Sicherungs–Verein. See PSVaG.
Pensionsversicherungsanstalt. See PVA.
Personal Retirement Savings Account. See PRSA.
Persson, Torsten 4, 5
Perustuslakivaliokunnan lausunto. See PeVL.

Perustuslakivaliokunta. See CC.
PESP 783, 798
PeVL 278, 283, 285, 291, 293
Pierson, Paul 487, 490, 514
pillar(s) 21–23
Pinto Balsemão, Francisco 618, 633
PIP 419, 420, 450
Plafonamento 22
Plaid Cymru [UK]. See PC.
Plan d'épargne individuel pour la retraite. See PEIR.
Plan partenarial d'épargne salariale volontaire pour la retraite. See PRESVR.
plans d'épargne–retraite d'entreprise 175, 185
PLI 405, 406, 411, 412, 431, 450
PNR 768, 778, 781–783, 801
PNV 509, 530, 548
Polizze Individuali Pensionistiche. See PIP.
Portugal 22, 32, 33, 605 ff.
    1993: Cutting the costs of pensions and preventing strategic behavior by pensioners–to–be 641, 642
    corporatism 607, 619, 622–625, 647
    Democratic Renovative Party 619, 654, 655
    electoral system 612, 615
    employers' organizations 622, 623, 652
    occupational pensions 627, 632, 635, 640
    parliament 610–622; role in pension politics 651
    party system 617–622
    pension system 624–632, 891–892; history 624–627
    pensioner organizations 622, 623, 652
    political institutions 610–622, 651
    political system 607–623
    politics of pension reform 1980 to present 633–650
    Portuguese Communist Party 617–619, 623, 634, 637, 645, 646, 649, 654, 657
    private pensions 607, 632, 640, 649, 653
    restructuring social security: The 2000 and 2002 social security framework laws and the issue of the plafonamento 645–650

Social and Democratic Center – Popular
  Party 617–619, 621, 629, 645–649, 653,
  657
Social Democratic Party 617–623, 634,
  636, 637, 639, 640, 642, 644–650,
  652–655, 658
Socialist Party 32, 617–623, 634, 636, 637,
  639, 640, 642, 644–650, 652–655, 658
the 1999 Measures to introduce a flexible
  retirement age, and to improve the
  benefits for dependent
  pensioners 644, 645
the creation of the second and third
  pillars of the Portuguese pension
  system in the second half of the
  1980s 639, 640
the white paper commission
  (1996–1998) 642–644
towards comprehensive social security:
  The creation of the non–contributory
  regime in 1980 and the social security
  framework law of 1984 633–639
unions 622, 623; role in pension
  politics 652
veto players 620
veto points 613, 614, 620
Powell, G. Bingham 4, 5
PP 31, 509–512, 517, 519, 522, 523, 525, 531,
  533, 534, 538–543, 545–548, 550
PPESVR 170, 173, 188, 195
PPF 62, 88
PPI 408, 412, 413, 450
PPM 362, 366, 383, 386, 390
PR 406, 409, 450
PRÄKO 565, 597
*Präsidentenkonferenz der
  Landwirtschaftskammer.* See PRÄKO
PRD 619, 654, 655
PREFON 168, 170, 173, 195
Premiepensionsmyndighet See PPM.
Premium Savings Fund [Sweden] 363, 386
presidential 5, 6, 25
PRI 405, 406, 411, 412, 450
Prinz, Christopher 584, 597, 602
PRL 305, 307, 322, 325, 342

problem pressure 16, 28
Prodi reform 429, 439, 444, 446
Prodi, Romano 412, 439, 440
Programme for Economic and Social
  Progress (1990). *See* PESP.
Programme for National Recovery (1987).
  See PNR.
Progressive Democrats. *See* PD.
proportional representation 5, 6, 9, 31, 34
Protestants Christelijke Ouderen Bond. See
  PCOB.
PRSA 771, 772, 775, 777, 790, 792–795, 798,
  799
PRSI 770, 771, 773, 776, 778–783, 788, 797,
  798, 801
PS [Belgium] 303, 304, 305, 307, 308, 327, 342
PS [Portugal] 32, 617–623, 634, 636, 637,
  639, 640, 642, 644–650, 652–655, 658
PSC 303, 304, 306–308, 322, 323, 325, 327,
  342
PSD 612, 617–623, 629, 633, 634, 637–642,
  644–646, 648–654, 657, 658
PSDI 405, 406, 410–412, 431, 450
PSF [France] 159, 161–163, 165, 174, 178–182,
  185–187, 189, 192, 195
PSF [Netherlands] 728, 731, 738, 747–749
PSI 405, 406, 408, 409, 411, 412, 424, 425,
  431, 450
PSOE 509–514, 517, 522, 526, 528, 530, 532,
  533, 537–540, 548, 549
PSVaG 675, 703
public–private mix 2, 18, 34
Pühringer, Josef 591, 592, 603
Puro report 285
Puro, Kari 277, 284, 285, 292
PVA 570, 597, 603
PVDA 34, 719–722, 724, 725, 730, 731, 736,
  793, 742, 744, 745, 752–754
PVV/VLD 303, 304, 308, 322, 324, 325, 326,
  327, 332, 342
Pym, Francis 74, 89

Quittkat, Christine 164, 198

Raffarin reform 175, 176

Raffarin, Jean-Pierre 163, 175, 176
Ragin, Charles 8
Rainwater, Lee 18
Rassemblement pour la République. See RPR.
RATP 166, 170, 175, 182, 183, 195
RAV 689, 703
RC 408, 427, 428, 439, 450
Reagan, Ronald 10
Redding, Vivian 827
Reformstau 660, 697
régime general 167
Regime geral. See RG.
Regimes Nao Contributivos o Equiparados. See RNCE.
régimes spéciaux 167
Reichhold, Mathias 590
Rein, Martin 16, 18, 38
remiss 352, 355, 359, 391
Rentenanpassungsverordnung. See RAV.
Rentendësch 822, 838–842, 852, 853
Rentenkorrekturgesetz 686
Reppas reform 121, 139, 140, 142
Reppas, Dimitris
retraites ouvrières et paysannes 166
retrenchment 2, 8–13, 17, 27, 30, 33, 34, 39
Reynolds, Albert 767, 787, 788
RFV 362, 365, 378, 384, 385, 386, 390, 391
RG 627–629, 635, 639, 654, 656, 657
Rhodes, Martin 13, 538, 554
RI 412, 413, 450
Richtlinienkompetenz 662, 663
Riester, Walter 677, 687–690, 692, 704
Riester-Rente 22, 674, 678, 693, 695, 696, 699, 700
Rifondazione Comunista. See RC.
Rijksdienst voor Arbeidsvoorziening. See RVA.
Rijksdienst voor Pensioenen. See RVP.
Rijksdienst voor Sociale Zekerheid. See RSZ.
Rijksdienst voor Werknemerspensioenen. See RWP.
Rijksinstituut voor ziekte- en invaliditeitsverzekering. See Riziv.
Rijkskas voor Rust en Overlevingspensioenen. See RROP.

Rijn, A. van 724
Riksförsäkringsverket. See RFV.
Rinnovamento Italiano. See RI.
Riziv 315, 342
RNCE 626, 627, 631, 633–638, 641–643, 645, 649, 652
Rocard, Michel 162, 174, 181, 189
Rokkan, Stein 38
Ross, Shane 793
Rothstein, Bo 359, 367, 394
RPR 161–164, 174, 175, 179, 181, 182, 185–187, 191, 192, 195
RROP 313, 314, 342
RSZ 313, 315, 342
Rürup Commission [Germany] 678, 694
Rürup Report 572, 584
Ruttenstorfer, Wolfgang 584
RV 457, 460, 461, 463, 476–481, 485, 486, 492
RVA 315, 342
RV-Nachhaltigkeitsgesetz 678, 693
RVP 314–316, 330, 341, 342
RWP 314, 326, 342

SACO 359, 375, 377, 379, 390, 393
Saerlige pensions Opparing. See SP.
SAF 359, 360, 378, 379, 390
SAK 263, 264, 266, 267, 282, 285, 292
Salaire annuel moyen. See SAM.
Salazar, António de Oliveira 607, 623–625, 650
SAM 172, 195
Sampaio, Jorge 606, 610, 612, 619, 621
Santana Lopes, Pedro 606, 619, 651
Santer, Jacques 813, 823, 824, 826
Santos, Boaventura S. 624, 659
SAP [Denmark] 466–469, 489, 491, 492
SAP [Sweden] 29, 350, 351, 357–362, 367–378, 380–383, 385–391
SAV/UPS 216, 244
Scalfaro, Oscar Luigi 436
Scharpf, Fritz W. 10
Schlüter, Poul 463, 475, 482
Schmidt, Manfred G. 9
Schmidt, Ulla 694
Schmidt, Vivien A. 17, 164

INDEX

Schmitter, Philippe 37
Schreiner, Ottmar 695, 704
Schröder, Gerhard 668, 669, 685, 686, 689, 690, 693, 695, 700, 710
Schultess Bill 218
Schulze, Isabelle 25, 28, 33, 35, 39
Schüssel, Wolfgang 564, 582, 586, 588, 590, 592, 595, 598
Schweizerische Gewerkschaftsbund/Union syndicale suisse. See SGB/USS.
Schweizerische Volkspartei/Union Démocratique du Centre. See SVP/UDC.
Schweizerischer Arbeitgeberverband/Union patronale suisse. See SAV/UPS.
Schweizerischer Gewerbeverband SGV/Union suisse des arts et métiers. See SGV/USAM.
Scott Committee [UK] 67, 68,3 70
Scottish National Party [UK]. *See* SNP.
SD 455–457, 460–463, 465, 466, 471, 472, 474–482, 485–490, 492, 493
SDI 408, 409, 413, 450
SDLP 55, 58, 88
SDP [Finland] 248, 249, 251, 252, 258–267, 274, 275, 278, 279, 281, 283–287, 289, 290, 292
SDP [Luxembourg] 811, 846, 847
SDP [UK] 24, 55, 58, 74, 85, 88, 89, 93, 95
SED 667, 669, 703
Seiler, Walter 32
Select Committee on Social Services [UK]
Self–employed 22, 35, 36
Sénat 152, 153, 155, 158, 160, 162, 174–176, 179, 182, 183, 185, 186, 189, 190, 196, 197
Seniority pensions [Italy] 29
sepcav 818, 846, 850
SER 723, 728, 730, 734, 735, 737–739, 746, 749, 753, 755
SERPS 50, 60–63, 65–69, 71–73, 75–80, 82, 84, 86, 88
Service central de la statistique et des études économiques. See STATEC.
Services, Industrial, Professional and Technical Union. *See* SIPTU.

SF [Denmark] 460, 485, 492
SF [Ireland] 765, 768
SFP 259–262, 274, 281, 282, 287, 292
SGB 671–675, 703
SGB/USS 214, 217, 231, 244
SGV/USAM 216, 244
SID 464, 492
SIF 360, 390
silver fund [Belgium] 28, 320, 337, 340
Simítis, Konstantinos 105, 107, 138, 142
Simonis, Heide 691
Sindacato Pensionati Italiani – CGIL. See SPI–CGIL.
single member districts 5, 26, 29, 33, 52, 53, 157, 400, 403, 410, 451
Sinn Féin. See SF.
SIPTU 786, 793, 798
SKDL 258–261, 282, 283, 292
SKP 258, 292
SMP 258–261, 292
SNCF 170, 174, 175, 182, 183, 195
SNP 55, 58, 88
Soares, Mário 610, 612, 618, 620–622, 639, 655
Sociaal–Economische Raad. See SER.
Social Democratic and Labour Party [UK]. *See* SDLP.
Social Democratic Party [UK]. *See* SDP.
Social Framework Law 319, 320, 335
Social Security Act 67, 69, 82, 84, 89–91
Social security ceiling. See SSC.
Social Security Committee [Switzerland] 212, 231, 234, 236, 237
Social Security Framework Law [Portugal] 606, 607, 633–639, 645, 651
Social Security Pensions Act 60, 73, 83, 86
Socialdemoktratief. See SD.
Socialistik Folkeparti. See SF.
Socialistische Partij [Belgium]. *See* SP.
Socialistische Partij [Netherlands]. *See* SP.
Société d'épargne–pension à capital variable. See SEPCAV.
Société Nationale des Chemins de Fer. See SNCF.

Solidaridad de Trabajadores Vascos. See ELA–STV.
Sosiaalivaliokunnan mietintö. See StVM.
Souflias Reform 1990 123–130
Souflias Reform 1992 120, 131–135
Souflias, Georgios 123
Sozialdemokratesch Partei. See SDP.
Sozialdemokratische Partei der Schweiz/Parti socialiste suisse. See SPS/PSS.
Sozialdemokratische Partei Deutschlands. See SPD.
Sozialdemokratische Partei Österreichs. See SPÖ.
Sozialgesetzbuch. See SGB.
Sozialistische Einheitspartei Deutschlands. See SED.
Sozialrechts–Änderungsgesetz 586, 587, 599
SP [Belgium] 303–305, 307, 308, 329, 330, 332, 342
SP [Denmark] 466–470, 473, 474, 484, 486, 488, 489, 491–493
SP [Netherlands] 719, 753
Spain 15, 17, 30, 31, 33, 41, 497 ff.
   1985 reform: Law of urgent measures for the rationalization of the structure and protective action of the Social Security system 522–529
   1987 reform: Law on regulation of pension plans and funds 529–532
   1990 reform: Law on non–contributory pensions of the Social Security system 532–534
   1997 reform: Law on consolidation and rationalization of the Social Security system 538–541
   2002 reform: Law on measures for the establishment of a system of gradual and flexible retirement 541, 542
   Basque Country and Liberty 502, 547, 548
   Basque Nationalist Party 509, 530, 548
   Communist Party of Spain 513, 548
   Convergence and Unity 509, 510, 522, 524, 534, 535, 538, 539, 547
   electoral system 507, 508, 544
   employers' organizations 513, 528, 530, 535, 539, 541, 543, 547
   Galician Nationalist Bloc 509, 547
   institutional solidness of the Toledo Pact 542–544
   occupational pensions 518, 522, 532
   parliament 502–512; role in pension politics 544, 545
   party system 509–511
   pension system 514–520, 887–888; history 514–516
   pensioner organizations 514, 548
   political institutions 502–510, 544, 545
   political system 501–514
   politics of pension reform 1980 to present 520–544
   Popular Democratic Party 530, 548
   Popular Party 509–512, 517, 519, 522, 523, 525, 531, 533, 534, 538–543, 545–548, 550
   private pensions 500, 516, 518, 524, 529–532, 537, 546, 550
   Republican Left of Catalonia 509, 511, 547
   Spanish Socialist Workers' Party 509–514, 517, 522, 526, 528, 530, 532, 533, 537–540, 548, 549
   Toledo Pact 534–538, 542–544
   unions 511–514; role in pension politics 545, 546
   United Left 509, 511, 548
   veto players 501, 511, 512, 545
   veto points 500, 503, 504–506, 512, 544
SPD 33, 661, 666–670, 672, 676, 677, 679–696, 698–700, 702–704
Specialarbejderforbundet i Danmark. See SID.
SPI–CGIL 410, 450
SPÖ 32, 555, 556, 561–566, 570, 572, 574–592, 594–599, 604
Spraos Committee 118, 120, 135, 136, 147
Spraos report 135–137
Spraos, Giannis 135
SPS/PSS 213–215, 231, 232
SSC 171, 195
SSP 50, 61–66, 77, 88
SSTP 292

St. Anna plan 318
Staaff, Karl 360
Ständerat 207, 210, 224, 225
State Earnings Related Pension Scheme. *See* SERPS.
State Earnings–Related Pensions 24, 60, 61, 63
State Second Pension. *See* SSP.
STATEC 805, 806, 846, 848, 853
Stephens, John 8
STK 263, 266, 267, 292
stock market 50, 87, 204, 222, 237–239, 269, 386, 491, 714, 729, 731, 738, 746–751, 897
Stoiber, Edmund 689, 690
Stoke, Lord Ashlee of 78, 79
Stoltenberg, Gerhard 681
Struck, Peter 688
Strukturanpassungsgesetze 580–583
STTK 263, 282, 285, 292
StVM 278, 281, 283, 286, 287, 292, 293
Suomen Ammattiyhdistysten Keskusliitto. See SAK.
Suomen Kansandemokraattinen Liitto. See SKDL.
Suomen Kommunistinen Puolue. See SKP.
Suomen Maaseudun Puolue. See SMP.
Suomen Sosialidemokraattinen Puolue. See SDP.
Suomen Sosialistinen Työväenpuolue. See SSTP.
Suomen Toimihenkilökeskusjärjestö. See STTK.
Suomen Työnantajien Keskusliitto. See STK.
Supplerende arbejdsmarkedspension for foertidspensionister. See SAP [Denmark].
Svenska Arbetsgivareföreningen. See SAF.
Svenska Folkpartiet. See SFP.
Svenska Industriförbundet. See SIF.
Sveriges Akademikers Centralorganisation. See SACO.
Sveriges Socialdemokratiska Arbetareparti. See SAP [Sweden].
SVP/UDC 213, 215, 216, 232, 234–237, 244
Swank, Duane 9

Sweden 2, 9, 13, 15–17, 22, 28–30, 347 ff.
1994/98 reform 372–386
buffer funds 369
Center Party 356, 357, 370, 376, 382, 391
Conservative Party 356, 357, 361, 370, 371, 375–377, 381, 391
constitutional history 351, 352
constitutional reform 350–353, 355, 357, 370
corporatism 359
county councils 353, 354
electoral system 353–355, 357, 359
employers 359, 360, 363, 364, 368, 369, 375, 376, 378, 379, 381, 382, 387, 390
employers' organizations 359, 360, 390
Left Party 356, 357, 371, 372, 374, 380
Liberal People's Party 352, 356–358, 361, 370, 375, 376, 382, 391
monarchy 352, 355, 390
municipalities 353, 354
nation–building 351, 352
New Democracy 356, 370–372, 374
occupational pensions 360, 362–364, 366, 369, 380, 383
parliament 352–359; role in pension politics 387, 388
partial pension cuts 371, 372
party system 356–359
pension system 360–367, 876–878, ; history 360–362
pensioner organizations 359, 360
political institutions 352–357
political system 351–360
politics of pension reform 367–386
premium pension 349, 362, 364, 366, 369, 376, 381–383, 385–387, 390
private pensions 363, 364, 366
Social Democracy 361
Social Democratic Party 350, 351, 357–362, 367–378, 380–383, 385–391
suspended indexing 371
unions 359, 360, 388; role in pension politics 388
veto players 350, 358, 371
veto points 350, 354, 358, 371, 379

Switzerland 2, 3, 5, 9, 10, 15, 23, 24, 26–28, 40, 42, 203 ff.
   10TH AHV/AVS revision 223, 224, 230, 233, 235, 237, 242
   11TH AHV/AVS revision 225, 233, 235, 237, 239
   1ST BVG/LPP revision 225, 226, 235, 237, 240
   Christian–Democratic Party 208, 213, 214, 215, 216, 232, 243, 244
   class interests 205, 229
   Communist Party 227, 228, 240, 242
   electoral system 209, 210
   employers' organizations 216, 244
   Evangelic Party 213, 243
   Green Party 213, 243
   Law on occupational pensions 212, 223, 224, 225, 226, 235, 237, 240, 243, 244, 246
   Liberal Party 213, 243
   occupational pensions 204, 212, 218–220, 222–229, 235, 237–240, 242
   parliament 205–215; role in pension politics 241, 242
   party System 213
   pension system 217–223, 866–868; history 217–219;
   political institutions 205–212, 241, 242
   political system 205–217, 241, 242
   politics of pension reform 223–239
   private pensions 241
   Radical Party 208, 213–215, 218, 231, 232, 244, 245
   Socialist Party 213–215, 231, 232
   Swiss People's Party 213, 215, 216, 232, 234–237, 244
   unions 216, 217; role in pension politics 240, 241
   veto players 209, 210, 215
   veto points 210, 211
SYN 104, 107, 133, 144
système de retraite par répartition 166

Tabellini, Guido 4, 5
TaEL 292
Taitelijoiden Eläkelaki. See TaEL.

Tangentopoli scandal 407, 431, 448
Taoiseach 760, 762, 783, 790, 792, 800
Tax deductions, deductibility 22, 34
Tax incentives 23, 269, 417, 420, 428, 429, 433, 438, 465, 530, 537, 544
Taxa Social Única. See TSU.
Taxes, taxation 6, 11, 20–23, 30, 31, 34
TCO 359, 360, 369, 372, 374, 376–379, 384, 385, 388, 390
TEL 266–272, 274, 278–280, 288, 292
TELA 271, 272, 283, 292
Teollisuuden työnantajien Keskusliitto. See TT.
Tfr 397, 398, 417–420, 426, 427, 429–431, 433, 441–445, 448, 450
TGWU 58, 88
Thatcher, Margaret 10, 24, 57, 58, 60, 67, 70–72, 74, 82, 84–87, 90, 95
Thomas law 184–187
Thullen, Peter 825, 828
tiers 21–23
Tjänstemännens Centralorganisation. See TCO.
Toimihenkilö–ja Virkamiesjärjestöjen Keskusliitto. See TVK.
Toledo Pact 31, 534–538, 542–544
Trades Union Congress [UK]. *See* TUC.
Transport and General Workers' Union [UK]. *See* TGWU.
Transports en Île-de-France. See RATP.
Trattamento di Fine Rapporto. See Tfr.
Travail.suisse 217
Tremonti, Giulio 443
Tsebelis, George 7, 8, 157, 160
TSU 629, 654
TT 264, 282, 292
TUC 58, 70–73, 75, 77, 78, 80, 88, 95, 96
TVK 263, 292
Työeläkevakuuttajat. See TELA.
Työntekijäin Eläkelaki. See TEL.

UDEUR 408, 409, 413, 450
UDF 159, 161–164, 174, 175, 179, 181, 182, 185–187, 189, 194, 192, 195
UDP 514, 548

UEL 815, 840, 846
UGT 513, 525, 528, 535, 538, 541, 545, 548, 550
UIL 410, 450
UJL 830, 846
Ulster Unionist Party [UK]. *See* UUP.
UMP 159, 161, 163, 189, 195
Unión Democrática de Pensionistas y Jubilados de España. See UDP.
Union des Entreprises Luxembourgeoises. See UEL.
Union des Journalistes Luxembourg. See UJL.
Union française de retraités 164
Unión General de Trabajadores. See UGT.
Union nationale des syndicats autonomes. See UNSA.
Union pour la Démocratie Française. See UDF
Union pour la Nouvelle République. See UNR.
Union pour un mouvement populaire. See UMP.
Union Wallonne des Entreprises. See UWE.
Unione Democratici per l'Europa. See UDEUR.
Unione Italiana dei Lavoratori. See UIL.
Unions 3, 11–14, 25, 27–32, 34, 35 [*See* also individual country entries]
United Kingdom 4, 24, 39, 49 ff.
  Child support pensions and social security act, 61, 67, 69, 79, 83, 91
  Conservative Party 50, 55–59, 67, 70–76, 80, 84, 85, 87, 89–91
  corporatism 58
  Democratic Unionist Party 55, 58, 87
  electoral system 52–54, 56–58, 84, 90, 93, 94
  employers' organizations 54, 58, 59, 86
  Labour Party 50, 55–60, 68, 70, 72, 75–80, 83–85, 88, 89, 91, 96
  Liberal Democratic Party 55, 58, 85, 88
  Liberal Party 50, 55, 56, 70, 88
  occupational pensions 50, 59–68, 70, 71, 73–78, 80–83, 86–88, 90
  parliament 51–58, 64, 65, 72, 75, 78, 84, 88, 91, 95; role in pension politics 83–85
  party system 50, 55–58, 84, 93, 94
  pension system 59–66, 856–859; history 59, 60;
  pensioner organizations 58, 59
  Pensions act 1995, 62, 65, 67, 68, 74–76, 83
  political institutions 52–58
  political system 51–59
  politics of pension reform 1980 to present 66–82
  private pensions 50, 62, 64, 66, 76, 81, 83, 90
  Scottish National Party 55, 58, 88
  Social Democratic and Labour Party 55, 58, 88
  Social Democratic Party 55, 58, 74, 85, 88, 89, 93, 95
  Social security act 1986, 67, 69, 82, 84, 89–91
  Ulster Unionist Party 55, 58, 88
  unions 58, 59; membership 58, 59, 72; role in pension politics 85, 86
  veto players 53, 57
  veto points 53, 57
  Welfare Reform and Pensions Act 1999 67, 68, 76–79, 83, 91
UNR 161, 195
UNSA 165, 176, 183, 188, 189, 195
UUP 55, 58, 88
UWE 342

V 460–463, 472, 477, 482, 484, 485, 488, 492
Vail, Mark I. 183
Vakcentrale voor middengroepen en hoger personeel. See MHP.
Vakuutusvalvontavirasto. See ISA
Valtion eläkelaki. See VEL.
Valtiopäivät. See Vp.
Vandenbroucke Law 320, 338
Vandenbroucke, Frank 338
VAT 20, 27
VB 723, 740, 747, 753
VBO 312, 341, 342
VDK 669, 670, 703
VDR 673, 679–681, 688, 691, 703, 707, 710
Veil, Simone 181

VEL 267, 269–271, 273, 280, 281, 287, 292
Venieris, Dimitris 110, 149
Venizelos, Eleutherios 98, 147
Venstre. See V.
Venstresocialisteme. See VS.
ver.di 670, 703
Verband der Kriegsbeschädigten, Kriegshinterbliebenen und Sozialrentner Deutschlands. See VDK.
Verband der Versicherungsunternehmen Österreichs. See VVÖ.
Verband Deutscher Rentenversicherungsträger. See VDR.
Verband österreichischer Banken und Bankiers. See VoeBB.
Verbond van Belgische Ondernemingen. See VBO.
Verdi (Partito dei). See GR.
Vereinigung österreichischer Industrieller. See VÖI.
Vereinigung schweizerischer Angestelltenverbände/Fédération Suisse des Sociétés d'Employés. See VSA/FSE
Vereinte Dienstleistungsgewerkschaft. See ver.di
Vereniging van Bedrijfstakpensioenfondsen. See VB
Vereniging van Nederlandse Ondernemingen. See VNO.
Vereniging van Nederlandse Ondernemingen–Nederlands Christelijk Werkgeversverbond. See VNO–NCW.
Vereniging van Ondernemingspensioenfondsen. See OPF.
Verhofstadt, Guy 308, 326, 327, 336
Verts, les [France] 159, 161, 186
veto players 7, 8 [*See* also individual country entries]
VEV 312
Vilrokx, Jacques 311
Visser, Jelle 720
Vlaams Economisch Verbond. See VEV.
VNO 722, 740, 753
VNO–NCW 722, 753
VoC 14, 15

VoeBB 566, 598
VÖI 598
Volkspartij voor Vrijheid en Democratie. See VVD.
vote bloquée 26, 153, 154
Vp 252–260, 288, 289
Vranitzky, Franz 564, 581, 583, 584
VS 460, 492
VSA/FSE 217, 243
VVD 719, 722, 724, 735, 736, 738–742, 744, 745, 748, 753, 754
VVÖ 566, 598

Waarden, Frans van 718, 723
wages 12–14, 19–21, 35
Wagner, Carlo 840, 849, 853
Wahlaltrnative Arbeit und soziale Gerechtigkeit. See WASG
WASG 661, 669, 703
Wassenaar Agreement 720, 723
Weaver, Kent 9, 11
Welfare Reform and Pensions Act 67, 68, 76–79, 83, 91
Welfare state 1, 2, 8–14, 28, 30, 33, 34, 37, 38
Westminster 4, 24, 49, 56, 83
Wet koppeling met afwijkingsmogelijkheid. See WKA.
Whelan, Brendan J. 771, 790, 797, 802
White paper commission [Portugal] 642–644, 647, 652
Widows', Orphans', and Old Age Contributory Pensions Act 59
Willockx, Freddy 319, 329–332, 334
WKA 727, 730, 739, 741, 753
Wolter, Michel 836
women 20, 27, 32, 38, 39
Woods, Michael 779, 784
World Bank 16, 17, 21, 144, 222, 454, 455, 466, 489, 491, 500, 696

YEL 266, 270, 271, 292
Yrittäjien Eläkelaki. See YEL.

Zapatero, José Luis Rodríguez 511, 512
Zilverfonds/Fonds de Vieillissement 337, 344